he

Prosecutor charges suspect with a crime

① Bail
② Appointment of counsel for poor
③ Preliminary hearing and/or grand jury review
④ Arraignment
⑤ Trial or guilty plea
⑥ Conviction
⑦ Pre-sentence investigation
⑧ Sentencing

Court Decisions

Not arraigned
Not indicted
Released on bail
Suspended sentence
Acquitted

Corrections Decisions

Community service
Fine
Probation
Restitution
Jail
Prison
Capital punishment

EXIT

Exits from criminal justice system

EXIT

EXIT

Criminal Justice

Fifth Edition

Criminal Justice

Fifth Edition

JOEL SAMAHA

University of Minnesota

Australia • Canada • Denmark • Japan • Mexico • New Zealand • Philippines • Puerto Rico
Singapore • South Africa • Spain • United Kingdom • United States

Executive Editor, Criminal Justice: Sabra Horne
Senior Development Editor: Dan Alpert
Assistant Editor: Shannon Ryan
Editorial Assistant: Ann Tsai
Marketing Manager: Christine Henry
Marketing Assistant: Ken Baird
Project Editor: Jennie Redwitz
Print Buyer: Karen Hunt
Permissions Editor: Robert Kauser
Production Service: Ruth Cottrell
Text Designer: Lisa Delgado
Photo Researcher: Meyers Photo Art
Copyeditors: Kevin Gleason, Lura Harrison
Illustrator: Nancy Wirsig McClure
Compositor: R&S Book Composition
Cover Designer: Laurie Anderson
Printer/Binder: Transcontinental Printing, Inc./Metropole

Printed in Canada

2 3 4 5 6 03 02 01 00

For permission to use material from this text, contact us by
web: www.thomsonrights.com
fax: 1-800-730-2215
phone: 1-800-730-2214

Library of Congress Cataloging-in-Publication Data
Samaha, Joel.
Criminal justice/Joel Samaha.—5th ed.
p. cm.
Includes bibliographical references and indexes.
ISBN 0-534-52264-5
1. Criminal justice, Administration of—United States. I. Title.
HV9950.S25 1999
345.73′05—dc21 99-30184

Instructor's Edition ISBN 0-534-52265-3

For more information, contact

Wadsworth/Thomson Learning
10 Davis Drive
Belmont, CA 94002-3098
USA
www.wadsworth.com

International Headquarters
Thomson Learning
290 Harbor Drive, 2nd Floor
Stamford, CT 06902-7477
USA

UK/Europe/Middle East
Thomson Learning
Berkshire House
168-173 High Holborn
London WC1V 7AA
United Kingdom

Asia
Thomson Learning
60 Albert Street #15-01
Albert Complex
Singapore 189969

Canada
Nelson/Thomson Learning
1120 Birchmount Road
Scarborough, Ontario M1K 5G4
Canada

For Doug

ABOUT THE AUTHOR

Professor Joel Samaha teaches Criminal Law, Criminal Procedure, Introduction to Criminal Justice, and the History of Criminal Justice at the University of Minnesota. He is both a lawyer and a historian whose primary research interest is the history of criminal justice. He received his B.A., J.D., and Ph.D. from Northwestern University. Professor Samaha also studied at Cambridge University, England (1969–1970), while doing research for his first book, *Law and Order in Historical Perspective* (1974), a quantitative and qualitative analysis of law enforcement in pre-industrial society.

Professor Samaha was admitted to the Illinois Bar in 1962. He taught at UCLA before coming to the University of Minnesota in 1971. At the University of Minnesota, he served as Chairman of the Department of Criminal Justice Studies from 1974 to 1978. Since then he has returned to teaching, research, and writing full-time. He has taught both television and radio courses in criminal justice, and has co-taught a National Endowment for the Humanities seminar in legal and constitutional history. He was named Distinguished Teacher at the University of Minnesota in 1974, a coveted award.

Professor Samaha is an active scholar. In addition to his monograph on pre-industrial law enforcement and a transcription with a scholarly introduction of English criminal justice records during the reign of Elizabeth I, he has written numerous articles on the history of criminal justice, published in such scholarly journals as *Historical Journal, American Journal of Legal History, Minnesota Law Review, William Mitchell Law Review,* and *Journal of Social History.* In addition to his best-seller, *Criminal Law,* Sixth Edition, he has written two other successful textbooks, *Criminal Procedure,* now in its fourth edition, and this fifth edition of *Criminal Justice* (all published by Wadsworth).

Contents

PART TWO / POLICE

PART FOUR / CORRECTIONS

Preface

Criminal Justice, Fifth Edition, presents a balanced description of criminal justice agencies, their personnel, and the decisions they make. This description is an essential foundation for all students whether they are—or hope to become—criminal justice professionals, or whether they want simply to be informed citizens. But description is not enough, even for an introductory course. Therefore, *Criminal Justice* uses this description to analyze and evaluate criminal justice policies and decision making.

Most students begin their study of criminal justice with a lot of information—much of it incorrect information. *Criminal Justice,* Fifth Edition, aims to dispel many myths that grow out of both a lack of information and incorrect information. When students have finished this course, they should have a solid basis for their opinions. This edition includes the major new developments in the increasingly vast literature of criminal justice. It also reflects major rethinking about criminal justice research regarding theory, policy, and practice.

APPROACH

Criminal justice is an enormous subject. *Criminal Justice* adopts a decision-making approach as a way to organize this vast subject of criminal justice. The decision making approach organizes the vast subject of criminal justice according to the formal and informal decision making in the major public agencies that make up the criminal justice system—police, courts, and corrections.

ORGANIZATION

Chapters and topics within chapters are organized chronologically according to when decisions are made regarding:

1. The definition, measurement, explanation, and reporting of crime.
2. The investigation, apprehension, prosecution, and conviction of criminal suspects and defendants.
3. The punishment and release of convicted offenders.

THE INFORMAL/FORMAL PERSPECTIVE

Criminal Justice, Fifth Edition, keeps a sharp focus on the decision-making process. Decision making is central to the systems paradigm that has dominated criminal justice analysis for the last half century. It has brought informal decision making into the forefront of empirical, theoretical, and policy research regarding criminal justice.

Chapters 1 through 4 introduce students to two major themes in the day-to-day operation of criminal justice:

1. The nature of formal and informal decision making in criminal justice.
2. The sociology, politics, economics, and law of criminal justice.

The remaining chapters analyze the nature and operation of the principal public agencies of crime control, beginning with the police, followed by the courts, and ending with corrections. A final chapter contains a brief overview of the structure and process of juvenile justice.

INTERDISCIPLINARY BALANCE

Every book to some extent reflects the individual experience and training of its author. *Criminal Justice,* Fifth Edition, is no exception. My training as a social scientist, historian, and lawyer definitely influenced both the content and the style of *Criminal Justice.* The emphasis on theoretical and empirical research in criminal justice reflects my social science training. The systems paradigm and the view of criminal justice as a series of decisions adopted as an organizing principle of the text stems from social science theory and research. My training as a lawyer draws me to issues and the possible alternatives to resolve them. The Use *Your* Discretion boxes and the presentation of varying views, conclusions, and research findings throughout the text reflect the tendency of lawyers to concentrate on critical thinking about issues and argument. Historians are trained to look for change and continuity in human experience as a fundamental aspect of their discipline. *Criminal Justice* shows some of that training. It emphasizes not only the continuing problems in criminal justice but it also recognizes change and development. Some new programs, policies, and institutions and enhanced training of criminal justice professionals demonstrate the possibility of a fairer, more humane, efficient, and effective criminal justice system. Much remains to be done, of course. These bright spots should not obscure the darkness that remains. *Criminal Justice* aims to strike a balance that acknowledges the shortcomings that make up the present reality of criminal justice and recognizes the hope that new developments promise for criminal justice in the 21st century.

STYLE

Criminal justice is a vast, complex subject, presenting challenges not only for students but also for authors of criminal justice textbooks. Writing a book of substance and style, one that both challenges and gives pleasure, and that engages students in active learning, is a major goal of *Criminal Justice,* Fifth Edition. I have written it with an eye not only toward accuracy and importance but also toward clarity and brevity. I have worked hard to strip the text of every unnecessary paragraph, sentence, clause, phrase, adverb, and adjective.

NEW FEATURES

Since the first edition, *Criminal Justice* has stressed interactive learning between the text and students. Like its predecessors, *Criminal Justice,* Fifth Edition, aims both to inspire and to challenge students to participate in the decision-making process. In doing so, students discover that studying criminal justice can be an interesting learning experience. Adopters have repeatedly affirmed the success of this aim. It is gratifying that instructors report that their students actually enjoy reading *Criminal Justice.*

- **Use *Your* Discretion Critical Thinking Boxes**

Critical thinking is essential to both criminal justice professionals and good citizens. And, it lies at the heart of interactive learning. The new feature, Use *Your* Discretion, builds on the unique You Decide feature of all four previous editions. *Criminal Justice,* Fifth Edition, includes 52 completely new critical thinking boxes called Use *Your* Discretion. It also updates and revises many more critical thinking boxes that used to be You Decides.

Most Use *Your* Discretion boxes present an issue based on empirical research findings that are conflicting, tentative, and/or incomplete. Students are asked to identify and summarize the findings. Then, they are asked critical thinking questions about the effectiveness, wisdom, legality, and policy implications of the positions they take regarding the issue. I believe that other students, like mine, will surprise instructors with their enthusiasm and with their increased understanding that comes from developing their critical thinking skills. In course evaluations, students consistently rank the critical thinking boxes their favorite feature. I have tried many of these boxes in my own introductory course in criminal justice—they really work!

- **Internet Exercises at Each Chapter End**

The vast resources of the Internet are now available to both students and instructors. *Criminal Justice,* Fifth Edition, provides students with specific research questions. It also includes specific instructions on how to find the answers to the research questions. For example, here are the questions in the exercise at the end of Chapter 1:

Exercise: This chapter discussed three types of criminal justice agencies: law enforcement, courts, and corrections. Using the Internet or InfoTrac College Edition, search for information about one of these agencies. What are the agency's primary functions? What services does it provide? What issues is it currently dealing with?

Suggested sites:

- Bureau of Justice Statistics: http://www.ojp.usdoj.gov/bjs (tip: click on "law enforcement," "courts and sentencing," or "corrections")
- Federal Bureau of Investigation: http://www.fbi.gov
- New York State Commission of Corrections: http://crisny.org/government/ny/nysscoc/index.html

InfoTrac College Edition: Run a key word search on the agency you want to investigate; for example, "state courts"

Please note that web site addresses ("URLs") are always subject to change. If you find that the address above is no longer working, use a search engine and enter key words to find an alternate address for your research topic.

- **Critical Thinking Questions Open and Close Every Chapter**

Every chapter opens with a question and an excerpt drawn from criminal justice research, a court case, or a popular news source. The opening question focuses students' attention on some major topic in the chapter. At the end of the chapter, the same question appears with a consideration of the answer to the question based on further information and on the content of the chapter.

- **Chapter Capsules at Each Chapter End**

Chapter Capsules identify the chapter's major points. Some of them review the highlights of the chapter, such as that for Chapter 3: "Explanations of criminal behavior focus on either the offender or the context." Others are inferences that the content of the chapter allows but which students may not have drawn, such as another capsule from Chapter 3: "We do not know the causes of crime."

MAJOR CHANGES AND ADDITIONS

Writing *Criminal Justice,* Fifth Edition, has provided me with the opportunity to keep myself and students abreast of the latest empirical research. In addition to updating the entire text with appropriate new research, I made major additions and revisions in *Criminal Justice,* Fifth Edition. Highlighted here are some of these major revisions and additions.

Chapter 1

- New Section: Demographics and criminal justice—with special emphasis on race, ethnicity, and gender.
- New Use *Your* Discretion box: "Justice for all" or "Just us"?

Chapter 2

- Covers the types, trends, and measurement of crime, and criminals and victims. Previous editions also included explanations of criminal behavior.
- New Use *Your* Discretion boxes: Did the crime rates really drop? Is the number of convenience-store robberies high? Are crime statistics objective measures or subjective constructions? Are surveys of defensive gun users accurate? Is it too early to make policy based on research about crime and drugs? Can we rely on the evidence of the career patterns of career criminals? Does gender matter in gay and lesbian victimization?

Chapter 3

- New chapter covering devoted solely to the explanations of criminal behavior
- New Use *Your* Discretion box: Is the economic explanation of crime convincing enough to support public policy?

Chapter 4

- New Use *Your* Discretion box: *Montana v. Egelhoff*, research and debate over the intoxication defense

Chapter 5

- New section on women police and women policing
- New Use *Your* Discretion boxes: What are the limits of the reform model? Is private security worth the cost? Does disorder cause serious crime? How much time do officers spend enforcing criminal laws?

Chapter 6

- New section on policing illegal drugs
- New Use *Your* Discretion boxes: Does the Kansas City Preventive Patrol Experiment prove that preventive motor patrol wastes police time and taxpayers' money? Are one-officer patrol units as effective as the San Diego study found? What's the controversy over crime attack strategies really about? Are crackdowns good policy? Should kids report parents to the police?

Chapter 7

- New Use *Your* Discretion boxes: Was the "no knock" entry legal? Was the confession voluntary? Does the exclusionary rule exact too high of a social cost?

Chapter 8

- New Use *Your* Discretion boxes: Does college education make "good" cops? Does broad field experience make "better" cops? Why do police abuse their power? Are police shootings affected by racism? What is the best policy regarding pursuits? Does civilian review work?

Chapter 9

- New Use *Your* Discretion boxes: Is speed necessarily bad? Is police-prosecutor cooperation worth the effort?

Chapter 10

- New Use *Your* Discretion boxes: Are public defenders ineffective? Is commercial bail a good idea? Can drug testing reduce pretrial misconduct?

Chapter 11

- New Use *Your* Discretion boxes: Is there a constitutional right to a jury of 12? Does race affect jury deliberations? Should race influence jury nullification decisions? Abolish plea bargaining?

Chapter 12

- New Use *Your* Discretion boxes: Is the indeterminate sentence responsible for disparity in sentences? Does the death penalty *increase* the number of murders?

Chapter 13

- New Use *Your* Discretion boxes: Is home confinement good policy? Do correctional boot camps "work"? Are community service sentences appropriate?

Chapter 14

- New Use *Your* Discretion box: Should we privatize prisons and jails?

Chapter 15

- New section on prisoners lifting weights and playing team sports
- New section on consensual sex in prison
- New section on life in women's prisons
- New Use *Your* Discretion boxes: Should prisoners be allowed contraband goods and services? Can we really know how widespread sex in prisons is? How much sexual assault in prison is there? What is the best policy for prison crowding? Should we expand prison industry programs? Does more women prisoners mean more female crime?

Chapter 16

- New Use *Your* discretion box: Does the success of parole depend on the kind of parole supervision?

Chapter 17

- New Use *Your* Discretion box: Should curfew laws be strictly enforced?

PEDAGOGICAL AIDS

- Chapter Key Terms identify the important items and concepts that all students should know.
- Knowledge and Understanding Check boxes are self-tests so students can tell if they have grasped the main points, remembered the important details, and grappled with the issues in the sections of each chapter. Students have reported repeatedly that these checks are a major aid to understanding the large amount of information in each chapter and definitely improve their scores on exams.

ACKNOWLEDGMENTS

Instructors from around the country have reviewed the previous editions of *Criminal Justice.* The book bears marks of their positive influence, marks that I hope they see and for which I am indebted to them. The list of my debtors is long and the mere mention of their names hardly repays my debt to them. The following instructors reviewed the fourth edition of *Criminal Justice* and provided thoughtful and serious evaluations of it:

Susan Brinkley, University of Tampa

Orman Buswell, Fairmont State College

Patricia Harris, University of Texas

Mark Jones, East Carolina University

Frank Lee, Middle Tennessee University

Robert McCormack, College of New Jersey

Allen Wagner, University of Missouri–St. Louis

John Watkins, University of Alabama

The instructors who reviewed previous editions include: James A. Adamitis, Bonnie Berry, John S. Boyd, Stephen Brown, Dave Camp, Paul V. Clark, Walt Copley, Jerry Davis, Dana C. DeWitt, Marlon T. Doss, Edna Erez, Walter M. Francis, Peter Grimes, John P. Harlan, Vincent Hoffman, Nicholas H. Irons, Michael Israel, Gary Keveles, Peter B. Kraska, Robert Lockwood, Matthew Lyones, Joseph Macy, Stephen Mastrofski, G. Larry Mays, William Michalek, JoAnn Miller, Robert Murillo, Gordon E. Meisner, Donald R. Morton, Charles E. Myers II, John Northrup, H. Wayne Overson, Gary Perlstein, Mario Peitrucci, Harry L. Powell, Joel Powell, Archie Rainey, Christine Rasche, Philip Roades, Ronald Robinson, Glenda Rogers, John Scarborough, William Selke, Edward Sieh, Stan Stodkovic, Kenrick Thompson, Myron Utech, Neil R. Vance, Timothy Vieders, Mervin White, Thomas Whitt, Warren M. Whitton, Keven Wright, and Stanley Yeldell.

It gives me great pleasure to acknowledge the deep obligation I owe my colleagues at the University of Minnesota and former students who are now criminal justice professionals who over the years have given so generously to the improvement of *Criminal Justice.* Professor David Ward, professor in the Department of Sociology, my loyal friend and colleague, knew all the answers to my questions about corrections research. The book is richer because of his knowledge, his experience, and his unlimited generosity in taking the time and energy to share that vast knowledge and experience with me. Professor Joachim Savelsberg, who read the entire book in earlier editions, made copious notes and discussed his experiences in using *Criminal Justice* as a text in an introductory course in criminal justice. Joachim offered not only editorial advice but has also continued to engage me in constructive thinking about the theory and sometimes not too subtle biases that appear in the text. I have not always taken his suggestions but the book is better because of his time and effort. Norm Carlson, former director of the Federal Bureau of Prisons and until his retirement my colleague at the University of Minnesota, has facilitated many visits to correctional facilities, helped me obtain information and other materials that I could not otherwise easily find, and praised and helpfully criticized the text. But more than that, he has set an example that all of us should follow—he has remained generous, optimistic, cheerful, and open-minded in the face of what would have soured many others in less challenging positions. His advice, encouragement, and example have all enriched *Criminal Justice,* Fifth Edition. His advice to me to "show the positive side of criminal justice," I took to heart.

Captain Greg Meyer, Los Angeles Police Department, has graciously shared with me his extensive knowledge of the use of force in particular and his perspectives on policing generally. His influence has definitely improved the chapters on policing. Lieutenant Richard Gardell, St. Paul Police Department; Sergeant James De Concini, Minneapolis Police Department; Martin Costello, Hughes and Costello; John Sheehy, Meshbesher and Spence; Judge Phil Bush; David Schwab, United States Probation Office; Deputy Commissioner of Minnesota Department of Corrections Dennis Benson; David Crist, warden of Stillwater State Prison, all former students and now experienced professionals, have helped me more than they know or than I can recognize. Following their careers, sharing their experiences, listening to their stories, and arguing with their positions, has kept me young in mind, in touch with the "real world," and inspired me to continue in the pursuit of knowledge, understanding, excellence, and improvement in criminal justice.

Stephen E. Brown, East Tennessee State University, has once again written an excellent Study Guide to accompany *Criminal Justice,* Fourth Edition. His careful, thorough, painstaking efforts have made the ancillaries to this edition a stronger package. Erik Larson, University of Minnesota, has helped me write the Instructor's Manual with Test Bank to accompany this edition. This part of the ancillary package is definitely better for his work.

Criminal Justice, Fifth Edition, owes much to the expertise, devotion, and effort of editors and others at or associated with Wadsworth Publishing Company. The warm and generous support and regular assurances of Criminal Justice Editor Sabra Horne and Senior Development Editor Dan Alpert has made my work much easier. Sabra and Dan provided excellent suggestions that surely improved the text. Dan read the first chapter line by line and the reduction in unnecessary words and the strength of his suggestions for transitions and re-organization not only improved Chapter 1 but also the entire text. Kevin Gleason and Lura Harrison deserve much credit for careful editing and excellent suggestions, especially since this edition involved major rewriting. Ruth Cottrell's calm efficiency, warm kindness, careful editing, and strong support during the production process were more important and welcome than she knows.

The book has also profited from the now thousands of students who have taken criminal justice courses from me at the University of Minnesota. Undergraduates, graduate students, law students, and criminal justice professionals who have taken the courses have changed in many respects over the years but in one important respect they have remained constant—they have challenged me to give them the most that I can and the best that I have. I hope the book goes some distance to meeting their challenge.

What would I do without Sally and Doug? My true friend Sally keeps on praising my work and me, even when I don't deserve it. And she finds books and other sources for my work that no else can or will find. Her discoveries have improved the text in ways that she cannot possibly know. My assistant Doug makes it possible for me physically to do the work required to write the books. But he does a lot more. He keeps me thinking critically by providing so many insights from a perspective that I could never acquire. His shrewd observations about life and people has improved the book more than he can know. And on top of all that, Doug puts up with my mercurial temperament on a daily basis. Friends and associates like these have made *Criminal Justice,* Fifth Edition, a better book. Whatever the book's failings, they are entirely mine.

Joel Samaha
University of Minnesota

We are grateful to the following individuals who responded to Wadsworth's recent marketing survey for the Introduction to Criminal Justice Course:

Edward Abair, Madonna University
Samuel Ackah, Delaware State University
Charles Adams, Savannah State College
Leanne Alarid, University of Missouri
R. B. Allen Anson Community College
James Amos, Alvernia College
Allen Anderson, Indiana University-Kokomo
William Arnold, University of Kansas
Kelly Asmussen, Peru State College
Thomas Austin, Shippensburg University
James Bachman, Bowling Green State University
Thomas Baker, University of Scranton
Gregg Barak, Eastern Michigan University
Tom Barclay, University of South Alabama
Allan Barnes, University of Alaska, Anchorage
Peter Barone, St. Thomas University
Thomas Barry, University of Texas at San Antonio
Elaine Bartgis, Fairmont State College
Lincoln Barton, Anna Maria College
Larry Bassi, State University of New York College at Brockport
Mary Ellen Batiuk, Wilmington College
Chris Beard, California State University-Sacramento
Frank Beck, College of the Sequoias
Joe Becraft, Portland Community College
Julia Beeman, University of North Carolina at Charlotte
Richard Bennett, American University
Charles Biggs, Oakland City University
Donna Bishop, University of Central Florida
John Bower, Bethel College
Gary Boyer, University of Great Falls
Chuck Brawner, Heartland Community College
Susan Brinkley, University of Tampa
Ronald Brooks, Clinton Community College
Paula Broussard, University of Southwestern Louisiana
Carolyn Brown, Fayetteville Technical Community College
Michael Brown, Ball State University
Joseph Bunce, Montgomery College
John Burchill, Kansas Wesleyan University
Tod Burke, Radford University
Michael Burnette, Southwestern Community College
Deborah Burris-Kitchen, University of LaVerne
Orman Buswell, Fairmont State College
Timothy Buzzell, Baker University
David Calihan, Longwood College
Paul Campbell, Wayne State College
Leon Cantin, Mount Marty College
Timothy Carboreau, University of Cincinnati
Joseph Carlson, University of Nebraska at Kearny
David Cary, Mary Baldwin College
William Castleberry, University of Tennessee at Martin
Darl Champion, Methodist College
Dae Chang, Wichita State University
Charles Chastain, University of Arkansas at Little Rock
Russ Cheothem, Cumberland University
Steven Chermak, Indiana University
Art Chete, Central Florida Community College
Steven Christiansen, Green River Community College
Charlie Chukwudolue, Northern Kentucky University
Monte Clampett, Asheville-Buncombe Technical Community College
Ray Clarkson, Kings River Community College
Kenneth Clontz, Western Illinois University
Jean Clouatre, New Hampshire Technical Institute
John Cochran, University of South Florida
Keith Coleman, Fayetteville State University
William Cook Jr., Westfield State College
Kim Cook, University of Southern Maine
Richard Cook, Evergreen Valley College
Tom Cook, Wayne State College
Walt Copley, Metropolitan State College of Denver
Gary Copus, University of Alaska at Fairbanks
David Corbett, Pensacola Christian College
Mark Correia, University of Nevada at Reno
Stephen Cox, Central Connecticut State University
Beverly Curl, Long Beach City College
Dean Dabney, Georgia State University
John Daly, Cazenovia College
Carol Davis, Indiana University Northwest
R. Davis, New Mexico State University
Peggy De Stefano, Bakersfield College
Tim Dees, Floyd College
Darrel Degraw, Delta State University
John Del Nero, Lane Community College
Tom Dempsey, Christopher Newport University
Holly Dershem-Bruce, Dawson Community College
John Doherty, Marist College
R. Dorsey, Shelby State Community College
Marion Doss, Jr., James Madison University
Yvonne Downes, Hilbert College
Daniel Doyle, University of Montana
Joyce Dozier, Wilmington College
J. C. Drake, Roanoke-Chowan Community College
David Duffee, State University of New York at Albany
Gary Dull, Mesa Community College
William Dunford, Erie Community College
Steve Dunker, Casper College
Tim Durham, Thomas College
Mary Ann Eastep, University Central Florida
Peter Eckert, Broward Community College
David Emmons, Richard Stockton College of New Jersey
Don Ernst, Joliet Junior College
Dave Evans, University of North Carolina
Tom Fields, Cape Fear Community College

Larry Field, Western New England College
Charles Fieramusca, Medaille College
Frank Fischer, Kankakee Community College
Terry Fisk, Grand Valley State University
Michael Foley, Western Connecticut State University
Walt Francis, Central Wyoming College
Carl Franklin, Cloud County Community College
Crystal Garcia, Indiana University
Barry Garigen, Genesee Community College
Godfrey Garner, Hinds Community College
Carole Garrison, University of Akron
Andrew Giacomazzi, University of Texas at San Antonio
John Gillespie, Pennsicola Christian College
J. Ginger, St. Mary's University
Mary Glazier, Millersville University
Dean Golding, West Chester University of Pennsylvania
Michael Goodman, Illinois State University
Dirk Grafton, Mt. Aloysius College
Charles Graham, Solano Community College
James Green, St. Thomas Aquinas College
Peter Grimes, Nassau Community College
Edmund Grosskopf, Indiana State University
Donald Grubb, Northern Virginia Community College
George Guay, Salem State College
Stephen Haas, California State University at Bakersfield
Jan Hagemann, San Jose State University
Sharon Halford, Community College of Aurora
Doris Hall, California State University at Bakersfield
Cynthia Hamilton, West Virginia State College
Hil Harper, Valdosta State University
Judith Harris, University of South Carolina-Spartanburg
Lou Harris, Faulkner University
Robert Harvie, St. Martin's College
Curtis Hayes, Western New Mexico University
Kay Henriksen, MacMurray College
Gary Hill, Cisco Junior College
Vincent Hoffman, Michigan State University
Joe Hogan, Central Texas College
Ronald Holmes, University of Louisville
John Homa, Murray State University
David Hough, University of Findlay
John Hudgens, Weatherford College
James Hudson, Bob Jones University
Wendelin Hume, University of North Dakota
G. Hunt, Wharton County Junior College
William Hyatt, Western Carolina University
Timothy Ireland, Niagara University
Michael Israel, Kean University
Mary Jackson, East Carolina University
Theron Jackson, Los Angeles Southwest College
Caron Jacobson, Wayne State University
J. D. Jamieson, Southwest Texas State University
Shirley Jarreo, Texas A & M University at Commerce
Denise Jenne, Montclair State University
H. Johnson, University of Iowa
Kathrine Johnson, Kentucky State University
Paul Johnson, Weber State University
W. Johnson, Sam Houston State University
Fred Jones, Simpson College
Ken Jones, Coastal Carolina Community College
Casey Jordan, Western Connecticut State University
Lamar Jordan, Southern Utah University
Judy Kaci, California State University-Long Beach
George Kain, Western Connecticut State University
Michael Kane, Coastal Bend College
Richard Kania, Guilford College
Mathew Kanjirathinkal, Texas A & M University at Commerce
Kimberly Kempf-Leonard, University of Missouri-St. Louis
Patrick Kinkade, Texas Christian University
Douglas Kirk, University of South Carolina-Aiken
Paul Kish, Elmira College
Dan Klotz, Los Angeles Valley College
F. Knowles, Jr., Central Methodist College
Junius Koonce, Edgecombe Community College
John Kozlowicz, University of Wisconsin-Whitewater
Fred Kramer, John Jay College of Criminal Justice
Pete Kraska, Eastern Kentucky University
Bob Kristic, College of the Redwood
A. Kuennen, Briar Cliff College
Karl Kunkel, Southwest Missouri State University
Lon Lacey, The Victoria College
Jerry Lane, Central Virginia Community College
Peter Lango, Gateway Technical College
Anthony LaRose, Western Oregon University
Michael Lauderdale, University of Texas at Austin
Deborah Laufersweiler-Dwyer, University of Arkansas at Little Rock
Alan Lavallee, Delaware Technical College
George Lawless, South Plains College
Richard Lawrence, St. Cloud State University
Nella Lee, Portland State University
Tazinski Lee, Mississippi Valley State University
Thomas Lenahan, Herkimer Community College
B. H. Levin, Blue Ridge Community College
Elizabeth Lewis, Waycross College
Walter Lewis, St. Louis Community College
Lee Libby, Shoreline Community College
Charles Linder, John Jay College of Criminal Justice
Bobby Little, University of North Alabama
Jay Livingston, Montclair State University
Robert Lockwood, Portland State University
Thomas Long, Vance-Granville Community College
Beth Lord, Louisiana State University
Albert Lugo, El Camino College
Dennis Lund, University of Nebraska at Kearney
Faith Lutze, Washington State University
Richard Mangan, Florida Atlantic University
Larry Marshall, Methodist College
Brad Martin, University of Findlay
William Mathias, University of South Carolina
Nancy Matthews, Northeastern Illinois University
Rick Matthews, Ohio University
Richard Mays, Cameron University

Michael Mc Morris, Ferris State University
Stephen McAndrew, Hessen College
Thomas McAninch, Scott Community College
William McCamey, Western Illinois University
James McCarten, Mt. Senario College
Kenneth McCreedy, Ferrum College
Susan McGuire, San Jacinto College North
Barry McKee, Bristol Community College
Maureen McCleod, Russell Sage College
M. McShane, Northern Arizona University
Jim Meko, Gannon University
D. Miller, Alvin Community College
Robin Miller, Sterling College
Al Miranne, Gonzaga University
John Mockry, Clinton Community College
Dale Mooso, San Antonio College
Karen Mullin, Southwest State University
William Muraskin, Queens College
Pat Murphy, State University of New York at Geneseo
Stephen Muzzatti, Clark College
Johnnie Myers, Morris Brown College
Alisa Nagler, Edgecombe Community College
Brian Nanavaty, Indiana University-Purdue University
Rebecca Nathanson, Housatonic Community College
Marc Neithercutt, California State University-Hayward
Steve Nelson, University of Great Falls
Robert Neville, College of The Siskiyous
Deborah Newman, Middle Tennessee State University
Frederica Nix, Missouri Western State University
Robert Nordvall, Gettysburg College
Paul North, Spoon River College
Patrick O'Guinn, Howard Community College
John O'Kane, Adirondack Community College
John O' Sullivan, Mt. San Antonio College
Robert Oatis, Indiana Wesleyan University
Willard Oliver, Glenville State College
Ihekwoaba Onwudiwe, University of Maryland-Eastern Shore
Kenneth Orr, College of the Albemarie
Alejandrina Ortiz, Catholic University of Puerto Rico
Gregory Osowski, Henry Ford Community College
Ted Paddack, Midwestern State University
Don Palmer, Union County College
Michael Palmioth, Wichita State University
Peter Parilla, University of St. Thomas
Dan Partrich, Mid America Nazarene University
Jill Payne, American International College
Michael Penrod, Ellsworth Community College
Francine Perretta, Mater Dei College
Morgan Peterson, Palomar College
Vincent Petrarca, Salve Regina University
Peter Phillips, University of Texas at Tyler
William Pitt, Del Mar College
Joy Pollock, Southwest Texas State University
Darrell Pope, Pensacola Christian College
Edward Porter, Halifax Community College
Harry Porter, Mississippi College
Wayne Posner, Los Angeles City College
Ronald Powell, Taylor University
Gary Prawel, Monroe Community College
Chester Quarles, University of Mississippi
Norman Raasch, Lakeland Community College
Alfred Reed Jr., Los Angeles Southwest College
Jack Reinwand, Ricks College
George Rengert, Temple University
Marylee Reynolds, Caldwell College
Jayne Rich, Atlantic Community College
Mark Robarge, Mansfield University
Matt Robinson, Appalachian State University
Herman Roe, The Victoria College
Darrell Ross, East Carolina University
Debra Ross, Buffalo State College
William Ruefle, University of South Carolina
Walter Ruger, Nassau Community College
Jeffrey Rush, Jacksonville State University
Gregory Russell, Washington State University
Carl Russell, Scottsdale Community College
Ronald Ryan, Bladen Community College
Julie Salazano, Pace University
Beth Sanders, Kent State University
Wayne Schaffter, Anderson University
Barry Schelzer, St. Ambrose University
Harry Schloetter, Napa State University
Patrick Schuster, El Centro College
Edward Selby, Southwestern College
Allen Settles, Mid-Plains Community College
Tim Sexton, University of Northern Iowa
Martin Seyler, San Antonio College
Stan Shernock, Norwich University
Daniel Simpson, Delaware Technical and Community College-Terry Campus
Barbara Sims, Pennsylvania State University
John Sloan, University of Alabama at Birmingham
Neal Slone, Bloomsburg University
Martha Smithey, University of Texas at El Paso
Beverly Smith, Illinois State University
Brian Smith, Northern Arizona University
Lynne Snowden, University of North Carolina-Wilmington
Diann Sollie, Meridian Community College
Ronald Sopenoff, Brookdale Community College
John Spiva, Walla Walla Community College
Phoebe Stambaugh, Northern Arizona University
Debra Stanley, Central Connecticut State University
Katherine Steinbeck, Lakeland Community College
Rick Steinmann, Lindenwood University
G. Stevens, Carteret Community College
Jeffrey Stewart, Howard University
Sandra Stone, State University of West Georgia
Thomas Stoney, Lees-McRae College
Danny Stover, Kaskaskia College
Gene Straughan, Lewis-Clark State College
David Struckhoff, Loyola University
Leslie Sue, Tacoma Community College
Thomas Sullenberger, Southeastern Louisiana University

Kathryn Sullivan, Hudson Valley Community College
Margaret Sylvia, St. Mary's University
Susette Talarico, University of Georgia
Michael Tatum, Ricks College
Carol Thompson, Texas Christian University
Shrund Thrower, University of Arkansas at Pine Bluff
George Tielsch, College of the Desert
Amy Tobol, Empire State College
James Todd, Tiffin University
C. Toler, Coastal Georgia Community College
Bonnie Toothaker, Mt. Wachusett Community College
Lawrence Travis, University of Cincinnati
Cecilia Tubbs, Jefferson State Community College
Jarrod Tudor, Kent State University-Stark Campus
Steve Turner, East Central University
Gary Uhrin, Westmoreland County Community College
Prabha Unnithan, Colorado State University
Dean Van Bibber, Fairmont State College
Ellen Van Valkenburgh, Jamestown Community College
Eddyth Vaughan, Hillsborough Community College
B. Vericker, Hano Community College
Kimberley Vogt, University of Wisconsin-La Crosse
Ron Walker, Trinity Valley Community College
Anthony Walsh, Boise State University
Thomas Ward, New Mexico Highlands University
Glenn Ware, North Harris College
Gene Waters, Georgia Southern University
John Watkins Jr., University of Alabama
Ralph Weisheit, Illinois State University
Karen Weston, Gannon University
Christine Westphal, Mt. Ida College
Giselle White, South Carolina State University
Martin White, Garland County Community College
Paul White, Quincy College
Stephanie Whitus, Sam Houston State University
Terri Wies-Haithcuck, Lima Technical College
Robert Wiggins, Cedarville College
Frank Williams, California State University-San Bernadino
Kathryn Williams, Southern Nazarene University
Deborah Wilson, University of Louisville
Deborah Wilson, Ohio State University
Michael Witkowski, University of Detroit-Mercy
Grace Witte, Briar Cliff College
Kevin Woods, Becker College
Alissa Worden, State University of New York at Albany
Robert Worden, State University of New York at Albany
John Wyant, Illinois Central College
Lisa Wyatt-Diaz, Nassau Community College
Bert Wyatt, University of Arkansas at Pine Bluff
Coary Young Sr., Jefferson College
Dawn Young, Bossier Parish Community College
Rosalie Young, State University of New York at Oswego
Steve Zabetakis, Hagerstown Junior College
Edward Zamarin, Catonsville Community College
Otho Zimmer Jr., Essex Community College
Glenn Zuern, State University of New York at Albany

CHAPTER 1

Criminal Justice in the United States

CHAPTER OUTLINE

Introduction

Formal and Informal Criminal Justice

Criminal Justice: Structure and Process

The Structure of Criminal Justice
The Process of Criminal Justice

The Criminal Justice "System"

Models of Criminal Justice

The Criminal Justice "Wedding Cake"
The Criminal Justice "Funnel"
The Crime Control Model
The Due Process Model
History of Crime Control and Due Process

Demographics and Criminal Justice

Crime and Punishment in New Haven: A Gender Gap?

The following cases occurred in New Haven, Connecticut, at about the same time.

Case 1

Time: February 1986 about 9:00 pm

Place: A prostitution stroll in New Haven

Facts: Kate, a white woman in her mid-thirties, waved down a man who was driving along the street. While Kate and the driver exchanged words, a second woman approached the car. Kate moved to the driver's side, opened the car door, and pulled the man out. The other woman put a knife to the man's back. Both women demanded his wallet and car keys. A police officer on patrol saw the three people and, recognizing Kate, stopped. As the officer approached, Kate told the victim she had a gun and showed it to him. Then the two women fled and the officer chased them. He was able to catch only Kate, whom he arrested.

Charge and prior record: Kate was charged with first-degree robbery. Three months later, she pled guilty to the charge. At the time, she had more than a dozen previous convictions, and had been in and out of prison since she was twenty years old.

Punishment: Sentenced to serve two years' incarceration.

Case 2

Time: February 1986, just after midnight

Place: An all-night convenience store in a poor neighborhood

Crime: Casey, a black man in his mid-twenties, entered the store and asked the clerk, a black woman in her early twenties, for an item. When she turned around, Casey hit the clerk on the back of the head with a blunt instrument, knocking her to the floor. When she came to, she saw Casey at the cash register and screamed. Casey took about $55. Another female employee heard the clerk's scream, saw the intruder, and called the police. The clerk was taken to the hospital and treated for neck and ear injuries. The second employee recognized Casey as being from the area and later identified him from a photo.

Charge and prior record: Arraigned in felony court for first-degree robbery; three months later, Casey pled guilty to first-degree robbery. He had more than a dozen previous convictions and has been in and out of prison since his late teens.

Punishment: Sentenced to serve ten years' incarceration.[1]

Both Kate and Casey were charged with identical crimes, in the same city, during the same month. Both had similar criminal histories. Yet, despite such strong surface similarities, New Haven's criminal justice system treated them differently. How do you explain these difference under a system that promises "equal justice for all"?

INTRODUCTION

Criminal justice, in the popular view, is a version of the age-old struggle between good and evil: good, law-abiding people and evil criminals. In this struggle, the police are supposed to catch the criminals, courts are supposed to try them and convict them, and corrections departments are supposed to punish them. On television and in movie theaters, these things are done most of the time. But, as Kate's and Casey's cases indicate, catching, convicting, and punishing criminals are more complex than movies and television suggest.

News accounts of criminals getting off on "technicalities" or getting off with a "slap on the wrist" frustrate and anger law-abiding people. These negative feelings are only aggravated by the perception that money, class, race, and gender—not the even-handed application of the law—determine who gets caught, who gets punished, and how much punishment they get.

This book distinguishes between criminal justice as it is portrayed by the media and as it actually is conducted in the real world. Most of the chapters concentrate on the main agencies of criminal justice—police, courts, and corrections—as they operate day to day. As students examine the parts of the criminal justice system, they can lose sight of the system as a whole: a case of not seeing the forest for the trees. This chapter introduces the idea that criminal justice is a complex system of interrelated parts—a theme that carries throughout the book. First, we examine the important difference between criminal justice "by the book" (decision making according to formal rules) and day-to-day decision making by criminal justice professionals (criminal justice in action). Next, we discuss some common models that criminologists use to describe the structure and the process of criminal justice. We will also explore the influence of race, gender, class, and other demographic variables on decision making in criminal justice. We also revisit the stories of Kate and Casey to perform a critical analysis of the difference in their sentencing.

FORMAL AND INFORMAL CRIMINAL JUSTICE

Criminal justice has two dimensions: **Formal criminal justice** is criminal justice "by the book"; **informal criminal justice** is criminal justice in action. Formal criminal justice is made up of written rules, including:

1. Provisions in the U.S. Constitution and state constitutions.
2. Statutes (written laws) created by the U.S. Congress, state legislatures, and city councils.
3. Rules of criminal justice agencies.
4. Court decisions

Formal criminal justice decision making is supposed to follow the written rules from these four sources, as the phrase "going by the book" implies. The process of formal decision making is public, and the decisions are usually published. One of the most famous examples of formal decision rule making is the case of *Miranda v. Arizona,* in which the Supreme Court created the Miranda warnings, establishing the formal rules for notifying suspects in custody of their rights. (See Chapter 6.)[2]

Informal criminal justice—criminal justice in action—consists of decision making by professional judgment based on specialized training and real-world experience; that is, based on **discretion.** Discretionary decision making lies at the heart of the day-to-day reality of criminal justice. You will notice that this book emphasizes informal criminal justice more than it does formal criminal justice. Remember, though, that *both* informal and formal decision making are important components of the reality of criminal justice. According to the distinguished scholar Donald J. Newman, criminal justice "rests on, indeed is created and enabled by . . . law."[3] (See Table 1.1.)

Newman's statement might lead us to believe that discretionary decision making is somehow not as "good" as formal decision making, but the contrary is closer to the truth. Discretion is indispensable to the operation of criminal justice, since real life is filled with exceptions to the rules. Three aspects of the real world of criminal justice complicate decision making:

1. The variety and complexity of problems faced by professionals.
2. The urgency of many problems professionals are called upon to solve.
3. The vague and often conflicting goals of criminal justice agencies.

In their daily work, criminal justice professionals face an almost endless array of individual circumstances that make decision making difficult. No neat set of written rules can tell police officers, prosecutors, judges, and corrections officers what to do to solve most of the problems they routinely encounter. Only good judgment that comes from training and experience will do. For example, should officers arrest a pregnant woman for speeding if she is rushing to the hospital to have her baby?

Furthermore, most situations that criminal justice professionals face—particularly law enforcement and corrections officers—do not allow professionals the luxury of reflection and research before they act. They have to decide what to do *right now,* because the situations they face are often emergencies or near-emergencies requiring immediate responses.

Decision making is made more difficult because the goals of criminal justice are vague and rarely defined, and those that are defined are not defined clearly. Also, criminal justice agencies have multiple goals that often conflict. The police are told to enforce the law, maintain order, and serve the public. Officers are expected to decide "right now," often with little or no guidance, what exactly these broad goals mean and what to do about them. Prosecutors, too, strive to

Table 1.1
Formal and Informal Decision Making

FORMAL RULES	INFORMAL DISCRETION
Constitutional Provisions 1. United States Constitution and Bill of Rights 2. State constitutions and bill of rights **Statutes** 1. United States Code 2. State codes **Court Decisions** Decisions of courts interpreting constitutional provisions and statutes **Rules of Procedure** 1. Federal Rules of Criminal Procedure 2. State rules of criminal procedure **Department and Agency Rules and Regulations** 1. Federal law enforcement agency rules 2. U.S. Attorney General rules 3. Federal Bureau of Prisons rules and regulations 4. State and local police departments rules and regulations 5. County and district attorneys rules and regulations 6. State and local prison and jail rules and regulations	**Police** 1. Do nothing 2. Investigate crime 3. Report and record crime 4. Arrest criminal suspect 5. Search criminal suspect 6. Interrogate criminal suspect 7. Release criminal suspect 8. Verbally warn criminal suspect 9. Use force against individuals 10. Intervene to maintain the peace by giving orders to people to "break it up," "move on," or "keep it quiet" 11. Provide service to people by recommending other social services, helping lost persons find their way, helping parents find their children **Prosecutor** 1. Take no action 2. Divert case or person to another agency 3. Charge suspect with a criminal offense 4. Recommend bail or detention 5. Negotiate a guilty plea 6. Go to jail 7. Recommend harsh or lenient sentence **Judge** 1. Bail 2. Pretrial detention 3. Accept negotiated plea 4. Reject negotiated plea 5. Suspend sentence 6. Sentence to probation 7. Minimum sentence 8. Maximum sentence **Probation Department** 1. Little or no supervision 2. Minimum supervision 3. Medium supervision 4. Maximum supervision 5. Report probation violations 6. Take little or no action regarding revocation of probation **Prisons** 1. Place minimum restrictions on prisoner liberty and privacy 2. Place medium restrictions on prisoner liberty and privacy 3. Place maximum restrictions on prisoner liberty and privacy 4. Issue disciplinary reports 5. Take disciplinary actions 6. Release prisoners **Parole Board** 1. Grant parole 2. Deny parole **Parole Department** 1. Little or no supervision 2. Minimum supervision 3. Medium supervision 4. Maximum supervision 5. Report probation violations 6. Take little or no action regarding revocation of probation

achieve multiple and conflicting goals. Formally, they are told to "do justice." However, they also pursue informal goals. They want to win cases, crack down on specific crimes, improve efficiency, save money, and divert cases from the criminal justice system. Judges have to decide the fates of defendants in the face of the conflicting goals of punishment and reform of convicted defendants. Probation officers are expected to provide both law enforcement and counseling. Corrections officers are supposed to maintain order and prevent escapes, discipline prisoners, and turn prisoners into people who can return to society ready and willing to work hard and play by the rules.

In addition to the need for immediate action and the vague and conflicting goals of criminal justice, a host of other factors add to the complexity and difficulty of decision making in criminal justice. Politics, budgetary constraints, social structure and processes, shifting ideology, and the professional ambitions and even personal needs of criminal justice professionals shape discretionary decision making. Many of the remaining chapters discuss in depth decision making in police departments, courts, and corrections agencies. For now, it is enough to remember this simple but essential truth about criminal justice as a whole: There are no simple solutions to the myriad of problems that criminal justice professionals are called upon to deal with "on the spot."[4]

Knowledge and Understanding CHECK

1. Why is formal criminal justice called criminal justice by the book and informal criminal justice called criminal justice in action?
2. List the characteristics of formal criminal justice in one column and the characteristics of informal criminal justice in a second column. Explain the differences.
3. Identify and briefly explain three reasons for the complexity and difficulty of criminal justice decision making.
4. Why is discretionary decision making indispensable?

CRIMINAL JUSTICE: STRUCTURE AND PROCESS

Criminal justice is both a structure and a process. The structure consists of a group of criminal justice agencies; the process consists of the decision makers in those agencies, the decisions they make, the factors that influence their decisions, and the effects of their decisions. The decision makers include law enforcement officers, prosecutors, judges, court professionals who are not lawyers, and corrections professionals. The process also includes the people whom the decisions directly affect, namely suspects, defendants, convicted offenders, and victims. See Figure 1.1 and the inside front cover for a graphic depiction of the criminal structure and process.[5]

The Structure of Criminal Justice

The criminal justice system consists of three types of government agencies:

1. *Law Enforcement:* municipal police departments and county sheriff's offices.
2. *Courts:* district lower criminal and trial courts and state courts of appeals.
3. *Corrections:* county and sometimes municipal jails, and state prisons.[6]

Law enforcement, courts, and corrections agencies exist at all three levels of government in the United States: local, state, and federal.

State and Local Agencies

The principal state and local criminal justice agencies include:

- *Law Enforcement:* municipal police departments and county sheriff's offices.
- *Courts:* lower criminal courts, criminal trial courts, state courts of appeal, and probation offices.
- *Corrections:* county and sometimes municipal jails, state prisons, and community corrections agencies.

Local agencies employ 60 percent of all criminal justice employees, most of them law enforcement officers.

Keep in mind that although state legislatures and city and town councils are not criminal justice agencies, legislatures create the vast bulk of criminal laws—murder, rape, and all other serious crimes. City and town councils also produce a large volume of criminal law, usually connected to or even duplicating state laws against minor offenses such as loitering, disorderly conduct, public drunkenness, and prostitution.

Federal Agencies

Although overshadowed by local agencies, federal criminal justice has grown steadily since the 1960s, and has shown especially strong growth during the 1980s and 1990s. This growth is due mainly to the creation of many new federal drug, gun, and violent crime laws.

The principal federal law enforcement agencies are:

- Federal Bureau of Investigation (FBI)
- Drug Enforcement Agency (DEA)
- Bureau of Alcohol, Tobacco, and Firearms (ATF)

The federal court system consists of the following:

- U.S. Attorney's offices: the federal prosecutors.

Figure 1.1
Decision Points and Decisions in Criminal Justice

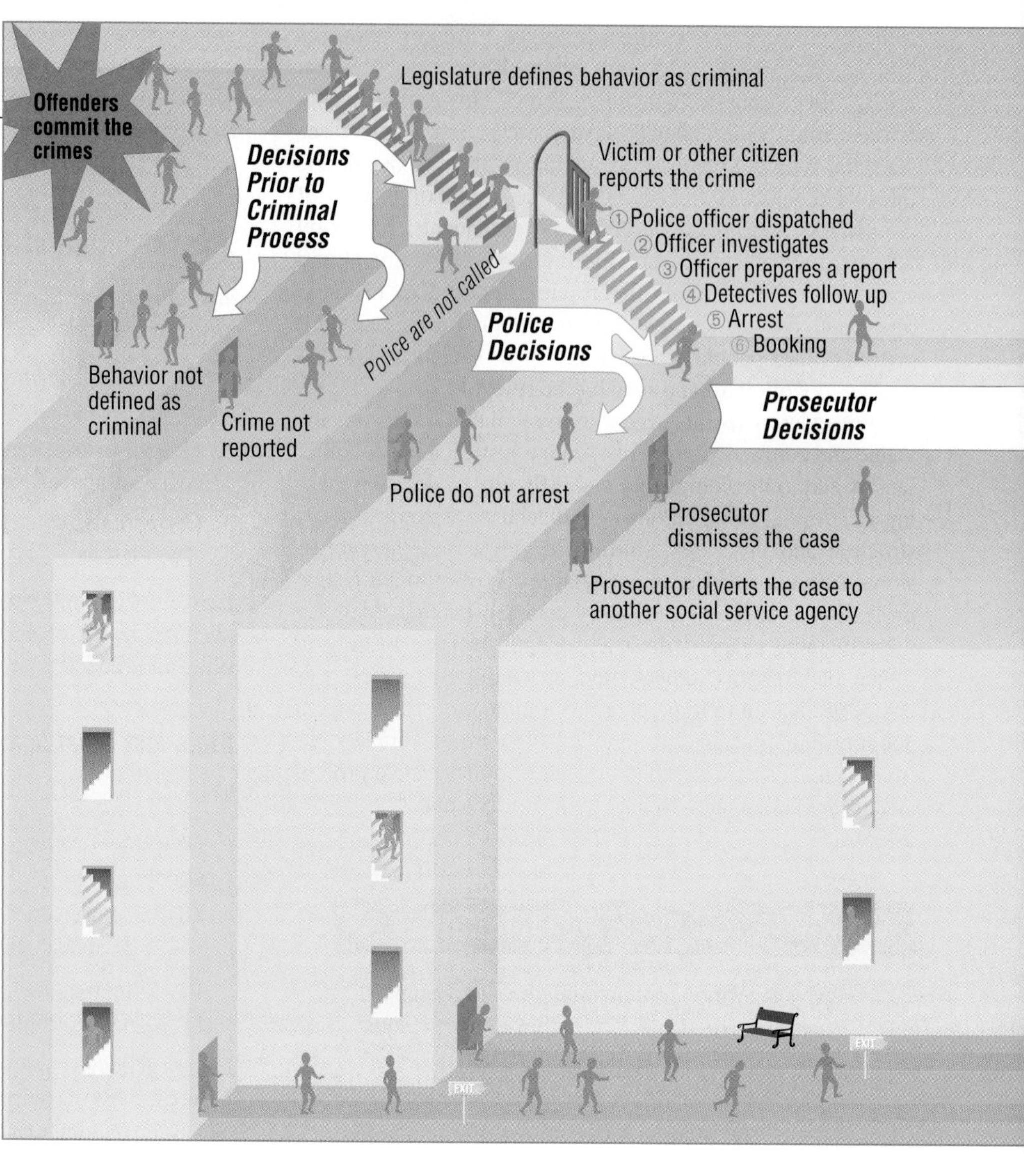

- U.S. marshals: the federal law enforcement officers responsible for transporting and supervising federal suspects and defendants.
- U.S. magistrates: judicial officers who issue warrants and conduct pretrial proceedings.
- United States District Courts: the federal criminal trial courts.
- U.S. Courts of Appeals: the federal intermediate courts of appeals, hear appeals both from federal district courts and often from state courts involving constitutional questions.
- U.S. Supreme Court: the nation's court of last resort.

The chief components of the federal correctional system are:

- U.S. Probation Office
- Federal Bureau of Prisons.

Both of these offices are responsible for persons convicted of federal offenses. As its name indicates, the Probation Office administers probation through its offices nationwide. The Bureau of Prisons administers the network of federal prisons throughout the United States.

The Process of Criminal Justice

Criminal justice is not only a structure but also a process—the process of decision making that takes place in all of the criminal justice agencies. This book examines decision

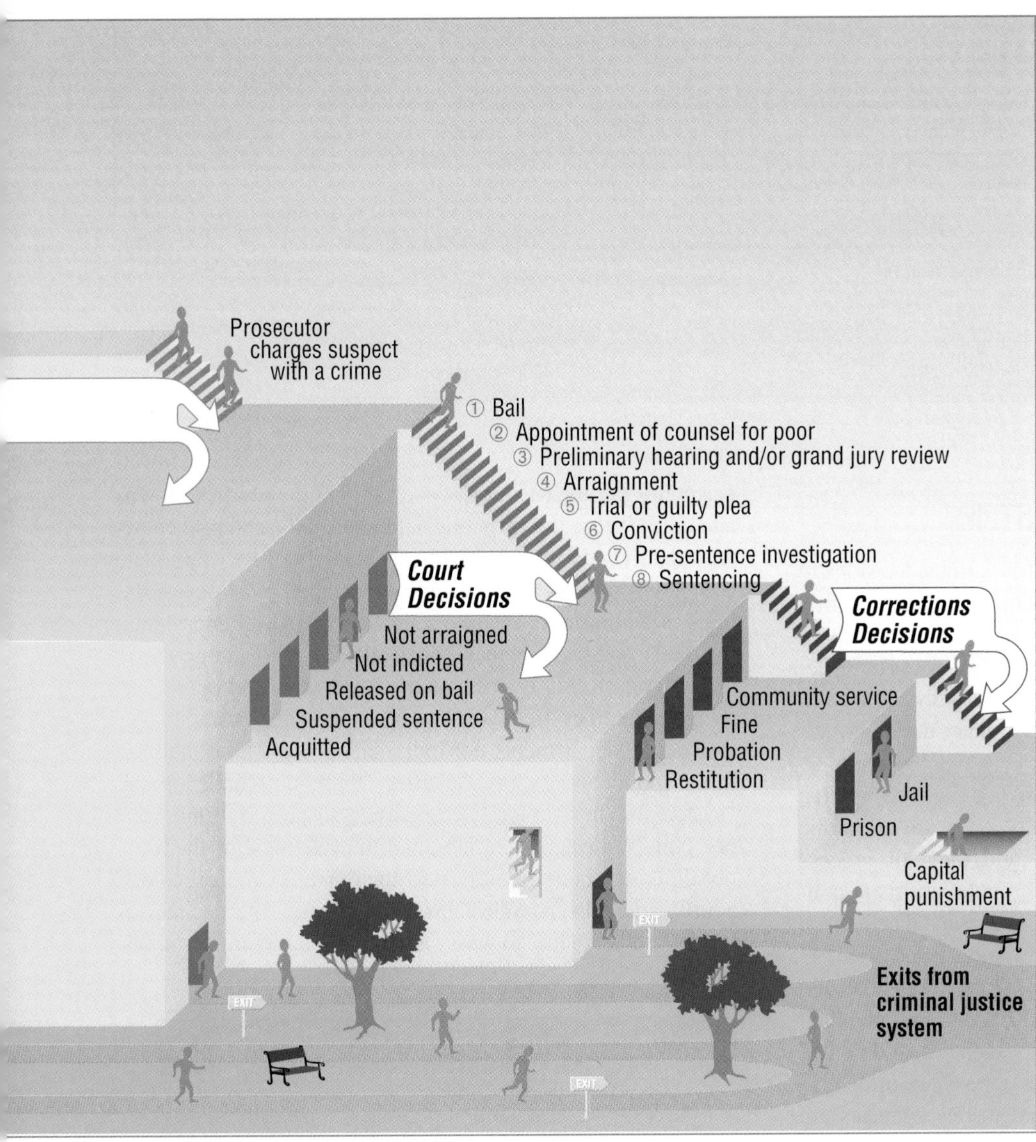

making at the major stages in the process. Law enforcement begins the process with decisions to investigate a crime and apprehend suspects. Prosecutors initiate the next stage by making the decision to charge suspects. At the following stage, prosecutors, defense counsel, and judges make decisions about the bail, disposition (trial or plea of guilty), and sentencing of offenders in court. The last stages involve decisions about the punishment, release, and community supervision of offenders released from state custody.

All of these decisions come down to deciding whether to move people further into the system, and when and under what conditions to remove them from it. Table 1.2 lists the major decision making stages through the criminal justice system and the agents who make them.

Knowledge and Understanding CHECK

1. Explain why criminal justice is both a structure and a process.
2. Identify and briefly describe the stages of decision making in criminal justice.
3. Who is responsible for each of these decision making stages?
4. What levels of government make up the structure of criminal justice?
5. List the three principal types of criminal justice agencies.
6. Identify the major functions of the three types of criminal justice agencies.

Table 1.2
Decision Making Stages and Agents

STEP	AGENT RESPONSIBLE
Detecting and investigating crime	Law enforcement agencies
Apprehending and arresting criminal suspects	Law enforcement agencies
Charging suspects with crimes	Prosecutors' offices
Detaining or bailing criminal defendants	Courts
Determining guilt	Courts and juries with participation by prosecutors and defense counsel
Sentencing	Trial judges and where appropriate sentencing commissions
Reviewing trial court decisions	Courts of appeals
Punishment	Corrections agencies
Release	Corrections agencies

THE CRIMINAL JUSTICE "SYSTEM"

Table 1.2 attributes the responsibility for various decisions to distinct individuals and agencies. But in fact, as this section will show, there is a great deal of interplay and interdependence among criminal justice agencies and agents. The structure and processes of criminal justice are usually referred to as the **criminal justice system.** The dictionary defines a system as a collection of parts that make up a whole. In important respects, the parts of criminal justice—police, courts, and corrections—do make up a whole: They are all public agencies engaged in crime control, and they all process people who have come in contact with public efforts to control crime—as suspects, defendants, and convicted offenders. Like most processes, decisions in criminal justice result in "products" at the various stages. The first product is the suspect in the police station. That suspect becomes a defendant in court, then an offender in corrections agencies, and finally, when released from supervision by the state, an ex-offender.[7]

Furthermore, because the criminal justice agencies are so interdependent, the decisions of one agency unavoidably affect other agencies. Say, for example, a legislature denies discretion to sentencing judges by fixing sentences by law. These fixed sentences do not eliminate discretion but only push sentencing discretion back to prosecutors in their charging and plea bargaining decisions. Or, if corrections officials release chronic offenders early, then local law enforcement agencies exercise their considerable discretion in controlling the parolees in the communities to which they returned. According to the criminologist Lloyd E. Ohlin, criminal justice is unavoidably "a system of complex individualization of justice, adaptively balanced, not easily controlled, and certainly not inevitably improved by attempts to mandate choices, remove discretion, or impose well-meaning but simplistic panaceas on such a highly complex process." This shifting of discretion from one agency to another is called the **hydraulic effect.** It means that when you compress discretion at one point in the system it will inevitably expand somewhere else.[8]

"System" is not an altogether accurate description of criminal justice. In some important respects, criminal justice agencies are independent bodies. Different agencies derive their authority and budgets from different sources. Police departments get their authority and funding mainly from towns and cities. Prosecutors, public defenders, jails, and trial courts are mainly countywide, with separate budgets. Appellate courts and prisons are statewide and funded by state legislatures. In addition to separate sources of authority and financing, these agencies set their own policies and to a large extent do not consciously coordinate their decisions and operations with one another. In day-to-day operations, for example, neither police departments nor individual officers base their actions and decisions on the effect these will have on the "system." When police officers arrest suspected drunk drivers, child molesters, burglars, and thieves, most of them are not thinking about the impact of their arrests on prosecutors, courts, and prisons. Why? Probably because the decision is too far down the line to worry about these larger implications.

Knowledge and Understanding CHECK

1. Why is criminal justice called a system?
2. List the major stages of criminal justice, the decisions made at each stage, and the agents and/or agencies responsible for making the decisions.
3. Why is the term criminal justice system not entirely accurate?
4. Describe and explain the "hydraulic effect."

MODELS OF CRIMINAL JUSTICE

Criminologists have described the structure and process of criminal justice by means of a variety of models. These models are simplified descriptions of reality, designed to expose the essential components of a system that are otherwise obscured by detail. Four of these models are:

- The criminal justice "wedding cake."
- The criminal justice "funnel."
- The crime control model.
- The due process model.

Figure 1.2
The Criminal Justice "Wedding Cake"

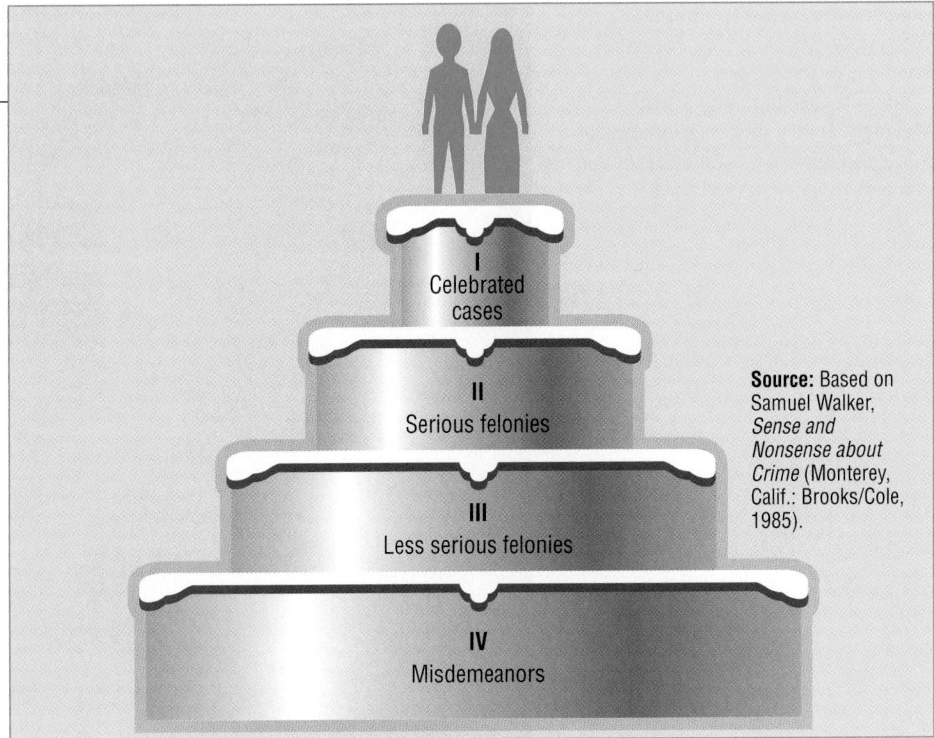

Source: Based on Samuel Walker, *Sense and Nonsense about Crime* (Monterey, Calif.: Brooks/Cole, 1985).

The wedding cake and funnel models apply only to decisions made by criminal justice officials concerning entry into and progress through the criminal justice system. Four decisions that affect criminal justice take place before anyone enters the system:

- Legislative decisions that define behavior as criminal.
- Offender decisions to commit crimes.
- Victim decisions to report crimes to the police.
- Police decisions regarding noncriminal justice matters; namely, maintaining order and performing public services.

The earliest chapters of this book focus on the decisions that take place either before the criminal justice process begins or instead of invoking the process at all. The remaining chapters focus on decisions that take place inside the criminal justice system.

The Criminal Justice "Wedding Cake"

The criminal justice "wedding cake" model was formulated by Lawrence M. Friedman and Robert V. Percival in their historical study of criminal justice in Alameda County, California. Historian Samuel Walker further elaborated on the model. The wedding cake model emphasizes that criminal justice officials informally rank criminal cases according to their perceived level of importance. Labels like "real crime," "garbage cases," and "bullshit cases" signify how criminal justice officials will deal with specific cases. Whether cases are classified as "real crimes" or "garbage" and "bullshit" depends on some or all of the following:

1. The seriousness of the charge.
2. The past criminal record of the offender.
3. The relationship of the victim to the offender.
4. Whether the victim was injured.
5. Whether the offender used a gun.

"Real crimes" get more attention at every stage of criminal justice than "garbage" cases, as we will see in detail in later chapters.[9]

A wedding cake may seem like an odd image for depicting the criminal justice process, but the idea arises more from its shape than its content: a wedding cake is usually made with several layers or tiers, narrow at the top and getting progressively wider toward the bottom (Figure 1.2). The wedding cake model of criminal justice divides cases into four types, each type represented by a tier:

1. A few "celebrated cases" in the smallest, top tier.
2. A somewhat greater number of "real crimes" in the second tier.
3. Most "ordinary felonies" in the third tier.
4. The vast number of misdemeanors in the fourth tier.

Felonies make up the top three tiers. **Felonies** are serious crimes usually punishable by more than one year of imprisonment. The "celebrated cases" in the top tier are those few that gain public attention because the crime is particularly grisly, a person involved is famous, or the case raises questions of current social concern. In the 1990s, a number of such cases stand out: Jeffrey Dahmer, convicted in Milwaukee of the cannibalistic murders of young men; William

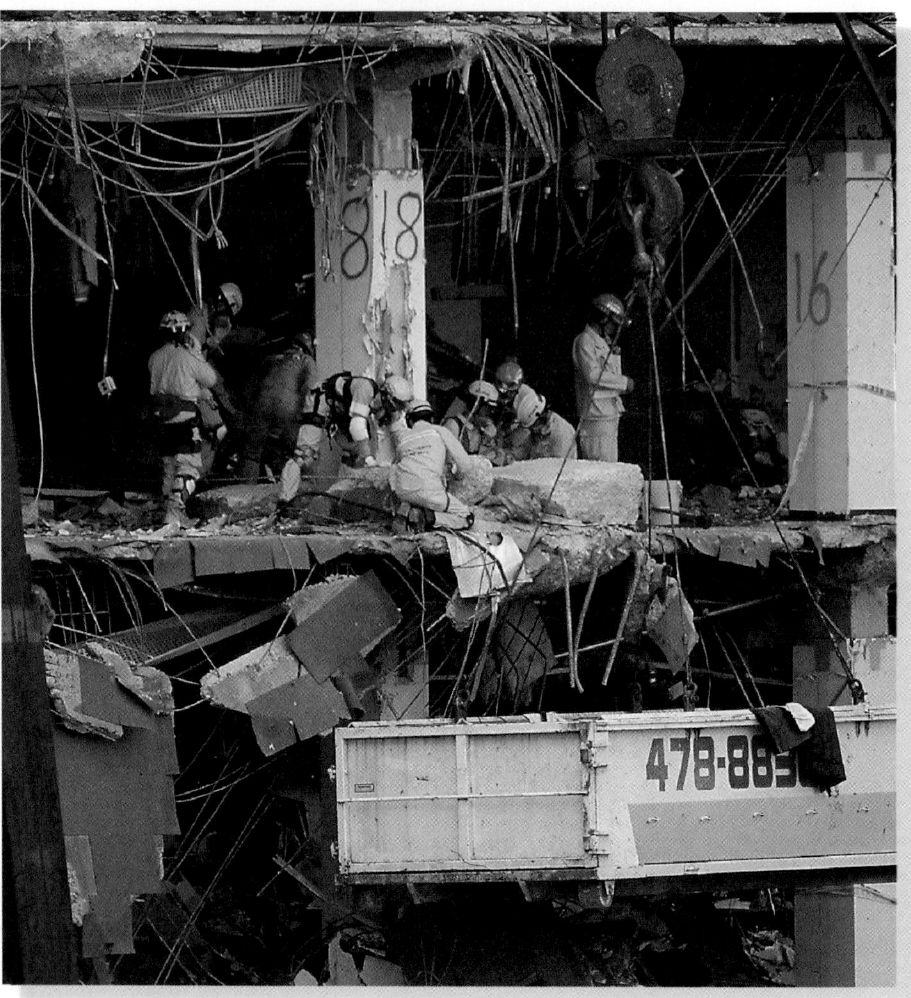

Rescue workers clean up and investigate following the terroristic bombing of the federal office building in Oklahoma by Timothy McVeigh. This is a good example of a "celebrated case" at the top of the criminal justice wedding cake.

Kennedy Smith, the socially prominent young medical student acquitted of date rape in Florida; Lorena Bobbitt, acquitted of cutting off her abusive husband's penis; Susan Smith, convicted of drowning her two young sons because her boyfriend did not want children; Timothy McVeigh, convicted of bombing the government building in Oklahoma City; Theodore Kaczinski, the serial pipe bomber; and, surely the most celebrated case of the decade, the trial and acquittal of O. J. Simpson. One more important point: The celebrated cases are also exceptional because they receive full formal processing, including a trial—the rarest event in real-life criminal justice.

The second layer consists of "real crimes"—serious felonies such as rape, aggravated assault, and armed robbery. Crimes are placed in this layer because they are committed by people who have past criminal records, are strangers to their victims, use guns to commit their crimes, and injure their victims. "Real crimes" are less likely than celebrated cases to go to full formal trial but more likely than less serious felony and misdemeanor cases.

"Ordinary felonies" make up the cases in the third layer of the wedding cake. There are more ordinary felonies than celebrated cases and real crimes. Ordinary felonies include burglaries, thefts, and robberies in which no weapons were used, no one was injured, and the victims were in some way related to the offenders. For example, some cases are, legally speaking, serious felonies, but the event is also a private dispute. Suppose Doug asks his roommate Eli for $25. When Eli gives Doug the money, Doug believes that Eli gave him the money as a gift. A few months later, Eli asks Doug for the money. When Doug refuses to pay, Eli grabs Doug's wallet and takes all the money in it, $40. "I'm taking the $25 plus the rest for interest." Police and prosecutors rarely treat this kind of case as a "real" robbery. It will probably be either diverted out of criminal justice or result in a plea of guilty to ordinary theft.

The fourth, and bottom, layer consists of the greatest number of cases. It is made up of the most common misdemeanors—simple assault, petty theft, shoplifting, and disorderly conduct. Walker labels this layer the "lower depths." Practically none of these cases go to trial; they are considered not worth the cost and effort of formal proceedings. Most are decided quickly either in preliminary proceedings in the lower criminal courts or in agreements among prosecutors, defendants, and lawyers. Many do not result in criminal charges at all; they are treated more as problems that the parties should settle themselves.[10]

The Criminal Justice "Funnel"

The shape of a funnel—wide at the top and narrow at the bottom—is the opposite of a wedding cake. But in criminal justice, both models represent the reality of day-to-day decision making. The wedding cake depicts how a few celebrated cases and serious felonies move through the whole formal criminal justice system and how the vast majority of misdemeanors are disposed of by informal discretion. The funnel emphasizes the reduction in numbers of cases at successive decision stages.

Some decisions remove people from the system either by diverting them into other agencies—such as drug and alcohol treatment or family counseling—or by releasing them outright. Other decisions send the remaining individuals on for further processing. At each stage, fewer individuals remain for sorting. Figure 1.3 depicts the funnel effect created by this sorting operation. More people are arrested than are charged with crimes; more people are charged with crimes than are convicted; more people are convicted than are sentenced to prison. Therefore, there are more suspects than defendants, more defendants than convicted offenders, and more convicted offenders than prisoners. Figure 1.4 shows a mordant socieconomic interpretation of the tunnel effect from 1912.

Until around 1950, the funnel effect—fewer cases at successive stages in the system—was called "case mortality." The term reflected the assumption that every arrest should and—barring corruption, incompetence, and softheartedness—could result in both conviction and punishment. This was a naive view, and considerable empirical research has demonstrated it to be a false assessment of criminal justice.

One main reason for **case attrition**—the reduction in the number of cases during the course between the reporting of crimes and conviction—is the law itself. According to the Constitution, the government has to back up every invasion and deprivation of the liberty, privacy, and property of individuals with sufficient facts. The greater the invasion and deprivation, the more facts are required to back it up. A brief stop on the street by a police officer requires only a few facts; a full-blown arrest requires more than a few facts to support it. Charging a suspect with a crime requires more facts than are required to stop and arrest. Conviction for a crime requires the greatest number of facts—proof beyond a reasonable doubt.

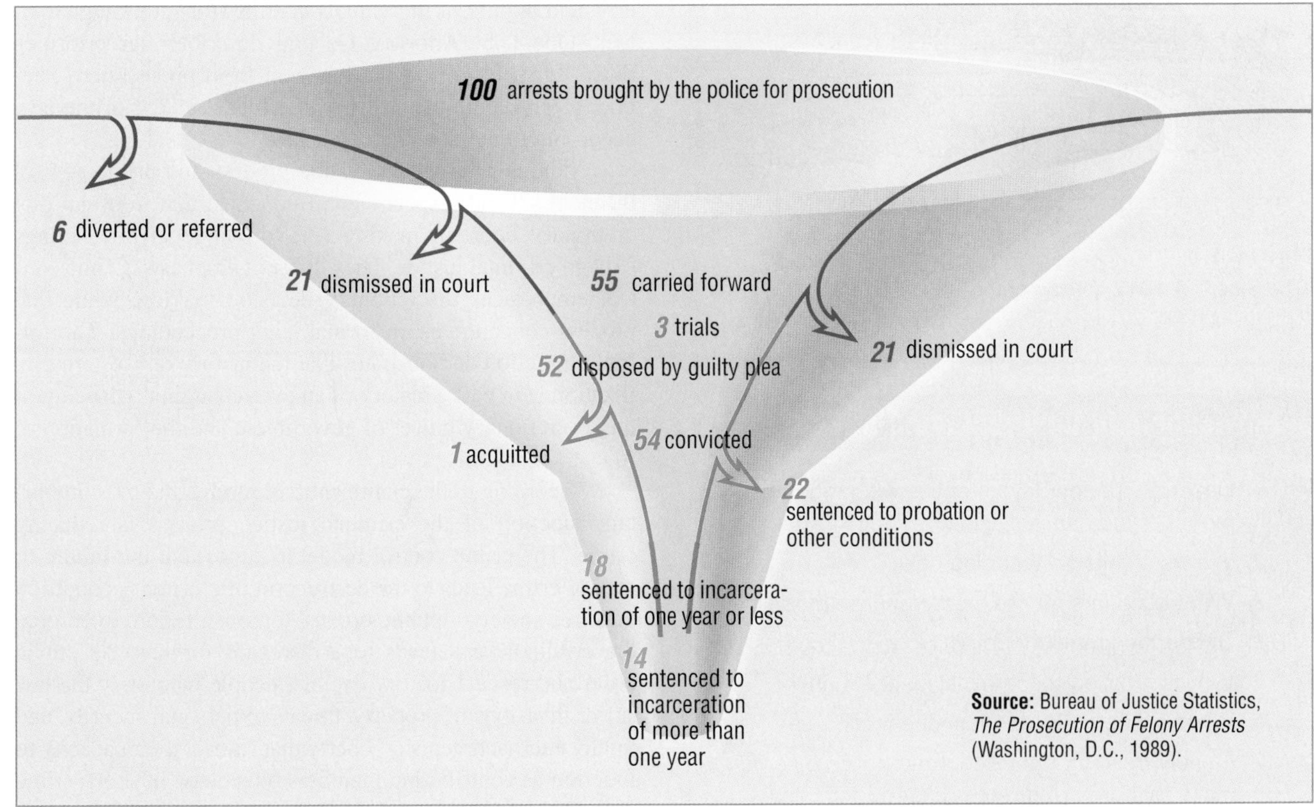

Figure 1.3
The Criminal Justice Funnel

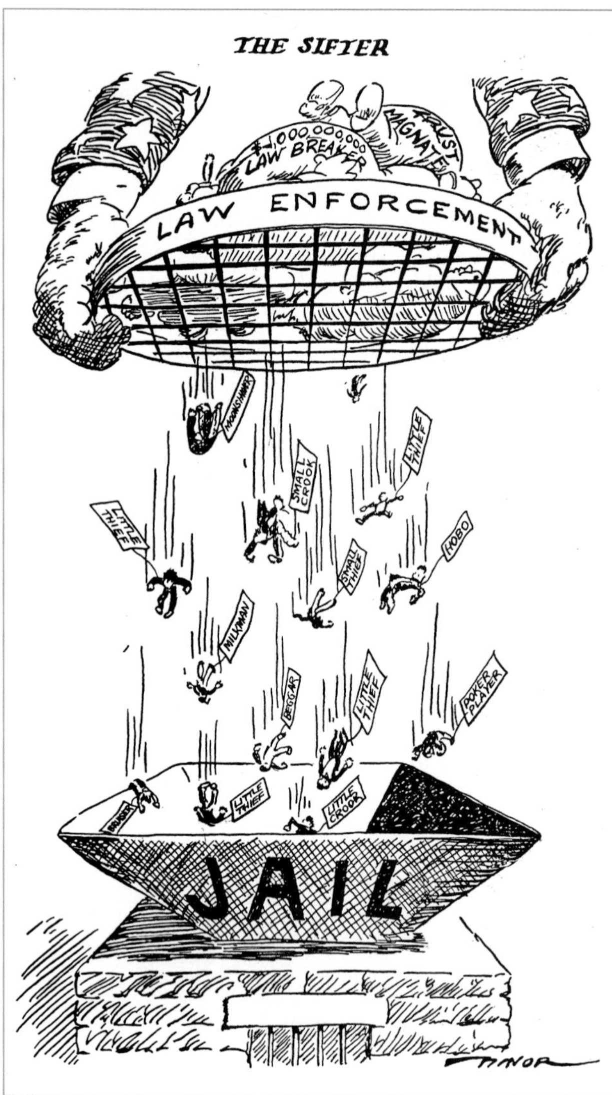

Figure 1.4
"The Sifter": A 1912 Version of the "Tunnel Effect"

Knowledge and Understanding CHECK

1. Describe the four layers of the wedding cake model of the criminal justice system.
2. Why is it called a wedding cake?
3. What accounts for the wedding cake model?
4. Define the funnel model.
5. Why is it called the criminal justice funnel?
6. What accounts for the funnel effect?
7. Identify the important decisions police officers make that are not directly related to criminal justice.
8. Identify three major decision makers whose decisions affect criminal justice.
9. When are these decisions made?

The Crime Control Model

Two basic and competing values lie at the heart of decision making in the criminal justice system: crime control and due process. In an influential article, "Two Models of the Criminal Process," Professor Herbert Packer of Stanford University explained how these values shape both the theory and practice of criminal justice. According to the value of crime control, the primary function of the criminal justice system is to reduce crime. The value of due process places a premium on the fairness of the procedures adopted to control crime. The tension between these two values is perhaps the single most pervasive influence on the way that Americans think about criminal justice and the way that criminal justice professionals perceive their roles.[11]

Most people put the control of crime high on their list of priorities. But most people reject the idea that we should control crime no matter how high the cost in money, privacy, and liberty. Most people who have lived through or have studied twentieth-century history know full well how dictators of police states can define crime as anything they oppose and then invoke the power of the state to enforce their will. They have the power to take property, invade homes, destroy human dignity, and snuff out life itself.

In the United States, how we define and respond to crime must remain consistent with the values of our constitutional, representative democracy. These values mandate that crime control practices respect the property, privacy, liberty, and dignity of individuals that the Constitution guarantees. One U.S. Attorney General describes her priorities thus: "First, to protect the innocent from prosecution. Second, to prosecute the guilty to the fullest extent of the law, according to the due process of law."[12]

Although the values of due process and crime control differ in several respects, both recognize that informal discretionary decision making and formal legal proceedings exist in criminal justice. They differ in emphasis. Crime control emphasizes discretionary decision making, while due process concentrates on formal legal proceedings. The following section demonstrates that the history of Western civilization is in part a history of an ever-changing balancing of the discretionary power of government and the formation of rules to check this power.[13]

According to the **crime control model,** the most important function of the criminal justice process is reducing crime. The crime control model assumes that the failure to reduce crime leads to the destruction of a primary condition of a free society—public order. Moreover, failure to enforce the criminal laws leads to a disregard for law. As public order and respect for law decline, people who obey the law suffer invasions of property, threats to personal security, and finally encroachments on liberty that restrict their capacity to function as contributing members of society. In short, crime control guarantees social freedom by protecting the security of people and their property. To fulfill this high purpose, the crime control model requires that the criminal justice process operate efficiently and quickly to screen suspects, determine guilt, and punish offenders.[14]

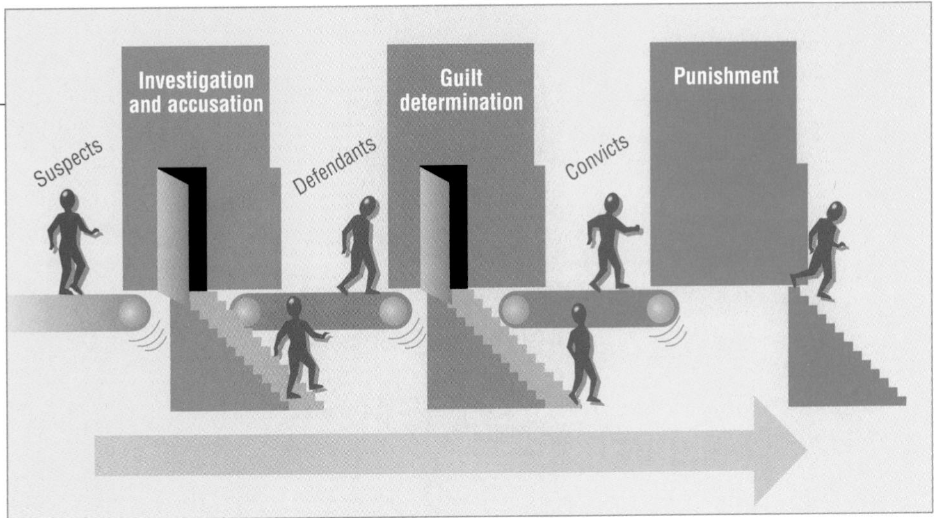

Figure 1.5
The Crime Control Conveyor Belt

Crime control puts a premium on speed and finality. With vast numbers of offenders and limited resources to process them, the value of crime control requires high apprehension and conviction rates. Informality is speedier and finality benefits from a minimum of challenges. Hence, in Professor Packer's words, "the process must not be cluttered up with [the] ceremonious rituals" of a formal legal contest. For example, the crime control model favors police interrogation because it uncovers facts faster than examination and cross-examination in formal trial proceedings. Informality, however, is not enough; the model also demands uniformity. It requires routine operations to process high numbers. According to Packer, the crime control model operates like

> an assembly line conveyer belt down which moves an endless array of cases, never stopping, carrying the cases to workers who stand at fixed stations and who perform on each case as it comes by the same small but essential operation that brings it one step closer to being a finished product, or, to exchange the metaphor, a closed file.[15]

According to the crime control model, therefore, criminal justice is a screening process that moves cases by routinized operations to successful conclusions: removing the innocent at the earliest possible stage and quickly convicting the guilty, with minimal opportunity for challenge. The crime control model includes a belief in the informal determination of guilt. The informal fact finding by law enforcement and prosecutors assures both the release of the innocent and the conviction of the guilty without unnecessary interference by formal legal proceedings. (See Figure 1.5.)

The crime control model operates according to a **presumption of guilt;** that is, those who remain in the criminal process are considered probably guilty. As we shall see in the discussion of the due process model, the presumption of guilt is not the opposite of the presumption of innocence—the idea that "you are innocent until proved guilty." The presumption of guilt is in effect a prediction that the person held is *probably* guilty.

The presumption of guilt leads to the belief that the criminal process should place few restraints on police and prosecutors. The courts should not "handcuff" the police in their efforts to get at the truth by throwing up too many formal barriers to apprehending, searching, and interrogating suspects. The crime control model puts most emphasis on the early stages in the process; namely, the role of the police and prosecutor. It places less emphasis on proceedings in court; in fact, these should be as short and simple as possible. In place of all the technical, time-consuming, expensive pretrial and trial proceedings, the crime control model favors the guilty plea.

Knowledge and Understanding CHECK

1. What major goals does the crime control model promote?
2. Identify and explain the model's major characteristics.
3. Why is the crime control model like a conveyer belt?

The Due Process Model

The **due process model** resembles an obstacle course rather than the assembly line of the crime control model. According to the due process model, each step in the criminal process should present as many impediments as possible to further involvement of the accused. These impediments are the formal procedural rules. Whereas the crime control model describes the day-to-day operation of criminal justice, due process describes the formal structure of the law. The due process model does not oppose crime control, but it does stress the unreliability of the informal fact-finding central to the crime control model. That is, it posits that the inaccuracy

Figure 1.6
The Due Process Obstacle Course

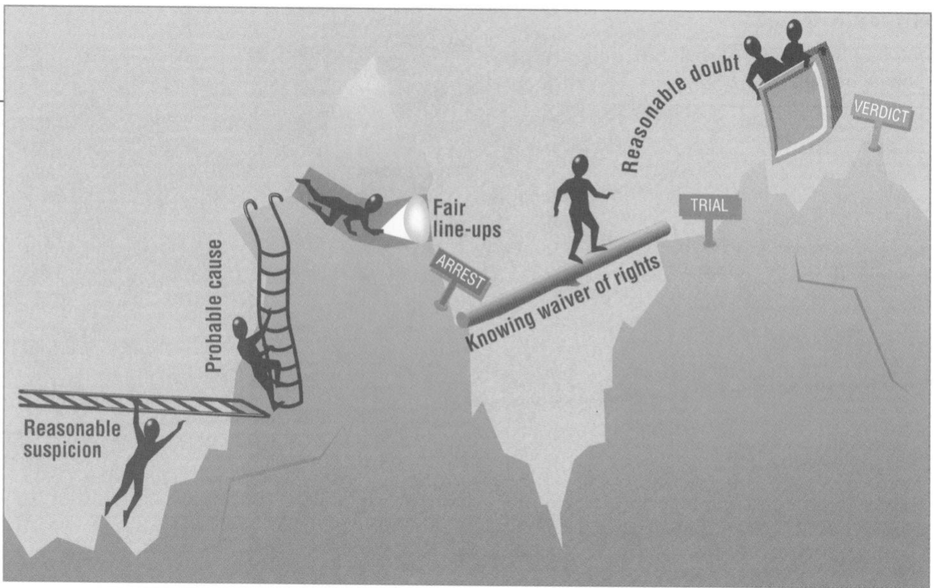

of human observation, the power of emotion, and the influence of bias all stand in the way of getting the truth informally. Formal, adversarial, public proceedings reduce the chance of mistake, for experts can examine and cross-examine witnesses before neutral judges and then submit the facts to impartial juries for the final determination of truth. (See Figure 1.6.)

The models differ in the relative value that each places on reliability and efficiency. The due process model puts the premium on reliability—obtaining the correct result by freeing the innocent and convicting the guilty. The crime control model accepts the potential for mistakes in order to achieve efficiency—quickly and economically handling large numbers of cases. (According to the model's adherents, very few mistakes occur.) The due process model rejects the emphasis on efficiency because it holds that criminal justice should aim as much to protect the innocent as to convict the guilty.

The due process model also emphasizes the primacy of individual suspects, defendants, and offenders. The stigma, loss of liberty and privacy, threats to employment, disruption of family, and general assault on personal dignity that accompany suspected criminal involvement result in the greatest possible deprivations and intrusions the government can inflict. Thus, according to the model, these deprivations and intrusions require strict formal controls at all stages, but especially in the early stages of police investigation of crime and apprehension of suspects.

According to the due process model, controlling the government requires that the criminal justice process operate according to the presumption of innocence: The process must treat all individuals as innocent until the government, following the formal rules of criminal procedure, proves guilt beyond a reasonable doubt. To punish an individual, the state must prove guilt by gathering, admitting, and presenting evidence according to the rules. A person may be guilty in *fact* but not *legally* guilty. For example, if the police seize evidence in an illegal search, the prosecutor cannot use the evidence, however reliable, to prove the guilt of the defendant. The evidence shows that the defendant committed the crime in fact; preventing its admission prevents the proof of guilt—by that evidence—at law. In such cases, juries, contrary to the many mispronouncements of journalists, do not find defendants "innocent." Their verdict says "not guilty," meaning not proven guilty according to the rules, but perhaps not innocent either. According to the due process model, the need to control the government and promote the rights of individuals outweighs the importance of obtaining the conviction of a guilty person in a specific case.

Equality is another feature of the due process model. According to the model, sociological influences (discussed later in this chapter) such as race, ethnicity, gender, age, social and economic status, or education should not determine the treatment individuals receive in the criminal justice process. Finally, whereas the crime control model favors the making of discretionary decisions by criminal justice professionals, the due process model adopts a more negative view. In the words of Professor Packer, the due process model harbors a "mood of skepticism about the morality and utility of . . . criminal" justice. Due process stresses all the imperfections possible in criminal justice—convicting the innocent; allowing racial, ethnic, and other prejudices to influence decisions; and relying on institutionalized punishment to control crime. Professor Paul Bator expresses that skepticism in stark terms: "The criminal law's notion of just condemnation and punishment is a cruel hypocrisy visited by a smug society on the psychologically and economically crippled."[16]

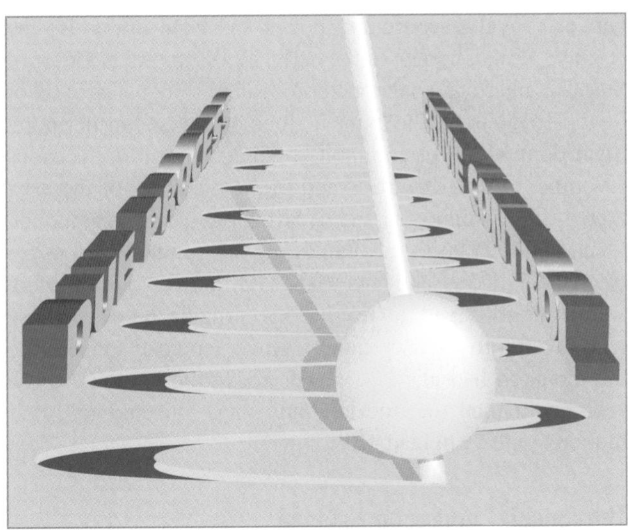

Figure 1.7
The Crime Control/Due Process Pendulum

Knowledge and Understanding CHECK

1. Describe the major goals of the due process model.
2. Describe the major characteristics of the due process model.
3. Why is the due process model called an obstacle course?

History of Crime Control and Due Process

The tension between the values of due process and crime control is not a recent phenomenon. In the broadest terms, the history of criminal justice in Western cultures reveals a pendulum swing between a commitment to crime control and a commitment to due process. (See Figure 1.7.) At one extreme is the fear of government abuse of power, which results in calls for formal control of that power. At the other extreme is the public fear of crime, leading to demands for more informal government power to eliminate it. Fear of government abuse of power has always resulted in demands for more rules and less discretion. Fear of crime has always produced calls for more discretion to enforce the law. No one has stated more eloquently the problem of crime control in a representative constitutional government than James Madison, during the debate over the Bill of Rights in 1787:

> If men were angels, no government would be necessary. If angels were to govern men, neither external nor internal controls on government would be necessary. In framing a government which is to be administered by men over men, the great difficulty lies in this: You must first enable the government to control itself. A dependence on the people is no doubt the primary control on the government; but experience has taught the necessity of auxiliary precautions.[17]

The Early History of Criminal Justice

In the ancient Roman republic, citizens enjoyed strong safeguards against government power. Despite threats of capital punishment in the criminal code, in practice the criminal law of the Roman republic "became . . . the mildest ever known in the history of mankind." Tribune Novius, victimized by a violent criminal, released him because "I will not follow the example of him with whom I find fault, and I will quash this sentence." In reaction to this mildness, during the later years of the Roman Empire, Rome went to the opposite extreme. The Emperor Hadrian boasted that merely sending a suspect to trial constituted conclusive proof of guilt.[18]

English history also reflects this shifting balance between unchecked discretionary power and the imposition of checks to it. In the period following the Norman Conquest, in 1066, the Norman kings wielded enormous power, which by 1185 the great Angevin king Henry II had consolidated and centralized. In the thirteenth century, a reaction occurred,

James Madison stressed the constitutional balance between the power of the government to control crime and the rights of the individual to privacy and liberty.

provoked by Henry II's unpopular, avaricious, and power-hungry son, John. In 1215, John's barons demanded that he accept several restraints on the royal authority. The king conceded much to the barons by signing the Magna Carta, or Great Charter, the famous antecedent to the U.S. Constitution. Among other constraints, John agreed to the restriction that "no freeman shall be taken or imprisoned . . . or in any wise destroyed, nor will we go upon him, nor will we send upon him, unless by the lawful judgment of his peers, or by the law of the land."[19]

These thirteenth-century limits on royal authority emboldened the English nobility to great lawlessness that went largely unchecked for more than two centuries. Finally, royal authority reemerged under the Tudor monarchs in the late 1400s and throughout the 1500s, especially during the reigns of Henry VII (1485–1509) and his son, Henry VIII (1509–1547). Complaints that the ordinary courts afforded criminals, rioters, and fomenters of disorder too much protection led to the creation of special royal courts known as the prerogative courts, the most famous of which was held in the Star Chamber. Unlike the period of Norman rule, however, the power of the Tudor monarchs was checked by a general commitment to the rule of law.[20]

The case, in 1575, of George Dibney, an Elizabethan gentleman, illustrates the balance between law and royal discretionary power. Queen Elizabeth suspected that Dibney had published seditious libels against Benjamin Clere, one of her supporters. She called on the local constables to go to Dibney's house in the borough of Colchester and search for the libels. When the constables arrived at his door, Dibney demanded to know what authority they had to search his house. They replied, "By the Queen's authority." Not good enough, Dibney replied, and lectured to them that according to the law they needed "probable cause" both to enter his house and to search it. The constables responded that they had probable cause. "Of what does it consist?" Dibney inquired. They answered that they were "credibly informed" that he had the libels in his house. Who credibly informed them? Dibney wanted to know. On hearing the name, Dibney scoffed that he, the constables, and everyone else knew that their informant was a "liar and a knave." Now impatient, the constables replied that they were coming in whether Dibney liked it or not. Dibney demanded to know everyone's name who was about to enter. When asked why he needed to know, Dibney replied so that when he sued them in the common-law courts he would be sure to collect damages for their illegal entry, just as he had done with the "last lot" who had illegally searched his house. Because the record ends at that point, we do not know whether the constables carried out their search or, if they did, whether Dibney sued them and collected damages. However, we do know that the Queen's suspicions were not sufficient legal grounds to allow her to send officers into a private home without probable cause to search.[21]

The resurgence of royal authority under the Tudors emboldened the Stuart monarchs in the 1600s to aggrandize their power. The Stuarts upset the precarious Tudor balance between royal discretionary power and legal limits. By the reign of King Charles, in the early 1600s, the royal Court of Star Chamber had abandoned procedural safeguards in favor of the royal power to punish troublemakers. Furthermore, royal domination of common-law judges ensured decisions favorable to royal interests and to the members of the aristocracy who supported the Stuart kings. This aggrandizement, and the abuses accompanying it, eventually led to the English Civil War, and later to the Glorious Revolution. Both were fought in part to resolve the struggle between those who favored royal discretionary power (some even claiming the monarch had absolute power above the law) and those who maintained that the law, not kings, queens, and their minions, ruled England.[22]

The Colonial American Balance

The first New England colonists came to America not only to establish their own church but also to escape the harsh Stuart criminal law and its arbitrary administration. They established the Massachusetts Body of Liberties, which reduced the number of capital offenses and guaranteed defendants several procedural safeguards. John Winthrop, the leading founder of the Massachusetts Bay Colony, devoted a major part of his life to working out the proper balance between the power of the government to enforce the criminal law and the rights of those charged with committing crimes.[23]

One of the most heated debates in the colony's earliest days was over criminal sentences. All agreed that the law alone conferred the power to punish. Some, however, maintained that the law must prescribe specific penalties, known as fixed or determinate penalties, for every offense, thereby eliminating judicial discretion in sentencing. Otherwise, these proponents of determinate sentencing argued, judges would abuse their authority. Others, Winthrop included, contended that discretion must always temper law in order to provide justice in individual cases. A "reproof entereth more into a wise man than 100 stripes into a fool," Winthrop wrote. The supporters of fixed penalties won the day, but the tension between law and discretion did not vanish; it still surfaces periodically, just as does the debate over determinate sentences.[24]

The Influence of the American Revolution

The American Revolution, fought in part over the American colonists' perception of George III's tyranny, led to the creation of a government of checks and balances, separation of powers, and constitutionally prescribed limits on government's power over individual citizens. All these actions bespoke a hostility to government power, expressed in Victorian historian Lord Acton's famous aphorism, "Power tends to corrupt and absolute power corrupts absolutely."

The authors of the Constitution believed that they could create in a written document a perfect balance between liberty and security, summed up in the Preamble: "insure the domestic tranquillity" *and* "secure the blessings of liberty." But many refused to trust the document unless it included specific guarantees that limited the power of the government to enforce the criminal law. These guarantees included the rights against unreasonable searches and seizures, self-incrimination, and cruel and unusual punishment, and the guarantees of the right to jury trial, to confront witnesses, and to counsel (see Chapters 3, 6, 8, 9, and 14). These guarantees appeared as amendments and are among those in the Bill of Rights.

The safeguards written into the Bill of Rights and into similar bills adopted by all the states for their own constitutions established a criminal procedure with strong formal safeguards against government power. This structure existed with minimal complaints as long as a relatively homogeneous, widely scattered, mainly agrarian population dominated American society and its institutions.[25]

Industrialization, Urbanization, and Immigration

Industrialization, urbanization, and immigration fundamentally transformed American society and its institutions during the nineteenth century. An agricultural society made up of farmers and small towns was transformed into a manufacturing society made up of wage laborers from widely differing cultural heritages, crowded into cities of teeming millions and causing enormous problems of public order. Although no one at the time was aware of it, the response to the growing disorder was the creation of what would later become the modern criminal justice system. The modern bureaucratic agencies of criminal justice—police, courts, and corrections—were begun in the nineteenth century (we will discuss the particular histories in the appropriate chapters on police, courts, and corrections). The United States was not unique in these responses to industrialization, immigration, and urbanization; most of the industrial nations of Western Europe and Japan formulated a similar response to similar historic developments.[26]

By the early years of the twentieth century, many influential Americans believed that they were in the midst of an epidemic crime wave. The widespread fear of crime led to the questioning of restrictions on the power of government to establish order, and to demands that police, prosecutors, and judges crack down on crime and criminals. Some, such as Samuel Untermeyer, a prominent New York attorney, advocated the abolition of the Fourth Amendment's protection against unreasonable searches and seizures and the Fifth Amendment's guarantee against self-incrimination. Others demanded harsher punishments for even minor offenses, such as life imprisonment and even death for hardened drunkards and prostitutes. This tough stance toward criminals, demands for the use of more government power, and calls for rules to restrain the discretionary power of criminal justice officials largely prevailed from the 1920s through the 1950s, when the public feared gangsters, mobsters, and juvenile delinquents more than they feared abuse of government power.[27]

The Due Process Revolution

Then came the due process revolution of the 1960s. Prior to this time, the U.S. Supreme Court had interpreted the Bill of Rights to apply only to federal, not state and local, criminal proceedings. During the 1960s the Court expanded the rights of criminal defendants in both federal and state proceedings, and substantially equated federal and state rights of criminal suspects, defendants, and convicted offenders (Chapter 3).

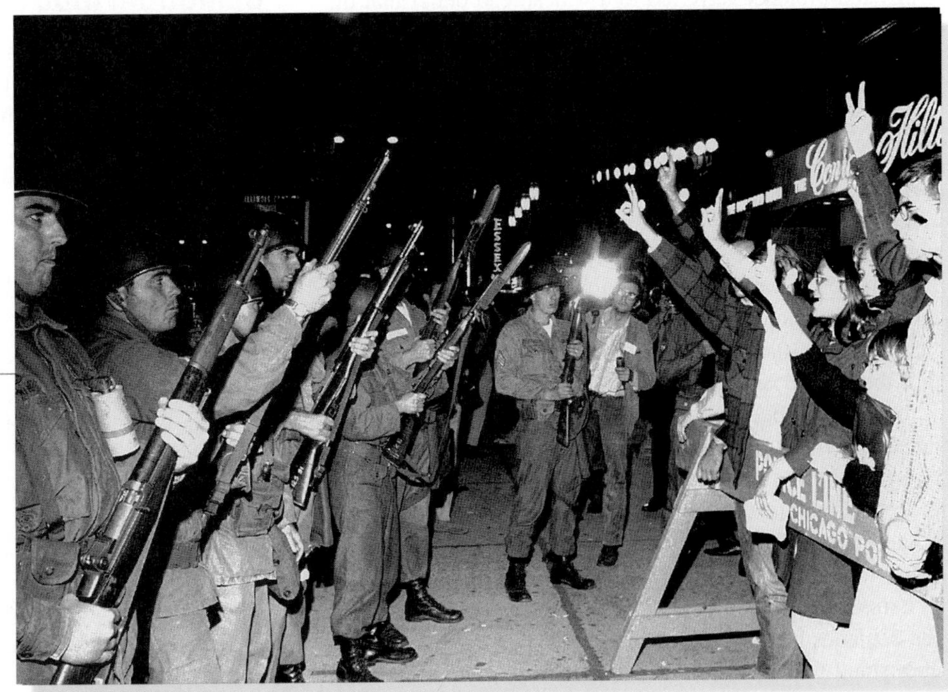

The due process revolution in the 1960s expanded the rights of criminal defendants, including the right against self-incrimination as decided by *Miranda v. Arizona*. But the '60s also saw soaring crime rates and a counterculture perceived as glorifying drug use and rioting, which may have spurred the resurgence of a commitment to crime control in later years.

The most famous example of this expansion of rights to state and local proceedings is the *Miranda v. Arizona.* In that case, the Court expanded the right against self-incrimination by requiring state and local law enforcement officers to warn suspects of their right to remain silent (Chapter 6).

During the 1960s, Americans also witnessed a series of challenges to their values, institutions, public policies, and programs. These included soaring crime rates; an increasingly militant civil rights movement; growing discord over an unpopular war in Vietnam; a highly publicized youth counterculture that supposedly glorified promiscuous sex, mind-altering drugs, and rock and roll, and attacked society's norms; and rioting in the streets and cities that left law-abiding citizens reeling. These events produced a litany of complaints about the administration of justice and prescriptions for its improvement—more power to enforce the criminal law and establish order, and harsher punishments for lawbreakers and rioters.[28]

The Return to Crime Control

One popular interpretation of the crisis in crime, law, and order in the 1960s was that a permissive society, compounded by too many safeguards for criminal defendants and too-lenient penalties had emboldened budding criminals to mock the standards of decency, hard work, and "playing by the rules." These "antisocial renegades" lived for sex, drugs, rock and roll, riot, and, eventually, for crime. The popular and political answer was to declare and fight an all-out "war on crime." The elements of this "war" consisted of more police, more punishment, and fewer rights for criminal defendants. This resurgence of a commitment to crime control continued relatively unabated through the 1980s and 1990s. There is ample demonstration that the fear of illegal drugs and violence have led to a widespread belief that the law-abiding public is still at war with crime, particularly violent crime and drugs.[29]

The pendulum swing between crime control and due process is closely connected to swings between law and discretion, as the history just outlined indicates. However, the swings between a reliance on rules and an emphasis on discretion are neither consistent nor systemwide. That is, they are not based on the broad principle that either discretion or rule is a better way to make criminal justice decisions generally. Those who called for rules instead of discretion in police decision making during the 1960s and 1970s claimed that their stand was based on a general commitment to the value of due process, such as when the U.S. Supreme Court decided *Miranda v. Arizona.* Those who called for the control of police discretion in the interest of due process also promoted judicial discretion in sentencing, to accomplish the rehabilitation of offenders.

On the other hand, not all rules support the same value systems. In periods when the value of crime control prevails, the demands for rules are mainly directed at limiting or even abolishing the discretion of prosecutors to plea bargain, of judges to decide the sentence of convicted offenders, and of corrections officials to release offenders before the end of their sentences. Those who favor the restriction of prosecutorial, judicial, and correctional discretion in the name of crime control also call for giving *more,* not less, discretion to the police to achieve the same goal. In criminal justice policy, both the means of discretion and rules can accomplish the ends of either crime control or due process.[30]

History suggests that the enduring conflict between crime control and due process will continue into the twenty-first century.

Knowledge and Understanding CHECK

1. Identify and define the values that underlie the crime control and due process models.
2. Compare and contrast the crime control and due process perspectives.
3. What decisions are made in these two models that are not made in the wedding cake and funnel models?
4. Identify and trace the developments of the major eras in the history of due process and crime control.
5. Describe specifically why the history of due process and control describes what are called pendulum swings.

DEMOGRAPHICS AND CRIMINAL JUSTICE

Criminal justice does not exist in a legal vacuum, as the pendulum swing between the emphasis on due process and crime control values demonstrates. Context plays a critical role in decision making; the historical context that we have briefly examined is an important element, but so, too, are a wide range of social, economic, political, ideological, and even personal elements. The most important of the nonlegal elements that influence decision making are the following:

- Geography: the time, place, and opportunity to commit crimes.
- Demography: the age, gender, race, ethnic origins, sexual orientation of offenders, victims, and criminal justice professionals.
- Status: the social class and the economic position of offenders, victims, and criminal justice professionals.
- Social structure: the social class of offenders, victims, and criminal justice professionals.
- Relationships: the interaction of individual offenders with family, friends, victims, associates, and criminal justice professionals.

Table 1.3
Rates of Violent Crime and Personal Theft, by Household Income, Marital Status, Region, and Location of Residence of Victims, 1997

		VICTIMIZATIONS PER 1,000 PERSONS AGE 12 OR OLDER						
		Violent crimes						
					Assault			
Characteristic of victim	Population	All*	Rape/sexual assault	Robbery	Total	Aggravated	Simple	Personal theft
Household income								
Less than $7,500	13,085,420	71.0	5.2	10.1	55.6	13.6	42.0	2.7
$7,500–$14,999	23,275,460	51.2	2.2	7.0	42.0	11.8	30.3	2.0
$15,000–$24,999	30,729,010	40.1	1.5	4.6	34.0	10.4	23.6	1.7
$25,000–$34,999	28,817,790	40.2	1.5	4.2	34.6	8.2	26.4	1.5
$35,000–$49,999	34,712,640	38.7	0.6	2.9	35.2	8.6	26.6	1.4
$50,000–$74,999	32,446,570	33.9	0.7	3.1	30.1	7.2	22.8	1.6
$75,000 or more	26,864,180	30.7	1.1	3.7	26.0	4.7	21.4	1.4
Marital status								
Never married	67,650,800	71.5	3.0	8.3	60.1	15.5	44.6	2.4
Married	113,762,150	19.0	0.3	1.7	17.0	4.2	12.8	1.0
Divorced/separated	23,451,480	62.8	2.8	7.3	52.7	13.9	38.8	2.5
Widowed	13,838,230	8.0	0.3	1.0	6.6	1.7	5.0	1.5
Region								
Northeast	41,935,440	34.6	1.2	4.1	29.3	5.5	23.8	2.4
Midwest	53,268,360	36.4	1.3	3.4	31.7	8.3	23.4	1.5
South	78,232,420	38.1	1.4	4.4	32.3	8.8	23.5	1.8
West	46,402,880	48.4	1.7	5.4	41.3	11.4	29.9	0.9
Residence								
Urban	64,609,030	51.2	2.0	7.4	41.8	12.4	29.4	2.8
Suburban	108,671,050	36.3	1.2	3.4	31.7	6.9	24.8	1.3
Rural	46,559,030	29.2	1.1	2.1	26.0	7.3	18.8	0.7

*The National Crime Victimization Survey includes as violent crime rape/sexual assault, robbery, and assault, but not murder and manslaughter.

Table 1.3 depicts how victimization varies according to sex, age, race, and Hispanic origin.

Acknowledging that these influences affect decisions in criminal justice contradicts a variety of deeply held beliefs. One is the belief in free will—the freedom to choose an action. But how can we say we have freely chosen our actions if the families who raised us, the neighborhoods in which we live, the job opportunities available to us, the education we received, and our race, ethnic origin, gender, sexual orientation, and social class to some degree determine our actions?

Another powerful belief is equality. It deeply offends our sense of fairness if we accept that race, ethnicity, gender, age, sexual orientation, class, and other influences that we cannot personally control affect official decisions such as whether we are stopped by the police, charged by prosecutors, convicted by juries, sentenced by courts, and punished by corrections authorities. Throughout this book, we examine two questions surrounding this controversy:

1. What, if any, disparities exist?
2. Are these disparities caused by discrimination, by something else, or by a combination of discrimination and something else?

Perhaps in no other area is a critical but open mind more important than on the sensitive and emotionally charged subjects of race and ethnicity. Virtually all serious scholars and nearly all empirical research have demonstrated that the percentage of racial and ethnic minorities in the criminal justice system consistently and sometimes greatly exceeds the percentage of these groups in the general population.

Some of the disparity is surely due to the bigotry of individual criminal justice professionals, but most of the evidence on the point is anecdotal. However, whether consciously discriminatory or not, disparate treatment can inflict considerable harm on those who experience it. African Americans, for example, suffer from what social welfare

Thomas Webb III shouts "Hallelujah, praise God, free at last" as he and attorney Irven Box (left) leave Cleveland County Court on Friday, May 24, 1996 in Norman, Oklahoma. Webb had spent more than thirteen years in Oklahoma's prisons after being wrongly convicted of rape. DNA tests finally excluded him as a suspect. What kinds of factors do you believe can contribute to the chances of a wrongful conviction?

scholars call **statistical discrimination;** that is, attributing to individuals the stereotypes of their group. According to Professor Michael Tonry, who has studied race and criminal justice, statistical discrimination in criminal justice means that "because young black men are members of a group in which crime is high, many people of all races react to the stereotype and unfairly judge individuals." Professor Tonry recounts the following incident:

> Early in 1993, Brian Roberts, a . . . law student in a three-piece suit, visiting a white St. Louis judge as part of a class project, was pulled over by the police soon after his rental car entered the judge's affluent neighborhood. He was then followed, the squad car leaving only after he was admitted to the judge's home.[31]

Many "privileged class" African Americans tell similar stories. Brent Staples, a member of the *New York Times* editorial board, has written of numerous instances in which he was stereotyped in college, graduate school, and afterwards. The journalist Ellis Cose, in *The Rage of a Privileged Class,* says that he was thrown out of a restaurant because the waiter mistook him for another African American who had caused trouble in the past. In *Race Matters,* the Harvard philosopher Cornel West relates that he was stopped on false charges of trafficking in cocaine while he was driving to Williams College and was stopped three times in his first ten days at Princeton "for driving too slowly in a residential neighborhood."[32]

Newark Judge Claude Coleman, a police officer turned judge, tells of how he was arrested while he was Christmas shopping in Bloomingdale's because of mistaken identity. Earlier that day, another African American had tried to use a stolen credit card. Even though Coleman bore no resemblance to the man, the police arrested him. When the officers arrived, Judge Coleman protested his innocence, asked to see his accusers, and showed identification. He was nonetheless handcuffed—tightly behind his back—and then dragged through crowds of shoppers to a police car. At the station house, he was chained to the wall and was prevented from calling a lawyer. Judge Coleman was eventually released. His response to the incident: "No matter how many achievements you have, you can't shuck the burden of being black in a white society."[33]

In addition to such individual cases, some local courts and bureaucracies are systematically discriminatory. Therefore, the general nondiscriminatory decision making that states as a whole practice does not mean much to those who meet pockets of discrimination in individual police departments, prosecutor's offices, courts, probation departments, jails, or prisons.

The weight of research on race-based discriminatory decision making in criminal justice indicates that most decisions are not based on conscious discrimination. Empirical research spanning more than 25 years, conducted by a wide range of scholars from all parts of the ideological spectrum, has repeatedly demonstrated that decisions throughout criminal justice—arrest, charge, conviction, sentence, punishment, and release from custody—are based mainly on three legitimate criteria. Listed in descending order of importance, they are:

1. The seriousness of the crime.
2. The amount of proof of guilt.
3. The past criminal record of the suspect and convicted offender.[34]

Another important point is that discriminatory decision making, when it occurs, is almost exclusively limited to minor offenses such as disorderly conduct, public drunkenness, and prostitution. The more serious the offense, the less race affects decision making. Few, however, deny that discrimination in numerous forms is a fact of life in the United States, not just in the criminal justice system. In fact, such social factors as education, job opportunities, family structure and dynamics, and class relate significantly to criminal behavior. These social factors undoubtedly influence legitimate criteria such as the seriousness of the crime and the criminal record of offenders. For example, a low-income African American teenager, denied access to a quality education and a good job, may turn to the "underground economy" of drugs in order to "get ahead." Explaining the disproportionate numbers of minorities compared to whites in the criminal justice system must still reckon with the history of discrimination, poor education, and the lack of good jobs.

Equally important, social factors—particularly education, job opportunities, families, and class—relate strongly to criminal behavior. Thus, although legitimate criteria such as seriousness of the offense, criminal history of the offender, and amount of proof probably explain most of the decision making that takes place inside the criminal justice system, nevertheless, class, family structure and dynamics, job opportunities, and education relate both to the seriousness of offenses and the criminal history of offenders.

Finally, the empirical research concerning discrimination in criminal justice deals with formal decisions—to stop and frisk, arrest, search, convict, sentence, and incarcerate. The finding that discrimination does not account for most of that decision making does not mean that criminal justice professionals are free of race, ethnic, gender, age, and class bias. William Wilbanks has surveyed most of the serious research on racism in criminal justice and has conducted some of his own. Even though he forcefully argues that a "racist criminal justice system" is a "myth," Wilbanks nonetheless concedes:

> To argue that there is no systematic bias against blacks in formal decisions does not speak to the issue of whether the police are more likely to "talk down" to black citizens or to show them less respect. The fact that a police officer may call a 40-year-old black man "boy" [however] does not necessarily mean that the officer will be more likely to arrest that man (or, if he does, that his decision is based primarily on the racist stereotype). Harassment of minorities by system personnel, less desirable work assignments, and indifference to important cultural needs could exist, but not be systematically reflected in formal criminal justice processing decisions.[35]

Knowledge and Understanding CHECK

1. Identify the five major extra-legal influences on criminal justice decision making.
2. According to most empirical research, what three factors account for most decision making in criminal justice?

CRITICAL THINKING

One major purpose of this book is to get you to think critically—that is, more deeply and carefully—about the basic concepts and the complex issues in criminal justice. To emphasize this theme, we have introduced a feature called Use Your Discretion. This feature is tied to chapter openers and to points throughout each chapter. The one that follows invites you to think critically about the empirical research on the effects of gender in criminal justice decision making. You are asked specific questions in each Use Your Discretion feature, but it is a good practice to follow these steps:

1. Identify the problem or issue to think critically about.
2. Summarize the evidence in support of the various possible conclusions regarding the issue or problem.
3. Form your conclusion.
4. Defend your answer with specifics from the Use Your Discretion feature.

Use *Your* Discretion

"Justice for all" or "Just us"?

Considerable research demonstrates that whites and blacks have very different views of the fairness of the criminal justice system. These two views of fairness are summed up by the title of this box. Most whites think that the system is fair; most blacks think that

Death penalty opponents demonstrate against the first execution of a woman in Texas since 1863. Karla Faye Tucker was convicted of murdering a Houston man with a pick axe in 1982; she was executed for this crime in 1998. The case received widespread attention, and there were many who wanted to spare Tucker the death penalty. Did Tucker's gender, appearance, and status as a born-again Christian affect public sympathy for her? Should she have been spared the execution?

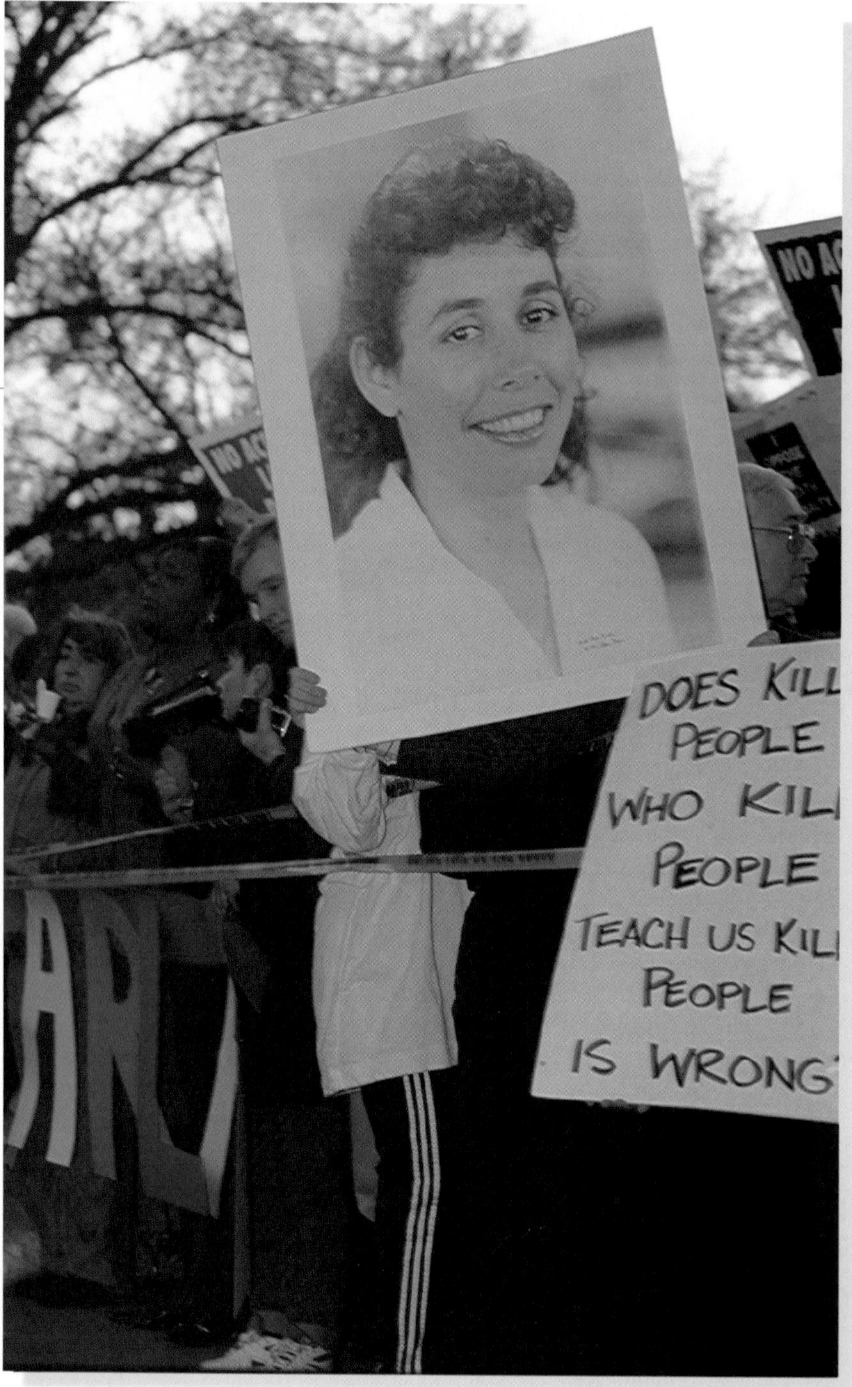

justice means "just us." Most empirical research backs up the ideal that our criminal justice system is "color blind." According to the research, it is not race (or incidentally social class, ethnicity, gender, or sexual orientation) that affects decision making in criminal justice, but, rather, in the vast majority of cases, two perfectly appropriate influences:

- The seriousness of the offense.
- The criminal record of the offender.

Professor John DiIulio, Jr. sums up the justice for all view: "The bottom line of most of the best research is that America's justice system is *not* racist. . . ."[36]

Think critically about how the following features of research on race and criminal justice can distort interpretation of the results:

- *Tunnel vision:* Examining only a part of the system and applying the findings to the entire system; for example, proving that racism plays no part in

Table 1.4
Indicators of Social Marginality

	White	Black
Arrests	4%	11%
Incarceration	<1%	1%
Nonmarriage births	22%	68%
Female head of household	14%	47%
Unemployment	6%	13%
Below poverty line	12%	33%

Source: National Urban League, *The State of Black America* (1995), reproduced in Katheryn K. Russell, *The Color of Crime* (New York: New York University Press, 1998), 30.

judges' sentencing does not prove that police officers' decisions to arrest and prosecutors and defense attorneys' plea bargaining are also not influenced by race.

- *Aggregate studies:* Lumping together the decisions of an entire police department or court system can hide the high levels of discrimination in some precincts or courtrooms.
- *Definition of disproportionality:* Most research defines disproportionality as the difference between a group's representation in the criminal justice system and its percentage of the general population. For example, blacks make up 12 percent of the general population, 30 percent of arrests, and 50 percent of prisoners. Some researchers criticize this approach on the ground that it works only if all groups are on an equal footing—which, of course, they are not. (See Table 1.4.) According to Professor Russell, "The empirical reality is that race, poverty, employment, crime, and education are interacting variables. Whether a group offends at a high or low rate typically reflects how it fares on other social indicators."
- *Formal and informal criminal justice:* Most research on disparity and discrimination focuses on the visible and recorded stages of criminal justice. These include arrest, bail, charges, sentences, and parole. Prejudice is difficult to detect in formal criminal justice, but may be more detectable in the low-visibility, unwritten, discretionary decision making of informal criminal justice. Analysis of the widespread informal criminal justice practices of police stops and frisks, prosecutors' decision to charge, and plea bargaining may yield different results from those for formal criminal justice. For example, police stops and frisks are serious invasions on the right to come and go as we please and on the right to be left alone by the government. Moreover, stops and frisks determine who the police arrest—and arrest is the gateway to the criminal justice system.

CRITICAL THINKING

1. Identify the findings reported in this box.
2. Do these findings support the view that justice in the United States means "just us" African Americans? Rely on the details included in the box to answer this question.
3. What is the significance of Table 1.4? Does it influence your opinion about racism in criminal justice? Defend your answer.
4. How can there be racism in criminal justice if most of the empirical research shows that decisions are based mainly on legitimate factors? Explain your answer.

Crime and Punishment in New Haven: A Gender Gap? Consideration

The information provided in the case excerpts presented at the beginning of the chapter came from the files available from the clerk of the court of New Haven. However, sociologist Kathleen Daly went beyond those files to find more information. Here is what she writes about the cases of Kate and Casey:

> The cases of Casey and Kate show the limits of quantification. From the information available in the files of the clerk of the court, their cases could have been coded identically for a statistical analysis. They were both accused and convicted of robbery at the same level of statutory severity; they both had a prior record of a similar level of seriousness; they were both incarcerated in the pretrial period; and both were represented by public defenders. Except for race and gender, then, the two cases would appear to be the same. Few data sets contain any more detail on an offense or offender. Upon gathering additional information on these cases, I learned that Kate's robbery differed from Casey's in the following ways: Although both victimized persons they did not know, Kate's victim was not injured; Kate's accomplice, not Kate, brandished the knife; and while Kate's story and the victim's conflict, it is likely he was looking for a prostitute and thus was not viewed as a completely innocent victim. At sentencing, for example, the prosecutor described the victim's presence in the area as "perhaps somewhat suspect." By contrast, the female victim in Casey's offense suffered both physical and psychological damage, saying that she was "afraid to go back to work. I can't go anywhere near [the] store; I get physically ill." Although Kate's previous record of convictions was substantial, almost all of them were misdemeanors and prostitution-related. Casey's record, on the other hand, was composed of more serious offenses, such as robbery and assault.[37]

Critical Thinking

1. Does the information that Professor Daly found affect your conclusion about whether there is a gender gap in criminal justice? Why?
2. If you changed your mind, what facts changed your mind?
3. What recommendations would you make concerning the use of quantitative analyses and case analyses in getting complete and accurate information?
4. Consider the following conclusions of Professor Daly's. What effect do they have on your assessment and their implications for making criminal justice policy? According to Professor Daly:

> The content and context of an offense, its perceived seriousness to victims and court officials, and the relation of a defendant's prior record to the current offense are not well captured by quantification. Indeed, the narrative detail resists capture and codification according to a uniform scheme. . . .
>
> I have conducted statistical studies . . . for more than a decade: if I am critical, it is because I know this method and its limits well. At the same time, I am critical of the ways in which journalists and legal advocates draw from selected or celebrated cases to illustrate disparity. . . . No information is provided on how the cases were selected nor on how typical they were. Instead, the method is to find the most egregious cases (or depending on one's aim, the least egregious) and to compare them. It is a deductive method whereby a conclusion is reached and then proved with selected examples. Case analyses have much to add, however; they bring depth and complexity to the meaning of crime and punishment. The problem is, then, not case analyses per se, but how particular cases are selected for analysis.[38]

After Professor Daly compared the statistical analysis with the case analysis of felony cases in New Haven, Connecticut, she concluded that the comparison suggested "two rather different stories about gender disparity in the New Haven felony court":

> With the . . . [case analysis], I was able to take note of differences in offense seriousness, prior record, and offender blameworthiness for the statutorily similar offenses in the deep

sample. In so doing, I identified just one of the forty pairs for which the disparity could not be explained. With the statistical analysis of the deep [more detail included about each case] and wide samples [basic information about each case], a greater level of gender-based disparity was evinced. My analysis leads me to conclude that traditional disparity studies may well give the misleading impression that women are favored in criminal court.[39]

CHAPTER CAPSULE

- There is a formal and an informal criminal justice.
- Formal justice consists of decisions "by the book"; informal criminal justice consists of discretionary decision making.
- Criminal justice is both a structure and a process, consisting of law enforcement, courts, and corrections agencies.
- Criminal justice is a system only in a loose sense.
- Various models describe criminal justice.
- Some decisions occur outside and before entry into the criminal justice system.
- The conflicting and competing values of crime control and due process underlie the criminal justice system.
- The history of criminal justice shows pendulum swings between the values of crime control and due process.
- Legal variables *and* nonlegal demographic variables influence decision making in criminal justice.

KEY TERMS

formal criminal justice
informal criminal justice
discretion
criminal justice system
hydraulic effect
felonies
case attrition
crime control model
presumption of guilt
due process model
statistical discrimination

INTERNET RESEARCH EXERCISES

You can use the vast resources of the Internet to learn more about topics in this textbook. Many "search engines" are available to help you start your research; some popular ones are http://www.yahoo.com, http://www.excite.com, and http://www.infoseek.com. If your textbook came packaged with access to the InfoTrac College Edition online library, you can conduct your research there.

Exercise: This chapter discussed three types of criminal justice agencies: law enforcement, courts, and corrections. Using the Internet or InfoTrac College Edition, search for information about one of these agencies. What are the agency's primary functions? What services does it provide? What issues is it currently dealing with?

Suggested sites:

- Bureau of Justice Statistics: http://www.ojp.usdoj.gov/bjs (tip: click on "law enforcement," "courts and sentencing," or "corrections")
- Federal Bureau of Investigation: http://www.fbi.gov
- New York State Commission of Corrections: http://crisny.org/government/ny/nysscoc/index.html

InfoTrac College Edition: Run a key word search on the agency you want to investigate; for example, "state courts"

Please note that web site addresses ("URLs") are always subject to change. If you find that the address above is no longer working, use a search engine and enter key words to find an alternate address for your research topic.

NOTES

1. Kathleen Daly, *Gender, Crime, and Punishment* (New Haven: Yale University Press, 1994), 1–2.
2. Samuel Walker, *Taming the System: The Control of Discretion in Criminal Justice,* 1950–1990 (New York: Oxford University Press, 1993), 18–20.
3. Lloyd E. Ohlin, "Surveying Discretion by Criminal Justice Decision Makers," and Donald J. Newman, "The American Bar Foundation Survey and the Development of Criminal Justice in Higher Education"; in Lloyd E. Ohlin and Frank J. Remington, eds., *Discretion in Criminal Justice: The Tension Between Individualization and Uniformity* (Albany: State University of New York Press, 1993), 279–349.
4. From a memo by Professor Remington quoted in Samuel Walker, "Origins of the Contemporary Criminal Justice Paradigm: The American Bar Foundation Survey, 1953–1969," *Justice Quarterly* 9 (1992): 47; Donald J. Newman, "The Development of Criminal Justice Higher Education," Lloyd E. Ohlin and Frank J. Remington, eds., *Discretion in Criminal Justice* (Albany: State University of New York Press, 1993), 279–280.
5. Keith Bottomly, *Decisions in the Penal Process* (South Hackensack, N.J.: Fred B. Rothman & Co., 1973), xiii.
6. *Report to the Nation on Crime and Justice* (Washington, D.C.: National Institute of Justice, 1983), 45.
7. Frank Remington et al., *Criminal Justice Administration* (Indianapolis: Bobbs-Merrill, 1969), 19–20.
8. Ohlin, "Surveying Discretion," 10.
9. Michael R. Gottfredson and Donald M. Gottfredson, *Decision Making in Criminal Justice: Toward the Rational Exercise of Discretion,* 2d edition (New York: Plenum Books, 1988); Lynn Mather, "Some Determinants of the Method of Case Disposition: Decision Making by Public Defenders in Los Angeles," *Law and Society Review* 8 (1974): 187–216; Cassia Spohn and Jerry Cederblom, "Race and Disparities in Sentencing: A Test of the Liberation Hypothesis," *Justice Quarterly* 8 (1991): 306.
10. Samuel Walker, *Sense and Nonsense about Crime and Drugs,* 3d edition (Belmont, Calif.: Wadsworth Publishing Company, 1994), 29–37.
11. Herbert L. Packer, "Two Models of the Criminal Process," *University of Pennsylvania Law Review* (1964), p. 113.
12. Remington et al., *Criminal Justice Administration* 3–4; Senate Confirmation Hearings for Janet Reno as Attorney General of the United States, 10 March 1993.
13. Herbert Packer, *The Limits of the Criminal Sanction* (Palo Alto: Stanford University Press, 1968), 155–57 and Chapter 8, upon which this discussion of the crime control and due process models is based.
14. Ibid., 158.
15. Ibid., 159.
16. Quoted in Packer, 170.
17. James Madison, "The Federalist No. 51," in Jacob E. Cooke, ed., *The Federalist* (Middletown, Conn.: Wesleyan University Press, 1961), 349.
18. Roscoe Pound, "The Future of the Criminal Law," *Columbia Law Review* 21 (1921): 1–16; James L. Strachen-Davidson, *Problems of the Roman Criminal Law* (Oxford: Clarendon Press, 1912), 114, 168.
19. Quoted in Theodore F. T. Plucknett, *A Concise History of the Common Law,* 5th ed. (London: Butterworth & Company, 1956), 24.
20. Geoffrey R. Elton, *England Under the Tudors,* 2d ed. (London: Methuen, 1974).
21. Joel Samaha, *Law and Order in Historical Perspective* (New York: Academic Press, 1974); for further development of how the law of criminal procedure afforded safeguards to Tudor subjects, see Joel Samaha, "Hanging for Felony: The Case of Elizabethan Colchester," *Historical Journal* (1979); and Geoffrey R. Elton, *Tudor Police and Policy* (Cambridge: Cambridge University Press, 1972).
22. Jack P. Kenyon, *The Stuart Constitution,* 2d ed. (New York: Cambridge University Press, 1986).
23. Samuel Walker, in *Popular Justice* (New York: Oxford University Press, 1980), has written about these and other themes in the history of American criminal justice.
24. Joel Samaha, "John Winthrop and the Criminal Law," *William Mitchell Law Review* 15 (1989): 217–253.
25. Pound, "Future of the Criminal Law."
26. Samuel Walker, *Popular Justice,* 2d edition (New York: Oxford University Press, 1998), 49–50.
27. American Academy of Political and Social Science, "Administration of Justice in the United States," *Annals of the American Academy of Political and Social Science* 36 (1910); Frederic C. Howe, "A Golden Rule Chief of Police," *Everybody's Magazine,* July 1910; Walker, *Popular Justice*; Craig M. Brown and Barbara D. Warner, "Immigrants, Urban Politics, and Policing in 1900," *American Sociological Review* 57 (1992): 296–305.
28. Thomas E. Cronin, Tania Cronin, and Michael Milakovich, *U.S. v. Crime in the Streets* (Bloomington: Indiana University Press, 1981); Jerome Skolnick, *Justice without Trial,* 3d edition (New York: Macmillan, 1994), 241; David Halberstam, *The Children* (New York: Random House, 1998).
29. Timothy J. Flanagan and Dennis R. Longmire, eds. *Americans View Crime and Justice* (Thousand Oaks, Calif.: Sage Publications, 1996); Elliot Currie, *Crime and Punishment in America* (New York: Metropolitan Books, 1998), 3–11.
30. The title of Walker's book is *Taming the System.*
31. Michael Tonry, *Malign Neglect: Race, Crime, and Punishment in America* (New York: Oxford University Press, 1995), 50–51.
32. Elliot Cose, *The Rage of a Privileged Class* (New York: Harper Perennial, 1995); Cornell West, *Race Matters* (New York: Vintage, 1994).
33. David Margolick, "Falsely Accused," *The New York Times,* 7 January 1994.
34. The literature on discrimination in the criminal justice system is voluminous, and we will refer to it in the chapters on crime, police, courts, and corrections. A few of the best overviews, and those on which I relied in writing this section, are: Gottfredson and Gottfredsen, *Decision Making in Criminal Justice*; Joan Petersilia, *Racial Disparities in the Criminal Justice System* (Santa Monica: Rand Corporation, 1983); William Wilbanks, *The Myth of a Racist Criminal Justice System* (Monterey: Brooks/Cole Publishing Company, 1986); and Tonry, *Malign Neglect.*
35. William Wilbanks, *The Myth of a Racist Criminal Justice System* (Monterey, Calif.: Brooks/Cole Publishing Company, 1987), 6.
36. Quoted in Katheryn K. Russell, *The Color of Crime* (New York: New York University Press, 1998), 29–30.
37. Kathleen Daly, *Gender, Crime, and Punishment* (New Haven: Yale University Press, 1994), 7.
38. Ibid.
39. Ibid., 254.

CHAPTER 2

Crime, Criminals, and Victims

CHAPTER OUTLINE

Is Fear of Robbery Racist?

> If I'm walking down a street in Center City Philadelphia at two in the morning and I hear some footsteps behind me and I turn around and there are a couple of young white dudes behind me, I am probably not going to get very uptight. I'm probably not going to have the same reaction if I turn around and there is the proverbial Black urban youth behind me. Now if I am going to have this reaction–and I'm a black male who has studied marshal arts for twenty some odd years and can defend myself–I can't help but think that the average white judge in the situation will have a reaction that is ten times more intense.[1]
>
> Comments of Judge Theodore A. McKee, an African American member of the United States Court of Appeals for the Third Circuit.

Jesse Jackson expressed similar sentiments:

> There is nothing more painful for me at this stage in my life than to walk down the street and hear footsteps and start to think about robbery and then look around and see it's somebody white and feel relieved.[2]

INTRODUCTION

Crime is a broad term that includes everything from serial murder to being drunk in public. Criminals vary from multiple rapists to one-time marijuana users. Some places have more crime than others, and some times of the day are more dangerous than others. The kinds of crimes offenders commit depend on their and their victims' gender, age, race and ethnicity, and social class. The sets of statistics that are collected and analyzed by various agencies to measure crime provide starkly different answers to how much crime there is and whether the numbers are rising or falling or holding steady.

This chapter examines the complex, tentative, and incomplete answers that research provides about the kinds, amounts, and trends of crime.

TYPES OF CRIME

A headline in the newspaper reads: "Serial Rapist Strikes Again." Local television news carries a story about a young man who was convicted of his first offense—shoplifting; a judge ordered him to walk up and down in front of the store wearing a sign that read: "I stole $5 from K-Mart." A young woman was thrown out of a bar when she became loud and obnoxious after drinking several bottles of beer. These are all crimes in the United States, because a crime is *any* behavior that breaks the law. One officer in Bloomington, Minnesota expressed his view of the extent of criminal law this way: "Welcome to Bloomington, you're under arrest." Why? "Because everything in Bloomington is a crime."

The incidents related in the last paragraph are examples of the three basic kinds of crime measured by the major criminal statistics in the United States:

1. **Violent or personal crime.** Actions that hurt or threaten to hurt people.
2. **Property crime.** Actions that take, damage, or destroy or threaten to take, damage, or destroy people's property.
3. **Other crimes.** Behavior such as disorderly conduct, public drunkenness, drug use, and prostitution.

All crimes inflict two harms—to the individual victims and to the community as a whole. For example, the serial rapist not only injures his victims but also undermines the community's sense of personal safety. Likewise, the shoplifter not only inflicts a property loss on K-Mart but also undermines the whole community's sense of the security of property. The unruly bar patron may not threaten individual victims so much as she undermines the community's sense of decency and order.

Putting particular crimes into a single one of the three basic categories is not easy. Two examples demonstrate this difficulty. Robbery—the felony of taking someone's property by force or the threat of force—is a crime against both persons and their property. Household burglary—the felony of breaking and entering someone else's house with the intent to commit a crime inside—not only invades the sanctity of the home but also creates fear for personal safety.

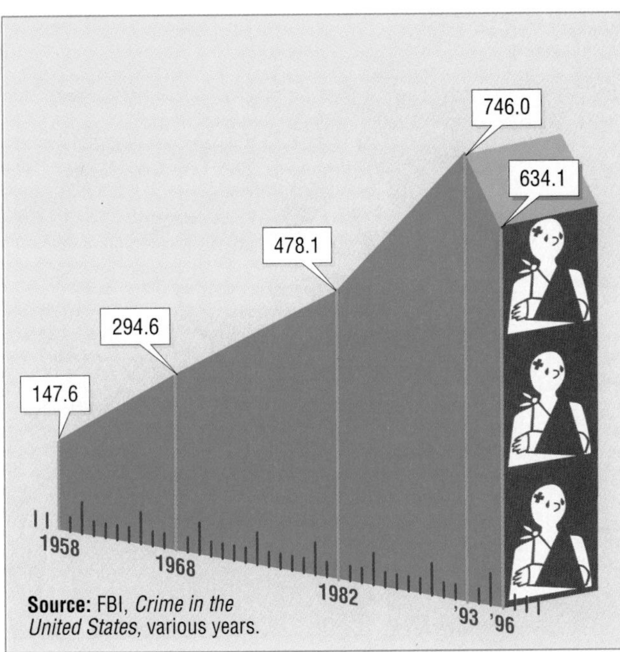

Figure 2.1
Violent Crime Rates per 100,000 People, 1958–1996

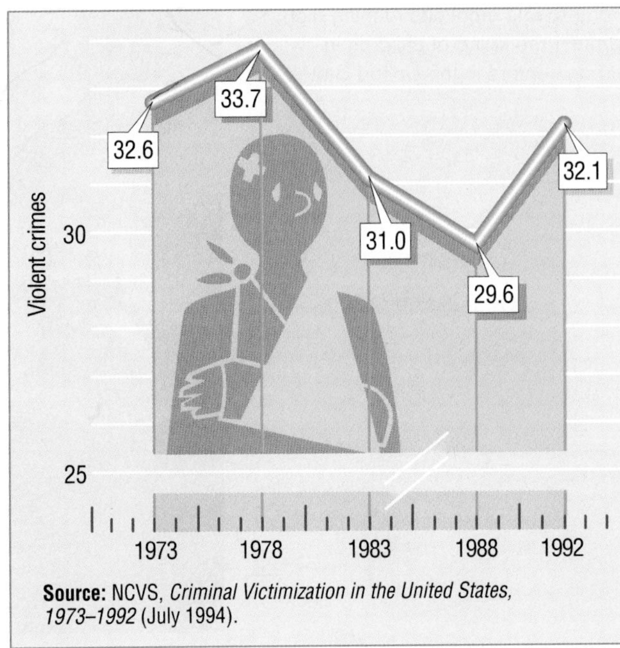

Figure 2.2
Violent Crime Trends NCVS per 1,000 Households

CRIME TRENDS

From the early 1970s to the early 1990s, the nation's two major collections of crime statistics—crimes known to the police and victim surveys—pointed in different directions. The FBI's Uniform Crime Reports (UCR), which report crimes known to the police, pointed to a steady increase in both the number and rates of crimes (Figure 2.1). In contrast, the Bureau of Justice Statistics' National Crime Victims Survey (NCVS) pointed to a relatively steady amount of crime reported by victims in its surveys (Figure 2.2).

What are we to make of these conflicting trends? The NCVS probably measures actual crime more accurately because it measures not only crimes that victims report to the police but also crimes that they do not report. UCR measures only crimes that local law enforcement agencies know about, record, and report to the FBI. The rise shown by UCR probably represents higher reporting and recording rates more than higher actual crime rates. In other words, the number of crimes reported by victims to interviewers for BJS has remained fairly steady, while the number of crimes entering the criminal justice system has increased markedly.[3]

In the mid-1990s, the statistical picture changed. UCR and NCVS statistics began to point in the same direction: both violent and property crimes were declining. Some experts argued that the change was dramatic, others maintained that it was insignificant, if not wholly nonexistent. Some said that it was evidence of a long-term trend and others said that it was only a temporary and brief drop in the trends depicted in UCR and NCVS of the past 25 years.

Use *Your* Discretion

Did the crime rates really drop?

At a meeting of criminologists and policy makers in the fall of 1995, New York City Police Commissioner William Bratton showed obvious pleasure when he announced that current crime statistics reflected a dramatic drop in crime rates in New York City (the so-called "crime capital of the world"). Some criminologists at the meeting agreed that the reductions were significant, if not dramatic. Others went further; Professor Jeffrey Fagan, director of the Center for Violence Research and Prevention at Columbia University, enthusiastically declared, "I'm flabbergasted. That's a very dramatic drop." Because both UCR and NCVS showed steady and sizable declines, "we can now have more confidence that we are in the midst of a trend, not simply a short-term or random fluctuation."[4]

Other criminologists were doubtful about the significance of the declines. James Allan Fox, dean of the College of Criminal Justice at Northeastern University, in Boston, urged that the figures suggesting a decrease in rape be treated cautiously because the number of rapes reported in the sample declined from 153 in 1995 to 94 in 1996. Although every rape is terrible, that number must be considered in relation to more than 280,000,000 people in the United States. "There really is a concern when we translate that small

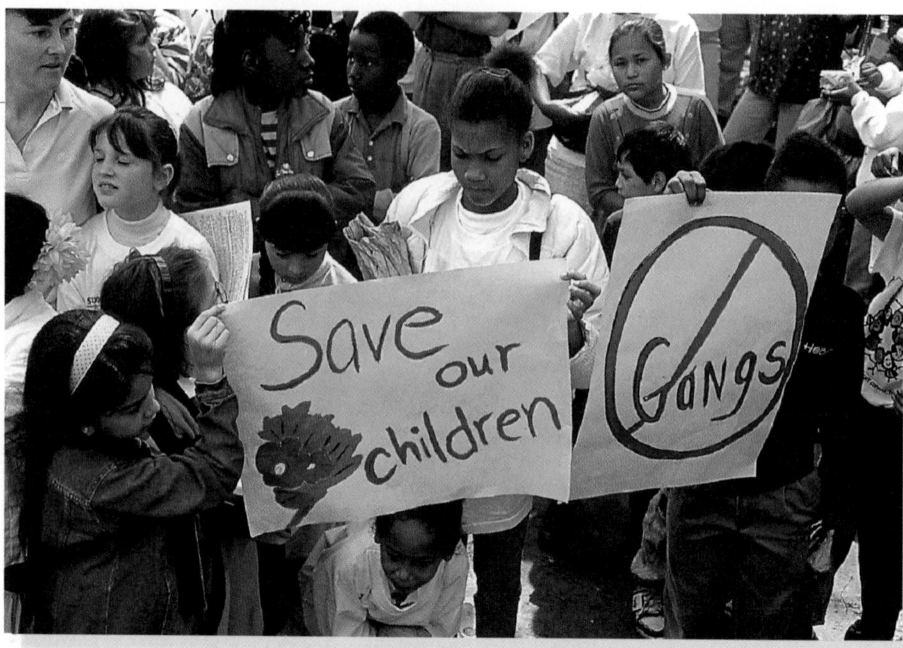

Youths, with emotions running high, protest the killing of children in urban centers in the United States.

sample into a national estimate." Dean Fox also questioned the true significance of the declines because, in all categories of crime, the declines were mainly in the less serious crimes. For example, the decline in simple assault, the least serious violent crime, was responsible for much of the decline in violent crime. Declines in thefts of less than $50, the least serious property offense, were responsible for most of the decline in property offenses. Dean Fox concluded, "It's good news that crime is down, but the numbers are not necessarily as good as you think."[5]

The debate was not only over *whether* the changes were significant and, if they were significant, *how* significant they were. There was an even greater debate about *why* the changes occurred.

In the same November as the New York meeting, Commissioner Bratton addressed 200 criminologists at the annual meeting of the American Society of Criminology, in Boston. There he explained why crime, especially violent crime, had dropped so dramatically in New York City over the past five years.[6] He quickly dismissed all explanations but one. As he had put it at the New York meeting,

> What we're engaged in, in New York City, is results-oriented management. The results I'm looking for in New York are, quite simply, reduced crime, reduced quality of life negatives such as disorderly behavior and, with that, reduced fear. We reorganized the New York Police Department to focus on producing those results. Not the 1, 2, 3 percent results that we were seeing in crime in the [early] '90s in New York City but now the 25 percent in our reduction in crime over the last 2 years. . . .

Bratton then took the opportunity to chastise the researchers and academics present:

> The writings of the last several years have raised a concern on my part that the police are discounted as an effective force in our ability to not only reduce crime where it was high . . . but to control it, keep it at manageable levels . . . Increasingly you are completely discounting the ability of the police and others—with the information you are providing—to make a difference. In that respect, you're scaring the hell out of people. There is a sense in this country now that no matter what we do over the last 5 years of this decade, [we] are going to [have] a blood bath. . . . You are doing a disservice to the public. . . .[7]

Criminologists saw the causes of the decline as more complex than did Bratton. Their explanations included:

1. Better law enforcement.
2. More prisoners behind bars.
3. Tougher gun control laws.
4. A good economy with less poverty.
5. Revulsion of inner city youths against the culture of drugs and guns that caused so much destruction in their neighborhoods.[8]

Professor Lawrence Sherman, chairman of the criminology department at the University of Maryland, offered another possible explanation for the declining crime rates. He said that in the mid-1980s the rise of crack cocaine use made drug dealing more profitable, and many younger people who might have become burglars and pickpockets had moved into robbery and drug dealing, thereby increasing the number of these more serious crimes. As the crack cocaine market stabilized, crack dealing became less violent and less accessible to young people. It was left to more experienced and older dealers. According to Sherman, "The long-term cumulative effect of this lack of recruitment may be sizable."[9]

Professor Fagan, however, was skeptical of all these explanations. He summed up his position succinctly: "nobody really knows why people stop committing crime, and criminologists are not very good at understanding why crime is going down."[10]

In early 1998, another conference was held to survey expert opinion on the cause of declining crime rates. UCLA Professor Eric Monkkonen, an expert on the history of crime, said, "The closer we look at the drop in crime, the more complex it gets. . . . " As for the drop in homicides specifically, Monkkenon commented, "It's like cancer. The more we know, the more what looks like one problem becomes a series of problems."[11]

Despite wide disagreement as to its causes, most criminologists believe—even though they cannot prove—that the decline was related to the steep increases in the 1980s, followed by an adjustment back to more "normal" levels in the early to mid-1990s. This the criminologists attribute to a change in the drug trade. Older, more established dealers took over the crack cocaine trade, driving out the younger dealers and reducing the need for violence. These older dealers were not willing to take the high risks of injury and death that younger, less experienced dealers accepted.[12]

Anthropologist Richard Curtis, of John Jay College of Criminal Justice, pointed to the change in the behavior of young people in inner-city neighborhoods. On the basis of ten years of observing residents and drug dealers in the Bushwick section of Brooklyn, Curtis said many young people were "frightened and sickened by the spate of drug deals, killings, arrests, and the epidemic of AIDS. So they have turned away from the violence of street life and found legitimate jobs in 1993." He gives little credit to the police for this change in attitude and behavior. He argues that the main effect of the repeated sweeps by the police and the frequent arrest of Bushwick's residents was to make young people angry.[13]

CRITICAL THINKING

1. What did criminologists have to say in favor of accepting the drop in reported crime rates at face value?
2. What did criminologists have to say against accepting the drop in reported crime rates at face value?
3. Did the crime rates drop dramatically? Use your responses to 1 and 2 to answer this question.
4. Referring to the remarks of Dean Fox, compare his figures with those in Table 2.1. How do you explain the differences?
5. Why has crime declined, according to Commissioner Bratton?
6. State the various explanations given by the criminologists.
7. On the basis of these conflicting explanations, what policies would you spend tax dollars to implement?

Knowledge and Understanding CHECK

1. Define the three main types of crime.
2. Who does crime hurt besides the victim?
3. Give two examples of crimes that are difficult to put neatly into one of the three types of crime.
4. What different trends did UCR and NCVS point to between the 1970s and early 1990s?
5. Describe the change that occurred in these statistics in the mid-1990s.
6. What did the experts say about the extent and the reasons for the mid-'90s shift?

MEASURING CRIME

For centuries, societies have kept track of crimes, although their reasons for doing so have varied over time.

1. *Measure the moral health of society.* The first crime statistics were intended to measure the "moral health" of society. Crime statistics were supposed to tell how "bad" a society was. The idea persists in the popular belief that rising crime rates indicate a breakdown in moral values and social civility.[14]
2. *Assess the effectiveness of the criminal justice system.* Another intended use of crime statistics is to assess the effectiveness of criminal justice agencies. Jeremy Bentham, the great eighteenth-century criminal law reformer, noted that accurate crime figures are a "political barometer, by which the effects of every legislative operation relative to [crime and punishment] may be indicated." Today, police departments, courts, and prison officials study crime rates to measure how effectively they are

Table 2.1
Arrests, Number and Rate, Regions, 1996

OFFENSE CHARGED	UNITED STATES TOTAL (9,666 AGENCIES; POPULATION 189,927,000)	NORTHEAST (2,165 AGENCIES; POPULATION 40,190,000)	MIDWEST (2,094 AGENCIES; POPULATION 37,198,000)	SOUTH (3,768 AGENCIES; POPULATION 60,270,000)	WEST (1,639 AGENCIES; POPULATION 52,269,000)
Total	**11,088,352**	**2,007,557**	**2,373,969**	**3,718,348**	**2,988,478**
Rate[1]	**5,838.2**	**4,995.2**	**6,382.0**	**6,169.5**	**5,717.5**
Murder and nonnegligent manslaughter	14,447	2,244	3,456	5,157	3,590
Rate	7.6	5.6	9.3	8.6	6.9
Forcible rape	24,347	4,750	5,792	8,145	5,660
Rate	12.8	11.8	15.6	13.5	10.8
Burglary	121,781	40,476	18,287	29,711	33,307
Rate	64.1	100.7	49.2	49.3	63.7
Aggravated assault	387,571	71,164	61,793	113,156	141,458
Rate	204.1	177.1	166.1	187.7	270.6
Burglary	264,193	43,661	41,444	88,720	90,368
Rate	139.1	108.6	111.4	147.2	172.9
Larceny–theft	1,096,488	176,081	237,482	369,204	313,721
Rate	577.3	438.1	638.4	612.6	600.2
Motor vehicle theft	132,023	20,186	30,913	34,457	46,467
Rate	69.5	50.2	83.1	57.2	88.9
Arson	13,755	2,329	3,155	4,045	4,226
Rate	7.2	5.8	8.5	6.7	8.1
Violent crime[2]	548,146	118,634	89,328	156,169	184,015
Rate	288.6	295.2	240.1	259.1	352.1
Property crime[3]	1,506,459	242,257	312,994	496,426	454,782
Rate	793.2	602.8	841.4	823.7	870.1
Crime Index total[4]	2,054,605	360,891	402,322	652,595	638,797
Rate	1,081.8	898.0	1,081.6	1,082.8	1,222.1
Other assaults	972,984	162,561	220,560	367,139	222,724
Rate	512.3	404.5	592.9	609.2	426.1
Forgery and counterfeiting	88,355	14,819	13,054	37,043	23,439
Rate	46.5	36.9	35.1	61.5	44.8
Fraud	324,776	66,052	49,384	185,143	24,197
Rate	171.0	164.4	132.8	307.2	46.3
Embezzlement	11,449	794	1,818	6,076	2,761
Rate	6.0	2.0	4.9	10.1	5.3
Stolen property; buying, receiving, possessing	111,066	24,886	24,246	26,744	35,190
Rate	58.5	61.9	65.2	44.4	67.3
Vandalism	234,215	51,061	60,412	57,442	65,300
Rate	123.3	127.1	162.4	95.3	124.9
Weapons; carrying, possessing, etc.	161,158	23,749	34,516	54,557	48,336
Rate	84.9	59.1	92.8	90.5	92.5
Prostitution and commercialized vice	81,036	18,046	20,778	14,296	27,916
Rate	42.7	44.9	55.9	23.7	53.4
Sex offenses (except forcible rape and prostitution)	70,619	11,960	14,446	18,804	25,409
Rate	37.2	29.8	38.8	31.2	48.6
Drug abuse violations	1,128,647	265,924	201,453	304,805	356,465
Rate	594.3	661.7	541.6	505.7	682.0
Gambling	16,984	7,451	4,120	3,224	2,189
Rate	8.9	18.5	11.1	5.3	4.2
Offenses against family and children	103,800	24,960	36,783	29,934	12,123
Rate	54.7	62.1	98.9	49.7	23.2
Driving under the influence	1,013,932	117,672	203,075	345,308	347,877
Rate	533.9	292.8	545.9	572.9	665.5

(continued)

Table 2.1
Arrests, Number and Rate, Regions, 1996 *(continued)*

OFFENSE CHARGED	UNITED STATES TOTAL (9,666 AGENCIES; POPULATION 189,927,000)	NORTHEAST (2,165 AGENCIES; POPULATION 40,190,000)	MIDWEST (2,094 AGENCIES; POPULATION 37,198,000)	SOUTH (3,768 AGENCIES; POPULATION 60,270,000)	WEST (1,639 AGENCIES; POPULATION 52,269,000)
Total	**11,088,352**	**2,007,557**	**2,373,969**	**3,718,348**	**2,988,478**
Rate[1]	**5,838.2**	**4,995.2**	**6,382.0**	**6,169.5**	**5,717.5**
Liquor laws	491,176	108,603	150,090	95,692	136,791
Rate	258.6	270.2	403.5	158.8	261.7
Drunkenness	522,869	26,124	40,354	328,879	127,512
Rate	275.3	65.0	108.5	545.7	244.0
Disorderly conduct	626,918	176,106	224,230	147,548	79,034
Rate	330.1	438.2	602.8	244.8	151.2
Vagrancy	21,735	6,680	2,104	4,684	8,267
Rate	11.4	16.6	5.7	7.8	15.8
All other offenses (except traffic)	2,767,751	496,757	602,366	947,818	720,810
Rate	1,457.3	1,236.0	1,619.4	1,572.6	1,379.0
Suspicion (not included in totals)	4,859	1,159	1,215	1,895	590
Rate	2.6	2.9	3.3	3.1	1.1
Curfew and loitering law violations	142,433	25,493	34,730	34,760	47,450
Rate	75.0	63.4	93.4	57.7	90.8
Runaways	141,844	16,968	33,128	55,857	35,891
Rate	74.7	42.2	89.1	92.7	68.7

[1]Rate: Number of arrests per 100,000 inhabitants
[2]Violent crimes are offenses of murder, forcible rape, robbery, and aggravated assault.
[3]Property crimes are offenses of burglary, larceny–theft, motor vehicle theft, and arson.
[4]Includes arson.
Population figures were rounded to the nearest thousand. All rates were calculated before rounding.
Source: FBI, *Crime in the United States,* 1997.

enforcing the law. The public tends to hold police, judges, corrections officers, and lawyers responsible for rising crime rates; however, these same agents seldom receive credit if crime rates fall.[15]

3. *Evaluate victimization.* Crime statistics are also a measure of victimization. The National Crime Victim Survey (NCVS), for example, concentrates on a range of variables related to victimization. The Bureau of Justice Statistics has even devised a "crime risk index" that measures the risk of becoming the victim of a crime.[16]
4. *Test criminal justice theory.* Measuring crime can help to develop and test criminal justice theory. Therefore, the kinds, amounts, and trends of crime shed light on theories about the decisions, practices, and policies of police, prosecutors, judges, and corrections officers.[17]

Crimes Known to the Police

The Uniform Crime Reports (UCR) are the product of a Federal Bureau of Investigation (FBI) program that began in 1929. UCR present **aggregate statistics:** total counts of crimes reported to the police and of arrests, containing no details about individual cases. UCR depend on the voluntary participation of local law enforcement agencies. Fortunately, participation is extensive, covering about 95 percent of the U.S. population. Local agencies collect and record the information from their jurisdictions and send it to the FBI. The FBI compiles the data about the following six topics and reports them annually in the publication *Crime in the United States:*[18]

1. Offenses known to the police
2. Index Crimes cleared by arrest
3. Persons arrested
4. Homicide patterns
5. Law enforcement personnel
6. Hate crimes[19]

Offenses known to the police—mostly reported to them by victims but also sometimes discovered by the police—provide the basis for the **Crime Index,** also called **Part I offenses.** Part I, or "index," offenses comprise the following eight:

1. Homicide
2. Forcible rape

3. Robbery
4. Aggravated assault
5. Burglary
6. Larceny–theft
7. Motor vehicle theft
8. Arson[20]

The Crime Index is the source of the most widely reported crime statistics. It is the only basis for most television, radio, and newspaper commentary on crime statistics in the United States. Also, criminal justice policymakers, legislators, sociologists, and politicians rely heavily on the statistics that the UCR publishes. The Index is based on the idea that crimes known to the police are the best measure of crimes actually committed. Therefore, the Crime Index is supposed to show the movement, fluctuations, and trends of the total U.S. crime rate.[21]

Use *Your* Discretion

Is the number of convenience-store robberies high?

The FBI reported that there were 26,000 convenience-store robberies in 1995. Researchers Anthony J. Petrosino and Dian Brensilber studied these robberies and found that:

> Convenience stores are especially targeted for robbery, since perpetrators regard them as an easy source of cash. Indeed both police and robbers refer to convenience stores as "stop & robs." These establishments are accessible, have varying amounts of cash on hand and are often viewed by potential offenders as being unprotected. Despite some recent decreases in reported crime, the Federal Bureau of Investigation still recorded approximately 26,000 convenience store robberies in 1995.[22]

H. E. Amandus and his colleagues analyzed the UCR data on the 26,000 robberies. They concluded that "the proportion of robberies that resulted in either a homicide or injury of an employee varied across selected metropolitan areas (.03 to .25)." In a more in-depth study of convenience-store robberies in Boston, Petrosino and Brensilber found that out of a sample of 20 owner and employee victims, six were injured. Three listed moderate to serious injuries (two concussions, one stab wound.). One victim reported being hospitalized for a day and received workmen's compensation. . . . [T]wo subjects reporting missing work, with one subject who received a concussion missing seven days.[23]

CRITICAL THINKING

1. Do you agree with Petrosino's and Brensilber's conclusion, as follows?

> Thus, even among this small sample, serious injuries were infrequent in Boston convenience stores. . . . Indeed, given that there are over 400 convenience stores in Boston alone, the risk of any single employee being injured in a robbery must be relatively small.[24]

2. Does the following quote by the Petrosino and Brensilber help you to determine what a "relatively small" rate of injury is?

> Recent statistics published by the federal government indicate that violence is the third leading cause of occupational death, and the primary cause of fatality for women on the job. These data also reveal that certain occupations are particularly vulnerable to death by violence. For example, convenience store . . . employees had the second highest rate of homicide (behind taxi cab drivers). . . . While convenience store workers are hurt or killed in other ways, most employee deaths occur during robbery events.[25]

UCR also collects data and reports about a number of **Part II offenses.** These cross a broad spectrum of less serious offenses, listed in Table 2.1, and are reported in raw numbers of arrests. UCR are not perfect; they can only report and record crimes that the police know about. The number of crimes not known or recorded is called the **dark figure in crime,** dark because these crimes are hidden from public view. According to Victoria W. Schneider and Brian Wiersema, informal policies within police departments dictate that officers overlook some crimes. For example, police may overlook minor drug offenses to avoid scaring away bigger dealers. Also, officers tend not to report crimes when suspects are related to their victims. Criminologist Marvin Wolfgang found that the police failed to report from 20 to 90 percent of all criminal events.

Another shortcoming is that the Crime Index overrepresents serious crime and underrepresents minor crimes because it includes both attempted and completed crimes. Moreover, people tend to report only the most serious crimes to the police, and the police tend to record only the most serious crimes reported to them. Finally, if several crimes occurred during one event, the UCR reporting procedures permit departments to record only the most serious index crime. Consider a victim who reports that a burglar took $3,000 in cash and several diamond rings, raped an occupant, and drove off in the family car. The victim has reported five Index crimes—one burglary, two larcenies, one rape, and one auto theft. The department records only one crime, rape, because the UCR rates it the most serious of the five Index crimes.[26]

Use *Your* Discretion

Are crime statistics objective measures or subjective constructions?

W. Gove, M. Hughes, and M. Geerken have argued that UCR objectively and accurately reflect what citizens and the police consider serious threats to society:

> It is important to note that if one defines crime as criminal acts serious enough to be reacted to by both citizens and the police, then . . . UCR are at least as valid and probably more valid than the data from the victimization surveys.[27]

Henry H. Brownstein, a professor of criminal justice at the University of Baltimore, sees it differently. Brownstein was in charge of collecting and disseminating crime statistics for the state of New York during the 1980s. He maintains that the official indices of crime are social constructions, not objective measures:

> Crime, even violent crime . . . is the social product of the decisions, interpretations, actions, and interactions of individuals with varying degrees of power and authority, each making claims about what crime is and how much of it there is. Crime is culturally defined in that those making claims about it use symbols and styles of culture and subculture to support their claims. . . .

One example that Brownstein uses to back up his claim is the collection of crime data:

> Theoretically, UCR data are voluntarily submitted . . . from . . . local law enforcement agencies. A staff of four data entry clerks, a supervisor, and an administrator receive around 800 completed forms each month. All UCR data are received on forms completed by hand. The data on these forms are verified by a senior clerk and entered into the agency computer by a data entry clerk. While staff work hard and try to maintain high data quality standards, even at this early stage in the construction of UCR statistics it is clear that these numbers are the product of . . . interpretations, decisions, and actions.
>
> Budget cuts in recent years forced an elimination of field staff who trained and assisted UCR clerks in local police agencies. Consequently, local law enforcement agency staff who prepare the forms to submit to the State are not trained, and can only get answers to questions about the forms and procedures for completing the forms from a handbook that had not been revised in almost two decades. . . . The people completing the forms, therefore, have to decide what to enter and how to enter it without having adequate training or support. . . .
>
> Four poorly paid clerks doing the tedious work of data entry with little or no possibility of overtime, which is discouraged because of budgetary constraints, often maintain a monthly backlog of as many as 1,000 submitted forms to enter. As FBI deadlines approach . . . the clerks and their supervisor scurry to enter as much as possible. Even diligent and hardworking people have difficulty maintaining their usual standard of quality control under these circumstances.[28]

Despite these and other criticisms, crimes known to the police are probably still the best available official crime statistics. More than a generation ago, the criminologist Thorsten Sellin noted that "the value of criminal statistics decreases as the procedures take us farther away from the offense itself." Although two steps removed from the crime (offenders and victims being first and second), the police are the criminal justice professionals closest to the crime.[29]

CRITICAL THINKING

1. What is the social construction of crime statistics?
2. Do Gove and his colleagues adequately defend the accuracy of UCR statistics? Explain.
3. Is Brownstein's case for the social construction of crime statistics convincing? Why? Why not?
4. What are the implications of Brownstein's arguments, if they are right?

To improve its statistics, UCR has adopted the **National Incident-Based Reporting System (NIBRS).** NIBRS collects details about two groups of offenses. Group A includes the eight UCR index crimes, with some changes in definition, and adds 14 others, including drug offenses, fraud, embezzlement, pornography, statutory rape and incest, and weapons law violations. Group B offenses include such crimes as writing bad checks, loitering, driving while intoxicated, nonviolent family offenses, Peeping Tomism, and a catchall known as "all other crimes."

NIBRS, as its name makes clear, is **incident-based reporting.** Incident-based reporting means that local law enforcement agencies collect detailed information about individual cases, including:

1. The offense. Attempts are kept separate from completed crimes.

Table 2.2
Uniform Crime Reports and the National Crime Victimization Survey

	UNIFORM CRIME REPORTS	NATIONAL CRIME SURVEY
Crimes measured:	(1) Homicide (2) Rape (3) Robbery (personal and commercial) (4) Assault (aggravated) (5) Burglary (residential and commercial) (6) Larceny (commercial and household) (7) Motor vehicle theft (8) Arson	(1) Rape (2) Robbery (personal) (3) Assault (aggravated and simple) (4) Household burglary (5) Larceny (personal and household) (6) Motor vehicle theft
Scope:	Crimes reported to the police; considerable flexibility in developing small-area data	Crimes both reported and not reported to the police; all data available for a few large geographic areas
Collection method:	Police departments report to FBI or to centralized state agencies who report to FBI	Survey interviews; periodically measures the total number of crimes committed by asking a national sample of 49,000 households that include 101,000 persons age 12 or older about their experiences as victims during specific time periods
Information:	(1) Offense counts (2) Crimes cleared by arrest (3) Persons arrested (4) Persons charged with crimes (5) Law enforcement officers killed and assaulted (6) Characteristics of homicide victims	(1) Victim age, sex, race, education, and income (2) Victim-offender relationship (3) Crime details, such as time and place, whether reported to police, use of weapons, physical injury, and economic loss
Sponsor:	Department of Justice Federal Bureau of Investigation (FBI)	Department of Justice research arm, the Bureau of Justice Statistics (BJS)

2. The victim. This includes information about age, sex, ethnicity, race, resident or alien status, type of injury, and relationship of victims to offenders.
3. Any property involved.
4. The offender. This includes details about age, sex, race, and ethnicity.
5. The arrestee. This includes information about the use of alcohol, narcotics, and other drugs.
6. Any witnesses.
7. A brief narrative describing the incident.

NIBRS separates attempts from completed crimes, and it includes information such as suspected use of alcohol, narcotics, or other drugs, or the use of a weapon in committing the crime. Offender data include age, gender, and race. Victim data include age, gender, race, ethnic origin, resident or nonresident status, type of injury sustained, and relationship of victim to offender.[30]

According to a joint project of the FBI and BJS, NIBRS has been slow to be implemented, "particularly in large law enforcement agencies."

> At present, [July, 1997] NIBRS reporting agencies represent approximately 5.7 percent of the United States population, and the Austin (Texas) Police Department is the only law enforcement agency serving a jurisdiction over 500,000 in population that is reporting NIBRS data to the FBI. Implementation of a program of this scope is an enormous undertaking, particularly so in that it relies so heavily on the internal information processing and reporting capabilities of local law enforcement agencies.[31]

Henry H. Brownstein, whose role in collecting UCR data for New York State was described earlier, adds the following reasons for the slow implementation of NIBRS:

> After years of development, implementation is slow at best because of limited support for the program, but also because the federal, state, and local governments cannot reach agreement about how the program should operate. For example, many local government agencies are still asking what value the program will have for their operation and at what cost.[32]

Victim Surveys

The **National Crime Victimization Survey (NCVS)** collects detailed information about the following crimes:

1. Rape and other sexual assaults
2. Robbery
3. Assault

Figure 2.3
Percent of Crimes Reported to Police, 1996

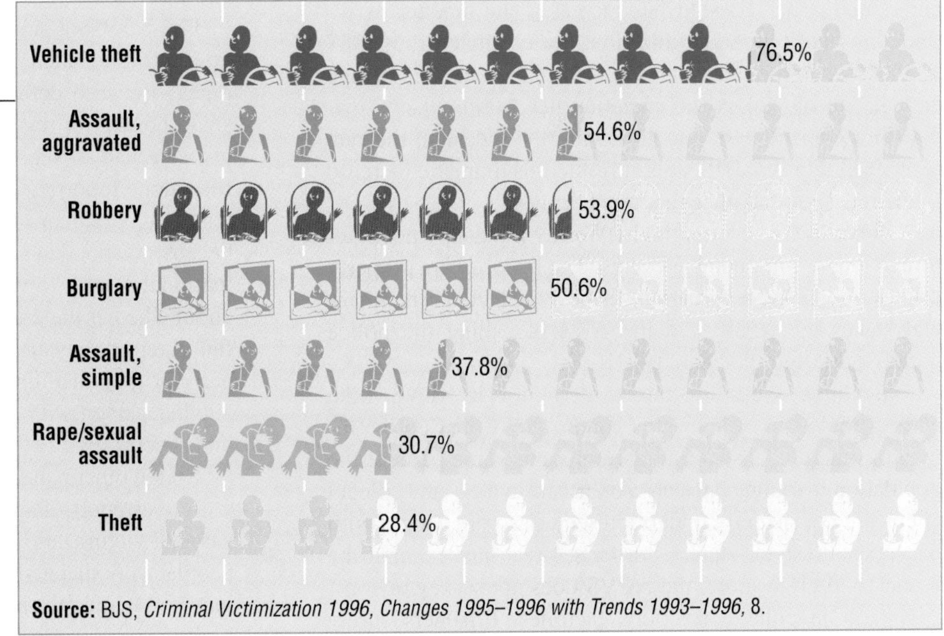

4. Household burglary
5. Theft
6. Motor vehicle theft

Sample data for NCVS are collected every year from approximately 50,000 households consisting of more than 100,000 individuals aged 12 or over. At six-month intervals, interviewers from the U.S. Census Bureau collect information about:

1. *Victimization:* Whether any household member over 12 years old was the victim of a crime within the past six months.
2. *Victims:* Age, race, sex, educational level, and income of victims.
3. *Crime:* Location, amount of personal injury, and economic loss suffered from the crime.
4. *Perpetrator:* Gender, age, race, and relationship to the victim.
5. *Reporting to the police:* Whether victims reported the crimes to the police, and the reasons why they did or did not do so.

NCVS is the only collection of national crime statistics that includes information about crimes that the police do not know about, and is the only national database on victims, their victimizers, and their victimization (see Table 2.2). According to James Garofalo, who has used the NCVS extensively in his own research, NCVS is "a potential information gold mine for researchers interested in the causes, trends, processes, and outcomes of crimes."[33]

The Bureau of Justice Statistics (BJS)—the administrator of NCVS—issues an annual report entitled *Criminal Victimization in the United States* that summarizes the findings of NCVS. BJS also publishes special bulletins and reports stemming from its surveys, such as *Violent Crime by Strangers, Households Touched by Crime*, and *Elderly Victims.* NCVS has demonstrated what researchers and policymakers have long suspected: Official crime statistics of the UCR underreport the actual amount of crime. NCVS has found that victims report only about 38 percent of all NCVS offenses. Moreover, they report violent crimes more often than property crimes, and completed crimes more than attempts. Figure 2.3 shows the percent of crimes that victims reported to the police in 1996.[34]

NCVS sheds some light on the dark figure in crime because it includes crimes reported to interviewers but not to the police. Nevertheless, like UCR, NCVS underreports the total number of crimes. Just as people do not report to the police all crimes that they know about, victims do not report to the interviewers all crimes committed against them. Their reasons for failure to report include:[35]

1. They are embarrassed or ashamed, fearing ridicule and contempt.
2. They distrust interviewers and so cover up the crime.
3. They are acquainted with or related to offenders.
4. They do not know they are concealing crimes.
5. They are apathetic.

Most of the failure to report, however, stems from simple forgetfulness. Six months can be too long to remember crimes, especially minor ones. One check showed that recall during the first three months is 70 percent, but between three and six months it falls to only 50 percent. Another survey showed a decrease of 61 percent in reporting crimes from the first to the last month of the survey.[36]

In 1993, BJS redesigned NCVS to produce more accurate reporting of violent crimes. The new survey replaces technical terms with words that describe violent crimes by the behavior involved. Respondents are also encouraged to talk about violent incidents even if they do not believe they are crimes. The redesign has increased the amount of reported violent crime victimization. For example, from 1987 to 1991, when the old system was still in effect, the average annual rate of violent victimization per 1,000 persons was 5.4; in 1993, the first year following the redesign, the rate rose steeply to 9.4. BJS staff attribute this dramatic increase to the redesign that uncovers more crimes.[37]

According to criminologist Wesley Skogan, "most victimizations are not notable events. The majority are property crimes in which the perpetrator is never detected. The financial stakes are small, and the costs of calling the police greatly outweigh the benefits."[38]

Sampling issues also distort the figures in NCVS. Like all household surveys, whether conducted by the Census Bureau or others, the NCVS underrepresents some parts of the population. Young African American males and illegal aliens are consistently underrepresented; so are people with particular lifestyles, such as drifters, street hustlers, and the homeless. Furthermore, the NCVS does not survey prisons, jails, and juvenile corrections facilities. Prisoners surely have higher victimization rates than the general population. Wealthy people, too, may escape the survey because they tend to insulate themselves from all kinds of interviews.[39]

Another sampling problem arises because there are so few raw numbers of serious crimes in the survey—rape, robbery, and aggravated assault. In 1994, the 160,000 households reported 160 rapes, 1,299 robberies, and 2,478 aggravated assaults. National estimates based on these low numbers subject NCVS to a considerable amount of sampling error.[40]

Use *Your* Discretion

Are surveys of defensive gun users accurate?

The number of law-abiding people who use guns to defend themselves against criminal attackers is regularly invoked in public policy debates as a benefit of widespread private ownership of firearms. Yet, there is considerable uncertainty about how many people use guns to defend themselves against criminals. NCVS estimates that 108,000 people do so annually. Private surveys, by groups with varying degrees of stakes in the results of their surveys, report that as many as 2.5 million people do so.

One random-digit-dial telephone survey estimated 4.7 million defensive gun uses. Households were selected by choosing a central telephone office, identified by the first six digits of the telephone number, and then selecting a household from every office. Sampling quotas were defined on the basis of race and gun ownership. People in the survey were asked how many times they used a gun, even if they did not fire it, to protect themselves or their property in the past 12 months.

Philip J. Cook and Jens Ludwig reviewed this survey and concluded that the estimates were "far too high." Because defensive gun use is a rare event, a small number of respondents who falsely report a gun use can lead to substantial overestimates of gun use. Inaccurate reporting can be either intentional or unintentional. Unintentional underreporting occurs usually because respondents forget that they used a gun. Intentional failure to report may be due to uncertainty about whether the use of the gun was legal. Those who fail to report may also have been carrying the gun illegally or they may not be sure it was legal to threaten another person with a gun. In either case, the result is underreporting.

On the other hand, it is more likely that respondents will overreport defensive gun use because, unlike cases of victimization and much other illegal behavior, people who successfully fight off an attacker with a gun are frequently hailed as heroes. One newspaper reported:

> An unidentified NRA member became famous throughout Texas as "The Hunter" when he and his son heard a distress call on their CB radio. Two college coeds saw a Waco man shoot Sammy Long, a Texas Department of Public Safety officer, and called for help. The hunter arrived on the scene too late to save Long's life, but killed the thug with a 6mm rifle. Upton County District Attorney Aubrey Edwards said the coeds and the hunter requested their names not be made public and said the hunter "deserved a medal" for his action.

Cook and Ludwig also found little information with which to determine whether defensive gun use provides a net benefit to society because it is difficult to determine whether such use is appropriate. Information is typically based on one side of the story—that of the gun user. "We are given little context with which to judge these reports and, of course, have no way to learn the other party's view of what happened."

> Further, alternative courses of action available to the respondent cannot be determined from the surveys. Claims about the benefits of defensive gun use assume that the firearm produces an outcome that is preferable to some (unobserved) alternative sequence of events. Citizens with access to firearms use their guns in situations where other effective response may be available. For example, in 16 of . . . 19 gun uses . . . the respondent reported that the encounter occurred "near the respondent's home" and also indicated that, when he first wanted to use his gun for protection, the gun was stored somewhere *in* the home. In other words, in about one-third of these events the respondent apparently had the option of staying inside and calling the police.

Finally, defensive gun use estimates cannot provide information about other important consequences of widespread gun ownership and carrying. Higher rates of gun ownership may increase the likelihood that criminals arm themselves. On the other hand, widespread gun ownership and carrying may deter criminal activity. Neither of these is reflected in defensive gun use estimates.[41]

CRITICAL THINKING

1. Why did Cook and Ludwig conclude that the estimates of defensive gun use were too high?
2. Why might instances of defensive gun use be overreported?
3. What important questions do estimates of defensive gun use, even if accurate, not answer?

Self-Reports of Crime

Self-reports are based on the idea that asking people about their criminal behavior is the best way to measure crime. James F. Short and F. Ivan Nye, in a pioneer self-report survey, asked anonymous juveniles about their delinquent acts. The reported offenses included driving without a license, truancy, defying parental authority, taking items worth less than two dollars, buying and drinking alcohol illegally, vandalism, and sexual relations with the opposite sex.

Nearly a third of those surveyed admitted to delinquent acts they had never reported. In another survey, college students admitted to similar unreported acts. And in a third survey, 60 percent of a sample of adult men between the ages of 20 and 30 admitted to driving while intoxicated, 44 percent to shoplifting, and 13 percent to breaking and entering. Sixty-nine percent of those who admitted to either public drunkenness or driving while intoxicated were not arrested, and 33 percent of the shoplifters escaped without arrest.[42]

In more recent times, self-reporting has focused on the criminal behavior of felons. Most of these surveys use prisoners as their subjects; a few have studied felons who are not in prison and are still active. Obstacles stand in the way of self-reports of felons. First, it is difficult to find substantial samples of active offenders not in prison. Researchers need connections with offenders, they need to gain their trust, and they face the ethical dilemma of expanding knowledge and letting known criminals remain free. Richard T. Wright and Scott H. Decker conducted an excellent and fascinating study of armed robbers, discussed later in the section on explanations of crime. The authors state that "most researchers remain unwilling to deal directly with offenders 'in the wild'. . . . everything from inclement weather to the possibility of grave personal injury mitigates against dealing with serious criminals in a real world setting."[43]

Samples of convicted offenders do not represent all criminals. The samples probably overrepresent multiple offenders or "unsuccessful" criminals—if it can be assumed that successful criminals do not get caught, or at least avoid imprisonment. Furthermore, even a representative sample does not guarantee accuracy concerning events that occurred on impulse, about which offenders may well not tell the truth. Offenders may exaggerate the professionalism of their actions and minimize the hurt they inflicted on their victims. They may not trust the researchers, or they may simply want to "play games" to fill up the boring and empty hours of life in prison. Whatever assurances they are given about confidentiality, prisoners may still think that what they say will affect their chances for release. They will paint the best possible picture of themselves.[44]

Despite these methodological shortcomings, researchers have conducted a number of surveys of convicted felons. One good example is James D. Wright's *The Armed Criminal in America*. Wright surveyed more than 1,800 convicted adult male felons incarcerated in 10 states. Men in the sample were asked how and why they obtain, carry, and use firearms, especially in committing crimes. Wright formulated a typology of criminals based on their use of weapons. The largest group (39 percent), unarmed criminals, had never committed any crime while armed. The "knife criminals" and "improvisers," armed with a variety of ready-to-hand weapons, constituted about 11 percent. Roughly the other half of the sample was made up of "gun criminals." More than half of these used a gun only once or sporadically; the rest (22 percent), consisting of "handgun predators" and "shotgun predators," committed nearly half of all the crimes reported.[45]

The gun criminals reported that guns made many crimes easier to commit and that they had lived around guns all their lives. Furthermore, the majority reported that they kept their guns loaded at all times and that they fired them regularly, often at other people. Half reported firing a gun at someone; half also reported someone had fired on them. Many reported that a man armed with a gun is "prepared for anything that might happen." When asked how they would respond to a ban on small, cheap handguns, they said they would carry bigger, more expensive handguns. Asked about their response to a total ban on handguns, a majority of gun criminals—and more than three-quarters of the "predators"—replied that they would carry sawed-off shoulder weapons.[46]

Like the UCR and NCVS, self-reports do not produce wholly accurate and complete crime statistics. This is so for two major reasons:

1. Some offenders, like some victims, forget and/or deceive interviewers.
2. Self-reports do not represent national samples. They survey particular groups, such as juveniles, college students, and felons, from specific regions or states.

The Canadian criminologist Gwynn Nettler had the following to say after reviewing self-surveys:

> Asking people questions about their behavior is a poor way of observing it. . . . It is particularly ticklish to ask people to recall their "bad" behavior. Confessional data are at least as weak as the official statistics they were supposed to improve upon.[47]

Measuring Occupational Crime

Measuring **occupational crime** (crimes committed by persons in the course of their employment) presents the greatest challenges to those who gather crime statistics. The UCR does not include occupational crimes, which individuals rarely report. The NCVS does not ask questions about occupational crime. Attempts to measure white-collar crime through victim surveys face several difficulties. There is often no identifiable, single victim. In many cases, individual victims do not feel a significant loss. Measuring **organizational crime** (crimes committed by corporate officers and managers under the authority of the corporation) by extracting data from official records of formal proceedings in white-collar crime cases has all the shortcomings of the UCR, plus one more. Isolated court cases do not reveal the widespread harm commonly suffered by many individuals affected by corporate crime.[48]

Measures of blue-collar crime are based on self-surveys of employees. These surveys concentrate on employee theft or other property misappropriation. In addition to interviews and questionnaires, blue-collar crime reporting relies on informants; that is, researchers who work in particular business places and report what they observe. Richard Hollinger and John P. Clark, for example, combined anonymous questionnaires and face-to-face interviews with both executives and employees in several industries and communities. To study employees' "cheating" at work, Gerald Mars interviewed more than 100 informants selected simply because they were available, rather than according to any rational selection criteria.[49]

Knowledge and Understanding CHECK

1. List and briefly describe the major characteristics of UCR.
2. Define "index crimes" and list the eight offenses included in the index.
3. Compare Part II offenses and the way they are reported with the Crime Index.
4. Identify the major shortcomings in UCR.
5. Define and list the major characteristics of the NIBRS.
6. What major details about individual cases does NIBRS collect?
7. Contrast NIBRS with UCR.
8. List the offenses about which NCVS collects details.
9. Describe the major features of NCVS.
10. How does NCVS collect data?
11. Contrast NCVS with UCR.
12. Identify and describe the major shortcomings of NCVS.
13. Define self-reports.
14. What is the major hypothesis from which self-reports originated?
15. Describe the major characteristics, advantages, and disadvantages of self-reports.
16. What were the principal findings of the gun criminals' self-reports?
17. Why does measuring occupational crime present a challenge to researchers?
18. Identify the source and describe the nature of measurements of blue-collar crime.

Crime rates vary among metropolitan areas, suburbs, and rural areas–and from neighborhood to neighborhood. What reasons would you guess account for geographical differences in crime rates?

GEOGRAPHY OF CRIME

Both UCR and NCVS report on the geographical distribution of crime and victimization. These regional and local breakdowns make clear that crime rates vary from one region of the country to another, from state to state, and from city to city. They also vary among metropolitan areas, cities outside metropolitan areas, and rural areas. Violent crime rates vary significantly in the same way. Although the phrase "high-crime areas" is vaguely defined and often misused to describe any low-income neighborhood in a large city, it is nonetheless true that crime is not evenly distributed among neighborhoods located even close to each other.[50]

SUBSTANCE USE AND CRIME

The link between the use of mind-altering substances and crime has been a constant theme in research, politics, and popular culture for nearly a century. But until the 1980s, little empirical evidence existed to help explain the link. Furthermore, the use of illegal drugs (mainly cocaine, heroin, and marijuana) has received most of the attention. Here we take a broader view, including both illegal substances and alcohol, the use of which is almost universally legal but which is nonetheless a mind-altering substance.

Illegal Drug Use and Crime

In 1970, criminologists Edward Sutherland and Donald Cressey wrote that "felons are overrepresented in the addict population, [and] crime rates are increased considerably by drug addiction." However, they conceded that the state of knowledge at that time had not established the reasons for the link. By 1980, substantially more was known about the connection between drugs and crime. Among the many findings were:

1. Many serious offenders were drug users who started using drugs as juveniles.
2. Many drug users became addicted before they began committing nondrug offenses and getting arrested.
3. Arrestees and prisoners who used drugs were more likely to have been arrested for property crimes than for violent crimes.
4. Among drug users, heroin addicts were most likely to commit numerous crimes.[51]

Some researchers and many policymakers concluded from these findings that the connection between drugs and crime is simple: Juvenile drug use progressed to heroin addiction, and heroin addiction caused addicts to commit **predatory crimes** (crimes such as prostitution and theft) in order to support their addiction. This belief was held despite two critical findings:

- Many heroin users are not addicted.
- Many heroin users do not commit crimes other than that of possessing and using heroin.[52]

By the 1990s, researchers had made clear that the connection between drugs and crime was considerably more complex than the prevailing view of the progression from drugs to crime. Jan and Marcia Chaiken cautiously reported that although *some* drug users progressed from heroin addiction to income-producing crimes, other behavior sequences applied more often than the drugs-to-crime sequence. According to the Chaikens, the behaviors of large groups of people in the aggregate demonstrate that "no coherent general patterns emerge associating drug use . . . with participation in predatory crime, age at onset of participation in crime, or persistence in committing crime." From their own research and a review of the findings of surveys of youths and prisoners and interviews with addicts who lived on the streets in New York, the Chaikens reported the following summary of findings:

1. People who have a long history of committing predatory crimes also commit other crimes and began their criminal careers when they were young.
2. Illicit drug users who use illegal drugs either often or in large quantities use a variety of drugs and began using them when they were adolescents.
3. Persistent offenders and persistent illicit drug users are not the same people. A few severely addicted people commit no crimes except for the possession and use of illegal drugs, and many criminals with long criminal histories do not use drugs.
4. No simple general relation between high rates of drug use and high rates of crime exists. Drug abuse and criminal behavior do coexist in some social groups, but the coexistence is due to external factors. For youths, these factors include physical abuse, lack of parental control, failure to participate in rewarding school activities, and irregular employment. For adults, these factors include irregular employment and absence of marital ties.
5. High-frequency drug users are likely to be high-frequency predators and also to commit a variety of crimes, including violent crimes. This is true for both youths and adults, for all races, and for men and women. One notable exception: high-frequency drug-using women commit fewer violent crimes than high-frequency drug-using men.
6. Drug *dealing* and criminality are *substantially* more closely linked than drug *use* and criminality.[53]

Use *Your* Discretion

Is it too early to make policy based on research about crime and drugs?

Dana E. Hunt, who studies the link between drugs and crime, had this to say about the sources available to study the link:

> In general, [most] . . . studies [of the link between drugs and crime] are studies of "accessible

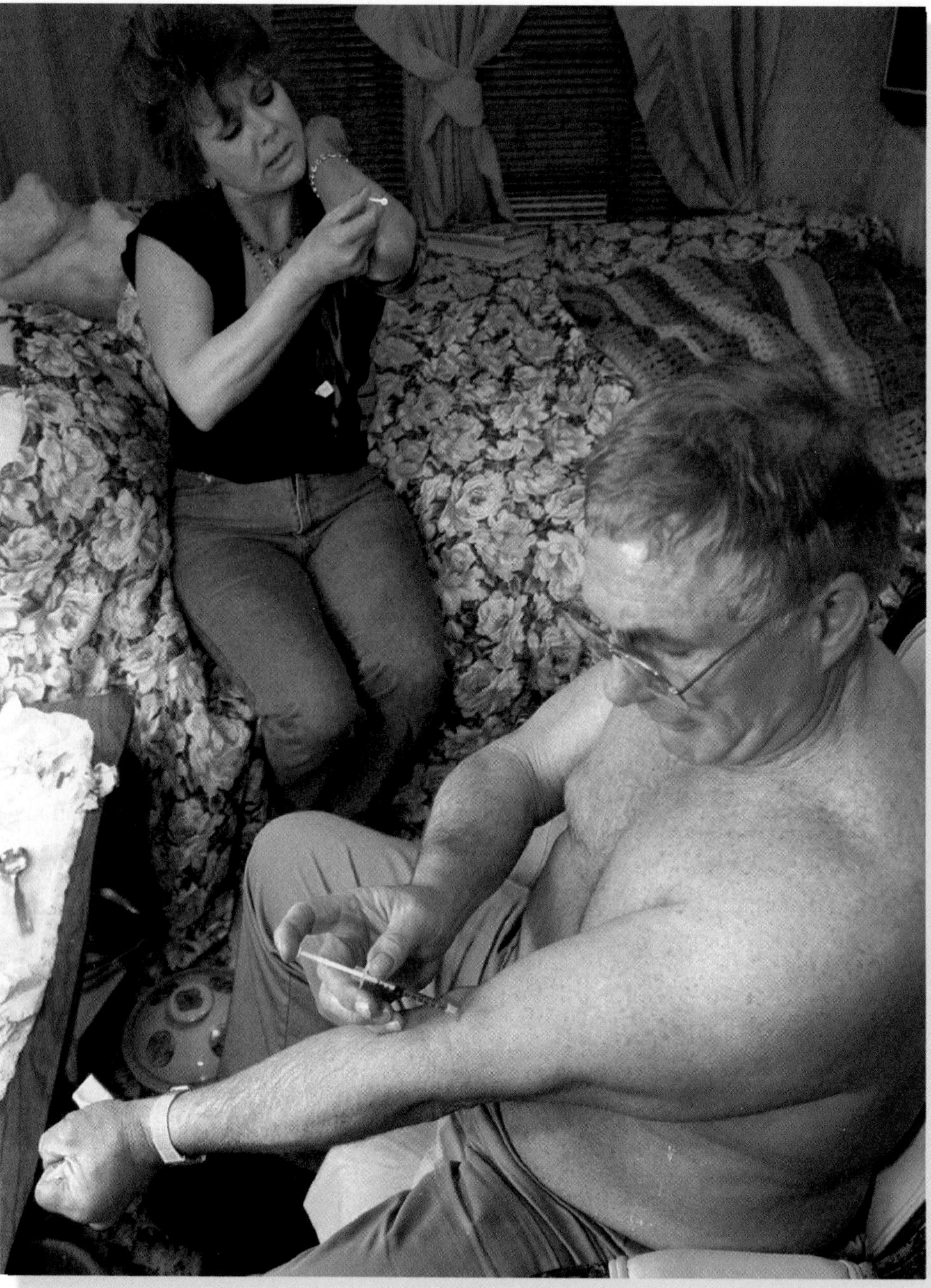

Researchers studying the links between drugs and crime face the problem that drug users and offenders are "hidden" populations, and it is difficult to pick subjects who are representative of all addicts and offenders.

populations," which are unlikely to be representative of all addicts and offenders. Both drug users and offenders are hidden populations; portions of both are inaccessible to research, and truly random samples are beyond the reach of most studies. Moreover, the few doors of ready access often lead to skewed populations. Access is possible to incarcerated populations, for example, but this sampling approach omits both users not involved in crime and the more successful addict offenders who have not yet been caught. Drug-treatment programs or hospitals provide handy "patient" populations, but samples from them overlook the broad range of addicts and addict offenders not currently seeking treatment.

Finally, samples of drug users are reached through field studies that enter the milieu of the drug world where researchers study small specialized groups of users through observation and interview. . . . However, [**ethnographic studies**, that is] . . . intensive field observation and interviews to gather data in the natural settings of the behavior under study from what is generally a nonrandomly selected sample . . . also has major limitations as a research tool. First, both by virtue of the design and size, the samples are not generalizable to the population of interest. Second, because the studies occur in natural settings, the control that is desirable for rigorous hypothesis testing is also often not possible. Therefore, these methods are not to be used to make causal inferences from the street scene. . . .[54]

CRITICAL THINKING

Would you be willing to make policy decisions based on the existing knowledge and the limitations of the sources available to study the link between drugs and crime? Explain your answer.

Alcohol Use and Crime

Empirical evidence has clearly demonstrated a link between drinking alcohol and criminal behavior. About half of all offenders have used alcohol within 72 hours of committing both violent and nonviolent crimes. This evidence is based on surveys of victims, people arrested, and prisoners. Figure 2.4 clearly demonstrates that more people drank than used illegal drugs before they committed crimes. Hence, the association between alcohol and criminal behavior is stronger than that between illegal drug use and criminal behavior. However, Jeffrey A. Greenfield, the statistician for the U.S. Bureau of Justice Statistics, cautions us to remember that "the vast number of those who consume alcohol do not engage in criminal behavior."[55]

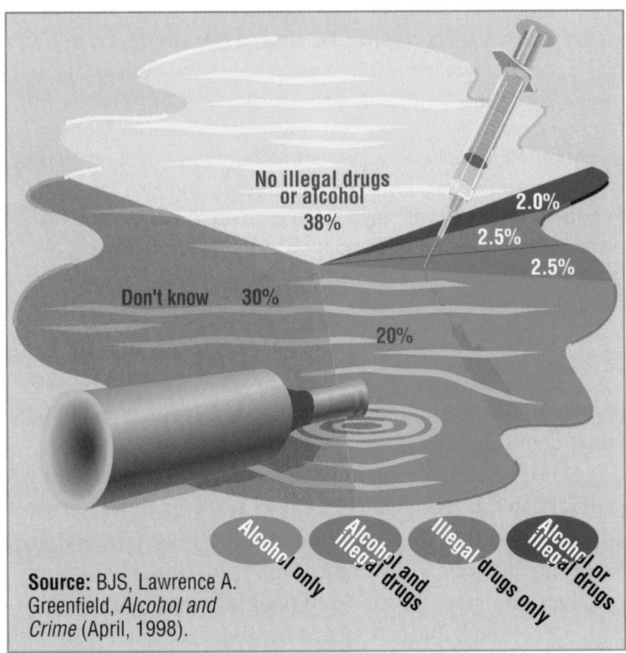

Source: BJS, Lawrence A. Greenfield, *Alcohol and Crime* (April, 1998).

Figure 2.4
Percent of Those Using Mind-Altering Substances Prior to Committing Crimes

Another important warning is needed: The association between alcohol use and criminal behavior is only that—an association. An association is not proof that alcohol use caused the criminal behavior, nor can it therefore prove that alcohol use increases the risk of criminal behavior, whether violent or nonviolent. To test the hypothesis that alcohol use increases the risk of criminal behavior, we need a benchmark—the number of people *not* involved in crime while they drink. A panel of experts could neither find nor construct this critical benchmark.[56]

Knowledge and Understanding CHECK

1. Describe the state of knowledge in 1970 about the link between drugs and crime.
2. Describe four findings resulting from increased knowledge about the drugs–crime link that had taken place by 1980.
3. Describe the simple connection between drugs and crime that some researchers and many policymakers drew from the findings described in question 1.
4. What had researchers made clear about the drug–crime connection by the 1990s?
5. Describe the six major findings that the Chaikens reported. Identify the sources of their findings.

CRIMINALS

Crime distribution varies not only according to geography but also according to:

1. The relationship between offenders and victims.
2. The sex of the offender.
3. The race and ethnicity of the offender.
4. Age.
5. Social class.
6. Education.
7. Other demographic characteristics.

Relationship of Offenders to their Victims

The major crime statistics and a host of other surveys and empirical analyses have well established that relationships matter in who commits crimes, how, and under what circumstances. The following relationships are relevant to criminal behavior (see Figure 2.5):

1. Intimates (spouses, ex-spouses, common law spouses, same-sex partners, boyfriends, girlfriends).

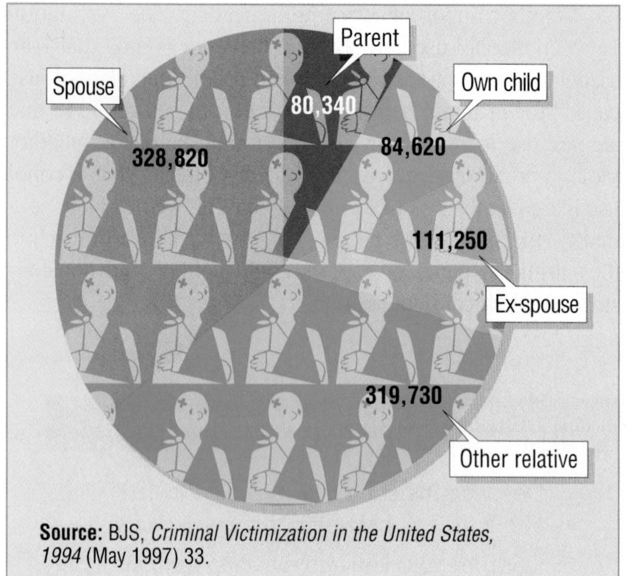

Source: BJS, *Criminal Victimization in the United States, 1994* (May 1997) 33.

Figure 2.5
Relationship of Offenders to Victims in Violent Crimes, by Numbers of Victimizations, 1994

2. Relatives (parents, children, siblings, grandparents, in-laws, cousins).
3. Acquaintances.
4. Strangers.

Crimes involving intimates, relatives, and acquaintances range across a wide spectrum of behavior, from the violent crimes of murder, rape, robbery, and assault to petty theft. Most people fear victimization by strangers when, tragically, the people they know are more likely to kill, rape, assault, and otherwise prey on them.[57]

Acquaintance crimes are difficult to measure because they usually take place in private and because victims hesitate to report them. For these reasons, crimes within families frequently do not enter the criminal justice system. According to one nationwide survey of crime victims, 48 percent of domestic violence incidents were not brought to police attention, mostly because the victims believed that violence within families is a private matter (49 percent), but also because the victims feared reprisal (12 percent). Even though such acts clearly violate the criminal law, victims rarely report crimes if they know their perpetrators. According to UCR, about 47 percent of the murders known to police were committed by intimates, relatives, and acquaintances. NCVS reports that in 1996 intimates committed 46 percent of all violent crimes.[58]

Murray A. Strauss and others interviewed more than 2,000 husbands, wives, children, brothers, and sisters. They found that 50 to 60 percent of all husbands assault their wives at least once during marriage. Although women are much less likely than men to be victims of violent crimes in general, they are much more likely than men to be victimized by their intimates (husbands and boyfriends). Seventy percent of intimate homicide victims are women. More than 90 percent of nonfatal violence victims are intimates.

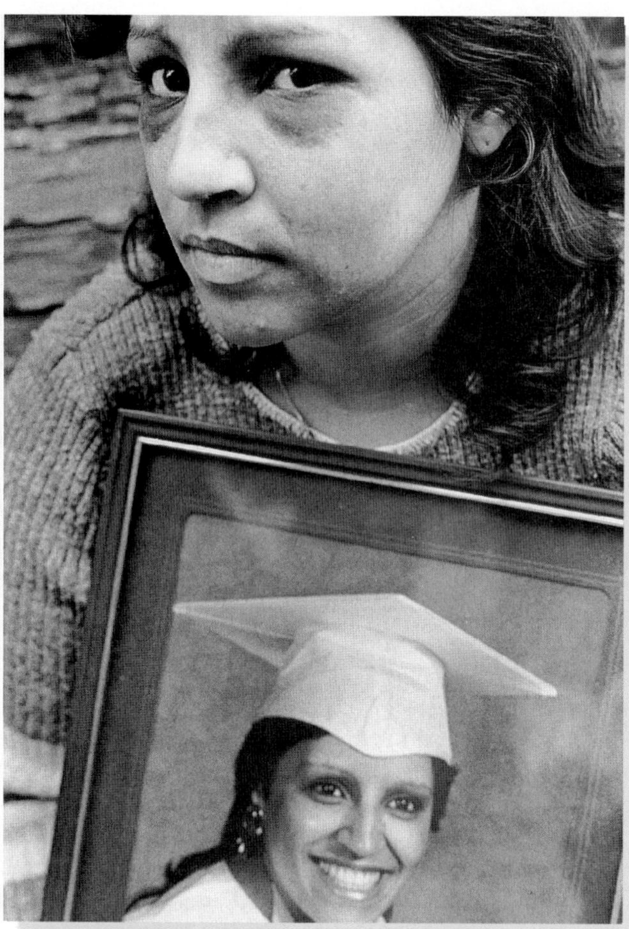

Husbands and boyfriends are major sources of interpersonal violence. When this woman returned home from her night shift in a Philadelphia hospital where she worked as a nurse, her husband was waiting for her. He accused her of cheating on him instead of working. He punched her in the eyes, smashed her face with the telephone, and broke her nose. The next day her son cried when he saw her: "You don't look like Mommy anymore." She pushed for protection from her husband, and he was ordered to keep away. Now divorced, she isn't interested in getting involved with anyone. "It's going to be hard on my own, but I don't want this again." She holds her high school graduation picture as a reminder of what she was like before the violent relationship.

Some researchers estimate that every year parents physically assault as many as 100,000 to 200,000 children, sexually abuse 60,000 to 100,000, and kill 5,000! Abuse varies according to social class. Stephen Brown used an anonymous questionnaire to survey 110 high school freshmen concerning parental abuse. The survey revealed that lower-class parents more frequently abused their children physically, while middle-class parents more commonly abused their children emotionally, for example, by making them feel guilty. Furthermore, although less frequent than parent–child crimes, crimes between siblings also occur.[59]

Figure 2.6
Murders Committed by Intimates, 1993–1996

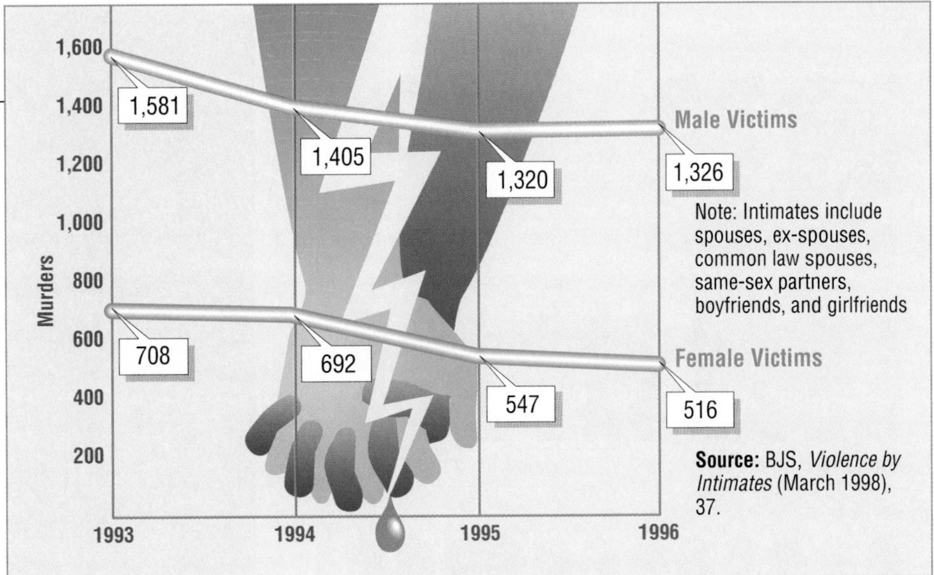

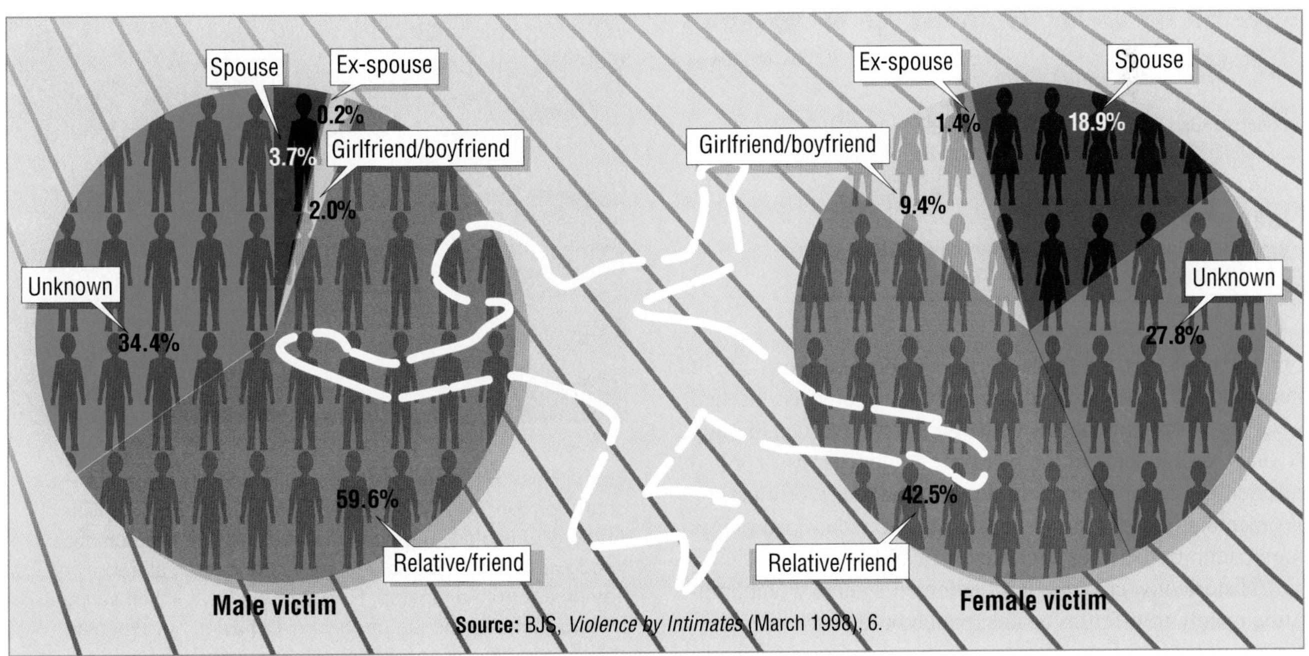

Figure 2.7
Victims of Murder by Intimates, 1976–1996

Family violence receives most of the attention, but property crimes also occur within families. In a pilot study, Alan J. Lincoln and Murray A. Strauss administered a voluntary anonymous questionnaire to 450 randomly distributed New England college students. The questionnaire asked about property crimes committed within their families against other family members. Among these college students, property crimes—including forgery, fraud, vandalism, and extortion by one family member against another—occurred in 73 percent of the families.[60]

The downward trend shown by NCVS and UCR discussed earlier extended to violence by intimates. According to a BJS special report, both the numbers and rates of violent crimes committed by intimates declined between 1993 and 1996 (see Figures 2.6 and 2.7).[61]

Male and Female Criminals

Many more men than women enter the criminal justice system. Figure 2.8 graphically illustrates the wide gap between men and women arrested for violent and property crimes. Early criminologists, criminal justice officials, and public policymakers believed that women committed crimes mainly having to do with sex. In the mid-1950s, for example,

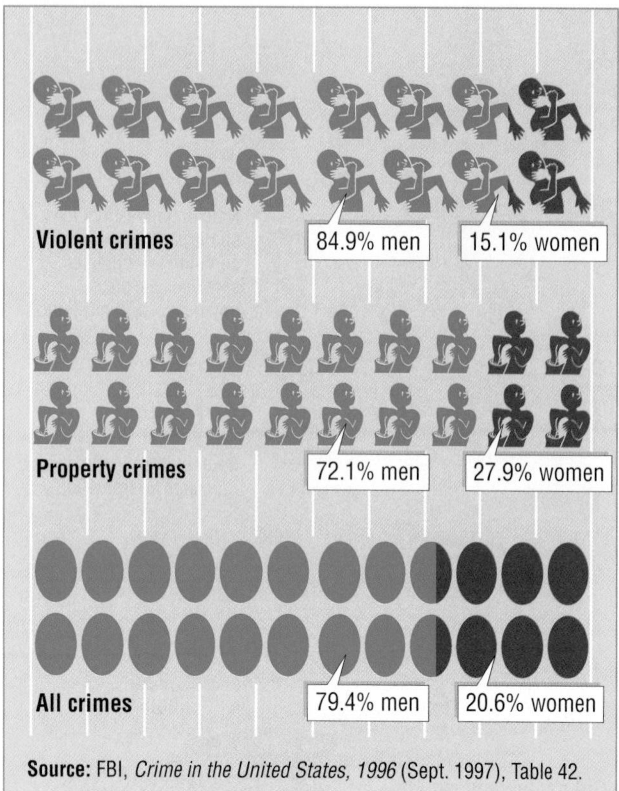

Figure 2.8
Percent of Male and Female Offenders by Type of Index Crime, 1996

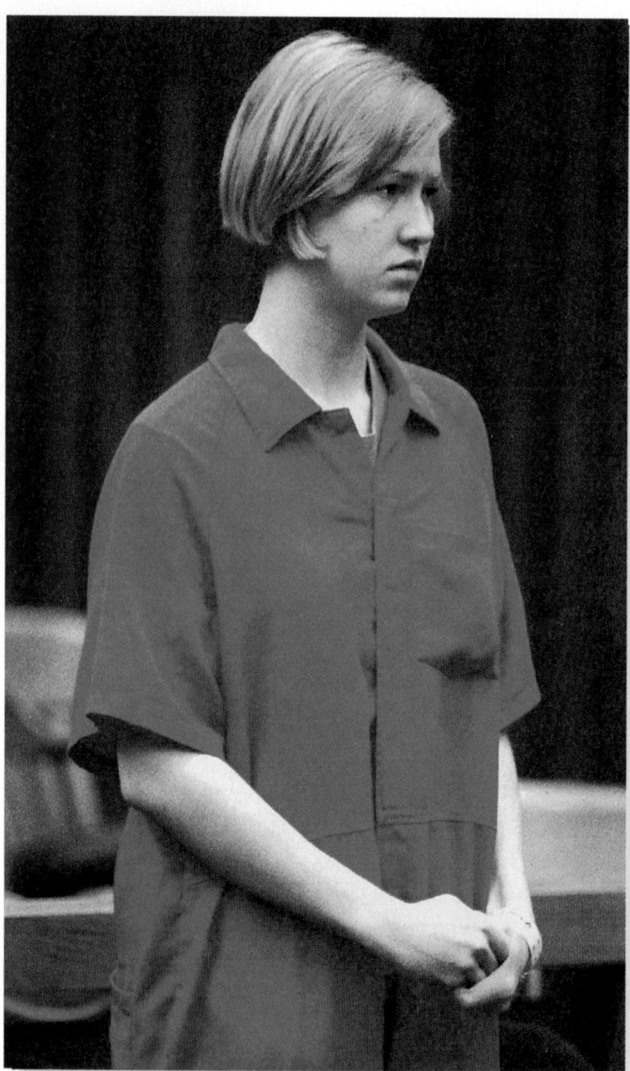

Emma Rose Freeman, 18, appears in a Santa Cruz, CA courtroom on Jan. 27, 1999. Freeman and an accomplice, Anthony Cristofani, are accused of using a semiautomatic handgun to rob a hair salon of $100 and later, stereo equipment from a Costco. Researchers have linked various factors to the incidence of criminal behavior, but Freeman defies many of the conventional stereotypes: she was a National Merit Scholar, a freshman at the University of California–Santa Cruz, and allegedly told police she needed money so "she could concentrate on her art."

one criminologist wrote that girls were beyond the scope of his theory of juvenile delinquency because boys committed a variety of delinquent acts while girls were overwhelmingly sexually delinquent. In the past, criminologists also applied different theories to explain female and male criminality. Women committed crimes because of individual pathology; men committed crimes because of social forces.

Historically, criminal laws enforced against women applied mainly to offenses against public order, such as prostitution, and nonviolent offenses, such as shoplifting and petty theft. According to some writers, this practice has changed dramatically. Some attribute the change to the women's movement and increased female emancipation. Freda Adler, in a widely cited book, *Sisters in Crime*, reported that in increasing numbers "women are using guns, knives, and wits to establish themselves as full human beings, as capable of violence and aggression as any man."[62]

Darrell Steffensmeier challenged Adler's "new female crime type" thesis. Surveying the Uniform Crime Reports from 1965 to 1980, Steffensmeier found that, according to official statistics, female crime had not changed in nature during those years. Although the police arrested women at a higher rate than men in 1980 than in 1965, petty theft accounted almost exclusively for the increase, with a slight increase in forgery, embezzlement, and fraud. Roy Austin also used the Uniform Crime Reports, but divided the period into shorter segments. He found that from 1968 to 1972, women committed more traditionally "female" crimes, as well as more robberies, burglaries, and auto thefts. Austin, using divorce and female employment rates as criteria, concluded that these were the years of women's "liberation."[63]

Self-report data show that women and men commit the same types of crimes, although at different rates. Criminologists Stephen E. Brown, Finn-Aage Esbensen, and Gilbert Geis summarized a group of self-report data thus: "female offending appears to be very similar to male criminality, except that the former occurs at a less frequent rate."[64]

Most assessments of female crime depend on the aggregate data in the national reports of crime in the United States, which seem to demonstrate that men commit crimes at higher rates than women do. But the picture gets considerably more complex when researchers disaggregate the data by geography, gender, and race. Deborah R. Baskin and Ira Sommers, for example, conducted interviews with community samples of 85 women who were active violent offenders, 43 women charged with violent felonies, and 42 women prisoners. Their findings challenged the gender gap between men and women offending. They found that complex relationships linked to neighborhood, peer groups, and addiction affect violent offending regardless of gender. For example, neighborhood poverty and weak social control strongly affected the initiation of adolescents into violent street crime. (See the beginning of Chapter 1, "Crime and Punishment in New Haven: A Gender Gap?")[65]

Knowledge and Understanding CHECK

1. Identify and define the relationships that are subject to criminal behavior.
2. Explain why relationship crimes are difficult to measure.
3. Summarize the major findings, method, and sources of Murray Strauss's research on relationships and crime.
4. Describe the importance of Lincoln and Strauss's study of relationships and crime.
5. Identify the differences between male and female criminals.
6. How did early criminologists explain these differences?
7. How has the government historically enforced the criminal laws against women?
8. Has this historical pattern of enforcement changed? Explain.
9. Explain Freda Adler's theory of female criminality.
10. Contrast Darrell Steffensmeier's view of "the new female crime type" with Freda Adler's.
11. Summarize the methods, sources, and finding of Deborah Baskin's and Ira Sommers' research.

Criminal Careers and Career Criminals

Literature and folklore have long recognized the professional, or career, criminal. Historical research supports these impressions. We now know, for example, that a criminal underworld existed in London from at least the mid-sixteenth century. Members of this "society" were the predecessors of the modern professional criminal—pickpockets, confidence game offenders, shoplifters, counterfeiters, fences, burglars, arsonists, and hired killers. Some empirical research also supports the idea of the professional criminal. According to this research, career criminals regard themselves as criminals, associate largely with other criminals, and make their living by criminal activity. In general, they take pride in their work and respect others who are professional criminals.[66]

A related but different idea is the **criminal career:** the idea that the career criminal's behavior has measurable characteristics:

1. *Onset:* when criminals commit their first crime.
2. *Frequency:* how often they commit crimes.
3. *Duration:* how long they continue to commit crimes.
4. *Desistance:* when they stop committing crimes.

Of particular interest is the so-called **violent predator,** the criminal who specializes in the use of violence for personal gain. Armed robbers and violent drug dealers are the prime examples. These violent predators represent only a small number of offenders, but they commit a disproportionately large number of offenses. One estimate of violent repeat offenders (offenders who had committed five or more offenses more serious than traffic offenses) reported that 25 percent of these offenders committed 61 percent of the homicides, 76 percent of the rapes, 73 percent of the robberies, and 65 percent of the aggravated assaults in Philadelphia.[67]

In a widely cited survey of prisoners in California, Texas, and Michigan, researchers at the Rand Corporation asked the prisoners about their criminal careers. The researchers found that violent predators frequently rob and assault other people to get money, by force if necessary. Nevertheless, violent predators do not *specialize* in violence. In fact, their nonviolent crimes far outnumber their violent crimes. They actively pursue burglary, theft, credit card forgery, and fraud. The most active 10 percent commit 135 robberies, more than 500 burglaries, 500 thefts, and 4,000 drug deals every year![68]

The Rand researchers found the following characteristics of violent predators:

1. They are under 23 years of age.
2. They have committed serious crimes for more than six years.
3. They begin to commit crimes well before they are 16.
4. They are likely to commit violent and property crimes by the time they are 18.
5. They have spent considerable time in juvenile institutions.
6. They have weak family ties or none.
7. They are unemployed or have difficulty keeping jobs.
8. They began to use "hard" drugs as juveniles and they continue to use them.[69]

In their study *Armed Robbers in Action*, Richard T. Wright and Scott H. Decker state:

> perhaps more than any other offense, [robbery] fuels the fear of crime that undermines the quality of life for urban residents. . . . Although the public certainly fears murder and rape, it is probably fear of robbery . . . that keeps them off the street, makes them avoid strangers, and leads them to lock their doors.[70]

But identifying the characteristics and tracing the careers of violent predators does not automatically translate into useful criminal justice policy and practice. The Rand researchers conducted their research in prisons, so their subjects were already identified and convicted. Furthermore, the felons reported information about crimes they had committed but that had not been discovered, information on their juvenile records, and employment and other personal data not readily accessible to researchers or decision makers. In practice, therefore, criminal justice practitioners cannot obtain such information when they most need it—*before* offenders commit crimes. Obviously, potential offenders are not going to reveal information that might lead to increased surveillance, arrest, prosecution, conviction, and, ultimately, punishment.

Singling out violent predators for more aggressive criminal justice attention also raises questions about both the fairness and the constitutional protections afforded all people before conviction. Police investigation and arrest methods may punish individuals before conviction, violating the presumption of innocence. Furthermore, singling out violent predators punishes individuals for their personal characteristics, not their behavior. This violates the law's requirement that guilt be based on offenders' actions, not on their status or condition. (See Chapter 3.)

Moreover, the evidence suggests that practitioners cannot accurately predict who will commit predatory crimes in the future. This inaccuracy renders unfair the designation of certain people as targets for intense police investigation and arrest efforts, more vigorous prosecution, and harsher penalties. Only a very few young men with long juvenile records, heavy drug habits, irregular employment, and weak family ties are violent predators.

Use *Your* Discretion

Can we rely on the evidence of the career patterns of career criminals?

Consider the following findings:

1. Alfred Blumstein and Jacqueline Cohen, who studied arrest records in Washington, D.C., and Detroit, estimated far fewer average robberies and burglaries than indicated by the Rand study.
2. Richard T. Decker and Scott H. Decker found that relying on their active robbers' memories of their past criminal behavior is highly risky:

> The difficulty of [determining the frequency and types of crimes committed] inheres in the inability of offenders to provide even modestly precise estimates. . . . [M]ost of the armed robbers we interviewed had only a vague notion of how many crimes they had carried out over the course of their careers. Similarly, few could recall accurately such things as the age at which they committed their first crime or the total amount of time they had spent "off the street" (and hence not at risk for lawbreaking) in jail or prison. . . . Estimates therefore are bound to be highly inexact, if not downright misleading.[71]

CRITICAL THINKING

1. On the basis of these warnings, would you agree with criminologists Michael Gottfredson and Travis Hirschi that criminal justice practitioners and academics should spend only a small portion of time and effort on the career criminal?[72]
2. Would you instead recommend spending more time and improving the methods of studying criminal careers?
3. Would you recommend that police, prosecutors, and judges stop devoting special efforts on young, unemployed, unattached, known offenders with drug problems until we are more sure of the numbers used to identify them and interfere with their lives?
4. Or do you believe that inconveniencing, even occasionally harassing, innocent young people on the basis of faulty information on their careers leads to the early apprehension, prosecution, and conviction of at least some violent predators?
5. How many innocent, nondangerous people in the general population are we willing to subject to intense criminal justice attention in order to identify a few highly dangerous, violent predators?
6. Would you favor adoption of the "sexual predator" law enacted by the state of Washington and a few other states? The Washington law authorizes the state to lock up indefinitely anyone who has committed at least one violent crime, if the person has a criminal history of sexual misconduct.

Crime and Occupation

In 1939, the sociologist Edwin H. Sutherland coined the phrase "white-collar" crime to describe crimes committed by "respectable" people, "or at least respected business and professional men." Sutherland was not the first sociologist to study crimes of the "respectable" classes. The French sociologist Emile Durkheim, in 1902, noticed that the most "blameworthy acts are so often absolved by success" that business people could escape liability for the harms they cause. A few years later, in 1907, the American sociologist Edward A. Ross complained that members of a new criminal class, which he called "criminaloid," used their prominent business positions to exploit consumers but escaped criminal liability because they did not fit the accepted definitions of criminals. Since their motive was profit, not injuring others, neither they nor the public considered their actions to be crimes.[73]

Today, criminologists use the broader term **occupational crime** to include not simply white-collar crime, but more generally the use of employment, occupation, or professional position to commit crimes. In this category are crimes committed by middle- and upper-class individuals, professionals, politicians, white-collar and blue-collar workers, corporations and other business enterprises, labor unions, and even government employees who illegally use their positions to secure gain, power, or advantage.

Some occupational crimes are committed for private, personal gain. Others, organization crimes, are committed to illegally enhance the power, prestige, and profits of organizations. A bank clerk who takes money from the bank in order to make payments on an expensive home has taken advantage of employment for purely private gain. Corporate executives who fix prices or mastermind illegal takeovers in order to enhance the power of their companies and raise their profits have committed organization crimes.[74]

Property crimes, what one expert calls "clever theft," are the most publicized occupation-related offenses. According to the criminologist and white-collar expert Marshall Clinard and his colleagues:

> White-collar crime is stealing—but not so plain and not so simple. It is clever theft, like that committed by a pickpocket, but is far more clever—because it operates in a manner which throws a smoke screen over the crime, either to hide the fact that there has been a crime at all, or to delay its discovery, or to insulate the receiver of the loot. And because the stealing is artful, proving criminal intent is usually made difficult by greater confusions than where a common thief is apprehended. The tools of crime are paper, pens, printing presses, advertising, glib talk, and even exploitations of government programs intended to protect the public from deception.[75]

Occupational and organization crimes also cause physical harm. Even if perpetrators do not intend physical harm in unlawfully pursuing profit and power, such crimes can make people ill or injure and even kill them. Traditionally, if the actions of corporations injured or killed people, victims sought redress either in tort actions or through government agencies. On the rare occasions when the government filed criminal complaints, it virtually always charged corporations with misdemeanors, not felonies. As a result, corporations have escaped assault and criminal homicide charges, being cited instead for violating safety and health codes.[76]

It is difficult to prosecute corporate crime, because the criminal law requires identifying specific wrongdoers and proving that they intended to hurt or kill their victims. Identifying individual wrongdoers in complex organizational structures is often impossible. Even if identified, most corporate wrongdoers did not intend to hurt or kill anyone. They sought only personal gain, organizational advantage, or both. In this respect, corporate and other organization crime differs from street and relational crime, in which the principles of criminal law and specific legal definitions of crime clearly apply: Identifiable perpetrators definitely intend to cause harm to their victims. In corporate crime, on the other hand, identifying perpetrators, proving criminal acts and criminal intent, and linking them through the causation requirement of the criminal law are frequently impossible. In the few instances where the government has prosecuted and obtained convictions, the punishment of corporations and their executives appeared mild in comparison to the harms suffered.

Employee theft is the most prevalent blue-collar crime. A survey of employees at 583 supermarkets revealed that 62 percent admitted to stealing cash or property. The average employee admitted to stealing $143 a year. Annual losses due to employee theft at these supermarkets were about $3,500,000. Employees also engaged in more indirect theft. Sixty-two percent admitted to some form of "time theft," such as sick-day abuse; and 87 percent admitted to some form of general counterproductivity, including wasting materials and supplies, arguing with customers, and working under the influence of drugs and alcohol. According to the Food Marketing Institute, "The typical employee thief worked the evening or night shift, was male, aged 16 to 20, reported having significantly more employers during the last year, and endorsed a set of attitudes that tended to rationalize and justify the legitimacy of employee theft."[77]

Richard Hollinger, Karen Slora, and William Terris tested the proposition that employee theft occurs more frequently in occupational settings that rely on "marginal" workers, especially those who are young and with little tenure and who believe that their employers treat them unfairly. Hollinger and his associates collected questionnaire data from 341 employees in fast-food corporations. Sixty percent admitted to some theft of company property in the past six months. Over one-third admitted to "altruistic" stealing, such as using employee discounts for friends. Eighty percent engaged in counterproductive activities, such as coming late to work and calling in sick when they were not sick. Hollinger and his associates found that employee theft was principally due to a combination of age (most "altruistic" thieves were under 21), perceived employer unfairness, and tenure. Counterproductive activities were due mainly to perceived employer unfairness, regardless of age or tenure.[78]

John Clark and Richard Hollinger found that employees steal in a variety of ways. Some "borrow money" from a cash register; others take merchandise home in handbags or briefcases, sell goods to friends for a kickback, or damage products in order to buy them at a discount. Employees who misappropriate their employers' property do not consider themselves criminals, nor do they call their misappropriation stealing.[79]

Knowledge and Understanding CHECK

1. What do literature, folklore, and some empirical research have to say about career criminals?
2. Distinguish between career criminals and criminal careers.
3. Identify and describe the four quantifiables in a criminal career.
4. What is a violent predator and why is the violent predator of special interest?
5. Summarize the eight main findings, the methods, and the sources of the Rand study of criminal careers.
6. According to Richard T. Wright and Scott H. Decker, what is the significance of armed robbers?
7. Give three reasons why knowledge about criminal careers is difficult to translate into criminal justice policy and action.
8. What did Edwin H. Sutherland mean by "white-collar" crime?
9. How have modern criminologists broadened Sutherland's definition?
10. Identify two reasons for committing occupational crimes.
11. Identify the two types of harm caused by occupational crime.
12. Why is it difficult to prosecute corporate crime?
13. Identify the most prevalent blue-collar crime and list specific details about it.
14. What proposition did Richard Hollinger and his colleagues test regarding employee theft? How did they test the proposition, and what did they find?
15. List the principal ways that employees steal.

CRIME VICTIMS

In 1996, NCVRS reported 43.6 million victimizations among residents in households who were aged 12 or older. Victims sustain physical injury in rapes, robberies, and assaults. They suffer financial losses from stolen, damaged, or destroyed property, lost income, medical expenses, and the cost of protection against crime. Victims' emotional distress ranges from fear and helplessness to anger and the desire for revenge. A husband and wife whose house was burglarized said:

> [Wife:] That made me angry inside, that someone would do that and upset my children. . . . It was somewhat revenge . . . anger toward that person and feeling like they had no business in my home. . . . The more I thought about it . . . the more revenge I felt.
> [Husband:] It's unfair that you work for something, like this lawn mower was nothing of value really, but you work hard for it and somebody takes it away from you when you're about to enjoy it or continue to enjoy it.

Another victim went even further:

> Six young men rob a teenager of his gold jewelry while he waits for a subway train. The next night the victim chances upon the offenders at the same station. He comes up to them and simply utters, "Remember me?" Although they don't recognize him and look puzzled he takes out a pistol and shoots three of them before fleeing.[80]

Crime victims may suffer not only from the actions of criminals but also from the reactions of employers. A bank teller found this out when she handed over money to a robber. The robber had handed her a note that read, "This is a stickup. Put all the money in a bag and no one will get hurt." In her panic she omitted to slip in a specially treated bundle of bills that would trigger an electronic beam at the entrance to the bank. The beam would have set off shots of red dye and tear gas at the robber when he tried to escape. The next morning her boss told her either to take a demotion and pay reduction or an unpaid indefinite leave of absence. She quit, saying, "I did what any normal person would do—I gave the man the money. For three years I've been a loyal employee and this is what I get."[81]

Crime victims may also suffer from the interventions of the criminal justice system. Police, prosecutors, and judges, although perhaps unintentionally, can treat victims as if they are at fault. Police officers may ask embarrassing questions. Prosecutors and court personnel do not always keep victims informed about the progress of their cases. Police and prosecutors withhold victims' property as evidence. Victims lose time from work and family to cooperate with police and prosecutors. Often not prepared to testify in court, victims may experience apprehension, fear, and other discomfort. Victims may also fear retaliation from those they testify against.[82]

Types of Victims

Victimization does not fall randomly over the general population. Most people never experience it, or do so only once; a minority experience frequent victimization. Does this mean that some people are more likely victims than others? Re-

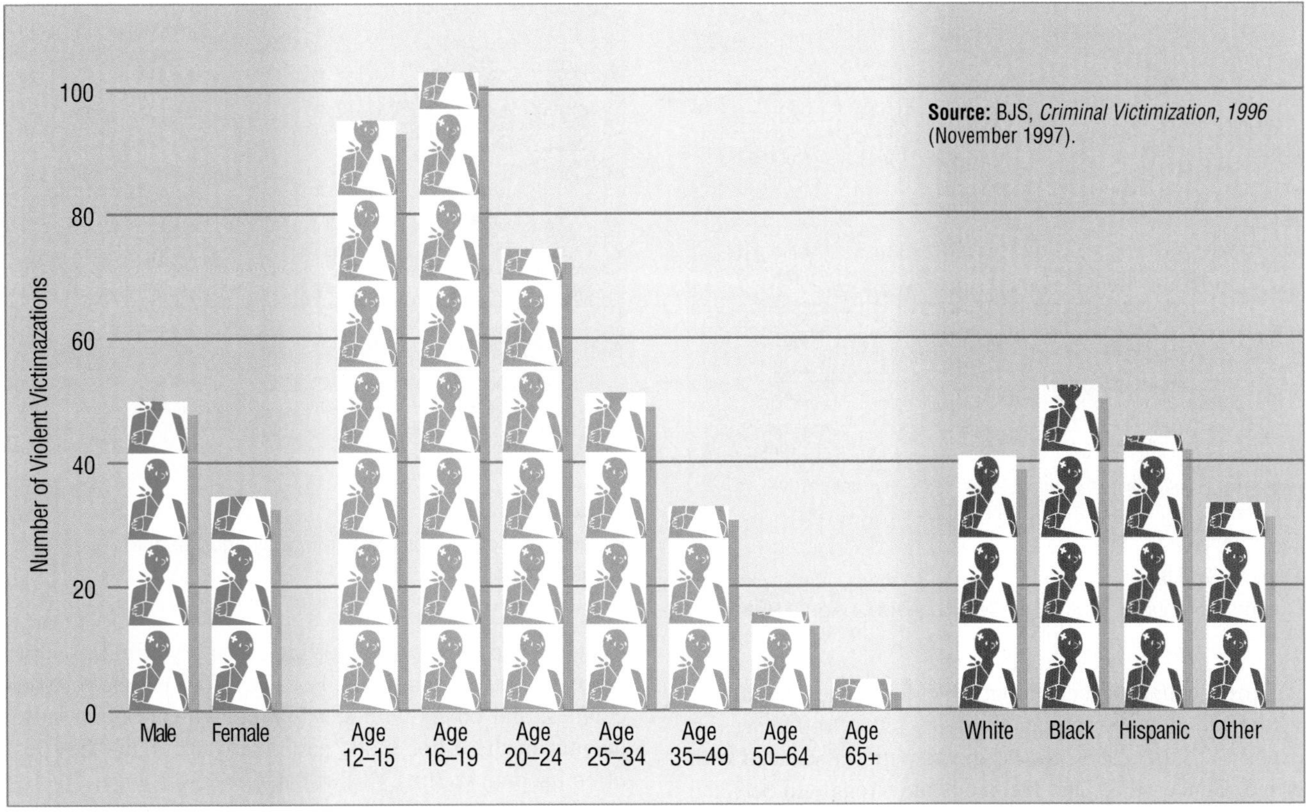

Figure 2.9
Violent Crime Victimizations per 1,000 Persons Age 12 or Older

search dispels the common perception that elderly and other vulnerable citizens suffer disproportionately from crime. In fact, for people aged 65 or over, violent crime claims victims five times less often; stolen car crimes, four times less often; and home burglaries, half as often. These numbers, of course, do not mean that the elderly do not suffer from crime. Victimization and fear of victimization may well traumatize the elderly more than they do younger victims. This fear erodes the quality of life for elderly citizens, forcing them to stay at home rather than venture outside (Figure 2.9).[83]

At the same time, empirical research has demonstrated some support for the notion of victim proneness, particularly for such crimes as rape, purse snatching, pocket picking, ordinary theft, burglary, and automobile theft; but not robbery and assault, with one notable exception. Marvin E. Wolfgang, Terence P. Thornberry, and Robert M. Figlio, in a follow-up to a self-report survey, asked birth cohorts (people of the same age) questions not only about their crimes but also about their victimizations between ages 12 to 18 and 18 to 26. The responses showed that a lifestyle within a subculture of crime involves becoming both a predator and a victim in personal, but not property, crimes.[84]

Occupation also has an effect on victimization. More than one million people a year are the victims of violent crime on the job. Every year, someone steals personal belongings from more than two million workers while they work, and the cars of another 200,000. These victimizations cost an average of about 3.5 days of work per person every year. Among those victimized while working, men are more likely to be the victims of violent crime, but women are just as likely to be the victims of theft. Race is also related to victimization. The National Institute for Occupational Health and Safety (OSHA) has found that the rate of work-related homicides for African Americans was nearly twice that of white workers during the 1980s. African American taxi drivers and gas station attendants have especially high homicide rates. Experts at OSHA speculate that the reason for the higher rates is that more African Americans work in dangerous neighborhoods than do white Americans.[85]

Perhaps the most significant finding of empirical research is that most crime victims resemble their perpetrators: They are young, poor, male, urban, and nonwhite. Victimization also strongly correlates with lifestyle. Criminologists have developed theories built around this correlation. The earliest of these theorists faced strong opposition on ideological grounds. During the 1970s, feminists and victims' advocates complained that such theories blamed the victims. Despite opposition, one of these theories, the **lifestyle-exposure theory,** has received considerable acceptance among criminologists.[86]

According to the basic premise of the lifestyle-exposure theory, introduced by Michael S. Hindaling, Michael Gottfredson, and James Garofalo, differences in the lifestyles of

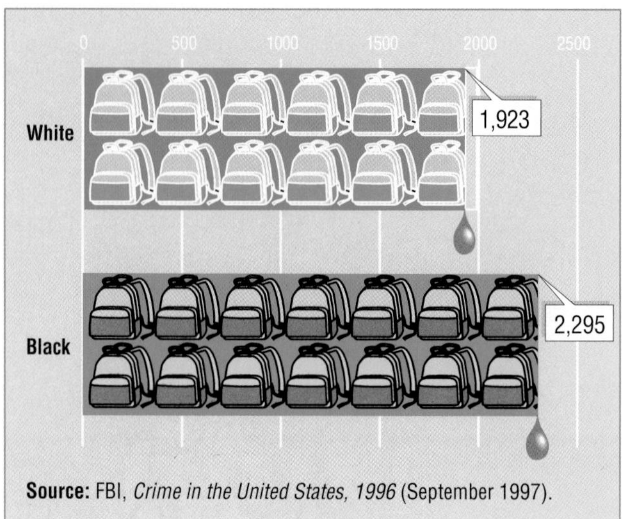

Source: FBI, *Crime in the United States, 1996* (September 1997).

Figure 2.10
Numbers of Murder Victims Under 22 Years of Age, 1996

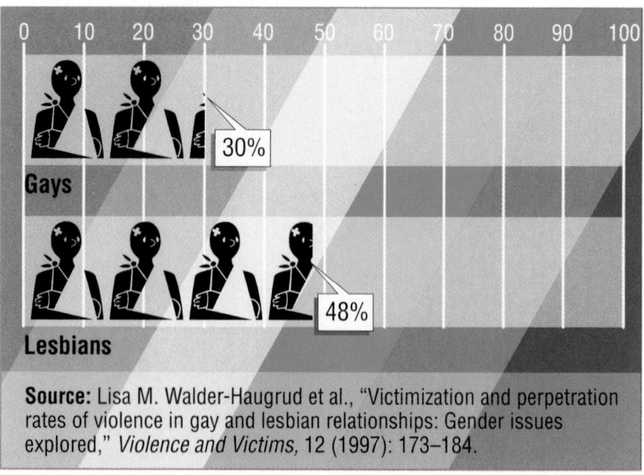

Source: Lisa M. Walder-Haugrud et al., "Victimization and perpetration rates of violence in gay and lesbian relationships: Gender issues explored," *Violence and Victims,* 12 (1997): 173–184.

Figure 2.11
Percent of Violent Victimization in Gay and Lesbian Relationships

victims account for the demographic differences in criminal victimization. Variations in lifestyles reflect differences in exposure to the places, times, and activities associated with crime. Gender, race, and income relate strongly to personal lifestyles and therefore to crime. According to the theory, crimes take place disproportionately against young, single, low-income African American men because this group spends more time outside the home at night, taking part in activities during which crimes often occur. Figure 2.10 shows the number of black and white murder victims under the age of 22. Notice that there are more black than white victims although blacks make up only 12 percent of the population.[87]

Use *Your* Discretion

Does gender matter in gay and lesbian victimization?

A sample of 283 gays and lesbians reported on their experience as victims and perpetrators of violence with their partners. (See Figure 2.11.)

CRITICAL THINKING

What more information would you need in order to rely on the results depicted in Figure 2.11?

By analyzing more than 300,000 emergency calls for one year in Minneapolis, Lawrence W. Sherman, Patrick R. Gartin, and Michael E. Buerger identified the locations where most crimes take place, which they called **"hot spots."** They found that these hot spots produce most calls to police and most calls reporting predatory crimes, such as robberies, rapes, and thefts. Because older people, married couples, and others with steady employment appear infrequently in these hot spots, particularly at night, they less often become victims.[88] (See Chapter 5.)

Attitudes Toward Victims

Americans hold ambivalent attitudes toward victimization. This ambivalence is reflected in American literature. Some fiction writers focus on victims' helplessness against outside forces. The novelist Saul Bellow, for example, says that literature "pits any ordinary individual against the external world and the external world conquers him, of course."[89]

Much literature pushes victims into the background, focusing attention on—and frequently engendering sympathy for—criminals. Truman Capote said of his *In Cold Blood*, which recounted a brutal Kansas murder:

> It's what I really think about America. Desperate, savage, violent America in collision with safe, insular, even smug America—people who have every chance against people who have none.

In the British film adaptation of the novel *A Clockwork Orange,* young thugs terrorize law-abiding people, but the real sympathy lies with Alex, one of the thugs, who becomes the "victim" of modern penological methods.

Some literature blames the victims. In *The Murdered One Is Guilty*, for example, the victim precipitated the crime. Many television crime dramas focus on "cops and robbers," pitting law enforcement agents against thugs, rapists, and drug dealers with no mention of the victims. Law enforcement, of course, always triumphs.[90]

Story lines that sympathize with victims sometimes go to the other extreme. Wronged individuals take the law into their own hands and wreak terrible revenge on their attackers, as in the film "Next of Kin," which reenacts a blood feud between residents of Appalachia and an Italian family responsible for a young man's death. The audience cheers as the avengers beat, stab, torture, torment, and kill the Italians in a virtual blood bath at the end of the film.

Protecting and Assisting Victims

The federal Victim and Witness Protection Act of 1982 protects and assists victims in federal crimes in the following ways:

1. Makes threatening victims and witnesses a felony.
2. Provides for the inclusion of victim impact statements in presentencing reports.
3. Gives trial judges authority to order offenders to make restitution to their victims.
4. Requires judges who do not order restitution to explain in writing why they did not.

In 1984, Congress passed the Victims of Crime Act, which created a $100 million crime victims' fund derived from criminal fines in federal offenses. The fund provides money for state victim-compensation programs and other programs that assist crime victims. States have also adopted legislation to assist crime victims. The most common statutes assisting victims of violent crime make citizens who report crimes and cooperate with investigation and prosecution eligible to receive from $10,000 to $15,000 for medical expenses, funeral expenses, lost wages, and the support of deceased victims' dependents. This low monetary cap, however, severely restricts the real help victims receive. Furthermore, most legislation does not allot money for psychotherapy or compensation for property loss.

Some states have established victim-witness assistance programs, usually supervised by prosecutors. These programs provide such services as:

1. *Personal advocacy:* helping victims receive all the services they are entitled to in both social service and criminal justice agencies.
2. *Referral:* recommending or obtaining assistance other than that given by the assistance programs.
3. *Restitution assistance:* urging judges to order, or probation authorities to collect, restitution, and helping violent-crime victims fill out the proper papers necessary to receive compensation.
4. *Court orientation:* helping victims and witnesses understand the criminal justice system and their participation in it.
5. *Transportation:* taking victims and witnesses to and from court, to social service agencies, and, if necessary, to shelters.
6. *Escort services:* escorting witnesses to court and staying with them during proceedings.
7. *Emotional support:* giving victims support during their ordeals with crime and with the criminal justice proceedings following it.[91]

Thirteen states have even written victim's rights provisions into their state constitutions. Typical provisions require that the criminal justice system

- Treat victims with compassion and respect.
- Inform victims of critical stages in the trial process.
- Invite victims to attend and comment on trial proceedings.

"I feel as if our movement is picking up the steam that it needs to carry through all 50 states," said Linda Lowrance, chairwoman of the Victims' Constitutional Amendment Network.

No one has comprehensively evaluated the effectiveness of these provisions, according to John Stein, deputy director of the National Organization for Victim Assistance. However, some individual studies have shown that victim impact statements make people "feel better" about the criminal justice system, even though the statements have little or no effect on sentencing or punishment of convicted offenders. Roberta Roper, whose daughter was raped and murdered, could not attend the trial of her daughter's murderers because Maryland has no victims' rights law. Forced to watch the trial by pressing her nose against the small pane of glass in a wooden courtroom door, Roper felt she had let her daughter down by not being in court. "By being a presence at the trial, we could as a family bear witness to the fact that Stephanie lived, and she mattered. We were denied that."[92]

At the time of the crime, however, victims must rely heavily on self-protection. According to NCVS, three-quarters of victims reported taking self-protective measures against offenders, including resisting, trying to capture, persuading, and running away. More than half of those who took self-protective measures reported that their actions had a positive effect. About 7 percent reported that the measures made the situation worse, while 6 percent reported that both positive and negative effects resulted. Figure 2.12 depicts the main ways in which crime victims protect themselves.

Knowledge and Understanding CHECK

1. Describe how much of our literature and popular culture treats victims.
2. Describe the role of victims in the criminal justice system.
3. Briefly describe the four ways in which the federal Victim and Witness Protection Act of 1982 protects and assists victims of federal crimes.
4. Summarize the purpose of the Victims of Crime Act enacted in 1984.
5. Identify and describe seven services provided by state victim-witness assistance programs.
6. Identify three common provisions in victims' rights provisions in state constitutions.

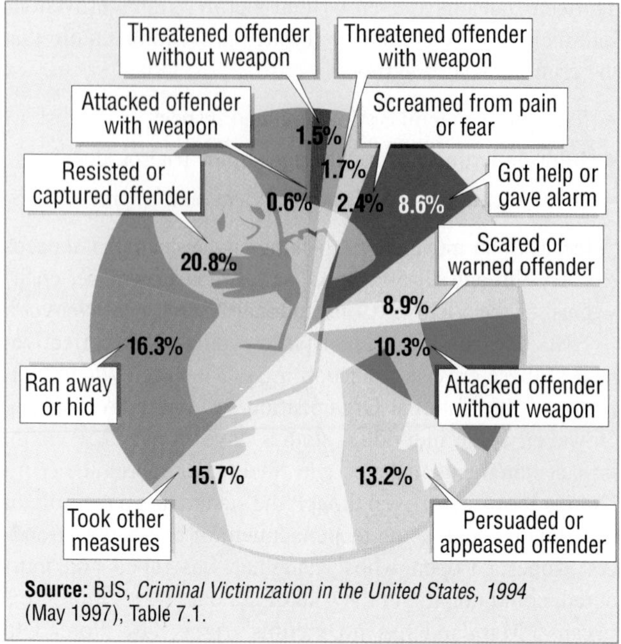

Source: BJS, *Criminal Victimization in the United States, 1994* (May 1997), Table 7.1.

Figure 2.12
Self-Protective Measures Taken by Victims, 1994, in Percentages

Victims and the Criminal Justice System

In colonial times, crime victims played a central part in criminal justice. They conducted their own investigations, secured warrants, paid witnesses, and hired private attorneys to prosecute their cases. Colonial law allowed victims to collect damages from offenders; it even authorized binding offenders in servitude to victims. Wealthy victims paid the government to incarcerate criminals. In other words, criminal justice was victim-centered and relied heavily on victims in its administration. By the early twentieth century, criminal justice had become society-centered. Punishment was calculated by the harm done to society, not to the individual victim. Victims lost most of their formal role in criminal justice, and offenders lost most of their legal responsibility to individual victims.[93]

Informally, the importance of the victim is quite a different matter. The government relies heavily on victims in identifying, apprehending, prosecuting, and convicting criminals. According to the political scientist James Q. Wilson, "The most important person in the criminal justice system may not be the judge, police officer, or prosecutor—it may be the victim." In appreciation of the victims' critical function in law enforcement, both federal and state governments have taken actions to improve treatment of victims. Crime victims are the gatekeepers of the criminal justice system. If victims do not report crimes to the police, those crimes do not receive official notice or response. Victims report or fail to report crimes for a variety of reasons described earlier. Reporting means getting involved in the criminal process. This means spending time, perhaps losing hours or days of work, and risking retaliation. After the time is spent the results may be frustrating, because the police could not apprehend the perpetrator, the penalty did not satisfy the victim, or the property was not recovered.[94]

The decision to report a crime also affects the criminal justice system. Without the report of the victim, the police do not know about the crime and cannot apprehend and arrest suspects in most property and violent crimes. If the police cannot arrest suspects, prosecutors cannot charge them with crimes, courts cannot convict them, and correctional facilities cannot punish them. On the other hand, if victims report all crimes, then the criminal justice system, already overloaded, may be asked to deal with many more crimes than it can manage.

The decision to report—or not to report—a crime also affects society. Will the highly discretionary, low-visibility decisions of victims satisfy a society that demands retribution and believes that apprehending and punishing more criminals will reduce crime? Furthermore, is it fair and just to allow victims to decide who enters the criminal justice system? Will they select only members of certain groups in society, or choose to report only some kinds of crime? Does society want victims to determine whether criminal justice officials devote scarce resources to the kinds of crimes victims report, or does society want money and time for other types of crimes (like organizational crime, family crimes, and drug offenses) that victims rarely report?

Knowledge and Understanding CHECK

1. Describe the ways crime victims suffer, giving examples.
2. What common misperceptions of victimization does empirical research dispel?
3. How do crime victims compare with their victimizers?
4. Summarize the findings of Lawrence W. Sherman and his colleagues regarding crime "hot spots."
5. Describe victim proneness.
6. Describe the effects of occupation on victimization.
7. Contrast the role of victims in colonial times with their role in the present.
8. Why is the crime victim perhaps the most important person in the criminal justice system?
9. Why do we call crime victims the gatekeepers of the criminal justice system?
10. How do victims' decisions to report or not to report crimes affect the criminal justice system and society?

Is Fear of Robbery Racist? Consideration

Consider the following excerpt from Richard T. Wright's and Scott H. Decker's *Armed Robbers in Action* concerning the fear of robbery:

> Racial prejudice undoubtedly accounts for some of the fear that robbery engenders in the population. Unlike other forms of criminal violence, armed robbery often is an interracial event in which a white victim is confronted by a black offender. The offense can both provoke and reinforce racial stereotypes in which blacks are perceived to be predatory and violent. . . . Robberies have done much to exacerbate racial tensions in American cities.[95]

Critical Thinking

1. If you had only this information, would you conclude that race is the reason for the fear of robbery, or is it the myth about robbery that generates the fear, or is it both?
2. What kinds of additional information would you need before you made any recommendations about what to do about the fear of robbery?

CHAPTER CAPSULE

- Crimes range across a wide spectrum of behavior.
- The distribution of crime varies according to time and place.
- Crime is also distributed differently according to demographic characteristics.
- It is difficult to tell whether the amount of crime is increasing, decreasing, or remaining steady.
- Crime is measured by crimes reported to the police, victim surveys, and self-reports of criminal behavior.

KEY TERMS

The Uniform Crime Reports (UCR)
aggregate statistics
Crime Index
Part I offenses
Part II offenses
dark figure in crime
National Incident-Based Reporting System (NIBRS)
incident-based reporting
National Crime Victimization Survey (NCVS)
occupational crime
predatory crimes
ethnographic studies
criminal career
violent predator
occupational crime
organizational crime
lifestyle-exposure theory
hot spots

INTERNET RESEARCH EXERCISES

Exercise: Using the Internet or InfoTrac College edition, find out what the national trend in crime statistics has been for the past four years. Has crime been rising or decreasing? What explanations can you find for this trend? Which do you find the most convincing? Find information on crime rates in your local geographic region. How do they compare to national crime rates? If there are differences, what explanations could you give?

Suggested sites:

- FBI Uniform Crime Reports: http://www.fbi.gov/ucr/ucreports.htm (tip: click on "Uniform Crime Reports" or "Crime in the United States")
- Bureau of Justice Statistics: http://www.ojp.usdoj.gov/bjs (tip: click on "Publications," then click on the most recent "Criminal Victimization" report you can found, then click on "ASCII file" to view the report to your computer.)

InfoTrac College Edition: Run a key word search on "criminal statistics" or "crime trends."

NOTES

1. Quoted in Randall Kennedy, *Race, Crime, and the Law* (New York: Vintage Press, 1998), 16.
2. Ibid., 15.
3. BJS, *Criminal Victimization in the United States*, 1990 (Washington, D.C.: Bureau of Justice Statistics, 1992), 8.
4. Fox Butterfield, "Number of Victims of Crime Fell Again in '96, Study Says," *New York Times*, 16 November 1997, Section 1, p. 18.
5. Ibid.
6. Henry H. Brownstein, *The Rise and Fall of a Violent Crime Wave* (New York: Harrow and Heston, 1996), 1–2.
7. National Institute of Justice, *Measuring What Matters, Part I* (Washington, D.C., December 1996), 11, 12.
8. Ibid.
9. Butterfield, "Number of Crimes Fell Again."
10. Ibid.
11. Fox Butterfield, "Reason for Dramatic Drop in Crime Puzzles the Experts," *The New York Times*, March 19, 1998, section 1, p. 16.
12. Ibid.
13. Ibid.
14. Richard Sparks, "Criminal Opportunities and Crime Rates," in *Indicators of Crime and Criminal Justice: Quantitative Studies*, Stephen E. Feinberg and Albert J. Reiss, Jr., eds. (Washington, D.C.: Bureau of Justice Statistics, June 1980), 18.
15. Ibid.
16. Patrick A. Langan and Christopher A. Innes, *The Risk of Violent Crime* (Washington, D.C.: Bureau of Justice Statistics, May 1985), 1.
17. Donald Black, "Production of Crime Rates," in *The Manners and Customs of the Police* (New York: Academic Press, 1980), 65–67; Richard F. Sparks, "A Critique of Marxist Criminology," in *Crime and Justice: An Annual Review of Research*, Norval Morris and Michael Tonry, eds. (Chicago: University of Chicago Press, 1980), 2: 159–210.
18. Henry H. Brownstein, *The Rise and Fall of a Violent Crime Wave* (New York: Harrow and Heston, 1996), 24; FBI, *Crime in the United States, 1996* (Washington, D.C.: Federal Bureau of Investigation, 1997).
19. Department of Justice, *The Nation's Two Crime Measures* (November 1995).
20. Yoshio Akiyama and Harvey M. Rosenthal, "The Future of the Uniform Crime Reporting Program: Its Scope and Promise," in Doris Layton MacKenzie, Phyllis Jo Baunach, and Roy R. Roberg, eds., *Measuring Crime: Large Scale, Long Range Efforts* (Albany: State University of New York Press, 1990), 49–50; Eugene C. Poggio et al., *Blueprint for the Future of the Uniform Crime Reporting Program, Final Report of the UCR Study* (Washington, D.C.: Bureau of Justice Statistics, May 1985), 1.
21. For a critique of the law enforcement bias in crime news, see Kenneth B. Nunn, "The Trial as Text: Allegory, Myth and Symbol in the Adversarial Criminal Process," *American Criminal Law Review* 32 (1995).
22. Anthony J. Petrosino and Dian Brensiller, "Convenient Victims—A Research Note," *Criminal Justice Policy Review* 8 (1997): 406.
23. Ibid., 409.
24. Ibid.
25. Ibid., 406.
26. Victoria W. Schneider and Brian Wiersema, "Limits and Use of the *Uniform Crime Reports*," in *Measuring Crime*, 21–27; Darrell Steffensmeier and Miles D. Harar, "Did Crime Rise or Fall During the Reagan Presidency? The Effects of an 'Aging' Population on the Nation's Crime Rate," *Journal of Research in Crime and Delinquency* 28 (1991): 333–35. Henry H. Brownstein, *The Rise and Fall of a Violent Crime Wave* (Guilderland, N.Y.: Harrow and Heston, 1996), 19–25.
27. W. Gove, M. Hughes, and M. Geerken, "Are Uniform Crime Reports a Valid Indicator of the Index Crime? An Affirmative Answer with Minor Qualifications" *Criminology* 23 (1985): 491.
28. Henry H. Brownstein, *The Rise and Fall of a Violent Crime Wave*, 20–22.
29. Thorsten Sellin, "The Significance of Records of Crime," *Law Quarterly Review* 67 (1951): 489–504.
30. "Structure and Implementation Plan for the Enhanced UCR Program," mimeograph (Washington, D.C.: Federal Bureau of Investigation, November 1988).
31. Bureau of Justice Statistics, *Implementing the National Incident-Based Reporting System: A Project Status Report* (Washington, D.C., July 1997).
32. Brownstein, *The Rise and Fall of a Violent Crime Wave*, 25.
33. BJS, *The National Crime Survey: Working Papers 1* (1981): 1; James Garofalo, "The National Crime Survey, 1973–86: Strengths and Limitations of a Very Large Data Set," in *Measuring Crime*, 75; Bureau of Justice Statistics, *Rape and Other Sexual Assaults Against Women*, (Washington, D.C., August 1995).
34. Bureau of Justice Statistics, Criminal Victimization in the United States, 1987 (Washington, D.C., October 1988); Bureau of Justice Statistics, *Criminal Victimization in the United States, 1990* (Washington, D.C., 1992), 100.
35. Bureau of Justice Statistics, *Criminal Victimization in the United States, 1990* (Washington, D.C., 1992), 100.
36. Wesley G. Skogan, "Poll Review: National Crime Survey Redesign," *Public Opinion Quarterly* 54 (1990): 256–272.
37. Ronet Bachman and Linda Salzman, *Violence Against Women: Estimates from the Redesigned Survey* (Washington, D.C.: Bureau of Justice Statistics, August 1995).
38. Wesley G. Skogan, "Poll Review," 256–72.
39. Garofalo, "The National Crime Survey," 81–82.
40. Bureau of Justice Statistics, *Criminal Victimization in the United States, 1994* (Washington, D.C., May 1997), Table 1.
41. Philip J. Cook and Jens Ludwig, "Defensive Gun Uses: New Evidence from a National Survey," *Journal of Quantitative Criminology*, 14 (1998): 111–31.
42. James F. Short and F. Ivan Nye, "Reported Behavior as a Criterion of Deviant Behavior," *Social Problems* 5 (1957–58): 207–13; John A. O'Donnell et al., Young Men and Drugs—A Nationwide Survey, monograph no. 5 (Washington, D.C.: National Institute on Drug Abuse, 1976).
43. Richard T. Wright and Scott H. Decker, *Armed Robbers in Action* (Boston: Northeastern University Press, 1997), 4–6.
44. Mike Hough, "Offenders' Choice of Target: Findings from Victim Surveys," *Journal of Quantitative Criminology* 3 (1987): 356; Richard T. Wright and Scott H. Decker, *Burglars on the Job: Streetlife and Residential Break-ins* (Boston: Northeastern University Press, 1994), 5–6.

45. James D. Wright, *The Armed Criminal in America* (Washington, D.C.: Bureau of Justice Statistics, November 1986).
46. Ibid.
47. Quoted in John Braithwaite, *Inequality, Crime, and Public Policy* (London: Routledge and Kegan Paul, 1979), 21.
48. Richard Sparks, *Testimony to House Subcommittee on Crime, Committee of the Judiciary, White Collar Crime, Second Session*, 95th Congress, June 21, July 12 and 19th, and December 1, 1978, 163–64.
49. Richard Hollinger and John P. Clark, *Theft by Employees* (Lexington, Mass.: Lexington Books, 1983); Gerald Mars, *Cheats at Work* (London: Allen and Unwin, 1982).
50. Samuel Walker, *Sense and Nonsense About Crime and Drugs*, 3rd edition (Belmont, Calif.: Wadsworth Publishing Company, 1994), 6.
51. Jan M. Chaiken and Marcia R. Chaiken, "Drugs and Predatory Crime," Michael Tonry and James Q. Wilson, eds. *Drugs and Crime* (Chicago, University of Chicago Press, 1990), 203–04.
52. Lee N. Robins et al., "Vietnam Veterans Three Years After Vietnam: How Our Study Changed our View," L. Brill and C. Winnick, eds., *Yearbook of Substance Abuse* (New York: Human Sciences Press, 1980)
53. Chaiken and Chaiken, "Drugs and Predatory Crime," 210–12.
54. Dana E. Hunt, "Drugs and Consensual Crimes," Tonry and Wilson, *Drugs and Crime*, 160, 162.
55. Albert J. Reiss and Jeffrey A. Ross, *Understanding and Preventing Violence* (Washington, D.C.: National Academy Press, 1993), 184–85; Lawrence A. Greenfield, *Alchohol and Crime* (Washington, D.C.: Bureau of Justice Statistics, 1998), 3.
56. *Understanding and Preventing Violence,* 184.
57. David Finkelhor et al., *The Dark Side of Families: Current Family Violence Research* (Beverly Hills: Sage Publications, 1983); Patrick A. Langan and Christopher Innes, *Preventing Domestic Violence Against Women* (Ann Arbor, Mich.: The Criminal Justice Archive and Information Network, Fall 1986); Walter Gove et al., "Are Uniform Crime Reports a Valid Indicator of the Index Crimes? An Affirmative Answer with Minor Qualifications," *Criminology* 23 (1986): 464–65; Bureau of Justice Statistics, Violence By Intimates (Washington, D.C., March 1998), 1.
58. Bureau of Justice Statistics, *Criminal Victimization in the United States, 1996* (Washington D.C.: 1997), 29.
59. Cited in Murray Strauss, Richard Gelles, and Suzanne Steinmetz, *Behind Closed Doors: Violence in the American Family* (New York: Doubleday, 1980), 49; Stephen E. Brown, "Social Class, Child Maltreatment, and Delinquent Behavior," *Criminology* 22 (1984): 259–78.
60. Alan J. Lincoln and Murray A. Strauss, *Crime and the Family* (Springfield, Ill.: Charles C. Thomas, 1985), 71–87.
61. Bureau of Justice Statistics Factbook, *Violence by Intimates* (Washington, D.C.: Bureau of Justice Statistics, 1998).
62. Barbara Raffel Price and Natalie J. Sokoloff, eds., *The Criminal Justice System and Women* (New York: Clark Boardman, 1982), 121–28; James A. Inciardi and Harvey A. Siegel, *Crime: Emerging Issues* (New York: Praeger, 1977), 138.
63. Darrell Steffensmeier, "Trends in Female Crime," *The Criminal Justice System and Women,* 117–129; Roy L. Austin, "Women's Liberation and Increases in Minor, Major, and Occupational Offenses," *Criminology* 20 (1982): 407–30.
64. Stephen E. Brown, Finn-Aage Esbensen, and Gilbert Geis, *Criminology: Explaining Crime and Its Content* (Cincinnati: Anderson Publishing Co., 1991).
65. Deborah R. Baskin and Ira B. Sommers, *Casualties of Community Disorder* (Boulder, Colo.: Westview Press, 1998).
66. John L. Macmullen, *The Canting Crew: London's Criminal Underworld, 1550–1700* (New Brunswick, N.J.: Rutgers University Press, 1984).
67. Alfred Blumstein et al., *Criminal Careers and "Career Criminals,"* Volume I (Washington, D.C.: National Academy Press, 1986), 1; Marvin Wolfgang, Robert Figlio, and Thorsten Sellin, *Delinquency in a Birth Cohort* (Chicago: University of Chicago Press, 1972); Paul E. Tracy, Marvin Wolfgang, and Robert Figlio, *Delinquency in Two Birth Cohorts* (Chicago: University of Chicago Press, 1985).
68. Jan M. Chaiken and Marcia R. Chaiken, *Varieties of Criminal Behavior: Summary and Implications* (Santa Monica: Rand Corporation, August 1982), 14.
69. Ibid., 18–19.
70. Richard T. Wright and Scott H. Decker, *Armed Robbers in Action* (Boston: Northeastern University Press, 1997), 7.
71. Wright and Decker, *Armed Robbers in Action*, 14.
72. Samuel Walker, *Sense and Nonsense About Crime*, 2d ed. (Pacific Grove, Calif.: Brooks/Cole Publishing Company, 1989), 59; Alfred Blumstein and Jacqueline Cohen, "Estimating Individual Crime Rates from Arrest Records," *Journal of Criminal Law and Criminology* 70 (1979): 561–85; Michael Gottfredson and Travis Hirschi, "The Value of Lambda Would Appear to Be Zero: An Essay on Criminals, Criminal Careers, Selective Incapacitation, Cohort Studies, and Related Topics," *Criminology* 24 (1986): 213–34.
73. Edwin H. Sutherland, "White-Collar Criminality," *American Sociological Review* 5 (1940): 1; Emile Durkheim, *The Division of Labor in Society* (New York: Free Press, 1964), 2; Edward A. Ross, "The Criminaloid," *Atlantic Monthly*, April 1907.
74. Albert J. Reiss and Albert D. Biderman, *Data Sources on White-Collar Crime* (Washington, D.C.: National Institute of Justice, 1980); Herbert Edelhertz, *The Nature, Impact and Prosecution of White Collar Crime* (Washington, D.C.: National Institute of Justice, 1970); Herbert Edelhertz et al., *A Manual for Law Enforcement Agencies* (Washington, D.C.: National Institute of Justice, 1977).
75. Marshall B. Clinard et al., *Illegal Corporate Behavior* (Washington, D.C.: National Institute of Law Enforcement and Criminal Justice, 1979).
76. Reiss and Biderman, *Data Sources*, 11–12; Richard Rashke, *The Killing of Karen Silkwood* (New York: Penguin Books, 1981).
77. Food Marketing Institute, "Picking Out the Bad Tomatoes," *Security Management* 36 (1992): 6–7.
78. Richard Hollinger, Karen Slora, and William Terris, "Deviance in the Fast-Food Restaurant," *Deviant Behavior* 13 (1992): 155–84.
79. Hollinger and Clark, *Theft by Employees*; Mars, *Cheats at Work.*
80. Martin S. Greenberg and R. Barry Ruback, *Social Psychology and the Criminal Justice System* (Dubuque, Iowa: Kendall/Hunt Publishing Company, 1991); first victim response quoted in Martin S. Greenberg, R. Barry Ruback, and David R. Westcott, "Seeking Help from the Police: The Victim's Perspective," in Arie Nadler, Jeffrey D. Fisher, and Bella M. DePaulo, eds., *New Directions in Helping*, Vol. 3 (New York: Academic Press, 1983), 81; second quote from Andrew Karmen, *Crime Victims*, 2d ed. (Pacific Grove, Calif.: Brooks/Cole Publishing Company, 1990), 2.
81. Karmen, *Crime Victims*, 2.
82. James Q. Wilson, moderator, *Crime File: Victims* (Washington, D.C.: Bureau of Justice Statistics, 1985).

83. Fay Lomax Cook, "Crime Among the Elderly: The Emergence of a Policy Issue," in *Reactions to Crime*, Dan E. Lewis, ed. (Beverly Hills, Calif.: Wadsworth, 1979), 123; Raymond A. Eve and Susan Brown Eve, "The Effects of Powerlessness, Fear of Social Change and Social Integration on Fear of Crime Among the Elderly," *Victimology* 9 (1984): 290; U.S. Congress, House of Representatives Select Committee on Aging, *In Search of Security: A National Perspective on Elderly Crime Victimization* (Washington, D.C.: U.S. Government Printing Office, 1977); Terance D. Miethe and Robert F. Meier, *Crime and Its Social Context: Toward an Integrated Theory of Offenders, Victims, and Situations* (Albany: State University of New York Press, 1994), 2.
84. Albert J. Reiss, Jr., "Victim Proneness in Repeat Victimization by Time of Crime," in *Indicators of Crime and Criminal Justice: Quantitative Studies*, Steven E. Feinberg and Albert J. Reiss, Jr., eds. (Washington, D.C.: Bureau of Justice Statistics, 1980), 47–57; Marvin E. Wolfgang, Terence P. Thornberry, and Robert M. Figlio, *From Boy to Man, From Delinquency to Crime* (Chicago: University of Chicago Press, 1987), chap. 13.
85. Bureau of Justice Statistics. *Violence and Theft in the Workplace, 1987–1992* (Washington, D.C., July 1994); "Death at Work," *The Wall Street Journal*, 22 March 1994.
86. Miethe and Meier, *Crime and Its Social Context*, 2.
87. Michael S. Hindaling, Michael Gottfredson, and James Garofalo, *Victims of Personal Crime* (Cambridge, Mass.: Ballinger Press, 1978); Robert F. Meier and Terance D. Miehe, "Understanding Theories of Criminal Victimization," in Michael Tonry, ed., *Crime and Justice: A Review of Research*, vol. 17 (Chicago: University of Chicago Press, 1993), 459–65.
88. Eduard Ziegenhagen, *Victims, Crime and Social Control* (New York: Praeger, 1977), 5; Kevin Wright, *The Great American Crime Myth* (Westport, Conn.: Greenwood Press, 1985), 57–62; Lawrence E. Cohen and Marcus Felson, "Social Change and Crime Rate Trends: A Routine Activity Approach," *American Sociological Review* 44 (1979): 588–608; Lawrence W. Sherman, Patrick R. Gartin, and Michael E. Buerger, "Hot Spots of Predatory Crime: Routine Activities and the Criminology of Place," *Criminology* 27 (1989): 27–55.
89. Elias, *The Politics of Victimization*, 14.
90. Ibid., 15.
91. *National Law Journal*, December 25, 1989–January 1, 1990, 12.
92. BJS, *The Redesigned National Crime Survey: Selected New Data*, Special Report (Washington, D.C.: Bureau of Justice Statistics, January 1989); "Victims' Rights Amendments Pass in 5 States," *New York Times*, November 8, 1992, 156.
93. Robert Elias, *The Politics of Victimization* (New York: Oxford University Press, 1986), 11–12.
94. Wilson, *Crime File: Victims*.
95. Ibid.

CHAPTER 3

Explanations of Criminal Behavior

CHAPTER OUTLINE

Why Do People Commit Crimes?

> For a man, pimping is a good way of making money, but the fastest way is narcotics, and the safest and best way of all is numbers. Even though my whores were making a lot of money, I just didn't like pimping that much. It ain't my style. . . . I missed stickup quite a bit. . . . What I really missed was the excitement of sticking up and the planning and getting away with it. . . . [As for numbers] I didn't really get into it, just like I didn't like pimping–there wasn't enough excitement in it. . . . [When I was a drug dealer] I was doing something like a grand worth of heroin a day. . . . I was rolling in drugs and rolling good. I'm well off. I'm dressing nice and keeping a knot in my pocket. I've got a nice ride. I've got me a stable of broads, so I'm cool.[1]
>
> John Allen, career robber

INTRODUCTION

The causes of criminal behavior have fascinated and puzzled moralists, political leaders, legislators, and policymakers for centuries. Criminologists consider the origins of criminal behavior fundamental to the discipline of criminology, but knowing the causes of crime is also of practical importance. Policymakers cannot control and reduce crime if they do not know what causes it. Unfortunately, criminologists have not discovered the *causes* of crime; they have, however, identified a number of factors that *correlate* with criminal behavior. Most of these explanations and correlations fall into two broad categories:

1. **Offender-focused explanations** focus on the individuals who commit crimes.
2. **Context explanations** focus on the situations in which crimes occur.

EARLY EXPLANATIONS OF CRIME

All of the early explanations of crime focused on individual offenders. The first of these offender-focused explanations of crime were religious. An ancient and long-standing belief held that criminals were possessed by demons, and that their behavior reflected this demonic possession. Some authorities believed that individuals chose to admit the demons; others contended that the individual could not control demonic possession.

The demonic possession theory began to lose its credibility during the eighteenth century, the "Age of Reason," or Enlightenment. The great English philosopher Jeremy Bentham, with considerable assistance from the ideas of Italian criminologist Cesare Beccaria, developed the utilitarian theory of crime causation. Bentham believed that individuals could choose between criminal and lawful behavior. He further believed in the principle of utility: Human beings seek pleasure and avoid pain. They choose crime because the pleasures of crime outweigh the potential pain of getting caught and punished. Although his rational theory made common sense, Bentham did not test his theory with scientific observations. Nevertheless, it had—and still has—an enormous impact on formal criminal law. The assumptions of free will and responsibility lie at the heart of the general principles of criminal law. Free will also influences a number of current explanations of criminal behavior.

During the nineteenth century, opposition to the idea that free will was the basis of human behavior grew. Nineteenth-century theories were based on the idea that forces beyond the control of individuals determine how people behave, hence the term **determinist theories of crime.** Criminals are born, not made, according to early biological theories. Crime originates in the very nature, or as we would say today, the genes, of criminals, not in their free choice.

Cesare Lombroso, a famous Italian psychiatrist turned criminologist, designed a crime causation theory based on skull shapes. As a young doctor at an asylum in Pavia, he performed an autopsy on an Italian version of Jack the Ripper. In the course of his examination, he detected an abnormality in the dead man's skull. Lombroso describes his discovery, which formed the core of what would later be called his "criminal anthropology":

> At the sight of that skull, I seemed to see all at once, standing out clearly illumined as in a vast plain under a flaming sky, the problem of the nature of the criminal, who reproduces in civilised times characteristics, not only of primitive savages, but of still lower types as far back as the carnivora.[2]

According to Lombroso, criminals have little or no control over their actions. They are atavistic, or "throwbacks" to lower-order creatures. Lombroso also believed it was possible to measure criminality scientifically by the physical characteristics of known criminals, particularly skull and body shapes.[3]

The psychoanalytic theory of crime also grew out of the nineteenth-century determinist intellectual tradition. Under the influence of the great Austrian psychoanalyst Sigmund Freud, psychoanalytic psychology became a significant force in the 1920s. It reached its high point during the 1950s and 1960s, after which it came under increasing attack from people who saw the theory as an excuse for brutalizing and reducing the dignity of individuals. During the 1980s, critics from all over the political and intellectual spectrum joined in the assault on psychoanalytic psychology. Conservative critics saw the theory as responsible for a soft and permissive attitude toward crime, providing an unacceptable excuse for antisocial behavior.

Freud himself rarely addressed the topic of crime, but his followers applied basic tenets of psychoanalytic theory to criminal behavior:

1. Aggression and sex are powerful drives that must be expressed.
2. The unconscious plays at least as important a role as the conscious in governing behavior.
3. All human behavior, rather than being chosen by the conscious, is determined by the unconscious forces of sex and aggression. (This concept of psychic determinism is the linchpin of the theory.)

If individuals do not develop "healthy" ways to express sex and aggression, a disorder known as neurosis (if relatively mild) or psychosis (if severe) results. These disorders can lead to aberrant violent and sexual behavior, much of which violates the criminal law. Aberrant behaviors arise through faulty early childhood development. According to Freudians, the most important formative period occurs in very early childhood, particularly in the first five years. Hence, according to psychoanalytic theory, disorder, not "badness," determines (that is, causes) crime. In its most extreme form, this theory takes the position that "all criminals are sick." One practical consequence of such determinist thinking is that we cannot blame or punish sick people for the behavioral consequences of their illness—their crimes.

Knowledge and Understanding CHECK

1. Identify the two major categories into which explanations of crime fall.
2. Describe the demonic possession explanation of crime.
3. Contrast the demonic possession theory with the principle of utility.
4. Describe the theories that arose from opposition to free will explanations of crime.
5. What is the significance of Cesare Lombroso in the development of explanations of crime?
6. Identify three elements of psychoanalytic psychology that were applied to the explanation of criminal behavior.

SOCIOLOGICAL THEORIES

Sociological explanations that focus on the societal context of criminal behavior dominate criminological research and writing. Neighborhood, social status, race, gender, age, education, and values loom much larger than mental illness, brain damage, and chemical imbalance as subjects for research into criminal behavior. The major sociological theories that link crime to conditions in society relate to the connection between crime and

- Social structure.
- Social process.
- Social control.
- Time and space.

SOCIAL STRUCTURE THEORIES

Social structure theories link individual criminal behavior to social conditions such as poverty, unemployment, poor education—that is, to the chief ways in which the social structure affects the individual's circumstances. According to social structure theorists, crime is located mainly in the lower-income classes because flaws in the social structure increase the odds that individuals in that part of society will commit crimes. The great nineteenth-century sociologist Emile Durkheim, in his theory of **anomie**, explained crime as the result of the weakening of social norms. Durkheim formulated the theory of anomie when France was undergoing transition from monarchy to democracy and from a rural, agricultural society to an industrialized nation. A society in transition, said Durkheim, weakens the bonds that ordinarily govern behavior. Social norms also weaken, and Durkheim believed this anomie contributes to criminal behavior.

Strain Theory

In 1938, during the Great Depression, the American sociologist Robert K. Merton, borrowing from Durkheim, formulated an American version of anomie in a paper entitled "Social Structure and Anomie." The sociologist Gilbert Geis has called Merton's paper "the single most influential formulation in the sociology of deviance, and . . . possibly the most quoted paper in modern sociology." According to Merton, society establishes goals toward which all strive, but at the same time the social structure makes it difficult or impossible for everyone to achieve these goals. In America, according to Merton, the goals are wealth, power, and prestige based on hard work. **Strain theory** explains why some people who work hard yet fail to attain the American dream commit crimes. The success story in America is the story of rags to riches. You may be a Burger King employee today, but if you work hard and stick to it, you will soon manage a Burger King, and eventually start your own chain of fast food restaurants. The trouble is, many people work hard and play by the rules, but obtain neither wealth, nor power, nor prestige. According to Merton, society praises only success. Winning, not fair play, is the goal.[4]

Not everyone who fails to attain the American dream turns to crime, and Merton accounts for this. According to Merton, people respond to strain in five ways: by conforming, ritualizing, retreating, innovating, or rebelling. Conformists continue to follow the rules even if they fail. Ritualists continue to go through the motions of following the rules, but they have given up; they no longer pursue the goals. Conformists and ritualists pose no problem for criminal justice. The others do. Retreatists drop out of society, neither aspiring to the goals nor following the rules. They become transients, homeless, and/or drug addicts. Although they commit few if any crimes against others, they do violate the laws of loitering, public drunkenness, and disorderly conduct. Moreover, they flout the work ethic so central to American values.

Innovators aspire to the legitimate goals of wealth, power, and prestige, but they are willing to use illegitimate means to obtain their goals. Savings-and-loan executives who risked others' savings for their own personal gain, burglars who steal VCRs, and students who cheat on tests all have acceptable goals, but they have chosen improper and illegal ways to reach them. Strain theory, as Merton states it, explains the criminal behavior of innovators mainly at the lower end of the social structure, because the legitimate means to success are less available there. Rebels reject both the goals and the means of society. Rebels replace acceptable goals with others. Street gangs, for example, might seek more members as an important goal and use violence and intimidation as the means of getting them.

Some theorists have extended strain theory to organization crime. Relative deprivation, that is, feeling deprived when compared to others around you who are doing better, causes strain for people in organizations who are not as successful as others. They may be doing exceptionally well by the standards of people below them, but they do not look down; they hunger for the position, salary, and prestige of those above them. This "anomie of affluence" leads some to put rules aside in order to reduce their deprivation (lack of success). Hence, the same strain that produces street crime in lower-income individuals leads to organizational crime in middle- and upper-income individuals. Their motivations are similar, even though manifestations differ.[5]

Emile Durkheim had earlier suggested that prosperity underlies crime. Prosperity expands economic opportunities, which in turn fosters the pursuit of material success. This heightened pursuit of economic success leads some people to commit crimes in order to obtain that success. To reduce crime, economic prosperity must be accompanied by the strengthening of noneconomic institutions, such as the family. These noneconomic institutions can provide alternative definitions of self-worth and achievement to those associated with material gain.[6]

Opportunity Theory

In 1960, Richard Cloward and Lloyd Ohlin introduced an expansion of strain theory called **opportunity theory.** Although they agreed with much of strain theory, they maintained that Merton overlooked the **illegitimate opportunity structure.** Access to illegitimate opportunities varies according to position in the social structure just as legitimate opportunities do. Cloward and Ohlin concluded that criminal behavior depends on the criminal opportunities available.[7]

In Clifford Shaw's classic book, *The Jack-Roller*, the delinquent youth Stanley describes a community with criminal opportunities:

> Stealing in the neighborhood was a common practice among the children and approved by the parents. Whenever the boys got together they talked about robbing and made more plans for stealing. I hardly knew any boys who did not go robbing. The little fellows went in for petty stealing, breaking into freight cars, and stealing junk. The older guys did big jobs like stick-up, burglary, and stealing autos. The little fellows admired the "big shots" and longed for the day when they could get into the big racket.[8]

SOCIAL PROCESS THEORIES

Social structure theory cannot explain all crime. After all, crime occurs in all social classes, and most people in the lower classes do not commit crimes. Other forces must operate to explain criminal behavior. Social process theories examine the experiences of individuals in families, peer groups, schools, and other social institutions responsible for establishing values and behavior. Abundant research establishes an association between the quality of one's experience with these institutions and criminal behavior. For example, most prison inmates come from single-parent homes, have relatives and friends who have served time in prison, are school dropouts or underachievers, and have poor work skills and employment records (see Chapter 14). Social process theorists agree that criminogenic forces in society affect behavior, but they disagree over how. **Social learning theories** maintain that individuals at birth are blank slates and can learn any values and behavior. **Social control theories** believe that everybody is born with the desire to break the rules. **Social conflict theories** maintain that the rich and powerful define criminal law and administer criminal justice in order to protect their property, safety, and values from less powerful groups in society.

Social Learning Theory

When I was a boy, a neighbor told her son to stay away from that Joel Samaha because, she warned, I would "put bad bugs in his head." The commonsense notion that people learn criminal behavior from others underlies social learning theory. This notion in turn depends on the assumption that at birth we are blank slates upon which our parents, friends, teachers, religious leaders, government, and other representatives of social institutions write the attitudes, beliefs, and values that determine our behavior.

Edwin Sutherland, the criminologist of white-collar crime, formulated the most prominent social learning theory: **differential association.** According to Sutherland, criminal behavior—like behavior in general—depends on the associations people have. If an individual has more associations with breaking the law than with obeying it, criminal behavior follows. Not all associations have equal influence. The most frequent and longest-lasting associations, such as with family and friends, are most important, and the most intense associations teach the most enduring lessons about how to behave. People in low-income neighborhoods who associate with "street criminals" learn to act like street criminals, not because people who live in poor neighborhoods are "bad" or by nature different from others, but because that is the way social beings behave. By the same reasoning, corporate criminals learn criminal behavior called white-collar crime.[9]

The following box examines the **cycle-of-violence hypothesis:** that a childhood history of physical abuse, neglect, or both predisposes the survivor to later violence.

Use *Your* Discretion

Do abused children become adult violent criminals?

The National Institute of Justice (NIJ) sponsored the most detailed study to date on the relationship between childhood abuse and adult criminal behavior. The study found that childhood abuse increased the odds of future delinquency and adult criminality by 40 percent.

Study design
The study followed 1,575 cases from childhood through young adulthood, comparing two groups:

1. A study group of 908 officially recorded cases of childhood abuse or neglect.
2. A comparison group of 667 not officially recorded as abused or neglected, matched to the study group according to sex, age, race, and approximate socioeconomic status.

The study design used the following definitions:

1. *Physical abuse:* injuries including bruises, welts, abrasions, lacerations, wounds, cuts, and bone and skull fractures.
2. *Sexual abuse:* assault and battery with the intent to satisfy sexual desires, fondling or touching in an obscene manner, rape, sodomy, and incest.
3. *Neglect:* extreme failure to provide adequate food, clothing, shelter, and medical attention.

Juvenile court records and probation records, and arrest data from federal, state, and local law enforcement records provided the information for abuse, neglect, and criminal records.

Study findings
The study findings are as follows:

1. *Juvenile record:* Abused or neglected persons faced a higher risk of beginning a life of crime at an earlier age, with more significant and repeated criminal involvement (see Figure 3.1).

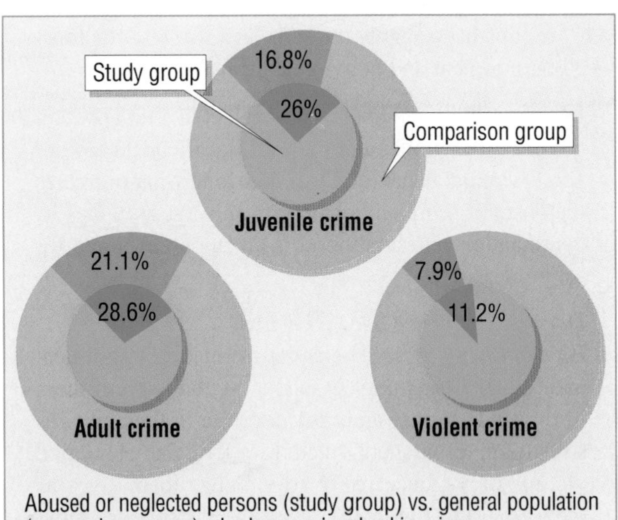

Abused or neglected persons (study group) vs. general population (comparison group) who became involved in crime.

Figure 3.1
Criminal Involvement of Abused and Neglected Children

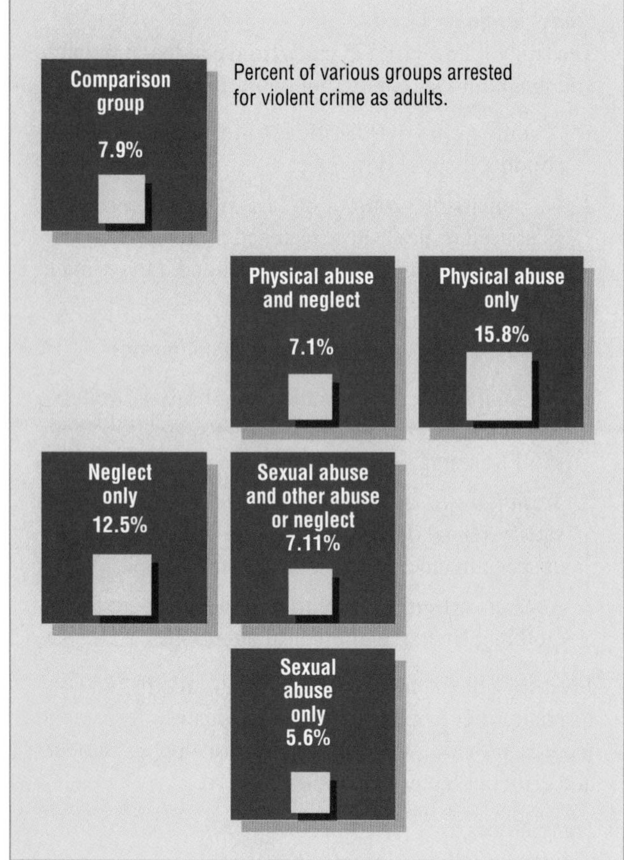

Figure 3.2
Abuse, Neglect, and Violence

2. *Adult record:* Abused or neglected persons were no more likely to continue a life of crime than other children. Both the study and the comparison groups had roughly the same arrests as adults for both violent and nonviolent crimes.

In short, childhood abuse and neglect had no apparent effect on the movement of juvenile offenders toward adult criminal behavior. Distinguishing what promotes the onset of criminal behavior from what promotes its continuation into adulthood is an important topic for future research.

Does only violence beget violence?
By examining violent behavior in relation to physical and sexual abuse, neglect, and a combination of them in the study group, and violent crime in the comparison group, researchers tested the notion that childhood victims of violence resort to violence themselves as they grow up. Physically abused children were more likely to face later arrest for violent crimes than children experiencing other forms of abuse or neglect. However, the neglected group followed close behind. Figure 3.2 illustrates the study results.

According to the NIJ, this finding offers persuasive evidence for the need to take concerted preventive action against child abuse and neglect. Nationwide, the incidence of neglect is almost three times that of physical abuse. Neglect is also potentially more damaging to the development of a child than abuse (provided the abuse involves no neurological impairment). In one study of the influence of early malnutrition on subsequent behavior, previously malnourished children had attention deficits, reduced social skills, and poorer emotional stability than a comparison group. The present study suggests that those differences include a greater risk of later criminal violence.

Policy recommendations
The NIJ recommends the following actions:

1. *Improved identification procedures.* It is imperative to improve the procedures for identifying child abuse and neglect, such as those for police response and follow-up.
2. *Outside-the-home placement.* Placement outside the home—including foster homes, guardianships, and special homes and schools—is one possible buffer for children. Although scholars and practitioners criticize these placements, the NIJ surveyed other research that showed no negative effects from removing abused and neglected children from their homes. The survey of this research, according to the NIJ, challenges the assumption that it is necessarily unwise to remove children from negative family situations. The instability caused by removal, especially if children move from one placement to another, is important but did not lead to a higher likelihood of arrest or violent criminal behavior.
3. *Follow-up and in-person interviews.* The present study demonstrates that abuse and neglect create an increased risk of juvenile delinquency, adult criminal behavior, and violent behavior. However, a large number of abused and neglected children did not later have official arrest records. Furthermore, the majority of abused and neglected children did not become delinquents, adult criminals, or violent offenders.

The NIJ has conducted a follow-up study. The interviews explore recollections of early childhood experiences, schooling, adolescence, undetected alcohol and drug problems, undetected delinquency and criminality, and important life experiences. Preliminary findings of the follow-up suggest that many study subjects experienced:

- Delinquency and criminality.
- Depression and suicide attempts.

- Alcohol and drug problems.
- Unemployment or employment in low-level service jobs.

CRITICAL THINKING

1. Do you think the evidence shows that abuse and neglect cause delinquency, adult crime, and violent crime?
2. Does the study prove the sociological theory of differential association in particular and social learning theory in general?
3. What does it have to say about social control theory?
4. On the basis of this study, what policy decisions do you recommend?
5. Would you recommend completion of the follow-up study first?
6. Would you recommend early intervention in neglect and abuse cases?
7. If so, what intervention? Out-of-home placement? Criminal prosecution of the abusers? Counseling of the victims? Anything else?

Andrew Golden, 13, charged with five counts of aggravated murder and 10 counts of aggravated battery in connection with shootings in the Westside Middle School in Jonesboro, Arkansas on March 24, 1998. This kind of case stimulates fears of a "teenage bloodbath" resulting from the increase in violent criminal behavior among teenagers.

Subculture Theories

The ideas of association and culture combine in the development of **subculture theories.** These theories vary greatly, but two exemplify their basic ideas. Albert Cohen has expanded Sutherland's and Merton's theories to explain juvenile delinquency. In American society, Cohen argues, the same pressures to succeed are placed on "lower-class boys" as on others, but these youths lack adequate legitimate avenues to that success. The boys band together with others in their predicament and make their own rules for success that allow them to win within their own subculture.[10]

Marvin Wolfgang and Franco Ferracuti, also elaborating on Sutherland's and Merton's theories, identified another subculture, the **subculture of violence**—one that in fact glorifies violence. According to Merton, recourse to violence is acceptable to certain groups—particularly Southerners, blacks, and lower-class males—when courage, manhood, or honor are challenged by insults, threats, or weapons.[11]

Corporations produce a **subculture of competition** in which the goal is success, measured in money, power, and prestige. Although there are broader, countervailing cultural values such as fairness and democracy, the premium is on success. This leads some members of the subculture to break the law to achieve success, a decision the subculture tacitly approves, encourages, and—some say—even demands.[12]

Knowledge and Understanding CHECK

1. To what do social structure theories link criminal behavior? Give some examples.
2. Explain Durkheim's theory of anomie.
3. Identify the major elements in Merton's strain theory.
4. Identify the five ways that people respond to strain.
5. How does strain theory explain organization crime?
6. Compare and contrast opportunity theory with strain theory. How do social process theories explain crime?
7. Identify the major social institutions that social process theories focus on.
8. What commonsense notion underlies social learning theory?
9. Identify the main elements of Sutherland's differential association theory.
10. What two ideas are combined in subculture theories?
11. Describe three subculture theories.

SOCIAL CONTROL THEORY

As we have just seen, social structure and social process theories treat crime as a morally neutral concept. According to these theories, children are clean slates at birth, born without any predisposition to commit crimes. Bad environment both creates the motivation and provides the opportunity to commit crimes. Social control theory assumes that people are rule breakers by nature. As Travis Hirschi, the leading proponent of social control theory, put it:

> control theory [is] a theory in which deviation is not problematic. The question "Why did they do it?" is simply not the question the theory is designed to answer. The question is, "Why don't we do it?" There is much evidence that we would, if we dared.[13]

People obey rules because of their ties to established institutions of social control. Families, peer groups, churches, and schools keep in check the natural desire to break rules and satisfy selfish interests. When ties to these institutions weaken, deviation and crime increase. Social bonds do not reduce the motivation to get what you want; they reduce the chance that you will give in to the motivation.[14]

Hirschi identified four elements in the social bond that curb the natural desire to break rules. First, attachment to others makes us sensitive to their opinions. According to control theorists, attachment to those whose opinions we respect—particularly parents, teachers, coaches, neighbors, and peers—is the best predictor of conformity to rules. The second element in the social bond is commitment to the conventional order. The greater the desire to get a job, take advantage of educational opportunities, and keep a good reputation, the greater the chances of conformity to rules. Involvement, the third element, means that the busier you are with conventional activities, the less time you have to get into trouble—according to the old adage, "idle hands are the devil's workshop." Finally, the stronger an individual's belief in the conventional order, the less likely he or she is to break the rules.

Hirschi reports the results of testing his theory in *Causes of Delinquency*. Data obtained from police reports, self-reports, and schools for more than 3,000 boys in a California youth project supported Hirschi's version of social control theory. Further empirical studies have yielded similar results.[15]

Control theory explains both street crime and organization crime. Organizations do not provide controls on deviance. Rules do not apply, especially at the very top. The ends justify the means. According to control theory, the rules are seen as obstacles to a greater goal. Hence, organizational criminals are freed from the bonds that lead to compliance with rules.[16]

LABELING THEORY

In his now classic *Outsiders,* Howard Becker developed the influential **labeling theory.** According to Becker, individuals do not commit crimes because they cannot manage the stresses in society, or because they associate with other criminals and learn crime from them. Rather, transitory deviant episodes are turned into criminal careers by outsiders—**moral entrepreneurs**—notably police, courts, and corrections officers, by attempting to suppress such behavior. In other words, the criminal justice system creates criminals. More broadly, society's response to crime defines some people as criminals and, by so doing, causes crime. Whether these people have broken the criminal law is immaterial. What is critical is that once this formal process has defined them as criminals, they start to act like criminals. Society's actions shape their self-image.[17]

Labeling theory endeavors to shift the emphasis from the behavior of the criminal to the behavior of those who operate the criminal justice system. It focuses on the actions, processes, and structures within criminal justice that cause, or at least contribute to, lawbreaking. Labeling theory has drawn attention to the harmful effects of contacts with criminal justice agencies, particularly with police and corrections officials. The theory had a direct influence on public policy during the 1960s and 1970s, in the creation of programs that diverted people out of the criminal justice system into alternative social programs.[18]

SOCIAL CONFLICT THEORIES

Another product of the 1960s was a group of social conflict theories that rejected the established explanations of crime—rational choice, biological, psychoanalytic, and sociological. In Chapter 4, we will explore the social conflict perspective as it applies to criminal law. Here we note that social conflict theories place the responsibility for criminal behavior on the power structure and on the control of society and its institutions by the rich and powerful. The rich and powerful define crime to protect their property interests, their safety, and their values. They use the power of government to preserve the status quo. Their influence over the definition of and responses to crime, whether consciously intended or not, has the effect of criminalizing the behavior of the poor, the weak, and the "different." According to social conflict theory, the causes of crime lie not in individual defects or in rational choice, but in the social structure and process that unevenly distribute the power to decide both what is criminal and how to respond to criminal behavior.

Knowledge and Understanding CHECK

1. Identify the ideas of social process and social structure that social control theories reject.
2. According to Travis Hirschi, why do people obey rules?

3. Identify the four elements of the social bond that curb the natural desire to break rules.
4. What types of crime do social control theories explain? According to Howard Becker, why do people commit crimes?
5. Who are the "outsiders" according to Becker?
6. What shift in emphasis does labeling theory attempt to accomplish?
7. Where do social conflict theories place the responsibility for criminal behavior?

ECONOMIC EXPLANATIONS

The theories and research of economists have led to a resurgence of the idea of free will as a central element in the explanation of criminal behavior. Since the late 1960s, several studies by economists have prompted criminologists to study a theory that many criminal justice personnel and the general public have subscribed to since at least the eighteenth century: People are rational and make decisions according to what they perceive is their self-interest. Some economists have taken these basic assumptions and refined them into highly sophisticated "econometric models" represented by complicated equations.

These models, far more comprehensive than anything social scientists had heretofore designed, share several basic propositions, including:

1. Individuals are rational.
2. Individuals are free to choose among a range of alternative courses of action.
3. Individuals are motivated by gain, both monetary and psychic.
4. Individuals will choose the course of conduct that produces the most gain (or, alternatively, results in the least loss).
5. Where illegal conduct produces more gain than legal conduct, illegal conduct will dominate.[19]

The economic being weighs the gains from illegal conduct against the risks of detection, arrest, conviction, and punishment. A rational person motivated by gain, therefore, will not commit a crime if the threat, or at least the perceived threat, of criminal justice action is great enough. The deterrent power of this action is not limited to actual punishment; it also includes the possibility of being convicted, presumably without actually suffering imprisonment; being arrested without prosecution; or even being discovered or detected without further action.[20]

Economic theorists do not restrict their explanations to property crimes. They claim that their theories have general application. In perhaps the most controversial application, the economist Isaac Ehrlich contends that the propositions outlined above apply to crimes against persons, and even to murder. Professor Ehrlich maintains that despite the

> abhorrent, cruel, and occasionally pathological nature of murder, there is no reason to expect that persons who hate or love others are less responsive to changes in costs and gains associated with activities they may wish to pursue than persons indifferent toward the well-being of others.[21]

If this explanation is correct, then it has significant implications for criminal justice policy. Ehrlich addresses one implication by applying economic theory to the deterrent effect of the death penalty. He asserts that for every person executed for committing murder between 1933 and 1967, eight innocent lives may have been saved. If Ehrlich is right, criminal justice policymakers should pay close attention to the economic explanation for criminal behavior and the free will, rationalist, self-interest assumptions underlying it.[22]

The economic theory of criminal behavior can lead to two different policy approaches to reducing crime. One is to raise the cost of illegal behavior to make crime less "profitable"; that is, make more arrests and convictions and levy stiffer punishments. This course has been followed in the past and is most widely recommended today. It also enjoys wide public support, as the perennial promises by politicians to "get tough on criminals" amply demonstrate. The second approach, to increase the gains from lawful behavior, has not enjoyed a great deal of support. It requires significant alterations—some even say unwarranted intrusions—into areas traditionally not matters for public regulation. For example, higher wages and better working conditions might make crime less attractive by making life less frustrating. If higher wages, better job security, and more chances for advancement make washing cars attractive enough, individuals will prefer washing cars—at least temporarily—to stealing them. But government interference to the degree required to bring about such changes is not acceptable in our free-market economy.

Use *Your* Discretion

Is the economic explanation convincing enough to support public policy?

Critics have found many faults with the economic theory of crime causation. Their objections cover a broad spectrum. Some have challenged the free will and rationalist assumptions on which the theory rests. Michael Gottfredson and Travis Hirschi maintain that one of the most serious failings of the economic analysis is that it treats criminal behavior as a job—the "illegitimate equivalent of labor-force participation." They contend that the decision to commit crimes, unlike the decision to go to work, does not have career characteristics such as specialization; it is not a source of lasting income; its pursuit is not compatible with legitimate activities; and criminals do not "respond to fluctuations in risk created by crime-control bureaucrats." Moreover, Gottfredson and Hirschi say that the data on property crime simply do not support the "view of crime derived from economic models of work." As an example, Gottfredson and Hirschi point out that data on burglars refutes the economic theory:

> The model age for burglars is about seventeen, and the rate of burglary declines rapidly with age. The most likely "pecuniary" outcome for a burglar is no gain, and his next offense is likely to be something else than burglary. Shoplifting of something he does not need and cannot use is high on the list of probabilities, or an offense likely to terminate his legitimate and illegitimate careers—such as rape, assault, or homicide—for (again) no pecuniary gain is also highly probable. In the unlikely event that he is legitimately employed, his most likely victim will be his employer, an act difficult to reconcile with maximization of long-term utility or the equation of legitimate work with risk avoidance. Because research shows that offenders are versatile, our portrait of the burglar applies equally well to the white-collar offender, the organized-crime offender, the dope dealer, and the assaulter; they are, after all, the same people.[23]

According to criminologists Ronald V. Clarke and Marcus Felson, "the economist's image of the self-maximizing decision maker, carefully calculating his or her advantage, did not fit the opportunistic, ill-considered, and even reckless nature of most crime."[24]

Others have criticized the economic model because self-interest is not the only motive for human behavior. According to Amitai Etzioni, "Individuals are simultaneously under the influence of two major sets of factors—their pleasure, and their moral duty. . . ." Robert H. Frank, in *Beyond Self-Interest,* argues that we often ignore our self-interest when we

> trudge through snowstorms to cast our ballots, even when we are certain they will make no difference. We leave tips for waitresses in restaurants in distant cities we will never visit again. We make anonymous contributions to private charities. We often refrain from cheating even when we are sure we would not be caught. We sometimes walk away from profitable transactions whose terms we believe to be "unfair." We battle endless red tape to get a $10 refund on a defective product. And so on.[25]

Mitchell B. Chamlin and John K. Cochran point out that

> the question remains . . . whether . . . downturns in the business cycle have much of an effect on the life-style choices of individuals. If . . . progressive transformations of the social, physical, and economic structure of post-World War II society have produced life-style patterns that embody a greater penchant for the consumption of consumer goods and the enjoyment of leisure activities away from the home . . . short-term downturns in the economy may have little effect on the day-to-day activities of individuals. Rather than abandoning behavioral patterns that have become ingrained over time, individuals may choose to maintain their life-styles but do so in a more frugal manner (e.g., eat more at fast-food restaurants and less so at more elegant establishments). . . .[26]

Others have attacked the highly sophisticated equations that are an essential element in econometric models, claiming that they are too mechanistic, too cold, calculated, and unemotional to reflect what most people are really like. Clarke and Felson maintain that "the formal mathematical modeling of criminal choices by economists often demanded data that was unavailable or could not be pressed into service without making unrealistic assumptions about what they represented." Still other critics find that even if these highly refined equations can accurately explain human behavior, they require much more sophisticated data than their creators have used up to this point. Ehrlich's startlingly specific findings about the deterrent effect of the death penalty on individuals relied on aggregate national statistics of reported murders. His opponents say conclusions assessing the highly complex psychology behind why murderers kill require more than a correlation between elaborate equations and crude reported crime rates.[27]

Despite these criticisms, the economic explanation of crime has forced criminologists to rethink basic questions about both the causes of crime and criminal justice policies based on those causes. It has, moreover, probably motivated other social scientists to design their research projects more carefully. Finally, the economic explanation of criminal behavior stemmed the tide of a century of "positivist" research that attacked both rationalist, free will assumptions and the policies of deterrence and retribution that had dominated social science research and criminal justice rhetoric, if not actual practice, since the eighteenth century.

CRITICAL THINKING

1. Summarize the major criticisms of the economic explanation of crime.
2. In light of these criticisms, would you recommend spending money on policies based on the economic

explanation of crime? Refer to specific criticisms in supporting your answer.

3. Would you ask for more research? If so, what would you specifically want to learn from this research?

Rational Choice Perspective

The rational choice perspective is another offender-focused explanation of criminal behavior. Drawing on the theories and empirical findings of a number of disciplines, including economics, political science, sociology, criminology, and law, the **rational choice perspective** assumes that criminal behavior is rational; that is, the product of reason. This behavior, though, need only be roughly rational; also allowed are both irrational and pathological components in criminal behavior.[28]

The interest in decision making and its relevance to criminal justice policy has spurred considerable research on the rational choice explanation of criminal behavior. Instead of emphasizing the differences between criminals and "the rest of us," rational choice stresses some of the similarities. The rational choice perspective consists of three elements:

1. A reasoning criminal.
2. A crime-specific focus.
3. Separate analyses for criminal involvement and criminal events.

The reasoning criminal perspective assumes that people commit crimes for a purpose, and that they make decisions to commit crimes on the basis of information. In the words of two rational choice proponents, Ronald V. Clarke and Marcus Felson,

> crime is purposive behavior designed to meet the offender's commonplace needs for such things as money, status, sex, and excitement. . . . meeting these needs involves the making of (sometimes quite rudimentary) decisions and choices, constrained as these are by limits of time and ability and the availability of relevant information.[29]

The perspective begins with the assumption that offenders seek to benefit themselves by committing crimes. Obtaining benefits requires rational decision making, however rough and affected by irrationality and pathology it may be. In short, criminals have specific goals, alternative means of obtaining them, and at least some information for choosing the best alternative to obtain their goals.

In addition, the rational choice perspective adopts a **crime-specific focus.** That is, decision making differs according to the crime being contemplated and committed. Crime-specific focus requires more refined definitions than do other crime theories. Burglary, for example, requires a different analysis than does robbery, and even burglary and robbery may require further definition. The decision to rob a convenience store, rob a bank, or "mug" a person on the street each requires its own special process of decision making. The decision to commit a commercial burglary is not the same as the decision to commit a residential burglary. Furthermore, the decisions about where to commit burglaries differ. Empirical research indicates that burglars targeting public housing, middle-class neighborhoods, and wealthy enclaves differ considerably in kinds of individuals, motivations, and methods. Similarly, bank robbers differ from street muggers, and car thieves from shoplifters (see Figure 3.3).

Finally, the rational choice approach requires making a distinction between criminal involvement and criminal events. Criminal involvement refers to the process of choosing to get involved in crime, continuing to be involved, and stopping one's involvement. The **criminal event** refers to the decision to commit specific crimes. The criminal event depends on three conditions:

1. Needs and desires for money, sex, friendship, status, and excitement.
2. Previous experience in committing specific crimes.
3. Opportunities to commit a specific crime at a particular time and place (see Figure 3.4).

Empirical research into a variety of crimes, including shoplifting, burglary, robbery, and illegal drug use, has demonstrated some support for all three elements in the rational choice perspective—the reasoning criminal, a crime-specific focus, and separate analyses for criminal involvement and criminal events. The research demonstrates a weak form of rationality. Criminals may not gather all possible information and use it to the greatest benefit, but they do consider risks and payoffs. According to one experienced safecracker:

> Usually, the assessment of economic value precedes the assessment of risk. A safecracker may, while on legitimate business, spot a particularly "easy" safe. He may then assess the probable economic value of the safe's contents. Whether the value is high or low, if the risks are low, he may "make" the safe. On the other hand, if both are high, he may also attempt the job.[30]

Richard T. Wright and Scott H. Decker studied burglars in St. Louis. Their sample of 105 residential burglars demonstrated that burglars have rational motives for committing burglaries. Wright and Decker concluded that both their sample and those of other researchers showed that

> In the overwhelming majority of cases, the decision to commit a residential burglary arises in the face of what offenders perceive to be a pressing need of cash. Previous research consistently has shown this to be so and the results of the present study bear out this point. More than nine out of ten of the offenders in our sample—95 out of 105—reported that they broke into dwellings primarily when they needed money.[31]

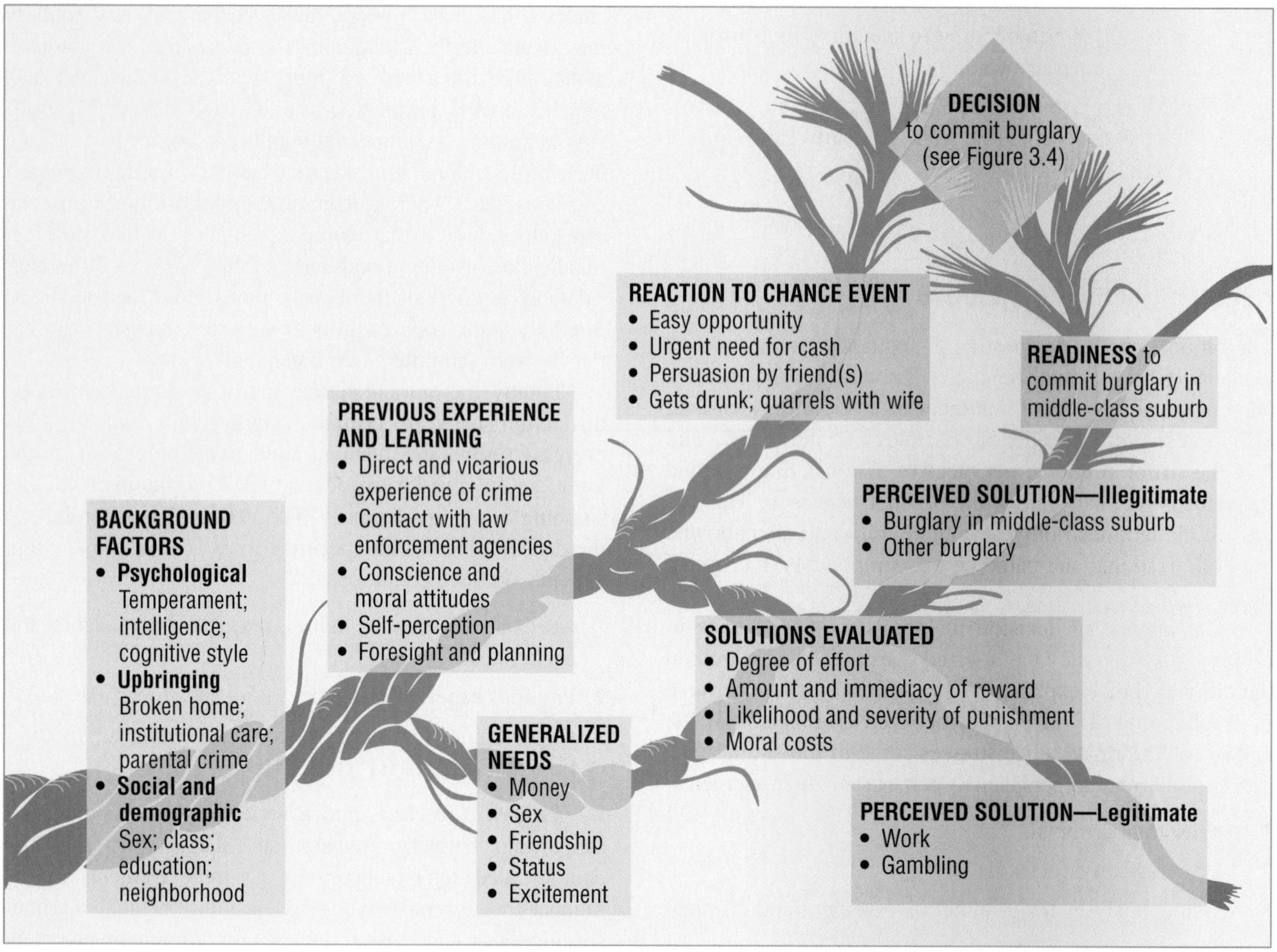

DECISION
to commit burglary
(see Figure 3.4)
REACTION TO CHANCE EVENT
• Easy opportunity
• Urgent need for cash
• Persuasion by friend(s)
• Gets drunk; quarrels with wife
READINESS to commit burglary in middle-class suburb
PREVIOUS EXPERIENCE AND LEARNING
• Direct and vicarious experience of crime
• Contact with law enforcement agencies
• Conscience and moral attitudes
• Self-perception
• Foresight and planning
PERCEIVED SOLUTION—Illegitimate
• Burglary in middle-class suburb
• Other burglary
BACKGROUND FACTORS
• Psychological
Temperament; intelligence; cognitive style
• Upbringing
Broken home; institutional care; parental crime
• Social and demographic
Sex; class; education; neighborhood
SOLUTIONS EVALUATED
• Degree of effort
• Amount and immediacy of reward
• Likelihood and severity of punishment
• Moral costs
GENERALIZED NEEDS
• Money
• Sex
• Friendship
• Status
• Excitement
PERCEIVED SOLUTION—Legitimate
• Work
• Gambling

Figure 3.3
Criminal Involvement: The Decision to Get Involved in Crime

Figure 3.4
The Criminal Event: The Decision to Commit a Specific Burglary

DECISION
to commit burglary
(see Figure 3.3)
REJECTED MIDDLE-CLASS AREA
• Unfamiliar
• Distant
• Neighborhood watch
• No public transport
SELECTED MIDDLE-CLASS AREA
• Easily accessible
• Few police patrols
• Low-security housing
• Larger gardens
HOME NOT BURGLED
• Nosy neighbors
• Burglar alarm
• No rear access
• Visible from street
• Window locks
• Dog
BURGLED HOME
• No one at home
• Especially affluent
• Detached
• Patio doors
• Bushes and other cover
• Corner site

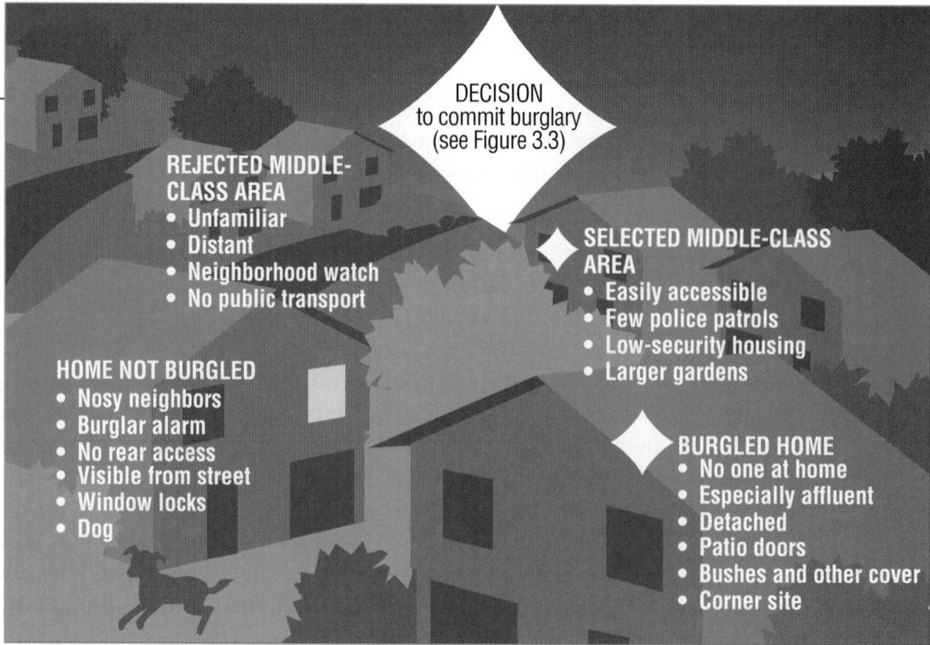

Studies have shown that in most cases the decision to commit a specific burglary arises from a perceived need of cash. Many times this money is needed to meet basic needs such as paying for rent or electricity or buying food. But often the money is needed to maintain a certain lifestyle in order to keep up with the demands of peer pressure.

Typical of this type of residential burglar was Larry William, who told the interviewers,

> Usually when I get in my car and drive around I'm thinking, I don't have any money, so what is my means for gettin' money? All of a sudden I'll just take a glance and say, "There it is! There's the house." . . . Then I get this feelin', that right moment, I'm movin' then.[32]

Wright and Decker found that burglars in their sample were not motivated "by a desire for money for its own sake." Rather, they wanted the money to "solve an immediate problem." Burglary for them was a "matter of day-to-day survival." According to two burglars in the sample,

> Usually what I'll do is a burglary, maybe two or three if I have to, and then this will help me get over the rough spot until I can get my shit straightened out. Once I get it straightened out, I just go with the flow until I hit that rough spot where I need money again. And then I hit it. . . . the only time I would go and commit a burglary is if I needed it in that point in time. That would be strictly to pay light bill, gas bill, rent. (Dan Whiting)

> You know how to stretch a dollar? I'll stretch it from here to the parking lot. But I can only stretch it so far and then it breaks. Then I say, "Well, I guess I got to go put on my black clothes. Go on out there like a thief in the night." (Ralph Jones)[33]

Of course, the need for cash is not always to meet such basic needs as food and rent. Sometimes it is to "keep the party going." When Wright and Decker asked the burglars in their sample what they spent the money for, almost 75 percent said for "high living." Most commonly, "high living" meant buying drugs. As Janet Wilson, one of the burglars put it, "Long as I got some money, I'm cool. If I ain't got no money and I want to get high, then I go for it." A substantial number of burglars "needed" money for "keeping up appearances" by buying status items, particularly brand-name clothes and high-status cars.[34]

Rational choice applies not only to the decision to commit a crime but also to the selection of a target—the person to rob or place to burglarize. Although in many cases, burglars do not indulge in high-level reasoning in planning their burglaries, a number of investigators have "shown that target decisions approximate simple common-sense conceptions of rational behavior." Wright and Decker found that among their sample of St. Louis burglars,

> a majority of the offenders typically had a potential residential burglary target already lined up. This involved not merely having a specific dwelling in mind, but also possessing reliable information about such things as the routine of its occupants. In most cases, the target initially had been located during the course of the offender's daily activities and then casually kept under surveillance for a period of time. Sometimes, though, the target was selected because the offender either knew the occupants personally or else had received a tip from someone with inside knowledge of the place.[35]

Finally, rational choice applies to assessing the risk of getting caught. Some researchers have concluded that burglars think little, if at all, of getting caught when they decide to commit burglary. Neal Shover and David Honaker, for example, interviewed a sample of Tennessee state prisoners who were repeat property offenders nearing the end of their prison terms. Most of the prisoners (62 percent) said they did not consider the risk of getting arrested; the remaining 38 percent said they gave some thought to arrest but easily dismissed the idea and got on with their planned burglaries. The following exchange took place between the interviewer and one of the burglars who never thought about getting caught:

> Q: Did you think about . . . getting caught?
>
> A: No.
>
> Q: [H]ow did you manage to put that out of your mind?
>
> A: [It] never did come into it.
>
> Q: Never did come into it?
>
> A: Never did, you know. It didn't bother me.

And the following exchange took place with one of the burglars who considered getting caught but easily dismissed the notion:

> Q: Did you worry much about getting caught? On a scale of one to ten, how would you rank your degree of worry. . . ?
>
> A: [T]he worry was probably a one. You know what I mean? The worry was probably one. I didn't think about the consequences, you know. I know it's stupidity, but it didn't—that [I] might go to jail, I mean—it crossed my mind but it didn't make much difference.[36]

Shover and Honaker concluded that their study of burglars and various other studies of property offenders demonstrate that "many serious property offenders seem to be remarkably casual in weighing the formal risks of criminal participation." One of their subjects summed up this conclusion: "you think about going to prison about like you think of dying."[37]

Kenneth Tunnell also questions the rationality of career property offenders. Tunnell maintains that rational decisions require the weighing of both the benefits and the risks of committing crimes. Tunnell interviewed 60 repeat property offenders in a Tennessee prison. Their crimes included everything from armed robbery to petty theft. The interviews showed that these offenders considered only the benefits, not the risks, of committing property crimes. They believed not only that they would not get caught, but also that if they did get caught they would receive only short prison sentences. They also believed that prison was not a threatening environment. According to Tunnell,

> the rationality of the respondents' decisions is debatable because they could not have considered realistically the possible outcomes of their actions. They were predisposed to calculate erroneously because they assessed the degree of punishment unrealistically.[38]

On the other hand, Julie Horney and Ineke Haen Marshall found that property offenders do consider and accurately perceive the risk of getting caught and punished for committing a wide range of crimes. They interviewed more than 1,000 convicted men sentenced to the Nebraska Department of Corrections. They asked them what they perceived to be the chances of getting arrested for a range of property crimes. Horney and Marshall found that experienced criminals have an accurate perception of the risk of getting punished for most crimes. They have learned through experience that "what actually happens when rules are violated is often nothing." They take this into account in their decision to commit crimes. This weighing the chances of getting caught supports the rational choice perspective.[39]

A sample of Washington, D.C., drug dealers may add further support to rational choice theory. Rand Corporation researchers selected a sample of persons charged with drug offenses in the District of Columbia between 1985 and 1987. They found that drug dealing was profitable, if not at the level that makes great fortunes. It does, however, pay a lot more than the legitimate work available to most urban youths with poor education and job skills. The Rand researchers estimated that drug dealers make an average of $30 an hour, including free drugs. The risks, of course, are also high. Drug dealers face an annual risk of a little more than a 1 in 100 chance of getting killed, a 7 percent chance of serious injury, and a 22 percent chance of going to prison. The real risks of death, injury, and imprisonment did not deter these Washington, D.C., residents from dealing drugs.[40]

This choice in favor of the profits from dealing drugs, against the known risks of death, injury, and imprisonment, may support rational choice theory, but it presents major problems for law enforcement agencies. "Drug selling is an important career choice and a major economic activity for many black males living in poverty," according to the Rand study. Improving employment prospects would probably do little to reduce drug selling, because many dealers have developed expensive drug habits. Raising legitimate wages by

50 percent, to about $10.50 an hour, is unrealistic in view of the low education and job skill level of most dealers. Besides, even $10.50 an hour falls far short of the $30 an hour they can make dealing drugs. According to researchers, society must teach young people to avoid the lure of short-term gains. The realities of frequent imprisonment and expensive drug dependency are not worth it.[41]

The benefits of committing crimes include a range of gains, not all of them related to money. Floyd Feeney examined the reasons why robbers committed crimes. He found that robbers had various motivations (see Table 3.1).

Definite goals are a critical element of rational decision making. Another critical element is the availability of alternatives to crime to achieve goals. Kenneth Tunnell, in his interviews with career robbery and burglary prison inmates referred to earlier, found that these offenders did not perceive any real alternative to committing crimes. Forty-two out of 60 believed they had no alternatives to committing robbery or burglary. Approximately equal numbers of the remaining inmates said that to avoid robbery and burglary, they had tried another crime, tried to borrow money, or tried to find a job.[42]

Rationality, of course, does not apply to all crimes, nor in equal measure. Crimes of passion *do* occur, and some criminals are psychotic or suffering from biological defects affecting behavior. Furthermore, rationality plays a larger role in the decision making of experienced criminals than of amateurs. Finally, criminals committing the same type of crime act with varying degrees of rationality. Contrast the following statements by robbers to Floyd Feeney as to why they committed a particular robbery:

> [ROBBER 1:] There wasn't no food in the house, you know. Scrounging. And I'm forced into having to do something like this. I know I was desperate. Besides, I was going out stealing anything I could get a hold of, get a little money to get some food.

Table 3.1
Motivation for Committing Robbery

MOTIVATION	PERCENT
Money	(57)
For drugs	17
For food and shelter	8
For other specific items	16
General desire for money	16
Other than Money	(24)
Excitement	6
Anger	6
Impress friends	6
Not sure; drunk or on drugs	6
Not Really a Robber	(19)
Recover money owed	5
Interrupted burglary	4
Fight turned into a robbery	4
Partner started robbery	6

> [ROBBER 2:] I have no idea why I did this. Well, guess it was for some money, but I didn't have no problem, really, then. You know, everybody got a little money problem, but not big enough to go and rob somebody. I just can't get off into it. I don't really know why I did it.[43]

Empirical studies also support the crime-specific element of the rational choice perspective. For example, while commercial burglars and robbers both planned their crimes, robbers were more determined to carry out their crime, and many more robbers were drunk or under the influence of some other drug at the time of the crime. Support for the crime-specific focus also appears within crime categories. Commercial robberies are more often planned than street muggings. Finally, the research supports the importance of distinguishing between involvement in crime generally and the decision to commit a specific offense.[44]

The rational choice perspective creates some methodological problems. Understanding the choices criminals make requires getting information from "real" criminals. Most real criminals likely to be interviewed are in prisons and jails, and so are not necessarily a representative sample. For instance, they may not tell the truth because of the implications for either the conditions or length of their imprisonment. Perhaps even more important, incarcerated offenders tend to be older, serious, and persistent criminals, which slants the data toward experience and planning. Attempting to interview ex-offenders or those not incarcerated adds the difficulty of identifying and contacting individuals. Gathering information about criminals also raises the issue of privacy. Finally, as with all interviews, researchers face the problem of accuracy.[45]

The "Seduction" of Crime

Another offender-focused perspective is what Jack Katz calls the seduction of crime. In his fascinating book, *Seductions of Crime,* Katz explores what he calls the foreground forces in crime, "the positive, often wonderful attractions within the lived experience of criminality." Rather than rejecting the "background" forces of traditional sociological theory, Katz's perspective elaborates on their explanations of criminal behavior. Thus, in addition to rational choices and economic motives for committing crimes, Katz explores other motivations, or foreground forces, particularly the thrill of committing crimes. Katz argues that traditional criminologists have neglected these foreground forces in favor of the background forces elaborated in sociological theories of crime:

> The social science literature contains only scattered evidence of what it means, feels, sounds, tastes, or looks like to commit a particular crime. Readers of research on homicide and assault do not hear the slaps and curses, see the pushes and shoves, or feel the humiliation and rage that may build toward the attack, sometimes persisting after the victim's death. How

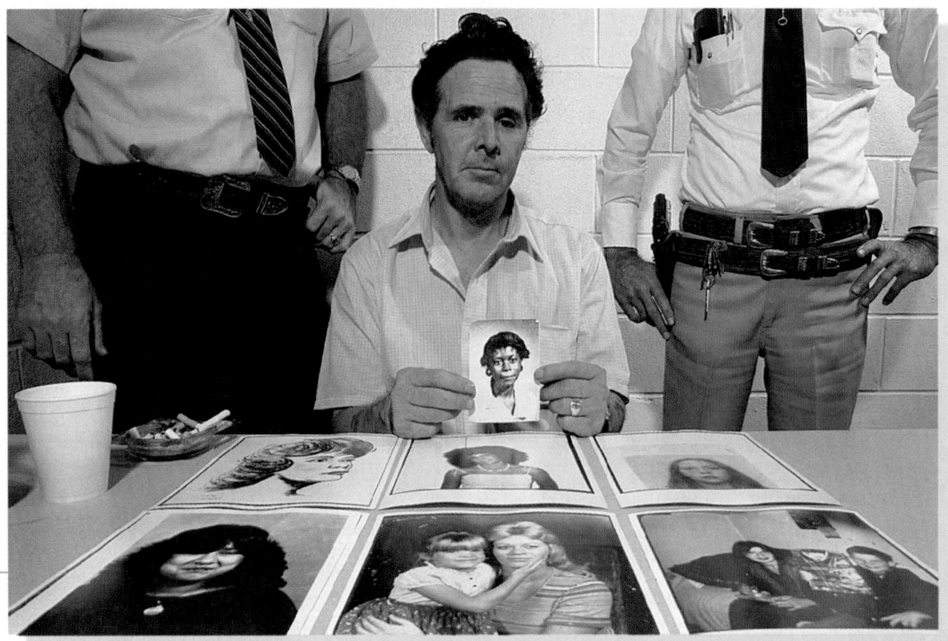

Serial killer Henry Lee Lucas (top) and his victims' families, all holding photos of Lucas's victims. Lucas was convicted of 10 homicides, many of them female hitchhikers, and at one time claimed to have killed as many as 600, though later recanted. Lucas claimed that robbery was never a motive; he is believed to have killed mainly because he enjoyed the experience. What types of theories would you posit to explain Lucas's criminal behavior? What kinds of questions would you ask about Lucas's background to investigate these theories?

adolescents manage to make shoplifting or vandalism of cheap and commonplace things a thrilling experience has not been intriguing to many students of delinquency. Researchers of adolescent gangs have never grasped why their subjects so often stubbornly refuse to accept the outsider's insistence that they wear the "gang" label. The description of "cold-blooded senseless murder" has been left to writers outside the social sciences. Neither academic methods nor academic theories seem to be able to grasp why such killers may have been courteous to their victims just moments before the killing, why they often wait until they have dominated victims in sealed-off environments before coldly executing them, or how it makes sense to kill them when only petty cash is at stake. Sociological and psychological studies of robbery rarely focus on the distinctive attractions of robbery, even though research has now clearly documented that alternative forms of criminality are available and familiar to many career robbers. In sum, only rarely have sociologists taken up the challenge of explaining the qualities of deviant experience.[46]

Katz maintains that the study of foreground forces may clear up some major deficiencies in existing theories of criminal behavior. Many, perhaps most, brain-damaged and psychotic people do not commit crimes. Many, probably most, who have suffered from the criminogenic forces created by the social structure and social processes of modern America do not commit crimes. At the same time, many who commit crimes have no physiological or psychological defects. Many criminals have escaped the criminogenic forces identified by theories of social structure, process, and control. Finally, many who fit the causal profiles of the biological, psychoanalytic, and sociological theories "go for long stretches without committing the crime to which theory directs them." "Why," asks Katz, "are some people who were not determined to commit a crime one moment determined to do so the next?"[47]

Katz maintains that the answer to his question lies in the "seduction," the "thrill" of crime; the foreground perspective explains not only crimes such as stickups or robbery, but also cold-blooded and passionate murder, theft, and probably most other crimes. The foreground approach requires finding out what was the distinctive restraint or seductive appeal, at the moment the person committed the crime, that the criminal's social, biological, and psychological background cannot explain.

According to Katz, at the moment of crime the criminal feels seduced, drawn to, compelled to commit the crime. Such feelings are not morally special to criminals—everyone feels them. What is unique is the seduction to commit a crime. Furthermore, feeling compelled does not mean that the crime was beyond the person's control; it was still a choice. At the moment of the crime, says Katz, there is a transition from the choice to commit crimes rationally to a compulsion to do so, driven by the seductive thrill of crime. This is not to say that the criminal has no control, because the criminal controls the *transition* from choice to compulsion.

Knowledge and Understanding CHECK

1. Briefly describe five propositions common to the economic explanations of crime.
2. Describe the two policy approaches that economic explanations of crime can apply.
3. What assumption about criminal behavior does rational choice make?
4. List the three major elements of the rational choice perspective.
5. Describe the crime-specific focus of the rational choice perspective.
6. List the three factors upon which the criminal event depends, according to the rational choice perspective.
7. Describe the form of rationality that the rational choice perspective posits.
8. According to Wright and Decker, what is the reason for committing burglary in most cases?
9. List the things burglars spend money on, and what they spend most of their money on.
10. Apply rational choice theory to burglars' selection of a place to burglarize.
11. Apply rational choice theory to burglars' assessment of the risk of getting caught.
12. Summarize the findings, identify the sources, and describe the methods of Tunnell's study of the rationality of property offenders.
13. Contrast Horney and Marshall's findings, sources, and methods with Tunnell's.
14. How do the findings of the Rand Corporation's study of Washington, D.C., drug dealers support rational choice theory?
15. List the motivations of armed robbers identified by Floyd Feeney's study.
16. Describe the methodological problems created by the rational choice perspective.

MODERN BIOLOGICAL THEORIES

Perhaps the most sensationalized modern offender-focused biological explanation of crime is that violent behavior is linked to abnormal chromosomes. Until 1960, it was widely accepted that males have two sex-linked chromosomes, one X and one Y. Using sophisticated methods, biologists discovered that some men have two or sometimes even three Y chromosomes. Then, in 1965, Scottish researchers reported an astonishing correlation: A high proportion of tall, violent, male mental patients had an extra Y chromosome.[48]

In a subsequent wave of studies in mental hospitals and prisons, researchers attempted to discover whether violence could be traced to these newly identified "supermales" with "chromosomes of criminality." These studies yielded decidedly mixed results: Some corroborated the chromosome-violence link; others contradicted it. A Danish study indicated that large men with extra Y chromosomes showed no special proclivity toward violence. However, it did show that in a large group of Danish men (more than 30,000), those with extra Y chromosomes committed more crimes than did men with normal chromosome configurations.

Such findings do not prove that abnormal chromosomes *cause* violent behavior; correlation is not causation. Causation means that one thing produces a result; in this case, that the XYY chromosome produces violent behavior. Correlation means only that two things are associated. An association of YY or YYY chromosomes with violence does not prove that YY or YYY chromosomes cause violence. Furthermore, important noninherited variables not measured in the study might also be associated with crime. The configuration of chromosomes may be only one, and not necessarily an important, explanation of criminal behavior. Other significant variables might include anything from nutrition to neighborhoods and family relationships.[49]

Twin studies are less dramatic than the XYY-chromosome theory, but they illustrate another attempt to link biology to crime. In one well-known study, Karl Otto Christiansen investigated all twins born in a particular part of Denmark between 1881 and 1910. He found that if one fraternal twin was a criminal, there was approximately a 12 percent chance that the other twin would be one, too. In identical twins, the chance jumps to about 35 percent. Although these links are weak, the study establishes a definite correlation between twins and the incidence of criminal behavior.[50]

Modern discoveries in brain research have also led to biological theories that link violent behavior to brain dysfunction. Research has placed the centers for rage and aggression in the limbic system. Theorists postulate that chemical imbalance in the limbic system, or damage to the limbic tissue itself—it is not clear which—results in violent behavior. According to the findings of brain researchers, many individuals who act violently have brain diseases that can be described, diagnosed, treated, and controlled—which is to say that violence is related to brain malfunction. Researchers also maintain that individuals who lose control of their anger, repeatedly attacking or injuring others and themselves, want and need medical help but are not getting it. In one study of 150 such people seen for treatment, nearly half had been driven to attempted suicide by their despair at what they had done. All of them felt anguish from the social and personal consequences of their acts; all had gone to doctors many times before for advice and aid. Most physicians are not aware of how often a brain abnormality may underlie violent behavior, and they are not accustomed to considering violence a medical problem. Consequently, they reject violent people as patients, dismissing them as incurable sociopaths or psychopaths when, say brain researchers, they should instead be looking for evidence of brain dysfunction.[51]

Despite the research of neurologists, psychiatrists, and biologists, criminologists are wary of biological theories of crime. Physiological theories discount sociological variables that might explain criminal behavior. Furthermore, physiological research does not explain—or even report on—the people in the population who have such dysfunctions but are not violent or do not commit crimes.

Some criminologists are now engaged in research that they hope can establish links between biology and crime. The results of this research have led to a variety of interesting but inconclusive links:

1. Jail inmates who consumed high levels of caffeine and sugar engaged in more antisocial conduct than those in a control group who did not consume these high levels.[52]
2. Hypoglycemia (low blood sugar levels) may contribute to violent behavior.[53]
3. Abnormal quantities of copper, zinc, chromium, and manganese have been found in violent offenders.[54]
4. Minimal brain dysfunctions due to as yet unestablished causes appear in some people subject to explosive rage.[55]
5. Premenstrual syndrome (PMS), caused by a deficiency of the hormone progesterone, has recently drawn attention as a possible cause of women's criminal behavior.

One case of PMS involved Sandie Craddock, a 29-year-old London bartender who attacked and killed a coworker. "While she was in prison awaiting trial," her physician recalls, "she was a good prisoner for twenty-eight days each month, and on the twenty-ninth day she would engage in what the prison psychiatrist called 'attention-getting behavior.' She tried to slash her wrists, she tried to strangle herself, she tried to set herself on fire." Craddock had an extensive arrest record that corresponded to a 29-day cycle.[56]

In women who are physiologically normal, progesterone imbalance does not cause severe distress. However, for those who, like Sandie Craddock, suffer other chemical imbalances, the problem can be severe, particularly if an endorphin imbalance in the brain results. Endorphins, the "natural tranquilizers," affect the function of the pituitary gland, which in turn influences mood, behavior, and premenstrual dysfunctions such as fluid retention and digestive problems. An endorphin imbalance can produce severe and dangerous mental disturbances—such as suicidal and murderous impulses, the two most relevant to criminal justice.

The National Research Council, research arm of the National Academy of Sciences, has given new credibility to the biological origins of crime. Its report, published as *Understanding and Preventing Violence,* compiles the work of 19 prominent scholars and scientists from a range of disciplines. The report calls for the consideration of biological and genetic factors, as well as the criminogenic forces in society, in the search for the causes of violence. A detailed survey of the present state of knowledge in sociology, psychology, psychiatry, law, genetics, and biology, the report recognizes the complexity of the causes of crime. According to the report:

> research strongly suggests that violence arises from interactions among individuals' psychosocial development, their neurological and hormonal differences, and social processes. Consequently, we have no basis for

considering any of these "levels of explanation" any more fundamental than the others.[57]

Mark Moore, professor of criminal justice policy at Harvard University, offered this bleak assessment of the National Research Council report on the link between violence and biology: "You come to the important point of view that the causes of violence are complex and therefore elusive. The hope that we might be able to base policy on definite knowledge of the causes of violence is receding." The report, like all biological theories of crime, also faces criticism by some that it reflects racism. Just a month before the council announced its report, the federal government, under pressure from protesters, withdrew financial support for a conference on the possible genetic causes of crime.[58]

Knowledge and Understanding CHECK

1. Explain the significance of the XYY chromosome in explaining criminal behavior.
2. Summarize the results of the XYY chromosome studies.
3. Summarize the results of Karl Otto Christiansen's twin study in explaining criminal behavior.
4. Summarize the modern discoveries of brain research and their implication for explaining criminal behavior.
5. List and briefly describe the findings of criminologists who have studied the link between criminal behavior and biology.
6. Summarize the results of the National Research Council's findings regarding the link between violence and biology.

SITUATION THEORIES

Situation theories of crime are context-based, not offender-focused. These theories reject, or at least minimize, the motivation of offenders as an explanation for criminal behavior. Situation theories have their intellectual roots not in the eighteenth-century Enlightenment but in the twentieth-century human ecology perspective. This perspective focused on plotting the distribution of crime geographically among neighborhoods and temporally according to time of day, day of the week, and month of the year. Situation theories study the "location of targets and the movement of offenders and victims in time and space." Central to situation explanations of crime are opportunity and temptation. Although situation theories assume that offenders are goal oriented, their decisions are "not calculated to maximize success, but rather to meet their needs with a minimum of effort." This explanation assumes that most criminals, like most other people, are "middling in morality, in self-control, in careful effort, in pursuing advantage." Therefore, criminal behavior depends on the situation—specifically, on time, space (perhaps more properly, place), opportunity, and temptation. Situation explanations look at the modus operandi of offenders "not merely as interesting material for undergraduate classes, but rather as central information for professional criminologists."[59]

In 1979, Lawrence E. Cohen and Marcus Felson introduced one of the best-known of the situation theories of crime, the **routine activities theory.** This theory focuses on the importance of time and place in the explanation of criminal behavior. According to Cohen and Felson,

> No matter at what level data were measured or analyzed, that approach kept returning . . . to specific points in time and space . . . and to changes from moment to moment and hour to hour in where people are, what they are doing, and what happens to them as a result.[60]

While routine activity theory brings time and space into the foreground, it pushes into the background both the individual motivation of criminals and the agencies of criminal justice. Whether money, power, status, sex, or thrills motivate offenders to commit crimes is not the significant inquiry; any motivation will do. According to Cohen and Felson, people are

> treated virtually as objects and their motivations scrupulously avoided as a topic of discussion, in stark contrast to the heavy motivational emphasis of virtually all contemporary criminology at that time [1970s]. . . . Thus, at the outset the approach distinguished clearly between criminal inclinations and criminal events and made that distinction a centerpiece rather than a footnote.[61]

Cohen and Felson argue that crime can be explained by the convergence of three elements:

1. A motivated offender (never mind what that motivation is).
2. A suitable target.
3. The absence of a capable guardian.

A likely offender is "anybody who for any reason might commit a crime." A suitable target of crime is "any person or object likely to be taken or attacked by the offender." In a sense, this means anyone or any property in the right place at the right time. The capable guardian is not usually a police officer or a security guard. Cohen and Felson offer this explanation for omitting the police as capable guardians:

> This was the result of a conscious effort to distance routine activity theory from the rest of criminology, which is far too wedded to the criminal justice system as central to crime explanation. . . . widespread media linkage of the police and courts to crime [is incorrect]. . . . in fact most crime involves neither agency. Indeed, the most likely persons to prevent a crime are not policemen (who seldom are around to discover crimes in the act) but rather friends, relatives, bystanders, or the owner of the property targeted.[62]

IMPLICATIONS OF THEORY FOR POLICY

Because the response to crime depends upon the explanation for the occurrence of criminal behavior, theories of crime have important implications for criminal justice policy. The criminal law, for instance, rejects sociological determinism, resting its principles on eighteenth-century concepts of individualism and free will and their modern counterparts. Also, the legal definitions of crime show a distinct bias against crimes committed by the "lower classes." After the adversary process has run its course, sociological theories may play some part in sentencing and in correctional programs.

Some sociological crime theories, especially those developed during the 1960s, suggest that neither formal nor informal criminal justice offers the best response to the crime problem. The best response is to remove the "root" causes of crime, causes deeply embedded in the social structure and processes of modern America. According to this view, the best response of society to crime might be to ameliorate those conditions and processes that cause crime. Some believe the entire social structure of capitalism must be altered. Others believe capitalism must be adjusted to allow for more equal distribution of wealth and opportunity. Still others believe the values that lead to unacceptably high levels of self-interest and pursuit of individual success must be changed. Whatever their particular program, all sociological theories commonly emphasize working to change society, on the grounds that criminogenic conditions in society cause crime.[63]

Unfortunately, society's criminogenic conditions stubbornly resist change. Furthermore, even if we knew how to alter families, peer groups, and other intimate groups, the mere attempt to do so would offend some of our deepest beliefs about freedom, privacy, and independence. Also, assuming that all these obstacles could be overcome, the results, although they might be enduring, would be a very long time in coming.[64]

Knowledge and Understanding CHECK

1. What is the importance of motivation in the situation theory of crime?
2. What exactly do situation theories study?
3. What assumptions do situation theories make about most criminals that apply as well to most people in general?
4. Describe the routine activity theory.
5. What elements does routine activity theory bring into the foreground and what does it push into the background?
6. What three factors must converge in routine activity theory, according to Cohen and Felson?
7. What is the relationship between the explanations of crime and criminal justice policies? Give examples.
8. Which theories of criminal behavior underlie current criminal law?

Why Do People Commit Crimes? Consideration

At the beginning of the chapter John Allen, a career robber from a poor neighborhood in Washington, D.C., explained why he preferred robbing to other crimes–not because of the money, but because robbery was more exciting.

1. Which theoretical perspective on criminal behavior does Allen's assessment of his own criminal life seem to most closely corroborate?
2. What other theory or theories, if any, might also apply to his assessment?

CHAPTER CAPSULE

- We do not know the causes of crime.
- Explanations of criminal behavior focus on either the offender or the context.
- Sociological explanations of criminal behavior look to social structure, social processes, and other forces outside the individual.
- Rational choice explanations focus on the offender's freedom to choose to commit crimes.

KEY TERMS

offender-focused explanations
context explanations
determinist theories of crime
anomie
strain theory
opportunity theory
illegitimate opportunity structure
social learning theories
social control theories
social conflict theories
differential association
cycle-of-violence hypothesis
subculture theories
subculture of violence
subculture of competition
labeling theory
moral entrepreneurs
rational choice perspective
crime-specific focus
criminal event
situation theories
routine activities theory

INTERNET RESEARCH EXERCISES

Exercise: Using the Internet or InfoTrac College Edition, come up with a list of possible explanations for why crime occurs. Which do you find the most convincing?

Suggested site:

- National Institute of Justice: http://www.ojp.usdoj.gov/nij/welcome.html (tip: click on "Publications and Products," then look for publications having to do with the causes of crime; you'll have to decide whether you prefer to view the publication you select as a summary, an ASCII file [suggested] or an Adobe Acrobat file [requires an Adobe Acrobat viewer installed on your computer].)

InfoTrac College Edition: Run a key word search on "causes of crime"

NOTES

1. Jack Katz, *Seductions of Crime: Moral and Sensual Attractions in Doing Evil* (New York: Basic Books, 1988), 166.
2. Gina Lombroso-Ferrero, *Criminal Man* (Montclair, N.J.: Patterson Smith, 1972), 6–7.
3. Juan B. Cortes with Florence M. Gatti, *Delinquency and Crime: A Biopsychological Approach* (New York: Seminar Press, 1972).
4. Emile Durkheim, *Suicide: A Study in Sociology* (New York: Free Press, 1951); Robert K. Merton, "Social Structure and Anomie," in *Social Theory and Social Structure*, enlarged ed. (New York: Free Press, 1968), 185–214.
5. William Simon and John H. Gagnon, "The Anomie of Affluence: A Post-Mertonian Conception," *American Journal of Sociology* 82 (1976): 356–78; Alex Thio, "A Critical Look at Merton's Anomie Theory," *Pacific Sociological Review* 18 (1975): 139–58.
6. Mitchell B. Chamlin and John K. Cochran, "Causality, Economic Conditions, and Burglary," *Criminology*, 36 (1998): 426.
7. Richard Cloward and Lloyd Ohlin, *Delinquency and Opportunity: A Theory of Delinquent Gangs* (New York: Free Press, 1960).
8. Clifford Shaw, *The Jack-Roller* (Chicago: University of Chicago Press, 1966), 54.
9. Edwin H. Sutherland and Donald R. Cressey, *Criminology*, 10th ed. (Philadelphia: J. Lippincott Co., 1978), 83–87.
10. Albert K. Cohen, *Delinquent Boys: The Culture of the Gang* (New York: Free Press, 1983); Albert K. Cohen, "Crime Causation: Sociological Theories," *Encyclopedia of Crime and Justice*, 1: 346.
11. Marvin Wolfgang and Franco Ferracuti, *The Subculture of Violence* (London: Tavistock, 1967).
12. James W. Coleman, *The Criminal Elite* (New York: St. Martin's Press, 1985), 202–04.
13. Travis Hirschi, *Causes of Delinquency* (Berkeley: University of California Press, 1969), 34.
14. Francis T. Cullen, *Rethinking Crime and Deviance Theory* (Totowa, N.J.: Rowman and Allenheld, 1983), 137–42.
15. This summary is based on Brown et al., *Criminology: Explaining Crime and Its Content*, 373.
16. Ezra Stotland, "White Collar Criminals," *Journal of Social Issues* 33 (1977): 179–96.
17. Cullen, *Rethinking Crime and Deviance Theory*, 123; Howard Becker, *Outsiders* (New York: Free Press, 1973).
18. Cullen, *Rethinking Crime and Deviance Theory*, 125–28.
19. Gary Becker, "Crime and Punishment: An Economic Approach," *Journal of Political Economy* 76 (1968): 169–217; Ann Dryden Witte, "Estimating the Economic Model of Crime with Individual Data," *Quarterly Journal of Economics* 91 (1980): 57–84.
20. Ann Dryden Witte, "Crime Causation: Economic Theories," *Encyclopedia of Crime and Justice*, Sanford Kadish, ed. (New York: Free Press, 1983), 319.
21. Isaac Ehrlich, "The Deterrent Effect of Capital Punishment: A Question of Life and Death," *American Economic Review* 65 (1975): 397–417.
22. Ibid., 398.
23. Michael Gottfredson and Travis Hirschi, *A General Theory of Crime* (Stanford: Stanford University Press, 1990), 74.
24. Ronald V. Clarke and Marcus Felson, eds., *Routine Activity and Rational Choice* (New Brunswick, N.J.: Transaction Publishers, 1993), 5.
25. Both Etzioni and Frank are quoted in Brian Forst, ed., *The Socio-Economics of Crime and Justice* (Armonk, N.Y.: M. E. Sharpe, 1993), 5–6.
26. Mitchell B. Chamlin and John K. Cochran, "Causality, Economic Conditions, and Burglary," *Criminology* 36(1998): 426–427.
27. Clarke and Felson, *Routine Activity and Rational Choice*, 5.
28. This section relies heavily on Derek B. Cornish and Ronald V. Clarke, eds., *The Reasoning Criminal: Rational Choice Perspectives on Offending* (New York: Springer-Verlag, 1986).
29. Clarke and Felson, *Routine Activity and Rational Choice*, 6.
30. P. Letkemann, *Crime as Work* (Englewood Cliffs, N.J.: Prentice-Hall, 1973), 151.
31. Wright and Decker, *Burglars On the Job*, 36.
32. Ibid.
33. Ibid., 37.
34. Ibid., 37–38.
35. Ibid., 101.
36. Neal Shover and David Honaker, "The Socially Bounded Decision Making of Persistent Property Offenders," *Howard Journal of Criminal Justice* 31 (1992): 279.
37. Ibid., 281.
38. Kenneth D. Tunnell, "Choosing Crime: Close Your Eyes and Take Your Chances," *Justice Quarterly* 7 (1990): 673–90.
39. Julie Horney and Ineke Haen Marshall, "Risk Perceptions Among Serious Offenders: The Role of Crime and Punishment," *Criminology* 30 (1992): 575–92.
40. Peter Reuter, Robert MacCoun, and Patrick Murphy, *Money from Crime* (Santa Monica: The Rand Corporation, 1990), viii–xix.
41. Ibid., xiv.
42. Kenneth D. Tunnell, "Property Criminals as the Lumpenproletariat: A Serendipitous Finding," *Nature, Society, and Thought* 3 (1990): 45.
43. Quoted in Floyd Feeney, "Robbers as Decision-Makers," in Cornish and Clarke, *The Reasoning Criminal*, 57; for similar findings, see Thomas Gabor et al., *Armed Robbery: Cops, Robbers, and Victims* (Springfield, Ill.: Charles C. Thomas Publisher, 1987), 62–69; Richard T. Wright and Scott H. Decker, *Armed Robbers in Action* (New York: Harrow and Heston, 1997) contains stories.
44. Cornish and Clarke, *The Reasoning Criminal*, 8.
45. Richard Wright, Scott Decker, Allison Redfern, and Dietrich Smith, "A Snowball's Chance in Hell: Doing Fieldwork with Active Residential Burglars," *Journal of Research in Crime and Delinquency* 29 (1992): 148–61; also see Richard T. Wright and Scott H. Decker, *Armed Robbers in Action*, Chapter 1, for an excellent discussion of these and other issues related to doing research about active offenders.
46. Katz, *Seductions of Crime*, 3.
47. Ibid., 4.
48. Ysabel Rennie, *The Search for Criminal Man* (Lexington, Mass.: Lexington Books, 1978), 224.
49. Sarnoff A. Mednick and Jan Volavka, "Biology and Crime," in *Crime and Justice: An Annual Review of Research* (Chicago: University of Chicago Press, 1980), 2: 92–94; Vicki Pollock et al., "Crime Causation: Biological Theories," in *Encyclopedia of Crime and Justice*, Sanford Kadish, ed. (New York: Free Press, 1983), 310–11.
50. "A Review of Studies of Criminality Among Twins," and "A Preliminary Study of Criminality in Twins," in *Biosocial Bases of Criminality*, Sarnoff Mednick and Karl Otto Christiansen, eds. (New York: Gardner Press, 1977).
51. Vernon H. Mark and Frank R. Ervin, *Violence and the Brain* (New York: Harper & Row, 1970), 5.

52. B. D'Asario et al., "Polyamine Levels in Jail Inmates," *Journal of Orthomolecular Psychiatry* 4 (1975): 149–52.
53. J. A. Yaryura-Tobias and F. Neziroglu, "Violent Behavior, Brain Dysrythmia and Glucose Dysfunction, A New Syndrome," *Journal of Orthopsychiatry* 4 (1975): 182–88.
54. Paul Cromwell et al., "Hair Mineral Analysis: Biochemical Imbalances and Violent Criminal Behavior," *Psychological Reports 64* (1989): 259–66; Louis Gottchalk et al., "Abnormalities in Hair Trace Elements as Indicators of Aberrant Behavior," *Comprehensive Psychiatry* 32 (1991), 229–37.
55. R. R. Monroe, *Brain Dysfunction in Aggressive Criminals* (Lexington, Mass.: D. C. Heath, 1978).
56. Robin Marantz Henig, "Dispelling Menstrual Myths," *New York Times Magazine,* March 7, 1982.
57. Albert J. Reiss, Jr., and Jeffrey A. Roth, eds., *Understanding and Preventing Violence* (Washington, D.C.: National Academy Press, 1993), 102.
58. Jack Katz, *Seductions of Crime,* 166; Fox Butterfield, "Study Cites Biology's Role in Violent Behavior," *New York Times,* 1992.
59. Clarke and Felson, *Routine Activity and Rational Choice,* 10–11.
60. Ibid., 3.
61. Lawrence E. Cohen and Marcus Felson, "Social Change and Crime Rate Trends: A Routine Activity Approach," *American Sociological Review* 44 (1979): 588–608; Ronald V. Clarke and Marcus Felson, eds., *Routine Activity and Rational Choice* (New Brunswick, N.J.: Transaction Publishers, 1993), 1–14; Marcus Felson, *Crime in Everyday Life,* 2d ed. (Thousand Oaks, California: Pine Forge Press, 1998), 2.
62. Clarke and Felson, *Routine Activity and Rational Choice*, 2–3.
63. The President's Commission on Crime, Law Enforcement and the Administration of Justice, *The Challenge of Crime in a Free Society* (Washington, D.C.: U.S. Government Printing Office, 1967); Jeffrey Reiman, *The Rich Get Richer and the Poor Get Prison,* 2d ed. (New York: John Wiley and Sons, 1984); Kevin Wright, *The Great American Crime Myth* (Westport, Conn.: Greenwood Press, 1985), discusses these broad issues in some detail.
64. James Q. Wilson, *Thinking About Crime*, rev. ed. (New York: Basic Books, 1983), especially chap. 3; Lloyd Ohlin, "The President's Commission on Law Enforcement and the Administration of Justice," in Mirra Komarovsky, ed., *Sociology and Public Policy* (New York: Elsevier, 1975), 93–115.

CHAPTER 4

Criminal Justice and the Law

CHAPTER OUTLINE

Should There Be a "Cultural Values" Defense to Criminal Behavior?

A Laotian refugee living in this country for approximately two years was convicted of intentionally murdering his Laotian wife of one month. At trial, he tried to enter a defense of "extreme emotional disturbance" to mitigate the homicide on the theory that the stresses resulting from his status of a refugee caused a significant mental trauma, affecting his mind for a substantial period of time, simmering in the unknowing subconscious and then inexplicably coming to the fore. Although the immediate cause for the defendant's loss of control was his jealousy over his wife's apparent preference for an ex-boyfriend, the defense argued that under Laotian culture the conduct of the wife in displaying affection for another man and receiving phone calls from an unattached man brought shame on defendant and his family sufficient to trigger defendant's loss of control. The trial court refused to admit information regarding Laotian culture.

INTRODUCTION

"No crime without law" and "No punishment without law" are two of the most ancient principles of our criminal law. Crime control in a constitutional democracy depends on these principles. A pure democracy is one in which the majority can do whatever it pleases. However, ours is not a pure democracy; it is a constitutional democracy. The U.S. Constitution establishes that crime control in a constitutional democracy such as ours has to operate within the framework—and only under the authority—of law. None of the behavior discussed in Chapter 2 can be criminal without a specific law defining it as a crime and prescribing a punishment for it. No action taken or decision made by any police officer, prosecutor, defense attorney, judge, jury, probation officer, corrections officer, or parole officer (discussed in the remaining chapters of this book) is allowed except by the authority of law. The sources of this authority are the national and state constitutions, federal and state statutes, and court decisions interpreting these constitutions and statutes.

Informally, the legal framework and authority is broad and flexible enough to allow ample room for discretionary decision making. Legal terms, like all other words, are at best imperfect symbols for what they represent. No written rule defining criminal behavior can precisely describe all the behavior it is intended to prohibit. No provision defining the power of criminal justice agencies can fully account for all the actions that power allows. No rule can cover all contingencies that may arise after it is written. Finally, no rule, however clear and predictive, can—or should—eliminate the influences of ideology, economics, social structure and processes, and individual personality. In short, the tension between formal rules and informal, discretionary decision making—between formal and informal criminal justice—also applies to criminal law and criminal procedure.

This chapter examines the constitutional and legal framework within which day-to-day criminal justice operations take place. Both criminal law and the law of criminal procedure affect these operations. The **criminal law** tells private individuals what behavior the law prohibits and prescribes the punishment for criminal behavior. In short, criminal law is the formal definition of crime and punishment, the primary source of the actions of criminal justice agencies. The **law of criminal procedure** defines the extent and limits of government power to enforce the criminal law in our constitutional democracy; it tells public officials what actions they are allowed to take to control crime and prescribes the consequences for official actions that violate the law.

Knowledge and Understanding CHECK

1. Recite the two ancient principles that are fundamental to a constitutional democracy.
2. What is the importance of law in controlling crime in a constitutional democracy?
3. Identify the sources of authority in controlling crime in our constitutional democracy.
4. Explain how and why discretionary decision making is important in crime control.
5. Explain the difference between criminal law and criminal procedure.

CRIMINAL LAW

In every society there are people whose behavior ought to be condemned. Some of this behavior causes considerable harm. However, no society makes crimes out of all offensive behavior. Criminal law distinguishes *reprehensible* behavior from *criminal* behavior. To put it bluntly, as a society we distinguish—as we should—between creeps and criminals. For example, it may be wrong to cheat on your girlfriend or boyfriend and to lie to your friends, but neither is a crime. Philanderers and liars deserve condemnation but not jail time. Why? Because criminal law is society's last resort against reprehensible behavior, and because it is expensive, cumbersome, and intrudes deeply into privacy and liberty, often with only limited effect. So, we rely on other social control mechanisms to discourage most misbehavior. These mechanisms include:

- Disapproval of family, friends, and others we love and respect.
- Informal discipline within social institutions like schools and places of employment.
- Private lawsuits.

Only when all of the following conditions apply can misbehavior become a crime:

1. A specific law gives clear and prior warning that the law prohibits the misbehavior.
2. The law prescribes a specific penalty for the prohibited conduct.
3. The particular law conforms to the general purposes and principles of criminal law.
4. The punishment does not violate the U.S. Constitution's prohibition against cruel and unusual punishment.

Knowledge and Understanding CHECK

1. What does it mean to say that society distinguishes between creeps and criminals?
2. Why do we distinguish between creeps and criminals?
3. Identify three social control mechanisms, beside criminal law, that are used to control misbehavior.
4. What four conditions are necessary for turning misbehavior into criminal behavior?

THE PRINCIPLES OF CRIMINAL LAW

"Welcome to Bloomington, you're under arrest." That's what one police officer told me ought to be printed on a billboard as you enter the city where he was a police officer. "Why?" I asked. "Because everything in Bloomington is a crime," he answered. He was referring to the broad scope of criminal law, not only in Bloomington but everywhere in the United States. Somewhere in the country, all of the following are crimes:

- Murder, rape, and robbery.
- Burglary and theft.
- Public drunkenness.
- Panhandling.
- Sleeping in public.
- Eating in buses.
- Spitting on the street.
- Returning books to the library late.
- Parking your own car on your own lawn.

The list is almost endless. And, "all of this," said one critic, "in the freest country in the history of the world." Therefore, the word "crime" by itself doesn't mean much. What most people mean by crime is violent acts and serious property offenses. But as students of criminal justice, we should always make clear exactly what kind of crime we are talking about. All crimes have one element in common: Legal definitions of crime have to comply with the general principles of criminal law. These principles are stated in:

1. U.S. and state constitutions.
2. Federal, state, and local laws.
3. General principles of criminal liability.
4. Principles of justification and excuse.

Knowledge and Understanding CHECK

1. What is the significance of the list of crimes at the end of the first paragraph of this section?
2. Why does the word "crime" have so little meaning by itself?
3. Identify the one thing that all crimes have in common.
4. Identify the four major places where the general principles of criminal law are stated.

CRIMINAL LAW AND THE CONSTITUTION

According to the U.S. Constitution, the government can punish people only when specific laws warn them in advance that their behavior is a crime, and prescribe a penalty. Three provisions in the Constitution concern advance warning.

First, Article I, Section 9: "No . . . ***ex post facto* law** shall be passed." An ex post facto law is a retroactive law. That is, it criminalizes conduct that was not criminal before the passage of a statute. For example, if a state passes a statute on January 5, 2000, that raises the drinking age from 18 to 21, it cannot prosecute a 19-year-old who bought a beer on New Year's Eve, 1999. In other words, people must know *before* they act that their actions are a crime.

The two other provisions concerning advance warning are the **due process clauses** of the Fifth and Fourteenth Amendments. The Fifth Amendment clause provides that "No person shall be . . . deprived of life, liberty, or property without due process of law. . . ." The Fourteenth Amendment due process clause provides that "No state shall . . . deny any person life, liberty, or property without due process of law." Thus, the Fifth Amendment clause applies to the federal government and the Fourteenth Amendment clause imposes a due process requirement on the states.

Due process consists of two types of protection. **Substantive due process** prohibits the enactment of laws that violate the constitutional protections of life, liberty, and property. For example, making it a crime to practice the Roman Catholic religion would violate substantive due process. **Procedural due process** refers to the constitutional limits on the means that the government uses to enforce the criminal law. We will discuss procedural due process in the section on criminal procedure. One major aspect of substantive due process is that statutes must define crimes precisely, or the courts will declare them **void-for-vagueness.** The U.S. Supreme Court has ruled that a statute

> which either forbids or requires the doing of an act in terms so vague that men [and women] of common intelligence must necessarily guess at its meaning and differ as to its application, violates the first essential of due process of law.[1]

The Nebraska supreme court applied the void-for-vagueness rule to a Lincoln, Nebraska, city ordinance that prohibited "any indecent, immodest, or filthy act in the presence of any person." A passerby saw a young man standing naked in front of his window eating a bowl of cereal for breakfast. The court ruled that the ordinance was void-for-vagueness:

> We know of no way in which the standards required of a criminal act can be met in those broad, general terms. There may be those few who believe persons of the opposite sex holding hands in public are immodest, and certainly more who might believe kissing in public is immodest.[2]

The Fourteenth Amendment also prohibits states from denying individuals the **equal protection of the laws.** The U.S. Supreme Court has interpreted this clause to prohibit *unreasonable* classifications, but not all distinctions. According to the Court, the equal protection clause prohibits government from separating persons by unacceptable criteria, such as gender, race, religion, ethnic background, and, in some instances, age. For example, a statute that made it a crime for women, but not men, to smoke in public violated the equal protection clause. On the other hand, the U.S. Supreme Court ruled that California's statutory rape law that applied only to men did not violate the equal protection clause. The Court gave the reason that California has a "compelling interest" in reducing "the tragic human costs of illegitimate teenage pregnancies." The Court reasoned that

> because the Equal Protection Clause does not demand that things which are different in fact . . . to be treated in law as though they were the same, this Court has consistently upheld statutes where the gender classification is not invidious, but rather realistically reflects the fact that the sexes are not similarly situated in similar circumstances.[3]

The Fourteenth Amendment due process clause also protects the controversial right of privacy. Although the word "privacy" is never mentioned in the U.S. Constitution, the U.S. Supreme Court has interpreted the Constitution to include a **right of privacy.** This right embodies the idea that a free society ought to maximize human autonomy. Therefore, the government should leave people alone in the privacy of their homes. The U.S. Supreme Court, in the important case of *Griswold v. Connecticut,* struck down a Connecticut statute that made it a crime for married couples to use contraceptives. Justice William O. Douglas wrote that the Constitution creates a "zone of privacy" around the "intimate relation of husband and wife," and that the statute had a "destructive impact upon the relationship."[4]

Although the Supreme Court created the right of privacy, it has always defined it narrowly. Some justices have consistently refused to accept that the Constitution implies a right of privacy at all. In 1986, for example, the Court upheld a Georgia sodomy law against a challenge that the right of privacy protected sexual acts in private between consenting adult homosexuals. In *Bowers v. Hardwicke,* police officers followed Hardwicke and his companion to the man's home. The two men went into the bedroom and closed the door. The police officer knocked on the door and awakened a house guest sleeping on a couch in the living room. The guest allowed the officer to enter the house. The officer surprised the two men in bed having sex. The Court ruled that the right to privacy does not protect the homosexual lifestyle.[5]

Several state constitutions have specific provisions protecting a right of privacy. The Alaska constitution, for example, provides that "the right of the people to privacy is recognized and shall not be infringed." Relying on the right to privacy provision in the Alaska constitution, the Alaska supreme court struck down an Alaska criminal code provision that made possession of marijuana a criminal offense. In the case of *Ravin v. State,* Ravin was convicted of possessing a small amount of marijuana for his personal use in his home. According to the court:

> The privacy amendment . . . was intended to give recognition and protection to the home. Such a reading

> is consonant with the character of life in Alaska. Our . . . state has traditionally been the home of people who prize their individuality and who have chosen to settle or to continue living here in order to achieve a measure of control over their own lifestyles which is now virtually unattainable in many of our sister states.[6]

Knowledge and Understanding CHECK

1. Describe the three provisions in the U.S. Constitution that are concerned with advance warning about what behavior is criminal.
2. Define substantive and procedural due process and describe the difference between them.
3. Describe and explain the void-for-vagueness doctrine.
4. How has the U.S. Supreme Court defined the equal protection clause of the Fourteenth Amendment?
5. Since the U.S. Constitution does not contain the word "privacy," how can the Court say that there is a constitutional right of privacy?
6. What reasons did the U.S. Supreme Court give for its ruling that consensual adult sodomy is not included in the right of privacy?
7. How do some state constitutions differ from the U.S. Constitution in the treatment of the right of privacy?

The Principles of Criminal Liability

All crimes consist of at least three elements that the prosecution has to prove beyond a reasonable doubt to convict persons charged with crimes. **Proof beyond a reasonable doubt** means that the prosecution has presented enough evidence legally obtained and properly presented that will convince an ordinary, reasonable person that the defendant is guilty. These three elements are:

1. A criminal act, called the physical element or ***actus reus.***
2. A criminal intent, called the mental element or ***mens rea***.
3. Union of the criminal act and the criminal intent, called **concurrence.**

Crimes of **criminal conduct**—the vast majority of all crimes—consist of these three elements alone. A few crimes, such as criminal homicide, require that the prosecution prove two additional elements beyond a reasonable doubt: **causation** and **harmful result;** namely, that criminal conduct causes a harmful result such as death in the crime of murder. Murder, for example, not only consists of the act of, say, shooting another person joined with the intent to kill, but also requires that the shooting cause the death of the victim.

Actus Reus

The principle of *actus reus* stresses the essential requirement of action. *Actus reus* excludes from criminal liability:

- Mere wishes, hopes, and intentions to act.
- Conditions or statuses.

In other words, criminal law does not punish people for who they are, what they think, wish, or merely *intend* to do. It punishes completed action and harm.

There are some exceptions to the requirement of completed action. Taking substantial steps toward completing a crime is called **attempt.** For example, a man chased his wife with a gun that he forgot to load. He caught up with her, pointed the gun at her head, and pulled the trigger several times. "It won't shoot! It won't shoot!" he shouted. He was convicted of attempted murder. He intended to kill his wife; he took substantial steps toward turning his intention into action. Except for the stroke of luck that the gun was not loaded he would have caused her death. The law of attempt is based on the idea that persons determined to commit crimes and whose actions go a substantial way toward completing the crimes should not escape criminal liability by a stroke of luck.

Other forms of uncompleted crimes also satisfy the *actus reus* requirement. Agreeing to rob a bank is the crime of **conspiracy** to commit robbery. Even asking another to commit a crime, such as a man who offered a friend $3,000 to kill his wife, is the crime of **solicitation** to commit murder. Furthermore, the possession of a wide range of items and substances, including weapons and drugs, and even the paraphernalia of drug use such as needles to shoot up heroin is a crime in all states and is a federal crime. Despite a completed crime, all of the offenses described above require at least some action—*pulling* the trigger, *agreeing* to commit murder, *asking* another to commit a crime, and *acquiring* possession. The law takes the position that we need not await actual harm in order to impose criminal liability. Action sufficient to demonstrate dangerousness—the determination to complete the crime—satisfies the *actus reus* requirement.[7]

Mens Rea

Mens rea, translated as "guilty mind," refers to four states of mind:

1. General intent.
2. Specific intent.
3. Transferred intent.
4. Constructive intent.

General intent can mean several things. Sometimes it means to intend to do something at an undetermined time. It can also mean an intent directed at an unspecified object, such as firing a gun into a crowd. It also can mean an intent to commit the *actus reus;* for example, taking and carrying away another's property, the *actus reus* of larceny. **Specific**

intent is the intent to do something in addition to the *actus reus.* For example, criminal homicide requires not only the general intent to shoot a gun but also the specific intent to cause the death of another person. **Transferred intent** is the intent to harm one victim but instead harming another. For example, if Mark aims and fires your gun at Michelle as she walks down the street with Doug, and the bullet hits and kills Doug instead of Michelle, the law transfers Mark's intent to kill Michelle to the intent to kill Doug. Sometimes, transferred intent is called "bad aim." However, transferred intent also refers to the intent to commit any similar crime, such as intending to burn down one house but instead burning another.

Constructive intent applies to those whose actions cause harms greater than they expect or intend; it extends criminal liability to cases in which actors did not intend harm, but their actions caused a result the criminal law prohibits. Constructive intent runs roughly parallel to what some prefer to call reckless and negligent wrongdoing. **Criminal recklessness** means to create high risks of harm purposely or consciously. Reckless wrongdoers may not intend to hurt anyone—in fact, they probably hope their actions hurt no one—but they risk causing harm anyway. If you intentionally leave your loaded gun lying within a two-year-old niece's reach, and, much to your horror, she picks it up, pulls the trigger, and kills herself while you are out of the room, you are reckless.

Negligent wrongdoers *un*consciously create risks. **Criminal negligence** means to unconsciously create a high risk of harm. Criminal negligence differs from ordinary negligence (the wrongful intent for liability in personal injury and product liability lawsuits between private parties). Criminal negligence is negligence that amounts to "a *gross* deviation from the standard of care that a reasonable person would observe." Negligence in personal injury and products liability cases means the lack of *ordinary* care that a reasonable person would exercise. Of course, the meanings of deviation, reasonable person, high risk, ordinary risk, and gross deviation all leave wide room for interpretation.[8]

Strict liability means liability without fault; that is, liability without *mens rea.* The prosecution has to prove only that defendants either engaged in prohibited conduct or caused a prohibited result. In strict liability, whether the defendants caused harm intentionally, recklessly, or negligently is irrelevant. The criminal law did not recognize strict liability until the transformations brought about by the Industrial Revolution. Public transportation, factories, and large-scale consumer purchasing created high risks to health and safety and made the requirement of personal and individual culpability meaningless. Large size and diffused managerial responsibility characterized these new enterprises. They created risks to victims whom they did not personally know, and whom they did not intend to injure. Under existing criminal law, the principle of *mens rea* excluded acts of exposing the public to serious injuries, incurable diseases, or deaths from criminal liability.

Legislatures responded by adopting a wide range of strict liability offenses, with two main justifications: necessity and lenient punishment. Strict liability offenses create high risks of serious harm to large numbers of people: those who need the services and employment associated with the high-risk behavior and who provide service and employment providers with large profits. Nevertheless, the penalties for strict liability result only in fines, not jail or prison time.

Concurrence

The **principle of concurrence** states that the *actus reus* has to join with the *mens rea.* In other words, intention to commit a crime has to set the criminal action in motion. For example, Lucy buys a VCR from Damien without knowing it is stolen. The next time he sees her, Damien tells Lucy that he stole the VCR from Lucy's enemy Catherine. Lucy is so delighted that Catherine suffered the loss that she decides to keep the VCR. She has not committed the crime of receiving stolen property because the intent to steal did not generate her action in buying the VCR in the first place. However, it is possible to have actions follow a bad state of mind and still satisfy the requirement of concurrence. For example, Corey hates Liza. He plans to kill her, but he changes his mind because he does not want to go to prison. As luck would have it, two months after he abandons his plan to kill Liza, Cordell accidentally runs Liza down with his car and kills her. When Corey hears about the fatality he is delighted. Corey is not guilty of murder because his intent to kill Liza did not set in motion Cordell's act of running Liza down.[9]

Causing a Harmful Result

In crimes that require a specific result, the conduct has to *cause* the result. The element of **causation** consists of two kinds of cause: cause in fact and legal cause. Cause in fact means that "but for" the actions of the defendant, the result would not have taken place. For example, Kibbe and his companion robbed Stafford and left him on a country road. Blake, a college student on his way to a class, accidentally ran Stafford down and killed him. "But for" Kibbe and his companion's leaving Stafford on the road, Blake would not have run Stafford down and killed him. Kibbe and his companion, therefore, were the cause in fact of Stafford's death.

Cause in fact is necessary but not sufficient to prove causation. There also must be legal cause. Legal cause asks the question: Is it fair to blame defendants for the results of actions that they set in motion? The answer depends on the relation of the result to the initiating actions: Is the result simply remote from the initial action, or does the result in fact come about through the intervention of someone or something else? For example, in a jealous rage Cameron stabs Rob. Rob refuses to go to the doctor because he does not want to spend the money. Finally, after nearly a day, he is so weak from loss of blood that he goes to an emergency room where he receives a transfusion. He develops an infection from an old needle that was accidentally used in the transfusion and dies three weeks later. The intervening actions—Rob's refusal to bind the wound and go to the doctor, and the actions of the hospital staff in using the dirty needle—were the *legal* cause of his death. Why? Because it is not fair to blame Cameron for Rob's death, even though in fact Rob would not have died if Cameron had not stabbed him.

General Principles and Specific Crimes

The general principles of *actus reus, mens rea,* concurrence, causation, and resulting harm do not define the elements of specific crimes. To define specific crimes, the general principles must be applied to particular conduct and harms. For example, the specific *actus reus* in burglary is breaking and entering, and the specific *mens rea* in first-degree murder is the intent to kill on purpose and with premeditation. Such elements of the specific crime are what the prosecution has to prove beyond a reasonable doubt in order to convict defendants.[10]

The elements of most serious crimes—criminal homicide, rape, aggravated assault, robbery, arson, burglary, and theft—contain highly refined definitions of all the material elements. In the lesser offenses, particularly crimes against public order and morals, definitions are broader and more relaxed with respect to the general principles. For example, statutes defining disorderly conduct, loitering, and begging rarely refer to the acts and the mental states that have to concur in order to qualify as criminal conduct.

Knowledge and Understanding CHECK

1. Define the three elements that the prosecution must prove to obtain a conviction in all crimes.
2. What two additional elements must the prosecution prove to obtain a conviction in criminal homicide and a few other crimes?
3. Define *actus reus* and identify two things that it excludes from criminal liability.
4. Define the three kinds of uncompleted crimes that qualify as crimes.
5. Explain how uncompleted crimes satisfy the *actus reus.*
6. Define *mens rea.*
7. Describe the four kinds of *mens rea.*
8. Explain criminal recklessness and criminal negligence.
9. In what essential respect does criminal recklessness differ from criminal negligence?
10. Define strict liability and explain how strict liability offenses came into the criminal law.
11. Explain the principle of concurrence.
12. Explain the difference between factual and legal causation.

Defenses to Crime

Defenses to crime allow defendants either to avoid criminal liability totally, as in **acquittal,** or to receive an alternative to conviction, such as commitment to a mental hospital in the defense of insanity, or a mitigated sentence. There are three main types of defenses:

1. **Alibi.** Defendants could not have committed the crime because they were in a different place when the crime was committed.
2. **Lack of a material element.** One of the elements is missing, such as in rape where the victim consented to the *actus reus* of sexual penetration.
3. Justification and excuse. All of the elements and the defendant are present at the time of the crime but defendants are either justified in committing the crime (for example, through self-defense) or excused from committing the crime (for example, by reason of insanity).

This section concentrates on the defenses of justification and excuse.

In **defenses of justification** defendants admit that they committed the crime but prove that under the circumstances what they did was right, or justified. Hence, in self-defense, a defendant argues: "I killed Cruz because he was about to kill me, so under the circumstances I was justified in killing him." Defenses of justification focus on the the rightness of the defendant's *actions.* In **defenses of excuse,** defendants admit that what they did was wrong but argue that under the circumstances they were not responsible. In the insanity defense, for example, defendants argue that although they were wrong to commit their crimes, they did so because of mental diseases or defects, and are therefore not legally responsible for their actions. The defenses of excuse focuses on *actors,* that is, the lack of responsibility of individuals.[11]

Defenses of Justification

The justifications for crimes include a cluster of defenses related to actions taken to protect people, their homes, and their property, and to carry out public duties. This chapter focuses on self-defense and the defense of homes and property. We save the defense of execution of public duties, including examples of criminal justice officers acting in the course of their professional responsibilities, for later chapters.

We usually think of killing in self-defense; however, the defense applies to any justified force. Self-defense includes self-protection. Self-protection does *not* include either preemptive strikes or retaliatory attacks.

Self-Defense

The right of self-defense justifies the use of force against attackers under the following circumstances:

1. The defendant did not provoke the attack.
2. The defendant reasonably believed that the use of force was necessary.
3. The attack was imminent.
4. The defendant used only the amount of force reasonably required to repel the attack.
5. The defendant intended only to defend against an imminent attack, not to prevent a future attack or to retaliate for a past attack.

Self-defense is not limited to defending yourself. It has always included the right to repel imminent attacks against members of your immediate family. Several states still require a special relationship between the defender and the person being defended against the attacker. Other states have abandoned this requirement, permitting the defense of any other person.

Two recent kinds of cases have raised questions about the application of the defense of self-defense. The first concerns battered women. Some women respond to long-term battering by eventually killing their batterers. When charged with criminal homicide, some of them argue that they killed in self-defense. In a New Mexico case, George Gallegos was a heavy drinker. Over the years, whenever he drank, he beat his wife. During one of the beatings when she was pregnant, he had thrown her against a wall, causing the premature birth of one of her children. Gallegos had frequently put a gun to his wife's head, threatening to kill her; had put a knife on her breasts, threatening to cut them off if they grew larger; and on the day of the killing had sodomized her against her will.

On that day, Mrs. Gallegos told her husband that she was tired of being hurt. When she threatened to leave, he drew his gun and told her that he would kill her if she tried. That evening, when he called her into the bedroom, Mrs. Gallegos testified that she was afraid, that she did not know whether her husband intended to kill, rape, or beat her. She picked up his loaded shotgun in the living room. While he was lying on the bed, she cocked the rifle and shot him, then stabbed him numerous times. The trial court refused Mrs. Gallegos's request to introduce evidence of self-defense to the jury, who convicted her of voluntary manslaughter. The appeals court reversed the decision, ordering a new trial so that she could introduce evidence of self-defense.[12]

A second problem of self-defense concerns people who become frightened by the brutal attacks they read about (particularly in large cities). As a result of this fear, some of them take measures to defend themselves. The box that follows includes an excerpt from the court case, *People v. Goetz*. Bernhard Goetz generated national attention when he shot four youths in a New York City subway in 1984. The case demonstrates some of the complexities of applying the law of self-defense, and of balancing the formal law of homicide against the jury's discretion to act according to informal influences outside the letter of the law.

Use *Your* Discretion

Can you shoot muggers when they approach? *People v. Goetz*, 68 N.Y.2d 96, 506 N.Y.S.2d 18, 497 N.E.2d 41 (1986)

A Grand Jury indicted Goetz for attempted murder, assault, and other charges arising out of his having shot and wounded four youths on a New York City subway train after one or two of the youths approached him and asked for $5. The lower courts dismissed the attempted murder, assault, and weapons possession charges. The New York Court of Appeals reversed the lower courts and reinstated all the counts of the indictment.

Facts

On Saturday afternoon, December 22, 1984, Troy Canty, Darryl Cabey, James Ramseur, and Barry Allen boarded an IRT express subway train in The Bronx and headed south toward lower Manhattan. The four youths rode together in the rear portion of the seventh car of the train. Two of the four, Ramseur and Cabey, had screwdrivers inside their coats, which they said were to be used to break into the coin boxes of video machines. Defendant Bernhard Goetz boarded this subway train at 14th Street in Manhattan and sat down on a bench towards the rear section of the same car occupied by the four youths. Goetz was carrying an unlicensed .38-caliber pistol loaded with five rounds of ammunition in a waistband holster. The train left the 14th Street station and headed toward Chambers Street.

It appears from the evidence before the Grand Jury that Canty approached Goetz, possibly with Allen beside him, and stated "Give me five dollars." Neither Canty nor any of the other youths displayed a weapon. Goetz responded by standing up, pulling out his handgun and firing four shots in rapid succession. The first shot hit Canty in the chest; the second struck Allen in the back; the third went through Ramseur's arm and into his left side; the fourth was fired at Cabey, who apparently was then standing in the corner of the car, but missed, deflecting instead off a wall of the conductor's cab. After Goetz briefly surveyed the scene around him, he fired another shot at Cabey, who then was sitting on the end bench of the car. The bullet entered the rear of Cabey's side and severed his spinal cord.

All but two of the passengers fled the car when, or immediately after, the shots were fired. The conductor, who had been in the next car, heard the shots and instructed the motorman to radio for emergency

Bernhard Goetz, charged with attempting to kill four youths on the New York subway, takes the subway to court.

assistance. The conductor then went into the car where the shooting occurred and saw Goetz sitting on a bench, the injured youths lying on the floor or slumped against a seat, and two women who had apparently taken cover also lying on the floor. Goetz told the conductor that the four youths had tried to rob him. While the conductor was aiding the youths, Goetz headed toward the front of the car. The train had stopped just before the Chambers Street station and Goetz went between two of the cars, jumped onto the tracks, and fled. Police and ambulance crews arrived at the scene shortly thereafter. Ramseur and Canty, initially listed in critical condition, have fully recovered. Cabey remains paralyzed and has suffered some degree of brain damage.

On December 31, 1984, Goetz surrendered to police in Concord, New Hampshire.... Later that day, after receiving Miranda warnings, he made two lengthy statements, both of which were tape recorded with his permission. In his statements, which are substantially similar, Goetz admitted that he had been illegally carrying a handgun in New York City for three years. He stated that he had first purchased a gun in 1981 after he had been injured in a mugging. Goetz also revealed that twice between 1981 and 1984 he had successfully warded off assailants simply by displaying the pistol.

According to Goetz's statement, the first contact he had with the four youths came when Canty, sitting or lying on the bench across from him, asked "How are you?" to which he replied "Fine." Shortly thereafter, Canty, followed by one of the other youths, walked over to the defendant and stood to his left, while the other two youths remained to his right, in the corner of the subway car. Canty then said "Give me five dollars." Goetz stated that he knew from the smile on Canty's face that they wanted to "play with me." Although he was certain that none of the youths had a gun, he had a fear, based on prior experiences, of being "maimed."

Goetz then established "a pattern of fire," deciding specifically to fire from left to right. His stated intention at that point was to "murder [the four youths], to hurt them, to make them suffer as much as possible." When Canty again requested money, Goetz stood up, drew his weapon, and began firing, aiming for the center of the body of each of the four. Goetz recalled that the first two he shot "tried to run through the crowd [but] they had nowhere to run." Goetz then turned to his right to "go after the other two." One of these two "tried to run through the wall of the train, but . . . he had nowhere to go." The other youth (Cabey) "tried pretending that he wasn't with [the others]" by standing still, holding on to one of the subway hand straps, and not looking at Goetz. Goetz nonetheless fired his fourth shot at him. He then ran back to the first two youths to make sure they had been "taken care of." Seeing that they had both been shot, he spun back to check on the other two. Goetz noticed that the youth who had been standing still was now sitting on a bench and seemed unhurt. As Goetz told the police, "I said '[Y]ou seem to be all right, here's another,'" and he fired the shot which severed Cabey's spinal cord. Goetz added that "if I was a little more under self-control . . . I would have put the barrel against his forehead and fired." He also admitted that "if I had had more [bullets], I would have shot them again, and again, and again."

After waiving extradition, Goetz was brought back to New York and arraigned on a felony complaint charging him with attempted murder and criminal possession of a weapon. The matter was presented to a Grand Jury in January 1985, with the prosecutor seeking an indictment for attempted murder, assault, reckless endangerment, and criminal possession of a weapon. . . . [T]he Grand Jury indicted defendant on one count of criminal possession of a weapon in the third degree for possessing the gun used in the subway shootings, and two counts of criminal possession of a weapon in the fourth degree. . . . It dismissed, however, the attempted murder and other charges stemming from the shootings themselves.

Several weeks after the Grand Jury's action, the People, asserting that they had newly available evidence, moved for an order authorizing them to resubmit the dismissed charges to a second Grand Jury. . . . [T]he second Grand Jury filed a 10-count indictment, containing four charges of attempted murder, four charges of assault in the first degree, one charge of reckless endangerment in the first degree, and one charge of criminal possession of a weapon in the second degree. . . . On October 14, 1985, Goetz moved to dismiss the charges contained in the second indictment alleging, among other things, that the evidence before the second Grand Jury was not legally sufficient to establish the offenses charged and that the prosecutor's instructions to that Grand Jury on the defense of justification were erroneous and prejudicial to the defendant so as to render its proceedings defective.

On November 25, 1985, while the motion to dismiss was pending before Criminal Term, a column appeared in the *New York Daily News* containing an interview that the columnist had conducted with Darryl Cabey the previous day in Cabey's hospital room. Cabey told the columnist in this interview that the other three youths had all approached Goetz with the intention of robbing him. . . . The court, after inspection of the Grand Jury minutes . . . held . . . that the prosecutor, in a supplemental charge elaborating upon the justification defense, had erroneously introduced an objective element into this defense by instructing the grand jurors to consider whether Goetz's conduct was that of a "reasonable man in [Goetz's] situation." The court . . . concluded that the statutory test for whether the use of deadly force is justified to protect a person should be wholly subjective, focusing entirely on the defendant's state of mind when he used such force. It concluded that dismissal was required for this error because the justification issue was at the heart of the case. . . . On appeal by the People, a divided Appellate Division affirmed Criminal Term's dismissal of the charges. . . .

Justice Asch, in a dissenting opinion in which Justice Wallach concurred, disagreed with both bases for dismissal relied upon by Criminal Term. On the justification question, he opined that the statute requires consideration of both the defendant's subjective beliefs and whether a reasonable person in defendant's situation would have had such beliefs. . . . Justice Wallach stressed that the plurality's adoption of a purely subjective test effectively eliminated any reasonableness requirement contained in the statute. Justice Asch granted the People leave to appeal to this court.

We agree with the dissenters.

Opinion

Penal Law article 35 recognizes the defense of justification, which "permits the use of force under certain circumstances." Penal Law § 35.15 (1) sets forth the general principles governing all such uses of force: "[a] person may . . . use physical force upon another person when and to the extent he reasonably believes such to be necessary to defend himself or a third person from what he reasonably believes to be the use or imminent use of unlawful physical force by such other person." Section 35.15 (2) provides: "A person may not use deadly force upon another person under circumstances specified in subdivision one unless (a) He reasonably believes that such other person is using or about to use deadly physical force . . . or (b) He reasonably believes that such other person is committing or attempting to commit a kidnapping, forcible rape, forcible sodomy or robbery."

Thus, consistent with most justification provisions, Penal Law §35.15 permits the use of deadly physical force only where requirements as to triggering conditions and the necessity of a particular response are met. As to the triggering of conditions, the statute requires that the actor "reasonably believes" that another person either is using or about to use deadly physical force or is committing or attempting to commit one of certain enumerated felonies, including robbery. As to the need for the use of deadly physical force as a response, the statute requires that the actor "reasonably believes" that such force is necessary to avert the perceived threat.

Because the evidence before the second Grand Jury included statements by Goetz that he acted to protect himself from being maimed or to avert robbery, the prosecutor correctly chose to charge the justification defense. . . . The prosecutor properly instructed the grand jurors to consider whether the use of deadly physical force was justified to prevent either serious physical injury or a robbery, and, in doing so, to separately analyze the defense with respect to each of the charges. . . .

When the prosecutor had completed his charge, one of the grand jurors asked for clarification of the term "reasonably believes." The prosecutor responded by instructing the grand jurors that they were to consider the circumstances of the incident and determine "whether the defendant's conduct was that of a reasonable man in the defendant's situation." It is this response by the prosecutor—and specifically his use of "a reasonable man"—which is the basis for the dismissal of the charges by the lower courts. As expressed repeatedly in the Appellate Division's plurality opinion, because section 35.15 uses the term "he reasonably believes," the appropriate test, according to that court, is whether a defendant's beliefs and reactions were "reasonable to him." Under that reading of the statute, a jury which believed a defendant's testimony that he felt that his own actions were warranted and were reasonable would have to acquit him, regardless of what anyone else in defendant's situation might have concluded. Such an interpretation defies the ordinary meaning and significance of the term "reasonably" in a statute, and misconstrues the clear intent of the Legislature, in enacting section 35.15, to retain an objective element as part of any provision authorizing the use of deadly physical force. . . .

We cannot lightly impute to the Legislature an intent to fundamentally alter the principles of justification to allow the perpetrator of a serious crime to go free simply because that person believed his actions were reasonable and necessary to prevent some perceived harm. To completely exonerate such an individual, no matter how aberrational or bizarre his thought patterns, would allow citizens to set their own standards for the permissible use of force. It would also allow a legally competent defendant suffering from delusions to kill or perform acts of violence with impunity, contrary to fundamental principles of justice and criminal law. We can only conclude that the Legislature retained a reasonableness requirement to avoid giving a license for such actions. The plurality's interpretation, as the dissenters . . . recognized, excises the impact of the word "reasonably."

Accordingly, the order of the Appellate Division should be reversed, and the dismissed counts of the indictment reinstated.

Note

Following the reversal, New York tried Goetz for attempted murder and assault. The jury acquitted him of both charges. The jury said Goetz "was justified in shooting the four men with a silver-plated .38-caliber revolver he purchased in Florida." They did convict him of illegal possession of a firearm, for which the court sentenced Goetz to one year in jail. Following the sentencing, Goetz told the court that "this case is really more about the deterioration of society than it is about me. . . . Well, I don't believe that's the case. . . . I believe society needs to be protected from criminals."[13]

Criminal law professor George Fletcher followed the trial closely. After the jury acquitted Goetz, Professor Fletcher noted that

> the facts of the Goetz case were relatively clear, but the primary fight was over the moral interpretation of the facts. . . . I am not in the slightest bit convinced that the four young men were about to mug Goetz. If he had said, "Listen, buddy, I wish I had $5, but I don't," and walked to the other side of the car, the chances are 60-40 nothing would have happened. Street-wise kids like that are more attuned to the costs of their behavior than Goetz was.[14]

CRITICAL THINKING

1. Do you agree with Professor Fletcher? Explain.
2. Or, do you agree with what Bernhard Goetz did? Why?
3. Did the jury apply the law of self-defense correctly, according to the standards set out in the text?
4. What influences outside the law swayed the jury to a verdict of acquittal?
5. Should the fear of city dwellers take precedence over narrow legal definitions? Explain.

Knowledge and Understanding CHECK

1. Identify three types of defense.
2. Explain the difference between defenses of justification and of excuse.
3. To what types of protective actions do the justifications usually refer?
4. List the three circumstances that justify the use of force in self-defense.
5. Besides protecting yourself, to what else does self-defense apply?
6. Describe two kinds of protective action that cause problems in self-defense.
7. Explain why these two protective actions create problems.

Defense of Home and Property

Killing nighttime intruders into homes was justifiable homicide in the earliest days of the **common law.** (The common law translated into legal rules, the traditions, customs, and values of the English community.) Modern law still follows the common-law rule by granting occupants the right to use force to defend their homes. For example, Colorado's "make-my-day law" grants immunity from all legal action—including criminal prosecution—to occupants of homes who use force, including deadly force, against "one who has made an unlawful entry into the dwelling."[15]

The make-my-day law generated controversy when David Guenther—who later killed his own wife—shot at his neighbors and killed one of them. David Guenther was unpopular in the neighborhood. He constantly got into altercations with neighbors, abused his wife in their sight and hearing, and generally annoyed them. One evening during a party, some neighbors decided to harass David Guenther. They banged on his car, shouted obscenities, and challenged Guenther to come out of his house. They left when Pam Guenther, David's wife, threatened to call the police. Later, when the party goers heard a loud noise at the front door, one of them ran to the door, saw no one, proceeded to the Guenthers, and knocked.

The evidence conflicted at this point, but shortly after the neighbor knocked on the door, David Guenther appeared, and from the doorway fired four shots from a Smith and Wesson .357 Magnum six-inch revolver. One shot wounded the person who had knocked, a second wounded another who was walking across the Guenthers' front yard to help, and a third killed Josslyn Volosin, who was trying to break up the fight. Colorado charged Guenther with second-degree murder and first-degree assault. The trial court dismissed the charges, ruling that the make-my-day law immunized Guenther from prosecution. The Colorado Supreme Court overruled the trial court, holding that the make-my-day law protects only against those who actually *enter* houses.[16]

Most states also permit the use of force to protect property other than homes. Texas, for example, authorizes the use of deadly force to "protect land or tangible property, and movable property . . . when and to the degree [they] reasonably believe the deadly force is immediately necessary . . ." to prevent the commission of serious felonies, such as robbery and arson, if they "reasonably believe" they cannot protect their property "by any other means," or if "the failure to use deadly force" would expose them or others to a "substantial risk of death or serious bodily injury."[17]

Knowledge and Understanding CHECK

1. How old is the right of occupants to kill intruders in their homes?
2. Describe Colorado's "make-my-day law."
3. How did the Colorado supreme court limit the defense of homes in the case involving David Guenther?

Defenses of Excuse

The criminal law recognizes a substantial list of defenses that focus on individual characteristics or conditions that excuse criminal liability. The defenses of excuse include:

1. Mistake of law and fact.
2. Age.
3. Duress.
4. Entrapment.
5. Intoxication.
6. Insanity.
7. Diminished capacity.
8. Mental and biological syndromes.

Mistake of Law and Fact

Mistake of law means that a defendant did not know a law or misunderstood it. **Mistake of fact** means that a defendant either did not know a fact at all or misinterpreted it. Mistake of law is not a defense to criminal liability in most instances. Everyone has heard the saying, "Ignorance of the law is no excuse." Suppose you find a $100 bill lying in the street. You take the money and spend it, believing in the old adage, "Finders keepers, losers weepers." Later, someone discovers your find and reports it to the police, who arrest you. You are charged and convicted of theft. You are guilty because the law does not authorize finders to keep lost property. Your ignorance of the law, despite your honest belief that the money you found belonged to you, is not a defense.

Sometimes mistake of law does excuse criminal liability, such as ignorance of the law following reasonable efforts to learn what the law is. For example, Harold Ostrovsky was convicted of fishing without a valid permit. He challenged the constitutionality of the statute requiring permits to fish. The trial judge ruled the statute unconstitutional. Ostrovsky then proceeded to fish again. The Alaska Supreme Court later reversed the trial judge's decision, ruling instead that the statute was constitutional. Alaska prosecuted Ostrovsky for violations of the statute occurring after the trial judge's ruling, but prior to the supreme court's reversal. Ostrovsky argued that the defense of mistake excused him because he had honestly and reasonably relied on the trial judge's ruling that the statute was unconstitutional. The court accepted his defense of mistake of law.

Mistake of fact, on the other hand, has always been a defense to criminal liability. Why? Because no *mens rea* sets the criminal acts in motion. For example, suppose you go to the coat room where you left your coat, pick up one identical to yours, put it on, and go home. In fact, the coat belongs to another person. You have satisfied all the requirements for the *actus reus* of larceny—taking and carrying away someone else's property. However, your state of mind does not satisfy the larceny *mens rea*—intending to deprive the owner permanently of possession. Your mistake of fact as to the ownership of the coat excuses your action.

Age

Immaturity has excused criminal liability since the earliest days of the English common law. The common law recognized three categories of maturity:

1. Individuals too young under all circumstances to be criminally responsible.
2. Individuals mature to the extent that they may or may not be criminally responsible.
3. Individuals mature enough to be criminally responsible in nearly all circumstances.

Modern law still recognizes these categories, but states vary as to the exact age that individuals reach these levels of maturity. Most states integrate the categories so that they coincide with the jurisdiction of the juvenile court. The modern age categories generally give juvenile courts exclusive jurisdiction up to age 15 or 16. Between 16 and 18, juveniles can be certified; that is, authority to hear their cases can be transferred to adult criminal courts. Usually, this occurs when juveniles are accused of murder, rape, aggravated assault, robbery, and drug-related offenses.

Old age has occasionally provided an excuse to criminal liability. In one case, a husband asked his wife of 50 years to get him some bagels. She forgot. According to the prosecutor, "The guy goes berserk and he axes his wife; he kills the poor woman with a Boy Scout-type ax!" The prosecutor did not charge the man, saying: "What do we do now? Set high bail? Prosecute? Get a conviction and send the fellow to prison? You tell me! We did nothing. The media dropped it quickly and, I hope, that's it." Incidentally, this case provides another excellent example of discretion adapting law to social reality. The formal law provided no excuse of advanced age. But the prosecutor exercised his independent judgment as to what justice required in this individual case, and how best to allocate scarce resources and balance the law and broad community values. (See Chapter 9 for the role of the prosecutor.)[18]

Duress

Sometimes, if another person forces you to commit a crime, you have the defense of **duress.** States vary as to what circumstances qualify you to claim duress. The circumstances relate to the following:

1. The crimes to which the defense applies.
2. The definition of duress.
3. The connection between the coercion and the completion of the crime.
4. The belief of the defendant regarding the coercion.

In some states, duress is a defense to all crimes except murder; in others, it excuses only minor crimes. States also differ as to the definition of duress. Some recognize only threats to kill if the defendant refuses to commit the crime; others accept threats to do serious bodily harm. Threats to damage reputation or to destroy property do not qualify. Most states require that defendants face immediate harm if they refuse to commit the crime. The degrees of immediacy, however, vary from state to state. Some require the threat of "instant death"; others accept imminent threats.

Entrapment

Entrapment occurs when law enforcement officers induce people to commit a crime for the purpose of prosecuting them. From the reign of Henry VIII to Hitler and Stalin, most police states have relied on government agents to repress political opponents. These police states paid no attention to the wise admonition of the great English prime minister William Gladstone, who said that government should make it *easy* to do right and *difficult* to do wrong. Nor did they consider the ancient entreaty in the Lord's Prayer to "lead us not into temptation, but deliver us from evil."[19]

The entrapment defense is a response to the difficulty law enforcement officers have in investigating crimes that have no complaining witnesses. These crimes include prostitution, gambling, pornography, official wrongdoing, and illicit drug offenses. In many cases, the only way to investigate these crimes is to use deception.

United States criminal law rejected the entrapment defense until the twentieth century because, as one court put it:

> We are asked to protect the defendant, not because he is innocent, but because a zealous public officer exceeded his powers and held out a bait. The courts do not look to see who held out the bait, but to see who took it.[20]

Singer George Michael was arrested on April 7, 1998, for engaging in "lewd conduct" in a park restroom in Beverly Hills. Michael argued entrapment–the officer involved was an undercover cop–but was convicted and served 80 hours of community service.

However, during the twentieth century, attitudes evolved from total indifference to limited sympathy toward entrapped defendants. At the same time, the law of entrapment reflects a growing intolerance of government pressures on law-abiding people to commit crimes. Present entrapment law attempts to catch habitual criminals, but not at the expense of innocent prosecuting innocent people.[21]

Entrapment does not prevent law enforcement officers from encouraging individuals to commit crimes. Encouragement allows law enforcement officers to:

- Act as victims, intending by their actions to encourage suspects to commit crimes.
- Communicate their encouragement to suspects.
- Have some influence on the commission of a crime.

Agencies adopt various techniques to enforce the laws against unsuspecting participants, including making requests to commit crimes, forming personal relationships with suspects, appealing to personal considerations, promising benefits as a result of committing crimes, and supplying and helping to obtain contraband.[22]

Courts use two tests to determine when officers cross the line between encouragement and entrapment: the predisposition test and the inducement test. Most courts follow the **predisposition test,** which focuses on the intent of defendants. According to this test, entrapment occurs only when the government induces defendants who were not predisposed—that is, had no desire—to commit crimes. The crucial question in the predisposition test is: Where did criminal intent originate? If it originated with the defendant, then the government did not entrap the defendant.

Sherman v. United States illustrates the predisposition test. In this case, a government undercover agent, Kalchinian, met Sherman in a drug treatment center, struck up a friendship with him, and eventually asked Sherman to get him some heroin. Sherman, an addict in treatment to control his addiction, at first refused. After several weeks of Kalchinian's pleading, Sherman broke down and obtained the requested heroin. The Supreme Court ruled that Kalchinian entrapped Sherman, because Sherman's reluctance and his being in treatment hardly predisposed him to commit the crime.[23]

A few courts adopt the **inducement test.** According to this test, if the government engages in conduct that would induce an ordinary, law-abiding person to commit the crime, the court should dismiss the case. The inducement test aims at deterring "unsavory police methods." Therefore, defendants' predisposition to commit a crime is not relevant.

There is no constitutional right against entrapment. Consequently, government can choose what they consider to be the best strategy for uncovering crime without stepping over the line into entrapment. However, government conduct may be so outrageous that it violates due process of law. According to retired Supreme Court Justice Lewis Powell, due process of law might "reverse the conviction of a . . . defendant," depending on "the outrageousness of police behavior." The following Use Your Discretion illustrates one tactic government agents use to encourage habitual criminals to commit crimes, and also shows how difficult it might be to draw the line between acceptable encouragement and prohibited entrapment."[24]

Use *Your* Discretion

Was the defendant entrapped?

An undercover FBI agent developed a sexual relationship with a target. After a period of sexual intimacy, she asked the target to sell illegal drugs to some "friends" who, unknown to the target, were FBI agents. The Ninth Circuit Court of Appeals said that it saw "no principled way to identify a fixed point along the continuum from casual physical contact to intense physical bonding beyond which the relationship becomes a violation of due process." The court rejected the claim that the FBI agent's sexual intimacy violated the due process clause.[25]

CRITICAL THINKING

1. Do you agree?
2. Can the formal law answer such questions?
3. Or, does the answer depend more on discretionary decision making to reflect the values lying behind the law and enforcement practices in question?

Intoxication

Johnny James was executed by lethal injection for kidnapping two women, forcing them to perform sex acts on each other, and then shooting them both in the head. One died, the other survived and identified James at trial. The criminal justice system turned a deaf ear to his claim that he had been too drunk to know what he was doing and did not deserve to die for the crime.[26]

According to Professor George Fletcher, the defense of intoxication is "buffeted between two conflicting principles":

1. *Accountability.* Those who get drunk should take the consequences of their actions. Someone who gets drunk is liable for the violent consequences.
2. *Culpability.* Criminal liability and punishment depend on blameworthiness.[27]

The common-law approach focused on the first principle:

> As to artificial, voluntarily contracted madness, by drunkenness or intoxication, which, depriving men of their reason, puts them in a temporary frenzy; our law looks upon this as an aggravation of the offense, rather than as an excuse for any criminal misbehavior.[28]

The Johnny James case illustrates that the common law principle is alive and well in 1997. John Gibeaut, who related the James case in an article entitled, "Sobering Thoughts," notes this contemporary emphasis on the principle of accountability in the subtitle to his article: "Legislatures and courts increasingly are just saying no to intoxication as a defense of mitigating factor." Between November 1996 and May 1997, at least ten states introduced bills that would abolish voluntary intoxication as a defense of excuse. According to a member of the Prosecution Function Committee of the American Bar Association's Criminal Justice Section, "The fight goes back to the ancient struggle over just how much free will one has."[29]

The debate surrounding the intoxication defense is directed only at *voluntary* intoxication. *Involuntary* intoxication remains a defense to criminal liability. Involuntary intoxication refers to the state of defendants who do not know they are taking intoxicants, or know but take them under duress. The defense applies only to *extreme* duress. According to one authority, "a person would need to be bound hand and foot and the liquor literally poured down his throat, or . . . would have to be threatened with immediate serious injury." For example, in one case an 18-year-old youth was traveling with an older man across the desert. The man insisted that the youth drink some whiskey with him. When the youth declined, the man became abusive. The youth, fearing the man would put him out of the car in the middle of the desert without any money, drank the whiskey, became intoxicated, and killed the man. The court rejected a claim of involuntary intoxication because the older man had not compelled the youth "to drink against his will and consent." [30]

The United States Supreme Court dealt with the constitutionality of state statutes that eliminate the defense of voluntary intoxication in *Montana v. Egelhoff.*

Use *Your* Discretion

Was he too drunk to intend to kill?
***Montana v. Egelhoff*, 116 S.Ct. 2013 (1996)**

Facts

In July 1992, while camping out in the Yaak region of northwestern Montana to pick mushrooms, respondent [Egelhoff] made friends with Roberta Pavola and John Christenson, who were doing the same. On Sunday, July 12, the three sold the mushrooms they had collected and spent the rest of the day and evening drinking, in bars and at a private party in Troy, Montana. Some time after 9 P.M., they left the party in Christenson's 1974 Ford Galaxy station wagon. The drinking binge apparently continued, as respondent was seen buying beer at 9:20 P.M. and recalled "sitting on a hill or a bank passing a bottle of Black Velvet back and forth" with Christenson.

At about midnight that night, officers of the Lincoln County, Montana, sheriff's department, responding to reports of a possible drunk driver, discovered Christenson's station wagon stuck in a ditch along U.S. Highway 2. In the front seat were Pavola and Christenson, each dead from a single gunshot to the head. In the rear of the car lay respondent, alive and yelling obscenities. His blood-alcohol content measured .36 percent over one hour later. On the floor of the car, near the brake pedal, lay respondent's .38 caliber handgun, with four loaded rounds and two empty casings; respondent had gunshot residue on his hands.

Respondent was charged with two counts of deliberate homicide, a crime defined by Montana law as "purposely" or "knowingly" causing the death of another human being. Mont.Code Ann. § 455102 (1995). A portion of the jury charge, uncontested here, instructed that "[a] person acts purposely when it is his conscious object to engage in conduct of that nature or to cause such a result," and that "[a] person acts knowingly when he is aware of his conduct or when he is aware under the circumstances his conduct constitutes a crime; or, when he is aware there exists the high probability that his conduct will cause a specific result." Respondent's defense at trial was that an unidentified fourth person must have committed the murders; his own extreme intoxication, he claimed, had rendered him physically incapable of committing the murders, and accounted for his inability to recall the events of the night of July 12. Although respondent was allowed to make this use of the evidence that he was intoxicated, the jury was instructed, pursuant to Mont.Code Ann. § 452203 (1995), that it could not consider respondent's "intoxicated condition . . . in determining the existence of a mental state which is an element of the offense." App. to Pet. for Cert. 29a. The jury found respondent guilty on both counts, and the court sentenced him to 84 years' imprisonment.

The Supreme Court of Montana reversed. It reasoned (1) that respondent "had a due process right to present and have considered by the jury all relevant evidence to rebut the State's evidence on all elements of the offense charged," and (2) that evidence of respondent's voluntary intoxication was "clear[ly] . . . relevant to the issue of whether [respondent] acted knowingly and purposely." Because § 452203 prevented the jury from considering that evidence with regard to that issue, the court concluded that the State had been "relieved of part of its burden to prove beyond a reasonable doubt every fact necessary to constitute the crime charged," and that respondent had therefore been denied due process. We granted certiorari.

Opinion

The cornerstone of the Montana Supreme Court's judgment was the proposition that the Due Process Clause guarantees a defendant the right to present and have considered by the jury "all relevant evidence to rebut the State's evidence on all elements of the offense charged." . . . [T]he proposition that the Due Process Clause guarantees the right to introduce all relevant evidence is simply indefensible. . . . Of course, to say that the right to introduce relevant evidence is not absolute is not to say that the Due Process Clause places no limits upon restriction of that right. But it is to say that the defendant asserting such a limit must sustain the usual heavy burden that a due process claim entails. . . .

Respondent's task . . . is to establish that a defendant's right to have a jury consider evidence of his voluntary intoxication in determining whether he possesses the requisite mental state is a "fundamental principle of justice."

Our primary guide in determining whether the principle in question is fundamental is, of course, historical practice. Here that gives respondent little support. By the laws of England, wrote Hale, the intoxicated defendant "shall have no privilege by this voluntarily contracted madness, but shall have the same judgment as if he were in his right senses." According to Blackstone and Coke, the law's condemnation of those suffering from dementia affectata was harsher still: Blackstone, citing Coke, explained that the law viewed intoxication "as an aggravation of the offence, rather than an excuse for any criminal misbehaviour." This stern rejection of inebriation as a defense became a fixture of early American law as well. The American editors of the 1847 edition of Hale wrote:

> Drunkenness, it was said in an early case, can never be received as a ground to excuse or palliate an offence: this is not merely the opinion of a

> speculative philosopher, the argument of counsel, or the obiter dictum of a single judge, but it is a sound and long established maxim of judicial policy, from which perhaps a single dissenting voice cannot be found. But if no other authority could be adduced, the uniform decisions of our own Courts from the first establishment of the government, would constitute it now a part of the common law of the land.

In an opinion citing the foregoing passages from Blackstone and Hale, Justice Story rejected an objection to the exclusion of evidence of intoxication as follows:

> This is the first time, that I ever remember it to have been contended, that the commission of one crime was an excuse for another. Drunkenness is a gross vice, and in the contemplation of some of our laws is a crime; and I learned in my earlier studies, that so far from its being in law an excuse for murder, it is rather an aggravation of its malignity. *United States v. Cornell,* 25 F. Cas. 650, 657658 (No. 14,868) (CC R.I. 1820).

. . .

Against this extensive evidence of a lengthy common-law tradition decidedly against him, the best argument available to respondent is [that] . . . over the course of the 19th century, courts carved out an exception to the common law's traditional across-the-board condemnation of the drunken offender, allowing a jury to consider a defendant's intoxication when assessing whether he possessed the mental state needed to commit the crime charged, where the crime was one requiring a "specific intent." . . . [However,] we find that fully one-fifth of the States either never adopted the "new common-law" rule at issue here or have recently abandoned it. . . .

It is not surprising that many States have held fast to or resurrected the common-law rule prohibiting consideration of voluntary intoxication in the determination of *mens rea,* because that rule has considerable justification—which alone casts doubt upon the proposition that the opposite rule is a "fundamental principle." A large number of crimes, especially violent crimes, are committed by intoxicated offenders; modern studies put the numbers as high as half of all homicides, for example. See, e.g., Third Special Report to the U.S. Congress on Alcohol and Health from the Secretary of Health, Education, and Welfare 64 (1978); Note, Alcohol Abuse and the Law, 94 Harv. L.Rev. 1660, 16811682 (1981). Disallowing consideration of voluntary intoxication has the effect of increasing the punishment for all unlawful acts committed in that state, and thereby deters drunkenness or irresponsible behavior while drunk. The rule also serves as a specific deterrent, ensuring that those who prove incapable of controlling violent impulses while voluntarily intoxicated go to prison. And finally, the rule comports with and implements society's moral perception that one who has voluntarily impaired his own faculties should be responsible for the consequences.

. . .

There is, in modern times, even more justification for laws such as § 452203 than there used to be. Some recent studies suggest that the connection between drunkenness and crime is as much cultural as pharmacological—that is, that drunks are violent not simply because alcohol makes them that way, but because they are behaving in accord with their learned belief that drunks are violent. See, e.g., Collins, Suggested Explanatory Frameworks to Clarify the Alcohol Use/ Violence Relationship, 15 Contemp. Drug Prob. 107, 115 (1988); Critchlow, The Powers of John Barleycorn, 41 Am. Psychologist 751, 754755 (July 1986). This not only adds additional support to the traditional view that an intoxicated criminal is not deserving of exoneration, but it suggests that juries—who possess the same learned belief as the intoxicated offender—will be too quick to accept the claim that the defendant was biologically incapable of forming the requisite *mens rea.* Treating the matter as one of excluding misleading evidence therefore makes some sense.

. . .

The people of Montana have decided to resurrect the rule of an earlier era, disallowing consideration of voluntary intoxication when a defendant's state of mind is at issue. Nothing in the Due Process Clause prevents them from doing so, and the judgment of the Supreme Court of Montana to the contrary must be reversed.

It is so ordered.

Dissent

Justice O'CONNOR, with whom Justice STEVENS, Justice SOUTER, and Justice BREYER join, dissenting.

. . .

Due process demands that a criminal defendant be afforded a fair opportunity to defend against the State's accusations. Meaningful adversarial testing of the State's case requires that the defendant not be prevented from raising an effective defense, which must include the right to present relevant, probative evidence. To be sure, the right to present evidence is not limitless; for example, it does not permit the defendant to introduce any and all evidence he believes might work in his favor, nor does it generally invalidate the operation of testimonial privileges. Nevertheless, "an essential component of procedural fairness is an opportunity to be heard. That opportunity would be an empty one if the State were permitted to exclude competent, reliable evidence" that is essential to the accused's defense. Section 452203 forestalls the defendant's ability to raise an effective defense by placing a blanket exclusion on the presentation of a type of evidence that directly negates an element of the crime, and by doing so, it lightens the prosecution's burden to prove that mental-state element beyond a reasonable doubt.

. . .

I would afford more weight to principles enunciated in our case law than is accorded in the Court's opinion today. It seems to me that a State may not first determine the elements of the crime it wishes to punish, and then thwart the accused's defense by categorically disallowing the very evidence that would prove him innocent.

. . .

The Due Process Clause protects those "principle[s] of justice so rooted in the traditions and conscience of our people as to be ranked as fundamental." At the time the Fourteenth Amendment was ratified, the common-law rule on consideration of intoxication evidence was in flux. The Court argues that rejection of the historical rule in the 19th century simply does not establish that the "new common law" rule is a principle of procedure so "deeply rooted" as to be ranked "fundamental." But to determine whether a fundamental principle of justice has been violated here, we cannot consider only the historical disallowance of intoxication evidence, but must also consider the "fundamental principle" that a defendant has a right to a fair opportunity to put forward his defense, in adversarial testing where the State must prove the elements of the offense beyond a reasonable doubt. As concepts of *mens rea* and burden of proof developed, these principles came into conflict, as the shift in the common law in the 19th century reflects.

. . .

CRITICAL THINKING

1. Was Egelhoff capable of forming the intent to commit murder? Back up your answer with facts from the case.
2. Summarize the arguments in favor of the power of states to abolish the defense of voluntary intoxication without violating the due process clause.
3. Summarize the arguments of the dissent that abolishing the defense of voluntary intoxication violates due process.
4. Which arguments persuade you?
5. Does your answer depend on the heinousness of the murder that Egelhoff committed?
6. Or does it depend on his capacity to form the intent to commit first-degree murder?
7. Or does it depend on whether he was capable of committing the voluntary act (*actus reus*) of first-degree murder?
8. Can you blame someone who is as intoxicated as Egelhoff was?
9. Which of the conflicting principles enunciated by Professor Fletcher at the outset of this section does the Court adopt?
10. Which does the dissent adopt?

Alcohol is the most widely used intoxicant, but it is not the only one qualifying defendants to claim the intoxication excuse. Most states include disturbing mental and physical capacities by introducing "substances" into the body. *State v. Hall* illustrates this point. Hall's friend gave him a pill containing LSD (lysergic acid diethylamide). Hall did not know this; he knew only that, as his friend assured him, it was only a "little sunshine" to make him feel "groovy." A car picked up the hitchhiking Hall. At that time, the drug caused Hall to hallucinate that the driver was a rabid dog. Under this sad delusion, he shot and killed the driver. The court recognized no legal distinction between the voluntary use of alcohol and the voluntary use of other intoxicants in determining criminal responsibility.[31]

Insanity

The insanity defense attracts a lot of public, philosophical, religious, and scholarly attention. However, it plays only a small part in the day-to-day operations of criminal justice. Most of what we know tells us that defendants rarely plead insanity, and rarely succeed if they do. The few defendants who plead insanity successfully do not automatically go free. In some jurisdictions, the verdict is "not guilty by reason of insanity"; in others, "guilty but insane." Guilty but insane means imprisonment but with the chance of treatment while incarcerated. Not guilty by reason of insanity means not guilty but not free to go. Special proceedings follow the verdict of not guilty by reason of insanity. Why? Because defendants have to be insane at the time that they committed the crime. The special proceedings after the verdict determine whether defendants are still insane, or mentally ill and dangerous. If courts find them to be mentally ill and dangerous—and virtually all courts find them to be—then courts order them confined to maximum security hospitals that are, in fact, prisons. They remain in these hospitals until they regain their sanity, which usually takes a long time and may not happen at all. John Hinckley, the attempted assassin of President Reagan in the early 1980s, is typical. He is still detained in a maximum security hospital (although as of January 1999, Hinckley is allowed weekend furloughs).

Insanity is a legal, not a medical, term. Hence, mental illness and insanity are not synonymous. The insanity defense requires that some mental disease or defect impairs

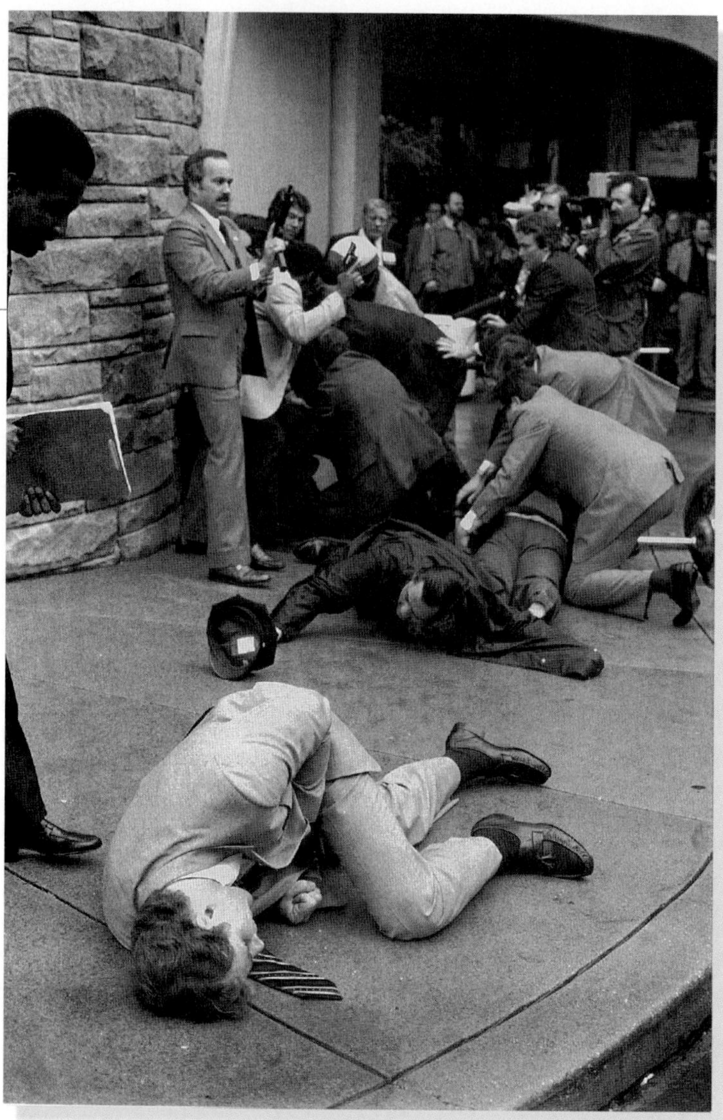

Secret Service agent Timothy J. McCarthy (foreground), Washington policeman Thomas K. Delanty (center), and presidential Press Secretary James Brady (background), lay wounded on a street outside a Washington, D.C. hotel after John Hinckley, Jr. pushed a pistol through a cluster of bystanders and fired six shots at President Ronald Reagan, one of which wounded the president. Hinckley later successfully pleaded insanity and is now confined to a maximum security hospital in Washington, D.C.

reason and/or will. So, mental illness or deficiency is a necessary but not sufficient component of insanity. The test for insanity depends on the jurisdiction where the defense of insanity is pleaded. Three tests are used to determine insanity:

1. The right-wrong test or *M'Naughten* rule.
2. The right-wrong test supplemented by the irresistible impulse test.
3. The substantial capacity or American Law Institute test.

The **right-wrong test** focuses on mental diseases and defects that damage the capacity to reason. The test, frequently called the *M'Naughten* rule, had its origins deep in history, but its present form derives from a famous English case during the reign of Queen Victoria. In 1843, Daniel M'Naughten had the paranoid delusion that the prime minister, Sir Robert Peel, had masterminded a conspiracy to kill him. M'Naughten shot at Peel in delusional self-defense, but mistakenly killed Peel's personal secretary. The jury acquitted M'Naughten. On appeal, the House of Lords—England's highest court of appeal—formulated the right-wrong test. The test consists of five elements: Defendants

1. at the time of the crime
2. suffered from a mental disease or defect
3. that so damaged their capacity to reason
4. that either they did not know what they were doing
5. or, if they knew what they were doing, did not know that what they did was wrong.[32]

Several jurisdictions have supplemented the right-wrong test with the **irresistible impulse test.** The irresistible impulse test focuses on mental diseases and defects that affect defendants' willpower, or the ability to control their actions, at the time of the crime. The irresistible impulse test requires that the defendant

1. at the time of the crime
2. suffered from a mental disease or defect

3. that caused the loss of power to choose between right and wrong.

In other words, defendants know right from wrong, but their mental disease or defect so affects their willpower that it has created the irresistible impulse to commit the crime.

The right-wrong test, supplemented in some states by irresistible impulse, remained the law in most states until the 1960s. At that time, the **substantial capacity test,** often called the ALI (American Law Institute) test, came into prominence. The substantial capacity test focuses on both reason and will. Formulated by the American Law Institute, the substantial capacity test requires that defendants

1. at the time of the crime
2. as a result of mental disease or defect
3. lacked substantial capacity
4. to appreciate the wrongfulness (criminality) of their conduct
5. or to conform their conduct to the requirements of the law.

Significantly, the test focuses on *substantial* capacity. In other words, the mental disease or defect need not totally destroy reason or will. It is enough that it substantially impairs reason or will.

John Hinckley's assassination attempt on former President Reagan, graphically captured and replayed hundreds of times on television, horrified the nation. In his trial, Hinckley pleaded insanity, claiming he shot at the president to gain actress Jodie Foster's attention. The jury acquitted Hinckley on a verdict of not guilty by reason of insanity. Despite Hinckley's confinement to a maximum security hospital, where he remains, a public outcry resulted from the belief that he had somehow "gotten away with" trying to kill a popular president. Criminal law professor Charles Nesson, for example, wrote:

> To many Mr. Hinckley seems like a kid who had a rough life and who lacked the moral fiber to deal with it. [But] lots of people have tough lives, many tougher than Mr. Hinckley's, and manage to cope. The Hinckley verdict let those people down. For anyone who experiences life as a struggle to act responsibly in the face of various temptations to let go, the Hinckley verdict is demoralizing, an example of someone who let himself go and who has been exonerated because of it.[33]

The Hinckley case produced a powerful reaction and a flurry of legislation regarding the insanity defense. Some jurisdictions shifted the burden of proving insanity from government to defendant, and raised the standard of proof, sometimes to proof beyond a reasonable doubt. Others, intending to ensure that defendants are labeled "guilty" and spend time incarcerated, revised the verdict from not guilty by reason of insanity to guilty but insane. Others returned to a strict right-wrong test of insanity. The irresistible impulse test had always generated criticism, never empirically demonstrated but powerfully felt, that it somehow contributed to weakening willpower.

California, for example, in a referendum overwhelmingly approved by the voters, returned to a pre-M'Naughten insanity definition, the "wild-beast" test. According to the wild-beast test, defendants must demonstrate the reasoning and willpower of wild beasts, that is, a mental disease or defect that has totally destroyed their capacity both to know right from wrong and to exercise any will power to control their actions. The California Supreme Court later rejected that formulation, interpreting the referendum to mean a return to right-wrong from the substantial capacity test that was in effect at the time the referendum passed.[34]

Diminished Capacity

Some defendants suffer from mental diseases or deficiencies that do not impair their reason and will sufficiently to satisfy the insanity tests. **Diminished capacity** provides a defense in some jurisdictions if the impairment affects the defendant's capacity to form *mens rea.* Many states reject this defense, maintaining that there is no middle ground: a person is either sane or insane. At the other extreme, the American Law Institute Model Penal Code recommends that evidence of diminished capacity should always be admissible to negate *mens rea.* The few jurisdictions that permit evidence of diminished capacity restrict its use to specific intent crimes of more than one degree—usually murder. Ordinarily, this means that defendants can show diminished capacity to premeditate a murder, thereby reducing charges from first- to second-degree murder.

Syndrome Defenses

Since the 1970s, a range of "syndromes" affecting mental states have led to novel defenses in criminal law. The most bizarre of these include the policeman's, love, fear, chronic brain, and holocaust syndromes. Law professor and defense attorney Alan Dershowitz has written a highly critical book; *The Abuse Excuse and Other Cop-Outs, Sob Stories, and Evasions of Responsibility* lists dozens of such syndromes. Dershowitz worries that these excuses are "quickly becoming a license to kill and maim." His is probably a needless worry because defendants rarely plead these excuses, and except for a few notorious cases picked up by television and the newspapers, defendants rarely succeed when they do plead syndromes and other "abuse excuses."[35]

When a San Francisco city official Dan White was tried for killing his fellow official Harvey Milk and Mayor George Moscone, the defense introduced the junk food syndrome, popularly called the "Twinkie defense." White's lawyer argued that junk food diminished White's mental faculties. One psychiatrist testified as follows concerning White's frequent depressions:

> During these spells he'd become quite withdrawn, quite lethargic. He would retreat to his room. Wouldn't come to the door. Wouldn't answer the phone. And during these periods he found that he could not cope with people. Any confrontations would cause him to kind of become argumentative. Whenever he felt things were not going right he would abandon his usual program of exercise and good nutrition and start gorging himself on junk foods. Twinkies, Coca Cola.
>
> Mr. White had always been something of an athlete, priding himself on being physically fit. But when something would go wrong he'd hit the high sugar stuff. He'd hit the chocolate and the more he consumed the worse he'd feel, and he'd respond to his ever-growing depression by consuming even more junk food. The more junk food he consumed, the worse he'd feel. The worse he'd feel, the more he'd gorge himself.[36]

The defense argued that these depressions, which junk food aggravated, sufficiently diminished White's capacity to reduce his responsibility. The jury returned a verdict of manslaughter, and White was sentenced to a relatively short prison term. After his release from prison, he committed suicide. No one has ventured to blame his suicide on junk food. During the White case, much public comment—most of it negative—was directed at the Twinkie defense. Despite that derision, substantial evidence exists to suggest that white sugar does indeed diminish capacity. Whether or not it does so to sufficiently reduce responsibility is a highly controversial and far-from-settled question.[37]

Defendants have, with limited success, relied on the battered spouse syndrome to justify killing spouses in self-defense, even though the defendants were not in imminent danger (see section on self-defense).

Occasionally, women have used premenstrual syndrome (PMS) to excuse their crimes. In a New York case, Shirley Santos called the police, telling them, "My little girl is sick." The medical team in the hospital emergency room diagnosed the welts on the girl's legs and blood in her urine as the results of child abuse. The police arrested Santos, who explained, "I don't remember what happened. . . . I would never hurt my baby. . . . I just got my period." At a preliminary hearing, Santos asserted PMS as a complete defense to assault and endangering the welfare of a child, both felonies. She admitted beating her child but argued that she had blacked out owing to PMS, hence she could not have formed the intent to assault or endanger her child's welfare. After lengthy plea bargaining, the prosecutor dropped the felony charges and Santos pleaded guilty to the misdemeanor of harassment. Santos received no sentence, not even probation or a fine, even though her daughter spent two weeks in the hospital from the injuries. The plea bargaining prevented a legal test of the PMS defense in this case. Nevertheless, the judge's leniency suggests that PMS affected the outcome informally.[38]

Three difficulties ordinarily stand in the way of proving the PMS defense:

1. Defendants have to prove that PMS is a disease; little medical research exists to demonstrate that it is.
2. The defendant has to actually suffer from PMS; rarely do medical records document the condition.
3. PMS must cause the mental impairment that excuses the conduct; too much skepticism still surrounds PMS to expect ready acceptance that it excuses criminal conduct.[39]

The years since the Vietnam War have revealed that combat soldiers suffered more lasting and serious casualties than physical injury. The war took a heavy emotional and mental toll on the veterans. The effects have created what some call a mental health crisis that has had a dramatic impact on the incidence of major crime. Medical research has established a complex relationship between the stress of the combat tour in guerilla-type warfare (as opposed to conventional warfare) and later antisocial conduct. At the same time, lawyers have begun to consider the effect the Vietnam Vet syndrome has on criminal responsibility.

Occasionally, defendants have sought to excuse their criminal liability by means of what might be called a **cultural norms defense.** This defense is based on the claim that some behavior called criminal in the United States is normal behavior in an immigrant's homeland. Therefore, although what they have done may be wrong, they are not responsible because they were acting according to their cultural norms.

Knowledge and Understanding CHECK

1. Differentiate between justifications and excuses.
2. List the major defenses that excuse criminal liability.
3. What is the difference between mistake of fact and mistake of law?
4. Which one excuses criminal liability? Why?
5. Under what circumstances is mistake of law a defense? Give an example.
6. Why is mistake of fact an excuse?
7. List the three categories of maturity at common law.
8. Are they still used today? Explain.
9. Is old age an excuse for crime? Explain.
10. Under what four circumstances is duress a defense to crime?
11. List the crimes that duress excuses.
12. How do states define duress differently?
13. What do the Lord's Prayer and the words of William Gladstone have to do with the defense of entrapment?

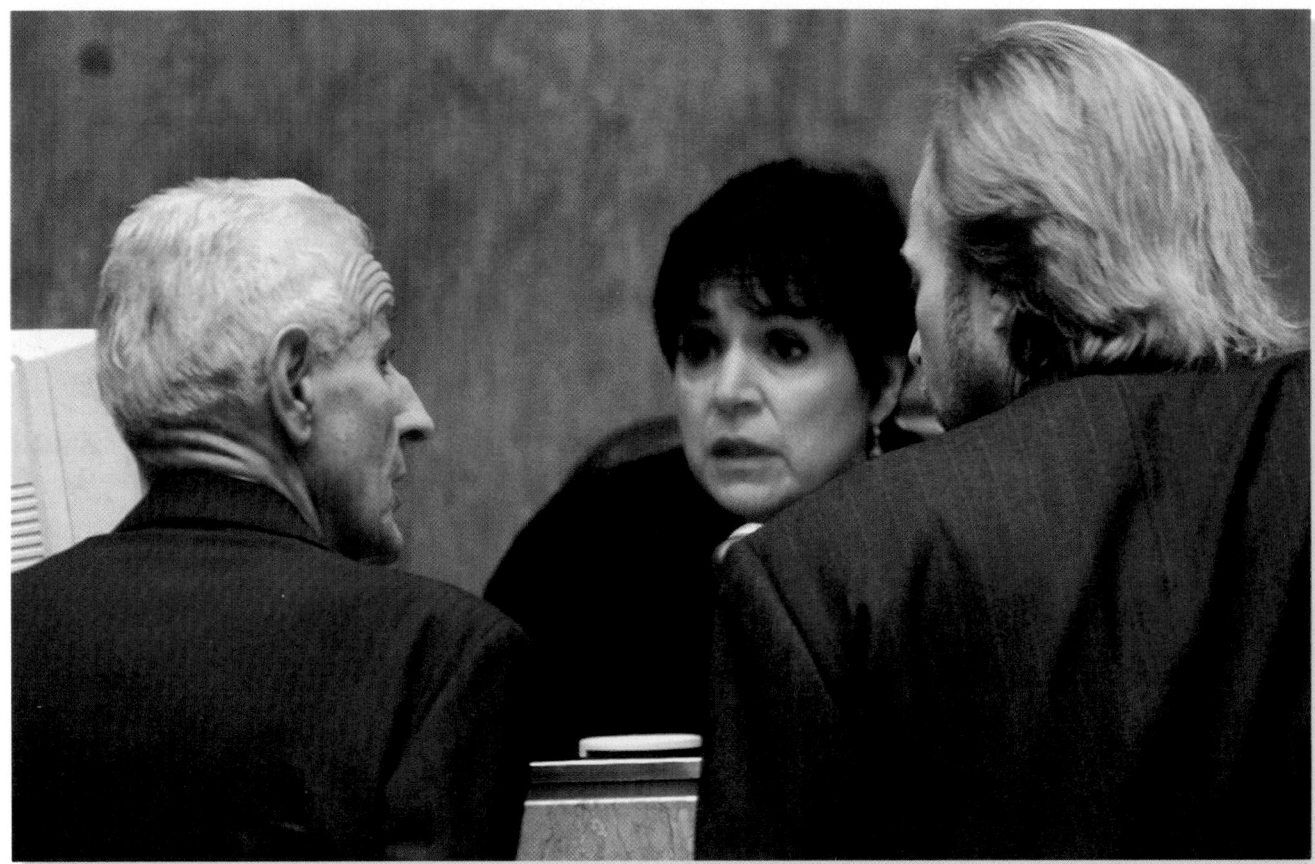

During Jack Kevorkian's murder trial in March of 1999, he argued unsuccessfully in his own defense that though he did indeed inject Thomas Youk with a dose of chemicals that ended his life, he was justified because he was acting not as a murderer but as a physician performing a medical treatment requested by the patient. Do you think that his defense of justification is viable?

14. What law enforcement difficulty does entrapment address?
15. Why did U.S. courts reject the defense of entrapment until the 20th century?
16. What changed the attitude of courts to entrapment?
17. What three kinds of government encouragement does the entrapment defense allow?
18. Describe and compare two tests that courts use to measure when government officers cross the line from encouragement to entrapment.
19. Between what two conflicting principles is the defense of intoxication buffeted?
20. Briefly describe the history of the application of these two principles.
21. To what kind of intoxication does defense apply? Why?
22. Explain the importance of the case of *Montana v. Egelhoff.*
23. Compare the attention the insanity defense receives publicly with the part the defense plays in day-to-day criminal justice operations.
24. What does it mean to say that insanity is a legal, not a medical term?
25. List the five elements of the right-wrong test of insanity.
26. Describe the irresistible impulse test of insanity and compare it with the right-wrong test.
27. List the five elements of the substantial capacity test of insanity.
28. Explain the effects of the Hinckley case on the defense of insanity.
29. Identify the kinds of syndromes that give rise to claiming excuses to criminal liability.
30. Identify the three difficulties that stand in the way of proving the PMS defense.
31. Describe the cultural norms defense.

CLASSIFICATIONS OF CRIMINAL LAW

Criminal laws can be classified according to the following criteria:

- Type and duration of punishment.
- "Evil" of the crime committed.
- Social harm inflicted.

Felony, Misdemeanor, and Violation

Crimes classified according to the type and duration of penalties are felonies, misdemeanors, and violations. These are ancient classifications, demonstrating how the past influences present criminal law. The great legal historian Frederic William Maitland maintained that the reasons for old classifications may have long since died, but their ghosts rule us from the grave. He meant that even when classifications have outlived their usefulness, they influence present practice. Dividing crimes into felonies and misdemeanors is one example. Historically, felonies were crimes punishable by death. Present law divides felonies into **capital felonies,** punishable by death or life imprisonment, and ordinary felonies, punishable by one year or more in prison. Therefore, the category includes both serial killers at one extreme and individuals who steal $500 at the other. The breadth of its scope makes the classification largely meaningless in any sociological sense. It serves mainly as an administrative device to determine who gets the death penalty, life imprisonment, or incarceration in a state prison.[40]

Misdemeanors include crimes punishable either by fines or up to one year in jail. Common misdemeanors include simple assaults and battery, prostitution, and disorderly conduct. Most jurisdictions divide misdemeanors into **gross misdemeanors,** punishable by jail terms from 30 days to one year, and **petty misdemeanors,** punishable by fines or up to 30 days in jail. A third category, **violation,** is punishable by a small fine and does not become part a criminal record. The most common violations are traffic offenses.

Mala in Se and *Mala Prohibita*

Another classification sorts crimes according to their perceived "evil." This old arrangement overlaps the felony, misdemeanor, and violation categories and defines some crimes as inherently bad (the Latin ***mala in se***). Crimes such as murder and rape fall into this category. Other behavior is a crime only because the law says so (the Latin ***mala prohibita***). Parking in a no-parking zone is *malum prohibitum.*

This ancient classification goes back to the roots of American criminal law in the religious and moral codes of England and colonial America. Although morality was frequently viewed as a preoccupation of the New England Puritans, the Anglicans of Virginia, Pennsylvania Quakers, and Maryland Catholics also infused criminal law with a moral component. The major felonies and the "morals" offenses—fornication, prostitution, sodomy, gambling, and public drunkenness—descend from this religious and moral heritage.[41]

In practice, no clear line separates *mala in se* and *mala prohibita* offenses. Despite legal theories that cling to the distinction, and notwithstanding talk of an ethical core in the criminal law, empirical research has demonstrated that offenders consider many crimes that are formally classified as *mala in se* "justifiable." That is, they consider their "criminal" actions as informal means to put right a deeply felt wrong. They may concede that their conduct "technically" violates formal criminal law, but they believe that what they did definitely was not really *evil.* According to sociologist Donald Black:

> There is a sense in which conduct regarded as criminal is often quite the opposite. Far from being an intentional violation of a prohibition, much crime is moralistic and involves the pursuit of justice. It is a mode of conflict management, possibly a form of punishment, even capital punishment. Viewed in relation to law it is self-help. To the degree that it defines or responds to the conduct of someone else—the victim—as deviant, crime is social control.[42]

Despite these empirical findings, legal theorists maintain that some crimes *are* inherently evil.[43]

Use *Your* Discretion

Are some crimes inherently evil?

The notion of inherently evil crimes suggests a consensus as to what serious crime is. Research does not confirm this conclusion. Not everyone agrees that activities such as drug use, gambling, and consensual adult sexual conduct are inherently evil, even if they are crimes. Consider these findings:

- More than one-third of all college men would rape if they thought they could get away with it.[44]
- Most murders are committed by people who think they are righting some wrong done to them.

According to Donald Black, "most intentional homicide in modern life is a response to conduct that the killer regards as deviant. Homicide is often a response to . . . matters relating to sex, love, or loyalty, to disputes about domestic matters (financial affairs, drinking, housekeeping) or affronts to honor, to conflicts regarding debts, property, and to child custody, and to other questions of right and wrong." For example, one youth killed his brother during an argument about the brother's sexual advances toward their younger sisters.[45]

- The vast majority of assaults occur between people who know each other.

In most cases, assailants believe they are redressing grievances. They take the law into their own hands in order to punish a wrongdoer. They do not believe that they were wrong in what they did, even though they may agree that it was against the law to do so. For example, some brothers attacked and beat their sister's boyfriend because he turned her into a drug addict. In another case, a gang member shot his gang leader for taking "more than his proper share of the proceeds from a burglary. Years later, the same individual shot someone who had been terrorizing young women—including the avenger's girlfriend—in his neighborhood. Though he pleaded guilty to 'assault with a deadly weapon' and was committed to a reformatory, not surprisingly he described himself as 'completely right' and his victim as 'completely wrong.'"[46]

- Many property offenders know their victims.

They have taken or destroyed their victims' property because they believe that their victims deserved it. For instance, a man broke into his ex-wife's apartment to take back property that he believed was rightfully his. A former burglar noted, "We always tried to get the dude that the neighbors didn't like too much or the guy that was hard on the people who lived in the neighborhood. I like to think that all the places we robbed, that we broke into, was kind of like the bad guys."[47]

- In many cases, vandalism turns out to be not wanton violence but an effort to punish what the vandals consider to be wrongdoing.

One young man found that someone had broken the radio antenna on his automobile. When he found out who did it, he slashed the culprit's tires in retaliation.[48]

According to the criminal codes of virtually all jurisdictions, all of these examples are crimes. Yet, none of the perpetrators considered what they did to be evil. Quite the contrary; although they are "criminals" according to the law, they believed that they were exercising justified social control over "wrongdoers." The criminals considered *themselves* victims because they believed that they were forced to commit crimes in order to rectify wrongs against them.[49]

CRITICAL THINKING

1. List and summarize the findings of the research summarized in the bulleted list.
2. Identify the behavior that you consider "inherently evil."
3. Explain the criteria you used to determine whether the situation describes "inherently evil" behavior.
4. If you need more information to decide, what would it be?

Crimes and Torts

Some harms can lead to legal actions even though they are not crimes. These private legal wrongs are called torts. Torts provide the grounds on which individuals sue each other, or engage in private litigation. They differ from criminal actions, at least formally, in several respects. In criminal cases, the government and the defendant are the parties to the case; hence, the title of the criminal case is *State* (or *United States,* or sometimes *Commonwealth*) *v. Simmons* (defendant), or *People v. Munckton.* In private personal injury actions (called **torts**) **plaintiffs** sue wrongdoers (defendants) to get money for their injuries (called **damages**); hence, *Chan v. Gonzalez.* Criminal cases rest on the notion that crime harms society generally, leaving individual injuries to tort actions. Almost all crimes against persons and property are also torts. A burglary, for instance, consists of the tort of trespass; a criminal assault is the tort by the same name.

Criminal prosecutions and tort actions may arise out of the same event, but criminal and tort proceedings are not mutually exclusive. Victims can sue for, and the government can prosecute, injuries arising out of the same conduct. For example, a burglary victim can sue the burglar for trespass and, at least theoretically, collect damages. The government can prosecute the burglar and, if it obtains a conviction, impose punishment.

Knowledge and Understanding CHECK

1. List the four criteria by which crimes are classified.
2. How do we currently define capital felonies?
3. Identify and compare two kinds of misdemeanors.
4. Contrast *mala in se* with *mala prohibita.*
5. What have empirical findings demonstrated about the *mala in se* and *mala prohibita* classifications?
6. Compare and contrast crimes and torts.

THE LAW OF CRIMINAL PROCEDURE

The criminal law defines what is a crime. The law of criminal procedure defines the power of the government to enforce the criminal law. The law of criminal procedure is the formal side of decision making in law enforcement agencies. It prescribes rules for decisions made at each step in the criminal process, from detecting crime to punishing offenders. These rules derive from several sources, including federal and state constitutions, statutes, court decisions, and the rules and regulations of criminal justice agencies. (See Chapter 1 for fuller discussion of these sources.)

Throughout the book, we examine the law of criminal procedure as it specifically affects the decisions and the actions of law enforcement, courts, and corrections. In this chapter, we focus on overarching principles of criminal procedure. Table 4.1 contains a list of the specific provisions in the Bill of Rights and the stages of the criminal process to which they relate.

Due Process of Law

The fundamental constitutional principle of the law of criminal procedure is "due process of law," guaranteed by the due process clauses of the Fifth and Fourteenth Amendments. As defined earlier in this chapter, the due process clauses provide that neither the federal government nor the states "shall deprive any person of life, liberty, or property without due process of law." (See also Chapter 1 on the tension between crime control and due process.)

Due process commands that the government cannot make decisions or take actions that deprive any person of life, liberty, or property without following established and usually written procedures. Furthermore, the same principles of federalism apply to the law of criminal procedure as apply to criminal law. As early as 1833, the Chief Justice of the U.S. Supreme Court, John Marshall, expressed the view that criminal procedure is a state and local matter. When Congress proposed the Bill of Rights, he wrote, if Congress had meant to take the extraordinary step of "improving the constitutions of the several states . . . they would have declared this purpose in plain . . . language." Therefore, Marshall concluded, the question of whether the Bill of Rights applied to state and local procedure is "of great importance, but not of much difficulty." He meant that the federal Bill of Rights did *not* apply to the states.[50]

Following the Civil War, a number of amendments were added to the U.S. Constitution. The original purpose of these amendments was to bring former slaves into full citizenship, particularly in the former Confederate states. Insofar as criminal justice is concerned, the due process clause of the Fourteenth Amendment is the most important of these "Civil War Amendments." The Fourteenth Amendment, among other things, specifically prohibits the *states* from depriving citizens of life, liberty, or property without due process of law. Despite this specific prohibition, courts did not apply the due process clause to the states until the 1930s.

It is probably not a coincidence that just as Hitler rose to power in Germany, the U.S. Supreme Court decided the landmark Scottsboro case, *Powell v. Alabama*. Both the German war machine during World War I and the rise of fascism had revived the fear of arbitrary government in the United States. This fear led to a reconsideration of whether not applying the Bill of Rights to state and local criminal procedure was appropriate. The Scottsboro case involved seven black male teenagers traveling on a train from Tennessee through Alabama. The seven youths got into a fight with seven white male teenagers. The black youths threw the white youths off the train, leaving behind two young white women. The women later accused the black youths of gang raping them. Before the train reached Scottsboro, Alabama, a sheriff's posse seized the black youths and took them and the young women to Scottsboro. A hostile mob met them in Scottsboro. The sheriff called up the militia, which guarded the prisoners, courthouse, and courthouse grounds from that point through the arraignment, trial, conviction, and sentencing. In fact, "the proceedings, from beginning to end, took place in an atmosphere of tense, hostile and excited public sentiment."[51]

The black youths were all young, illiterate, and far from home with no friends, relatives, or acquaintances nearby. They were confined under close guard without a lawyer during the few days following the incident until they were found guilty. The court did not appoint a lawyer for them until the morning of the trial. Within minutes, the jury found all seven defendants guilty and the court sentenced them all to death. The U.S. Supreme Court decided—at least in these circumstances—that the Fourteenth Amendment due process clause applied to the states. For the Court, Justice Sutherland wrote:

Table 4.1
The Bill of Rights and Criminal Justice

The Police
Fourth Amendment
(1) Guarantee against unreasonable search and seizure.
Fifth Amendment
(2) Right to a grand jury indictment.
(3) Right against double jeopardy.
(4) Right to due process.
(5) Right against self-incrimination.

The Courts
Sixth Amendment
(6) Right to a speedy and public trial.
(7) Right to an impartial jury.
(8) Right to notice of charges.
(9) Right to confront witnesses.
(10) Right to a lawyer.

Courts and Corrections
Eighth Amendment
(11) Prohibition against excessive bail.
(12) Prohibition against cruel and unusual punishments.

Samuel B. Liebowitz (left), a brilliant New York lawyer of his day, defends Heywood Patterson in the famous Scottsboro case. Patterson and seven other African American men were charged with raping two Caucasian women in Decatur, Alabama, in 1931. After the defendants' initial convictions, the U.S. Supreme Court ordered new trials on the grounds that the defendants had not received adequate legal representation. Liebowitz became involved when the new trials began in 1933, and in 1935 a historic Supreme Court decision ruled that the defendants' constitutional rights were violated because African Americans had been systematically excluded from the jury rolls (a landmark opinion that spurred a battle to include African Americans on the jury rolls). Despite this ruling, the defense team remained unable to have any of the defendants released from jail until 1937; the last defendant was not released until 1950.

> It has never been doubted by this court . . . that notice and hearing are preliminary steps essential to the passing of an enforceable judgment, and that they, together with a legally competent tribunal having jurisdiction of the case, constitute the basic elements of the constitutional requirement of due process of law. The words of [the great lawyer, Daniel] Webster . . . that by "the law of the land" is intended "a law which hears before it condemns" have been repeated . . . in a multitude of decisions. . . . [T]he necessity of due notice and an opportunity of being heard is . . . among the "immutable principles of justice which inhere the very idea of free government which no member of the Union may disregard."[52]

The Fundamental Fairness Doctrine

The U.S. Supreme Court has formulated two constitutional doctrines by which to apply the provisions of the Bill of Rights to the states. *Powell v. Alabama* represents the application of the **fundamental fairness doctrine,** or substantive due process doctrine. The fundamental fairness doctrine focuses on the *substance* of fairness, rather than on the **form** of procedure. According to fundamental fairness, due process might include the protections of the Bill of Rights, but it is not equivalent to the Fourth, Fifth, Sixth, and Eighth Amendments. In other words, due process derives its meaning independent of the Bill of Rights. Supreme Court Justice Felix Frankfurter, the doctrine's major proponent, said that fundamental fairness means "those canons of decency and fairness which express the notions of justice of English-speaking peoples even toward those charged with the most heinous offenses."[53]

To determine fundamental fairness, the Court decided on a case-by-case method what offended those "notions of justice." For example, in *Rochin v. California,* sheriff's deputies unlawfully entered Rochin's house and forced open his bedroom door. Inside, they found Rochin partially dressed, sitting on the bed with his wife. The officers noticed two capsules on the nightstand. When they asked, "Whose stuff is this?" Rochin grabbed the capsules and put them in his mouth. The officers "jumped upon him" and tried to pull the capsules out of his mouth, but he swallowed them. The police took him to a hospital and forced him to submit to stomach pumping. The vomiting produced by the stomach pumping produced the two capsules, which contained morphine. In reversing Rochin's conviction, the Supreme Court wrote:

> The proceedings by which this conviction was obtained do more than offend some fastidious squeamishness or private sentimentalism about combating crime too energetically. This is conduct that shocks the conscience. Illegally breaking into the privacy of the petitioner, the struggle to open his mouth and remove what

was there, the forcible extraction of his stomach's contents . . . are methods too close to the rack and screw.[54]

The Incorporation Doctrine

According to the **incorporation doctrine,** the due process clause guarantees procedural regularity in all cases. Procedural regularity means the procedures specifically spelled out in the Bill of Rights. Therefore, the due process clause of the Fourteenth Amendment *incorporated* the safeguards in the Fourth, Fifth, Sixth, and Eighth Amendments, requiring state proceedings to adhere to them. Some jurists, such as Supreme Court Justice Hugo Black, maintained that the due process clause incorporated all of the Bill of Rights, but the Court never accepted this reading. Instead, during the 1960s, the Court opted for a **selective incorporation doctrine.** The selective incorporation doctrine looked at whether the particular provision in the Bill of Rights was *fundamental* to fair procedure. As of this writing, the Court has incorporated the rights against unreasonable seizures, against self-incrimination, to assistance of counsel, to confront opposing witnesses, to compulsory process to obtain witnesses, and to the prohibition against cruel and unusual punishment. It has *suggested,* but has not specifically ruled, that public trial, notice of charges, and prohibition of excessive bail are also incorporated. It has ruled that due process does *not* require indictment by a grand jury.

Once a right is incorporated, it applies in the entirety of its meaning to state proceedings. As one of the doctrine's critics, Associate Supreme Court Justice John Marshall Harlan, Jr., put it, the incorporated right applies to the state, "jot for jot and case for case."[55]

Almost every state has a bill of rights in its constitution that parallels, if not specifically duplicates, the federal Bill of Rights. States cannot *reduce* the state standards below those guaranteed in the federal Bill of Rights; the federal standard represents a constitutional minimum. However, states can *raise* the state standard above the federal standard, and occasionally they have done so. For example, in one leading case, the Michigan Supreme Court differed with the U.S. Supreme Court on whether the Fourth Amendment search and seizure clause permits states to conduct DWI (driving while intoxicated) checkpoints at which all motorists are stopped and checked for signs of intoxication. Although upheld by the U.S. Supreme Court, these "seizures" are not supported by probable cause or reasonable suspicion, which the Fourth Amendment ordinarily requires. (See Chapter 7 on police and the law.)

A motorist challenged Michigan's DWI checkpoint law on the grounds that it violated both the unreasonable search and seizure clause in the Fourth Amendment and the parallel clause in the Michigan constitution. The Supreme Court held that the stops were reasonable Fourth Amendment seizures, even though they were not backed up by any facts suggesting that the stopped motorists were intoxicated. The Michigan Supreme Court ruled, however, that stops without reasonable suspicion of intoxication were unreasonable seizures under the Michigan constitution. In raising the minimum standard, Michigan in effect expanded the right against unreasonable searches and seizures for people in Michigan beyond their rights under the United States Constitution. According to the Michigan court,

> our courts are not obligated to accept what we deem to be a major contraction of citizen protections under our constitution simply because the United States Supreme Court has chosen to do so. . . . This court has never recognized the right of the state, without any level of suspicion whatsoever, to detain members of the population at large for criminal investigatory purposes. . . . In these circumstances, the Michigan Constitution offers more protection than the United States Supreme Court's interpretation of the Fourth Amendment.[56]

Knowledge and Understanding CHECK

1. What is the difference between criminal law and the law of criminal procedure?
2. State the fundamental principle of the law of criminal procedure.
3. What does due process command to the government?
4. How did the Fourteenth Amendment due process clause affect the principle of due process?
5. What is the connection between the rise of Adolf Hitler to power and the case of *Powell v. Alabama*?
6. Describe the facts and the decision in *Powell v. Alabama.*
7. Describe the two doctrines that the U.S. Supreme Court adopted to apply the Bill of Rights in the U.S. Constitution to individual states.

SOCIAL THEORIES OF CRIMINAL LAW AND PROCEDURE

Criminal law and procedure do not exist in a value-neutral state that is distinct from society. They are living institutions that respond to political and ideological influences. Stating the principles of criminal law and procedure does not explain how and why they originated. Analyzing the words of statutes, court decisions, and legal principles does not explain why legislatures enact particular criminal codes, does not reveal the reasons for courts' interpretations of these codes, and does not account for why the criminal law excludes many social harms from its scope. Social scientists do not accept the proposition that specific statutes simply apply neutral principles of criminal law. They search instead for the influences that create society's demands to write its wishes into criminal law.[57]

Furthermore, examining formal criminal law does not reveal how the criminal law operates in practice; it does not explain discretion. Nonlegal interests influence which crimes citizens decide to report to the police; who the police select for arrest, prosecutors choose for prosecution, juries decide to convict, or judges proceed to sentence; who gets incarcerated; and what decisions are made in corrections agencies. Law reflects the societal values and interests that determine these choices. Law upholds these values and interests, prohibits conduct that threatens them, and authorizes punishment for those who violate them. In other words, law is not a set of moral absolutes; it is a social institution, shaped by time, place, and circumstance.[58]

Consensus and Conflict Perspectives

Our pluralistic society has greatly influenced both the creation of criminal law and the administration of criminal justice. The diverse values of racial, ethnic, and cultural groups make it impossible to explain criminal law and its enforcement without accounting for the influence of pluralism. This requires an exploration of the connection between society and criminal law and procedure.

Throughout history, two contrasting views of the nature of society and social change have prevailed among social theorists. According to the **consensus perspective,** a general agreement regarding values exists in society, and the state protects these common values. To the extent that conflict exists, the state mediates among groups with competing values. According to the consensus theory, the state represents the values and interests of the whole society, not those of any particular group or groups. According to the **conflict perspective,** conflict—not consensus—is normal. Conflict is not always violent and out of control. Revolution and civil war only rarely resolve conflict; more frequently, debate and consultation do. Society is composed of groups with conflicting values and interests. The dominant group usually wins the revolutions, civil wars, debates, and consultations. The state represents the values and interests of the group or groups with enough power to control social institutions.[59]

Consensus Theory

Consensus theory has an ancient heritage, going back at least to Plato and Aristotle. Its modern version owes much to Emile Durkheim, the great nineteenth-century French sociologist whose ideas have greatly influenced the sociology of law and have contributed to criminal justice theory. Durkheim enunciated two fundamental propositions relevant to understanding the sociology of criminal law:

1. Crime is conduct "universally disapproved of by members of each society. Crimes shock sentiments which, for a given social system, are found in all healthy consciences."
2. "An act is criminal when it offends strong and defined states of the collective conscience."[60]

Based on these ideas, Durkheim suggested two broad hypotheses of the consensus theory:

1. Criminal law is a synthesis of a society's essential morality, based on values that are shared by all "healthy consciences."
2. Society creates crime in order to establish moral boundaries that, if violated, threaten society's basic existence. In other words, the definition of behavior as criminal notifies ordinary people how far they can go without undoing social order.[61]

The American sociologist Kai Erikson's classic study, *Wayward Puritans,* tested Durkheim's boundary hypothesis. Erikson studied witchcraft among seventeenth-century New England Puritans. He analyzed evidence about creating, prosecuting, and punishing witchcraft, concluding that the community created "crime waves" to solidify moral boundaries in order to keep the community from disintegrating. Puritans needed witchcraft to keep society from wandering outside settled behavioral boundaries.[62]

Empirical evidence from modern times also supports Durkheim's synthesis hypothesis. Blacks and whites, men and women, rich and poor, young and old, well-educated and poorly educated people agree about what conduct amounts to serious crime. In 1983, researchers asked a selected sample to rank the seriousness of various crimes. The answers displayed broad consensus on the following: Violent crimes were considered most serious, property crimes less serious, and public-order crimes least serious. This compares favorably with rankings in most criminal codes. Table 4.2 contains the results of this comprehensive survey of American opinion concerning the seriousness of offenses. Do your own rankings agree with these findings?[63]

Conflict Theory

Consensus theory dominated mainstream criminology in the 1940s and 1950s. Then, in the late 1950s, social conflict theories reemerged. The conflict theorists challenged the notion that consensus is the "normal" state of society. Instead, conflict theory—which enjoys a history in social thought as old as consensus theory—assumes that conflict is the normal state of society. It assumes further that social control requires active constraint, sometimes in the form of coercion. Common values and interests do not produce social control, because they do not exist in real societies. Society is divided into competing classes and interest groups, the most powerful

Table 4.2
Consensus on the Seriousness of Crimes

Severity Score	Offense–10 Most Serious
72.1	Planting a bomb in a public building (the bomb kills 20 people)
52.8	Forcibly raping a woman, who dies from the injuries
43.2	Robbing a victim at gunpoint, who dies from the robber's shots when the victim struggles
39.2	Husband stabbing a wife to death
35.7	Stabbing a victim to death
35.6	Intentionally injuring a victim, who dies as a result
33.8	Running a drug ring
27.9	Wife stabbing her husband to death
26.3	Skyjacking a plane
25.9	Forcibly raping a woman with no *physical* injury resulting
Severity Score	**Offense–10 Least Serious**
1.1	Disturbing the neighborhood with noisy behavior
1.1	Taking bets on the numbers
1.1	Group hanging around a street corner after police tell them to move on
0.9	Running away from home when under 16
0.8	Being drunk in public
0.7	Breaking the curfew law when under 16
0.6	Trespassing in the backyard of a private home
0.3	Being a vagrant
0.2	Playing hooky from school when under 16

of which dominate social institutions, including legislatures, criminal justice agencies, and their processes. The dominant group writes criminal laws that attempt to further their interests and impose their values on the whole society. These laws then become an instrument enabling the dominant classes and interest groups to retain their dominance, and to prevent conflict.[64]

Conflict theory has many variants, but all shift the emphasis from law *breaking* to law *making* and law *enforcing.* Until modern conflict theory reemerged in the late 1950s, most criminologists began their study with criminal law already in place. They considered *criminals,* not criminal *law,* to be the social problem. Conflict theory changed all that. The emphasis on law making and law enforcing led to an examination of criminal law and its enforcement in a new and different light. Conflict theory maintains that criminal law does not reflect absolute, agreed-on principles or universal moral values. Instead, criminal law defines, and criminal justice agencies preserve and protect, the interests and values of the dominant social groups. Criminal law and procedure are means of preserving the dominant group or groups' definition of social order.[65]

Radical Theory

Dissatisfaction with both consensus and conflict theory, and with mainstream criminology and criminal justice in general, contributed to the creation of a "new," or radical, criminology in the 1960s. It was not, however, exactly new. It drew on the long tradition of social conflict theory discussed in the last section and on Marxist theory. Radical criminology maintains that mainstream criminologists and criminal justice professionals are apologists, if not lackeys, for a capitalist ruling class that dominates the state. Radicals disagree over whether the dominant class consciously exploits the working class, or whether the structure of capitalist society inevitably determines their exploitative actions. Instrumentalists contend that the ruling class consciously decides to exploit. Structuralists maintain that capitalists do not exploit by conscious design, but rather because capitalism by its nature requires exploitative class relationships and class conflict. They believe that the capitalist social and economic structure requires exploitation to operate; criminal law forms but an instrument of that structure. Although the rhetoric often ran high in the 1960s and 1970s, radical criminologists developed a criminal justice theory based on the following propositions:

1. The state's primary purpose is to protect the dominant class in society.
2. This requires controlling the lower classes.
3. The ruling class exploits the working class by wringing profit from overworked laborers.
4. Criminal law controls workers so capitalists can get richer and secure protection for their accumulated riches.
5. Brute force is not always necessary to protect these interests and control the workers.
6. Capitalists sometimes have to commit crimes in order to maintain the existing power arrangements. So, police officers violate individuals' rights, government abuses its power, corporations fix prices, and so on. They try not to do this too often because it threatens the myth that law is neutral, evenhanded, and fair.
7. Workers commit crimes mainly out of necessity. They prey on other workers, and sometimes capitalists, in order to survive: They steal what they cannot earn. Or, out of frustration with existing unjust arrangements, they erupt in violence against others. Occasionally, they commit

"heroic crimes," like attacking the power structure. Their crimes are not bad or evil; they are utilitarian actions necessary to survive in capitalist society.[66]

These brief descriptions oversimplify the consensus, conflict, and radical social theories. Consensus theorists do not maintain that harmony and negotiation always prevail in politics and society; nor do they claim that their theories explain everything in criminal justice. Conflict theorists do not demand an interpretation of social interaction that totally excludes agreement and social cohesion. Radical criminologists do not contend that class determines all laws or that capitalists always win and workers always lose. Consensus, conflict, and radical theorists do maintain that criminal law reflects their theoretical view of social reality.

Knowledge and Understanding CHECK

1. What does it mean to say the criminal law and procedure are living institutions?
2. Describe the shortcomings of examining only formal law.
3. Define and then contrast the consensus and conflicts in criminal law and procedure.
4. Define and describe the importance of radical theory in criminal law and procedure.
5. Identify the seven propositions underlying the radical theory of criminal justice.

THE POLITICS OF CRIMINAL LAW AND PROCEDURE

The consensus, conflict, and radical theories suggest but do not elaborate on the political process involved in legislating criminal law and criminal procedure. The decisions to define certain behavior as a crime and to establish rules of criminal procedure depend not only on the ideological approaches to law, but also on the interaction of individuals, public and private interest groups, and criminal justice professionals. Scholars long ago revised the theory that laws reflect the unaltered will of the majority. Sometimes public outrage does get translated relatively unaltered into criminal law. During the 1940s, outrage over a few heinous sex crimes led to the enactment of sexual psychopath laws. In the 1990s, a spate of carjackings spurred Congress and the president into rare quick action when they passed specific federal legislation dealing with taking cars by violence.

An interest group theory has replaced the pure democracy explanation of criminal law and procedure enactments. According to this theory, public and private groups, led by moral entrepreneurs, or reformers, put pressure on legislators by a variety of means to purify society. Prohibition and anti-prostitution crusades are two examples of how the theory can explain the politics of criminal law. However, neither public outrage nor moral crusades explain the enactment of the bulk of criminal law or the law of criminal procedure. Recent research shows that criminal justice professionals decide the content of run-of-the-mill legislation; that is, the majority of criminal law and criminal procedure. This happened in the revision of most states' and the federal government's criminal procedure codes that took place during the 1960s and 1970s. Barton Ingraham, in an analysis of the enactments of these revisions, concluded:

> Legislative reform of criminal procedure . . . is usually initiated by some agency or official of the state with law-making or law-enforcing authority. The job of drafting the new code is then placed in the hands of a group consisting mostly of lawyers, judges, and law professors.[67]

Timothy Lenz reached a similar conclusion in a detailed analysis of sentencing reform in Indiana, Minnesota, and Mississippi. He found that although conditions might bring legislation into public view and generate heated opposition, the public "is not constantly watching over" the legislative process. As a result, "policy is usually the domain of a narrow set of political and professional interests." Richard Hollinger and Lonn Lanza-Kaduce examined the enactment of computer crime legislation that rapidly spread throughout the country during the 1970s. They found that, except for one organization linked to the private security industry and the American Bar Association, few interest groups influenced this legislation. They concluded that neither interest groups nor moral entrepreneurs were responsible for most computer crime legislation. Instead, computer crime experts and legislators wrote most of the laws.[68]

Knowledge and Understanding CHECK

1. What is the importance of the will of the majority to criminal law and procedure?
2. Describe the interest group theory and explain its significance in criminal law and procedure.
3. Summarize the findings of Timothy Lenz regarding interest groups and criminal justice legislation.

Should There Be a "Cultural Values" Defense to Criminal Behavior?

At the beginning of the chapter you read a brief description of the trial of a Laotian refugee who murdered his wife. Here are excerpts from the case:
People v. Aphaylath, 68 N.Y.2d 945, 502 N.E.2d 998, 510 N.Y.S.2d 83 (1986)

Facts

Defendant, a Laotian refugee living in this country for approximately two years, was indicted and tried for the intentional murder of his Laotian wife of one month. At trial, defendant attempted to establish the affirmative defense of extreme emotional disturbance to mitigate the homicide (Penal Law § 125.25[1][a]) on the theory that the stresses resulting from his status of a refugee caused a significant mental trauma, affecting his mind for a substantial period of time, simmering in the unknowing subconscious and then inexplicably coming to the fore. Although the immediate cause for the defendant's loss of control was his jealousy over his wife's apparent preference for an ex-boyfriend, the defense argued that under Laotian culture the conduct of the victim wife in displaying affection for another man and receiving phone calls from an unattached man brought shame on defendant and his family sufficient to trigger defendant's loss of control.

Opinion

The defense was able to present some evidence of the Laotian culture through the cross-examination of two prosecution witnesses and through the testimony of defendant himself, although he was hampered by his illiteracy in both his native tongue and English. Defendant's ability to adequately establish his defense was impermissibly curtailed by the trial court's exclusion of the proffered testimony of two expert witnesses concerning the stress and disorientation encountered by Laotian refugees in attempting to assimilate into the American culture. It appears from the record before us that the sole basis on which the court excluded the expert testimony was because "neither one . . . was going to be able to testify as to anything specifically relating to this defendant." It is unclear from this ruling whether the Trial Judge determined that she had no discretion to allow the testimony because the experts had no knowledge of this particular defendant or that she declined to exercise her discretion because of the experts' lack of knowledge of the defendant or his individual background and characteristics. Under either interpretation, however, the exclusion of this expert testimony as a matter of law was erroneous because the admissibility of expert testimony that is probative of a fact in issue does not depend on whether the witness has personal knowledge of a defendant or a defendant's particular characteristics. Whether or not such testimony is sufficiently relevant to have probative value is a determination to be made by the Trial Judge in the exercise of her sound discretion.

Accordingly, because the court's ruling was not predicated on the appropriate standard and the defendant may have been deprived of an opportunity to put before the jury information relevant to his defense, a new trial must be ordered.

Critical Thinking

1. Should defendants be allowed the "opportunity to put before the jury" information about cultural norms? Why or why not?
2. A variation of the cultural norms defense is what Alan Dershowitz calls the "urban survival syndrome." This excuse is that some neighborhoods are so dangerous as to require living by the motto, "Kill or be killed." In one Texas case, a lawyer used the defense. Although it did not produce a "not guilty" verdict, it nevertheless caused a hung jury.[69] Should the conditions of your neighborhood excuse your criminal liability? Act as both prosecutor and defense attorney and argue your case.

CHAPTER CAPSULE

- Criminal law defines criminal behavior and prescribes punishments for it.
- Criminal procedure prescribes the rules for enforcing the criminal law.
- All crimes require a union of action (*actus reus*) and intention (*mens rea*).
- Some crimes contain two additional elements: causation and a resulting harm.
- Defenses to criminal liability are either justifications or excuses.
- Due process limits both criminal law and criminal procedure.
- The Fifth Amendment due process clause prohibits the federal government from denying any person life, liberty, or property without due process of law.
- The Fourteenth Amendment prohibits state and local governments from denying individuals life, liberty, or property without due process of law.
- Social influences create demands to write social values into criminal law and its enforcement.
- Both consensus and conflict in our pluralistic society have shaped the content of criminal law and procedure.

KEY TERMS

criminal law
law of criminal procedure
ex post facto law
due process clauses
substantive due process
procedural due process
void-for-vagueness
equal protection of the laws
right to privacy
proof beyond a reasonable doubt
actus reus
mens rea
concurrence
criminal conduct
attempt
conspiracy
solicitation
general intent
specific intent
transferred intent
constructive intent
criminal recklessness
criminal negligence
strict liability
principle of concurrence
causation
acquittal
alibi
lack of a material element
defenses of justification
defenses of excuse
common law
mistake of law
mistake of fact
duress
entrapment
predisposition test
inducement test
insanity
irresistible impulse test
substantial capacity test
diminished capacity
capital felonies
misdemeanors
gross misdemeanors
petty misdemeanors
violation
mala in se
mala prohibita
torts
plaintiffs
damages
fundamental fairness doctrine
consensus perspective
conflict perspective

INTERNET RESEARCH EXERCISES

Exercise: Using the Internet or InfoTrac College Edition, search for information about "the intoxication defense." What do you find? Can you find any cases that are using this defense? How successful was this defense?

Suggested site:
- FindLaw: http://www.findlaw.com (tip: click on "Law: Cases and Codes," then click "Supreme Court Opinions." Under "Party's Name," type in "Egelhoff" and read the case.)

InfoTrac College Edition: Run a key word search on "intoxication defense"

NOTES

1. *Lanzetta v. New Jersey,* 306 U.S. 451, 453 (1939).
2. *State v. Metzger,* 319 N.W.2d 459 (Neb. 1982).
3. *Michael M. v. Superior Court of Sonoma County,* 450 U.S. 464 (1981).
4. *Griswold v. Connecticut,* 381 U.S. 479 (1965).
5. *Bowers v. Hardwicke,* 478 U.S. 186 (1986).
6. *Ravin v. State,* 537 P.2d 494 (Alaska 1975).
7. *State v. Damms,* 100 N.W.2d 592 (Wis. 1960) (attempted murder); *State v. Furr,* 235 S.E.2d 193 (N.C. 1977) (solicitation to commit murder).
8. American Law Institute, *Model Penal Code,* Section 2.02(2)(d).
9. See Wayne R. LaFave and Austin W. Scott, Jr., *Criminal Law,* 2d ed. (St. Paul: West Publishing Co., 1986), 267–277.
10. Ibid.
11. Ibid.
12. Douglas N. Husak, "Justifications and Accessories," *Journal of Criminal Law and Criminology* 80 (1989): 496–497; George Fletcher, *Rethinking Criminal Law* (Boston: Little, Brown, 1978), 759.
13. *New York Times,* 14 January 1989.
14. Quoted in *New York Times,* 23 January 1989; see also George Fletcher's interesting book on the Goetz trial, *A Crime of Self-Defense: Bernhard Goetz and the Law on Trial* (New York: Free Press, 1988).
15. *Colorado Statutes,* Section 18-1-704.5, 8b, C.R.S. (1986).
16. *People v. Guenther,* 740 P.2d 971 (Colo. 1987).
17. *Texas Criminal Code,* Section 9.42.
18. Fred Cohen discusses the case in *Criminal Law Bulletin* 21 (1985): 9.
19. Jonathan C. Carlson, "The Act Requirement and the Foundations of the Entrapment Defense," *Virginia Law Review* 73 (1987): 1011.
20. *People v. Mills,* 70 N.E. 786, 791 (N.Y. 1904).
21. Paul Marcus, "The Development of Entrapment Law," *Wayne Law Review* 33 (1986): 5.
22. Lawrence P. Tiffany et al., *Detection of Crime* (Boston: Little, Brown, 1967).
23. *Sherman v. United States,* 356 U.S. 369 (1958).
24. Concurring in *Hampton v. United States,* 425 U.S. 484 (1976).
25. *United States v. Simpson,* 813 F.2d 1462 (9th Cir. 1987).
26. Related in John Gibeaut, "Sobering Thoughts: Legislatures and courts increasingly are just saying no to intoxication as a defense or mitigating factor," *American Bar Association Journal,* May 1997, 56.
27. Fletcher, *Rethinking Criminal Law,* p. 846.
28. Blackstone, *Commentaries,* pt. IV, pp. 25–26.
29. Gibeaut, "Sobering Thoughts," pp. 56–57.
30. *People v. Penman,* 271 Ill. 82, 110 N.E. 894 (1915); Hall, *General Principles of Criminal Law,* p. 540; *Burrows v. State,* 38 Ariz. 99, 297 P. 1029 (1931).
31. 214 N.W.2d 205 (Iowa 1974).
32. *M'Naughten's Case,* 8 Eng. Rep. 718 (1843).
33. Ibid., 82; Bureau of Justice Statistics, *Sourcebook of Criminal Justice Statistics—1993* (Washington, D.C.: Bureau of Justice Statistics, 1994), Table 3.2.
34. Technical Report, *New Directions for the National Crime Survey* (Washington, D.C.: Bureau of Justice Statistics, March 1989).
35. Alan Dershowitz, *The Abuse Excuse and Other Cop-Outs, Sob Stories, and Evasions of Responsibility* (Boston: Little, Brown, 1994), p. 3.
36. Mike Weiss, *Double Play: The San Francisco City Hall Killings* (Reading, Mass.: Addison-Wesley, 1984), pp. 349–350.
37. Ibid.
38. "Not Guilty Because of PMS?" *Newsweek* (November 8, 1982): 111.
39. "Premenstrual Syndrome: A Criminal Defense," *Notre Dame Law Review* 59 (1983): 263–269.
40. Stephen E. Brown, "Involuntary Smoking: A Case of Victims Without Crime," 1984 Meeting of Mid-South Sociological Association; Thomas Simmons, "Should the Library Throw the Book at 'Em?" *New York Times,* 23 February 1985.
41. David Flaherty, "Law and the Enforcement of Morals in Early America," in *Law in American History,* Donald Fleming and Bernard Bailyn, eds. (Boston: Little, Brown, 1971), 203–253.
42. Donald Black, "Crime as Social Control," *American Sociological Review* 48 (1983): 34–45.
43. Rollin M. Perkins and Ronald Boyce, *Criminal Law,* 3d ed. (Mineola, N.Y.: Foundation Press, 1982), 88.
44. Donald Black, "Crime as Social Control," 34–36.
45. Ibid., 36.
46. Ibid., 37.
47. Ibid.
48. Ibid.
49. Peter Rossi et al., "The Seriousness of Crimes: Normative Structure and Individual Differences," *American Sociological Review* 39 (1974): 224–37.
50. *Barron v. Baltimore,* 32 U.S. 7 Pet. 243, 250 (1833).
51. Francis A. Allen, "The Law as a Path to the World," *Michigan Law Review* 77 (1978): 157–58; James E. Goodman, *Stories of Scottsboro* (New York: Pantheon Books, 1994).
52. *Powell v. Alabama,* 287 U.S. 45 (1932).
53. *Rochin v. California,* 342 U.S. 165 (1952).
54. Ibid.
55. Jerold H. Israel, "Selective Incorporation Revisited," *Georgetown Law Journal* 71 (1982): 274; Justice Harlan concurring in *Duncan v. Louisiana,* 391 U.S. 145 (1968).
56. *Michigan v. Sitz,* 496 U.S. 444 (1990); *Sitz v. Department of State Police,* 506 N.W.2d 209 (Mich. App. 1993), 218.
57. Lawrence Friedman, *A History of American Law,* 2d ed. (New York: Simon and Schuster, 1985).
58. For a good introduction to the enormous body of literature on the relation of law to society, see Friedman, *A History of American Law,* 36–56.
59. Ralf Dahrendorf, "Out of Utopia: Toward a Reorientation of Sociological Analysis," *American Journal of Sociology* 64 (1958): 126; Thomas J. Bernard, *The Consensus-Conflict Debate: Form and Content in Social Theories* (New York: Columbia University Press, 1983); William J. Chambliss, *Criminal Law in Action* (Santa Barbara: Hamilton Publishing Company, 1975), vii; Douglas Hay, "Crime and Justice in Eighteenth- and Nineteenth-Century England," in *Crime and Justice: An Annual Review of Research,* Norval Morris and Michael Tonry, eds., 2 (1980):45–84.
60. Emile Durkheim, *The Division of Labor in Society* (New York: Free Press, 1933), 73–80.
61. William Chambliss and Robert Seidman discuss this in *Law, Order, and Power,* 2d ed. (Reading, Mass.: Addison-Wesley Publishing, 1982), 171–206.
62. Kai T. Erikson, *Wayward Puritans: A Study in the Sociology of Deviance* (New York: John Wiley & Sons, 1966).

63. Rossi, "The Seriousness of Crimes," 227–37.
64. William J. Chambliss, *Criminal Law in Action,* 2d ed. (New York: Macmillan, 1984), 16–31.
65. David Greenberg, ed., *Crime and Capitalism: Readings in Marxist Criminology* (Palo Alto: Mayfield Publishing Co., 1981), 1–26, 190–94.
66. Richard Quinney, *Class, State, and Crime: On the Theory and Practice of Criminal Justice* (New York: David McKay Co., 1977).
67. Barton L. Ingraham, "Reforming Criminal Procedure," in Alvin W. Cohn and Benjamin Ward, eds., *Improving Management in Criminal Justice* (Beverly Hills: Sage Publications, 1980), 28.
68. Timothy Lenz, "Group Participation in the Politics of Sentencing Reform" (University of Minnesota, Ph.D. dissertation, 1986), 282; Richard C. Hollinger and Lonn Lanza-Kaduce, "The Process of Criminalization: The Case of Computer Crime Laws," *Criminology* 26 (1988): 101.
69. Dershowitz, *Abuse Excuse,* p. 73.

CHAPTER 5

The Missions and Roles of the Police

CHAPTER OUTLINE

What Are the Police?

1. The police are a body of handsome young men and women . . . who bravely fight the forces of evil to make the world safe for decent people. [This definition was offered by a handsome and humorous young man who worked for the campus police.]
2. The police are a bunch of hot shots who get their kicks from hassling blacks, students, and most other people who are trying to have a good time. [This definition was the effort of a tall, thin, hairy fellow with a widely advertised appetite for controlled substances.]
3. The police are an agency of government that enforces the law and keeps the peace. [This one came from a very serious young woman who always sat in the front row. She remembered it from another class.]
4. The police are a weapon the state uses to oppress the working classes, the poor, and minorities. [The author of this definition was an intense young Marxist.]
5. The police are the people who come into my father's restaurant to get free food. [This from a second-generation Eastern European student.]
6. The police are the people who drive police cars. [The effort of one of the brightest students I have ever taught. She went on to become a lawyer.][1]

These are definitions of police offered by some of Professor Carl Klockars' criminal justice students, together with his comments in brackets.

INTRODUCTION

Every profession has a mission. The mission of armies is to win wars, of doctors to cure the sick, of teachers to educate the young. To fulfill these missions, professionals play roles, become part of organizations, adapt to the culture of the group, and engage in a range of strategies. Of course, the mission is not so clear and focused as these statements suggest. Armies are sometimes dispatched to keep the peace, and soldiers play the role of "peacekeepers." Doctors may pursue the mission of ending suffering, playing the role of "ministers of mercy" by allowing or even helping terminally ill patients to die. Teachers sometimes go beyond their traditional mission, helping students through crises by assuming the role of counselor. All these added missions, roles, and strategies can be sources of controversy. Perhaps no profession has more missions than policing. Perhaps none has faced more controversy both from inside and outside as to what police missions should be.

To the public, to politicians, in most of the news media, and on television and movie dramas, the police mission is simple and clear: criminal law enforcement, especially against murder, rape, robbery, aggravated assault, burglary, theft, and drug law violations. In reality, the police spend far more time playing roles other than fighting crime.

HISTORY OF POLICE

Sometime around 1500 B.C., Egypt and Mesopotamia established police forces that were efficient and effective, but tortured suspects to obtain confessions and mistreated prisoners. In 27 B.C., the Roman Emperor Augustus appointed an urban officer armed with the power to maintain public order. By A.D. 6, the Romans had established a large police force that patrolled the streets of Rome 24 hours a day.[2]

English Origins

In early medieval England, about A.D. 900, law enforcement became the responsibility of local inhabitants. After the Norman Conquest, in 1066, King William instituted true community policing. The "frankpledge" required every male over 12 years of age to form a group of 10 members, called a tithing. All members swore to apprehend, hold, bring to court, and testify against members of their tithing who committed crimes, and to report rumors and information that raised suspicions about the behavior of members. Heavy fines were levied against breaches of frankpledge. Ten tithings made up the next level of organization, called the hundred, under the charge of a constable appointed by a local noble. Hundreds were in turn grouped into shires (counties), supervised by shire reeves (sheriffs).[3]

The frankpledge system never worked effectively. Most tithingmen had plenty to do just to survive by working at their own occupations, with little or no time left for watching other tithing members. Furthermore, sheriffs could not supervise constables, who were widely scattered and linked if at all by poor, dangerous, and frequently impassable roads. In 1285, the Statute of Westminster remodeled the frankledge into the parish constable-watch system. Every parish—the smallest unit of government—appointed two constables, either by lot or by some form of freeholder election. Constables, who served without pay for one year, selected watchmen to aid them in their three primary duties:

1. *Maintaining order* by patrolling town and village streets from dusk until dawn, ensuring that all local people were indoors and quiet, that no strangers were wandering about, and that, as they proclaimed periodically, "All's well!"
2. *Providing services,* such as lighting street lamps, clearing garbage from the streets, and dousing fires.
3. *Enforcing the criminal law* by apprehending suspects.

Constables and other members of the watch practiced both proactive and reactive policing. **Proactive policing** means that the police themselves initiate action to control crime. **Reactive policing** means that the police respond to calls for help from victims and witnesses. Proactively, they looked for wrongdoing by patrolling streets, lanes, and alleys. Reactively, they raised and administered the "hue and cry"—the loud outcry used to enlist help in pursuit of suspects who were caught "red-handed" (literally, with blood on their hands); the police and those helping pursued suspects to the parish border.

Colonial America

The American colonies adopted the English watch system with few if any modifications. The police mainly reacted to calls for help, seldom acting proactively. Although they were frequently admonished to take such initiative, stories of their failings to do so abound. The evidence shows that only considerable pressure could rouse them to do anything; they were after all unpaid amateurs compelled to perform a thankless task after hours (they served only during the night). Criminal investigation was a private matter. Colonial America had no counterparts to the modern detective; victims built their own cases. Constables' crime-fighting responsibilities ended with the hue and cry.[4]

The Nineteenth Century

The local parish constable-watch system endured both in England and the United States until 1829. During the late 1700s and the early 1800s, rapid population increases, crowded cities, and industrialization produced fundamental and rapid social change and dislocations. Riot, general disorder, and increased crime, particularly property offenses, rendered the watch system virtually unworkable. Calls to replace it with various substitutes began as early as the mid-1700s. Sir John Fielding and Henry Fielding (author of the classic English novel *Tom Jones*), Patrick Colquhoun, a London magistrate, and Jeremy Bentham, the philosopher and law reformer, called for a revolutionary proactive police. Henry Fielding, when he became chief magistrate in Bow Street, appointed about a half dozen "thief takers," known as the Bow Street Runners. This roving band of former London constables pursued lawbreakers, broke up criminal gangs, and arrested suspects.[5]

In 1829, under the leadership of Prime Minister Sir Robert Peel, Parliament mandated publicly funded police forces (ever since called "Bobbies") throughout England. Like the old constabulary, the Bobbies were reactive police forces that were charged with accomplishing the same three missions as the constable-watch system: maintaining order, providing services (the street lights still needed lighting), and enforcing the criminal law.

The new departments were organized differently from the local informal community frankpledge of hundred, parish, and county. The Mets, as the new London police were called, were organized into "chains of command." These chains were capable of deployment in large and small groups. They were also better trained, better paid, and considerably more numerous than the parish constables. All of these changes generated great ideological controversy. Critics said the police were not appropriate for a free society, only for authoritarian governments, such as that of France, with its gendarmes.[6]

In 1845, New York organized a police force modeled on the British constabulary. Philadelphia and Boston quickly followed suit. By 1855, cities as far inland as Milwaukee had adopted English-style police departments. Their principal organization consisted of a chief, assisted by a deputy, who headed citywide departments, subdivided into precincts, patrolled by paid officers. Officers eventually wore uniforms and carried guns as well as "nightsticks," or batons as they were called then. Police work ceased to be a duty; it became a job.

The police in the United States differed in one critical respect from the London police. The national government controlled the latter; municipalities controlled police in the United States.[7] As a result of municipal control, the police were arms of the dominant political machines. Police departments participated in partisan politics, and that participation was often corrupt—manipulating ballot boxes, for example. Departments also were corrupted by the lure of money from making deals with vice operations, like houses of prostitution, saloons, and gambling establishments. These deals were highly profitable to police departments. In New York City, for example, an officer who was assigned to the vice section of the city was delighted because before he came to the district he could only afford chuck steak but now he'd be eating tenderloin. After that, districts with high amounts of vice came to be known throughout the country as "tenderloins."[8]

Despite these weaknesses, the new police claimed a number of strengths. For example, they:

1. Enjoyed community support because officers were almost always from the neighborhoods that they policed.
2. Assumed responsibility for "whatever emergencies and crises that crossed their paths."
3. Provided various needed services: ambulance services, soup kitchens, garbage collection, and homeless shelters.

According to Malcolm K. Sparrow, Mark H. Moore, and David M. Kennedy, in their excellent book on the police: "In a time before widespread and well-supported social work and social programs, and before municipalities had assumed many of their routine obligations, the police often filled important vacuums."[9]

The Reform Era, 1895–1950

A wave of reform swept the United States at the turn of the century. This reform wave inspired a series of investigations in cities throughout the United States from about 1895 to 1920. These investigations clearly demonstrated that most of the major city police departments were plagued with both incompetence and corruption. Departments were seen as:

1. Fragmented.
2. Unable to control crime.
3. Unwilling to clamp down on vice.
4. Out of control.
5. Corruptly linked with politicians.[10]

As the twentieth century opened, the typical urban police officer in the United States was a poorly paid, low-status white male, a recent immigrant with little or no education, appointed by a local politician and expected to enforce the law according to the ward's wishes. According to Richard A. Staufenberger,

> They knew who put them in office and whose support they needed to stay there. Their job was to manage their beat; often they became completely enmeshed in the crime they were expected to suppress. Corruption, brutality, and racial discrimination, although not universal, were characteristic of most big city departments.[11]

In the 1920s, three California police chiefs, August Vollmer, O. W. Wilson, and William Parker, sponsored the **reform model of policing.** According to this model, the police are the front end or, as some say, the gatekeepers of the criminal justice system. Indeed, virtually all criminal proceedings begin with arrest; if police do not arrest suspects, the criminal process does not start. The reform proponents adopted an agenda that was supposed to *uplift* the police, not belittle them. Thus they proposed that police decision making exhibit three characteristics:

1. *Independence:* that it be based on special police expertise.
2. *Competence:* that it be determined by special skills and training.
3. *Correctness:* that it be governed by law, not discretion.

Finally, the sole mission of the police was crime control by means of enforcing the laws against the FBI's Index Crimes.[12]

Major changes followed the reformers' proposals. By the 1950s, all of the following elements in the reform agenda had become a reality:

1. *Centralization of police authority:* police chiefs began to really run their departments.
2. *Shift from foot to motorized patrol:* the days of the squad cars patrolling neighborhoods began slowly and then snowballed.
3. *Use of technological advances:* the automobile, two-way radios, and the telephone call box allowed fewer officers to cover more territory.
4. *Paramilitary organization:* chiefs were in charge of a strictly disciplined hierarchy with formal authority descending from the top through the ranks to patrol officers.
5. *Specialized units:* most common were centralized vice squads to control what was believed to be the major source of police corruption.
6. *UCR data:* use of FBI Uniform Crime Reports data (described in Chapter 2) as the measure of police performance.
7. *Reactive, incident-driven policing:* the distinctive method of policing.
8. *Restriction on police discretion:* such as department rules regarding use of force and high speed chases.
9. *Focus on criminal law enforcement:* as opposed to maintaining order and providing service.[13]

The last of these—crime control by means of criminal law enforcement—was immediately popular with not only police officers but also the public and politicians. According to Malcolm K. Sparrow and his colleagues:

> The reformers produced a conception of policing whose purpose has been largely focused on crime control and whose methods have been limited to law enforcement. Every discussion of the purpose of the police begins with crime control. For many the discussion ends there as well. Crime control is widely taken, both inside and outside the police, as the only important police function, with everything else they might do not only secondary but a dangerous and wasteful distraction. This is not in itself new; much thinking about the police has taken more or less this form for the last century. But the degree to which the reform model . . . has narrowed the debate unprecedented. . . .[14]

Use *Your* Discretion

What are the limits of the reform model?

Public confidence in the reform model remains high and support from police professionals and politicians remains strong but not unchallenged. A small band of police chiefs around the country are fighting the reform model. These chiefs and their supporters in academic circles cite the following factors as having undermined their confidence in the model.

1. Despite some reduction in the mid to late 1990s, crime rates taken in the long run remain at historic highs (see Chapter 2).
2. Criminal justice is ineffective because even if the police arrest suspects, the likelihood is small that they will serve time in prison (see Chapter 11).
3. Police tactics such as patrol, rapid response, follow-up investigation, and arrest do not work well to either control crime or reduce fear.
4. Private security is outpacing public police as a means to control crime, fear, and disorder. (See section on private policing later in this chapter.)[15]

In spite of these shortcomings, three police experts, Malcolm K. Sparrow (experienced police officer and administrator) Mark H. Moore (teacher of police executives, consultant to police departments, and student of the police), and David M. Kennedy (professional field observer of the police and the public), have concluded:

> Regarding police departments almost exclusively as the front end of the criminal justice system continues to make a great deal of sense to police and public alike. That definition, in turn, continues to restrict the role the police can play in the life of cities. Their proper task is widely seen to be enforcing the criminal law against murderers, rapists, robbers, burglars, and auto thieves. It might be nice to have police help with other urban problems, but anything that takes away from these urgent tasks misuses their resources and leaves the cities vulnerable to increased criminal victimization. That, at least, is what the police often argue, and they tend to find a sympathetic audience.[16]

CRITICAL THINKING

1. Does reason number 1 for objecting to the reform model underestimate the value of crime reduction during the mid-1990s? Explain your answer by referring to discussions in Chapter 2.
2. On what assumption is the relationship between arrest and imprisonment based? Is it sound? Explain.
3. Consider the concluding assessment of the reform model. Do you support it or do you believe it is time for a change? Explain your answer.

The 1960s

During the 1960s, a predominantly urban, industrial, pluralist United States challenged the values of white Anglo-Saxon Protestant men and their dominance. The challengers demanded to share the promises of American life—material abundance, freedom, and justice. Their hopes were raised and quickly dashed. The belief that a "quick fix" could assure everybody an opportunity to share the good life evaporated. Understanding the police in the 1960s requires appreciating the false hopes and the resulting frustration, anger, destruction, and, ultimately, realistic goals that resulted from this turmoil.[17]

Liberals called for "professional police" while riots raged and reports of street crime rates soared, especially in the nation's largest cities. In those cities, it was becoming increasingly difficult to deny that poverty, race, and gender created a chasm between the promise and reality of American life. The disorder and destruction created by riots and the fear and frustration brought on by street crime in major cities focused attention on the police, whose responsibility it was to maintain order. The police became easy scapegoats in cities plagued with riot, crime, and disorder. Of course, it was clear to any thoughtful observer that the police could not remove or even significantly reduce the fundamental causes of disorder embedded in the deeper social and economic realities of American life. These deep-seated problems did not arise from police actions; they were only brought into sharp and painful focus during those troubled days.

"Law and order" was a major theme of the 1964 presidential election campaign. The significance of the Republican nominee Barry Goldwater's appeals for law and order were not lost on Lyndon Johnson, despite his landslide victory. In the aftermath of the election, President Johnson created the President's Commission on Law Enforcement and the Administration of Justice. The Crime Commission, as it was called, gave serious attention to six police problems:

1. Multiple missions of the police.
2. Fragmented nature of law enforcement.
3. Poor training and minimal education of police officers.
4. Police corruption, brutality, and prejudice.
5. Separation of the police from the communities they serve.
6. Diminution in the public support on which effective policing ultimately depends.[18]

By the late 1960s, police officers were frustrated, angry, and fed up with the highly publicized and unrelenting criticism of the reformers. But they also had other complaints, including poor pay, dictatorial chiefs, urban riots, unrealistic demands that they solve the nation's social problems, and Supreme Court opinions that "handcuffed the police instead of the criminal." These complaints had one lasting effect—police unionization. Regardless of whether their complaints were justified and whether unions were the answer to their complaints, departments in almost all large cities, except those in the South, became unionized.

Unionization had a major impact on police administration. It wrought a revolution by reducing the power of police management. Police chiefs now had to share their power by negotiating with unions over many issues. Furthermore, according to historian of the police Samuel Walker, the union movement "won dramatic improvement in salaries and benefits for officers along with grievance procedures that protected the rights of officers in disciplinary hearings." Not everyone favored unionization—and it still has its share of critics. Some reformers believed unions "resisted innovation and were particularly hostile to attempts to improve police community relations." Nevertheless, the union movement represents a major concrete result of the troubled 1960s.[19]

The Legacy of Twentieth-Century Reform

The achievements of all reform movements fall short of promise, and this was surely true of twentieth-century police reform movements. A new federal agency, the Law Enforcement Assistance Agency (later, Administration), or LEAA, was created to accelerate reform in criminal justice. Ideological conflict swirled around it from the beginning. Liberals wanted more expenditures for reform, training, and innovative programs; conservatives defended the expenditures on local police hardware as necessary to preserve order in a rapidly disintegrating society. Social scientists challenged LEAA's effectiveness in either reducing crime or preserving order. Furthermore, academics criticized LEAA's failure both to evaluate existing programs and to create new, experimental programs. Amidst a gradual disillusionment with government programs in general, Congress gradually reduced the funding of LEAA; it was finally dissolved by President Jimmy Carter in 1980.[20]

In the more than 30 years since President Johnson's Crime Commission issued its report, we have witnessed considerable progress, despite problems that have plagued American policing since colonial times. The government awarded early grants to local police departments to improve police-community relations and to upgrade hardware, such as radios and other equipment. In 1969, President Richard Nixon launched a major effort to aid local police departments that had or wanted to begin programs to reduce specific crimes, such as robbery and burglary. Education and training have increased. Police have formulated and adopted more and better-articulated policies, and they have developed rules governing police practices. Finally, we have enormously advanced our knowledge of policing. More than courts and corrections, police departments have willingly participated in evaluations of their work, even when research has found police practices deficient. They have also established experiments that have led to changes in policies and practices. These advances demonstrate that the legacy of the 1960s includes more than riot, disorder, and dislocation.[21]

Knowledge and Understanding CHECK

1. List the three primary missions that remained more or less constant throughout the entire history of policing.
2. Trace the shifts between proactive and reactive policing that have occurred during the history of policing.
3. Trace the developments in police organization throughout the history of policing.
4. Identify three strengths of the "new" police in the nineteenth century.
5. List five images of police that emerged from the investigations of police departments on the late nineteenth and early twentieth centuries.
6. Identify three characteristics of police decision making supported by the reformers of the early 20th century.
7. List the nine major elements of the reform agenda that had become a reality by 1950.
8. Identify six police problems that President Johnson's Crime Commission focused on.
9. Summarize the legacy of 20th century police reform.

History of Policewomen and Women Policing

It is difficult to weave the important history of policewomen and women policing into the general history sketched above. This is partly because until 1900 there were no policewomen, and since then there have been relatively few women, and these few played minor roles in policing. But in the 1990s excellent histories of policewomen and women policing have appeared. Thanks to these histories and the growing numbers of women police officers with responsibilities equal to those of policemen, it is possible to outline the major developments in the history of women police officers.

In 1930, an unidentified woman wrote the following editorial in a Midwestern newspaper.

> There is to most of us something highly distasteful in the idea of a women walking a beat, carrying a billy [club] and going into all sorts of low places. . . . Though we may feel ourselves equally capable as the

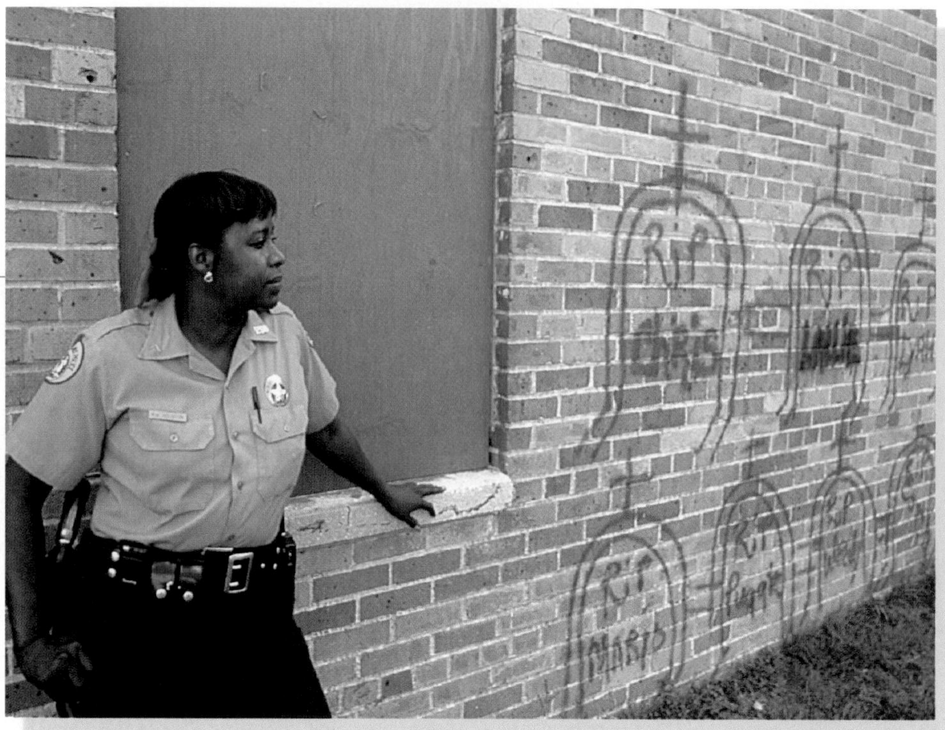

This community-oriented policewoman on foot patrol in a New Orleans public housing project shows that women police officers and the police force itself have come a long way since the days of Alice Stebbing Wells, one of the women pioneers in the field.

> men in many ways, it is better that we do our work well than to try to do men's poorly. Women have great power as law enforcers. But that power should be used in the home. . . . We can still do more good . . . as mothers and teachers than as policewomen.[22]

The idea that police work is "man's work" is a central idea in the history of police in the United States, even though women have worked in law enforcement since 1820, when they commonly served as matrons in jails and prisons. And police work throughout U.S. history has included much that is not "masculine," such as helping lost children, running soup kitchens, and providing lodging for the destitute and the homeless. Helping the helpless may have been the public image of women's work but it was not the reality in U.S. police departments.[23]

By 1900, a new attitude about women law enforcement was developing. One of the pioneers in women policing was Alice Stebbing Wells. In 1910, Wells told her family and friends that she wanted to become a police officer. Wells hardly fit the popular image of a police officer (working-class, heavy-drinking, Irish Catholic men with lots of muscle). Wells was a middle-class, Protestant, college educated, five-foot-tall member of the Women's Christian Temperance Union.[24]

Police Women as Social Workers, 1900–1930

The women pioneers in police work advocated that the compassionate nature of women qualified them to accomplish the mission of crime prevention, in such areas as juvenile delinquency and female criminals. The pioneers contended that the best women for police work were middle-class women social workers. They were good role models and were trained in the improvement of people, particularly women and juveniles. Their argument in favor of this crime prevention model of policing was:

1. The highest form of police work is social work.
2. Prevention is the most important mission of police work.
3. Therefore, women's nature suited them best to prevent crime by means of social work.[25]

As a result of the efforts of the pioneers, hundreds of middle-class women had become police officers during the 1910s and 1920s.[26] In her excellent history of women policing, *Policing Women,* the historian Janis Appier wrote:

> despite women's presence in police departments, the anticipated gender- and class-based transformation of police work never took place. Instead, year after year, pioneer policewomen remained a tiny, beleaguered minority within police work, resented and even despised by most of their colleagues. . . . the . . . entry of women into police work during the 1910s and 1920s fundamentally changed the nature and gendered representation of law enforcement in unintended ways. Whereas prior to the 1910s, the occupation of police work was presumed to be sex-specific (only men could be police officers), during the 1910s and 1920s it became an occupation with an array of gender-linked functions. According to pioneer policewomen and their advocates, men were best at performing certain police duties, while women were best at performing other police duties.[27]

Knowledge and Understanding CHECK

1. List all of the limits of women policing mentioned by Appier.
2. Identify the unintended consequences of policewomen as social workers.
3. Considering your answers to both 1 and 2, were the pioneers successful or not? Defend your answer.

From Social Workers to Crimefighters, 1930–2000

Policing underwent major changes during the Depression of the 1930s. FBI Director J. Edgar Hoover and the reform chiefs August Vollmer and O.W. Wilson led the way in deemphasizing the social service mission of policing, stressing criminal law enforcement as the sole mission of the police. At the same time, working women were viewed less favorably than they had been during the prosperous 1920s, and feminism no longer commanded the public support it once had. The Depression reinforced more traditional roles for women. According to historian Susan Ware:

> Women were strongly encouraged to limit their aspirations to husband, family, and domesticity; work outside the home, especially for married women, was discouraged. Working women were considered selfish and greedy, who took money away from men—the real breadwinners.[28]

Women returned to police work during World War II, when there was a shortage of male officers. However, they remained social service officers at a time when most departments minimized the social service mission because of the commitment to crimefighting. Women's reentry into policing does not compare to women's entry into the general workforce. "Rosie the Riveter" really did replace male riveters who were in the armed forces. But there was no comparable "Connie the Crimefighter" in police work. Women did not replace male crimefighters who served in World War II.[29]

The 1950s are commonly viewed as a time when the place of women was in the home. However, it was a time of growth for policewomen. Women's role was shifting from social worker to crimefighter. Women worked with men in undercover operations; they wore uniforms for the first time, and they were trained to use and were expected carry firearms.[30]

By 1968, the woman crimefighter was a reality. Betty Blankenship and Elizabeth Coffel were assigned to patrol in Indianapolis. They became the first female officers "to wear uniforms, strap gun belts to their waists, drive a marked car, and answer general purpose police calls on an equal basis with policemen."[31]

In the mid-1990s Dorothy Moses Schulz declared:

> Today's women police officers, like their male colleagues, are primarily working class high school graduates who enter policing for its salary, benefits, and career opportunities. Their demands no longer reflect the upper middle class, educated roots of the past, but reflect working-class concerns about pay, promotions, and pensions. Their law enforcement concept is also similar to that of their male peers; as crimefighters, they enforce the law, maintain order, and provide for the public safety, just as men do. Thus, not only is the role of women in the police service radically different from its historical roots, the women are also radically different from their foremothers.[32]

Schulz added some qualification to these observations about the advances of women policing:

> Although women are slowly moving up the ranks of police departments . . . women frequently do not avail themselves of promotion opportunities both for personal reasons but also because systemic discrimination against them still exists. The personal reasons women list involve not wanting to give up positions with daylight hours due to family and childrearing requirements. Systemic reasons involve lack of assignments to high-profile units, weighted seniority beyond the minimal eligibility requirements, negative supervisory evaluations, and general attitudes of male co-workers that psychologically discourage ambition. Sexual harassment and male resentment over affirmative action hiring goals and what many officers see as a dilution of physical standards are also of concern. These systemic reasons belie the legal equality women have achieved and highlight issues pertaining to the subtle discrimination women face as they compete with men on terms defined by and for men.
>
> Women police chiefs are a rarity. Although Penny E. Harrington, a 20-year veteran member of the Portland, Oregon, Police Department, served as chief of the 940-member department for seventeen months . . . [in the mid-1980s] exceedingly few women have reached the top of all but small agencies. As of 1994, only two additional women had served as police chiefs in major cities. . . .
>
> Feminist criminologists . . . are asking whether advocates of gender-neutral policing—including police managers—are doing themselves and other women a disservice and should, instead, be stressing their differences from, rather than their similarities to, the men who make up the overwhelming majority of the police.[33]

Knowledge and Understanding CHECK

1. Trace the major developments and accomplishments of women policing in the 20th century.
2. List the qualifications that Schulz applies to accounts of advances.
3. Do the advances and the qualifications indicate that equality has been achieved—or can ever be? Defend your answer.

LAW ENFORCEMENT ORGANIZATION

Police organization in the United States conforms to our federal system of government. (See Chapter 4.) That is, law enforcement operates on federal, state, county, and municipal levels. Law enforcement also conforms to the constitutionally mandated separation of powers; that is, law enforcement agencies are under the jurisdiction of the executive branch of federal, state, county, and municipal government. Law enforcement agencies enjoy a large amount of autonomy in their operations.

Formally, law enforcement agencies are **quasi-military organizations:** Their officers wear uniforms and are subject to a hierarchical command structure, the ranks of which have military-sounding names—chief, commander, captain, lieutenant, sergeant, patrol officer; orders come from the chief, and subordinates are formally obligated to obey them. Insubordination leads to disciplinary action. Slogans to describe the police mission are also borrowed from the military. The police frequently refer to law enforcement as a "war" on crime, and criminals as the "enemy."

The following description of the New York City Police Academy nicely captures the quasi-military view of police:

> "Attention," the drill sergeant yelled at 200 men and women. One man slouched. Another saluted with his left hand. "About face." A few turned the wrong way. A few more stumbled. The sergeant was not amused. "This is unbelievable!" the sergeant bellowed at a new crop of police recruits on their first day of gym class at the Police Academy. "Look straight ahead when you're at attention. Do things in unison." "You're not civilians anymore," he told them. "You're in a semi-military outfit."[34]

The formal, bureaucratic side of police department organization calls for considerable routine and conformity to prescribed procedures that frustrate police officers and lead some experts to conclude that bureaucracy turns the police officer from a self-directed professional to an "hourly worker." Officers work fixed shifts, punch in and out, and carefully watch exactly how many hours they work. Jerome H. Skolnick and David H. Bayley refer to this bureaucratic dimension of police work and the frustration it causes some officers in *The New Blue Line:*

> They discuss endlessly among themselves their accumulated sick days, the amount of overtime worked, and vacation rotations. They live in a tightly supervised, formalistic environment, constantly checking what they do against set rules. Perhaps the most telling item of equipment patrol officers carry is a small bottle of "white-out," . . . used for correcting errors in the reports they write, fitting them exactly to the form demanded by the department. "Who's got the white-out?" is heard more often in patrol circles than "Let's be careful out there."[35]

The quasi-military model of policing describes the formal, outward appearance of police organization, not the informal reality of day-to-day operations. Soldiers wait for orders from officers before they take action, and most of the time they follow the orders closely. Police officers, on the other hand, have wide discretion and are left largely on their own to make decisions. They can decide whether or not to issue traffic tickets, arrest disorderly citizens, stop suspicious persons, or help lost people. Soldiers cannot and do not decide whether to move into an area, shoot at the enemy, or take other actions.

The military model creates problems for the police. If they are akin to the military and are engaged in a "war" against crime and drugs, then they have an enemy. Since "all's fair in war," some police officers might use excessive force or otherwise illegally invade the privacy and liberty of anyone they consider the "enemy." The "enemy"—in this case, people in the community—may adopt the same maxim, putting the police in danger. According to Skolnick and Fyfe:

> However stirring this call [for a war on crime], it relies upon an inexact analogy and is far more likely to produce unnecessary violence and antagonism than to result in effective policing. The lines between friend and foe were clear in the Arabian desert, but police officers on American streets too often rely on ambiguous cues and stereotypes in trying to identify the enemies in their war. When officers act upon such signals and roust people who turn out to be guilty of no more than being in what officers view as the wrong place at the wrong time—young black men on inner-city streets at night, for example—the police may create enemies where none previously existed.[36]

Federal Law Enforcement Agencies

Federal law enforcement agencies, legally part of the executive branch of the U.S. government, are independent of other law enforcement agencies and of legislative and judicial agencies (see Chapter 1). The following are among the major federal law enforcement agencies:

- *U.S. Marshal's Service.* The Marshal's Service is a separate agency within the Department of Justice. The marshals protect the federal courts, judges, and jurors; guard federal prisoners from arrest to conviction; investigate violations of federal fugitive laws; serve summonses; and control custody of money and property seized under federal law.
- *U.S. Customs Service.* Customs inspectors examine all cargo and baggage entering the country. Special agents investigate smuggling, currency violations, criminal fraud, and major cargo frauds. Special customs patrol officers concentrate on contraband, such as drugs and weapons, at official border crossings, seaports, and airports.
- *Bureau of Alcohol, Tobacco, and Firearms (ATF).* ATF deals with the criminal use of explosives and with arson.

Working with state and local police, it investigates arson cases. ATF has also pursued motorcycle gangs, such as the Hell's Angels, that violate federal firearms and explosives laws and federal laws against drug trafficking.

- *Immigration and Naturalization Service (INS).* INS administers immigration and naturalization laws. Border patrol agents patrol more than 8,000 miles of land and coastal boundaries to the United States. INS takes into custody and arranges for the deportation of illegal aliens entering or residing in the country.
- *Drug Enforcement Administration (DEA).* DEA enforces all federal narcotics and dangerous drug laws.
- *Federal Bureau of Investigation (FBI).* The FBI investigates more than 200 categories of federal crime. In addition, the FBI assists other federal, state, and local agencies through its extensive fingerprint files and other records. The FBI National Academy provides aid for some enforcement agencies throughout the country.

State Law Enforcement Agencies

Some states have state police agencies with statewide authority. These state police forces originated with the Texas Rangers, who in the early 1800s patrolled the Texas settlements. Following the Civil War, Massachusetts and Connecticut created state police agencies to combat vice. In the wake of labor-management strife resulting from rapid industrialization, Pennsylvania adopted a state police agency to quell industrial violence. These states overcame resistance generated by a fear that centralized state police agencies threatened both civil liberties and local autonomy.

In the years following 1910, when the number of motor vehicles proliferated, the need for highway traffic control generated new calls for state police. States such as Texas, Pennsylvania, Connecticut, and Massachusetts added a state trooper division to their existing organization. Most states never overcame the opposition to a centralized state police agency, but they did adopt special state highway patrol agencies with authority limited to traffic law enforcement. State highway patrol officers have only limited authority to perform general law enforcement duties, such as investigating crimes occurring in a state trooper's presence or on or near state highways.

Governors appoint the directors of state police or state highway patrols. Technological advances in traffic devices, alcohol testing, and communications systems all require officers to have greater ability and more training than their predecessors. Increasing numbers of states are setting statewide entry requirements and training standards for police officers, either through agency-established academies or in conjunction with institutions of higher learning. Following training, line officers advance in rank through either civil service or merit plans. In addition to enforcement agencies and training institutions, most states maintain "crime lab" or "criminalistics" services; some support investigative units.

County Law Enforcement Agencies

Sheriffs' departments enforce the criminal law in most rural and unincorporated portions of the more than 3,000 counties in America. In most instances, sheriffs do not interfere in municipal law enforcement because most incorporated towns and cities have their own police forces. In addition to county law enforcement, sheriffs' departments have two other major duties. They maintain the county jails, which hold pretrial detainees and most persons sentenced for misdemeanors. Finally, the sheriff is an officer of the county court. The sheriff's office supplies bailiffs to provide security and management of detainees on trial, transport prisoners to and from court, and serve a range of court papers, such as summonses, forfeiture and eviction notices, and court judgments.

Municipal Police Departments

Local police departments make up the great bulk of law enforcement agencies in the United States. The New York City Police Department employs more than 37,000 officers. But most local police departments employ only a few people. Ten thousand of the nation's departments employ fewer than 10 sworn officers. Many, such as the one in Empire, California, employ a single officer. In most of these small towns, crime is not a major problem.[37]

Private Police

The first private security officer, Allan Pinkerton, in the mid to late nineteenth century worked mainly for railroads and factory owners, providing security and combating industrial violence during strikes. Modern private security has also grown mainly in response to business needs. However, residents in large-city apartment complexes and condominiums and suburban gated communities have also stepped up their use of private security guards. Private security is a for-profit industry. It provides personnel, such as guards, investigators, couriers, and bodyguards. It also supplies equipment, including safes, locks, alarm systems, and closed-circuit television. In addition, it furnishes services, including monitoring, employee background checks, polygraphs, and drug testing. Businesses or others can either hire private security directly or contract for specific services and equipment.[38]

Many states grant private security personnel the authority to make felony arrests. Unlike sworn police officers, private police need not give arrestees the Miranda warnings. Private security guards cannot detain suspects or conduct searches without suspects' consent. Some states have special legislation authorizing private security to act as "special police" within a specific jurisdiction such as a plant, store, or university campus.[39]

Some jurisdictions require private security firms to obtain licenses. Sworn police officers may "moonlight" for

Private security officers guard the Taj Mahal gambling casino in Atlantic City, New Jersey. These private security guards are one example of what have become the nation's "primary protective force."

private security firms during their off-duty hours; most police departments permit moonlighting. Some departments contract with private concerns to provide personnel and use the revenue for department needs. For example, Miami and St. Petersburg, Florida, allow off-duty police officers to work armed and in uniform; the departments even arrange jobs for their officers.[40]

New York City allows companies to form "business districts" that pay special taxes for private security. A number of private security forces patrol various parts of the city to augment public police. For example, 29 uniformed but unarmed security guards patrol a 50-block section of Manhattan. A former police borough commander directs the force, and a surtax imposed by property owners on themselves pays for it. Security guards start at about $10 an hour, take a special 35-hour training course at John Jay College of Criminal Justice, and spend two more weeks training on the street. Squads patrol from 8 A.M. to midnight. Similar private security forces patrol other areas: A 285-member unit patrols Rockefeller Center; a 49-member unit patrols South Street Seaport; Roosevelt Island has an unarmed 46-member force commanded by a former police official. New York City police officers are allowed to moonlight, but not in the department's uniform.[41]

Public police protection grew rapidly during the 1960s and 1970s but stabilized during the 1980s. Private security, on the other hand, continued to grow. By 1990, private security had become the "nation's primary protective force," outspending public law enforcement by 73 percent and employing two and a half times the workforce. Spending for private security in 1990 reached $52 billion; private security agencies employed 1.5 million people. Public law enforcement spent $30 billion and employed 600,000. Public expenditures for law enforcement are expected to reach $44 billion by the year 2000; private security expenditures will dwarf them at $104 billion. The annual rate of expenditure of private security will double that of expenditures for public law enforcement (see Figure 5.1).[42]

In some precincts, more off-duty police than on-duty officers are performing police functions. Because they wear uniforms, off-duty employment swells both the availability and visibility of police officers. On the other hand, off-duty employment raises concerns about conflict of interest in serving private interests, fears of corruption, and possible lawsuits for alleged misconduct. To reduce the risk of these problems, department orders and regulations frequently limit the kinds of employment officers can accept.[43]

Use *Your* Discretion

Is private security worth the cost?

The following story was written by freelance writer Brae Canlen, based in San Diego.

> If I watched TV news more often, maybe . . . like many of my neighbors in San Diego, I'd install a burglar alarm and contract for an "armed response." I might even buy the full-service package: A guard would meet me in front of my house

Figure 5.1
Public Law Enforcement vs. Private Security

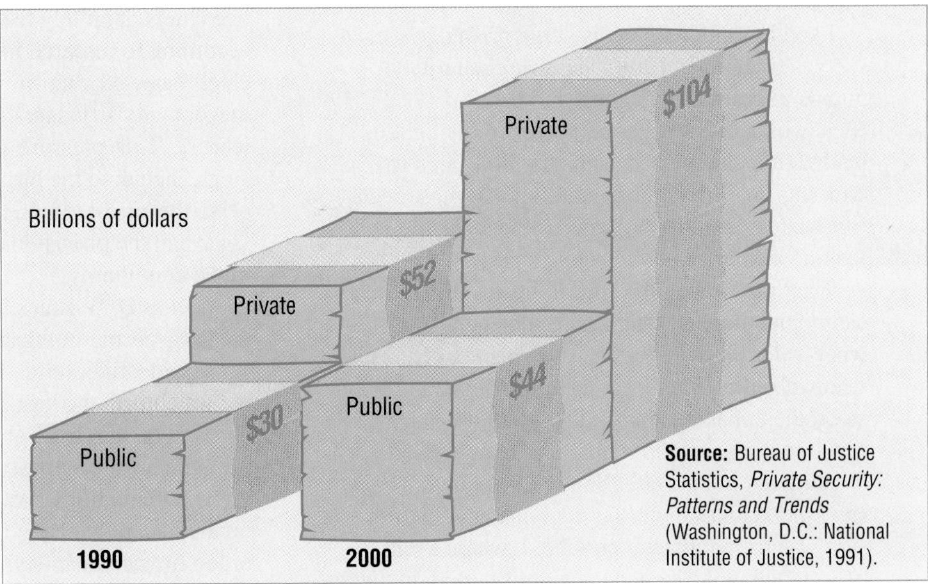

Source: Bureau of Justice Statistics, *Private Security: Patterns and Trends* (Washington, D.C.: National Institute of Justice, 1991).

every night and escort me in the door. This option is only available in Southern California, according to the private security firm I spoke to. "There wasn't much demand for it in Northern California," a representative explained. "People seem to think differently about crime up there." At least half of the state is sane.

Granted, I've never been the victim of a predatory crime or had my house broken into. If either were the case, I'm sure I'd feel more vulnerable. But this doesn't fully explain the collective angst in my corner of the country. San Diego homeowners install residential security systems more often than they paint the house, replace the carpet or fix up the bathroom, according to one market research firm. In Los Angeles, burglar alarms also rank first among home improvement projects.

Meanwhile, criminal activity is in a slump all over the state. Some people might see an inverse relationship between security and crime, but home burglar alarms don't stop murders, assaults and armed robberies. They don't even catch burglars. Police departments across the country, angry and overwhelmed at the high percentage of false alarms, have begun ignoring these calls—or at least responding to them with something less than lightning speed. In Los Angeles, the average police response time to a residential-alarm call is 55 minutes—almost enough time to roll up the rugs and empty out the clothes closets.

A surer bet, for many residents, is a private security firm that dispatches armed guards. It's a reassuring prospect, except that security officers rarely encounter a burglary in progress. What they do come across is the family dog, who naturally tries to bite them. At one California security company, its armed guards have not shot at an intruder for 12 years, according to their records. They have killed two dogs, however.

Some of the wealthier California neighborhoods boast of having their own private police patrols. These are not gated communities with guarded entrances, but places like Beverly Hills, Brentwood and Santa Monica, where residents wish they could erect walls against the common rabble. Security companies have so many subscribers in these areas that they "dedicate" a patrol car to roam the streets 24 hours a day, checking on all those little lawn signs that notify would-be felons of their services.

Homeowners aren't the only ones protecting their flanks; businesses are also trying to cover their assets. Not from burglars or thieving employees, but from customers, tenants and employees who sue after they become crime victims. These "negligent security" lawsuits have resulted in an army of security guards who serve primarily as window dressing. They don't have guns and they've been instructed not to use force, lest they get sued for providing too much security. If anything bad happens, all they can do is call the real police.

The illusion of safety is a hot commodity. The money spent on private security products and services in this country exceeds the combined budgets of all law enforcement agencies, local, state and federal. Security officers now outnumber police officers three to one; in California, it's four to one.

Even law enforcement is going private. Cities such as Oceanside, Calif., are hiring security guards to transport prisoners and patrol parks. Meanwhile, off-duty police officers moonlight in banks, shopping centers and bars. So what's wrong with this ubiquity? Maybe nothing. All those security guards, working on the private nickel, are making a contribution to public safety.

They may not be the arm of the law, but they can point a finger. Their square footage is a (somewhat) safer place to be. The supermarket guard who walked me to my car the other night, and stood there making small talk while I unloaded my groceries, wasn't on the flirt. Before he left, he muttered to himself, "You're O.K. now." The supermarket was my last errand that day; my first stop was my daughter's preschool, where I said hello to the uniformed guy always standing in the foyer. At lunchtime I dropped off a video at the rental place, where I passed by another security guard.

Had I visited the gym, the mall or even the ballpark, I'd have crossed through several more private security jurisdictions. Was there any point where I stood on public land? Yes. When my foot touched the sidewalk next to my car. "This is California," I keep reminding myself. "More is always better." But part of me longs for a patch of unprotected space, where no one is watching over me.[44]

CRITICAL THINKING

1. List the shortcomings the author ascribes to private security.
2. Specifically, what does she say about the gap between the promise and the reality of private security?
3. How much confidence can we place in this one story? Explain your answer.

Police Management Styles

For all of the visible bureaucratic formality of law enforcement agencies, individual departments vary in management style according to the following community characteristics:

- The community they serve.
- The goals their chiefs set.
- The values and ambitions their individual officers hold.

In other words, the formal structure of police departments adapts to serve the professional, ideological, political, and societal needs of its personnel and the community. Police chiefs definitely feel the pressure from political sources, according to research findings. A survey of Kentucky police chiefs showed that 56 percent felt political pressure from mayors, city managers, city council members, and business leaders. This pressure is related to a broad range of decisions, including the hiring, promotion, and demotion of officers; the arrest of offenders; the enforcement of specific laws; and the provision of special services to specific groups in the community.[45]

James Q. Wilson's landmark *Varieties of Police Behavior* emphasized the political dimensions of police organization. Wilson identified three basic styles in police departments—the watchman, the legalistic, and the service styles. The style depends on the political culture of the community.[46]

The **watchman style of policing** originated in immigrant communities. Watchman-style officers are decidedly nonbureaucratic. They focus on caretaking and maintaining order. In watchman-style departments, the police commonly ignore minor violations, exercising discretion to determine not what behavior violates the criminal law, but what may threaten order in the community. Watchmen-style officers avoid formal arrest; they settle disputes informally according to "street justice."

The **legalistic style of policing** predominated in Yankee-Protestant, or "good government," communities. Legalistic departments emphasize criminal law enforcement. Uniform, impartial arrests for all violations of law characterize the legalistic style. This style places a premium on the formal side of criminal justice; it concentrates on reducing discretion to an absolute minimum.

The third major management style, the **service style of policing,** also originated in "good government" communities. Service-style departments, like legalistic-style departments, rely on a bureaucratic formalism. They take all requests for service seriously, regardless of whether they stem from criminal law violations, maintaining order, or simply providing information. Officers often intervene but rarely arrest, particularly for minor violations. Instead, they counsel, issue written warnings, or make referrals to social service agencies.

Which style is best? That depends on the goals of the department. If the goal is to enforce the criminal law and serve the will of the community, then the legalistic style that minimizes discretion and emphasizes formal rules is best. If the goals are service and maintaining order, then the police are expected to rely on their professional judgment, not on prescribed rules for every situation. These goals require an emphasis on informal discretion, not formal rules.[47]

Knowledge and Understanding CHECK

1. Describe the quasi-military organization of the police.
2. Describe the frustrations that arise out of the bureaucratic side of police organization.

3. Contrast the informal reality of police work compared to the formal quasi-military side.
4. List and describe the major federal, state, county, and local law enforcement agencies.
5. Describe the nature and importance of private policing, and the trend in its prevalence.
6. Compare and contrast public and private police and policing.
7. Identify the three community characteristics that determine the style of policing that departments adopt.
8. Explain the three styles of policing that James Q. Wilson identified.

POLICE MISSIONS

"The police in modern society . . . have an "impossible task," wrote police expert Peter K. Manning in 1977. This remains true, as does his additional comment:

> To much of the public the police are seen as alertly ready to respond to citizen demands, as crime-fighters, as an efficient, bureaucratic, highly organized force that keeps society from falling into chaos. The policeman himself considers the essence of his role to be the dangerous and heroic enterprise of crook-catching and the watchful prevention of crimes. . . . They do engage in chases, in gunfights, in careful sleuthing. But these are rare events.[48]

This "rare" side of police work refers only to formal policing. Formal policing dominates the public mind; radio and television coverage of crime news; and in popular culture as reflected in television crime drama, movies, and novels. Formal policing definitely affects day-to-day actions and decision making in "serious" crimes. It is in the enforcement of laws against serious crimes that arrests, searches, interrogation, and identification procedures play a major role. (See Chapter 6.)

But there is much more to policing than formal initiation of the criminal process. Police officers spend far more time and their departments expend far more resources on informal policing—the other two historic missions of maintaining order and providing other services to communities. For this much larger side of police work, informal, discretionary decision making dominates, in both defining disorder and responding to it. Police departments are the only public service agency on call 24 hours a day, 365 days a year. People call the police to solve all kinds of problems, from fights, drunkenness, rowdy youths, prostitutes, and panhandlers on the street, to domestic disturbances, noisy parties, lost children, and animals in distress, to directions to the nearest hospital, post office, or school. Police departments touch the lives of more people in more ways than any other public agency. The police also consume the largest share of criminal justice expenditures (see Figures 5.2 and 5.3).

In maintaining order, law enforcement officers in their day-to-day activities on the street must balance *conflicting* interests in enforcing *vaguely* defined standards. They use their judgment to "do the right thing," without clear guidelines and with little consensus as to what the right thing is. In all three of their missions, they have the power to back up their decisions with force. This so-called monopoly of force is the defining feature of the police in U.S. society.[49]

According to Jerome H. Skolnick, sociologist of the police, and James J. Fyfe, former New York City police officer and now professor of criminal justice,

> the risk of physical injury is greater in many lines of industrial work than in policing, but cops are the ones to whom society accords the right to use, or to threaten

Figure 5.2
Direct Expenditure for Each of the Major Criminal Justice Functions (Police, Corrections, Judicial)

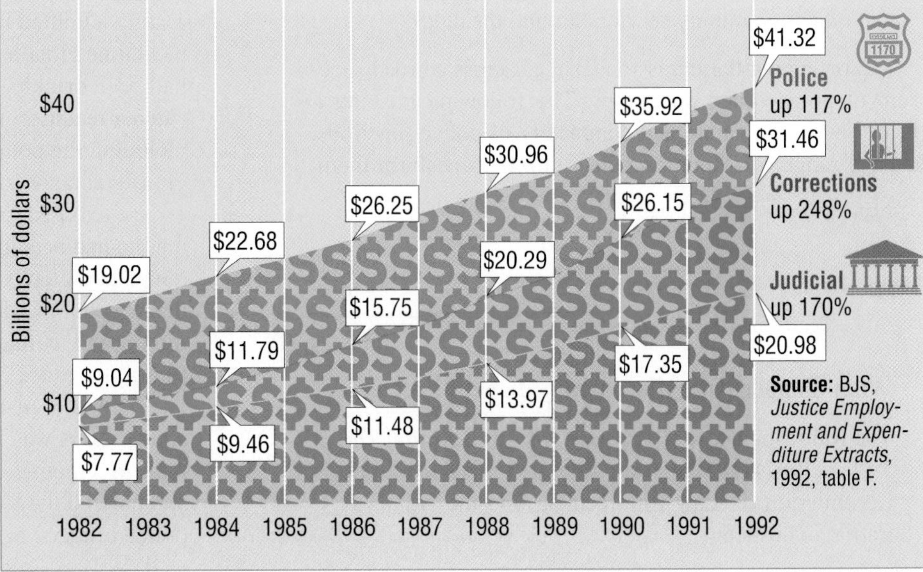

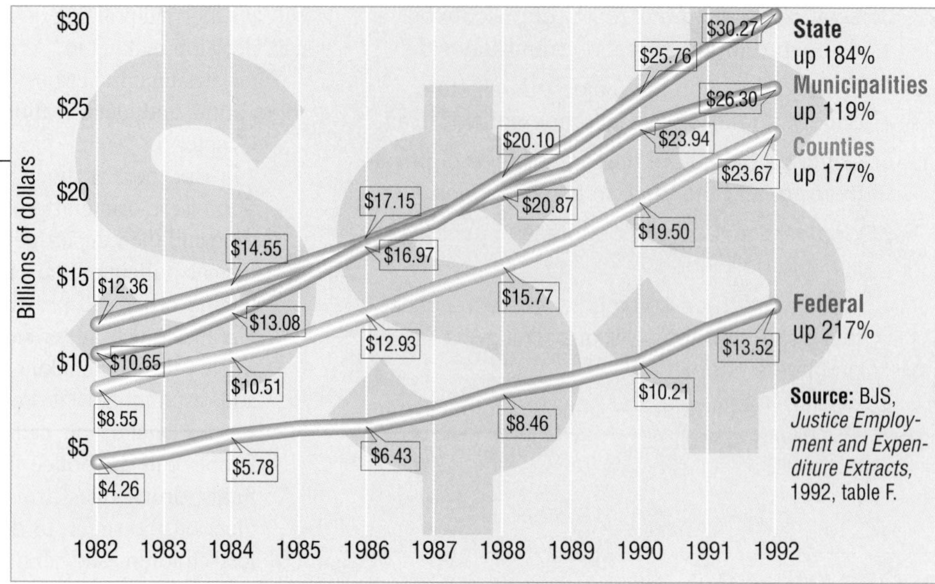

Figure 5.3
Expenditures for Criminal Justice by States, Municipalities, Counties, and the Federal Government

to use, force. This assignment and the capacity to carry it out are said to be the central feature of the role of police in society.[50]

In the United States, people place enormous demands on their local police. Society expects the police to solve most problems and to solve them *now.* This unreasonable expectation is not new. Brand Whitlock, the reform mayor of Toledo, Ohio, recognized it in 1910. He complained that when anything, however minor, "bothered" people, their first reaction is, "It's time to call the police."[51]

As we have seen in the section on the history of police, the police have three missions:

1. Crime control: enforcing criminal law.
2. Maintaining order: maintaining minimum standards of public behavior.
3. Community service: providing emergency, informational, and other community services around the clock.

Carrying out these missions ranges across a broad spectrum of policies and operations. The following box introduces you to the nature and complexity of police functions, and the range of responses police utilize to perform them.

Use *Your* Discretion

What do police do? How do they do it?

The following account of police work is based on *The Police* (1967), a Task Force Report of the President's Commission on Law Enforcement and the Administration of Justice:

After receiving routine instructions at the roll call held at the precinct station, Officers Garcia and Ranello started out for the area in which they would spend their tour of duty. The officers soon received instructions from the dispatcher to handle a fight in an alley. Upon arrival, they found a group of young men surrounded by their parents, wives, and children. One of the young men, A, had a couple of knives in his hand. While the knives were within legal limits, Officer Garcia took them (and later disposed of them in a trash can). Another of the young men, B, stood by his mother. The third, C, stood by A, from whom the knives had been taken.

The mother of B was the complainant. She claimed that C had attacked her son with a knife, and she demanded that C be arrested and jailed. C readily admitted he had been fighting with B, but he claimed that he had just tried to protect A. C had been drinking and was belligerent. He indicated a readiness to take on anyone and everyone, including the police. He kept shouting and was obviously antagonizing the officers.

A attempted to explain the situation. He stated that he had been the one originally fighting B, and that C had merely come to his aid. B concurred in this account of what had taken place, though he did not reflect much concern as the supposed victim of the attack.

A's mother-in-law interrupted at this time to claim that A was innocent; that the fight was B's fault. B's mother did not stand for this accusation and entered the fray. The confusion spread. Other police officers, in the meantime, had arrived at the

Joanne Curley is led by county sheriffs from the Luzerne County Courthouse in Wilkes Barre, Pennsylvania, July 17, 1997. Curley admitted that she slowly murdered her husband by spiking his drinks with rat poison. Most people would agree that officers should enforce the law fully in a case such as this—what other kinds of criminal acts should be immune from selective enforcement?

scene, and the number of observers had grown. Officers Garcia and Ranello decided to take the participants to the precinct station, where conditions would make it possible to conduct a more orderly inquiry.

At the station, the families and participants were separated and talked with individually. The mother of B insisted on signing a complaint against C and A, but finally relented toward A when he promised not to allow C to come to his apartment.

C was then formally arrested and charged with disorderly conduct. A and B were sent home with their wives and mothers. By charging C with disorderly conduct rather than a more serious crime, the officers observed that they were saving themselves some paperwork. They felt that their action in letting the mother sign a complaint against the "loudmouthed" C had served to pacify her. After filling out the arrest reports on C, Officers Garcia and Ranello notified the dispatcher that they were available and resumed patrolling.

Within a few minutes they were dispatched to another beat to handle a domestic situation. A young American Indian woman met them at the door. There obviously had been a fight; the place was a shambles. Furniture was broken, food was on the floor, and beer cans were scattered everywhere. The woman gave an explanation to which the police officers were very much accustomed—her husband had gotten drunk, had become angry, and had gone on the "warpath." When she told the officers that her husband had been behaving in this manner for five years, any sympathy they had for her disappeared. They explained that they were not in a position to do anything for her, since her husband was not there. They advised her to go to court to obtain either a warrant for his arrest or to arrange for the issuance of a peace bond.

On reporting back in service with the dispatcher, Garcia and Ranello were assigned a domestic problem involving a couple who had been married for twenty-seven years. The couple had only recently begun to have trouble getting along. But when the difficulty started, it was serious. The wife had been attacked by the husband a week previously and had suffered a concussion. She was now back from the hospital and wanted her husband locked up. The woman led the officers to the apartment, but the husband had, in the interval, left. They then went through the ritual of telling the wife the procedure by which she could obtain a warrant or a peace bond. They also told her to call back if she had any more trouble.

After this call, there was a lull in activity, during which the officers patrolled the southeast corner of their assigned area. They were then told to see a complainant at a designated address. The complainant, it turned out, was a landlord. One of his tenants had a child who had been bothering other tenants. The mother had been told to quiet the child down, but she apparently had not done so. In addition, the mother was behind in the rent. The landlord had attempted to serve her with an eviction notice but had not been able to find her at home. The mother was at work at a bar, and the landlord asked the officers to serve the eviction notice on her there. The officers explained that they would not be able to do so, since the bar was outside the district to which they were assigned. The landlord countered this by contending that he had been a friend of the police, and that he had helped them in the past. He also stressed that he was a taxpayer. Officer Ranello reacted by requesting the dispatcher to assign a police officer to meet the landlord at the bar and help him in serving the notice. The officers, in this manner, disposed of the incident.

Garcia and Ranello were next dispatched to investigate a noisy party. When they arrived at the scene, they found the party was going "full blast." They knocked and, when the door was answered, Officer Garcia asked for the host. He told the person who then came to the door that someone had complained, and that they would have to "hold the noise down." The host and others who were listening readily agreed. When Officer Ranello notified the dispatcher that the party had been quieted, the men were dispatched to another. The officers could not find the second party and could hear no loud noise at the address that had been given. Officer Ranello requested the apartment number from the dispatcher. Both officers then went to the apartment. When the hostess came to the door, Officer Garcia told her that someone had complained about a loud party. He told her that while the party seemed quiet enough at the moment, she should be careful because she evidently had some touchy neighbors.

Garcia and Ranello stopped for a Coke before placing themselves back in service. While they were parked, Officer Ranello spotted a "drunk" in the doorway of the office occupied by the city council member representing the area. They called for a patrol wagon. They then went over to the drunk, awakened him, and asked him some questions. He had been sleeping and eating wherever he could, having slept the previous night in a "flophouse" downtown. When the wagon arrived, the drunk was placed in it and taken to jail.

When the officers reported back in service, they were immediately assigned to a juvenile disturbance at a hot-dog stand. They did not rush to the scene, since they had been there numerous times in the past. The owner of the hot-dog stand would not force the youths to leave, letting them stand about until the whole parking area was congested. He would then call the police. Garcia and Ranello dispersed the crowd. One youth started to resist, but moved on when Officer Ranello threatened him with jail.

The officers informed the dispatcher that they had handled the problem at the hot-dog stand and then resumed patrol. They had traveled several blocks from the hot-dog stand when they observed a driver running a red light. The officers chased and pulled the vehicle over to the side of the street. The driver, it was revealed, had just returned from Somalia, and Officer Garcia felt that he deserved a break. He released him with a suggestion that he be more careful. While Officer Garcia was talking to the veteran, Officer Ranello spotted a fight between two youths. He ran over, broke it up, and talked to the combatants. He sent them on their way with a warning.

The officers requested permission from the dispatcher to take time out to eat, but he responded by sending them back to the first party that they had quieted. A great deal of damage had been done by the time they arrived. The youths had gotten drunk and loud. They had created a disturbance when the party broke up, and the manager of the building had called the police. The officers advised the manager to exercise more care in deciding on the people to whom she rented her apartments. Since the persons causing the disturbance had already gone, there was nothing else that the officers could do; they departed.

They again asked permission to take time for food, but were instead dispatched to the scene of a stabbing. They hurried to the location, which turned out to be a new public swimming pool. Three persons were present—two lifeguards and a watchman. One of the lifeguards had been knifed. The officers placed him in the police car and started off for the nearest hospital. On the way, the victim told the officers that a man had tried to go swimming in the pool after it had been closed for the night. When the lifeguard attempted to stop the intruder, he was stabbed during the scuffle. The other lifeguard called the police. At the hospital, the officers made out their reports while the victim received medical care. They later returned to the scene, but found no additional information or people who would assist in identifying the assailant. The reports were turned in for attention by the detectives.

The officers then—without asking—took their meal break, after which they reported that they had completed their work on the stabbing.

They were dispatched to a party disturbance. When they arrived, they encountered a youth walking out of the building carrying a can of beer. He was stopped and questioned about the party. Officer Garcia told him that "this is not Kentucky," and drinking on the street was not allowed. The fellow agreed to take the officer up to the party. When he turned to lead the way, Officer Ranello observed a knife in the youth's back pocket. He took the knife away. There was not much going on at the party. Those present were admonished to keep it quiet.

Back on patrol, the officers cruised for a short period. It was soon quitting time, so they headed in the direction of the precinct station. As they turned a corner, Officer Garcia saw a couple of youths drinking on the street, but rather than get involved at that time, the officers did nothing.[52]

CRITICAL THINKING

Notice how officers Garcia and Ranello move from one problem to another, dealing with each in a different way.

1. Identify the formal law enforcement duties and the informal order maintenance and service duties that the officers performed.
2. Did they use different responses for each category? Explain.
3. Do you think Garcia and Ranello responded properly to enforce the law, maintain order, and provide service? Defend your answers with specific details.

Criminal Law Enforcement

The law enforcement mission entails four duties:

1. Preventing crime.
2. Investigating crime.
3. Apprehending criminal suspects.
4. Assisting in criminal prosecution.

Laws and written police department rules require **full enforcement;** thus, law enforcement officers are formally required to enforce all criminal statutes with equal vigor. Informally, however, in their day-to-day performance, officers never make the futile—and also unwise—effort to enforce every criminal statute all of the time. As we have already seen in Chapter 3, legislatures routinely enact criminal laws, reflecting the popular attitude that "there oughta be a law" to deal with every social and moral problem, however minor. Instead, officers practice **selective enforcement:** They use their discretion, enforcing *some* laws *sometimes* against *some* people. Selective enforcement is not distributed evenly across all types of crimes. Discretion increases as crimes decrease in severity. Practically everyone agrees that the police should arrest suspected murderers, rapists, and armed robbers. Most people also agree that the police should not arrest everyone who attends a noisy party, comes out of a bar drunk, begs on the street, or fails to signal a left turn, even though these are criminal offenses in most jurisdictions. How to respond to these "technical crimes" is best left to the judgment of the officer or officers on the scene. The following box addresses some issues surrounding discretion and selective enforcement.[53]

Use *Your* Discretion

Which laws should the police enforce?

The following incidents took place in Chicago:

1. A 19-year-old youth fired three shots from the street at a woman standing in her doorway. Several neighbors witnessed the shooting. The woman asked the police not to arrest the youth.
2. A police officer witnessed an armed robbery. The victim asked him not to arrest the robber.

3. A police officer witnessed a shoplifting. The store owner asked the officer not to arrest the shoplifter.
4. An officer caught a juvenile throwing rocks through large windows. The youth agreed to pay for the damages he caused.
5. A patrol officer saw a juvenile drinking.
6. The police witnessed a man paying a prostitute for her services.
7. Anyone over 12 who rides a bicycle on the sidewalk is guilty of a misdemeanor. A patrol officer saw a 21-year-old woman riding her bicycle on the sidewalk.
8. A city ordinance makes it a crime to smoke in nonsmoking sections of restaurants. An officer saw patrons smoking at a designated nonsmoking table.
9. Gambling is a crime. A group of neighbors gathered in an apartment for a Saturday night poker game for money. A police officer, in the building on another call, saw this game in progress through an open door.
10. Spitting on the sidewalk is a petty misdemeanor. Two patrol officers saw a man spit on the sidewalk.
11. Fornication is a crime. Two patrol officers came upon a young couple having sexual intercourse in their car while parked in a city park.
12. A patrol officer caught a 21-year-old man smoking marijuana. The man had no marijuana in his possession other than what he was smoking when he was caught.
13. The police caught a cocaine user with cocaine in her possession. She was well known among big drug dealers and would make an excellent "snitch" (informant).
14. Homosexual sodomy is a crime. The police witnessed two professionals, a physician and a lawyer, engaging in homosexual sodomy.

The police arrested none of the people involved in the incidents just related, even though a state law, a city ordinance, police board rules, and general orders issued by the chief of police required the police to enforce all the laws and city ordinances.[54]

CRITICAL THINKING

1. Which of the people in the incidents related should the police have arrested? Why? Why not?
2. Who should decide whether to arrest?
3. What should be the source of authority for the decision?

Selective law enforcement does not mean that police officers can do as they please in choosing when, how, and against whom to enforce the criminal laws. The U.S. Constitution, the state constitutions and statutes, city ordinances, and department orders all curb free choice in police law enforcement (see Chapter 6). This is especially true of decision making about serious felonies. As gatekeepers of the criminal justice system, law enforcement officers feel strong informal pressure to always "open the gates" to murder, rape, aggravated assault, robbery, burglary, and major thefts. In fact, arrest is the appropriate action for serious felonies. In the less serious felonies, and in misdemeanors and violations, decision making is more discretionary and criminal proceedings are initiated less often.

Maintaining Order

The mission of **maintaining order** calls upon the police to "do something right now to settle problems." Notice three major differences between maintaining order and criminal law enforcement.

1. "Do something" calls for a wide range of discretionary decision making about problems that extend beyond arrest.
2. "Settle problems" also allows a wide range of discretionary decision making. Problems include more than crimes, and "settle" means more than initiating criminal proceedings.
3. "Right now" means to settle the problem immediately. By contrast, criminal law enforcement embraces a broader time span stretching from investigation before arrest, through arrest, and to follow-up investigation (see Chapter 6).

There are many definitions of order, but we define **disorder** as breaches of minimum standards of decent behavior on public sidewalks, in streets, and in parks that fail to comport with minimum community standards of civility. To maintain order police officers must decide how to respond to highly complex problems involving emotion-charged behavior arising out of personal relationships. This kind of decision requires individual judgment based more on experience, community standards, and personal values than on the mechanical application of rules found in manuals, ordinances, statutes, constitutions, and court decisions. Officers cannot say, "Hold everything until I check the book on this one."

Surveys show a strong consensus in all kinds of neighborhoods and across the spectrum of age, sex, race, ethnicity, and class that disorderly conduct threatens the quality of life. Only a minority of the public believes that police enforcement of minimum standards threatens the individual liberty and privacy that our constitutional democracy guarantees. Business people complain that disorderly conduct by homeless and other street people is "bad for business." Shoppers may find them annoying or fear being attacked, civil libertarians maintain that they have the right to live on the streets, and social justice experts contend that social injustice has created these groups. Business owners, shoppers, civil libertarians, and social justice experts all agree that the police should arrest street people who mug and attack pedestrians. They begin to part company, however, when the "things" to "settle" include panhandling, urinating and defecating in the street, and the mere presence of homeless people in public. In such examples, officers do not ask the legal question, Was a crime committed? They rely instead on their discretionary judgment to determine how they can maintain or restore order.

The list of the kinds of behavior that most people agree does not comport with civilized standards is long. It includes:

- Public drinking and drunkenness.
- Begging and aggressive panhandling.
- Threatening behavior and harassment.
- Obstruction of streets and public places.
- Vandalism and graffiti.
- Street prostitution.
- Public urination and defecation.
- Unlicensed vending of most kinds, including the more aggressive forms such as "squeegeeing"—washing the windshields of stopped cars and demanding money for the "service."

The varied responses of officers Garcia and Ranello described in Use Your Discretion, "What Do Police Do? How Do They Do It?" illustrate the use of discretionary judgment. Consider the following decisions Garcia and Ranello made during one work day:[55]

1. Did nothing when they saw two men drinking in the street.
2. Told a battered woman they were not in a position to do anything for her and advised her to go to court.
3. Told another battered woman how to get a warrant and peace bond against her husband and advised her to call back if she had any more trouble.
4. Requested the dispatcher to assign a police officer to help a landlord serve an eviction notice to a tenant outside the district.
5. Told some people at a noisy party to hold the noise down.
6. Told the hostess of another party she should be careful because she evidently had some touchy neighbors.
7. Told the manager whose tenants had a rowdy party at which considerable damage was done that she should be more careful about whom she rented apartments to.
8. Broke up a disturbance by teenagers near a hot-dog stand.
9. Threatened a teenager at a disturbance with jail if he did not leave.
10. Dispersed the crowd at the hot-dog stand where the disturbance occurred.
11. Took a knife from a youth at a noisy party.
12. Took some people from a fight to the station.
13. Questioned the same people at the station.
14. Arrested and charged one participant in the fight.

These 14 responses, arranged from the least to the most coercive action taken, range from doing nothing to arresting and charging an individual with a crime. In between are verbal responses (giving advice, warnings, and orders or asking questions) and physical responses (dispersing a crowd, detention, and taking property).

Use *Your* Discretion

Does disorder cause serious crime?

The controversy over quality of life crimes has generated heated debate since the early 1980s. Two prominent scholars sensed a deep public yearning for what seemed to be a lost sense of decency and order in national life, particularly as manifested in public misbehavior on the sidewalks, streets, and parks in the nation's largest cities. Professors James Q. Wilson and George L. Kelling suggested that what were labeled "petty crimes" not only upset law-abiding people, but could also lead to a rise in serious crime. The article—and the name given to the authors' theory as to a cause of crime—was entitled "Broken Windows."[56]

According to Kelling, research conducted since the article was written in 1982 has demonstrated "a direct link between disorder and crime. . . ." Wilson described the broken windows theory in 1996 more cautiously. In the foreword to a book written by Kelling and Catherine M. Coles, entitled *Fixing Broken Windows,* Wilson wrote:

> We used the image of broken windows to explain how neighborhoods might decay into disorder and even crime if no one attends faithfully to their maintenance. If a factory or office window is broken, passersby observing it will conclude that no one cares or no one is in charge. In time, a few will begin throwing rocks to break more windows. Soon all the windows will be broken, and now passersby will think that, not only is no one in charge of the building, no one is in charge of the street on which it faces. Only the young, the criminal, or the foolhardy have any business on an unprotected avenue, and so more and more citizens will abandon the street to those they assume prowl it. *Small disorders lead to larger and larger ones, and perhaps even to crime.*[57] [emphasis added]

One mission of policing is to maintain order, one example of which is controlling public drunkenness. This mission is based on the "broken windows theory," which suggests that if relatively minor offenses like vandalism, broken windows, or public drunkenness go unchecked, offenders will feel at liberty to commit more serious crimes. In this light, maintaining order is one way of curbing more serious offenses.

Professor Wesley G. Skogan, the author of some of the research on which Kelling relies, has also characterized his and others' research more cautiously than Kelling:

> Our concern with common crime is limited to whether disorder is a cause of it. . . . neighborhood levels of disorder are closely related to crime rates, to fear of crime, and the belief that serious crime is a neighborhood problem. This relationship could reflect the fact that the link between crime and disorder is a causal one, or that both are dependent on some third set of factors (such as poverty or neighborhood instability).[58]

To be fair, Skogan added that his data "support the proposition that disorder needs to be taken seriously in research on neighborhood crime, and that both directly and through crime, it plays an important role in neighborhood decline."[59]

Whatever the relationship between crime and disorder, the attention given to quality of life crimes differs significantly between national and local debate, as public opinion surveys have revealed. The national debate on crime focuses on major Index felonies—murder, rape, aggravated assault, robbery, burglary, arson, theft, and auto theft. Of course, mayors and the residents of communities worry about murder, rape, burglary, and theft. But they also care a great deal about order on their streets and in their parks and other public places. A representative sample of residents of 40 high- and low-crime neighborhoods scattered throughout the country's major cities placed public drinking, followed closely by loitering youths, at the top of their list of worries. Survey participants also listed begging (particularly aggressive panhandling), street harassment, noisy neighbors, vandalism, street prostitution, illegal vending, and, in New York City, "squeegeeing."[60]

CRITICAL THINKING

1. Identify the discrepancy between national debate and local concerns regarding serious crime and disorder.
2. What accounts for this discrepancy?
3. Should public opinion dictate how order is maintained? Explain your answer.

Policing Domestic Disturbances

Domestic disturbances are especially challenging to police discretionary judgment. One officer summed up his frustration with family disturbances this way: "I hate those [domestic disputes]. There's not a thing you can do with them." In one survey, nearly half the officers asked what they would do about a husband who beat his wife, admitted there is little they can do.[61]

Police officers also believe that intervention in domestic cases is the most dangerous part of their job. The available evidence, however, suggests that domestic cases are no more dangerous than other cases. Joel Garner and Elizabeth Clemmer used observational studies to compute the risk of death in police-citizen encounters. They found no evidence that police were killed more often in domestic disturbances than in other kinds of incidents. Mary Rose Stanford and Bonney Lee Mowry gathered data on 349 domestic disturbance calls and 534 general disturbance calls received by the Tampa, Florida, Police Department. They found that domestic disturbance calls accounted for less than 5 percent of all calls handled by the dispatch system. The danger of assault was approximately 2.6 out of 1,000 domestic disturbance calls, lower than the danger in general disturbance calls.[62]

Whatever the real danger police officers face, the perceived danger shapes their attitudes toward intervention in domestic disturbances. According to Lawrence W. Sherman:

> Whatever the truth may be, the widespread police belief that domestic work is dangerous may influence their decision to make arrests. Anticipating a higher risk of police injury from any attempt to make an arrest may make avoiding arrest seem more attractive.[63]

The Police Foundation and the Minneapolis Police Department collaborated in the most publicized experiment to determine whether mediation, separation, or arrest works best to prevent future incidents in domestic violence cases. In the years since the results of the Minneapolis study were announced in the *New York Times,* they have been published in over 300 newspapers, broadcast by three networks in prime-time documentaries, and commented on in numerous nationally syndicated columnists and editorials.[64]

Designed by Lawrence W. Sherman, the Minneapolis experiment was conducted between 1980 and 1983. Minneapolis police officers agreed to give up their discretion in domestic calls. Instead, a random system dictated whether they arrested, mediated, or separated domestic partners in minor domestic disturbances. Researchers interviewed victims they were able to contact every two weeks for six months following domestic incidents. Repeat violence was also measured by tracking all official records. Both official records (arrests and convictions) and interviews with victims demonstrated that arrested individuals were about half as likely to repeat their violence as those who were not arrested—18 percent of all offenders repeated their violence, while only 10 percent of the arrested offenders repeated theirs.[65]

The Minneapolis Domestic Violence Study changed both the law and police policy on domestic cases throughout the country, dramatically demonstrating the effect that experimental research can have on criminal justice policy. The U.S. Attorney General's Task Force on Family Violence endorsed the Minneapolis findings and recommended that state and local agencies adopt a policy of arrest in domestic violence cases. Fifteen states and the District of Columbia enacted mandatory arrest laws in misdemeanor domestic violence cases. By 1988, 90 percent of police agencies either encouraged or required arrest in minor domestic assault cases. Arrests for minor assaults increased a dramatic 70 percent between 1984 and 1989.[66]

The Minneapolis experiment was not the only reason for this major change in policy. The highly publicized case of Tracey Thurman probably also contributed to the change. She won a $2.5 million damage award in a lawsuit against the Torrington, Connecticut, Police Department. Police officers ignored months of complaints by Tracey Thurman against her husband, Charles Thurman. Responding to her final call, several officers stood by while Charles Thurman beat and kicked Tracey Thurman while holding the bloody knife he had already used to stab her in the chest, neck, and throat. Only when he approached her while medics were carrying her away on a stretcher did the police finally arrest Charles Thurman, who turned out to be a short-order cook at a cafe frequented by the police.[67]

The widespread adoption of the policy of arresting suspects in minor domestic assault cases took place in the favorable social context provided by the 1980s. That social context included an increasingly "get tough on crime" attitude, a disillusionment with rehabilitation of criminals, a heightened awareness of domestic violence, the victims' rights movement, and the vehemence of advocacy groups. James Meeker and Arnold Binder suggested that this context was more important than the Minneapolis experiment in changing police policy in domestic assault cases. They asked a regionally balanced sample of rural and urban police departments to rank eight separate influences on changes in domestic violence policy. The respondents (54 percent of the total) ranked the Minneapolis experiment last.[68]

Police officers strongly support the arrest policy in domestic violence cases, according to one survey of a Midwestern community of about 60,000 that adopted a spouse arrest policy. A survey of 115 patrol and command officers, conducted by Paul Friday, Scott Metzger, and David Walters, found that officers supported the policy because it gave them more power, even though they were uncertain of the effect of the policy. Arrest data for the two years following the first arrest showed that initial arrest had little effect on subsequent calls.[69]

Only half the victims responded to follow-up efforts to determine whether violence was repeated. The follow-up continued only for six months; researchers had difficulty contacting many of the victims, and no data exist for recurrence of violence after this period. Moreover, after the initial crackdown, Minneapolis police officers reduced compliance with the policy. University of Nebraska researchers surveyed 100 Minneapolis police officers after the new policy was adopted. Ninety-nine of the 100 said that they "should make their own decisions about problems that arise on duty," 77 officers responded that they "usually do what they think necessary even if their supervisors disagree," and 43 said that they "should use their own standards of police work even when department procedures prohibit them from doing so."[70]

Crime Control Institute criminologist Michael Buerger described one of these deliberate refusals to follow the policy of arrest:

> Two officers responded to a "heavy domestic" call, and were met in the hall by the victim. She had sustained obvious injuries; one description was that "the side of her face was like hamburger." Her assailant was still at the scene when the officers arrived. Instead of arresting the suspect, the officers yelled at the woman (some alleged that derogatory remarks were made to her), and told her not to waste their time by calling again. The officer told the male assailant to go back into the apartment, take a shower, and cool off. Then the officers left, clearing the call as GOA (Gone On Arrival), which ordinarily means that they had no contact with the offender because he was gone before the squad [car] arrived.[71]

Furthermore, according to Sherman, "What the Minneapolis experiment did *not* prove . . . was that arrest would work best in every community, or for all kinds of people." Replications of the experiment in Omaha; Charlotte, North Carolina; Milwaukee; Miami; and Colorado Springs challenge the initial conclusion drawn from Minneapolis that arrest works best. In three cities, according to Sherman, arrest "backfired"; that is, it actually increased incidents of future domestic violence. A survey of the experiments in the six cities yielded several major conclusions:

- Arrest increases domestic violence from those who have nothing to lose, especially the unemployed.
- Arrest deters domestic violence in cities with higher white and Hispanic populations.
- Arrest deters domestic violence in the short run (30 days), but escalates violence later in cities with higher proportions of unemployed black suspects.
- A small but chronic group of violent couples produces most of the domestic violence.
- Offenders in Omaha who flee the police are deterred by arrest.[72]

The debate over arrest policy in domestic violence cases is far from over. Just as the replications called the policy into question, some researchers are now challenging the replications. Joel Garner, Jeffrey Fagan, and Christopher Maxwell have concluded that these were not true replications but only studies that resembled the Minneapolis research. They concluded that "the available findings do not offer a single replication of the measures and analysis used in the Minneapolis study." For example, the Minneapolis experiment included "threats of violence and property damage as failures equivalent to actual violence. . . . None of the . . . [replications] uses these outcome criteria. . . ."[73]

Garner and his associates not only challenge whether the studies are replications, but they also criticize the characterizations of the studies by other researchers:

> Once made public, the findings from the SARP [Spousal Abuse Replication Programs] experiments have been interpreted in ways that on occasion conflict with the original authors. For instance, Sherman summarizes SARP findings in the following manner:
>
> > The best way to compare the findings across experiments is still to focus on the effects of arrest compared to nonarrest, the central policy issue for state legislatures and police agencies. The most important finding for them is that arrest increased domestic violence in Omaha, Charlotte, and Milwaukee.
>
> He also reports
>
> > There is evidence that arrest had a deterrent effect in Minneapolis, Colorado Springs, and Metro-Dade [Miami] but the cumulative evidence is somewhat mixed.
>
> Notably, these statements about an escalation effect in Omaha and Charlotte are not the conclusions of the original authors of the Omaha and Charlotte experiments. . . . This fact warrants emphasis since the Sherman interpretation has become a commonly accepted representation of the published results.[74]

Use *Your* Discretion

Is arrest the best policy for all people?

Consider the following cases drawn from a study of domestic violence:

Chuck Switzer, a white, middle-aged resident of a Minneapolis suburb and a long-term wife beater was raised in a Great Plains farmhouse, where his father's brutal physical discipline included killing Switzer's dog and sticking Switzer's fingers in an electrical socket. Switzer began to beat his wife on their wedding night, because Mrs. Switzer failed to have an orgasm. His subsequent beatings were prompted by such failures as dinner not being ready on time, children making too much noise, or other disruptions of normal routine. His wife finally sought relief from police, and Mr. Switzer was arrested. His reaction was to thank her for helping him to confront his problems, for which he went on to receive counseling. By both their accounts, the arrest broke the pattern of repetitive violence. Switzer's arrest shamed him, but his middle-class life and employment helped to reintegrate him into that world as a repentant and recovering abuser.[75]

"William Smith," a white, unemployed, 24-year-old in Milwaukee, like Chuck Switzer, was abused as a child and beat his first lover. Unlike Switzer, Smith had both a juvenile and adult arrest record, for nondomestic crimes. He also had no steady job and no home, living with women supported by Aid to Dependent Children. He beat at least three different women over a three-year period in which Milwaukee police kept records on domestic violence. After he was arrested for beating one woman, he reacted with anger and a desire to "get even." He beat her twice as often in the next six months as he had in the preceding six months. He then beat other women, with a total frequency of domestic violence that was higher than police had detected before the first arrest. Being arrested created no shame in him—only rage. It sent no message from people he cared about that his conduct was an important failure to achieve self-control. Rather, Smith lived in a world where self-control was not expected, and arrest was no different from any other challenge to his "toughness."[76]

The following theories have been offered to explain why police arrest (or fail to) in domestic cases.

Stake in conformity theory

Rutgers University sociologist Jackson Toby explained the delinquent behavior of "hoodlums" according to a theory he called the stake in conformity theory: "For those with social honor, disgrace is a powerful sanction. For a boy disapproved of already, there is less incentive to resist the temptation to do what he wants when he wants to do it." Toby applied his stake in society theory to places as well as people. According to Toby, "communities differ in the proportion of defeated people. A community with a high concentration of them has an even higher crime rate than would be expected by adding up the predispositions of its individual members." According to police expert Lawrence S. Sherman, who applied Toby's stake in society theory to domestic violence cases, "individuals with a higher stake in conformity would fear arrest more than those with a lower stake, regardless of the neighborhood they live in. Yet the disgrace of arrest is likely to be lower in neighborhoods with a lower average stake in conformity—or *higher* where, as in Minneapolis, the average stake in the community is quite high."[77]

Social control theory

According to social control theory, everyone has a natural tendency to commit crimes. Only strong bonds to conventional society keep people from committing crimes. Failure to develop these strong bonds at an early age causes crime, according to this theory. In other words, the greater their bonds to conventional society, the greater people's resistance to committing crimes. People with strong ties to or involvement in family, church, school, and job demonstrate bonding that inhibits their desire to commit crimes. Sherman noted a

> conflict between the implications of the [social control] theory and standard police and public conceptions of justice. *Those with the most conventional lifestyles would be most deterred by arrest; those with the least attachment to convention would be least deterred or worse.* [Emphasis added] . . . If the control theory of crime is correct, and if it interacts with sanctions so that more socially bonded people are more deterrable, then the unfairness [of arrest based on deterrability] will seem great indeed. Those who would be *most* highly recommended for arrest would be those most involved with the church, family, community organizations, and the labor force. Those *least* likely to be recommended for arrest would be the marginal characters of low "moral worth" that police love to punish: the unemployed, unmarried, nonchurchgoing riffraff.[78]

Shame theory

The Australian sociologist John Braithwaite devised a theory that puts shame at the center of causing and preventing crime. Braithwaite argues that communitarian societies such as Japan have low crime rates because of the powerful influence of shaming in the prevention of socially unacceptable behavior. Western societies, on the other hand, have separated criminal punishment from public shaming. He argues that this separation has contributed to the increase of crime in Western societies. Kirk R. Williams and Richard Hawkins conducted a survey of predominantly white, employed males in a national sample that seems to lend support to the theory as an explanation for domestic violence. Their data showed that humiliation was the most highly rated consequence of arrest for wife assault, *not* losing jobs or going to jail. In other words, arrest deters wife beating because of the fear of shame, not the fear of going to jail.[79]

Too much shame, according to Braithwaite, will have a similar effect to not enough shame—it can cause crime. Lawrence S. Sherman has applied Braithwaite's theory and Williams's and Hawkins's survey results to domestic violence. According to Sherman,

> The dilemma that shaming theory raises is that the effectiveness of legal sanctions may depend on a foundation of informal social control. If formal sanctions can only deter socially interdependent people, what can be done about people who are not well bonded to others? If exercise can only strengthen a well-fed body, more exercise would be a foolish prescription for a starving body. Yet that may be just what punishment does to people who are not enmeshed in a stable social network committed to conventional social institutions. More legal sanctions may simply push them beyond Braithwaite's tipping point of "too much" stigma, causing them to commit more crime than they would if left unpunished. Yet these are usually the same people who commit the most crimes and most "deserve" punishment as a matter of justice or fairness.[80]

Ghetto poverty theory

The Harvard sociologist Lee Rainwater, in his classic study of the Pruitt-Igoe housing project in St. Louis, concluded that shame was used too much. According to Rainwater,

> Children are shamed for not doing the right thing, but they are also shamed by parents and peers for not being tough enough to cope with their problems. . . . As the child grows up he increasingly acquires an awareness that nothing he can do will protect him from danger or attack, whether from his parents for failure to meet their standards, or from his caretakers (e.g., school teachers and police) who always seem to want something from him other than what he is doing.[81]

Applying Rainwater's findings to domestic violence, Sherman suggests that this much shame is "well past the hope of using shame to mold behavior to comply with social norms." Pride becomes the adaptive strategy, which in the case of arrest for domestic assault can lead to more, not less, violence. "If someone is shamed when a lover or spouse has him arrested, the pride response may require retaliation against that lover, or more violence against other lovers in the future." Therefore, arrest of a person overdosed on shame may create a strategy of "*defiance* for avoiding the shame of arrest by a proudly assertive posture of 'knowing no shame.'"[82]

CRITICAL THINKING

1. Considering the theories outlined above, is arrest the best policy in domestic violence cases?
2. Assume you are a police administrator: Would you adopt a policy of arresting all people where there is probable cause to believe they had committed a minor assault? Or would you adopt a policy of arresting respectable, employed people but not those who are unemployed and not respectable? Or would you leave arrest to the discretion of individual police officers, after explaining to them the results of the research on the theories outlined above? Explain your decision.

Community Service

Community service consists of providing both information and physical assistance to people in need. People routinely call the police for information: Where is the football stadium? How do I find the nearest hospital? Why are the sirens

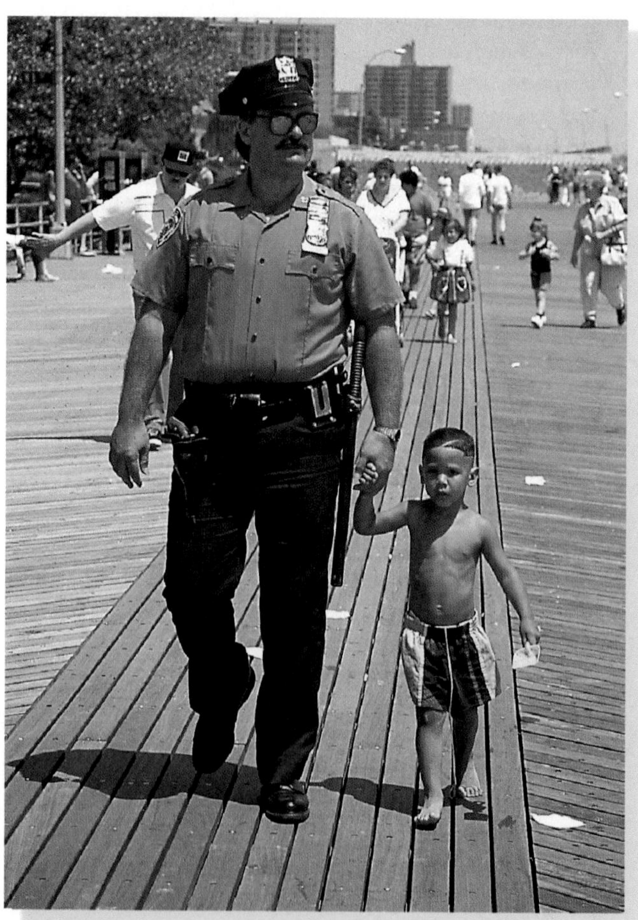

Foot patrol officers perform an often overlooked police service: helping people.

blaring? They also call on the police to help them, for example, find lost children and pets or rescue a drowning person. The police have cared for the "down and out," particularly people who were intoxicated, poor, and mentally ill, throughout police history.[83]

In settling problems, the police do not sort criminal law enforcement, maintaining order, and community service into neat categories. They draw on whatever means they believe are appropriate to the time and circumstances. In both public drunkenness and cases involving the mentally ill, the police combine community service with peacekeeping and criminal law enforcement.[84]

Policing Public Drunkenness

Until the 1920s, jails offered temporary lodging for intoxicated, destitute, and roaming mentally ill people that police officers brought to them. This service died out after the 1920s, and some jurisdictions decriminalized public drunkenness. Reformers hoped that decriminalization would shift the responsibility for public drunkenness to public service agencies, freeing the police to devote time to "real crimes." Decriminalization did not, however, produce the hoped-for results. Since the police cannot allow intoxicated individuals to lie in the street, instead of taking them to jail the police now transport such persons to detoxification centers for sobering up and treatment. Cumbersome entry procedures mean that commitment for treatment may take more time than an arrest.[85]

Patrol officers have conflicting attitudes toward intoxicated individuals. Some act with considerable compassion, making arrests to protect them from muggers or from freezing on winter nights. Other officers harass intoxicated people, particularly if they are annoying "respectable citizens," driving them away from businesses or middle-class shoppers. The varied police response to public drunkenness demonstrates how the police can use the legal power to arrest as a tool to perform community service functions. They take drunk people to jail both to protect them and to keep the streets clear and orderly.

Policing the Mentally Ill

Most states have statutes authorizing the police to manage mentally ill persons, even when they have not broken the law. Two alternative procedures call this service into operation. One results from court orders directing the police to find particular mentally ill individuals and take them to a hospital. The other grants the police emergency power to initiate steps to confine a person who officers believe is "mentally ill and because of his illness is likely to injure himself or others if not immediately hospitalized."[86]

The police spend as much time serving the mentally ill as arresting major felony suspects. Mental health reforms favoring community treatment place a heavy burden on the police. Community treatment often means putting mentally ill people "on the streets," where police must deal with problems arising from their outpatient status. The police exercise broad discretion in their response to emergency mental health service. Their responses range, at one extreme, from taking people to psychiatric hospitals under civil (noncriminal) statutes or arresting them for some criminal offense, to neither arresting nor committing them at the other extreme. Although statutes strictly govern both arrest and emergency apprehension for mental illness, the law does not control the initial decision not to arrest or apprehend.[87]

Sometimes the police do not select a caretaker; they administer "psychiatric first aid" instead. For example, one agitated mentally ill woman told officers that neighbors were pursuing her, attempting to attack her with an imaginary weapon. Her highly vocal distress not only disturbed her, but also had potential for causing considerable turmoil in the neighborhood. Police listened patiently to her story, never questioning its veracity. After an hour spent searching her house for the evidence they knew they would never find, they kindly advised her how to call the police if she had any more trouble and further convinced her not to question the suspected neighbors. She was calm and satisfied when they left. They had "handled the problem" and restored peace to the area.[88]

Police refer some people to emergency psychiatric service. According to a survey of referrals to such service in the Cincinnati Hospital, police referrals account for 22 percent of the total. People referred by police were among the most likely to be diagnosed by professionals as a danger to themselves or others. More than half required restraints, and one-quarter required medication; half of those requiring medication were diagnosed as psychotic. Therapists, according to the survey, believed that police make more appropriate referrals than others who refer persons to psychiatric emergency service.[89]

Overlap of Missions

Police functions do not fall easily into separate compartments. As demonstrated by problems of public drunkenness, mental outpatients, and domestic disputes, police functions overlap and blend to a considerable degree. Perhaps more important, they reinforce each other. As James Q. Wilson observes:

> Though the law enforcement, order maintenance, and service provision aspects can be analytically distinguished, concretely they are thoroughly intermixed. Even in a routine law enforcement situation (for example, arresting a fleeing purse snatcher), how the officer deals with the victim and the onlookers at the scene is often as important as how he handles the suspect. The victim and onlookers, after all, are potential witnesses who have to testify in court; assuring their cooperation is as necessary as catching the person against whom

> they will testify. The argument about whether "cops" should be turned into "social workers" is a false one, for it implies that society can exercise some meaningful choice over the role the officer should play. Except at the margin, it cannot.[90]

Others have suggested that the crime-fighter image lends effectiveness to the peacekeeping and community service work. For example, police effectiveness depends on respect for police authority, in particular the ultimate police authority to use force. A wife beater less willingly obeys an unpleasant order given by a service-oriented police officer than one issued by a crime fighter who shows a willingness to arrest and put him in jail. So, too, individuals "needing help" listen more to a crime fighter's orders than to those of a community service agent.[91]

According to police expert Herman Goldstein:

> We've learned that what the police do in their "order maintenance" function may have a very important bearing on their capacity to deal with crime; that citizen attitudes and cooperation are heavily influenced by the effectiveness of the police in providing the wide range of services that the public has come to expect from them.[92]

Possible Shifts in Mission Priorities

Some evidence suggests that the myth of the crime-fighting mission may be losing its supremacy. Professor James Q. Wilson notes that at least some police administrators are aware of, and willing to talk openly about, the precedence of maintaining order and providing services over law enforcement. A study based on observing three California departments reports that patrol officers willingly, even eagerly, nurture their community service functions, from which they derive considerable satisfaction. Some departments issue clear policy statements regarding the importance of maintaining order and providing service.[93]

Twenty years ago, police expert George Kelling offered the following excellent summary of the complex police function, a summary that still holds true and probably will continue to well into the twenty-first century:

> Although the crime-related functions of the police were historically important and continue to be so, it is insufficient to define the police either predominantly or exclusively on the basis of those functions. Their functions are far broader, and consist of peace-keeping and management functions essential to urban life. Taking this point of view the police are not just a part of the criminal justice system, but also are a key element of urban government. They are the primary contact citizens have with government. . . . police services constitute more than 30% of the cost of city government. The police are available 24 hours a day. They resolve conflicts between families, groups, interests and individuals. All police rhetoric about crime fighting aside, it is clear, from observing the needs of citizens and what the police actually do, that the order and service functions are the functional heart of policing.[94]

Not everyone agrees that the police should perform such a wide variety of services. Instead, many criminal justice professionals, the public, and politicians call for the police to narrow their focus to concentrate on serious crime. Thirty years ago Professors Gordon Hawkins and Norval Morris wrote what still holds true to a large degree today:

> the immense range of police obligations and duties must be drastically reduced. A variety of means are suggested here [transferring traffic control, most misdemeanors, and minor violations to other agencies] for both diminishing the range of their responsibilities and enabling the more effective use of their resources in the prevention and control of serious crime [murder, rape, robbery, and burglary in particular].[95]

Use *Your* Discretion

How much time do officers spend enforcing criminal laws?

Empirical research to determine exactly how much time police officers spend on criminal law enforcement gives mixed results. Most studies completed between the late 1960s and the mid 1980s showed that the police spend less than 25 percent of their time enforcing the criminal law. However, one study conducted in 1991 cast doubt on that percentage. Police scholars Carl B. Klockars and Stephen D. Mastrofski studied how Wilmington, Delaware, police officers spend their time. Merely replicating earlier studies, they found about the same distribution of effort among law enforcement, order maintenance, and public service. However, when they removed officer free time (the time officers spend on patrol between calls) and added police-initiated actions, they concluded that the police spend almost half their time fighting crime. Still, this falls far short of the crime-fighting image so prominently displayed on television and in the newspapers, and encouraged in the public mind.[96]

CRITICAL THINKING

1. What accounts for the difference between the findings of most studies and those of the Klockars and Mastrofski study?
2. Is the difference significant? Explain your answer.

Knowledge and Understanding CHECK

1. Identify and describe the three major police missions.
2. On which mission do police spend most of their time?
3. List the four aspects of the law enforcement mission.
4. Contrast formal and informal criminal justice as they apply to the requirements of criminal law enforcement.
5. Describe the three major differences between criminal law enforcement and maintaining order.
6. What do public opinion surveys reveal about the importance of enforcing minimum standards of behavior in public?
7. List the kinds of behavior that most people believe do not comport with minimum standards.
8. What dangers do domestic violence cases pose for the police?
9. Describe the methods and results of the Minneapolis Domestic Violence Study.
10. Summarize the methods and results of research since the Minneapolis experiment.
11. List the major conclusions of a survey of domestic violence in six cities.
12. Explain the conflicting attitudes of police toward the policing of public drunkenness.
13. What two procedures call the policing of the mentally ill into action?
14. Describe the various ways that the police respond to the mentally ill.
15. Explain why police actions do not fall neatly into one of the three police missions.
16. Summarize George Kelling's summary of the complexity of police functions.

What Are the Police? Consideration

The definitions of police at the beginning of the chapter were written by students in an introductory police course. After reading the chapter:

1. Which definition do you think is correct?
2. Have you changed your answer after reading this chapter?
3. Exactly how has your definition of the police mission and role changed?

CHAPTER CAPSULE

- Policing has developed from a medieval neighborhood public duty to a government function operating at all governmental levels.
- Police have performed three missions throughout history: law enforcement, maintaining order, and providing public services.
- There were no policewomen before 1900. Since then there have been relatively few women police officers, most of whom have been allowed to play only minor roles in policing.
- Police spend most of their time maintaining order and providing public service.

KEY TERMS

proactive policing
reactive policing
reform model of policing
quasi-military organizations
watchman style of policing
legalistic style of policing
service style of policing
full enforcement
selective enforcement
maintaining order
disorder
community service

INTERNET RESEARCH EXERCISES

Exercise: Using the Internet or InfoTrac College Edition, search for information on police departments. How are police departments organized? What are their stated missions? What differences do you see between local police departments and U.S. State police departments? Bonus question: What differences do you see between police departments in the United States and police departments in other countries?

Suggested sites: There are numerous sites on the Internet with information about local and state police departments, as well as police departments in other countries. Using a search engine like http://www.yahoo.com, search for sites by using the key words "police departments." Sample sites—

- Duluth, Georgia Police Department: http://www.duluthpd.com/
- Illinois State Police: http://www.state.il.us/isp/isphpage.htm
- Royal Canadian Mounted Police: http://www.rcmpgrc.gc.ca/html/rcmp2.htm

InfoTrac College Edition: Run a subject search on "police departments"

NOTES

1. Carl B. Klockars, *The Idea of Police* (Beverly Hills: Sage Publications, 1986), 7–8.
2. Patrick B. Adamson, "Some Comments on the Origin of the Police," *Police Studies* 14 (1991): 1–2.
3. This section rests on my own research into English law enforcement, some of which appears in Joel Samaha, *Law and Order in Historical Perspective* (New York: Academic Press, 1974); David H. Bayley, "Police: History," in *Encyclopedia of Crime and Justice,* Sanford H. Kadish, ed., Vol. 3 (New York: Free Press, 1983), 1120–25; Thomas A. Critchley, *A History of Police in England and Wales, 900–1966* (London: Constable, 1967); Roger Lane, *Policing the City* (New York: Atheneum, 1975); Sidney L. Harring, *Policing a Class Society: The Experience of American Cities, 1865–1915* (New Brunswick, N.J.: Rutgers University Press, 1983); Robert Fogelson, *Big-City Police* (Cambridge, Mass.: Harvard University Press, 1977); James F. Richardson, *The New York Police: Colonial Times to 1901* (New York: Oxford University Press, 1970); Eric Monkkonen, *Police in Urban America, 1860–1920* (Cambridge: Cambridge University Press, 1981); Samuel Walker, *A Critical History of Police Reform: The Emergence of Professionalism* (Lexington, Mass.: D.C. Heath and Company, 1977); Malcolm K. Sparrow, Mark H. Moore, and David M. Kennedy, *Beyond 911: A New Era for Policing* (New York, Basic Books, 1995), Chapters 1–2.
4. Evelyn Parks, "From Constabulary to Police Society," in *Criminal Law in Action,* 2d ed., William Chambliss, ed. (New York: Macmillan, 1984), 209–22; Roger Lane, "Urban Crime and Police in Nineteenth-Century America," in *Crime and Justice: An Annual Review of Research,* Norval Morris and Michael Tonry, eds., Vol. 2

(Chicago: University of Chicago Press, 1980), 1–45; Mark H. Moore and George L. Kelling, "Learning from Police History," *The Public Interest* (Spring 1983): 51.
5. Thomas Critchley, *The Conquest of Violence: Order and Liberty in England* (London: Constable and Company, 1970), 69.
6. David Taylor, *The New Police in Nineteenth-Century England* (Manchester, England: Manchester University Press, 1997).
7. Lane, *Policing the City,* is an excellent history of the creation and development of the Boston police.
8. *Beyond 911,* 33–34.
9. Ibid., 34.
10. Ibid., 34–35.
11. Richard A. Staufenberger, *Progress in Policing: Essays on Change* (Cambridge, Mass.: Ballinger Publishing Company, 1980), 8-9; Janis Appier, *Policing Women* (Philadelphia: Temple University Press, 1998), 9.
12. *Beyond 911,* 37–38.
13. Ibid., 38–40.
14. Ibid., 41.
15. Ibid., 44–50.
16. Ibid., 44.
17. We are deluged with good writing about the 1960s. Two excellent places to start are the general summary of the political tensions and turmoil of the period in Allen J. Matusow's, *The Unraveling of America: A History of Liberalism in the 1960s* (New York: Harper & Row, 1984), and the thorough examination of the liberal and conservative criminal justice response in Thomas E. Cronin et al., *U.S. vs. Crime in the Streets* (Bloomington: Indiana University Press, 1981).
18. Crime Commission Report, *The Police* (Washington, D.C.: Government Printing Office, 1967); Staufenberger, "The Role of the Police," in *Progress in Policing,* 13–18.
19. Samuel Walker, *The Police in America,* 2d ed. (New York: McGraw-Hill, 1992), 27–28.
20. Malcolm M. Feeley and Austin D. Sarat, *The Policy Dilemma: Federal Crime Policy and Enforcement,* 1968–1978 (Minneapolis: University of Minnesota Press, 1980); Staufenberger, *Progress in Policing.*
21. Ibid.
22. Janis Appier, *Policing Women* (Philadelphia: Temple University Press, 1998), 2.
23. Ibid.
24. Ibid.
25. Ibid., 3.
26. Ibid.
27. Ibid.
28. Dorothy Moses Schulz, *From Social Worker to Crimefighter* (Westport, Conn.: Praeger, 1995) 80–81.
29. Ibid., 98–99.
30. Ibid.
31. Ibid., 5.
32. Ibid.
33. Ibid., 5–6.
34. "Police Academy Adapts to Changing New York," *New York Times,* 6 February 1987.
35. Jerome H. Skolnick and David H. Bayley, *The New Blue Line* (New York: Free Press, 1986), 125.
36. Skolnick and Fyfe, *Above the Law,* 114.
37. FBI, *Crime in the United States, 1996* (Washington, D.C.: Federal Bureau of Investigation, September 1997).
38. BJS, *Report to the Nation on Crime and Justice,* 2d ed. (Washington, D.C.: Bureau of Justice Statistics, 1988), 66.
39. Ibid.
40. Ibid.
41. Ralph Blumenthal, *New York Times,* 22 August 1989; "Security Guards Are Hired Increasingly to Fight Crime on the Streets," *Wall Street Journal,* 22 March 1994.
42. William C. Cunningham, John J. Strauchs, and Clifford W. Van Meter, *Private Security: Patterns and Trends* (Washington, D.C.: National Institute of Justice, 1991).
43. Albert Reiss, Jr., *Public Employment of Private Police* (Washington, D.C.: Bureau of Justice Statistics, 1988).
44. Brae Canlen, "A Golden State of Siege." *Newsday,* July 26, 1998.
45. Kenneth Tunnel and Larry K. Gaines, "Political Pressures and Influences on Police Executives: A Descriptive Analysis," *American Journal of Police* 11 (1992): 10.
46. Wilson, *Varieties of Police Behavior.*
47. Robert H. Langworthy, "Organizational Structure," in *What Works in Policing,* Gary W. Cordner and Donna C. Hale, eds. (Cincinnati: Anderson Publishing, 1992), 103.
48. Peter K. Manning, "The Police: Mandate, Strategies, and Appearances," reprinted in Victor E. Kappeler, *The Police and Society: Touchstone Readings* (Prospect Heights, Ill.: Waveland Press, Inc., 1995), 103.
49. Egon Bittner, *The Functions of the Police in Modern Society* (1970), 36-47; James Q. Wilson, *Varieties of Police Behavior* (Cambridge, Mass.: Delgeschlager, Gunn and Hain: Harvard University Press, 1968), 4-5.
50. Jerome H. Skolnick and James J. Fyfe, *Above the Law: Police and the Excessive Use of Force* (New York: Free Press, 1993), 94.
51. Brand Whitlock, *Forty Years of It* (New York: D. Appleton and Company, 1914), 239.
52. Adapted from the President's Commission on Law Enforcement and the Administration of Justice, Task Force Report: *The Police* (Washington, D.C.: U.S. Government Printing Office, 1967), 15–16.
53. Goldstein, *Policing a Free Society,* chapters 3 and 4.
54. Most of these examples were taken from Kenneth Culp Davis, *Police Discretion* (St. Paul: West Publishing Company, 1975), 3–7.
55. Wesley G. Skogan, *Disorder and Decline* (New York: Free Press, 1990), Chapter 2.
56. James Q. Wilson and George L. Kelling, "Broken Windows," Atlantic Monthly, March 1982.
57. James Q. Wilson, "Foreword," George L. Kelling and Catherine M. Coles, *Fixing Broken Windows* (New York: Free Press, 1996), xiv.
58. Wesley G. Skogan, *Disorder and Decline* (New York: Free Press, 1990), 10.
59. Ibid., 75.
60. Ibid., chapter 2.
61. Donald Black, *The Manners and Customs of the Police* (New York: Academic Press, 1980), 146; Brown, *Working the Street,* 289.
62. Joel Garner and Elizabeth Clemmer, *Danger to Police in Domestic Disturbances—A New Look* (Washington, D.C.: Bureau of Justice Statistics, November 1986); Mary Rose Stanford and Bonney Lee Mowry, "Domestic Disturbance Danger Rate," *Journal of Police Science and Administration* 17 (1990): 244–49.
63. Lawrence W. Sherman, *Policing Domestic Violence: Experiments and Dilemmas* (New York: Free Press, 1992), 31.
64. Joel Garner, Jeffrey Fagan, and Christopher Maxwell, "Published Findings from the Spouse Assault Replication Program: A Critical Review," *Journal of Quantitative Criminology* 11 (1995): 4.
65. Vera Institute of Justice, *Felony Arrests* (New York: Longman, 1981); BJS, *Intimate Victims: A Study of Violence Among Friends*

and Relatives (Washington, D.C.: Bureau of Justice Statistics, January 1980); Walker, *The Police in America,* 130.
66. Lawrence W. Sherman and Richard A. Berk, *The Minneapolis Domestic Violence Experiment* (Washington, D.C.: The Police Foundation, 1984); "The Specific Effects of Arrest for Domestic Assault," *American Sociological Review* 50 (1985): 262–63; Lawrence S. Sherman and Ellen G. Cohn, "The Impact of Research on Legal Policy: The Minneapolis Violence Experiment," *Law and Society Review* 23 (1989): 117–44; Police Report on Domestic Violence: A National Survey (Washington, D.C.: Crime Control Institute, 1986); Sherman, *Policing Domestic Violence,* 1–2, 14, 104.
67. *Thurman v. City of Torrington,* 595 F. Supp. 1521 (D. Conn. 1984).
68. James Meeker and Arnold Binder, "Reforms as Experiments: The Impact of the 'Minneapolis Experiment' on Police Policy," *Journal of Police Science and Administration* 17 (1990): 147–53.
69. Paul C. Friday, Scott Metzger, and David Walters, "Policing Domestic Violence: Perceptions, Experience, and Reality," *Criminal Justice Review* 16 (1991): 198–213.
70. Michael Steinman, "Anticipating Rank and File Police Reactions to Arrest Policies Regarding Spouse Abuse," *Criminal Justice Research Bulletin* 4 (1988): 1–5, as summarized in Sherman, *Policing Domestic Violence,* 113.
71. Michael E. Buerger, ed., *The Crime Prevention Casebook: Securing High Crime Locations* (Washington, D.C.: Crime Control Institute, 1992), 231.
72. Sherman, *Policing Domestic Violence,* 2–5.
73. Garner et al., "Published Findings from the Spouse Assault Replication Program," 9, 24–25.
74. Ibid., 7.
75. Sherman, *Policing Domestic Violence,* 162.
76. Ibid., 163.
77. Ibid., 159–60.
78. Ibid., 161.
79. Kirk R. Williams and Richard Hawkins, "Perceptual Research on General Deterrence: A Critical Review," *Law and Society Review* 20 (1986): 545–72.
80. Sherman, *Policing Domestic Violence,* 161–63.
81. Lee Rainwater, *Behind Ghetto Walls: Black Families in a Federal Slum* (Chicago: Aldine Publishing Co., 1970), 229, as quoted by Sherman, *Policing Domestic Violence,* 164.
82. Sherman, *Policing Domestic Violence,* 164–65, 170.
83. Donald J. Black, *The Manners and Customs of the Police* (New York: Academic Press, 1980), 29–32.
84. Ibid.
85. Raymond Nimmer, *Two Million Unnecessary Arrests: Removing a Social Service Concern from the Criminal Justice System* (Chicago: American Bar Foundation, 1971); Edwin M. Schur and Hugo Adam Bedau, *Victimless Crimes: Two Sides of a Controversy* (Englewood Cliffs, N.J.: Prentice-Hall, 1974); Charles W. Weis, *Diversion of the Public Inebriate from the Criminal Justice System* (Washington, D.C.: National Institute of Law Enforcement and Criminal Justice, 1973).
86. Egon Bittner, "Police Discretion in Emergency Apprehension of Mentally Ill Persons," *Social Problems* 14 (1967): 279.
87. Herman Goldstein, "Improving Policing: A Problem-Oriented Approach," *Crime and Delinquency* (April 1979): 254.
88. Bittner, "Police Discretion," 286, 288.
89. Gary N. Sales, "A Comparison of Referrals by Police and Other Sources to a Psychiatric Emergency Service," *Hospital and Community Psychiatry* 42 (1991): 950–51.
90. James Q. Wilson, *Thinking About Crime,* rev. ed. (New York: Basic Books, 1983), 111–12.
91. Elaine Cumming et al., "Policeman as Philosopher, Guide and Friend," *Social Problems* 12 (1965): 285.
92. William O. Douglas Institute, *The Future of Policing* (Seattle: William O. Douglas Institute, 1984), 11.
93. Wilson, *Varieties of Police Behavior,* ix–x; Brown, *Working the Street,* 236.
94. The Police Foundation, *The Newark Foot Patrol Experiment* (Washington, D.C. The Police Foundation, 1981), 112.
95. Norval Morris and Gordon Hawkins, *The Honest Politician's Guide to Crime Control* (Chicago: University of Chicago Press, 1967), 9.
96. Egon Bittner, "Florence Nightingale in Pursuit of Willie Sutton: A Theory of the Police," *The Potential for Reform in Criminal Justice,* Herbert Jacob, ed. (Beverly Hills: Sage Publications, 1974), 27–31; John A. Webster, "Police Task and Time Study," *The Journal of Criminal Law, Criminology, and Police Science* 61 (1970): 94–100; Black, *Manners and Customs of the Police;* Eric J. Scott, *Calls for Service: Citizen Demand and Initial Police Response* (Washington, D.C.: National Institute of Justice, July 1981); Jack R. Greene and Carl B. Klockars, "What Do Police Do?" in Carl B. Klockars and Stephen D. Mastrofski, eds., *Thinking About Police,* 2d ed. (New York: McGraw-Hill, 1991), 281.

CHAPTER 6

Policing Strategies

CHAPTER OUTLINE

Is Police Investigation Worth the Effort?

Several studies underscore the crucial role of private individuals in effective criminal law enforcement. Information provided by private individuals to the police leads to the solution of far more crimes and to the apprehension of many more perpetrators than elaborate police detective work. The awareness of private individuals and their prompt, complete, and accurate reports to the police–not magical police genius and super weapons–are instrumental in apprehending and convicting suspects.

According to police experts Jerome H. Skolnick and David H. Bayley:

> Crimes are not solved–in the sense of offenders arrested and prosecuted–through criminal investigations conducted by police departments. Generally, crimes are solved because offenders are immediately apprehended or someone identifies them specifically–a name, an address, a license plate number. If neither of these things happens, the studies show, the chances that any crime will be solved fall to less than one in ten. Despite what television has led us to think, detectives do not work from clues to criminals; they work from known suspects to corroborating evidence. Detectives are important for the prosecution of identified perpetrators and not for finding unknown offenders.[1]

INTRODUCTION

All organizations adopt strategies (plans or methods) to accomplish their missions. As organizations, police departments resemble other organizations. The two main strategies of modern policing are visible patrol and criminal investigation (Table 6.1).

From at least the sixteenth century, English and American police have relied on both proactive and reactive strategies (Chapter 4). All modern police operations derive from three ancient strategies: walling, wariness, and watching. **Walling** consisted of building walls surrounding entire towns to control entry. Today, locks, barred windows, alarms, fences, and other individual security devices have replaced city walls. However, in some places, walling in the old sense seems to have returned. Whitley Heights in Los Angeles is where famous movie stars like Marlene Dietrich, Rudolph Valentino, and Judy Garland once lived. Today, just two blocks away is the high-crime Hollywood Boulevard. In 1992, residents of Whitley Heights each contributed $3,000 to erect electronic gates to the streets leading into the neighborhood. "There have been rapes, robberies, muggings, even murders. We just feel like we're under siege." Opposing this modern walling of Whitley Heights is long-time resident Jon Jay who argues, "Los Angeles could become a gated city."[2]

Table 6.1
Distribution of Police Resources

STRATEGY	PERCENT
Patrol	65
Criminal investigation	15
Traffic	9
Administration	8
Crime prevention	<1

Source: David H. Bayley, *What Works in Policing?* (New York: Oxford University Press, 1998), 71.

Until the 1800s, **wariness** took the form of curfews enforced to keep people at home and out of trouble and to protect strangers from becoming the object of unwarranted suspicion. Over time, wariness has come to mean staying home at night, exercising care around strangers, and avoiding "dangerous" places. Walling and wariness are mainly individual and private responsibilities, although police departments and private security forces increasingly support these private efforts.

Historically, **watching** was a joint effort between civilians and police officers. Residents spent most of their time at or near home; hence, they were more likely to notice suspicious people and circumstances. With the advent of the automobile, two-income families, single-adult households, and heavily populated cities and suburbs, however, residents spend less time at home and know few, if any, neighbors. They do not know who "belongs" in the neighborhood and who does not.[3]

Beginning in the early 1800s, two strategies dominated policing: preventive patrol and criminal investigation. Uniformed police officers patrolled the streets to prevent and interrupt crime and apprehend suspects. Whatever crimes that uniformed officers did not prevent from occurring in the first

Figure 6.1
Calls for Service

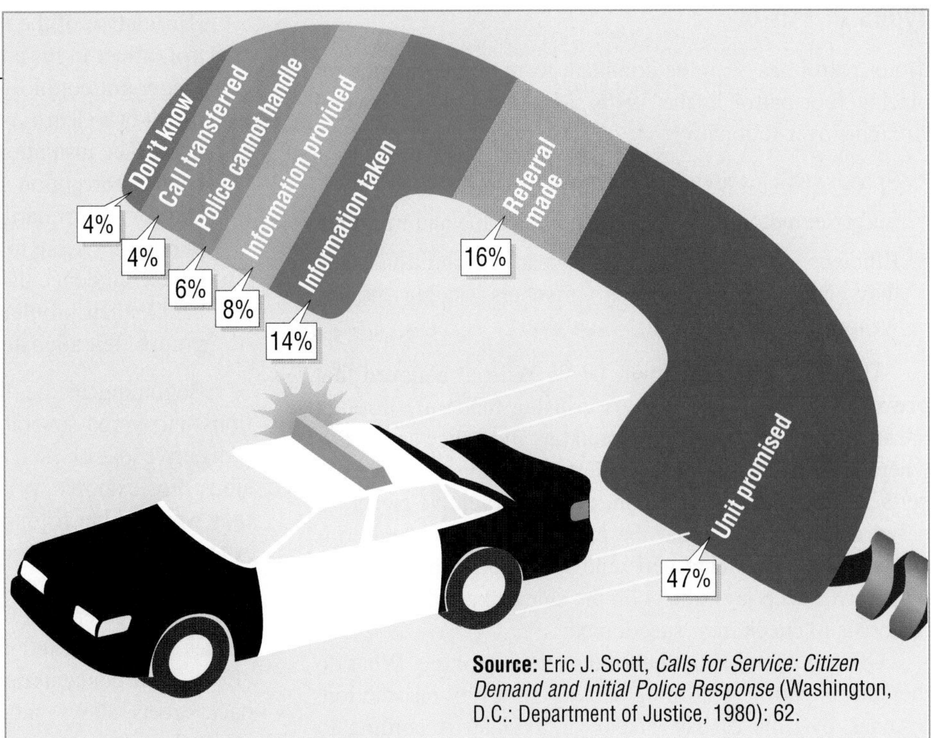

Source: Eric J. Scott, *Calls for Service: Citizen Demand and Initial Police Response* (Washington, D.C.: Department of Justice, 1980): 62.

place, detectives followed up by questioning victims, witnesses, and suspects. The police applied preventive patrol and follow-up investigation to all problems, whatever their nature. Research since the 1960s has demonstrated the limits of both traditional patrol and follow-up investigation in controlling crime.[4]

Limits demonstrated by research, growing public frustration and anger over illegal drugs and violence, fear of crime, and impatient demands to "do something" to control crime led to insistence that the police adopt more aggressive proactive strategies to "attack" crime. The police responded with various crime-attack strategies, including aggressive field investigation, decoys, undercover operations, roadblocks, drug raids, and saturation patrol. Crime-attack strategies raise empirical questions regarding their effectiveness. They also raise ethical questions about what kind of policing is appropriate to a constitutional democracy that values privacy and liberty. Despite such questions, crime-attack strategies are major police strategies in the late twentieth century.

PATROL: THE BACKBONE OF POLICING

The medieval word *patrol* meant "to walk or paddle in mud or dirty water." Today, patrol officers move through the streets, sometimes on foot, but usually in vehicles. Patrol cars, aptly named "prowlers," either move slowly (prowling) in order to prevent crime, or speed through the streets, sirens screaming and red lights flashing, in the pursuit of suspected lawbreakers. The slow prowler suggests the reactive watching strategy of patrol; the high-speed chase demonstrates the proactive strategy used to apprehend criminals.[5]

Mobilizing Patrol

In 90 percent of all cases, the police only respond when private individuals call them to report crimes. In the remaining 10 percent of cases, officers take the initiative by looking for crimes and other misbehavior. Police mobilization takes place in five stages:

1. Victims and witnesses call the police.
2. Police operators—usually untrained civilian employees—answer calls. Operators have enormous discretion to cut off or confer police services. About half the callers will never get beyond the operators. Most of these discretionary decisions are never reviewed. However, the more serious the crime the more likely operators will confer service. (See Figure 6.1.)
3. Operators forward calls to dispatchers.
4. Dispatchers decide whether to mobilize the police. Dispatchers have wide discretion in classifying calls as violent crime, domestics, and so on. Ultimately, they decide whether to assign cars at all, and if they do, what priority the calls receive.
5. Patrol officers respond to the calls from the dispatchers. Patrol officers, like operators and dispatchers, have wide discretion. They can drop some calls, hurry to the scene in others, or proceed with no particular urgency, depending on their reading of the situation.[6]

Types of Patrol

Motor patrol has been the dominant form of patrol since replacing foot patrol in the 1940s. Motor patrol has several strengths over foot patrol:

- Speed: vehicles are obviously faster than walking.
- Surprise: motor patrol is both unpredictable and irregular.
- Efficiency: cars operate in all weather conditions, and they facilitate transporting prisoners, stolen goods, weapons, and equipment.

The famous reform chief, O. W. Wilson, believed that **preventive patrol**—police cars cruising randomly through the streets—creates the impression that the police are everywhere and can appear at any time. According to police experts Jerome Skolnick and James Fyfe, preventive patrol "is based on the premise that the presence of uniformed cops and marked police cars will send would-be criminals elsewhere, will keep jaywalkers on the sidewalk, and will cause motorists to check their speedometers."[7]

Officers spend about half their time patrolling. What do they do on patrol? Patrolling activity varies by jurisdiction, by beat, by time of day, and by individual. According to Gary Cordner and Robert Trojanowicz:

> Patrolling can be stationary or mobile; slow-, medium-, or high-speed; and oriented toward residential, commercial, recreational, or other kinds of areas. Some patrol officers intervene frequently in people's lives by stopping cars and checking out suspicious circumstances; other officers seem more interested in . . . parked cars and the security of closed businesses; still other officers rarely interrupt their continuous patrolling. Some officers devote all of their uncommitted time to loafing or personal affairs.[8]

Technology—vehicles, telephones, two-way radios, and computers—has contributed to making the police more mobile and in reducing the time it takes them to respond to calls. But these technologies also have a downside. They have changed the fundamental nature of policing from a personal operation of individuals with direct knowledge of communities into a bureaucratic, mechanical, centralized operation. Computers have further isolated the police. Computers can pinpoint the exact location of patrol cars at all times. Computer terminals—now present in most patrol cars—provide rapid access to all kinds of information.

For all of its advantages, technology has contributed to poor police-community relations. This is especially true in poor urban neighborhoods where many residents think of the police as a hostile occupational force that dominates the people on the fringes of "respectable" society. Isolated in their temperature controlled "rolling fortresses," with windows rolled up to protect them from the smells and dangers of the areas they patrol, the police "seem unable to communicate with the people they presumably serve."[9]

The eminent police sociologist Professor Albert J. Reiss, Jr., concluded:

> [I]nsulation of the police came at a high price. The patrol officer in his air-conditioned and heated car no longer got out of the police vehicle to do preventive patrol or to learn more about the community being policed. The insulation of the police from the public to control corruption and to respond rapidly to their calls had served primarily to insulate the police from the public they were to serve. No longer did the public have confidence that the police were handling, or could handle their problems, and many, particularly minority groups, felt alienated from the police.[10]

Beginning in the 1970s, a series of empirical evaluations uncovered several deficiencies in the effectiveness of preventive patrol as a strategy to accomplish police missions. For example, prisoners admitted to interviewers that they were neither frightened nor deterred by police presence. Attempts to increase perceived police presence by permitting officers to use squad cars for their personal use had little, if any, deterrent effect. Moreover, patrol does not affect crimes committed indoors. Even when preventive patrol is effective, it concentrates on main streets, leaving side and back streets, alleys, and even the rears of buildings on main streets largely unattended.[11]

These evaluations also indicated that crimes of passion are largely beyond the reach of preventive patrol. Enraged or demented individuals, hardly aware of anyone's presence when they give vent to explosive impulses, do not consider whether patrol officers will observe or catch them. In addition, skilled criminals quickly discover where the police concentrate their efforts; they avoid those places, or at least wait until a squad car passes before they make their moves.[12]

Andrew Halper and Richard Ku reported that according to one police administrator:

> Patrolmen in uniform are expected to be highly visible and thus deter crime by their conspicuous presence. But given the cost of personnel and the resources available to the city, it is inconceivable that enough uniformed patrolmen could be employed to completely cover the city in this way. Indeed, if the entire municipal budget were directed for this purpose it would still be inadequate. In any event, a patrolman in uniform, while a reassuring sight to many, is not the deterrent to crime that many people assume him to be. In a sense he performs the functions of a scarecrow, which is to say that he can only be effective within the short range of his ability to effectively observe and respond to criminal activity. In this respect his presence can be as reassuring to criminals as to the law-abiding. The potential felon, knowing where a policeman is, can safely deduce where he is not, and guide himself accordingly.[13]

Kansas City Preventive Patrol Experiment

The most famous and perhaps the most influential study of preventive patrol, the **Kansas City Preventive Patrol Ex-**

periment, tested the effectiveness of preventive patrol under carefully controlled conditions. Researchers divided 15 beats into three groups matched for similar crime rates and demographic characteristics. For one year, the police applied three distinct patrol strategies to each group. In the control group, they applied traditional preventive patrol; one car drove through the streets whenever it was not answering calls. In group two, proactive patrol, they greatly increased patrol activity; cars drove through the beats two to three times more often than in the control group. In group three, designated reactive patrol, they eliminated preventive patrol entirely; a patrol car entered the streets only in response to calls.

Before, and again following the experiment, interviewers asked business people and neighborhood residents if they had been crime victims, their opinion about the quality of law enforcement, and about their fear of crime. To the surprise of many, the experiment revealed that no matter what the strategy, there was little or no change in any of the following:

- Crime rates.
- Rates of reporting crime to the police.
- People's fear of crime.
- Opinion about the effectiveness of police services.

However, the experiment detected two changes:

1. Respect for the police increased in the control beats.
2. Fear of crime increased in the proactive beats.[14]

According to policing expert, David H. Bayley, the report of the Kansas City Preventive Patrol Experiment

> came like a thunderclap in policing, shaking the very foundations of traditional strategic thought. Police professionals immediately criticized its findings as being contrary to common sense, and scholars criticized them on methodological grounds. Viewed historically, however, the impact of the Kansas City research has been puzzling.[15]

Use *Your* Discretion

Does the Kansas City Preventive Patrol Experiment prove that preventive motor patrol wastes police time and taxpayers' money?

Some critics have rushed to that conclusion. However, Cordner and Trojanowicz caution that the Kansas City study merely "demonstrated that varying the level of motorized patrol between zero cars per beat and 2–3 cars per beat, for one year in one city, had no effect." James Q. Wilson, author of the influential *Varieties of Police Behavior,* warns that the experiment did not prove that adding police presence of all kinds is useless in controlling crime. It only showed that random, preventive motor patrol in marked cars did little good, regardless of whether it was proactive, reactive, or a little of both. Results might have differed substantially had officers responded to calls more quickly, in unmarked cars or on foot. Reported crime declined in Flint, Michigan, for example, when the Flint Police Department adopted foot patrols.[16]

The Kansas City Preventive Patrol Experiment had several definitely positive effects. It demonstrated the willingness of police departments to engage in research to evaluate the effectiveness of their programs. According to police expert Herman Goldstein, the experiment also "demonstrated that the police can undertake complex experiments that require altering routine operations with results that are beneficial to the agency . . . and to the entire police field." The experiment also opened up the possibility of freeing expensive patrol resources for other police activities; administrators might be able to divert as much as 60 percent to investigation, surveillance, and community service without diminishing the effectiveness of patrol. Finally, by challenging traditional practices, according to J. L. Ray LeGrande of the Miami Beach Police Department, "It was a breakthrough in research—as important as using the police radio for the first time."[17]

The Kansas City Preventive Patrol Experiment was widely accepted—and still is—as true. Nevertheless, according to policing expert David H. Bayley:

> Motorized patrol is still the mainstay of policing, with police departments continuing to assign the bulk of their personnel to random motor patrolling. . . . In sum, the Kansas City preventive patrol research is famous; its findings are generally accepted as being true; its research strategy is considered to be seriously flawed; it has never been replicated; it has not lessened appreciably the reliance of the police on random patrolling, but it has encouraged a rethinking of police purposes and methods. The curiously mixed, indeed paradoxical impact of the Kansas City research represents a failure, in my view, of police professionals, as well as social scientists. One group or the other should have acted on it, and neither really has.

CRITICAL THINKING

1. Summarize the findings of the evaluations of preventive patrol.
2. List the positive and negative findings regarding preventive patrol.
3. Do you favor preventive patrol as a strategy? Defend your answer.

Response Time

Until empirical research demonstrated otherwise, police departments assumed that **response time**—the length of time it took officers to get to a crime scene—determined their chances of apprehending and convicting offenders. Preventive patrol relied on two basic tactics to shorten the length of response time:

1. The emergency 911 telephone number.
2. Computer-assisted automobile vehicle monitoring (AVM) system.

Dialing 911 permits people to contact the police quickly; AVM facilitates rapid police response to these calls.[18]

Neither "911" nor AVM alone reduces crime. Researchers have demonstrated that the length of time it takes private individuals to call the police—not how fast the police respond to the call—is the important time measure. Most people are too upset to call the police immediately. When they finally call, it is usually their family and friends first, and then the police. Of great importance, researchers have also discovered that *police response time has no effect on apprehension, charge, and conviction rates.* Getting to the scene of the crime does not automatically translate into either getting information needed to apprehend suspects or finding evidence required to charge and convict them. Finally, researchers have found that the level of callers' satisfaction with the police does not depend on response time.[19]

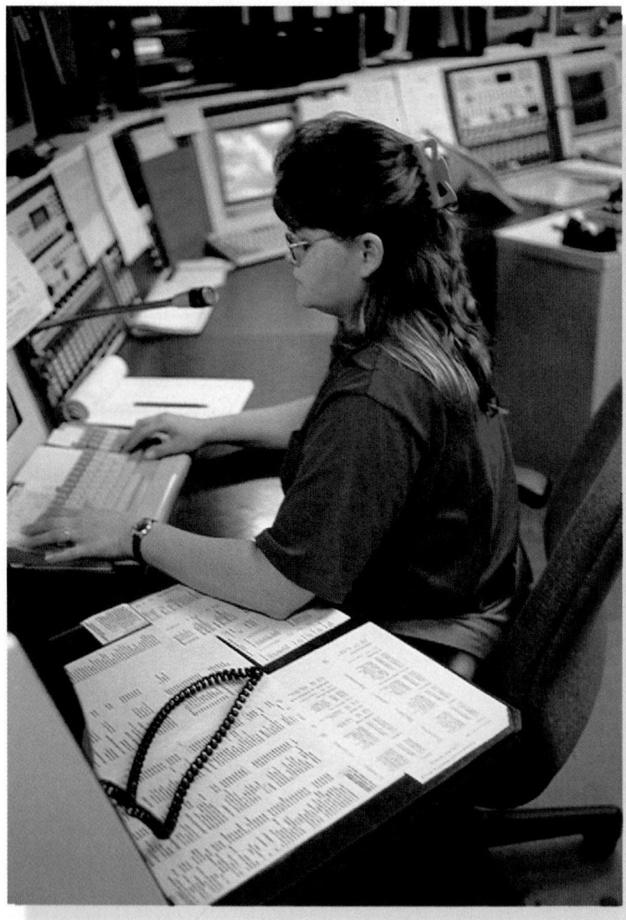

Patrol is the "backbone" of police strategies, and 911 is an integral part of making patrols more effective by increasing police response and the time it takes them to do so. The newest 911 systems rely increasingly on computer-run emergency response. The computer can locate and process more emergency calls more quickly than prior systems, helping police respond to emergencies in a shorter amount of time.

These discoveries led police departments to consider the possibility of **differential response.** Differential response means responding according to the type of crime involved. Rapid response should be the tactic for serious crimes such as rape and robbery. Minor offenses do not require getting a squad car to the scene of the crime immediately, if at all. Police departments in Wilmington, Delaware, and Birmingham, Alabama, participated in a differential response study to determine how many noncritical calls the police received and to discover if people were willing to accept delayed responses to these noncritical calls. About 15 percent of the calls involved serious crimes, whereas 55 percent were about less serious crimes. People who called the police about noncritical problems, reported that responses other than a patrol car coming to the scene would have satisfied them. What does this mean? Simply put, the arrival of a squad car is not required to satisfy people who call the police about noncritical issues.[20]

The National Institute of Justice (NIJ) funded a test of the **Management-of-Demand (MOD) System** in Wilmington, Delaware. MOD required that officers handle noncritical calls with alternatives to getting a patrol car on the scene as soon as possible. The alternatives included:

- 30-minute delays to on-the-scene responses.
- Telephone reporting.
- Walk-in reporting.
- Scheduled appointments.

Michael F. Cahn and James Tien assessed both crime rates and victim satisfaction before and after MOD went into effect. They found that:

1. Crime rates did not increase under MOD.
2. Citizen satisfaction with the police continued.
3. MOD freed resources for other police activities.[21]

The respected Police Executive Research Forum (PERF) designed a model response system. In this model, civilian complaint-takers answer all citizen calls, classify them as critical or noncritical, and transfer the critical calls to dispatchers for immediate response. Complaint-takers stack the noncritical calls, asking callers to file reports later. The Wilmington Police Department in Delaware implemented the model, and the Police Executive Research Forum evaluated it. The evaluation reported that the system saved police resources and allowed the department to handle more calls without increasing the number of police officers.[22]

Evaluation of a refined version of the model response system (tested in Toledo, Ohio; Greensboro, North Carolina; and Garden Grove, California) found:

- Fast police response accounted for less than 5 percent of arrests for serious crimes.
- Most service calls do not require fast response by patrol units.
- Different responses do not alienate people if they know in advance how the police will handle their calls.
- Differential response saved the Garden Grove Police Department 8,000 person hours, or more than $223,000 during the first year.[23]

Foot Patrol

The old practice of patrolling on foot returned to policing in the 1970s and 1980s. **Foot patrol** increases contact with neighborhood residents. This increased contact both enables officers to see, appreciate, and intervene in minor disturbances and to enhance people's sense of security in their neighborhoods. According to Stephen Mastrofski,

> Imbued with a proprietary interest in the neighborhood's well-being and armed with a rich knowledge of its people and places, the officer is expected to enlist citizens' assistance and thus reinforce the informal social control mechanisms of the community. Ultimately these efforts are expected to contribute to more positive police-community relations, less fear of crime and disorder, and an actual reduction in crime and disorder.[24]

Evaluations showing the benefits of foot patrol have encouraged a number of police departments to adopt foot patrol as part of their operations. Some, such as Boston, Massachusetts; Flint, Michigan; and Newark, New Jersey, have shifted substantially toward foot patrol. The evaluation in Flint showed that foot patrol reduced both the fear of crime and actual crime rates. Foot patrol in Flint was so popular that despite severe financial problems, the city voted three times for special tax increases to maintain and expand the program. The Newark Foot Patrol Experiment, the other major evaluation, produced mixed results. It showed reduced fear of crime but no decrease in the amount of crime.[25]

Single-Officer Patrol

Patrol is labor-intensive; that is, it relies heavily on people, not labor- and cost-saving equipment. Salaries make up 80 percent of police budgets, making patrol the most expensive police operation. This is particularly true of two-officer patrol, which prevailed in American policing until the 1980s. Faced with declining budgets, the cost effectiveness of one-officer patrol appealed to budget-conscious administrators. Administrators saw the chance to reduce the cost of patrol officers by half by moving from the traditional two-officer patrol to one. However, many officers strongly opposed it. They believed that partners who backed each other up in dangerous situations enhanced their safety. The Police Executive Research Foundation evaluated one-officer patrol in San Diego. The study reported that one officer patrol units:

- Were more cost effective.
- Were less often involved in resisting arrest situations.
- Resulted in fewer assaults against officers.
- Resulted in fewer injuries to officers.
- Generated fewer citizen complaints.
- Showed similar levels of proactivity as two-officer units, including traffic warnings, field interrogation, business checks, arrests, and crime report filing.[26]

Use *Your* Discretion

Are one-officer patrol units as effective as the San Diego study found?

Although other studies have supported most of these findings, one study suggests that one-officer units are less likely to make arrests and file serious charges. According to Mastrofski, who conducted a major survey of police operations:

> It seems reasonable to postulate that the greater efficiency of one-officer units creates a facilitative environment for higher "productivity" [by] policing in the areas that departments typically monitor (arrests, citations and field interrogations), but how that available time is actually used will be heavily influenced by departmental policies that affect officers' incentives to conform their actions to departmental priorities.[27]

CRITICAL THINKING

1. What exactly is Mastrofski arguing with respect to one-officer patrol?
2. Do you think he has a point? Defend your answer.
3. If you think this is not enough information to answer the questions, what specifically would you like to know before answering? Explain.

Knowledge and Understanding CHECK

1. Trace the development of walling, wariness, and watching from their origins to the present.
2. List and briefly describe the five stages of police patrol mobilization.

3. List three advantages of preventive patrol.
4. Describe the basic assumption underlying preventive patrol.
5. List the advantages and disadvantages of preventive patrol.
6. List the findings of empirical research regarding the effectiveness of preventive patrol.
7. List the findings of and explain the importance of the Kansas City Preventive Patrol Experiment.
8. Identify the two main tactics used in preventive patrol.
9. Explain the importance and the effect of empirical research regarding response time.
10. Describe and discuss the importance of the Management-of-Demand System in Wilmington, Delaware.
11. List the results of the evaluations of foot patrol.
12. List the findings of the evaluation of San Diego's one-officer patrol.
13. Why do officers oppose one-officer patrol? Are they right? Explain.

PROACTIVE POLICING

The shortcomings in preventive patrol, police concern over career criminals who return to the streets, public anger, and fear over violence and illegal drugs have led police departments to turn to new tactics and strategies. One survey indicates that nearly half the departments surveyed have instituted some form of police-initiated mobilization, or proactive police operations. **Proactive police operations,** usually in the form of special crime-attack units, focus on the concentration of crime problems among small proportions of offenders, places, and victims. Crime-attack operations include the following tactics:

- Decoys
- Undercover patrol
- Saturation patrol
- Raids
- Roadblocks
- Informants
- Field interrogation
- Targeting repeat offenders
- "Hot spot" policing, or policing repeat-complaint addresses to maintain order

Crime-attack units focus on two kinds of targets:

1. *Trouble spots,* sometimes called "hot spots," such as restaurants where "known suspects hang out," neighborhoods with particularly high burglary rates, bars where disturbances are common, or addresses from which a large number of calls come.
2. *Troublemakers,* such as known criminals or repeat offenders.[28]

Researchers have demonstrated that a few people account for the lion's share of arrests. In Kansas City, Missouri, for example, 2.7 percent of the 500,000 persons arrested two or more times in 1990 accounted for 60 percent of all arrests. Similarly, a few addresses account for most calls for police service. A major study of these hot spots in Minneapolis showed that 5 percent of the 115,000 street addresses and intersections accounted for 100 percent of the calls to police to report criminal sexual conduct, robbery, and auto theft.[29]

Use *Your* Discretion

What's the controversy really about?

Crime-attack tactics generate considerable controversy, much of it based on ideology. Opponents contend that proactive policing of all kinds threatens individual rights in a free society; some even contend that it makes America a police state. These critics maintain that responses to citizen calls must befit life in a democracy. On the other hand, many individuals and groups—especially those who believe crime-attack strategies might reduce violence, illegal drugs, and the number of chronic offenders in the community—strongly favor aggressive tactics. Liberty and privacy cannot exist, supporters of crime-attack operations maintain, in communities ravaged by violence, drugs, and career criminals. Supporters also believe that court restrictions on law enforcement practices have forced the police to rely on decoys, informants, and other crime-attack tactics.[30]

CRITICAL THINKING

1. State the precise nature of the controversy over crime-attack tactics.
2. On which side of the controversy are you? Explain why. Do you just "feel" this way, or do you have specific information to support your position?

The end of spring term classes has often led to rioting by Akron, Ohio, college students. Akron police officers relied on their strong presence to prevent students getting out of control: officers on bikes in large numbers headed down Wheeler Street, a popular celebration point. They believe that their strong presence contributed to a calmer celebration. Despite this example of police presence preventing disorder, the empirical proof of the success of this tactic is not conclusive.

Hot Spots Patrol

"Hot spot" patrol differentiates the kind of police response based on location. Hot spots are determined by a well-established conclusion: Crime is not evenly distributed geographically. Over half the crimes in one city come from only 3 percent of the addresses. Furthermore, crime in these "hot spots" is further concentrated into "hot" days of the week and times of the day. Therefore, says Lawrence W. Sherman, expert on police strategies, "most addresses, and even most blocks, in any city go for years without any crime—even in high-crime neighborhoods."[31]

Hot spot response is based on the idea that some addresses at certain times need more police response than others. The traditional strategy of evenly distributed patrol—that is, giving every resident an equal share of patrol whether they need it or not—is not the best use of police resources. Evaluations of experiments in which police have concentrated patrol visibility on high crime times and places are modest, but positive. Hot spot patrol can reduce—or at least displace—identified crime problems.

In a major experiment, the Minneapolis Hot Spots Patrol Experiment, "three hours a day of intermittent, unpredictable police presence was applied to" a random selection of the "worst" hot spot intersections in the city. Robbery fell 20 percent, and crimes overall fell 13 percent in these intersections. The number of fights and disturbances was cut in half in the experimental areas. The success of hot spot patrol may depend on what the police do when they get to the hot spots. The Minneapolis police officers did little except drive around. They rarely got out of their cars to talk to people or to interrogate suspects. According to Sherman, who conducted the experiment, "More aggressive efforts may have reduced crime even further—or made it worse."[32]

Aggressive Field Investigation

Aggressive field investigation means that the police themselves decide to check out suspicious circumstances, places, and people; they do not wait for people to call them. Police action can take various forms, including checking locks on buildings; shining spotlights through windows; watching, following, stopping, questioning, and sometimes frisking suspicious persons for weapons, stolen property, or contraband. Suspicious people might be in cars, standing in a public place, walking down the street, or just "hanging around." Aggressive field investigation, however, rarely extends to entering homes.[33]

Numerous circumstances lead officers to engage in field investigations. People out too late at night arouse police suspicions, although what is "too late" differs from place to place. In small towns, it might mean after 10:00 P.M.; in cities, it could be an hour after the bars close. Location is also important. Three men in their twenties who are huddled near a jewelry store's side entrance at 1:30 A.M. certainly make a seasoned officer wary. A shiny, clean car displaying old, dirty license plates suggests a stolen car with switched plates. Six suspicious-looking young people of mixed races parked in a car near a recently robbed store, or two young men pacing up and down in front of a clothing store in a high-crime area suggest that delinquents are "casing the joint." Hence, a variety of circumstances might lead officers to believe that places or people do not "look right." Crime attack calls for officers to probe these suspicious circumstances.[34]

Undercover Police Work

Covert, meaning **undercover, police operations** are not unique to the turn of the twenty-first century. Authoritarian kings and modern dictators have relied heavily on them. Henry VIII used them during the 1520s to enforce the English Reformation. Hitler, Stalin, and Saddam Hussein are well-known twentieth- century counterparts to Henry VIII in using informants to accomplish their missions. For at least a century, U.S. police departments have used such tactics extensively to fight vice and political crime. However, since 1970, undercover police activity has expanded and changed its form. According to criminologist Gary T. Marx, an expert on the subject, undercover work

> is now invoked to attack street crimes and even to go after white collar crime and official corruption. All this is very controversial, at least among some groups, but the latter two seem to inspire particularly pronounced rancor. Undercover police tactics such as Operation Greylord uncovered corruption among Chicago judges, the ABSCAM Operation discovered bribe taking by members of Congress, and the sting operation against the mayor of Washington, D.C. showed that the mayor used illegal drugs. Police have used these same tactics to uncover other white-collar and organization crimes.[35]

Use *Your* Discretion

When is undercover police work ethical?

Gary T. Marx, who has written extensively on undercover police, tells of the following real incidents involving ethical issues raised by undercover police work.

1. The case of a San Francisco police officer and 16 of his fellow officers raises the issue of "[t]he conflict of goals between preventing crime and encouraging it in order to apprehend criminals." [The 17 officers] patrolled the streets in plainclothes looking for parking violators and meter jammers. The officer reported that his unit was effective because "if you have a uniformed officer there, no one is going to wipe off their tires." To which the skeptic might respond, "Isn't that what we want uniformed officers for—to prevent violations? Do we really want to encourage people to break the rules because we want them to think no one is there?" Underlying the officer's remark is the need to write citations in order to meet productivity goals. The unstated assumption here is, "We want to create a situation in which, because they never know whether or not a police officer is watching, persons won't wipe off their tires." This "myth of surveillance" comes with other costs, but it is believed to be more efficient than obtaining that result only when a uniformed officer is actually present. From the standpoint of empirical impact, we don't know if it is a myth.
2. The issue of the sometimes conflicting goals of preventing crimes and making arrests can also be seen in the case of Malcolm X's daughter, Quiblah Shabazz, who was accused of hiring a pretend hit man to avenge her father's death. When the informant was asked why he didn't try to discourage the plot, he said, "I'm supposed to sound like a murderer, remember? A hit man wouldn't agree to kill someone and then say it's wrong." When a suspect is hesitant (for example, Shabazz indicated that she was leery, wanted to put the plot on hold, and missed a planned meeting), should the informant respect this apparent withdrawal or ambivalent intent, or persist? In this case, 38 of 40 phone calls were initiated by the informant, and he appears to have done most of the talking on the tapes.
3. The issue of when undercover police should intervene to prevent a crime has continued to raise moral and practical questions. Thus, in Dallas an undercover officer watched a woman being raped by a group he had infiltrated. He pretended to be sick to avoid participating. He stated, "You don't

the coming times. If we can show the future managers and building owners that working proactively will reduce the problems at an address, the whole experiment will have been a success.

The RECAP final report announced, among others, the following findings:

- The residential locations, relative to the control group, showed a 21 percent reduction in assault, a 12 percent reduction in disturbances, and a 15 percent reduction in calls related to drunkenness.
- Commercial targets showed a 9 percent reduction in theft calls; and a 21 percent reduction in shoplifting calls at seven stores participating in a special program.
- Residential burglaries were up 27 percent compared to controls.
- Calls for commercial predatory crime (criminal sexual conduct, robbery, and kidnapping combined) were up 28 percent at the experimental addresses relative to controls.[69]

[Reprinted with permission from: Buerger, Michael E., ed., *The Crime Prevention Casebook: Securing High Crime Locations* (Washington, D.C.: Crime Control Institute, 1992), copyright 1992.]

CRITICAL THINKING

The officers in RECAP describe the problems, their responses to them, and their assessment of the success or failure of their efforts.

1. Were they successes or failures?
2. How would you evaluate the decisions made and the problems faced?
3. Put yourself in the place of the officers. What decisions would you have made? Defend your decisions.
4. Do these findings indicate that community-oriented policing is good policy? Explain your answer.
5. How do you define "good" policy? Some experts argue that the goals set for problem-oriented policing are too high. According to the experimenters, these

> mixed results . . . suggest that merely focusing police attention on chronic problems cannot guarantee their solution . . . the results of a test with objective target selection seem far more modest than results of quasi-experiments using subjective target selection. When the most troublesome addresses in a city are intentionally selected as targets, perhaps a more appropriate goal would be "managing" rather than "solving" problems.[70]

6. Do you agree? Defend your answer.

Participant observer Michael Buerger concluded that the experiment may be more useful than it might appear at first glance. He listed the following reasons:

1. Every new program is successful when measured in the short term. Then, due to declining officer and citizen satisfaction, displacement of problems, or return of problems to the "reclaimed" area, the success wears off. RECAP measured calls and results for a full year, longer than the few months or weeks of most "successful" programs.
2. As police departments "open up more of their prioritization to citizen input, they may well end up with problem addresses similar to those worked on by RECAP."
3. The rhetoric of problem solving frequently oversells the possibility of its success. "Possible outcomes are promoted as if they were automatic, painless, and inevitable, when in fact they are not."
4. Unrealistic rhetoric leads to unrealistic expectations. When these expectations are not fulfilled, they "can lead to burnout and bail-out of formerly committed officers whose enthusiasm is a critical element of the successes, small or otherwise."
5. "The prime benefit to others of the RECAP experience may well be to make the exercise of problem solving more real, and to more fully engage the participation of police officers who are grounded in what *is,* not what *ought* to be."[71]

Knowledge and Understanding CHECK

1. Identify the two main strategies used in community-oriented policing.
2. Describe the major aspects of the strategies used in community-oriented policing.
3. List the major elements of community-oriented policing.
4. List the advantages and disadvantages of community-oriented policing.
5. Identify three reasons for the alarm that prompted the re-emergence of community-oriented policing.
6. Describe the DARE program and describe the findings of empirical research evaluating DARE.
7. State and explain your own assessment of community-oriented policing.

Is Police Investigation Worth the Effort? Consideration

According to crime novels, television and the movies, detectives solve most crimes. The empirical research discussed in the chapters suggests that reality is considerably more complex than fiction and popular conceptions on the matter of who is responsible for "solving" crimes, Summarize the findings reported in the "Criminal Investigation" section of this chapters. How does this research compare with popular opinion and fiction.

Critical Thinking

On the basis of these findings (and the remaining chapter discussion), how would you answer the question that opens the chapter? Explain your answer.

CHAPTER CAPSULE

- Modern strategies originated in the ancient practices of walling, wariness, and watching.
- From 1850 until the 1990s, preventive patrol and criminal investigation were the dominant police strategies.
- Ninety percent of all police actions are reactive—namely, responses to victims' and witnesses' calls.
- Police operators, dispatchers, and patrol officers enjoy wide discretion in how they respond to calls.
- Crime-attack tactics—"hot spots" patrol, aggressive field investigation, undercover police work, and police crackdowns—raise questions about the proper balance between crime control and individual liberty and privacy.
- Patrol officers—not detectives—account for most arrests.
- Community-oriented police strategies shift the emphasis from responding to single incidents to drawing on public and private agencies and services, as well as on line officers' expertise, not only to control crime but also to reduce disorder and fear.

KEY TERMS

walling
wariness
watching
preventive patrol
Kansas City Preventive Patrol Experiment
response time
differential response
Management-of-Demand (MOD) System
foot patrol
proactive police operations
hot spot patrol
aggressive field investigation
undercover police operations
police crackdown
displacement
Hawthorne principle
preliminary investigations
incident reports
follow-up investigations
community-oriented policing
DARE

INTERNET RESEARCH EXERCISES

Exercise: Using the Internet or InfoTrac College Edition, search for information about SWAT teams as a police strategy. What are the missions of SWAT Teams? How are they organized? What are the criteria for selecting officers for the teams?

Suggested site:

- Directory of Police SWAT Teams: http://www.policeguide.com/swat.htm

InfoTrac College Edition: Run a key word search on "SWAT teams."

NOTES

1. Jerome H. Skolnick and David H. Bayley, *The New Blue Line* (New York: Free Press, 1986), 5.
2. Sally Ann Stewart, "L.A. Residents Seek Security in Gates," *USA Today,* 23 December 1992.
3. Lawrence W. Sherman, "Patrol Strategies for the Police," in *Crime and Public Policy,* James Q. Wilson, ed. (New Brunswick, N.J.: Transaction Books, 1983), 163.
4. Lawrence W. Sherman, "Police in the Laboratory of Criminal Justice," in *Critical Issues in Policing,* Roger G. Dunham and Geoffrey P. Alpert, eds. (Prospect Heights, Ill.: Waveland Press, 1989), 48.
5. Lawrence W. Sherman, "Attacking Crime: Police and Crime Control," in *Modern Policing,* Michael Tonry and Norval Morris, eds. (Chicago: University of Chicago Press, 1992), 172.
6. Eric J. Scott, *Calls for Service: Citizen Demand and Initial Police Response* (Washington, D.C.: U.S. Department of Justice, 1980), 59–67.
7. Jerome H. Skolnick and James J. Fyfe, *Above the Law: Police and the Excessive Use of Force* (New York: The Free Press, 1993), 251–52.
8. Gary W. Cordner and Robert C. Trojanowicz, "Patrol," in *What Works in Policing?* Gary W. Cordner and Donna C. Hale, eds. (Cincinnati: Anderson, 1992), 5.
9. Police Foundation, *Newark Foot Patrol Experiment,* 11; Skolnick and Fyfe, *Above the Law* (New York: Free Press, 1993), 240.
10. Albert J. Reiss, Jr., "Police Organization," in *Modern Policing,* 53.
11. George L. Kelling et al., *The Kansas City Preventive Patrol Experiment: A Summary Report* (Washington, D.C.: The Police Foundation, 1974), 9–10; Herman Goldstein, *Policing a Free Society* (Cambridge, Mass.: Ballinger, 1977), 49–54.
12. Ibid.
13. Andrew Halper and Richard Ku, *An Exemplary Project: New York City Police Department Street Crimes Unit* (Washington, D.C.: U.S. Government Printing Office, 1975), 1–2.
14. Kelling, *Kansas City Preventive Patrol Experiment.*
15. David H. Bayley, *What Works in Policing?* (New York: Oxford University Press, 1998), 26.
16. James Q, Wilson, *Thinking About Crime,* rev. ed., (New York: Basic Books, 1983), 65–66; Flint Study cited in Sherman, "Patrol Strategies for the Police," 153–54.
17. Goldstein, *Policing a Free Society,* 52; Joan Petersilia, "Influence of Research on Policing," in *Critical Issues in Policing,* 232.
18. The National Advisory Committee on Criminal Justice Standards and Goals, *Police* (Washington, D.C.: U.S. Government Printing Office, 1973), 193.
19. U.S. Department of Justice, *Response Time Analysis: Executive Summary* (Washington, D.C.: U.S. Government Printing Office, 1978); Brian Forst et al., *What Happens After Arrest* (Washington, D.C.: National Institute of Law Enforcement and Criminal Justice, 1977), chaps. 3, 5; George L. Kelling and David Fogel, "Police Patrol—Some Future Directions," in *The Future of Policing,* Alvin W. Cohn, ed. (Beverly Hills, Calif.: Sage, 1978), 166–67; Brian Forst et al., *Arrest Convictability as a Measure of Police Performance* (Washington, D.C.: National Institute of Justice, 1982); Sherman, "Patrol Strategies for the Police," 153; Petersilia, "Influence of Research on Policing," 233.
20. Petersilia, "Influence of Research on Policing," 234.
21. Michael F. Cahn and James Tien, *An Alternative Approach in Police Response: Wilmington Management of Demand Program* (Washington, D.C.: National Institute of Justice, 1981).
22. Ibid.
23. Reported in Petersilia, "Influence of Research on Policing," 235.
24. Stephen D. Mastrofski, "The Prospects for Change in Police Patrol: A Decade of Review," *The American Journal of Police* 9 (1990): 37.
25. Cordner and Trojanowicz, "Patrol," 10.
26. Mastrofski, "Prospects for Change in Police Patrol," 31.
27. Lee A. Daniels, "How Many Does It Take to Staff a Squad Car," *New York Times,* 6 December 1991; Walker, *Police in America,* 89.
28. Wilson, *Thinking About Crime,* 68–74; Susan E. Martin and Lawrence W. Sherman, "Selective Apprehension: A Police Strategy for Repeat Offenders," *Criminology* 24 (1986): 155–73.
29. Lawrence W. Sherman, Dennis Rogan, and Robert Velke, "The Menagerie of Crime: Targets for Police Crime Control Strategies," Unpublished manuscript (Washington, D.C.: Crime Control Institute, 1991); Sherman, "Attacking Crime: Police and Crime Control," *Modern Policing,* 178.
30. Richard Staufenberger, ed., *Progress in Policing* (Cambridge, Mass.: Ballinger, 1980), 69.
31. Lawrence W. Sherman, "The Police," in *Crime,* James Q. Wilson and Joan Petersilia, eds. (San Francisco: Institute for Contemporary Studies, 1995), 331.
32. Ibid., 333–34.
33. Goldstein, *Policing a Free Society,* 49–54.
34. Jonathan Rubenstein, *City Police* (New York: Farrar, Straus and Giroux, 1973), chap. 6.
35. Geoffrey R. Elton, *Tudor Policy and Police* (Cambridge, England: Cambridge University Press, 1973); Gary T. Marx, "Who Really Gets Stung? Some Issues Raised by the New Police Undercover Work," *Crime and Delinquency* (April 1982): 165; Gary T. Marx, *Undercover: Police Surveillance in America* (Berkeley: University of California Press, 1988); Gerald M. Caplan, ed., *ABSCAM Ethics: Moral Issues and Deception in Law Enforcement* (Washington, D.C.: The Police Foundation, 1983).

36. Gary T. Marx, "Recent Developments in Undercover Policing," in *Punishment and Social Control: Essays in Honor of Sheldon L. Messinger,* Thomas G. Blomberg and Stanley Cohen, eds. (New York: Aldine de Gruyter), pp. 101–102.
37. Sherman, "The Police," in *Crime,* 332.
38. Ibid.
39. Lawrence W. Sherman, "Police Crackdowns," *NIJ Reports* (March/April 1990), 2–6.
40. Robert E. Worden, Timothy S. Bynum, and James Frank, "Police Crackdowns on Drug Abuse and Trafficking," in *Drugs and Crime,* Doris Layton MacKenzie and Craig D. Uchida, eds. (Thousand Oaks, Calif.: Sage Publications, 1994), 95–97.
41. Ibid., 101–103.
42. Quoted in Staufenberger, *Progress in Policing,* 80.
43. Ibid.
44. John E. Eck, "Criminal Investigation," in *What Works in Policing?* 19; Steven G. Brandl and James Frank, "The Relationship Between Evidence, Detective Effort, and the Disposition of Burglary and Robbery Investigations," *American Journal of Police* XIII (1994): 149–68.
45. Forst et al., *What Happens After Arrest?* 24–32; Forst et al., *Arrest Convictability.*
46. See Peter W. Greenwood and Joan Petersilia, *The Criminal Investigation Process,* Vols. I–III (Santa Monica, Calif.: The Rand Corporation, 1975); Peter Greenwood, Jan Chaiken, and Joan Petersilia, *The Criminal Investigation Process* (Lexington, Mass.: D.C. Heath, 1977); John E. Eck, *Solving Crimes: The Investigation of Burglary and Robbery* (Washington, D.C.: Police Executive Research Forum, 1983); and Brandl and Frank, "Relationship Between Evidence."
47. Greenwood, Chaiken, and Petersilia, *Criminal Investigation Process.*
48. John E. Eck, *Solving Crimes,* quoted in Brandl and Frank, "Relationship Between Evidence," 149; David H. Bayley, *What Works in Policing?* 71.
49. Brandl and Frank, "Relationship Between Evidence," 163–64.
50. Petersilia, "Influence of Research on Policing," 240.
51. Jerome H. Skolnick and David H. Bayley, *The New Blue Line* (New York: Free Press, 1986), 5.
52. Skolnick and Fyfe, *Above the Law,* 251.
53. Skolnick and Bayley, *New Blue Line,* 53–55.
54. Robert Yin et al., *Patrolling the Neighborhood Beat: Residents and Residential Security* (Santa Monica, Calif.: Rand Corporation, 1976); Sherman, "Patrol Strategies for the Police," 145.
55. Mark H. Moore, "Problem-Solving and Community Policing," in *Modern Policing,* 123; Dennis P. Rosenbaum and Arthur J. Lurigio, "An Inside Look at Community Policing: Definitions, Organizational Changes, and Evaluation Findings," *Crime and Delinquency* 40 (1994): 301.
56. "Community Policing in the 1990s," *National Institute of Justice Journal* (August 1992): 3–4.
57. David Hayselip, Jr. and Deborah Weisel, "Local Level Drug Enforcement," in *What Works in Policing?* (Cincinnati: Anderson, 1992), 36–37.
58. Robert Rheinhold, "Police, Hard Pressed in Drug War, Are Turning to Preventive Measures," *New York Times,* 28 December 1989.
59. Ibid.
60. Joseph Pereira, "In a Drug Program, Some Kids Turn in Their Own Parents," *Wall Street Journal,* 20 April 1992; Lewis Donohew, Howard Sypher, and William Bukoski, eds., *Persuasive Communication and Drug Abuse Education* (Hillsdale, N.J.: Erlbaum Associates, 1991).
61. Dennis P. Rosenbaum et al., "Cops in the Classroom: A Longitudinal Evaluation of Drug Abuse Resistance Education (DARE)," *Journal of Research in Crime and Delinquency* 31 (1994): 1–31.
62. Quoted in Periera, "In a Drug Program."
63. Ibid.
64. Dennis P. Rosenbaum and Arthur J. Lurigio, "An Inside Look at Community Policing Reform: Definitions, Organizational Changes, and Evaluation Findings," *Crime and Delinquency* 40 (1994): 304.
65. Ibid.
66. Michael E. Buerger, "The Problems of Problem-Solving: Resistance, Interdependencies, and Conflicting Interests," *American Journal of Police* XIII (1994): 2.
67. Ibid., 4.
68. Ibid., 3.
69. Ibid., 5–6.
70. Spelman and Eck, *Problem-Oriented Policing.*
71. Buerger, "Problems of Problem-Solving," 28–29.

CHAPTER 7

Police and the Law

CHAPTER OUTLINE

Is Eyewitness Testimony Reliable?

Eyewitness testimony is among the most damning of all evidence that can be used in a court of law. When an eyewitness points a finger at a defendant and says, "He did it! I saw him! I was so shocked I'll never forget that face!" the case is as good as over. "Cast-iron, brass-bound, copper-riveted," as one prosecutor put it. The defendant sits helpless, without hope, eyes wide, fear turning into panic. Only someone who has been accused of a crime he didn't commit can know just how devastating the experience can be. I once heard a falsely accused person say, "I'd rather have terminal cancer than go through this. . . . Innocent people continue to be convicted based on faulty eyewitness testimony. Some of them are eventually set free, but sadly, not until they have spent years of their lives in prison."[1]

Elizabeth Loftus, leading authority on eyewitness identification and author of Eyewitness Testimony, *read by lawyers, psychologists, and students all over the world.*

INTRODUCTION

Formal criminal justice requires getting evidence to back up government interference with two basic rights:

1. *Locomotion:* the right of people to come and go as they please.
2. *Privacy:* the right to be left alone by the government.

So, if the police want to get cases into court, they have to gather information that prosecutors and courts will accept. This information is called **admissible evidence.** It is admissible only if the police gathered it according to the requirements of the U.S. and state constitutions. According to police expert Carl B. Klockars,

> What the courts offer to police is the opportunity, if they wish to take advantage of it, to seek the state's capacity to punish. In effect, the courts say to the police that if they wish to make use of that capacity, they must demonstrate to the courts that they have followed certain procedures in order to do so. . . . Only on those occasions that the police wish to employ the state's capacity to punish do the two institutions [courts and police] have any relationship of any kind. Despite the enormous growth in police law in the past quarter century, the courts have no more "control" over the police than local supermarkets have over the diets of those who shop there.[2]

In the day-to-day reality of police work, the police often do not take advantage of the opportunity to bring cases to prosecutors and courts. Critical to understanding the role of the law in police work is that the law plays a much less significant part than might appear from the attention it receives in courts, on television, and in the news. W. F. Walsh, for example, demonstrated that police officers arrest only a few people for felonies, even where felony offense rates are high. Forty percent of the officers assigned to a high-crime area in New York City did not make a single felony arrest in an entire year; 68 percent of the officers in the area made only three arrests in the same year. Furthermore, according to sociologist Donald J. Black, the police frequently do not arrest even when they have plenty of admissible evidence to back up the arrest. Black found that the police decided to arrest in only 27 percent of the cases of violent felonies where they had ample evidence to do so. Exercising the wide discretion they have ready to hand, officers frequently decide not to initiate formal criminal justice.[3]

This surprising finding must be seen in context. A number of constraints operate to explain it. A fragmented criminal justice system, scarce resources, community norms, and order maintenance and public service responsibilities all contribute to police decision making (see Chapter 4). In many instances, bringing cases into the criminal justice system is not even the object of police actions.

Practically speaking, constitutional rights and other legal rules are only relevant if the object of law enforcement officers is to have suspects charged with crimes. In these cases, the police face numerous formal limits. First are the general principles embodied in the rule of law, separation of powers, and federalism (discussed in Chapter 4). In addition, specific provisions in the U.S. Constitution, state constitutions, federal and state statutes, court decisions, and administrative rules all prescribe guidelines for gathering evidence and dealing with suspects.

According to the courts, the balance between the public interest in both criminal law enforcement and individual privacy and liberty does not require, nor should we expect, mechanical application of formal rules. Individual police officers and their departments need room to make discretionary judgments. However, just as private citizens must face punishment if convicted of crimes, sanctions follow from police violations of constitutional commands. Courts can exclude evidence illegally obtained. Individuals can sue police officers, chiefs, departments, or other governmental agencies for the violation of constitutional rights. Police departments may discipline offending officers, even removing them from the force in serious cases.

Police officers, guns in hand, prepare to use force if necessary to enter an apartment and search and seize persons and evidence. The Constitution requires that all such invasions of liberty and privacy be backed up by facts.

LAW ENFORCEMENT AND THE CONSTITUTION

To enforce the criminal law, the police need information, which they obtain by a variety of operations—surveillance, stop and frisk, arrest, searches, interrogation, and identification procedures. All of these coercive government actions against the lives, property, liberty, and privacy of individuals require facts to back them up—called technically an **objective basis.** Hunch, whim, or mere suspicion are not enough. Coercive action covers a wide spectrum, ranging from brief stops on the street entailing slight loss of liberty to capital punishment, the ultimate deprivation of life itself. The requirement of facts differs only in degree. A few facts are enough to back up a street stop; conviction demands proof beyond a reasonable doubt (see Chapter 10).

The objective basis requirement controls police discretion in criminal law enforcement. Prosecutors rely on the police to gather enough facts to prove guilt beyond a reasonable doubt. However, police cannot get facts for proof of guilt without an objective basis to back up the seizures, searches, interrogations, and identification procedures. It is not an exaggeration to say that facts control the formal criminal process. Naturally, the police would like the power to manage the discovery and the use of this information. Suspects and defendants, of course, would like to manage if, when, what, and how the police get the information. And innocent people, understandably, want the assurance that the police will not coercively interfere with their liberty, privacy, and property unless they have enough information to back up their actions.

The U.S. Constitution creates a balance between the interest of government in criminal law enforcement and the rights of individuals in liberty, privacy, and property. The U.S. Supreme Court arbitrates conflicts that arise over this general balance. Four provisions apply specifically to balancing police power and the rights of individuals—the Fourth, Fifth, Sixth, and Fourteenth Amendments to the U.S. Constitution:

- *Amendment IV:* The right of the people to be secure in their persons, houses, papers, and effects, against unreasonable searches and seizures, shall not be violated, and no warrants shall issue but upon probable cause, supported by oath or affirmation, and particularly describing the place to be searched, and the persons or things to be seized.
- *Amendment V:* No person . . . shall be compelled in any criminal case to be a witness against himself, nor be deprived of life, liberty, or property, without due process of law. . . .
- *Amendment VI:* In all criminal prosecutions, the accused shall enjoy the right . . . to be confronted with the witnesses against him . . . and to have the assistance of counsel for his defense.
- *Amendment XIV:* No state shall make or enforce any law which shall abridge the privileges or immunities of citizens of the United States; nor shall any state deprive any person of life, liberty, or property, without due process of law; nor deny to any person within its jurisdiction the equal protection of the laws.

These provisions do not define themselves; they require interpretation. We discussed the meaning of due process and the Supreme Court's interpretation of it in Chapter 4. The following examples illustrate the application of the Fourth, Fifth, and Sixth Amendments to real-life situations:

1. Police officers pat down the outer clothing of a citizen who they think might have a weapon and drugs. Have the police searched the person? If so, was the search "unreasonable"?

2. Police approach a citizen on the street and ask, "What are you doing here?" Have they "seized" the citizen? If so, was the seizure "unreasonable"?
3. Police officers receive an anonymous tip that a black man wearing a red cap has just carried a concealed weapon into Jean's bar. Do the police need "probable cause" to search a man who fits the description? Do they have probable cause?
4. Police officers tell a suspect that if he does not confess to a murder, they will arrest his mother as an accomplice. The suspect confesses. Have the police "compelled" the suspect to be a witness against himself?
5. Is issuing a traffic ticket a criminal "case" or criminal "prosecution"?
6. Is an arrest for rape a criminal "case" or criminal "prosecution"?
7. Are lineups and show-ups "confrontations" between witnesses and the accused?

Who interprets these terms? Sometimes, legislatures enact laws to define them. More frequently, courts define their meaning. Most important, courts, especially the U.S. Supreme Court, decide whether to leave the interpretation to the discretionary judgment of individual police officers; whether the police have to get prior judicial approval for proposed actions; or whether police officers can take initial action subject to later review by the courts. Regardless of who interprets them, the Fourth, Fifth, and Sixth Amendments require balancing society's interests in criminal law enforcement against society's interest in individual autonomy, liberty, and privacy. Furthermore, it is police officers who determine the application of provisions to day-to-day actions on the street and at the police station.

One way to view the history of criminal procedure as a whole is as the gradual **formalization** of—that is, application of legal and administrative rules to—government actions. At first, formal rules controlled only the procedures during a criminal trial. Since the 1600s, developments have diminished discretion and have subjected proceedings both before and after a criminal trial to formal rules. We save discussion of the formalization of proceedings during and following trial for Chapters 8 through 12. In examining the formalization of police procedures, we have to distinguish between two stages in the criminal process:

1. Procedures that take place on the street before the police formally invoke the criminal process by arrest.
2. Actions that take place in the police station following arrest.

During the 1960s, the U.S. Supreme Court, led by a former California prosecutor, Chief Justice Earl Warren, began to reduce police discretion in law enforcement. First, the Court restrained police actions in the station regarding suspects in custody. Then, it applied the Fourth and Fifth Amendments to police-citizen encounters on the street and in other public places outside the police station. All these extensions of constitutional rights and their consequent restraints on police discretion generated heated controversy. Many police, lawyers, and members of the public believed that legal restraints on police discretionary decision making prevented effective crime control. At the same time, others hailed the restraints as a bulwark against police abuse and a step toward guaranteeing individual liberty and privacy in an increasingly authoritarian world.

During the 1970s under Chief Justice Warren Burger, and then during the 1980s under Chief Justice William Rehnquist, the Supreme Court returned some of the discretion lost to the police during the 1960s. However, the Supreme Court has remained committed to the principle of applying the Constitution to both police-citizen contacts outside, and police practices inside, the police station. In the first half of the 1990s, the Supreme Court continued to balance the need for government power to enforce the criminal law against the societal interest in restraining the government from subjecting citizens to unwarranted intrusions and deprivations. However, it is important to point out that that application has almost always *expanded*—not *reduced*—the power of the police.[4] (See Chapter 4.)

Knowledge and Understanding CHECK

1. Identify the two main rights that government evidence gathering interferes with.
2. How important to the police is bringing cases to court?
3. Identify the constraints that explain why frequently the police do not bring cases to court.
4. Practically speaking, in what kinds of cases are constitutional rights important?
5. What role does discretion play in the decision to bring cases into the criminal justice system?
6. Of what importance is information in criminal law enforcement?
7. Identify and describe the four provisions in the U.S. Constitution that apply to balancing law enforcement and individual liberty and privacy.
8. Describe one way to view the history of criminal justice.
9. Identify the two stages in the criminal process that are relevant in examining the formalization of police practices.
10. Describe the Warren, Burger, and Rehnquist courts' approach to police discretion.

ARREST

To determine whether government actions are Fourth Amendment seizures, courts have adopted a three-step analysis. (Notice that the Fourth Amendment applies only to government—not private—actions.)

1. Is the action a seizure by the government? If not, the Fourth Amendment does not apply at all.
2. If the government action is a seizure, is it unreasonable?
3. If the seizure is unreasonable, what are the remedies for unreasonable seizures?

The Definition of Arrest

Police actions affecting the freedom of movement of individuals range from voluntary encounters to forcible detentions. Police officers who approach people to ask them questions have not "seized" the individuals they approach. Police officers who stop people against their will have seized them, although they have not necessarily arrested them. Whether police officers make a Fourth Amendment **arrest** of the people that they have detained depends on three qualities of the detention:

1. The *duration* of the detention (that is, how long does it last?).
2. The *location* of the detention (was the individual involuntarily moved from the place of detention?).
3. The *invasiveness* of the detention (that is, how much of an invasion was it?). Sometimes called the *subjective dimension* of the seizure, it refers to the fear and surprise generated by the detention.

Clearly, police officers have arrested people when they say, "You're under arrest," transport them to the police station, book them, and then detain them overnight. However, many other cases do not so easily satisfy the three requirements. For example, officers who release suspects after 15 minutes without taking them to the police station, and spend the 15 minutes in friendly questioning present a more difficult case. The opinions in *Florida v. Royer,* decided by the U.S. Supreme Court and excerpted in the Use Your Discretion case that follows, introduce you to the difficulties that can arise in determining when a contact between police officers and individuals is a "seizure," and if it is, when the seizure is an arrest.

When did the police arrest Royer?
***Florida v. Royer,* 460 U.S. 491 (1983)**

Facts

Detectives Johnson and Magdalena, plainclothes narcotics detectives, observed Royer at Miami International Airport. They believed that his mannerisms, luggage, and actions fit the "drug courier profile." The detectives approached Royer on the concourse, identified themselves, and asked if he had a "moment" to talk to them; Royer answered, "Yes." On request, but without saying he consented, Royer produced his airline ticket and driver's license. When asked why his driver's license bore the name Royer and his ticket and luggage, Holt, Royer said a friend had bought the ticket. The detectives then told Royer they were narcotics investigators and that they suspected him of transporting narcotics. The detectives did not return Royer's ticket and identification and asked him to accompany them to a room, approximately 40 feet away. Royer said nothing but accompanied the officers to the room. Detective Johnson described the room as a "large storage closet," containing a desk and two chairs. Fifteen minutes later, after obtaining Royer's luggage, opening it with a key Royer supplied, and finding marijuana in it, the officers told Royer he was "under arrest."

Opinion

Law enforcement officers do not violate the Fourth Amendment by merely approaching an individual on the street or in another public place, by asking him if he is willing to answer some questions, by putting questions to him if the person is willing to listen. . . . Nor would the fact that the officer identifies himself as a police officer, without more, convert the encounter to a seizure. . . . Asking for and examining Royer's ticket and his driver's license were no doubt permissible in themselves, but when the officers identified themselves as narcotics agents, told Royer that he was suspected of transporting narcotics, and asked him to accompany them to the police room, while retaining his ticket and driver's license and without indicating in any way that he was free to depart, Royer was effectively seized for the purposes of the Fourth Amendment. These circumstances surely amount to a show of official authority such that a reasonable person would not have believed he was free to leave. . . .

At the time Royer produced the key to his suitcase, the detention to which he was then subjected was a more serious intrusion on his personal liberty than is allowable on mere suspicion. By the time Royer was informed that the officers wished to examine his luggage, he had identified himself when approached by the officers and had attempted to explain the discrepancy between the name shown on his identification and the name under which he had purchased his ticket and identified his luggage. The officers were not satisfied, and they informed him they were narcotics agents and had reason to believe that he was carrying illegal drugs. They requested that he accompany them to a police room. Royer went with them. He found himself in a small room—a large closet—equipped with a desk and two chairs. He was alone with two police officers who again told him that they thought he was carrying narcotics. He also found that the officers, without his consent, had retrieved his checked luggage from the airlines. What had begun as a consensual inquiry in a public place had escalated into an investigatory procedure in a police interrogation room, where the police, unsatisfied with previous explanations, sought to confirm their suspicions. The officers had Royer's ticket, they had his identification, and they had seized his luggage. Royer was never informed that he was free to board his plane if he so chose, and he reasonably believed that he was being detained. At least as of that moment, any consensual aspects of the encounter had evaporated.... As a practical matter Royer was under arrest.

Dissent

The public has a compelling interest in detecting those who would traffic in deadly drugs for personal profit.... In my view, the police conduct in this case was minimally intrusive. Given the strength of society's interest in overcoming the extraordinary obstacles to the detection of drug traffickers, such conduct should not be subjected to the requirement of probable cause.... The key principle in the Fourth Amendment is reasonableness—the balancing of competing interests.... On the one hand, any formal arrest, and any seizure having the essential attributes of a formal arrest, is unreasonable unless it is supported by probable cause.... In my view, it cannot fairly be said that, prior to the formal arrest, the functional equivalent of an arrest had taken place.... Royer was not taken from a private residence, where reasonable expectations of privacy perhaps are at their greatest. Instead, he was approached in a major international airport where, due in part to extensive antihijacking surveillance and equipment, reasonable privacy expectations are of significantly lesser magnitude.... Royer was not subjected to custodial interrogation.... Instead, the officers first sought Royer's consent to move the detention forty feet to the police room.... The question is whether the move was voluntary.... Royer consented voluntarily to this change of locale.... Certainly, the intrusion on Royer's privacy was not so extreme as to make the countervailing public interest in greater flexibility.... I do not understand why the [Court] fails to balance the character of the detention and the degree to which it intruded upon Royer's privacy against its justification as measured by . . . the law enforcement interest.... The intrusion was short-lived and minimal. Only fifteen minutes transpired from the initial approach to the opening of the suitcases. The officers were polite, and sought and immediately obtained Royer's consent at each significant step of the process....

The [Court] concludes that somewhere between the beginning of the forty-foot journey and the resumption of the conversation in the room the investigation became so intrusive that Royer's consent evaporated, leaving him as a practical matter under arrest. But if Royer was legally approached in the first instance and consented to accompany the detectives to the room, it does not follow that his consent went up in smoke and he was arrested upon entering the room.... Other than the size of the room . . . there is nothing . . . which would indicate that Royer's resistance was overborne by anything about the room. Royer, who was in his fourth year of study at Ithaca College . . . simply continued to cooperate with the detectives as he had from the beginning of the encounter. Absent any evidence of . . . coercion . . . the size of the room does not transform a voluntary consent into a coerced consent.

CRITICAL THINKING

1. Consider the duration, intensity, and location of the police contact with Royer. At what point, if at all, did the police arrest Royer?
2. What specific facts support your conclusion?
3. If you had this encounter, at what point would you "not feel free to leave"? Do you think the answer to these questions depends on your perspective? For example, would police officers and defense attorneys answer these questions differently? Should the answers to these constitutional questions depend on the biases created by these "perspectives"? Explain your answer.

The "Reasonableness" Requirement

The reasonableness of an arrest depends on two factors:

1. *Objective basis:* the facts to back it up.
2. *Manner of execution:* the way the officer made the arrest.

Probable Cause as the Objective Basis

The Fourth Amendment requires probable cause as the objective basis required to back up arrests. **Probable cause to arrest** means that officers possess enough facts and circumstances that would lead a reasonable officer to *believe* the person arrested *has* committed, *is* committing, or *is* about to commit a crime. These facts or circumstances must be **articulable facts and circumstances;** that is, officers can put them into words specific enough for a judge to weigh their contents and make an independent judgment as to whether they add up to probable cause. Probable cause denotes quantity. It stands somewhere between zero facts and all the facts. More technically, probable cause stands between a hunch, whim, or mere suspicion that someone has committed a crime and absolute proof that a person has committed a crime. According to the prestigious American Law Institute's *Model Code of Pre-Arraignment Procedure,* written by lawyers, police administrators, judges, scholars, and other criminal justice experts:

> In determining . . . [probable cause] to justify an arrest . . . a law enforcement officer may take into account all information that a prudent officer would judge relevant to the likelihood that a crime has been committed and that a person to be arrested has committed it, including information derived from any expert knowledge which the officer in fact possesses and information received from an informant whom it is reasonable under the circumstances to credit, whether or not at the time of making the arrest the officer knows the informant's identity.[5]

Firsthand or direct information, secondhand information or hearsay, or a combination of both can satisfy the probable cause requirement. **Direct information** consists of facts and circumstances personally known to the officers. It is information that officers see, hear, touch, or smell themselves. For example, an officer who sees a suspect pace up and down and peer in a window has direct information. **Hearsay** consists of facts or circumstances that officers learn from someone else. The "someone else" is ordinarily a victim, a witness, another police officer, or an informant. For example, a witness who calls a police officer and says, "I saw a man walking up and down peering in a jewelry store window" has provided hearsay information.

Probable cause requires more than mere suspicion or hunches, but it does not mean legal guilt (proof beyond a reasonable doubt is discussed in Chapter 11), or even that suspects are more guilty than not. The police might have probable cause to arrest but not proof beyond a reasonable doubt to convict. Arrest, in the legal sense, allows the police to detain suspects or "freeze" a situation long enough for prosecutors to decide whether they have enough evidence to charge suspects. Juries, or in some cases judges, decide if the government has proof of guilt beyond a reasonable doubt. One of the most common errors in the public mind is the belief that either judges are "soft on crime" or "technicalities" account for half of all arrests not leading to convictions. The truth is that there is probable cause to arrest suspects but no proof beyond a reasonable doubt to convict them.[6]

Use *Your* Discretion

Did the officers have probable cause to arrest?

In *People v. Washington,* the defendant, Michael Washington, appealed the judgment entered in the Superior Court of the City and County of San Francisco revoking his probation and sentencing him to three years in prison. The revocation of probation and the sentence were based on the finding that Washington possessed cocaine. On appeal, Washington argued that the cocaine used against him at the probation revocation hearing was the product of an illegal arrest because the officers did not have probable cause to arrest him. The following is taken from the court's opinion:

> Officers Lewis and Griffin were in the vicinity of 1232 Buchanan Street. They observed defendant along with four other individuals in a courtyard area between 1133 Laguna and 1232 Buchanan. Defendant and the others were observed talking in a "huddle" formation with "a lot of hand movement" inside the huddle, but the officers could not see what was in the hands of any member of the group. The officers then walked toward the group, at which point everyone looked in the officers['] direction, whispered, and quickly dispersed. When defendant saw the officers, he immediately turned around and started walking at a fast pace through the lobby of 1232 Buchanan. The officers followed him for a quarter of a block when Officer Griffin called out to defendant. Defendant replied, "Who me?" Officer Griffin answered, "Yes," and defendant immediately ran away. The officers gave chase. Two minutes later, while still chasing defendant, Officer Lewis saw defendant discard a plastic bag containing five white bundles. Officer Lewis scooped up the bag as he continued to give chase. Shortly thereafter, the officers apprehended defendant.
>
> During the probation revocation hearing, Officer Lewis testified that during the four years he had been a patrolman he had made at least 100 arrests concerning cocaine in the area frequented by defendant that night. On cross-examination, Officer Lewis answered in the affirmative when asked if most of the black men he saw in the area usually had something to hide if they ran from police. The officer stated that prior to the chase he saw no contraband, nor was anything about the group's dispersal significant. Nor did the officer explain why they singled out defendant to follow. The trial court denied defendant's motion to suppress and revoked the defendant's probation.

Opinion

Prior to defendant's abandonment of the cocaine, the police lacked the "articulable suspicion that a person has committed or is about to commit a crime." The officers spotted the group of men in an open courtyard at 6:15 P.M.; the men made no attempt to conceal themselves and did not exhibit any furtive behavior. The hand gestures were, on the police officer's own testimony, inconclusive and unrevealing. Furthermore, the time at which the detention occurred is not the "late or unusual hour . . . from which any inference of criminality may be drawn." The fact that defendant was seen in what was a high crime area also does not elevate the facts into a reasonable suspicion of criminality. Courts have been "reluctant to conclude that a location's crime rate transforms otherwise innocent-appearing circumstances into circumstances justifying the seizure of an individual."

Once the officers made their approach visible, they gave no justification for their decision to follow defendant apart from the others in the group. Neither officer knew defendant or knew of defendant's past criminal record, nor did Officer Lewis testify that defendant appeared to be a principal or a leader in the group. Further, the defendant had the right to walk away from the officers. He had no legal duty to submit to the attention of the officers; he had the freedom to "go on his way," free of stopping even momentarily for the officers. By walking at a brisk rate away from the officers, defendant could have been exercising his right to avoid the officers or avoid any other person, or could have simply walked rapidly through sheer nervousness at the sight of a police officer.

We see no change in the analysis when defendant decided to run from the officers. Flight alone does not trigger an investigative detention; rather, it must be combined with other objective factors that give use to an articulable suspicion of criminal activity. No such factors existed, nor does Officer Lewis's assertion that the "black men [they] see in the project usually have something to hide when they run" justify a detention. "[M]ere subjective speculation as to the [person's] purported motives . . . carries no weight." Thus, prior to defendant's abandonment of the contraband, the circumstances of defendant's actions were not reasonably consistent with criminal activity. . . .

. . . [T]he officers conceded they had no objective factors upon which to base any suspicions that the group was involved in illegal activity, and the officers offered no explanation why they singled out defendant to follow. Indeed, the only justification for engaging in pursuit was that defendant was a black male, and that it was the officer's subjective belief that black men run from police when they have something to hide. Thus, a single factor—the defendant's race—triggered the detention.[7]

CRITICAL THINKING

1. What were the facts on which Officers Lewis and Griffin based their arrest?
2. Assume you are the prosecutor in the case. How would you try to convince the judge that the arrest was legal?
3. Now assume you are the defense counsel. How would you argue that the arrest was illegal? Now you are the judge. How would you decide the case? Write an opinion explaining your decision.

The Manner of Arrest–Entering Homes and Using Force

The reasonableness of an arrest depends not only on probable cause but also on the manner in which the police execute the arrest. The reasonableness of the manner of arrest arises primarily in two situations:

1. When the police enter private homes to make arrests.
2. When the police use force against people to make arrests.

The Fourth Amendment requires officers to get a warrant before they enter private homes to arrest suspects. The Fourth Amendment also requires that officers follow the **knock-and-announce rule.** As the name implies, the rule requires that officers knock and announce their presence before they enter. Also, officers have to allow occupants at least a brief time to get to the door. They need not wait for long; suspects might either flee out the back door, grab a weapon, or destroy evidence or contraband. So, police officers have not unreasonably seized a suspect if they obtain a warrant, knock on the door saying, "Open up, police"; wait 15 seconds; and then knock down the door, enter, and arrest the suspect named in the warrant.

Police use of force is a controversial, and difficult, subject. We leave the problem of police use of force generally to Chapter 8. Here, we discuss only when the use of deadly force by the police is an unreasonable seizure. The U.S. Supreme Court has ruled that the Fourth Amendment requires that police officers can only use reasonable force before, during, and after arrests. Historically, the **fleeing felon doctrine** governed the use of force. Under that doctrine, law enforcement officers could, if necessary, use deadly force to apprehend any fleeing felony suspect. The fleeing felon doctrine made sense in medieval England where there were few felonies, all of them capital; guns were rare; and lack of technology made it difficult to apprehend criminals. In the centuries that followed, a long list of noncapital, nonviolent felonies was enacted, applying the doctrine to many more crimes. Also, police forces armed with guns were created, making the chance of killing fleeing suspects more likely. Finally, advances in communications technology increased the tools police could use to apprehend escaped felony suspects. Despite these fundamental changes, most American states retained the fleeing felon doctrine until the 1960s.

The civil rights movement, the corresponding heightened concern for the rights of criminal defendants, and the loss of life during the urban riots of the 1960s coalesced to cause a reevaluation of the fleeing felon doctrine. Changes in the doctrine occurred formally by means of statutes, administrative rules, and court decisions. Most statutes limited the doctrine to "forcible felonies." By 1985, about half the states had adopted statutes limiting the use of deadly force.

In 1985 the U.S. Supreme Court, in the landmark case of *Tennessee v. Garner,* ruled that the fleeing felon doctrine is unconstitutional. Because half the states had already outlawed its use and most urban departments had already restricted the doctrine, the decision affected primarily medium-sized and small towns and rural areas. The following Use Your Discretion case, "Can the police shoot to kill a fleeing burglar?" examines the Supreme Court's reasons for striking down the fleeing felon doctrine.

Use *Your* Discretion

Can the police shoot to kill a fleeing burglar?
***Tennessee v. Garner,* 471 U.S. 1 (1985)**

Facts

At about 10:45 P.M. on October 3, 1974, Memphis police officers Elton Hymon and Leslie Wright were dispatched to answer a "prowler inside call." On arriving at the scene they saw a woman standing on her porch and gesturing toward the adjacent house. She told them she had heard glass breaking and that "they" or "someone" was breaking in next door. While Wright radioed the dispatcher to say that they were on the scene, Hymon went behind the house. He heard a door slam and saw someone run across the backyard.

The fleeing suspect, Edward Garner, stopped at a six-foot-high chain link fence at the edge of the yard. With the aid of a flashlight, Hymon was able to see Garner's face and hands. He saw no sign of a weapon and, though not certain, was "reasonably sure" and "figured" that Garner was unarmed. He thought Garner was 17 or 18 years old and about 5′5″ or 5′7″ tall. [In fact, Garner was a 13-year-old eighth grader, 5′4″ tall, weighing somewhere between 100 and 110 pounds.] While Garner was crouched at the base of the fence, Hymon called out "Police! Halt!" and took a few steps toward him. Garner then began to climb over the fence. Convinced that if Garner made it over the fence he would elude capture, Hymon shot him. When asked at trial why he fired, Hymon stated:

> Well, first of all it was apparent to me from the little bit that I knew about the area at the time that he was going to get away because, number 1, I couldn't get to him. My partner then couldn't find where he was because, you know, he was late coming around. He didn't know where I was talking about. I couldn't get to him because of the fence here. I couldn't have jumped this fence and come up, consequently jumped this fence and caught him before he got away because he was already up on the fence. Just one leap and he was already over the fence; and so there is no way I could have caught him.

Hymon also stated that the area beyond the fence was dark, that he could not have gotten over the fence easily because he was carrying a lot of equipment and wearing heavy boots, and that Garner, being younger and more energetic, could have outrun him. The bullet hit Garner in the back of the head. Garner was taken by ambulance to a hospital, where he died on the operating table. Ten dollars and a purse taken from the house were found on his body.

In using deadly force to prevent the escape, Hymon was acting under the authority of a Tennessee statute and pursuant to police department policy. The statute provides that "[i]f, after notice of the intention to arrest the defendant, he either flees or forcibly resists, the officer may use all the necessary means to effect the arrest." The department policy was slightly more restrictive than the statute, but still allowed the use of deadly force in cases of burglary. The incident was reviewed by the Memphis Police Firearm's Review Board and presented to a grand jury. Neither took any action.

Opinion

The use of deadly force to prevent the escape of all felony suspects, whatever the circumstances, is constitutionally unreasonable. It is not better that all felony suspects die than that they escape. Where the suspect poses no immediate threat to the officer and no threat to others, the harm resulting from failing to apprehend him does not justify the use of deadly force to do so. It is no doubt unfortunate when a suspect who is in sight escapes, but the fact that the police arrive a little late or are a little slower afoot does not always justify killing the suspect. A police officer may not seize an unarmed, nondangerous suspect by shooting him dead. The Tennessee statute is unconstitutional insofar as it authorizes the use of deadly force against such fleeing suspects.

Dissent

Although the circumstances of this case are unquestionably tragic and unfortunate, our constitutional holdings must be sensitive both to the history of the Fourth Amendment and to the general implications of the Court's reasoning. By disregarding the serious and dangerous nature of residential burglaries and the longstanding practice of many states, the Court effectively creates a Fourth Amendment right allowing a burglary suspect to flee unimpeded from a police officer who has probable cause to arrest, who has ordered the suspect to halt, and who has no means short of firing his weapon to prevent escape. I do not believe that the Fourth Amendment supports such a right, and I accordingly dissent.

CRITICAL THINKING

1. Do you agree with the majority or the dissent in the case? What arguments persuaded you?
2. In an investigation of the impact of the decision, Abraham N. Tennenbaum found a significant reduction (approximately 16 percent) in the number of homicides committed before and after the decision. This reduction was more significant in states

that declared their laws regarding police use of deadly force to be unconstitutional after the *Garner* decision. Evidence suggests that the reduction is due not only to a general reduction in shooting fleeing felons but also to a general reduction in police shootings.[8]

3. What impact, if any, do the findings of Tennenbaum have on your position? Explain.

Shooting suspects draws the most public attention, but other means to arrest occur more frequently. Some of these have caused considerable debate. The Supreme Court has not decided whether the use of choke holds, Mace, and stun guns are Fourth Amendment "seizures." Some lower courts have held that they are not. In determining their reasonableness, courts have examined whether officers have applied excessive force. If they have, excessive force amounts to unreasonable seizures. Using this test, a federal appeals court found the use of Mace reasonable to subdue an intoxicated suspect who refused to remain in a small room near the booking area in a police station.[9]

Knowledge and Understanding CHECK

1. To whose actions does the Fourth Amendment apply?
2. Identify and explain the three-step analysis of the Fourth Amendment.
3. Identify the three qualities that determine whether a government action is an arrest.
4. Identify the two factors that determine the reasonableness of an arrest.
5. What are the major sources of direct and indirect information to back up arrests?
6. Explain the U.S. Supreme Court's interpretation of the Fourth Amendment in cases involving police entry into homes.
7. Identify the major exceptions to the requirement of warrants to enter homes.
8. Identify the two major situations in which the manner of arrest usually arises.
9. What is the law regarding the reasonableness of choke holds, Mace, and stun guns?

SEARCHES

The right against unreasonable **searches** is ancient. The Babylonian Talmud of the Jews recognized the need to be left alone by prohibiting putting up buildings that could allow looking into others' dwellings. Cicero in 57 B.C. spoke of citizens' homes as "sacred . . . hedged about by every kind of sanctity." Under the Code of the Byzantine Emperor Justinian in 533 A.D., a "freeman could not be summoned from his house" because it is "everyone's safest place, his refuge and his shelter." The roots of the right against government searches run deep in British history and in the history of the United States. In 1505, John Fineux, chief justice of the Court of King's Bench in England, held that "the house of a man is for him his castle and his defence."[10]

Despite the long tradition lauding the *right* to be free from unreasonable searches, the exercise of the *power* to search has also had a long history. In England, searches were used extensively. One major area of controversy began with the invention of the printing press. The fear of the vicious verbal attacks in the form of seditious libels against English monarchs led to the use of the power to search to stamp out this type of objectionable speech. By the 1700s, seditious libels had increased because of the low respect the English had for their imported German kings, the four Georges of the House of Hanover. General warrants, or writs of assistance, gave a range of officials blanket authority to break into shops and homes to look for seditious libels. These warrants were valid for the life of the monarch, so a person holding one could enter any house at any time for years. The practice was to issue the writs at the beginning of a new monarch's reign; they were valid until the reigning monarch died.

General warrants were also used to combat smuggling of a growing list of taxable goods. Writs of assistance authorizing the search of houses and shops for smuggled goods were common in the American colonies, but they generated considerable controversy. In the English House of Commons, William Pitt, the Earl of Chatham, spoke the most famous words ever uttered against the power of government to search:

> The poorest man may in his cottage bid defiance to all the forces of the Crown. It may be frail; its roof may shake; the wind may blow through it; the storm may enter; but the king of England may not enter; all his force dare not cross the threshold of the ruined tenement without a lawfull warrant.

In America, the great colonial trial lawyer James Otis argued a widely publicized writs of assistance case in Boston. Otis argued that writs of assistance were illegal, maintaining that only searches with specific dates, naming the places or persons to be searched and seized, and based on probable cause were lawful where free people lived. Young John Adams attended the trial. Many years later Adams recalled how moved he was by Otis's words. He wrote, "There was the Child Independence born." Despite the great oratory hurled against writs of assistance, colonial governors continued to use them widely. But hostility toward general warrants led the drafters of the Bill of Rights to write the Fourth Amendment right against "unreasonable searches and seizures."

The purpose of the Fourth Amendment "unreasonable searches" clause is to make sure the government gathers the information it needs to control crime without conducting "unreasonable searches." But it leaves the government with considerable power to conduct searches. According to former prosecutor John Wesley Hall, Jr.:

> The raw power held by a police officer conducting a search is enormous. An officer wielding a search warrant has the authority of the law to forcibly enter one's home and search for evidence. The officer can enter at night and wake you from your sleep, roust you from bed, rummage in your drawers and papers and upend your entire home. Even though the particularity clause of the warrant defines the scope of the search, the search, as a practical matter, will be as intense as the officer conducting a stop or warrantless search chooses to make it. The power of an officer conducting a stop or warrantless search is also quite intense. Nothing can be more intimidating or frightening to a citizen than being stopped by the police and being asked or told to submit to a search.[11]

Use *Your* Discretion

Was the search "reasonable"?

Drug officers got a tip from an informant that retirees Marian and William Hauselmann were operating a methamphetamine lab. A SWAT team in ski masks went to the Hauselmanns' home, kicked in the door, and held them at gunpoint for 45 minutes while they searched for evidence. "They put a pillowcase on my head and handcuffed me and forced me to stay on the floor," said Mrs. Hauselmann. "My husband and I tried to speak and they screamed to shut up. It was the worst thing that ever happened to us." William Hauselmann, 64, who suffers from a heart condition, said the officers stepped on his back and cut his face while wrestling him to the floor.

The officers found nothing. The Hauselmanns say the worst vice they have is eating too much bratwurst. They live on 20 acres for their cows and enjoy their eight grandchildren. Mrs. Hauselmann complains of sore wrists from the heavy plastic handcuffs. "Funny thing is, after they realized their mistake, they had to ask us for something to cut them off with," she said. The Hauselmanns say they can't sleep and are tense. "But we're not going to a shrink. I think we'll be O.K. It's those police who need psychiatrists." The officers apologized to the Hauselmanns and offered to pay for the doors they kicked in. "We all feel very badly," said Sheriff's Lieutenant Richard McFarren.[12]

CRITICAL THINKING

1. Was the search reasonable; that is, did the informant's tip amount to probable cause?
2. Was kicking in the door reasonable?
3. Was the action once inside reasonable? How do you decide what is reasonable?
4. Should the officers have gotten a warrant?
5. Does knowing that the police made a mistake affect your answer? Legally, only what officers know *before* they search can be taken into account in determining probable cause. Defend your answer.

Searches with Warrants

According to the U.S. Supreme Court, the Fourth Amendment refers to two types of searches:

1. Searches *with* warrants.
2. Searches *without* warrants.

The Court has ruled that the Fourth Amendment states a clear preference for searches based on warrants. Only searches that fall within a list of well-defined exceptions are reasonable without warrants. The reasonableness of a search based on a warrant depends on:

1. *The particularity of the warrant:* that is, on how adequately the warrant describes the places and persons to be searched, and things or persons to be seized.
2. *Probable cause to search:* that is, an accompanying **affidavit** (sworn statement) lists facts and circumstances that would lead a reasonable officer to believe that the places or persons searched will yield the items or persons named in the search warrant.
3. *Knock and announce:* that is, this must be done before entering a home to search.

The attitudes of police officers toward the warrant requirement varies. L. Paul Sutton found that:

> a few [officers] acknowledged that the warrant requirement is appropriate for everyone's protection. Many seem to accept the requirement as a necessary part of law enforcement. Some are begrudgingly resigned to it as a reality that has to be dealt with. Others appear to regard the requirement as one of a long series of unnecessary intrusions of the court into what they consider to be the exclusive province of law enforcement; to these officers, the requirement is largely something to be gotten around.[13]

Sutton found that these attitudes stem from a variety of origins. According to a veteran officer, the search warrant is another "game" the courts have created. He assured researchers that the game was easy for the officers to win. "One way or another . . . cops would get what they wanted." Others complain about the frustration and delay in getting warrants. It takes several hours between the time officers decide they need a warrant and when they actually have one in hand. According to one deputy sheriff narcotics detective:

> We will go out to a yard and see marijuana plants growing in the back of the yard. Then what we have to do is go get a judge to sign a warrant stating that you have seen the marijuana plants there, which all seems a waste of time since they always sign the warrant if we have seen the marijuana plant, and since we know that they are going to sign the warrant. We still have to go through the rigmarole.[14]

Officers also complain about the inconsistencies of the judges who issue the warrants. One detective said, "You get a lot of different rulings from different judges; judges don't all see the law exactly the same. . . . One judge might make a ruling . . . and one judge might throw it out. Another expressed exasperation: "We went through everything—search warrants, etc.—all the way down the line. We got to the [misdemeanor] court, and [his/her] royal highness thought [he/she] knew more than the U.S. Supreme Court who ruled on a case identical to [ours] and [the misdemeanor court judge] said [what we had done] wasn't good enough."[15]

Underlying the officers' frustration over delay and inconsistency is a conflict between the values of due process and law enforcement (Chapter 1). Police officers see their job as enforcing the criminal law and controlling crime; they want to do so with the least amount of hassle and the greatest degree of efficiency. Judges stress the need for *due process,* the legal procedures whereby officers collect the evidence for criminal prosecutions.

Use *Your* Discretion

Was the "no knock" entry legal?
***U.S. v. Ramirez,* 91 F.3d 1297 (1996)**

> Before: REINHARDT, KOZINSKI, and FERNANDEZ, Circuit Judges.
>
> Opinion by Judge Fernandez; Dissent by Judge Kozinski.
>
> FERNANDEZ, Circuit Judge:

Hernan Ramirez was indicted for being a felon in possession of firearms. 18 U.S.C. § 922(g)(1). The district court determined that the firearms had been discovered in connection with a violation of Ramirez's rights under the knock-and-announce law. 18 U.S.C. § 3109. It, therefore, suppressed the evidence of the weapons, and the United States appealed. We affirm.

Facts

On November 5, 1994, Ramirez and his wife awoke out of their peaceful slumbers to a series of unusual sounds, including the breaking of a window. Their child, too, awoke and started crying. They feared that they were being attacked by burglars. They were not, but by the end of the day Ramirez found himself in the custody of federal agents and charged with a crime—felon in possession of a firearm—which could lead to a lengthy period of incarceration. How he found himself in that predicament takes some telling.

Just three days before, Alan Laurence Shelby had knocked a deputy sheriff down and escaped from custody. He was then facing a term of federal imprisonment of 248 months and had declared that he would not do federal time. He had tried to escape before. One time he had struck an officer, kicked out a jail door, stolen an automobile, and rammed a police vehicle as he attempted to get away. Another time he had attempted to escape by using a rope made from torn bedsheets. At some time in the past he had also threatened to kill witnesses; and, it was said, he had tortured someone with a hammer.

The authorities were understandably anxious to get Shelby back, so they sent out a press release. Almost immediately, on November 3, 1994, a reliable confidential informant contacted Bureau of Alcohol, Tobacco and Firearms Special Agent George H. Kim and told him that he had seen a person he believed to be Shelby at Ramirez's home the day before. Agent Kim and the informant then drove out to the area, and from some distance away they saw a person who was "very similar to" a photo of Shelby and noted that the man was wearing a blue jumpsuit and was clean-cut. That was the person the confidential informant had seen there the day before. Thereupon, a deputy marshal also went out, and from 1,000 yards away he saw a clean-cut man wearing blue sweats come out of the house. The marshal decided that the man was the person whom Agent Kim had seen.

In the afternoon of the next day, a warrant to arrest Shelby at Ramirez's home was obtained, and that led to the early morning raid on November 5, which brought Ramirez, but not Shelby, into the clutches of the law.

Ramirez's fateful day unfolded in this way. In the predawn hours of November 5, Ramirez, his wife, and their three-year-old child were asleep in their abode. The main house had three bedrooms, a living room, an activity room, and a kitchen, which led into a small utility room, which, in turn, led into an attached garage. The informant, who said that Shelby was at the house, also "indicated there were supposed to be several guns in the garage." Apparently there were not, and apparently the informant had never seen them there. Nevertheless, that is what he had said.

At 6:15 A.M., 45 armed officers converged on the property. The group included SWAT teams of state, county, and city officers. The officers set up a portable loudspeaker system and began announcing that they had a search warrant, but without waiting for a response they broke the window of the garage and began waving a gun through that window—a maneuver that was not too efficacious because a curtain got in the way.

The Ramirezes had no idea that police were outside their home, but they did hear the disturbance, did hear the breaking of glass, and did think that they were being burglarized. They feared for their safety and for the safety of their three-year-old child. Thus, to frighten the intruder off, Mr. Ramirez obtained a pistol from a utility closet and fired it toward the ceiling of the garage. The officers fired back and shouted "Police." At that point, and only at that point, the occupants of the house realized that it was law enforcement officers who had broken into the home. Ramirez "ran to the living room, threw away the firearm across the floor, and threw himself on the floor in a prone position, shaking from fright." By 6:35 A.M., he and his wife, with their child in her arms, had walked out of the house and into police custody. These householders were the only persons captured in the raid. Shelby was nowhere to be found, although Ramirez acknowledged that a photo of Shelby looked like a person who might have been there on November 3.

Based on what occurred at the house that morning, a second warrant was obtained, the gun that Ramirez had fired and another one were seized, and Ramirez found himself in the toils of the law.

Opinion

The fear of a smashing in of doors by government agents is based upon much more than a concern that our privacy will be disturbed. It is based upon concern for our safety and the safety of our families. Indeed, the minions of dictators do not kick in doors for the mere purpose of satisfying some voyeuristic desire to peer around and then go about their business. Something much more malevolent and dangerous is afoot when they take those actions. It is that which strikes terror into the hearts of their victims. The Fourth Amendment protects us from that fear as much as it protects our privacy. . . .

As concerned citizens we also fear the needless injuries that might be inflicted upon police officers, or upon a homeowner, as a result of the homeowner's mistaken belief that miscreants are invading his little castle. So it was here. Had Ramirez been less reasonable, the officer at the window might have been killed; had Ramirez been less wise, he or his family might have been killed. As it was, his property was needlessly damaged when his home was broken into.

When the officers executed the warrant they brushed aside the wisdom of history and elicited a response which, if not strictly intended, should have been reasonably foreseen. They seek to excuse their conduct on the grounds that the dangerousness of Shelby resulted in an exigency which permitted them to break into the home of Ramirez without following knock-and-announce requirements.

. . . The 45 officers did not fear any of the actual residents of the house and were not attacking a gang or cult hangout where they might be met by a fusillade of gunfire. They were concerned about one person, Shelby, who might be on the premises. But Shelby was not known to have ever shot or shot at anyone. He was an escape artist, who said he would not go to federal prison. He had knocked people down in his escape attempts, and he had stolen a car and run into a police vehicle. His violence towards law enforcement had not extended beyond that, even though he had obviously been arrested on some occasions. Perhaps his degree of dangerousness bespoke a mild exigency. Certainly it did not bespeak more. . . .

There is no suggestion that the police presence was known, no confirmation that Shelby was on the premises, and, more importantly, no indication that Shelby was armed and would resist with deadly force.

Police must have some leeway in balancing the demands of the knock-and-announce requirement against other safety considerations. Nevertheless, the courts must ultimately determine whether the police struck that balance properly. We think it clear that the police did not do so in this case. . . .

The flame of our Fourth Amendment liberties is bright and strong—that should come as no surprise. It has been tended by lovers of liberty for over two centuries. While it burns, it keeps our homes free from unlawful intrusions by the government. Still, it is just a flame, and it will be quickly quenched if it is not protected. Should that occur, a tenebrific atmosphere would envelop our liberties and our homes. That must not happen.

We hold that Ramirez's statutory and Fourth Amendment rights were violated when government agents broke into his home in the early morning hours without complying with the knock-and-announce requirements. We also hold that the district court correctly suppressed use of the seized weapons as evidence against him.

AFFIRMED.

Dissent

KOZINSKI, Circuit Judge, dissenting.

There is much rhetoric in the opinion about the sanctity of every man's "little castle," but the principal reason we can sleep safely at night is that the men and women of law enforcement put their lives on the line to keep our castles from being invaded by brutal criminals. When police track down "a major methamphetamine manufacturer, [who] has had access to large caches of weapons" and a history of torture and other violent conduct, they are entitled to take precautions. A castle, little though it be, often looks like a fortress from the outside; police cannot know what's lurking within. It's easy enough, sitting in our well-guarded offices, and with the benefit of hindsight, to issue pronouncements about what the police should or could have done, but this provides little useful guidance to police in the field who must make difficult judgments in unknown territory and [are] subject to unpredictable developments. What if the police had adopted the majority's rosy view of Shelby and had politely tapped at the door and asked if he would come along, but Shelby had seized the guns in the garage, taken the Ramirez family hostage and precipitated a shoot-out? No doubt, we would then have issued a similarly smug opinion, this time lecturing the police that they were not free to ignore the words and warnings of their CRI, and affirming the payment of compensation to the Ramirezes or anyone else harmed in the altercation.

My guess is that, had any of us been in charge of this operation—had we been responsible for the lives and safety of dozens of law enforcement officers and the family sleeping inside—we would have done just what the police here did. To have done less would have been foolhardy (my colleagues' high-fallutin' rhetoric notwithstanding); to have done more would have been excessive. The police properly balanced the homeowner's privacy and property interests against the dictates of security. See *Wilson v. Arkansas,*— U.S.—,—, 115 S.Ct. 1914, 1918, 131 L.Ed.2d 976 (1995) ("The Fourth Amendment's flexible requirement of reasonableness should not be read to mandate a rigid rule of announcement that ignores countervailing law enforcement interests."); *United States v. Bustamante-Gamez,* 488 F.2d 4, 10 (9th Cir. 1973) ("[I]t has never been suggested that the [no-knock] requirement is an inflexible one; both at common law and in the constitutional context the courts have acknowledged that the interests [protected by the rule] may give way to other considerations."), cert. denied, 416 U.S. 970, 94 S.Ct. 1993, 40 L.Ed.2d 559 (1974). They deserve to be congratulated, not chastened and ridiculed.

CRITICAL THINKING

1. List the facts relevant to determining whether the entry here required the use of the knock-and-announce rule.
2. Give the reasons for the majority's and the dissent's opinions.
3. Do you favor the majority or the dissent? Defend your answer, relying on the facts and the arguments in the opinion.

Knowledge and Understanding CHECK

1. Describe the right and the reality of the right to be free from unreasonable searches.
2. Why is it important to know about how searches were made during the American Revolution?
3. Identify the two basic types of search.
4. Which of the two types is used more and why?
5. Identify the three main elements upon which the reasonableness of search warrants is determined.
6. Summarize the attitudes of police officers toward search warrants.

Searches Without Warrants

In day-to-day law enforcement, the vast majority of searches take place without warrants. The Supreme Court has created a number of exceptions to the warrant requirement. The major exceptions include:

- Searches accompanying arrests
- Consent searches
- Searches of vehicles
- Plain-view searches
- Stops and frisks

The U.S. Supreme Court has held that warrantless searches are reasonable if they satisfy what is called the **balancing test of reasonableness.** According to this test, courts look at the facts of each case to balance the following interests:

1. Criminal law enforcement
2. Individual privacy

The balancing test requires that courts look at all of the facts on a case-by-case basis. This look at all of the facts in each individual case is called the **totality of circumstances.** If the totality of circumstances demonstrates that the government's need to invade the privacy of individuals and their homes outweighs the degree of invasion of the individual's privacy, then the search is reasonable.

Searches Incident to Arrest

In day-to-day criminal law enforcement, the most common searches are those that accompany arrest. Searches accompanying arrests are known as **searches incident to arrest.** These warrantless searches are reasonable if there is probable cause to *arrest* the suspect.

Officers can search only to the extent necessary to protect officers, prevent escape, and/or preserve evidence. The

The right against unreasonable searches is upheld by the Fourth Amendment. However, most searches are made without warrants; they are validated by the list of exceptions to warrant requirement established by the Supreme Court. Obviously, the circumstances officers face are ambivalent in many situations. When do you think searches or arrests cross the line and become "unreasonable"?

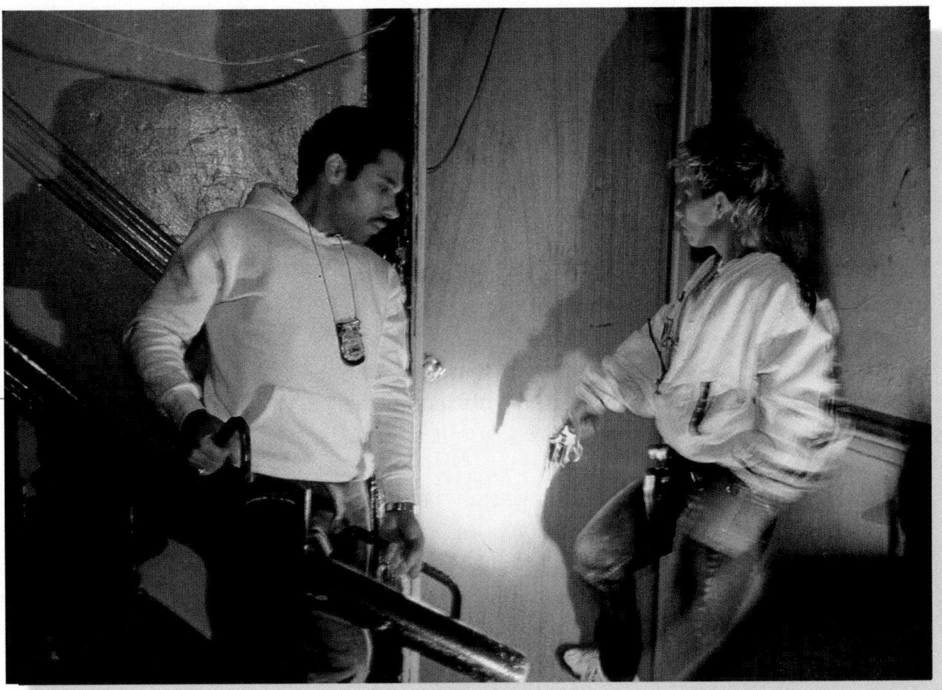

Supreme Court applied the balancing test of reasonableness to warrantless searches incident to arrests in the landmark case *Chimel v. California.* Police officers arrived at Chimel's house with an arrest warrant, but not a search warrant. They asked if they could "look around." When Chimel refused to let them, the police searched the house anyway. In a bedroom dresser drawer, they found coins Chimel had stolen during the burglary of a coin shop. Chimel challenged the search's reasonableness, but the trial court and two California appeals courts upheld his conviction. When Chimel appealed to the Supreme Court, the Court balanced the invasion of Chimel's home against the government interest in catching a burglar. To do this, the Court had to decide how extensively the police could reasonably search accompanying (or "incident to") Chimel's lawful arrest. In deciding that the search was "unreasonable," the Court wrote:

> When an arrest is made, it is reasonable for the arresting officer to search the person arrested in order to remove any weapons that the latter might seek to use in order to resist arrest or effect his escape. Otherwise, the officer's safety might well be endangered, and the arrest itself frustrated. In addition, it is entirely reasonable for the arresting officer to search for and seize any evidence on the arrestee's person in order to prevent its concealment or destruction. And the area into which an arrestee might reach in order to grab a weapon or evidentiary items must, of course, be governed by a like rule. A gun on a table or in a drawer in front of one who is arrested can be as dangerous to the arresting officer as one concealed in the clothing of the person arrested. There is ample justification, therefore, for a search of the arrestee's person and the area "within his immediate control"—construing that phrase to mean the area from within which he might gain possession of a weapon or destructible evidence. . . .
>
> The search here went far beyond the petitioner's person and the area from within which he might have obtained either a weapon or something that could have been used as evidence against him. . . . The scope of the search was, therefore, "unreasonable" under the Fourth and Fourteenth amendments, and the petitioner's conviction cannot stand.[16]

Consent Searches

The second most common kind of day-to-day searches are the **consent search.** Consent searches are those that individuals agree to allow the police to conduct. Consent searches do not require warrants, probable cause, or a legitimate purpose. In consent searches, people give up their constitutional right against unreasonable searches. They can give up their right only if their consent is voluntary. Formally, the U.S. Supreme Court has ruled that the government has a heavy burden to prove that the totality of circumstances in each case shows that the person searched voluntary consented.

In the leading consent search case, *Schneckcloth v. Bustamonte,* police officers asked if it was "okay to look in the trunk of the car." The driver replied, "Sure, go ahead." According to the Supreme Court, the police legally seized stolen checks they found in the trunk because the driver voluntarily consented to the search.[17]

Critics maintain that most people believe they are obliged to comply with the requests of police officers. In other words, ordinary people treat the requests of police officers as implied commands. Therefore, consent to police requests is not truly voluntary. To meet this objection, some say that the Fourth Amendment requires that before officers can search without warrants or probable cause, they must not only obtain voluntary consent but also a specific waiver of the right against unreasonable searches, similar to the situation involving confessions. (See the following section on interrogation.) According to this position, police officers have to advise people that they do not have to consent to the request to search. If people do consent, the officers can seize any incriminating evidence they find and use it against the person consenting or others.

The Supreme Court specifically rejected this call for a waiver test in *Schneckcloth v. Bustamonte.* Instead, the law assumes that people know they have rights; and to claim their rights, people have to assert them. But, asserting rights carries risks because officers might read a refusal to consent "as evidence of guilt, perhaps even sufficient to establish probable cause to search." The courts have not solved this "damned if you do, damned if you don't" problem. However, the Supreme Court has held that mere refusal to cooperate with police officers is not enough to add up to probable cause.

Searches of Vehicles

The reasonableness of warrantless vehicle searches also depends on balancing the government interest in law enforcement and the privacy interest of individuals. There are two reasons for the elimination of the warrant requirement in vehicle searches:

1. Mobility of vehicles.
2. Reduced expectation of privacy in vehicles.

The mobility of vehicles increases the risk of both the escape of suspects and the destruction of evidence. Requiring a warrant to search the vehicle, therefore, places too heavy a burden on law enforcement. By the time officers could obtain the warrant, the vehicle would be gone. Furthermore, the Supreme Court has held that people have a reduced privacy interest in their vehicles as opposed to that they have in their homes. For these reasons, searches of vehicles are reasonable without warrants, if they are based on probable cause. According to the Supreme Court, the danger to the public of using vehicles as instruments of crime, the reduced privacy interest of individuals in their vehicles, and the probable cause to support them justify searches of vehicles without warrants. Despite the use of mobile homes and some vans as temporary or even permanent residences, the Supreme Court has also held that the government interest in law enforcement outweighs the individual privacy interest in these "hybrid" vehicles.[18]

Plain-View Searches

Plain-view searches allow law enforcement officers to seize weapons, contraband, stolen property, or evidence that is in plain view. Plain *view* is really an incorrect term, because the rule applies to discoveries by any of the ordinary senses—sight, smell, hearing, and touch. Plain view, plain smell, plain hearing, and plain touch searches are reasonable under the following conditions:

1. Discovery by means of *ordinary* senses.
2. Discovery by *inadvertent* means.
3. Discovery by officers who had a lawful right to be where they were and were doing only what they had a legal right to do.

Use *Your* Discretion

Were they plain-view searches?

1. Officers stop a car for running a red light. They see a plastic bag full of marijuana lying on the front seat.
2. Officers use a high-powered telescope to see into the apartment of a suspect hundreds of feet away.
3. Officers see a television set that they suspect is stolen. They turn the set upside down to get its serial number, check out the serial number to find out if it is stolen, and learn from the check that it is stolen.

CRITICAL THINKING

1. Which of the three searches is a plain-view search. Which is not?
2. Give reasons for your answer, relying on the requirements for plain-view searches.
3. According to the U.S. Supreme Court, the first search was a plain-view search but the second and third were not. Can you figure out the reasons?
4. Here is what the Court said: In the first search, officers used only their ordinary sense of sight to make the discovery. They have inadvertently discovered the marijuana by virtue of their being in a position to see it without any further action on their part. They have a legal right to stand outside the car on a public road where they have lawfully stopped a driver for a traffic violation. In the second case, officers relied on a technological enhancement of their sense of sight to look into the apartment. In the third case, the discovery was not inadvertent because the officers had to take further actions to discover that the television set was stolen.[19]

Stop and Frisk

In the course of normal duty, patrol officers encounter large numbers of people. Individuals frequently initiate these contacts because they want information or help, or because they want to report trouble. Less frequently, patrol officers themselves witness suspicious activity, and they initiate contact with individuals who may either be involved or know something about the activity. These field investigations are known as **stop and frisk.** Usually, a stop and frisk involves officers approaching, questioning, and sometimes patting down individuals. The objective basis for stops and frisks is less than probable cause; it is called **reasonable suspicion.** The definition of reasonable suspicion is facts and circumstances that would lead a reasonable officer in the light of her training and experience to *suspect* that a crime *may* be afoot. (Compare this definition with probable cause in which there must be enough facts and circumstances to *believe* that a crime *is* being committed.) "Suspect" is not as strong a conclusion as "belief"; and, of course, "may" is not as certain as "is."

Police can also lawfully frisk persons under two conditions:

1. The individual is lawfully stopped.
2. The officer suspects that the officer may be armed.

Stopping suspicious persons and demanding to know who they are and why they are out and about is an old practice. Ancient statutes and court decisions empowered English constables to detain "suspicious nightwalkers" and hold them until morning in order to investigate their suspicious behavior. Until the mid-1960s, police-initiated contacts with people on the street and in other public places did not arouse controversy. These encounters were left to the discretion of individual officers. During the 1960s, the police discretionary power to stop and frisk became a matter of public concern.[20]

The due process revolution (discussed in Chapter 4) led reformers to call for extending constitutional protections to all contacts between officers and individuals and to subjecting those encounters to review by the courts. This resulted in a formalization of the period of criminal investigation occurring before the arrest of suspects. This formalization caused—and still causes—bitter controversy. The police and their supporters argue that police expertise and professional independence require that discretion, not formal rules, govern street encounters prior to arrest. Civil libertarians, on the other hand, maintain that citizens, especially those on the "fringes of society," need—and a free society requires—the Constitution to follow them wherever they go.

For complex reasons not yet sorted out, the courts, led by the Supreme Court, formalized stop and frisk during the 1960s. Despite strong opposition at the time, and some modification over the years since then, this formalization has remained intact. Furthermore, what happens in the police station—which until the 1960s was another sanctuary from formal judicial interference—has also come under constitutional protection.

Patrol officers regularly confront suspicious circumstances that call for further information from someone seen on the street or in a car, persons unknown to the officers and whom they will probably never see again. To enforce the criminal law effectively, officers need the discretion to "freeze the situation" briefly to check out suspicious circumstances and people. These suspicions frequently do not amount to probable cause. Also, if officers approach citizens and detain them, the citizens may endanger officers. If they suspect persons may be carrying a weapon, they pat them down for weapons. Courts and legislatures, who are neither experts nor present during these contacts, rarely second-guess the decisions of officers on the street to stop and frisk citizens. In most cases, officers decide quickly whether they have probable cause to arrest; if not, they release the detained person.

Encounters between individuals and police officers occur far more often on the street or in cars than inside police stations. In San Diego, for example, during one six-month period, the police recorded more than 21,000 stops on the street. They arrested only 392, or less than 2 percent, of the citizens they stopped. Since police do not record stops if they absolve citizens immediately, virtually no stops result in arrests.[21]

The 1960s reform wave focused attention on street encounters between citizens and the police. Some legislatures, such as New York's, passed stop-and-frisk laws specifically authorizing the police to approach citizens, detain them briefly to check out suspicions, and frisk them for weapons if necessary. In 1968, the U.S. Supreme Court took the opportunity to decide whether stops were arrests and frisks were seizures. The landmark case *Terry v. Ohio* balanced the interests of law enforcement and the rights of individuals to go about without interference from the government.

Terry and a companion walked up and down a Cleveland street, peering into a men's clothing store. Officer McFadden, a 37-year veteran of the Cleveland Police Department, observed them from across the street. He suspected that they were "casing" the store in preparation for a robbery, but he lacked probable cause to arrest them. So he approached them, asking their names and the reason they were there. When Terry mumbled in response, McFadden spun him around and ran his hands quickly over Terry's outer clothing. Feeling something hard in Terry's overcoat pocket, McFadden reached inside the coat and removed a gun. The Supreme Court had to decide whether police officers can stop citizens on the street and pat them down without probable cause to arrest them. The Court had three choices:

1. Stops are not seizures, and frisks are not searches; therefore, they fall within the realm of informal police discretion and decision making.
2. Stops are arrests, and frisks are full-body searches; therefore, they must satisfy the formal constitutional requirement of probable cause and other aspects of reasonable search and seizures.
3. Stops are seizures but lesser ones than full arrests; frisks are searches but lesser ones than full body searches. Therefore, they require only reasonable suspicion, not full probable cause, to back them up.[22]

There is a clear difference between a search and a seizure. In the first photo, the search consists of feeling the outside of the man's clothing. The second photo depicts the seizure through the removal of the weapon.

The Supreme Court chose the third option. The Court brought stop and frisk within the formal law of search and seizure but relaxed the probable cause standard. The Court acknowledged that good police work requires officers to stop citizens on the street to investigate suspicious circumstances and prevent crime. If Officer McFadden had not checked out Terry and his companion, they might have robbed the clothing store. To protect citizens from unwarranted stops, the Court extended the Fourth Amendment's protection to both stops and frisks. The justices refused to engage in a semantics battle—they simply agreed that stops constitute seizures, and frisks searches, within the meaning of the Fourth Amendment. Stops are lesser deprivations than full-blown arrests—and frisks are less intrusive than full-body searches—so they require fewer facts than probable cause. Instead, they require reasonable suspicion, facts that lead officers to suspect that crimes may be afoot and that suspects may be armed.

Stop and frisk has strong critics, who claim that it arouses hostility and therefore harms good police relations with the community. They argue that the price paid in hostility is not worth the benefit derived from crimes the practice might prevent or criminals it might lead to apprehending. Some research challenges these conclusions. In a study sponsored by the respected Police Foundation, John E. Boydstun evaluated stop and frisk in San Diego. The city was divided into three areas. In the control area, stops and frisks were conducted without any changes in police activities. In the Special Field Interrogation Area, only officers trained to reduce potential friction between subjects and officers conducted stops and frisks. In the No Field Interrogation Area, stops and frisks were suspended for the nine-month experimental period. The results of the experiment showed that San Diego's aggressive field interrogations had at least some deterrent effect without raising much community hostility.[23]

Use *Your* Discretion

Are police sweeps good policy?

Consider the following articles. The first describes a proposal by the Republican governor of Minnesota to introduce police sweeps in Minneapolis. The second describes the elements of the Minnesota Senate Democrats' anti-crime proposals. The third describes the police stop practices in Beverly Hills. The final two selections comment on the outcome of police sweeps in public housing units in Chicago.

"Governor Proposes $20 Million Anticrime Program," by Conrad deFiebre, *Minneapolis Star Tribune* (December 29, 1995)

A tough-talking Gov. Arne Carlson announced a $20 million proposal Thursday to fight crime in the Twin Cities, including state funding to extend a controversial Minneapolis police tactic of street sweeps to much of the metro area. Carlson said increased stop-and-frisk efforts modeled after Minneapolis' Operation Safe Streets will hit hard at criminals coming to Minnesota "from Illinois or elsewhere. . . . We're going to harass them out of here, and I mean it."

Under the governor's plan, which requires approval from the Legislature, up to $5 million in state money would pay overtime to officers from the State Patrol and 11 metro jurisdictions. The officers would "sweep neighborhoods of any kind of illegality, period," Carlson said. Carlson also urged using $15 million in state bonding money to buy sophisticated equipment to link fragmented metro police radio communications across city and county lines.

The centerpiece of his proposal, however, is an apparently unprecedented level of state involvement in local law enforcement in Minnesota—and specifically in support of police tactics that some have called unfair and indiscriminate. In the police sweeps envisioned by Carlson, officers would saturate targeted high-crime neighborhoods, making arrests for traffic and curfew violations, loitering, truancy and other minor offenses in an effort to find and seize guns and drugs.

"It's zero tolerance," said Don Davis, former Brooklyn Park police chief who is now Carlson's deputy commissioner of public safety. "It's a very, very drastic step. I'm apologizing in advance to the good citizens who might get caught in this, but it's a technique that has to be used."

Minneapolis police say their efforts last summer led to the seizure of more than 160 guns and a marked reduction in reports of shots fired, although the city's number of homicides has already set a record. Some black men have complained of being repeatedly stopped simply because of their skin color. But the state must step in now with money and police for "a very serious crackdown," Carlson said, because crime has become a major concern to all Minnesotans.

"The bulk of Minnesota citizens no longer feel safe, no matter where they live," the governor said. "That's a first and a serious red flag. . . . When safety is placed in jeopardy, everything else is in jeopardy." Fear of crime is even impeding efforts to improve the state's economic climate, transportation and education, he said.

Carlson announced his initiative at the Minneapolis police precinct station on Plymouth Av. with dozens of officers lined up behind him. Officials from several agencies that would benefit from the plan voiced enthusiastic support for it. With the state money, said Minneapolis Police Chief Robert Olson, "we hope we'll be able to double our efforts." Richard Eckwall, St. Paul deputy chief, said his department intends to apply for the state money, even though its crime-fighting efforts differ from those in Minneapolis.

Meanwhile, a group of St. Paul and Minneapolis DFL [Democrat Farmer Labor party] legislators plan to announce today another set of crime-fighting ideas, including state matching funds to help cities pay for so-called "Clinton cops"—new officers hired with federal assistance. But Sen. Allan Spear, DFL-Minneapolis, chairman of the state Senate Crime Prevention Committee, said he also expects to back Carlson's plan. "If this involves putting more law enforcement officers on the streets, that's a concept I support," Spear said.

In addition to Minneapolis and St. Paul, Carlson's program would include officers from Bloomington, Brooklyn Center, Brooklyn Park, Burnsville, Columbia Heights, Maplewood, St. Louis Park and Hennepin and Ramsey counties. State troopers may participate under provisions allowing them to do local police work at the request of local authorities, said State Patrol Chief Col. Mike Chabries.

"Anybody who violates the law, we're going to harass," Carlson said. "I don't want one single criminal to feel comfortable in the state of Minnesota." (Reprinted with permission of Minneapolis StarTribune, Copyright 1995.)

"Senate DFL Presents Anticrime Package," by Conrad deFiebre, *Minneapolis Star Tribune* (December 30, 1995)

DFL legislators presented their prescription for Minnesota's burgeoning crime problems Friday, urging equal parts of stepped-up law enforcement and help for kids before they can become hardened criminals. A day after Republican Gov. Arne Carlson proposed a tough state-backed crackdown on crime in the Twin Cities, the DFLers said his ideas would complement their own. But they also criticized Carlson's plan as one-dimensional and too meddlesome in local affairs.

"We should not be planning police strategy at the Capitol," said Sen. Allan Spear, DFL-Minneapolis. "The governor is a latecomer to the crime issue. We're glad he's now on board, but there's a sense of a quick fix in his proposal. There just is no quick fix for problems like the homicide rate in Minneapolis." That comment set off a round of sniping between Republican and DFL leaders, an indication that crime may be one of the most volatile issues of the 1996 political season.

State Republican Chairman Chris Georgacas blamed Spear and other Minneapolis DFL officials for allowing the city's crime to flourish. Rep. Wes Skoglund, DFL-Minneapolis, then scolded Carlson for advocating reduced sentences for some drug and property offenders.

The DFL plan includes these proposals:

- A $2.5 million state appropriation to provide local matching funds for 100 federally subsidized "Clinton cops," new officers who would concentrate community policing efforts in high-crime areas. (Carlson's plan calls for $5 million to pay overtime to existing officers for neighborhood sweeps and expanded block club programs.)
- About $1 million for 11 new early childhood programs intended to break cycles of family violence that can lead to later crime. Included are home visits by nurses to newborns and their parents, crisis nurseries and youth programs.

- All-day kindergartens at elementary schools in impoverished neighborhoods. Proponents cited research showing that graduates of high-quality preschool programs are at least four times less likely to become repeat criminals.
- Intensive supervision and support for juvenile offenders after their release from detention centers, using college interns as in a successful Missouri program.

Cost estimates were not available for the last two components, but Sen. Randy Kelly, DFL-St. Paul, said the entire proposal would require $6 million to $8 million. The DFLers proposed footing the bill with up to $5 million a year in savings in the state prison system. They said that could be done by sending 200 inmates to the low-cost city-run Prairie Correctional Facility in Appleton, Minn., doubling the number of inmates eligible for shortened "boot camp" sentences and making prison industries more profitable.

Corrections officials say these notions are already being studied or implemented, and Georgacas accused the DFLers of expropriating Republican ideas of prison industry privatization. But that was just the warmup for Georgacas' broadside. "Minneapolis probably would not have a record homicide rate if Spear had not fought Republican ideas like 'three strikes, you're out' . . . if DFLers had not made welfare eligibility requirements and benefits levels so attractive for non-Minnesotans, and if [DFL] Hennepin County Attorney Mike Freeman had not made plea-bargaining an all-too-common practice," he said.

Spear, however, said the DFL plan is a more comprehensive and tight-budgeted approach to fighting crime. Noting that the state is planning a $100 million prison in Rush City, he said: "We need to prevent the need for another prison after that. Building prison after prison is a budget-buster. . . . We know there's a significant correlation between the well-being of kids and the crime rate. If we can help at-risk kids, these are the things we need to do now to help keep ourselves safe in the future." (Reprinted with permission of Minneapolis StarTribune, Copyright 1995.)

"Stops Prompt Suit by Blacks: Cops Target Us in Beverly Hills," by Sally Ann Stewart, *USA Today* (November 11, 1995)

BEVERLY HILLS—People who know Pat Earthly can't understand why he has been repeatedly stopped and interrogated by Beverly Hills police officers. "Anyone who meets Pat would be impressed with what an even-headed and bright individual he is," says Sharon Davis, a foundation executive who's married to the lieutenant governor. Earthly, 29, sexton at All Saints' Episcopal Church in this glittery city of palm trees, pricey designer boutiques and luxury cars, is certain he knows why he's been stopped: He's black.

Today, Earthly joins five teen-age boys—including four Beverly Hills High School football players—in filing a federal lawsuit against the city and police department, saying their civil rights were violated. Earthly, who says he has been illegally stopped or searched four times, and the others are seeking money and an end to what they say is police harassment of young black men. "I want to see a change and have some type of justice for people who look like myself," says Earthly, an aspiring singer-songwriter-pianist. "I don't think police should be able to stop people just because we're black."

They don't, says Frank Salcido, spokesman for the 126-officer force in the town of 31,971. "Our practice is to treat everyone with respect and to meticulously respect the rights of individuals." Earthly doesn't buy that. He recalled once being forced by police officers to lie on the ground in handcuffs in front of his church colleagues. His offense: Police say Earthly's car was missing a brakelight.

Ralph and Cheryl Jones understand. They say that in January their 15-year-old son, Moacir, was walking with three other boys to a video store near the family's apartment. En route, a police officer stopped and ordered the boys to place their hands against a wall. At least five other police cars and a motorcycle officer also responded. The boys were handcuffed and interrogated about where they were going and where they lived. And when Moacir slumped his shoulders, Ralph Jones says, one police officer became so enraged that he threw Moacir against a storefront wall. Eventually, the boys were released—without being charged with anything. "They not only didn't apologize, but they really were very arrogant about the whole thing," says Ralph Jones, a church choir director and a Santa Monica–Malibu School District music teacher. "One officer even said to me, 'You're lucky this is all that happened.'"

Civil rights lawyer Leo Terrell, who's not involved in the case, says he expected such a federal suit. Police mistreatment of black men, he says, "has been whispered about for years. Young black men know that if they are in Beverly Hills, they're going to be followed. The only unique thing about this case is that 99% of the time the police get away with it." Lawyer Robert Tannenbaum, a former Beverly Hills mayor, says he expects the trial to begin by spring. "When I was mayor, if I'd ever known anything like this was going on, I would have put a stop to it. It's critical that people in this community clean their house." Although City Manager Mark Scott made a personal, verbal apology to Earthly in April, All Saints parish administrator Sam Williamson says, "We see no change in their policy."

Chicago introduced "Operation Clean Sweep," a program of police sweeps into the Cabrini Green public housing units, in 1989. They conducted house-to-house searches and required residents to show their identification in order to enter the projects. Responding to complaints that their actions were illegal searches, the chairman of the Chicago Public Housing Authority responded, "We are not infringing on rights. We are restoring our citizens' rights to a safe and decent environment."[1] (Copyright 1995, USA Today. Reprinted with permission.)

"Judge to Rule on Chicago Gunsweeps," by Robert Davis, *USA Today* (April 4, 1994)
A federal judge is expected to decide this week whether Chicago police may search public housing projects for guns without a warrant. Critics say the searches infringe on residents' rights, and U.S. District Judge Wayne Andersen put a temporary end to the practice in February, calling it "a greater evil than the danger of criminal activity."

But then came more gunfire, death and rhetoric. Mayor Richard Daley fought for the sweeps, arguing that "public housing is owned by the people," and the people "do not want guns, gangbangers and drugs in their building." Harvey Grossman of the American Civil Liberties Union, which opposes the sweeps, says: "You simply cannot toss out the Constitution."

As the city and the ACLU fight in public and in the court, gunfire continues to crack. During the last weekend of March, for example, police were called for 300 reports of shots fired at Robert Taylor Homes, a 6-story public housing project on the South Side. "It was like Vietnam," says Tammera Evans, 48, who has lived there since 1983. "It was H-E-L-L with a gun. You couldn't go in front of a window or take the garbage out." Now the city, which broke a record for killings in March with 88 dead, wants to again sweep apartments for guns. Police began searching homes without warning or warrants after a 7-year-old boy was killed by a sniper in 1992. The ACLU, which sued to stop the searches, now wants a permanent ban. But many scared residents want police to continue.

"The people I represent want security," says Thomas Sullivan, a former U.S. attorney who is fighting the ACLU on behalf of some complex residents. "They are sick and tired of the kind of violence they are subjected to. These are fine people who are just being terrorized." The fear has left many residents willing to give up some of their constitutional rights. "Go ahead, invade my privacy. I give you permission. Hurry up," says Evans. "The way it is now, I can't go out to the store; the mailman doesn't want to come in here. It's like I'm in a prison." Police can "look in my drawers, under my sink, wherever they want to look" to get the guns out of her building, the violence out of her face, says Evans. "I want my safety."

Sullivan, who is representing project residents for free, says "reams of rhetoric" over the gun sweep have "missed the point" of the problem. Lousy security means "anybody can just walk right into those buildings." He wants security changed the way the Secret Service recommended to the Housing and Urban Development Department last year, including simple tasks like building a sturdy fence. "The sweeps are really just a . . . fix that doesn't get down to the real problems," says Sullivan. "These tenants don't want gangs in their building."

In court last week, Andersen said the problem ultimately may be up to politicians to fix. "There are no magically right answers," he said. "Everything is imperfect." (Copyright 1994, USA Today. Reprinted with permission.)

"Residents' Hopes Rise as Murders Decline in CHA [Chicago Housing Authority] Sites," by Flynn McRoberts, *Chicago Tribune* (January 7, 1995)
The death of Eric Morse last October refocused attention on Chicago Housing Authority developments as places of great peril for children. To make matters worse, there was this inescapable irony: CHA preventive programs are headquartered in the Ida B. Wells high-rise from which Eric was dropped to his death, allegedly because he wouldn't steal candy for two 10- and 11-year-old boys. Yet 1994 was a substantially safer year for most CHA children, at least judging from statistics that show four of them, including Eric, under age 15 were murdered last year. The year before, that figure was 10, and in 1992 it was 14 out of the nearly 35,000 kids in that age group living in CHA housing.

No one knows exactly why the number is declining, or if it is just a statistical anomaly. But there are those who live in and work in or for CHA who believe it is more than that; for them it's a glimmer of hope after years of bad news. Residents, police and authority personnel point to a range of factors that might help explain the lower death toll.

Those include better cooperation between police and residents and an emerging number of resident leaders who have helped push some criminal activity to other neighborhoods—good news for

[1] *New York Times,* 16 October 1989.

Police sweeps of public housing are controversial but many support them because of the high levels of violence in the units. This Chicago Housing Authority building was the scene of the killing of 5-year-old Eric Morse. Morse was killed when two boys ages 10 and 11 dropped him from a fourteenth floor window when he refused to steal candy for them.

them, if not for the city as a whole, which recorded 930 homicides in 1994, the third-highest total in its history. People like Melanie Thomas, grandmother of 18 and a 17-year resident of CHA's Washington Park development, say they can't help but notice a difference. "It used to look like an Easter parade of people wanting to buy drugs," said Thomas, the captain of the tenant patrol for her South Side building. Now, there are just "a few teenagers who wanna be" dealing, she said.

Brenda Stephenson, a member of the West Side Rockwell Gardens' resident council, said the gunplay has "decreased drastically over here" in the last year and a half. One reason, she said: Gang members "are not hanging out as much as they used to. So that gives other gang members fewer targets to shoot at." In addition, she said, the Nation of Islam affiliate that is helping to privately manage the development has "sort of talked the gangs into putting the guns down and fistfighting when they get into discrepancies. So that's a plus, at least over here in Rockwell."

Though the crime statistics show a gradual, albeit small, decrease in crime throughout CHA developments, neighborhoods without large CHA developments, such as Englewood, have suffered more violence in the last year or two. But in areas where young children have not been killed by gunfire or abuse, the murder statistics don't necessarily give the whole picture. For example, things appear to be safer now than they were last spring when a flurry of gang-related shootings tore through the Robert Taylor Homes, said Kweli Kwaza, a program supervisor for CHA's preventive programs. But he said, "Sometimes when crime is high, people keep their kids inside."

While pinpointing reasons for the statistical decline in crime isn't easy, police attribute some of it to the cooperation of residents and a law enforcement mix of security sweeps and community policing. The greater presence of city and CHA police walking the buildings "seems to have shifted a lot of this crime out of the developments," said Robert Guthrie, commander of the Chicago police public housing division. "They're all walking and talking in the halls and stairwells. And it's been a deterrent to some of the crime we've had in public housing." Guthrie said the sniper death of 7-year-old Dantrell Davis in October 1992 at the Cabrini-Green complex caused more CHA residents to unite with police in crime-fighting efforts. "They started working with the police," he said. "They had had enough." He dismisses the belief of many residents that gang truces are responsible for much of the drop in shootings. "If there's a gang truce, how come there are so many murders in South Chicago and South Shore? The same gangs are there that are in the developments. . . . It seems like these gang truces coincide with law enforcement efforts."

The impact of other possible factors on the decline of deaths among the young is difficult to quantify. For instance, no figures are available on the number of children in CHA developments who have been taken into protective custody by state authorities. But anecdotal evidence suggests that number might be declining because of new intensive family preservation programs such as those funded through the Illinois Department of Children and Family Services.

Barbara Reynolds, supervisor of such a program run by the Children's Home and Aid Society, said that of the 32 cases it has handled since January 1994, children have gone into protective custody in only two instances. DCFS is monitoring the other 30, but the children are still with their families. The program is a "last-chance effort to preserve the family unit," Reynolds explained, in which therapists with just two cases apiece provide a minimum of 10 to 20 hours a week of basic parenting instruction and other services. The society's 28-day program, which gets 95 percent of its cases from CHA, expects to save the state money by "reducing the number of children who are being placed in foster care or group homes," she said.

For their part, CHA administrators and resident leaders say the decline in the number of murdered children shows that efforts to get tenants to work together are finally starting to pay off. Bernita Lucas, the authority's acting director of preventive programs, said she hopes the new Republican-controlled Congress keeps that in mind. "I hope they take great caution and care in what social programs they may slash or cut out," she said, "because these programs raise social consciousness both outside and inside the fishbowl" that is public housing. "These programs are about helping people become self-sufficient," Lucas said, pointing out that some members of the CHA's 600-member tenant patrol no longer participate because they have gotten jobs and moved out of public housing.

Similarly, the CHA's resident management program—aimed at eventually turning over buildings to tenants—has helped create a growing number of people with "a heightened sense of value in their community," according to Lucas. "It's not luck," she said of the declining numbers of child homicides in CHA developments. "It happens because people in the community are committed to a change." That means people like Thomas, who said the visibility of CHA tenant patrols, with their trademark navy blue jackets and yellow lettering, has discouraged some of the drug dealing in her building. "Just putting on your jacket and doing those walk-downs, that is what has stopped (much) of the crime that was going on."

Also gone are the days when she simply remained quiet, figuring "if you keep to yourself, you stay out of trouble." Or, as Lucas put it, now there are "folks who can never go back home and just stay inside." (Copyright 1995, Chicago Tribune. Reprinted with permission.)

CRITICAL THINKING

1. What are the advantages Governor Carlson sees in his proposed police sweep policy for Minneapolis?
2. Why did the governor propose the policy? Is what happened in Beverly Hills the implementation of a policy? Is it the effect of deliberate race discrimination?
3. What are the reasons for the decline in the murders of children in the Chicago Public Housing units, according to the article?
4. How important are the complaints that Operation Clean Sweep violates people's rights?
5. In what ways, if any, does police sweep policy in Minneapolis relate to the Beverly Hills stop practices and the actions of the Chicago Housing Authority?
6. Suppose you are a criminal justice policy advisor to Governor Carlson. What policy would you recommend, having read about Beverly Hills and Chicago?

Knowledge and Understanding CHECK

1. How important are searches without warrants?
2. List the major exceptions to the warrant requirement.
3. Identify the two interests that are balanced in deciding the reasonableness of searches without warrants.
4. Explain how the balance must be struck to satisfy the test of reasonableness.
5. List the three main requirements to make searches incident to arrest reasonableness.

6. Describe the limits of searches incident to arrest.
7. What is the constitutional effect of a consent search?
8. Why do some critics argue that there is no such thing as a consent to search?
9. What do critics recommend may reduce the chances of involuntary consent?
10. Compare the voluntariness and the waiver tests of consent searches.
11. List two reasons for the elimination of the warrant requirement in vehicle searches.
12. Why is "plain view" an incorrect term?
13. List the three conditions in which plain-view searches are valid.
14. What does a stop and frisk usually involve?
15. Contrast reasonable suspicion with probable cause.
16. Identify the two conditions under which police can frisk people.
17. Describe the facts and explain the significance of *Terry v. Ohio.*
18. List the three choices open to the U.S. Supreme Court in deciding *Terry v. Ohio.* Which option did the Court adopt? Do you agree with the choice? Explain your answer.
19. Describe the gist of the criticisms of stop and frisk.

INTERROGATION

The Fifth Amendment provides that "no person shall be compelled to be a witness against himself in any criminal case." Many police interrogators, prosecutors, and judges believe that **interrogation** (the questioning of suspects) is a crucial—indeed, indispensable—part of criminal investigation. They assert that many cases would go unsolved if officers could not interrogate suspects. Others maintain that police interrogation goes against the values of a free society and that the government should not convict people with evidence out of their own mouths. Supporters of interrogation reply that interrogation not only helps to convict the guilty but also aids in freeing the innocent. Critics argue that the police use unethical tactics, including lying, deceit, and tricks to get confessions.

Police interrogation has provoked more debate since the early 1970s than perhaps any other police practice. The controversy revolves around three issues:

1. The importance of confessions in solving crimes and convicting criminals.
2. The kinds and amount of pressure used in police interrogation.
3. The extent of the abuse of interrogation.

Empirical data will probably never fully resolve these issues. In *Miranda v. Arizona,* Chief Justice Earl Warren—himself an experienced former prosecutor—acknowledged the problems of getting information about what really happens in interrogation rooms:

> Interrogation still takes place in privacy. Privacy results in secrecy and this in turn results in a gap in our knowledge as to what in fact goes on in the interrogation room.[24]

Some empirical research from the late 1990s is closing this gap. Sociologist Richard Leo spent more than 500 hours inside the interrogation rooms of a major urban police department, and he also analyzed videotaped custodial interrogations from two other departments. He made the following important discoveries:

- Very few interrogations are coercive.
- One in five suspects invokes one or more of their *Miranda* rights to avoid cooperating with the police.
- Interrogators use tactics advocated in police training manuals (fabricated evidence, "good guy–bad guy") to undermine the confidence of suspects and overbear their rational decision making.
- Interrogators have become increasingly skilled in eliciting incriminating evidence during custodial interrogation.
- The overwhelming majority of custodial interrogations last less than one hour.
- Suspects who provide incriminating information are likely to be treated differently at every stage of the criminal process than suspects who do not.[25]

Police interrogation and resulting incriminating statements raise not only empirical questions but also controversial constitutional and ethical issues:

1. When do suspects acquire their right against self-incrimination?
2. What does interrogation mean?
3. How do citizens waive their right against self-incrimination?
4. When may officers question citizens without warning them of their right against self-incrimination?
5. What is a voluntary confession?

Miranda v. Arizona

In 1966, in the case of *Miranda v. Arizona,* the U.S. Supreme Court tried to answer these questions in perhaps the most controversial and famous case ever decided involving the police and criminal law enforcement. The Court ruled that the Fifth Amendment protects suspects against coercive custodial police interrogation. The Court said that confessions extracted by physical brutality were not the only form of coercive incrimination. According to a majority of the Court, simply being in a police station was sufficiently intimidating to call for Fifth Amendment protection. To secure that protection, the Court devised rules to cover *custodial interrogation,* meaning interrogation while a suspect is in custody "at the station or otherwise deprived of his freedom of action in any significant way."[26]

Before law enforcement officers can interrogate suspects who are in custody, the police have to read suspects the ***Miranda* warnings.** According to the Court, officers who interrogate suspects in custody must do all of the following, to assure the voluntariness of incriminating statements obtained during the custodial interrogation:

1. *Warn* suspects in clear and certain terms that they have the right to remain silent.
2. *Explain* to suspects that the government can and will use anything said against them.
3. *Inform* suspects that they have the right to consult with a lawyer during interrogation.
4. *Assure* suspects that the government will appoint a lawyer if they cannot afford to hire one.

The Court also made the following rulings that are not part of the required warnings:

1. If at any time during interrogation, suspects express a desire to remain silent, the interrogation must cease immediately.
2. If no lawyer is present, a heavy burden rests on the prosecution to prove that suspects voluntarily and knowingly waived their rights.
3. No evidence obtained in violation of these rules is admissible in court.
4. No suspect may be penalized for asserting the right to remain silent. Therefore, the prosecution may not use silence at trial to show suspects had something to hide.[27]

Court decisions since *Miranda* have clarified several points left vague in the original decision. When or where does the suspect have the right to warnings? What if police interrogate a suspect at home, in the presence of family and friends? The courts have decided the warnings are not required in familiar surroundings that are not likely to intimidate the suspect. On the other hand, simply because questioning takes place at the station does not automatically require the police to warn suspects. What if a suspect comes to the station in response to a note from an officer left at the suspect's apartment saying, "I want to discuss something with you"? The U.S. Supreme Court ruled that the questioning that followed at the station did not require *Miranda* warnings because the suspect was "invited," not "taken," to the station. Furthermore, the Court has ruled that not all police questioning requires the warnings. For example, police who stop and briefly question people on the street during field investigation do not have to give the warnings. Nor does *Miranda* protect against routine questions asked at booking, such as "What is your name?" "Where do you live?" and "Are you married?"[28]

The *Miranda* decision stirred a bitter debate about the balance between police power and the rights of suspects. Those who opposed *Miranda* claimed that it handcuffed the police in their fight against crime. Some extremists even blamed the decision for the rapidly rising recorded crime rates of the 1960s. Others defended the decision as a major stride toward true liberty. *Miranda* became a pawn in the political issue of law and order. Congress joined the fray and in 1968 repealed the decision in the Safe Streets Act that President Nixon signed into law. As a result, under the law, police are not constitutionally required to give the warnings. As this book goes to press, the constitutionality of this law is being questioned.[29]

Voluntariness of Confessions

Even if officers read the required warnings to suspects in custody whom they intend to interrogate, incriminating statements that follow a valid waiver must be given voluntarily and knowingly. The Fifth Amendment prohibits the police from *compelling* suspects to confess. Voluntariness, according to the U.S. Supreme Court, is a legal question that depends on the totality of the circumstances of each individual case. A confession is compelled under the voluntariness test if all of the circumstances in the case show two things:

1. *Coercion* by law enforcement officers.
2. *Causal link*—that is, that the coercion by law enforcement officers caused the incriminating statements.

According to Chief Justice Rehnquist, writing for a majority of the U.S. Supreme Court in the leading confession case of *Colorado v. Connelly:*

> [T]he cases considered by this Court over . . . 50 years . . . have focused on the crucial element of police overreaching. While each confession case has turned on its own set of factors justifying the conclusion that police conduct was oppressive, all have contained a substantial element of coercive police conduct. Absent police conduct causally related to the confession, there is simply no basis for concluding that any state actor has deprived a criminal defendant of due process of law. . . . [A]s interrogators have turned to more subtle forms of psychological persuasion, courts have found the mental condition of the defendant a more significant factor in the "voluntariness" calculus. But this fact does not justify a conclusion that a defendant's mental condition, by itself apart from its relation to official coercion, should ever dispose of the inquiry into constitutional "voluntariness."[30]

The most common circumstances that courts consider in determining whether coercive law enforcement action has caused people to confess include:

- Number of interrogators.
- Length of the questioning.
- Place of questioning.
- Denial of food, water, and toilet facilities.
- Threats, promises, lies, and tricks.
- Denial of access to a lawyer.
- Characteristics of the suspect, such as age, gender, race, physical and mental condition, education, and experience with the criminal justice system.

The Use Your Discretion case, "Was the confession voluntary?" includes an excerpt from the confession case of *Colorado v. Connelly,* from which the preceding quote by Chief Justice Rehnquist is taken.

Use *Your* Discretion

Was the confession voluntary?

Facts

Francis Connelly approached a uniformed Denver police officer and began confessing to a murder. Taken aback by these statements, the officer asked Connelly if he had ever undergone therapy for a mental disorder. Connelly responded that he had. The officer gave Connelly the *Miranda* warnings, after which Connelly continued to give details of the murder. After Connelly offered to show the police where the murder took place, the Denver police held him overnight. The next morning Connelly became visibly disoriented and spoke of voices that ordered him to come to Denver to confess to the murder. At the trial, a state hospital psychiatrist testified that Connelly had been in a psychotic state the day before he confessed and suffered from chronic schizophrenia. Connelly had told the psychiatrist that the "voice of God" told him he had either to confess or to commit suicide.

Both the trial court and the Colorado Supreme Court had said "no"; but in *Colorado v. Connelly,* the U.S. Supreme Court ruled that the confession was admissible. For the Court majority, Chief Justice William Rehnquist held that some form of police coercion is absolutely essential to violate due process on the grounds of an involuntary confession. In other words, although the totality of circumstances surrounding confessions is relevant to determine voluntariness, police coercion stands as a necessary circumstance in a finding of involuntariness. Justice Brennan dissented, writing:

> Today the Court denies Mr. Connelly his fundamental right to make a vital choice with a sane mind, involving a determination that could allow the State to deprive him of liberty or even life. . . . Surely in the present stage of our civilization a most basic sense of justice is affronted by the spectacle of incarcerating a human being upon the basis of a statement he made while insane. Because I believe that the use of a mentally ill person's involuntary confession is antithetical to the notion of fundamental fairness embodied in the due process clause, I dissent.

CRITICAL THINKING

1. Was the confession voluntary?
2. Apply the criteria from the text and case to back up your answer to (1).
3. Do you agree with Rehnquist or Brennan?
4. Was the confession voluntary because it was without coercion?
5. Was it involuntary because Connelly was insane? Explain your reasons.

Voluntary does not mean totally free of influence. The *Miranda* warnings were intended to remove coercion from police custodial interrogation. They were not meant to eliminate all pressure on criminal suspects. According to one commentator:

> At trial, after establishing probable cause of guilt and when the defendant enjoys the protection of a neutral bench, a personal advocate, and public scrutiny, the government may not so much as put a polite question to the defendant. But, between arrest and commitment, the police may badger, trick, and manipulate the suspect in an environment solely within their control and to which no other witness is admitted. With respect to confessions, society insists on enjoying "at one and the same time the pleasures of indulgence and the dignity of disapproval."[31]

Knowledge and Understanding CHECK

1. List the reasons for the conclusion that interrogation is an indispensable part of criminal investigation.
2. List the arguments against interrogation.
3. Identify the three issues that have generated controversy over police interrogation.
4. List the findings and describe the methodology of Richard Leo's study of police interrogation.

5. List the major constitutional and ethical issues raised by interrogation.
6. List the major warnings that are required by *Miranda v. Arizona.*
7. List the other holdings of *Miranda* that are not part of the warnings.
8. What two things show that a confession was not voluntary?
9. Identify the most common circumstances that courts consider in determining whether coercive law enforcement action has caused people to confess.
10. What exactly does voluntary mean in the context of incriminating statements?

IDENTIFICATION PROCEDURES

Proving that a crime was committed is easier than identifying the perpetrator. In some cases, of course, identification is not a major problem. Some suspects are caught red-handed; victims and witnesses personally know other suspects; others confess. Technological advances have led to the increasing use of novel scientific evidence to identify criminals. Bitemark evidence helped to convict the notorious serial rapist and murderer Ted Bundy. Fiber evidence helped to convict Wayne Williams of the murder of 2 out of 30 murdered young African Americans in Atlanta.

We will examine the best-known "novel scientific evidence": DNA (deoxyribonucleic acid) testing. DNA testing lifts samples of body fluid from the victim, much like lifting fingerprints, and then matches these samples with the body fluids of the suspect. Heralded as the "single greatest advance in the 'search for truth' . . . since . . . cross-examination," many courts have found DNA evidence admissible. However, researchers have uncovered problems that have led some courts to rethink their initial enthusiasm.

The Dangers of Mistaken Identifications

The most common—and probably most problematic—cases are those that rely on the eyewitness identification of *strangers.* (Obviously, eyewitness identification is not a problem where witnesses know the suspect.) The police rely on three major procedures to help eyewitnesses identify suspects. In **lineups,** witnesses try to identify a suspect standing in a line with other individuals. In **show-ups,** witnesses attempt to identify suspects without other possible suspects present. This may be in the police station or elsewhere. Police officers may take witnesses to observe suspects at work or in other places. In both lineups and show-ups, a confrontation occurs between suspects and the witnesses who may incriminate them. Suspects may not actually see witnesses, but witnesses look directly at suspects, perhaps through a one-way mirror. In **photo identification,** witnesses look at a picture or pictures—"mug shots"—to identify suspects. Identification procedures are critical in many cases; in some, they are the only evidence available. The procedures are also fraught with the danger of identifying the wrong person.

Witness identification of strangers is notoriously low in reliability, even in ideal settings. The most common identification procedures—lineups and photographic identification—are not ideal and, hence, render eyewitness identification still less reliable. According to one expert, faulty identifications present the "greatest single threat to the achievement of our ideal that no innocent man shall be punished." Best guesses (reliable exact figures are not available) are that about half of all wrongful convictions are due to eyewitness error. To take but one example, seven eyewitnesses swore that Bernard Pagano, a Roman Catholic priest, robbed them with a small, chrome-plated pistol. In the middle of Pagano's trial, Ronald Clouser admitted that he, not Father Pagano, had committed the robberies.[32]

Misidentification occurs because of three normal mental processes taking place at three points in time:

1. *Perception:* the information taken in by the brain at the time of the original event.
2. *Memory:* the information retained from the original event in the interval between the event and the lineup, show-up, or photographic array.
3. *Recall:* the information retrieved at the time of the lineup, show-up, or photographic array.

Improper suggestive measures used by law enforcement probably account for some errors in identification. However, according to the widely accepted findings of psychologists who have studied perception, memory, and recall, the great majority probably are attributable both to the inherent unreliability of human perception and memory and to human susceptibility to unintentional, and often quite subtle, suggestive influences.[33]

For about a century, psychologists have demonstrated that the eye is not a camera that records exact images on the brain. Cameras have no expectations. However, people do; these expectations influence perceptions. Like beauty, the physical characteristics of perpetrators of crimes are in the eye of the witness. The brain cannot process all that the eye sees because of natural human limits on perception. Furthermore, even trained observers pay only *selective* attention to the events that they experience. They notice only certain features, leaving later gaps in memory. The accuracy of initial impressions depends on five circumstances:

1. *Length of time* the witness observed the stranger.
2. *Distractions* during the observation.
3. *Focus* of the observation.
4. *Stress* to the witness during the observation.
5. *Race* of the witness and the stranger.

It is true that the longer the witness observes the stranger, the more reliable the perception. However, distractions such as other activity going on during the observation reduce reliability. Witnesses who gain a general impression, such as a whole face, are more reliable than those who focus on a single characteristic, such as a scar. But many witnesses focus on other details, such as what experts call "weapon focus," where they may remember a gun but not the person who carried it. The perceptions of highly stressed witnesses are less reliable than those of witnesses under low stress. Distractions and stress play a particularly large role in criminal events—that is, in the events where accuracy is most important. According to Martin Yant, an identification expert who conducted one study:

> Many of the cases we have identified involve errors by victims of robbery and rape, where the victim was close enough to the offender to get a look at him—but under conditions of extreme stress. . . . Such stress can significantly affect perception and memory and should give us cause to question the reliability of such eyewitness testimony.[34]

Identifying a stranger of the same race is more reliable than identifying someone of a different race. In one famous experiment, researchers showed observers a photo of a white man brandishing a razor blade in an altercation with an African American man on a subway. When asked immediately afterward to describe what they saw, over half the observers reported that the African American man was carrying the weapon.

> [C]onsiderable evidence indicates that people are poorer at identifying members of another race than of their own. Some studies have found that, in the United States at least, whites have greater difficulty recognizing blacks than vice versa. Moreover, counterintuitively, the ability to perceive the physical characteristics of a person from another racial group apparently does not improve significantly upon increased contact with other members of that race. Because many crimes are cross-racial, these factors may play an important part in reducing the accuracy of eyewitness perception.[35]

The problem of cross-race identifications is aggravated by findings that African Americans identify whites better than whites identify African American and other racial groups; that is, whites are most susceptible to the "they all look alike" phenomenon. Curiously, accuracy does not improve with increased contact with members of the other race.[36]

Memory fades over time. It fades most during the first few hours following the identification of a stranger, then remains stable for several months. What happens during the lapse of time, however, can dramatically affect the reliability of memory. Curiously, witnesses' confidence about their recall grows as time passes; while, in fact, actual memory is fading. The confidence of witnesses is highly unreliable, despite the heavy weight accorded this confidence by judges and juries. The dangers of suggestion are high following an event. The mind combines everything about the event, whether the witness learned it at the time or later, and stores all the information in a single "bin." According to psychologist and respected eyewitness research expert Elizabeth Loftus, witnesses added to their stories depending on how she described an incident. Later, they drew this information out of the "bin" during the identification process.[37]

Steven Penrod, identification researcher at the University of Wisconsin, says that this embellishment is natural to all of us. "A witness tells his story to the police, to the family, then to friends, then to the prosecutor." As the story gets retold, it becomes less reality and more legend. "[Witnesses] feel very confident about what they now think happened and that confidence is communicated to the jury."[38]

Outside influence and witness self-confidence affect the accuracy of identification in lineups, show-ups, and photographic displays. Witnesses tend to treat these situations as multiple-choice tests without a "none of the above" choice. They feel they have to choose the "best" likeness. Witnesses are afraid they might look foolish if they "don't know the answer," or they respond easily to suggestion, particularly in uncomfortable or threatening situations. Suggestions—mostly not intended, it should be stressed—by authority figures, such as the police, aggravate these tendencies. For example, witnesses will feel pressure simply because the police have arranged an identification procedure. Witnesses believe the police must have found the culprit—why else would they have arranged the identification event? So, the witnesses believe that the culprit must be among the people in the lineup or photographic array.

Once witnesses identify a stranger, it is difficult to shake their conclusion, even if it is wrong. This fact is extremely important for at least three reasons. First, a convincing amount of research runs counter to the commonsense idea that confidence bespeaks accuracy. Quite the contrary, according to the research confidence says little if anything about accuracy. It might even show less accuracy. Second, the confidence of a witness identification plays a major role in the decisions of jurors. Most jurors believe a confident identification and readily dismiss other evidence in the face of it. Thus, the confident, but wrong, identification of a suspect is particularly damning.[39]

Finally, despite the dangers of faulty identification, the courts rarely reject eyewitness identification testimony. For example, during trials, prosecutors often ask victims or other witnesses if they see the person who committed the crime in the courtroom. If witnesses answer yes, which they invariably do, then prosecutors ask them to point to that person, which they also invariably do. Courts also regularly admit evidence of prior identifications, such as those made during lineups. One court said,

> We think it is evident that an identification of an accused by a witness for the first time in the courtroom

> may often be of little testimonial force, as the witness may have had opportunities to see the accused and to have heard him referred to by a certain name; whereas a prior identification, considered in connection with the circumstances surrounding it, serves to aid the court in determining the trustworthiness of the identification made in the courtroom.[40]

The possibility of misidentification has led to efforts to reduce its likelihood. (Of course, no rules and procedures can reduce the inherent human limits on perception and memory. The only part of the identification process that law enforcement agencies and courts can affect is the recall of information during identification procedures.) These efforts may take the form of police department rules regarding the number of persons required to participate in lineups and the number of photographs required in arrays; the kinds of people who participate in lineups and the characteristics and quality of photographs in arrays; and the conditions under which witnesses participate in lineups, show-ups, and photographic arrays. Sometimes the effort involves the testimony of expert witnesses or the instructions of judges to juries during trial regarding the problems of reliability in identification procedures.

Identification Procedures and the Constitution

The U.S. Supreme Court relies on the Sixth Amendment right to counsel and the due process clauses of the Fifth and Fourteenth Amendments in deciding identification procedure cases. The Court has repeatedly ruled that the constitutional requirements governing identification procedures are intended to promote the interest in accurate fact-finding in particular cases. In short, the Constitution requires that the purpose of identification procedures is to convict the guilty and to free the innocent. According to the Court, the government violates the right to counsel and due process only if police misconduct in identification procedures leads to an incorrect result.

Identification procedures take place three times:

1. Prior to charges.
2. Between the beginning of judicial proceedings and trial.
3. At trial.

The right to counsel applies only after adversary proceedings against the accused begin (see Chapter 10), and it applies only to identification procedures involving a *confrontation* between the accused and witnesses. Witnesses face accused people in lineups and show-ups but not in photographic displays. The due process clause, on the other hand, applies to all identification procedures—lineups, show-ups, and photographic displays—whenever they occur. The right to counsel cannot, of course, improve at all the witness's perception and memory of the original event. Furthermore, it is doubtful that the presence of a lawyer can detect *un*intentional suggestive influences of lineups and show-ups.

Lineups and show-ups after the initiation of formal proceedings represent the smallest number of identification cases. Most take place before prosecutors decide to charge suspects with crimes; these make up the next largest number of identification cases. The most frequent identification procedure is photographic identification where no right to counsel exists at all because photographic displays are not confrontations, according to the Supreme Court's interpretation of the confrontation clause in the Sixth Amendment. The right to counsel, therefore, applies to the fewest number of cases. In lineups and show-ups before formal proceedings begin and in all photographic displays whenever they take place, the police can proceed without the presence of a defense attorney.

The due process clauses of the Fifth and Fourteenth Amendments provide the basis for ensuring correct identification at lineups and show-ups before trial, and photographic identification whenever it occurs. In early decisions, the Supreme Court seemed to indicate that the focus of the due process protection was on deterring police from misconduct in the administration of lineups, show-ups, and photographic arrays. But, by the 1970s, the Court had made it clear that the primary purpose of the due process clauses is to protect against the denial of life, liberty, or property based on evidence of unreliable identification. The U.S. Supreme Court has established a two-stage inquiry to determine whether identification procedures violate the due process rights of defendants. Due process requires that courts determine if the totality of circumstances in each case show that:[41]

1. The procedure was unnecessarily suggestive.
2. The unnecessarily suggestive procedure caused a "very substantial likelihood of . . . misidentification."[42]

Lineups

Lineups depend for their reliability on making sure of two things:

1. There are enough participants.
2. The participants share similar characteristics.

The International Association of Chiefs of Police (IACP) recommends the following four standards for lineups that will produce accurate identification:

1. Five or six participants.
2. Same gender, race, and nearly the same age.
3. Similar height, weight, skin color, hair color, and body build.
4. Similar clothing.

In reality, lineups consist mainly of police officers and inmates of the local jail. As a result, suspects usually stand out from the others. This is not usually because of intended suggestiveness by the police, but rather because police officers and jail inmates are ordinarily the only people available. Courts rarely exclude evidence based on lineups that do not meet the requirements of the IACP.

Show-ups

Show-ups, or identifications of a single person, are considerably more suggestive and substantially less reliable than lineups. The main reason for their unreliability is the suggestiveness of presenting a single person to identify. Despite this, courts usually admit testimony derived from show-ups in several circumstances. For example, if show-ups take place within a few hours of a crime, two reasons justify admitting them into evidence:

1. Solving crimes quickly.
2. Fresh eyewitness identifications.

Show-ups take place in several situations:

1. When witnesses accidentally confront suspects, as in courthouse corridors.
2. When they occur in emergencies, such as when witnesses are hospitalized.
3. When suspects are at large, such as when police cruise crime scenes with witnesses.
4. When external circumstances "prove" the identification accurate, such as when the witness already knows the suspect.[43]

Photographic Identification

The least reliable form of identification is a photograph, which is only two-dimensional, and thus not entirely true to life. Also, the fewer photos used, the less reliable the identifications. Furthermore, photographs in which the suspect stands out are highly suggestive. In addition, police can make remarks—such as, "Is this the one?" or "The suspect is in this group of photos"—that lead to particular conclusions. Despite their recognized unreliability and the urging of commentators that courts should exclude them if lineups and show-ups can be substituted, photographs are the most widely used means of identification. Courts accept photographic identification regularly. They have the approval of the U.S. Supreme Court, which said, "[T]his procedure has been used widely and effectively in criminal law enforcement." Courts generally have rejected defendants' claims of the unreliability of photographic identification, even the least accurate of all—the single-photograph identification.[44]

DNA Testing

DNA (deoxyribonucleic acid) testing can potentially identify or exclude suspects in cases either where suspects have left DNA at the scene of a crime or where victims have left DNA on items traceable to perpetrators. This capacity to use DNA to identify criminal suspects has come about because of rapid advances in molecular biology in the past 15 years. DNA is a long, double-stranded molecule found in everyone's chromosomes. Chromosomes are carried in the nucleus of body cells that have nuclei, including white blood cells, sperm cells, cells surrounding the hair roots, and saliva cells. DNA testing involves comparing the DNA samples in the nuclei of cells found at crime scenes with either similar DNA samples taken from the nuclei of cells of suspects, or DNA samples left by victims on items traceable to perpetrators.

The most widely used test is called DNA fingerprinting, or *DNA profiling.* In this test, long sections of DNA are broken into fragments. Fragments that tend to vary from person to person are measured. If samples from crime scenes have different lengths from those of the suspect, they exclude the suspect. If the sample at the scene and that of the suspect have the same lengths, the samples might have a common source. However, they might also match by chance. To reduce the element of chance, laboratories measure six or more distinct fragments. Two commercial laboratories, Cellmark Diagnostics Corporation and Lifecodes Corporation, and the FBI are the major sites for DNA testing in the United States.[45]

DNA testing quickly entered the legal system, heralded by one court as "the greatest advance in crime fighting technology since fingerprinting." Then a serious scientific controversy broke out over DNA testing. Some challenged the theory of DNA itself; others challenged the testing methods. Most, however, accepted the soundness of the theory and the testing technology, but attacked the admission of the tests. According to Professor Edward Imwinkelried of the University of California Davis Law School:

> My reading of the proficiency studies of forensic DNA testing laboratories is that the most common cause of error is not the inherent limitations of the technique, but the way in which the specific test was conducted. What the courts don't understand is that no matter how impressive studies are of the validity of a scientific technique, they are worthless as a guarantee of reliability unless you replicate the variables of the experiment.[46]

In 1989, knowledgeable defense counsel obtained the aid of disinterested scientists to successfully challenge DNA evidence in *People v. Castro.* Lifecodes, the laboratory that did the testing, violated its own rules and was charged with scientific fraud. In the face of unanimous scientific opinion, including experts hired by the prosecution, Lifecodes admitted that the testing did not amount to a match. The wide coverage the case received in both the popular and the scientific press led to a full-scale debate. So heated did the controversy become, according to John Hicks, head of the FBI Laboratory Division, that "[t]his is no longer a search for the truth, it is a war."[47]

The correct identification of criminal suspects by means of DNA testing depends on the answers to the following three questions and the inferences jurors or other fact finders make about them:

1. Is a reported match between the sample at the scene of the crime and the sample from the suspect a true match?
2. Is the suspect the source of the trace of DNA left at the scene of the crime?
3. Is the suspect the perpetrator of the crime?

A reported match strongly suggests a true match. However, mistakes in DNA processing do occur. Technical errors, such as enzyme failures, salt concentrations, and dirt spots, can produce misleading patterns. Human errors, including contaminations, mislabelings, misrecordings, misrepresentations, case mix-ups, and errors of interpretation also occur. Assuming the match is true, it strongly suggests that the suspect is the source of the trace of DNA left at the scene of the crime. However, the match might be coincidental. The coincidence depends on the frequency of matching traits among the population, usually the ethnic group of the suspect. However, the validity of this reference population depends on the correct ethnic group identification. Source probability errors also occur.

Prosecutors, experts, and jurors often exaggerate the weight given to the match between the trace and the suspect by speaking in terms of odds. According to one trial transcript, for example, after testifying that the blood of a victim matched a sample from a blanket, the following exchange took place:

> Q [Prosecutor]: And in your profession and in the scientific field, when you say match what do you mean?
>
> A [Expert]: They are identical.
>
> Q [Prosecutor]: So the blood on the blanket . . . Can you say it came from [the victim]?
>
> A [Expert]: With great certainty I can say that those two DNA samples match and they are identical. And with population statistics we can derive a probability of it being anyone other than the victim.
>
> Q [Prosecutor]: What is the probability in this case?
>
> A [Expert]: In this case that probability is that it is a one in 7 million chance that it could be anyone other than that victim.

According to Professor Jonathan Koehler at the University of Texas at Austin, it is misleading to suggest that general population statistics can prove the probability that a specific victim was not the source.[48]

Finally, evidence that the suspect is the source of the trace is also evidence that the suspect committed the crime. But it does not necessarily prove that the suspect committed the crime. After all, the suspect could have left the trace innocently, either before or after the commission of the crime. The use of the match to prove guilt depends on an inference, perhaps a fair inference but not automatic or always correct. Whatever the problems and criticisms of the use of DNA testing to identify suspects and link them to crimes, the impact of DNA (and other scientific evidence, too, for that matter) is substantial. According to one researcher, about 25 percent of jurors said they would have voted not guilty if it were not for the introduction of scientific evidence. In another survey, 75 percent of judges and lawyers throughout the United States said they believed judges accorded scientific evidence more credibility than other kinds of evidence, and 70 percent said they believed jurors did the same.[49]

Knowledge and Understanding CHECK

1. Describe the reliability of eyewitness identification.
2. List the normal mental processes that lead to misidentification.
3. How does the human eye compare to a camera?
4. Identify the five circumstances that affect the accuracy of initial impressions.
5. Summarize the major reasons for misidentification.
6. How do courts treat eyewitness testimony?
7. At what three points does eyewitness occur, and what provisions in the Constitution apply to the points?
8. Rank the reliability of lineups, show-ups, and photographic arrays.
9. List the two steps in determining whether identification procedures violate due process of law.
10. Describe the elements that are thought to make lineups, show-ups, and photographic arrays more reliable.
11. Describe the strengths and weaknesses of DNA testing.

THE EXCLUSIONARY RULE

Everyone knows that when private persons break the law they are supposed to get caught and punished. However, most people are not so clear about what should happen when government officials break the law. Mechanisms to enforce the constitutional standards and values that underpin the law of criminal procedure range across a broad spectrum. They consist of three types of actions:

1. *Legal and administrative actions against individual officers,* including criminal prosecution, civil lawsuits, and disciplinary action within the officer's agency or department. (See Chapter 8.)
2. *Civil actions against the heads of criminal justice agencies, the agencies themselves, or the government units responsible for the agencies,* including suits for damages and court orders (injunctions) prohibiting specific conduct. (See Chapter 8.)
3. *Process remedies that affect the outcome of criminal cases,* including dismissing cases, reversing convictions, and excluding or suppressing evidence.[50]

Chapter 8 examines the remedies of criminal prosecution and suing the police, departments, and other government units. This chapter examines the major process remedy: excluding illegally obtained evidence from judicial proceedings. For now, it is enough to note that these three types of remedies are not mutually exclusive; injured parties don't have to choose one out of three. They are all available in the same case. For example, the state might prosecute a police officer for breaking and entering to illegally search a house. The individual whose house the officer illegally entered can sue the officer for the damages incurred in the illegal breaking and entering. The officer's department can suspend the officer for the wrongful act. Finally, a court trying the defendant whose house was the object of the illegal entry may apply the **exclusionary rule** that excludes the evidence obtained from the illegal search and, in some instances, may dismiss the case against the victim of government lawbreaking—even if the defendant is clearly guilty! This rarely happens in practice, but it could; the law does not require that injured parties choose one action above others.

Controversy over the Exclusionary Rule

Throwing out "good" evidence that might convict "bad" criminals is a highly controversial consequence of illegal government action. But that is what the exclusionary rule does: It forbids the government to use confessions obtained in violation of the right against self-incrimination guaranteed by the Fifth Amendment, and it prohibits the use of physical evidence gathered through unreasonable searches and seizures prohibited by the Fourth Amendment. The rule also excludes evidence obtained in violation of the Sixth Amendment right to counsel, and eyewitness identifications obtained by procedures so suggestive that their unreliability violates the due process clauses of the Fifth and Fourteenth Amendments. Occasionally, the Supreme Court has also extended the rule to include statutory violations, such as those involving federal wiretapping legislation.[51]

The exclusionary rule excludes *good evidence* because of *bad practices.* It puts the truth second to the means that police use to obtain the truth. In other words, the exclusionary rule stands for the proposition that the ends (finding the truth) do not justify the means (constitutional procedures) in criminal law enforcement. In our constitutional democracy we support criminal law enforcement, but not at any price. Violating proper procedures is simply too high a price to pay for obtaining convictions. If the government does not obey the law, the public loses confidence in the law. That lost confidence, in turn, breeds contempt for and hostility to the law. In the end, both law and order suffer.[52]

In 1929, in the famous U.S. Supreme Court case *Olmstead v. United States,* Justice Oliver Wendell Holmes, recognizing the dilemma of having to exclude reliable evidence that could convict guilty defendants, wrote the following defense of the exclusionary rule:

> [W]e must consider two objects of desire, both of which we cannot have, and make up our minds which to choose. It is desirable that criminals should be detected, and to that end that all available evidence should be used. It also is desirable that the Government should not itself foster and pay for other crimes, when they are the means by which the evidence is to be obtained. . . . For my part, I think it is less evil that some criminals should escape than that the Government should play an ignoble part.[53]

Social Costs and Deterrent Effects

By the 1980s, a majority of the Supreme Court applied a deterrence rationale for exclusion of evidence. The Court weighed the social cost of letting criminals go free by excluding evidence of guilt against the possible deterrent effect such exclusion has on law enforcement officers. The deterrence rationale definitely limited the number of cases in which evidence was excluded. If the social costs outweighed the deterrent effect (which in virtually every case the Court found that it did), then the evidence was admissible.[54]

The questions of the social cost incurred by lost convictions and of the effectiveness of the exclusionary rule in deterring unconstitutional police behavior have generated heated debate among scholars. A majority of the Supreme Court has held the view that the social cost outweighs the deterrent effect of the rule. However, empirical research does not support that conclusion.

In an extensive study of the exclusionary rule among Chicago narcotics officers, Myron W. Orfield, Jr., reported several important findings:

- Chicago narcotics officers are *always* in court when judges suppress the evidence.
- They *always* understand why the court excluded the evidence.
- This experience has led them to seek search warrants more often and to be more careful when they search for and seize evidence without warrants.

Prior to the decision in *Mapp v. Ohio* (which applied the exclusionary rule to state and local law enforcement), police officers rarely obtained warrants. By 1987, in the narcotics division of the Chicago Police Department at least, "virtually all preplanned searches that are not 'buy busts' or airport-related searches occur with warrants."[55]

Orfield's study also demonstrated that the exclusionary rule "punishes" officers. The Chicago Police Department initiated an officer rating system in response to the exclusionary rule, making the loss of evidence due to exclusion a personal liability to police officers. Suppression of evidence can negatively affect both assignments and promotions. Orfield also found that some police officers still lie in court to avoid the suppression of illegally seized evidence. This in-court police perjury limits the effectiveness of the exclusionary rule. However, strong responses to police perjury by both the police department and the courts have reduced the impact of perjury on the practical application of the exclusionary rule. Finally, Orfield reported that every officer believed the courts should retain the rule. They all saw the rule as a positive development with just about the right amount of a deterrent element, although they would like a "good faith" exception to warrantless searches. They believed that a tort remedy (discussed in Chapter 8) would "overdeter" the police in their search for and seizure of evidence.[56]

The social costs of letting guilty criminals go free by excluding credible evidence that would convict them are not nearly so high as is commonly thought. Researchers have found that the exclusionary rule affects only a minuscule number of cases in an extremely narrow range of crimes. The rule does not affect prosecutions of murder, rape, robbery, and assault; primarily, illegal drug dealing, gambling, and pornography prosecutions suffer from it. In California, for example, the rule is overwhelmingly connected to drug offenses, not violent felonies. How many cases do courts dismiss because of the exclusionary rule? Available evidence suggests only a few. In California, illegally seized evidence led to dismissals in a mere 0.8 percent of all criminal cases and only 4.8 percent of felonies. Less than one-tenth of 1 percent of all criminal cases will be dismissed because the police seized evidence illegally. The rule leaves violent crimes and serious property offenses virtually unaffected.[57]

Use *Your* Discretion

Does the exclusionary rule exact too high a social cost?

According to Thomas Y. Davies, who studied the exclusionary rule in California, prosecutors practically never reject cases involving *violent* crimes because of the exclusionary rule. He found that prosecutors rejected for prosecution 0.06 percent of homicide, 0.09 percent of forcible rape, and 0.13 percent of assault cases because of illegal searches and seizures. They rejected less than one-half of 1 percent of theft cases and only 0.19 percent of burglary cases. The largest number of cases rejected for prosecution due to illegal searches and seizures involved the possession of small amounts of drugs (see Figure 7.1). Other studies reached similar conclusions; that is, that the exclusionary rule affects only a small portion of cases, and of that small number, most are not crimes against persons. Furthermore, not all cases rejected or lost because of illegally obtained evidence are lost because of the exclusionary rule. Peter F. Nardulli, for example, found that in some cases of drug possession, the police

Figure 7.1
The Exclusionary Rule in California

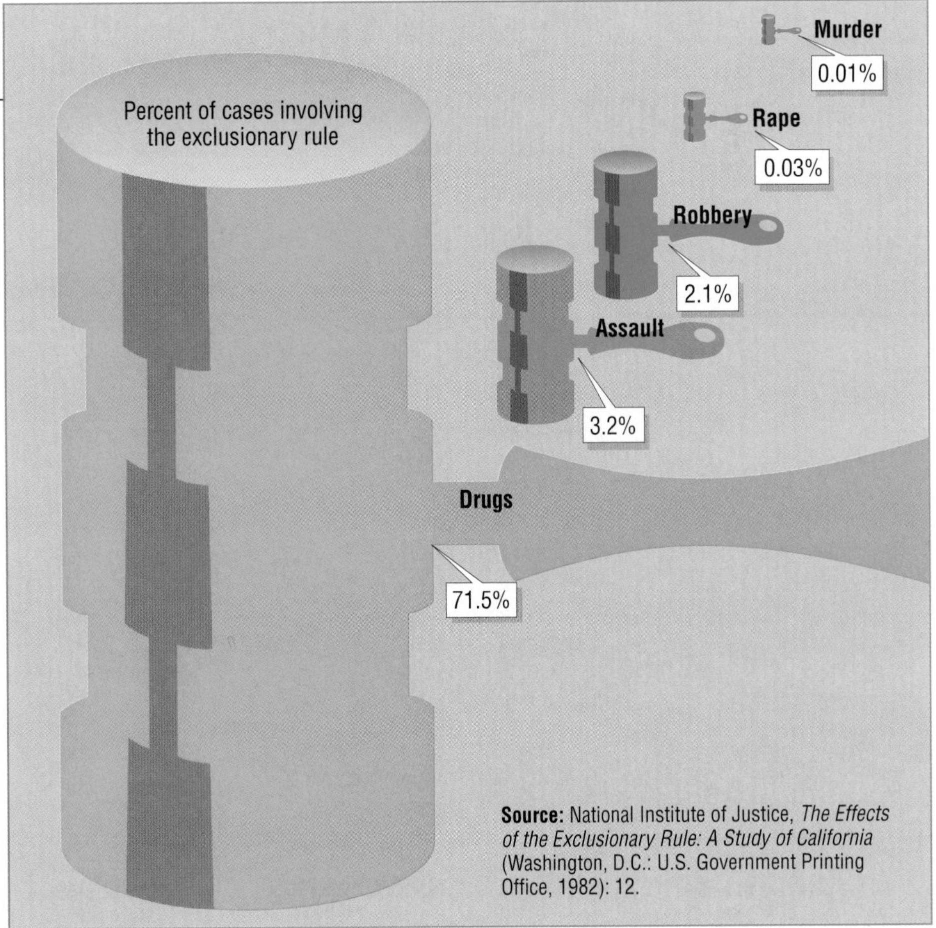

Source: National Institute of Justice, *The Effects of the Exclusionary Rule: A Study of California* (Washington, D.C.: U.S. Government Printing Office, 1982): 12.

were not interested in successful prosecution but rather in getting contraband off the street.[58]

My own view is that because of its limited application, restrictions on the exclusionary rule hardly seem adequate cause either for critics to rejoice or supporters to lament. Perhaps its strongest claim as a policy instrument is that it helps to ensure judicial integrity. Courts, by excluding illegally obtained evidence, keep the criminal justice system pure. The exclusionary rule exacts the price of setting a few criminals free to maintain the rule of law. It sacrifices the correct result in an individual case for the general interest in constitutional government.[59]

CRITICAL THINKING

1. Is letting even one criminal go free, no matter what the crime, worth the cost of excluding illegally obtained evidence? Explain your answer.
2. Is the judicial integrity rationale for the exclusionary rule a good rationale, even though the U.S. Supreme Court has rejected it? Explain your answer.

Knowledge and Understanding CHECK

1. Identify the three types of actions open to individuals who have suffered unconstitutional invasions conducted to obtain evidence.
2. Describe the rationale of the exclusionary rule.
3. Summarize the research on the social costs of the exclusionary rule.

Eyewitness Testimony Consideration

According to Professor Loftus,

> We have no clear method for estimating the frequency of wrongful accusations based on faulty eyewitness testimony. Even if percentage-wise the frequency is low, the absolute number of known cases of wrongful convictions is sizable. More than one thousand people are known to have been wrongfully convicted prior to 1986, and some of them were, tragically, executed. Moreover, some reliable estimates of the number of wrongful convictions in the United States alone in a single year are staggering–exceeding eight thousand. As important as it is to minimize the devastation that befalls an innocent person, it is, of course, also important to identify those who have actually committed crimes and punish them appropriately. Clearly, accurate identification and conviction of perpetrators is in all of our interests. After all, who wants to live in a world where criminals don't get identified, don't get caught, and continue to rob and rape?[60]

Critical Thinking

1. After reading this chapter, do you think the problem of misidentification can be solved?
2. How do you explain the willingness of courts to accept eyewitness identification in view of Professor Loftus's remarks?

CHAPTER CAPSULE

- The law of criminal procedure balances the need for criminal law enforcement and the privacy and liberty interests of individuals.
- All police invasions of privacy and liberty require an objective basis to back them up.
- The greater the invasion the higher the amount of objective basis required to back up the invasion.
- Searches and seizures are not supposed to be right or pleasant; they are supposed to be reasonable.
- The inherent limits of human perception, memory, and recall cause misidentifications.
- The exclusionary rule prohibits the use of good evidence because of bad practices in obtaining it.

KEY TERMS

admissible evidence
objective basis
formalization
arrest
probable cause to arrest
articulable facts and circumstances
direct information
hearsay
knock-and-announce rule
fleeing felon doctrine
search
affidavit
balancing test of reasonableness
totality of circumstances
search incident to arrest
consent search
plain-view search
stop and frisk
reasonable suspicion
interrogation
Miranda warnings
lineups
show-ups
photo identification
DNA (deoxyribonucleic acid) testing
exclusionary rule

INTERNET RESEARCH EXERCISES

Exercise: Using the Internet or InfoTrac College Edition, search for information on searches incident to arrest. Answer the question: Can police officers search people's cars for drugs after they have arrested the driver for a minor traffic violation?

Suggested site:

- The Oyez Project at Northwestern University, http://oyez.nwu.edu/ (tip: Click on "Cases," then "Search by title." Enter the title word "Whren." The case *Whren v. United States* deals with searches for drugs following arrests for traffic offenses. Read the case. If you have RealAudio on your computer, you can also listen to the oral arguments. If you don't, you can download RealAudio at http://www.realaudio.com/)

InfoTrac College Edition: Run a key word search on "pretext searches." You should find a lot of information about the subject, particularly as it relates to the case of *Whren v. U.S.*

NOTES

1. Elizabeth Loftus, *Eyewitness Testimony* (Cambridge, Mass.: Harvard University Press, 1996), v–vi.
2. This is Carl B. Klockars's paraphrase of Egan Bittner's position in "The Rhetoric of Community Policing," *Thinking About Police,* 2d ed., Carl B. Klockars and Stephen D. Mastrofski, eds. (New York: McGraw-Hill, 1991), 532.
3. W. F. Walsh, "Patrol Officer Arrest Rates: A Study of the Social Organization of Police Work," *Justice Quarterly* 2 (1986): 271–90; Donald J. Black, *Manners and Customs of Police* (New York: Academic Press, 1980); both cited in Klockars, "The Rhetoric of Community Policing," 532.
4. Herbert Packer, *The Limits of the Criminal Sanction* (Palo Alto: Stanford University Press, 1968), chaps. 8–12.
5. American Law Institute, *A Model Code of Pre-Arraignment Procedure, Proposed Official Draft, Complete Text and Commentary* (Philadelphia: American Law Institute, 1975), 13–14.
6. Floyd Feeney et al., *Arrests Without Conviction: How Often They Occur and Why* (Washington, D.C.: National Institute of Justice, 1983); Brian Forst et al., "Prosecution and Sentencing," in *Crime and Public Policy,* James Q. Wilson, ed. (New Brunswick, N.J.: Transaction Books, 1983), 165–68; Vera Institute of Justice, *Felony Arrests* (New York: Longman, 1981); Donald J. Black, *The Manners and Customs of the Police* (New York: Academic Press, 1980), chap. 4; *The Prosecution of Felony Arrests 1980* (Washington, D.C.: Bureau of Justice Statistics, 1985), 7–17.
7. *People v. Washington,* 236 Cal.Rptr. 840 (1987).
8. Abraham N. Tennenbaum, "The Influence of the *Garner* Decision on Police Use of Deadly Force," *Journal of Criminal Law and Criminology* 85 (1994): 241.
9. *Justice v. Dennis,* 834 F.2d 380 (4th Cir. 1987).
10. William J. Cuddihy, "The Fourth Amendment: Origins and Original Meaning, 602-1791" (unpublished dissertation, Claremont Graduate School, 1990), xc–xcvi.
11. John Wesley Hall, Jr., *Search and Seizure,* 2d ed. (Deerfield, Ill.: Clark, Boardman, 1991), ix.
12. Maria Goodavage, "But '180 Degrees' Wrong," *USA Today,* 1 December 1992.
13. "Getting Around the Fourth Amendment," *Thinking About Police,* 434–35.
14. Quoted in "Getting Around the Fourth Amendment," 436.
15. Ibid.
16. *Chimel v. California,* 395 U.S. 752 (1969).
17. *Schneckcloth v. Bustamonte,* 412 U.S. 218 (1973).
18. *California v. Carney,* 471 U.S. 386 (1985).
19. Joel Samaha, *Criminal Procedure,* 4th ed. (Monterey, Calif.: Wadsworth, 1999), 75–78 and cases cited therein.
20. Loren G. Stern, "Stop and Frisk: An Historical Answer to a Modern Problem," *Journal of Criminal Law, Criminology, and Police Science* 58 (1967): 532; Frank Remington, "The Law Relating to 'On the Street' Detention, Questioning, and Frisking of Suspected Persons and Police Arrest Privileges in General," *Journal of Criminal Law, Criminology, and Police Science* 50 (1960): 390.
21. John E. Boydstun, *San Diego Field Interrogations: Final Report* (Washington, D.C.: Police Foundation, 1975), 45; *Terry v. Ohio,* 392 U.S. 1 (1967).
22. *Terry v. Ohio,* 392 U.S. 1 (1967).
23. American Law Institute, *Model Code of Pre-Arraignment Procedure,* 273–76; Boydstun, *San Diego Field Interrogations,* 40–64.
24. 384 U.S. 436 (1966), 448.
25. Richard Leo, "Inside the Interrogation Room," *Journal of Criminal Law and Criminology,* 86 (1996): 266, 302.
26. *Miranda v. Arizona,* 384 U.S. 436 (1966).
27. Ibid.
28. *State v. Anderson,* 332 So.2d 452 (La.1976); *Oregon v. Mathiason,* 429 U.S. 492 (1977); *United States ex rel Hines v. LaVallee,* 521 F.2d 1109 (2d Cir. 1975).
29. U.S. Senate, Committee on the Judiciary, Subcommittee on Criminal Laws and Procedures, *Hearings, Controlling Crime Through More Effective Law Enforcement* (Washington, D.C.: U.S. Government Printing Office, 1967).
30. *Colorado v. Connelly,* 479 U.S. 157 (1986).
31. Donald A. Dripps, "Foreword: Against Police Interrogation and the Privilege Against Self-Incrimination," *Journal of Criminal Law and Criminology* 78 (1988): 701.
32. "Pagano Case Points Finger at Lineups," *National Law Journal* (September 10, 1979): 1.
33. "Notes: Did Your Eyes Deceive You? Expert Psychological Testimony on the Unreliability of Eyewitness Identification," *Stanford Law Review* 29 (1977): 970.
34. Quoted in Martin Yant, *Presumed Guilty: When Innocent People Are Wrongly Convicted* (Buffalo: Prometheus Books, 1991), 99.
35. Samuel R. Gross, "Loss of Innocence: Eyewitness Identification and Proof of Guilt," *Journal of Legal Studies* 16 (1987): 398–99; "Notes: Did Your Eyes Deceive You?" 982–83.
36. "Notes: Did Your Eyes Deceive You?" 982.
37. Cited in Yant, *Presumed Guilty,* 100.
38. Ibid.

39. "Notes: Did Your Eyes Deceive You?" 969; David Bazelon, "Eyewitness News," *Psychology Today* (March 1980): 102–104; LaFave and Israel, *Criminal Procedure* 1:551–53; Gross, "Loss of Innocence," 401.
40. *Basoff v. State,* 208 Md. 643, 119 A.2d 917 (1956).
41. *Manson v. Braithwaite,* 432 U.S. 98, 97 S.Ct. 2243, 53 L.Ed.2d 140 (1977).
42. *Rodriguez v. Young,* 906 F.2d 1153 (7th Cir. 1990).
43. LaFave and Israel, *Criminal Procedure,* 590–91.
44. Ibid., 588–90.
45. Kenneth R. Kreiling, "DNA Technology in Forensic Science," *Jurimetrics Journal* 33 (1993): 449; William C. Thompson, "Evaluating the Admissibility of New Genetic Identification Tests: Lessons from the 'DNA War,'" *Journal of Criminal Law and Criminology* 84 (1993): 26–27.
46. Quoted in Stephanie Goldberg, "A New Day for DNA?" *American Bar Association Journal* 78 (April 1992): 85.
47. *People v. Wesley,* 140 Misc.2d 306, 533 N.Y.S.2d 643 (Cty.Ct.1988), affirmed 183 A.D.2d 75, 589 N.Y.S.2d 197 (1992) ("greatest advance" and "war" quoted in Thompson, "Evaluating the Admissibility," 23); *People v. Castro,* 144 Misc.2d 956, 545 N.Y.S.2d 985 (Bronx Cty.1989); Kreiling, "DNA Technology in Forensic Science," 449.
48. Quoted in Jonathan J. Koehler, "Error and Exaggeration in the Presentation of DNA Evidence at Trial," *Jurimetrics Journal* 34 (1994): 21.
49. Koehler, "Error and Exaggeration"; surveys of jurors, judges, and lawyers reported in Paul C. Giannelli, "Criminal Discovery, Scientific Evidence, and DNA," *Vanderbilt Law Review* 44 (1991): 794.
50. Jon O. Newman, "Suing the Lawbreakers: Proposals to Strengthen the Section 1983 Damage Remedy for Law Enforcers' Misconduct," *Yale Law Journal* 87 (1978): 447–67.
51. *Mapp v. Ohio,* 367 U.S. 643, 81 S.Ct. 1684, 6 L.Ed.2d 1081 (1961); *Miranda v. Arizona,* 384 U.S. 436, 86 S.Ct. 1602, 16 L.Ed.2d 694 (1966); *United States v. Wade,* 388 U.S. 218, 87 S.Ct. 1926, 18 L.Ed.2d 1149 (1967); *Gelbard v. United States,* 408 U.S. 41, 92 S.Ct. 2357, 33 L.Ed.2d 179 (1972); *United States v. Caceres,* 440 U.S. 741, 99 S.Ct. 1465, 59 L.Ed.2d 733 (1979).
52. William A. Schroeder, "Deterring Fourth Amendment Violations," *Georgetown Law Journal* 69 (1981): 1361, 1378–86.
53. 277 U.S. 438, 470, 48 S.Ct. 564, 575, 72 L.Ed.2d 944 (1928).
54. Schroeder, "Deterring Fourth Amendment Violations."
55. Myron W. Orfield, Jr., "The Exclusionary Rule and Deterrence: An Empirical Study of Chicago Narcotics Officers," *University of Chicago Law Review* 54 (1987): 1017–18, 1029.
56. Ibid., 1027–28.
57. National Institute of Justice, *The Effects of the Exclusionary Rule: A Study of California* (Washington, D.C.: U.S. Government Printing Office, 1982), 12.
58. Thomas Y. Davies, "A Hard Look at What We Know (and Still Need to Learn) About the 'Social Costs' of the Exclusionary Rule: The NIJ Study and Other Studies of 'Lost' Arrests," *American Bar Foundation Research Journal* (1983): 640; Peter F. Nardulli, "The Societal Costs of the Exclusionary Rule Revisited," *University of Illinois Law Review* (1987): 235.
59. Yale Kamisar, "Does (Did) (Should) the Exclusionary Rule Rest on a 'Principled Basis' Rather Than on 'Empirical Propositions?'" *Creighton Law Review* 16 (1983): 565.
60. Loftus, *Eyewitness Testimony,* vi.

CHAPTER 8

Issues in Policing

CHAPTER OUTLINE

Do Rules Against the Use of Force Make a Difference?

Following LAPD officers' use of force against Rodney King, the Independent Commission of the Los Angeles Police Department said, "The problem of excessive force in the LAPD is fundamentally a problem of supervision, management, and leadership." William B. Waegel examined shootings in Philadelphia to assess the effectiveness of a statute that changed the old law giving police officers the right to shoot *any* fleeing felony suspect, to the more restrictive rule authorizing officers to shoot only fleeing *violent* felony suspects.[1]

INTRODUCTION

"We did things differently then, things that we've outgrown," said a Savannah, Georgia, police sergeant, explaining why police officers no longer shoot people as often as they did in the 1970s. "Back then, we used to routinely point our guns at unarmed people." By the early 1980s, such practices were almost unheard of in his department, the sergeant said. According to police researcher Lawrence W. Sherman, this sergeant's remark captures a fundamental shift in policing in the United States:

> This change in police culture is nothing short of extraordinary. For generations big-city police departments maintained a culture of policing that placed little restriction on firearms use. The long-term persistence of that pattern is not surprising, since corporate cultures are easier to maintain than to change. Some academic critics in the 1970s announced what they concluded was the failure of a broad social movement for police reform over a half century. To the contrary . . . the essence of policing, the distribution of coercion in the community, [has changed dramatically].[2]

This shift in police culture is due to a variety of causes. First, criminal justice research has demonstrated the informal discretionary nature of police work (Chapters 5–7). Second, police work involves order maintenance more than criminal law enforcement (Chapter 4). Third, research demonstrated that neither preventive patrol nor crime attack strategies had much, if any, effect on crime rates (Chapter 5). Finally, community-oriented policing has affected the view of policing in some departments (Chapter 4). This chapter examines three main issues in police work in police culture at the turn of the twenty-first century:

- The police working personality.
- Recruitment, training, socialization, and career advancement.
- Review of police conduct and decision making.

THE POLICE WORKING PERSONALITY

"The day the new recruit walks through the doors of the police academy he leaves society behind to enter a profession that does more than give him a job; it defines who he is. For all the years he remains, he will always be a cop." This is what the highly respected James Ahern, the late police chief of New Haven, Connecticut, said about the police working personality.[3]

The police are "one of the strongest vocational subcultures" in the United States. It is a subculture pervaded by norms of unity, loyalty, perceptions of danger, and suspicion. There is wide consensus that the police subculture has a distinct **police working personality.** Early researchers reported mostly unflattering attributes of this personality, including:

- Authoritarian
- Suspicious
- Racist
- Hostile
- Insecure
- Conservative
- Cynical

Later research reports more complex findings. Officer styles are not monolithic; they vary. William Muir, in his excellent study of the police working personality, *Streetcorner Politicians,* applied the famous sociologist Max Weber's attributes of *passion* and *perspective* to the police working personality. Passion consists of the capacity to recognize both the need for force and the willingness to use it. Police officers with passion can deal with situations in which they must coerce others to achieve just ends. Perspective consists of the capacity of officers to understand human suffering and the limits of the police in dealing with that suffering. These officers have the "tragic perspective." They know that issues are not either absolutely right or wrong, or good or bad; life is more complex to them.[4]

In cross-tabulating the attitudes of 28 patrol officers in a California city, Muir found four ideal types of the police working personality:

1. *Professionals* possess both passion and perspective. They use force when necessary, but they also understand the suffering of others. They are the "good cops" who know they cannot solve all the problems they encounter, but they try to provide fair, humane law enforcement.
2. *Enforcers* have passion, that is, they have no reservation about using force. But they lack perspective; they do not understand the complexity of human nature. They like to lock people up. They are the cynical, authoritarian type that early research stressed.
3. *Reciprocators* have perspective, but they hesitate or cannot use force when necessary. They are lenient; they want to help, not hurt. They are social workers.
4. *Avoiders* lack perspective and passion. They suffer from low skills and low self-esteem. They avoid the responsibility of providing quality service of any kind.[5]

John Broderick concluded that, based on his own research and his surveys of all the major research, Muir's findings applied to all size departments in all parts of the United States.[6]

J. Snipes and Stephen Mastrofski found that the police working personality was even more complex than that Muir had reported. The police working personality does not depend solely on attitudes of individual police officers but also upon the situations in which they find themselves. For example, a police officer may readily use force in a robbery but not in a shoplifting case. Officers in crime-attack situations may rely on force but not when answering a call about a loud party. Police officers may rely on force in some neighborhoods and not in others, or with some kinds of people and not others. In other words, police style is not wholly a matter of personality; it depends on the type, manner, and circumstances of encounters between officers and private individuals.

Stephen M. Cox and James Frank distributed hypothetical situations to patrol officers. One proactive and one reactive scenario took place in a high-crime area of an inner city, followed by one proactive and one reactive situation in a high-income suburban neighborhood. The researchers found that officers changed their style depending on the type of intervention and, to a lesser extent, on the neighborhood.[7]

Social scientists have disagreed about whether the police working personality derives from innate character traits, or from the socialization process of training, street experience, and the police subculture. At first, researchers concluded that the police personality was inherently different from other groups. The majority of later studies found that to the extent that police possess a working personality, it derives from socialization through the police academy, field training, and patrol experience.[8]

Knowledge and Understanding CHECK

1. List the unflattering characteristics of the police working personality identified by early researchers.
2. Identify the major findings on the complexity of the police working personality.
3. List and describe Muir's four ideal types of police working personality.
4. Compare Muir's findings with those of Snipes and Mastrofski.

RECRUITMENT, TRAINING, AND PROMOTION

Two major influences have brought about changes in the selection, training, and promotion of police officers:

1. President Lyndon Johnson's Crime Commission Report (Chapter 1).
2. Application of federal civil rights law to state criminal justice (Chapter 4).

Until these changes, most police officers were white men from blue-collar backgrounds. Most police departments, at least publicly, focused on their law enforcement mission. In 1967, President Johnson's Crime Commission documented widespread police corruption, discrimination, and failure to respond to the needs and demands of communities. The commission challenged the assumptions that the "manly virtues" and the capacity to obey orders—the qualities sought in traditional police forces—were the qualities most needed to make a "good" police officer. The commission rejected the prevailing requirements of height, financial credit history, and the absence of *any* criminal record that were supposed to screen for competent officers. Instead, the commission argued, those requirements effectively, if not consciously, excluded large segments of society from police work. As a result, the most visible form of law enforcement did not represent women or African Americans, Native

Americans, Asian Americans, or Hispanics. The commission recommended the adoption of screening devices that eliminate arbitrary and exclusionary effects.

In 1972, federal legislation extended the 1964 Civil Rights Act to prohibit race, gender, religious, and national origin discrimination in public employment.[9]

Disagreement about the definition of "good" police officers added to the challenges of the Crime Commission and civil rights legislation. To some segments of society, good police officers maintain the status quo; to others, they change it. To some segments, good police officers aggressively fight crime; to others, they help people in trouble. To some, good officers follow the letter of the law; to others, they bend the rules to get results.

Despite such disagreements, no one denied that personality, recruitment, training, and advancement affect both the effectiveness of police operations and the degree of police deviance, such as corruption and brutality. Robert D. Meier and Richard E. Maxwell reported a growing consensus that psychological testing can determine the emotional and psychological fitness of recruits. More than half the nation's police departments now use some form of psychological testing.

Unfortunately, psychologists and psychiatrists disagree on what makes a good police officer and, therefore, do not agree on what they are looking for and how to find it in the tests. Furthermore, a growing body of empirical research casts doubt on the accuracy of predictions of future officer performance based on psychological testing. Benjamin Wright, William Doerner, and John Speier analyzed data from the Tallahassee Police Department to test the relationship between preemployment psychological test results and performance of recruits during their initial field training. The results showed no relationship between the results of the Minnesota Multiphasic Personality Inventory or the California Personality Inventory and field performance. The researchers concluded that the results suggest a need to reshape the police selection process.[10]

Traditional selection procedures and training methods, and socialization into the police subculture following training, favored the creation of a homogeneous conservative, authoritarian, punitive, and cynical police working personality. Most traditional departments maintained stringent physical, mental, and character requirements. The minimum 5′8″ height and 150-pound weight requirements made it difficult for women to enter police work. Traditional civil service examinations favored whites. Physical agility tests—timed runs, carrying weights, and repeat trigger-pulling—favored men. Character investigations that eliminated potential recruits with even the most minor criminal records favored whites. Oral interviews allowed gender and race to affect judgments. Traditional screening produced a homogeneous group of recruits: young, white men with blue-collar backgrounds and high school diplomas who entered police work because it promised job security. Furthermore, recruits did not reveal authoritarian, punitive, or cynical personalities *before* becoming officers. Instead, the working personality developed from the teaching in the police academy, field training, and street experience *after* entering police work.[11]

A 1990 survey of police departments throughout the country found that 75 percent still used a physical performance test in recruiting officers; 20 percent used it in selecting graduates from basic training. Seventy-one percent screened for substance abuse in recruiting officers; 20 percent used the screen in selecting graduates. Most used written tests that the departments evaluated for validity. Somewhat less than 40 percent failed basic training.[12]

All of the following aspects of the changes during the 1960s and 1970s put pressure on traditional ideas about the "right" police personality:

- The complexity of our pluralistic society.
- Demands for equal opportunity by women and by ethnic and racial minorities.
- Recognition of the multiple missions of police.
- The large part discretion plays in performing police missions.
- The limits of preventive patrol and other traditional police operations in reducing violence, illegal drugs, and other problems.
- The popularity of community-oriented policing among researchers and reformers.

The "manly virtues" and obeying the orders of police managers were no longer considered enough to meet the challenges of policing. For example, community policing and problem-oriented policing require great skills in recognizing, selecting, and solving community problems; in drawing on a wide array of resources in the community; and in working with residents and groups in the community (see Chapter 6). This kind of work requires officers who are sensitive to neighborhoods, aware of the varying interests within neighborhoods—or even in buildings within neighborhoods—and who have the skills to communicate, the capacity to seek solutions, and the knowledge of where to look. In short, this work requires the exercise of good judgment. It calls for the development and exercise of wise discretion.

Police expert Egon Bittner, in discussing the qualities of problem-oriented police officers, writes:

> The question that would . . . be asked of a performance is not if it complied with rules and regulations, but whether it showed adequacy of skill, knowledge, judgment, efficiency and other relevant criteria of good work. Moreover, such judgment would not be passed by one's administrative superiors, although their judgment need not be ruled out entirely, but by one's professional colleagues.[13]

Education

The demands for police officers who possessed more than physical strength and the capacity to obey orders did not begin with the recognition of the complexity of society and the police mission. August Vollmer, the famous reform police chief of Berkeley, California, recommended higher education for police officers as early as 1920. Little movement in that direction occurred until the 1960s, when training and education became the foremost measures to "upgrade" the police. In 1989, the Police Executive Research Forum reviewed research, surveyed 502 departments, and visited 7 departments to determine the present state of police officer education in the United States. They reported that the national average educational level had risen from 12.4 years in 1967 to 13.6 years in 1989. Seventy-two percent of African Americans and 73 percent of Hispanics employed had attended college. Nearly two-thirds of departments had a formal policy in favor of higher education.[14]

A number of police chiefs in the 1990s have commented on the importance of police education. Neil Behan, chief of police in Baltimore County, said, "When I was a rookie 43 years ago, we knew where we stood as officers. In those days, you spent an entire career in the same department with that department's same mind-set. It took a very special person to break away." Now Behan tells his 1,545-member department that he will promote no one to senior management without a college degree "or the imminent prospect of one." Charlie Johnson, chief of police in the Denver suburb of Lakewood, said: "I want disciplined, dedicated, tolerant people who understand how society works and want to solve problems, not just answer distress calls." Allen H. Andrews, Jr., chief of police in Peoria, Illinois, maintained that "society is more complicated now. Society and I expect officers not just to be law enforcers but to be the grease on the wheels of solving social conflicts." Andrews sends all recruits to special courses on courtesy and body language so they can read people's movements and focus on their own attitudes and intentions.[15]

According to the Police Executive Research Forum, higher education can benefit police officers in many ways. It:

- Develops a broader base of information for decision making.
- Provides additional years and experience for increasing maturity.
- Inculcates responsibility through course requirements and achievement.
- Teaches the history of the country, the democratic process, individual rights, and the values of a free society.
- Engenders the ability to handle difficult and ambiguous situations with creativity and innovation.
- Teaches the "big picture" of the criminal justice system and provides a fuller understanding and appreciation of prosecution, courts, and corrections.
- Develops a greater empathy for minorities and discrimination.
- Encourages tolerance and understanding of differing lifestyles and ideologies.
- Helps officers communicate with and respond to people and their problems in a competent, civil, and humane manner.
- Develops officers who can deal innovatively and flexibly with problem-oriented and community policing.
- Helps officers develop better communications and community relations skills.
- Engenders more "professional" demeanor and performance.
- Enables officers to cope with stress.
- Makes officers less authoritarian and cynical.
- Prepares officers to accept and adapt to change.
- Helps reduce the number of lawsuits against police departments, because college-educated officers know the law better.[16]

An increase in the numbers of college-educated officers does not automatically translate into improved quality and effectiveness. Despite a growing nationwide emphasis on training, and with some departments and even state laws requiring higher education, a growing body of research supports the conclusion of one researcher that "there is growing doubt that training in its present form achieves the objectives its proponents hold out for it." Robert Worden measured the attitudes and performance of officers who obtained bachelor's degrees before entering police work, officers who became police officers before obtaining a degree, and officers without college degrees. He surveyed both officers and private individuals in 24 police departments in three metropolitan areas: St. Louis, Rochester, and Tampa-St. Petersburg. He found only marginal differences in both attitudes and performance among the three groups:

> Although college-educated officers may be superior from the perspectives of supervisors, who find that such officers are more reliable employees and better report writers, they are not superior from the perspective of police clientele, who are concerned principally with effective and courteous contacts with police. Therefore this analysis suggests that patrol officers' performance and morale will be affected neither by policies that encourage in-service education nor by entry requirements that include college education.[17]

In another study, Worden relied on data collected from observations of more than 5,000 police-citizen encounters. He looked at a number of officer characteristics and their relationship to the use of force. He found that officers who earned bachelor's degrees were *more* likely to use force generally. However, Worden also found that officers with bachelor's degrees were *less* likely to use *excessive* force.[18]

Victor Kappeler, Allen Sapp, and David Carter, in an analysis of citizen complaints against officers in a medium-sized department, found that officers with college degrees produced fewer citizen complaints for rudeness than officers without college degrees. However, they had more departmental complaints of rules violations.

Use *Your* Discretion

Does college education make "good" cops?

The results of these and other similar studies do not necessarily prove that college education has no positive effect on police attitudes and performance. They do suggest the need for more research. In a major review of the research on the increase in the numbers of college-educated police officers, Stephen Mastrofski concluded that whether the increase has significantly affected police practice "remains mostly unanswered." He called for more data that demonstrate the relationship between the personal characteristics of officers, the kind of education received, and the willingness of departments to encourage and facilitate the skills and lessons of college education. Despite increased education, Mastrofski wonders, "Can one teach old cops new tricks, or is there an experiential threshold beyond which few officers respond to new approaches?"[19]

Clearly defined training goals cannot be established unless departments have defined police missions. However, not everyone agrees on what those missions should be. Some take a broad view of training and advanced education, even going so far as to claim as a goal that they will bolster the general social status of police officers as educated professionals in the community. Others take a much narrower view; they believe that training should stick to preparing police officers to carry out the mission of effective and fair criminal law enforcement. Still others view training as an opportunity to reform police administration, such as reducing the emphasis on law enforcement and enhancing order maintenance and public service functions. Others hope that training will develop in officers a better capacity to make judgments and solve problems that will enhance the strategies of community and problem-oriented policing.[20]

Complicating the answer to the question of whether education and training "work," administrators and researchers do not agree on what training and education police officers *should* receive. Examine your answers to the questions that follow. Are your conclusions based on "gut reactions"? Or, do you have specific knowledge to support them?

CRITICAL THINKING

1. Should instructors teach by lecturing, the most efficient, economical educational method?
2. Discretion requires judgment, so should teachers utilize discussion and problem-solving methods to encourage recruits to think critically? Should police officers have a college or university degree?
3. Should it be a liberal arts degree or a specialized criminal justice major?
4. In regard to training, how many hours does adequate training require?
5. Is vicarious classroom learning enough, or should recruits have field training as well?
6. What priority should training receive in the whole police operation?
7. What purpose should training serve, and does training accomplish that purpose?[21]

The Police Academy

Researchers have consistently found that "the transition from civilian to police officer is a long and complicated series of stages, inviting much upheaval and self doubt." For most officers, this transition begins in the **police academy,** which socializes recruits by both formal and informal means. Formally, recruits learn the written rules of the academy, namely, the laws of search, seizure, interrogation, and identification; technical skills, including crime scene preservation, pursuit driving, weapons use, self-defense, and report writing. Rules govern virtually everything in police academies, and military-like officers attempt to enforce them. Rules focus on punctuality, neatness, order, attentiveness, and obedience to authority.[22]

Police recruits also learn the unwritten informal rules about how police officers are supposed to behave. Two important informal rules that recruits learn include:

1. Rules are something to "get around."
2. Administrators are punishers.

Neither the rules of the traditional academy nor the formal laws of criminal procedure answer recruits' most pressing questions:

- "What is it really like out there on the streets?"
- "How do I arrest someone who doesn't want to be arrested?"
- "Exactly when do I use my nightstick, and how do I do it?"
- "What do the other patrol officers think of me?"

Recruits learn some of the answers from instructors or other experienced officers in the form of **police war stories.** Most of these stories, such as that told by Jonathan Rubenstein stress two themes: **police defensiveness** and **police depersonalization:**[23]

> A jack is a beautiful weapon, but it is very dangerous, fellas. I remember once we were looking for a guy

Figure 8.1
Rate of Death per 100,000 in Various Occupations

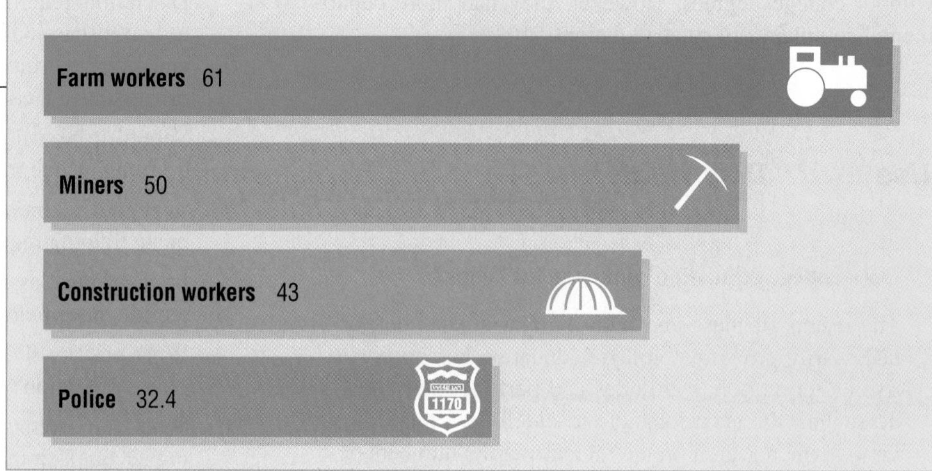

who had beaten up a policeman and escaped from a wagon. I found him hiding under a car. To this day I don't know if he was coming out to surrender or to attack me, but he was just coming out before I told him to move. He was a real big guy and I didn't wait. I had my jack ready, and as he came up I hit him as hard as I could. I thought I killed him. He was O.K., but since then I haven't carried a jack unless I was going on some dangerous job. I don't want to beat someone to death, and with a jack you can never be sure. You should get yourself a convoy and use it in your fist. If you punch for a guy's heart, the whipping action of the spring will snap it forward and break his collarbone. Then you've got him.[24]

This war story portrays both themes. Officers learn they not only need to defend themselves but also to develop defensiveness. They learn not to trust "outsiders." According to Richard Harris, a journalist who attended a police academy in New York City, instructors told recruits that politicians do not know what they are doing; African Americans and other minorities are criminal threats who deny the work ethic; reporters will distort all police stories; women cause special problems by false accusations of sexual assault; and, in general, "anyone who was not a law enforcement officer was not to be trusted."[25]

The story of using the blackjack also illustrates how the traditional academy encourages recruits to depersonalize individuals, as this instructor did by describing the use of force in such a cold, matter-of-fact manner. The themes of defensiveness and depersonalization stem in large part from the perceived danger of police work. In fact, other occupations carry greater risk of death and injury than police work does (see Figure 8.1). Police deaths and injuries, however, usually arise from willful, deliberate attacks. Furthermore, as respected police experts David H. Bayley and Egon Bittner note:

Police continually deal with situations in which physical constraint may have to be applied against people who are willing to fight, struggle, hit, stab, spit, bite, tear, hurl, hide, and run. People continually use their bodies against the police, forcing the police to deal with them in a physical way. While police seem to be preoccupied with deadly force, the more common reality in their lives is the possibility of a broken nose, lost teeth, black eyes, broken ribs, and twisted arms. Few officers are ever shot or even shot at, but all except the rawest rookie can show scars on their bodies from continual encounters with low-level violence.[26]

Field Training

New police officers finish their academy training insecure about whether what they have learned will help them on the street. Departments usually require **field training,** which places rookies in the hands of older officers who are supposed to help their transition from the academy and learn the craft of policing. But training involves more than learning skills and techniques. According to James Fyfe:

Everything that supervisors do or tolerate, every interpretation of broad departmental philosophy, every application of specific rules and policies is a training lesson that has at least as much impact on officers' performance as what they may have learned in their rookie days.[27]

Field training officers are fabled for telling rookies, "Forget what they told you in the police academy, kid; you'll learn how to do it on the street." When they do that, says Fyfe,

formal training is instantly and irreparably devalued. Worse, when officers actually see firsthand that the behavioral strictures in which they are schooled are routinely ignored in practice, formal training is neutralized and the definitions of appropriate behavior are instead made in the secrecy of officers' locker rooms.[28]

In teaching rookies the craft of policing, experienced officers emphasize that "real" policing involves "heavy" calls, such as "man with gun," "shots fired," and "officer needs assistance." The true test of a good officer, according to the traditional standards, is the ability and willingness to risk injury in these situations.[29]

Some older officers are experienced in field training, and some departments establish structured field training and evaluation. In other departments, the officers have had little or no training in evaluating rookies. William G. Doerner and E. Britt Patterson describe field training in Tallahassee, Florida, before a court case prompted the department to improve its field training:

> [P]ost-academy training consisted of a thirty-day observation period with a senior patrol officer. The veteran officer imparted words of wisdom as needed and answered any questions that the rookie had. At the end of the assignment, the senior officer would submit a recommendation. . . . [T]here were no . . . standardized training modules. A sound performance rating system, particularly one anchored in actual job tasks, was absent. What this practice amounted to was an indefensible extension of the antiquated "good old boy" system.[30]

Use *Your* Discretion

Does broad field experience make "better" cops?

Some departments provide broader educational experience than the traditional academy and field training. Some accept courses that are supposed to improve critical thinking because administrators believe that such courses improve the capacity of police officers to make sound discretionary judgments. Some departments accept liberal arts courses, and even degrees, as satisfying both entry and advancement criteria. Instructors in some law enforcement courses have adopted problem-solving approaches, the case method, and discussion to enhance prospective officers' ability to make judgments. Experienced officers sometimes act as guest lecturers, interacting with students who hope to become officers and with other students. The interaction can prove enriching to students, instructors, and officers.

Field experiences that broaden the perspectives of new officers are supposed to improve their understanding and effectiveness. Community service internships offer recruits the opportunity to gain a broader perspective on crime and criminal law enforcement. To improve understanding of the criminal justice system beyond the police department, some officers spend time in prosecutors' offices to appreciate the complexities of charging suspects; in public defenders' offices getting the defense point of view; and in judges' chambers learning about the difficulties of sentencing. Some departments give officers the opportunity to learn more about the cultural diversity in their district by assigning them to hospital emergency rooms, alcoholic detoxification clinics, psychiatric wards, welfare offices, and schools.[31]

The San Diego Police Department introduced an innovative field experience aimed at sensitizing police officers to the authority they wield by subjecting them to it. Trainees and their supervisors traveled to San Jose, California, for the field training phase. In a stimulating and educational session, officers were placed in situations designed to attract the attention of the local police. The exercise attempted to give officers firsthand experience of police interrogation from a nonpolice perspective. Some officers felt they were harassed; others felt they were subjected to unnecessary physical handling or illegal arrest. However, not all the contact experiences were negative; some very good interrogations were conducted. The San Diego officers in training had to think about what they had done to attract the attention of the local police. This led the trainees to examine their own motives for selecting particular individuals for field interrogations.[32]

Training in improving discretionary decision making, whether by means of courses in critical thinking or field experiences, works best when departments recruit applicants adaptable to these innovations. Almost everyone agrees that police work requires officers intelligent enough to grasp difficult problems and to decide quickly on a response. Beyond that, controversy lies. Some want to improve the effectiveness of discretionary decision making generally, because it plays such a large role in all police missions—maintaining order, enforcing the criminal law, and providing other services. Others want to focus strictly on producing more effective crime fighters. John E. Boydstun, who studied field interrogation in San Diego, expresses the broad view of training:

> [R]ecruits should be able to understand the cosmopolitan nature of an urban area and appreciate differences between cultures. They must learn to tolerate unconventional behavior and respect divergent life-styles. They must be able to appreciate the meaning of freedom and be sensitive to the awesome consequences stemming from the unbridled use of authority. They must take on the commitment to protect constitutional guarantees. They must subscribe to the value our society attaches to limiting the use of force, and they must learn to appreciate the controls exercised over the use of police powers and the role of the community in directing and reviewing police conduct.[33]

CRITICAL THINKING

1. Do the studies described here prove the value of broad field experience on police behavior? Or, do they provide little helpful "hard" knowledge about its impact?
2. Would you recommend further study on, more experimenting with, or forgetting about new field training experiences? Explain your answer.

Knowledge and Understanding CHECK

1. Identify and explain the two major influences in bringing about changes in the selection, training, and promotion of officers.
2. Identify two effects of personality, recruitment, training, and advancement on police and policing. Then, summarize the findings on these effects.
3. How do police departments use physical performance in recruiting officers?
4. List the changes during the 1960s and 1970s that put pressure on traditional ideas about the desirable police personality.
5. List the qualities that are required of problem-oriented police officers, according to Egon Bittner.
6. List the ways in which higher education can benefit police officers, according to the Police Executive Research Forum.
7. Summarize the findings of Robert Worden on the effect of a college degree on the attitudes of, performance of, and the use of force by police officers.
8. Identify the formal and informal ways that the police academy socializes officers.
9. Identify the two most important informal rules recruits learn in the academy.
10. List the most important questions recruits have that the academy does not answer.
11. Identify and explain the two major themes of most police stories.
12. Describe and explain what recruits learn from field training.

WOMEN AND MINORITY OFFICERS

We have learned from the history of police (outlined in Chapter 5) that women police, and policing, have received little attention by researchers. And, we have learned from the preceding sections that adequate training and intelligent recruits do not by themselves produce "good" police officers and effective policing. However, we do know that police departments perform best when they secure strong public support. Hiring competent personnel who reflect the cultural diversity and gender division of the community is one way to assure public support. Calls for establishing closer connections between the police and the community, the law requiring affirmative action and equal employment opportunity, and the values of an open and diverse society all encourage hiring and advancing women and minorities in policing. Successfully recruiting minorities and women has challenged police administrators for decades. Empirical and impressionistic evidence suggest a weakening, but by no means a removal, of barriers in police departments based on race, ethnic origin, and gender.[34]

Women Officers

Susan E. Martin of the Police Foundation has found that the available evidence on women in policing presents a "mixed picture." A 1973 survey of cities serving populations of 250,000 or more found that women comprised 2 percent of sworn law enforcement personnel; and that nearly all departments excluded these women from patrol duties. By 1979, 87 percent of departments serving populations of more than 50,000 assigned women to patrol; women comprised 3.38 percent of the sworn officers in those cities. Very few women, however, had risen above the entry rank of patrol officer. Some experts maintained that limited seniority accounted for the failure of women to advance during the 1970s.[35]

During the 1980s, the percent of sworn women officers continued to rise; by 1985 it had reached 7.5 percent of sworn officers in departments serving more than 50,000, and 8.6 percent in departments serving more than 250,000; and in suburban departments it reached 10 percent. In 1989, Susan E. Martin, who conducted the survey that reported these results, wrote that the bad news is that women officers, despite these gains, compose "only a token proportion of all police personnel." The FBI reported that by October 1994, sworn women officers had risen to 11.85 percent of total sworn officers in departments serving more than 50,000 people. In cities serving more than 250,000 people, the percent reached 14.2. The trend is definitely up, but the proportion of women sworn police officers still is far below the percentage of women in the total population.[36]

The skepticism among traditional police departments and officers, and among the public, about women police officers generated considerable research during the 1990s about their effectiveness. Nine surveys representing a broad cross section of the country's police departments demonstrated that women patrol officers perform as well as men patrol officers. For example, performance ratings of women after their first year in the Washington, D.C., Police Department were similar to those of men in their first year of service. Women stood up to difficult circumstances as well as

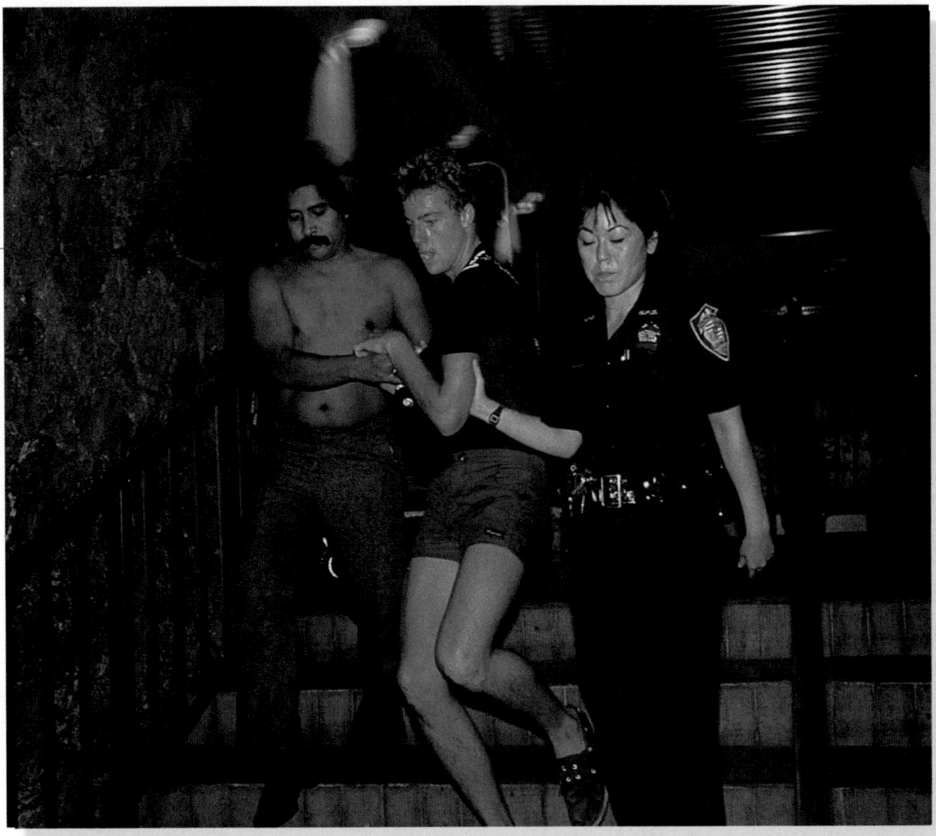

The number of women in policing has increased in the last two decades, but women still make up only a small percentage of all officers in the U.S. Despite research to the contrary, prejudices that women are "not up to" the job of policing remain.

men. They resigned or were terminated at about the same rate as men. According to former Police Chief Cullinane of Washington, D.C., "It's an accomplished fact. Some cities are still in court, saying women can't do the job—that you can't put women on patrol. Well, you can go out on the streets of the District of Columbia any time, day or night, and watch women do the job."[37]

The empirical research regarding the *performance* of women police officers led to questions and research about their *attitudes.* One theory explaining the attitudes of women police officers is the **gender model of police attitudes.** The gender model predicts differences in attitude between women and men police officers because of their different early socialization into gender roles. According to Carol Gilligan, women develop a "morality of care," which depicts "society as an interdependent and interconnected web of personal relationships." The theory predicts that the morality of care leads women to take a broad view of the police mission—that is, to provide service. Men, on the other hand, the theory predicts, develop a "morality of justice," which concentrates on law enforcement, hierarchy, rules, and discipline.[38]

A second theory, the **job model of police attitude,** predicts that women and men do not differ in their attitudes toward police work because socialization to work overrides prior socialization into gender roles. In other words, women may come into police work with attitudes that differ from men's, but after attending the academy, going through field training, and especially after working as police officers for a period of time, the attitudes of men and women converge into a similar police officer attitude. Alissa Pollitz Worden tested these theories by measuring attitudes in a large data set that surveyed 1,435 police officers in 24 police departments. She found that women and men officers had similar attitudes on a range of subjects concerning policing. Both favored uniform over selective law enforcement; women did not define the police mission in broader terms than men; the longer women worked, the more their views of people converged with the views of men; the views of women and men also converged over time with respect to their willingness to accept legal restrictions on their work. According to Worden,

> The most striking finding in this study is the failure of gender to explain much or any variation in the array of attitudes examined, even when potentially confounding variables are controlled. Overall, female as well as male police officers were predictably ambivalent about restrictions on their autonomy and the definition of their role, only mildly positive about their public clientele, complimentary of their colleagues, and unenthusiastic about working conditions and supervisors. What should one conclude from this about theories of gender differences and their applicability to policing? . . . [T]aken as a whole, these findings offer little support for the thesis that female officers define their role or see their clientele differently than do males, and one must therefore remain skeptical . . . about claims that women bring to their beats a distinctive perspective on policing.[39]

Figure 8.2
Percent of Sworn Police Officers Who Are African American

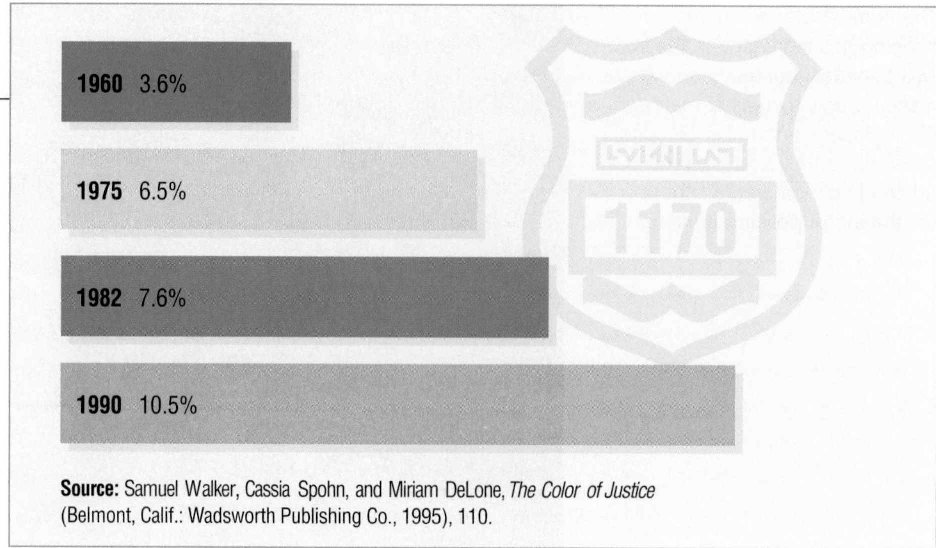

Source: Samuel Walker, Cassia Spohn, and Miriam DeLone, *The Color of Justice* (Belmont, Calif.: Wadsworth Publishing Co., 1995), 110.

Minority Officers

Dr. Elysee Scott, executive director of the National Organization of Black Law Enforcement Executives (NOBLE), remembers that as she was growing up in a small Louisiana town in the 1950s, African American police officers rode around in police cars marked "Colored Only." African American officers could arrest only "colored" people; if a white person committed a crime in an African American neighborhood, African American officers had to call for a white officer to make the arrest. Beginning in the 1960s, following brutality by white officers against African Americans, civil rights legislation, lawsuits brought by African Americans, and demands for minority hiring, the position of African American and other minority officers began to change.[40]

Since the 1960s, the number of African American police officers has grown (see Figure 8.2). However, these aggregates are misleading because some departments reflect the racial makeup of their communities better than others. In 1992 in New York City, for example, African Americans made up 11.4 percent of the police force but 28.7 percent of the population. In Los Angeles in 1992, on the other hand, the percent of African American police officers and the African American population of the city were identical—14 percent. In that same year, Rodney King was beaten and the Christopher Commission documented a racist climate in the Los Angeles department. Obviously, merely employing minority police officers is not enough to eliminate problems.[41]

Samuel Walker surveyed police departments in the nation's 50 largest cities. He found that between 1983 and 1988, those departments "made uneven progress in the employment of African American and Hispanic officers." While nearly half the big-city departments made significant progress in employing African American officers, another 17 percent reported declines in the percent of African American officers. Similarly, 42 percent of the departments hired more Hispanics, whereas 11 percent reported declines. Affirmative action plans play a significant role in police employment trends, according to Walker. Nearly two-thirds of the departments reported operating under such plans. Twenty-three of the plans were court ordered, seven voluntary. Despite the unevenness of the progress in hiring African American and Hispanic officers, a survey of all police departments in the country revealed that the numbers of African American and Hispanic police officers roughly compared with their representation in the general population (see Figure 8.3).[42]

A *New York Times* survey showed that despite efforts by the New York Police Department to recruit more women and minorities, most NYPD officers are white males who grew up in the suburbs or in low-crime neighborhoods in the city. Seventy-five percent of the men are Roman Catholics. Most of them followed friends or relatives into the department. The survey, along with interviews with graduates of the department's police academy, "suggests that a resilient network of whites, born of the Irish, Italian, and German immigrant streams of a much older New York, has built an enduring cultural pipeline into the department."

Vincent Gerard, 21, is a product of the pipeline. He grew up in Whitestone, Queens, went to Holy Cross High School in Bayside and earned a two-year associate's degree in criminal justice at St. John's University. He is Sicilian-Irish, he said, and his mother's father was a police officer who died in a fire in the line of duty.

"I took the test when I was a junior in high school," he said. "My mother saw the announcement in the newspaper. I also took the housing police test, the transit police test and the fireman's test. My next-door neighbor is a housing detective. He would tell me stories about cops."[43]

African American police chiefs have increased significantly in numbers since the 1960s. In 1976, Hubert Williams, chief of the Newark, New Jersey, Police Department, was the only African American police chief in the country. By 1990, African Americans headed one-quarter of the 50 largest city police departments, including New York, Chicago, Philadel-

Figure 8.3
Racial Makeup: Police vs. General Population

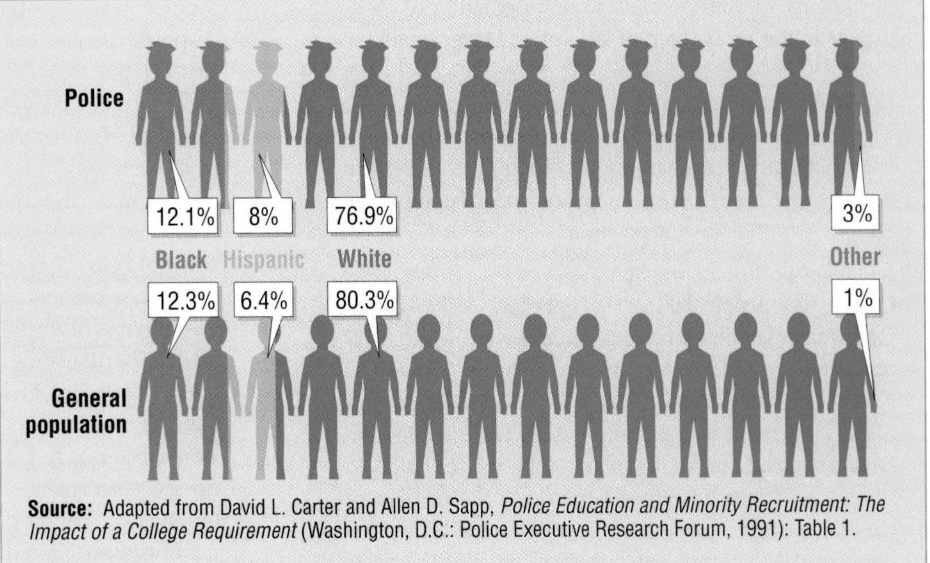

Source: Adapted from David L. Carter and Allen D. Sapp, *Police Education and Minority Recruitment: The Impact of a College Requirement* (Washington, D.C.: Police Executive Research Forum, 1991): Table 1.

phia, Baltimore, Detroit, Washington, and Miami. The Use Your Discretion case on race, ethnic, and gender hiring asks you to assess the value of quotas to establish more racially balanced police departments. [44]

Use *Your* Discretion

Should courts establish hiring quotas?

In a long, drawn-out court battle that dates back to 1973 and that the parties finally settled in 1989, Chief Judge Curtin found the hiring practices of the Buffalo, New York, Police Department discriminatory. He fashioned a remedy based on quotas of women, Hispanics, and African Americans. This case resembles many that courts have already decided, and numerous others still in progress. Do you agree with Judge Curtin's orders? Why? How would you alter them?

Opinion
United States of America v. City of Buffalo, 633 F.2d 643 (2d Cir. 1988).
CURTIN, Chief Judge
The United States government challenged the employment practices of the Buffalo Police Department in a lawsuit originally filed in August 1973. The action sought to enforce Title VII of the Civil Rights Act of 1964, as amended by the Equal Employment Opportunity Act of 1972. Section 703(a) of Title VII, 42 U.S.C. Sec. 2000e-2(a) states the central premise of the Act:

> It shall be an unlawful employment practice for an employer (1) to fail or refuse to hire or to discharge any individual, or otherwise to discriminate against any individual with respect to his compensation, terms, conditions, or privileges of employment, because of such individual's race, color, religion, sex, or national origin. . . .

The act proscribes not only overt discrimination but also practices that are fair in form, but discriminatory in operation. The touchstone is business necessity. If an employment practice which operates to exclude Negroes cannot be shown to be related to job performance, the practice is prohibited.

I. General population statistics
Census figures show that the population of the City of Buffalo is 20.4 percent Black and between 3.2 percent to 3.9 percent Spanish-surname Americans (hereinafter "SSA"). In addition, the labor force in the City is 17.5 percent Black and 40.6 percent Female. In 1973, the police department employed 1,395 uniformed personnel of whom 36 (2.6 percent) were black males, 2 (0.1 percent) were black females, 3 (0.2 percent) were SSA males, and 16 (1.1 percent) were white females. As of the same date the department employed 911 patrolmen of whom 24 (2.6 percent) were black males and 3 (0.3 percent) were SSA males. No women were employed in the patrolman position. Meanwhile, of the 42 police cadets employed by the Department at that time, 3 (7.1 percent) were black males.

At that time the Police Department also employed 95 full-time nonuniformed personnel (clerks, typists, cleaners, etc.). Of these, 45 (47.4 percent) were white females, 2 (2.1 percent) were black males, and 5 (5.2 percent) were black females. Of the 7 blacks employed, 5 were cleaners or charwomen.

Here the evidence indicates a substantial disparity between the general black, SSA, and female population in the City of Buffalo and the representation of those groups in the work force of the Police Department.

II. Written examinations

The Government argues that the Police Department uses written examinations in their job selection process that have a discriminatory impact upon black and SSA candidates for positions.

A. Disproportionate impact

Of the 621 people taking the February 1973 written patrolman examination, 86.6 percent were white, 11.7 percent were black, and 1.6 percent were SSAs. The New York State Department of Civil Service designated 70 percent as a passing grade. The examination results showed that 43.4 percent of the whites received at least a 70 percent grade while only 8.2 percent of the blacks and 10 percent of the SSAs achieved a passing score. The significant disparity between the passing grades of whites and both black and SSA candidates establishes a case of discrimination in the Police Department testing programs.

B. Relation to job performance

Such tests are impermissible unless "predictive of or significantly correlated with important elements of work behavior which comprise or are relevant to the job or jobs for which candidates are being evaluated." Although the examiner admits that numerous critical areas of work behavior are involved in the patrolman job, only three areas were tested: good judgment, preparation of written material, and the understanding and interpretation of reading material. The court finds that the defendants have failed to show the validity of the 1973 written patrolman examination. As such, it stands in violation of Title VII.

III. Height requirements

Prior to and including the last competition for patrolman in 1973, persons applying for appointment were required to be at least 5′9″ in height. During the last competition for police cadet, applicants were required to be at least 5′7″ in height; prior to that they were required to be at least 5′9″ in height. Applicants meeting these minimum physical requirements were then permitted to take written and physical agility examinations.

A. Minimum height standards

The government has introduced statistical findings to show a case of discrimination against both women and SSA individuals through the use of the absolute height requirements of 5′9″ for police patrolman and of 5′7″ for police cadet. According to a U.S. Department of Health, Education, and Welfare publication, males between the ages of eighteen and twenty-four average 68.7″ (5′8.7″) in height, while females in the same age group average only 63.8″ (5′3.8″) in height. This necessarily eliminates the vast majority of American women from job selection as a patrolman and has a disproportionate effect on them. Furthermore, statistics for the New York and New Jersey geographical area introduced by the government show that the 5′9″ standard eliminates 80.6 percent of SSA males aged seventeen to twenty-six as compared to only 48.5 percent of non–SSA males. The 5′7″ standard eliminates 54.7 percent of SSA males aged seventeen to twenty-six, but only 21.3 percent of non–SSA males. These disparities certainly establish a case of discrimination through use of absolute height requirements.

The burden now falls to the defendants to justify the absolute height requirements as job related. They have introduced the testimony of Police Commissioner Blair as to the importance of height in successful job performance by police officers. He stated that the average height of males eighteen to thirty-four in the northeast United States is 5′10″ and that approximately 60 percent of the male arrestees in the City of Buffalo are 5′9″ or taller. Furthermore, it was his opinion that the height of police officers serves as a deterrent to the need for use of force by the police since it will keep people from engaging in antisocial acts and will enable the police to obtain submission with minimum use of force. Although the opinions of the commissioner are to be accorded substantial weight due to his experience in the field of crime control, standing alone they do not provide sufficient justification to uphold minimum height requirements.

IV. High school diploma requirement

In addition to the age, height, weight, and vision requirements, an applicant for either the police or fire departments must possess a high school diploma or equivalency diploma. The government challenges this requirement as another violation of Title VII . . . I find that a high school education is a bare minimum requirement for successful performance of the policeman's responsibilities. This reasoning has been followed by several courts to uphold the high school requirement.

V. Sex discrimination

At completion of trial, there had never been a single woman patrolman [or] cadet. Furthermore, not a single woman was on the eligibility lists for any of these positions. No attempt had ever been made to recruit women for these positions. Under Title VII the purpose of the sex discrimination provisions is to eliminate disparate treatment of female employees and to provide equal access to the job market for both men and women. The act rejects the notion of "romantic paternalism" toward women and seeks to put them on an equal footing with men. . . . In order to discriminate lawfully on the basis of sex, an employer must show that sex is a bona fide occupational qualification (bfoq) reasonably necessary to the operation of that employer's business.

Looking to the evidence presented in this case, we find not only a case of sex discrimination but an absolute bar to the hiring of women for the positions in the Buffalo Police Department. Defendants present no evidence to establish a bfoq that would justify this absolute bar. Plaintiff, on the other hand, has provided the court with substantial evidentiary materials in the form of statistical studies and job evaluations that demonstrate the ability of women to act as patrolmen, as well as their current active status in these positions in other police and fire departments throughout the United States. Furthermore, they demonstrate the existence of a large, qualified pool of women in the Buffalo area who have shown an interest in this field of work. This court finds that the Police Department has failed to show the necessary bfoq to justify its total failure to hire women for the position of patrol officer.

VI. Relief

1. The city shall seek to achieve the long-term goal of reaching a minority composition in the ranks of uniformed personnel within the Police Department comparable to that of the work force within the city as a whole, according to the most recent census.
2. The city shall adopt and seek to achieve the interim goal of making 50 percent of all entry-level and/or police officer appointments from among qualified black and SSA applicants.
3. In addition, the defendants shall take affirmative steps to recruit and hire women in numbers commensurate with their interest and with their ability to qualify on the basis of performance-related criteria for positions as police officers. Within eighteen months following December 11, 1978, the court shall, upon motion of plaintiff and after evidentiary hearing, consider the entry of specific long-term and interim hiring goals for women in this position.
4. No long-term goal for hiring females in the police department shall be set at this time. However, the defendants shall adopt and seek to achieve an interim goal of making 25 percent of all entry-level and/or police officer appointments from among qualified women applicants. A minority woman shall count toward both interim goals.
5. The interim hiring goal for minorities shall remain in effect until the minority composition of the uniformed personnel of the police department and fire department is at least equal to the percentage of minorities in the labor force of the City of Buffalo according to the most recent census, or until this court has found, after a hearing, that all proposed selection procedures for entry-level and/or police officer positions have been validated in accordance with the Uniform Guidelines on Employee Selection Procedures, and that no further interim goals are appropriate.

CRITICAL THINKING

1. What precisely were the prejudicial practices?
2. What arguments did the court give for their unfairness? Do you agree?
3. Give the arguments for and against quotas. Would you impose hiring quotas on police departments? Defend your answer.

Knowledge and Understanding CHECK

1. What is the importance of public support to police departments?
2. Identify and describe the findings of available evidence on women in policing.
3. Summarize the findings of empirical research regarding the effectiveness of women in policing.
4. Describe the two major theories used to explain the attitudes of women police officers.
5. Summarize the findings of empirical research regarding minority police officers.

POLICE STRESS

Stress plays a part in the lives of everyone. Some stress is not only inevitable, it can be good. For example, the physical stress of "working out" improves your cardiovascular system, and feeling pressure that causes you to study harder for an exam can improve your score. **Police stress,** however, refers to the *negative* pressures related to police work. Police officers are not superhumans. According to Gail Goolkasian and others, research shows that they are affected by their daily exposure to human indecency and pain; that dealing with a suspicious and sometimes hostile public takes its toll on them; and that the shift changes, the long periods of boredom, and the ever-present danger that are part of police work do cause serious job stress.[45]

Dr. Hans Selye's classic *The Stress of Life* describes the effect of long-term environmental threats he calls "stressors." Dr. Selye maintains that the unrelieved effort to cope with stressors can lead to heart disease, high blood pressure,

Dealing with a sometimes hostile public is clearly a situation that introduces "stressors" into police officers' jobs. Which of the stressors listed in the text would an officer have to cope with in this situation? Can you think of others?

ulcers, digestive disorders, and headaches. Stressors in police work fall into four categories:

1. Stresses inherent in police work.
2. Stresses arising internally from police department practices and policies.
3. External stresses stemming from the criminal justice system and the society at large.
4. Internal stresses confronting individual officers.[46]

Police stress arises from several features of police work. Alterations in body rhythms from monthly shift rotation, for example, reduce productivity. The change from a day to a swing, or graveyard, shift not only requires biological adjustment but also complicates officers' personal lives. Role conflicts between the job—serving the public, enforcing the law, and upholding ethical standards—and personal responsibilities as spouse, parent, and friend act as stressors. Other stressors in police work include:

- Threats to officers' health and safety (see Figure 8.4).
- Boredom, alternating with the need for sudden alertness and mobilized energy.
- Responsibility for protecting the lives of others.
- Continual exposure to people in pain or distress.
- The need to control emotions even when provoked.
- The presence of a gun, even during off-duty hours.
- The fragmented nature of police work, with only rare opportunities to follow cases to conclusion or even to obtain feedback or follow-up information.[47]

Administrative policies and procedures, which officers rarely participate in formulating, can add to stress. One-officer patrol cars create anxiety and a reduced sense of safety. Internal investigation practices create the feeling of being watched and not trusted, even during off-duty hours. Officers sometimes feel they have fewer rights than the criminals they apprehend. Lack of rewards for good job performance, insufficient training, and excessive paperwork can also contribute to police stress.[48]

The criminal justice system creates additional stress. Court appearances interfere with police officers' work assignments, personal time, and even sleeping schedules. Turf battles among agencies, court decisions curtailing discretion, perceived leniency of the courts, and release of offenders on bail, probation, or parole also lead to stress. Further stress arises from perceived lack of support and negative attitudes toward police from the larger society. (Most public opinion surveys, however, show strong support for and positive attitudes toward police.) Stress also stems from distorted and/or unfavorable news accounts of incidents involving police. The inaccessibility and perceived ineffectiveness of social service and rehabilitation agencies to whom officers refer individuals act as further stressors.[49]

Women and minority officers face additional stressors. They are more likely to face disapproval from fellow officers and from family and friends for entering police work. Supervisors, peers, and the public question women officers' ability to handle the emotional and physical rigors of the job, even though research indicates women can do so. The need to "prove themselves" to male officers and to the public constitutes a major stressor for women officers.

Stress contributes not only to the physical disorders previously mentioned, but also to emotional problems. Some research suggests that police officers commit suicide at a higher rate than other groups. Most investigators report unusually high rates of divorce among police. Although

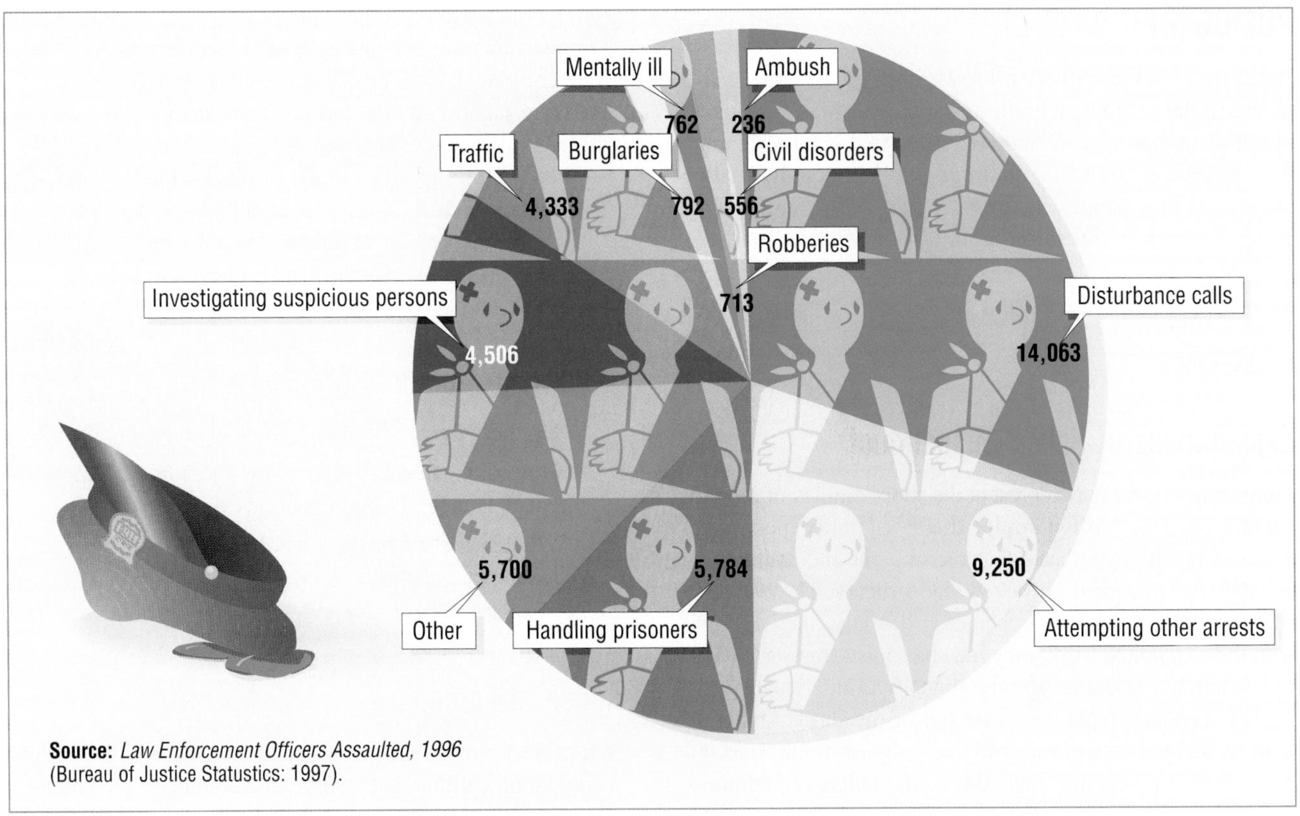

Source: *Law Enforcement Officers Assaulted, 1996* (Bureau of Justice Statustics: 1997).

Figure 8.4
Officers Assaulted in 1996, Distributed by Circumstances at Time of Assault

some maintain that researchers have exaggerated the divorce rate among police, interview surveys demonstrate that police stress reduces the quality of family life. A majority of officers interviewed reported that police work inhibits nonpolice friendships, interferes with scheduling family social events, and generates a negative public image. Furthermore, they take job pressures home, and spouses worry about officers' safety. Systematic studies do not confirm the widely held belief that police suffer from unusually high rates of alcoholism, although indirect research has established a relationship between high job stress and excessive drinking. Finally, officers interviewed cited guilt, anxiety, fear, nightmares, and insomnia following involvement in shooting incidents.[50]

In the past, departments either ignored officers with problems or dealt with them informally by assigning them to desk jobs. During the 1950s, some departments began to formalize their responses, usually by incorporating officer-initiated Alcoholics Anonymous groups made up exclusively of alcoholic officers. In the 1970s, departments instituted "employee assistance" programs to deal with problem officers, particularly those suffering from alcoholism. These programs have expanded into a broad range of responses to police stress. Some programs focus on physical fitness, diet, relaxation, and biofeedback to cope with stress. Others emphasize family counseling to involve spouses in reducing police stress, such as Kansas City's Marriage Partner Program or Minnesota's Couple Communications Program.

Knowledge and Understanding CHECK

1. List the major sources of police stress, according to the research of Gail Goolkasian and her colleagues.
2. Identify the stressors in police work, according to Dr. Hans Selye.
3. Identify the administrative procedures that can add to police stress.
4. Explain how the criminal justice system creates stress for police officers.
5. Identify the additional stressors faced by women and minority officers.
6. Identify the physical and emotional disorders created by police stress.
7. Describe efforts by police departments to help officers cope with stress.

POLICE MISCONDUCT

Police misconduct covers a broad range of behavior, so it means little without definition. It can mean something as minor as accepting a free cup of coffee in a local restaurant, or as serious as trafficking in drugs and intentionally beating up and killing people. In this section, we examine three major forms of **police misconduct:**

- Abuse of force
- Discrimination
- Corruption

Explanations of Police Misconduct

Police misconduct may represent the shortcomings of individual officers. This **"rotten apple" theory** of police misconduct is based on the hypothesis that recruitment and training inevitably fail to screen out a few bad officers. These "rotten apples" have deep-seated characteristics that they brought with them to police work; they may be sadists, racists, sexists, or any number of things peculiar to them as individuals.

Misconduct might also arise out of the shortcomings of training and police work itself. "Bad" officers might start out as idealists but become "bad" due to the failures of administrative rules, leadership, and the socialization processes of education, training, and field experiences. In some instances, police training and socialization might contain the message that the police cannot do their job by following the book. To serve what they and much of the public call "justice," these officers resort to "dirty means." They fabricate evidence, intimidate, and sometimes even torture suspects because they believe they have to get around such obstacles to justice as the exclusionary rule. This is the only way, they believe, that they can prove someone that they "know" is guilty has committed a crime. Professor Carl Klockars calls this the **Dirty Harry problem,** derived from the Clint Eastwood *Dirty Harry* movie. In the film, Harry Callahan, the tough detective, tortures a clearly guilty suspect because he will not tell where he has buried alive a young rape-kidnapping victim. In such cases, officers achieve what they consider a good end by illegal means. Responsibility for police misconduct, if it is even considered misconduct, lies with the institution, not the individual.[51]

Use *Your* Discretion

Why do police abuse their power?

Based on his observations of U.S. police and police in the Caribbean and South America from the 1960s to the 1990s, Chevigny describes the dynamics of police abuse of power:

> [One of the dynamics is] that defiance of police orders would provoke a sanction from the police, perhaps violence, but at least an arrest. Another was that the police would put together a story, consistent with legal requirements, to account for any sanction they imposed. Thus anyone who defied the police—especially if he was part of an outcast group, like hippies or blacks, the very existence of which was a sort of defiance—was likely to be roughed up, and then charged with disturbing the peace and resisting arrest. I began to refer to these petty crimes as "cover charges."[52]

CRITICAL THINKING

1. Do these dynamics fit your view of abuse of power?
2. How did you reach your view? Reading? Experience? Hunch? Explain your answer.
3. What more would you want to know before you reached a conclusion on this subject?

Abuse of Force

In a perfect world there would be no need for police. There would be no conflict, and everyone would obey the law. In a second-best world, people who broke the law would voluntarily comply with police requests. However, in the real world both obedience to the law and voluntary compliance with police are far from complete. Therefore, police must use force to do their job; hence, the defining characteristic of police is the **legitimate use of force.** According to Egon Bittner, "[T]he capacity to use coercive force lends thematic unity to all police activity in the same sense in which . . . the capacity to cure illness lends unity to everything that is ordinarily done in the field of medical practice."[53]

Uneasiness about the police use of force has an ancient history. The Romans asked, "Sed quis costodiet ipsos custodes?" (Who will watch the watchmen?) As we saw in the history of police in Chapter 5, the establishment of professional police forces faced stiff opposition. Once established, the English "bobbies" were allowed to carry only truncheons, and they had to keep those concealed except to defend themselves against physical assault. In the United States, departments did not openly approve the use of weapons until some years after the establishment of public police departments. But the use of force was common, even necessary, because of the difficulty in arresting suspects. Officers faced a generally disrespectful public and other difficulties as well. Most arrests were for drunkenness and public disorder, which required that officers use physical force to subdue the people they arrested. Once officers subdued people, they faced the difficulty of transporting them, on foot, back to the station house.

In the twentieth century, the *perception,* if not the *reality,* of the **abuse of force** has contributed to some of the worst riots in American history—Harlem in 1935, Watts in 1965, Miami in 1980, and Los Angeles in 1992. These riots were not just about police use of force generally, but about the perceived or real use of excessive force against African Americans specifically. The question of race is inescapably connected to the problem of police use of excessive force.[54]

After the riots in Los Angeles sparked by the acquittal in 1992 of the police officers accused of beating Rodney King, the ambivalence about the use of force came into bold relief. By chance, a young man trying out his newly acquired camcorder recorded Los Angeles police officers beating King following a high-speed chase in which King tried to elude capture. The sight of many officers using clubs, boots, and other means to keep King down was etched into the public mind by repeated showings of the tape on television, night after night. There followed a great debate over the use of force by the police.

The beating, the acquittal, and the death and destruction that followed revealed three critical points:

1. The defining characteristic of police work—the *legitimate* use of coercive force—is critical to effective police work.
2. The need for *legitimate* use of force creates the central problem of police misconduct—the *excessive* use of coercive force.
3. Much of the perception, if not the reality, of the excessive use of force is held by (against) members of racial minority groups. [55]

Bringing these points out into the open produced a rich discussion and generated considerable research that tried to tell us what we know—and don't know—about the kinds and amounts of police use of force; about policies and practices regarding the use of force; and about the effectiveness of these policies and practices.

The debate over police use of force hardly began with Rodney King. New York journalist Lincoln Steffens opened the twentieth century with a series of articles reporting the wanton brutality of Patrolman "Clubber Williams" of the New York Police Department. The Wickersham Commission lamented the abuse of force by police officers in 1930. The President's Commission on Law Enforcement repeated the lament in 1967. The debate provoked by the beating of Rodney King, the initial acquittal of the officers, the ensuing riots, the later conviction of the officers, and their ultimate release promises to continue in the 21st century.

Types and Amounts of Force

The basic idea of the use of force is to bring resisting or fleeing suspects under control as quickly as possible, with the minimum force necessary and minimum injury to both suspects and officers. Officers are trained to use an escalating level of responses to accomplish this. The Los Angeles Police Department uses ten tactics listed here from least to most force used:

1. Firm grip (tightly grabbing a suspect's arm).
2. Compliance holds (applying bending and twisting pressure to sensitive tendon and joint areas of the hands and arms).
3. Batons or nightsticks (or flashlights as substitutes).
4. Pushing and shoving.
5. Karate kicks and punches.
6. A swarm (organized tackle by several officers).
7. Spraying with chemical irritants (tear gas).
8. TASER (stun gun).
9. Choke holds (upper body control holds).
10. Shooting.[56]

Every time a Los Angeles police officer uses nondeadly force, the department requires the officer to document the incident on a Use of Force Report. In an extensive survey of these reports, Greg Meyer, a police tactics consultant and member of the Los Angeles Police Department, found that the Los Angeles police used less-than-deadly force in about one out of every 89 arrests. That means that Los Angeles police officers used force approximately ten times a day. About seven times a day, the police used enough force to "cause the suspect to fall to the ground," called **knockdown force.**[57]

In a comparison of various knockdown tactics, Meyer's data showed that the TASER, an electronic immobilization device, was as (or more) effective than most traditional knockdown tactics. More important, it was much safer. Meyer's data showed that TASERS and tear gas produced no injuries to either suspects or police officers (Figure 8.5). On the basis of his analysis, Meyer concludes:

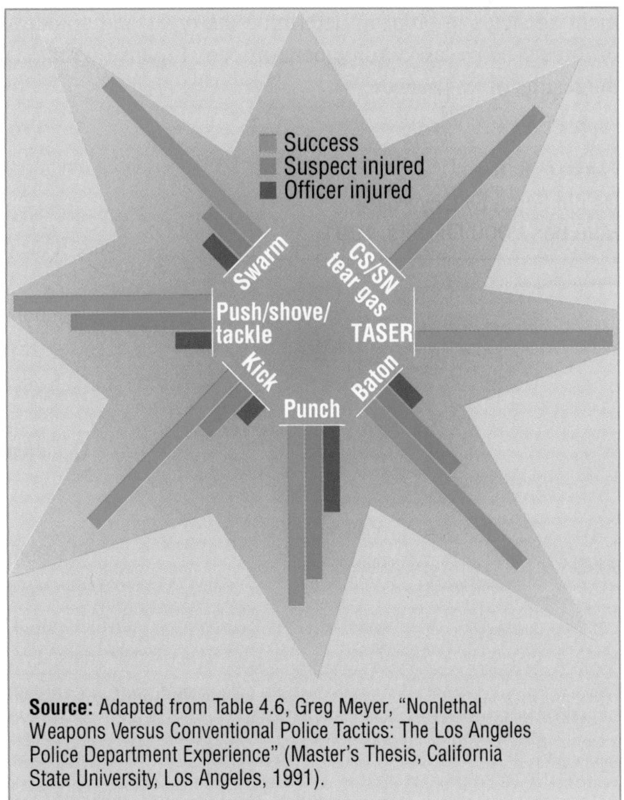

Source: Adapted from Table 4.6, Greg Meyer, "Nonlethal Weapons Versus Conventional Police Tactics: The Los Angeles Police Department Experience" (Master's Thesis, California State University, Los Angeles, 1991).

Figure 8.5
Knockdown Tactics: Success and Safety

> Expanded use of nonlethal weapons and the development of the next generation of such devices ["Star Trek–style ray guns"] would lead to fewer and less severe injuries to suspects and officers, reduced civil liability claims and payments, and an improved public image for law enforcement.[58]

Others agree. James K. Stewart, former director of the National Institute of Justice, noted that:

> Law enforcement officials have long recognized that a wide and dangerous gap exists in the range of tools that are available to them. The most common law enforcement tools, the nightstick and the gun, may be either too weak or too strong a response to many police situations. In violent confrontations, officers may be obliged to choose an unnecessarily strong response for lack of an effective alternative weapon.[59]

According to unpublished work by the Police Foundation, the benefits of more weapons like TASERs, stun guns, and tear gas sprays include "fewer citizen injuries and deaths, fewer officer injuries and deaths, improved police-community relations, reduced exposure to departmental liability for wrongful police actions, and improved police morale."[60]

The Police Foundation, a Washington-based research organization devoted to police reform and improved policing conducted the most thorough and detailed study yet of the kinds and amounts of police use of force. Researchers surveyed a sample of state, county, and municipal law enforcement agencies in order to determine the types and amounts of force used by law enforcement officers. Figure 8.6 reflects the results of this survey.[61]

It is difficult to define, measure, and evaluate the use of force. According to Carl B. Klockars, "No one knows what excessive force is. . . . [I]t follows that all the talk of wanting to reduce or eliminate it is largely meaningless. . . . Needless to say, if no one knows what excessive force is, it also follows that empirical research that accurately measures it or its reduction is nonexistent."[62]

Nevertheless, there is some consensus that police use of force can be classified according to four groups:

- Nondeadly and deadly
- Violent and nonviolent
- Reasonable and excessive
- Necessary and unnecessary

The distinction between nondeadly and deadly force is that **deadly force** can cause serious bodily injury or death. Shooting at suspects, even if they do not die or even if the shots miss them, is an exercise of deadly force. *Violent force* means the use of physical force; *nonviolent force* means verbal coercion such as orders, advice, warnings, and persuasion. Reasonable and excessive are legal terms. *Reasonable force* means the amount of force necessary to accomplish compliance with legitimate police authority; *excessive force* means more force than is required to accomplish the legitimate purpose. Reasonable force is lawful; excessive force is illegal.

Necessary and *unnecessary force* are expansions of the other classifications. These categories were created by James Fyfe, who explains that both necessary and unnecessary force are lawful. Unnecessary violence occurs when "police officers who know better cause bloodshed in situations that

Figure 8.6
Use of Force by City Police, Rate per 1,000 Officers, 1991

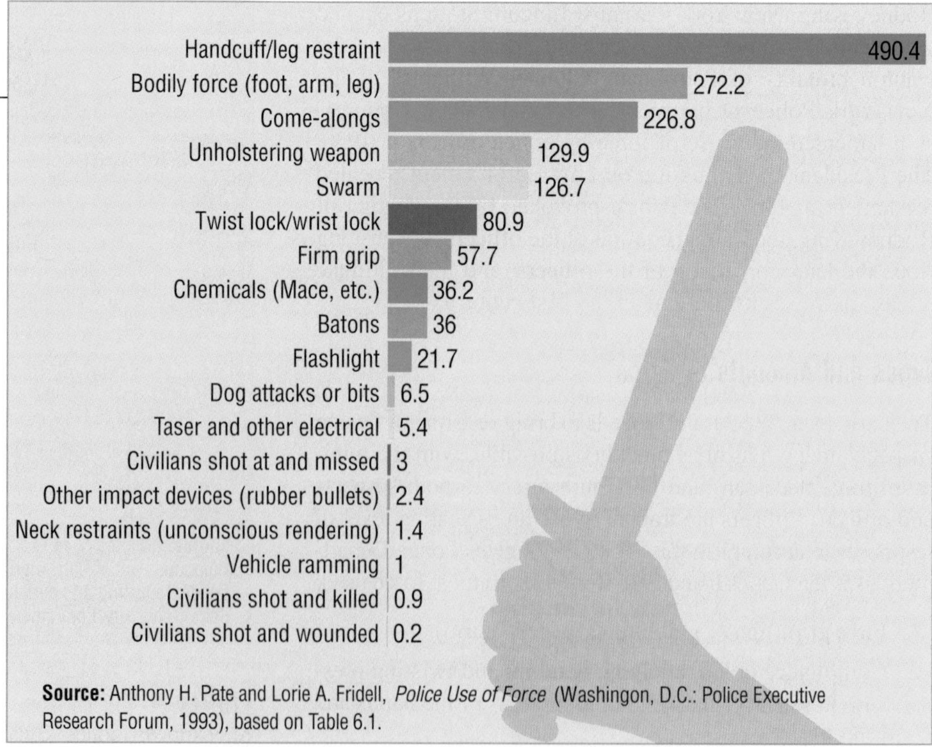

Source: Anthony H. Pate and Lorie A. Fridell, *Police Use of Force* (Washington, D.C.: Police Executive Research Forum, 1993), based on Table 6.1.

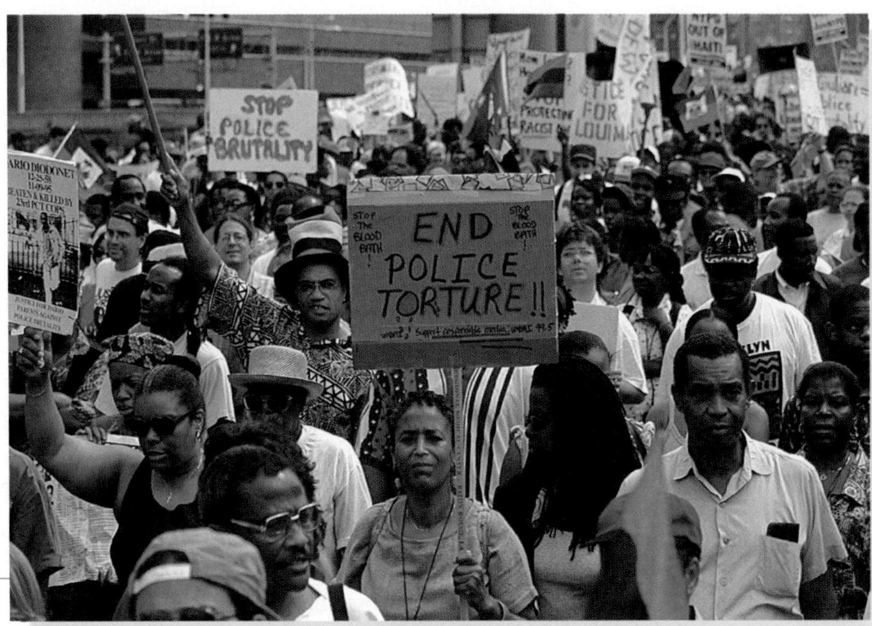

Police brutality made headlines in August of 1997, when 30-year old Haitian immigrant Abner Louima was hospitalized after being beaten and sodomized with a bathroom plunger by police at a Brooklyn, NY precinct. Louima was exiting a Brooklyn club when police arrived on the scene in response to a fight that had broken out between two women. In the ensuing melee, Louima, a bystander, was pushed to the ground, handcuffed, and driven two blocks from the club, where he was beaten. He was then taken to a police precinct where his ordeal continued. The case received widespread attention and generated protest and debate about police abuses of force.

might have been resolved peaceably and bloodlessly by more capable officers." Fyfe warns that "unnecessary force is far more likely than brutality to generate either widespread resentment of the police or civil liability for the police."[63]

For 30 years, observers have reported that the police use force infrequently. Estimates cover a broad range. Robert E. Worden reported that the police used force in only 60 out of 5,688 (1.05 percent) police-citizen encounters. Ross Lundstrom and Cynthia Mullen, on the other hand, reported that the police used force in 1,750 out of 11,989 (14.6 percent) of incidents where officers arrested and transported people to detox centers and mental hospitals.

Situations vary from place to place, situation to situation, and probably by race. Angus Campbell and Howard Schuman asked people in 15 cities about their negative experiences with the police. Two percent of a sample of whites said that police had "roughed them up"; 7 percent of the African Americans said the police had "roughed them up."[64]

How often do police abuse the use of force? Little is known on this point. One reason is that it is difficult to measure. Most studies suffer validity and reliability problems. Observational studies usually generate too little data for generalizing, and they suffer from officers being influenced by having someone watching them work. Surveys and interviews of civilians measure *perceptions* of excessive force that may differ substantially from reality. Surveys and interviews of police officers also suffer from perception problems, and police officers may give socially desirable responses. Data from agency records reflect more the perspectives of the agency than actual behavior. Furthermore, departments willing to allow researchers access are probably the most progressive. Official agency records measure excessive force indirectly; they contain information only about complaints that civilians bring to them and, thus, not all the incidents of excessive force.[65]

Deadly Force

It has always been unlawful for police officers to use unnecessary force in their work. The courts, statutes, and police department rules have always limited the use of force to that which is reasonable under the circumstances. However, this vague directive does not give much guidance to police officers. During the 1970s, as a result of a number of influences, law enforcement agencies began to draft administrative rules outlining policies and practices regarding the use of force. Most of these rules were limited to the use of *deadly* force only. For example, some rules allowed the use of deadly force only to apprehend suspected violent felons. Others restricted the use of deadly force to suspects whom officers believed would endanger community safety unless they were apprehended immediately. A few forbade the use of deadly force except in the defense of the life of officers or other innocent people. Most departments that adopted rules restricting deadly force were urban departments.[66]

The Police Foundation studied the deadly force rules of police departments in Birmingham, Alabama; Detroit, Michigan; Indianapolis, Indiana; Kansas City, Missouri; Oakland, California; Portland, Oregon; and Washington, D.C. The authors of the study recommended two policy changes:

1. Adoption of deadly force rules formulated by police administrators and other public officials, private individuals, and especially officers who actually use guns.
2. Use of deadly force only to defend officers and to apprehend suspects committing specifically identified deadly or potentially deadly felonies, such as armed robbery and aggravated assault.[67]

Formulating, implementing, and enforcing deadly force rules is difficult. Line officers suspect proposed changes, and police unions oppose them. Administrators hesitate to put firearms policies in writing because they might provide the grounds for lawsuits. Some courts have held departments legally liable for violating their own rules. The California Supreme Court, for example, permitted the written firearms policy of the Los Angeles Police Department to be used as evidence in a wrongful death action involving an officer who deviated from the rules.[68]

Compelling reasons lie behind adopting rules that tighten firearms use. Researchers estimate that police kill about 600 people every year, shoot and wound another 1,200, and fire at, but miss, another 1,800. The numbers vary from city to city. For example, from 1974 to 1978, Chicago and Los Angeles police fatally shot about the same number of people: Chicago, 132, and Los Angeles, 139. However, Chicago police wounded 386 people, whereas Los Angeles police wounded only 238. Chicago police fired on 2,876; Los Angeles police fired on 611. Furthermore, the incidence of police shootings varies from neighborhood to neighborhood within cities. Chicago's Near West Side, for example, is 27 times more likely than the Near North Side to experience a police shooting in an average year. Rates also vary from city to city. New Orleans police are 10 times more likely to kill people than are Newark police.[69]

Deadly force not only kills suspects; officers die as well. In 1995, 162 police officers died while on duty. Contrary to public perceptions, it is not always suspects who kill officers. In a substantial number of fatalities, officers accidentally shoot other officers. Departments with effective deadly force rules show sharp decreases not only in citizen deaths but also in officer deaths. In Kansas City, Missouri, for example, after the department adopted a rule that prohibited police from shooting juveniles except in self-defense, the number of youths under 18 shot by the police dropped dramatically. James Fyfe showed that not only did police shootings drop sharply following New York City Police Department adoption of a strict deadly force rule, but the numbers of police officers shot at also dropped. Hence, deadly force rules appear to reduce not only citizen but also police fatalities and woundings.[70]

According to researchers, the following techniques to control shooting show promise:

1. Limit the discretionary use of shooting.
2. Train officers to abide by a "shoot only as a last resort" policy.
3. Use modern communications equipment and interagency cooperative arrangements that enable officers to summon whatever assistance they need.
4. Use protective equipment, such as lightweight soft-body armor and "less lethal weapons," including TASERs (electronic dart guns), stun guns (compact cattle prods), and rubber bullets.
5. Increase supervision of line officers, and enforce fair but firm accountability up the chain of command for inappropriate officer aggressiveness and for deficient firearms training, procedures, and practices.
6. Counsel officers who want help in dealing with job and other stresses and with post-shooting trauma.
7. Train officers to be sensitive to ethnic, religious, or other group traits that might have a bearing on an officer's appraisal of a suspect's dangerousness.
8. Adopt departmental reward systems that honor both an officer's decisiveness in using deadly force when necessary and his or her ability to resolve situations by less violent means when that option is available. (See above on Types and Amounts of Force section.)[71]

Frequency of Deadly Force

How many shootings is too many? Compared with the total number of contacts police have with individuals, shootings are rare. Figure 8.7 depicts the number of years an average police officer would have to work, statistically, before being forced to kill a suspect. A study of New York City patrol officers found that officers used force of any sort in less than one-tenth of 1 percent of all encounters with private individ-

Figure 8.7
Number of Years (Statistically) for Officer to Kill a Suspect

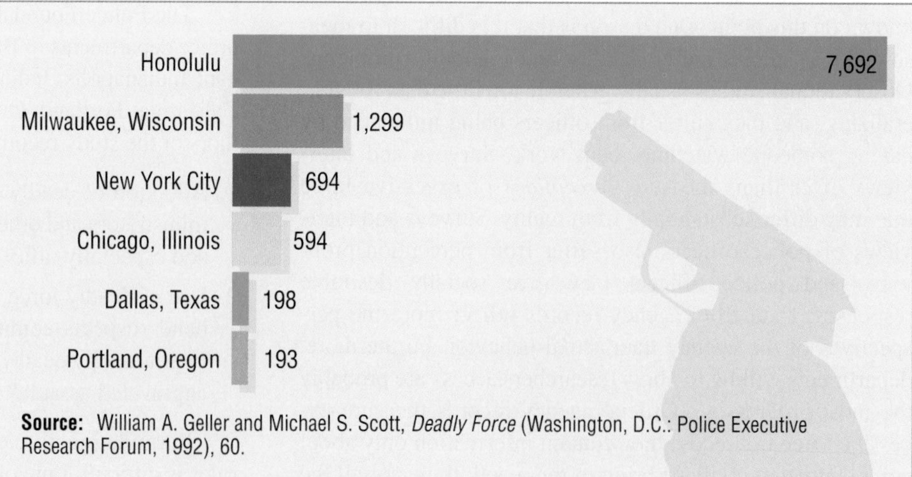

Source: William A. Geller and Michael S. Scott, *Deadly Force* (Washington, D.C.: Police Executive Research Forum, 1992), 60.

uals. They shot at civilians 5 times out of 1,762 times that observers saw officers use any physical force.[72]

Race and Deadly Force

Whom do the police shoot? According to a survey of all studies on deadly force over the past 30 years, the typical shooting is described by William A. Geller and Michael S. Scott:

> The most common type of incident in which police and civilians shoot one another in urban America involves an on-duty, uniformed, white, male officer and an armed, black, male civilian between the ages of 17 and 30 and occurs at night, in a public location in a high-crime precinct, in connection with a suspected armed robbery or a "man with a gun" call.[73]

Nearly all the studies report that the police shoot at more African Americans than whites. Here is a sample of the findings:

- Chicago police officers shot at African Americans 3.8 times more than at whites during the 1970s.
- New York City police officers shot at African Americans 6 times more than at whites during the 1970s.
- Dallas police officers shot at African Americans 4.5 times more than at whites during the 1970s and 1980s.
- St. Louis police officers shot at African Americans 7.7 times more than at whites from 1987 to1991.
- Memphis police officers fatally shot at African Americans 5.1 more times than at whites from 1969 to 1974; 2.6 times more from 1980 to 1984; and 1.6 times more from 1985 to 1989. Considering only property crime suspects, Memphis police officers were 9.4 times more likely to shoot at African Americans than at whites from 1969 to 1974 and 13 times more from 1980 to 1984; and African Americans were the only property crime suspects shot at from 1985 to 1989.[74]

Use *Your* Discretion

Are police shootings affected by racism?

The shooting of *fewer* African Americans by the police has accounted almost exclusively for a reduction in shootings over the past few decades. A survey of 57 cities showed that the ratio of African American to white killings fell from 7 to 1 in 1971 to 2.8 to 1 in 1979. Do the racial disparities in shooting indicate racism among the police? Researchers have theorized that the difference may lie in other factors, such as poverty and violent crime. The Dallas Police Department, in a report on the disproportionate number of African Americans and Hispanics shot at, addressed these factors:

> This is not to say that Blacks and Hispanics are more likely to attack the police officers or are more criminally inclined because of race or heritage. On the contrary, violent crime is well recognized as being a lower socio-economic class phenomenon. Blacks and Hispanics comprise a large majority of this lower socio-economic group because of discrimination in education and employment in previous decades. Typically, in large cities, the majority of individuals in these lower socio-economic classes are Black or Hispanic. (In the city of Dallas, the percent of families below the poverty level is 5.2% for Whites, 17.7% for Hispanics, and 21.7% for African Americans).[75]

Lawrence Sherman, who has conducted major research on all aspects of the policing, disagrees:

> In the absence of more conclusive evidence, the demonstrably higher rates of police homicide for blacks strongly suggests racial discrimination on a national basis. Although such patterns are quite likely to vary from one city to the next, such a variation would support the argument that present procedures allow police homicide to be administered in a discriminatory fashion.[76]

Some research suggests that most police officers shoot for reasons other than race. Figure 8.8 depicts the reasons for why officers use deadly force. However, most of that research suffers from methodological problems. Often, the only information available about police shootings is the written report of the officer who fired the shots. According to Michael E. Donahue of the Savannah, Georgia, Police Department and Frank S. Horvath of Michigan State University:

> It is naive to believe that such written reports always reflect exactly what took place during such an incident. That is not to say, however, that either police officers or other witnesses deliberately lie about such events—even though it is likely that some do—but that these events usually occur quite quickly, and that even the best recollection of what was observed may not always square with the facts.[77]

One study by James Fyfe shows that there is racial discrimination in some types of shootings. Fyfe studied shootings by the Memphis Police Department (the department involved in the case excerpted in the Chapter 7 Use Your Discretion case, "Can police shoot to kill a fleeing burglar?"). He reviewed the data for six years, 1969 to 1974, and concluded that

> the data strongly support the assertion that police [in Memphis] did differentiate racially with their

Figure 8.8
Reasons Why Police Officers Shoot

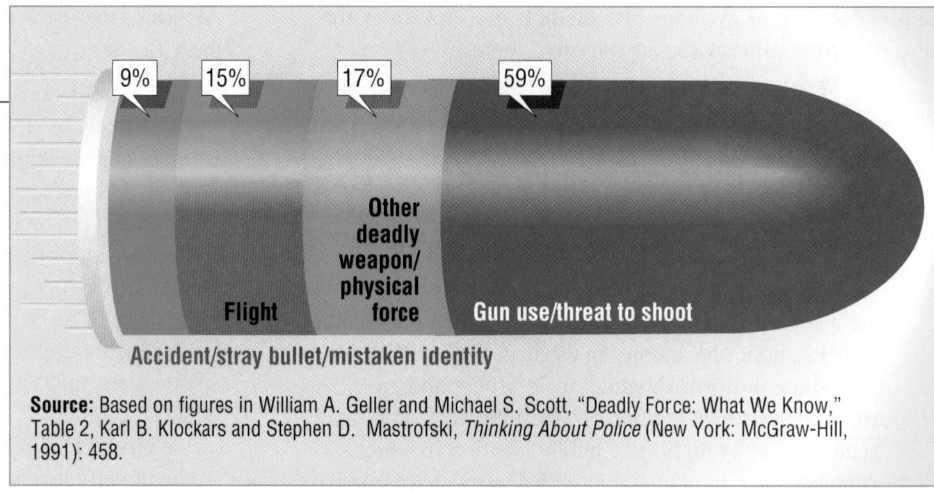

Source: Based on figures in William A. Geller and Michael S. Scott, "Deadly Force: What We Know," Table 2, Karl B. Klockars and Stephen D. Mastrofski, *Thinking About Police* (New York: McGraw-Hill, 1991): 458.

> trigger fingers, by shooting blacks in circumstances less threatening than those in which they shot whites. . . . [The] black death rate from police shootings while unarmed and non-assaultive (5.4 per 100,000) . . . is 18 times higher than the comparable white rate (0.3).[78]

Following the shooting of 13-year-old Edward Garner (described in Chapter 7), Memphis adopted a more restrictive shooting policy to allow the use of deadly force only to prevent the commission of "dangerous felonies." Following the Supreme Court decision in *Tennessee v. Garner,* Memphis restricted its shooting policy still further. According to the new policy, shooting was justified only if the suspect had committed a "violent felony" and posed "a threat of serious physical harm to the officer or to others unless he is immediately apprehended." Jerry R. Sparger and David J. Giacopassi reviewed records of police shootings in Memphis during each succeeding shooting policy. Following each restriction on the fleeing felon doctrine, a review of incidents showed a marked reduction in the total number of police shootings. Furthermore, "the apparently discriminatory shooting practices which occurred under the prior deadly force policies have been eliminated almost entirely." Moreover, the number of African American deaths resulting from shooting has steadily declined. However, despite the apparent end of discriminatory shooting *practices,* and the reduction in the number of fatalities, Sparger and Giacopassi report that the *rate* of African American deaths from police shootings remains 56.5 percent higher than the rate of white deaths.[79]

Despite the mixed results of studies of disparities in the shooting of nonwhites by the police, few deny that race influences some shootings. According to an African American police officer who testified to the Independent Commission on the Los Angeles Police Department in the course of investigating police use of force in the Rodney King case:

> There are many fine white officers who are doing their job and do not harbor racist sentiments. However, there is still a significant group of individuals whose old line, deep-seated biases continually manifest themselves on the job.[80]

CRITICAL THINKING

1. Describe the findings of researchers on the racist element in police shootings.
2. Which of the findings is most persuasive? Explain your answer.
3. What, if any, policy changes would you make on the basis of these findings?
4. If you need more information in order to answer the question, what would that information be?

High-Speed Chases

Shooting suspects is not the only form of police use of force; despite its high visibility, shooting actually is the rarest form of force. High-speed chases, a controversial means to apprehend suspects, are more common than shootings and, according to some experts, are a form of deadly force. Jerome Skolnick and James Fyfe explain why some officers initiate high-speed chases:

> During our years in police cars, we have been at the cop's end of more than thirty high-speed chases. Younger cops, hotshot cops, aggressive cops, relish the exhilaration of these pursuits. People who haven't ridden in patrol cars for a full shift cannot appreciate how tedious policing can be even in the world's most

Figure 8.9
Results of Police Pursuits, Metro-Dade County Police Department, 1985–1987

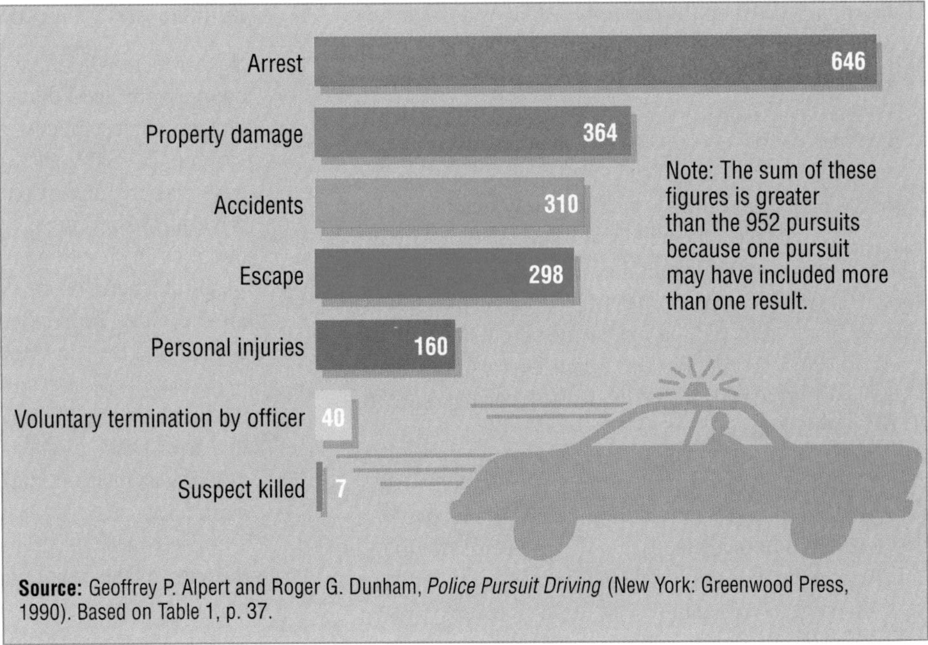

Source: Geoffrey P. Alpert and Roger G. Dunham, *Police Pursuit Driving* (New York: Greenwood Press, 1990). Based on Table 1, p. 37.

crime-ridden cities. Patrol policing, like military combat and the lives of cowboys, consists mostly of periods of boredom, broken up by interludes of excitement and even of terror. For police, a chase is among the most exciting of all work experiences: the sudden start of a chase is a jolt not unlike that experienced by the dozing fisherman who finds suddenly that he has a big and dangerous fish on the other end of his line.[81]

Geoffrey P. Alpert and Roger G. Dunham studied police pursuits based on pursuit-reporting forms and supporting documents by officers in Florida's Metro-Dade County Police Department. He found that 54 percent of pursuits were initiated for traffic infractions; 32 percent for suspected felony stops; 12 percent because of calls "to be on the lookout for" a specific offender; and 2 percent to make stops for reckless driving while intoxicated (DWI). Figure 8.9 depicts the results of these pursuits. Accidents occurred in more than half the pursuits in which officers arrested suspects. At the same time, failure to chase might permit a suspect to escape apprehension. Alpert found that many traffic pursuits resulted in arrests for serious felonies not related to the traffic offense.[82]

Use *Your* Discretion

What is the best policy regarding pursuits?

Publicity over accidents, injuries, and deaths from high-speed chases has brought pursuits under scrutiny. Pursuits demand the exercise of discretion; the law guides police discretion to engage in high-speed chases. Researchers have drawn contradictory policy implications from recent studies of police pursuits. The California Highway Patrol, following a pursuit study, represents one point of view:

> Attempted apprehension of motorists in violation of what appear to be minor traffic infractions is necessary for the preservation of order on the highways of California. If approximately 700 people will attempt to flee from officers who participated in this six-month study, knowing full well that the officers will give chase, one can imagine what would happen if the police suddenly banned pursuits. Undoubtedly, innocent people may be injured or killed because an officer chooses to pursue a suspect, but this risk is necessary to avoid the even greater loss that would occur if law enforcement agencies were not allowed to aggressively pursue violators.[83]

On the other hand, Stone and DeLuca, authors of a police administration textbook, maintain that

> one of the major areas of controversy . . . is the practice of pursuing fugitives at high speed. High-speed pursuit is an exceedingly dangerous kind of police operation. It is dangerous not only for the police officer and the fugitive, but equally so for innocent citizens who happen to be in their path. . . . More often than not, a high-speed pursuit ends only when either the fugitive or the officer is involved in a collision, often a fatal one.[84]

High-speed police pursuits, a form of deadly force, raise several policy issues. According to police specialist

Gordon E. Misner, "If the circumstances don't reasonably permit the use of deadly force, they also do not warrant engaging in a high-speed chase!" However, most police departments, according to a survey Misner conducted, did not generally equate deadly force and police pursuits. Several did use a deadly force analogy in cases of "ramming," or deliberately touching a pursued vehicle to "alert the driver that the pursuing officer is serious about stopping!"[85]

Pursuits also raise issues of peer group pressure, the idea that chases put the machismo of pursuing officers on the line. Lee P. Brown, when he was chief of the Houston Police Department, in a cover message to a new pursuit policy, wrote:

> Remember the criminals will continue to be out there in the future and they can be found and arrested by other means. So if you decide not to chase based on the risks involved, you will not be subject to criticism. However, if you decide that you should chase, we will support you and offer acceptable standard operating procedures to assist you. The safety and well-being of our officers and the public we serve is the first and foremost priority in our minds, and we will continue to work toward that end with you.[86]
>
> A Houston officer referred to the importance of altering organizational culture from "Chase them until the wheels fall off" to "Why risk your life to chase some traffic violator?"[87]

The Louisiana State Police caution their officers as follows regarding chases:

> When the violator begins to seriously endanger the lives of innocent persons upon the highway, by passing on curves or in the face of oncoming traffic, the trooper should discontinue the pursuit except as follows:
> a. The violator is a felon who has committed a crime which endangered life; or
> b. The actions of the violator are such that the trooper reasonably believes that his continued freedom would seriously jeopardize the lives of others.[88]

CRITICAL THINKING

1. Summarize the possible policies regarding pursuits excerpted here.
2. Which is the best policy? Back up your answer with information in the paragraphs.
3. Which is the worst policy? Back up your answer with information.
4. If you cannot decide, what more information would you want to have to make a decision?

Policies and Practices Regarding Force

Researchers who have evaluated police use of force policies have emphasized that simply making rules is not enough to change what happens in day-to-day police decision making. Jerome H. Skolnick and James J. Fyfe surveyed several cities where unwritten rules "overwhelmed" written rules governing shootings. Lawrence W. Sherman argues that reductions in shootings following the adoption of rules do not mean that rules alone can reduce the use of deadly force. In all the cities he studied, Sherman said, the rules were accompanied by "intense public criticism of the police and an increasingly severe administrative and disciplinary posture toward shooting." Fyfe maintains that the adoption of a new Firearms Discharge Review Board to enforce a new shooting policy was instrumental in the reduction of shootings in New York City.

Two projects dramatically illustrate the importance of training in the reduction of force. Psychologist Hans Toch and two colleagues, J. Douglas Grant and Ray Galvin, assembled a group of officers, some of whom had histories of violent encounters and others whose supervisors had identified them as "good" officers. The group was allowed to define the problem of police-citizen violence, identify its causes, develop a strategy for dealing with it, and put the strategy into operation.

The officers started by creating a Violence Prevention Unit. The unit reviewed the files of officers whose records indicated frequent incidents of violence. The unit then conducted an investigation, collecting information about the officers with violence problems from supervisors and fellow officers. A study group reviewed the information and developed questions to ask at a meeting with violence-prone officers. The meeting explored the key incidents of violence, allowed the subject to summarize the incidents, and then discussed how the pattern of incidents led to violence. Alternatives that might avoid violence were then discussed. Before participation in the discussions, the most violence-prone officers engaged in conflicts four times more often than other officers. Following participation, the incidents were cut in half![89]

A scandal arising out of an incident prompted a violence-reduction training program in the Metro-Dade County Police Department. Several police officers beat an African American insurance agent into a coma following a chase for a traffic violation. To make the injuries look like they were caused by a traffic spill (the man was on a motorcycle), the officers drove their squad car over the motorcycle. The man died four days later. When the officers' cover-up was discovered, they were tried for manslaughter. A jury acquitted them, and a riot followed the acquittal. But out of the tragedy came a success story: the Metro-Dade Police/Citizen Violence Reduction Project.

The project was designed to defuse potentially violent situations between police and private individuals. A task force of police officers, investigators, supervisors, and trainers analyzed reports of 100 encounters between private individuals and police that culminated in the use of force, injuries to officers, or complaints against officers. From their analyses, the task force drew up detailed lists of "Dos and Don'ts" for the four most frequent potentially violent encounters: traffic stops, stops of suspicious vehicles, responses to reported crimes, and disputes. The lists were built into a training program. In the year and a half following completion of the training program, the use of force by officers, injuries to officers, and complaints against officers all dropped by between 30 and 50 percent.[90]

Knowledge and Understanding CHECK

1. Identify the four major types of police abuse.
2. Summarize the major explanations for police misconduct.
3. Describe the importance of the use of force in police work.
4. Describe the "Dirty Harry" problem.
5. List the three major points discovered following the Rodney King case.
6. List and describe the types and amounts of force used by the police.
7. How often do police use force in their work?
8. Why is so little known about how often the police abuse the use of force?
9. Describe the two policies on the use of deadly force recommended by the Police Foundation.
10. Explain why formulating, implementing, and enforcing deadly force rules is difficult.
11. List the reasons why it is a good idea to tighten the rules on the use of firearms.
12. Who does the use of deadly force usually injure or kill?
13. Identify the ten techniques to control shooting that show promise.
14. How many shootings is too many? Explain your answer.
15. Whom do the police shoot?
16. What do high speed chases have to do with the use of force?
17. Summarize the findings of researchers regarding high-speed chases.
18. Explain why making rules is not enough to change the behavior of officers on the street.

Police Corruption

Police corruption is a form of occupational crime: misusing police authority for private gain. Corruption varies. It might affect only one or two officers or pervade a whole department. The definition of corruption also varies. It can include everything from a top official regularly extorting thousands of dollars a month from vice operations to a patrol officer accepting a free cup of coffee from a neighborhood restaurant. According to former New York Police Commissioner Patrick Murphy, "Except for your paycheck, there is no such thing as a clean buck."[91]

The most common corrupt practices include:

- *Mooching:* free meals, alcohol, groceries, or other items.
- *Chiseling:* demands for free admission to entertainment.
- *Favoritism:* gaining immunity from traffic violations.
- *Prejudice:* giving nonwhites less than impartial treatment.
- *Shopping:* picking up small items from stores left unlocked after business hours.
- *Extortion:* demanding money in exchange for not filing traffic tickets.
- *Bribery:* receiving payments of cash or "gifts" for past or future assistance in avoiding arrest, or in falsifying or withholding evidence.
- *Shakedown:* taking expensive items for personal use and attributing their loss to criminal activity when investigating a break-in or burglary.
- *Perjury:* lying to provide an alibi for fellow officers apprehended in illegal activity.
- *Premeditated theft:* executing a planned burglary to gain forced entry in order to acquire unlawful goods.[92]

When police officers engage in the same conduct that they are sworn to prevent, it corrodes public confidence and breeds resentment. Police officials who preach obedience to the law and then break it themselves can hardly rely on citizen cooperation in maintaining an orderly society. Police corruption also impairs effective policing from within the police department. Officers who are "on the take" have less time to spend on police duties. In fact, they frequently resent having to perform their police responsibilities, particularly when these interfere with their pursuit of private gain. Corrupt sergeants, captains, inspectors, and other supervisors weaken administrative control over patrol officers. A commander taking payoffs is not an effective supervisor. Weak supervision also leads officers "typically [to] respond more slowly to calls for assistance, avoid assigned duties, sleep on the job, and perform poorly in situations requiring discipline."[93]

The causes of corruption run deeper than simple greed. In their normal work days, police officers deal with some not very nice people. Repeated contacts with these types of people and their problems lead many officers to conclude that everybody is "on the take." Also, police officers often view criminal justice mainly as an exercise in futility. They watch masses of offenders pass haphazardly through undignified lower courts; and they see prosecutors, defense attorneys, and judges get their share of dirty money. Officers bitterly recognize that the corruption of prosecutors and judges is largely immune from scandalous exposure. From this arises the belief that everybody is on the take, but only the police are scandalized. In the end, this steady diet of ineffectiveness and wrongdoing leads some police officers to conclude that their own corruption is no worse than, perhaps not even as bad as, that of others. Furthermore, they come to believe it really makes no difference anyway, considering the inability of the criminal process to reform what, to the police, is largely a corrupt society.[94]

Police discretion also permits many decisions *not* to enforce laws to go without review. Furthermore, corruption is addictive. Officers frequently spend graft-augmented income on large new purchases, such as homes and cars. To keep up the payments, the increased income becomes a necessity that leads to dependence on money acquired by corrupt practices.

Exposing and correcting corruption are difficult. In most departments, "a code of silence brands anyone who exposes corruption a traitor. . . . [I]t is easier for . . . [a rookie] to become corrupt than to remain honest." This leads to two attitudes:

1. Suspicion of and hostility toward outside interference.
2. Desire to be loyal to the department.[95]

Knowledge and Understanding CHECK

1. Why is police corruption a form of occupational crime?
2. List the most common corrupt practices. Rank them according to your own opinion of the seriousness of the practice. Defend your ranking.
3. Identify and briefly describe the causes of police corruption.
4. Why is it difficult to expose and correct police corruption?

ACCOUNTABILITY FOR MISCONDUCT

We all know what happens—or should happen—when ordinary people break the law. They are supposed to be apprehended, prosecuted, and punished. The same notion should apply to police officers who break the law. We examine in this section four forms of punishment for officers who break the law:

1. Criminal punishment.
2. Money damages for injuries to individuals.
3. Disciplinary action inside police departments.
4. Disciplinary action outside police departments.

Criminal Punishment

Most police abuse of force is not only a violation of police rules but is also a crime. For example, a police officer who *illegally* shoots a person and the person dies has committed some form of criminal homicide, depending on the intent and surrounding circumstances. Suppose the worst kind of case: a police officer abuses her authority to use deadly force and intentionally but unnecessarily shoots and kills a man because she is prejudiced against African American men. This is murder; however, this form of criminal behavior by police rarely occurs. Most common are the illegal searches and arrests that may amount to burglary, criminal trespass, false imprisonment, and kidnapping.

How likely is it that police officers whose misconduct is criminal behavior will be charged with crimes, convicted, and punished? Not very (see Figure 8.10). First, the invasions of life, liberty, and property that result from police misconduct are often not accompanied by the criminal intent required as a material element in the crime. Furthermore, it is difficult to prove guilt beyond a reasonable doubt, even though officers may have in fact committed the crime. Witnesses may not exist; or if they do, they may not be credible. Even if they are credible, they may not be sympathetic. Many people who are subjects of police misconduct are themselves "marginal"—that is, they may have criminal histories. Rarely will a prosecutor or a jury (or, for that matter, the public) side with a "real" criminal over police officers who, after all, are "only trying to do their job."

Civil Lawsuits

Plaintiffs, individuals who sue the police, seek one of two legal remedies:

1. **Damages:** money compensation.
2. **Injunctions:** court orders requiring individual police officers and departments to do or stop doing something.

There are both federal and state sources for civil lawsuits. Most illegal actions by police officers are state **torts;** that is, they violate duties imposed on all people. State law provides that injured parties can sue and obtain money from the party who injures them. Many torts are civil versions of crimes. For example, illegal searches and seizures (discussed in Chapter 7) may include all of the following state torts for which plaintiffs can sue for damages: wrongful death, assault, battery, false arrest, false imprisonment, trespass, and breaking and entering.

The difference between torts and crimes is that the standard of proof for crimes is "beyond a reasonable doubt," as

Figure 8.10
Number of Criminal and Civil Cases per 1,000 Sworn Officers Involving Excessive Use of Force, 1991

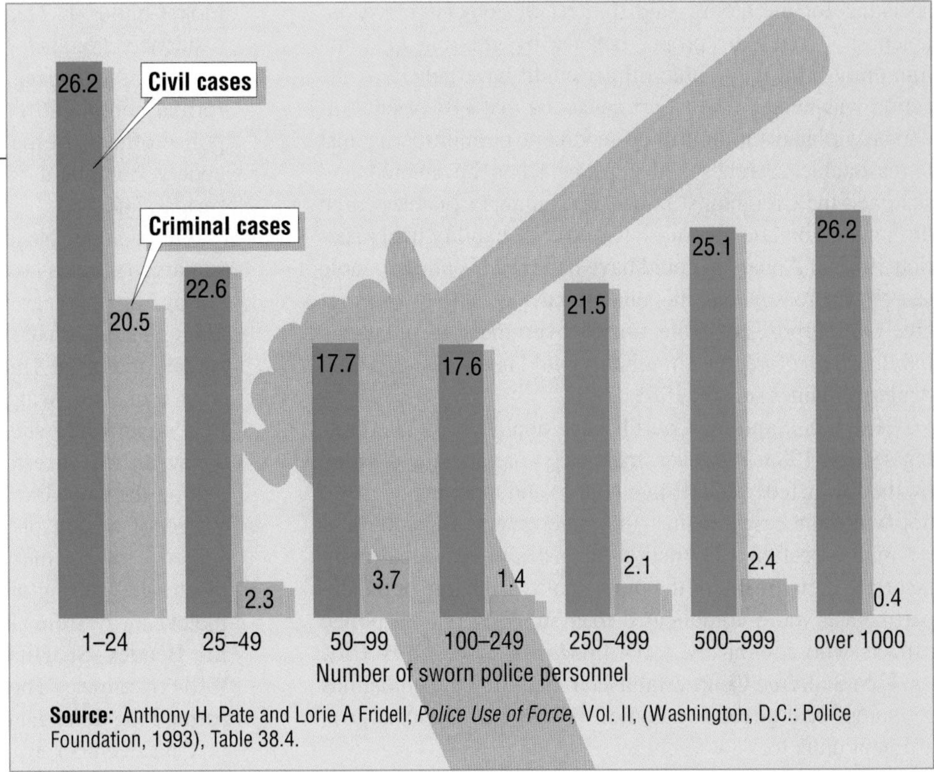

Source: Anthony H. Pate and Lorie A Fridell, *Police Use of Force*, Vol. II, (Washington, D.C.: Police Foundation, 1993), Table 38.4.

opposed to the preponderance of evidence required to win a tort case (see Chapter 11). The result in a criminal case is that convicted defendants either pay a fine, go to jail or prison, or get probation; defendants in tort cases pay damages to plaintiffs out of their own pockets.

The **doctrine of official immunity** limits the liability of police officers for their torts. According to the doctrine, police officers cannot be legally liable for exercising their discretion unless they engage in intentional and malicious wrongdoing. According to the Minnesota Supreme Court, for example, "[t]o encourage responsible law enforcement . . . police are afforded a wide degree of discretion precisely because a more stringent standard could inhibit action." Therefore, according to the court, a police officer was not liable for the death of a small boy killed during a high-speed chase in which the officer was attempting to apprehend a fleeing shoplifter. Official immunity protected the officer; otherwise, the court maintained, officers in the future might hold back in their vigorous enforcement of the law. The **doctrine of *respondeat superior*** imposes liability on state and local governments and their agencies for the torts of individual police officers; that is, individuals can sue the departments or local governments responsible for the police.[96]

In addition to state tort law, federal law enforcement officers who violate the constitutional rights of individuals violate the federal Civil Rights Act of 1871. This act allows individuals to sue state and local governments, their agencies, and their agents for violations of rights guaranteed by the U.S. Constitution. Suits under the Civil Rights Act are commonly called **section 1983 actions,** because these actions arise under Chapter 42, section 1983 of the United States Code. Section 1983 provides:

> Every person who, under color of any statute, ordinance, regulation, custom, or usage, of any State or Territory, subjects, or causes to be subjected, any citizen of the United States or other person within the jurisdiction thereof to the deprivation of any rights, privileges, or immunities secured by the Constitution and laws, shall be liable to the party injured in an action at law, suit in equity, or other proper proceeding for redress.[97]

State and local officers and agencies are not liable for all violations of the federal constitutional rights of individuals. The U.S. Supreme Court has created a **defense of qualified immunity** for officers whose actions are "objectively reasonable." Qualified immunity shields officers from "liability for civil damages insofar as their conduct does not violate clearly established statutory or constitutional rights of which a reasonable person would have known." Qualified immunity, according to the Court, strikes a balance "between the interests in vindication of people's constitutional rights and in public officials' effective performance of their duties."

The leading qualified immunity case is *Anderson v. Creighton,* in which FBI agents searched the Creightons' home without a warrant and without probable cause, looking for one of the Creightons' relatives. Justice Antonin Scalia, speaking for the Court, said the test of "objective reasonableness" strikes the proper balance by granting qualified immunity if "a reasonable officer could have believed" the action was lawful. The Court conceded that FBI Agent Anderson violated the Fourth Amendment prohibition against unreasonable searches and seizures when he entered and searched the Creightons' house. But an unreasonable search does not automatically translate into civil liability under section 1983. If Anderson could have believed his unreasonable search was reasonable, this qualified as "objectively reasonable" for purposes of protecting a government agent against liability. Therefore, the Creightons could not prevail in suing Anderson under section 1983.[98]

The U.S. Supreme Court has the final word in interpreting section 1983. However, most cases are actually decided by the lower federal and state courts, and most plaintiffs do not win their cases against the government. Bringing and winning a section 1983 action against a police department head, the department, or the municipality in charge of the department is more complicated than suing individual police officers who commit the torts. In *Monell v. New York City,* the U.S. Supreme Court established the following guidelines for suing local governing bodies. People can sue local government units for:

1. Unconstitutional actions that "implement or execute a policy statement, ordinance, regulation, or decision officially adopted and promulgated by that body's officers."
2. Unconstitutional actions taken pursuant to "custom, even though such a custom has not received formal approval through the body's decision making channels."
3. Government units are liable only if their unconstitutional actions "caused a constitutional tort."[99]

The Use Your Discretion case, "Is the city liable?" examines some of the issues in suing a city for the torts of its police officers.

Use *Your* Discretion

Is the city liable?

***Thurman v. City of Torrington,* 595 F.Supp. 1521 (D.Conn. 1984)**

Facts

In October 1982, Charles Thurman attacked plaintiff Tracey Thurman at the home of Judy Bentley and Richard St. Hilaire in the City of Torrington. Mr. St. Hilaire and Ms. Bentley made a formal complaint of the attack to one of the unnamed defendant police officers and requested efforts to keep the plaintiff's husband, Charles Thurman, off their property. On or about November 5, 1982, Charles Thurman returned to the St. Hilaire–Bentley residence and using physical force took Charles J. Thurman, Jr. [their child] from said residence. Plaintiff Tracey Thurman and Mr. St. Hilaire went to Torrington police headquarters to make a formal complaint. At that point, unnamed defendant police officers of the City of Torrington refused to accept a complaint from Mr. St. Hilaire even as to trespassing.

On or about November 9, 1982, Charles Thurman screamed threats to Tracey Thurman while she was sitting in her car. Defendant police officer Neil Gemelli stood on the street watching Charles Thurman scream threats at Tracey Thurman until Charles Thurman broke the windshield of plaintiff Tracey Thurman's car while she was inside the vehicle. Charles Thurman was arrested after he broke the windshield, and on the next day, November 10, 1982, he was convicted of breach of peace. He received a suspended sentence of six months and a two-year "conditional discharge," during which he was ordered to stay completely away from the plaintiff Tracey Thurman and the Bentley–St. Hilaire residence and to commit no further crimes. The court imposing probation informed the defendant of this sentence.

On December 31, 1982, while plaintiff Tracey Thurman was at the Bentley–St. Hilaire residence, Charles Thurman returned to said residence and once again threatened her. She called the Torrington Police Department. One of the unnamed police officer defendants took the call, and, although informed of the violation of the conditional discharge, made no attempt to ascertain Charles Thurman's whereabouts or to arrest him.

Between January 1 and May 4, 1983, numerous telephone complaints to the Torrington Police Department were taken by various unnamed police officers, in which repeated threats of violence to the plaintiff by Charles Thurman were reported and his arrest on account of the threats and violation of the terms of his probation was requested.

On May 4 and 5, 1983, the plaintiff Tracey Thurman and Ms. Bentley reported to the Torrington Police Department that Charles Thurman had said that he would shoot the plaintiff. Defendant police officer Storrs took the written complaint of plaintiff Tracey Thurman, who was seeking an arrest warrant for her husband because of his death threat and violation of his "conditional discharge." Defendant Storrs refused to take the complaint of Ms. Bentley. Plaintiff Tracey Thurman was told to return three weeks later on June 1, 1983, when defendant Storrs or some other person connected with the police department of the defendant City would seek a warrant for the arrest of her husband.

On May 6, 1983, Tracey Thurman filed an application for a restraining order against Charles Thurman in the Litchfield Superior Court. That day, the court issued an *ex parte* restraining order forbidding Charles

Many districts are starting to recognize the need for special training for police officers who deal with domestic crimes, in part as a result of incidents like the one described in the Thurman case.

Thurman from assaulting, threatening, and harassing Tracey Thurman. The defendant City was informed of this order. On May 27, 1983, Tracey Thurman requested police protection to get to the Torrington Police Department, and she requested a warrant for her husband's arrest upon her arrival at headquarters after being taken there by one of the unnamed defendant police officers. She was told that she would have to wait until after the Memorial Day holiday weekend and was advised to call on Tuesday, May 31, to pursue the warrant request.

On May 31, 1983, Tracey Thurman appeared once again at the Torrington Police Department to pursue the warrant request. She was then advised by one of the unnamed defendant police officers that defendant Schapp was the only policeman who could help her and that he was on vacation. She was told that she would have to wait until he returned. That same day, Tracey's brother-in-law, Joseph Kocsis, called the Torrington Police Department to protest the lack of action taken on Tracey's complaint. Although Mr. Kocsis was advised that Charles Thurman would be arrested on June 8, 1983, no such arrest took place.

On June 10, 1983, Charles Thurman appeared at the Bentley–St. Hilaire residence in the early afternoon and demanded to speak to Tracey Thurman. Tracey, remaining indoors, called the defendant police department asking that Charles be picked up for violation of his probation. After about 15 minutes, Tracey went outside to speak to her husband in an effort to persuade him not to take or hurt [their child] Charles Jr. Soon thereafter, Charles began to stab Tracey repeatedly in the chest, neck, and throat.

Approximately 25 minutes after Tracey's call to the Torrington Police Department and after her stabbing, a single police officer, the defendant Petrovits, arrived on the scene. Upon the arrival of Officer Petrovits at the scene of the stabbing, Charles Thurman was holding a bloody knife. Charles then dropped the knife and, in the presence of Petrovits, kicked the plaintiff Tracey Thurman in the head and ran into the Bentley–St. Hilaire residence. Charles returned from within the residence holding the plaintiff Charles Thurman, Jr. and dropped the child on his wounded mother. Charles then kicked Tracey in the head a second time. Soon thereafter, defendants DeAngelo, Nukirk, and Columbia arrived on the scene but still permitted Charles Thurman to wander about the crowd and continue to threaten Tracey. Finally, upon approaching Tracey once again, this time while she was lying on a stretcher, Charles Thurman was arrested and taken into custody.

It is also alleged that at all times mentioned above, except for approximately two weeks following his conviction and sentencing on November 10, 1982, Charles Thurman resided in Torrington and worked there as a counterman and short order cook at Skie's Diner. There he served many members of the Torrington Police Department, including some of the named and unnamed defendants in this case. In the course of his employment Charles Thurman boasted to the defendant police officer patrons that he intended to "get" his wife and that he intended to kill her.

Opinion

The City brings a motion to dismiss the claims against it. The City . . . argues that the equal protection clause "only prohibits intentional discrimination that is racially motivated." The defendant City's argument is clearly a misstatement of the law. The application of the equal protection clause is not limited to racial classifications or racially motivated discrimination. . . . Classifications on the basis of gender will be held invalid under the equal protection clause unless they are substantially related to strike down classifications which are not rationally related to a legitimate governmental purpose.

In the instant case, the plaintiffs allege that the defendants use an administrative classification that manifests itself in discriminatory treatment violative of the equal protection clause. Police protection in the City of Torrington, they argue, is fully provided to persons abused by someone with whom the victim has no domestic relationship. But the Torrington police have consistently afforded lesser protection, plaintiffs allege, when the victim is (1) a woman abused or assaulted by a spouse or boyfriend, or (2) a child abused by a father or stepfather. The issue to be decided, then, is whether the plaintiffs have properly alleged a violation of the equal protection clause of the Fourteenth Amendment.

. . . City officials and police officers are under an affirmative duty to preserve law and order, and to protect the personal safety of persons in the community. This duty applies equally to women whose personal safety is threatened by individuals with whom they have or have had a domestic relationship as well as to all other persons whose personal safety is threatened, including women not involved in domestic relationships. If officials have notice of the possibility of attacks on women in domestic relationships or other persons, they are under an affirmative duty to take reasonable measures to protect the personal safety of such persons in the community. Failure to perform this duty would constitute a denial of equal protection of the laws.

. . . The plaintiffs have alleged that there is an administrative classification used to implement the law in a discriminatory fashion. It is well settled that the equal protection clause is applicable not only to discriminatory legislative action, but also to discriminatory governmental action in administration and enforcement of the law. Here the plaintiffs were threatened with assault in violation of Connecticut law. Over the course of eight months the police failed to afford the plaintiffs protection against such assaults, and failed to take action to arrest the perpetrator of these assaults. The plaintiffs have alleged that this failure to act was pursuant to a pattern or practice of affording inadequate protection, or no protection at all, to women who have complained of having been abused by their husbands or others with whom they have had close relations. Such a practice is tantamount to an administrative classification used to implement the law in a discriminatory fashion.

. . . A man is not allowed to physically abuse or endanger a woman merely because he is her husband. Concomitantly, a police officer may not knowingly refrain from interference in such violence, and may not "automatically decline to make an arrest simply because the assaulter and his victim are married to each other." Such inaction on the part of the officer is a denial of the equal protection of the laws.

In addition, any notion that defendants' practice can be justified as a means of promoting domestic harmony by refraining from interference in marital disputes has no place in the case at hand. Rather than evidencing a desire to work out her problems with her husband privately, Tracey Thurman pleaded with the police to offer her at least some measure of protection. Further, she sought and received a restraining order to keep her husband at a distance. . . . Accordingly, the defendant City of Torrington's motion to dismiss the plaintiff Tracey Thurman's complaint on the basis of failure to allege violation of a constitutional right is denied. . . .

While a municipality is not liable for the constitutional torts of its employees on a *respondeat superior* theory, a municipality may be sued for damages under section 1983 when "the action that is alleged to be unconstitutional implements or executes a policy statement, ordinance, regulation, or decision officially adopted and promulgated by the body's officers" or is "visited pursuant to governmental 'custom' even though such a custom has not received formal approval through the body's official decision-making channels." *Monell v. New York City Department of Social Services,* 436 U.S. 658, 690, 98 S.Ct. 2018, 2035, 56 L.Ed.2d 611 (1978).

Some degree of specificity is required in the pleading of a custom or policy on the part of a municipality. Mere conclusory allegations devoid of factual content will not suffice. As this court has pointed out, a plaintiff must typically point to the facts outside his own case to support his allegation of a policy on the part of a municipality. In the instant case, however, the plaintiff Tracey Thurman has specifically alleged in her statement of facts a series of acts and omissions on the part of the defendant police officers and police department that took place over the course of eight months. From this particularized pleading a pattern emerges that evidences deliberate indifference on the part of the police department to the complaints of the plaintiff Tracey Thurman and to its duty to protect her. Such an ongoing pattern of deliberate indifference raises an inference of "custom" or "policy" on the part of the municipality. Furthermore, this pattern of inaction climaxed on June 10, 1983 in an incident so brutal that under the law of the Second Circuit that "single brutal incident may be sufficient to suggest a link between a violation of constitutional rights and a pattern of police misconduct." Finally, a complaint of this sort will survive dismissal if it alleges a policy or custom of condoning police misconduct that violates constitutional rights and alleges "that the City's pattern of inaction caused the plaintiffs any compensable injury."

For the reasons stated above, the City's motion to dismiss the complaint for failure to allege the deprivation of a constitutional right is denied . . . ; the City's motion to dismiss claims against it for failure to properly allege a "custom" or "policy" on the part of the City is denied. . . .

SO ORDERED.

CRITICAL THINKING

1. What constitutional rights did the city allegedly violate?
2. What facts did the plaintiff allege to demonstrate the unconstitutional acts?
3. What facts demonstrate a "custom" or "policy"?
4. Did these facts cause injury to Tracey Thurman? Explain.
5. Is the lack of sufficient police training ever official policy? Is a pattern of non-discipline for the actions of officers official policy? Wayne LaFave, an expert on criminal procedure and the author of many leading works on the subject, has commented that the rule that requires courts to determine whether an unconstitutional action was caused by the "execution of a government's policy or custom" raises difficult questions. Is a directive in a police department manual official policy?[100]

Internal Review

Criminal cases against the police are rare. The discretionary judgments of prosecutors are affected by their beliefs that prosecuting police officers is both difficult and unwise. Civil suits against the police are also difficult to bring, and they are sporadic as well because they depend on the resources and the will of complainants. By far the most pervasive and systematic review of police misconduct is internal review. Most large and mid-sized departments have **internal affairs units (IAU),** special units within the police department, usually attached to the office of the chief.[101]

According to Professor Douglas W. Perez, a former deputy sheriff, "most cops do not like internal affairs." They view IAU skeptically, at best. Some even consider IAU investigators traitors. Nevertheless, most officers believe that IAU operations are necessary. In some measure, internal review is a defense against external review, which police officers believe threatens police control of their own profession and operations. The famed Chicago chief of police, O. W. Wilson, said, "It is clearly apparent that if the police do not take a vigorous stand on the matter of internal investigation, outside groups—such as review boards consisting of laymen and other persons outside the police service—will step into the void."[102]

Internal affairs operations consist of four stages:

1. Intake
2. Investigation
3. Deliberation
4. Disposition

The Internal Affairs Section of the Oakland, California, Police Department is considered an excellent unit; we will use it as an example of how internal review should proceed through these four stages. The unit is housed in the department building. The department intake policy is that "anyone anywhere should accept a complaint if a citizen wishes it taken." Oakland takes most complaints at the department, but it also accepts telephone and anonymous complaints. All complaints alleging excessive force, police corruption, and racial discrimination are followed up. Supervisors have the discretion not to follow up anonymous complaints believed to be hoaxes. Furthermore, the unit has the discretion not to follow up on complaints of "such a minor nature that the unit or person first contacted can dispose of the incident *to the satisfaction of the complainant* without the necessity of a formal investigation." Seventy-eight percent of internal review units surveyed encourage the handling of complaints informally.[103]

Someone other than the intake officer is assigned to investigate the complaint. The investigator gathers documentary evidence and interviews witnesses, usually interviewing the officer against whom the complaint is filed last. If officers refuse to respond, they are subject to discipline, which might include dismissal for refusing a direct order of the chief.

Figure 8.11
Disposition of Internal Review Excessive Force Complaints

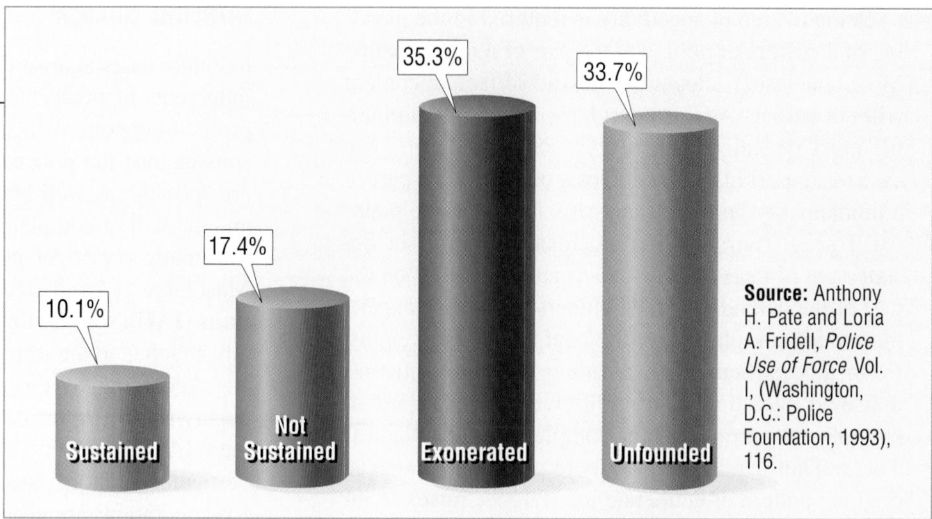

Source: Anthony H. Pate and Loria A. Fridell, *Police Use of Force* Vol. I, (Washington, D.C.: Police Foundation, 1993), 116.

The completed investigation then goes to the supervisor of the Internal Affairs Section. If the supervisor is satisfied, it goes to the decision-making or deliberation stage. The case usually goes up the chain of command, beginning with the immediate supervisor of the officer under investigation. The supervisor discusses the case with the officer and gives one of four possible dispositions:

1. *Unfounded:* The investigation proved that the act did not take place.
2. *Exonerated:* The acts took place, but the investigation proved that they were justified, lawful, and proper.
3. *Not sustained:* The investigation failed to gather enough evidence to clearly prove the allegations in the complaint.
4. *Sustained:* The investigation disclosed enough evidence to clearly prove the allegations in the complaint.[104]

If the disposition is unfounded, exonerated, or not sustained, the case is closed. If it is sustained, the supervisor makes a disciplinary recommendation. (See Figure 8.11 for a survey of the dispositions of internal review cases concerning excessive force.) These recommended disciplinary actions can include:

- Reprimand
- Written reprimand
- Transfer
- Retraining
- Counseling
- Suspension
- Demotion
- Fine
- Dismissal

After the initial disposition, the case goes up the chain of command for review until it finally reaches the chief. In about half the cases, there is a discrepancy between the chief's recommendations and those of the immediate supervisor. These discrepancies are important because the immediate supervisor, usually a sergeant of patrol, works on the street with other patrol officers. The supervisors of sergeants usually go along with the recommendations of sergeants. Chiefs of police, on the other hand, are removed from the day-to-day street operations of patrol officers and their immediate supervisors. They have departmentwide perspectives and are responsible to "local political elites" for their department's performance. So chiefs may find the disciplinary penalty too light and make it heavier. According to Perez, "Oakland chiefs are often seen from below as abusive of police officers, always increasing punishments, never going along with the lighter recommendations." Oakland, however, may not be typical in this respect. (Figure 8.12 depicts the disciplinary measures taken in a national sample of city police departments.)[105]

External Review

The fundamental objection to internal review is that the police cannot police themselves. To the question, "Who will watch the watchmen?" the answer is, "Not the watchmen!" Hence, we have seen the growth of external review procedures. **External review of police misconduct** is a procedure in which individuals or others who are not sworn police officers participate in the review of complaints against the police. Usually called *civilian review,* it has generated controversy for nearly half a century. The central issue in external review is whether civilians should participate in the complaint process of police misconduct. The police have opposed external review because it invades their professional autonomy; because they have no confidence in outsiders knowing enough about police work to review it; and because they know that outside scrutiny would pierce the "blue cur-

Figure 8.12
Percent of Discipline Administered in Sustained Complaints in City Police Departments

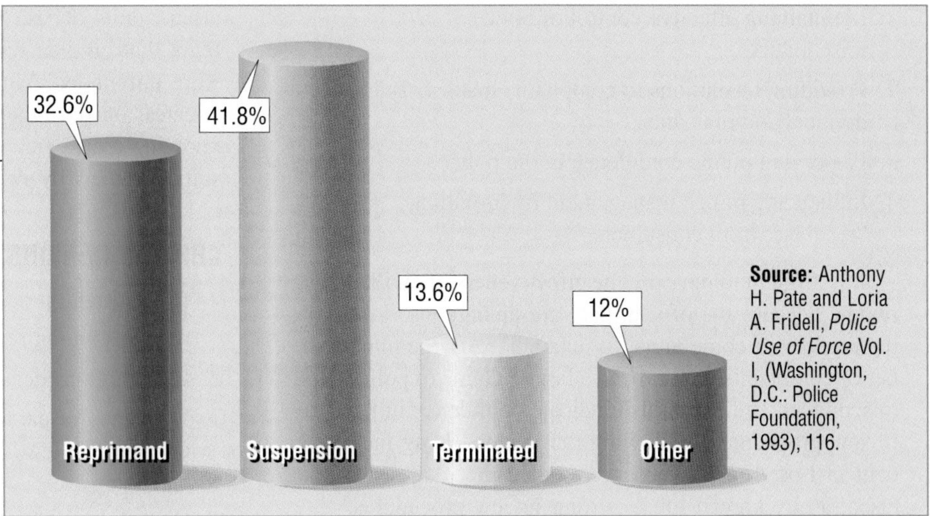

tain" that hides their "real" work from public view. Strong police unions, chiefs who opposed external review, and the creation of internal review procedures (discussed in the last section) successfully prevented external review during the 1960s, when it became a popular proposal of some liberal reformers and citizen groups.[106]

However, by 1994, 72 percent of the 50 largest cities had created civilian review procedures of some sort. The growth of civilian review became possible, in part, because the opposition of police unions and chiefs either lessened or was overcome, and because internal review did not change public *perceptions,* especially among African Americans in large cities, that police misconduct, particularly the use of excessive force, was still a major problem. The beating of Rodney King added further momentum to the movement to create civilian review procedures.[107]

Types of External Review

The differences among civilian review procedures all turn on the degree of participation in the decision-making process by people who are not sworn police officers. "Degree of participation" means the point in the process when unsworn officers take part in the review procedures. These points are:

1. The initial investigation to collect the facts.
2. The review of the investigation reports.
3. The recommendation for disposition to the chief.
4. The review of decisions made by the chief.

A survey of the civilian procedures of the 50 largest U.S. cities, conducted by Samuel Walker and Vic W. Bumphus, identified three major types of review procedures, based on the four points in the decision-making process:

1. *Class I systems:* Individuals who are not sworn police officers conduct the initial fact-finding investigation. Their reports go to a person or panel, also not sworn officers, who recommend action to the chief.
2. *Class II systems:* Sworn officers conduct the fact-finding investigation. Civilians recommend action to the chief.
3. *Class III systems:* Sworn officers conduct the initial fact-finding investigation. Sworn officers also recommend action to the chief. If complainants are not satisfied with the disposition of the complaint, they can appeal the decision to a panel of civilians.[108]

Despite differences, all three systems share three important characteristics. First, they can only *recommend* disciplinary action to police chiefs. Under civil service laws, only police chiefs can actually decide on disciplinary action against police officers. Second, all existing review procedures were established either by municipal ordinance or state statute. Therefore, they are all on a solid legal footing that makes it more difficult to alter or abolish them. Third, civilian review enjoys broad public support. A Louis Harris poll reported that 80 percent of adults favored review by a mixture of civilians and sworn police officers. Only 15 percent favored review by civilians alone, and a mere 4 percent supported review by sworn officers alone.[109]

Use *Your* Discretion

Does civilian review work?

The answer depends both on the *definition* of effectiveness and the *measures* of effectiveness. *Effectiveness* can mean at least four things, all of which are important in determining the value of civilian review procedures:

1. Maintaining effective control of police misconduct.
2. Providing resolutions to complaints that satisfy individual complainants.
3. Preserving public confidence in the police.
4. Influencing police management by providing "feedback from consumers."[110]

It is difficult to measure the effectiveness of civilian review because the official data are ambiguous. Take the number of complaints, for example. A large number of complaints might mean a large volume of police misconduct. But it can also indicate confidence in the review procedures. Following the Rodney King incident in Los Angeles, observers noted that San Francisco, a city known for its strong review procedures, received more complaints than the much larger city of Los Angeles. The Independent Commission heard a number of citizen complaints that the LAPD created "significant hurdles" to filing complaints, that they were afraid of the process, and that the complaint process was "unnecessarily difficult or impossible." The ACLU collected evidence suggesting that the LAPD "actively discouraged the filing of complaints." The beating of Rodney King, in fact, would never have come to public attention without the video, according to the Independent Commission. This is because, according to the Commission, the efforts of Rodney King's brother Paul to file a complaint following the beating were "frustrated" by the LAPD.[111]

The numbers and rates of complaints are also difficult to assess because we do not know the numbers of incidents about which people do not file complaints. In one national survey, of all the people who said that the police mistreated them, only 30 percent said they had filed complaints. One thing, however, seems clear. Misconduct is not distributed evenly among individuals and neighborhoods. In one survey, only 40 percent of the addresses in one city had any contact with the police in a year. Most contacts between private individuals and the police occur in neighborhoods in which poor people live. In New York City, the rate of complaints ranges from 1 to 5 for every 10,000 people, depending on the neighborhood.

Official data have consistently indicated that racial minority males are disproportionately represented among complainants. Thus, the perception of a pattern of police harassment is a major factor in conflict between the police and racial minority communities.[112]

Whatever the ambiguity of numbers and rates in the official statistics, observers have noted that civilian review procedures sustain complaints against police officers at a low rate. Furthermore, the rates of complaints that are sustained in civilian review do not substantially differ from the rates of sustained complaints by internal affairs units. These similar rates suggest that police fears that civilian review will be a "kangaroo court" were unfounded. Minority groups and civil rights advocates, on the other hand, ought to take comfort in knowing that review by civilians produces similar results to review by sworn police officers.[113]

CRITICAL THINKING

1. Explain why it is difficult to measure the effectiveness of civilian review.
2. Do you consider this a serious problem? Explain.
3. What has research discovered regarding race and civilian review? Of what importance is this discovery?
4. How do civilian review outcomes compare with internal review outcomes?
5. Should this comparison affect policymaking? How, if at all, would you change policy on the basis of the comparison? Explain.

Other Responses to Misconduct

One positive approach to dealing with police misconduct relies on training and other socialization measures to improve police-community relations. For example, advocates for the positive approach argue the effectiveness of convincing officers to use unflappable responses to unpleasant behavior. Taking an insult without reaction wins more respect and obedience than responding emotionally to insults. James Q. Wilson, a supporter of the positive approach, recommends that recruitment, training, and the police subculture should aim at producing police officers

> who can handle calmly challenges to their self-respect and manhood, are able to tolerate ambiguous situations, have the physical capacity to subdue persons, are able to accept responsibility for the consequences of their own actions, can understand and apply legal concepts in concrete situations, and are honest.[114]

Knowledge and Understanding CHECK

1. Identify and compare the four main remedies against police officers who break the law.
2. Explain the remedy of criminal punishment and its effectiveness.
3. Identify the two major remedies granted in civil lawsuits.
4. Identify the sources of authority for civil lawsuits.

5. Describe and explain the significance of the doctrine of immunity.
6. List and explain the requirements of section 1983 actions.
7. Why is it more difficult to obtain relief from government units than from individuals?
8. Who has the final word in interpreting section 1983, and where are most 1983 actions brought?
9. List the requirements for suing local governing bodies.
10. Explain the nature of and the differences between internal and external review.
11. Identify the four stages of internal review.
12. Identify the four possible results of internal review procedures.
13. List the nine types of disciplinary actions that departments can take if complaints against the police are sustained.
14. Describe the review process following the initial disposition of complaints.
15. What is the fundamental objection to internal review?
16. Identify the central issues in external review.
17. Who favors and who opposes external review? Explain why.
18. Identify the points when unsworn officers might take part in external review.
19. Identify the three types of external review procedures.
20. List the three characteristics that are common to all three procedures.
21. Describe the positive approach to dealing with police misconduct.

Do Rules Against the Use of Force Make a Difference? Consideration

The number of unlawful shootings in Philadelphia remained high after the change restricting the use of force. Waegel concluded that changes in laws may not be enough. Reductions in unlawful shootings require changes in police behavior. Changes in police behavior will not take place unless police leadership insist, and by their example demonstrate, that they demand compliance with the rules. Consider the information in the "Policies and Practices Regarding Force" section. Do you favor simply the use of rules to regulate force or rules in addition to something else? Explain your answer.

CHAPTER CAPSULE

- The police have a strong working personality.
- The findings regarding recruitment, training, and promotion are mixed.
- Women police officers perform similarly to men officers.
- Minority and women officers have made advances since the 1960s but have not achieved equality with white men officers.
- Force is the defining characteristic of police work.
- Excessive force, not the use of force, is the problem in policing.
- Force includes everything from tightly grabbing a suspect's arm to shooting a suspect.
- Accountability for police misconduct can take the forms of criminal punishment, damages and injunctions, and disciplinary actions within the department.
- Few people win lawsuits against either individual police officers, police departments, or local government units.

KEY TERMS

police working personality
police academy
police war stories
police defensiveness
police depersonalization
field training
gender model of police attitudes
job model of police attitude
police stress
police misconduct
"rotten apple" theory
Dirty Harry problem
legitimate use of force
abuse of force
knockdown force
deadly force
police corruption
plaintiffs
damages
injunctions
torts
doctrine of official immunity
doctrine of *respondeat superior*
section 1983 actions
defense of qualified immunity
internal affairs units (IAU)
external review of police misconduct

INTERNET RESEARCH EXERCISES

Exercise: In your opinion, when is the use of police non-deadly force justified? When is it not? Search for information about the case of *Smith v. Mattox.* Was Officer Mattox guilty of police misconduct when he broke Anthony Smith's arm while arresting him?

Suggested site: *Smith v. Mattox,* http://www.law.emory.edu/11circuit/nov97/96-6648.opa.html

InfoTrac College Edition: Run a key word search on "Smith versus Mattox"

NOTES

1. Skolnick and Fyfe, *Above the Law;* Lawrence W. Sherman, "Reducing Police Gun Use: Critical Events, Administrative Policy and Organizational Change," in *The Management and Control of Police Organizations,* Maurice Punch, ed. (Cambridge: MIT Press, 1983), 98–125; *Report of the Independent Commission of the Los Angeles Police Department* (1991); William B. Waegel, "The Use of Lethal Force by Police: The Effect of Statutory Change," *Crime and Delinquency* 31 (1984): 121–40; all cited and discussed in Pate and Fridell, *Police Use of Force,* 26–27.
2. Lawrence W. Sherman et al., *Citizens Killed by Big City Police, 1970–1984* (Washington, D.C.: Crime Control Institute, 1986), 15.
3. Quoted in Jerome H. Skolnick and James J. Fyfe, *Above the Law: Police and the Excessive Use of Force* (New York: Free Press, 1993), 91.
4. William K. Muir, *Streetcorner Politicians* (Chicago: University of Chicago Press, 1977).
5. Summarized from John J. Broderick, *Police in a Time of Change,* 2d ed. (Prospect Heights, Ill.: Waveland Press), 10–11.
6. Ibid.
7. J. Snipes and Stephen Mastrofski, "An Empirical Test of Muir's Typology of Police Officers," *American Journal of Criminal Justice* 16 (1990): 268–96; Stephen M. Cox and James Frank, "The Influence of Neighborhood Context and Method of Entry on Individual Styles of Policing," *American Journal of Police* 11 (1992): 1–23.
8. Edward A. Thibault, Lawrence M. Lynch, and R. Bruce McBride, *Proactive Police Management* (Englewood Cliffs, N.J.: Prentice-Hall, 1985), 21; Richard J. Lundman, *Police and Policing* (New York: Holt, Rinehart & Winston, 1980), 73; Milton Rokeach et al., "The Value Gap Between Police and Policed," *Journal of Social Issues* 27, no. 2 (1971): 155–71; Bruce N. Carpenter and Susan M. Raza, "Personality Characteristics of Police Applicants: Comparisons Across Subgroups and with Other Populations," *Journal of Police Science and Administration* 15 (1987): 10–17.
9. President's Commission on Law Enforcement and the Administration of Justice, *The Challenge of Crime in a Free Society* (Washington, D.C.: U.S. Government Printing Office, 1967); Egon Bittner, "Some Reflections on Staffing Problem-Oriented Policing," *American Journal of Police* 9 (1990): 189–95.
10. Robert D. Meier and Richard E. Maxwell, "Psychological Screening of Police Candidates: Current Perspectives," *Journal of Police Science and Administration* 15 (1987): 210–15; Alan W. Benner, "Psychological Screening of Police Applicants," in *Critical Issues in Policing,* Roger C. Dunham and Geoffrey P. Alpert, eds. (Prospect Heights, Ill.: Waveland Press, 1989), 73; Geoffrey P. Alpert, "Hiring and Promoting Police Officers in Small Departments—The Role of Psychological Testing," *Criminal Law Bulletin* 27 (1991): 261–69; Benjamin S. Wright, William G. Doerner, and John C. Speier, "Pre-employment Psychological Testing as a Predictor of Police Performance During an FTO Program," *American Journal of Police* 9 (1990): 65–84.
11. Lundman, *Police and Policing,* 75–76.
12. International City/County Management Association, *Police Personnel Recruitment.*
13. Bittner, "Some Reflections on Staffing," 195.
14. David L. Carter, Allen D. Sapp, and Darrel W. Stephens, *The State of Police Education: Policy Direction for the 21st Century* (Washington, D.C.: Police Executive Research Forum, 1989).
15. All quoted in *New York Times,* 23 April 1990.
16. David L. Carter and Allen D. Sapp, *Police Education and Minority Recruitment: The Impact of a College Requirement* (Washington, D.C.: Police Executive Research Forum, 1991), 2–4; David L. Carter and Allen D. Sapp, "Higher Education as a Policy Alternative to Reduce Police Liability," *Police Liability Review* 2 (1990): 1–3.
17. Lawrence W. Sherman et al., *The Quality of Police Education* (San Francisco: Jossey-Bass, 1978); Robert E. Worden, "A Badge and a Baccalaureate: Policies, Hypotheses, and Further Evidence," *Justice Quarterly* 7 (1990): 565, 588–90.
18. Robert E. Worden, "The 'Causes' of Police Brutality," in *And Justice for All: Understanding and Controlling Police Use of Force,* William A. Geller and Hans Toch, eds. (Washington: Police Executive Research Forum, 1995), 45.
19. Victor E. Kappeler, Allen D. Sapp, and David L. Carter, "Police Officer Higher Education: Citizen Complaints and Rule Violations," *American Journal of Police* 11 (1992): 37–54.
20. Richard N. Harris, "The Police Academy and Professional Self-Image," in *Policing: A View from the Street,* Peter K. Manning and John Van Maanen, eds. (Santa Monica: Goodyear Press, 1978), 273–91; Lieutenant Gene Berry, "The Uniformed Crime Investigator," *Law Enforcement Bulletin* (March 1984): 1.
21. Herman Goldstein, *Policing a Free Society* (Cambridge, Mass.: Ballinger, 1977), 272.
22. William G. Doerner and E. Britt Patterson, "The Influence of Race and Gender upon Rookie Evaluations of Their Field Training Officers," *American Journal of Police* XI (1992): 31; Lundman, *Police and Policing,* 78–80.
23. Lundman, *Police and Policing,* 81–82.
24. Jonathan Rubenstein, *City Police* (New York: Farrar, Straus, and Giroux, 1973), 282.
25. Richard Harris, *The Police Academy: An Inside Story* (New York: John Wiley and Sons, 1973), 53.
26. David H. Bayley and Egon Bittner, "Learning the Skills of Policing," in *Critical Issues in Policing,* 93.

27. James J. Fyfe, "Training to Reduce Police-Civilian Violence," in *And Justice for All,* 164.
28. Ibid.
29. Ibid.
30. Doerner and Patterson, "Influence of Race and Gender," 25.
31. Michael S. McCampbell, *Field Training for Police Officers: State of the Art* (Washington, D.C.: National Institute of Justice, 1986).
32. John E. Boydstun, *San Diego Field Interrogation: Final Report* (Washington, D.C.: U.S. Government Printing Office, 1975), 11.
33. Boydstun, *San Diego Field Interrogation,* 263.
34. *Critical Issues in Policing,* 311.
35. Susan E. Martin, *Women on the Move? A Report of the Status of Women in Policing* (Washington, D.C.: Police Foundation, May 1989); U.S. Department of Justice, *Crime in the United States 1994* (Washington, D.C.: U.S. Government Printing Office, November 19, 1995), Table 74, p. 294.
36. Ibid.
37. Martin, "Female Officers," 316; The Police Foundation, *Policewomen on Patrol: Final Report* (Washington, D.C.: The Police Foundation, 1974); Catherine H. Milton, "The Future of Women in Policing," in *The Future of Policing,* Alvin W. Cohn, ed. (Beverly Hills, Calif.: Sage Publications, 1978), 196.
38. Alissa Pollitz Worden, "The Attitudes of Women and Men in Policing," 205–206.
39. Ibid., 228–29.
40. Peggy S. Sullivan, "Minority Officers: Current Issues," in *Critical Issues in Policing,* 331.
41. Samuel Walker, Cassia Spohn, and Miriam DeLonc, *The Color of Justice: Race, Ethnicity, and Crime in America* (Belmont, Calif.: Wadsworth, 1996), 110.
42. Samuel Walker, "Employment of Black and Hispanic Police Officers, 1983–1988: A Follow-up Study" (Omaha: University of Nebraska, Center for Applied Urban Research, February 1989).
43. *New York Times,* 10 September 1994.
44. Arlene Williams, National Organization of Black Law Enforcement Executives, *New York Times,* 23 April 1990.
45. Gail A. Goolkasian et al., *Coping with Police Stress* (Washington, D.C.: National Institute of Justice, 1985), 1.
46. Hans Selye, *The Stress of Life* (New York: McGraw- Hill, 1976).
47. Goolkasian, *Coping with Police Stress.*
48. Harold E. Russell and Alan Biegel, *Understanding Human Behavior for Effective Police Work,* 2d ed. (New York: Basic Books, 1982), 280–98.
49. Goolkasian, *Coping with Police Stress.*
50. Cited in Goolkasian, *Coping with Police Stress.*
51. James J. Fyfe, "The Split-Second Syndrome and Other Determinants of Police Violence," in *Critical Issues in Policing,* 465–79; Carl B. Klockars, "The Dirty Harry Problem," in *Thinking About Police,* 2d ed., Carl B. Klockars and Stephen D. Mastrofski, eds. (New York: McGraw-Hill, 1991), 413–23.
52. Paul Chevigny, *Edge of the Knife: Police Violence in the Americas* (New York: The New Press).
53. Anthony M. Pate and Lorie A. Fridell, *Police Use of Force: Official Reports, Citizen Complaints, and Legal Consequences,* Vol. I (Washington, D.C.: PERF, 1993), 5; Bittner quote on page 17.
54. Hubert Williams, "Foreword," 6–7, Anthony M. Pate and Lorie A. Fridell, *Police Use of Force: Official Reports, Citizen Complaints, and Legal Consequences,* Vol. I (Washington, D.C.: PERF, 1993).
55. Wayne A. Kerstetter, "Who Disciplines the Police? Who Should?" in *Police Leadership in America: Crisis and Opportunity,* William A. Geller, ed. (New York: Praeger, 1985), 149–82.
56. Los Angeles Police Department, *Training Bulletin* (September 1986).
57. Ibid., 5–6.
58. Greg Meyer, "Nonlethal Weapons Versus Conventional Police Tactics: The Los Angeles Police Department Experience" (Master's Thesis, California State University, Los Angeles, 1991), 59.
59. Quoted in Meyer, "Nonlethal Weapons," 20.
60. Quoted in Meyer, "Nonlethal Weapons."
61. Anthony M. Pate and Lorie A. Fridell, *Police Use of Force: Official Reports, Citizen Complaints, and Legal Consequences* (Washington, D.C.: Police Foundation, 1993), 21–25, 73–78.
62. Carl B. Klockars, "A Theory of Excessive Force and Its Control," in *And Justice for All,* 11–12.
63. James J. Fyfe, "Training to Reduce Police-Citizen Violence," in *And Justice for All,* 165.
64. Robert E. Worden, "The Causes of Police Brutality: Theory and Evidence," in *And Justice for All,* 31–60; Ross Lundstrom and Cynthia Mullen, "The Use of Force: One Department's Experience," *FBI Law Enforcement Bulletin* (January 1987): 6–9; Angus Campbell and Howard Schuman, "Racial Attitudes in Fourteen American Cities," *Supplemental Studies for the National Advisory Committee on Civil Disorders* (Washington, D.C.: U.S. Government Printing Office, 1969).
65. Ibid., 24.
66. Mark Blumburg, "Controlling Police Use of Deadly Force: Assessing Two Decades of Progress, " in *Critical Issues in Policing,* 443–44.
67. Ibid.
68. *Grudt v. Los Angeles,* 2 Cal.3d 575 (1970).
69. Lawrence O'Donnell, *Deadly Force* (New York: William Morrow Co., 1983), 14; Geller and Scott, *Deadly Force,* 59–60.
70. O'Donnell, *Deadly Force,* 14; William A. Geller, *Crime File: Deadly Force* (Washington, D.C.: National Institute of Justice, 1985); Milton, *Police Use of Deadly Force,* 10; James Fyfe quoted in O'Donnell, *Deadly Force,* 14; *Criminal Justice Newsletter,* 15 February 1996, 5.
71. Geller, *Crime File: Deadly Force.*
72. William A. Geller and Michael S. Scott, *Deadly Force: What We Know* (Washington, D.C.: Police Executive Research Foundation, 1992), 60; New York State Commission on Criminal Justice and the Use of Force, "Report to the Governor," Vol. I, (1987), reported in Geller and Scott.
73. Geller and Scott, *Deadly Force,* 143.
74. Ibid., 147–48.
75. Quoted in Geller and Scott, 152–53.
76. Ibid., 155.
77. Michael E. Donahue and Frank S. Horvath, "Police Shooting Outcomes: Suspect Criminal History and Incident Behaviors," *American Journal of Police,* 10 (1991): 21.
78. James J. Fyfe, "Blind Justice: Police Shootings in Memphis," *Journal of Criminal Law and Criminology* 73 (1982).
79. Jerry R. Sparger and David J. Giacopassi, "Memphis Revisited: A Reexamination of Police Shootings After the *Garner* Decision," *Justice Quarterly* 9 (1992): 211–25.
80. Independent Commission on the Los Angeles Police Department ("Christopher Commission"), *Report of the Independent Commission on the Los Angeles Police Department* (Los Angeles: Independent Commission on the Los Angeles Police Department, 1991), 80.
81. Skolnick and Fyfe, *Above the Law,* 11.
82. Geoffrey P. Alpert and Roger G. Dunham, *Police Pursuit Driving: Controlling Responses to Emergency Situations* (New York:

Greenwood Press, 1990), 38; Geoffrey P. Alpert, "Questioning Police Pursuits in Urban Areas," *Journal of Police Science and Administration* 15 (1987): 298–306.

83. Geoffrey P. Alpert, "Police Pursuits—Linking Data to Decisions," *Criminal Law Bulletin* 24 (1988): 453.

84. Quoted in Alpert, "Police Pursuits," 453–54.

85. Gordon E. Misner, "High-Speed Pursuits: Police Perspectives," *Criminal Justice, the Americas* (December/January 1990): 15.

86. Quoted in Misner, "High-Speed Pursuits."

87. Ibid.

88. Ibid., 17.

89. Hans Toch and J. Douglas Grant, *Police as Problem Solvers* (New York: Plenum Press, 1991), 214.

90. Discussed in Skolnick and Fyfe, *Above the Law,* 181–84.

91. Lawrence W. Sherman, *Scandal and Reform* (Berkeley: University of California Press, 1978), 30–31; Murphy quoted in Goldstein, *Policing a Free Society,* 201.

92. Ellwyn R. Stoddard, "Blue Coat Crime," in *Thinking About Police,* 340–41.

93. Goldstein, *Policing a Free Society,* chap. 2, 190–92.

94. Goldstein, *Policing a Free Society,* 197–99; Rubenstein, *City Police,* 382–83; Commission to Investigate Allegations of Police Corruption and the City's Anti-Corruptional Procedures, *Commission Report* (New York: Braziller, 1972), 5–6.

95. Commission to Investigate Allegations of Police Corruption.

96. *Susla v. State,* 311 Minn. 166, 247 N.W.2d 907, 912 (1976); *Pletan v. Gaines et al.,* 494 N.W.2d 38, 40 (Minn. 1992).

97. 42 U.S.C.A. sec. 1983 (1976).

98. 483 U.S. 635, 107 S.Ct. 3034, 97 L.Ed.2d 523 (1987).

99. *Monell v. New York City Department of Social Services,* 436 U.S. 658, 98 S.Ct. 2018, 56 L.Ed.2d 611 (1978).

100. Wayne R. LaFave, *Search and Seizure,* 2d ed. (St. Paul: West, 1987), 1:248–49.

101. David B. Griswold, "Complaints Against the Police: Predicting Dispositions," *Journal of Criminal Justice* 22 (1994): 215–21; Kerstetter, "Who Disciplines the Police?" in *Police Leadership in America: Crisis and Opportunity,* 149–82; Douglas W. Perez, *Common Sense About Police Review* (Philadelphia: Temple University Press, 1994), 87–88.

102. Perez, *Common Sense About Police Review,* 88–89.

103. Ibid., 92–93.

104. Ibid., 96.

105. Ibid., 96–97.

106. Samuel Walker and Vic W. Bumphus, "The Effectiveness of Civilian Review: Observations on Recent Trends and New Issues Regarding the Civilian Review of the Police," *American Journal of Police* XI (1992): 1.

107. Walker and Bumphus, "The Effectiveness of Civilian Review," 3–4.

108. Ibid., 4

109. Ibid.

110. Ibid., 8.

111. Pate and Fridell, *Police Use of Force,* 39.

112. Walker and Bumphus, "The Effectiveness of Civilian Review," 10.

113. Ibid., 16–17.

114. James Q. Wilson, *Thinking About Crime,* rev. ed. (New York: Basic Books, 1983), 112.

CHAPTER 9

Courts and Courtroom Work Groups

CHAPTER OUTLINE

Should "Guilty" Clients Have a Lawyer?[1]

According to the famous defense lawyer and commentator on the criminal justice system, Alan Dershowitz:

> Attorneys who defend the guilty and the despised will never have a secure or comfortable place in any society. Their motives will be misunderstood; they will be suspected of placing loyalty to clients above loyalty to society; and they will be associated in the public mind with the misdeeds of their clients. They will be seen as troublemakers and gadflies. The best of them will always be on the firing line, with their licenses exposed to attack.
>
> There will never be a Nobel Prize for defense attorneys who succeed in freeing the guilty. Indeed there are few prizes or honors ever bestowed on defense lawyers for their zealousness. The ranks of defense attorneys are filled with a mixed assortment of human beings from the most noble and dedicated to the most sleazy and corrupt. It is a profession that seems to attract extremes. The public sometimes has difficulty distinguishing between the noble and the sleazy; the very fact that a defense lawyer represents a guilty client leads some to conclude that the lawyer must be sleazy. Being so regarded is an occupational hazard of all zealous defense attorneys.

INTRODUCTION

Following arrest, if they are charged with crimes, suspects become defendants; decision making shifts from the police station to the criminal courts; and, lawyers play the leading roles and make most of the decisions. Formally, courts are legal institutions. They are "palaces of justice." In their courtrooms, aggressive prosecution and vigorous defense, umpired by judges applying the rule of law, are supposed to ensure that truth and justice will win out.[2]

Informally, most decision making takes place in the corridors and behind closed doors; and courts are political and social, as much as they are legal, institutions. Courts pay attention to and respond to the needs and demands of the public, interest groups, and individuals. Witness the enormous increase in drug offense cases that reach the criminal courts, due in large part to public demands to "crack down on drug dealers." Courts rely upon discretionary decision making to balance the law and extralegal professional, organizational, political, and societal goals. This discretionary decision making affects and often circumvents formal decision making. In reality, formal court proceedings merely ratify what lawyers and other criminal justice personnel have already decided informally. The visible, open, publicized formal court proceedings governed by the rule of law mask the leading role that discretionary decision making plays in the courts.[3]

CRIMINAL COURTS

Criminal courts are arranged into three tiers (Figure 9.1):

Lower criminal courts: courts with the power to decide minor cases and to conduct pretrial proceedings.

Trial courts: courts with the power to conduct pretrial and trial proceedings in all criminal cases.

Appellate courts: courts with the authority to review the decisions of trial and lower criminal courts.

Lower Criminal Courts

Lower criminal courts are called by various names, such as superior, municipal, county, justice of the peace, and magistrate's courts. They are courts of **limited jurisdiction,** meaning that their authority is limited to trying misdemeanor cases and conducting preliminary proceedings in felony cases. Formally, defendants in lower criminal courts have the same rights as defendants in trial courts. In practice, however, judges try most cases less formally than trial courts; and they try them without juries. Lower criminal courts are not **courts of record**—that is, they do not keep written records of proceedings unless defendants pay for them.

The lower courts decide the great bulk of criminal cases, which consist of minor crimes, such as traffic offenses, drunk and disorderly conduct, shoplifting, and prostitution. Hence, they are the first and, in most instances, the only contact most

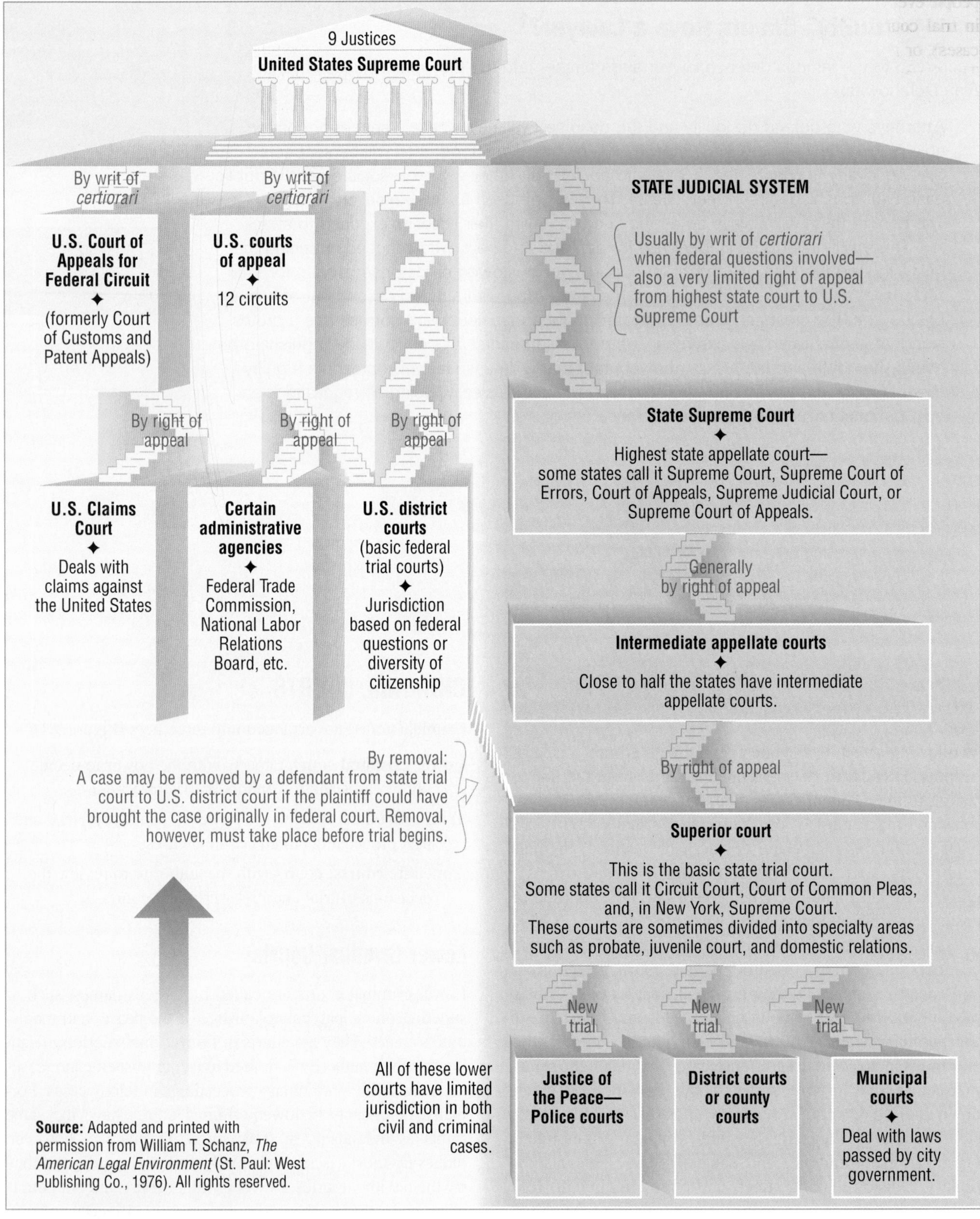
9 Justices
United States Supreme Court
By writ of certiorari
By writ of certiorari
STATE JUDICIAL SYSTEM
U.S. Court of Appeals for Federal Circuit ✦ (formerly Court of Customs and Patent Appeals)
U.S. courts of appeal ✦ 12 circuits
Usually by writ of certiorari when federal questions involved—also a very limited right of appeal from highest state court to U.S. Supreme Court
By right of appeal
By right of appeal
By right of appeal
State Supreme Court ✦ Highest state appellate court—some states call it Supreme Court, Supreme Court of Errors, Court of Appeals, Supreme Judicial Court, or Supreme Court of Appeals.
U.S. Claims Court ✦ Deals with claims against the United States
Certain administrative agencies ✦ Federal Trade Commission, National Labor Relations Board, etc.
U.S. district courts (basic federal trial courts) ✦ Jurisdiction based on federal questions or diversity of citizenship
Generally by right of appeal
Intermediate appellate courts ✦ Close to half the states have intermediate appellate courts.
By removal: A case may be removed by a defendant from state trial court to U.S. district court if the plaintiff could have brought the case originally in federal court. Removal, however, must take place before trial begins.
By right of appeal
Superior court ✦ This is the basic state trial court. Some states call it Circuit Court, Court of Common Pleas, and, in New York, Supreme Court. These courts are sometimes divided into specialty areas such as probate, juvenile court, and domestic relations.
New trial
New trial
New trial
All of these lower courts have limited jurisdiction in both civil and criminal cases.
Justice of the Peace—Police courts
District courts or county courts
Municipal courts ✦ Deal with laws passed by city government.
Source: Adapted and printed with permission from William T. Schanz, The American Legal Environment (St. Paul: West Publishing Co., 1976). All rights reserved.

Figure 9.1
State Judicial System

people ever have with the criminal courts. Defendants appear in trial courts only for criminal trials (about 2 out of 100 cases), or rarer still, in appellate courts on criminal appeals. The lower criminal courts also perform a number of other tasks, including:

- Decide bail.
- Assign lawyers to indigent defendants.
- Conduct pretrial proceedings, including preliminary hearings to test the government's case against defendants, and hearings to decide the legality of confessions, searches, and seizures.

Lower criminal courts vary greatly across the country and even within jurisdictions. Some limits are formally created by state legislatures. Most states limit the jurisdiction of lower courts to misdemeanors. Forty-two percent of lower criminal courts can impose a maximum $500 fine; 39 percent can set fines in excess of $500; 19 percent can levy fines of only up to $100. Informally, community standards, local politics, city size, and local culture create differences in proceedings from one jurisdiction to another, from one court to another in the same jurisdiction, and even from one courtroom to another in the same courthouse. Disorderly conduct and drunk driving may predominate in some courts; prostitution may take up the time of others. Some courtrooms may conduct only first appearances, and others only preliminary hearings.[4]

In about two-thirds of lower court systems, judges are not required to be members of the bar. Some states require these judges to attend training courses or pass an examination. However, the judges in lower courts will have less training than the least experienced lawyers who appear before them. Some states require only a high school diploma to qualify for membership on the bench of the lower courts. The Constitution does not require that lower criminal court judges have legal training.

In *North v. Russell,* the Supreme Court held that trials before nonlawyer judges do not deny defendants charged with misdemeanors due process of law. In that case, Lonnie North was tried, convicted, and sentenced to a term of imprisonment in a Kentucky criminal trial presided over by Judge C. B. Russell, "a coal miner without any legal training or education whatever," who testified that he had only a high school education, was not familiar with the Kentucky rules of criminal procedure, and did not know the rights guaranteed to criminal defendants by the U.S. Constitution. Nevertheless, the Supreme Court ruled that the proceeding did not deny North his right to due process of law. According to David A. Harriss, "many lower court judges are marginally qualified to rule on complex legal issues, decide guilt or innocence, and pass sentence."[5]

Trial Courts

The criminal trial receives the most public attention, even though it is the rarest of all judicial events. (Chapter 11 discusses the criminal trial.) These trials take place in courts known variously as district or circuit courts. Trial courts are courts of **general jurisdiction,** meaning that they have the authority to hear and decide all criminal cases from capital felonies to petty misdemeanors. Trial courts decide felony cases, over which they have both exclusive and original jurisdiction. **Original jurisdiction** means that **adjudication** (court proceedings) begins in trial courts. **Exclusive jurisdiction** means that only the trial courts can adjudicate these cases. Trial courts adhere to formal rules more than lower criminal courts do. They permit only members of the bar to preside as judges; and they are courts of record.

Appellate Courts

Appellate courts hear and decide appeals of trial court decisions. Proceedings in the appellate court are the most formal of all three levels of courts. The federal judiciary and 39 states have a two-tiered appellate structure. Intermediate appellate courts hear most initial appeals. They decide whether the government has proved all elements of crimes beyond a reasonable doubt, and whether defendants have carried their burden in establishing their defenses. Supreme courts, or courts of last resort, review intermediate appellate court decisions, complicated questions of law, and the constitutional rights of criminal defendants.

There is no *constitutional* right to a review of lower court decisions. But, all jurisdictions by law allow defendants to have the decisions of lower courts reviewed by courts of appeals. Many states allow the automatic appeal of death sentences. Overturning the decisions of the lower courts does not automatically end the matter. The government can retry defendants. State appellate courts decide about 80 percent of all appeals.

The U.S. Supreme Court decides about 150 cases a year complete with a full written opinion. The principal mechanism for review in federal cases is by writs of *habeas corpus* and *certiorari.* The petition for a **writ of *habeas corpus,*** meaning, literally, "you have the body," asks for review on the grounds that a detention facility has unlawfully detained a prisoner. These reviews rarely succeed.[6]

In the petition for a **writ of *certiorari,*** literally, an order "to certify the record" of a lower court, defendants ask appellate courts to review proceedings of lower courts. The U.S. Supreme Court practices the **rule of four** in petitions for *certiorari.* If four justices decide that the Court should grant the petition and issue the writ, then the Court will hear the case. The Court usually agrees to review cases for two reasons:

1. There is a conflict among the U.S. Circuit Courts (the intermediate federal appellate courts).
2. There is an important constitutional question that has not been resolved.

CRIMINAL COURT MISSIONS

Society demands much of its criminal courts. They are supposed to balance the demands for justice according to the rule of law and the demands of professional, organizational, political, and societal interests. The formal demands include the expectation that the criminal court will, according to the great, early twentieth-century jurist Roscoe Pound,

> meet society's demand that serious offenders be convicted and punished, and at the same time it is expected to insure that the innocent and the unfortunate are not oppressed. It is expected to control the application of force against the individual by the state, and it is expected to find which of two conflicting versions of events is the truth. And so the court is not merely an operating agency, but one that has a vital educational and symbolic significance. It is expected to articulate the community's most deeply held, most cherished views about the relationship of the individual and society. The formality of the trial and the honor accorded the robed judge bespeak the symbolic importance of the court and its work.[7]

In day-to-day operations, informal professional, organizational, and societal goals receive higher priority than the formal goals outlined in the quote from Roscoe Pound. Since the middle of the nineteenth century, observers have noted that the lower criminal courts in particular fail to live up to their high formal responsibilities. In the courts of large cities, cramped, noisy, and undignified courtrooms hurry defendants through important decisions in the most perfunctory manner.[8]

In the 1950s, Professor Caleb Foote observed one Philadelphia magistrate who decided 55 cases in 15 minutes. Four defendants were tried, convicted, and sentenced in 17 seconds! The magistrate accomplished this by merely reading off the defendant's name, taking one look at him, and saying, "Three months." In the 1970s, in another city, magistrates decided 72 percent of the cases before them in less than a minute each, according to a sociologist who systematically observed the court's proceedings for three months. Most reports indicate that things have not changed much since these observations.[9]

According to Professor Harry I. Subin, the New York criminal court in 1993 was

> overwhelmed by a flood of cases . . . [and, therefore] accomplishes very little. It does not dispense justice. It simply disposes of each day's business in any way it can, so it can be ready to dispose of the next day's business. And because substantive action would slow things down, the court very rarely conducts legal proceedings or imposes punishment on the guilty.[10]

Nothing much has changed since Professor Foote's study. During the 1990s, the Manhattan lower criminal court disposed of most cases in less than 4 minutes.[11]

Use *Your* Discretion

Is speed necessarily bad?

Observers express conflicting views regarding this emphasis on informality and speed. According to one experienced trial judge, "For many years I have been dismayed by the fact that [most criminal] cases were allocated only fifteen to twenty minutes." The emphasis on speed, according to critics, has produced "assembly-line justice," not the deliberation that justice requires.

But Stephen J. Schulhofer, who observed lower criminal courts in Philadelphia for several months, reached a different conclusion. After allowing for individual differences in judges, prosecutors, and defense attorneys, he found that magistrates conduct misdemeanor trials according to genuine adversarial proceedings. Even though it took only 25 minutes on the average, and often less than 10 minutes, to decide these cases, Schulhofer concluded that they received all the time needed to decide them fairly and accurately. Judges listened carefully to witnesses, often taking notes.[12]

Judges and attorneys, according to Schulhofer, took the rules of evidence seriously. Attorneys raised objections, and judges often sustained them [the objections] at the price of slowing down the trial. In a simple assault case, Judge KA sustained several defense objections to the form of the prosecutor's direct examination. At the end of the trial, KA made much of the prosecutor's ineptitude and said he found it "hard to believe that this case went on for half an hour or an hour." (In fact, the trial had consumed 22 minutes.)[13]

Thomas W. Church, Jr., observed four criminal courts in the Bronx, Detroit, Miami, and Pittsburgh. He found the adversary system alive and well in the local legal culture of those courts:

> by observing the obvious distaste many lawyers working in a prosecuting attorney's office seem to have for the defense side in general, a feeling often reciprocated by defense attorneys. (Possibly the most graphic evidence of this antipathy came during the summer I was conducting interviews in Miami when the annual prosecutor-public defender softball game degenerated into a fist fight.) After years of scholars' debunking the "adversary myth," it may be that the adversary system is in need of . . . bunking."[14]

CRITICAL THINKING

1. List all of the facts and conclusions regarding speed in the criminal courts.
2. Do you believe that speedy decisions hurt criminal defendants? Use the facts and conclusions from the list you made to back up your answer.

Due Process

The due process mission of the criminal courts consists of making sure that all proceedings are fundamentally fair. This commitment to due process originated in the abuses of royal power in colonial America. The founders of our constitutional system were charged with a heavy dose of suspicion about the power of government (Chapter 1). They wrote into the U.S. Constitution principles intended to impose strict rules of procedure governing criminal procedures because they believed that following the rules is more important than obtaining the right result in individual cases. The old saying, "It is better that ten guilty persons go free than to punish one innocent person," expresses the idea in popular terms.[15]

Due process is also based on the **adversary system,** sometimes called the "sporting theory of justice." Prosecutors represent the government, and defense attorneys represent the accused. Both fight vigorously for the victory of their sides. As adversaries on opposite sides of a case, each presents only his or her side. However, they are not allowed to win at any cost. They have to fight according to the rules set out in the laws and constitutions of the state and federal governments. In this struggle or, more politely, contest or game, judges preside as umpires, impartially enforcing the rules. Juries, armed with the instructions in the law as explained by judges and their own common sense, sort out facts from fiction. This image reflects the highest ideals of American justice—an open, fair, impartial, dignified conflict that sorts out the guilty from the innocent, punishing one and vindicating the other.[16]

The adversary system assumes that through free and open competition over the facts, the truth will triumph. However, these time-consuming legal functions cannot easily take place in the face of pressures to achieve countervailing informal goals. The adversary system never operated fully according to its ideals. Its emphasis on individual rights and limited government power secured by judicial proceedings not only differed from eighteenth-century practices, but was also cumbersome, inefficient, and slow. Formal judicial proceedings were rigid and, ironically, did not allow for individual differences.

Even in rural, sparsely populated, homogenous eighteenth-century America, the adversary system presented major drawbacks. The problems worsened when society became predominantly urban and industrial, when immigrants of many different ethnic origins crowded into cities and factories, and when values shifted from extolling individual rights to meeting the demand for order. The state was no longer an object of suspicion, but instead became an instrument for social order and the "reform" of individuals. Courts that convicted innocent people were no longer the problem, critics warned; rather, the problem was a legal system that set criminals free because of individual rights that made it virtually impossible to convict them.[17]

By the early twentieth century, the due process functions of the criminal courts faced increasing challenges from societal demands for order, the growing need for efficient, economical administration, and the expanding requirements of a complex, modern criminal court bureaucracy. As a result, informal action more consistent with achieving crime control, efficiency, economy, and internal organizational goals began to supplant formal due process goals in criminal courts.[18]

Crime Control

Due process emphasizes the individual interest in privacy, liberty, and property. Crime control gives primacy to society's interest in crime control (see Chapter 3). Formal legal rules limit the crime control mission of courts, but these rules by no means eliminate it. Thus, friction between formal due process and informal crime control often arises. Crime control assumes a harsher image than due process. It is based on the idea that the "nasty, brutish" side of life gets portrayed in criminal courts. Courts are supposed to punish thieves, muggers, rapists, and burglars because of the pain and suffering they have already wrought in the lives of their victims and the fears they have spawned in those who might be next.

One typical judge said, "There's no use kidding yourself. We have a particular type of clientele in this court: The criminal court is a cesspool of poverty." The public expects criminal justice to punish these "bad" people. Prosecutors are supposed to be ruthless, defense lawyers should not be allowed to "get their clients off on technicalities," and judges should not be "soft on criminals" or "handcuff the police" in their fight against crime (Chapter 1).[19]

Organizational

Neither the due process nor the crime control missions completely describes the reality of criminal courts. Criminal courts are complex organizations in which neither due process nor crime control triumphs as the ultimate goal. Due process and the whole rubric of formal rules and procedures cannot work precisely as legal theorists say. Justice is a vague goal, subject to widely differing interpretations. The due process goals that favor criminal defendants often conflict with the crime control goals that call for enforcing the law and protecting society. Moreover, no agreed-on method can achieve all these goals, even if their definitions were clear and not in conflict. No one really knows for sure what "works" to control crime, protect society, and restrain individuals all at the same time.

In addition, the courts operate within a constantly shifting and uncertain environment not entirely under their control. The public changes its mind about what it wants from courts; budgets shrink and expand unpredictably; and, most of all, different types of people come before the courts. In such circumstances as multiple and conflicting goals, unproved and uncertain methods, and a shifting and unpredictable environment, making decisions according to uniform rules and procedures is impossible. Informality permits necessary flexibility to make discretionary judgments in these fluid situations.[20]

Bureaucratic

Courts are bureaucratic organizations. Bureaucracies place high premiums on administrative values, especially efficiency, economy, and speed. The pride some judges take in managing case dispositions well reflects this high regard for bureaucratic values. A New York State chief judge's summary of his achievements shows his pride and satisfaction:

> New York has become one of the few states where the courts are disposing of more cases than they are taking on. We've made the courts more manageable. The courts are working much better than they did, they're producing much more, and they're more nearly up to date than they were six years ago.[21]

Social Service

In addition to their legal and organizational functions, courts also act as social service agencies. In this capacity, they seek what is "best" for the victims and offenders who appear in court. As one Pittsburgh judge put it, "We don't sentence the crime, we sentence the offender; so you have to consider the person first." Another said, "You have to consider what type of person [the defendant] is. I try to glean from the background, the kind of woman he is married to, from the nature of his offense, from his relationship to his children and from his associations." Adopting this approach, one judge granted probation to an armed robber because he learned that the victim provoked the defendant. Furthermore, he was also favorably impressed because the defendant's wife was a "neatly dressed woman in her twenties who appeared mature and seemed to have a settling effect on the defendant."[22]

Using this **substantial justice approach,** judges look at each case individually to award "meaningful justice." The substantial justice approach emphasizes informal criminal justice. According to the approach, formal rules can actually impede doing substantial justice; individual cases do not always fit the prescribed rules of criminal law and criminal procedure. Extenuating and aggravating circumstances and differing individual needs call for different procedures and results, so the substantial justice approach relies heavily on discretion.[23]

Sometimes, the social service and legal functions of courts are integrated. The tension between law and discretion usually prevents bringing these functions into the open. However, the extraordinary growth in the caseload of drug cases led Dade County, Florida, to establish a special Drug Court. The Miami Drug Court Model is a hybrid that combines "elements of both criminal justice and drug treatment." According to John S. Goldkamp and Doris Weiland, guiding the creation of the drug court was the "notion that an effective and flexible program of court-supervised drug treatment could reduce demand for illicit drugs and hence involvement in crime and reinvolvement in the court system."[24]

The Miami Drug Court accepts only defendants without prior convictions who are charged with third-degree felony drug possession. Goldkamp and Weiland examined a sample cohort of defendants for a period of 18 months. Their research produced a number of positive findings, including:

- Far fewer Drug Court defendants than other felony drug and nondrug defendants were sentenced to incarceration for longer than one year.
- Drug Court defendants generated far fewer rearrest rates than other felony drug defendants.
- When Drug Court defendants were rearrested, the length of time to their first rearrest averaged from two to three times longer than that of comparison groups.
- Drug Court defendants had a higher rate of failure to appear for court appearances, but this was due to the far higher number of times that the court required Drug Court defendants to appear.[25]

COURTHOUSE WORK GROUP

The major organizational mission of the criminal courts is the efficient, economic, and quick disposition of cases. Harmony within the court organization is also a goal. Discretion and negotiation, not the adversary process according to written rules, are the means to achieve these goals. Prosecutors, judges, and defense attorneys form a **courthouse work group,** or "courtroom elite," whose primary mission is the disposition of criminal cases. The large number of cases in most criminal courts makes this goal difficult to achieve, particularly in cumbersome formal adversary proceedings. Legally prescribed "speedy trial" requirements aggravate the pressures created by heavy caseloads.[26]

Case disposition takes place within a close working and personal environment. Judges, prosecutors, and defense attorneys see each other regularly, have similar backgrounds, and many have similar career aspirations. They have much more in common than the adversary process suggests. According to Peter F. Nardulli, who has extensively studied the courtroom work group:

> In many [Chicago] courtrooms daily sessions were frequently preceded (as well as followed) by "coffee klatches" held in the judge's chambers. The coffee klatches were usually attended by the judge, public defender, the two assistant attorneys and a handful of private defense attorneys, who may or may not have had a case in that courtroom on the day in question. Conversations ranged from the fate of the Blackhawks or Bulls the night before, the potential impact of some changes in criminal law or procedure, the cases scheduled for that day, to what happened in the annual football game between the state's attorney's office and the public defender's office. "War stories" concerning unusual criminal cases in which the various participants had been involved were also related frequently, and occasionally some political gossip was exchanged. Oftentimes these klatches evolved into plea bargaining

> sessions involving concerned participants, with opinions and comments by bystanders freely registered. In short, these sessions were not unlike those that might take place in any office or shop.[27]

After interviewing more than 500 judges, prosecutors, and defense attorneys in major cities throughout the country, Paul B. Wice concluded:

> Despite their locations in a hectic urban setting, the criminal courts which I visited seemed like traditional villages. The high level of intimacy and frequency of interaction between nearly all of the courtroom work group made many defendants and outsiders unfamiliar with the court's inner workings incredulous as to the possible existence of adversary proceeding. Although the "kibitzing" is curtailed during the time when court is in session, it is never completely absent. In the hallways, around the snackbars, in the courtrooms during recesses, and before and after the day's business, the friendly joshing never seems to end. Whether this exaggerated conviviality serves as a type of necessary social lubricant to disguise actual tensions, or is an accurate measure of their camaraderie, is difficult to discern. Whichever purpose it serves, it is an omnipresent style of interaction that typified almost every city visited.[28]

Amid the relationships of the courtroom work group, defendants are alien even to their lawyers who, like the judges and prosecutors, rarely question their clients' guilt. Particularly if cases have gone beyond the charging state (Figure 1.1), judges, prosecutors, and defense lawyers usually agree that defendants have committed some offense. All they have left to do is agree on a punishment. The desire to dispose of cases stems from a variety of reasons:

- The large volume of cases, all with deadlines.
- The large number of routine cases.
- The preference for amicable negotiation and settlement to haggling and dispute.
- The pull of other business.

In view of these common goals, due process and crime control have to share with informal missions of the courtroom work group. The common goal to dispose of cases and the desire and need to maintain a continuing positive work group relationship softens formal role conflicts among prosecutors, defense counsel, and judges.[29]

Herbert Jacob and James Eisenstein describe the desire for "group cohesion" and some of its consequences:

> Pervasive conflict is not only unpleasant; it also makes work more difficult. Cohesion produces a sense of belonging and identification that satisfies human needs. It is maintained in several ways. Courtroom work groups shun outsiders because of their potential threat to group cohesion. The work group possesses a variety of adaptive techniques to minimize the effect of abrasive participants. For instance, the occasional defense attorney who violates routine cooperative norms may be punished by having to wait until the end of the day to argue his motion; he may be given less time than he wishes for a lunch break in the middle of a trial; he may be kept beyond usual court hours for bench conferences. Likewise, unusually adversarial defense or prosecuting attorneys are likely to smooth over their formal conflicts with informal cordiality. Tigers at the bench, they become tame kittens in chambers and in the hallways, exchanging pleasantries and exuding sociability.[30]

The "justice" negotiated behind the scenes in the courthouse corridors, judges' chambers, or even the restrooms overshadows the criminal trial that looms so large on television and movie screens. "Justice by consent"—so important to a smooth-functioning organization—dominates the criminal courts, not the much-touted criminal trial. This informal reality, in which crime control and due process share the work group's own agenda and relationships, confuses citizens, often to the point of resentment and bitterness. "Deals" that prosecutors and defense attorneys make and that judges approve are inconsistent, or so they appear to be, with both due process and crime control.[31]

As parts of an organization, judges, prosecutors, and defense attorneys do not oppose each other in competition for the truth. They are a team, negotiating the best settlement possible with minimal dispute and maximum harmony within the courtroom work group. They have the largely thankless task of doing what they can to balance an array of competing, often irreconcilable, demands and values. Such balancing rarely satisfies anyone because no one gets everything he or she wants—that is the meaning of settlement, as opposed to victory. In the adversary system, the goal is victory, and there is always a winner, or at least it seems that way from the outside. In the negotiation process, the goal is settlement, and the result is always at best "only half a loaf." Negotiation and settlement should not suggest injustice. They can represent the best resolution to a complex problem.[32]

Judges

"The decision as to who will make the decisions affects what decisions will be made," Jack Peltason, scholar of federal courts, wrote more than 40 years ago. The statement is still true. Even though we pride ourselves on being a "government of laws" and not individuals, judges play a major policymaking role in American criminal justice. Since the personal characteristics of judges affect decision making, it is important to know something about these characteristics.[33]

The personal characteristics of judges vary significantly. In a major study of urban criminal court judges, Martin A. Levin compared judges in Minneapolis and Pittsburgh. In Minneapolis, middle-class, Protestant men, who before becoming judges had practiced law in firms representing business and corporate interests, dominate the bench. They have had little or no outside experience with the clients who dominate the criminal courts. They are deeply committed to uniform, predictable rules and procedures. Most Pittsburgh judges, on the other hand, have mainly working-class, ethnic backgrounds. They have had direct life contact with the typical court client. Pittsburgh judges favor informal justice that tailors decisions to the needs of individual defendants. Judges in Pittsburgh tailor justice to societal interests, and interpret legal rules to do so. Despite these differences, most judges are upper middle-class, white, male Protestants with a better than average education.[34]

Jurisdictions select judges by three methods: popular election, appointment, and the merit plan. Thirty-two states elect judges—some in partisan, others in nonpartisan elections. Thirty-seven states and the federal government appoint judges; the president nominates and the Senate approves federal judges; governors appoint state judges. Twenty-two states select judges according to the merit system or the Missouri Bar Plan. (Missouri created the merit plan idea in 1940 to overcome the widespread use of political patronage in judicial selection.) In the merit system, lawyers, citizens, and an incumbent judge make up a commission that draws up the list of nominees. From this list, governors appoint judges to their brief initial term. After that, judges must face the electorate. The ballot asks simply whether to retain sitting judges. If approved, judges serve until the next election.[35]

Minneapolis typifies the merit system, Pittsburgh the election system. Minneapolis judges appear on the ballot, but they do not campaign. The governor appoints them to an interim term; the voters approve their appointment at the next election. Governors may appoint judges from their own party, but they generally choose nominal Democrats or Republicans who do not actively participate in party activities. Campaign literature never mentions judges' party affiliations. Pittsburgh judges run for office in the traditional way. Billboards advertise their candidacy; they openly and vocally run as Democrats or Republicans.[36]

Controversy over the merit and election systems can run high. For example, Chief Justice John Hill of the Texas Supreme Court proposed a merit system for Texas in 1987. Pressures from the development of a two-party system, the increasing specialization of the bar, and the growth of urban counties spurred the chief justice to act. The proposal failed. Some attorneys, politicians, minority and women's groups, and the populist tradition of electing most state officials blocked the plan.[37]

Supporters of the merit system argue that selection based on party loyalty precludes impartial judging. Competence in the law and the ability to judge according to it are the only acceptable criteria for judgeships. Supporters of the elective system promote its democracy. Elected judges are responsive and responsible to the community they serve. If they fail to meet community needs and standards, the voters will remove them. Judicial decisions ought to reflect politically sensitive judgments about community values.[38]

A variety of interest groups—political parties, bar associations, businesses, police unions, civil rights organizations—debate and try to influence the selection of judges because of the power of judges to shape criminal justice policy. These groups want that policy shaped to benefit their particular interests. Members of women's and minority groups, like other interest groups, seek the appointment of women and minority judges who will represent their interests. Minority groups especially feel the need for representation on state courts because they are most likely to come in contact with state criminal justice.

Figure 9.2
Year African American State Court Judges Received Judgeship

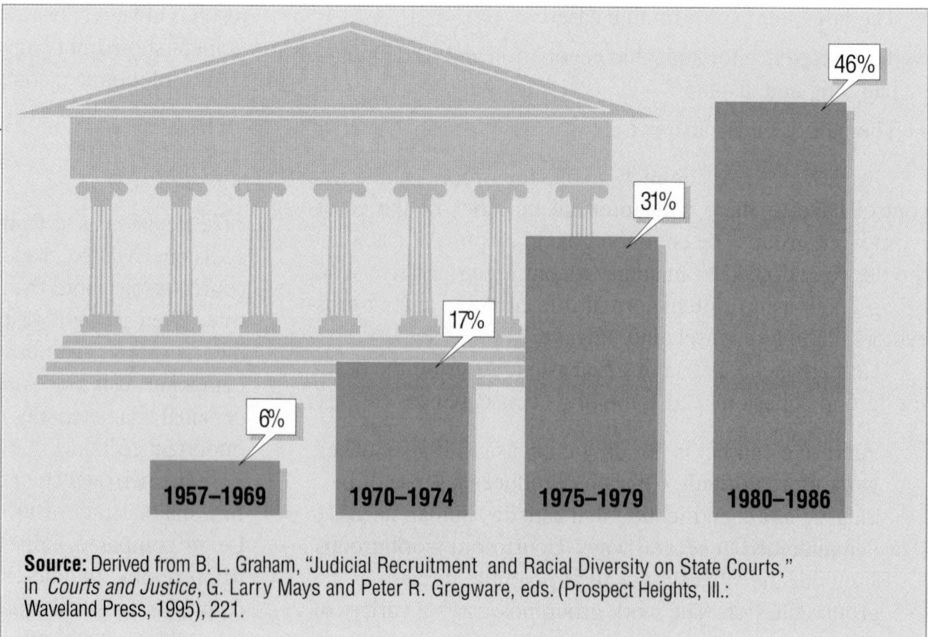

Source: Derived from B. L. Graham, "Judicial Recruitment and Racial Diversity on State Courts," in *Courts and Justice*, G. Larry Mays and Peter R. Gregware, eds. (Prospect Heights, Ill.: Waveland Press, 1995), 221.

The number of women judges is growing. Though little research has been done on the possible effects of gender on judicial decision making, one study has found that in criminal cases female judge's decisions differed little from those of their male counterparts.

Barbara Luck Graham analyzed data derived from a list of African American judges compiled by the Joint Study for Political Studies and the Judicial Council of the National Bar Association and from information provided by the clerks and administrators of state courts of general and limited jurisdiction. She found that African American judges are underrepresented on state courts, making up about 3.6 percent of all seats. She also found that most African American judges either serve on the lower criminal courts or are quasi-judicial officials. However, she also found that the rate of appointment for African American judges is improving (Figure 9.2).

It is not clear whether the explanation for the underrepresentation of African Americans on state courts is due to structural or other reasons. Some research suggests that judicial selection procedures favor the selection of white judges. Other research suggests that the relatively small number of African American attorneys explains the small number of African American judges. Whatever the reason, despite the significant gains that African American attorneys have made in securing selection to state courts, they are still significantly underrepresented.[39]

Women have served as lower court judges since 1870. The first woman was elected to a trial court in 1921. By 1940, 21 states had women judges; by 1950, the number had risen to 29. The best estimates indicate that by 1991, about 8 percent of state and 9 percent of federal judges were women. By the year 2000, estimates are that women will make up nearly 50 percent of all lawyers and that the number of women judges will also increase. Little empirical research, however, indicates what effect gender has on judicial decision making. The only available research suggests that male judges sentence women defendants more leniently than they do men. One study found that although women were more "liberal" in sex discrimination cases, their decisions in criminal cases differed little from the decisions of men.[40]

Prosecutors

Prosecutors may be the most powerful member of the courtroom work group. Why? According to Professor of Criminal Justice Candace McCoy:

> The prosecutor is the government's representative and advocate in all phases of criminal adjudication. Except for the daily operations of public police, prosecution is the most powerful component of the criminal justice process because of the number of offenders and victims it affects and because it dominates decision making about the legal course of every case. In the United States, the prosecutor reviews the cases of all defendants arrested by the police, exercises independent investigatory powers, determines the factual and legal sufficiency of each case and whether to dismiss or pursue it, officially files the charges, negotiates the conditions of guilty pleas, and serves as the trial attorney whose client is the state.[41]

Prosecutors are a vital link between police and courts, and courts and corrections. Police in nearly every jurisdiction in the country bring arrests to prosecutors' offices, not to courts. Prosecutors, not judges, decide whether these cases ever get to court. Enormous power results from this nexus. Prosecutors can bring police work to a halt and render courts and corrections powerless by failing to charge. Even when they charge, they shape the course of events by what specific offenses they choose to prosecute, by what arrangements they make with defense attorneys, and by what sentences they recommend to judges.[42]

Prosecution in the United States is extremely local. Counties elect local prosecutors. In 1996, the latest available figures, 2,343 local prosecutors' offices employed about 71,000 attorneys, investigators, and support staff—an increase of 25 percent over 1992. About 75 percent of chief prosecutors held full-time positions.[43]

There are two reasons why U.S. prosecution is local:

1. American colonists resisted appointment of prosecutors by English kings.
2. The colonists opposed private prosecutors because they flouted the principle of equal access to justice.

So, following the Revolution, the United States implemented public prosecution—locally elected prosecutors paid for by public funds were put in charge of law enforcement. American prosecutors are unique in that they are wholly public officials.[44]

The federal system, in contrast, includes an attorney general appointed by the president who appoints a U.S. Attorney in charge of the 94 federal districts. Despite this uniform centralized formal system, informally, practice varies dramatically among the districts. Especially, in Professor McCoy's words, "considering that the U.S. attorneys in each district are drawn from the ranks of the party faithful with close ties to local political constituencies."[45]

Missions

Prosecutors pursue multiple and conflicting missions. Formally, they are the chief law enforcement officer in the criminal courts. More than 60 years ago, U.S. Supreme Court Justice Sutherland described their function in a classic statement:

> The mission of the prosecutor is not that he shall win a case, but that justice shall be done. As such, he is in a peculiar and very definite sense the servant of the law, the twofold aim of which is that guilt shall not escape or innocence suffer. He may prosecute with earnestness and vigor—indeed, he should do so. But, while he may strike hard blows, he is not at liberty to strike foul ones.[46]

Prosecutors are also office administrators—forming policy and managing cases and their office staff. Further, they are also careerists. As such, they prepare to run for higher public office, enter lucrative and prestigious private practice, or simply maintain comfortable working conditions until they retire. These formal legal goals and informal organizational and personal goals are not always in harmony. They require prosecutors to perform multiple functions, as well as to relate to various other criminal justice agencies, each of which has different goals and priorities.

The informal missions of prosecutors revolve around their role as head of an independent criminal justice agency, the prosecutor's office, or variously the county, district, and city attorneys' offices. Heads of prosecutors' offices hold exclusive power to charge arrested suspects with crimes, to divert them into some social service agency such as drug or alcohol counseling, or to drop the matter altogether, thus effectively terminating the criminal justice process. We discuss these largely discretionary decisions in Chapter 10. The formal role of prosecutors centers on their position as officers of the court, bound by the rules governing adjudication. To understand prosecutors fully, remember that they act as administrative heads of organizations with broad discretion and as officers of the court are subject to judicial supervision following charges.[47]

Law Enforcement

Prosecutors choose what crimes and suspects to prosecute, and they decide how to measure successful prosecution. For example, they may decide that welfare fraud deserves high priority and measure their success in dealing with it by either the number of convictions, the ratio of convictions to acquittals, or the types and lengths of sentences they achieve. Whatever crimes they choose to prosecute most vigorously, and however they measure their law enforcement success, prosecutors are influenced by public opinion. As elected officials, some respond to community pressure more readily than others. If prosecutors see themselves as the people's representatives, they take their cues from public opinion on particular crimes and punishments, "try[ing] primarily to reflect community opinion." Hence, if welfare recipients who are "ripping off the taxpayers" bother the public, prosecutors will fight welfare-related offenses. If the community believes drunk drivers are "getting off too easy," the representative-of-the-people-type prosecutors will seek a high conviction rate and harsh sentences for drunk drivers. The heightened prosecution of drug offenses is the most dramatic current example of the exercise of prosecutorial discretion in response to public pressure.[48]

Other prosecutors believe that their law enforcement role requires them not only to satisfy public wishes but also to control crime. Such prosecutors see themselves more as experts elected by the public to use their best professional judgment to decide which crimes to prosecute, what sentences to request, and how to measure success. As public interest lawyers they work for the community's best interest, not simply to satisfy the public's desires. When asked how he views the public, one prosecutor who considers himself a trustee of the public's best interest replied, "with a jaundiced eye."[49]

Prosecutors do not always enjoy harmonious relationships with police. Sixty years ago, the National Commission on Law Observance and Enforcement found "frequent and characteristic want of cooperation between investigating and prosecuting agencies in the same locality." Both police and prosecutors are law enforcement officers on the same side in controlling street crime. Nevertheless, they have frequently clashed. Prosecutors and police generally come from different backgrounds. Prosecutors have advanced training in law that most police officers lack. Furthermore, prosecutors have assimilated values from law school and the courts that can lead them to overemphasize their importance to the criminal justice system.[50]

Prosecutors work in different surroundings from the police. The police work on the streets. Prosecutors work in and around the criminal courts with other lawyers. Prosecutors

The strength of the prosecution's case depends on evidence; physical evidence is often the most compelling. Here, prosecutor Sharlene Honnaka holds what she claims is a murder weapon during closing arguments in the trail of Charles Ng in Santa Ana, California, in February 1999. Ng, a Hong Kong native, was charged with murdering two infants, three women, and seven men.

focus on legal guilt—that is, getting sufficient constitutionally admissible evidence to win cases. Traditional police officers act on factual guilt—that is, on individuals they "know" are guilty. Police can view legal rules and the legal subculture prosecutors live in not only as a personal rebuke to police work, but also as a system that compromises the interests of victims, police, and the public by making "deals" that lead to reduced charges, diversions, and light sentences. For prosecutors, whose work world is the courts, conviction for a crime less than factual guilt suggests may suffice. Police who work the streets do not consider convictions for crimes less serious than factual guilt an appropriate end to criminal justice. They believe the government should prosecute, convict, and punish street criminals for the crimes they actually commit, not for some lesser offense.[51]

Use *Your* Discretion

Is police-prosecutor cooperation worth the effort?

In some places, police-prosecutor teams have overcome some of the problems arising out of their different interests. The teams, consisting of police investigators and prosecutors, work closely from the early stages of investigation all the way to conviction to establish legal guilt. In 1987, Maine created an entirely new agency, the Bureau of Intergovernmental Drug Enforcement. In unprecedented language, the statute charged the agency with the responsibility for "the integration and coordination of investigative and prosecutorial functions in the State with respect to drug law enforcement." For the first time, state law "mandates that prosecutors and investigators team up to create a more efficient and effective drug law enforcement strategy." "It's not an investigation and then a trial; it's a unitary process, a case throughout," according to Assistant U.S. Attorney for Maine, John Gleason.[52]

The agency has reduced basic misunderstandings arising out of the different vantage points of police and prosecutors. Bureau supervisor Dan Ross said,

> We have had to change some of our ideas because the attorney's perspective is that of the courtroom. Officers may not be concerned with how things appear in court because they tend to concentrate on just the facts. But the attorney has to care because appearances are so important in getting a conviction.[53]

For example, to obtain evidence, investigators frequently rely on informants. Prosecutors hesitate to call informants as witnesses. Despite their persuasiveness to police investigators, prosecutors know that such witnesses negatively impress jurors. Investigators now realize this and gather additional evidence. Prosecutors also benefit from the teamwork because, as one prosecutor observed, "The insights I have gained into case investigation translate into better courtroom performance." As prosecutors work closely with investigators, they learn that officers must make quick decisions to search based on limited information. Knowing this, prosecutors can make more effective arguments for the good faith exception to the search warrant requirement, an area, according to one prosecutor in Maine, "where prosecutors are sometimes weak."[54]

Laconia, New Hampshire, has adopted police-prosecutor cooperation to test its effectiveness in misdemeanors, order maintenance problems that rarely receive publicity but account for the largest expenditures of police resources. In Laconia, a prosecutor with an office in the police department prosecutes all misdemeanor arrests. Officers consult with the prosecutor about filing criteria and investigative practices, and the prosecutor provides timely information on case dispositions. This information leads to police decisions that close legal loopholes in cases of driving while intoxicated (DWI), disorderly conduct, theft, and assault. According to the chief of police in Laconia, the close contact between police and prosecutors has also reduced the number of lawsuits against the police. The chief says, "A higher degree of legal awareness has developed and it is reflected in the officers' actions on the street."[55]

A New York program adopted to decrease felony case attrition by improving the coordination between police and prosecutors in preparing cases produced mixed results. James Garofolo examined felony arrests and interviewed prosecutors and liaison officers in a sample of six county prosecutor's offices and the New York State Police. Four of the counties instituted the liaison program and two did not. The liaison program had little effect on felony case attrition; liaison officers had little effect on whether cases resulted in conviction. However, liaison officers did affect the amount of case "slippage"—that is, a conviction for an offense less than the charge, such as from a Class E felony to a Class A misdemeanor. It also simplified the communication channels between prosecutors and arresting officers.[56]

CRITICAL THINKING

1. Summarize the findings of the studies discussed.
2. List those that favor cooperation and those that don't.
3. What would you recommend as a wise public policy regarding cooperation. Why? Why not? Support your answer with information you have acquired.

Officers of the Court

In addition to law enforcement officers, prosecutors are supposed to do justice. They are supposed to uphold and protect defendants' constitutional rights even as they prosecute them for crimes. Prosecutors are supposed to tailor the law to suit individual defendants' needs as well as apply the law evenhandedly. These are difficult functions to perform because so little is known about exactly what "suits" individuals and what punishment satisfies the purposes of criminal law. Further, no one agrees about the purposes of punishment: should it be merely to punish, deter others from committing crimes, or rehabilitate offenders (Chapter 12)? In addition, as officers of the court with responsibility for protecting the constitutional rights of defendants, prosecutors are legally bound to enforce laws and other rules controlling police conduct. This either brings them into direct conflict with police or forces them to balance their formal public duty and their informal relationships with police.[57]

Administrative Officers

Prosecutors are also administrators of organizations in which missions not related to law enforcement or court proceedings are paramount. Prosecution offices, especially large ones, have basic organizational goals: efficiency, economy, and smooth-working relations among staff and between staff and outside agencies, such as police, public defenders, and courts. As administrators, prosecutors strive to further the organization's effective, efficient, economical, and speedy dispatch of business, often by using limited public resources in the most cost-effective manner. Accordingly, prosecutors may put a premium on cases and crimes that produce the greatest impact for the quickest and most economical processing. Prosecutors as administrators also favor rules that foster routine, regular, predictable results. Here, prosecutors may emphasize the uniformity of cases, rather than the uniqueness of individuals.[58]

Careerists

Finally, prosecutors are careerists. They seek to advance in the legal profession, not necessarily as prosecutors or even judges, but as private practitioners. If they want to be career prosecutors, they build amicable relationships with their superiors and with members of related agencies, mainly the police, public defenders, and judges. If they aspire to higher public office, local political interests influence their actions. If private practice appeals to them, they seek the goodwill of members of private law firms.[59]

Not all prosecutors perform their various functions with equal vigor. They develop prosecutorial styles, much as the police develop policing styles. Some prosecutors favor their role as chief law enforcer and, as a result, stress conviction rates. Others lean toward the role of court officer, emphasizing the need to prosecute only according to rules that do not violate defendants' rights. Still others are concerned mainly with running efficient, economical organizations where cases are processed rapidly with minimal obstruction or difficulty. Some treat prosecution as only a stepping stone to a higher political office or more lucrative law practice, or as "just a job" in which hassles are to be minimized and material benefits gained. Others are career prosecutors who work to establish good working relationships with the other criminal justice agencies, particularly courts, police, and defense counsel.[60]

Structure and Management

Prosecution management varies greatly according to jurisdiction size, geography, resources, and technology. Every jurisdiction has a chief prosecutor, an elected officer, usually with a four-year term. In small jurisdictions, prosecutors work alone or with a few assistants who know each other personally and who work together closely. Such prosecutors often have private practices also. In large jurisdictions, prosecutors' offices are large agencies with many assistants whom chief prosecutors rarely see, or may not even know. Chief prosecutors—usually called district attorneys in states, and U.S. attorneys in federal jurisdictions—rarely appear in court. They set general office policy, deal with the public, and manage relations with other criminal justice agencies. Some chief prosecutors are career prosecutors, but most eventually enter private practice, become judges, or run for higher political office.[61]

Assistant prosecutors are young attorneys, frequently recent law school graduates. They are appointed to office on the basis of not only their professional credentials but also their political connections. Democrats usually appoint Democratic assistant prosecutors; Republicans appoint Republicans. Assistant prosecutors do not often make prosecution a career. Most stay fewer than five years and then enter private practice. According to one New York City assistant prosecutor, "You're not supposed to stay too long. Sixty percent leave after three years. The longer you stay the less career value is the ADA [assistant district attorney] experience."[62]

Former assistant prosecutors rarely enter prestigious corporate law firms. They usually remain in low-status criminal law practice, often becoming defense attorneys. A few become judges, but former assistant prosecutors rarely run for political office. Rising salaries for assistant prosecutors and shrinking opportunities in private practice have reduced high prosecutor turnover.[63]

Assistant prosecutors work according to two basic modes. Under the zone system, or horizontal case assignment, assistants manage different phases of the criminal process. Some assistants draft complaints; others go to court for arraignment, others to try cases, and still others to argue cases on appeal. The case system, or vertical case management, links assistants to particular cases; assistants manage individual cases from arraignment through trial. Zone system assistants become experts in criminal procedure (arraignment, preliminary hearing, pretrial motions, and trial); case system assistants become experts in criminal law (homicide, rape, burglary). The most prominent current use of the case system is in career-criminal units. To target repeat offenders, assistant prosecutors in a specialized career-criminal unit have adopted police-prosecutor teams, such as those discussed in the section on the law enforcement function of prosecutors. If the police arrest career criminal suspects, assistants in the career unit prosecute the cases.[64]

Chief prosecutors in large urban areas cannot know the individual cases on their dockets. They deal with several judges with different ideologies. Assistants do not know in detail the office's policies and, by the time they do, they have probably entered private practice. Therefore, effective management of large prosecutors' offices demands that chief prosecutors set clear goals and establish statistical and accounting mechanisms for measuring whether policy goals are met and for determining whether to alter current policies. Prosecutors resist quantifying their work, displaying an occupational antipathy for statistics, efficiency, or accounting. Typical of many prosecutors, one told William F. McDonald in his study of prosecutors, "I'm a lawyer. I don't have to be quantified. I make my judgment, exercise my discretion in accordance with what my perception of the public needs are and whether I think they should be satisfied. My assistants are professionals."[65]

This approach leads to perceptions inconsistent with reality for individual assistant prosecutors with varying degrees of insight, experience, and maturity. In the words of one former chief prosecutor:

> Such an office, characterized by unchecked exercise of discretion directed toward no discernible goal, leads to knee-jerk reactions to daily problems, the solution of which is never predictable. This type of office can best be characterized as exemplifying management by crisis. In this office there exists very little paperwork; and what little there is, when it depends on a lawyer to complete it, is very nearly never done.[66]

Information management technology has altered management in the offices of some prosecutors. PROMIS (Prosecutors' Management Information Service) was developed by the Institute for Law and Social Research (INSLAW), a nonprofit research and development corporation in Washington, D.C. It composes the "richest source of criminal justice facts ever gathered." Its database includes 150 facts about "street crime" cases and defendants that allow prosecutors to track cases from arrest to conviction.[67]

PROMIS data have led to a number of significant findings:

- Most arrests for serious crimes end in dismissal.
- Police officers poorly trained in collecting and preserving evidence, *not constitutional restrictions,* account for most dismissals.
- A few police officers account for most arrests resulting in conviction.
- A small subset of defendants, career criminals, commits many robberies and burglaries.
- Cases against career criminals are just as likely to result in dismissal as cases against other defendants.
- Many dismissals result from witnesses' failure to appear in court to testify.[68]

PROMIS research projects have led to changes in prosecution policies and practices in some jurisdictions. Many prosecutors' offices now have career offender programs that use PROMIS data to prosecute offenders responsible for large numbers of street crimes and to seek maximum sentences for those they convict. In other offices, victim witness programs notify witnesses about court appearances, assure that they appear for them, and counsel witnesses on courtroom procedure. PROMIS has also affected the creation and effectiveness of police-prosecutor teams.[69]

Defense Counsel

Criminal defense attorneys, like all other criminal justice professionals, have both formal and informal functions. The best known and most public is the formal mission of defending the rights of the accused. Informally, obtaining guilty pleas and getting along with the courtroom work group are equally fundamental missions.

Formal Functions

Formally, criminal defense attorneys are advocates who zealously represent their clients. As champions of the accused, their role in the adversary system is to challenge the government at every point in its effort to convict defendants. Defense counsel has the formal responsibility to see to it that the government proves every element of the case beyond a reasonable doubt and only by means of evidence legally obtained and presented in court.

Criminal defense lawyers, therefore, according to Rodney J. Uphoff, who has both practiced and studied criminal defense, "may actually frustrate the search for truth. Indeed, defense counsel may be ethically required to do so."[70] This responsibility to zealously defend their clients exists even when counsel knows that the defendants they represent are guilty. The opening question "Should 'Guilty' Defendants Have a Lawyer?" deals with this frequently misunderstood and criticized responsibility to defend the guilty.

Informal Missions

Experts disagree about whether the reality of day-to-day practice conforms to the formal functions of criminal defense lawyers. In the 1960s, Abraham Blumberg called the practice of criminal defense law "a confidence game." According to Blumberg, organizational pressures generated by the courtroom work group lead criminal defense lawyers to abandon the role of zealous advocate for the accused. Instead, they "help the accused redefine his situation and restructure his perceptions concomitant with a plea of guilty." Relationships with judges and prosecutors, according to Blumberg, outweigh the needs of clients. To maintain good relations, judges, prosecutors, and defense lawyers join together in an "organized system of complicity."[71] Blumberg describes the relationship this way:

> Accused persons come and go in the court system schema, but the structure and its occupational occupants remain to carry on their respective career, occupational and organizational enterprises. The individual stridencies, tensions, and conflicts a given accused person's case may present to all the participants are overcome because the formal and informal relations of all the groups in the court setting require it. The probability of continued future relations and interaction must be preserved at all cost.[72]

Defense attorneys are a critical element in all criminal cases. Most are public defenders but some defense lawyers gain fame and fortune for satisfying the constitutional guarantee of a lawyer in criminal cases. F. Lee Bailey, shown here defending O. J. Simpson, is one of these wealthy and famous defense lawyers.

Criminal defense lawyers vary greatly individually, but the criminal defense bar can be divided into three general types:

1. Elite defense attorneys.
2. Private defense counsel.
3. Public defenders.

Elite, private defense lawyers such as Johnnie Cochran, Gerry Spence, and F. Lee Bailey have highly lucrative criminal law practices that bring them great wealth, fame, and prestige. Few criminal defense lawyers, however, fall into this elite category. Most private defense attorneys have little prestige or glory; instead, they eke out a barely adequate living by "haunting the courts in hope of picking up crumbs from the judicial table." These lawyers have given rise to the unflattering terms "shyster" and "ambulance chaser." Much of their business arises from walking the halls of jails and lower courts, where they find their clients—suspects or defendants who need lawyers immediately. The largest group of criminal defense attorneys are public defenders, funded by the government and working in established public defender's offices. In 1993, public defenders represented 80 percent of all criminal defendants.[73]

Defense counsel, like all criminal justice professionals, play a number of roles. Some adhere to their formal role as guardian of their clients' rights and their formal duty to defend vigorously their clients' interests. According to one defense lawyer in Arthur Lewis Wood's classic study of the defense bar:

> It's a criminal lawyer's function to get a criminal off or help him get a lighter sentence. He's helping him preserve his freedom. Whether it's good for society to have a criminal loose is another question. It may not be good for society, but that is the lawyer's job. It's his duty to the client; everybody knows it. His job is to preserve his client's freedom.[74]

Other criminal defense lawyers enjoy the conflict that criminal trial work provides. These competitors' commitment to the constitutional principles underlying criminal defense work takes second place to the satisfaction they derive from courtroom drama and fighting for the underdog. Another lawyer in Arthur Wood's study noted that "Criminal law offers a wonderful chance to fight injustice and to help people." The competitor role does not necessarily conflict with the defender role, particularly when lawyers who love to compete also believe deeply in the rights of defendants. The elite, private criminal defense lawyers most readily fall into this category.[75]

Criminal defense lawyers, particularly public defenders, play informal roles that do give rise to potential conflict with their formal defender role. Public defenders, and to a lesser extent other lawyers for the poor, are not only lawyers, but constitute an integral part of the courthouse work group. They know, work with, need to get along with, and socialize with prosecutors and judges on a continuing basis. As such, attorneys for the indigent act not only as their clients' lawyers but also as agents of the government, "surrogates of the prosecutor, a member of their 'little syndicate.'" The government pays public defenders, so some people, not surprisingly, view them as agents of the government—a suspicion apparently widely held among indigent defendants. The "friendly adversary" relationship between defense counsel and prosecutors, their supposed opponents, feeds this suspicion. Opponents are not supposed to be friends.[76]

According to David W. Neubauer, who has studied day-to-day decision making in criminal justice systems in "middle America,"

> If they are friendly adversaries, then we begin to suspect something is amiss. For example, if you visit most courtrooms, you will see the prosecution and defense exchange pleasantries before, after, and during the court appearances. You may even see two lawyers strenuously arguing their case in court, and then having lunch together. Some commentators interpret such actions to mean that the defense has closer ties to the prosecution than to the client, and the client suffers.[77]

Can lawyers vigorously defend clients whom they have never seen before and probably will never see again, especially when it may antagonize professional peers with whom defense attorneys have ongoing relationships? Recent empirical evidence suggests that defense attorneys wage a hard fight in the adversary system, drive a hard bargain in plea-negotiating sessions, and still maintain close professional, peer, and personal relationships with prosecutors and judges. In other words, defense lawyers do not take personally either the fights over defending clients in court or the arguments for clients out of court. They treat them as simply part of their job of defending clients.[78]

Law practice involves unwritten norms of conduct. In a profession based on conflict in court, rules have developed to keep the conflict confined to court. There is enough disagreement without adding bad personal relations among the attorneys. For this reason, lawyers are expected to confine their disputes to the courtroom. As one judge commented, "Yesterday two lawyers started arguing about their case in the corridor after the hearing. That just shouldn't happen. Lawyers have to know how to channel disagreement." Thus, if defense and prosecution are on good terms, this does not mean that the adversary process has broken down. It may be only a reflection of the normal rules of conduct expected of lawyers. The "cooperation" of defense and prosecution is a product of these general expectations about how lawyers should conduct themselves. We should not equate effective advocacy with hostility.[79]

Some criminal defense lawyers primarily commit themselves neither to their formal role of upholding constitutional rights nor to their informal role of maintaining good working relationships with prosecutors and judges. They focus merely on making a living. In fact, according to one study,

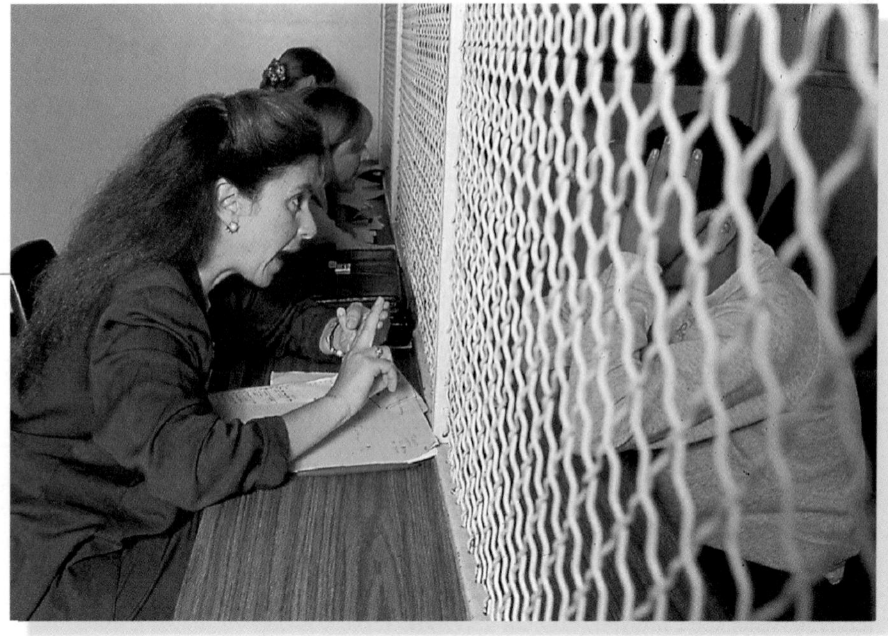

Criminal defense lawyers perform both the formal mission of upholding constitutional rights and an informal mission of maintaining good working relationships with other members of the courtroom work group. Part of both missions is consulting with clients, which is not always private or convenient.

most criminal defense lawyers practice criminal law because it is the only way they can get by financially. Not at the top of their law school classes, they could not command top jobs in large law firms or in corporations. They entered general practice and let minor criminal work help pay their bills. This is especially true of the majority of private criminal defense attorneys. These lawyers form an outer ring, beyond the elite corporate lawyers and the less elite but still middle-status lawyers such as personal injury and labor lawyers who oppose corporations.[80]

Generally, these lawyers neither like their work nor believe it accomplishes anything noble for anybody. One of them said:

> It's not a very acceptable way of earning a living—at least according to many other lawyers. You are always dealing with shady characters. I take criminal cases but I would just as soon get away from it.[81]

Others view defense work, particularly the trial experience gained as a public defender, as a good credential to obtain positions in prestigious corporate law firms. In a sense, these lawyers treat criminal defense work as an apprenticeship for private law practice. Except in high-paying public defender's offices like the one in Los Angeles, where some attorneys earn close to $100,000 a year, most public defenders leave public defense work after a few years and go on to private practice. The same pattern exists for prosecutors, many of whom go on to the same private law firms that defenders enter. This trial work apprenticeship and their later close association in private practice draw defense lawyers and prosecutors closer together than their formal adversary relationship indicates. The pull of the work group and the apprenticeship is considerably stronger than the formal roles of prosecutor and defense counsel.[82]

Knowledge and Understanding CHECK

1. Identify and describe the three tiers of criminal courts.
2. Describe the formal and informal dimensions of the lower criminal courts.
3. Describe the formal and informal dimensions of the trial courts.
4. Explain the constitutional status and the reality of appellate court review.
5. Compare *habeas corpus* and *certiorari*.
6. List and describe the missions of criminal courts.
7. Identify the major members of the courtroom work group.
8. List and explain missions of the courtroom work group.

Should "Guilty" Clients Have a Lawyer? Consideration

In addition to the opening quote, Dershowitz also wrote:

> The zealous defense attorney is the last bastion of liberty—the final barrier between an overreaching government and its citizens. The job of the defense attorney is to challenge the government; to make those in power justify their conduct in relation to the powerless; to articulate and defend the right of those who lack the ability or resources to defend themselves. (Even the rich are relatively powerless—less so, of course, than the poor—when confronting the resources of a government prosecutor.)
>
> One of the truest tests of a free country is how it treats those whose job it is to defend the guilty and the despised. In most repressive countries there is no independent defense bar. Indeed, a sure sign that repression is on the way is when the government goes after the defense attorneys. Shakespeare said, "The first thing we do, let's kill all the lawyers." Hitler, Stalin, the Greek colonels, and the Chinese Cultural Revolutionaries may not have killed all the lawyers first, but they surely placed defense attorneys—especially vigorous and independent ones—high on their hit lists.
>
> One of the surest ways of undercutting the independence of defense attorneys is to question the propriety of their representing the guilty. Those who argue that defense attorneys should limit their representation to the innocent, or indeed to any specific group or category, open the door to a system where the government decides who is, and who is not, entitled to a defense. Granting the power to the government, to the bar, or to any establishment, marks the beginning of the end of an independent defense bar—and the beginning of the end of liberty.
>
> The role of the defense attorney who defends guilty clients is the hardest role in the criminal justice system to explain to the public. In 1980 I traveled to China to advise the People's Republic on its criminal justice system. Most Chinese lawyers seemed to understand the need for free and independent judges and prosecutors. But hardly anyone—even those lawyers who had suffered most under the Cultural Revolution—seemed willing to justify the actions of a defense attorney representing a client whom he knew to be guilty and "counter-revolutionary." (Every society has its own favorite epithets for those it most despises.) "Why should our government pay someone to stand in the way of socialist justice?" was the question I was most often asked. I tried to explain that justice—whether socialist, capitalist, or anything else—is a process, not only an end; and that for the process to operate fairly, all persons charged with crime must have the right to a defense. Since not all defendants are created equal in their ability to speak effectively, think logically, and argue forcefully, the role of a defense attorney—trained in these and other skills—is to perform those functions for the defendant. The process of determining whether a defendant should be deemed guilty and punished requires that the government be put to its proof and that the accused have a fair opportunity to defend.
>
> I also tried to explain to the Chinese lawyers that laws that are today directed against counterrevolutionaries may tomorrow be directed at them. As H. L. Mencken once put it: "The trouble about fighting for human freedom is that you have to spend much of your life defending sons of bitches; for oppressive laws are always aimed at them originally, and oppression must be stopped in the beginning if it is to be stopped at all."
>
> To me the most persuasive argument for defending the guilty and the despised is to consider the alternative. Those governments that forbid or discourage such representation have little to teach us about justice. Their systems are far more corrupt, less fair, and generally even less efficient than ours. What Winston Churchill once said about democracy can probably also be said about the adversary system of criminal justice: It may well be the worst system of justice, "except [for] all the other [systems] that have been tried from time to time."
>
> The late Supreme Court Justice Felix Frankfurter once commented that he knew of no title "more honorable than that of Professor of the Harvard Law School." I know of none more honorable than defense attorney.

Critical Thinking

1. What reasons does Dershowitz give for being a defense attorney? Do you agree? A common question people ask defense attorneys is, "How can you defend these people?"
2. Does Dershowitz answer the question? Would you defend a guilty person? Why? Why not? Defend your answer.
3. Refer to the Defense Counsel section. Would you defend a guilty person? Why? Why not? Defend your answer.

CHAPTER CAPSULE

- Formally, courts are "palaces of justice." Informally, most decision making takes place in the corridors and behind closed doors; and courts are political and social, as much as they are legal, institutions.
- Courts pay attention to and respond to the needs and demands of the public, interest groups, and individuals.
- In reality, formal court proceedings only ratify what lawyers and other criminal justice personnel have already decided informally.
- The visible, open, publicized formal court proceedings governed by the rule of law mask the leading role that discretionary decision making plays in the courts.

KEY TERMS

lower criminal courts
trial courts
appellate courts
limited jurisdiction
courts of record
general jurisdiction
original jurisdiction
adjudication
exclusive jurisdiction
writ of *habeas corpus*
writ of *certiorari*
rule of four
adversary system
substantial justice approach
courthouse work group

INTERNET RESEARCH EXERCISES

Exercise: What are the issues involved in allowing videotaped or audiotaped confessions in a court case? What were the issues that arose surrounding the use of a videotaped confession in the case of *DeLisle v. Rivers*?

Suggested site: FindLaw, http://www.findlaw.com (tip: Click on "Laws: Cases and Codes," then click on "Sixth Circuit" under Courts of Appeals. Under "Party Name Search," type in "Delisle" and click the search button. Select the case dated 12/8/97.)

InfoTrac College Edition: Search using the key words "Lawrence DeLisle"

NOTES

1. Alan Dershowitz, *The Best Defense* (New York: Random House, 1982).
2. Arthur Rosett and Donald R. Cressey, *Justice by Consent: Plea Bargains in the American Courts* (Philadelphia: J. Lippincott, 1976), 1; Peter F. Nardulli, James Eisenstein, and Roy B. Flemming, *The Tenor of Justice* (Urbana: University of Illinois Press, 1988), 211–14.
3. Frances Kahn Zemans, "In the Eye of the Beholder: The Relationship Between the Public and the Courts," in *Courts and Justice,*

G. Larry Mays and Peter R. Gregware, eds. (Prospect Heights, Ill.: Waveland Press, 1995), 7–8.

4. James J. Alfini, *Misdemeanor Courts* (Washington, D.C.: U.S. Department of Justice, 1981), 13.

5. Doris M. Provine, *Judging Credentials: Nonlawyer Judges and the Politics of Professionalism* (Chicago: University of Chicago Press, 1986), xi; *North v. Russell,* 427 U.S. 328 (1976); David A. Harriss, "Justice Rationed in the Pursuit of Efficiency," in *Courts and Justice,* 72.

6. BJS, *Report to the Nation on Crime and Justice: The Data* (Washington, D.C.: Bureau of Justice Statistics, October 1983).

7. Roscoe Pound, "The Administration of Justice in American Cities," *Harvard Law Review* 12 (1912).

8. Alfini, *Misdemeanor Courts,* 14.

9. Caleb Foote, "Vagrancy-Type Law and Its Administration," *University of Pennsylvania Law Review* 104 (1956): 605; Maureen Mileski, "Courtroom Encounters: An Observation Study of a Lower Criminal Court," *Law and Society Review* (May 1971): 479; Lois Forer, *Money and Justice* (New York: W. W. Norton, 1984), 3; President's Commission on Law Enforcement and the Administration of Justice, *The Challenge of Crime in a Free Society* (Washington, D.C.: U.S. Government Printing Office, 1967), 128.

10. Harry I. Subin, "230,000 Cases, Zero Justice," *New York Times,* 19 December 1991.

11. "Rising Caseload in Manhattan Courts," *New York Times,* 16 February 1987; Barbara Boland and Brian Forst, "Prosecutors Don't Always Aim to Pleas," *Federal Probation* 49 (1985): 11; Elliot Spitzer, "Faster Justice in New York," *New York Times,* 1 March 1993; Paul B. Wice, *Chaos in the Courthouse: The Inner Workings of the Urban Criminal Courts* (New York: Praeger, 1985), 18.

12. Stephen J. Schulhofer, "Justice Without Bargaining in Lower Criminal Courts," *American Bar Foundation Research Journal* (1985): 562.

13. Ibid.

14. Thomas W. Church, Jr., "Examining Local Legal Culture," *American Bar Foundation Research Journal* (1985): 453.

15. James Eisenstein, Roy B. Flemming, and Peter F. Nardulli, *The Contours of Justice* (Boston: Little, Brown, 1988), 5.

16. Pound, "The Administration of Justice," 302–28.

17. Everett P. Wheeler, "Reform in Criminal Procedure, " *Annals of the American Academy of Political and Social Science* (1910): 185–89.

18. Sheldon Glueck, ed., *Roscoe Pound and Criminal Justice* (Dobbs-Ferry, N.Y.: Oceana Publications, 1965): Rosett and Cressey, *Justice by Consent,* 53–55.

19. Martin A. Levin, *Urban Politics and the Criminal Courts* (Chicago: University of Chicago Press, 1977), 60.

20. Charles Perrow, *Complex Organizations: A Critical Essay,* 2d ed. (Glenview, Ill.: Scott, Foresman, 1979).

21. *New York Times,* 30 December 1984.

22. Levin, *Urban Politics and the Criminal Courts,* 129–30.

23. Levin, *Urban Politics and the Criminal Courts;* John F. Padgett, "The Emergent Organization of Plea Bargaining," *American Journal of Sociology* 90 (1985): 753–800.

24. John S. Goldkamp and Doris Weiland, *Assessing the Impact of Dade County's Felony Drug Court: Final Report* (Philadelphia: Crime and Justice Research Institute, 1993).

25. Ibid.

26. Peter F. Nardulli, *The Courtroom Elite* (Cambridge, Mass.: Ballinger, 1978).

27. Ibid.,179.

28. Wice, *Chaos in the Courthouse,* 48.

29. Ibid., 110–13, 152; see also Peter F. Nardulli, "Organizational Analyses of Criminal Courts: An Overview and Some Speculation," in *The Study of Criminal Courts: Political Perspectives,* Peter F. Nardulli, ed. (Cambridge, Mass.: Ballinger, 1979); James Eisenstein and Herbert Jacob, *Felony Justice* (Boston: Little, Brown, 1977), 27.

30. Eisenstein and Jacob, *Felony Justice,* 24–25.

31. Levin, *Urban Politics and the Criminal Courts,* 3; Rosett and Cressey, *Justice by Consent,* 2.

32. Nardulli, Eisenstein, and Flemming, *Tenor of Justice,* 373–74.

33. Peltason quoted in Elliot E. Slotnik, "Review Essay on Judicial Recruitment and Selection," in *Courts and Justice,* 200.

34. Levin, *Urban Politics and the Criminal Courts;* David W. Neubauer, *America's Courts and the Criminal Justice System,* 3d ed. (Pacific Grove, Calif.: Brooks/Cole, 1988), 170.

35. BJS, *Report to the Nation,* 64.

36. Levin, *Urban Politics and the Criminal Courts.*

37. Anthony Champagne, "Judicial Reform in Texas," *Judicature* 72 (1988): 146–59.

38. Stuart S. Nagel, *Improving the Legal Process* (Lexington, Mass.: Lexington Books, 1975), 31–32; William Hall and Larry Aspin, "What Twenty Years of Judicial Retention Elections Have Told Us," *Judicature* 70 (1987): 340; John M. Scheb II, "State Appellate Judges' Attitudes Toward Judicial Merit Selection and Retention: Results of a National Survey," *Judicature* 72 (1988): 170–74.

39. Barbara Luck Graham, "Judicial Recruitment and Racial Diversity on State Courts," in *Courts and Justice,* 216.

40. Edited transcript of American Judicature Society Annual Meeting, August 4, 1990, "Different Voices, Different Choices?" in *Courts and Justice,* 230–32.

41. Candace McCoy, "Prosecution," Michael Tonry, ed., *The Handbook of Crime and Punishment* (New York: Oxford University Press, 1998), 457.

42. Peter W. Greenwood et al., *Prosecution of Adult Felony Defendants in Los Angeles County: A Policy Perspective* (Santa Monica: Rand Corporation, March 1973); Joan Jacoby, *The American Prosecutor: A Search for Identity* (Lexington, Mass.: D. C. Heath, 1980); John Buchanan, "Police-Prosecutor Teams: Innovations in Several Jurisdictions," *National Institute of Justice Reports* (May/June 1989): 2–8.

43. BJS, *Prosecutors in State Courts, 1996* (Washington, DC: BJS, July 1998).

44. McCoy, "Prosecution," 458.

45. Ibid.

46. *Berger v. United States,* 195 U.S. 78 (1935).

47. David W. Neubauer, *Criminal Justice in Middle America* (Morristown, N.J.: General Learning Press, 1974), chap. 3; Lief H. Carter, *The Limits of Order* (Lexington, Mass.: Lexington Books, 1974).

48. Neubauer, *Criminal Justice in Middle America,* 45; Leonard Mellon, Joan Jacoby, and Marion Brewer, "The Prosecutor Constrained by His Environment: A New Look at Discretionary Justice in the United States," *Journal of Criminal Law and Criminology* 72 (1981): 52.

49. Mellon, Jacoby, Brewer, "The Prosecutor Constrained."

50. *Prosecution* (Washington, D.C.: U.S. Government Printing Office, 1931), 17; Brian Forst, *Improving Police-Prosecutor Coordination* (Washington, D.C.: Institute for Law and Social Research, 1981), 1–3.

51. Malcolm M. Feeley and Mark H. Lazerson, "Police-Prosecutor Relationships: An Interorganizational Perspective," in *Empirical*

Theories About Courts, Keith O. Boyum and Lynn Mather, eds. (New York: Longman, 1983), 229–32; Floyd Feeney, *Case Processing and Police-Prosecutor Coordination* (Davis, Calif.: University of California, Davis, Center on Administration of Criminal Justice, 1981), 4–6.
52. Buchanan, "Police-Prosecutor Teams," 2–3.
53. Ibid.
54. Ibid., 4.
55. Ibid., 7.
56. James Garofolo, "Police, Prosecutors, and Felony Case Attrition," *Journal of Criminal Justice* 19 (1991): 439–49.
57. Wayne R. LaFave, *Arrest: The Decision to Take a Suspect into Custody* (Boston: Little, Brown, 1965), 515.
58. *The Study of Criminal Courts,* 108–11.
59. Carter, *The Limits of Order,* 71–74.
60. Ibid., 62–75; Neubauer, *Criminal Justice in Middle America,* chap. 3.
61. BJS, *Prosecutors in State Courts, 1990* (Washington, D.C.: Bureau of Justice Statistics, 1992), 1.
62. Herbert Jacob, *Crime and Justice in Urban America* (Englewood Cliffs, N.J.: Prentice-Hall, 1980), 76–77; Malcolm M. Feeley, *The Process Is the Punishment* (New York: Russell Sage Foundation), 70–71; William F. McDonald, ed., *The Prosecutor* (Beverly Hills, Calif.: Sage, 1979), 251.
63. *The Prosecutor,* chap. 9; Wice, *Chaos in the Courthouse,* 63.
64. Jacob, *Crime and Justice in Urban America,* 78–79; BJS, *Prosecutors in State Courts,* 3.
65. *The Prosecutor,* 138.
66. Ibid., 139
67. Brian Forst et al., *What Happens After Arrest* (Washington, D.C.: National Institute of Law Enforcement and Criminal Justice, 1977), v.
68. *The Prosecutor,* 127.
69. Ibid., 127–34.
70. Rodney J. Uphoff, "The Criminal Defense Lawyer: Zealous Advocate, Double Agent, or Beleaguered Dealer?" in *Courts and Justice,* 16.
71. Abraham Blumberg, "The Practice of Law as Confidence Game: Organizational Co-Optation of a Profession," *Law and Society Review* 1 (1967): 20, 22.
72. Ibid., 20.
73. Jack Ladinsky, "The Impact of Social Backgrounds of Lawyers on Law Practice and the Law," *Journal of Legal Education* 16 (1963): 128; Wice, *Chaos in the Courthouse,* 63–64; Andy Court, "Is There a Crisis?" *The American Lawyer* (January/February 1993), 46.
74. Quoted in Arthur Lewis Wood, *Criminal Lawyer* (New Haven, Conn.: College and University Press, 1967), 67; Lynn M. Mather, "The Outsider in the Courtroom: An Alternative Role for Defense," in *The Potential for Reform in Criminal Justice,* Herbert Jacob, ed. (Beverly Hills, Calif.: Sage, 1974), 263–89, makes a good case for the importance of this role and its existence, despite pressures to adopt the informal roles; William F. McDonald, *The Defense Counsel* (Beverly Hills, Calif.: Sage, 1983).
75. Wood, *Criminal Lawyer.*
76. Jonathan D. Casper, *American Criminal Justice* (Englewood Cliffs, N.J.: Prentice-Hall, 1972), 107, 110–11.
77. Neubauer, *Criminal Justice in Middle America,* 78.
78. Lisa J. McIntyre, *The Public Defender* (Chicago: University of Chicago Press, 1987), 148 ff.
79. Ibid.
80. Ladinsky, "The Impact of Social Backgrounds of Lawyers," 128.
81. Ibid., 64.
82. Anthony Platt and Randi Pollock, "Channeling Lawyers: The Careers of Public Defenders," in *The Potential for Reform in Criminal Justice;* Emily Barker, "Paying for Quality," *The American Lawyer* (January/February 1993), 83.

CHAPTER 10

Proceedings Before Trial

CHAPTER OUTLINE

Was This a Vindictive Prosecution?

Nathaniel Williams was charged with two counts of distributing "crack" cocaine, a felony offense under Virginia law. On September 23, 1993, Williams and his defense attorney appeared for the preliminary hearing. The prosecutor, Michael Cummings, discussed the case with Williams's attorney and advised that he would refer Williams's case for federal prosecution unless he pled guilty to the two state charges and agreed to cooperate with the state. The prosecutor warned that federal prosecution would subject Williams to a much more severe mandatory minimum sentence.

When asked how much cooperation would be required, the prosecutor directed Williams's attorney to Detective Robert Christian of the Virginia Beach Police Department. Christian explained that the state would expect Williams to make several undercover drug purchases, to testify before grand juries and in open court, and to disclose all information of any criminal activities known to him. However, the defense counsel advised the prosecutor that Williams would not cooperate with the police because he feared for his safety and life, and for the safety of his family.

A federal grand jury then indicted for the same offenses that had been charged in state court. When the state prosecutor presented the case to the federal grand jury, Williams moved to dismiss the indictment on grounds of vindictive prosecution.[1]

INTRODUCTION

Only one out of ten people arrested for committing a felony goes to prison (see Figure 10.1). Why? This and the following chapters tell us what happens to the 90 percent of felony arrests that do not result in imprisonment. Both the law and discretion play a large role in reducing the number of cases between arrest and incarceration. (See Chapter 1 for an explanation of the funnel effect in general.) Table 10.1 depicts the major decisions and the decision makers who determine whether arrested persons go free or are subjected to further processing and describes the nature and consequences of that processing.

THE DECISION TO CHARGE

The late Supreme Court Justice Robert Jackson, a former prosecutor, maintained that the power to charge people with crimes bestows on prosecutors "more control over life, liberty, and reputation than any other person in America." The power *not* to charge confers even greater power on the prosecutor, as most defendants are not charged. Prosecutors do not have absolute power to charge. They share the **decision to charge,** or not, with other decision makers, including:

- Citizens who complain to the police.
- Patrol officers who respond to the complaints.
- Detectives who investigate complaints to gather evidence and witnesses.
- Victims and other witnesses who provide testimony and other information.
- Judges who conduct the first appearance and other preliminary proceedings.
- Grand jurors who hand up indictments.
- Defendants who agree to plead guilty, or refuse to plead guilty, to a specific crime.[2]

The police take cases directly to prosecutors shortly after arrest in most jurisdictions. However, in a few cities, police screen arrests first. For example, Los Angeles police drop or refer to social service agencies nearly half the arrests they make. Prosecutors never see these cases. And, in a few cities, police file cases directly with criminal courts. Prosecutors for more than a century have had "unfettered discretion" in making three vital decisions:

1. To charge or not—namely, to **initiate formal proceedings.**
2. The specific crime to charge.
3. **Diversion**—to transfer the case from the criminal justice system to social services.[3]

Formal court proceedings (**adjudication**) begin when prosecutors file charges. In the stages before trial or guilty pleas, prosecutors participate in pretrial release and detention decisions. They appear at all preliminary hearings, preside over grand jury proceedings, and present the government's case against defendants at trials. Prosecutors also par-

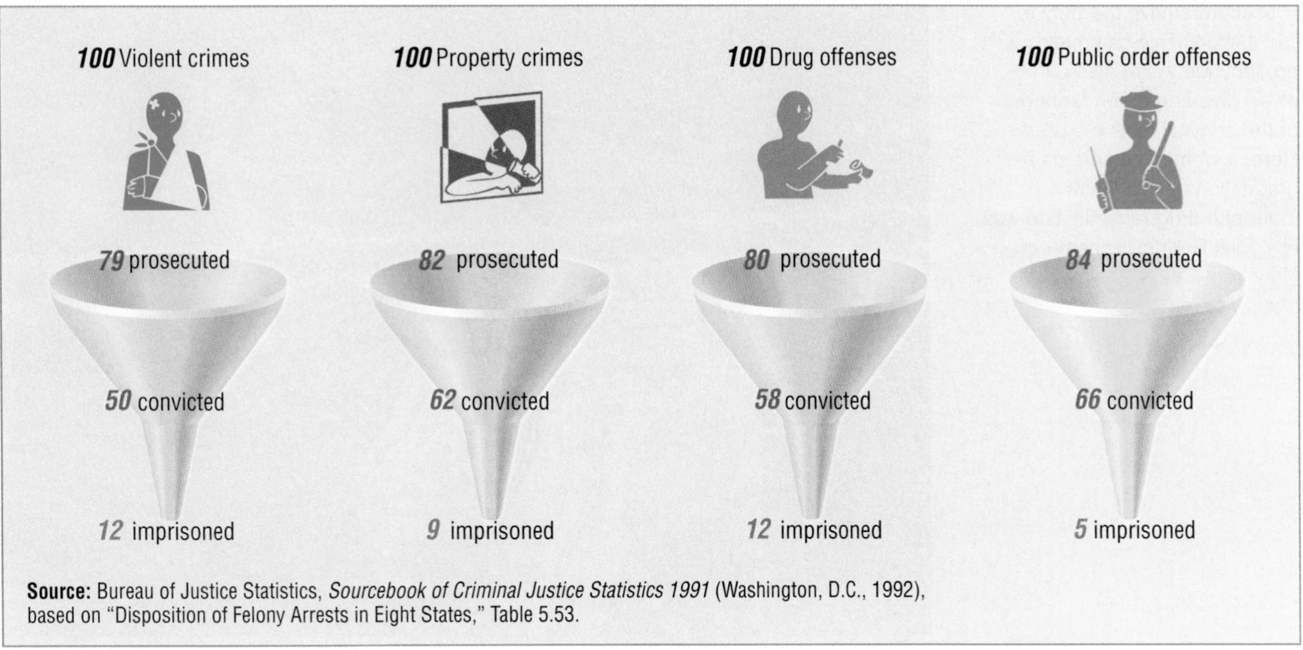

Figure 10.1
The Funnel Effect After Arrest

ticipate in plea bargaining and sentencing. In 1967, President Lyndon Johnson's Crime Commission called prosecutors the "key administrative officer[s] in the processing of cases." They still are.[4]

Consequences of the Decision to Charge

The decision to charge has far-reaching consequences. The decision to file cases marks the formal entry of suspects into the judicial system. At this point, criminal suspects become criminal defendants. Even though charges do not amount to convictions, penalties accompany them. Defendants can suffer:

- Loss of work time and even the loss of their job.
- Loss of freedom if they are denied bail.
- Damage to their reputations.

Defendants are not the only ones who suffer. Families experience hardship, and the community may be burdened with unemployment compensation, the expense of treatment programs, and eventually welfare payments.[5]

Becoming a criminal defendant is a form of "degradation ceremony," to borrow Erving Goffman's phrase. According to Abraham S. Blumberg:

> The accused is confronted by definitions of himself which reflect the various worlds of the agent-mediators yet are consistent for the most part in their negative evaluation of him. The agent-mediators have seized upon a wholly unflattering aspect of his biography to reinterpret his entire personality and justify their

Table 10.1
Decisions and Decision Makers from Arrest to Prison

DECISION MAKERS	DECISIONS
Prosecuter	• Charge with a crime • Divert to social service agency • Dismiss case • Test case by grand jury or judge • Plea-bargain • Try case • Recommend sentence
Judge	• Set bail • Assign counsel • Bind defendant over for trial • Rule on motions and objections before, during, and after trial • Sentence defendants
Bail bondsman	• Put up money bail • Pursue defendants who fail to appear
Grand jury	• Indict • "No bill" or dismiss charge
Defense counsel	• Advise defendant how to plead • Plea-bargain with prosecutor • Develop strategy to defend client's interest
Defendant	• Plead guilty or not guilty • Accept plea bargain
Court personnel	• Conduct bail investigation • Conduct pre-sentence investigation and report
Trial Jury	• Convict • Acquit

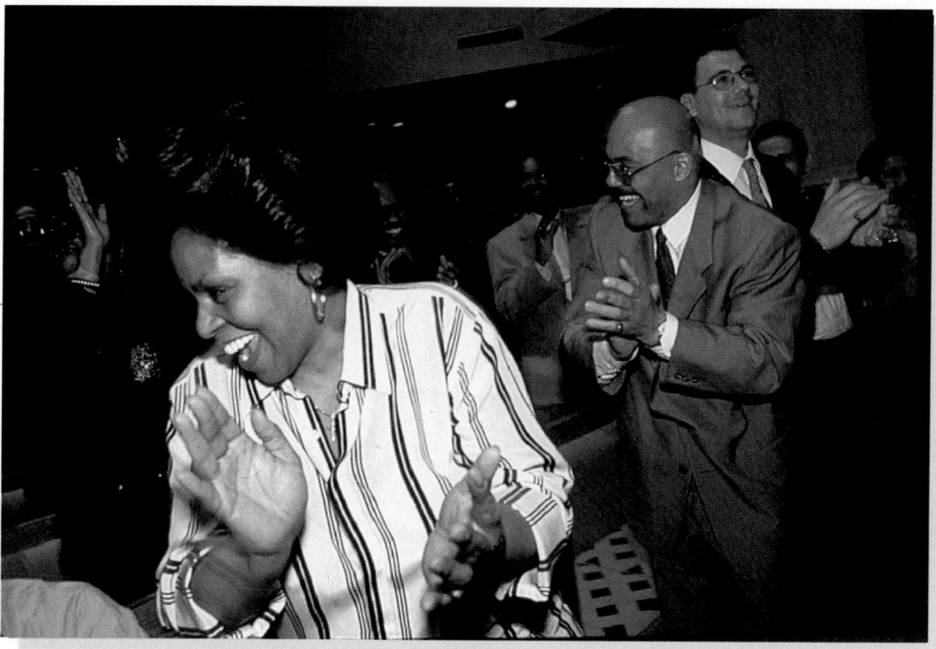

Prosecutors have the duty to "do justice." This can mean prosecution, but it also can mean diverting defendants out of the criminal justice system. Here, a woman celebrates her graduation from a Victory Outreach drug rehabilitation and HIV Risk Reduction home in New York City.

> present attitude and conduct toward him. Even an individual with considerable personal and economic resources has great difficulty resisting pressures to redefine himself under these circumstances. For the ordinary accused of modest personal, economic and social resources, the group pressures and definitions of himself are simply too much to bear. He willingly complies with the demands of agent-mediators, who in turn will help "cool him out."[6]

The power to decide what specific crimes to charge enjoys wide latitude. For example, prosecutors can decide to charge first-degree murder, second-degree murder, voluntary manslaughter, or involuntary manslaughter. They can charge aggravated assault, attempted murder, or simple assault and battery. They can charge armed robbery, simple robbery, larceny from the person, or simply larceny. Because the penalties vary for each of the specific crimes, prosecutors in effect set the upper limits of criminal punishment. However, prosecutors rarely decide to *reduce* a crime involving violence to one that does not—simple theft instead of armed robbery.

Influences on the Decision to Charge

The charging decision is an excellent example of how both law and sociology influence decision making. "Let the punishment fit the crime," the eighteenth-century Italian criminal reformer Caesere Beccaria argued. In other words, criminal justice ought to focus on the *legal* elements in crimes and fit the punishment to criminal behavior. Modern prosecutors have turned the eighteenth-century idea around and instead maintained that the crime should fit the punishment. Informally, prosecutors decide how much punishment the "badness" of the act and the "sinisterness" of the suspect deserve, and then they look for a crime to fit the deserved punishment. Criminal punishment has to meet two legal requirements:

1. The presence of the material elements of the crime in the facts surrounding the case (Chapter 4).
2. The availability of enough admissible and reliable evidence to prove the elements of the crime beyond a reasonable doubt (Chapter 11).

Legal Influences

Based on qualitative analysis of interviews with prosecutors and quantitative data that tracks defendant movement through the criminal process, Barbara Boland, Paul Mahanna, and Ronald Sones uncovered several legal factors that explain why prosecutors drop cases. Most frequently, the lack of evidence to prove guilt explains why cases are dropped. The lack of proof is due mainly to problems with witnesses and physical evidence. Some witnesses fail to appear; others are reluctant or refuse to testify. Some lack credibility because of illegal drug use and alcoholism or criminal histories. Some are not attractive enough. Empirical research has demonstrated that personal characteristics, such as attractiveness, race, and sex make witnesses undesirable to jurors. Some cases lack more than one credible witness; conviction frequently requires two or more. Physical evidence problems include missing or questionable fingerprints; the absence of stolen property or weapons recovered; and the failure to obtain medical evidence.[7]

Prosecutors practically never—in less than one-tenth of 1 percent of all cases—decide *not* to charge because law enforcement officers have violated the constitutional rights of suspects. This small number contradicts the widely held belief that constitutional safeguards against unreasonable searches and seizures present a major stumbling block to prosecution. It is failure to collect enough "good" evidence, not illegally collecting it, that accounts for most of the decisions not to charge suspects with crimes. For every case dropped because of the violation of constitutional rights, 20 are dropped because the police failed to obtain sufficient evidence to charge and convict.[8]

Furthermore, the law of evidence does not dominate charging decisions; informal influences also affect the decision to charge.[9] Brian Forst, who has studied the decision to charge for two decades, concluded from a survey of prosecution:

> In short, whether an arrest ends in conviction depends in the first place on factors over which the prosecutor has no control: the strength of the evidence as presented to the police officer, the effectiveness of the officer in bringing the best available evidence (both tangible and testimonial) to the prosecutor, and the seriousness of the offense. Nonetheless, prosecution resources and practices and the exercise of discretion—do play a significant role in determining whether arrests lead to conviction.[10]

Extralegal Influences

Extralegal considerations also affect the decision to charge. Sociologist Donald Black calls these influences the **social structure of the case.** According to Black, "the strength of the case is a sociological as well as a legal question." Therefore, prosecutors must ask:

> Who allegedly killed whom? That is, what were the characteristics of the alleged victim and the accused? Was this an upward or a downward murder (was the social status of the accused below or above the social status of the victim)? Or was it a lateral murder (between equals)? If lateral, at what status level were the principals: low, intermediate, or high? And what was the relational structure of the crime? Were the victim and the accused acquainted? If so, how well? Who are the witnesses for each side? . . . Anyone who ventures into the legal world without knowing how to assess the sociological strengths and weaknesses of a case has a disadvantage. Any law school that does not offer a course on this subject is denying its students valuable knowledge about how the law actually works.[11]

The major sociological influences on the decision to charge include:

- The seriousness of the offense.
- The sinisterness of the offender.
- The organizational pressure on prosecutors to "win" cases.

The reality of criminal justice justifies the wide discretion of prosecutors to charge. Most statutes cannot account for variations in individual cases. Legislatures pass many criminal laws, making a crime out of virtually everything that "bothers" particular groups without regard to enforceability. Some prosecutors believe that criminal codes are "society's trash bin." The charging process gives prosecutors a way to scour it. Also, prosecutors have to "individualize justice." Possessing 1 ounce of marijuana is not the same as possessing 150 ounces. Prosecutors do, and probably should, respect the wishes of victims who want to forgive those who have harmed their persons and property. Burglars who break into stores to steal compact disc players have not caused the same harm as those who break into homes in the dead of night, terrorizing occupants in their beds.

Not prosecuting suspects can sometimes serve justice better than prosecuting them. A minor property offender willing to return a stolen television set and pay for the inconvenience to the victim probably fares better if not prosecuted. Scarce resources demand that prosecutors set priorities because they cannot prosecute all cases. Accordingly, they prosecute the most serious crimes and, among the most serious crimes, pick the most "dangerous" offenders.

Lisa Frohman observed the screening process in more than 300 sexual assault cases in two branch offices of a West Coast metropolitan district attorney's office. One office served a white middle- to upper-class community, the other an African American and Hispanic lower-class community. Frohman found that the organizational pressure to win cases influenced the screening process. The promotion policy in the prosecutor's office encourages prosecutors to accept only "strong" or "winnable" cases. Promotions are based on conviction rates, and the office gives more credit to convictions than to guilty pleas. The stronger the case, the better the chance for a guilty verdict, the better the "stats" for promotion. The office discourages taking risks on weaker cases. It treats high ratios of not guilty verdicts as an indicator of incompetence. On the other hand, it gives credit to prosecutors for the number of cases they reject, because the rejections reduce the caseload of an overworked court.[12]

The Use Your Discretion case "When should prosecutors charge?" asks you to weigh the legal and sociological factors prosecutors consider important in charging rape.

Use *Your* Discretion

When should prosecutors charge?

Charging Factors in Rape

Professor Susan Estrich of the Harvard Law School relates the following incident in *Real Rape,* Estrich's essay on sexual assault and the legal system:

> The man telling me this . . . story is an assistant district attorney in a large Western city. He is in his thirties, an Ivy League law school graduate, a liberal, married to a feminist. He's about as good as you're going to get making decisions like this. This is a case he did not prosecute. He considers it rape—but only "technically." This is why.

The victim came to his office for the meeting dressed in a pair of tight jeans. Very tight. With a see-through blouse on top. Very revealing. That's how she was dressed. It was, he tells me, really something. Something else. Did it matter? Are you kidding!

The man involved was her ex-boyfriend. And lover; well, ex-lover. They ran into each other on the street. He asked her to come up and see *Splash* on his new VCR. She did. It was not the Disney version—of *Splash,* that is. It was porno. They sat in the living room watching. Like they used to. He said, "Let's go into the bedroom where we'll be more comfortable." He moved the VCR. They watched from the bed. Like they used to. He began rubbing her foot. Like he used to. Then he kissed her. She said no, she didn't want this, and got up to leave. He pulled her back on the bed and forced himself on her. He did not beat her. She had no bruises. Afterward she ran out. The first thing she did was flag a police car. That, the prosecutor tells us, was the first smart thing she did.

The prosecutor pointed out to her that she was not hurt, that she had no bruises, that she did not fight. She pointed out to the prosecutor that her ex-boyfriend was a weight lifter. He told her it would be nearly impossible to get a conviction. She could accept that, she said; even if he didn't get convicted, at least he should be forced to go through the time and expense of defending himself. That clinched it, said the D.A. She was just trying to use the system to harass her ex-boyfriend. He had no criminal record. He was not a "bad guy." No charges were filed.

Someone walked over and asked what we were talking about. About rape, I replied; no, actually about cases that aren't really rape. The D.A. looked puzzled. That was rape, he said. Technically. She was forced to have sex without consent. It just wasn't a case you prosecute.[13]

Table 10.2 shows the rank order of factors that prosecutors interviewed by researchers at the Battelle Law and Justice Study Center considered most important in deciding whether to charge suspects with rape or a lesser charge.

Notice that more than half the prosecutors considered important the use of force, the proof of penetration, the promptness of reporting, the extent of suspect identification, injury to the victim, the circumstances of the initial contact, the relationship of the victim and the accused, the use of a weapon, and resistance by the victim. Four of these factors relate to resistance to force. Prosecutors weighed factors related to consent as less important. They considered least important personal characteristics of the victim and the offender, such as age, race, occupation, and criminal record.

Table 10.2
Factors in Filing Rape Charges

Rank	Factor	Percent Choosing
1	Use of physical force	82.0
2	Proof of penetration	78.0
3	Promptness of reporting	71.3
4	Extent of suspect I.D.	67.3
5	Injury to victim	63.3
6	Circumstances of initial contact	61.3
7	Relationship of victim and accused	60.7
8	Use of weapon	58.0
9	Resistance by victim	54.0
10	Witnesses	36.0
11	Suspect's previous record	31.3
12	Age of victim or suspect	24.7
13	Alcohol or drug involvement	12.7
14	Victim's previous arrest record	10.7
15	Sexual acts other than intercourse	9.3
16	Location of offense	4.0
17	Accomplices	3.4
18	Race of victim and suspect	0.7
19	Occupation of suspect	0.7

CRITICAL THINKING

1. Do you agree with the rankings in Table 10.2?
2. Do they indicate that prosecutors take mainly formal or informal legal factors into account when charging rape?
3. Do you agree with the prosecutor's decision in the case Professor Estrich relates?
4. Consider the factors prosecutors take into account in charging rape. Which of these factors do you consider important?
5. Legally, rape requires the intent to penetrate sexually against the will and without the consent of the victim. Does the charging decision in rape indicate that prosecutors follow the law, or do organizational, community, professional, and other informal interests mainly influence their decisions?
6. What factors should prosecutors consider? In what order of importance? Defend your answer.[14]

Violent crime suspects frequently know their victims; they are their victims' spouses, lovers, friends, or casual acquaintances. Prosecutors, even in serious bodily injury felonies, consider relational crimes unattractive. Victims either cooperate reluctantly or, worse, decide after charging that they do not want prosecution to continue. In stranger assault, New Orleans prosecutors, for example, charge within a day or two of arrest. If victims know their attackers, prosecutors routinely delay the charging decision for a week because so many victims change their minds after a suspect's arrest. Prosecutors reject assault charges between family members at the rate of 40 percent, three times greater than the rate at which they reject stranger assault cases.

In a sample drawn from New York City, more than half of the cases of assault in which the offenders and victims had some prior relationship (24 of 46) were dismissed; in 22 (92 percent) of these dismissals, the primary reason given in interviews was the victim's refusal to cooperate with the prosecution. An assistant district attorney described one of them:

> This woman was charged on the complaint of her common-law husband. She then filed a complaint against him for assault. I don't know which of them called the police first. The charge against her was reduced in the Complaint Room to assault in the third degree [a misdemeanor]. Because they were both complainants in court, I was able to speak to them both. They told me they did not wish to continue prosecution. They told me that they were both drinking and apparently they both started to insult each other. It wasn't clear who struck first, but the common-law husband struck his wife with a shovel, hitting her in the eye, and she struck him in the arm with an exacto knife, causing injury. Neither said they were injured seriously, though the arresting police officer had written up her assault against her husband as assault in the second degree, while his assault against her was a third-degree assault. She was also charged with possession of a weapon as a misdeameanor, which was also dropped because the husband refused to testify as to how the knife was used. The knife was not classified as a dangerous instrument *per se.*
>
> When I had satisfied myself that neither had been injured seriously, I looked at their past records. He had one previous arrest ten years ago, I don't recall for what, and she had no prior arrests. I felt that since there had not been problems with the law, and neither one had any sort of record, there was no reason to keep this case in court.[15]

This case is typical of prior relationship assaults in a number of ways: first, the victim was not interested in pressing for a conviction and was reconciled with the assailant after the arrest had been made; second, the victim was not entirely innocent; and third, the passion of the relationship led to infliction of injuries in the attack, but the injuries were not so obviously serious that the attack fit the definition of assault in the second degree, thus justifying a felony charge.[16]

Race and gender affect the decision to charge only slightly. Celesta A. Albonetti found no effect of race or gender in the decision to reduce burglary and robbery charges. Barbara Boland and others reported mainly legal considerations in the decision to charge in the jurisdictions they surveyed. W. Boyd Littrell found little evidence of race or gender influencing the decision to charge in the New Jersey jurisdictions he examined. Of course, even slight prejudice in charging is serious, although perhaps impossible to avoid.[17]

Knowledge and Understanding CHECK

1. What percent of people arrested for a felony actually go to prison?
2. Who do prosecutors share the power to charge with?
3. Describe the amount of and limits on the power of prosecutors to charge people with crimes.
4. What three decisions does the decision to charge comprise?
5. What decisions do prosecutors participate in between charging and trial?
6. Identify and describe the consequences of the decision to charge.
7. Explain how both law and sociology influence the decision to charge.
8. List both the legal and extralegal influences on the decision to charge.
9. What does the sociologist Donald Black mean by the "social structure of the case"?

THE FIRST APPEARANCE

After prosecutors file charges, defendants appear in lower criminal courts for their **first appearance.** For defendants detained in jail, the first appearance takes place within a day (or weekend) following the filing of charges. **Bailiffs** (a court officer who keeps order and has custody of jurors and prisoners) escort detained defendants into court. Judges perform three functions at the first appearance:

1. Read the charges against defendants and inform them of their rights.
2. Appoint lawyers for indigent defendants.
3. Decide whether to bail or detain defendants prior to trial, and set the initial terms for bail or detention.

Appointment of Defense Counsel

The U.S. Constitution guarantees the right to a lawyer. However, the Constitution says nothing about how this right should be put into practice.

The Right to Counsel

The Sixth Amendment to the U.S. Constitution provides that "in all criminal prosecutions, the accused shall enjoy the right to have the assistance of counsel for his defense." The right to counsel provision raises several questions that the amendment does not answer:

1. At what point in the criminal proceedings does the right to counsel take effect?
2. Do poor people have a right to free counsel?
3. How poor is poor?
4. Do defendants have the right to a lawyer in all crimes, no matter how petty?

Originally, courts interpreted the Sixth Amendment right to counsel to mean that defendants could have lawyers only if they could either afford to hire them or could find a lawyer to represent them without pay (**pro bono assistance**). The lawyer's code of professional ethics has traditionally required lawyers to represent the poor without fees, on the theory that lawyers are not only champions of their clients but also officers of the court, bound to see that justice is done. But does the Sixth Amendment *require* that free legal counsel be given to indigent criminal defendants? If so, who should assign or appoint counsel for the indigent? In 1942, in *Betts v. Brady,* the U.S. Supreme Court ruled that indigent criminal defendants in federal courts have a right to free counsel. The states, however, were left to fashion their own rules.[18]

In 1963, the Supreme Court expanded the right to counsel to apply to state as well as federal cases. The landmark case *Gideon v. Wainwright,* arose in Florida, where only indigent defendants charged with death penalty offenses had the right to assigned counsel. Florida prosecuted Gideon with breaking and entering a poolroom "with intent to commit a misdemeanor," a felony in Florida at the time. Appearing in court without funds and without a lawyer, Gideon asked the court to appoint or assign counsel to represent him. This exchange followed:

> The Court: Mr. Gideon, I am sorry, but I cannot appoint Counsel to represent you in this case. Under the laws of the State of Florida, the only time the court can appoint Counsel to represent a defendant is when that person is charged with a capital offense. I am sorry, but I will have to deny your request to appoint Counsel to defend you in this case.
>
> The Defendant: The United States Supreme Court says I am entitled to be represented by Counsel.[19]

In a jury trial, Gideon conducted his own defense. He made an opening statement to the jury, cross-examined the state's witnesses, presented witnesses in his own defense, declined to testify himself, and made a short argument "emphasizing his innocence to the charge contained in the information filed in this case."[20]

The jury found him guilty, and the court sentenced Gideon to five years in the state prison. Gideon filed a habeas corpus petition (Chapter 9) in the Florida Supreme Court attacking his conviction and sentence on the grounds that the trial court's refusal to appoint counsel for him denied him rights "guaranteed by the Constitution and the Bill of Rights by the U.S. Government." The Florida Supreme Court, without an opinion, denied all relief. Gideon then appealed to the U.S. Supreme Court.[21]

The U.S. Supreme Court reasoned that the failure to provide a lawyer to all defendants made equal justice impossible. The government has prosecutors to present its case to the best advantage. To decide cases fairly, lawyers also have to present defendants' sides of the story. According to the Court, "the right to be heard would be, in many cases, of little avail if it did not comprehend the right to be heard by counsel."[22]

Gideon v. Wainwright did not clarify the specific kinds of crimes that the right to assigned counsel included. In 1972, in *Argersinger v. Hamlin,* the U.S. Supreme Court extended the right to counsel to misdemeanors in which defendants faced jail sentences. According to the Court, the framers of the Constitution intended to include all criminal defendants who actually faced incarceration, not just defendants charged with felonies. Furthermore, the Court ruled that justice requires that defendants must have counsel *before* they plead guilty, which is how most cases are disposed of (see Chapter 11). The Court reasoned that the enormous pressure to decide misdemeanor cases in a hurry makes representation by a lawyer necessary to guarantee fairness. This is especially true, said the Court, because defendants with lawyers fare much better in court than those without lawyers.[23]

Argersinger left an important question unanswered. Does the right to counsel extend to indigent defendants in petty misdemeanor cases that do not require jail sentences as penalties? The U.S. Supreme Court answered that question in *Scott v. Illinois.* The Court ruled that the right to counsel applies only to cases in which defendants are subject to an *actual* jail term, not just the possibility of going to jail. According to the Court, requiring appointed counsel in all criminal cases "would create confusion and impose unpredictable, but necessarily substantial, costs on fifty quite diverse states." In a strong dissent, Justice Brennan argued that the Sixth Amendment covers all criminal cases. Furthermore, he maintained that the government cannot sacrifice constitutional rights to administrative convenience and budgetary considerations. According to Justice Brennan, "This Court's role in enforcing constitutional guarantees for criminal defendants cannot be made dependent on the budgetary concerns of state governments."[24]

The constitutional right to a lawyer for defendants who cannot afford a lawyer—the great bulk of criminal defendants (see Figure 10.2)— is carried out in three ways:

1. **Public defenders,** supported by public funds are full-time defenders of poor defendants.
2. **Assigned counsel,** lawyers in private practice, are on lists from which judges select individual lawyers on a rotating basis to represent indigent defendants on a case-by-case basis, either for a fee or pro bono.
3. **Contract attorneys,** private attorneys operating under contracts with local jurisdictions, represent indigent defendants for an agreed-upon fee.

About 75 percent of all state prison inmates and 80 percent of all defendants charged with felonies in the nation's

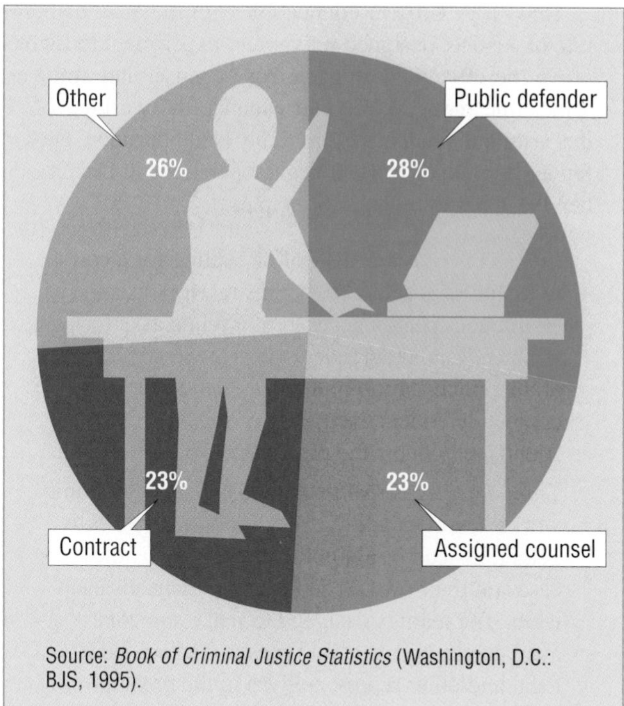

Figure 10.2
Types of Defense for the Indigent

largest counties relied on either a public defender or on assigned counsel for legal representation. Standards for determining indigence vary among the states. About half of all felony defendants qualify as indigent. Fewer misdemeanor defendants qualify, because most states impose higher standards for defendants charged with minor crimes.[25]

Criminal Defense in Practice

In practice, criminal justice does not completely satisfy the right to counsel. To be sure, defendants with sufficient means to hire top criminal defense lawyers obtain effective representation. These defendants demand and make the proverbial "phone call" to summon their lawyers to police stations to protect their rights. Private attorneys stand by their clients through every step in the criminal process, fighting for their clients and watchdogging every prosecutorial move to ensure that the government remains within constitutional bounds. Defendants with adequate resources rarely suffer abuse in police, prosecutorial, or judicial actions.

The same is not true where public defenders represent poor defendants. One-third of all indigents rely on assigned, unpaid counsel, and only half the public defender systems in existence are well-staffed offices. Lack of money and personnel make it impossible to implement the constitutional right to counsel. Only 5 percent of all indigent defendants see a lawyer prior to their first appearance before a magistrate. Thus, defendants' encounters with the police are effectively without counsel. Furthermore, most public defenders are inexperienced and receive no special training. Less than 2 percent of assigned counsel have had any training beyond a law degree. Thus, the most inexperienced and least-trained lawyers defend indigent clients.[26]

Bill Kennedy heads one of the best public defender's offices in the country. According to Kennedy, the number of serious felonies handled by public defenders mushroomed in the 1990s. The number of appeals that his office handled

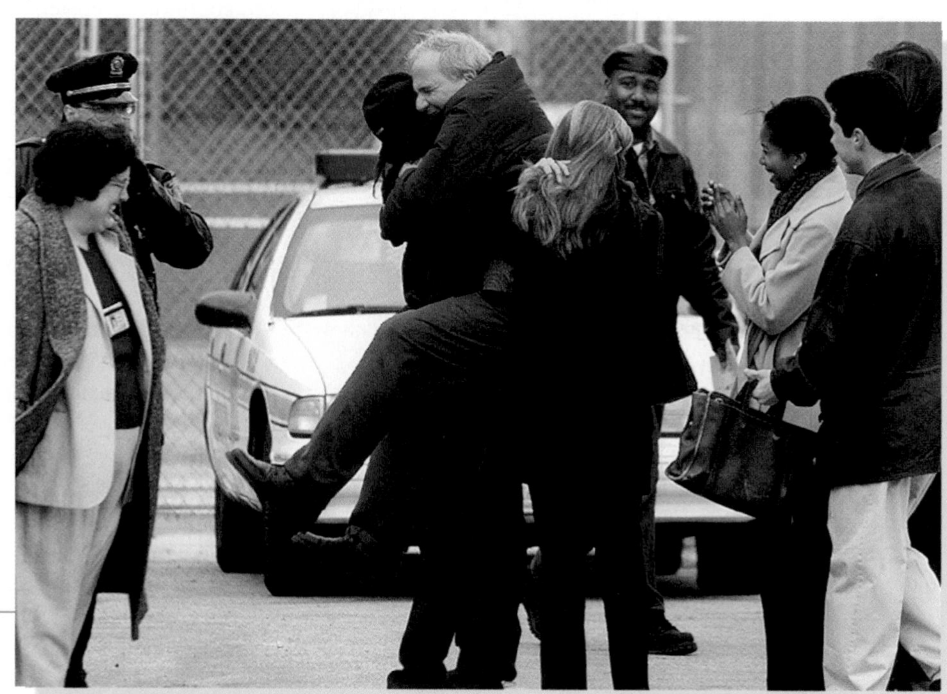

For those defendants who cannot afford to hire private defense attorneys to represent them, chances are high that the counsel he or she will be assigned will not have enough training or enough time to adequately prepare a defense. The consequences for defendants can be severe: Anthony Porter spent 16 years in prison after being wrongfully convicted of multiple murders. Here he hugs David Protess, a journalism professor from Northwestern University, who, with several of his students (also pictured), was instrumental in gaining Porter's release in February of 1999.

representation to which [our clients] are legally entitled. It's alarming, demoralizing and, ultimately, not legal."[27]

Use *Your* Discretion

Are public defenders ineffective?

Despite the apparently discouraging conclusions summarized in the text, considerable empirical evidence suggests that public defenders do as well for their clients as private defense counsel do for theirs. Sociologist Lisa J. McIntyre concluded that "numerous empirical studies have failed to find any evidence that clients of public defenders fare worse (at least in terms of case outcomes) than defendants who are represented by private lawyers."[28]

Roger A. Hanson, Brian J. Ostrom, William E. Hewitt, and others analyzed a random sample of 4,000 felony cases from nine courts and interviewed 125 defense attorneys. They found that public defenders

- Disposed of their cases as fast as privately retained lawyers.
- Were as successful as privately retained counsel at obtaining favorable outcomes for their clients.
- Were compensated, trained, and received about the same level of support as prosecutors in the same jurisdictions.[29]

Robert Spangenberg, who has conducted major studies of criminal defense, challenges the validity of Hanson and his colleagues' study, labeling it "a sloppy piece of research." And, Spangenberg says, the study suffers from a selective hypothesis fallacy. According to Spangenberg, Hanson "went to the jurisdictions in the country that were among the best-funded public defense systems . . . and he's drawing conclusions based on those sites."[30]

David Lynch, former public defender, after studying defense lawyers in two counties, reports that the courtroom work group and the collusion that occurs within it corrupts the relationship between public defenders and their clients:

> I have witnessed countless criminal defendants who claimed they were being "sold out" by their lawyers. Many asked the court, almost always unsuccessfully, to appoint new counsel. Some later filed collateral attacks, alleging coercion, to the entry of their guilty pleas. These allegations were almost always found to be unsubstantiated. Like mental institution inmates yelling "conspiracy," prison inmates yelling "conspiracy" were never taken credibly, even though the similarities of their tales of woe should have made people wonder.[31]

New York City, in connection with the Vera Institute of Justice, designed a five-year experiment to improve the effectiveness of defense counsel and at the same time reduce costs and enhance the working of the criminal justice system. The Neighborhood Defender Service of Harlem began operations in December 1990, based on three principles:

- *Early intervention:* Instead of waiting for a court to assign counsel, NDS begins its work as soon as an indigent person accused of a crime asks for assistance. Public defenders interview many clients at the police station immediately after arrest. Some contact defenders even earlier, if relatives or friends tell clients the police are looking for them.
- *Team defense:* Small teams of lawyers, community workers, and an administrative assistant work together, instead of assigning lawyers to handle cases on their own. A senior attorney heads each team. The team is designed to make someone available to clients at all times, to include both legal and other representatives in the preparation of cases, and to provide emotional support and professional training for staff.
- *Client-centered representation:* Representation is designed around all the legal consequences of the accusation of a crime, not simply the resolution of a particular case. These other consequences include forfeiture of cars, cash, and leaseholds; eviction; termination of parental rights and welfare benefits; and deportation.[32]

The Neighborhood Defender Service has put these features at the core of its experiment. Its office is located in a building in central Harlem, nowhere near a courthouse. Posters on the street and in subways advertise the availability of its services, "telling Harlem residents how to handle themselves if arrested and to call NDS [Neighborhood Defender Service] immediately if they cannot afford a private lawyer." The office itself is also unusual. It contains "teams of lawyers and nonlawyers working together in an open-space plan." The large percentage of nonlawyers reflects the priority given to investigation and social services. Most of the nonlawyers—administrative assistants, interns, and community workers—work in teams alongside the lawyers. The community workers (mostly young college graduates) handle most of the investigation—not retired police officers, who are usually found in charge of investigation in the offices of public defenders. The NDS attorneys represent their clients in many courthouses in all stages of the criminal process and even in civil cases, particularly in the growing instances of forfeitures in drug cases.[33]

The principles of early intervention, increased investigation, and total representation seem to work, according to an interim evaluation. At the end of the first year, the Vera Institute of Justice evaluated the experiment. Vera matched clients in NDS with similar clients defended by the regular public defender's office in Manhattan.[34]

According to the Vera researchers:

> The results in the NDS cases are striking when compared to those in the matched cases handled by traditional defenders. Despite the fact that the arrests, charges, prior records, and personal characteristics of the defendants were similar, the NDS cases resulted in less pretrial detention, fewer convictions, fewer sentences of incarceration, and shorter sentences when incarceration was imposed.
>
> These outcomes, moreover, were the results of decisions made by the same prosecutors and judges applying the same laws and policies to both samples of cases. None of the cases in the NDS sample, and only three of the matched cases, resulted in trial, so juries were almost irrelevant to these results.
>
> By representing clients in their new way, the NDS teams were able to persuade prosecutors and judges that the decisions they made in these cases should be different, and significantly less severe and costly, than the decisions they made in similar cases handled by traditional defenders.[35]

CRITICAL THINKING

1. Summarize the findings of the empirical research by the Vera Institute of Justice.
2. Does the research prove its point about the effectiveness of public defender assistance? Explain.
3. What policy changes, if any, would you make in view of these findings and the Vera Institute's experiment? Defend your answer.

Knowledge and Understanding CHECK

1. List the three functions performed at the first appearance.
2. What does the Sixth Amendment say–and not say–about having a lawyer?
3. Briefly trace the development of the interpretation of the right to counsel.
4. Summarize the holdings of *Gideon v. Wainright, Argersinger v. Hayes,* and *Scott v. Illinois.*
5. Identify and describe the three types of defense available to the poor.
6. Describe how the right to counsel operates in practice.

BAIL AND DETENTION

Almost all misdemeanor defendants and nearly two-thirds of all felony defendants are released prior to conviction. **Bail,** the release of defendants pending the final disposition of their cases, is an ancient practice. More than two thousand years ago, the Greek philosopher Plato wrote that prosecutors must

> demand bail from the defendant [who] shall provide three substantial securities who guarantee to produce him at the trial, and if a man be unable or unwilling to provide these securities, the court must take, bind and keep him, and produce him at the trial of the case.[36]

The practice that Plato described prevailed until about one hundred years ago. Then, individuals who guaranteed that defendants would appear in court all but disappeared. Financial guarantees—that is, money—replaced personal guarantees. At first, defendants had to deposit whatever

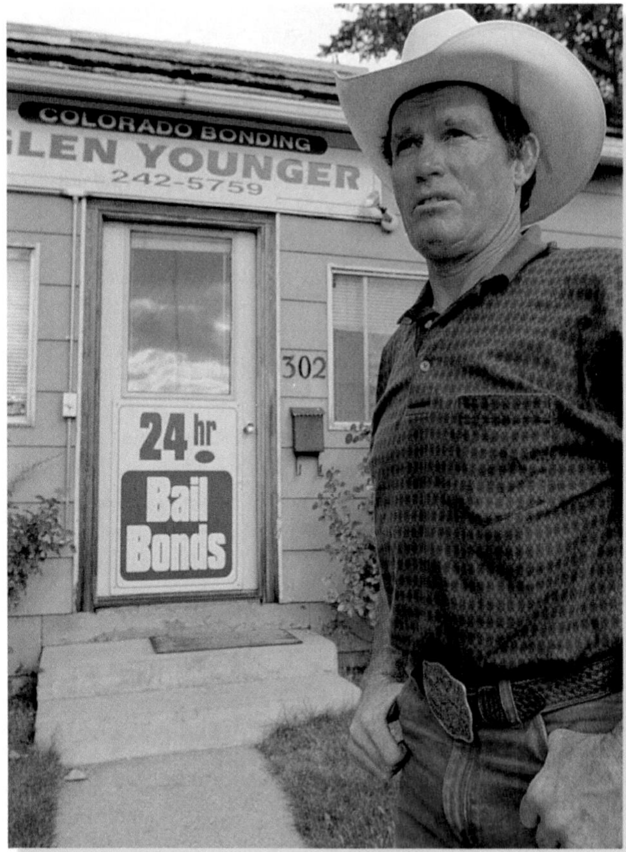

Bail is an ancient practice, dating back at least 1000 years. It is also controversial. Nevertheless, most criminal defendants are released on bail. Here, Glen Younger stands in front of his bail bond company in Grand Junction, Colorado. "Up front, you know that everyone who comes into your office has a problem," says Younger, who is also a rancher, outfitter, auctioneer, and runs a construction company. "I am optimistic about people. If I wasn't, I wouldn't be here."

Figure 10.3
Percent of Felony Defendants Released and Detained in 75 Most Populous Counties, 1992

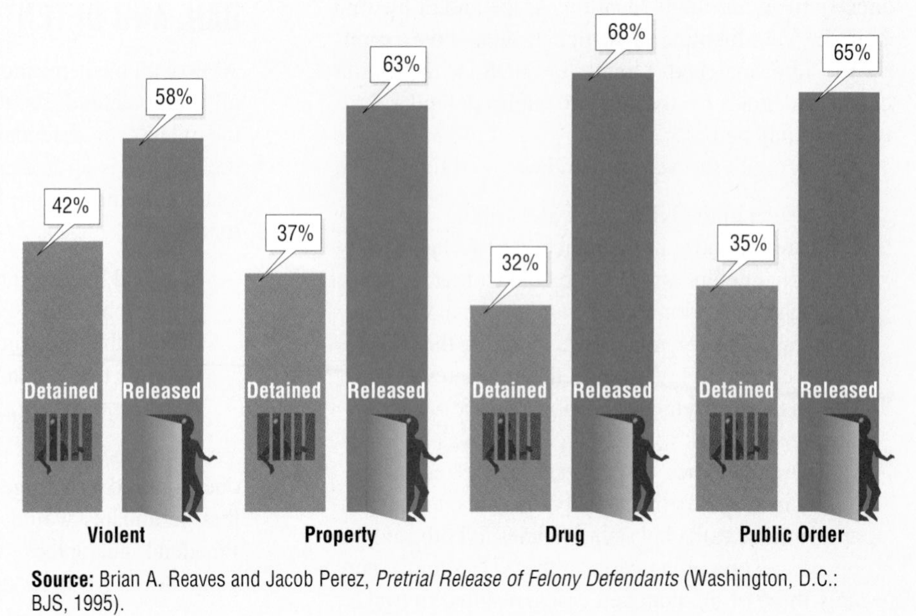

Source: Brian A. Reaves and Jacob Perez, *Pretrial Release of Felony Defendants* (Washington, D.C.: BJS, 1995).

amount judges decided was necessary to ensure that defendants appeared in court. If defendants appeared as scheduled, the court returned their money. **Commercial bail,** or the bail bond system, has replaced direct financial surety. During the 1960s, many jurisdictions established pretrial release programs that relied on nonfinancial release conditions. Fear of crime and consequent concern for public safety led to a return to pretrial detention. Nevertheless, the number of defendants released before conviction or acquittal remains large.[37] (See Figure 10.3.)

The U.S. Constitution, bail statutes, and court cases formally govern bail. However, formal law does not explain the day-to-day operations of pretrial release and detention. Informally, bail bond offices and pretrial release agencies operate the system.

Commercial Bail

Until the 1960s, most jurisdictions in the United States required money bail. *Commercial bail* (bail bonding as a private business) still plays the major role in pretrial release. Judges set the bail amount, and defendants pay a fee to the bondsmen, usually 10 percent of the bail amount. Bondsmen guarantee to pay *forfeitures*—the face amount of the bail bond—if defendants do not appear.

Fees paid by defendants are bondsmen's livelihood. Suppose a court sets bail at $1,000. If a defendant secures a bail bond for a 10 percent fee, the bondsman retains the $100 (10 percent of the bail amount). If, on the other hand, a defendant has the money to deposit the $1,000 with the court, the court returns the full amount when the defendant appears.

Use *Your* Discretion

Is commercial bail a good idea?

Andy Hall, in his survey of pretrial release programs, listed all of the following objections to commercial bail:

- Commercial bail discriminates against poor defendants.
- It is impossible to translate the risk of flight and/or danger into money values.
- The premise that money will secure appearance is questionable because bondsmen keep the money paid.
- Judges may set bail high to punish defendants prior to conviction.
- Commercial bail transfers the release decision from judges to bail bondsmen.
- It provides for little or no supervision of defendants.
- It fosters corrupt and abusive practices.
- Pretrial detention informally punishes poor defendants prior to legal proof of guilt.[38]
- Commercial bail discriminates, either directly or indirectly, against racial minorities.[39]

As a result of these and other criticisms, some states have abolished the private bail bond system. In these states, defendants generally pay their 10 percent directly to the court. If they appear, the court returns their deposits. Defendants who fail to appear forfeit their deposits; they also remain legally liable for the full remaining amount of bail.

Technically, when defendants fail to appear on private bail bonds, courts can collect the full amount from the bondsmen; bondsmen can recoup the amount paid from defaulting defendants. In practice, this rarely happens. Elaborate and entrenched informal rules ensure that bondsmen will not forfeit the amount of bail bonds.

Bondsmen in Connecticut, for example, avoid forfeiture in several ways. They can compromise or come to an agreement with the court to reduce the forfeited amount. They can secure continuances from the court for a period during which they look for defendants. Finally, they can attempt to find and bring their customers to court. From his observations in a Connecticut lower court, Malcolm M. Feeley concluded that bondsmen lost only about 3 percent of the face amount of bond forfeitures.[40]

CRITICAL THINKING

1. Compare the private and public bail systems.
2. Which is better? Why?
3. Would you recommend that your jurisdiction adopt public or private bail? Why?

Competing Bail Policies

Bail involves two fundamental and conflicting public policies:

1. Public safety.
2. Protecting innocent people from incarceration.

Freeing defendants until trial may endanger public safety. Also, guilty bailed defendants might escape conviction. Furthermore, while free, they may commit more crimes. In addition, bailed defendants can injure, threaten, and intimidate victims and witnesses.[41]

However, detaining innocent defendants encroaches on their liberty. Pretrial detention disrupts theirs and their family's lives. It also interrupts, and sometimes terminates, employment. Furthermore, it impairs the capacity of accused persons to aid in their own defense; they have difficulty contacting witnesses and talking with their lawyers. Detention also lessens the bargaining power of defendants, either when pleading or at sentencing. More seriously, pretrial detention amounts to incarceration before trial. Legally, defendants are innocent until prosecutors prove them guilty beyond a reasonable doubt. Poor jail conditions exacerbate the punitive aspects of pretrial detention.

Pretrial detention also is expensive. The direct economic costs of detaining suspects in jail, paying welfare benefits to their dependents, and providing public defense counsel, along with the loss of tax revenue from the wages of defendants, "are enormous," says Steven R. Schlesinger, former director of the Bureau of Justice Statistics. According to Schlesinger, "A defendant who is detained on a petty theft involving a few dollars may cost the government thousands of dollars."[42]

Crime control and public safety conflicts with pretrial liberty and economy in government. Balancing crime control, individual rights, and economy never satisfies everybody. The prospect of bailed defendants committing more crimes disturbs many. Incarcerating innocent defendants troubles others. Fiscal conservatives demand that taxpayers get the most for their tax dollars and object to spending money that is not demonstrably effective in controlling crime.

The Law of Bail

The Eighth Amendment to the U.S. Constitution says that "Excessive bail shall not be required." Notice that the Eighth Amendment does not outlaw detention prior to trial. What it does do is prohibit the imposition of *excessive* bail.

In the landmark bail case *Stack v. Boyle,* the U.S. Supreme Court defined "excessive bail." Twelve people were charged with conspiring to advocate overthrowing the government by force, a federal crime. The trial court set bail at $50,000 for each defendant. The defendants protested that the amount was excessive and submitted evidence that their financial resources, family relationships, health, prior criminal records, and other information all indicated that less money would ensure their appearance. The trial court ignored this information, accepting instead a government statement that four other defendants in similar circumstances had fled the jurisdiction of the court. The Supreme Court held that the "proper method" is to determine the amount necessary to ensure the defendants' appearance at trial.[43]

In another case, *United States v. Abrahams,* Abrahams was arrested for defrauding the federal government, a felony punishable by up to five years' imprisonment. A federal magistrate set bail at $100,000. Abrahams posted the bail, was released, and jumped bail by failing to appear for a hearing to remove the case to another jurisdiction. When Abrahams was charged before a U.S. district court, the government prosecutor took the position that he should be held without bail, for the following reasons:

- Abrahams had three previous convictions in both federal and state courts.
- He was an escaped state prisoner from New Jersey.
- He had given false information at the previous bail hearing.
- He had failed to appear on January 18, 1978, as ordered by Magistrate Pierce.
- Using the name Layne, he had failed to appear in a California case and was a fugitive from the courts of that state.

- He had used several aliases in the past.
- He had transferred 1.5 million dollars to Bermuda in 1976 and 1977.[44]

The prosecutor argued:

> The record before us depicts a man who has lived a life of subterfuge, deceit and cunning. He is an escaped felon. He did not hesitate to flee to Florida and forfeit $100,000 to avoid the removal hearing. There is nothing in the record that suggests that bail will result in his appearance at trial. Every indication is to the contrary. This is the rare case of extreme and unusual circumstances that justifies pretrial detention without bail.[45]

Abrahams presents one extreme of money bail—where no amount can secure a defendant's appearance. At the other extreme, indigent defendants cannot pay even $50 to secure their release. The U.S. Supreme Court has never squarely decided that money bail amounts to excessive bail for indigents. However, a federal appeals court reviewed Florida's bail procedure as it applies to indigents. A group of indigent defendants brought an action challenging Florida's bail practices. They argued that money bail was unconstitutional for indigents, who were jailed to await their cases' outcomes simply because they were poor.[46]

In the midst of the lawsuit, Florida adopted new rules that provided alternatives to money bail for those released prior to disposition. These nonmonetary alternatives are almost identical to the ones in effect under the federal Bail Reform Act. However, unlike federal law, Florida law neither established priorities among the alternatives nor indicated any presumption favoring nonmonetary conditions over money bail.

The same indigents challenged the new Florida rules on grounds similar to their reasons for challenging the old Florida pure money bail practice. The court said:

> At the outset we accept the principle that imprisonment solely because of indigent status is invidious discrimination and not constitutionally permissible. The punitive and heavily burdensome nature of pretrial confinement has been the subject of convincing commentary.[47]

However, the court went on to hold that indigence did not require Florida either to establish a presumption in favor of nonmonetary bail for indigents or to create priorities among various bail conditions. The court said each case must be decided individually and left it to the discretion of magistrates to determine what condition or combination of conditions best serves the interests of society and poor defendants. In short, indigent defendants do not have a constitutional right to nonmonetary bail and are not unconstitutionally discriminated against simply because they are required to advance money bail.[48]

Those who cannot make bail face pretrial detention and a disadvantage in future proceedings. Pretrial detention makes it difficult for defendants to help their lawyers build the strongest defense against the government's case. Jailed defendants pose serious obstacles for defense counsel. They cannot help locate witnesses or evidence. Attempting to confer in crowded jails with restricted hours impedes the development and implementation of an effective defense strategy. Time spent in jail often adversely affects defendants' demeanor and appearance in court. Their complexion looks pallid, their clothing rumpled, and they exhibit a "jailed look." If convicted, a detained defendant who has lost a job and been separated from family and other relationships has a much poorer chance for probation than one "who has earned money, kept his job, and maintained strong family ties."

The Federal Bail Reform Act

Since the passage of the Judiciary Act of 1789, defendants in federal courts have had a statutory right to bail. According to that statute, defendants in federal courts *shall* be bailed, except in capital cases. The Bail Reform Act of 1966 favored nonmonetary release if it was sufficient to ensure the appear-

Although most bailed defendants abide by the conditions of their release, bail is always a risk. Here, the body of Leroy George Brown is a sad reminder of that risk. This boy was the only witness to his mother's boyfriend's murder who was willing to testify. The suspect, out on bail, shot him and his mother in January 1999 in spite of police promises of protection.

Figure 10.4
Types of Release in 75 Largest U.S. Counties, 1992

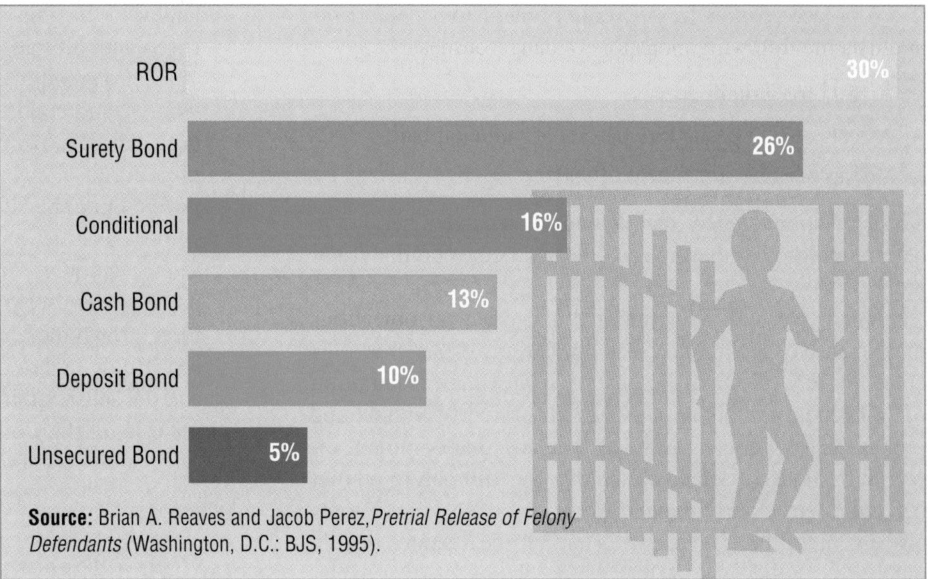

ance of defendants. The most common form of nonmonetary release is ROR (or simply OR)—**release on recognizance**—which releases defendants solely on their promise to appear at trial. A second form is **conditional release,** in which judges can impose a range of nonmonetary conditions, including maintaining regular contact, either by telephone or in person, with a pretrial program; reporting for regular drug monitoring or treatment; and being placed in the custody of a third party. Another form, release on unsecured bonds, does not require putting up any money, but it results in a bail forfeiture if defendants fail to appear. (See Figure 10.4.)[49]

Despite the emphasis on nonmonetary release, bonds requiring at least some cash advances are common (see Figure 10.4). All monetary releases are based on bonds of various types. In full cash bonds, defendants have to put up the entire amount either in cash or in collateral. In the deposit bond, defendants usually put up 10 percent of the cash amount. In the surety bond, bail bondsmen put up 10 percent of the cash amount of bail.

The 1966 Bail Reform Act also specifies what information the court may use to determine the conditions of release, including:

- Nature of the offense charged.
- Amount of evidence against the defendant.
- Past criminal record of the defendant.
- Ties of the defendant to the community, such as family, property owned, and job.
- Mental condition of the defendant.
- Length of residence of the defendant in the community.
- Failure of the defendant to appear at required court proceedings.[50]

Defendants who are denied release can demand that judges promptly reconsider the conditions. If judges reaffirm their initial decisions not to release defendants, they must provide written reasons for the conditions imposed. The act prescribes potentially severe penalties for defendants who fail to appear. Bail jumpers forfeit any security pledged and are subject to as much as a $5,000 fine or a maximum of five years in prison. In short, the courts can release defendants on liberal conditions but reserve the right to punish them severely for failure to appear.[51]

State Bail Statutes

State bail statutes vary widely, but since the 1970s they have reflected a shift from emphasizing the rights of defendants to protecting community safety. A Florida law, for example, states clearly that "it is the intent of the legislature that the primary consideration be the protection of the community from risk of physical harm to persons." Ten state statutes briefly list gross criteria, leaving the bail decision to judges as "a matter of sound discretion." Others resemble the federal act and list release conditions in detail.[52]

Most judges base their decisions to bail on three legal criteria:

1. The seriousness of the charges against defendants.
2. The strength of the prosecution's case against defendants.
3. The prior criminal history, or "rap sheet," of defendants.

Few judges give any weight to community ties or to defendants' background and character.[53]

Preventive Detention

Preventive detention allows courts to order the detention of defendants who might endanger either public safety generally or specific victims and other witnesses. Preventive detention is an ancient practice but the modern basis for it began when the U.S. Congress enacted the Bail Reform Act of 1984.

That act permits the detention of dangerous defendants and lists the following indicators of dangerousness:

- Arrests for violent crimes.
- Arrests during probation, parole, or while on bail.
- Multiple arrests for repeat offenders.

The act also guarantees that defendants receive a hearing to determine whether their release endangers the community or individuals.[54]

There are both constitutional and practical objections to preventive detention. Civil libertarians argue that it is cruel and unusual punishment; it violates the presumption of innocence; and, it deprives citizens of liberty without due process of law. Social scientists maintain that empirical research has clearly demonstrated that it is difficult to predict behavior, particularly dangerous behavior. Social scientists also maintain that preventive detention incarcerates people unnecessarily because of the overprediction of dangerousness. Decision makers don't want to free someone who might commit a crime. For example, judges overpredict defendants' potential dangerousness, despite consistent evidence indicating that a minority of defendants released on bail commit crimes while they are free. One survey found that 86 percent of freed defendants were not arrested while they are on bail. And, only 5.1 percent of those arrested were convicted.[55]

However, the Supreme Court rejected these arguments, upholding the act's preventive detention provisions in *United States v. Salerno.* The government charged Salerno with 29 counts of racketeering and conspiracy to commit murder. At his arraignment, the government asked the judge to detain Salerno because no release condition could ensure community safety. At a detention hearing, the government presented evidence that Salerno was the "boss" of the Genovese organized crime family. Wiretaps showed that Salerno had participated in conspiracies to commit murder. Witnesses corroborated the wiretap evidence. Salerno provided character witnesses, presented evidence of a heart condition, and challenged the government's evidence, but the trial judge allowed the detention. The Supreme Court ruled that preventive detention does not constitute punishment; it amounts to a regulatory device to ensure public safety. The Constitution allows for balancing individual liberty and community safety; in this case, according to the Court, the need for public safety outweighed Salerno's right to freedom pending legal determination of his guilt.[56]

Justice Marshall strongly dissented:

> It is a fair summary of history to say that the safeguards of liberty have frequently been forged in controversies involving not very nice people. Honoring the presumption of innocence is often difficult; sometimes we must pay substantial social costs as a result of our commitment to the values we espouse. But at the end of the day the presumption of innocence protects the innocent; the shortcuts we take with those whom we believe to be guilty injure only those wrongfully accused and, ultimately, ourselves.
>
> Throughout the world today there are men, women, and children interned indefinitely, awaiting trials which may never come or which may be a mockery of the word, because their governments believe them to be "dangerous." Our Constitution, whose construction began two centuries ago, can shelter us forever from the evils of such unchecked power. Over 200 years it has slowly, through our efforts, grown more durable, more expansive, and more just. But it cannot protect us if we lack the courage and the self-restraint to protect ourselves. Today, a majority of the Court applies itself to an ominous exercise in demolition.[57]

Predicting Misconduct on Bail

Two reports showed that pretrial release grew in most cities between 1962 and 1980. Between 1962 and 1971, felony releases increased from 48 to 67 percent and misdemeanor releases from 60 to 72 percent. By 1980, release rates had risen to 80 percent in many jurisdictions, and the average dollar amount of bail had declined. These two developments allowed the release of large numbers of defendants who would previously have been denied bail.[58]

Researchers also found that "only a few bail violators become real fugitives from justice; most eventually return." More than 87 percent of all released defendants appeared for every scheduled appearance. In addition, most defendants who failed to appear were not fugitives from justice. Their failure to appear was inadvertent; they forgot a date, got confused about where they should go, or missed the scheduled time. Sometimes they were given the wrong time, date, or courtroom. All these registered as failures, but they differ from defendants who intentionally stayed away to avoid judicial proceedings. All but about 2 percent who did not appear for their first appearance eventually did show up in court.[59]

Originally, evaluators believed that selecting defendants with the closest community ties produced these impressive results. For example, the Manhattan Bail Project used an objective release system based on an elaborate **bail point system** that determined community ties by assigning points for employment, residence, family, and other relationships with the community. Most other bail projects around the country adopted similar point scales.[60]

John S. Goldkamp evaluated the point system in Philadelphia. He concluded, in an elaborate regression analysis, that

> no decision criteria—including community ties, charging seriousness, or any others promulgated . . . have been found to do what presumably they are employed to do; that is, they cannot predict risk of flight or pretrial dangerousness.[61]

Use *Your* Discretion

Can drug testing reduce pretrial misconduct?

Britt, Gottfredson, and Goldkamp studied the value of monitoring the use of drugs by defendants on bail as a means to reduce not only their use of drugs but also their pretrial misconduct. They relied on a computerized case-tracking system in Pima and Miracopa counties in Arizona to select a control group and an experimental group of similar defendants on bail. The computerized system included information about prior record, court appearance history, offense, living arrangements, bail decision, failure to appear, and criminal behavior while on bail. The control group received normal supervision; the experimental group received drug monitoring during pretrial release.[62]

No significant differences in failure to appear or rearrest rates between the two groups occurred in Pima County, except that members of the monitored group were slightly less likely to get rearrested for the possession of drugs. In Miracopa County, arrests and failure to appear rates were *higher* in the monitored group than in the control group. On the basis of their findings, the authors concluded that

> systematic drug testing and monitoring in the pretrial setting . . . is not likely to achieve significant or major reductions in pretrial misconduct. At the same time that these programs fail to achieve their stated goal of reducing rates of pretrial misconduct, they carry a heavy price tag. In both Pima County and Miracopa County the cost of drug testing programs averaged from $400,000 to $500,000 per year. Given the high financial costs of these programs, including the testing and staffing required to accomplish them, it seems reasonable to question the effectiveness and cost-effectiveness of drug testing the released pretrial population.[63]

CRITICAL THINKING

1. Summarize the method and findings of the research on drug testing and bail.
2. On the basis of this research, would you recommend adopting drug testing? Why? Why not?

Race and Gender Bias in Bail Decisions

Some research has suggested that bail decisions suffer from race and gender discrimination. E. Britt Patterson and Michael J. Lynch examined the compliance of judges with the bail schedule of a large western city. They found that the schedule did not remove race and gender disparities in bail decisions. Whites, particularly white women, were more likely to receive bail below the schedule than nonwhites. When they controlled for other variables that might affect the outcome of the bail decision, such as the seriousness of the offense and the dangerousness of the defendant, they found that nonwhites and men were no more likely than whites and women to receive bail in *excess* of the schedule. However, whites and women were significantly more likely than nonwhite men to receive bail *below* the schedule. (See Figure 10.5.) Patterson and Lynch

Figure 10.5
Race and Gender Differences in Bail Schedule

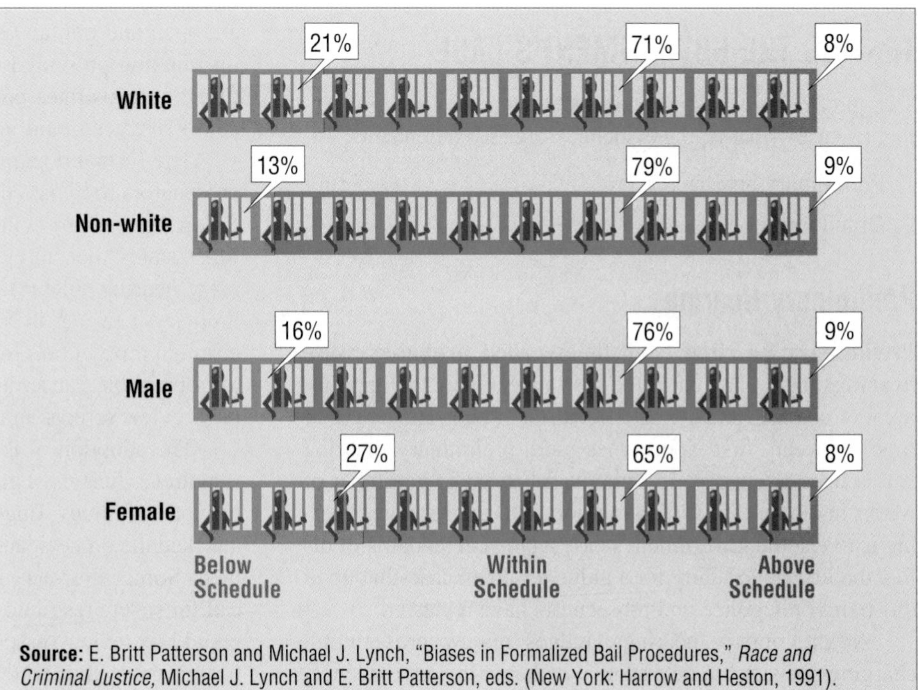

Source: E. Britt Patterson and Michael J. Lynch, "Biases in Formalized Bail Procedures," *Race and Criminal Justice,* Michael J. Lynch and E. Britt Patterson, eds. (New York: Harrow and Heston, 1991).

concluded that "although minorities were not treated more harshly than whites, they were discriminated against because they were not given the same benefit of the doubt as were whites."[64]

Knowledge and Understanding CHECK

1. Describe the bail system that Plato advocated (which operated until about a century ago).
2. Identify and explain the effects of the two conflicting public policies regarding bail.
3. Does the Eighth Amendment create a right to bail? Explain your answer.
4. List the provisions of and explain the importance of the Federal Bail Reform Act of 1986.
5. Describe the shifts in state bail statutes since the 1970s.
6. List the three legal criteria that most state judges base their bail decisions on.
7. List the pros and cons of preventive detention.
8. According to the studies that evaluated prediction of misconduct by defendants on bail, what is the danger of failure to appear and the commission of crimes while on bail?
9. Describe specifically the effects of gender and race on bail decisions.

TESTING THE GOVERNMENT'S CASE

Two pretrial proceedings test the strength of the government's case—that is, the evidence—against defendants:

1. Preliminary hearings
2. Grand jury review

Preliminary Hearing

Preliminary hearings, sometimes called **probable cause hearings,** take place after the first appearance, the appointment of counsel, and the determination of bail. The length of time between first appearance and preliminary hearing varies from a few days in some jurisdictions to a number of weeks in others. The formal mission of the preliminary hearing is to test the government's case against defendants. It offers the first opportunity for a judge to screen casesthat up to this point only police and prosecutors have reviewed.

At preliminary hearings, judges review prosecutors' charging decisions to determine whether sufficient evidence, or probable cause, exists to warrant further proceedings. If judges decide that cases deserve further action, they **bind over defendants;** that is, judges send the case to trial. If judges determine that the prosecution's case lacks probable cause, they dismiss charges. Although prosecutors *can* charge the case again, they rarely reopen cases dismissed at preliminary hearings.[65]

Indictment and Information

The government can also initiate criminal proceedings and test probable cause by issuing an **indictment,** a formal written accusation by the grand jury; this is an ancient practice originating in medieval England. Grand jury proceedings can be held in place of preliminary hearings, or they can follow preliminary hearings as a second screening device. Dismissals at preliminary hearings do not prevent grand juries from reconsidering probable cause to send a case to trial. If magistrates dismiss cases, prosecutors can bring them to grand juries for another try, in the hope of winning a more favorable outcome. On the other hand, even if judges bind cases over, grand juries can decide not to indict.

Grand juries are composed of private citizens chosen to serve from one to several months. Traditionally, 23 people sat on a grand jury; today, as few as 6 make up grand juries, with 12 to 16 most common. Compared with the unanimous verdict usually required to convict, it takes a simple majority of grand jurors to indict.

Indicting by grand jury screening and binding over in preliminary hearings both rest on the same objective basis—probable cause. However, major differences separate preliminary hearings from grand jury proceedings. Grand jury hearings are not adversary proceedings; only the government presents evidence. Defendants can neither offer evidence nor appear before grand juries. Furthermore, grand jury proceedings are secret and closed; preliminary hearings are open and public. Grand jurors or others who "leak" any information presented to grand juries face severe penalties. Finally, magistrates preside in preliminary hearings; prosecutors oversee grand jury proceedings.[66]

The formal document known as an **information** allows prosecutors to bypass the grand jury and initiate proceedings following the prosecutor's own review of probable cause. Most states that allow informations require that a preliminary hearing follow the filing of an information. The preliminary hearing in information jurisdictions prevents a criminal prosecution from proceeding solely on the prosecutor's probable cause determination; it screens what a grand jury review screens in indictment jurisdictions.

The adoption of the information process followed longstanding criticisms of grand jury review. In the eighteenth century, the famous English law reformer Jeremy Bentham attacked the process, and objections to it have continued since then. Some reformers demand its outright abolition; others call for severe restrictions on its power. Abolitionists consider grand jury review "essentially worthless." They agree with the former prosecutor who said he could "indict anybody, at any time, for almost anything before a grand jury."[67]

This criticism depicts grand juries as rubber stamps for prosecutors; and statistics indicate that grand juries rarely disagree with prosecutors. Between January 1, 1974, and June 30, 1977, 235 cases were presented to the San Francisco grand jury, and indictments were returned in all 235. The ratio has not changed significantly since then. Also, according to critics the grand jury "is costly in terms of space, manpower and money," and it delays case processing because grand juries are not as accessible as magistrates.[68]

Despite criticism, supporters of grand jury review claim several advantages. They maintain that grand juries effectively screen criminal cases. According to supporters—who count prosecutors among their numbers—grand jurors do have minds of their own. The low rate of refusals to indict has little or nothing to do with prosecutors dominating the grand jury room; instead, the many indictments result from careful preliminary screening. Prosecutors bring only strong cases that persuade the grand jury to indict. In fact, prosecutors say they present cases for which they have not only probable cause but also proof beyond a reasonable doubt. The high ratio of indictments to convictions—more than 98 percent result in conviction—supports this conclusion.

The preliminary hearing, indictment, and information represent different ways to test the government's case against defendants before trial. The preliminary hearing places the decision in the magistrate's or judge's hands; the information, in the prosecutor's; and the indictment, in the community's representatives—the grand jurors. Each has a check on its authority to initiate the criminal process. The grand jury can review and reverse a preliminary hearing bind over or an information; and magistrates can review grand jury indictments. Despite its tenacious and occasionally truculent critics, the grand jury remains an alternative to informations and preliminary hearings in serious and sensitive cases. In these cases, prosecutors can share the responsibility with the grand jury, a body that represents the community.

ARRAIGNMENT AND PRETRIAL MOTIONS

Criminal courts have the authority to dispose of cases either by trial or by guilty pleas. **Arraignment** consists of bringing defendants to open court, reading the charges against them, and demanding that they plead either not guilty, guilty, or **nolo contendere** (no contest) to the charges. The arraignment and plea to charges formally set the stage for the criminal trial. Informally, they provide the opportunity either to start, continue, or ratify a plea agreement.

If the defense and prosecution want to make pretrial motions, they can do so between arraignment and trial. Most states require the defense by pretrial motion to object to the indictment or information; to request the prosecution's evidence (known as **discovery**); and to object to the government's evidence (fruits of illegal searches and seizures or forced confessions). The government can also request discovery in the form of a pretrial motion.

Pretrial motions and hearings occur in only 10 percent of all felony cases and in less than 1 percent of misdemeanor prosecutions. They usually occur in cases involving noncomplaining victims, such as in drug-related felonies. Politicians and the press greatly exaggerate the numbers of violent—or even nonviolent—criminals set free by pretrial motions to exclude evidence illegally obtained under the search and seizure clause (see Chapter 7). Courts dismiss practically no misdemeanor cases and only about 5 percent of felony cases in pretrial hearings arising out of objections in pretrial motions.[69]

Knowledge and Understanding CHECK

1. Identify the two pretrial proceedings that test the strength of the government's case.
2. Make a table listing differences between preliminary hearings, indictments, and informations.
3. What is arraignment, and what is its purpose?
4. Identify and describe the major pretrial motions.
5. Describe the extent to which pretrial motions are used in practice.

Was This a Vindictive Prosecution? Consideration

The district court filed an order dismissing the federal indictment, reasoning that a criminal defendant has the right to enter an unconditional plea of guilty to charges in an indictment. The prosecutor had demanded that Williams plead guilty and cooperate with the police to avoid a more severe federal prosecution. However, according to the district court, Williams had the right to refuse to cooperate with the police and to enter an unconditional plea of guilty to the state charges. By referring Williams's case for federal prosecution, the prosecutor was retaliating against Williams for exercising his lawful right to enter an unconditional plea to the state charges. According to the district court, the prosecutor's actions amounted to prosecutorial vindictiveness and violated Williams's Fifth Amendment due process rights.

After the district court denied the government's motion for reconsideration, the government appealed to the U.S. Court of Appeals. The government argued that prosecutors' threats were constitutionally permissible in the context of plea bargaining and did not arise to prosecutorial vindictiveness under the Supreme Court's precedents. The Court of Appeals agreed with the government's position and reversed the district court's dismissal of the federal indictment against Williams.[70]

CHAPTER CAPSULE

- Prosecutors possess wide discretion in deciding whether to charge suspects and which crime to charge them with.
- The right to counsel works better for people with high incomes than it does for people of ordinary means.
- Public safety is the major policy driving bail and pretrial detention.
- Indictment tests the government's case by secret proceedings controlled by prosecutors.
- Preliminary hearings test the government's case by public adversary proceedings controlled by judges.
- Motions to suppress evidence are rare.

KEY TERMS

decision to charge
initiate formal proceedings
diversion
adjudication
social structure of the case
first appearance
bailiff
pro bono assistance
public defenders
assigned counsel
contract attorneys
bail
commercial bail
release on recognizance (ROR)
conditional release
preventive detention
bail point system
preliminary hearing
probable cause hearing
bind over defendants
indictment
grand jury
information
arraignment
nolo contendere
discovery

INTERNET RESEARCH EXERCISES

Exercise: Using the Internet or InfoTrac College Edition, search for information about state prosecuted cases. How many cases were closed by state prosecutors last year? How many of these cases resulted in conviction? How many prosecutors were threatened with harm? How often did prosecutors' offices use DNA evidence? What was the breakdown among felony and misdemeanor cases, and what specific offenses fell into these two categories?

Suggested site:

- Bureau of Justice Statistics, http://www.ojp.usdoj.gov/bjs/ (tip: Click on "Prosecution," then "Publications," then "Prosecutors in State Courts, 1996," then "Acrobat File" if you have the Acrobat Reader. If not, click on "ASCII text file.")

InfoTrac College Edition: Search using the key words "state prosecution cases."

NOTES

1. *U.S. v. Williams,* 47 F.3d 658 (1995).
2. *Journal of the American Judicature Society* 34 (1940): 18–19; W. Boyd Littrell, *Bureaucratic Justice: Police, Prosecutors, and Plea Bargaining* (Beverly Hills: Sage, 1979), 32–33.
3. Barbara Boland et al., *The Prosecution of Felony Arrests, 1986* (Washington, D.C.: Bureau of Justice Statistics, June 1989); *People v. Wabash, St. Louis and Pacific Railway,* 12 Ill. App. 263 (1883); Celesta A. Albonetti, "Criminality, Prosecutorial Screening, and Uncertainty: Toward a Theory of Discretionary Decision Making in Felony Case Processings," *Criminology* 24 (1986): 624; William F. McDonald, *Plea Bargaining: Critical Issues and Common Practices* (Washington, D.C.: National Institute of Justice, July 1985), 11–15.
4. President's Commission on Law Enforcement and Administration of Justice, *The Challenge of Crime in a Free Society* (Washington, D.C.: U.S. Government Printing Office, 1967), 10; McDonald, *Plea Bargaining,* 26ff.
5. Boland et al., *Prosecution of Felony Arrests;* U.S. Department of Justice, *Principles of Federal Prosecution* (Washington, D.C.: U.S. Department of Justice, 1980), i.
6. Abraham S. Blumberg, *Criminal Justice* (Chicago: Quadrangle Books, 1970), 69.
7. Andrea deSantis and Wesley A. Kayton, "Defendants' Characteristics of Attractiveness, Race, and Sex and Sentencing Decisions," *Psychological Reports* 81 (1997): 679–83.
8. Brian Forst et al., "Prosecution and Sentencing," in Crime and Public Policy, James Q. Wilson, ed. (New Brunswick, N.J.: Transaction Books, 1983), 367, note 17, 588.
9. Peter F. Nardulli, James Eisenstein, and Roy B. Flemming, *The Tenor of Justice* (Urbana: University of Illinois Press, 1988), chap. 7; Forst et al., "Prosecution and Sentencing," 367.
10. Forst et al., "Prosecution and Sentencing," 367–68.
11. Donald Black, *Sociological Justice* (New York: Oxford University Press, 1989), 24.
12. Lisa Frohman, "Discrediting Victims' Allegations of Sexual Assault: Prosecutorial Accounts of Case Rejections," *Social Problems* 38 (1991): 213–26.
13. Susan Estrich, *Real Rape* (Cambridge: Harvard University Press, 1987), 8–9.
14. Battelle Law and Justice Study Center, *Forcible Rape: A National Survey of the Response by Prosecutors,* vol. 3 (Washington, D.C.: National Institute of Law Enforcement and Criminal Justice, 1977), 18–19.
15. Vera Institute of Justice, *Felony Arrests: Their Prosecution and Disposition in New York City's Courts* (New York: Vera Institute of Justice, 1977), 31–32.
16. Ibid.
17. Albonetti, 623–44.
18. *Betts v. Brady,* 316 U.S. 455 (1942).
19. *Gideon v. Wainwright,* 372 U.S. 335 (1963).
20. Ibid.
21. Ibid.
22. Ibid.
23. *Argersinger v. Hamlin,* 407 U.S. 25 (1972).
24. *Scott v. Illinois,* 440 U.S. 367 (1979).
25. BJS, *Indigent Defendants* (Washington, D.C.: Bureau of Justice Statistics, February 1996).
26. Andy Court, "Is There a Crisis?" *The American Lawyer* (January/February, 1993).
27. "Defenders Make Their Case," *Sessions Weekly* (Minnesota State Legislature, 1993), 11.
28. Lisa J. McIntyre, *The Public Defender: The Practice of Law in the Shadows of Repute* (Chicago: University of Chicago Press, 1987), 3.
29. Roger A. Hanson et al., *Indigent Defenders Get the Job Done and Done Well* (Williamsburg, Va.: National Center for State Courts, 1992).
30. Court, "Is There a Crisis?" 46.
31. David Lynch, "The Impropriety of Plea Bargaining," *Law and Social Inquiry* 19 (1994): 124.
32. Court, "Is There a Crisis?" 3.
33. Ibid.
34. Ibid., 11–14.
35. Vera Institute of Justice, *The Neighborhood Defender Service of Harlem: Research Results from the First Year* (New York: Vera Institute of Justice, December 1992).
36. Brian A. Reaves and Jacob Perez, *Pretrial Release of Felony Defendants, 1992* (Washington, D.C.: Bureau of Justice Statistics, 1995), 1; Plato, *Laws* (Cambridge, Mass.: Harvard University Press, 1926), 2:261.
37. John S. Goldkamp, "Danger and Detention: A Second Generation of Bail Reform," *Journal of Criminal Law and Criminology* 76 (1985): 1–75.
38. Andy Hall et al., *Pretrial Release Program Options* (Washington, D.C.: National Institute of Justice, June 1984).

39. Samuel Walker, Cassia Spohn, and Miriam DeLonc, *The Color of Justice: Race, Ethnicity, and Crime in America* (Belmont, Calif.: Wadsworth, 1996), 128.
40. Malcolm M. Feeley, *The Process Is the Punishment* (New York: Russell Sage, 1979), 96–111; see also Steven R. Schlesinger, "Bail Reform: Protecting the Community and the Accused," *Harvard Journal of Law and Public Policy* 9 (1986): 182.
41. Schlesinger, "Bail Reform," 173–202.
42. Ibid., 178–79.
43. *Stack v. Boyle,* 342 U.S. 1 (1951).
44. *United States v. Abrahams,* 575 F.2d 3 (1st Cir. 1978).
45. Ibid.
46. *Pugh v. Rainwater,* 557 F.2d 1189 (5th Cir. 1977).
47. *Pugh v. Rainwater,* on rehearing, 572 F.2d 1053 (5th Cir. 1978).
48. Ibid.
49. 18 United States Code Ann., secs. 3146–3151; Reaves and Perez, *Pretrial Release of Felony Defendants,* 1992.
50. 18 U.S. Code Ann., sec. 3146.
51. Ibid., secs. 3146, 3150.
52. Fla. Stat. Ann. Sec. 907.041(1) (St. Paul: West, 1985); Ga. Code Ann. Sec. 27–901(a) (1983 & Supp. 1985).
53. Paul Wice, *Freedom for Sale* (Lexington, Mass.: Lexington Books, 1974); Wayne R. LaFave and Jerold H. Israel, *Criminal Procedure* (St. Paul: West, 1984), 2:114; Goldkamp, "Danger and Detention," 8–9.
54. BJS, *Pretrial Release and Detention: The Bail Reform of 1984* (Washington, D.C.: Bureau of Justice Statistics, February 1988).
55. John Monahan, *The Clinical Prediction of Dangerousness* (Rockville, Md.: U.S. Department of Health and Human Services, Public Health Service, Alcohol, Drug Abuse, and Mental Health Administration, National Institute of Mental Health, 1981); Henry J. Steadman and Joseph J. Cocozza, *Careers of the Criminally Insane: Excessive Social Control of Deviance* (Lexington, Mass.: Heath, Lexington Books, 1974); David J. Rabinowitz, "Preventive Detention and *United States v. Edwards:* Burdening the Innocent," *The American University Law Review* 32 (1982): 201.
56. *United States v. Salerno,* 481 U.S. 739 (1987).
57. Ibid.
58. Wayne H. Thomas, *Bail Reform in America* (Berkeley: University of California, 1976); Mary A. Toborg, *Pretrial Release: A National Evaluation of Practices and Outcomes* (Washington, D.C.: National Institute of Justice, 1981).
59. Mary A. Toborg, *Pretrial Release: A National Evaluation of Practices and Outcomes* (Washington, D.C.: National Institute of Justice, 1981); BJS, *Pretrial Release and Detention;* Goldkamp, *Two Classes of Accused,* 221.
60. Goldkamp, *Two Classes of Accused,* 53–59.
61. Ibid., 221.
62. Chester L. Britt III, Michael R. Gottfredson, and John S. Goldkamp, "Drug Testing and Pretrial Misconduct: An Experiment on the Specific Deterrent Effects of Drug Monitoring Defendants on Pretrial Release," *Journal of Research on Crime and Delinquency* 29 (1992): 62–78.
63. Ibid., 77.
64. E. Britt Patterson and Michael J. Lynch, "Biases in Formalized Bail Procedures," in *Race and Criminal Justice,* Michael J. Lynch and E. Britt Patterson, eds. (New York: Harrow and Heston, 1991); discussed in Walker, Spohn, and DeLonc, *The Color of Justice,* 129.
65. Kathleen B. Brosi, *A Cross-City Comparison of Felony Case Processing* (Washington, D.C.: Law Enforcement Assistance Administration, 1979); LaFave and Israel, *Criminal Procedure,* 2:253–54.
66. *Hawkins v. Superior Court,* 22 Cal.3d 584 (1978).
67. Ibid.
68. Ibid.; LaFave and Israel, *Criminal Procedure,* 2:283.
69. LaFave and Israel, *Criminal Procedure,* 1:27.
70. *U.S. v. Williams,* 47 F.3d 658 (1995).

CHAPTER 11

Trial and Guilty Pleas

CHAPTER OUTLINE

Can an Innocent Defendant Plead Guilty?

Alford was indicted for first-degree murder, a capital offense under North Carolina law, punishable by death unless the jury recommends life imprisonment. The trial court appointed an attorney to represent [Alford], and this attorney questioned all but one of the various witnesses who Alford said would back up his claim of innocence. The witnesses, however, did not support Alford's story, instead giving statements that strongly indicated his guilt. Faced with strong evidence of guilt and no substantial evidentiary support for the claim of innocence, Alford's attorney recommended that he plead guilty, but left the ultimate decision to Alford. The prosecutor agreed to accept a plea of guilty to a charge of second-degree murder, and Alford pleaded guilty to the reduced charge.

Before the plea was finally accepted by the trial court, the court heard the sworn testimony of a police officer who summarized the state's case. Two other witnesses besides Alford were also heard. Although there was no eyewitness to the crime, the testimony indicated that shortly before the killing, Alford took his gun from his house, stated his intention to kill the victim, and returned home declaring that he had carried out the killing. After the summary presentation of the state's case, Alford took the stand and testified that he had not committed the murder but that he was pleading guilty because he faced the threat of the death penalty if he did not do so.

After giving his version of the events of the night of the murder, Alford stated:

> I pleaded guilty on second degree murder because they said there is too much evidence, but I ain't shot no man. . . . We never had an argument in our life and I just pleaded guilty because they said if I didn't they would gas me for it, and that is all.

In response to questions from his attorney, Alford affirmed that he had consulted several times with his attorney and with members of his family and had been informed of his rights if he chose to plead not guilty. Alford then reaffirmed his decision to plead guilty to second-degree murder. The trial court sentenced him to thirty years' imprisonment, the maximum penalty for second-degree murder.[1]

INTRODUCTION

The criminal trial is the high point of formal criminal justice. It attracts attention because criminal trials are visible and public, and because it contains moments of high drama and sometimes gory details about the many horrors that people can inflict on each other. However, only a few select cases are decided by formal trials. Informal, low-visibility, private negotiations between prosecutors and defense counsel determine the outcome of most criminal cases. The proceedings in court merely ratify formally and publicly what the parties have already decided informally in private.

You have already read about the formal-informal relationship in police actions on the street and in police departments, in prosecutors' offices prior to filing charges, and during the first appearance. You will read more about these informal relationships after conviction both at sentencing and in correctional administration in later chapters. In this chapter, we examine the most dramatic form of this dichotomy—the formal criminal trial and the informal pleas of guilty and plea bargaining.

DISPOSITION BY TRIAL

Fewer than 3 out of 100 felony arrests ever reach trial. Practically no misdemeanor arrests do so. In most cases, before trial, courts have dismissed charges, or defendants have pleaded guilty. (Figure 11.1 depicts the reasons why prosecutors negotiate.) Nevertheless, just as courts represent the formal centerpiece of criminal justice institutions, trials are the high point of the formal criminal process. Legally, every action from arrest through pretrial motion aims at trial.

The impact of formal trials extends beyond the number of cases that make it to trial. Trials affect the informal deci-

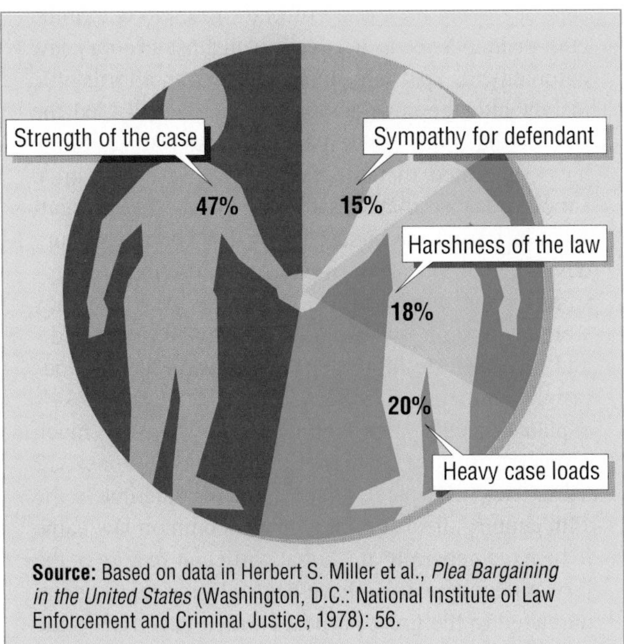

Source: Based on data in Herbert S. Miller et al., *Plea Bargaining in the United States* (Washington, D.C.: National Institute of Law Enforcement and Criminal Justice, 1978): 56.

Figure 11.1
Reasons Why Prosecutors Negotiate

sions of police, prosecutors, defense attorneys, and corrections officers and administrators. They all look to trial outcomes as defining boundaries within which informal criminal justice operates. So, formal rules limit informal discretion, even if they do not wholly control it.

The criminal trial has several missions. First, it is a symbol of justice. Criminal trials are supposed to show that crime does not pay, that the innocent receive vindication, and that the criminal justice system effectively punishes the guilty. Of course, the "wrong" outcomes can teach the opposite—a public display of *in*justice, proving that the wicked win and the innocent lose. Moreover, the triumph of the powerful and the rich proves that those who have the resources to hire "fancy lawyers" can influence who gets convicted and who goes free. This lesson breeds contempt for criminal justice. For good or ill, then, the trial teaches a public, visible, and potent lesson about the integrity, fairness, and effectiveness of the criminal justice process.

Second, criminal trials are elaborate fact-finding proceedings. According to strict rules, they ferret out the facts that prove *legal* guilt so that the truth prevails. Note, however, an important distinction: **Legal guilt** means guilt that the government has proved beyond a reasonable doubt by evidence that is admissible only according to the U.S. Constitution (see Chapter 7). On the other hand, **factual guilt,** demonstrates that defendants have actually committed a crime. Therefore, absence of legal guilt means, as the verdict says, "not guilty "; absence of factual guilt means *innocent*—the defendant really did not commit the crime. Criminal trials are supposed to ensure that fact-finding proceeds fairly and according to due process of law (see Chapter 4 on due process). Changes of venue, jury selection, obtaining and presenting evidence, speedy trial, and proof beyond a reasonable doubt are procedures that are intended to ensure accurate fact-finding fairly.

Third, trials are supposed to influence the conduct of the vast majority of cases that never reach the trial stage. Expectations about what a judge and jury might do shape police decisions to arrest, prosecutorial decisions to charge, defense counsel willingness to negotiate, and defendants' decisions to plead guilty. These agents base their expectations and predictions on what judges and juries have done in cases that have gone to trial. Police, prosecutors, and judges are all aware that "juries do not merely determine the outcome of the cases they hear; their decisions profoundly influence the 90 to 95 percent of cases that are settled through informal means."[2] Juries can become popular representatives in the "halls of justice," guarding against undue, improper, and vindictive government action. Leading jury experts have called this the "halo effect."[3]

Jury Trial

Trial by jury has ancient roots. In the Magna Carta of 1215, King John promised that "no free man shall be taken or imprisoned or in any way destroyed except by the lawful judgment of his peers." The Sixth Amendment to the U.S. Constitution provides that defendants "in all criminal prosecutions" have the right to trial "by an impartial jury of the State and district" where the crime was committed. In *Duncan v. Louisiana,* the U.S. Supreme Court ruled that the due process clause of the Fourteenth Amendment requires states to provide a jury trial in criminal prosecutions.[4]

Trials decide two kinds of questions:

1. Questions of law
2. Questions of fact

Formally, the law says that juries decide the facts and judges decide the law in jury trials. The questions of fact, which include the testimony of witnesses and physical evidence, all have to do with proof of guilt beyond a reasonable doubt. It is the duty of the jury to decide whether the government has proved its case by weighing both the quantity and the truth of the testimony and other evidence presented. Judges decide the legal questions, including the rules of evidence, the rules of procedure, and the definition of crimes. Not all criminal trials are jury trials. **Bench trials** are trials without juries in which judges decide both the legal and the fact questions.

The Supreme Court has not only ruled that there is no constitutional right to a 12-member jury, but it has also declared that the right to jury trial does not include the right to a unanimous verdict. The Court has decided, for example, that neither 11-to-1 nor 10-to-2 votes to convict in felony cases violate the Sixth Amendment. The reason, according to the Court in *Apodaca v. Oregon:* the commonsense judgment of peers does not depend on whether all jurors agree to convict. The jury has served its purpose in guarding against unfair government prosecution even in less-than-unanimous votes:

> [The court could] perceive no difference between juries required to act unanimously and those permitted to convict by votes of 10-to-2 or 11-to-1. [In] either case, the interest of the defendant in having the judgment of his peers interposed between himself and the officers of the state who prosecute and judge him is equally well served.[5]

In a companion case, *Johnson v. Louisiana,* the Court rejected the argument that proof beyond a reasonable doubt required a unanimous verdict; it decided that a 9-to-3 guilty verdict in a robbery case complied with the right to an impartial jury. According to the Court,

> Nine jurors—a substantial majority of the jury—were convinced by the evidence. Disagreement of the three jurors does not alone establish reasonable doubt, particularly when such a heavy majority of the jury, after having considered the dissenters' views, remains convinced of guilt.[6]

Critics of the *Apodaca* and *Johnson* decisions argue that unanimity instills confidence in the system, ensures participants' careful deliberation, and guarantees the hearing of minority viewpoints. Furthermore, unanimity prevents government oppression and supports the established legal preference for freeing 100 guilty persons rather than convicting one innocent individual. Finally, unanimity comports better with the requirement that criminal conviction rest on proof beyond a reasonable doubt.[7]

Use *Your* Discretion

Is there a constitutional right to a jury of 12?
***Williams v. Florida,* 399 U.S. 78 (1970)**

Johnny Williams was convicted of robbery in a Florida state court by a jury of 6. He was sentenced to life in prison. Williams appealed because, he argued, the Sixth Amendment right to jury trial includes the right to the ancient tradition of juries of 12 members.

Justice White for the majority
The question in this case is whether the constitutional guarantee of a trial by "jury" necessarily requires trial by exactly 12 persons, rather than some lesser number—in this case six. We hold that the 12-man panel is not a necessary ingredient of "trial by jury," and that respondent's refusal to impanel more than the six members provided for by Florida law did not violate petitioner's Sixth Amendment rights as applied to the States through the Fourteenth.

The history of trial by jury in criminal cases shows a long tradition attaching great importance to the concept of relying on a body of one's peers to determine guilt or innocence as a safeguard against arbitrary law enforcement. That same history, however, affords little insight into the considerations that gradually led the size of that body to be generally fixed at 12. Some have suggested that the number 12 was fixed upon simply because that was the number of the presentment jury from the hundred, from which the petit jury developed. Other, less circular but more fanciful reasons for the number 12 have been given, "but they were all brought forward after the number was fixed," and rest on little more than mystical or superstitious insights into the significance of "12." Lord Coke's explanation that the "number of twelve is much respected in holy writ, as 12 apostles, 12 stones, 12 tribes, etc.," is typical. In short, while sometime in the 14th century the size of the jury at common law came to be fixed generally at 12, that particular feature of the jury system appears to have been a historical accident, unrelated to the great purposes which gave rise to the jury in the first place. The question before us is whether this accidental feature of the jury has been immutably codified into our Constitution.

The purpose of the jury trial is to prevent oppression by the Government. Given this purpose, the essential feature of a jury obviously lies in the interposition between the accused and his accuser of the commonsense judgment of a group of laymen, and in the community participation and shared responsibility that results from that group's determination of guilt or innocence. The performance of this role is not a function of the particular number of the body that makes up the jury. To be sure, the number should probably be large enough to promote group deliberation, free from outside attempts at intimidation, and to provide a fair possibility for obtaining a representatives cross section of the community. But we find little reason to think that these goals are in any meaningful sense less likely to be achieved when the jury numbers six, than when it numbers 12—particularly if the requirement of unanimity is retained. And, certainly the reliability of the jury as a factfinder hardly seems likely to be a function of its size.

It might be suggested that the 12-man jury gives a defendant a greater advantage since he has more "chances" of finding a juror who will insist on acquittal and thus prevent conviction. But the advantage might just as easily belong to the State, which also needs only one juror out of twelve insisting on guilt to prevent acquittal. What few experiments have occurred—usually in the civil area—indicate that there is no discernible difference between the results reached by the two differentsized juries. In short, neither currently available evidence nor theory suggests that the 12-man jury is necessarily more advantageous to the defendant than a jury composed of fewer members.

Similarly, while in theory the number of viewpoints represented on a randomly selected jury ought to increase as the size of the jury increases, in practice the difference between the 12-man and the sixman jury in terms of the cross section of the community represented seems likely to be negligible. Even the 12-man jury cannot insure representation of every distinct voice in the community, particularly given the use of the peremptory challenge. As long as arbitrary exclusions of a particular class from the jury rolls are forbidden, the concern that the cross section will be significantly diminished if the jury is decreased in size from 12 to six seems an unrealistic one.

We conclude that the fact that the jury at common law was composed of precisely 12 is a historical accident, unnecessary to effect the purposes of the jury system and wholly without significance "except to mystics." To read the Sixth Amendment as forever codifying a feature so incidental to the real purpose of the Amendment is to ascribe a blind formalism to the Framers which would require considerably more evidence than we have been able to discover in the history and language of the Constitution or in the reasoning of our past decisions. We do not mean to intimate that legislatures can never have good reasons for concluding that the 12-man jury is preferable to the smaller jury, or that such conclusions—reflected in the provisions of most States and in our federal system—are in any sense unwise. Legislatures may well have their own views about the relative value of the larger and smaller juries, and may conclude that, wholly apart from the jury's primary function, it is desirable to spread the collective responsibility for the determination of guilt among the larger group. In capital cases, for example, it appears that no State provides for less than 12 jurors—a fact that suggests implicit recognition of the value of the larger body as a means of legitimating society's decision to impose the death penalty. Our holding does no more than leave these considerations to Congress and the States, unrestrained by an interpretation of the Sixth Amendment that would forever dictate the precise number that can constitute a jury. Consistent with this holding, we conclude that petitioner's Sixth Amendment rights, as applied to the States through the Fourteenth Amendment, were not violated by Florida's decision to provide a sixman rather than a 12-man jury. The judgment of the Florida District Court of Appeal is affirmed.

Dissent

Since I believe that the Fourteenth Amendment guaranteed Williams a jury of 12 to pass upon the question of his guilt or innocence before he could be sent to prison for the rest of his life, I dissent from the affirmance of his conviction.

I adhere to the holding of *Duncan v. Louisiana,* that "(b)ecause . . . trial by jury in criminal cases is fundamental to the American scheme of justice . . . the Fourteenth Amendment guarantees a right of jury trial in all criminal cases which—were they to be tried in a federal court—would come within the Sixth Amendment's guarantee." And I agree with the Court that the same "trial by jury" is guaranteed to state defendants by the Fourteenth Amendment as to federal defendants by the Sixth. "Once it is decided that a particular Bill of Rights guarantee is 'fundamental to the American scheme of justice' . . . the same constitutional standards apply against both the State and Federal Governments."

At the same time, I adhere to the decision of the Court in *Thompson v. Utah,* 170 U.S. 343, 349, 18 S.Ct. 620, 42 L.Ed. 1061 (1898), that the jury guaranteed by the Sixth Amendment consists "of twelve persons, neither more nor less." As I see it, the Court has not made out a convincing case that the Sixth Amendment should be read differently than it was in Thompson even if the matter were now before us de novo—much less that an unbroken line of precedent going back over 70 years should be overruled. The arguments made by Mr. Justice Harlan in Part IB of his opinion persuade me that Thompson was right when decided and still states sound doctrine. I am equally convinced that the requirement of 12 should be applied to the States.[8]

According to Professor Peter W. Sperlich:

> Nearly all commentators on *Williams* regarded the Court's reasoning and sense of evidence as bizarre. A close reading of Justice Byron White's opinion made it clear that there was no constitutional or factual support for the ruling. The Court cited several items of "evidence" to support its assertion of functional equivalence—ranging from a statement that "it could be argued that there would be no differences" to a trial judge's thoughts on the economies of smaller juries. None of the items were competent evidence and most of them were not even relevant to the issue at hand.
>
> The reviews of *Williams* were scathing. The only difference of opinion was whether the Court had been willfully or naively ignorant. Three years later, in *Colrove v. Battin,* which authorized six-person civil juries, the Court answered for the question in favor of willfulness. It boldly reasserted the *Williams* proofs, added further flawed materials to the evidentiary array, and rebuked the critics of *Williams* as unpersuasive. For whatever reasons, the Court wanted smaller juries and got them.[9]

In addition to these criticisms, a number of empirical evaluations of jury decisions have concluded that six-member juries are less reliable, do not save time, and are less likely to represent a cross section of the community.[10]

CRITICAL THINKING

1. How did the Court back up its decision that the Sixth Amendment does not guarantee the ancient right to 12-member juries?
2. Do you agree? Explain your answer.
3. Summarize Professor Sperlich's and the critics' positions on the case. Do you agree? Explain your reasoning.

The Political Nature of Juries

According to the respected nineteenth-century French commentator on American government Alexis de Tocqueville, "the jury is, above all, a political institution, and it must be regarded in this light in order to be understood." De Tocqueville's observation is still true; but it must be qualified. In clear-cut cases, law not politics governs. However, in cases that can go either way, extralegal influences enter the jury room and affect jurors' deliberations and decisions.[11]

Research has shown that jurors try hard to get at the truth. "I just stuck to the facts," most say when asked how they decided. And they are not lying. Their reliance on extralegal considerations is subconscious. Jurors operate according to a **liberation hypothesis,** in which their value judgments unconsciously affect their finding of the facts in close cases.

According to Harry Kalven and Hans Zeisel in their classic study of the jury, determining the truth and making value judgments are intertwined. The facts in close cases are ambiguous. Trial heightens the possibility of reading ambiguous facts in at least two starkly contrasting ways. The prosecution argues forcefully for the interpretation that supports conviction; the defense counsel argues equally strongly for that which supports acquittal. So, two things permit extralegal factors to influence deliberations:

1. Ambiguities in the evidence.
2. The adversary process.

Close cases "liberate" jurors to decide cases according to their own values. They resolve doubts in favor of their sentiments.[12]

Personal prejudice may determine the sentiments of jurors. But most frequently their sentiments reflect the values of their community, which they represent in the jury room. These values range across a broad spectrum, including

- Views concerning the crime problem and the value of punishment.
- Values and positions regarding gender, race, and ethnicity.
- Conflicts in moral standards.
- Beliefs about law and social problems such as self-defense, euthanasia, police power, drug use, the homeless, and the environment.[13]

Use *Your* Discretion

Does race affect jury deliberations?

The verdicts in cases involving the use of force by the police reflect the influence of community values. In communities with strong sentiments about law and order, jurors rarely convict the police on charges of police brutality. The Southern California community of Simi Valley, where police officers were tried for using force against Rodney King, is an example. The jury acquitted the officers, despite what looked like a clear case of excessive force to most people who watched videotape of the incident. The jurors accepted the argument that the police are a "thin blue line" between respectable citizens and violence and disorder. Unpleasant as the use of force was, the police were using it to protect law-abiding citizens from criminals.

In other communities, the use of force by police looks different. In the Bronx, where juries are more than 80 percent African American and Hispanic, juries acquit African American defendants 47.6 percent of the time, nearly three times the national rate of acquittal. This is true even though most crime victims are also African American and Hispanic. In one case, Larry Davis, an alleged major drug dealer and multiple murderer, was acquitted twice during a time when he was the most wanted fugitive in New York City. Davis's case and others like it led a Bronx prosecutor to comment, "It's bizarre. Everything here is truly stood on its head. The jurors are overwhelmingly suspicious of cops. If you have a case involving cops, you are almost certain to lose." The Larry Davis case led to an article entitled, "Bronx Juries: A Defense Dream, a Prosecutor's Nightmare."[14]

The acquittal of O. J. Simpson raised a spate of commentary about race influencing the decisions of

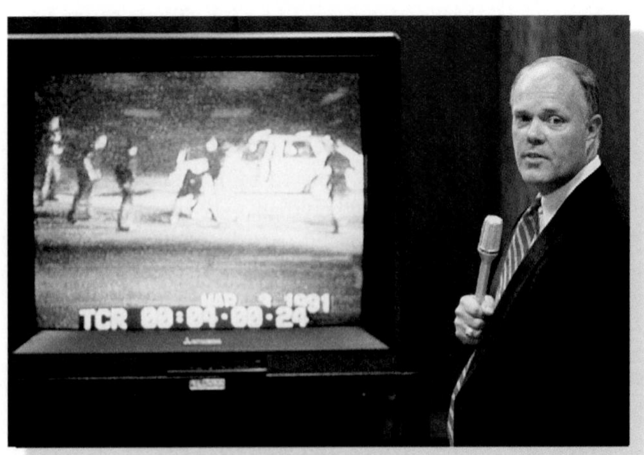

Sergeant Stacey Koon explains his actions during the beating of Rodney King while a video of the incident plays for the court.

juries. Commentators argue that the evidence, far more than race, determines verdicts. Jury watchers say otherwise. According to Benjamin A. Holden, Laurie P. Cohen, and Eleena de Lisser, "[R]ace plays a far more significant role in jury verdicts than many people involved in the justice system prefer to acknowledge." Race-based verdicts, of course, are not by any means limited to African American juries deciding in favor of African American defendants. All-white juries in the South for centuries convicted African Americans accused of committing crimes against whites no matter what the evidence, while whites who raped and killed African Americans were acquitted. In death penalty cases, whites acquit white defendants accused of killing African Americans more often than they acquit African Americans accused of killing whites.[15]

CRITICAL THINKING

1. How do you account for the differences in the outcomes of the Simi Valley and the Bronx cases?
2. What would you need to know in addition to the outcomes of these cases to decide whether race affected these jury deliberations?

Jury nullification, the power of juries to ignore the law and decide cases according to informal extralegal considerations, "fits neatly into a tradition of political activism by U.S. juries" and enjoys a long heritage in both English and U.S. history. William Penn benefited from nullification in 1670 when an English jury acquitted him for following his conscience in practicing his Quaker beliefs, a crime under English law. During colonial times, John Peter Zenger also violated the law by publishing material that criticized the British government. Zenger's lawyer told the jury they had the right "beyond all dispute to determine the law and the fact[s]." The jury followed his suggestion and acquitted Zenger.[16]

Use *Your* Discretion

Should race influence jury nullification decisions?

Paul Butler, a professor of criminal law who is studying jury activism among African Americans, maintains that African American jurors should "presume in favor of nullification." According to Professor Butler:

> Jury nullification is power that black people have right now and not something that Congress has to give them. Black people have a community that needs building, and children who need rescuing, and as long as a person will not hurt anyone, the community needs him there to help.[17]

Critics maintain that juries who disregard the law by acquitting defendants guilty beyond a reasonable doubt set a bad example; it breeds lawlessness in society generally. Ahmet Hisim, an assistant state's attorney in Baltimore says, "It's terrible and sad that juries will base their opinions on race bias rather than facts." Nevertheless, the courts have sustained jury nullification, upholding acquittals in criminal cases against all attack. Juries have an absolute right to acquit; neither the government nor defendants can appeal against it. Evidence suggests that juries exercise this power, particularly if they know about and understand it. Irwin Horowitz studied the effects of juror knowledge of nullification on 144 prospective jurors. He found that when juries received full nullification information from a judge or defense attorney, they were more likely to acquit a sympathetic defendant; when they did not receive the information, they were likely to judge a dangerous defendant more harshly. Knowledge of nullification definitely reduced the value of formally presented evidence and increased the discretionary power of juries.[18]

CRITICAL THINKING

1. What is Professor Butler's point?
2. Do you agree that jurors should use nulllification to serve greater missions when African American defendants are on trial? Explain.

Jury Selection

The Sixth Amendment guarantees trial by an impartial jury. The Federal Jury Selection and Service Act requires that jurors be selected at random, from a "fair cross section of the community." The act also prohibits exclusion from jury service based on race, color, religion, sex, national origin, or economic status. Most states have followed this general outline in ensuring an impartial criminal trial jury.[19]

To fulfill the random selection requirement, jurisdictions can compile a master roll of names using voter registration lists, actual voter lists, tax rolls, telephone directories, or even lists of driver's license registrations. Lists made up from these sources disqualify minors, people unable to speak or write English, convicted felons, and recent residents. Poor health, old age, hardship, and distance also excuse citizens from jury duty. Members of some occupations, such as doctors, government workers, and members of the armed forces, do not appear on jury lists; the law in most jurisdictions exempts them from jury duty.[20]

Martin A. Levin has argued that jurors cannot represent a cross section of the community because they are drawn from unrepresentative lists, and because attorneys can remove prospective jurors by peremptory challenge. Multiple

Juries are supposed to represent community values. The extent to which they do so depends on the jury selection process. The Constitution guarantees trial by an "impartial jury." Laws require that jurors be selected so as to represent a "fair cross section" of the community. Exclusion from juries cannot be based on race, religion, or national origin.

prospect lists, including voters, public utility customers, driver's licenses, telephone directories, and tax rolls, would produce more representative jurors.[21]

The **jury panel** consists of those people called for jury duty, except for those excused and exempted. These prospective jurors make up the **voir dire** (examination of prospective jurors by judge and lawyers) and subsequent selection of the actual jury. The voir dire gives prosecutors and defense counsel the means to impanel jurors whom they find suitable and to exclude those whom they consider undesirable. They can remove jurors either by challenge for cause or peremptory challenge.

In the **challenge for cause,** both prosecution and defense can object to as many prospective jurors as they like, as long as they can demonstrate prejudice to the judge's satisfaction, such as women in rape cases, bar owners in drunk-driving cases, and white men in a black gang-rape case. The prosecution and the defense also have a specified number of **peremptory challenges,** in which they may remove prospective jurors without cause or explanation. Peremptory challenge is an old practice; even in Elizabethan England, at one time defendants could peremptorily remove 35 prospective jurors.[22]

The jury selection process has given rise to a great deal of litigation. Two questions dominate this litigation:

1. Is the jury a randomly selected, fair cross section of the community?
2. Alternatively, have particular groups been systematically or intentionally excluded from jury panels and juries?

The Supreme Court has ruled that "selection of a petit jury from a representative cross section of the community is an essential component of the Sixth Amendment right to a jury trial." However, the Court also has made clear that impartiality does not require that juries "mirror the community and reflect the various distinct groups in the population." For example, a jury need not contain 8 percent Hispanics simply because the community has an 8 percent Hispanic population. The Constitution, according to the Court, bars the intentional or systematic exclusion of recognized racial groups or genders from a chance to participate; it does not require that they actually sit on juries. Defendants have no constitutional right to have poor people, rich people, African Americans, Caucasians, young people, baby-boomers, or old people represented on the jury.[23]

Fair Trial

Fair trials require an atmosphere that does not prejudice the jury against defendants. In a notorious case, the State of Ohio tried Dr. Sam Sheppard for brutally murdering his socialite wife. The newspapers were filled with "evidence" (actually rumors) about Sheppard's "guilt"; nearly all editorials were against him, and reporters even disrupted the trial proceedings in their efforts to scoop "sensational" stories. Although the jury convicted him, the U.S. Supreme Court ruled that Sheppard could not receive a fair trial in such a "carnival atmosphere."[24]

Trial judges bear the primary responsibility for ensuring that defendants get fair trials. They may grant motions for a *change of venue,* the transfer of a trial to a new location. Judges can also sequester the jury to ensure fairness. When judges order sequestration, they isolate jurors from the public so that they cannot receive news about the trial from outside the courtroom. Generally, juries are sequestered in hotels where they cannot read newspapers, watch television, or otherwise receive news about the trial. Sequestration occurs only in sensational trials that receive a lot of public attention and reporting in newspapers and on television and radio.[25]

Trial judges can also restrict trial publicity by curtailing news reports, limiting what lawyers can say to the press, and barring reporters from the courtroom. These restrictions on publicity all raise questions concerning the First Amendment guarantee of free press. Most press restrictions are permissible only when trial publicity seriously jeopardizes chances for a fair trial.

Finally, judges have wide discretion to control courtroom behavior. They can remove "unruly" spectators and "troublesome" members of the press if their behavior interferes with the decorum of the courtroom. Judges have less freedom to deal with disruptive defendants, because the Sixth Amendment guarantees defendants the right to be present at their own trials. Nevertheless, judges can remove defendants who make it impossible to proceed. Short of removal, judges have ordered bailiffs to gag and bind unruly defendants to ensure orderly proceedings.[26]

Proving Guilt

The criminal trial is a highly formal mechanism to determine guilt. The prosecution follows a set procedure to present physical evidence, such as murder weapons and bloodstained clothing; to examine and cross-examine witnesses; to argue cases to the jury (or judge in a bench trial, a trial without a jury); and to rebut the opposition's arguments. The formal purpose of this highly popularized sparring is to determine the legal guilt of the accused according to a long-entrenched standard, **proof beyond a reasonable doubt.**

In criminal cases, prosecutors must prove guilt to the degree that it is completely consistent with the guilt of the defendant and inconsistent with any other plausible conclusion. All evidence the state presents serves that purpose, or at least formally is supposed to serve it. The state must find, arrange, present, and support the case against defendants. The defense has no obligation to aid the state in its case; defendants do not need to prove their innocence. They are, to use the well-worn phrase, innocent until proven guilty. Therefore, the defense role in criminal trials is essentially negative: to cast doubt on the prosecution's case, not to create a case on its own.[27]

According to the Supreme Court in the landmark case *In re Winship,* the Constitution requires the reasonable doubt standard. The standard's role in "the American scheme of criminal procedure" is "vital" because it reduces the risk of mistakenly convicting innocent people. The Court decided that criminal defendants have at risk such vital interests—loss of property, liberty, and sometimes life, as well as the stigma attached to conviction—that reasonable doubt about guilt should prevent such consequences from befalling a citizen in a free society. Placing a heavy burden on the prosecution, it is believed, reduces the margin of error in criminal convictions. The reasonable doubt standard also "command[s] the respect and confidence of the community in applications of the criminal law." A lesser standard of proof reduces the law's moral force and leaves citizens uncertain about the capacity of courts to condemn the guilty and to vindicate innocent people.[28]

In trying to help jurors come to a decision, courts have struggled to define proof beyond a reasonable doubt. Here are some common definitions, extracted from the cases:

- A doubt of about 7½ on a scale of 10.
- A doubt that would cause prudent persons to hesitate before acting in a matter of importance to themselves.
- A doubt based on reason and common sense.
- Not frivolous or fanciful doubt.
- Substantial doubt.
- Persuasion to a moral certainty.[29]

Use *Your* Discretion

Was there reasonable doubt?
***State v. Dewitt,* 611 A.2D 926 (1993)**

A Connecticut statute provides that:

> [A]ny person who manufactures, distributes, sells, prescribes, dispenses, compounds, transports with the intent to sell or dispense, possesses with the intent to sell or dispense, offers, gives or administers to another person any controlled substance which is a hallucinogenic substance other than marihuana, or a narcotic substance, except as authorized in this chapter, for a first offense, shall be imprisoned not more than fifteen years and may be fined not more than fifty thousand dollars or be both fined and imprisoned; and for a second offense shall be imprisoned not more than thirty years and may be fined not more than one hundred thousand dollars, or be both fined and imprisoned; and for each subsequent offense, shall be imprisoned not more than thirty years and may be fined not more than two hundred fifty thousand dollars, or be both fined and imprisoned.

Facts

At about 8:45 P.M., Officers Nicholas Ortiz and John Losak of the Bridgeport Police Department were assigned to conduct a narcotics investigation at Father Panik Village, building 13. They drove into the courtyard between buildings 9 and 13 in an unmarked police car and parked near a dumpster. The well-lighted area was known for high narcotics trafficking, especially cocaine and crack. The officers observed the defendant standing about four feet from them in the courtyard between concrete traffic barriers and the dumpster. There were other individuals in the area who left when the uniformed officers exited the car. The defendant had not been observed approaching anyone or conducting any transactions.

The defendant saw the officers and placed a clear plastic bag containing several red objects in his mouth. Ortiz testified that narcotics are often placed in plastic sandwich bags and that street level dealers place the bags in their mouths hoping that the police will not see the drugs. The defendant turned his back on the officers just before he was seized. They removed the bag from his mouth and found it to contain forty-four plastic vials with red caps. A field test indicated that a white substance in the vials was cocaine. No significant amount of money was seized from the defendant.

Ortiz indicated that each of the vials of cocaine would be worth $5 and would allow a user to be high for fifteen to twenty minutes. Ortiz testified that a typical buyer would purchase between one and five vials at a time. Losak testified that buyers typically purchased one or two vials at a time, but he had arrested buyers who had purchased five to ten vials at once. A state toxicologist testified that each vial tested contained between 42.9 and 58.6 milligrams of cocaine that was 82.2 to 86.9 percent pure. This, he said, was typical of crack cocaine seized in the Bridgeport area. The defendant testified that the forty-four vials of cocaine were for his and a friend's use and that he had no intention of selling them.

Opinion

The defendant claims that the evidence presented by the state prior to his motion for a judgment of acquittal was insufficient to sustain a conviction on the charge of possession with intent to sell narcotics because the state failed to prove his intent to sell. The defendant's argument is that the forty-four vials found in his possession do not allow an inference of his intent to sell, but rather would allow an inference that he intended the vials for personal use. He argues, therefore, that the trial court should have granted his motion for acquittal. We disagree.

We ascertain whether a jury could REASONABLY have concluded that the cumulative effect of the established evidence, and the inferences REASONABLY drawn from those evidentiary FACTS, established guilt BEYOND a REASONABLE DOUBT. Where a group of FACTS are relied upon for PROOF of an element of the crime it is their cumulative impact that is to be weighed in deciding whether the standard of PROOF BEYOND a REASONABLE DOUBT has been met and each individual FACT need not be proved in accordance with that standard. Thus, each essential element of the crime must be proven beyond a reasonable doubt; and a jury may not speculate or resort to conjecture but may draw only reasonable, logical inferences from the proven facts.

In this case, Ortiz and Losak testified that the defendant was standing in an area known for high narcotics trafficking, that he was in possession of a large quantity of narcotics packaged in a manner used by street dealers, and that, when police officers approached, he hid the narcotics in his mouth in a manner used by street level dealers. On the basis of the officers' testimony about quantities purchased by typical buyers, the jury could have concluded reasonably that the amount possessed by the defendant was not intended for his personal use. A trier of fact could have concluded reasonably at the close of the state's case, without any consideration of the defendant's evidence, that the state had proven beyond a reasonable doubt that the defendant possessed narcotics with an intent to sell them. The trial court, therefore, properly denied the defendant's motion for a judgment of acquittal.

The judgment is affirmed.

CRITICAL THINKING

1. Suppose you are on the jury in this case. Did the prosecution prove its case "beyond a reasonable doubt"?
2. If so, define proof beyond a reasonable doubt, and list the facts in this case proving that the defendant possessed cocaine with the intent to sell it.
3. If not, explain what a reasonable doubt is and why you have a reasonable doubt that DeWitt possessed the cocaine with the intent to sell it.

Opening Statements

Opening statements allow both prosecution and defense to present juries with their respective overviews of the case. The lawyers make their opening statements after jury selection but before presenting any evidence. Although prosecutors present no evidence at this point, opening statements can impress juries with the nature and gravity of the charges against defendants. In introducing their case, prosecutors can enlighten juries about how the prosecution intends to develop its case. This helps juries to make more sense of testimony and physical evidence that do not always appear in logical order. Juries also have less tendency to become bored, frustrated, and irritated if they can follow the case. Finally, opening statements allow prosecutors to persuade juries. Lawyers have only two opportunities to address the jury directly without interruption: during the opening statements and closing arguments.

Calling and Examining Witnesses

In the adversary system, lawyers determine which witnesses to call. Both defense and prosecution have broad powers to **subpoena,** meaning to command witnesses by court order to appear in court to present relevant testimony. Ordinary witnesses receive travel money and a small daily fee that, incidentally, rarely compensates them for time lost from work. Expert witnesses, such as fingerprint specialists and psychiatrists, receive full compensation for their court time. Although broad, the subpoena power cannot violate either the Fifth Amendment protection against self-incrimination or a range of privileged relationships, such as lawyer-client, doctor-patient, and sometimes husband-wife.

The prosecution calls government witnesses first. After the prosecution has completed its case, the defense calls its witnesses. First, the side who called the witness conducts the **direct examination.** Following the direct examination, the lawyer on the other side conducts the **cross-examination** of the witness. Occasionally, re-direct and re–cross-examination follow.

The manner of questioning differs in direct and cross-examination. A proper direct examination question is, "Where were you on October 8 at about 8:00 P.M.?" In direct examination, lawyers cannot ask **leading questions,** questions that steer witnesses to desired answers. For example, they cannot ask the defendant, "You were at the victim's house on October 8, at about 8:00 P.M., weren't you?" However, leading questions—that is, questions that essentially tell the witness how to answer—are proper and typical in cross-examination. Witness answers in direct examination require narration, sometimes in considerable length. Yes or no answers typically suffice in cross-examination.

Direct and cross-examination questioning differ for two main reasons. First, unless they are **hostile witnesses** (defense witnesses favorable to the prosecution and prosecution witnesses favorable to the defense), witnesses favor the side that called them. Witnesses usually give answers damaging to the other side, and opposition lawyers have not had the opportunity to learn what these witnesses will say. Second, direct witnesses have discussed what they know with the lawyer who calls them to testify.

George P. Fletcher, professor of criminal law at Columbia University and a respected writer on criminal law, attended the trial of Bernhard Goetz, who pleaded self-defense to a charge of attempted murder for shooting four youths in a New York subway (see the Use Your Discretion in Chapter 4). In his book about the Goetz trial, Fletcher observes that

> lawyers at trial are directors as well as performers in presenting their client's version of the truth. They make theatrical decisions about the order in which to present their witnesses, they coach them like directors in rehearsal, and they lead their witnesses gently through their parts. Their presentation of the truth reflects art and rhetoric as well as rational argument.
>
> Their role [in direct examination] stops short of prompting their witnesses when they do not perform as expected. Prompting falls under the ban against asking "leading questions." A lawyer disappointed in his witness may not try to put words in his mouth. He cannot ask (assuming that the witness would be prepared to answer "yes"), "Isn't it true that you saw the gunman smiling as he was shooting?" He must try to elicit this testimony without giving away the script.
>
> But when they turn into critics on cross-examination, lawyers can ask all the leading questions they want and insist, often contemptuously, that the witness answer "yes" or "no."[30]

Fletcher describes defense attorney Barry Slotnick's skill in leading witnesses in cross-examination. Slotnick wanted to establish that Goetz fired the shots against the youths in rapid succession, not pausing between shots:

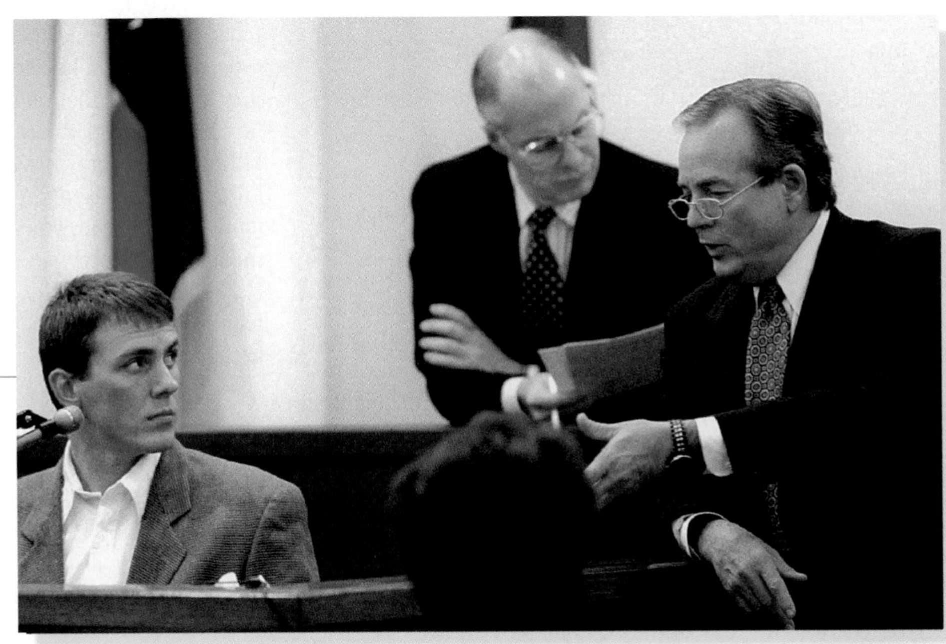

Part of criminal trials is vigorous cross-examination of witnesses. Here, Jay Guild is cross-examined by defense attorney John Linebarger, right, during testimony in the Diane Zamora trial in Fort Worth, Texas, February 1998. Diane Zamora, a Naval Academy midshipman, was eventually convicted of capital murder for the killing of 16-year-old Adrianne Jones.

> The tactic became clear on the cross-examination of . . . Victor Flores, who claimed actually to have seen Goetz fire at two of the youths as they were running toward him and away from Goetz. He heard four shots "one after another."
>
> On cross-examination, Slotnick took advantage of his legal option to restate Flores's testimony in his own language and ask Flores to answer "yes" or "no" whether that was his view of what happened. Thus he reformulated Flores's first statement about the pattern and rapidity of the shots by asking, "And the three shots or the four shots . . . that you hear in rapid succession after the first shot, were all going in your area, is that correct?" Having gained Flores's assent to the phrase "rapid succession," Slotnick began using the label over and over again in cross-examination. The jury heard Flores say "yes" to this description so often–five more times–that the words came to seem like his own.[31]

The case that Slotnick was eliciting on cross-examination became clear in a question that he put solely for the jury's benefit:

> So it is fair to say that as far as your witnessing what occurred, the fact that he might have walked over to a rear seat and shot somebody and said something to them, like "you don't look bad, here's another," something like that, that really never happened?[32]

Admission of Evidence

Evidence is either physical evidence—such as weapons, stolen property, and fingerprints—or testimonial—the words of witnesses. Admissible evidence must be:

- Relevant
- Material
- Nonprejudicial
- Reliable
- Legally obtained (see Chapter 7 on illegally obtained evidence)

Relevant evidence is evidence that relates to the elements of the crime. In robbery, for example, relevant evidence is evidence proving that the defendant, by force or the threat of force, took something of value from the victim. Relevant evidence that can prove these material elements is **material evidence** (sometimes called probative evidence). The court excludes evidence, even if relevant and material, if it unfairly prejudices jurors against defendants. For example, evidence that a defendant on trial for murder has committed previous assaults and other violent crimes, although clearly relevant and material because it shows the defendant is capable of committing violent crimes, can also lead the jury to conclude, perhaps erroneously, that the defendant must have committed this murder. The prejudice to the defendant outweighs the probative value of the evidence.

Courts also exclude **hearsay evidence**—information not directly known by the witness that is offered for its truth at trial—even if relevant, material, and not prejudicial to defendants. For example, a police officer who did not see a robbery gives hearsay evidence when she testifies that a bank teller told her the defendant entered the bank with a gun and ordered the teller to turn over all the money. Only the bank teller saw the robbery firsthand, and only the teller can testify in court. Hearsay is unreliable, and therefore excluded, because juries cannot weigh hearsay as firsthand knowledge, and lawyers cannot cross-examine the actual eyewitnesses about it.

Closing Arguments

The experienced prosecutor Steven Phillips explains the importance of the closing argument:

> It is one of the few arts left in which time is of no consequence. Standing before 12 people, a lawyer can be brief or lengthy—the choice is his own; there are no interruptions, and a captive audience. All that matters are those 12 people; they must be persuaded, or everything that has gone before is in vain. Summation is the one place where lawyers do make a difference; if an attorney can be said to "win" or "lose" a case, the chances are that he did so in his closing argument to the jury.[33]

Charging the Jury

Following the closing arguments, judges instruct, or "charge," the jury. **Jury instructions** explain to the jury the law governing the case. Judges begin by explaining the jury's role in the case: the court decides the law; the jury decides the facts. For example, in a murder trial, the judge explains the legal meaning of *premeditation* required for a first-degree murder conviction. The jury decides whether the facts prove beyond a reasonable doubt that the defendant *premeditated* the killing. Hence, the judge may instruct the jury that premeditation in this state means *any* lapse of time, however brief, between the intention to kill and the act of killing. Therefore, if you the jury find that the defendant killed the deceased even instantaneously following her intention to kill him, you may find the defendant guilty of premeditated murder.

The long, complex, and technical legal definitions and requirements found in judge's instructions often demand a great deal from juries:

> A judge's charge to the jury is an amazing exercise in optimism. For two or three hours he reads to twelve laymen enough law to keep a law student busy for a semester. Twelve individuals, selected more or less at random, sit there, unable to take notes or ask questions. Somehow, just by listening, it is presumed everything spoken by the judge will take root in their collective intelligence.[34]

Jury Deliberations

Following the charge, the jury retires to a designated place to deliberate. They may ask for clarification in the instructions, further review of the evidence, and sometimes just rereading of some of the testimony. When they have reached their decision, all parties return to the courtroom for the familiar scene endlessly depicted on television and movie screens and described in written works. After the jury verdict, the most formal public event in criminal justice ends. Adjudication sometimes continues in criminal appeals, but the high drama of adjudication effectively ends with the jury verdict.

Knowledge and Understanding CHECK

1. Why do criminal trials attract attention?
2. How do trials compare with guilty pleas?
3. Identify and explain the missions of the criminal trial.
4. Explain the difference between factual and legal guilt.
5. Identify and contrast the two questions answered by trials.
6. Explain why 12 member juries and unanimous verdicts are not required by the U.S. Constitution.
7. Describe the political nature of juries and the impact it has on jury verdicts.
8. Identify two factors that are extralegal factors that influence jury deliberations.
9. Identify the broad spectrum of values that appear in jury rooms.
10. Define jury nullification.

DISPOSITION BY GUILTY PLEA

Only a tiny minority of persons charged with murder, rape, and armed robbery go to trial. The vast majority of defendants plead guilty before trial. The numbers of guilty pleas, or informal dispositions, as with most other decisions in criminal justice, vary from a minority of dispositions in some jurisdictions to virtually all in others. For example, in New York City, 97.5 percent of felony defendants plead guilty, while in Philadelphia, only 26 percent do so. Even more misdemeanor defendants plead guilty. In New Haven, Connecticut, in 1975 not one trial took place out of 1,640 cases filed in the lower criminal courts![35]

As early as 1557, English criminal court records show that an overwhelming number of criminal defendants pleaded guilty. A survey of 1920s Cleveland, Ohio, showed that guilty pleas disposed of half the felony cases scheduled for criminal court. It was not until the 1960s, however, that the guilty plea acquired widespread attention and became subject to careful scrutiny and considerable criticism.[36]

Why do so many defendants plead guilty? Some claim that the plethora of rights given criminal defendants and the adversary system that places a premium on argument and procedure cannot deal with the great numbers of criminal cases. Others point to the lack of resources to hire judges and other staff to manage criminal trials. Others focus on rising crime rates that have placed too heavy a burden on criminal courts. Some researchers of formal organizations and many judges and lawyers argue that efficiency and economy demand disposition by guilty plea. Others interpret guilty pleas as the inevitable outcome of the courtroom work group's desire for harmony and the natural human desire for predictability. Some maintain that the costs of pleading not guilty are too high in time, money, and the risk of longer sentences or higher fines. Others maintain that guilty pleas, especially in large urban areas, are part of a system of imposing discipline on "dangerous" lower-class people. Some combination of these reasons explains the prevalence of the guilty plea. Whatever the reasons, the guilty plea emphasizes the significance of informal decision making in the disposition of criminal cases.[37]

Straight Pleas

Guilty pleas are not all alike. Some guilty pleas, called **straight pleas,** do not result from negotiations. Some defendants want to plead guilty, or at least their lawyers want them to do so. **Negotiated pleas,** or the "copped" pleas of ill repute, do involve bargaining and trade-offs. Research has not yet revealed how many defendants enter straight guilty pleas, although available information suggests large numbers. According to Michael L. Rubenstein, Steven Clarke, and Theresa Wright, who analyzed court documents and interviewed judges, prosecutors, and defense attorneys in Alaska, "most defendants ple[a]d guilty even when the state offer[s] them nothing in exchange for their cooperation." After examining several jurisdictions, political scientist Milton Heumann concluded, "Most court personnel (regardless of ideological persuasion) will readily admit that in many cases there are simply no contestable factual or legal issues." Barbara Boland and Brian Forst estimated that "the majority of pleas in the United States may involve no negotiation at all." Perhaps defendants plead guilty because they know they are guilty, or because they believe that a trial would be hopeless or, worse, might lead to harsher punishment. (See the opening discussion "Can an Innocent Defendant Plead Guilty?")[38]

Rubenstein, Clarke, and Wright obtained data from police, jail, and court records. They interviewed every judge, prosecutor, and criminal defense attorney in Anchorage, Fairbanks, and Juneau to determine the effects of a ban on plea bargaining in Alaska. They asked why defendants give up their right to jury trial without getting concessions in return.

The quotes in this and other sections drawn from their study typify the group interviewed. One experienced defense lawyer gave the following representative answer:

> Well, where you've got a nineteen-year-old kid who's ripped off somebody else's stereo and he confessed to it, what do you gain from going to trial? You can go to jury trial and your client gets on the stand and says, "I didn't do it," and you say, "Well, you confessed to it, and we found the stereo in your house." You know what's going to happen then? I mean, your client is either going to have to perjure himself, or he's not going to take the stand. And, if he doesn't take the stand, and if it takes you four days to try the case, you have nothing to argue at the end. The judge is going to say, "What happened here? Why did you waste thousands of dollars putting us all through this?" You know, they're going to pay a price for this—it's only natural.[39]

Dead-bang cases, cases of virtually certain conviction, most often lead to straight pleas, but so do cases involving particularly gory evidence or sympathetic victims. Defendants fare worse in trials where judges and juries listen and see the evidence and witnesses for several hours or days. Some defendants plead guilty without a bargain because their lawyers believe putting up a fight will ruin a "previous posture of compliance and cooperation."[40]

> Now if the guy is a "boy scout" [said one defense lawyer] I might advise him to enter a guilty plea. Keep the image consistent that way. Take this guy charged with a first-offense burglary in a dwelling. He confessed when he was arrested and he helped the cops retrieve the property. He had no real defenses. If he had exercised all his constitutional rights it would have hurt him. He'd have gone to jail. I could advise him that if he continued in the cooperative mode in which he had already begun when I started representing him he'd have the best chances of probation. He got straight probation and a suspended imposition of sentence. He could never have gotten that disposition if he had exercised his constitutional rights.[41]

Straight pleas do not always originate for such noble reasons. Defense attorneys admit that occasionally the advantages from guilty pleas accrue not to their clients but to themselves. Some guilty pleas help lawyers "avoid the three or four grueling courtroom days usually required for a felony trial, not to mention more time spent in pretrial preparation." As one assistant public defender put it:

> You really have to watch yourself if you have three or four trials scheduled over the next month, and you are picking up new cases. If a case looks bad you may automatically say, "Well, that person is going to plead guilty." There is only so much you can take. As a defense attorney you have a wide range of rationalizations for not going to trial. The defense attorney does not misrepresent, so much as he comes up with rationalizations why clients shouldn't go to trial. And it isn't difficult to do this in any given case.[42]

Sometimes a lawyer will advise a client to plead guilty because of the only too human reluctance to appear foolish in public. According to one typical defense attorney, "fear of embarrassment was one of the big things that I have had to get over as a trial attorney [one defense lawyer admitted candidly]. Some cases are just embarrassing."[43]

Another lawyer said:

> You know, that's got to be the toughest thing, when you just don't have very much to argue at all, and you're sitting through a trial just searching for something to say at the end of the case. There are a lot of attorneys that wouldn't subject themselves to that, who would rationalize that their clients would gain something by entering their pleas.[44]

Defense attorneys also believe—and empirical findings support their belief—that insisting on a trial results in harsher penalties. In the words of one assistant public defender:

> In violent crimes the judge sees the victim and hears the whole ugly story. Naturally he's going to give a tougher sentence. In fraud cases the judge has a chance to sit and think, "Boy, this guy really premeditated this fraud; he's too slick to trust."[45]

One judge bluntly revealed:

> The defendant played the odds; they went against him. He played and he declined to plead. He put the state to the burden of proof, and the state won. There is nothing wrong with [giving him a harsher sentence for losing the gamble].[46]

Finally, going to trial is expensive. Those who can afford a lawyer can measure that cost in dollars. According to one defense attorney, private lawyers "simply have to inform their client how much it will cost them to pursue their claim of innocence at trial. This causes a lot of defendants to sober up." Not even indigent defendants want to draw out their cases for months. They want to get the case over with as soon as possible for the perfectly understandable reason that it makes life easier.[47]

Negotiated Pleas

In negotiated pleas, defendants plead guilty in exchange for concessions from the government. Straight pleas and plea bargains stem from similar self-serving motives. Defendants plead guilty because they—or their lawyers—want to save time, money, hassle, embarrassment, defeat, and harsher penalties.[48]

Plea bargaining is negotiating of guilty pleas in exchange for concessions made by the government. In **express**

bargaining, prosecutors, defendants, defense lawyers, and sometimes trial judges meet face to face to work out specific concessions. Express bargaining prevails in most jurisdictions. Implicit bargaining involves no direct meetings. Instead, local practice, sometimes called the going rate for guilty pleas, determines concessions. According to Milton Heumann, the going rates vary from one community to another, and are

> products of the individual courthouse and community, and are not primarily shaped by state or national considerations. In one jurisdiction an armed robber may receive eight years after a trial and five years if he pleads; in another, the comparable figures may be seven and four, or ten and eight, and so on.[49]

In **implicit bargaining,** defense attorneys can fairly assume that if their clients plead guilty to "normal" crimes, they will receive concessions in line with the going rate. According to one Detroit judge familiar with the practice, "The system operates in terms of defense attorney and defendants' expectations—what is widely known as a rate. It's an expectation model."[50]

Implicit bargaining should not mean unclear consequences. The consequences are, says Heumann,

> usually made very explicit! That is, defendants are told clearly by someone—usually their lawyers, but sometimes by judges, prosecutors, police officers, or others—that they had better plead guilty or they will be punished more severely if they go to trial.[51]

Concessions in negotiations usually take three forms. In **charge bargaining,** prosecutors drop some charges and/or file charges less serious than the facts justify in exchange for defendants' guilty pleas. For example, a defendant who has committed a first-degree murder carrying a mandatory life term might plead guilty to second-degree murder with a term of 20 years to life. The plea to second-degree murder gives the judge discretion to sentence the defendant to less than life imprisonment.

In **sentence bargaining,** pleading guilty "on the nose," defendants plead guilty to charges actually warranted by the facts in the case, but with the understanding that the judge will grant, or at least the prosecutor will request, a lenient sentence, such as probation.

In **slow pleas,** defendants go to trial, but the trial is short and superficial. The government and defense agree to set aside the rules of evidence, and they stipulate, or agree, not to argue over guilt; conviction becomes a foregone conclusion.[52]

Plea bargaining varies from community to community. **Local legal culture** (attitudes, values, and expectations regarding law and the legal system) determines whether charge bargaining, sentence bargaining, or slow pleas predominate. History and tradition contribute to that culture. In Detroit, for example, sentence bargaining rarely takes place; charge bargaining predominates because the courts historically have prohibited prosecutors from participating in sentencing. In Washington, D.C., sentence bargaining predominates. There, the prosecution historically has had to address the court to make a "pitch" for a particular sentence. In Los Angeles, slow pleas have enjoyed a long tradition.[53]

Public opinion also shapes local legal culture. Plea bargaining disposes of run-of-the-mill cases, cases that do not attract public attention. In highly visible, sensational cases generating great public interest, trials occur more frequently. Research suggests that public opinion favors trial over bargaining in such spectacular cases, and that prosecutors and courts follow that opinion. The distinguished former U.S. Attorney General Edward Levi recommended the following to U.S. attorneys:

> [Consider] what the public attitude is toward prosecution under the circumstances of the case. There may be situations where the public interest might be better served by having the case tried rather than by being disposed of by means of a guilty plea—including situations in which it is particularly important to permit a clear public understanding that "justice is done" or in which a plea agreement might be misconstrued to the detriment of public confidence in the criminal justice system. For this reason, the prosecutor should be careful not to place undue emphasis on factors which favor disposition of a case pursuant to a plea agreement.[54]

According to James Eisenstein and Herbert Jacob, the courtroom work group also contributes to the local legal culture's influence on plea bargaining. They found that defense attorneys, prosecutors, and judges have established practices, values, and norms concerning not only the "going rates" for crimes but also the "way things are done." The work group rarely acts outside this social organization context. If they do, they proceed with considerable discomfort.[55]

The Prosecutor and Plea Bargaining

Plea bargaining varies according to the roles its key participants—prosecutors, defense counsel, and judges—play. Prosecutors' discretion in charging and sentencing decisions conditions their role in plea bargaining. Discretion not only affects decisions in individual cases, but also orders general charging policies in prosecutors' offices. In small or rural jurisdictions, individual case discretion, not general charging policies, constitutes the norm. In large, urban jurisdictions, however, general charging policy includes plea bargaining.

Urban and rural policy differences have historical roots. As jurisdictions grow and become more complex, a transformation occurs; plea bargaining changes with it. Delaware County, Pennsylvania, for example, grew from a small, rural jurisdiction to a large, suburban one in about 20 years. Plea bargaining changed too, from implicit bargaining with heavy judicial participation in the 1950s to explicit bargaining between prosecutors and defense counsel with little or no judicial participation by the 1970s.[56]

Decision to Negotiate

Early impressionistic and anecdotal evidence and recent quantitative analyses have shown broad agreement on the five major influences on prosecutors' decisions to negotiate pleas:

- Seriousness of the offense.
- Criminal history of the defendants.
- Strength of the government's case.
- Reputation of defense counsel.
- Heavy caseloads.[57]

The weight given to each of these reasons varies (Figure 11.1). Herbert S. Miller, William McDonald, and James Cramer, in a random 10 percent sample of all jurisdictions with populations of more than 100,000, interviewed judges, prosecutors, public defenders, private defense attorneys, clerks, probation officers, and police officers. Several of the quotes from individuals in this section represent typical answers to questions in their survey. Miller and his associates asked prosecutors what most influenced their decisions to prosecute.[58]

In determining the strength of their case, prosecutors examine both the source and the quality of information available to them. As a primary source of that available information, the police investigation significantly influences plea bargaining. A senior prosecutor in Delaware County, Pennsylvania, said that prosecutors ask the arresting officer who brings them the case jacket "whether [or not] this guy is [in] trouble." Sometimes the officer "[will] tell you that although he looks like trouble, [he really is not a bad guy or vice versa]. Sometimes [the police can] tell you [that] he is a known troublemaker [in their jurisdiction]."[59]

Prosecutors do not always take police officers at their word or automatically accept their recommendations. A senior prosecutor from Dade County, Florida, explained:

> If the policeman says I don't like this guy and want to bust his ass and doesn't explain himself any further, I am not satisfied that he really tried to make the case. But on the other hand if the policeman reports that this guy is only the wheel man and won't give us the names of the two robbers who pulled the job, then I am willing to go along with a request for a tougher deal. Or if they say, the defendant told one story to the policeman at the crime scene and is now telling a different story, then I'll take this information into account as a legitimate concern of the police.[60]

Victims also supply information to prosecutors. What victims say affects prosecutors' assessments of offense seriousness and/or the dangerousness of defendants. Again, as the Dade County chief prosecutor explains:

> If an employee stabs his employer in the back or brings his employer close to bankruptcy as a result of embezzlement or other violations of trust, then I feel that the victim's request for a tough sentence should be respected. Also, if a victim tells me that he has been calling the police about this defendant for two years and the police have never arrested him before and that during that time this guy has been making a lot of trouble, then that would count heavily with me. I would go along with his request for a tough plea deal.[61]

The "Right" Bargain

How do prosecutors know what charges to press and what sentences to recommend? What is a "good deal" from prosecutors' perspectives? How do they know they are not "giving away the store" or, conversely, demanding too much? The answer begins with the going rates, or local "market values," for particular crimes. Market values rarely mirror statutory penalty prescriptions; and they vary from court to court within particular jurisdictions. For example, in Pennsylvania, first-degree burglary, a felony carrying prison time, informally has a going rate of much less. In Montgomery County it receives only a few days in jail, while in neighboring Philadelphia it gets automatic probation. In addition to market value, a "good bargain" also considers the seriousness of the offense, defendant dangerousness, and the strength of the government's case.[62]

Learning the market values and how to integrate them with offense seriousness, offender dangerousness, and case strength to arrive at the "right" bargain is difficult but critical for prosecutors who hope to survive and do well. Values not only vary across jurisdictions, but they also differ within specific jurisdictions according to particular judges' ideas about the seriousness of individual crimes and the dangerousness of individual criminals.

To deal with these particular variations, new prosecutors learn to incorporate into their decisions those informal, but nonetheless powerful, work-group standards in effect at the local courthouse. Senior staff rarely aid junior prosecutors in this respect. In Delaware, Pennsylvania, the senior prosecutor instructed new prosecutors only to:

> Protect yourself. You're a lawyer first and a prosecutor second. Check with somebody. Don't be Mr. Nice-Guy. Don't make a fool of yourself or a reputation of poor judgment. Don't bring stuff into a judge and have it rejected.[63]

Prosecutors do not like either surprises or losses. They can avoid both if they refrain from striking bargains for less than the going rates. Young prosecutors learn quickly that they cannot automatically bargain outside the going rates. Pressures from defense counsel, judges, and even other prosecutors urge the newcomer to be "reasonable." One new prosecutor learned this the hard way. In his first bargained case, he asked for the maximum sentence. Amid laughter, a senior prosecutor stepped up, took the file from the novice's hand, and made clear to the judge that the state wanted considerably less (in other words, the going rate, not the maximum penalty).[64]

Strength of the Case

Prosecutors consider case strength the single most important ingredient in plea bargaining. Miller and his associates report that "virtually all prosecutors regard weak cases as prime targets for plea negotiations." Plea-bargaining guidelines in one jurisdiction permit negotiated pleas "when the state has a weak case and the odds of conviction are not great." William F. McDonald, who interviewed prosecutors in 31 jurisdictions, found only one exception to this view. In Kalamazoo, Michigan, prosecutors adopted a policy of "plead the gold and take the dogs to trial."[65]

What makes a case strong is a complicated matter. A defendant might have committed the crime, but the government may not have sufficient or solid enough evidence to ensure conviction; the government can establish factual guilt outside court, but not legal guilt in court. A St. Louis prosecutor had charged a defendant with murder on no more evidence than a photograph a pawnbroker took of the suspect pawning the victim's television set the day after her apartment was burglarized and she was murdered. When asked if he was worried that the defendant might be innocent, he replied he knew the defendant was guilty because:

> I sent two of my best investigators who are black and competent men out on the street to check out the case. They went down to the section of town where this guy hangs out and they talked to the people down there about his involvement in this crime. They found out that the street talk says he's guilty. The guys down there on wise-guy alley say he did it, so I know he is guilty.[66]

Prosecutors may speak confidently about their ability to determine the strength of a case, sometimes coming up with as much as a 50 percent probability of conviction, but their confidence does not always reflect empirically sound judgments. The Institute for Law and Social Research (INSLAW) studied the Superior Court in the District of Columbia. It concluded that prosecutors—at least inexperienced ones—made unreliable estimates about a defendant's chances for conviction. Presumably, inexperienced prosecutors "guesstimate" or use "common sense," not empirical data, to draw conclusions about criminal cases.[67]

Four things weaken the government's case against criminal defendants:

1. Only shaky evidence connects defendants to crimes.
2. Defendants have committed criminal acts but lacked requisite intent. Absent mens rea, a material element in most serious crimes, defendants cannot be convicted.
3. Defendants have committed acts with requisite intent, but other legal flaws mar the case. For example, police illegally seized evidence needed to convict; the government cannot use it to prove guilt.
4. Evidence available at charging has disappeared or weakened. Witnesses die or leave town; victims lose resolve, forget, or decide they do not want the defendant to suffer after all.[68]

If any one or a combination of the preceding conditions weakens cases, many prosecutors make **sweet deals,** sometimes called settling for half a loaf. Those who justify this practice claim it is better to get convictions on lesser charges without trials than to go to trial on the "right" charge and risk losing totally by acquittal. "Hard-liners" do not agree. One prosecutor argued that the law should protect only factually innocent defendants; if defendants committed crimes, prosecution should follow, and "legal technicalities should not stand in the way."[69]

Seriousness of the Case

In determining offense seriousness, prosecutors go beyond the crude outlines of the technical crime charged and consider defendants' actual behavior. For example, burglary includes a wide range of actions, from something as serious as breaking into a sleeping woman's bedroom at night with the intent of raping her to the more minor crime of entering a locked office with the intent of stealing a typewriter. Some embezzlements are worse than others; for example, consider an embezzler who takes an employer's money wrongfully, but does not threaten the business's very existence. One prosecutor remembered a case he had overestimated. He charged a man with attempted murder for breaking into his ex-girlfriend's apartment and shooting up the place with a shotgun. If the prosecutor had a similar case today, he would be more flexible. He would not look at the case as one of attempted murder; instead, he would call it some domestic disturbance offense because the man never pointed the gun at his ex-girlfriend.[70]

Prosecutors cite defendants' prior criminal record as the most frequently used determinant of offender seriousness. Defendants' "bad records," however, matter less in measuring their seriousness as offenders than whether they are "bad persons."[71]

Herbert S. Miller quotes an experienced prosecutor on the point:

> I've got the police department record. I can see where the kid lives, what kind of neighborhood it is. I find out the place where the guy is hanging around and whether there are other scum in the area. I've got his prior arrests and their dispositions.[72]

Prosecutors do not look at case strength and at offense and offender seriousness in isolation. In weak cases involving serious offenses and "bad news" offenders, prosecutors will probably seek a bargain for some conviction, even if it is only half a loaf. In Miller and his associates' national survey of plea bargaining, one prosecutor reflected this attitude in the admission that he would not dismiss murder, drug, and robbery cases, even lacking evidence to convict, because of their seriousness.

According to sociologist Howard Daudistel, in practice prosecutors blur the distinction between case strength and offender seriousness. Weighing evidence, a highly subjective exercise, permits offender seriousness to determine case strength inappropriately, Daudistel found. Prosecutors' character evaluations often influence the way they evaluate the evidence against defendants; they sometimes associate either bad character with strong cases or "good citizens" with weak cases. In other words, personal character colors the evidence; prosecutors do not weigh it independently.[73]

Influence on Plea Bargaining

Prosecutors play four principal roles in plea bargaining, each with different and sometimes conflicting goals:

- Administrator
- Advocate
- Judge
- Legislator

Each role affects plea bargaining differently. As *administrators,* prosecutors primarily manage caseloads, which most consider too heavy. Prosecutors seek the administrative goal of rapid, efficient, and smooth case disposition. "We are running a machine here. We know we have to grind them out fast," said one Los Angeles trial assistant. A Manhattan prosecutor observed, "Our office keeps eight courtrooms extremely busy trying 5 percent of the cases. If even 10 percent of the cases ended in a trial, the system would break down. We can't afford to think very much about anything else."

Administrative concerns have varying effects on plea bargains, depending on the actual or perceived pressure of case backlogs. A Los Angeles prosecutor who had earlier refused to bargain approached defense counsel the day before the case was scheduled for trial and said, "Look, I'm awfully tired, and I have a bad calendar for tomorrow. Do you still want that deal you suggested?"[74]

Although prosecutors contend, and no doubt believe, that heavy caseloads force them to plea bargain, empirical research casts doubt on their contention. No simple relationship exists between caseload pressure and guilty pleas. Comparing trial rates in districts with extremely high volume and those with minimal caseload pressures showed no significant differences in the percentage of cases disposed of by trial and those disposed of by guilty plea. In Connecticut, where court caseloads were cut in half with no corresponding reduction in personnel, numbers of guilty pleas did not decline at all.[75]

Not all prosecutors emphasize administrative considerations most. In fact, an overwhelming number consider their *advocate* role most important; as advocates, they fight crime by convicting criminals. In the broadest sense, the prosecutor represents the general public. However, victims, their families, and the entire law enforcement community look toward prosecutors in particular as their advocates in criminal justice. As advocates, prosecutors seek the maximum number of convictions; case strength weighs most heavily in plea bargaining. "Half a loaf is better than none" expresses the advocate's philosophy. A Chicago prosecutor said, "When we have a weak case for any reason, we'll reduce to almost anything rather than lose."[76]

Advocacy can lead to disparate treatment for similar defendants. One defense lawyer in Chicago said that

> when a prosecutor has a dead-bang case he is likely to come up with an impossible offer like thirty to fifty years. When the case has a hole in it, however, the prosecutor may scale the offer all the way down to probation. The prosecutor's goal is to get something for every defendant, and the correctional treatment the defendant may require is the last thing on their minds.[77]

Informally, prosecutors can act as *judge* and *legislator.* According to the doctrine of separation of powers, they cannot legally judge or legislate; so they become quasi judges, or quasi legislators. As informal judges, prosecutors seek to do the right thing for defendants. If defendants plead guilty to a charge, prosecutors let their particular circumstances and need for proper correctional treatment take priority, so the state can provide the "right" treatment. As legislators, prosecutors may grant concessions because they consider the law too harsh according to current public opinion. Conversely, prosecutors in their formal advocate role seek the maximum penalty, or even refuse a "deal" if they believe the public demands severe punishment for certain crimes, such as welfare fraud, child sexual abuse, and, currently, drug-law violations. As quasi legislators, prosecutors place heavy emphasis on going rates and current market values in making plea bargains.

Defense Counsel and Guilty Pleas

Formally, defendants are wholly responsible for the decision to plead guilty. In practice, criminal defense lawyers play a crucial role in the decision. A manual for defense lawyers says that they[78]

> may and must give the client the benefit of counsel's professional advice on this crucial decision; and often counsel can protect the client from disaster only by using a considerable amount of persuasion to convince the client that a plea which the client instinctively disfavors is in fact in his or her best interests. This persuasion is most often needed to convince the client that s/he should plead guilty in a case in which a not-guilty plea would be totally destructive.[79]

Straight Pleas

Defense attorneys consider circumstances similar to those that prosecutors consider when advising clients to plead guilty. First, if the prosecution has a strong case and there is no good defense against it, defense counsel are likely to recommend that their clients plead guilty. Second, circumstances that will prejudice the trier of fact (jury, or judge in bench trials) can lead defense counsel to recommend a straight plea. These circumstances may include violent sex crimes, especially brutal crimes even in the absence of sexual assaults, crimes against children, and, currently, virtually all drug-law violations. Defense counsel usually favor guilty pleas when confronted with abrasive defendants; sympathetic defendants, on the other hand, recommend themselves for not guilty pleas. Also, the criminal records of defendants, especially if long and offensive, will prejudice juries against defendants. Finally, unfavorable, heavy news coverage will lead defense counsel to avoid trial.

Some circumstances might make a trial disadvantageous for the accused at sentencing. Defendants who plead guilty generally receive lighter sentences for their cooperation. But defense counsel have an obligation to apprise defendants of both the possibility and consequences of conviction, including the maximum penalties for the offense charged; mandatory minimum sentences for the offense charged; rules regarding probation and parole, particularly actual prison or jail time; forfeiture statutes that permit confiscation of cars and other paraphernalia used to commit liquor, gambling, and narcotics offenses; civil rights restrictions imposed on convicted felons; and privately imposed sanctions, such as higher insurance rates and restrictions on employment, barred admission to some professions, and forfeiture of admission to some educational institutions. Defendants weigh these factors in deciding whether to plead guilty immediately, enter into plea bargaining, or plead not guilty and go to trial.

Negotiated Pleas

The consequences that defendants face if they are convicted influence the plea-bargaining decisions of defense counsel. Thus, most defense lawyers view plea bargaining as integral to serving their clients well. As one expert put it:

> Experienced criminal lawyers know that one of defense counsel's most important functions, perhaps the most important, is working out with the prosecutor the best possible disposition of a client's case in situations in which there is no realistic prospect of acquittal. The lawyer not only may properly do this, but s/he violates the obligation to represent the client adequately if s/he does not.[80]

Defendants who can afford private attorneys receive the time and attention they deserve. Criminal defendants who rely on public defenders spend little, if any, time working out the proper plea with their lawyers. According to one survey, defendants spend "a total of five to ten minutes conferring" with their public defender lawyers, "usually in rapid, hushed conversations in the courthouse."[81]

Defense counsel play conflicting roles in criminal justice. Their most widely known and accepted formal role involves a vigorous defense of their clients' interests, but defense counsel also have informal obligations to the courthouse work group. As such, they want to dispose of cases with minimum friction and disruption. Like prosecutors and judges, they do not like surprises or losses, and negotiated pleas minimize both. Nor do they, or any other members of the courtroom elite, want bad relations with colleagues they encounter daily. Defendants are in adjudication only once and will then probably never return, at least not to the same work group's bailiwick. Prosecutors, defense attorneys, and judges, on the other hand, stay in the work group long after defendants leave.

David Lynch, who worked both as a prosecutor and a public defender, in his description of "workgroup pathologies," reveals how much closer to the work group public defenders feel than they do to most of their clients:

> Part of "doing time" was having to put up with the constant stress and abuse heaped on us by ill-tempered and antisocial clients, whose sole audience for their angry outbursts against "the system" was their public defenders, whom they often considered to be incompetent, hired cronies of the state. . . . This was the sort of individual we public defenders were expected to represent to the best of our abilities. This was the sort of individual who caused us to become cynical about our role as "liberty's last champion" (the logo on our office's baseball team shirts) and who tended to alienate us from our work. This was the sort of individual who made us love plea bargaining. Plea bargaining unfortunately plays right into the hands of alienated public defenders. . . . It makes cases "go away," taking with them some of the stress, work, combat, and (very important) the client—whose "companionship" one often wishes to minimize and whose guilt one often believes (correctly or incorrectly) to be so obvious.[82]

Clients

The pressure to plea bargain arises from the work-group relationship—that is, the urge to "go along in order to get along." Attitudes of lawyers toward defendants also favor negotiation over adjudication. In particular, defense lawyers usually believe that their clients are guilty of something; otherwise, the police would not have arrested them in the first place, nor would prosecutors have charged them with crimes after reviewing the arrest. Such an attitude directly contradicts the formal "presumption of innocence" that supposedly enshrouds every criminal defendant in the system prior to conviction. It replaces the formal presumption with its informal opposite, "the presumption of guilt," which far more often affects the defense counsel's decisions. "The public defender learns to view most of his clients as wrongdoers who should be convicted of some crime and punished, rather than as presumably innocent men who should be defended."[83]

Defense lawyers who operate on such a belief may "lean on" their clients to plead guilty to ensure a more lenient sentence. Even when lawyers believe their clients are innocent, they may pressure them to plead guilty because they think it is better to accept a lenient sentence than to risk conviction at trial and harsher punishment. Leaning on defendants may arise from a combination of the belief in clients' guilt, the belief that defendants can get a better deal by pleading guilty, and the desire to comply with the norms of the courtroom work group.

Former public defender and prosecutor David Lynch who later wrote of his experiences, reveals this combination of motives in his description of the process of "client control":

> Defense attorneys knew all too well that if they brought too many cases to trial, they would be seen as either unreasonable and worthy of professional ostracism or as a fool who was too weak to achieve "client control." Many attorneys I knew became masters of the fine art of "chair therapy," in which a client who insists on a trial is made to sit in the hall of the courthouse (or in the courthouse lockup) for days on end during the courthouse trial terms, waiting for his day in court, until he accepts a deal. Some (usually unintentionally) resorted to "good cop/bad cop" routines, in which a resistant defendant is subjected to the screams of his or her attorney, followed by the lawyer's associate, who tries to calmly help the accused see the light. Usually, however, defense attorneys, aware that incredible trial penalties were attached to the "right" to a jury trial, only needed to tell a defendant of the unconscionable sentences that had been meted out to others who dared to create work for a judge.[84]

Defendants in plea-bargaining jurisdictions may do better without lawyers, for several reasons. Asking for a lawyer might send out a signal that defendants are troublemakers. Judges may rule more leniently when defendants are not represented by counsel. In weak cases, prosecutors are more likely to charge defendants represented by counsel during screening. One prosecutor admitted that "if defense counsel were present when certain weak cases were about to be screened out, the prosecutor might first offer a plea deal to the attorney."[85]

Judges and Plea Bargaining

Judges enter into plea bargaining in one of two ways. They may either participate during the negotiations or supervise after lawyers have struck bargains. Sometimes they do both. About one in four judges participates in plea bargaining in felony cases, and one in five participates in misdemeanor plea bargaining. Judges play a supervisory role that is widely accepted as proper; but strong controversy exists over whether judges ought to participate in shaping plea bargaining.[86]

Judicial participation in plea bargaining varies according to individual judges' styles and from jurisdiction to jurisdiction. By observing, interviewing, and surveying judges in several jurisdictions, Miller and his associates found six types of participation by judges:

- No participation in any way.
- Gently leaning on participants, or facilitating the bargaining process.
- Implicit bargaining.
- Implicit bargaining and heavily pressuring participants to "force" guilty pleas.
- Explicit bargaining and making *general* sentence recommendations.
- Explicit bargaining and making specific sentence recommendations.[87]

Judges who refuse to participate at all oversee what prosecutors, defense counsel, and defendants have already decided. These judges believe they cannot effectively and impartially supervise a process in which they participate. In these "pure" jurisdictions, judges seldom second-guess the actual arrived-at bargain. They accept the prosecutor's dominant role in recommending a sentence. In fact, in most cases prosecutors and judges agreed on sentencing 100 percent of the time and never less than 95 percent of the time, leading some to conclude that judges have relinquished their sentencing powers.

One judge admitted he had never changed a prosecutor's recommendation. If he did not like the recommendation, he might tell the prosecutor that the sentence was not in line with current rates, so the prosecutor would think about it for future cases, but the judge would not change the recommendation in the current case.[88]

Judges who avoid both explicit and implicit participation do not pressure defendants indirectly by punishing them more severely if they go to trial. These "pure" judges who remain aloof from the bargaining process preside, almost without exception, in felony courts. In misdemeanor courts, judges feel that the sheer number of cases demands that they "encourage" defendants to plead guilty.[89]

Judges who lean on participants try to keep the flow of cases moving as smoothly and swiftly as possible. They stress administrative-bureaucratic values, believing, as one Oregon judge put it, that they have "to keep the pleas coming in." One Alaska judge said some cases should never go to trial. For instance, cases in which defendants have no legal defense and where there are no real questions of factual or legal guilt waste the time and money of prosecutors, defendants, and defense lawyers and squander badly needed court dates as well.

According to Miller and his associates, this led some judges to "facilitate" guilty pleas

> by speaking with defense attorneys or prosecutors regarding the case. If a particular prosecutor insisted on trying such cases the judge would in various informal ways indicate displeasure and would even go so far as to question why the case was in trial at all.[90]

These judges encourage bargaining in dead-bang cases (those where guilt appears obvious) to preserve court time for complicated cases. A judge in Colorado Springs said that if he had several hard cases and several easy ones, "he felt obligated to make time for the troublesome cases by clearing out those where there was little question as to guilt."[91]

Few judges exert harsh pressure to force bargaining toward guilty pleas; most merely lean on prosecutors and defense counsel. These judges cite heavy caseloads as the single most important reason for pressuring prosecution and defense. According to one observer, judges in this category made sure "no stone was left unturned to arrive at a plea of guilty. This included arm twisting, forcing, jerking the defense attorney around, and coming down on the defendant."[92]

A judge presiding over a burglary case in New York City's criminal courts provides an excellent example of arm twisting. When the case was called, one of the two defendants did not have a lawyer. Rather than continue the case, the judge appointed an attorney from among those present in the courtroom. The district attorney immediately offered a two- to four-year sentence in return for a guilty plea. The judge said, "After today, it's 3 to 6, after that it's 4 to 8. If they're ever going to plead, today is the time to do it." When the defendant rejected the bargain (the judge had appointed the lawyer only moments before), the judge said, "We'll make it very easy. It's 4 to 8 after today. Let's play hardball."[93]

These pressures included assigning defense attorneys to tough judges, denying continuances, overruling motions, and using other judicial techniques to force prosecutors and defense counsel to bargain. No judges in this group said they punished defendants for going to trial, but they did point out that going to trial created the risk that information adverse to defense and prosecution might surface and influence their sentencing decisions.[94]

Judges bargain implicitly when they systematically impose heavier sentences on convicted defendants who demand a trial. Such judges justify differential sentencing on several grounds. Defendants who admit their guilt show remorse and have, therefore, taken the first step toward rehabilitation; they deserve a lesser penalty. Other judges abide by the slogan, "If you want to win big, you'd better be prepared to lose big," meaning that defendants who put the state to the burden of a trial will pay a price if the state wins. One Chicago judge feels that defendants who "waste" taxpayers' money and the court's time "deserve more time in jail for the problems [they] create." Judges who sentence publicly after a trial often apply differential sentencing because they are under considerably more pressure to sentence harshly than are judges who do so in the obscurity of the plea-bargaining process.[95]

Judges who bargain explicitly and make general sentence recommendations enjoy considerable flexibility. In general, they specify only that they will give prison time as opposed to probation, or the upper instead of lower range of time incarcerated. Judges who bargain explicitly and indicate general sentences do so because they consider predictability critical to the criminal justice system: defendants should have a good idea of what will happen to them if they plead guilty, and lawyers ought to have indications of what will result from their work. At the same time, these judges show concern about retaining judicial independence. If they promise an exact sentence, they feel they have abdicated their primacy in sentencing.[96]

The most active judges not only bargain explicitly concerning pleas but also commit themselves to specific sentences following the negotiation process. Explicit bargaining might take place in formal pretrial negotiating conferences, such as those in Alameda County, California, and Cook County, Illinois. It might be done informally in judges' chambers, or even in court with the defense counsel and the prosecutor huddling with the judge at the bench. Such informal bargaining sessions are common in Dade County, Florida, and El Paso County, Colorado.[97]

Judges specify caseload pressure as their single most frequent reason for participating in plea negotiations, saying they have to "keep things from getting bogged down." One Hartford, Connecticut, judge admitted that

> he became in fact a prosecutor when 835 cases were backlogged. He reduced the backlog to 299 cases by ordering the prosecuting attorney to select his two best assistants and setting up conferences at five-minute intervals day and night for six days. He enforced attendance of the prosecutor and defense attorney under threat of an arrest warrant. Under these conditions defense attorneys went to prosecutors and disposed of easy cases. The judge then ordered them into his chambers to discuss "sticky cases" and make a plea recommendation. They then marched back into court to recite the recommended disposition onto the record. He observed, somewhat ironically, that this practice "stinks" because a judge becomes a prosecutor. He did, however, indicate pleasure with the results.[98]

According to the American Bar Association Committee on Professional Ethics, judges "should not be a party to advance arrangements for the determination of sentence whether as a result of a guilty plea or a finding of guilty based on proof." The American Bar Association Standards asserts that the "trial judge should not participate in plea discussions."[99]

Some jurisdictions prohibit judicial participation by statute or court rule. Under the Federal Rules of Criminal Procedure, for example, the "court shall not participate in any such discussions." One court interpreted this rule to mean that

> the sentencing judge should take no part whatever in any discussion or communication regarding the sentence to be imposed prior to the entry of a plea of guilty, conviction, or submission to him of a plea agreement.[100]

Guilty Pleas and the Constitution

Three constitutional provisions require judges to supervise the entering of guilty pleas:

1. Fifth Amendment protection against self-incrimination.
2. Sixth Amendment guarantee of a jury trial.
3. Fourteenth Amendment requirement that no state shall deprive a citizen of life, liberty, or property without due process of law.

These provisions require judges to make sure defendants plead guilty knowingly and voluntarily.

According to these criteria, judges have to ensure that defendants:

1. Understand the charges against them, meaning the material elements of the crime charged.
2. Fully appreciate that pleading guilty waives their rights against self-incrimination and to a jury trial.
3. Appreciate that they know the maximum and minimum sentences awarded the crime.

Judges determine that defendants' pleas are voluntary and knowing by a formal discussion called the **colloquy.** The colloquy consists of the following:

1. Judges ask defendants if bargaining produced their guilty pleas.
2. If they did, defendants have to reveal the terms of the agreement to the judge.

Then judges advise defendants of the possible consequences of their guilty pleas.

Judges also determine whether sufficient facts support guilty pleas. The Federal Rules of Criminal Procedure, for example, provide that judges cannot "enter a judgment upon such a plea without a factual basis for the plea." Generally, judges question prosecutors and defendants and examine presentence reports to make sure that guilty pleas are backed up by sufficient evidence of guilt.[101]

Inquiring into factual bases of guilty pleas has several functions. It protects defendants against pleading guilty to crimes the facts do not fit. For example, one defendant pleaded guilty to four counts of interstate transportation of stolen money orders when he had crossed state lines only once. The judge's failure to inquire into the factual basis of the plea led to conviction on four crimes when, on the basis of the facts, the defendant had committed only one. Inquiring into the evidence also helps judges determine defendants' willingness to plead guilty and their understanding of the charges against them. It generates a fuller and more adequate record, making later review more accurate and successful challenges to the agreed-on plea bargain less likely.[102]

Plea-Bargaining Reform

Despite its widespread practice, plea bargaining has generated great controversy. It has both many supporters and many critics. Those who favor it point to the benefits it confers on the whole criminal justice system, on taxpayers, and on defendants. These benefits include:

- Creates administrative efficiency by controlling court calendars and moving cases swiftly through the criminal process after arrest.
- Saves tax dollars because negotiating costs less than trying cases, especially with a jury.
- Ensures prompt correctional measures for defendants.
- Promotes rehabilitation of defendants by requiring them to admit their guilt.
- Reduces the humiliation and misery to defendants that can accompany a public trial.
- Results in lesser punishment.

Opponents point to reasons why plea bargaining should be either totally abolished or at least substantially curtailed. They maintain that informal discretionary bargaining is inherently wrong in our adversary system. Furthermore, plea bargaining corrodes public confidence in criminal justice because it smacks of corruption, "deals," and evading punishment for crime. According to criminal law professor George P. Fletcher, in his interesting book *With Justice for Some:*

> Though roughly 90% of all cases are disposed of consensually without trial, there is something unseemly about the prosecution's trading a lower charge in return for the defendant's cooperating and waiving his right to trial. The very idea that the authorities cut special deals with particular defendants offends the rule of law. Many legal systems on the Continent, Germany most strongly, have long rejected this kind of discretionary justice. . . . Germans refer to American-style discretionary justice as the . . . principle of expediency as opposed to the . . . principle of legality, which demands prosecution according to the extent of the perceived legal violation. Even-handed justice under the law should mean that everyone receives the same treatment: no leniency for those who promise something in return.[103]

Whether or not these claims are in fact true, the public believes them.

Critics also point to the unfairness of plea bargaining. Guilty defendants escape the full consequences of their wrongdoing by pleading guilty to crimes less serious than those they have actually committed. Innocent defendants, on the other hand, feel compelled to plead guilty when they have committed no crime at all. For example:

> San Francisco defense attorney Benjamin Davis . . . represented a man charged with kidnapping and forcible rape. The defendant was innocent, Davis says, and after investigating the case Davis was confident of an acquittal. The prosecutor, who seems to have shared the defense attorney's opinion on this point, offered to permit a guilty plea to simple battery. Conviction on this charge would not have led to a greater sentence than thirty days' imprisonment, and there was every likelihood that the defendant would be granted probation. When Davis informed his client of this offer, he emphasized that conviction at trial seemed highly improbable. The defendant's reply was simple: "I can't take that chance."[104]

Critics of plea bargaining consider such a situation repugnant to the very notion of justice.

Bargaining, according to critics, also distributes lenient sentences unevenly and unfairly. It reduces the law's deterrent effect because it results in lower sentences for guilty defendants. It impairs correctional measures because it curtails judges' sentencing discretion. It punishes defendants who go to trial: considerable research demonstrates that defendants who insist on trial are punished more harshly if they are convicted than if they had pleaded guilty to the same charge.[105]

Despite criticism, calls for change and plea-bargaining research did not begin in earnest until the 1960s. Lyndon Johnson's Crime Commission took a harsh view of plea-bargaining practices. Furthermore, although the Supreme Court approved plea bargaining as a "necessity" in 1971, in 1973 the prestigious National Advisory Commission on Criminal Justice Standards and Goals, appointed by Richard Nixon, recommended that "As soon as possible, but in no event later than 1978, negotiations between prosecutors and defendants—either personally or through their attorneys—concerning concessions to be made in return for guilty pleas should be prohibited."[106]

Use *Your* Discretion

Abolish plea bargaining?

In 1975, Alaska Attorney General Avrum Gross surprised criminal justice practitioners in his own state and aroused the interest of professionals and scholars nationwide when he banned plea bargaining in Alaska. A follow-up study to determine the ban's effects revealed several startling conclusions.[107]

Courts in Alaska did not collapse under a crush of criminal trials; defendants continued to plead guilty at about the same rate, for the reasons already reviewed. The ban did not affect sentences for violent crimes (murder, rape, robbery, and felonious assault). On the other hand, "clean kids," young defendants with no criminal record, convicted of the least serious property felonies—burglary, larceny, or receiving stolen property—received longer sentences. Plea bargaining no longer provided an opportunity for first-time property offenders to receive probation or lighter prison sentences.[108]

Attorney General Gross's ban also returned sentencing to trial judges where, formally, it has always been. Prior to the ban, judges routinely accepted the recommendations of prosecutors, meaning that informally prosecutors sentenced convicted offenders. Without plea bargaining, routine cases were disposed of more rapidly. Time spent bargaining over the sentences of nonviolent criminals prior to the ban was no longer necessary; they continued to plead guilty without negotiation. "In short, prosecutors learned that they could achieve the same results under the attorney general's new system, but with less time spent on routine cases."[109]

Alaska's plea ban has had mixed results. It has destroyed some well-entrenched myths concerning plea bargains, showing that drastically reducing plea bargaining does not break down the criminal justice system. On the contrary, the ban actually hastened case dispositions, at least in routine, nonviolent felonies. It gave prosecutors and defense attorneys more, not less, time to try cases. Banning plea bargaining, however, was not a panacea: Evils once attributed to plea bargaining continued unabated following the plea ban. Defendants' incomes still affected the quality of pretrial dispositions and trials. Defendants who went to trial still received harsher sentences than those who pleaded guilty. Race, income, and employment status remained telling determinants on sentences. Furthermore, according to law professors Franklin Zimring and Richard Frase, the ban sometimes caused undue rigidity, particularly for first-time, nonviolent property offenses. "A shaky prosecution witness, a faulty police investigation, or an attractive defendant may provide irresistible inducements to bargain, and make negotiated settlement[s] seem by far the most sensible recourse."[110]

The finding that the abolition of plea bargaining did not break down the criminal justice system by overburdening the courts with trials supports the caseload hypothesis. According to the caseload hypothesis—widely held by criminal justice practitioners but disputed by a number of empirical studies—the pressure to dispose of large numbers of criminal cases requires plea bargaining to keep the courts working at a reasonable, efficient, economical pace.

Some research, however, supports the caseload hypothesis. Malcolm D. Holmes, Howard C. Daudistel, and William A. Taggart reviewed the ban on plea bargaining in El Paso, Texas, using data published by the Texas Judicial Council Annual Reports. These data include annual numbers of felony cases pending at the beginning of each year; the number of cases added each year; jury trial dispositions each year; and convictions each year. Holmes and his associates found that following the ban on plea bargaining in El Paso the

- Majority of defendants still pled guilty.
- Number of jury trials increased.
- Rate of dispositions fell.
- Number of convictions remained mostly unchanged.

Using a quasi-experimental time-series design, the researchers concluded that the caseload pressure hypothesis does have some validity. Following the ban on plea bargaining, even a small increase in adversariness increased the time it took to dispose of cases;

going to trial in place of plea bargaining definitely slows the disposition rate.

The El Paso study indicates an important truth about criminal justice research: What may be true for one place and time may not be true for another. The differences between the circumstances in El Paso, Texas, and Alaska may explain the difference in outcome. It may also, however, point to another truth: The methodology followed in the El Paso study (a time-series analysis) contrasted with a single point in time analysis—once before and once after the ban in Alaska—may explain the difference in support for the caseload pressure hypothesis.[111]

CRITICAL THINKING

1. Summarize the findings and methods of the Alaska and El Paso studies of plea bargaining.
2. Which, if any, is the better study? Explain.
3. On the basis of these studies would you recommend the abolition of plea bargaining? Explain.
4. If you need further information to decide, what would that information be? Explain.

Pretrial Settlement Conferences

Plea bargaining excludes some people with a vital interest in the case—victims, defendants, police officers, and judges. To meet this deficiency, researchers conducted a field experiment in Dade County, Florida. They established pretrial settlement conferences to restructure plea bargaining. In these conferences, all negotiations took place before judges, and defendants, victims, and police officers were invited to attend.[112]

The experiment tested several hypotheses about conferences:

- Increased participation by judges, victims, defendants, and police officers would make plea bargaining more "open and seemly."
- Increased citizen participation would enhance citizen satisfaction with plea bargaining.
- Police satisfaction with case dispositions would improve by making the police knowledgeable participants in the plea-bargaining process.
- Police presence would increase police understanding of the process and lead to greater support for case dispositions that they might otherwise have criticized as too lenient.
- Judicial participation would protect the public interest in criminal case disposition instead of putting most control in the hands of prosecutors and defense lawyers.
- The participation of victims would focus attention on their legitimate concerns about the criminal status of the offender and their claims to compensation for injury or damage.
- Victims have both a moral right and a psychological need to participate in criminal case dispositions that involve them.
- Defendants have a right to have their interests protected at sentencing.

As to the rights and needs of victims, the criminologist Norval Morris wrote:

> At present, victims of crimes are treated very shabbily by our criminal justice system. The system appears to serve its functionaries more than the public. Victims are repeatedly interrogated; they make too many trips to pretrial and trial hearings, at most of which they sit and do nothing, unable to hear the proceedings, forbidden to talk or read, bewildered as to what is going on, wondering if they are the wrongdoers or not, and reflecting on their lost wages and other costs. If the criminal process is the taking over by the state of the vengeful instincts of the injured person—buttressed by the recognition that harm to the victim is also harm to the state—then it would seem, at first blush, that the victim at least has a right to be informed of, and where appropriate involved in, the processes that have led to whatever is the state settlement of the harm that has been done to him. . . . [I]t is a matter of courtesy and respect for the individual victim.[113]

All in all, the field experiment was designed to test whether, and to what extent, changing the structure of plea bargaining would have positive results.

The Dade County pretrial settlement conferences took place in judges' chambers. Judges wore business suits instead of the forbidding black robes. Participants sat around the room or gathered about a table in an atmosphere more like a conference than a court proceeding. Generally, conference sessions were brief, averaging about 10 minutes, with some lasting 25 minutes. Conference topics most often included the facts of the case, recommendations, and defendants' prior records. The personal backgrounds and circumstances of victims and defendants became subjects of discussion somewhat less frequently. Because most conferences generally lasted about 10 minutes, they covered matters only superficially.

Judges were the most active participants in the proceedings and made the most frequent contributions to every topic. In 40 percent of the cases, prosecutors said nothing about the facts of the case, and in over half the cases, prosecutors said nothing about defendants' prior records. Defense attorneys discussed defendants' prior records—usually to clear up misunderstandings—and defendants' personal characteristics in more than one-third of the cases. Police officers contributed facts relating to the crime in about 70 percent of the cases; they added to information about defendants' backgrounds in more than half the cases.

Victims were passive in the conferences they attended. Occasionally, they commented on the facts but practically never expressed views about disposition, except occasionally to approve what judges and lawyers recommended. The often-expressed fear that victims would demand maximum sentences simply did not materialize. In fact, victims and defendants played a minor role in the deliberations overall. Furthermore, victim attendance was disappointing: only 32 percent of invited victims ever came to the conferences. Defendants attended pretrial conferences at a higher rate—66 percent—but only minimally participated in them. If they commented at all, they usually contributed information about either the facts of the case or their background. They rarely said anything about disposition or recommended sentences.

Conferences did not noticeably affect case dispositions. Cases went to trial at similar rates, sentences remained comparable, and the time and expense involved in processing cases stayed about the same. However, the conferences did modify victims' and police attitudes toward plea bargaining and the criminal justice system. Slightly more than half the victims and police expressed greater approval and understanding of plea bargaining and the criminal process after the experiment.

The Dade County efforts to restructure plea bargaining, therefore, only slightly altered the results of plea bargaining. The pretrial settlement conference did enhance, if only marginally, victims' and police confidence in plea bargaining; it was not a panacea.

Administrative Rule Making

Some experts have recommended reforming plea bargaining by subjecting it to written guidelines established by those who participate in it. Although not a widespread practice, formal administrative rules are increasingly used as a device to control discretion in the bargaining process. The American Bar Association's *Standards Relating to Pleas of Guilty* include rules for prosecutors, defense attorneys, and judges. The standards permit prosecutors to bargain over charges and sentence recommendations. They require defendants' approval to all plea bargains, and demand that defense counsel clearly outline to defendants all the alternatives available in the case. Although they prohibit judges from participating in plea bargaining, they allow prosecutors and defense counsel to submit written agreements to judges prior to guilty pleas. If judges initially accept agreements but later reject them, defendants can change their pleas.[114]

Knowledge and Understanding CHECK

1. List the reasons why so many defendants plead guilty.
2. Distinguish between straight and negotiated guilty pleas.
3. According to research in Alaska, identify the reasons that defendants enter straight pleas.
4. Identify and explain the types of negotiation for guilty pleas.
5. Identify and describe the three forms that concessions take in plea bargaining.
6. Explain the nature and significance of local legal culture on plea bargaining.
7. Describe the role of the prosecutor in plea bargaining.
8. Identify and describe the weight given to the five major influences on the prosecutor on plea bargaining.
9. Explain the importance of "going rates" on plea bargaining.
10. How do prosecutors' estimates of their ability to determine the strength of cases compare with reality?
11. Identify four things that weaken the government's case against criminal defendants.
12. Identify and explain how prosecutors determine the seriousness of offenses.
13. Identify the four roles prosecutors play in plea bargaining, and explain how these roles influence their decisions.
14. Describe the influence of caseload pressures on plea bargaining.
15. What circumstances do defense counsel consider in deciding whether to recommend straitght pleas to their clients?
16. Explain how the work group relationship affects plea bargaining.
17. Identify the two ways in which judges enter plea bargaining.
18. Identify six types of participation that characterize the role of judges in plea bargaining.
19. Identify three constitutional provisions that require judges to supervise the entering of guilty pleas.
20. Identify and explain the reforms that critics of plea bargaining support.

Can an Innocent Defendant Plead Guilty? Consideration

According to the U.S. Supreme Court, which reviewed Alford's conviction:

> Ordinarily, a judgment of conviction resting on a plea of guilty is justified by the defendant's admission that he committed the crime charged against him and his consent that judgment be entered without a trial of any kind. . . . Here Alford entered his plea but accompanied it with the statement that he had not shot the victim. . . .
>
> State and lower federal courts are divided upon whether a guilty plea can be accepted when it is accompanied by protestations of innocence. . . . Some courts, giving expression to the principle that "[o]ur law only authorizes a conviction where guilt is shown," require that trial judges reject such pleas. But others have concluded that they should not "force any defense on a defendant in a criminal case," particularly when advancement of the defense might "end in disaster." They have argued that, since "guilt, or the degree of guilt, is at times uncertain and elusive . . . [a]n accused, though believing in or entertaining doubts respecting his innocence, might reasonably conclude a jury would be convinced of his guilt and that he would fare better in the sentence by pleading guilty." As one state court observed nearly a century ago, "[r]easons other than the fact that he is guilty may induce a defendant to so plead, [and] [h]e must be permitted to judge for himself in this respect."
>
> [We can perceive no] material difference between a plea that refuses to admit commission of the criminal act and a plea containing a protestation of innocence when . . . a defendant intelligently concludes that his interests require entry of a guilty plea and the record before the judge contains strong evidence of actual guilt. Here the state had a strong case of first-degree murder against Alford. Whether he realized or disbelieved his guilt, he insisted on his plea because in his view he had absolutely nothing to gain by a trial and much to gain by pleading. . . . Confronted with the choice between a trial for first-degree murder, on the one hand, and a plea of guilty to second-degree murder, on the other, Alford quite reasonably chose the latter and thereby limited the maximum penalty to a thirty-year term. When his plea is viewed in light of the evidence against him, which substantially negated his claim of innocence and which further provided a means by which the judge could test whether the plea was being intelligently entered, its validity cannot be seriously questioned. In view of the strong factual basis for the plea demonstrated by the state and Alford's clearly expressed desire to enter it despite his professed belief in his innocence, we hold that the trial judge did not commit constitutional error in accepting it.[115]

Critical Thinking

1. How does the Court justify allowing innocent defendants to plead guilty?
2. Do you agree that this is a voluntary and intelligent plea? Explain your answer.
3. Which courts have the better argument regarding innocent people who plead guilty: those that allow innocent defendants to plead guilty or those that prohibit it? Defend your answer.

CHAPTER CAPSULE

- Most criminal cases do not go to trial.
- Most people plead guilty without even plea bargaining.
- Jurors reflect a cross section based on telephone directories and voter registration lists.
- Jurors try hard to be objective but the values of their neighborhood affect their verdicts.

- Most decisions regarding guilty pleas have to do with the seriousness of the offense, and the previous record of the offender, and the strength of the evidence, not race, sex, or ethnic origins.
- Judges and prosecutors may support harsher penalties for those who exercise their right to a trial and are found guilty.
- Caseload pressure does not affect bargaining, even if prosecutors and judges believe that it does.

KEY TERMS

legal guilt
factual guilt
bench trial
liberation hypothesis
jury nullification
jury panel
voir dire
challenge for cause
peremptory challenge
proof beyond a reasonable doubt
subpoena
direct examination
cross-examination
leading questions
hostile witness
relevant evidence
material evidence
hearsay evidence
jury instructions
straight pleas
negotiated pleas
dead-bang cases
express bargaining
implicit bargaining
charge bargaining
sentence bargaining
slow pleas
local legal culture
sweet deals
colloquy

INTERNET RESEARCH EXERCISES

Exercise: Using the Internet or InfoTrac College Edition, search for information on plea bargaining. Based on your research and what you have learned in this chapter, are you in favor of plea bargaining or would you ban it?

Suggested sites:

- Alaska's Plea Bargaining Ban: http://www.ajc.state.ak.us/Reports/pleafram.htm
- Core Concerns of Plea Bargaining: http://www.law.emory.edu/ELJ/volumes/spg98/guido.html

InfoTrac College Edition: Search on the key words "plea bargaining reform."

NOTES

1. *North Carolina v. Alford,* 400 U.S. 25 (1970).
2. Harry Kalven, Jr. and Hans Zeisel, *The American Jury* (Chicago: The University of Chicago Press, 1966), 31–32; Charles Silberman, *Criminal Violence, Criminal Justice* (New York: Random House, 1978), 283.
3. Ibid.
4. *Duncan v. Louisiana,* 391 U.S. 145 (1968); James J. Gobert, "In Search of the Impartial Jury," *Journal of Criminal Law and Criminology* 25 (1988): 669–742.
5. *Apodaca v. Oregon,* 406 U.S. 404 (1972).
6. *Johnson v. Louisiana,* 406 U.S. 356 (1972).
7. Wayne R. LaFave and Jerold H. Israel, *Criminal Procedure* (St. Paul: West, 1984), 2:698.
8. *Williams v. Florida,* 399 U.S. 78 (1970).
9. Peter W. Sperlich, "*Williams v. Florida,*" in Kermit Hall, ed., *The Oxford Companion to the United States Supreme Court* (New York: Oxford University Press, 1992), 931–32.
10. Wayne R. LaFave and Jerald H. Israel, *Criminal Procedure* (St. Paul: West, 1984), 2:695–96.
11. De Tocqueville quote from James P. Levine's excellent book *Juries and Politics* (Pacific Grove, Calif.: Brooks/Cole, 1992), 14.
12. Kalven and Zeisel, *The American Jury,* 163–67.
13. Levine, *Juries and Politics,* 16.
14. Levine, *Juries and Politics,* 128; Benjamin A. Holden, Laurie P. Cohen, and Eleena de Lisser, "Color Blinded? Race Seems to Play an Increasing Role in Many Jury Verdicts," *Wall Street Journal,* 4 October 1995; John Kifner, "Bronx Jurors: A Defense Dream, A Prosecutor's Nightmare," *New York Times,* 5 December 1988.
15. Holden, Cohen, and de Lisser, "Color Blinded?"
16. Ibid.
17. LaFave and Israel, *Criminal Procedure,* 2:700.
18. Hisim quoted in Holden, Cohen, and de Lisser, "Color Blinded?"; Irwin A. Horowitz, "Jury Nullification: The Impact of Judicial Instructions, Arguments, and Challenges on Jury Decision Making," *Law and Human Behavior* 12 (1988): 439–53.
19. 28 U.S.C.A., secs. 1861–69.
20. LaFave and Israel, *Criminal Procedure,* 2:708.

21. Martin A. Levin, "The American Judicial System: Should It, Does It, and Can It Provide an Impartial Jury to Criminal Defendants?" *Criminal Justice Journal* 11 (1988): 89–124.
22. William Lambarde, *Eirenarcha* (London: n.p., 1581).
23. *Taylor v. Louisiana,* 419 U.S. 522 (1975); *Holland v. Illinois,* 493 U.S. 474 (1990).
24. *Sheppard v. Maxwell,* 384 U.S. 333 (1966).
25. Steven Phillips, *No Heroes, No Villains: The Story of a Murder Trial* (New York: Random House, 1977), 218.
26. *Illinois v. Allen,* 397 U.S. 337 (1970).
27. Henry Campbell Black, Black's Law Dictionary, 5th abridged ed. (St. Paul: West, 1983), 635; *In re Winship,* 397 U.S. 358 (1970).
28. *In re Winship.*
29. Joel Samaha, *Criminal Procedure* (St. Paul: West, 1999), 597.
30. George P. Fletcher, *A Crime of Self-Defense: Bernhard Goetz and the Law on Trial* (New York: Free Press, 1988), 116, 231.
31. Ibid., 121–22.
32. Ibid.
33. Phillips, *No Heroes, No Villains,* 196–97.
34. Ibid., 213.
35. Stephen J. Schulhofer, "Is Plea Bargaining Inevitable?" *Harvard Law Review* 97 (1984): 1061–62; BJS, *Report to the Nation on Crime and Justice* (Washington, D.C.: Bureau of Justice Statistics, 1988), 83; *Malcolm Feeley, The Process Is the Punishment* (New York: Russell Sage, 1979), 310.
36. Joel Samaha, *Law and Order in Historical Perspective* (New York: Academic Press, 1974); Roscoe Pound and Felix Frankfurter, eds., *Criminal Justice in Cleveland* (Cleveland: The Cleveland Foundation, 1922), 93; Arthur Rosett and Donald R. Cressey, *Justice by Consent* (New York: Harper & Row, Publishers, 1976); Albert W. Alschuler, "Plea Bargaining and Its History," *Law and Society Review* 13 (1979): 211; Joseph Sanborn, "A Historical Sketch of Plea Bargaining," *Justice Quarterly* 3 (1986): 111.
37. Peter F. Nardulli, James Eisenstein, and Roy B. Flemming, *The Tenor of Justice: Criminal Courts and the Guilty Plea* (Urbana, Ill.: University of Illinois Press, 1988); Mike McConville and Chester Mirsky, "Guilty Plea Courts: A Social Disciplinary Model of Criminal Justice," *Social Problems* 42 (1995): 216–34.
38. Michael L. Rubenstein, Steven Clarke, and Theresa Wright, *Alaska Bans Plea Bargaining* (Washington, D.C.: U.S. Government Printing Office, 1980), 81; Milton Heumann, "Author's Reply," *Law and Society Review* 13 (1979): 651; Barbara Boland and Brian Forst, "Prosecutors Don't Always Aim to Pleas," *Federal Probation* 49 (1985): 10–15. For contrasting views see Schulhofer, "Is Plea Bargaining Inevitable?" 1044, and Feeley, *The Process Is the Punishment,* 168–75.
39. Rubenstein, Clarke, and Wright, *Alaska Bans Plea Bargaining,* 81.
40. Ibid., 82.
41. Ibid., 85.
42. Ibid., 86.
43. Ibid., 87.
44. Ibid., 88.
45. Ibid., 91.
46. Ibid., 92.
47. Defense attorney quoted in Feeley, *The Process Is the Punishment,* 186.
48. William F. McDonald, "From Plea Negotiation to Coercive Justice: Notes on the Respectification of a Concept," *Law and Society Review* 13 (1979): 385–92.
49. Milton Heumann, "Thinking About Plea Bargaining," in *The Study of Criminal Courts,* Peter F. Nardulli, ed. (Cambridge, Mass.: Ballinger, 1979), 208, 210.
50. Ibid., 9.
51. Ibid., 7.
52. Lynn M. Mather, "Some Determinants of the Method of Case Disposition: Decision-Making by Public Defenders in Los Angeles," *Law and Society Review* 8 (1974): 187.
53. Lawrence M. Friedman, *American Law* (New York: W. W. Norton, 1984), 6; Heumann, "Thinking About Plea Bargaining," 211–12; Thomas W. Church, Jr., "Examining Local Legal Culture," *American Bar Foundation Research Journal* 3 (1985): 449–518.
54. Heumann, "Thinking About Plea Bargaining," 213–14.
55. James Eisenstein and Herbert Jacob, *Felony Justice* (Boston: Little, Brown, 1977), 286. See also Nardulli, Eisenstein, and Flemming, *The Tenor of Justice,* for more recent assessments to similar effect.
56. Herbert S. Miller et al., *Plea Bargaining in the United States* (Washington, D.C.: National Institute of Law Enforcement and Criminal Justice, 1978), 56; and, more recently, Nardulli, Eisenstein, and Flemming, *The Tenor of Justice.*
57. Albert W. Alschuler, "The Prosecutor's Role in Plea Bargaining," *University of Chicago Law Review* 36 (1968): 50; Miller et al., *Plea Bargaining in the United States,* 60–61; Lynn Mather, *Plea Bargaining or Trial? The Process of Criminal Case Disposition* (Lexington, Mass.: Lexington Books, 1979); Celesta A. Albonetti, "Race and the Probability of Pleading Guilty," *Journal of Quantitative Criminology* 6 (1990): 316–18; Dean J. Champion, "Private Counsels and Public Defenders: A Look at Weak Cases, Prior Records, and Leniency in Plea Bargaining," *Journal of Criminal Justice* 17 (1989): 253–63; Brian Forst, "Prosecution and Sentencing," in *Crime,* James Q. Wilson and Joan Petersilia, eds. (San Francisco: Institute for Contemporary Studies Press, 1995), 366–68.
58. Miller et al., *Plea Bargaining in the United States,* 62.
59. Ibid., 67–68.
60. Ibid.
61. Ibid., 71–72.
62. Ibid., 80.
63. Ibid., 82.
64. Ibid., 83.
65. Ibid., 101–102; William F. McDonald, *Plea Bargaining: Critical Issues and Common Practices* (Washington, D.C.: National Institute of Justice, 1985), 65.
66. Quoted in Miller et al., *Plea Bargaining in the United States,* 93.
67. Cited, ibid., 103.
68. Ibid., 106–107.
69. Ibid., 108.
70. Ibid., 117–18.
71. Institute for Law and Social Research (INSLAW), *Curbing the Repeat Offender* (Washington: INSLAW, 1977).
72. Miller et al., *Plea Bargaining in the United States,* 119.
73. Howard Daudistel, "Deciding What the Law Means: An Examination of Police Prosecutor Discretion," Ph.D. dissertation, University of California, Santa Barbara, 1976, 162–64.
74. Quoted in Franklin E. Zimring and Richard S. Frase, *The Criminal Justice System* (Boston: Little, Brown, 1980), 506–07.
75. Milton Heumann, *Plea Bargaining: The Experience of Prosecutors, Judges and Defense Attorneys* (Chicago: University of Chicago Press, 1978), 29–31.
76. Ibid., 507.
77. Ibid., 508.
78. *Jones v. Barnes,* 51 U.S.L.W. 5151 (July 5, 1983). 463 U.S. 745.
79. Anthony Amsterdam, *Trial Manual for the Defense of Criminal Cases* (Philadelphia: American Law Institute, 1984), 1:229.

80. Ibid., 235.
81. Jonathan D. Casper, *American Criminal Justice* (Englewood Cliffs, N.J.: Prentice-Hall, 1972), 10.
82. David Lynch, "The Impropriety of Plea Agreements," *Law and Social Inquiry* 19 (1994): 121–22.
83. Miller et al., *Plea Bargaining in the United States,* 168.
84. Lynch, "The Impropriety of Plea Agreements," 123.
85. Ibid., 185–86.
86. LaFave and Israel, *Criminal Procedure,* 2:627.
87. Miller et al., *Plea Bargaining in the United States,* 230–31, 243–44.
88. Ibid., 244–45.
89. Ibid., 246.
90. Ibid., 246–48.
91. Ibid., 248.
92. Ibid., 249.
93. Quoted in Stephen J. Schulhofer, "No Job Too Small: Justice Without Bargaining in the Lower Criminal Courts," *American Bar Foundation Research Journal* 3 (1985): 585, note 234.
94. Miller et al., Plea Bargaining in the United States, 249–50.
95. Ibid., 263–64.
96. Ibid., 260.
97. Ibid., 250.
98. Ibid., 252.
99. LaFave and Israel, *Criminal Procedure,* 2:626.
100. *United States v. Werker,* 535 F.2d 198 (2d Cir. 1976), certiorari denied 429 U.S. 926.
101. LaFave and Israel, *Criminal Procedure,* 2:652–53.
102. *Gilbert v. United States,* 466 F.2d 533 (5th Cir. 1972); LaFave and Israel, *Criminal Procedure,* 2:652–53.
103. George P. Fletcher, *With Justice for Some: Victims' Rights in Criminal Trials* (Reading, Mass.: Addison-Wesley, 1995), 191.
104. Zimring and Frase, *The Criminal Justice System,* 523.
105. Ibid., 542–63.
106. National Advisory Commission on Criminal Justice Standards and Goals, *Courts* (Washington, D.C.: U.S. Government Printing Office, 1973), standard 3.1, 46.
107. The material on the Alaska ban on plea bargaining is derived from Rubenstein, Clarke, and Wright, *Alaska Bans Plea Bargaining,* 219–43.
108. Michael L. Rubenstein and Teresa J. White, "Alaska's Ban on Plea Bargaining," *Law and Society Review* 13 (1979): 374–77.
109. Ibid.
110. Zimring and Frase, *The Criminal Justice System,* 684.
111. Malcolm D. Holmes, Howard C. Daudistel, and William A. Taggart, "Plea Bargaining Policy and State District Court Loads: An Interrupted Time Series Analysis," *Law and Society Review* 26 (1992): 139–53.
112. This section relies on Wayne A. Kerstetter and Anne M. Heinz, *Pretrial Settlement Conference: An Evaluation* (Washington, D.C.: U.S. Department of Justice, 1979).
113. Norval Morris, *The Future of Imprisonment* (Chicago: University of Chicago Press, 1974), 55–56.
114. American Bar Association, *Standards Relating to Pleas of Guilty* (Chicago: American Bar Association, 1968).
115. *North Carolina v. Alford,* 400 U.S. 25 (1970).

CHAPTER 12

Sentencing

CHAPTER OUTLINE

What Is the "Right" Sentence?[1]

Mirna Rivera transported about one pound of cocaine, from New York to Providence, with intent to distribute it, in violation of a federal statute. The U.S. Sentencing Guidelines provide a sentence of 33 to 41 months' imprisonment for a first time offender who has engaged in this conduct. Rivera argued to the district court that it should reduce sentence for the following reasons:

1. She has three small children, ages 3, 5, and 6, who need a mother's care.
2. She lives solely on welfare, receiving no financial aid from her former husband.
3. She has virtually no contact with any other family member (except for a sister, with five children, also on welfare).
4. She has never before engaged in any criminal activity.
5. She committed this single offense because of an unwise wish to obtain money for Christmas presents for her children.

The district court decided not to depart. Rivera claims that this decision reflects the court's incorrect belief that it lacked the legal authority to depart. And, she asks us to order a new proceeding.

INTRODUCTION

Twice a year in eighteenth-century England, the scarlet-robed royal judges of Assize put on their "black caps of death" and rode circuit throughout all the county towns in the kingdom. They displayed their power surrounded by pomp and ceremony, and wielded their authority by means of speeches, rulings, grand jury charges, and other pronouncements. And they did it all in public, accompanied by the local gentry in the midst of large crowds of ordinary people gathered to witness the spectacle.

Nowhere was the royal judicial power more evident than in the public pronouncement of the court's judgment of punishment—the sentence. Judges held the power of life and death over convicted felons, because all felonies from murder to larceny were capital offenses. The royal judges rarely sentenced felons to hang. Most of the time, they took full advantage of the public proceedings to strike terror by pronouncing the death sentence. Then, at the last minute, they tempered justice with mercy by sparing repentant convicts from the hangman's noose in a dramatic stay of execution.

> Methinks I see him [recalled one observer in 1785] with a countenance of solemn sorrow, adjusting the cap of judgment on his head. . . . He addresses in the most pathetic terms, the consciences of the trembling criminals . . . shows them how just and necessary it is, that there should be laws to remove out of society, those, who instead of contributing their honest industry to the public good and welfare of society, have exerted every art that the blackest villainy can suggest, to destroy both. . . . He then vindicates both the mercy, as well as the severity of the law, in making such examples, as shall not only protect the innocent from outrage and violence, but also deter others from bringing themselves to the same ignominious end. He acquaints them with the certainty of speedy death and consequently with the necessity of speedy repentance. And on this theme he may so deliver himself, as not only to melt the wretches at the bar into contrition, but the whole auditory into the deepest concern. Tears express their feelings. . . . [M]any of the most thoughtless among them may . . . be preserved from thinking lightly of the first steps into vice. . . . The dreadful sentence is now pronounced. Every heart shakes with terror.[2]

Modern judges do not have as much power as the eighteenth-century English judges. The U.S. Constitution and state constitutions prohibit "cruel and unusual punishments"; the denial of life, liberty, or property without due process of law; and the denial of the equal protection of the laws. Furthermore, sentencing authority is distributed among legislatures, sentencing guidelines commissions, prosecutors' offices, judges, and corrections departments.

Moreover, sentencing no longer culminates with the fanfare of public ceremonies conducted in the center of town with crowds gathered to watch and hear. Nevertheless, the judgment of punishment still fascinates us. Sentencing also affects public policymakers, particularly during times of heightened concern about crime. Since the 1970s, politicians, criminologists, reformers, and the public have subjected sentencing to scrutiny. The public has demanded that we "get tough" on violence, illegal drugs, and juvenile crime. And, crime rates have risen steeply until the late 1990s. As a result of these influences, almost all legislatures have enacted some kind of sentencing reform laws.

Most of the reforms include:

- Shifts in the philosophy of punishment from rehabilitation to retribution and incapacitation.
- Increases in the severity of punishment.
- Transfers of sentencing authority from courts to legislatures and prosecutors.
- Restrictions on discretionary indeterminate sentencing.
- Expansion of fixed sentencing.

HISTORY OF SENTENCING

The question of whether to fit sentences to the crime or tailor them to individual criminals has vexed officials, academics, and the public for more than a thousand years. In **determinate sentencing** (sometimes called fixed sentencing) legislatures "fix" or "determine" the specific punishment (usually incarceration). Fixed sentences are supposed to fit the punishment to the crime. In **indeterminate sentencing** legislatures set only the outer limits of possible penalties. The actual time served and what kind of "treatment" offenders receive depends on corrections officials. Indeterminate sentences are supposed to tailor the punishment to suit individual offenders. As early as 700 A.D., the Roman Catholic Church's penitential books revealed a tension between prescribing penance strictly according to the sin and tailoring it to suit individual sinners.

Like Roman Catholic penance, judicial discretion also has an ancient heritage. Arguments abound in the history of sentencing not only over what sentences to impose, but also over who should impose them. These early arguments regarding sinners and penance, judges and punishment, strikingly resemble current thought about the proper authority, aims, and types of criminal sentencing.[3]

In U.S. history, the controversy over fixed and indeterminate sentencing began during the 1630s in the Massachusetts Bay. Political rivals of the great Puritan "father," John Winthrop, criticized him for what they called his excessive use of discretion in sentencing criminals. Winthrop tailored many penalties to suit individual offenders. Winthrop maintained that be both fair and just, judges had to take into account individual circumstances such as hardship and contrition. The disparity and leniency in Winthrop's sentences disturbed his critics. Particularly offensive to his critics was Winthrop's leniency toward serious wrongdoers.

Lenient sentences did not trouble Winthrop. He said that the law defined crimes broadly. It was left to judges to apply those broad definitions to specific cases. Each sentence, he said, depends on a combination of the facts of the case, the background and character of the defendant, and the general needs of the community. Hence, he argued, poor people should pay lower fines than rich people, religious leaders should suffer harsher penalties than laypersons for committing morals offenses, and powerful colonists should receive more severe penalties for breaking the law than weak individuals.

According to Winthrop, the appointment of wise judges whose personal prejudices do not influence their sentencing is the remedy for abuse of judicial discretion. Not convinced, the Massachusetts Bay Colony legislature enacted a determinate sentencing statute that prohibited judges from fitting sentences to individual offenders. Winthrop, who was the governor of the colony, had to accept the law, much to his displeasure.[4]

Fixed sentencing based on crime and not criminals was the norm from the seventeenth until the latter part of the nineteenth century. Then, a shift toward indeterminate sentences tailored to fit individual criminals became common. However, neither fixed nor indeterminate sentences have ever totally dominated criminal sentencing. The tension between the needs for certainty and flexibility is inherent in sentencing as it is in all rule enforcement. This is so because both predictability in sentences and a degree of flexibility toward individual needs are necessary. Shifting ideology and other informal influences ensure that neither fixed nor indeterminate sentences will ever wholly dominate.

Following the American Revolution, fixed but moderate penalties became the norm. States abolished the death penalty for many offenses. Rarity of use in practice rendered corporal punishment (whipping), mutilation (cutting off ears and slitting tongues), and shaming (the ducking stool) obsolete. Imprisonment, up to that time used mainly to detain accused persons before trial, had become the dominant form of criminal punishment by 1850. Statutes fixed prison terms for most felonies. In practice, liberal use of pardons, early release for "good time," and other devices permitted judges to use informal discretionary judgment in altering formally fixed sentences.[5]

The modern history of sentencing—with important echoes from the past—grew out of dissatisfaction with legislatively fixed harsh prison sentences. Reformers complained that prisons were no more than warehouses for the poor, immigrants, and other "undesirables" at the lower end of society. Furthermore, prisons did not work. Crime continued at unacceptably high rates no matter how many offenders were locked up, and those who were released soon proved how futile imprisonment was by quickly returning to prison. Many public officials and concerned citizens agreed. Particularly instrumental in demanding reform were prison administrators and other criminal justice officials.

A high point in the debate about the ineffectiveness of fixed prison sentences was the National Prison Congress held in 1870 in Cincinnati. Its "Declaration of Principles" was based on the idea that sentencing should reform criminals, not simply punish them; hence, fixed sentences should be replaced with indeterminate sentences. "Mere lapse of time" to "pay" for past crimes, the transactions of the Congress proclaimed, should not determine sentence length. Rather, "satisfactory proof of reformation" ought to determine how long convicted criminals remain in prison.[6]

According to one conference leader, Zebulon Brockway,

> all persons in a state, who are convicted of crimes or offenses before a competent court, shall be deemed wards of the state and shall be committed to the custody of the board of guardians, until, in their judgment, they may be returned to society with ordinary safety and in accord with their own highest welfare.[7]

Even before the conference, Brockway, who was superintendent of the Detroit House of Correction, played an instrumental role in the enactment of the nation's first indeterminate sentencing law. A prototype statute appeared in Michigan in 1869. The statute authorized judges to sentence prostitutes to three years in houses of correction, but permitted inspectors to terminate such sentences if, in their discretion, a prostitute "reformed."[8]

New York enacted the first truly indeterminate sentencing law in 1878. The statute provided:

> Every sentence to the reformatory of a person convicted of a felony or other crime shall be a general sentence to imprisonment in the New York State reformatory at Elmira and the courts of this state imposing such sentence shall not fix or limit the duration thereof. The term of such imprisonment of any person so convicted and sentenced shall be terminated by the managers of the reformatory, as authorized by this act; but such imprisonment shall not exceed the maximum term provided by law for the crime for which the prisoner was convicted and sentenced.[9]

By 1922, all but four states had adopted some form of indeterminate sentencing law. According to Lucy Flower, the famous Chicago criminal justice reformer, the system should focus on the offender and not the offense. Reforming offenders was based on the confident belief that professionals could help offenders to transform their lives of crime into lives of productive work.

A dedicated core of middle-class reformers accepted the findings (in fact they were more beliefs than scientific findings) of contemporary social and physical scientists, which argued that both basic human "drives" and social "forces" controlled human behavior. According to these "findings," individuals did not choose their actions freely; their heredity, physical characteristics, psyche, and environment thrust their behavior on them.[10]

Reform-minded proponents of indeterminate sentences were by no means "bleeding hearts." Far from it. According to the rehabilitation experts of the time, criminals were either corrigible or incorrigible. The corrigibles—under 30 years old—were resilient enough to respond to reformative measures. The incorrigibles—over 30—were hardened criminals beyond hope of reformation. The corrigibles required stern measures to turn them into good citizens. Strict rules of conduct and highly programmed daily schedules of hard work, study, exercise, and healthy living habits were the order of the day. Harsh punishment, including solitary confinement on a diet of bread and water, paddling, and other forms of corporal punishment, were regularly administered to "reform" prisoners. This transformation from criminal to productive citizen usually required years of imprisonment followed by a long period of parole.

Corrigible prisoners had to prove that they had reformed by the outward display of following prison rules. Long periods of perfect behavior were often required before parole was granted. Parolees had to clinch the proof by keeping a job, living a clean life, and staying out of even minor trouble with the law. Prison officials, parole officers, and reformers believed that prisoners and parolees could easily fake reformation. Although they believed most prisoners were stupid, officials and reformers also had no doubt that prisoners were cunning.

The incorrigibles, on the other hand, could not reform, no matter how strong the efforts. The reformers, however, were not about to let the incorrigibles "get away" without working. They recommended that incorrigibles stay in prison for life, where they would be forced to work to support themselves–because they could or would not voluntarily work for a living outside prison. If they could not be forced into earning their keep, then they should be killed.[11]

According to reformers, judges trained in the narrow, rigid rules of law were not qualified to exercise the discretionary judgment required to decide either who was corrigible and incorrigible or when corrigibles could safely return to society. Only criminologists, physicians, psychiatrists, social workers, corrections officials, and other experts had the training to classify, treat, and proclaim the reformation of criminals.[12]

When the indeterminate sentence became the prevailing practice, administrative sentencing by parole boards and prison officials took precedence over legislative and judicial sentence fixing. At its extreme, judges set no time on sentencing, leaving it wholly to parole boards and corrections officials. More commonly, judges were free to grant probation, suspend sentences in favor of alternatives to incarceration such as community service, or pick confinement times within minimums and maximums prescribed by statutes. Parole boards and corrections officers determined the exact release time.

Indeterminate sentencing remained dominant until the 1970s, when several forces coalesced to oppose it. Prison uprisings, especially at Attica and the Tombs in New York in the late 1960s, dramatically portrayed rehabilitation as little more than rhetoric, and prisoners as deeply and dangerously discontented. Individual rights advocates challenged the widespread and unreviewable informal discretionary powers exercised by criminal justice officials in general and judges in particular. Demands for increased formal accountability spread throughout the criminal justice system. Courts required public officials to justify their decisions in writing and empowered defendants to dispute allegations against them at sentencing. Formalization even reached prisons in requirements that they publish their rules and grant prisoners the right to challenge rules they were accused of breaking (see Chapter 15).

Disillusionment with rehabilitation became widespread among professionals during the late 1960s. One reason was that several statistical and experimental studies showed significant discrimination in sentencing. In particular, some research strongly suggested that poor people and African Americans were sentenced more harshly than whites and more affluent Americans. Also, crime rates were increasing sharply. As a result of the disillusionment and scientific studies, a distinguished panel of the National Research Council was created to review sentencing practices. The panel concluded that by the early 1970s, a "remarkable consensus emerged among left and right, law enforcement officials and prisoners groups, reformers and bureaucrats that the indeterminate sentencing era was at its end."[13]

Critics called indeterminate sentencing ineffective. Despite what they perceived as all-out efforts to treat and rehabilitate criminals, crime continued to increase. Political scientist James Q. Wilson, in his best-selling *Thinking About Crime,* reported that the public widely believed sentences were too lenient—that soft-hearted, weak-willed judges were "letting too many criminals off with a slap on the wrist." Hence, critics argued, swift, certain, and more severe penalties ought to replace existing open-ended sentences.[14]

Others argued that rehabilitation simply did not work, no matter how long prison sentences were. In the early 1970s, sociologist Robert Martinson headed a major study surveying rehabilitation programs in the United States. Martinson's study gained wide readership and characterized both pessimistic attitudes about reforming criminals and renewed confidence in retribution and incapacitation. Distorting Martinson's findings, critics concluded that "nothing works" when it comes to rehabilitation programs. As a result, these critics rejected the whole underlying rehabilitative premise on which indeterminate sentencing rested, leading one author to entitle an article "The Rehabilitation of Punishment" as an apt description of penal policy during the 1970s.[15]

A distinguished panel from the National Research Council of the National Academy of Sciences surveyed rehabilitation research and considerably softened Martinson's conclusions. The panel concluded that

> although there is little in the reported literature that demonstrably works, the conclusion that "nothing works" is not necessarily justified. It would be more accurate to say instead that nothing yet tried has been demonstrated to work. This is true because many plausible ideas have not been tried and because the research done so far, even when theoretically informed, has not been carried out satisfactorily. The research has been flawed by limitations in the evaluation of programs, the questionable degree to which treatments are actually implemented, and the narrow range of approaches actually attempted.[16]

By the late 1970s, rehabilitation had lost ground, and retribution, deterrence, and incapacitation had gained renewed popularity. The growing weakness of rehabilitation was due to a powerful alliance between civil libertarians and conservatives who agreed that the aim of sentencing practices ought to be swift and certain punishment. But there was a rift in their thinking that eventually destroyed the alliance. They differed as to the *length* and the *nature* of sentences. To civil libertarians, determinate sentencing meant short, fixed sentences; with programs to prepare prisoners for playing by the rules and paying their way in life. To conservatives, punishment meant long, fixed uncomfortable sentences; jails and prisons are not "country clubs," they're supposed to be hard and unpleasant. In the end, a debate ensued as to the purpose of confinement that went far beyond the confining bounds of liberalism and conservatism. As we shall see in Chapter 15, the debate was whether offenders are sent to prison *as* punishment or *for* punishment.

Several researchers have concluded that ineffective programs, not rehabilitation itself, have accounted for the failures of rehabilitation. Most programs lacked adequate resources. Most adequately funded programs labeled "treatment" in fact relied on coercion and punishment. The few truly rehabilitative and adequately funded programs have registered promising results. These few successful programs suggest that some types of programs for some kinds of offenders show considerable promise.[17]

Two programs directed at helping ex-prisoners survive financially illustrate this point. Peter Rossi and others conducted an experiment with released felons in Texas and Georgia. The control group was released with no financial help. An experimental group was given up to six months of financial assistance, roughly equivalent to unemployment insurance. Called the Transitional Aid Research Project (TARP), the experiment showed that the prisoners who received financial assistance were arrested less frequently than those in the control group. In another study, Ann Dryden Witte found that North Carolina prisoners who were part of a work-release group in prison committed less serious offenses after they were freed than those who were not part of the work-release group.[18]

Despite criticism, rehabilitation still enjoys support. Surveys indicate that although the public and some criminal justice professionals demand harsher punishment, most also want to rehabilitate offenders.[19] By the 1980s, three ideas had come to dominate thinking about sentencing:

- Serious crimes deserve severe punishment.
- Repeat career offenders need severe punishment to incapacitate them.

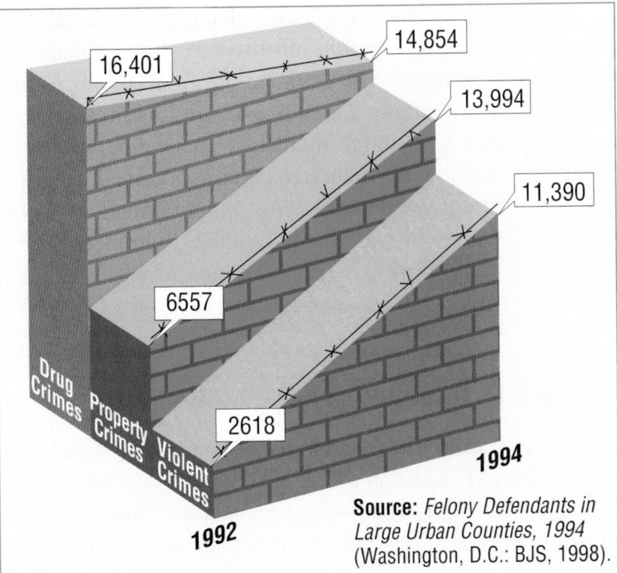

Figure 12.1
Federal Sentencing Trends, 1992 and 1994 Number of Offenders

- All crimes deserve some punishment because it demonstrates the deterrent potency of the criminal law.

According to the National Council on Crime and Delinquency,

> by 1990, the shift in goals of sentencing reform was complete. Virtually all new sentencing law was designed to increase the certainty and length of prison sentences to incapacitate the active criminal and deter the rest.[20]

Harsher penalties since the 1980s have accompanied the shift in the philosophy of punishment just outlined. Public support for the death penalty grew after the U.S. Supreme Court ruled that it was not cruel and unusual punishment. Courts began to sentence more people to death. States once again actually executed criminals sentenced to death. In non–death penalty cases, judges sentenced more people to prison than to probation; and, they sentenced them to longer prison terms. By 1996 the United States was sentencing more people to prison for longer terms than almost any other country in the world. Figure 12.1 depicts the results of this shift in attitude and sentencing practice in state courts.

Knowledge and Understanding CHECK

1. List five changes in sentencing that have taken place from 1970 to 2000.
2. Identify the question that has vexed sentencing throughout its history.
3. List the arguments in favor of and against both fixed and indeterminate sentencing made by John Winthrop and his opponents in the Massachusetts Bay Colony.
4. What caused the dissatisfaction with fixed sentencing during the nineteenth century?
5. Describe the significance of the National Prison Congress held in 1870.
6. Why did middle-class reformers support the indeterminate sentence in the late nineteenth and early twentieth centuries?
7. Were the middle-class reformers "bleeding hearts"? Explain your answer.
8. Identify the forces of the 1970s that caused a swing from indeterminate to fixed sentences.
9. Identify the major arguments for and the research findings regarding the effectiveness of rehabilitation.
10. List the three ideas that came to dominate thinking about sentencing during the 1970s.

REVIVAL OF FIXED SENTENCING

The shift from rehabilitation to retribution, incapacitation, and deterrence led to a revival of the idea of fixed sentencing. Three variations of fixed sentencing are in operation as a result of sentencing reform during the 1970s:

1. Fixed (or determinate) sentencing laws.
2. Mandatory minimum sentencing.
3. Sentencing guidelines.

Determinate Sentencing Laws

Determinate sentencing laws limit judicial discretion by prescribing a narrow range of penalties from which judges can choose in sentencing offenders. In determinate sentencing, defendants learn their release date at the time they are sentenced. California, a pioneer in *in*determinate sentencing and rehabilitation, broke new ground in its 1976 determinate sentencing law. In an abrupt about-face, the state enacted the Uniform Determinate Sentencing Law, which proclaimed that "the purpose of imprisonment is punishment," not treatment or rehabilitation. The California law reflected widespread national dissatisfaction with the indeterminate sentencing system to rehabilitate offenders. In a pattern that was followed nationally, conservatives who believed that indeterminate sentencing was too lenient forged a formidable political alliance with liberals who believed that indeterminate sentences were too severe and that they discriminated racially. The alliance successfully removed what both believed was a proven failure.[21]

The California law created four categories of offenders, each with a small range of penalties:

1. *Category 1:* sixteen months, two years, and three years.
2. *Category 2:* two, three, and four years.
3. *Category 3:* three, four, and five years.
4. *Category 4:* five, six, and seven years.

According to the law, "When a judgment of imprisonment is ordered, the court shall order the middle of the three possible prison terms, unless there are circumstances in mitigation or aggravation of the crime."[22]

Under the old indeterminate sentencing system, judges could impose high maximum penalties, but the parole board determined the actual time served, which was supposed to depend on the rehabilitation of individual offenders. Formally, the new law drastically reduced the authority of judges to impose sentences, and it removed the enormous power of the parole board to determine actual time served. However, in practice, the new system imposes sentences similar to those under the old laws. *Presumptive sentences,* or the discretion of judges to sentence within the narrow range, explain the limited effect of the statute. Based on the average time served under the old system, presumptive sentences allow judges and others tied to the courtroom work group to continue practices in effect prior to the change and to reach similar results.[23]

The law also has had some undesired results; it decreased sentence uniformity. Under the old system, the parole board, called the Adult Authority, a centralized state agency, tended to decide like cases similarly, no matter what the law permitted. The new system places most of the sentencing power in the hands of the prosecutor. Because the new law restricts the authority of judges to sentence and that of the Adult Authority to release, the charging discretion of the prosecutor and plea bargaining act as mechanisms that provide flexibility. Furthermore, although commitments to prison have increased (in place of probation), the length of time actually spent in prison has decreased.

Substantial regional variations also have resulted: "There was at least as much variation in the use of imprisonment, between counties, as there had been before the law came into effect—which is to say, quite a lot." These variations reflect an important dimension to all attempts to reform criminal justice by legislation—the "propensities of local officials" to serve their own interests and to reflect the "going rates" for criminal punishment as the "local legal culture" determines them.[24]

On the positive side, California's determinate sentencing law may have enhanced racial equity in sentencing. Stephen P. Klein, Susan Turner, and Joan Petersilia reviewed California sentencing based on official records of 11,553 persons convicted of assault, robbery, burglary, theft, forgery, and drug offenses. Using a combination of defendant and crime characteristics and criminal justice processing variables, they found no relation between race and sentence types, particularly prison or probation, or sentence length.[25]

California's experience with determinate sentencing contains an important lesson. Informal pressures, habits, and relationships among local work groups, along with formal objectives in criminal sentencing and punishment, create obstacles to changing long-established sentencing practices. Sentencing requires both enough certainty derived from formal controls to generate confidence in its fairness and sufficient flexibility to provide for individual differences. These differences arise from the facts and circumstances of each case; informal discretion furnishes that flexibility.

Mandatory Minimum Sentencing Laws

Mandatory minimum sentence laws are truly fixed sentences. They require that offenders convicted under the laws serve at least some time—the "mandatory minimum"—in prison. They deny to judges discretionary power; judges can neither suspend the mandated minimum sentence nor substitute probation for it. Prison and parole authorities cannot release offenders before the statutory minimum period has passed.

Mandatory penalties have a long history. The Old Testament sentences of "an eye for an eye" and "a tooth for a tooth" are mandatory penalties. The Anglo-Saxon king Alfred prescribed a detailed mandatory penalty code, including such provisions as "If one knocks out another's eye, he shall pay 66 shillings, 6⅓ pence. If the eye is still in the head, but the injured man can see nothing with it, one-third of the payment shall be withheld." As early as 1790, mandatory penalties were established for capital crimes. Throughout the nineteenth century, Congress enacted mandatory penalties—usually short prison sentences—for a long list of crimes, including refusal to testify before Congress, failure to report seaboard saloon purchases, or causing a ship to run aground by use of a false light.[26]

Until the 1950s, the use of mandatory minimum penalties was only an occasional occurrence in the twentieth century. Fear of crime and drugs in the 1950s, brought on in part, it was believed, by a Communist plot to get Americans "hooked" on especially potent "pure Communist heroin" from China, led Congress to enact the Narcotic Control Act of 1956. The Boggs Act signaled a shift to a heavier reliance on mandatory minimum sentences. The Senate Judiciary Committee explained why Congress needed a mandatory minimum sentence drug law:

> [T]here is a need for the continuation of the policy of punishment of a severe character as a deterrent to narcotic law violations. [The Committee] therefore recommends an increase in maximum sentences for first as well as subsequent offenses. With respect to the mandatory minimum features of such penalties, and prohibition of suspended sentences or probation, the committee recognizes objections in principle. It feels, however, that, in order to define the gravity of this class of crime and the assured penalty to follow, these features of the law must be regarded as essential ele-

ments of the desired deterrents, although some differences of opinion still exist regarding their application to first offenses of certain types.[27]

The statute imposed stiff mandatory minimum sentences for narcotics offenses, requiring judges to pick within a range of penalties. Judges could not suspend sentences or put convicted offenders on probation. Offenders were not eligible for parole if they were convicted under the act. For example, the act punished the first conviction for selling heroin by a term of from 5 to 10 years of imprisonment. Judges had to sentence offenders to at least 5 years in prison; they could not suspend the sentence or put the offender on probation; offenders were not eligible for parole for at least the minimum period of the sentence. For second offenders, the mandatory minimum was raised to 10 years. The penalty for the sale of narcotics to persons under 18 years of age ranged from a mandatory minimum of 10 years to a maximum of life imprisonment or death.[28]

In 1970, Congress retreated from the mandatory minimum sentence approach. In the Comprehensive Drug Abuse Prevention and Control Act of 1970, Congress repealed virtually all the mandatory minimum provisions adopted in the 1956 act, saying that the increased sentence lengths "had not shown the expected overall reduction in drug law violations." Among the reasons for the repeal were that mandatory minimum penalties for drug law offenses:

- Alienated youth from the general society.
- Hampered rehabilitation of drug offenders.
- Infringed on judicial authority by drastically reducing judicial discretion in sentencing.
- Reduced the deterrent effect of drug laws because even prosecutors thought the laws were too severe.

> According to the House Committee considering the bill:
>
> The severity of existing penalties, involving in many instances minimum sentences, have led in many instances to reluctance on the part of prosecutors to prosecute some violations, where the penalties seem to be out of line with the seriousness of the offenses. In addition, severe penalties, which do not take into account individual circumstances, and which treat casual violators as severely as they treat hardened criminals, tend to make conviction more difficult to obtain.[29]

However, the retreat from mandatory minimum sentences was short-lived, as public concern about violence and drugs rose to the top of the national agenda. The public and legislatures blamed rising crime rates, in part at least, on the uncertainty and "leniency" of indeterminate sentences. So, beginning in the early to mid-1970s, the states and federal government enacted more and longer mandatory minimum prison sentences. By 1991, 46 states and the federal government had enacted mandatory minimum sentencing laws. Although the list of such laws is long (the U.S. Criminal Code contains at least 100), the main targets of mandatory minimum sentences are drug offenses, violent crimes, and crimes committed with a weapon.[30]

Mandatory minimum sentences are supposed to satisfy basic aims of criminal punishment: retribution, incapacitation, and deterrence. They promise that serious crimes will receive severe punishment. Violent criminals, criminals who use weapons, and drug offenders cannot harm the public if they are in prison. Furthermore, the knowledge that committing mandatory minimum crimes will bring certain, severe punishment should deter other potential offenders.

Evaluations suggest that mandatory minimum penalties in practice do not always achieve the goals their proponents hoped they would. The National Institute of Justice assessed two mandatory minimum sentence laws, one in New York and one in Massachusetts. In 1973, the New York legislature enacted "the nation's toughest drug law." For example, the possession of two ounces of heroin or the sale of a single ounce carried a minimum 15 to 25 years in prison. A second conviction for the unlawful possession of any "stimulant, hallucinogen, hallucinogenic substance, or LSD," with intent to sell carried a minimum term of 1 to 813 years. Conviction for the possession of one ounce of marijuana carried a 1- to 5-year minimum prison sentence.

The results of the New York drug law were disappointing. Drug offense conviction rates dropped 30 percent. Heroin use following enactment was as widespread as before. Serious property crime—the kind generally believed to be linked to drug use—increased sharply, despite the tough legislation. The law probably did not deter convicted felons from committing further crimes. A rigorous Department of Justice evaluation concluded that "the threat embodied in the words of the law proved to have teeth for relatively few offenders" because "mandatory sentencing laws directly affect only an end product of a long criminal justice process—the convicted offender." The statute also had some serious side effects. It slowed down the criminal process and worked a real hardship in some cases. One 38-year-old woman with no prior criminal record, for instance, was sentenced to life imprisonment for possessing one ounce of heroin.[31]

In 1974, Massachusetts enacted the Gun Control Act. The law imposed a mandatory minimum one-year sentence on anyone who failed to comply with the state's long-time requirement that handgun owners license their weapons. The law allowed no chance of reducing the minimum by probation, parole, or judicial manipulation. The National Institute of Justice evaluation showed more positive results from the Massachusetts gun control law than from the New York drug law. Despite widespread predictions that the law would not work, officials did not evade the law and more persons were imprisoned for violating it. Finally, fewer people carried firearms as a result of the stiff new penalties.[32]

Why these mixed results in Massachusetts and New York? First, the number of gun control cases was very small—the Massachusetts law increased the overall caseload by only about 70 cases a year, whereas the New York drug act covered thousands of cases. Second, the Massachusetts law enjoyed much more support than did the New York law.

Mandatory minimum sentences, it seems from these results, depend for their effectiveness on the conditions in which they are implemented.

Research on Michigan's Felony Firearm Statute further complicates matters. Michigan's gun law mandated an additional two-year minimum sentence for carrying a gun during the commission of a felony. A popular law because it distinguished between lawful and unlawful use of guns (which the Massachusetts law did not), the Michigan statute enjoyed wide support. The statute does not prohibit plea bargaining; nevertheless, the Wayne County prosecutor initiated a policy forbidding negotiations regarding the law. In a combined qualitative and quantitative analysis relying on interviews with judges, prosecutors, and defense attorneys, and on case dispositions in Detroit (Wayne County), Milton Heumann and Colin Loftin found that the law had little impact on the severity of sentences.[33]

In 1990, Congress ordered the U.S. Sentencing Commission to evaluate the rapidly increasing number of mandatory minimum sentencing cases in the federal system. The results of the Sentencing Commission's study provided little empirical support for the success of mandatory minimum sentencing laws. To determine the reasons for the support of mandatory minimum sentences, researchers first reviewed legislative history, statements made by the executive branch, and views expressed in academic literature. The commission also conducted and analyzed field interviews with judges, assistant U.S. attorneys, defense lawyers, and probation officers. They found, among others, the following reasons for supporting mandatory minimum sentences:

- *Equality:* Mandatory minimum penalties ensure that the same offenses receive the same sentences.
- *Certainty:* Mandatory minimum penalties ensure truth in sentencing because both the public and offenders know that offenders will really serve the minimum time in prison the sentence imposes.
- *Just deserts:* Violent and drug offenders, habitual criminals, and criminals who use guns to commit crimes deserve mandatory long prison terms.
- *Deterrence:* Mandatory prison sentences deter crime by sending the strong message that those who commit mandatory minimum offenses will go to prison.
- *Incapacitation:* Mandatory prison terms protect public safety by locking up drug dealers and violent armed criminals.[34]

The commission evaluated federal mandatory minimum sentencing statutes. They used data from three major sources: presentence reports prepared by probation officers; data derived from sentencing hearings, plea agreements, and sentencing guideline worksheets; and an in-depth analysis of a random sample of 12.5 percent of drug and firearms cases. These were cases that extracted information about the amount of drugs by type and the facts regarding "using and carrying" firearms that triggered the mandatory minimum sentences.

The findings included:

- Only a few of the mandatory minimum sentencing provisions are ever used. Nearly all those used relate to drug and weapons offenses.
- Only 41 percent of defendants whose characteristics and behavior qualify them for mandatory minimum sentences actually receive them.
- Mandatory minimum sentences actually introduce disparity in sentencing. For example, the commission found that race influences disparity in a number of ways. Whites are less likely than African Americans and Hispanics to be indicted, or convicted at the mandatory minimum. Whites are also more likely than African Americans and Hispanics to receive reductions for "substantial assistance" in aiding in the prosecution of other offenders.

The mandatory minimum sentence laws allow an exception for offenders who provide "substantial assistance" in investigating other offenders, but only on the motion of prosecutors. Substantial assistance also leads to disparities quite apart from race. It tends to favor the very people the law was intended to reach—those higher up in the chain of drug dealing—because underlings can offer less assistance to the government. In one case, for example, Stanley Marshall, who sold less than one gram of LSD, got a 20-year mandatory prison sentence. Jose Cabrera, on the other hand, who the government estimated made more than $40,000,000 from importing cocaine and who would have qualified for life plus 200 years, received a prison term of 8 years for providing "substantial assistance" in the case of Manuel Noriega. According to Judge Terry J. Hatter, Jr., "The people at the very bottom who can't provide substantial assistance end up getting [punished] more severely than those at the top."[35]

Mandatory minimum sentences do not eliminate discretion; they merely shift it from judges to prosecutors. Prosecutors can use their discretion in a number of ways, including manipulation of the "substantial assistance" exception and the decision not to charge defendants with crimes carrying mandatory minimum sentences, or to charge them with mandatory minimum crimes of lesser degree. New York prosecutors gave three reasons why they avoided mandatory minimum sentence laws: First, because of limited resources, charging every drug courier with a mandatory minimum crime would overwhelm the courts. Second, most couriers have limited culpability; therefore, they do not deserve mandatory prison sentences. Third, judges do not like sentencing low-level couriers to prison.[36]

The commission recommended further study before drawing any final conclusions about the effectiveness of mandatory penalties. But their findings, along with other research, suggest that mandatory minimum penalties are not the easy answer to the crime problem that politicians promise and the public hopes.[37]

Use *Your* Discretion

Was the mandatory minimum sentence appropriate?
***United States v. Brigham*, 977 F.2d 317 (7th Cir. 1992)**
Easterbrook, Circuit Judge

Facts

Steep penalties await those who deal in drugs. Buying or selling 10 kilograms of cocaine—even agreeing to do so, without carrying through—means a minimum penalty of 10 years' imprisonment, without the possibility of parole (21 U.S.C. §841(b)(1)(A), 846). The "mandatory" minimum is mandatory only from the perspective of judges. To the parties, the sentence is negotiable. Did a marginal participant in a conspiracy really understand that a 10-kilo deal lay in store? A prosecutor may charge a lesser crime, if he offers something in return. Let's make a deal. Does the participant have valuable information; can he offer other assistance? Congress authorized prosecutors to pay for aid with sentences below the "floor." Let's make a deal.

Bold dealers may turn on their former comrades, setting up phony sales and testifying at the ensuing trials. Timorous dealers may provide information about their sources and customers. Drones of the organization—the runners, mules, drivers, and lookouts—have nothing comparable to offer. They lack the contacts and trust necessary to set up big deals, and they know little information of value. Whatever tales they have to tell, their bosses will have related. Defendants unlucky enough to be innocent have no information at all and are more likely to want vindication at trial, losing not only the opportunity to make a deal but also the two-level reduction the sentencing guidelines provide for accepting responsibility.

Mandatory minimum penalties, combined with a power to grant exceptions, create a prospect of inverted sentencing. The more serious the defendant's crimes, the lower the sentence—because the greater his wrongs, the more information and assistance he has to offer to a prosecutor. Discounts for the top dogs have the virtue of necessity, because rewards for assistance are essential to the business of detecting and punishing crime. But what makes the post-discount sentencing structure topsy-turvy is the mandatory minimum, binding only for the hangers on. What is to be said for such terms, which can visit draconian penalties on the small fry without increasing prosecutors' ability to wring information from their bosses?

Our case illustrates a sentencing inversion. Such an outcome is neither illegal nor unconstitutional, because offenders have no right to be sentenced in proportion to their wrongs (*Chapman v. United States*, ___ U.S. ___, 111 S.Ct. 1919, 1928–29, 114 L.Ed.2d 524 (1991)). Still, meting out the harshest penalties to those least culpable is troubling, because it accords with no one's theory of appropriate punishments.

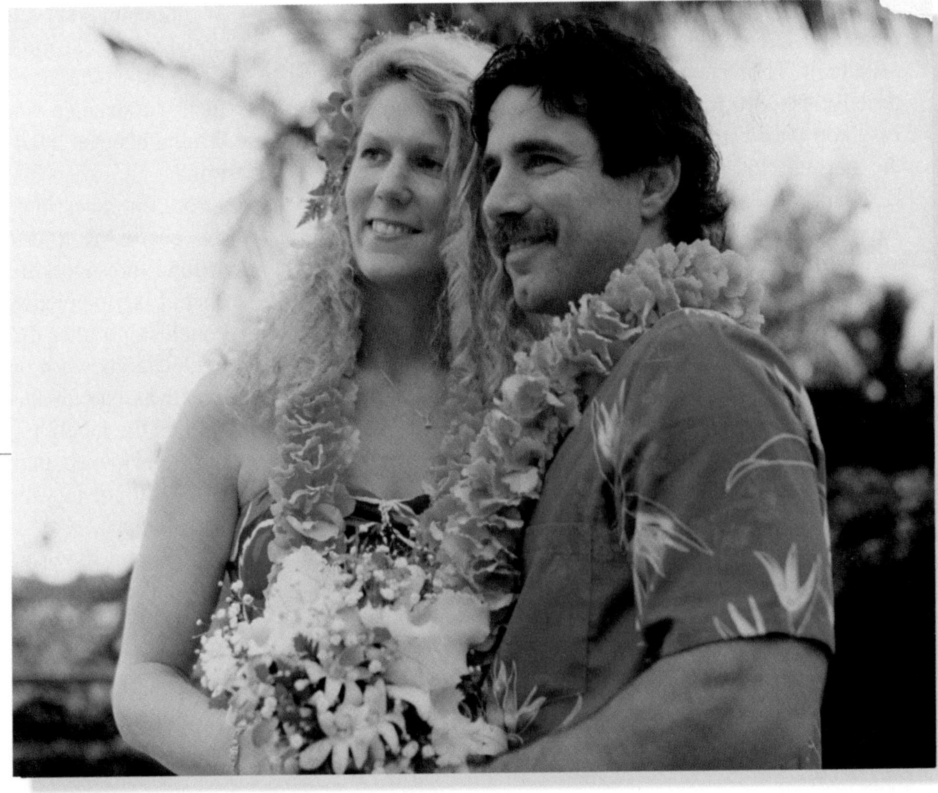

Steven Treleaven and some friends grew small marijuana plants for his brother, who used it to relieve the effects of AIDS. Treleaven and his friends received 10-year sentences–even though guidelines determined a much shorter sentence–because of the federal mandatory sentencing law. Treleaven was a contractor, has a wife and child, coached sports teams, and was well-liked in the community. His brother died of AIDS while he was in prison.

Agents of the Drug Enforcement Agency learned from an informant that Craig Thompson was in the market to buy 10 kilograms of cocaine. The DEA's undercover agents feigned willingness to supply him. During negotiations, Thompson said that he had just sold 17 kilograms and needed 10 more that very day to tide his organization over until the arrival of a shipment that he was expecting. Thompson and the agents did not trust one another. Jeffrey Carter, one of Thompson's goons, searched an agent; the agent's gun, normal in the business, did not trouble Carter, but a transmitter or recorder would mean big trouble. Carter was not very good at his job; he didn't find the concealed recorder. Thompson ultimately agreed to pay $30,000 per kilogram, a premium price for quick service. After the agents let on that they didn't trust Thompson any more than Thompson trusted them, Thompson agreed to let the agents hold his Rolls Royce as collateral until payment. In the agents' presence, Thompson called Tyrone Amos and told him to pick up "ten of those things today" at a suburban motel. Thompson and Carter would hand over the Rolls in a different suburb.

At the appointed time, less than five hours after the agents first met Thompson, one team descended on a restaurant to receive the Rolls Royce and another decamped to the motel to "deliver" the cocaine. Amos arrived at the motel in a car driven by Anthony Brigham. Amos and the agents at the motel had a conversation; Brigham stayed in the car. Carter had not appeared at the restaurant with the Rolls Royce, so everyone settled down to wait. Brigham looked around the parking lot but scrunched down in his seat when the agents' Corvette drove slowly by. At the restaurant, Thompson and the agents discussed future deals of 50–100 kilograms per month. At the motel, Brigham paced nervously in the lobby. After touring the parking lot again, lingering over the Corvette, Brigham joined Amos at a nearby gas station, where Amos placed a phone call. The two had a conversation and returned to the motel, where Amos told the agents that Carter and the Rolls were still missing. While Amos and one agent were dining together some distance from the motel, Thompson paged Amos with news that the Rolls had arrived. Back at the motel, the agents went through the motions of delivering cocaine. As Amos headed for the agents' car to retrieve the drugs from the trunk, Brigham moved his car to a location from which he could keep the delivery in sight. But there was no cocaine. Before Amos could open the trunk other agents moved in, arresting Amos and Brigham, just as they pinched Thompson and Carter at the restaurant.

All but Brigham pleaded guilty and provided valuable assistance to prosecutors. All but Brigham were sentenced to less than the "mandatory" minimums. Thompson received 84 months' imprisonment and Amos 75 months, after the prosecutor made motions under §3553(e). Carter, who was allowed to plead to a charge that did not carry a minimum term, received 4 years' probation, 4 months of which were to be in a work-release program run by the Salvation Army. That left Brigham, who went to trial, was convicted, and received the "mandatory" term of 120 months' imprisonment.

Opinion

Judge Easterbrook

Was the evidence sufficient? Appellate judges do not serve as additional jurors. After a jury convicts, the question becomes whether any sensible person could find, beyond a reasonable doubt, that the defendant committed the crime. That is a steep burden, for 12 persons, presumably sensible and having a more direct appreciation of the evidence than the written record affords to appellate judges, have unanimously found exactly that.

Brigham emphasizes that "mere" presence at a crime does not implicate the bystander in that offense. Conspiracy is agreement, and what proof of agreement did the prosecutor present? Brigham arrived with Amos, conferred with Amos, and was in position to watch an exchange occur. No one testified that Brigham had any role in the exchange or Thompson's organization. Although the prosecutor portrayed Brigham as a lookout, he asks: What kind of lookout would be unarmed, without radio, pager, cellular phone, or any other way to give or receive alerts? What countersurveillance operative would hunker down in the car rather than keep a hawk-eyed watch? Thompson, Carter, and Amos, who reaped rewards for their assistance, were conspicuously absent at Brigham's trial. Had they no evidence to offer against him?

No one questions the rule that "mere presence" at the scene of a crime does not prove conspiracy. "Mere" presence differs from, say, "revealing" presence. Like many a weasel word, "mere" summarizes a conclusion rather than assisting in analysis. When the evidence does not permit an inference that the defendant was part of the criminal organization, the court applies the label "mere presence." So we must examine the evidence, taking inferences in the light most favorable to the jury's verdict, rather than resting content with slogans.

Brigham shows up on short notice with Amos, who the jury could conclude was there to receive 10 kilograms of cocaine from strangers whom Thompson and Amos do not trust. Is Amos likely to come alone? Is a companion apt to be ignorant of the nature and risks of the transaction? For almost three hours Brigham remains at the motel, generally observant and generally nervous; he follows Amos to a pay phone where a telephone call and conversation ensue. Amos reveals the contents of this conversation to the agents; the jury could conclude that he revealed it to Brigham too. While Amos and an agent go to dinner, Brigham keeps watch. After Amos returns, eye contact and a nod from Amos lead Brigham to take up position where he can watch the trunk of the agents' car. Just what was Brigham doing for three hours in the lobby and parking lot of the motel, if not assisting Amos? He was not exactly passing through while a drug deal went down around him. Brigham did not testify, and his lawyer offered no hypothesis at trial. At oral argument of this appeal the best his counsel could do was to suggest that Brigham might have believed that Amos was picking up counterfeit money rather than drugs. Tell us another! The jury was entitled to conclude that Brigham knew about, and joined, a conspiracy to distribute cocaine.

Thin the evidence was, but it was also sufficient. Evidence at sentencing shows that the jury drew the right inference. Amos related that he brought Brigham as a lookout. Brigham told the prosecutor that he was part of the organization and had been involved in some big-stakes transactions. But he was unable to provide enough information to induce the prosecutor to make the motion under §3553(e) that unlocks the trap door in the sentencing "floor." Pleading guilty would have produced the 10-year minimum term, so Brigham went to trial; he had nothing to lose and some chance of being acquitted. The evidence at sentencing showed that Brigham knew that Thompson's organization dealt in multi-kilogram quantities, which supports the judge's conclusion that Brigham qualifies for the 10-year minimum. All that remains is Brigham's argument that the judge should have invoked U.S.S.G. sec 5K2.0 to give him a break. Section 5K2.0 describes appropriate departures from the guidelines, but Brigham needed a departure from a minimum sentence prescribed by statute. That was available only on motion of the prosecutor under sec 3553(e). Brigham does not contend that in declining to make the motion the prosecutor violated the Constitution. . . . Wise exercise of prosecutorial discretion can prevent egregious sentencing inversions. How that discretion is to be exercised is a subject for the political branches. Brigham joined the conspiracy and received a sentence authorized by Congress. His judicial remedies are at a close.

AFFIRMED.

Dissent

Judge Bauer

I respectfully dissent. Taking all the evidence as described in the majority opinion as absolutely true, and viewing it in the light most favorable to the government, I still do not find that any sensible juror could find Brigham guilty of the crime of conspiracy beyond a reasonable doubt. At oral argument, counsel for Brigham could only suggest, in answer to a question from the bench as to what explanation he could give for Brigham's actions on the day in question, "that Brigham might have believed that Amos was picking up counterfeit money rather than drugs." An unbelievable scenario. The fact is, no one testified as to what exactly Brigham was doing or why he was doing it; no one, in spite of the marvelous totally cooperating witnesses who, if the government's theory is correct, could have nailed Brigham's hide to the jailhouse wall. But they didn't. And it is not Brigham's missing explanation that is fatal; it is the government's inability to explain that creates the problem.

Tell us another, indeed, but only if it is the government tale; the accused has absolutely no burden to explain anything. The government accuses, the defendant says "prove it," and the government says the suspicious activity is enough to convince and convict. And so it proved.

I would have directed a verdict of "not guilty" had I been the trial judge and I construe my role in review to be the same. I do not believe the evidence sufficient to convince a sensible juror of proof beyond a reasonable doubt. The existence of cooperating witnesses who knew all and told nothing virtually implies the missing witness analysis: you had the control, you didn't produce, I infer the testimony would have been adverse to you.

I would reverse.

CRITICAL THINKING

1. What exactly are Judge Easterbrook's objections to the mandatory minimum sentence he was obliged to impose in this case?
2. Do you agree? Defend your answer.

Despite the shortcomings of mandatory minimum sentences discussed in the last section, mandatory minimum sentences remain popular with the public and some professionals. The **"three strikes and you're out"** mandatory sentence laws are especially popular. The basic thrust of these "three strikes" laws is to lock up for life dangerous offenders who habitually prey on innocent people.

The catchy phrase may be new, but the idea of the three-strikes laws is nearly 500 years old. In sixteenth-century England and in the American colonies, statutes imposed harsh penalties on criminals who committed identical crimes a particular number of times. By the late eighteenth century, these habitual felon laws were expanded to target repeat offenders of multiple but not identical crimes. New York, in

Figure 12.2
Percent Distribution of Three-Strikes Cases by Race in Los Angeles, 1994

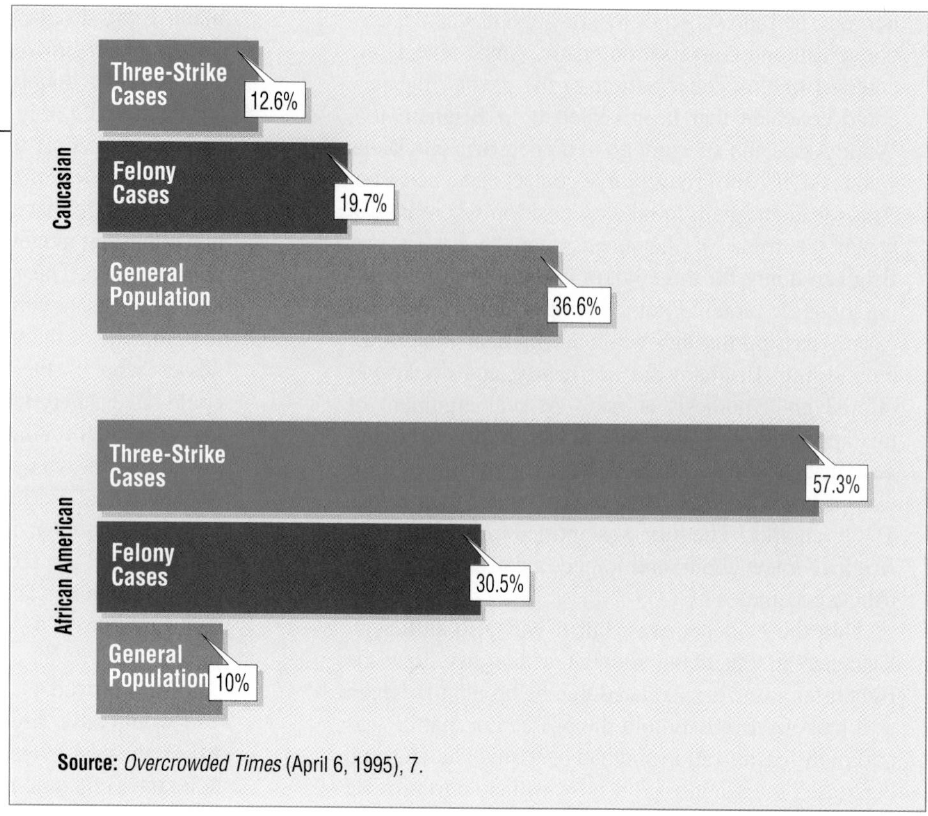

Source: *Overcrowded Times* (April 6, 1995), 7.

1797, enacted the first of these broader habitual offender laws. The New York law ordered a sentence of mandatory life imprisonment "at hard labor or in solitude, or both" for all offenders convicted of their second felony—no matter what that second felony was. Despite the move toward the indeterminate sentence in the period from 1870 to 1970, habitual felon statutes flourished. By 1968, every state had some form of habitual felon statute.[38]

The three-strikes laws are little more than habitual felon laws with a new name. By 1995, 37 states had proposed some form of three-strikes legislation. Liberals and conservatives, Democrats and Republicans, the public and politicians all favor them. Michael G. Turner, Jody L. Sundt, Brandon Applegate, and Francis T. Cullen surveyed the enactment of three-strikes legislation. They found that conservatives were only slightly more enthusiastic about three-strikes laws than were liberals, and that Republicans sponsored such laws only slightly more frequently than did Democrats in state legislatures. They speculate that the reason for the widespread popularity and consequent legislation is due to:

- General public dissatisfaction with the criminal justice system.
- The "panacea phenomenon"—the promise of a simple solution to a complex problem.
- The appeal of the catchy phrase—putting old habitual offender statute ideas into the language of modern baseball: "Three strikes and you're out."[39]

The effectiveness of three-strikes legislation in reducing crime is not clear. Joan Petersilia, in a study of California's "get tough on crime" strategy, concluded that "the much higher imprisonment rates in California had no appreciable effect on violent crime, and only slight effects on property crime." Conversely, according to a RAND Corporation study, three-strikes legislation in California might reduce "serious crime" by as much as 25 percent. However, the cost would be high: $5.5 billion, or $300 per taxpayer annually.

According to a report issued by California's Center on Juvenile and Criminal Justice, during the first six months after the enactment of California's three-strikes law, the statute disproportionately affected African Americans. The report was based on an analysis by the Los Angeles Public Defender's Office, which looked at overall felony filings and three-strikes felony filings against whites and African Americans. Using data from the California Department of Finance, the general population of African Americans and whites was compared with felony and three-strikes filings. Figures 12.2 and 12.3 depict this disparity.[40]

Sentencing Guidelines

Sentencing guidelines are designed to balance the need for both certainty and flexibility in sentencing. Seventeen states and the federal government have adopted some form of sentencing guidelines that establish ranges within which judges

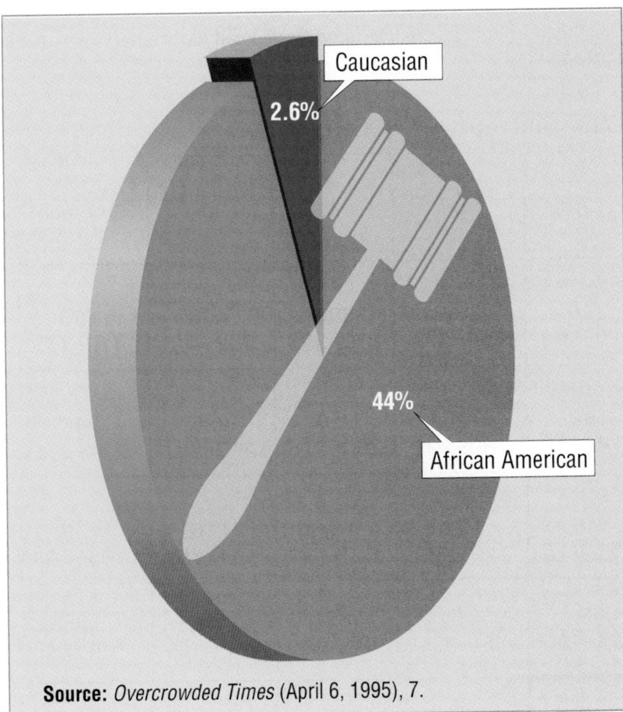

Source: *Overcrowded Times* (April 6, 1995), 7.

Figure 12.3
Rate of Three-Strikes Cases per 100,000 People by Race in Los Angeles County, 1994

can sentence offenders. Most guidelines have at least four major purposes:

- *Uniformity:* improving the chances that similar offenders who have committed similar offenses will receive similar penalties.
- *Neutrality:* reducing the chances that race, gender, ethnicity, age, and class affect sentencing by restricting the type and length of sentence to the seriousness of the offense and the criminal history of the offender.
- *Truth:* ensuring that the type and length of sentences that offenders actually serve nearly equal the sentences judges impose; that is, "You do the crime, you do the time."
- *Control:* preventing rapidly growing prison populations from overtaking prison space and state resources.

In **presumptive sentencing guidelines,** either legislatures or special commissions set the types and ranges of sentences. Judges have to contain their sentences within the prescribed ranges, unless they can justify in writing their departures from the guidelines according to criteria usually prescribed in a guidelines manual. **Voluntary sentencing guidelines** merely suggest possible sentences. Judges can, and often do, follow the suggested sentences, but they are not legally bound to do so. The specific types and exact ranges of sentences are either descriptive or prescriptive. In **descriptive sentencing guidelines,** the guidelines are based on existing sentencing practices within the state; the guidelines merely put in writing what judges have actually been doing. **Prescriptive sentencing guidelines** develop new sentencing norms, based on what decision makers decide the type and range of penalties should be.

Minnesota, a pioneer guidelines state, adopted its guidelines to reduce judicial discretion and sentencing disparity without increasing prison populations. The Minnesota guidelines incorporate a "modified deserts sentencing model"; they base sentences on a combination of the severity of the convicted offense and the criminal history of the offender. The guidelines regulate both disposition—that is, the decision to impose a sentence of incarceration or probation—and the length of jail and prison terms. Figure 12.4 reproduces the Minnesota grid, or matrix as it is sometimes called, for determining sentences under the modified deserts model.

The rows on the grid contain offenses and the columns represent a score for criminal history. The bold line, called the *disposition line,* represents the boundary separating presumptive stayed sentences—that is, those cases in which judges suspend prison sentences for the number of months specified in the grid. The numbers above the bold line are the presumptive executed sentences—that is, those cases in which judges sentence offenders to prison. The numbers in the cells present the range of months as guides to the sentence a judge may choose. For example, a first-time aggravated robbery conviction carries a recommended sentence of 48 months, but the judge can choose either 44 or 52 months without formally departing from the guidelines. Permitting judges to choose within a range without departing from the guidelines builds flexibility into the system, allowing for differences in individual cases. Characteristics, such as the amount of money stolen, the extent of personal injury inflicted, and the criminal history of the offender can affect the sentence judges impose without undermining the basic goals of uniformity and equity.

According to the Minnesota Sentencing Guidelines Commission, judges can depart from the presumptive range when the "individual case involves substantial and compelling circumstances." The following are reasons for departing downward:

- The victim was the aggressor in the crime.
- The offender played a minor role in the crime.
- The offender lacked the capacity of judgment due to physical or mental impairment.

Reasons for departing upward include:

- The victim was vulnerable.
- Cruelty to the victim was involved.
- The crime involved a major drug offense.
- The offender committed the crime for hire.

If judges depart from the presumptive range, they must give written reasons for their departures. If judges depart upward, defendants can appeal the departure. If judges depart downward, the prosecution can appeal the departure.[41]

Terance D. Miethe and Charles A. Moore evaluated the impact of the Minnesota sentencing guidelines. They noted a

Italicized numbers within the grid denote the range within which a judge may sentence without the sentence being deemed a departure. Offenders with nonimprisonment felony sentences are subject to jail time according to law.[1]

SEVERITY LEVEL OF CONVICTION OFFENSE		CRIMINAL HISTORY SCORE 0	1	2	3	4	5	6 or more
Murder, 2nd Degree (intentional murder; drive-by-shootings)	X	306 *299–313*	326 *319–333*	346 *339–353*	366 *359–373*	386 *379–393*	406 *399–413*	426 *419–433*
Murder, 3rd Degree Murder 2nd Degree (unintentional murder)	IX	150 *144–156*	165 *159–171*	180 *174–186*	195 *189–201*	210 *204–216*	225 *219–231*	240 *234–246*
Criminal Sexual Conduct, 1st Degree Assault, 1st Degree	VIII	86 *81–91*	98 *93–103*	110 *105–115*	122 *117–127*	134 *129–139*	146 *141–151*	158 *153–163*
Aggravated Robbery 1st Degree	VII	48 *44–52*	58 *54–62*	68 *64–72*	78 *74–82*	88 *84–92*	90 *94–102*	108 *104–112*
Criminal Sexual Conduct 2nd Degree (a) & (b)	VI	21	27	33	39 *37–41*	45 *43–47*	51 *49–53*	57 *55–59*
Residential Burglary Simple Robbery	V	18	23	28	33 *31–35*	38 *36–40*	43 *41–45*	48 *46–50*
Nonresidential Burglary	IV	12[2]	15	18	21	24 *23–25*	27 *26–28*	30 *29–31*
Theft Crimes (Over $2,500)	III	12[2]	13	15	17	19 *18–20*	21 *20–22*	23 *22–24*
Theft Crimes ($2,500 or less) Check Forgery ($200–$2,500)	II	12[2]	12[2]	13	15	17	19	21 *20–22*
Sale of Simulated Controlled Substance	I	12[2]	12[2]	12[2]	13	15	17	19 *18–20*

☐ Presumptive commitment to state imprisonment. First Degree Murder is excluded from the guidelines by law and continues to have a mandatory life sentence. See section II.E. Mandatory Sentences for policy regarding those sentences controlled by law, including minimum periods of supervision for sex offenders released from prison.

■ Presumptive stayed sentence; at the discretion of the judge, up to a year in jail and/or other nonjail sanctions can be imposed as conditions of probation. However, certain offenses in this section of the grid always carry a presumptive commitment to a state prison. These offenses include Third Degree Controlled Substance Crimes when the offender has a prior felony drug conviction, Burglary of an Occupied Dwelling when the offender has a prior felony burglary conviction, second and subsequent Criminal Sexual Conduct offenses, and offenses carrying a mandatory minimum prison term due to the use of a dangerous weapon (e.g., Second Degree Assault). See sections II.C. Presumptive Sentence and II.E. Mandatory Sentences.

[1]Those who receive nonfelony sentences are subject to jail time; they are not required to get it.

[2]One year and one day

Minnesota Sentencing Guideline Commission, 1998.

Figure 12.4

Minnesota Sentencing Guidelines Grid: Presumptive Sentence Lengths in Month, Effective August 1, 1998 shift in prison populations from property offenders to violent criminals, an outcome consistent with the intent of the Minnesota legislature to move property offenders into community corrections. They also noted that, despite its rigorous and systematic construction, the system allows ample opportunity for sentencing disparity.

Presumptive standards restrict the direct introduction of socioeconomic biases into sentencing decisions but do not prevent their indirect entry. Judges can continue to hide biases within their departures, despite the requirement that they give written reasons for departing. Also, the guidelines shift the more open form of discretion exercised by judges at sentencing to the less visible discretionary decision making of prosecutors in selecting charges and in plea bargaining. In summary, the guidelines cannot eliminate the influence of socioeconomic, gender, and racial biases from either judicial departures or prosecutorial discretion in charging and plea bargaining.[42]

Miethe and Moore compared dispositions before and after the guidelines were implemented. They found that offense severity, criminal history, weapon use, and personal crimes predicted both whether and how long judges sentenced convicted offenders to prison. The guidelines did reduce the direct impact of social and class attributes. However, gender, marital status, and employment status continued to affect sentencing indirectly; they significantly relate to the severity of the type of conviction and criminal history. Employment status continues to affect charging and plea-bargaining decisions.[43]

Joachim Savelsberg also examined the changes effected by the implementation of the Minnesota sentencing guidelines. He noted that the Minnesota Sentencing Guidelines Commission tried to change the existing practice of sentencing property offenders to longer terms than violent offenders, as reflected in the grid shown in Figure 12.4. At first, Savelsberg discovered, the sentencing guidelines did change the practice. However, because prosecutors disagreed with the new policy, they tried to establish the old practice: harsher penalties for property offenders. They succeeded by "defining charges for property offenders in a more detailed way so that the criminal history score of property offenders added up faster." The guidelines merely shifted discretion and the influence of sociological factors from judges to the charging discretion of prosecutors. According to Savelsberg, the powerful, informal social, organizational, and ideological influences impeded, if they did not entirely defeat, the formal goal of sentencing according to the severity of the crime.[44]

The impact of sentencing guidelines on sentencing reform remains uncertain. Descriptive guidelines have little effect on judicial discretion. Voluntary guidelines depend on cooperation and support from all participants. Presumptive/prescriptive guidelines may have more effect, but sociological variables still affect the sentencing decision, as Savelsberg demonstrated in Minnesota. Political pressures also affect sentencing under guidelines. In Minnesota, for example, a combination of general demands for harsher punishment and a few highly publicized, gruesome rape-kidnapping-murders spurred the legislature to increase the severity levels of most crimes during the late 1980s and early 1990s. Sentencing guidelines, like all sentencing practices, must contend with contemporary political pressures, well-entrenched practices, and the need to balance certainty and predictability with flexibility and individual needs. They are, as they should be, a product of the society that creates them and in which they operate.[45]

Use *Your* Discretion

Was the sentence departure justified?

Facts

Robert Adamo

Mr. Adamo was convicted of embezzling about $100,000 belonging to the union Health and Welfare Fund of which he was a fiduciary, in violation of 18 U.S.C. §664. He accepted responsibility for the crime (U.S.S.G. §3E1.1). It was his first offense. The [federal sentencing] Guidelines provided a minimum prison term of fifteen months. See U.S.S.G. secs, 2E5.2, 2B1.1, 3B1.3 (base offense level of 4; increase of 8 points for amount of loss; 2 level enhancement for more than minimal planning; 2 level enhancement for fiduciary); U.S.S.G. Ch. 5, Pt. A (sentencing table). The district court, departing downward from the Guidelines, sentenced Mr. Adamo to probation alone, without any imprisonment.

The court gave the following reasons for its downward departure:

> When I look at these cases of sentencing, the first thing I ask myself is, "What sentence would I impose if there were no guidelines?" That's what I did for more than 20 years. And then I ask myself, "What's a just sentence in these circumstances? Am I going to be limited by these artificial guidelines made by people who have no idea of what kind of a case I'm going to have to decide?" No two cases are the same. . . . So that's where justice is in this case, having restitution made to this Health & Welfare Fund. If I send this defendant to prison I think it's foreordained that restitution will not be made. It may be made in some respect, but I'm sure the defendant would lose both his jobs and would find it very difficult to have employment which would allow him to make restitution. And a time in prison would serve no useful purpose in this case. The only factor in sentencing which would be accomplished is punishment, but the defendant has been punished just by being here—just being here and what's he's gone through in the last six months, and the notoriety of this. So, imprisonment serves no useful purpose in

this case. It certainly isn't a matter of deterrence. I'm sure the defendant will never do anything like this again. Here is a man who has lived an exemplary life, he's worked two jobs to take care of his family. His wife has worked, and although they were making in the range of $70,000 a year, the problem of educating two children came up. It's a problem that everyone faces. This is where the error of judgment comes in. He took this money, not out of greed, not out of desire to own a fancy car or a palatial home and a boat, but to educate his children. He didn't think about the other alternatives. His daughter wanted to go to an expensive private school, instead of going to a local state school of some sort, and he thought that's what she should have. He didn't consider loans and other types of programs. This money was available, he took it—a terrible mistake. But that's the only mistake that he seems to have made, and I just don't think he should spend time in prison because of this one mistake. I want restitution made, so I'm going to exercise my best judgment in these circumstances. My best judgment is to have as long a term of probation as possible so that restitution can be made with the guidance of the probation office. So, I'm going to depart downward and impose a term of probation of five years. That's the maximum that I can impose. And one of the conditions of probation will be, and is, that the defendant shall pay restitution in the amount of $91,125.62 to the Health & Welfare Fund of the Building Service Employees International Union, AFL-CIO Local 334.

Opinion

The basic theory of the [federal] Sentencing Guidelines is a simple one. In order to lessen the degree to which different judges imposed different sentences in comparable cases, an expert Sentencing Commission would write Guidelines, applicable to most ordinary sentencing situations. In an ordinary situation, the statutes, and the Guidelines themselves, would require the judge to apply the appropriate guideline—a guideline that would normally cabin, within fairly narrow limits, the judge's power to choose the length of a prison term. Should the judge face a situation that was not ordinary, the judge could depart from the Guidelines sentence, provided that the judge then sets forth the reasons for departure. A court of appeals would review the departure for "reasonableness." . . .

The Sentencing Statute itself sets forth the basic law governing departures. It tells the sentencing court that it shall impose a sentence of the kind, and within the range. . . . established for the applicable category of offense committed by the applicable category of defendant as set forth in the Guidelines. . . . The statute goes on immediately to create an exception for departures by adding that the sentencing court shall "impose" this Guidelines sentence unless the court finds that there exists an aggravating or mitigating circumstance of a kind, or to a degree, not adequately taken into consideration by the Sentencing Commission in formulating the Guidelines that should result in a sentence different from that described. If the sentencing court makes this finding and sentences "outside the [Guidelines] range," it must state in open court . . . the specific reason for the imposition of a sentence different from that described [in the Guidelines]. The defendant may then appeal an upward departure, and the Government may appeal a downward departure. On appeal, if the court of appeals determines that the sentence . . . is unreasonable, . . . it shall state specific reasons for its conclusions and . . . set aside the sentence and remand the case for further sentencing proceedings with such instructions as the court considers appropriate. . . .

The Guidelines deal with departures in four basic ways.

1. *Cases Outside the "Heartland."* The [U.S. Sentencing] Commission intends the sentencing courts to treat each guideline as carving out a "heartland," a set of typical cases embodying the conduct that each guideline describes. The Introduction goes on to say that when a court finds an atypical case, one to which a particular guideline linguistically applies, but where conduct significantly differs from the norm, the court may consider whether a departure is warranted. . . . [A] case that falls outside the. . . . guideline's "heartland" is a candidate for departure. It is, by definition, an "unusual case." And, the sentencing court may then go on to consider, in light of the sentencing system's purposes, whether or not the "unusual" features of the case justify departure. . . . Thus, (with a few exceptions) the law tells the judge, considering departure, to ask basically, "Does this case fall within the 'heartland,' or is it an 'unusual case'"?
2. *Encouraged Departures.* In certain circumstances, the Guidelines offer the district court . . . special assistance, by specifically encouraging departures. Part 5K [of the Guidelines] lists a host of considerations that may take a particular case outside the "heartland" of any individual guideline and, in doing so, may warrant a departure. The individual guidelines do not take account, for example, of an offender's "diminished capacity," which circumstance, in the Commission's view would normally warrant a downward departure. Nor do certain guidelines (say, immigration offense guidelines) take account of, say, use of a gun, which circumstance would remove the situation (the immigra-

tion offense) from that guideline's "heartland" and would normally warrant an upward departure. . . .

3. *Discouraged Departures.* The Guidelines sometimes discourage departures. Part 5H, for example, lists various "specific offender" characteristics, such as age, education, employment record, family ties and responsibilities, mental and physical conditions, and various good works. The Guidelines say that these features are "not ordinarily relevant" in determining departures. . . . At the same time, the Commission recognizes that such circumstances could remove a case from the heartland, but only if they are present in a manner that is unusual or special, rather than "ordinary." It may not be unusual, for example, to find that a convicted drug offender is a single mother with family responsibilities, but, at some point, the nature and magnitude of family responsibilities (many children? with handicaps? no money? no place for children to go?) may transform the "ordinary" case of such circumstances into a case that is not at all ordinary. Thus, a sentencing court, considering whether or not the presence of these "discouraged" factors warrants departure, must ask whether the factors themselves are present in unusual kind or degree. The Commission, in stating that those factors do not "ordinarily" take a case outside the heartland, discourages, but does not absolutely forbid, their use.
4. *Forbidden Departures.* The Commission has made several explicit exceptions to the basic principle that a sentencing court can consider any "unusual case" (any case outside the heartland) as a candidate for departure. The Guidelines state that a sentencing court "cannot take into account as grounds for departure" race, sex, national origin, creed, religion, and socioeconomic status. The Guidelines also state that "lack of guidance as a youth" cannot justify departure, that drug or alcohol abuse is not a reason for imposing a sentence below the Guidelines range, and that personal financial difficulties and economic pressure upon a trade or business do not warrant a decrease in sentence. Thus, even if these factors make a case "unusual," taking it outside an individual guideline's heartland, the sentencing court is not free to consider departing. But, with these . . . exceptions, the sentencing court is free to consider, in an "unusual case," whether or not the factors that make it unusual (which remove it from the heartland) are present in sufficient kind or degree to warrant a departure. The court retains this freedom to depart whether such departure is encouraged, discouraged, or unconsidered by the Guidelines. . . .

If the district court decides to depart, the defendant may appeal (an upward departure) or the Government may appeal (a downward departure). The statute then provides the appellate court with two important instructions. First, the court of appeals must decide if the resulting sentence is "unreasonable, having regard for" the sentencing court's reasons and the statute's general sentencing factors. Second, the court of appeals must (as it ordinarily does) give "specific reasons" for its decision. . . .

We now apply our "departure" analysis to . . . that of Mr. Robert Adamo. . . .

The court's explication of its reasons is useful, for it produces understanding and permits evaluation, both by appellate courts and by the Commission. We nonetheless believe the analysis does not permit the departure before us.

First, we believe . . . that the embezzlement guidelines encompass, within their "heartland," embezzlement accompanied by normal restitution needs and practicalities (i.e., the simple facts that restitution is desirable and that a prison term will make restitution harder to achieve). It would seem obvious, and no one denies, that the embezzlement guidelines are written for ordinary cases of embezzlement, that restitution is called for in many such cases, and that prison terms often make restitution somewhat more difficult to achieve. Moreover, the embezzlement guideline reflects the Commission's intent to equalize punishments for "white collar" and "blue collar" crime. Yet, as the Sixth Circuit has pointed out, a rule permitting greater leniency in sentencing in those cases in which restitution is at issue and is a meaningful possibility (i.e., generally white collar crimes) would . . . nurture the unfortunate practice of disparate sentencing based on socioeconomic status, which the guidelines were intended to supplant. Further, the district court itself, stating that it did not wish "to be limited by these artificial guidelines," and that "no two cases are alike," seemed to disregard, rather than to deny, the scope of the embezzlement guideline. For these reasons, we join the Fourth and Sixth Circuits, in holding that ordinary restitution circumstances of this sort do not fall outside the embezzlement guideline's "heartland," and therefore do not warrant a downward departure.

Second, we recognize that a special need of a victim for restitution, and the surrounding practicalities, might, in an unusual case, justify a departure. But, we cannot review a district court determination to that effect here, for the district court made no such determination. . . . We mention this fact because the defendant has pointed to one unusual feature of the case. The record before us contains a suggestion that Mr. Adamo could keep his job (and therefore remain able to make restitution) were his prison term only one year, but he could not keep his job (and thus would lose his ability to make restitution) were he sentenced to the Guidelines prison term of one year and three months. We can imagine an argument for departure resting upon a strong need for restitution, an important practical advantage to the lesser sentence, and a departure limited to three months.

We are not arguing such a departure or saying that we would eventually find it lawful. We mention the special circumstance to underscore the need for reasoned departure analysis, sensitive to the way in which the Guidelines seek to structure departure decisions and to the role that such departures, and their accompanying reasons, can play in the continued development of the Sentencing Guidelines. . . . The district court, in Mr. Adamo's case, may wish to conduct such an analysis in light of the special features of the case to which the defendant has pointed. We therefore remand this case for new sentencing proceedings.

So ordered.

CRITICAL THINKING

1. What is the basic philosophy of the federal sentencing guidelines?
2. Explain the difference between "heartland" and "unusual" cases and its effect on sentencing under the guidelines.
3. Would you grant the departure in the case of Adamo? Give reasons why or why not.

Knowledge and Understanding CHECK

1. List and describe the types of sentences judges can impose.
2. Identify the major findings on California's fixed sentencing.
3. Describe mandatory minimum sentences, and list the major findings on their effectiveness.
4. Explain the effect of mandatory minimum sentences on discretion.
5. Describe the nature and effectiveness of "three strikes and you're out" laws.
6. Identify and describe the four major purposes of sentencing guidelines.
7. Describe the Minnesota Sentencing Guidelines scheme, and list the major findings on it.

DISTRIBUTION OF SENTENCING AUTHORITY

Under indeterminate sentencing, sentencing guidelines, and fixed sentencing (both mandatory and less rigid fixed sentencing statutes), the law distribute sentencing power among several public agencies. Legislatures enact statutes that prescribe penalties for crimes. These statutes typically grant judges some range within which they can choose the exact sentence. Statutes sometimes allow judges to choose between sentences of fines or jail terms, or within a range of years in prison. Occasionally, the law allows judges to sentence offenders to probation, restitution, or community service. However, since the 1970s, legislatures have increasingly restricted the discretion of judges.[46]

You have already learned that police departments and prosecutors' offices play a major role in building cases against defendants (Chapters 7 and 11). Police influence sentencing in two ways. First, people that the police do *not* arrest will not be sentenced at all. Second, the police influence sentencing by strength of the cases they bring to prosecutors (Chapter 7). Strong cases lead to more severe sentences than weak cases.

Prosecutors influence sentencing in three ways. First, defendants whom prosecutors do not charge are beyond the sentencing authority of judges. Second, prosecutors choose what crimes to charge defendants with. The maximum and minimum penalties prescribed for these charges confine judges' sentences within these limits. Third, prosecutors influence sentencing in guilty pleas, particularly negotiated pleas (Chapter 11). Prosecutors often recommend, and in some jurisdictions promise, specific penalties; and judges rarely, if ever, reject penalties that prosecutors recommend.

Probation officers also affect sentencing. They conduct *presentence investigations* that judges use to sentence offenders. Parole boards also play a major role in the sentencing process, particularly in **"bark-and-bite" sentencing.** The parole board's informal "bite" (the actual time served) reduces the judges' formal "bark" (the sentence pronounced in court).

Prison officials also affect sentencing. They manage the prisons and affect the length of the actual sentence (Chapter 16). They advise parole boards concerning the release of prisoners, and parole boards do not often ignore their advice. Corrections officials also control **"good time"**—that is, the number of days deducted from sentences for good behavior. Most jurisdictions deduct one day of time served for every three days of good time. So, the power to decide rule violations also affects the actual time served.

State governors and U.S. presidents also have the power to alter sentences. **Executive clemency,** the power to pardon (forgive a criminal punishment) or **commute** (reduce a penalty, such as from execution to life imprisonment), provides yet another powerful limit to judicial sentencing authority.

This complex distribution of the sentencing authority reflects the structure, distribution, and operation of governmental power in general. The doctrines of separation of powers and of checks and balances render official decisions provisional: Prosecutors can overrule police decisions; judges can dismiss prosecutors' charges; and parole boards, corrections officials, governors, and presidents can alter the sentences of judges.

Because of this separation of authority, these same officials engage in frequent second-guessing among themselves. They attempt to anticipate and then counter the decisions of other officials. If prosecutors want defendants to serve no more than two years in prison and know that particular judges routinely sentence defendants in similar cases to five, prosecutors may well accept plea bargains carrying a maximum of two years in anticipation of such sentences. For example, to ensure that convicted defendants actually serve three years, judges sentence them to nine years because they know that prisoners become eligible for release after serving one-third of their sentence. Parole boards, who know defendants plead guilty to offenses less serious than those they actually commit, base their release decisions on actual offense behavior to adjust for the bargain on the charge.[47]

Distributing sentencing authority does more than serve as a formal means of checks and balances and separation of powers. Informally, particularly in unpopular cases, the diffused responsibility for imposing sentence takes the onus off any one institution. For example, no one wants sole charge of sentencing—or releasing—a child abuser. Diffused decision making spreads sentencing responsibility among several officials, thereby permitting a practical solution to an unpleasant and difficult problem.[48]

DETERMINANTS OF SENTENCING

Formally, the norms expressed in the philosophies of punishment—retribution, rehabilitation, incapacitation, deterrence, and restitution—determine the sentence imposed. Informally, a range of personal, professional, organizational, political, and social influences affect the outcome of the case. Therefore, the sentence actually imposed depends on the legal, social, and even individual structure of particular cases.

Formal Determinants

Punishment rests on either retribution or utility. **Retribution** looks backward to the crime committed. **Utility** looks forward in time to prevent future crimes. Retribution focuses on the crime, whereas utility emphasizes the offender.

The ancient maxim "an eye for an eye" embodies the essence of retribution: criminals deserve punishment. Retribution assumes a natural human urge expressed in this simple example: If you bump your shin on the table leg, you want to kick the table. Punishment satisfies this assumed natural impulse toward revenge or, more politely, retribution. Retribution assumes free will—that is, that individuals can and do choose either to commit crimes or to refrain from doing so. If they choose to commit crimes, then they deserve punishment. Retribution advocates the moral rightness of punishing wrongdoers.

Retribution does not look backward entirely; it also performs a utilitarian function. Nothing causes more public anger, breeds more resentment and contempt for law, and more deeply offends the sense of justice than when wrongdoers escape punishment. Retribution—in this sense, formalized vengeance—satisfies the demand for justice. It channels public outrage into an acceptable form—the criminal sentence. If criminal sentences do not satisfy this demand for justice, angry citizens may lose respect for law and even, on occasion, take it into their own hands.

Except for the late nineteenth century until the 1960s, retribution has been the dominant sentencing objective

Punishments based on retribution seek to satisfy the demand for justice. When the public perceives that wrongdoers have escaped punishment, they lose faith in the law. Their outrage is often expressed by flaunting the laws that they believe have failed them.

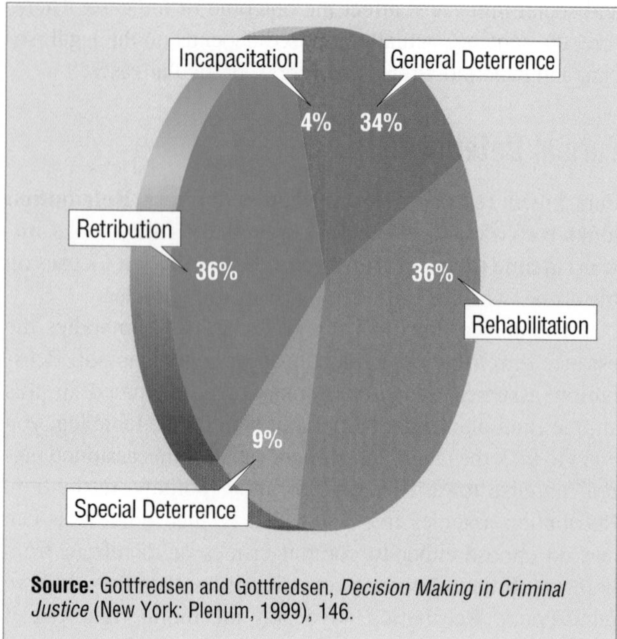

Source: Gottfredsen and Gottfredsen, *Decision Making in Criminal Justice* (New York: Plenum, 1999), 146.

Figure 12.5
Purposes Cited by Judges for Sentencing

(Figure 12.5). The idea is that justice demands retribution (**just deserts,** or the **justice model**). According to Andrew von Hirsch, in his influential *Doing Justice,*

> we should punish criminals simply for the crime committed. We should not do it either to reform them, or to deter them, or to deter others. In other words, punishment should fit the crime already committed, not the criminal—nor the crimes either the criminal or others might commit in the future. The justice model responds to a general sense of justice but raises the difficult question: How much pain and in what form satisfies retribution? For example, how many years in prison is a rape worth?[49]

Informal influences make it impossible to fix sentences entirely according to the justice model. Joachim Savelsberg, in his analysis of the adoption and implementation of the Minnesota and federal sentencing guidelines, has demonstrated the effects of these informal influences on the formal structure and process of the justice model of sentencing. Savelsberg found that the same social, organizational, and political realities that led to the creation of the indeterminate sentence are today impeding the implementation of the determinate sentence.[50]

The four major utilitarian strategies include:

- General deterrence
- Incapacitation
- Rehabilitation
- Restitution

General deterrence looks forward to people in the general population who are thinking about committing crimes. In theory, sentencing individuals who have already committed crimes "sends a message" to potential criminals, in effect threatening to punish them if they commit crimes. Deterrence, like retribution, assumes free choice. It assumes further that people seek pleasure and avoid pain. We cannot measure exactly the effectiveness of general deterrence, because we do not know how many people avoid committing crimes mainly because they fear punishment. Some researchers suggest that threats of punishment more effectively deter white-collar criminals than street criminals.[51]

Deterrence raises a question similar to the one asked about retribution: How much and what kind of pain will prevent potential offenders from committing crimes? In theory (from the time of Jeremy Bentham, the great English utilitarian philosopher who devised it), deterrence rested morally and practically on inflicting only the amount of pain necessary to change behavior.

Early deterrence researchers focused on measuring deterrence by aggregate data—that is, by crime rates and conviction and imprisonment rates. More recently, researchers have turned their attention to individuals in the general population. For example, JoAnn L. Miller and Andy B. Anderson surveyed 751 individuals in Baltimore in the crime-prone group between ages 15 and 36. They distributed booklets containing 50 scenarios describing a potential crime opportunity, including an offense, possible economic gain from the crime, risk of getting caught, chance of getting convicted, and specific punishment imposed. They found that "men, especially white men, are more strongly influenced than black men or black women" by the certainty and severity of punishment.[52]

Incapacitation, sometimes called **specific deterrence,** also looks forward; but it focuses on preventing specific offenders from committing crimes. Its basic idea is simple: criminals removed from society cannot victimize innocent persons. Incapacitation can result from three methods:

- Capital punishment.
- Mutilation, such as castration and amputation.
- Incarceration.

Capital punishment, although on the increase since the late 1970s, takes place infrequently. Mutilation, almost extinct, has returned in a few jurisdictions. Incarceration stops criminal behavior of prisoners *outside* but not *inside* prisons. Furthermore, it cannot incapacitate *after* release from prison.[53]

Rehabilitation, like incapacitation, targets individual offenders. However, rehabilitation tailors penalties to suit criminals, not crimes. Rehabilitationists consider punishment distasteful, preferring instead to call the objective of criminal sentencing "treatment." The **medical model** of criminal justice—treating instead of punishing criminals—stems from the idea that training, therapy, and teaching can change criminals into law-abiding citizens. In the medical idiom, treatment cures the disease of criminality.[54]

Restitution obliges offenders to pay for their crimes. A sentence to restitution orders offenders to repay a victim. Frequently, restitution includes repaying the state for its losses. Although meant primarily to compensate victims, restitution has won support on the grounds that it rehabilitates criminals and prevents them from returning to lives of crime. The rehabilitative and preventive effects of restitution depend on whether direct payment makes offenders realize the loss their crimes have caused to their victims.[55]

Use *Your* Discretion

How does philosophy affect sentences?

The general philosophies of punishment affect sentences, but exactly how is difficult to assess because the philosophies are so varied and, in some cases, contradictory. For instance, sentencing highly intelligent muggers to learn legitimate ways to acquire money at Harvard Business School may satisfy the rehabilitative ends of punishment. However, most judges (and certainly the public) do not believe that attending college will satisfy the aims of retribution; imprisonment is more appropriate. Furthermore, judges rarely articulate their general philosophical aims in ways that social scientists can accurately measure. Judges may say the purpose of their sentence is to rehabilitate—and may believe what they say—when in fact they are incapacitating or punishing offenders.[56]

CRITICAL THINKING

1. List the reasons why it is difficult to assess the effects of punishment philosophy on sentences.
2. Summarize the results of the survey of judges in Figure 12.5.
3. With this in mind would you favor changes in the use of philosophy in sentencing? Exactly what changes do you favor? Explain your answer.

Informal Determinants

Informally, it is mainly the social structure of individual criminal cases that affects sentencing. Both the facts and the characteristics of offenders influence the sentences that judges impose. The legal definitions in criminal codes leave room for judicial discretion to take social characteristics into account in sentencing. Nevertheless, most research on sentencing confirms the pattern that we have noted with regard to other decisions in criminal justice: seriousness of the offense and dangerousness of the offender as reflected in criminal history weigh most heavily in sentencing. Interviews with judges, for example, support the conclusion that judges consider offense seriousness the most important determinant in their sentencing, even though individual judges may define seriousness variously and imprecisely.[57]

Most judges said that the seriousness of the offense followed by the criminal record of the offender influences their decisions the most. However, the data rarely permit measuring what judges include as criminal records. Some count juvenile records. Others consider arrests part of a prior criminal record. Some judges count only prior convictions. Judges freely apply their own standards to the policy question: What should judges include? In this freedom, judicial discretion expresses informal determinants in sentencing.[58]

As in police decisions to stop and arrest, prosecutors' decisions to charge, and the courtroom work group's decisions to plea bargain, the social status of offenders and victims, their relationship to each other, and the specific characteristics of each affect judges' definitions of seriousness and, consequently, the sentences they impose. Age, family relationships, employment status, and demeanor affect sentencing. For example, judges don't give the same sentence to young first offenders with families to support as they give to multiple offenders with no family or employment ties. Offenders with well-established employment records ordinarily do not receive sentences identical to those with little or no work record. Judges treat guilty pleas more leniently than convictions at trial. Status also affects sentencing. Low-status offenders who commit crimes against high-status victims receive the harshest sentences. Low-status offenders who victimize low-status persons receive more lenient sentences than high-status offenders who victimize high-status persons. High-status offenders who victimize low-status individuals receive the most lenient sentences. Similar outcomes may also characterize interracial and intraracial crimes, and crimes involving gender differences.[59]

Organizational determinants also affect sentences. Heavy caseloads prevent giving careful individual attention to each case, and sentencing takes on a routinized character to keep cases moving. Crowded prisons and jails lead judges to sentence fewer offenders to incarceration and more to noninstitutional alternatives, such as probation, restitution, and community service. Judges ordinarily sentence offenders in ways that do not unduly upset courtroom work group relationships. Public opinion and political pressures also influence sentencing. Famous defendants, prominent victims, or victims who generate sympathy cause judges to tailor sentences to suit the facts of the case. Heavy media attention also affects sentencing.

Personal and behavioral characteristics of individual victims and offenders also affect sentencing. Attractive female victims sometimes induce harsher sentences. On the other hand, individual characteristics can soften a penalty. In Wisconsin, a judge imposed no penalty on a convicted rapist because "the victim's enticing dress and the general aura of permissiveness provoked the offender." Victims who acted provocatively, used excessive self-defense, consented, or were negligent can also reduce a judge's sentence. Contrite, submissive, clearly remorseful offenders can reduce sentences. Unrepentant ones can aggravate sentences. One judge ignored a defense request for probation instead of prison time because a physician convicted of involuntary manslaughter for recklessly providing a young patient with barbiturates that killed her refused to accept responsibility for his actions.[60]

Despite these important individual, organizational, and social influences on sentencing in particular cases, offense seriousness and offender dangerousness remain the dominant influences. After thoroughly reviewing all the available research on sentencing, a distinguished panel of the National Academy of Sciences concluded:

> Using a variety of different indicators, offense seriousness and offenders' prior record emerge consistently as the key determinants of sentencing. The more serious the offense and the worse the offender's prior record, the more severe the sentence. The strength of this conclusion persists despite the potentially severe problems of pervasive biases arising from the difficulty of measuring—or even precisely defining—either of these complex variables. This finding is supported by a wide variety of studies using data of varying quality in different jurisdictions and with a diversity of measures of offense seriousness and prior criminal record.[61]

PRESENTENCE INVESTIGATION

Judges need adequate information to sentence defendants. The **presentence investigation (PSI)** and the **presentence report (PSR)** based on it are supposed to provide this information. Presentence investigation focuses on the three things about defendants:

1. Prior criminal record
2. Social history
3. Psychiatric evaluation

Most professional groups associated with sentencing have recommended mandatory PSIs. The federal government led the way in adopting the PSI, and most states have followed its lead.[62]

The first part of PSRs enumerates the facts of the case based on both the police report and the defendant's version of what happened. As might be expected, police and defendant versions often diverge widely. Judges usually accept the police version, which critics argue treats defendants unfairly. The second part deals with prior criminal record, including prior convictions, dropped charges, and arrests. Controversy exists over whether criminal histories should count arrests, because arrests require only probable cause and convictions demand proof beyond a reasonable doubt. Social histories include such things as family history, employment record, and education of offenders. According to judges, social histories enable them both to determine defendants' potential for rehabilitation and to predict their future behavior. When available, psychiatric evaluations, although done infrequently, are also included.

The presentence investigation and report can cause problems. The quality of information in PSRs is one of these problems. Overburdened probation officers, responsible for conducting most PSIs, have to collect information while supervising convicted criminals on probation. Always pressed for time, probation officers cannot always verify information, and judges may unwittingly eventually use this erroneous information to sentence defendants.

Another problem is that probation officers have less influence on sentencing than their reported wide agreement with judges suggests. One study challenges the probation officer's central role in sentencing. Based on his 15 years of experience as a probation officer and on qualitative interviews with other probation officers, Professor John Rosecrance concluded that they write presentence reports for three audiences: the court, the prosecutor, and the probation supervisor. They use the report to maintain their credibility, looking for cues from these audiences and providing them with recommendations that are what they want to hear. Probation officers make ballpark recommendations not to influence their audiences' perceptions of defendants, but to legitimate their own claim to being "reasonable."[63]

Knowledge and Understanding CHECK

1. List the public agencies that participate in sentencing.
2. List and describe the five formal determinants of sentencing.
3. Identify three methods of incapacitation.
4. Identify and explain the major informal influences on sentencing.
5. According to the National Academy of Sciences, what are the major influences on sentencing?
6. List the main elements of presentence investigations, and explain their importance.

TYPES OF SENTENCES

Judges can impose several types of sentences. Most dramatically, they can sentence convicted murderers to either death or mutilation. At the other end, they can also sentence convicted offenders to shaming, Shame-based punishment creates public attention in the hope that the public will respond with shaming.[64]

Use *Your* Discretion

Is shaming good policy?
***Illinois v. Meyer,* 680 N.E.2d 315 (1997)**

Facts

On February 25, 1995, Gary Mason visited the defendant's farm in order to return some vehicle parts that he purchased from the defendant. Mason and the defendant began to quarrel over whether the parts were functioning properly. During the argument the defendant swung one of the parts at Mason, striking him in the nose and eye, causing several injuries.

At the defendant's sentencing hearing, evidence was presented in aggravation and mitigation. On behalf of the State, Tim Belford testified that in September 1986, he went to the defendant's farm in order to collect monies for two insufficient fund checks issued by defendant to Belford's employer, the First National Bank of Pittsfield. Belford stated that the defendant eventually gave him the money, but then kicked him and ordered him off the farm. Belford acknowledged that a jury acquitted the defendant of aggravated battery charges stemming from this incident.

Next, Harry Dyel testified that in May of 1990, he went to the defendant's farm on behalf of his employer, Shelter Insurance Company, in order to investigate a claim filed by the defendant. Dyel testified that the defendant became hostile because he was annoyed by the company's failure to process his claim promptly. Dyel stated that after he attempted to comply with the defendant's demands for payment, the defendant pushed him down and kicked him several times, causing injuries to his torso, arms, face and head. The defendant was convicted of the aggravated battery of Dyel. Finally, Gary Mason, the victim in the present case, testified regarding the defendant's actions on February 25, 1995.

Several witnesses testified in mitigation. Kenwood Foster testified that he is a licensed clinical social worker who operates a private counseling service. The defendant began seeing Foster in the fall of 1991. Foster testified that doctors at several different clinics have diagnosed the defendant as having "major depressive disorder" or clinical depression. Foster further stated that he believes that the defendant may also suffer from a condition similar to a type of posttraumatic stress disorder. He indicated that the defendant has been taking prescription medication known as Zoloft, to control his illness.

Foster further testified that certain stresses, such as a perceived threat to the defendant or his family, could trigger a change in the defendant's behavior. Foster acknowledged that the defendant may perceive certain behavior as threatening, even if the average individual would not feel threatened under similar circumstances.

Friends of the defendant, Gregg Smith, David Gratton, and Bruce Lightle, also testified. All three described the defendant's good character and reputation within the community.

Mary Meyer, the defendant's wife of 36 years, testified that the defendant's elderly mother relies on the defendant, her only child, for care and assistance. Mrs. Meyer stated that she teaches high school, and has always relied on the defendant to manage the farm. She indicated that her family would suffer great hardship if the defendant were incarcerated. Mrs. Meyer also testified regarding the defendant's prolonged psychological illness and his efforts to control his sickness with medication.

In addition to the testimony of the witnesses, 20 letters were submitted by individuals from throughout the defendant's community. These letters chronicle examples of the defendant's generosity and willingness to assist friends and neighbors in need. The letters contain many descriptions of the defendant's good character and reputation.

Additionally, the presentence investigation report contains a detailed description of the defendant's mental health history. Several psychological evaluations of the defendant, dating from 1989, show that he suffers from major depressive disorder and possibly an additional psychological malady.

Upon evaluating all of the evidence in mitigation and aggravation, the trial court sentenced the defendant to 30 months' probation. The court considered the defendant's family members and the adverse impact that incarceration would have upon them. The court stated that it considered that the defendant was 62 years old, his mother's age and ill-health, and Mary Meyer's need to have the defendant care for the farm, in deciding to sentence the defendant to probation instead of prison.

The court conditioned defendant's probation on the following: (1) payment of $9,615.95 in restitution, (2) payment of a $7,500 fine, (3) payment of a $25 monthly probation services fee, (4) psychological psychiatric evaluation and treatment, (5) oneyear home confinement and (6) the placement of a "violent felon" warning sign at each entrance to the defendant's property for the duration of the probation period. With respect to the sign requirement, the court stated that it believed that "maybe [the sign] will protect society." The court's supplemental order regarding the sign provides: "As a condition of probation defendant shall erect and maintain at each entrance of his property a 4′ × 8′ sign with clearly readable lettering at least 8″ in height reading: 'Warning! A Violent Felon lives here. Enter at your own Risk!' To be erected by 8-11-95."

The defendant appealed his sentence, arguing that the sign was an improper condition of probation. The appellate court determined that section 5-6-3(b) authorized the trial court to order the sign as a reasonable condition of probation, and affirmed the trial court on this issue. We granted the defendant leave to appeal.

Opinion

The sole issue presented to us for review is whether the trial court was authorized to order the violent felon warning sign as a condition of probation. The defendant maintains that the trial court acted outside of the scope of its sentencing authority because the sign is not a reasonable condition of probation within the meaning of the Unified Code of Corrections (730 ILCS 5/5-6-3(b) (West 1994)). Section 5-6-3(b) of the Code lists 16 permissible probation conditions that the trial court may impose "in addition to other reasonable conditions relating to the nature of the offense or the rehabilitation of the defendant as determined for each defendant in the proper discretion of the Court" (730 ILCS 5/5-6-3(b) (West 1994)). The defendant maintains that the warning sign is not a reasonable condition of probation because it does not comport with traditional notions of punishment or probation in Illinois, and instead is an unauthorized "shaming penalty" or a scarlet letter type of punishment. The defendant argues that nothing in the Code supports the subjection of probationers to public ridicule as a goal of probation.

The State responds that while the sign may embarrass the defendant, it is not intended to subject him to public ridicule. Rather, the State and the amicus curiae, the American Alliance for Rights and Responsibilities, contend that this condition of probation furthers the goals of probation because it protects the public and serves to rehabilitate the defendant.

The State maintains that the sign protects the public by warning against provoking the defendant and by reducing the number of guests or business invitees who visit the farm. The State and the amicus argue that the goal of rehabilitation is fostered by the sign because it reminds the defendant that society disapproves of his criminal conduct. The amicus further argues that because the sign reminds the defendant of his offense, the defendant will modify his behavior and will be less likely to commit acts of violence in the future. Finally, both the State and the amicus argue that the trial court acted within its discretion by carefully fashioning the conditions of probation to correspond to the needs of the defendant and the public.

This court has recognized repeatedly that the purpose of probation is to benefit society by restoring a defendant to useful citizenship, rather than allowing a defendant to become a burden as an habitual offender. Probation simultaneously serves as a form of punishment and as a method for rehabilitating an offender. Protection of the public from the type of conduct that led to a defendant's conviction is one of the goals of probation.

Although the sign may foster the goals of probation to the extent that it punishes the defendant and protects the public, furtherance of these two goals alone does not render the condition reasonable. Indeed, we are persuaded by defendant's contention that the sign, in fact, may hamper the goal of rehabilitation, and that the erection of the sign is inconsistent with the conditions of probation listed in section 5-6-3(b). We recognize that the trial court labored arduously and sincerely to develop a sentence which would serve the needs of society and simultaneously avoid incarceration of the defendant. Nonetheless, we hold the sign condition of probation imposed in this case was unreasonable and did not serve the purposes of section 5-6-3(b).

We hold that section 5-6-3(b) of the Code did not authorize the trial court to require the sign as a condition of the defendant's probation. The sign contains a strong element of public humiliation or ridicule because it serves as a formal, public announcement of the defendant's crime. Thus, the sign is inconsistent with the conditions of probation listed in section 5-6-3(b), none of which identify public notification or humiliation as a permissible condition. Further, we determine that the sign may have unpredictable or unintended consequences which may be inconsistent with the rehabilitative purpose of probation.

Finally, the nature and location of the sign are likely to have an adverse effect on innocent individuals who may happen to reside with the defendant. At the time of sentencing in this case, the defendant's wife was living on the premises where the violent felon sign was to be displayed. The defendant's elderly mother also intended to live there. The record shows that the defendant has two adult children who visit the farm, as well as young grandchildren. We believe that the manner in which the sign affects others also renders it an impermissible condition of probation.

Conditions which label a defendant's person or property have a stigmatizing effect and are considered shaming penalties. D. Kahan, What Do Alternative Sanctions Mean? 63 U. Chi. L.Rev. 591 (1996); Comment, Sentenced to Wear the Scarlet Letter: Judicial Innovations in Sentencing—Are They Constitutional? 93 Dick. L.Rev. 759 (1989); Comment, The Modern Day Scarlet Letter: A Critical Analysis of Modern Probation Conditions, 1989 Duke L.J. 1357 (1989). Although a probationer may experience a certain degree of shame from a statutorily identified condition of probation, shame is not the primary purpose of the enumerated conditions.

The judicially developed condition in the case at bar does not reflect present penological policies of this state as evidenced by our Unified Code of Corrections. The authority to define and fix punishment is a matter for the legislature. The drastic departure from traditional sentencing concepts utilized in this case is not contemplated by our Code. Therefore, we determine that the erection of the sign as a condition of probation was unreasonable, and may be counterproductive to defendant's rehabilitative potential.

For the above stated reasons, we conclude that the trial court exceeded its authority and abused its discretion under section 5-6-3(b) when it ordered the defendant to place the violent felon sign at the entrance to his farm. This condition was not reasonable. Because the sign has already been in place for more than half the period of the defendant's probation, and in order that the issue may not become moot by the further passage of time, we hereby order that the disputed condition of probation is vacated instanter.

The judgment of the appellate court is reversed and the judgment of the circuit court is affirmed in part and vacated in part. Appellate court judgment reversed; circuit court judgment affirmed in part and vacated in part.

CRITICAL THINKING

1. List all the facts in the case that are relevant to the punishment of Meyer.
2. Summarize the state's and the defendant's arguments for and against the shaming punishment.
3. Summarize the reasons why the court rejected the state's arguments and accepted the defendant's argument.
4. Do you agree or disagree with the decision. Explain your answer.
5. If you disagree with the court, what would you do in this case? Defend your answer.

Judges can also sentence offenders to community service, such as working in hospitals, jails, or other public institutions, or to perform menial work, such as cleaning streets or collecting trash. These punishments, although they attract attention, rarely occur in day-to-day criminal sentencing.

The most frequent sentence that judges impose is probation, followed in frequency by incarceration. Offenders convicted of less serious crimes, but not sentenced to probation, go to jail; convicted felons go to prison. In most jurisdictions, local jails house offenders with short sentences, usually less than one year, frequently for 30 days or less. Most convicted felons serve some time in prison, where sentences exceed one year. However, up to one-quarter of felons receive probation in some jurisdictions, and about one-fifth receive a split sentence, time in jail followed by release on probation for the remainder of the sentence. Judges also impose fines for many petty crimes.

Use *Your* Discretion

Are castration and electric shock appropriate sentences?

Castration

While he was on probation for molesting a 7-year-old girl, Steven Allen Butler, a 28-year-old with a wife and child of his own, was convicted of aggravated sexual assault for repeatedly raping a 13-year-old girl. Butler, who shines shoes for a living, and who was in the Houston jail awaiting trial, asked the court to sentence him to castration instead of life imprisonment. At the sentencing hearing, Judge Michael McSpadden agreed to allow the castration in return for a plea of guilty to the charges of aggravated sexual assault. In return, Judge McSpadden said he would sentence Butler to 10 years probation, after which, if the probation was successfully completed, the conviction would be removed from his record. Butler's wife agreed to the castration. So did the parents of the victim.

Doctors who treat sex offenders, as well as advocates of victims' rights, criticize the castration of sex offenders. They say castration is a "simplistic and questionable solution to a complex problem." "This is

Steven Allen Butler, a 28-year-old with a wife and child, was convicted of aggravated sexual assault for repeatedly raping a 13-year-old girl. Butler asked the court to sentence him to castration instead of life imprisonment. Judge Michael McSpadden agreed to allow the castration in return for a plea of guilty to the charges of aggravated sexual assault.

not the answer," says Cassandra Thomas, president of the National Coalition Against Sexual Assault. "It sounds good. It makes you feel good, but in the long haul it doesn't deal in any way with the basic issues of sexual assault." Surgical castration—the removal of the testicles—reduces the sex drive but does not necessarily eliminate the capacity to get an erection. Chemical castration—the use of drugs to suppress the sex drive—is less drastic.

Other countries offer castration as an alternative to prison. During the 1960s, Denmark castrated about 2,000 men, according to the distinguished criminologist Marvin Wolfgang. Wolfgang says, however, "I don't think castration is necessary. In Germany and Italy, they have used anti-androgens, which have been very effective in reducing the sex drive." Anti-androgens suppress the male hormones and are also used in the United States. Dr. John Money, who has worked with anti-androgens since 1966, says, "I know of several cases in which people chose to be treated with drugs, usually Depo-Provera, rather than go to jail. Usually it's a condition of probation. I know people call it chemical castration, but it's reversible, and it's not castration at all."

Judge McSpadden advocates castration because traditional punishment does not work. "We're all painfully aware," he says, "that present laws in Texas and elsewhere neither protect society nor effectively treat sex offenders. I've been on the bench 10 years, and I've seen over and over, the moment these people are released back into society, the violence begins again. Here in Harris County, we had 2,500 children raped last year, and these are just reported rapes. If we dare call ourselves a civilized society, we can't tolerate that and other daily violence we see."

But Cassandra Thomas argues that castration "buys into the myth that sexual assault is about sex. I think it ignores the issues of power, control, feelings of anger that are prime motivators." Dr. Michael Cox, director of the sexual abuse treatment center at Baylor College of Medicine in Houston, opposed the castration of Steven Allen Butler. "It's being held up as some sort of panacea that's somehow going to reverse the violent crime problem we have. I think it's a scary precedent. It purports to offer a simple and very primitive biological solution to a very complex social problem."

Legal experts say castration raises questions of coercion. "It's clear that mandatory castration, or any other corporal mutilation, would be cruel and unusual punishment," says Stephen Schulhofer, professor of criminal law at the University of Chicago. "So the question is, if the state can't directly take away your sexuality, should they be able to do it by the back door like this? But the other view is, if the defendant thinks it's a better choice, why should we take it away?"

CRITICAL THINKING

1. What are the arguments for and against castration?
2. Do you favor compulsory surgical castration?
3. Under what conditions? Why?
4. Do you oppose castration of any kind? Defend your answer.
5. Do you favor voluntary chemical castration? Defend your answer.

Electric Shock

The acute punishment of electric shock is easily demonstrated to be superior in every respect to our current punishment practices. Compare a typical occurrence in today's courtroom with what we would have in the future if only we could get it straight that it is pain, pure and simple, that is the essence of punishment.

The judge peers out over his glasses at the pathetic woman who sits across the courtroom. In a violent outburst she has just called him a heartless tyrant or something to that effect. The public defender and a courtroom guard restrain her.

"Mrs. Washington," says the judge. "This is your third shoplifting offense. You leave me no choice." He hesitates, expecting another outburst. Mrs. Washington's three-year-old daughter sits next to her, eyes wide and watery. The judge tries to avoid her gaze. "Mrs. Washington, it is the judgment of this court that you be sentenced to a minimum of six months in the penitentiary and a maximum of one year. Your daughter will be turned over to the care of the Department of Youth, since the presentence report indicates that you have no husband or relatives who could care adequately for her."

The mother is led, crying, out of the courtroom. The child pulls at her mother's skirt, crying "Mama! Mama!" But the hands of the court are upon her, and an innocent child is about to be punished for the crime of having a guilty mother.

Every day, all across America, many, many families and relatives of offenders suffer in this way. This means that literally thousands of people are punished for other people's crimes.

Now an example of what punishment of the future could be like. Twenty-year-old John Jefferson stands along with his lawyer, the public defender. "John Jefferson," says the judge, "the court has found you guilty of burglary in the first degree. Because this is your first offense, but the damage you did was considerable, I sentence you to . . ." The judge pushes a few buttons at his computer console. The average sentence for similar cases to Jefferson's flashes on the display: five shock units. "You will be taken immediately to the punishment hall to receive five shock units. Court dismissed."

The victim of this crime is sitting at the back of the court. He approaches the court clerk, who directs him to the punishment hall where he will be able to watch the administration of the punishment. Jefferson's wife and child are ushered to the waiting room where they will await Jefferson's return after he has been punished. Meanwhile, in the punishment hall, Jefferson is seated in a specially designed chair. As part of the arrest procedure he has already received a medical examination to establish that he was fit to receive punishment.

In addition to the victim, a few members of the press are seated on the other side of the glass screen. The punishment technician, having settled the offender in the chair, returns to an adjoining room where he can observe the offender through a one-way screen. A medic is also present. The technician sets the machine at the appropriate pain level, turns the dial to 5, and presses the button. Jefferson receives five painful jolts of electricity to his buttocks. He screams loudly, and by the time the punishment is over, he is crying with pain. The technician returns and releases the offender. "Stand and talk a little," he says. Jefferson walks around, rubbing his buttocks. A shade drops over the spectators' screen.

"Do you still feel the pain?" asks the medic. "Goddam, I sure do! But it's getting better. Can I go now?" "Just sign here, and you've paid your dues." Jefferson sighs happily and asks, "Which way to the waiting room?" "Straight down the passage and second left." Jefferson enters the waiting room where his wife rushes into his arms, crying, "I'm so glad it's over! Thank goodness you weren't sent to prison."

We see in this example that only the guilty person is punished. The punishment administered is clean, simple, and, most importantly, convincingly painful. It is over in a brief time, and the offender is able to return to his family and his job. Punishment is confined only to the guilty. The side effects of punishment are minimized. (Graeme Newman, *Just and Painful,* 2d ed., New York: Harrow and Heston Publishers, 1995. Reprinted with permission.)

CRITICAL THINKING

1. What arguments in favor of corporal punishment do you see in this excerpt?
2. What arguments against it do you see?
3. What formal and informal purposes of punishment does it serve?
4. Do you agree judges should use it? Why? Why not? Defend your answer.

INDETERMINATE SENTENCING, DISPARITY, AND DISCRIMINATION

Sentencing discrimination means the use of unacceptable criteria, usually race or gender, to determine sentences. **Sentencing disparity** includes inequality of three different types:

1. *Different sentences imposed on similar offenders.* For example, two burglars the same age, with similar records, break into stores after hours and each takes $100 from the cash register. One burglar goes to prison, the other gets probation.
2. *Similar sentences imposed on different offenders.* For example, a five-time burglar gets the same sentence as a first-time burglar.
3. *Similar offenders receiving different sentences for unimportant differences.* For example, an armed robber who takes $1,000 receives a sentence twice as long as an armed robber who takes $750.[65]

Use *Your* Discretion

Is the indeterminate sentence responsible for disparity in sentences?

Beginning with Lyndon Johnson's Crime Commission's report in 1967, a storm of popular criticism has blamed the indeterminate sentence for arbitrary and inconsistent penalties. One group of critics has focused on the amount of racial discrimination in sentencing. Researchers have tried to explain why in a general population of 11.5 percent adult African American males in the United States, the sentenced population includes nearly 50 percent adult African American males. As early as 1928, critics asserted that judges imposed more severe sentences on African Americans than on whites. Early critics also charged that women benefited from reverse discrimination in sentencing. Women, it was reported, received probation and suspended sentences more frequently than did men.[66]

Later studies challenged these early findings. For example, according to some research, taking seriousness of offense and criminal records into account removed the disparity among minorities, women, and white adult men. Early research on the connection between race and sentencing suffered from two shortcomings. First, most sentencing research depended on aggregate sentencing data—that is, combined data from diverse localities. Aggregate data often obscure local differences. For instance, conclusions based on all sentences in a state might hide racially determined sentences in particular counties, or the use of aggregate data for one jurisdiction might obscure the racism of individual judges.[67]

A study in Georgia demonstrates the importance of disaggregating data. Martha A. Myers and Susette M. Talarico studied the impact of race on sentencing in a random sample of 16,798 Georgia felons. They compared these data with those from a comparable random sample of 1,685 Georgia felons from Fulton and DeKalb counties. They found little systemwide discrimination against African Americans.

> We expected that sanctions would be more severe in counties characterized by pronounced inequality, a sizeable percentage of black unemployed residents, and relatively high crime rates. In actuality, we found little evidence to support these expectations. . . . We found no consistent relationship with punitiveness in sentencing. Nor did the presence of large economically subordinate populations, whether black or unemployed, foster more severe sanctions.[68]

Second, when Myers and Talarico looked more closely at different communities, courts, and times, however, they found that "the absence of evidence of system-wide discrimination does not mean that all courts and judges are blind in the administration of criminal law. Interactive analysis revealed context-specific patterns of discrimination." As a result, they found significant differences in sentencing to prison, depending on the seriousness of the crime combined with the racial composition of the community. They also found that African Americans were incarcerated longer than whites on the average, no matter what the racial makeup of the community. Disparity could, however, result in leniency as well as severity:

> Importantly, however, there were many instances in which blacks receive disproportionately lenient punishment. Although this pattern may suggest a paternalism that is just as discriminating as disproportionate punitiveness, it nevertheless indicates that courts in Georgia do not have a heavy hand with black defendants in the general systemic sense or in every context where differential treatment is observed.[69]

Researchers clearly have not settled the problem of the degree and nature of racial discrimination and disparity in sentencing. The prestigious National Academy of Sciences panel on sentencing research, after surveying all the research on discrimination in sentencing, concluded:

> Despite the number and diversity of factors investigated as determinants of adult sentences in different statistical studies, two-thirds or more of the variance in sentence outcomes remain unexplained. The literature indicates that offense seriousness and offender's prior record are the key determinants of sentences. Factors other than racial discrimination in sentencing account for most of the disproportionate representation of blacks in U.S. prisons, although racial discrimination in sentencing may play a more important role in some regions or jurisdictions, for some crime types, or in the decisions of individual participants. The evidence of discrimination on grounds of social and economic status is uncertain; the evidence on the role of sex in sentencing is only preliminary. The strongest and most persistently found effect of case processing variables is the role of guilty pleas in producing less severe sentences.[70]

Most research has not separated race from other characteristics such as gender, poverty, offense seriousness, and prior criminal record. Joan Petersilia of the RAND Institute in Santa Monica, California, studied convicted felons in California, Texas, and Michigan, hoping to sort out the important factors that influence sentencing. Controlling for these other influences, Petersilia found that more African Americans and Hispanics were sentenced more frequently to longer prison terms than were whites. In a replication relying on a larger database, however, Petersilia, along with Stephen Klein and Susan Turner, found race not related to sentencing. Cassia Spohn and her associates, on the other hand, found that African American males are sentenced to prison at a rate 20 percent higher than that for white males.[71]

According to Spohn and her colleagues:

> Judges in Metro City apparently do discriminate against black males in deciding between incarceration and lengthy probation. White males are more likely to receive probation, black males a short prison term.[72]

Furthermore, John H. Lindquist and his associates examined judicial processing of 2,859 men and women prostitutes in a southwestern Texas city, based on computerized judicial files in criminal district courts. They found that women, repeaters, and nonrepeater minorities were more frequently convicted. Heterosexual offenders and minorities were more frequently jailed. Minorities were sentenced most harshly.[73]

Gary D. LaFree analyzed 755 defendants in Tucson and El Paso, whose most serious charge was robbery and burglary. He found major differences between the two cities. In Tucson, no significant differences appeared in the sentencing of Hispanics and non-Hispanics. In El Paso, on the other hand, Hispanics received longer sentences. Interviews with criminal justice officials suggested that the established Hispanic population in Tucson, versus the less-established Mexican American and Mexican national populations in El Paso, accounts for the difference in treatment. According to one El Paso prosecutor:

> We're sitting here on a border. Across the river from us, which is nothing more than an oversized mud puddle, is the city of Juarez, with over a million and a quarter residents. . . . Our police force is geared to the size of this city and what it can afford. El Paso does not have the economic base to support the city itself. In other words, we perceive El Paso as the city north of the Rio Grande, but bullshit, we're talking about another million and a quarter people that go back and forth like a tide.[74]

Another difference between the cities is the aggressive, adversarial stance toward prosecutors taken by Tucson public defenders, an attitude not found in other Arizona cities. In contrasting the public defenders of Tucson and Phoenix, for example, one Tucson public defender said of the relationship with prosecutors, "It's more of a combat mentality here." Another said that public defenders in Phoenix "are much more prone to plead a case out than we are." Texas, however, has no public defender system. Judges assign defenders from a list of private attorneys. As a result, indigent El Paso defendants get lawyers without trial experience.[75]

Finally, LaFree found significant differences in the language assistance provided by Tucson and El Paso. Both cities provide translators for defendants who cannot speak English. However, because of El Paso's high Hispanic population (more than 60 percent, compared with 21 percent in Tucson) and the cost of providing translators (El Paso is a poorer community than Tucson), El Paso defendants suffer from inadequate translation, "a major block to equal treatment for southwestern Hispanics."[76]

The research in race, gender, and status discrimination in sentencing demonstrates that methodology and local variation account for much of the mixed results reported by researchers. Further research based on sophisticated methodology such as the sampling reviewed here, drawn from a greater variety of settings, should add to the incomplete state of our knowledge as of this writing. Research to date suggests disparities and discrimination in some places under some conditions. Answers to how extensive it is, how deliberate, and how linked to other factors await further research.

The broad range of sentencing options—such as one to five years, thirty years to life, or even one year to life—that is common under indeterminate sentencing statutes has also received major criticism as a factor in creating disparity. These sentences place no real limits on judicial discretion in sentencing—hence, the perceived *lawlessness* in sentencing. In a stinging rebuke to lawless sentencing, the distinguished federal judge Marvin E. Frankel, in his widely read and acclaimed *Criminal Sentences,* wrote:

> [T]he almost wholly unchecked and sweeping powers we give to judges in the fashioning of sentences are terrifying and intolerable for a society that professes devotion to the rule of law. Federal trial judges, answerable only to their varieties of consciences, may and do send people to prison for terms that may vary in any given case from none at all up to five, ten, thirty, or more years. This means in the great majority of federal criminal cases that a defendant who comes up for sentencing has no way of knowing or reliably predicting whether he will walk out of the courtroom on probation, or be locked up for a term of years that may consume the rest of his life, or something in between.[77]

CRITICAL THINKING

1. What is the difference between sentencing discrimination and sentencing disparity?
2. Identify and describe the three types of sentencing disparities.
3. State the major findings of the preceding studies.
4. Compare and contrast the findings.
5. Which is the most persuasive to you? Explain your answer.
6. How do methodology and location affect the findings on sentencing differences?
7. On the basis of these findings, what recommendations would you make for future sentencing research and sentencing policies? Defend your recommendations.

DEATH SENTENCES

Perhaps no sentence has generated greater debate than the sentence of death. The U.S. Supreme Court has ruled that the death penalty is not cruel and unusual punishment (prohibited by the Eighth Amendment); does not deny individuals due process of law (Fifth and Fourteenth Amendments); and does not deny equal protection of the law (Fourteenth Amendment) if the administration of the death penalty meets three conditions:

- The sentence is for murder.
- Both mitigating and aggravating circumstances were considered before imposing the sentence of death.
- The sentence was not discriminatory according to race or other unacceptable criteria.

To meet these requirements, most states that authorize the death penalty have enacted **guided discretion death penalty statutes.** These statutes require juries to administer capital punishment according to statutory guidelines on mitigating and aggravating circumstances. Defendants charged with capital crimes under guided discretion statutes receive **bifurcated trials.** The first stage, the traditional trial, determines guilt. If the verdict is guilty, then the second stage, sentencing, takes place to decide death or life imprisonment. During this second stage, statutory guidelines listing aggravating and mitigating circumstances guide the jury's discretion. The principal aggravating circumstances include killings during felonies; previous convictions for homicide; killing strangers; and killing multiple victims. Mitigating circumstances include no prior criminal history; mental or emotional stress; victim participation in the crime; and, playing only a minor part in the murder.

The Supreme Court has also decided that the Constitution permits the execution of persons who committed murder while they were juveniles, and of retarded persons who do not qualify for the insanity defense. For example, when he was 15, William Wayne Thompson, with three older persons, shot his brother-in-law twice, cut his throat, chest, and abdomen, and broke his leg. The attackers then chained the body to a concrete block and threw it in a river. Thompson was convicted and sentenced to death. The Supreme Court ruled that the Constitution did not prevent his execution. Johnny Paul Penry raped, beat, and then stabbed Pamela Carpenter with a pair of scissors. She died a few days later. Dr. Jerome Brown testified that Penry was mentally retarded, probably due to brain damage at birth, that he had the mental age of a 6½-year-old and the social maturity of a 9- or 10-year-old. Penry was convicted and sentenced to death. The Supreme Court ruled that mental retardation could not prevent his execution.[78]

Facts About the Death Sentence

Although 36 states authorize the death penalty, and juries convict and courts sentence increasing numbers of murderers to death row, states execute few of them. This has led to an unprecedented number of death row inmates, but relatively few executions every year. In 1997, 74 prisoners were executed; the most since the 76 executed in 1955. Since 1930, when the government began collecting statistics, the federal and state governments in the United States have executed 4,016 individuals, most of them prior to the 1950s. The numbers dwindled to zero from 1967 to 1977. Then, on January 17, 1977, a Utah firing squad executed Gary Gilmore.[79]

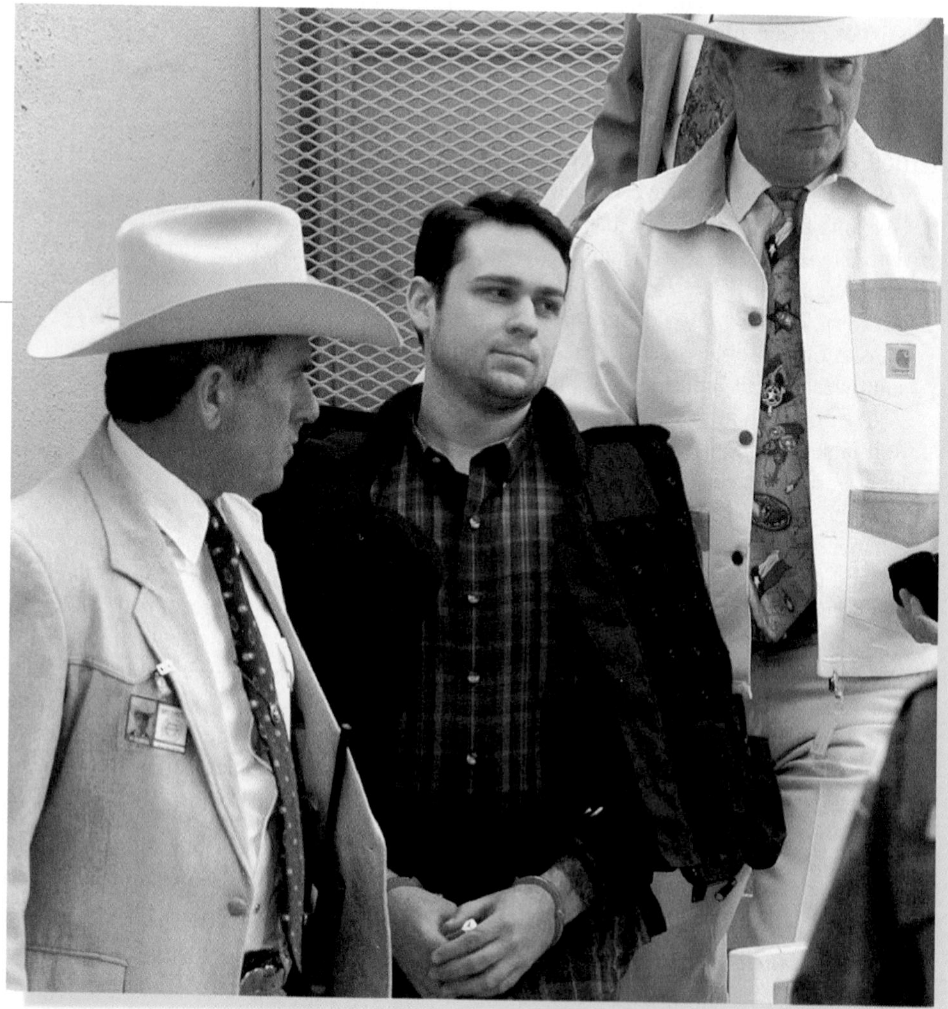

Convicted killer John William King, center, is escorted from the Jasper County, Texas, courthouse after being sentenced to die by lethal injection for the capital murder of James Byrd, Jr. on June 7, 1998. King killed his African-American victim by dragging him behind a pickup truck.

Figure 12.6
Number of Persons under Sentence of Death, 1956–1996

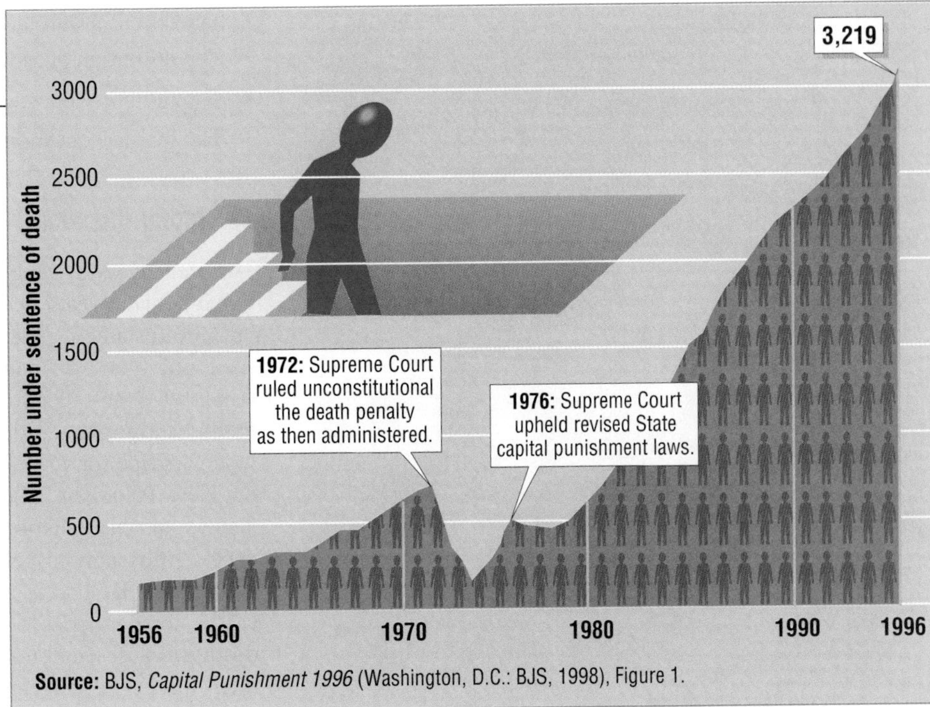

Source: BJS, *Capital Punishment 1996* (Washington, D.C.: BJS, 1998), Figure 1.

Gilmore's execution was a major media event, producing both a cover story in *Newsweek* and a Norman Mailer best-seller. On January 27, 1993, the state of Missouri executed Marsay Bolder by lethal injection, the 191st execution since Gary Gilmore's in 1977. By contrast, the story was carried in a small article deep in the national news section of the *New York Times*.

It took two unusually sensational back-to-back executions to bring capital punishment back onto the front pages of newspapers and the top of television news. On January 25, 1996, Utah child rapist-killer John Albert Taylor became the first prisoner to face the firing squad since Gary Gilmore. On January 26, Delaware double-murderer Billy Baily became the first person in that state to die by hanging since 1946. Both prisoners chose the old-fashioned firing squad or noose over lethal execution. Taylor said he wanted to put Utah to the greater expense and embarrassment of the firing squad. Baily said, "I was sentenced to hang. Asking a man to choose how to die is more barbaric than hanging." Figure 12.6 depicts the number of prisoners on death row at the end of 1996.[80]

All death-row prisoners now awaiting death are convicted murderers. In 1996, two-thirds of the prisoners on death row had prior felony convictions; 8 percent had prior homicide convictions. There were 2,793 white prisoners on death row; 2,278 African American; 306 Hispanic; and 387 others. Executed prisoners spend an average of seven years on death row. Most death-row inmates are undereducated and poor.[81]

Public Attitudes Toward the Death Sentence

Since 1930, the majority of Americans have supported the death penalty. Only in 1996 did opponents begin to slightly outnumber supporters with support for the death penalty standing at a record high of 75 percent. Educating people about issues surrounding the death penalty has little or no effect on attitudes. From this, researchers have concluded that background has more influence on attitudes than knowledge. Race and political ideology are important background influences; gender, community size, and choice of major have little influence according to a survey of 307 criminal justice students in a medium-sized southern college. Surveys of the general population show the same. Maria Sandys and Edmund McGarrel found that white male conservatives are the strongest supporters.[82]

The Cost of the Death Sentence

A popular argument "Kill them! Why spend the money on keeping killers alive in prison for life?" The reality is that the death sentence is expensive. Texas leads the nation in both death-row population (almost 400) and executions (almost 20). It takes about 7½ years between the trial and the execution of a death-row prisoner, a cost to the taxpayers of about $2.3 million for every capital case. By contrast, to imprison someone in a single cell at the highest security level in a Texas prison for 40 years costs $750,000.[83]

Dallas lawyer Vincent Perini, chairman of the Texas Bar Association's committee on representing death-row inmates, argues, "There's some things that a modern American city and state have got to have. You have got to have police and fire and public safety protection. You have to have a criminal justice system. You don't have to have a death penalty."[84]

Allen Hightower, a Texas politician, said that although life without parole would save millions of dollars, "From a

Debate over the death penalty has raged for centuries. On a visit to the United States in 1999 Pope John Paul II ignited controversy by calling on the governor of Missouri to stay the execution of a prisoner scheduled to die during the pope's visit to St. Louis.

correctional practice standpoint, if someone needs to go to prison for life, I'm for gassing them. The end result is that with no chance or hope of getting out, no matter how you behave . . . there's no reason not to stab a guard and no reason not to kill or rape another inmate." Hightower favored saving money by limiting appeals of death sentences. "Will we ever convict a person in the state that's not guilty? Sure. We've done it before, and we'll do it again. But our criminal justice system is the fairest system in the world." Texas Assistant Attorney General Bob Walt, who complained that defense tactics are the cause of the problem, also supports the death penalty despite its cost. "We have no shortage of violent characters in this state," he said. "The death penalty is something Texans want."[85]

Issues in Death Sentencing

The U.S. Supreme Court settled the *legal* argument over the death penalty, but it cannot settle the issues of morality, fairness, and effectiveness that surround this ancient punishment of death:

- The moral question: Is it right?
- The utilitarian question: Does it work?
- The fallibility question: Does it kill innocent people?
- The fairness question: Does it discriminate?

The Moral Question

The debate over capital punishment is fundamentally a moral debate. Death penalty proponents point to two familiar Old Testament passages: one from Genesis, "Whoever sheds the blood of man, by man shall his blood be shed" (Gen. 9:6); the other from Exodus, "Eye for eye, tooth for tooth, hand for hand, foot for foot, burn for burn, wound for wound, stripe for stripe" (Ex. 21:24–25). Opponents invoke the New Testament, alluding to the death of Christ to save sinners and his calls to forgive enemies and turn the other cheek. Jesus admonishes the crowd before the stoning of an adulteress: "He that is without sin among you, let him first cast a stone at her" (John 8:7). Punishment will come after death, because God alone can punish. Even the Old Testament teaches, "Vengeance is mine" (Deut. 32:35). Capital punishment is inconsistent with the merciful, redemptive aspect of both Judaism and Christianity, yet the Bible provides justification both to support and to condemn it. Amnesty International moves beyond scriptures to a more general moral condemnation: "The death penalty violates the right to life and the right not to be subjected to cruel, inhumane or degrading treatment."

Supporters of capital punishment also rely on general moral grounds to bolster their arguments. They maintain that it is right to hate criminals and to base punishment on our outrage at heinous crimes. It is as morally right to punish criminals for their wicked deeds as it is to praise heroes for their courageous deeds. If it is noble for soldiers in wartime to give their lives for their country, then it is morally right in a peaceable society to claim the lives of murderers for killing innocent people. According to Professor Ernest van den Haag:

> The life of each man should be sacred to each other man. . . . [I]t is not enough to proclaim the sacredness and inviolability of human life. It must be secured as well, by threatening with the loss of their own life those who violate what has been proclaimed as inviolable—the right of innocents to live.[86]

In the end, the moral debate over capital punishment is not a matter of either science or logic; it is a question of values. Some people deeply believe that it is wrong for the state to kill anyone for any reason; others believe just as deeply that it is wrong not to execute heinous criminals.

The Deterrence Question

Popular belief has it that the harsher the punishment, the greater its deterrent effect. Accordingly, the death penalty must have the greatest deterrent effect. Would-be murderers will hesitate if they believe execution awaits them. Criminal justice professionals, policymakers, and scholars, however, do not agree on the death penalty's deterrent effect. Indeed, nothing in recent years has generated more controversy concerning the death penalty than whether it prevents crime.

Since at least the sixteenth century, long before modern social science, observers have questioned the capacity of capital punishment to prevent crime. Lord Coke, the English judge never known for his compassion for criminals, said it made him "weep" that after sending 500 criminals to their deaths on the gallows in one year, no reduction in crime resulted; crime actually increased. In the eighteenth century, both the Italian criminologist Cesare Beccarria and the American reformer Benjamin Rush argued that capital punishment did not reduce crime; in fact, the death penalty probably encouraged crime by its example.

Not until the past 30 years has social science developed research methods that could accurately measure the deterrent effect of the death penalty. The debate has shifted dramatically as a result of studies either conducted or inspired by criminologist Thorstin Sellin and economist Isaac Ehrlich. Sellin and his followers compared capital crime rates in states having the death penalty with the rate in neighboring, similar states that did not. In general, they found no significant difference in the capital crime rate between states that had the death penalty and those that did not. They concluded from this that the death penalty was not a significantly greater deterrent than life imprisonment. Of course, such a conclusion rests on the assumption—not proven—that other influences on the homicide rates did not account for the figures.[87]

These studies seemed to settle the empirical question until Isaac Ehrlich's provocative capital punishment study appeared in 1975. Ehrlich used a highly technical statistical device called regression analysis to measure the death penalty's deterrent effect. Regression analysis tests the relationship between the death penalty and the capital crime rate. It uses a complex mathematical formula to isolate the death penalty's effect on the capital crime rate from other influences, such as the age of the capital offenders. Regression analysis incorporates the multiple factors that influence the rate, so that the influence of capital punishment will not be exaggerated. Ehrlich applied regression analysis to FBI homicide figures from 1934 to 1969 and concluded that "an additional execution per year" may have resulted in "seven or eight fewer murders" annually. During the 1980s, economists made even bolder claims. Steven K. Layson, in another elaborate econometric analysis based on homicide data from 1936 to 1977, concluded that every execution prevents 18 murders.[88]

Ehrlich's study set off a firestorm of debate. The U.S. Solicitor General used it to support the constitutionality of the death penalty. President Richard Nixon's administration hailed it as scientific proof that the death penalty did in fact deter capital crimes. Because Ehrlich's findings ran counter to prevailing evidence that the death penalty did not deter capital crimes, it generated a host of follow-up studies. These follow-up studies uncovered serious flaws in his research. One criticism charged that Ehrlich's conclusions hold up only if the regression equation is in one of its more unusual forms, called logarithmic. If it is put in the more conventional linear regression, the deterrent effects of the death penalty disappear, and Ehrlich's findings do not hold up.[89]

The worst blow to Ehrlich's research came from a study of the use of the death penalty during the 1960s. Ehrlich had made much of the figures that showed capital crime rates soared when the death penalty was on hold during the 1960s. But, was it the failure to execute capital criminals that caused rising capital crime rates, or was the relationship only coincidental. Brian Forst developed a rigorous test for Ehrlich's findings. Instead of aggregate data for the whole United States, Forst compared states having the death penalty with those that did not. He found that capital crime rates in all jurisdictions rose about the same amount, whether they had the death penalty or not. States that had never executed criminals and states that had recently decided not to execute showed similar increases in capital crimes during the 1960s. On the basis of this comparative state analysis and some other more complicated matters, Forst concluded that capital punishment did not deter homicide. The debate continued without resolution into the 1990s.[90]

Use *Your* Discretion

Does the death penalty *increase* the number of murders?

A long line of research has examined the effects of the death penalty. The two principal types of effects studies are

1. *Deterrence:* Examines whether the death penalty *reduces* the number of murders.
2. *Brutalization:* Examines whether the death penalty *increases* the number of murders.

Most of this research has found no consistent relationship between the death penalty and either the increase or decrease in the number of murders, as the discussion about deterrence in this section demonstrates. These studies are all based on aggregated data—that is, general homicide rates, not particular types of homicide such as stranger and acquaintance homicides. For example, William C. Bailey compared monthly homicide rates with the publicity that executions received on television from 1976 through 1987. Bailey found support for neither the deterrence nor the brutalization thesis. Homicides were related neither to the amount nor to the type of publicity given to executions.[91]

John K. Cochran and his colleagues found support for the brutalization thesis in disaggregated execution data from Oklahoma. In September 1990, Oklahoma executed its first murderer in 25 years. An immediate increase in the number of killings of some types of strangers followed the execution of Charles Troy Coleman. But, the increase did not occur in all stranger homicides, such as murders during the course of committing felonies such as robbery. Cochran and his colleagues contend that executions do not deter killings; they actually *incite* others to kill.[92] Bailey used the same data but he controlled for

> [I]f inhibitions against the use of lethal violence to solve problems created by "unworthy others are reduced by executions, such a brutalization effect is most likely to occur in . . . [situations] where inhibitions against the use of violence are already absent or considerably relaxed."[93]

Bailey studied the same data, but he focused on the effects of media coverage and some other variables. Using this disaggregated data, he found even stronger support for the brutalization thesis: There was a significant increase both in total killings and in all kinds of stranger killings. Moreover, he found that the death penalty did not reduce the number of homicides. According to Bailey,

> It is a mistake for criminologists to treat the deterrence/brutalization question as a dead issue. It is equally a mistake for death penalty examiners to be content with "testing" deterrence/brutalization arguments by simply examining general homicides. Rather, detailed combinations of homicide circumstances and victim-offender relationships must be considered, as well as the possibility that the deterrent/brutalization impact of capital punishment may differ for different dimensions of capital punishment.
>
> I recommend that the next round of deterrence/brutalization research extend this analysis by considering additional and more diverse jurisdictions, and more extended time periods. Besides Oklahoma, a number of other states have returned to capital punishment in the past few years. . . . In addition, a number of jurisdictions that have not conducted an execution for decades have large death row populations. The former and the latter jurisdictions (when executions resume) can be examined as additional quasi-natural experiments to both clarify and determine the generalizability of the findings for Oklahoma.[94]

CRITICAL THINKING

1. Are you convinced that executions *incite* killings? Explain your answer.
2. Would you call for reconsidering the death penalty in light of the research summarized here?
3. What more would you like to know before making a final decision about executions as a deterrent or incitement to crime? Explain.

Clearly, the death penalty incapacitates or specifically deters the executed person from killing again. Some cases demonstrate the importance of this effect. In *Tison v. Arizona,* for example, the defendants helped their father (serving a life sentence for murdering a prison guard) to escape from prison. He killed four more persons. Life without parole, an alternative to capital punishment receiving increasing attention, does not prevent killings in the prison environment.[95]

The Fallibility Question

Fallibility means that wrongfully convicted people are executed. These wrongful convictions arise in two ways:

1. Convictions were obtained by illegal means, such as by forced confessions or unreasonable searches and seizures.
2. Innocent people are convicted.

The fallibility issue demands an answer to the question of how many mistakes are acceptable. Abolitionists say none, maintaining that the irrevocability of the death penalty puts innocent people at too high a risk. To proponents, the paucity of innocent people killed out of the thousands sentenced to death implies the death penalty is almost perfect. They claim further that the last innocent person was executed in the 1930s, demonstrating that even the few mistaken executions took place a long time ago. They say it cannot happen in modern times.

Abolitionists counter that the numbers cited are minimum figures and therefore represent the fewest innocent people executed. Some people executed may not deserve it even though they are technically guilty. Joey Kagebien, for instance, was sentenced to death for first-degree murder. He was one of several teenage boys who killed an Arkansas farmer, but he did not do the actual killing. Although that made no difference legally, it distinguished him from other first-degree murderers who receive death sentences. Therefore, Joey Kagebien does not appear among the innocent people sentenced to death; nor does Clifford Hallman, convicted of killing a woman in Tampa, Florida. After Hallman was on death row, authorities established that his victim died not from Hallman's attack, but from improper medical attention at Tampa General Hospital.

Cases do come to light periodically. The release of Randall Adams, who spent years on death row for a murder he did not commit (depicted in the docudrama *The Thin Blue Line*), clearly demonstrates that human error occurs in death sentences. It seems to demonstrate also that errors come to

Freddie Pitts smiles as he and Wilbert Lee receive compensation checks for being wrongfully imprisoned for 12 years (nine of which were on death row). The two men were convicted twice of the murders of two white gas station attendants by all-white juries, and were finally released when another man confessed to actually committing the crimes. Do you think that cases like this of error in sentencing provide a strong enough argument against the death penalty?

light in the review process, even if it takes years for them to do so. No matter how few or many mistaken capital convictions and executions exist, cases like that of Wilber Lee and Freddie Pitts are important:

> After twelve years in jail for someone else's crime, Freddie Pitts and Wilber Lee walked out of prison here today, into the bright autumn sunshine and new lives as free men. The state, which twice convicted them of murder and kept them on death row for nine years after another man confessed to the crime, gave them an executive pardon and $100 and sent them on their way. They did not look back. "Is it over, Freddie?" Mr. Lee asked softly as the gates of the Florida State Prison hummed and buzzed and then opened electronically in front of them. "It's over, man," said Mr. Pitts as they strode through together. "It's really over."[96]

The Fairness Question

The fairness question arises mainly because capital punishment falls most heavily on poor African American men. Women are rarely sentenced to death, even though they commit almost 20 percent of all criminal homicides. Neither are middle-class people. Since John Webster, a famous professor of medicine at the Harvard Law School, was put to death in 1850, businesspeople, professors, lawyers, and doctors have escaped the ultimate penalty. Instead, as numerous studies have demonstrated, poor, undereducated, underemployed men face execution in America. According to Peter W. Lewis, all the death-row inmates in Florida are blue-collar workers—"truck drivers, laborers, carpenters, dishwashers, private security guards"—and other unskilled workers. According to Charles L. Black, "All or almost all . . . [death row inmates] are poor, at least in the frame of reference wherein the expenses of effective defense against crime are to be calculated."[97]

Adalberto Aguirre, Jr., and David V. Baker reviewed a wide range of empirical research on racial disparities in the death penalty. According to their research, the death penalty is imposed on African Americans in a "wanton" and "freakish" manner, despite the efforts of the Supreme Court in *Furman v. Georgia* and *Gregg v. Georgia* to eliminate racial discrimination in its use. The research surveyed by Aguirre and Baker also showed that "blacks who victimize whites consistently have the highest probability of receiving a capital sentence." This finding supports the claim that capital punishment "protects (through deterrence) that class of individuals (whites) who are least likely to be victimized."[98]

Knowledge and Understanding CHECK

1. According to the U.S. Supreme Court, under what conditions is the death penalty constitutional?
2. Identify the major facts about the death penalty.
3. Summarize public attitudes toward the death penalty.
4. Identify the major issues in death sentencing.
5. Summarize the arguments for and against each of the major issues you identified in the last question.

What Is the "Right" Sentence? Consideration

United States v. Rivera, 994 F.2d 942 (1st Cir. 1993)

After reviewing the record of the sentencing proceeding, we conclude that Rivera is correct. The district court's analysis of the nature of its power to depart is not consistent with the view of departures that we set forth in this opinion. We recognize a difference between "forbidden departures," and "discouraged departures." And, we believe that the district court did not realize that it had the legal power to consider departure, where departure is discouraged (but not forbidden), if it finds features of the case that show it is not ordinary.

At the sentencing hearing, the district court said:

> With respect to Defendant's argument that the Defendant's family situation, economic situation, warrants a departure, I must say that the guidelines are drawn to apply to everyone in exactly the same way, that it is clear from the guidelines that the economic situation and the family situation of the Defendant is not a consideration. There are those who certainly would disagree with that, but that is the principle that is embodied in the guidelines. They are age blind, they are sex blind, they are blind to family circumstances, and can result in their application in a certain amount of cruelty. But, that isn't a basis for making a departure. It's a situation where somebody tries to draw a straight line that applies to every situation that can possibly arise and this Court is without discretion to take what might well be thought by most people, at least, legitimate concerns into consideration. Simply put, I can't do that because the guidelines do not permit me to do that. So that Defendant's objection or request to make a downward departure is denied. . . . Your Counsel says that a court somewhere observed that these guidelines are not a straightjacket for a District Court. Well, I don't agree with that. Here is a circumstance where I'm satisfied that the reason you did this was to buy toys for your children at Christmas. It was a serious mistake. The pre-sentence report says this: There is no information suggesting that Ms. Rivera had any previous participation in a similar type criminal activity. The Defendant's lifestyle is not indicative of that of a drug dealer who has profited from ongoing criminal activity. Rather she appears destitute, relying on public assistance to support herself and her children. . . . If I had the authority to do it, I would not impose the sentence that I am about to impose. I would impose a lesser sentence because I think that these guidelines simply are unrealistic when applied to real-life situations like this. They may work in many circumstances, but they certainly don't work here.

In these statements, the court repeatedly said that it lacked the legal power to depart; it characterized the case before it as different from the "many circumstances" where the Guidelines might work; it added that it would depart if it could; it set forth several circumstances that might make the case a special one; and it described as identical ("sex blind" and "blind to family circumstances") guidelines that, in fact, differ significantly, the former involving a "forbidden" departure, and the latter a "discouraged" departure. Taken together, these features of the case warrant a new sentencing proceeding, conducted with the district court fully aware of its power to depart in "unusual cases" and where family circumstances are out of the "ordinary.". . .

. . . The upshot is a difficult departure decision. On the one hand lie a host of quite special circumstances (though many are of the "discouraged" sort), and on the other hand lies the simple fact that Ms. Mirna Rivera did transport a pound of cocaine from New York to Providence. This is the kind of case in which, if the district court departs, its informed views as to why the case is special would seem especially useful and would warrant appellate court "respect."

We remand the case for further proceedings.

Critical Thinking

1. What specific facts justify the departure in the case of Rivera?
2. Would you allow the departure in Rivera's case? Argue the case for and against the departure, and then give your reasons for departing or not departing.

CHAPTER CAPSULE

- Neither harsh penalties nor rehabilitation has much impact on either crime rates or imprisonment rates.
- Mandatory minimum sentencing sounds good, but there is little convincing solid evidence that it reduces crime.
- Fixed sentences do not allow enough discretionary judgment, whereas indeterminate sentences allow too much discretionary judgment.
- Sentencing guidelines are probably the best hope for fair and effective sentences, if they balance criminal behavior and past criminal records and keep a careful watch on prison capacity.
- The justice, effectiveness, fairness, and cost of the sentence of death are all open to heated debate.
- Belief in the death penalty seems to be related to race and political ideology.
- Despite a lot of talk about the need for alternative sentences, either incarceration or probation is still the most often imposed sentence.

KEY TERMS

determinate sentencing
indeterminate sentencing
mandatory minimum sentence laws
"three strikes and you're out"
presumptive sentencing guidelines
voluntary sentencing guidelines
descriptive sentencing guidelines
prescriptive sentencing guidelines
"bark-and-bite" sentencing
good time
executive clemency
commute
retribution
utility
just deserts
justice model
general deterrence
incapacitation
special deterrence
rehabilitation
medical model
restitution
presentence investigation (PSI)
presentence report (PSR)
sentencing discrimination
sentencing disparity
guided discretion death penalty statutes
bifurcated trials

INTERNET RESEARCH EXERCISES

Exercise: What are the pros and cons of "mandatory minimum" sentences? Explain your answer based on the information you find.

Suggested site:

- There are several sites on the Internet with articles concerning mandatory minimum sentences. Using any search engine, type in the key words "mandatory minimum sentences" and report on the results of your research. Some sample sites:
- NACDL—Mandatory Minimum Sentences, http://www.criminaljustice.org/LEGIS/leg15.htm
- RAND study on Mandatory Minimum Drug Sentences, http://mall.turnpike.net/~jnr/randstud.htm

InfoTrac College Edition: Search on key words "mandatory minimum sentences"

NOTES

1. *United States v. Rivera,* 994 F.2d 942 (1st Cir. 1993)
2. Quoted in Douglas Hay, "Property, Authority and the Criminal Law," in *Albion's Fatal Tree,* Douglas Hay et al., eds. (London: Allen Lane, 1975), 17–19.
3. Joel Samaha, "Discretion and Law in the Early Penitential Books," in *Social Psychology and Discretionary Law,* Richard Abt, ed. (New York: W. W. Norton, 1978).
3. Joel Samaha, "Fixed Sentences and Judicial Discretion in Historical Perspective," *William Mitchell Law Review* 15 (1989): 217–53.
4. Ibid.
5. David Rothman, *The Discovery of the Asylum* (Boston: Little, Brown, 1971).

6. *Transactions of the National Congress of Prisons and Reformatory Discipline* (Albany, N.Y.: American Correctional Association, 1971).
7. Zebulon Brockway, *Fifty Years of Prison Service* (New York: Charities Publication Committee, 1912), 401.
8. Twentieth Century Fund, *Fair and Certain Punishment* (New York: McGraw-Hill, 1976), 95.
9. Ibid.
10. Janis Appier, *Policing Women: The Sexual Politics of Law Enforcement and the LAPD* (Temple University Press, 1998), 16–17.
11. Based on the author's summary of reformatory records of Stillwater Prison and St. Cloud Reformatory in Minnesota, 1900–1920.
12. Edward Lindsey, "Historical Sketch of the Indeterminate Sentence and Parole Systems," *Journal of Criminal Law and Criminology* 16 (1925): 18, 96.
13. Alfred Blumstein et al., *Research on Sentencing: The Search for Reform* (Washington, D.C.: National Academy Press, 1983), 48–52.
14. James Q. Wilson, *Thinking About Crime,* 2d ed. (New York: Basic Books, 1983), chaps. 7–10.
15. Robert Martinson, "What Works?: Questions and Answers About Prison Reform," *The Public Interest* 35 (1974): 22–54; Ted Palmer, "Martinson Revisited," in *Rehabilitation, Recidivism, and Research,* Robert Martinson et al., eds. (Hackensack, N.J.: National Council on Crime and Delinquency, 1976), 41–62; Marc F. Plattner, "The Rehabilitation of Punishment," *The Public Interest* (Summer 1976): 104–14.
16. Susan E. Martin, Lee B. Sechrest, and Robin Redner, eds., *New Directions in the Rehabilitation of Criminal Offenders* (Washington, D.C.: National Academy Press, 1981), 3.
17. Francis T. Cullen and Karen E. Gilbert, *Reaffirming Rehabilitation* (Cincinnati: Anderson, 1982); Donald R. Cressey, "Criminological Theory, Social Science, and the Repression of Crime," *Criminology* 16 (1978): 171–91; Seymour Halleck and Ann Witte, "Is Rehabilitation Dead?" *Crime and Delinquency* 23 (1977): 372–82; Elliott Currie, *Confronting Crime* (New York: Pantheon, 1985).
18. Peter Rossi et al., *Money, Work and Crime: Experimental Evidence* (New York: Academic Press, 1980); Ann Dryden Witte, *Work Release in North Carolina: An Evaluation of Its Post-Release Effects* (Chapel Hill, N.C.: Institute for Research in Social Science, University of North Carolina at Chapel Hill, 1975).
19. Cullen and Gilbert, *Reaffirming Rehabilitation,* 257–60.
20. National Council on Crime and Delinquency, *Criminal Justice Sentencing Policy Statement* (San Francisco, NCCD, 1992), 6.
21. *California Penal Code,* sec. 1170(a) (St. Paul: West, 1980).
22. *California Penal Code,* sec. 1170(b).
23. Jonathon D. Casper, David Brereton, and David Neal, *The Implementation of the California Determinate Sentence Law* (Washington, D.C.: National Institute of Justice, 1981); Pamela Utz, *Determinate Sentencing in Two California Courts* (Berkeley, Calif.: Center for the Study of Law and Society, 1981), 32–135; Sandra Shane-DuBow, Alice P. Brown, and Erik Olsen, *Sentencing Reform in the United States: History, Content and Effect* (Washington, D.C.: National Institute of Justice, 1985), 33–39.
24. Ibid.; Malcolm M. Feeley, *Court Reform on Trial* (New York: Basic Books, 1983), 143–45; John Monahan and Laurens Walker, *Social Science in Law* (1985), 54–59, 80–81.
25. Stephen P. Klein, Susan Turner, and Joan Petersilia, *Racial Equity in Sentencing* (Santa Monica: RAND Corporation, 1988).
26. Henry Scott Wallace, "Mandatory Minimums and the Betrayal of Sentencing Reform: A Legislative Dr. Jekyll and Mr. Hyde," *Federal Probation* (September 1993): 9.
27. U.S. Sentencing Commission, *Mandatory Minimum Penalties in the Federal Criminal Justice System* (Washington, D.C.: U.S. Sentencing Commission, August 1991), 5–7. For a discussion of the alleged Communist role in the perceived increased use of illicit drugs, see U.S. Congress, Senate, Committee on the Judiciary, *Hearing Before the Subcommittee to Investigate Juvenile Delinquency,* Miami, Florida, 83d Cong., 2d sess., 1954, 7.
28. U.S. Sentencing Commission, *Mandatory Minimum Penalties,* 6.
29. H. Rep. No. 1444, 91st Cong., 2d Sess. 11 (1970).
30. Judith A. Lachman, "Daring the Courts: Trial and Bargaining Consequences of Minimum Penalties," *Yale Law Journal* 90 (1981): 597–631.
31. National Institute of Justice, *Mandatory Sentencing: The Experience of Two States* (Washington, D.C.: National Institute of Justice, 1982); quotes from Samuel Walker, *Sense and Nonsense About Crime,* 2d ed. (Monterey, Calif.: Brooks/Cole, 1989), 89; Feeley, *Court Reform on Trial,* 118–28.
32. Wilson, *Thinking About Crime,* 135–36.
33. Feeley, Court Reform on Trial, 131; Milton Heumann and Colin Loftin, "Mandatory Sentencing and the Abolition of Plea Bargaining: The Michigan Firearm Statute," *Law and Society Review* 13 (1979): 393–430.
34. U.S. Sentencing Commission, *Mandatory Minimum Penalties.*
35. Wallace, "Mandatory Minimums," 11.
36. Ibid.; *Criminal Justice Newsletter,* November 15, 1993, 5.
37. Stephen J. Schulhofer, "Rethinking Mandatory Minimums," *Wake Forest Law Review,* 28 (1993): 199; Campaign for an Effective Crime Policy, "Evaluating Mandatory Minimum Sentences" (Washington, D.C.: Campaign for an Effective Crime Policy, unpublished manuscript, October 1993).
38. Michael G. Turner et al., "'Three Strikes and You're Out' Legislation: A National Assessment," *Federal Probation* (September 1995): 16.
39. Ibid., 18, 32–33; Peter J. Benekos and Alida V. Merlo, "Three Strikes and You're Out!: The Political Sentencing Game," *Federal Probation* (March 1995): 3.
40. Benekos and Merlo, "Three Strikes," 7; "'Three Strikes'—Serious Flaws and a Huge Price Tag," *Overcrowded Times* (October 1995): 3; Vincent Schiraldi, "Blacks Are Targets of 57 Percent of 'Three Strikes' Prosecution in Los Angeles," *Overcrowded Times* (April 1995): 7.
41. Minnesota Sentencing Guidelines Commission, *Minnesota Sentencing Guidelines and Commentary,* revised August 1998, 21–25.
42. Terance D. Miethe and Charles A. Moore, "Socioeconomic Disparities Under Determinate Sentencing Systems: A Comparison of Preguideline and Postguideline Practices in Minnesota," *Criminology* 23 (1985): 339.
43. Ibid., 357–61.
44. Joachim Savelsberg, "Laws That Do Not Fit Society: Sentencing Guidelines as a Neoclassical Reaction to the Dilemmas of Substantive Law," *American Journal of Sociology* 75 (1992): 1372.
45. See Richard Sparks, "The Construction of Sentencing Guidelines: A Methodological Critique," and Susan E. Martin, "The Politics of Sentencing Reform: Sentencing Guidelines in Pennsylvania and Minnesota," in *Research on Sentencing,* vol. 2, Alfred Blumstein et al., eds., for interesting and thorough discussions of sentencing guidelines; Richard Frase, "The Role of the Legislature, the Sentencing Commission, and Other Officials Under the Minnesota Sentencing Guidelines," *Wake Forest Law Review* 28 (1993): 345, 359–64.

46. Michael H. Tonry, "Sentencing," *Encyclopedia of Crime and Justice,* Sanford Kadish, ed. (New York: Free Press, 1983), 4:1436.
47. Ibid.
48. *Fair and Certain Punishment,* 117.
49. Andrew von Hirsch, *Doing Justice: The Choice of Punishments* (New York: Hill and Wang, 1976); Alexis Durham, "Crime Seriousness and Punitive Severity: An Assessment of Social Attitudes," *Justice Quarterly* 5(1998): 131–53.
50. Savelsberg, "Laws That Do Not Fit Society, 1346–81.
51. Alfred Blumstein et al., eds., *Deterrence and Incapacitation: Estimating the Effects on Crime Rates* (Washington, D.C.: National Academy of Sciences, 1978).
52. JoAnne Miller and Andy B. Anderson, "Updating Deterrence Doctrine," *Journal of Criminal Law and Criminology* 77 (1986): 426–27, 437.
53. Blumstein et al., *Deterrence and Incapacitation.*
54. Martin, Sechrest, and Redner, eds., *New Directions.*
55. Charles F. Abel and Frank H. Marsh, *Punishment and Restitution* (Westport, Conn.: Greenwood Press, 1984).
56. Blumstein et al., *Research on Sentencing,* chap. 2.
57. Ibid.
58. Ibid.
59. Donald Black, *Sociological Justice* (New York: Oxford University Press, 1986), chaps. 1, 6.
60. Robert Elias, *The Politics of Victimization* (New York: Oxford University Press, 1986), 156–59; *Commonwealth v. Youngkin,* 427 A.2d 1356 (Pa. 1981).
61. Quoted in Michael R. Gottfredson and Don M. Gottfredson, *Decision Making in Criminal Justice: Toward a Rational Exercise of Discretion,* 2d ed. (New York: Putnam, 1990), 153.
62. John Rosecrance, "The Probation Officers' Search for Credibility: Ball Park Recommendations," *Crime and Delinquency* 31 (1985): 539–54; Patrick D. McAnany, "Sentencing: Presentence Report," *Encyclopedia of Crime and Justice* 4: 1472–75.
63. Rosecrance, "Probation Officers' Search"; John Rosecrance, "Maintaining the Myth of Individualized Justice: Probation and Presentence Reports," *Justice Quarterly* 5 (1988): 236–56.
64. David R. Karp, "The Judicial and Judicious Use of Shame Penalties," *Crime and Delinquency* 44 (1998): 281.
65. Vincent O'Leary, "Criminal Sentencing: Trends Tribulations," *Criminal Law Bulletin* 20: 417–29; Barbara Boland et al., *Prosecution of Felony Arrests, 1980* (Washington, D.C.: BJS, 1985), 28–29; Stephen J. Schulhofer, "Assessing the Federal Sentencing Process: The Problem Is Uniformity, Not Disparity," *The American Criminal Law Review* 29 (1992): 835–36.
66. Thorsten Sellin, "Race Prejudice in the Administration of Justice," *American Journal of Sociology* 41 (1935): 212–17.
67. Stuart S. Nagel and Lenore J. Weitzman, "Women as Litigants," *Hastings Law Journal* 23 (1971): 171–98; "Alabama Law Review Summer Project 1975: A Study of Differential Treatment Accorded Female Defendants in Alabama Criminal Courts," *Alabama Law Review* 27 (1975): 676–746; Candace C. Kruttschnitt, "Sex and Criminal Court Dispositions: The Unresolved Controversy," *Journal of Research in Crime and Delinquency* 21 (1984): 213–32; Kathleen Daly, "Neither Conflict nor Labeling nor Paternalism Will Suffice: Intersections of Race, Ethnicity, Gender, and Family in Criminal Court Decisions," *Crime and Delinquency* 35 (1989): 136–68; Joan Petersilia, "Racial Disparities in the Criminal Justice System: A Summary," *Crime and Delinquency* 31 (1985): 15–35.
68. Martha A. Myers and Susette M. Talarico, *The Social Contexts of Criminal Sentencing* (New York: Springer-Verlag, 1987), 80–81.
69. Ibid., 170–71.
70. Blumstein et al., *Research on Sentencing.*
71. Joan Petersilia, "Racial Disparities," 21. For a general summary of the conflicting conclusions about race and sentencing, see Daniel Nagin and Luke-Jon Tierney, "Discrimination in the Criminal Justice System," in *Research on Sentencing,* Blumstein et al., eds.
72. Cassia Spohn et al., "The Effect of Race on Sentencing: A Re-Examination of an Unsettled Question," *Law and Society Review* 16 (1981–82): 86.
73. John H. Lindquist et al., "Judicial Processing of Males and Females Charged with Prostitution," *Journal of Criminal Justice* 17 (1989): 277–91.
74. Quoted in Gary D. LaFree, "Official Reactions to Hispanic Defendants in the Southwest," *Journal of Research in Crime and Delinquency* 22 (1985): 228.
75. Quotes are from LaFree, "Official Reactions," 229.
76. Ibid.
77. Marvin E. Frankel, *Criminal Sentences: Law Without Order* (New York: Hill and Wang, 1973), 5, 7.
78. *Thompson v. Oklahoma,* 487 U.S. 815 (1988); Penry v. Lynaugh, U.S. (109 S.Ct 2934)(1989).
79. BJS, *Capital Punishment* 1996 (Washington, D.C.: BJS, December 1997).
80. "Prisoner Is Executed After Supreme Court Won't Hold Hearing," *New York Times,* 28 January 1993; *USA Today,* 24 January 1996.
81. BJS, *Capital Punishment 1996* (Washington, DC: BJS, December 1997, Table 11).
82. Brian K. Payne and Victoria Coogle, "Examining Attitudes About the Death Penalty," *Corrections Compendium,* April 1998, 1.
83. "High Cost of Death Row," *Houston Chronicle,* 9 March 1992.
84. Quoted in "High Cost of Death Row."
85. Ibid.
86. Amnesty International, *Proposal for a Presidential Commission on the Death Penalty in the United States of America* (London: Amnesty International Publications, 1980); Van den Haag quoted in Bedau, *Death Penalty in America,* 331.
87. Thorstin Sellin, *The Penalty of Death* (Beverly Hills, Calif.: Sage Publications, 1980).
88. Isaac Ehrlich, "The Deterrent Effect of Capital Punishment: A Question of Life and Death," *American Economic Review* 65 (1976): 397–417; Steven K. Layson, "Homicide and Deterrence: A Reexamination of the United States Time-Series Evidence," *Southern Economics Journal* 52 (1985): 68.
89. Bedau, *Death Penalty in America,* 95.
90. Brian Forst, "The Deterrent Effect of Capital Punishment: A Cross-State Analysis of the 1960s," reported in Bedau, *Death Penalty in America,* 131–32; Stephen J. Markman and Paul G. Cassell, "Protecting the Innocent: A Response to the Bedau-Radelet Study," *Stanford Law Review* 41 (1988): 121, 155; Hugo Adam Bedau and Michael L. Radelet, "The Myth of Infallibility: A Reply to Markman and Cassell," *Stanford Law Review* 41 (1988): 161, 168; Hans Zeisel, "The Deterrent Effect of the Death Penalty: Facts Versus Faith," in Bedau, *Death Penalty in America,* 132–33.
91. William J. Bowers and Glenn L. Pierce, "Deterrence or Brutalization: What Is the Effect of Executions?" *Crime and Delinquency* 26 (1980): 453; William C. Bailey, "Murder, Capital Punishment, and Television," *American Sociological Review* 55 (1990): 628–33.
92. William C. Bailey, "Deterrence, Brutalization, and the Death Penalty: Another Examination of Oklahoma's Return to Capital Punishment," *Criminology* 36 (1998): 711–33.

93. Quoted in ibid., 712.
94. Ibid., 731–732.
95. William Weld and Paul Cassell, *Report to the Deputy Attorney General on Capital Punishment and the Sentencing Commission* 28 (February 13, 1987).
96. *New York Times,* 20 September 1975.
97. Peter W. Lewis, "Killing the Killers: A Post-Furman Profile of Florida's Condemned," *Crime and Delinquency* 25 (1979): 203–204; Charles L. Black, Jr., *Capital Punishment: The Inevitability of Caprice and Mistake,* 2d ed. (New York: W. W. Norton, 1981), 94.
98. Adalberto Aguirre, Jr., and David V. Baker, "Empirical Research on Racial Discrimination in the Imposition of the Death Penalty," *Criminal Justice Abstracts* 22 (1990): 147–48.

CHAPTER 13

Community Corrections

CHAPTER OUTLINE

Was This an Appropriate Punishment?

Roy Letterlough was convicted of felony DWI and was placed on probation for five years. One of the conditions of Letterlough's probation was that he attach a florescent sign reading "CONVICTED DWI" to the license plates of any vehicle he drove. Letterlough appealed, claiming that the florescent sign requirement violated his constitutional rights.

INTRODUCTION

Once convicted criminals are sentenced, they move to the next agency in the criminal justice system—corrections. The term **corrections** derives from the idea that the state can "reform" or "correct" criminals. The principal mission of corrections agencies is to supervise convicted criminals while they are in state custody. This takes place in three settings:

1. The community.
2. Jails and prisons.
3. A combination of incarceration and community supervision.

Incarceration—particularly in prisons—receives the lion's share of both public and research attention. However, most people convicted of crimes in the United States are not in prison. More than 3.9 million adult men and women were on probation at the end of 1997 (see Figure 13.1). In addition to straight probation, a relatively small number offenders are given intermediate punishments, such as paying fines, performing community service, undergoing intensive probation, attending correctional boot camps, and wearing electronic monitors. This chapter examines straight probation and intermediate punishments. The following chapters take up incarceration and parole.[1]

Probation is often confused with parole, which in some ways it resembles. Both are forms of community supervision with somewhat similar aims and operations. The principal difference is that probation *replaces* incarceration. **Parole,** on the other hand, *follows* incarceration. Also,

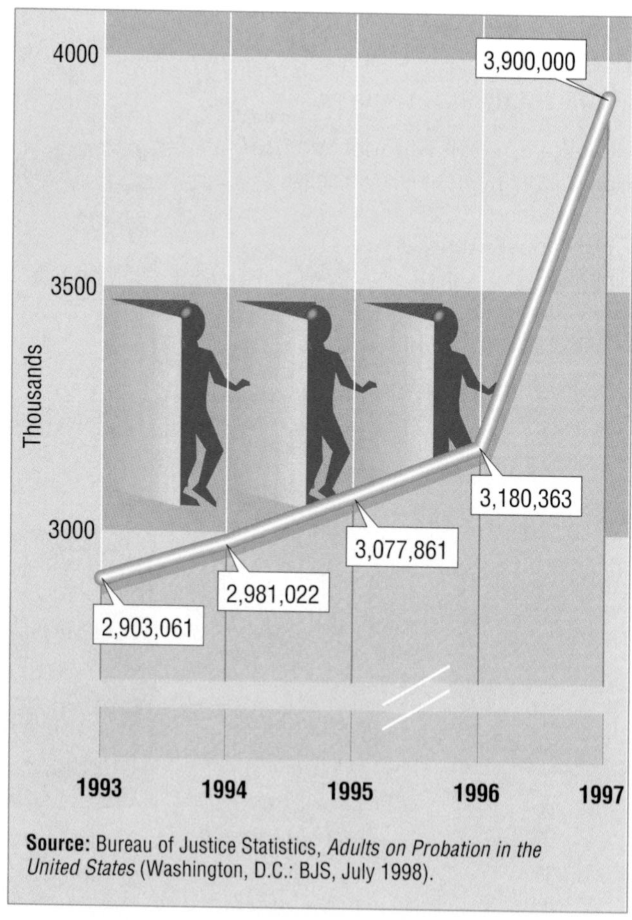

Figure 13.1
Number of Probationers, 1993–1997

counties usually administer probation, whereas states are responsible for the administration of parole. Intermediate punishments "exist somewhere between incarceration and ordinary probation." Typically, intermediate punishments replace both incarceration and probation, with offenders remaining in the community under stricter supervision than ordinary probationers.

Modern intermediate punishments resulted from a combination of developments during the 1980s:

- Rapidly expanding prison populations.
- Shrinking government budgets.
- Shifting penal policies from rehabilitation to retribution and incapacitation.
- Yearning for a middle ground between the "either or choices" of incarceration and probation.

Intermediate punishments quickly became the latest corrections panacea. However, a growing body of empirical research points to the need for further experimentation and evaluation before pronouncing intermediate sanctions a success.[2]

Community corrections pursue at least eight missions:

1. Punishment of offenders.
2. Protection of the community.
3. Reduction of crime.
4. Saving money.
5. Prevention of prison crowding.
6. Rehabilitation of offenders.
7. Reintegration of offenders into the community.
8. Providing humane treatment of offenders.

There is controversy over both the priority and the effectiveness of the missions.

PROBATION

The basic idea of probation is to substitute community supervision for incarceration. Community supervision is an ancient practice. Justices of the peace in sixteenth-century England commonly released minor offenders from custody if the offenders promised to "be of good behavior" and if they provided "sureties"—that is, friends or family—to both enforce their promise and secure their appearance in court. If they broke their promise or did not appear in court at the scheduled time, they were put in jail. The "good behavior bond" continued as a common practice in colonial America and in the new United States.

Also, until about 1800 in England, first-time property offenders could gain community supervision by pleading "benefit of clergy." A successful plea of benefit of clergy meant that the offender could recite the 51st Psalm that began with the words "Have mercy on me . . ." The plea of clergy was an instrument of leniency at a time when all felonies were punishable by death.[3]

In the mid-1800s, a Boston shoemaker, John Augustus, earned the title of "first probation officer" in the United States by expanding on this old Elizabethan idea. In 1841, Augustus visited the Boston police court, where "a ragged and wretched looking man" charged with being a "common drunkard" begged Augustus to save him from the House of Correction. In return, the man promised Augustus, he would never drink again. Deeply moved by the episode, Augustus asked the magistrate to release the man into his custody for 30 days. During that time, Augustus fed the man and found him a job. The man stopped drinking and supported himself after that.[4]

Encouraged by his success, Augustus abandoned shoemaking and devoted the remainder of his life to "saving" Boston criminals. Over the years, magistrates released two thousand people into his custody, mainly drunks, prostitutes, juveniles, and gamblers. Augustus worked with them as he did with the first man, taking them into his home, finding them work, and encouraging them to lead "pure" lives. He claimed enormous success in reforming them, a success probably due to his devotion and to his selectivity. He gave all his energy to his newfound career. Equally important, he agreed to work only with "good risks," usually first-time, minor offenders who showed promise of success.[5]

Early in the twentieth century, probation became immensely popular. In the great Progressive reform wave of that time, probation became an integral part of American corrections. It was a favorite of reformers, and courts increasingly used it as an alternative to incarceration. By 1930, the federal government and 36 states had enacted probation legislation. By 1940, all but the most rural areas in the country had embraced probation.[6]

The Missions of Probation

Up to the end of World War II, judges granted probation only to first-time, minor offenders as an act of leniency. After the war, authorities began to doubt that incarceration was "correcting" offenders. As a result, judges began to grant probation to repeat and violent offenders as a way to reform them. Judges attached special conditions to probation to enhance the chances of rehabilitation.

However, beginning in the 1970s, there arose a growing backlash against probation. The demands for more punishments and greater public safety generated an intolerance toward "felons on the streets." These demands ran counter to another public concern over a rapidly growing prison population at great public expense. According to Todd R. Clear and Anthony A. Braga:

> Since the mid-1980s, disquiet about offenders under community supervision has maintained a collision course with an equivalent dismay over burgeoning prison populations. On the one hand, it has bothered policy makers that so many offenders, some of whom

stand convicted of serious crimes, receive so little in the way of official control over traditional probation and parole methods. Yet the alternative, ever-expanding prison capacity, seems equally unpalatable in times of strained tax revenues.[7]

In spite of worries about probation and the availability of intermediate punishments, probation is still the punishment of choice. According to Joan Petersilia and her colleagues:

> When the prison population began to overwhelm existing facilities, probation and "split sentences" (a jail sentence followed by a term on probation) became the de facto disposition of all misdemeanors. As prison overcrowding becomes a national crisis, the courts are being forced to use probation even more frequently. Many felons without criminal records are now sentenced to probation.[8]

The conflicting goals of rehabilitation and leniency, punishment and controlling prison populations, sometimes have led to vaguely defined and frequently conflicting missions. Edward J. Cosgrove, a federal probation officer, has nicely explained these missions:

> When Gannon and Friday were the role models for police officers, probation officers were an extension of the law. We kept "order" by seeing that people just did the right things. In the '70s, rehabilitation was the goal of supervision. The medical model taught us to diagnose a problem and then provide treatment. Help meant counseling; understanding the hardships of poverty, illiteracy, and broken homes; rendering the necessary support to address these symptoms; and coping with the bad feelings and making changes.
>
> As client needs seemed ever expanding, the '80s brought us the philosophy of reintegration. Probation officers could not expect to service all needs; so, the answer became brokering services: identify the problem and make the appropriate referral. By the end of the '80s, the pendulum had swung from primary care to clients to listening to the needs of the community. Mercy was not to be forgotten, but disparity must be eliminated. Guidelines achieved this with a focus on retributive justice, with scant attention focused to rehabilitation of the individual. The offender will be held accountable. Society will be protected. The Probation Service responded with the development of Enhanced Supervision. The goals were ranked: enforce court orders, provide risk control, address the correctional treatment needs of the offender.
>
> What does a probation officer do? To this day, I suffer a violent visceral pain whenever I hear some visiting academic discuss the "two hats" of the probation officer: cop or counselor. At last count, we wear at least 33 hats and the number is growing.[9]

The tensions between control and service, the interests of society and the needs and rights of probationers, and punishment and rehabilitation have led social scientists to identify a number of probation officer roles:

- Law enforcement officer.
- Social worker.
- Bureaucrat.
- Social service broker.
- Bill collector.

The law enforcement role is played by **punitive probation officers** who consider themselves "guardians of middle-class morality." The punitive officer, according to Patrick D. McAnany and his colleagues,

> attempts to coerce the offender into conforming by means of threats and punishment, and emphasizes control, the protection of the community against the offender and the systematic suspicion of those under supervision.[10]

The social worker role is played by **welfare probation officers.** According to McAnany and his associates, the welfare officer's ultimate goal is

> the improved welfare of the client, achieved by aiding him in his individual adjustment within limits imposed by the client's capacity. Such an officer believes that the only genuine guarantee of community protection lies in the client's personal adjustment since external conformity will only be temporary, and in the long run, may make a social adjustment more difficult. Emotional neutrality permeates his relationships. The diagnostic categories and treatment skills which he employs stem from an objective and theoretically based assessment of the client's needs and capacities.[11]

Protective probation officers combine the law enforcement and social worker roles by trying to balance the interests of clients and society. According to McAnany and his colleagues, protective officers

> vacillate literally between protecting the offender and protecting the community. His tools are direct assistance, lecturing, and alternately, praise and blame. He is perceived as ambivalent in his emotional involvement with the offender and others in the community as he shifts back and forth in taking sides with one against the other.[12]

Bureaucratic probation officers take their cues from the bureaucratic emphasis on efficiency, economy, and orderly procedure. They try to minimize interruption or interference from either clients or outsiders. **Time-server probation officers** try to reduce the "hassle" from both clients and supervisors; collect their salary; and take advantage of their fringe benefits. Time-servers "don't make the rules; they just work here."[13]

Social service brokers mark a shift in the mission of probation that arose during the late 1960s, when reintegrating offenders into the community became a popular probation

Despite the shift in focus in the '90s toward a stronger law enforcement role for probation officers, many still fill the social worker role as well, helping their probationers to find the skills and counseling they need to be able to hopefully function in society without returning to a pattern of crime.

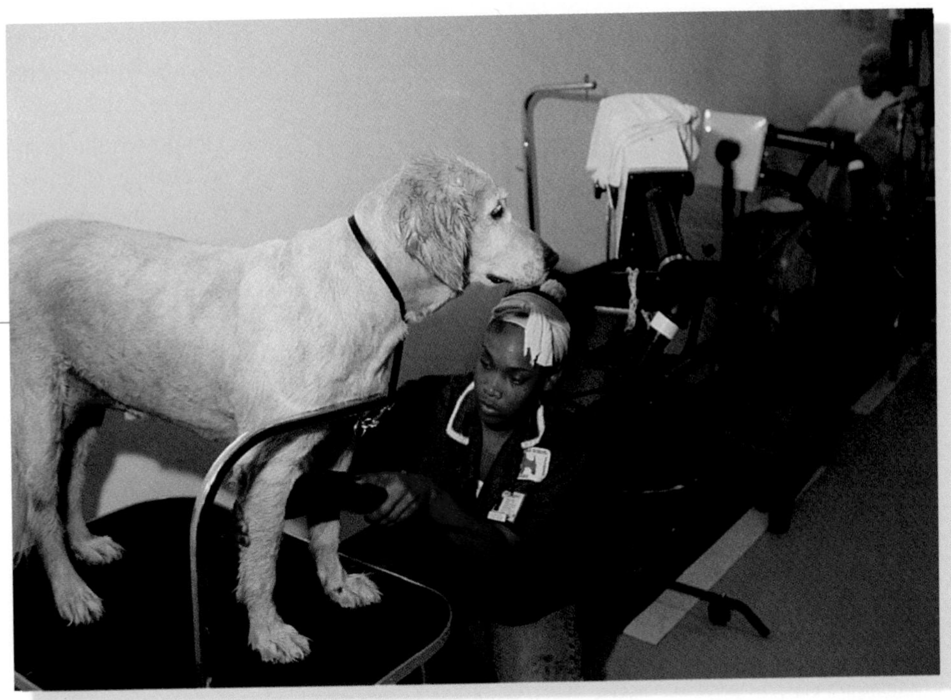

policy goal. The mission of reintegration came about because of a shift in beliefs about the origins of crime from a focus on individual pathology to social problems like poverty, racism, unemployment, and lack of opportunity. Social service brokers focused less on providing direct psychological counseling and more on putting clients in touch with community social service agencies that could help them become law-abiding, productive members of their communities.[14]

In the 1990s, yet another mission for probation arose—seeing to it that probationers pay at least part of the cost for the "privilege of being on probation." This mission is based on the idea that probation is not a right, but a "break" for offenders, and so, they ought to pay for it. The **probation bill collector** has to collect these fees. Unfortunately, it is a lot easier to charge the fees than to collect them. Only about 40 percent of the fees are in fact collected. Furthermore, according to critics, probation officers pay more attention to collecting fees than they do to their clients. Nevertheless, probation fees bring in millions of dollars every year to support probation services.[15]

The multiple missions of probation and multiple roles for probation officers are all still present to some extent. However, as rehabilitation and the rights of offenders receded in the 1980s, retribution, public safety, and economy have become the dominant missions of probation. Hence, the law enforcement role for probation officers has overtaken the social worker and social service broker role.[16]

The Nature and Types of Probation

Formally, probation is a criminal sentence. Probationers are in the custody of the state—legally accountable to the state, and subject to conditions that limit their freedom and privacy. The sentencing court retains the authority to change the conditions of probation and to revoke probation if probationers violate conditions. Informally, probation consists of a combination of discretionary decision making to achieve the goals of leniency, treatment, reintegration, punishment, public safety, bill collection, control of prison populations, and saving of tax dollars.

Probation is often confused with the suspended sentence. Unlike probation, suspended sentences do not impose conditions and do not require supervision. Judges can suspend sentences in two ways: (1) they can sentence offenders to jail or prison and then suspend only the execution of the sentence; or, (2) they can withhold both the imposition and the execution of the sentence. In both cases, offenders remain free, but they have incarceration "hanging over their heads." At any time, judges can revoke the suspension and impose and execute the sentence by sending them to jail or prison.[17]

The sentence of probation is carried out mainly in the community, not in prisons or jails. However, probation sometimes combines supervision in the community with incarceration. In **split-sentence probation,** judges sentence offenders to a some time in jail or prison, followed by some time on probation. In **shock incarceration**—like correctional "boot camps"—judges sentence offenders to incarceration. Then, following a period of confinement, offenders can petition the court for probation. Shock incarceration gives offenders a "taste" of imprisonment to "shock" them into staying out of trouble. Probation tests whether confinement has sufficiently "shocked" offenders into becoming people who work and play by the rules. In **intermittent incarceration,** probationers work, go to school, perform community service, and sometimes receive drug or other

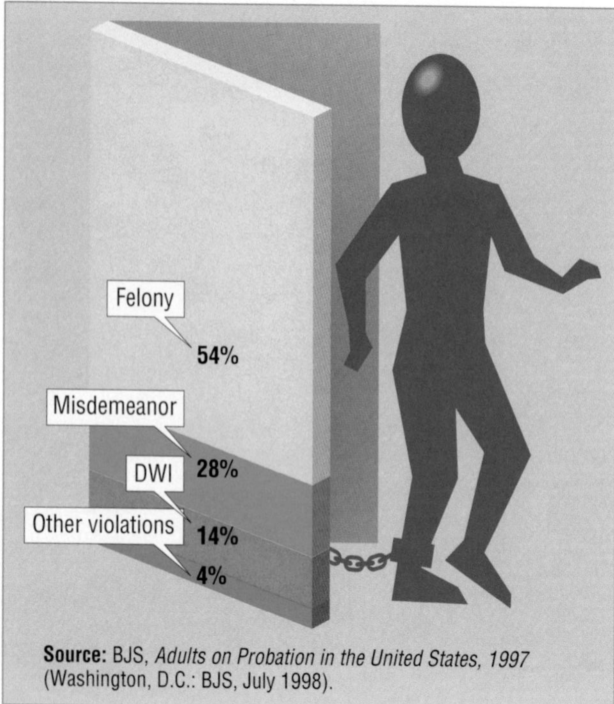

Source: BJS, *Adults on Probation in the United States, 1997* (Washington, D.C.: BJS, July 1998).

Figure 13.2
Percent of Probationers by Type of Offense

treatment during the day. They spend their nights and weekends in jails, workhouses, and, occasionally, in halfway houses.

Felony Probation

Most minor offenders receive probation because they are not considered a high risk to public safety. But minor offenders make up only about half of the offenders on probation (Figure 13.2). The other half consists of felons who have committed violent and serious property offenses. Probation was not intended for nor is it set up to deal with repeat felony offenders. According to Joan Petersilia and her colleagues who examined felony probation in California:[18]

> [C]an probation accommodate more serious offenders, supervise them appropriately, and prevent them from threatening public safety? The most vital and fundamental question is whether traditional probation—based principally on the treatment/service role—should even be considered a legitimate sentencing alternative for convicted felons.[19]

The Conditions of Probation

The typical conditions of probation require probationers to:

- Obey the law.
- Possess no weapons or explosives.
- Work, go to school, or get vocational training.
- Pay child support.
- Obtain written permission from the probation officer to change residence.
- Obtain written permission from the probation officer for all changes of employment.
- Notify the probation officer of any arrests or criminal investigations.
- Refrain from traveling outside the community without written permission.
- Refrain from using or selling illegal drugs.[20]

Felony probationers usually have to fulfill special conditions in addition to the typical conditions. These special conditions include at least one of the following:

- Drug testing.
- Drug treatment.
- Alcohol treatment.
- Community service work.
- Mental health counseling.
- Residence in a community facility.
- Daytime reporting.
- House arrest.
- Paying probation fees to help pay the cost of probation.[21]

Figure 13.3 depicts the conditions of probation used by the U.S. District Courts for federal probationers.

The Revocation of Probation

Probation ends either when probationers successfully complete the terms of their probation or when a court revokes (cancels) their probation. **Revocation** results when probationers violate the terms of their probation. Revocation can result when probationers are either arrested for or convicted of a new crime (**recidivism**), or when they break probation rules that are not crimes (**technical probation violations**), such as failing to notify their probation officer of a change of address.

About half of all probationers commit technical violations. However, only about 20 percent of technical violations result in the revocation of probation. This has led to criticism of the gap between violations and actual revocation. According to Todd R. Clear and Anthony A. Braga, critics portray an image of wanton disregard for program rules followed by little or no sanction from program managers. The result, it is sometimes argued, is a continuing breach of community safety.[22]

Clear and Braga conclude that despite the surface appeal of the critics' argument, the link between technical violations and public safety is not that simple. First, the number of rules is growing and the surveillance capacity to enforce the rules is increasing, particularly by means of urine testing for drugs. Second, technical violations may point to a lack of discipline, but lack of discipline does not necessarily translate into threats to public safety; the failure of probationers to

PROB 7A
(Rev. 6/90)©

Conditions of Probation and Supervised Release

UNITED STATES DISTRICT COURT
FOR THE
____

Name ______________________ Docket No. ______________________
Address ______________________

Under the terms of your sentence, you have been placed on probation/supervised release (strike one) by the Honorable ______________________, United States District Judge for the District of ______________________. Your term of supervision is for a period of ______________________, commencing ______________________.

While on probation/supervised release (strike one), you shall not commit another Federal, state, or local crime and shall not illegally possess a controlled substance. Revocation of probation and supervised release is mandatory for possession of a controlled substance.

CHECK IF APPROPRIATE:

☐ As a condition of supervision, you are instructed to pay a fine in the amount of ____________; it shall be paid in the following manner ______________________.

☐ As a condition of supervision, you are instructed to pay restitution in the amount of ______________________ to ______________________; it shall be paid in the following manner ______________________.

☐ The defendant shall not possess a firearm or destructive device. Probation must be revoked for possession of a firearm.

☐ The defendant shall report in person to the probation office in the district to which the defendant is released within 72 hours of release from the custody of the Bureau of Prisons.

It is the order of the Court that you shall comply with the following standard conditions:

(1) You shall not leave the judicial district without permission of the court or probation officer;

(2) You shall report to the probation officer as directed by the court or probation officer, and shall submit a truthful and complete written report within the first five days of each month;

(3) You shall answer truthfully all inquiries by the probation officer and follow the instructions of the probation officer;

(4) You shall support your dependents and meet other family responsibilities;

(5) You shall work regularly at a lawful occupation unless excused by the probation officer for schooling, training, or other acceptable reasons:

(6) You shall notify the probation officer within seventy-two hours of any change in residence or employment;

(7) You shall refrain from excessive use of alcohol and shall not purchase, possess, use, distribute, or administer any narcotic or other controlled substance, or any paraphernalia related to such substances, except as prescribed by a physician;

(8) You shall not frequent places where controlled substances are illegally sold, used, distributed, or administered;

(9) You shall not associate with any persons engaged in criminal activity, and shall not associate with any person convicted of a felony unless granted permission to do so by the probation officer;

(10) You shall permit a probation officer to visit you at any time at home or elsewhere, and shall permit confiscation of any contraband observed in plain view by the probation officer;

(11) You shall notify the probation officer within seventy-two hours of being arrested or questioned by a law enforcement officer;

(12) You shall not enter into any agreement to act as an informer or a special agent of a law enforcement agency without the permission of the court;

(13) As directed by the probation officer, you shall notify third parties of risks that may be occasioned by your criminal record or personal history or characteristics, and shall permit the probation officer to make such notifications and to confirm your compliance with such notification requirement.

The special conditions ordered by the court are as follows:

Upon a finding of a violation of probation or supervised release, I understand that the Court may (1) revoke supervision or (2) extend the term of supervision and/or modify the conditions of supervision.

These conditions have been read to me. I fully understand the conditions, and have been provided a copy of them.

(Signed) ______________________ ______________________
Defendant Date

______________________ ______________________
U.S. Probation Officer/Designated Witness Date

Figure 13.3
Conditions of Probation

report an address change does not mean they are going to commit crimes.[23]

Probation and the Law

Probationers are convicted offenders. Because they have committed crimes, they have fewer rights than people who are not in state custody. According to the U.S. Supreme Court, probationers "do not enjoy the absolute liberty to which every citizen is entitled, but only . . . conditional liberty properly dependent on observance of special restrictions." These restrictions are legal as long as they ensure that "probation serves as a period of genuine rehabilitation and that the community is not harmed by the probationer's being at large." So, according to the Court, "supervision is a 'special need' of the State permitting a degree of impingement upon privacy that would not be constitutional if applied to the public at large."[24]

Probationers may have fewer rights than people who are not in state custody, but they are not totally devoid of rights. For instance, the U.S. Supreme Court ruled in *Morrissey v. Brewer* and *Gagnon v. Scarpelli* that probationers are entitled to due process of law in the revocation of their probation. The due process clause provides that the state cannot take away persons' "life, liberty, or property" without "due process of law." According to the Court, "Revocation deprives an individual, not of absolute liberty to which every citizen is entitled, but only of the conditional liberty properly dependent on observance of special . . . [probation] conditions." Probationers are entitled to the protection of the due process clause; however, because the liberty is conditional, they are not entitled to the same process to which fully free people are entitled.[25]

The lesser "process" that is "due" to probationers before the state can deprive them of their conditional liberty demands "some orderly process, however informal." That orderly process must provide "an effective but informal hearing" to ensure that "the finding of a . . . violation will be based on verified facts and that the exercise of discretion will be informed by an accurate knowledge of the . . . [probationer's] behavior." The hearing involves two stages: a preliminary hearing and a revocation hearing.

The Preliminary Hearing

According to the U.S. Supreme Court, due process requires a **preliminary hearing.** This hearing determines whether there is probable cause to proceed to an actual revocation hearing. The preliminary hearing is a

> minimal inquiry . . . at or reasonably near the place of the alleged . . . violation or arrest and as promptly as is convenient after arrest while information is fresh and sources are available. Such an inquiry should be seen as in the nature of a "preliminary hearing" to determine whether there is probable cause or reasonable ground to believe that the arrested person has committed acts that would constitute a violation of . . . [probation] conditions.[26]

"Disinterested persons" means that judges are supposed to determine whether reasonable grounds exist to believe probationers have violated their probation and that probable cause exists to arrest them. Judges do not personally have to determine probable cause. They can rely on the judgment of disinterested probation officers (officers who did not report the actual violations).[27]

Probationers have the right to receive notice that there will be a hearing, of the date it will take place, and that its purpose is to determine whether reasonable grounds exist to believe that they have violated the conditions of their probation. The notice lists the specific alleged violations. Probationers can attend the hearing, tell their side of the story, and bring "letters, documents, or individuals" who can provide relevant information. Probationers can question individuals who have provided information upon which the alleged violations are based. If the hearing officer determines that "an informant would be subjected to risk of harm if his identity is disclosed, he need not be subjected to confrontation and cross-examination."[28]

The Revocation Hearing

The U.S. Supreme Court has ruled that probationers have a right to a second hearing. This **revocation hearing** performs two functions:

1. It decides contested facts.
2. It decides whether revoking probation is justified.

In the revocation, according to the Court, the probationer

> must have an opportunity to be heard and to show, if he can, that he did not violate the conditions, or, if he did, that circumstances in mitigation suggest that the violation does not warrant revocation. The revocation hearing must be tendered within a reasonable time after the . . . [probationer] is taken into custody.
>
> We cannot write a code of procedure; that is the responsibility of each State. . . . Our task is limited to deciding the minimum requirements of due process. They include (a) written notice of the claimed violations . . . ; (b) disclosure . . . of the evidence against him; (c) opportunity to be heard in person and to present witnesses and documentary evidence; (d) the right to confront and cross-examine adverse witnesses (unless the hearing officer specifically finds good cause for not allowing confrontation); (e) a 'neutral and detached' hearing body . . . members of which need not be judicial officers or lawyers; and (f) a written statement by the factfinders as to the evidence relied on and reasons for revoking . . . [probation].[29]

The Supreme Court has placed further limits on the constitutional rights of probationers. In *Minnesota v. Murphy*, the Court ruled that probation officers do not need to give probationers the *Miranda* warnings when they question them about crimes they may have committed while on probation. The Use Your Discretion case "Are probationers' homes their 'castles'?" deals with the Court's definition of the rights of probationers against "unreasonable searches and seizures."

Use *Your* Discretion

Are probationers' homes their "castles"?
***Griffin v. Wisconsin,* 483 U.S. 868, 107 S.Ct. 3164, 107 S.Ct. 3164**
97 L.Ed.2d 709, 55 USLW 5156 (1987)

Facts

On September 4, 1980, Griffin, who had previously been convicted of a felony, was convicted in Wisconsin state court of resisting arrest, disorderly conduct, and obstructing an officer. He was placed on probation. Wisconsin law puts probationers in the legal custody of the State Department of Health and Social Services and renders them "subject . . . to . . . conditions set by the court and rules and regulations established by the department."

One of the department's regulations permits any probation officer to search a probationer's home without a warrant as long as his supervisor approves and as long as there are "reasonable grounds" to believe the presence of contraband—including any item that the probationer cannot possess under the probation conditions. The rule provides that an officer should consider a variety of factors in determining whether "reasonable grounds" exist, among which are information provided by an informant, the reliability and specificity of that information, the reliability of the informant (including whether the informant has any incentive to supply inaccurate information), the officer's own experience with the probationer, and the "need to verify compliance with rules of supervision and state and federal law."

Another regulation makes it a violation of the terms of probation to refuse to consent to a home search. Still another forbids a probationer to possess a firearm without advance approval from a probation officer.

On April 5, 1983, while Griffin was still on probation, Michael Lew, the supervisor of Griffin's probation officer, received information from a detective on the Beloit Police Department that there were or might be guns in Griffin's apartment. Unable to secure the assistance of Griffin's own probation officer, Lew, accompanied by another probation officer and three plainclothes police officers, went to the apartment. When Griffin answered the door, Lew told him who they were and informed him that they were going to search his home. During the subsequent search—carried out entirely by the probation officers under the authority of Wisconsin's probation regulation—they found a handgun.

Griffin was charged with possession of a firearm by a convicted felon, which is itself a felony. He moved to suppress the evidence seized during the search. The trial court denied the motion, concluding that no warrant was necessary and that the search was reasonable. A jury convicted Griffin of the firearms violation, and he was sentenced to two years' imprisonment. The conviction was affirmed by the Wisconsin Court of Appeals, 126 Wis.2d 183, 376 N.W.2d 62 (1985). On further appeal, the Wisconsin Supreme Court also affirmed. . . . 131 Wis.2d 41, 52—64, 388 N.W.2d 535, 539–544 (1986).

Opinion

We think the Wisconsin Supreme Court correctly concluded that this warrantless search did not violate the Fourth Amendment. . . . As his sentence for the commission of a crime, Griffin was committed to the legal custody of the Wisconsin State Department of Health and Social Services, and thereby made subject to that Department's rules and regulations. The search of Griffin's home satisfied the demands of the Fourth Amendment because it was carried out pursuant to a regulation that itself satisfies the Fourth Amendment's reasonableness requirement under well-established principles.

A probationer's home, like anyone else's, is protected by the Fourth Amendment's requirement that searches be "reasonable." Although we usually require that a search be undertaken only pursuant to a warrant (and thus supported by probable cause, as the Constitution says warrants must be), we have permitted exceptions when "special needs, beyond the normal need for law enforcement, make the warrant and probable-cause requirement impracticable." Thus, we have held that government employers and supervisors may conduct warrantless, work-related searches of employees' desks and offices without probable cause, and that school officials may conduct warrantless searches of some student property, also without probable cause. We have also held, for similar reasons, that in certain circumstances government investigators conducting searches pursuant to a regulatory scheme need not adhere to the usual warrant or probable-cause requirements as long as their searches meet "reasonable legislative or administrative standards."

A State's operation of a probation system, like its operation of a school, government office, or prison, or its supervision of a regulated industry, likewise presents "special needs" beyond normal law enforcement that may justify departures from the usual warrant and probable-cause requirements. Probation, like incarceration, is "a form of criminal sanction imposed by a court upon an offender after verdict, finding, or plea of guilty." Probation is simply one point (or, more accurately, one set of points) on a continuum of possible punishments ranging from solitary confinement in a maximum-security facility to a few hours of mandatory community service. A number of different options lie between those extremes, including confinement in a medium- or minimum-security facility, work-release programs, "halfway houses," and probation—which can itself be more or less confining depending upon the number and severity of restrictions imposed. . . . To a greater or lesser degree, it is always true of probationers (as we have said it to be true of parolees) that they do not enjoy "the absolute liberty to which every citizen is entitled, but only . . . conditional liberty properly dependent on observance of special . . . restrictions."

These restrictions are meant to assure that the probation serves as a period of genuine rehabilitation and that the community is not harmed by the probationer's being at large. These same goals require and justify the exercise of supervision to assure that the restrictions are in fact observed. Recent research suggests that more intensive supervision can reduce recidivism [see Petersilia, "Probation and Felony Offenders," 49 Fed. Probation 9 (June 1985)] and the importance of supervision has grown as probation has become an increasingly common sentence for those convicted of serious crimes. Supervision, then, is a "special need" of the State permitting a degree of impingement upon privacy that would not be constitutional if applied to the public at large. That permissible degree is not unlimited, however, so we next turn to whether it has been exceeded here.

In determining whether the "special needs" of its probation system justify Wisconsin's search regulation, we must take that regulation as it has been interpreted by state corrections officials and state courts. As already noted, the Wisconsin Supreme Court—the ultimate authority on issues of Wisconsin law—has held that a tip from a police detective that Griffin "had" or "may have had" an illegal weapon at his home constituted the requisite "reasonable grounds." Whether or not we would choose to interpret a similarly worded federal regulation in that fashion, we are bound by the state court's interpretation, which is relevant to our constitutional analysis only insofar as it fixes the meaning of the regulation. We think it clear that the special needs of Wisconsin's probation system make the warrant requirement impracticable and justify replacement of the standard of probable cause by "reasonable grounds," as defined by the Wisconsin Supreme Court.

A warrant requirement would interfere to an appreciable degree with the probation system, setting up a magistrate rather than the probation officer as the judge of how close a supervision the probationer requires. Moreover, the delay inherent in obtaining a warrant would make it more difficult for probation officials to respond quickly to evidence of misconduct—see *New Jersey v. T.L.O.,* 469 U.S., at 340, 105 S.Ct., at 743—and would reduce the deterrent effect that the possibility of expeditious searches would otherwise create. By way of analogy, one might contemplate how parental custodial authority would be impaired by requiring judicial approval for search of a minor child's room. And on the other side of the equation—the effect of dispensing with a warrant upon the probationer: Although a probation officer is not an impartial magistrate, neither is he the police officer who normally conducts searches against the ordinary citizen. He is an employee of the State Department of Health and Social Services who, while assuredly charged with protecting the public interest, is also supposed to have in mind the welfare of the probationer (who in the regulations is called a "client"). The applicable regulations require him, for example, to "[p]rovid[e] individualized counseling designed to foster growth and development of the client as necessary," and "[m]onito[r] the client's progress where services are provided by another agency and evaluat[e] the need for continuation of the services." In such a setting, we think it reasonable to dispense with the warrant requirement. . . .

We think that the probation regime would also be unduly disrupted by a requirement of probable cause. To take the facts of the present case, it is most unlikely that the unauthenticated tip of a police officer—bearing, as far as the record shows, no indication whether its basis was firsthand knowledge or, if not, whether the firsthand source was reliable, and merely stating that Griffin "had or might have" guns in his residence, not that he certainly had them—would meet the ordinary requirement of probable cause. But this is different from the ordinary case in two related respects: First, even more than the requirement of a warrant, a probable-cause requirement would reduce the deterrent effect of the supervisory arrangement. The probationer would be assured that so long as his illegal (and perhaps socially dangerous) activities were sufficiently concealed as to give rise to no more than reasonable suspicion, they would go undetected and uncorrected. The second difference is well reflected in the regulation specifying what is to be considered "[i]n deciding whether there are reasonable grounds to believe . . . a client's living quarters or property contain contraband." The factors include not only the usual elements that a police officer or magistrate would consider, such as the detail and consistency of the information suggesting the presence of contraband and the reliability and motivation to dissemble of the informant, but also "[i]nformation provided by the client which is relevant to whether the client possesses contraband," and "[t]he experience of a staff member with that client or in a similar circumstance.". . . We deal with a situation in which there is an ongoing supervisory relationship—and one that is not, or at least not entirely, adversarial—between the object of the search and the decisionmaker.

In such circumstances it is both unrealistic and destructive of the whole object of the continuing probation relationship to insist upon the same degree of demonstrable reliability of particular items of supporting data, and upon the same degree of certainty of violation, as is required in other contexts. In some cases—especially those involving drugs or illegal weapons—the probation agency must be able to act based upon a lesser degree of certainty than the Fourth Amendment would otherwise require in order to intervene before a probationer does damage to himself or society. The agency, moreover, must be able to proceed on the basis of its entire experience with the probationer, and to assess probabilities in the light of its knowledge of his life, character, and circumstances. . . .

The search of Griffin's residence was "reasonable" within the meaning of the Fourth Amendment because it was conducted pursuant to a valid regulation governing probationers. This conclusion makes it unnecessary to consider whether, as the court below held and the State urges, any search of a probationer's home by a probation officer is lawful when there are "reasonable grounds" to believe contraband is present. For the foregoing reasons, the judgment of the Wisconsin Supreme Court is Affirmed.

Dissent

Justice BLACKMUN, with whom Justice MARSHALL joins and as to Parts I-B and I-C, Justice BRENNAN joins and, as to Part I-C, Justice STEVENS joins, dissenting.

In ruling that the home of a probationer may be searched by a probation officer without a warrant, the Court today takes another step that diminishes the protection given by the Fourth Amendment to the "right of the people to be secure in their persons, houses, papers, and effects against unreasonable searches and seizures." In my view, petitioner's probationary status provides no reason to abandon the warrant requirement. The probation system's special law enforcement needs may justify a search by a probation officer on the basis of "reasonable suspicion," but even that standard was not met in this case.

The need for supervision in probation presents one of the "exceptional circumstances in which special needs, beyond the normal need for law enforcement," . . . justify an application of the Court's balancing test and an examination of the practicality of the warrant and probable-cause requirements. The Court, however, fails to recognize that this is a threshold determination of special law enforcement needs. The warrant and probable-cause requirements provide the normal standard for "reasonable" searches. "[O]nly when the practical realities of a particular situation suggest that a government official cannot obtain a warrant based upon probable cause without sacrificing the ultimate goals to which a search would contribute, does the Court turn to a 'balancing' test to formulate a standard of reasonableness for this context." The presence of special law enforcement needs justifies resort to the balancing test, but it does not preordain the necessity of recognizing exceptions to the warrant and probable-cause requirements.

My application of the balancing test leads me to conclude that special law enforcement needs justify a search by a probation agent of the home of a probationer on the basis of a reduced level of suspicion. The acknowledged need for supervision, however, does not also justify an exception to the warrant requirement, and I would retain this means of protecting a probationer's privacy. Moreover, the necessity for the neutral check provided by the warrant requirement is demonstrated by this case, in which the search was conducted on the basis of information that did not begin to approach the level of "reasonable grounds." . . .

I do not think . . . that special law enforcement needs justify a modification of the protection afforded a probationer's privacy by the warrant requirement. The search in this case was conducted in petitioner's home, the place that traditionally has been regarded as the center of a person's private life, the bastion in which one has a legitimate expectation of privacy protected by the Fourth Amendment. . . . The Court consistently has held that warrantless searches and seizures in a home violate the Fourth Amendment absent consent or exigent circumstances. . . . "It is axiomatic that the 'physical entry of the home is the chief evil against which the wording of the Fourth Amendment is directed.' " And a principal protection against unnecessary intrusions into private dwellings is the warrant requirement imposed by the Fourth Amendment on agents of the government who seek to enter the home for purposes of search or arrest. It is not surprising, therefore, that the Court has recognized, as a "basic principle of Fourth Amendment law[,]" that searches and seizures inside a home without a warrant are presumptively unreasonable. . . .

A probationer usually lives at home, and often, as in this case, with a family. He retains a legitimate privacy interest in the home that must be respected to the degree that it is not incompatible with substantial governmental needs. The Court in *New Jersey v. T.L.O.* acknowledged that the Fourth Amendment issue needs to be resolved in such a way as to "ensure that the [privacy] interests of students will be invaded no more than is necessary to achieve the legitimate end of preserving order in the schools." The privacy interests of probationers should be protected by a similar standard, and invaded no more than is necessary to satisfy probation's dual goals of protecting the public safety and encouraging the rehabilitation of the probationer. . . .

There are many probationers in this country, and they have committed crimes that range widely in seriousness. The Court has determined that all of them may be subjected to such searches in the absence of a warrant. Moreover, in authorizing these searches on the basis of a reduced level of suspicion, the Court overlooks the feeble justification for the search in this case.

I respectfully dissent.

Justice STEVENS, with whom Justice MARSHALL joins, dissenting.

Mere speculation by a police officer that a probationer "may have had" contraband in his possession is not a constitutionally sufficient basis for a warrantless, nonconsensual search of a private home. I simply do not understand how five Members of this Court can reach a contrary conclusion. Accordingly, I respectfully dissent.

CRITICAL THINKING

1. How did the Court reduce the rights of probationers when it comes to the right against "unreasonable searches" of homes?
2. What reasons does the majority of the Court give for this reduction?
3. Why do the dissenting justices disagree with the majority decision?
4. Which of the opinions—the majority or the dissent—do you agree with? Should probationers have any rights against searches by their probation officers? Defend your answer.

The Effectiveness of Probation

Half of all probationers complete probation without violating the conditions of their sentence. Success rates, however, vary, from 88 percent in New Hampshire to 37 percent in Virginia. Success is highest among young, new offenders and lowest among older, hardened offenders. Furthermore, failure increases with the length of time after release from probation. However, evidence suggests that close monitoring in the community, including surprise drug tests for addicts, reduces rearrest rates among advanced offenders. For low-risk offenders, the amount of supervision does not seem to affect failure rates.[30]

Probation is at least as effective as imprisonment in preventing future offenses. Some evidence suggests that probation might be even more effective. Joan Petersilia and others studied 511 offenders on probation and 511 offenders released from prison. The two groups matched each other closely in year they were sentenced, gender (male), county of conviction (Los Angeles or Alameda), and conviction crime (assault, robbery, burglary, theft, or drug sale/possession). The study found *associations,* but not *causal relations,* among prison, probation, and recidivism. Among the findings of the two-year study:

- Released prisoners had higher recidivism rates than probationers.
- 72 percent of the released prisoners were rearrested.
- 63 percent of probationers were rearrested.
- 53 percent of the prisoners had new charges filed against them.
- 38 percent of the probationers had new charges filed against them.
- 47 percent of the prisoners returned to prison later.
- 31 percent of the probationers were later imprisoned.
- Prisoners' new offenses were no more serious than those of probationers.

The Bureau of Justice Statistics examined the results of felony probation by conducting the largest ever national follow-up survey of adult felony probationers. The survey used official records to track the progress of a sample of probationers (in 17 states) through their first three years on probation. Within three years of sentencing:

- 62 percent of the probationers were either arrested for a new felony or charged at a hearing with a violation of the conditions of their probation.
- 43 percent were arrested for a felony within three years.
- 49 percent had a disciplinary hearing for a violation of probation.[31]

Figure 13.4 depicts the detailed progress of 100 felons based on the sample.

Use *Your* Discretion

Should felons be put on probation?

The combination of failure rates found in the BJS study and demands that we "get tough" have led to a heated policy debate about the use of probation, particularly for felons. This debate led Michael R. Geerken and Hennessey D. Hayes to examine the impact of probationer crime on the overall crime rates. They analyzed data on arrest, incarceration, and probation supervision for burglary and armed robbery in New Orleans. To determine probationers' impact on these data, Geerken and Hayes "examined the percent-

Figure 13.4
Recidivism of Felons on Probation

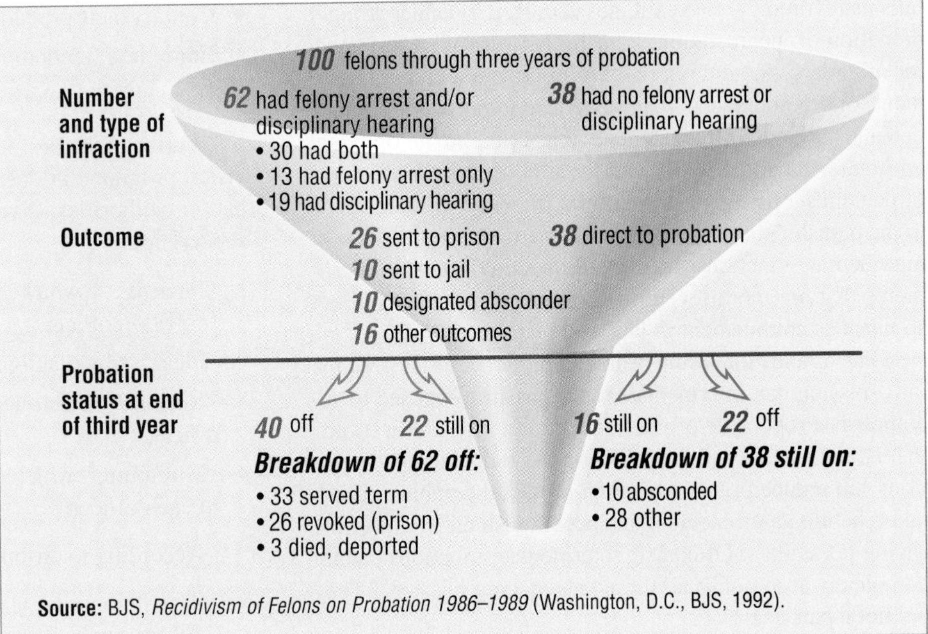

Source: BJS, *Recidivism of Felons on Probation 1986–1989* (Washington, D.C., BJS, 1992).

age of all burglary and armed robbery arrests . . . that involved persons on probation. . . ." They found that probationers accounted for 8 percent of all adult arrests for burglary and armed robbery. According to Geerken and Hayes,

> These percentages are contrary to expectations and surprisingly low. They suggest that even the complete elimination of probation . . . would have a very negligible effect on the burglary and armed robbery rates since more than 90 percent of all burglaries and armed robberies were committed by persons not on probation . . . at the time of the arrest. . . . We argue . . . that since a low percentage of all burglary and armed robbery arrests are of persons on probation . . . at the time, policy changes tightening or eliminating . . . [probation] can affect only a small percentage of these crimes.[32]

CRITICAL THINKING

1. Describe the specific findings of the research.
2. In view of these findings, what policy recommendations would you make. Give reasons for your answer.

Knowledge and Understanding CHECK

1. Identify the eight missions of community corrections.
2. Identify the basic idea of probation.
3. Briefly trace the history of probation.
4. Why is probation the punishment of choice in the United States?
5. List the conflicting goals of probation.
6. Identify and describe the major probation officer roles.
7. Identify the informal and formal nature of probation.
8. Explain why felons receive probation.
9. List the usual conditions of probation.
10. Under what conditions can probation be revoked?
11. How successful is probation?
12. Describe the legal nature of probation.
13. Identify and describe the two stages of revocation proceedings.
14. What are the criteria for measuring the effectiveness of probation?
15. Using these criteria, how effective is probation?

INTERMEDIATE PUNISHMENTS

For most of the twentieth century, the United States followed an **either-or punishment** practice; that is, convicted offenders were either incarcerated or put on ordinary probation. The wide range of actual criminal behavior, however, rarely falls neatly into the two extremes provided by either straight probation or incarceration. Punishment was often too harsh for offenders who did not deserve imprisonment and too lenient for offenders who were sentenced to probation. Justice demands a range of punishments that fit the range of actual criminal behavior. The demand for a more appropriate range of penalties—the application of the principle of just deserts to the punishment of offenders—is one reason for the rise of intermediate sanctions. **Intermediate sanctions** are punishments that are more severe than ordinary probation but not so harsh as confinement in jails and prisons.

The application of the principle of just deserts is not the only mission that intermediate sanctions are supposed to accomplish. Proponents of intermediate sanctions have "sold" them to legislators and the public on the claims that the sanctions can reduce prison crowding, protect the public, punish and rehabilitate offenders—and accomplish all of this while saving tax dollars. Of course, intermediate sanctions cannot completely accomplish all these far-reaching missions. They are not a panacea.[33]

Intermediate punishments are not new. The ideas for intermediate punishments that have attracted the attention of a number of academics, some of the general public, a handful of politicians, and a less-enthusiastic few criminal justice professionals have a long history. Home confinement is as old as recorded history. Henry VIII confined Catherine of Aragon for years in various palaces in England. Intensive supervised probation arose in the 1960s.

The interest in principled grading of punishments arises out of a long-standing dissatisfaction with the either-or, in-out choice between incarceration and probation. A major shift from rehabilitation to retribution and community safety has generated demands for a richer variety of humane punishments that do not threaten community safety. Prison crowding and budgetary restraints increase the attractiveness of community alternatives that are more punitive and safer than ordinary probation.[34]

Local, state, and federal governments adopted a variety of intermediate sanctions programs in the 1980s and 1990s:

- Intensive Supervised Probation (ISP).
- Home confinement (often called house arrest or home detention).
- Shock incarceration (correctional boot camps).
- Community service.
- Day reporting centers.
- Fines.

Intensive Supervised Probation (ISP)

Crowded prisons, budget crunches, and the perceived threat to public safety led to the adoption of intensive supervised probation (ISP). **Intensive supervised probation** is a tougher version of traditional probation in several respects. ISP probationers

- Contact their probationers more often.
- Enjoy less freedom and privacy.
- Have either to work, get treatment, or go to school.

In one of the best-known evaluations of intensive supervision programs in operation during the 1960s, federal probation authorities divided offenders into four levels of supervision:

1. "Intensive," which assigned only 20 offenders to each probation officer.
2. "Ideal," which assigned 50 offenders to each officer;
3. "Normal," which assigned 70 to 130 offenders to each officer.
4. "Minimum," which assigned several hundred offenders to each officer.

> According to Arthur J. Lurigio and Joan Petersilia:
>
> After two years, it was shown that smaller caseloads did little except generate more technical violations. Crime rates were about the same for all categories of supervision. . . . As similar evidence accumulated, federal funding for criminal justice projects began to evaporate. . . . Under these circumstances, most of the earlier IPS projects were dismantled; they remained dormant until the early 1980s.[35]

Curiously, proponents of intensive supervised probation have largely ignored this finding. Intensive supervised probation is now the most popular and the most widely used intermediate punishment. Every state and the federal government has adopted some form of ISP (see Figure 13.5).[36]

Intensive supervised probation has several ambitious aims:

- Reducing prison crowding.
- Increasing community protection.
- Rehabilitating offenders.
- Proving that probation can work and that probation is punishment.
- Saving money.

It also serves a number of hidden missions:

- *Institutional:* Probation has an image problem; it is often regarded as a "slap on the wrist." ISP claims to be "tough" on criminals and promises to protect the community.
- *Professional:* ISP is supposed to generate more money for probation departments. Therefore, probation officers "get to do probation work the way it ought to be done," and they "work closely with just a few people so [they] can make a difference in their lives."
- *Political:* ISP allows probation departments to get in tune with the public "get tough on crime and criminals" attitude. This harmony with the public makes probation—and probation budgets—more saleable to the public.[37]

Figure 13.5
Probationers Under ISP and Electronic Monitoring, 1992

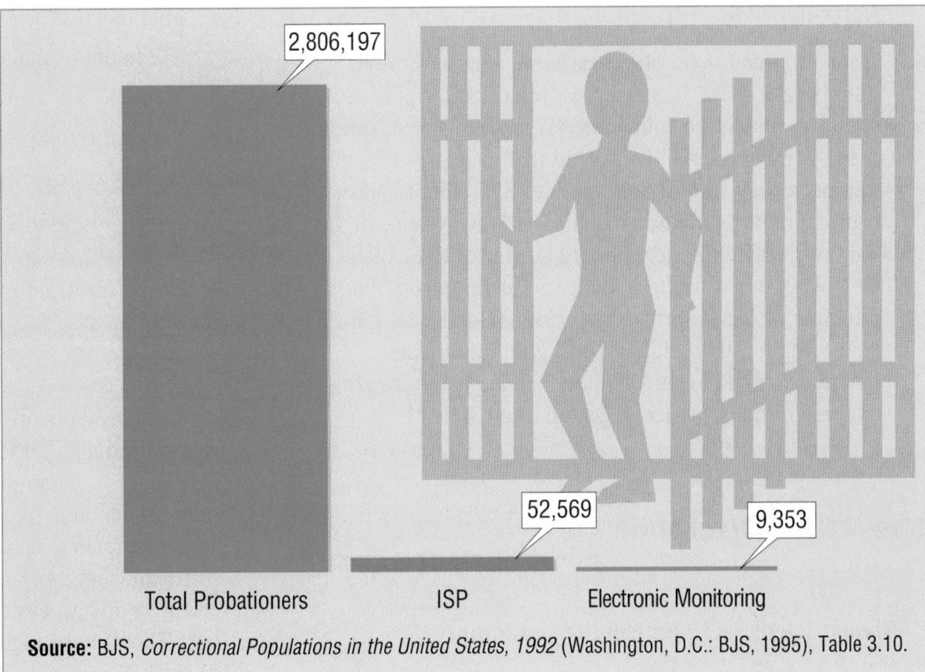

Source: BJS, *Correctional Populations in the United States, 1992* (Washington, D.C.: BJS, 1995), Table 3.10.

Most ISP programs include:

- Frequent alcohol and other drug testing.
- Unannounced visits by probation officers.
- Intolerance of even minor violations of the conditions of probation.
- Daily contact with probation officers.[38]

ISP programs sometimes mix community supervision with incarceration. For example, New Jersey has an ISP program that includes an element of shock incarceration. Prisoners can apply for the ISP program only after serving a minimum of 60 days in prison. The median prison time served is about three-and-a-half months. New Jersey has accepted more than 1,460 offenders into its ISP program. Most offenders chosen are already sentenced to prison, represent an acceptable risk to the community, and have not committed a violent offense. A risk assessment instrument is used to screen them. The majority of those selected fall into the category of nonviolent property offenders, with a large number of alcohol and other drug-related offenders included in the program.[39]

In the New Jersey ISP program, probation officers carry a caseload of 16 probationers. Contacts average one daily, including 12 face-to-face meetings, seven curfew checks, and four urinalyses a month during the first six months in the program. Program rules include work requirements, curfew, abstinence from alcohol and other drugs, and payments of fines, restitution, and child support. Participants who violate even minor program rules return to prison.

By 1989, of participants who entered New Jersey's program prior to December 31, 1985, 58 percent graduated from the program and 40 percent returned to prison because of violations. Urinalysis accounted for many returns to prison, misconduct that would remain undetected in ordinary supervision. Twelve percent of program participants were convicted of another offense at the end of two years, compared with 23 percent of a control group who served their normal prison terms.

In 1987, the Bureau of Justice Statistics provided funding for a rigorous experimental evaluation of intensive supervised probation. Seven jurisdictions in five states developed programs that were stricter than ordinary probation but less harsh than prison and jail. The programs identified serious repeat drug offenders on probation or parole, randomly assigning them to either the ISP or a control group. This ensured that differences in outcome would not come from the participants but from the programs. The data indicated that both the experimental and control groups were similar in background and had committed similar offenses. Participants in the ISP group were tested more frequently for drug use, and they had more contacts with their probation officers than participants who were assigned to the control group.

A 12-month follow-up study found

> no significant variations . . . among the ISP and routine probationers . . . in terms of (a) the proportion rearrested, (b) the average number of arrests during the follow-up period, (c) the nature of the new offenses, or (d) the rate of arrests, controlling for street time (i.e., time not incarcerated).[40]

Despite these disappointing results regarding recidivism, Joan Petersilia, Susan Turner, and Elizabeth Piper Deschennes concluded that the seven programs did accomplish another important mission of ISP—administering just deserts.

According to the researchers,

> [T]he programs were able to achieve another of their stated goals, that of imposing an intermediate punishment, for which the court-ordered sanctions were more credibly monitored and enforced than was possible with routine supervision. It appears that ISP, rather than rehabilitating the offender, rehabilitated the system. In the long run, such intermediate sanctions should escalate the cost of crime to the offender and help restore the principle of just deserts to the criminal justice system. And bridging the middle ground with intermediate sanctions should eventually enhance the deterrent effectiveness of the sentencing system as a whole.[41]

Use *Your* Discretion

Should felons serve time in the community?

According to a Bureau of Justice Statistics assessment, Georgia's intensive supervised probation program, an alternative, intermediate form of punishment . . . changes the perception of probation as a "slap on the wrist" to that of a viable alternative to imprisonment. The core of such an alternative must be intensive surveillance, coupled with substantial community service and/or restitution. It must be structured to satisfy public demands that the punishment fit the crime, to show criminals that crime really doesn't pay, and to control potential recidivists.[42]

Georgia's . . . program, implemented in 1982, has stirred nationwide interest among criminal justice professionals because it seems to satisfy two goals that have long appeared mutually contradictory:

- *Restraining the growth* of prison populations and associated costs by controlling selected offenders in the community.
- *Satisfying the demand* that criminals be punished for their crimes.

The basic question here is whether or not prison-bound offenders can be shifted into intensive probation supervision without creating a threat to public safety. The National Institute of Justice funded a study that suggests that intensive supervision provides greater controls than regular probation and costs far less than incarceration.

The program, located in Georgia, was called the Intensive Probation Supervision (IPS) program and began in 1982. A pilot study, it focused on 13 of Georgia's 45 judicial sentencing circuits. By the end of 1985, it had expanded to 33 circuits and had supervised 2,322 probationers. Georgia's IPS is one of the most stringent in the nation. Requirements include:

- Five face-to-face contacts per week.
- 132 hours of mandatory community service.
- Mandatory curfew.
- Mandatory employment.
- Weekly check of local arrest records.
- Automatic notification of arrest elsewhere in the state.
- Crime Information Network listing.
- Routine and unannounced alcohol and drug testing.

Requirements are enforced by a team of probation and surveillance officers. The team supervises 25 probationers. In some jurisdictions, a team of one probation officer and two surveillance officers supervises 40 probationers. The standards are designed to provide sufficient surveillance to control risk to the community and give a framework to treatment-oriented counseling. The counseling is designed to help the offender direct his energies toward productive activities, to assume responsibilities, and to become a law-abiding citizen.

Most offenders chosen for the pilot program were already sentenced to prison, presented an acceptable risk to the community, and had not committed a violent offense. A risk assessment instrument was used to screen offenders. While the majority of those selected fell into the category of nonviolent property offenders, a large number of individuals convicted of drug- and alcohol-related offenses also were included as the program developed. Some of these offenses also involved personal violence. Of the 2,322 people in the program between 1982 and 1985, 370 (or 16 percent) absconded or had their probation revoked. The remaining 1,952 were successfully diverted from prison into some form of probation.

According to one evaluation of the program, the IPS pilot program played a significant role in reducing the flow of offenders to prison. Among the findings were:

- The percentage of offenders sentenced to prison decreased, and the number of probationers increased.
- The kinds of offenders diverted were more similar to prison inmates than to regular probationers.
- IPS probationers committed less serious crimes during their probation than either comparable groups of regular probationers or probationers released from prison.
- The cost of IPS, while much greater than regular probation, is considerably less than the cost of a prison stay, even when construction costs are not considered.

- Society received thousands of hours of community service from IPS offenders.

Criminal justice practitioners accepted IPS as real, fair, and proportional punishment. Judges particularly liked it because it allowed them to choose something between traditional probation and imprisonment.[43]

One negative result of ISP is **net widening.** [Net widening means that offenders who would be sentenced to ordinary probation if imprisonment were the only alternative are sentenced to intermediate punishments when they are available.] For example, Georgia judges report "backdooring" by sentencing borderline offenders to prison while announcing they will "welcome an application for intensive supervision."

Furthermore, intensive supervised probation does not necessarily reduce either prison population or costs. For example, one participant originally sentenced to one year in prison violated a rule on intensive supervised probation. They returned the offender to prison—for five years!

Intensive supervision also can backfire. Some participants who could succeed with less supervision react negatively to intense supervision. Joan Petersilia cautions that what might work in Georgia, a state with a high incarceration rate (that sends to prison offenders that other states might place on probation), might not work elsewhere.[44]

CRITICAL THINKING

1. On the basis of the Bureau of Justice Statistics' description and assessment of Georgia's intensive probation supervision program, would you introduce a similar program in your community? Defend your answer.
2. What specific facts, findings, and arguments from the Georgia experience convince you—or do not convince you—to recommend an ISP program for your community? Explain.

Home Confinement: Electronic Monitoring

Home confinement—sentencing offenders to remain in their homes—is an old practice. As mentioned, Henry VIII confined his wife, Queen Catherine of Aragon, to home confinement and twentieth-century dictators did the same to many of their political enemies. During the 1980s, home confinement became popular with advocates of intermediate punishments. Most people sentenced to home confinement have committed misdemeanors—DWI, for example.[45]

The benefits of home confinement include:

- Reducing the stigma of incarceration while still punishing offenders.
- Maintaining family ties and occupational roles that improve chances for rehabilitation.
- Saving money from reduced jail and prison maintenance and construction costs and from payments by offenders.
- Protecting the public by keeping offenders "off the street."
- Meeting the demand for punishment.[46]

Some critics of home confinement claim that it violates the right to privacy and the rights against self-incrimination,

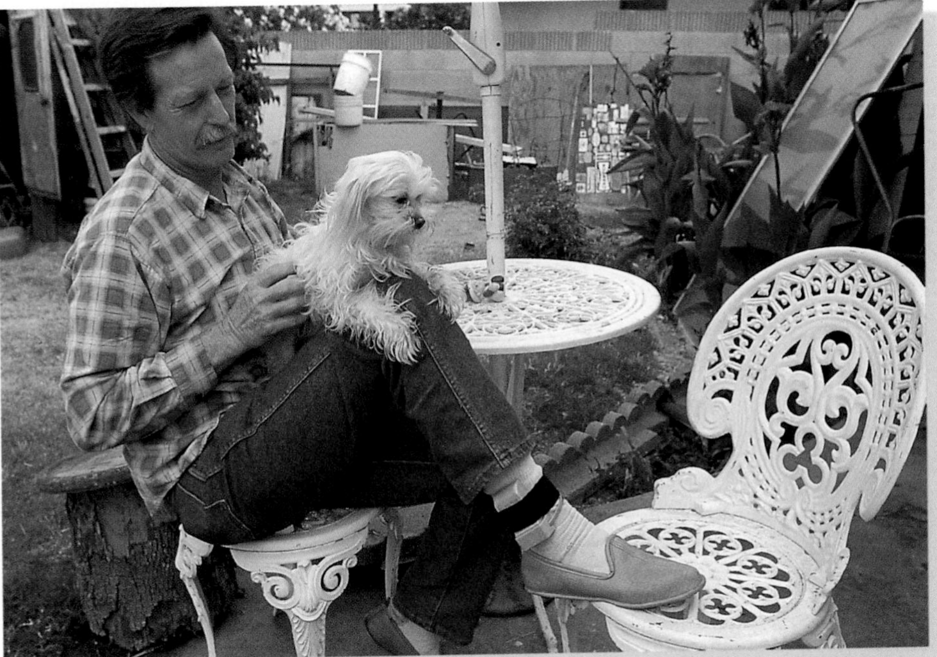

Home confinement is not a cure-all, but when it is used as a real alternative to incarceration it can both save money and protect society.

search and seizure, and cruel and unusual punishment. However, since 1929, the U.S. Supreme Court has ruled that electronic surveillance does not violate the Constitution. This is especially true under the doctrine that convicted offenders enjoy only diminished constitutional rights.

Use *Your* Discretion

Is home confinement good policy?

Florida adopted a statewide home confinement program in the 1980s. The program provided round-the-clock surveillance. The Palm Beach Sheriff's Department operates one type of home confinement: a battery-powered, waterproof transmitter securely fastened by riveted straps to an offender's ankles emits a signal at regular intervals, with a maximum range of 100 feet to a receiver/dialer at the offender's home telephone. The unit monitors the transmitter and automatically dials a host computer, describing the time offenders go beyond the range of the unit or tamper with, or remove, the transmitter. The host computer, a small PC at the sheriff's office, contains offenders' personal data, home address, telephone number, and weekly schedule, reflecting times offenders can leave home. The program prints a violation message for every unauthorized "left home," tampering, or removal.[47]

The program selects its participants from jail prisoners already in a work-release program. To qualify, prisoners have to meet the following conditions:

- Offenders have to complete part of the work-release program in jail.
- They leave work during the day and return to the jail at night and on weekends.
- Offenders' families have to consent to their participation.
- Offenders have to live in Palm Beach.
- Offenders have to have telephone.
- Offenders have to return to jail every day, and the last day of every workweek.
- Offenders have to pay the program cost of nine dollars for each day in the program.
- The sheriff's department has to make sure that the transmitter is working.[48]

More than 5,000 offenders have participated in Florida home confinement programs. A surveillance team maintains a caseload of 20. According to officers, team surveillance enables them to keep offenders "off guard," and provides personnel for night and weekend surveillance. Team surveillance illustrates the emphasis on the surveillance and supervision functions of probation officers. Responding to this emphasis, Florida trains home confinement officers in surveillance, self-defense, and search and seizure.[49]

Thomas G. Blomberg and Carol Bullock, in a statewide survey of officers, offenders, and offenders' families, found that officers indicated that most offenders either found employment or retained existing employment while on home confinement. Employers reported positive experience with offenders. Spouses reported that husbands were providing their families with full paychecks. All family members reported that participants showed more interest and involvement in their families and homes. Married and mature offenders did better than young offenders. Younger participants frequently failed to fulfill the home confinement program's requirements.[50]

Home confinement is not a panacea. It has not significantly reduced jail and prison populations. Net widening occurs and many offenders cannot qualify, particularly those without homes and telephones. The technology also creates problems. Some telephone lines cannot transmit signals. Windstorms and thunderstorms can interrupt or send false signals. External radio signals can interfere with signals on transmitters. Iron and steel can block signals or create electromagnetic fields.

When used as a true alternative to incarceration, however, home confinement costs less than jail, even when taking into account the costs of electronic surveillance devices. Moreover, it represents an intermediate punishment that allows for a principled approach to grading sanctions. It also provides for community safety while allowing offenders to maintain and perhaps strengthen family ties and employment.[51]

CRITICAL THINKING

1. Identify the conditions of the Florida home confinement program.
2. List the findings of Blomberg and Bullock on home confinement.
3. Would you recommend home confinement on the basis of the information provided here? Explain your answer.

Correctional Boot Camps

Correctional boot camps, a form of shock incarceration, provide an alternative to prison for young, first-time, nonviolent offenders, particularly drug offenders. They are based on the assumption that they deter and rehabilitate offenders

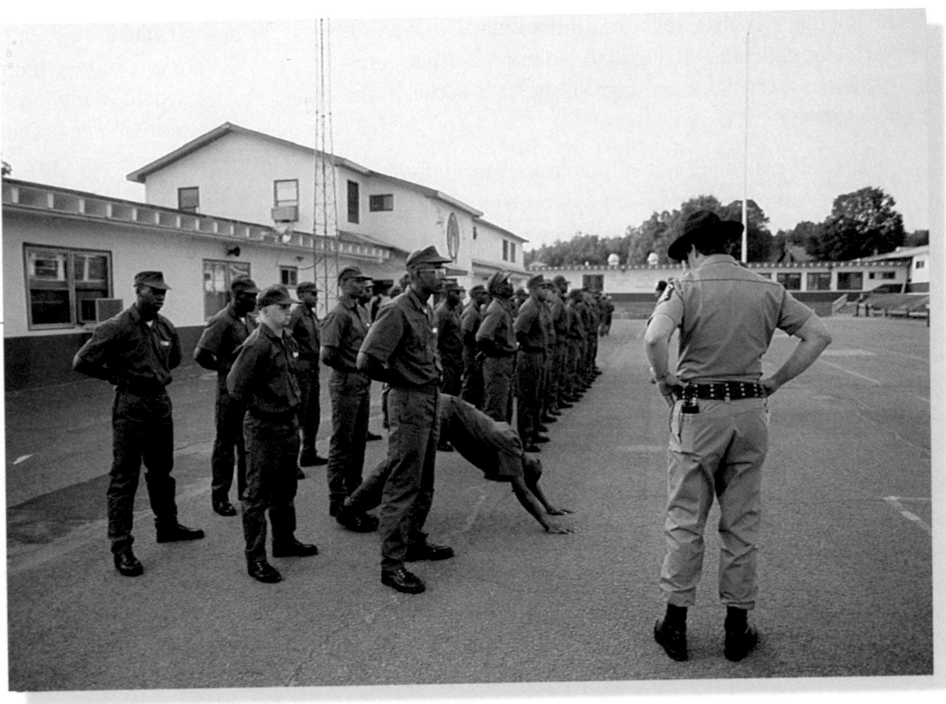

Correctional boot camps are a popular rehabilitative strategy with the public. However, research indicates that they do not appear to be effective in reducing rates of recidivism. Why do you think shock incarceration does not effectively "scare" criminals into not committing crimes again?

more effectively than prisons. In 1994, 28 states were operating 43 boot camps; other states were planning to start them. Boot camps are modeled on basic training in the military. Like other intermediate punishments, correctional boot camps are a response to the combined influences of prison crowding, the demand for more severe punishment, and budgetary restraints.

Correctional boot camps stress a number of features in common with military boot camps:

- Strict discipline.
- Physical training.
- Drill and ceremony.
- Military bearing and courage.
- Physical labor.
- Summary punishment for minor misconduct.

According to a camp sergeant in a Georgia correctional boot camp, "Here being scared is the point. You have to hit a mule between the eyes with a two-by-four to get his attention . . . and that's exactly what we're doing with this program."[52]

The use of militarism, hard labor, and fear in prisons has a long history. In 1821, John Cray, deputy keeper of Auburn prison, turned away from solitary confinement because of the high rates of suicide and mental breakdowns. He replaced it with the requirement of downcast eyes, the lockstep, no talking, and long hours of hard work under close supervision. At Elmira Reformatory, Zebulon Brockway adopted Auburn's basic idea, with some "modern" twists, in the 1890s.

Use *Your* Discretion

Do correctional boot camps "work"?

Correctional boot camps have received wide publicity. They are extremely popular with the public and, therefore, with state and national politicians. Even presidents have repeatedly advocated correctional boot camps as part of their crime control programs. One political candidate produced an effective commercial promising that young offenders who did not want to obey the law would "wind up breaking up rocks" in a correctional boot camp instead.

Empirical evidence, however, does not support the conclusion that correctional boot camps deter offenders through their use of fear, or that you can "scare offenders straight." After surveying a considerable amount of the available research, Mary Morash and Lila Rucker concluded that

> the boot camp model is unlikely to provide a panacea for . . . the pressures arising from the problems of both prison overcrowding and public demands for severe punishment. Whether the point is to provide rehabilitation, to deter, or to divert people from prison, alternatives other than boot camp should be given careful consideration.[53]

The General Accounting Office, the National Institute of Justice, and several states have independently evaluated boot camps. After interviewing officials and reviewing NIJ data regarding boot camps in Florida and Georgia, the General Accounting Office concluded, somewhat more cautiously than Morash and Rucker, that

> available data are not sufficient to determine if boot camps reduce prison overcrowding, costs, or recidivism. . . . Boot camps may reduce prison overcrowding and prison costs if they involve offenders who would have otherwise been sent to prison, the offenders are incarcerated for a shorter time, and they are not readmitted to prison after their release at a greater rate than prisoners sentenced to regular prisons. However, the possibility that some offenders sent to boot camps would have been put on probation if they had not been sent to boot camps would affect any potential savings.[54]

Dale K. Sechrest reviewed shock incarceration reports based on National Institute of Justice research and gave boot camps the most negative assessment:

> Regardless of the media hype, there is no evidence that shock incarceration "works" for the offenders that need to be reached any more than scared straight or shock probation worked to any great degree. None. Yet these types of "quick-fix" solutions linger on. Shock programs like scared straight and boot camps appear to be "right" methods based on our middle-class understanding of how punishment works. The American Correctional Association [however] notes that "This deeply-rooted social problem cannot be eradicated by exposing [young criminals] to threats of force, intimidation, verbal abuse, or other practices that are meant to shock youths out of [undesired] behavior."[55]

Doris Layton MacKenzie, Robert Brame, David McDowall, and Claire Souryal found mixed results at best when they compared boot camp graduates with comparison samples of prison parolees, probationers, and boot camp dropouts in eight states (Florida, Georgia, Illinois, Louisiana, New York, Oklahoma, South Carolina, and Texas). All the programs were chosen because they contained the core components of boot camps—military drill and ceremony, hard labor, physical training, strict rules, and discipline. The programs, however, differed in other respects that can affect recidivism, including length of stay and the amount of time devoted each day to treatment. MacKenzie and her colleagues measured recidivism in a number of ways, including arrest, revocation for technical violations, and revocation for committing new crimes.[56]

Using regression analysis and other measures of the performance of boot camp graduates and comparison groups, MacKenzie and her colleagues concluded:

> If [the core] components [of boot camp] effectively reduce the recidivism of offenders, we would likely have observed a consistent pattern across states. That pattern would be one of lower recidivism rates for boot camp graduates in contrast to those of comparison groups. *This did not occur* [emphasis added]. As a result, we conclude that these components in and of themselves do not reduce the recidivism of participating offenders.[57]

MacKenzie and her colleagues suggest why boot camp graduates of some programs do better than others. One possibility is the selection process. Boot camp identifies and selects

> offenders who were at lower risk of recidivism in the first place. That is, boot camp completers may be at lower risk than the dropouts for some unanswered reason at the start of the program, and the boot camp program merely separates those who are low risks (the completers) from those who are higher risks (the dropouts).[58]

It may be that the key to boot camp success is not the military drill, strict discipline and rules, hard labor, and heavy physical exercise. Georgia, where boot camp graduates did worse than the comparison groups, had little treatment in the daily schedule. Louisiana boot camp graduates had the lowest arrest rate of all the programs in the study, fewer revocations than either parolees or dropouts, fewer crimes than parolees, and fewer technical violations than dropouts. One possible explanation is that the Louisiana program devoted three or more hours every day to treatment. The researchers call for more research on this aspect of boot camps and ask the critical question: Would programs that incorporate treatment without the military atmosphere do as well as those with the military atmosphere?[59]

In a related study of some of the boot camps just discussed, MacKenzie and Brame tried to answer that question. They compared a sample of those who completed boot camp and those who dropped out of boot camp with groups who were eligible for boot camp but did not attend. The researchers subjected the data collected from the samples to several statistical evaluations. They found "little conclusive evidence that" boot camps "had a positive effect on offender behavior." However, they did find that "supervision intensity plays an important role in shaping offenders' activities during community supervision." They conclude:

> The relatively weak association between shock incarceration [boot camp] and positive adjustment [meaning avoiding illegal activities, obtaining work and education, and meeting financial and family responsibility] should give policymakers reason for pause. While efforts to identify circum-

stances where shock incarceration is effective might be useful, it seems that the evidence weighs against concluding that shock incarceration programs are broadly effective at enhancing the ability of offenders to adjust more successfully in the community.[60]

In 1998, Sheldon X. Zhang reviewed a wide range of evaluations of the effectiveness of shock incarceration by means of boot camps. He concluded:

> Although some have found positive changes in participants' attitudes, few program evaluations have found "hard" evidence of the effectiveness of these camps in terms of rehabilitation or reducing recidivism. According to the most comprehensive study to date [MacKenzie and her colleagues discussed above], based on a comparative analysis of programs in eight states, no clear-cut statements can be made about the effectiveness of boot camps. In general, boot camp graduates do not fare better or worse after release than their counterparts in the conventional correctional system. . . . Empirical efforts have also failed to produce consistent findings on other program effectiveness indicators such as increased prosocial behavior, reduction in technical violations, or reduced drug involvement of camp graduates. At present, the only summarizing statement one can make about boot camps is the lack of any consistent effect either positive or negative.[61]

CRITICAL THINKING

1. Summarize the details of the findings reviewed here.
2. Divide the findings into support and lack of support for the effectiveness of boot camps.
3. Summarize how each study defined effectiveness.
4. On the basis of these findings would you recommend more boot camps, fewer boot camps, or more evaluations?
5. If you would like more research, just what would you want the research to show?

Fines

Fines are monetary punishment that date back to the Old Testament notion of "an eye for an eye." Fines prevailed in England for much of the early part of the Middle Ages, when a price was put on all kinds of offenses, including maiming and murder. Fines have much to recommend them as appropriate criminal punishment. They are clearly aimed at both retribution and deterrence. They emphasize accountability by requiring offenders to pay their "debt to society" literally, in the form of money. All these aims are consistent with current sentencing policies. Fines also fulfill the aims of fairness and proportionality in punishment by allowing the size of the debt to society to be adjusted to the seriousness of offenses in our criminal law. The flexibility of monetary penalties also allows for the adjustment of the fine to the ability of the offenders to pay. Moreover, fines are already a current sentencing option in all American courts, whether large or small, urban or rural. Finally, and far from least important, fines generate revenue.[62]

Fines are consistent with basic American values. According to Michael Tonry and Kate Hamilton:

> It seems odd, in a country where economic incentives and rational calculation are so widely celebrated, that monetary penalties play so small a part in punishment of offenders. Although in practice fines are generally set in amounts too small to be commensurate to the seriousness of nontrivial crimes, in principle they can vary from small change to economic capital punishment. Although in practice fines are often collected haphazardly or not at all, in principle they can be collected with the same vigor and solicitude that characterize our friendly neighborhood finance companies. Although in practice increased use of fines seems to be unfair to the poor and unduly lenient to the rich, in principle amounts can be tailored to individuals' assets and incomes so as to constitute roughly comparable financial burdens.[63]

Why have fines not figured prominently in the repertoire of intermediate punishments? According to Sally T. Hillsman and Judith A. Greene:

> Among American criminal justice practitioners, there lingers a deep skepticism about the usefulness of fine sentences that focuses on the absolute size of the fine: Don't fines need to be large in order to be punitive and to deter? This emphasis on large fines leads to further issues about the fairness of fine sentences: If fines are large enough to punish and deter, how can they be collected from the majority of offenders who come before American courts? And if only those who can pay sizable amounts are fined, are not these more affluent offenders buying their way out of the more punitive sentences to imprisonment?[64]

According to some experts, the answer to problems with fines is a system that most European countries have put into effect—the day fine. **Day fines** base fines on the daily income of offenders. The imposition of day fines is a two-step process. In the first step, judges assign fine units. The more serious the offense, the more units are assessed. In the second stage, monetary amounts are attached to the units. The amount of money each unit costs depends on offenders' daily income.[65]

Lower criminal courts have always been the primary users of fines. To determine the usefulness of day fines in the

United States, an experiment was established in New York's Staten Island Criminal Court. The experiment was developed by a planning group comprising judges, prosecutors, public and private defense attorneys, court administrators, and planners from the Vera Institute of Justice. The planning group assigned fine units according to the seriousness of the offenses for which the court imposed sentences. They then created a method for attributing a monetary value to the fine units, basing the monetary value on a "fair share" of the daily, after-tax income of offenders. Fair share takes into account the offender's number of dependents and whether the offender's income is below the poverty line. According to Sally T. Hillsman:

> Using this method, the day-fine amounts in the Staten Island court could range from as low as $25 for a welfare recipient with three children who was convicted of the least serious offense in the court's jurisdiction, to $4,000 for a single offender with no dependents and a gross income of $35,000 who was sentenced for the most serious offense.[66]

The results of an interim evaluation of the experiment were promising. The court implemented day fines smoothly: virtually all fixed fines were replaced with day fines during the pilot year of the experiment. Revenue from fines rose 14 percent during the experiment because of the larger day fines imposed on affluent offenders. Despite the higher fines, collection rates did not decrease; they remained as good under the experiment with day fines as they were under the old fixed-fine system. The court enforced the sentences of 84 percent of day-fine offenders. Most offenders paid their fines, or a substantial part of them. Thirteen percent originally sentenced to day fines were returned to court for resentencing because they did not pay. These offenders were usually sentenced to community service or to jail.[67]

Community Service

Community service sentences order offenders to work at projects for the benefit of the public. These sentences hark back to two ancient practices. The first is **restitution**—paying back victims for the injuries and other losses caused by offenders. The laws of the ancient Babylonians, Greeks, Romans, and Jews, and the laws of medieval Europe all provided for specific compensation that offenders had to pay their victims. When victims lost their central place in criminal justice (see Chapter 2), the use of restitution fell into disuse. Society as a whole took the place of individuals as the victim of crime. Community service orders took the place of restitution. Community service orders are sentences that order offenders "to work without pay at projects that . . . benefit the public or . . . public charities." Second, "offenders could avoid worse punishment if they performed hard manual labor on public projects (such as road building) or manned oars on galleys."[68]

Community service orders are most often used in lower criminal courts where the predominant business is traffic violations and other misdemeanors. However, community service orders receive the most publicity in "celebrity cases." Michael Milken, a notorious "junk bond" trader during the 1980s, was ordered to work in a charity full time for three years after his term in federal prison. Oliver North, who ran an illegal covert military operation out of the Reagan White House, and Zsa Zsa Gabor, the Hollywood celebrity who slapped a police officer when he stopped her for a traffic offense, also received community service sentences. There

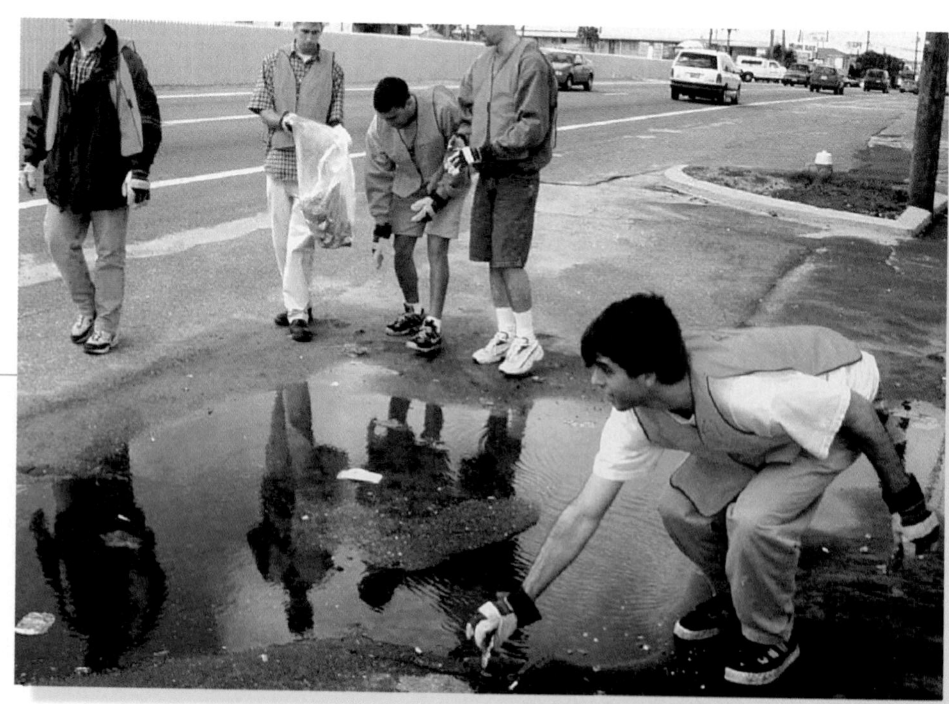

Rob Schlaeger picks up trash along a highway in Panama City Beach, Florida. He and other "spring breakers" have been required to perform eight hours of community service as punishment for misdemeanor charges. How effective do you think community sentences are as forms of restitution? How effective do you think they are as rehabilitative measures?

was talk in 1998 that President William J. Clinton should perform community service for lying under oath while he was president.[69]

Community service has several underlying purposes that have varied over time. During the 1970s, community service was acclaimed as a mechanism to serve a variety of utilitarian purposes. It was touted as a form of restitution; instead of paying back individual victims, however, community service paid back the entire community. Furthermore, community service was supposed to rehabilitate offenders. Reformers hoped that by working beside law-abiding people, offenders would develop a sense of responsibility. Judge Dennis Challeen, a booster of community service sentences, argued that

> they require offenders to make efforts toward self-improvement, thus removing them from their roles as losers and helping them to address their personal problems and character defects that alienate them from the mainstream of society.[70]

These practical, or utilitarian, justifications for community service began to sound outdated in the atmosphere of tougher attitudes toward crime and criminals that began in the 1970s. The philosophy of "just deserts" replaced utilitarian aims such as rehabilitation. Community service came to be seen mainly as a way to punish criminals who deserve intermediate punishment; that is, they deserve to suffer more than ordinary probationers, but not so much as offenders in jails and prisons.[71]

Use *Your* Discretion

Are community service sentences appropriate?

This question boils down to both an empirical and a value assessment. Empirically, little evidence exists on the effectiveness of community service. The Vera Institute of Justice tried to estimate the crime control effects of community service sentences in its community service sentencing project. The project provided judges in the criminal courts of Manhattan, Brooklyn, and Queens the option of choosing between traditional short jail terms (90 days or less) and community service for chronic misdemeanor property offenders. Community service was not pleasant—and was not supposed to be. It was not intended to humiliate offenders, but it was definitely intended to punish them. Offenders worked 70 hours a week in crews, painting senior citizen centers and nursing homes, cleaning neighborhood lots, and renovating dwellings for low-cost housing.[72]

Six months later, between 39 and 51 percent of a sample of offenders sentenced to community service had been rearrested for some kind of property crime. This rearrest rate was identical to similar offenders who were sentenced to short jail terms. Hence, community service neither rehabilitated nor deterred property offenders in these New York City boroughs any more effectively than jail terms. Furthermore, given that offenders cannot commit crimes in the community if they are in jail, those sentenced to community service may pose a greater risk to society. The project directors estimated that about 15 out of every 100 offenders sentenced to community service committed crimes because they were not in jail. However, community service did yield other benefits. The community received about 60,000 hours of useful work, some of which would probably not have been done at all if community service had not "donated" it.[73]

According to Douglas C. McDonald of the research team at the Vera Institute of Justice, the values reason is more compelling than the utilitarian reason for community service orders:

> My own view is that a more compelling reason for considering community service, as well as other intermediate sanctions, is that it provides a means of more finely matching deserved punishments with the severity of offenses. This suggests the importance of developing guidelines to determine how much unpaid labor, and of what sort, should be given for crimes of differing severity, although there may be compelling practical reasons for a fixed "dose" of hours or days to be served by all.[74]

CRITICAL THINKING

1. Summarize the findings of the Vera Institute of Justice on the crime control effects of community service sentences.
2. According to Douglas C. McDonald, why is the values reason more compelling than the effectiveness of community service orders?
3. Would you support spending more on community service programs? Explain your answer.

Day Reporting Centers

A handful of states have introduced day reporting centers. **Day reporting centers** can reduce jail and prison crowding by requiring offenders to report every day instead of confining them. Day reporting centers "combine high levels of surveillance and extensive services, treatments, or activities." Their clients include:

1. Defendants denied bail before conviction.
2. Prisoners released conditionally from prison.

3. Offenders sentenced to day reporting instead of confinement in jails.

Dale G. Parent gives one example of (3): The Connecticut Prison Association reviewed "Frank's" case and recommended that the judge release him to Alternative Incarceration Center (AIC) in Hartford. The judge agreed:

> [H]e ordered Frank to report to the AIC every morning and to file an itinerary showing where he would be, and how he could be contacted, for each hour of each day. The judge ordered Frank to look for a job (Frank used the association's employment project to find a job as a custodian in a local factory) and to attend drug-use counseling sessions at AIC. Finally, the judge ordered Frank to submit to random drug-use tests.[75]

Jack McDevitt and his colleagues evaluated the Metropolitan Day Reporting Center (MDRC) in Boston, Massachusetts. The center deals with inmates released early from jails. The researchers used the records of inmates and interviews with both inmates and staff members. MDRC found that

- "MDRC inmates were twice as likely to remain crime-free as those released directly from a jail."
- Only 1 percent committed a crime while they were in the program.
- Nearly 80 percent were either working or looking for a job.
- Most inmates were suffering from serious alcohol or other drug abuse.
- About 60 percent of MDRC clients who had been incarcerated three or more times in the past did not commit new crimes.[76]

Use *Your* Discretion

Do intermediate sanctions punish offenders enough?

Joan Petersilia, when she was the director of the Criminal Justice Program at the RAND Corporation, suggested that we take seriously offenders' attitudes toward community punishments. Petersilia writes:

> Are community sanctions punitive enough to convince the public that the "punishment fit the crime"? Having studied the development of these intermediate sanctions, I have discovered that some serious offenders feel that ISPs are at least as punitive as imprisonment—if not more so. If this is true, then offenders' perceptions should be considered in structuring sanctions and in making sentencing decisions.
>
> Why is this issue worth studying? The most pragmatic reason is that ISPs offer some hope of relieving prison overcrowding—without draining the public purse. If it can be shown that other—less expensive—sanctions also have punitive qualities, then perhaps the public might accept that community-based sanctions are appropriate and quite consistent with their demand to "get tough" and hold criminals accountable for their crimes. If this link were made, the criminal justice system could save money and operate a system with more rehabilitation potential.
>
> More theoretical, but possibly more compelling, these hypotheses question some basic assumptions that underlie sentencing decisions, the structure of sanctions, and resource allocation in the criminal justice system. Consequently, those assumptions may be partly responsible for today's "crisis in corrections." It would probably have been salutary to question these assumptions long ago, but under present circumstances it is imperative to do so.
>
> *Punishment for Whom?*
> This country bases assumptions about "what punishes" on the norms and living standards of society at large. This practice overlooks two salient facts: First, most serious offenders neither accept nor abide by those norms—otherwise, they wouldn't be offenders. Second, most of the people who even "qualify" for imprisonment today come from communities where conditions fall far below the living standards most Americans would recognize. If their values and standards differ, why should their perceptions of punishment be the same? Nevertheless, criminal sanctions reflect society's values—negatively. The demand that serious criminals go to prison implies that prison imposes conditions that are intolerable and frightening to the law-abiding citizen. The belief that community sanctions are too lenient implies that no matter what conditions probation or parole impose, remaining in the community is categorically preferable to imprisonment.
>
> When crime rates were lower and minor crimes could land a person in prison, many offenders might have shared these perceptions. Apparently, feelings are different among offenders who face prison sentences today. In several states, given the option of serving prison terms or participating in ISPs, many offenders have chosen prison. Pearson reports that about 15 percent of offenders who apply to New Jersey's ISP program retract their applications once they understand the conditions and requirements. Under the New Jersey structure, this means that they will remain in prison on their original sentences.

One of the more striking examples comes from Marion County, Oregon, which has been cooperating with researchers from the RAND Corporation in a randomized field experiment. Selected nonviolent offenders were given the choice of serving a prison term or returning to the community to participate in ISP. These offenders have been convicted, and the judge has formally imposed a prison term. After conviction, they were asked if they would agree to return to the community and participate in ISP, rather than go to prison. During the one-year study period, about a third of those eligible for the experiment have chosen prison instead of ISP.

What accounts for this seeming aberration? Why should anyone prefer imprisonment to remaining in the community—no matter what the conditions? Can we infer from this that prison conditions seem less "punishing" than ISP requirements to these offenders? To consider this possibility, we first need to understand why imprisonment may have lost some of its punitive sting.

Has the Punitive Power of Imprisonment Diminished?

Zimring and Hawkins note that sanctions are most likely to deter if they meet two conditions: "the social standing is injured by the punishment," and "the individual feels a danger of being excluded from the group." It is hard to imagine that prison terms have either of these attributes for repeat criminals. Possessing a prison record is not as stigmatizing as in the past, because so many of the offender's peers (and other family members) also have "done time." A recent survey shows that 40 percent of youths in state training schools have parents who have also been incarcerated. Further, about a quarter of all U.S. black males will be incarcerated during their lives, so the stigma attached to having a prison record is not as great as it was when it was relatively uncommon.

In fact, far from stigmatizing, imprisonment evidently confers status in some neighborhoods. Particularly for gang-affiliated and career criminals, a prison sentence enhances status when the offender returns to his neighborhood, especially in the inner cities. California's Task Force on Gangs and Drugs reported that during public testimony, gang members themselves "repeatedly stated that incarceration was not a threat because they knew their sentences would be minimal." Further, some gang members considered the short period of detention as a "badge of courage, something to brag about when they return to the streets." And according to the California Youth Authority, inmates steal state-issued prison clothing for the same reason. Wearing it when they return to the community lets everyone know they have "done hard time."

As for employment opportunities, imprisonment has had increasingly less effect for the people in question. As William Julius Wilson makes painfully clear in *The Truly Disadvantaged,* employment opportunities have been shrinking for people of lower economic status, especially in urban areas, so the effect of a prison record may not be as dramatic as it was when jobs were more plentiful.

Some have argued that for poor people, prison may be preferred, but few scholars take such discussions seriously. It is undoubtedly true, however, that the quality of a person's lifestyle when free certainly has some bearing on the extent to which imprisonment is considered undesirable. The grim fact—and national shame—is that for most people who go to prison, the conditions inside are not all that different from the conditions outside. The prison environment may be far below the ordinary standards of society, but so is the environment they come from. As the quality of life that people can expect when free declines, the relative deprivation suffered while in prison declines.

Social isolation is another presumably punitive aspect of imprisonment. Again, the values of society surface in the belief that when a person goes to prison he is "among aliens." In prison, he is isolated from the kinds of people he would customarily (and by preference) be among. For today's inmates, that is less likely to be true. The newly admitted inmate will probably find friends, if not family, already there.

The warden of Pontiac Penitentiary described it thus: "When a new guy comes up here it's almost a homecoming—undoubtedly there are people from his neighborhood and people who know him. . . ." He goes on to recall how a ranking gang member, upon entry to prison, received a "letter from the ranking chief welcoming him into the family." As for real family, the warden in a Washington, D.C. jail recently noted that his facility currently contained three generations of a particular family at once. He remarked that, "It was like a family reunion for these guys." Some even suggest that prison serves as a buffer for offenders who find the outside world particularly difficult. One man, just released from a Massachusetts prison, said:

> I have literally seen guys who have been released walk out the door and stand on the corner and not know which direction to go. And they eventually go back to prison. As horrible as it is, prison provides some sort of community.

And, finally, the length of time an offender can be expected to actually serve in prison has

Overcrowded prisons can result in offenders serving shorter terms than they were sentenced to. Here, prisoners await transfers from a county prison to a state prison because of overcrowding at the county level.

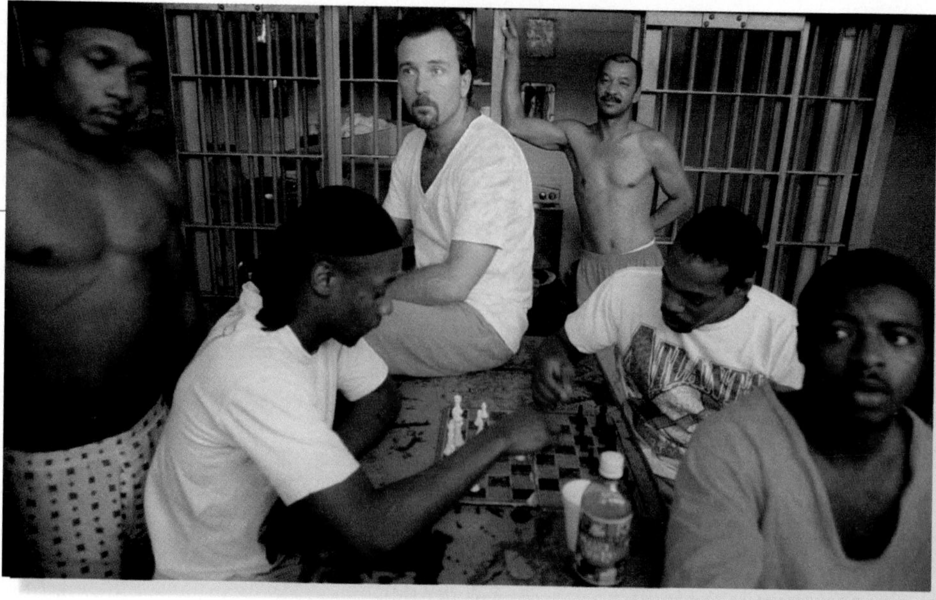

decreased—from eighteen months in 1984 to twelve months in 1987. But more to the point, for marginal offenders (those targeted for prison alternatives), the expected time served can be much less. In California, Texas, and Illinois, two- to three-year prison terms often translate into less than six months actually served. In Oregon, prison crowding has created a situation in which a five-year sentence can translate into three to four months of actual time served. Particularly when the prison system is the subject of a court order and offenders are released because of a "cap," prison terms can be quite short. Offenders on the street seem to be aware of this, even more so with the extensive media coverage such issues are receiving.

For the above reasons, then, it seems at least plausible that prison terms (on average) are not perceived as being as severe as they were historically. No one has ever surveyed prisoners or ex-convicts to find out how punitive they think imprisonment is. However, one could say their actions answer that question implicitly: More than 50 percent of today's prison inmates have served a prior prison term. Add prior jail sentences, and the percentage rises to 80 percent. Knowing what it's like, 80 percent of them evidently still think that the "benefits" of committing a new crime outweigh the "costs" of being in prison. This implies a lot about how punitive prison is for these offenders. However, it does not explain why they would choose imprisonment over intensive probation.

Why Would Offenders Choose Prison Over ISPs?
For many offenders, it may seem preferable to get that short stay in prison over rather than spend five times as long in an ISP. But what about the relative conditions? If the speculations above have any validity, better a short time in conditions that differ little from your accustomed life than a long time in conditions that are very different from the "ordinary standards" of your community.

Taking Marion County, Oregon, as an example, consider the alternatives facing convicted offenders:

IPS
The offender will serve two years under this sanction. During that time, the offender will be visited by a probation officer two or three times per week, who will phone on the other days. The offender will be subject to unannounced searches of his home for drugs and have his urine tested regularly for alcohol and drugs. He must strictly abide by other conditions set by the court—not carrying a weapon, not socializing with certain persons—and he will have to perform community service and be employed or participate in training or education. In addition, he will be strongly encouraged to attend counseling and/or other treatment, particularly if he is a drug offender.

Prison
A sentence of two to four years will require that the offender serve about three to six months. During his term, he is not required to work nor will he be required to participate in any training or treatment, but may do so if he wishes. Once released, he will be placed on two years routine parole supervision, where he sees his parole officer about once a month.

For these offenders, as for any of us, freedom is probably preferable to imprisonment. However, the ISP does not represent freedom. In fact, it may stress and isolate repeat offenders more than imprisonment does. It seems reasonable that when offenders return to their communities, they expect to return to their old lives. The ISP transforms those lives radically.

Their homes can be searched and they must submit regularly to urine testing. Offenders may well consider such invasions of their homes and lives more intrusive and unbearable than the lack of privacy in prisons—where it is an expected condition of life. The same is true of discipline and social isolation. By definition, imprisonment limits freedom of movement and activity, but once a person is in his own community, curfew and other restrictions may seem harder to take. Ironically, he may be less socially isolated from his peers in prison than in ISP.

Why Do Offenders' Perceptions Matter?
Having established the counter-intuitive fact that some serious offenders prefer imprisonment to ISPs, what are we to make of it? Whatever else, it does argue for reconsidering the range of sanctions this country has and the assumptions they reflect. The point is not to insist that on any absolute scale ISP is "worse" than prison. Rather, it is to suggest that the scale we currently use needs reexamining.

For the people who are likely to come under either sanction, how society at large views those sanctions is largely irrelevant. How offenders view punishment ought at least to be considered.[77]

CRITICAL THINKING

1. Why should the views of offenders about punishment matter?
2. What do offenders' attitudes suggest about the value of community punishments?
3. What would you recommend as a result of Petersilia's arguments?

Knowledge and Understanding CHECK

1. What does either/or punishment mean in the United States?
2. List the major intermediate punishments.
3. Identify the major missions of intermediate punishments.
4. How frequently are intermediate sanctions used?
5. Identify the major ways that ISP differs from ordinary probation.
6. Identify the major visible and hidden aims of ISP.
7. Identify and describe the major characteristics of most ISP programs.
8. Summarize the major findings on the evaluations of ISP.
9. Identify the benefits of home confinement.
10. How effective is home confinement?
11. Describe the nature of correctional boot camps.
12. Identify the major characteristics of boot camps.
13. How effective are correctional boot camps?
14. Identify the major strengths and weaknesses of fines.
15. Describe the nature of day fines.
16. Describe the nature and extent of community service sentences.
17. What are day reporting centers, and how extensively are they used?
18. Why would offenders choose prison over ISP?

Was This an Appropriate Punishment? Consideration

The appeals court denied Letterlough's appeal. The court held that the legislature intended that trial courts were supposed to tailor DWI sentences to individual DWI offenders. The sentences were supposed to both punish offenders and prevent them from driving while drunk in the future. The condition was supposed to be "especially unpleasant" so that it would accomplish the legislature's intent.[78]

CHAPTER CAPSULE

- Probation and intermediate punishments are ancient practices.
- Most probationers complete their probation successfully.
- Most probationers do not return to prison when they violate the conditions of their probation.
- Probation is about as effective as imprisonment.
- There are a variety of intermediate punishments, but they are not often used in practice.
- There is little empirical support for the effectiveness of intermediate punishments.

KEY TERMS

corrections
probation
parole
punitive probation officers
welfare probation officers
protective probation officers
bureaucratic probation officers
time-server probation officers
social service brokers
probation bill collector
split-sentence probation
shock incarceration
intermittent incarceration
revocation
recividism
technical probation violations
preliminary hearing
revocation hearing
either-or punishment
intermediate sanctions
intensive supervised probation (ISP)
net widening
home confinement
correctional boot camp
fines
day fines
community service sentences
restitution
day reporting centers

INTERNET RESEARCH EXERCISES

Exercise: What are some of the current issues in probation? What solutions have been proposed to resolve them? How can examples from other countries help U.S. probation?

Suggested sites:

- Bureau of Justice Statistics, Probation and Parole Populations, http://www.ojp.usdoj.gov/bjs/abstract/papp97.htm
- Findlaw, http://laws.findlaw.com/US/000/97-634.html (tip: Read the case of *Pennsylvania Department of Corrections v. Yeskey*)

InfoTrac College Edition: Search using the key word "probation issues"

NOTES

1. BJS, *Adults on Probation, 1997* (Washington, D.C.: BJS, 1998).
2. Belinda R. McCarthy, ed., *Intermediate Punishments: Intensive Supervision, Home Confinement, and Electronic Surveillance* (Monsey, N.Y.: Willow Tree Press, 1987), 1; James M. Byrne, Arthur J. Lurigio, and Joan Petersilia, eds., *Smart Sentencing: The Emergence of Intermediate Sanctions* (Newbury Park, Calif.: Sage Publications, 1992); Norval Morris and Michael Tonry, *Between Prison and Probation: Intermediate Punishments in a Rational Sentencing System* (New York: Oxford University Press, 1990).
3. Joel Samaha, "The Recognizance in Elizabethan Law Enforcement," *American Journal of Legal History* 25 (1981): 189–204; Joel Samaha, *Law and Order in Historical Perspective* (New York: Academic Press, 1974).
4. Dean J. Champion, *Felony Probation: Problems and Prospects* (New York: Praeger, 1988), 1–3.
5. John Augustus, *First Probation Officer,* reprint (New York: National Probation Association, 1983).
6. David Rothman, *Conscience and Convenience* (Boston: Little, Brown, 1980), 82–83.
7. Todd R. Clear and Anthony A. Braga, "Community Corrections," in *Crime,* James Q. Wilson and Joan Petersilia, eds. (San Francisco: Institute for Contemporary Studies, 1995), 422.
8. Joan Petersilia et al., *Granting Felons Probation* (Santa Monica: RAND Corporation, 1985), 1; Joan Petersilia, "A Crime Control Rationale for Reinvesting in Community Corrections," *The Prison Journal* 45 (1995): 479, 481.
9. Edward J. Cosgrove, "ROBO-PO: The Life and Times of a Federal Probation Officer," *Federal Probation* (September 1994): 29.
10. Patrick D. McAnany et al., *Probation and Justice: Reconsideration of Mission* (Cambridge, Mass.: Oelgeschlager, Gunn & Hain, 1984), 43.
11. Eric W. Carlson and Evalyn C. Parks, *Critical Issues in Adult Probation* (Washington, D.C.: U.S. Department of Justice, LEAA), 43–44.
12. Ibid., 43.
13. Carlson and Parks, *Critical Issues in Adult Probation,* 46.
14. Todd R. Clear and George F. Cole, *American Corrections,* 3d ed. (Belmont, Calif.: Wadsworth, 1994), 176.
15. Ibid., 176–77.
16. Vincent O'Leary, "Probation: A System in Change," *Federal Probation* 51 (1987): 8–11.
17. Harry E. Allen et al., *Probation and Parole in America* (New York: The Free Press, 1985), 81.
18. BJS, *Correctional Populations in the United States, 1996* (Washington, D.C.: Bureau of Justice Statistics, 1997).
19. Petersilia et al., *Granting Felons Probation,* 2.
20. Harry E. Allen and Clifford E. Simonson, *Corrections in America,* 4th ed. (New York: Macmillan, 1986), 154; Daniel Glaser, "Supervising Offenders Outside of Prison," in *Crime and Public Policy,* James Q. Wilson, ed. (New Brunswick, N.J.: Transaction Books, 1983), 213; Champion, *Felony Probation;* Fredrick A. Hussey and David E. Duffee, *Probation, Parole and Community Field Services: Policy, Structure and Process* (New York: Harper & Row, 1980), 10.
21. BJS, *Recidivism of Felons on Probation, 1986–1989* (Washington, D.C.: Bureau of Justice Statistics, 1992), 2–4.
22. Clear and Braga, "Community Corrections," 439.
23. Ibid.
24. *Griffin v. Wisconsin,* 483 U.S. 868 (1987). 874–875.
25. *Morrissey v. Brewer,* 408 U.S. 471 (1972), 480; *Gagnon v. Scarpelli,* 411 U.S. 778 (1973).
26. *Morrissey v. Brewer,* 485–486.
27. Ibid.
28. Ibid.
29. Ibid., 487–89.
30. BJS, *Correctional Populations in the United States, 1995* (Washington, D.C.: BJS, 1997), Table 3.6, 4; Glaser, "Supervising Offenders Outside of Prison," 225–27.
31. Ibid., 5.
32. Michael R. Geerken and Hennessey D. Hayes, "Probation and Parole: Public Risk and the Future of Incarceration Alternatives," *Criminology* 31 (1993): 557.
33. Byrne, Lurigio, and Petersilia, *Smart Sentencing,* ix, xiii–xiv.
34. Norval Morris and Michael Tonry, "Between Prison and Probation—Intermediate Punishment in a Rational Sentencing System," *National Institute of Justice Reports* (January/February 1990): 8–10; *Crime and Delinquency,* Special Issue: Intensive Probation Supervision 36 (1990); McCarthy, *Intermediate Punishments.*
35. Arthur J. Lurigio and Joan Petersilia, "The Emergence of Intensive Probation Supervision Programs in the United States," in *Smart Sentencing,* 7–8; Joan Petersilia, "A Decade of Experimenting with Intermediate Sanctions: What Have We Learned?" *Federal Probation* 62 (December 1998): 3–9.
36. Todd R. Clear and Patricia Hardyman, "The New Intensive Supervision Movement," *Crime and Delinquency* 36 (1990): 43–45; Lurigio and Petersilia, "Emergence of IPS Programs," 5–6; Joan Petersilia, Susan Turner, and Elizabeth Piper Deschennes, "Intensive Supervision Programs for Drug Offenders," in *Smart Sentencing,* 18.
37. Conversation with David A. Ward, 30 March 1990.
38. Ibid., Raymond Holt, "Marion: Separating Fact from Fiction," *Federal Prisons Journal* 2 (1991): 33–34.
39. Frank S. Pearson and Alice Glasel Harper, "Contingent Intermediate Sentences," *Crime and Delinquency* 36 (1990): 75–86.
40. Petersilia, Turner, and Deschennes, "Intensive Supervision Programs for Drug Offenders," 19.
41. Ibid., 35.
42. Petersilia et al., *Granting Felons Probation,* 65.
43. Billie S. Erwin and Laurence A. Bennett, "New Dimensions in Probation: Georgia's Experience with Intensive Probation Supervision (IPS) " (Washington, D.C.: Bureau of Justice Statistics, January 1985).
44. Tonry, "Stated and Latent Functions of ISP," *Crime and Delinquency* 36 (1990): 175–76; Clear and Hardyman, "The New Intensive Supervision Movement"; Joan Petersilia, "Georgia's Intensive Probation: Will the Model Work Elsewhere?" in *Intermediate Punishments,* McCarthy, ed., 15–30.
45. Richard A. Ball, C. Ronald Huff, and J. Robert Lilly, *House Arrest and Correctional Policy: Doing Time at Home* (Beverly Hills: Sage Publications, 1988), 34, chap. 1.
46. Annesley K. Schmidt and Christine E. Curtis, "Electronic Monitoring," in McCarthy, *Intermediate Punishments,* 141–42.
47. Palm Beach Sheriff's Department, "Palm Beach County's In-House Arrest Work Release Program," in McCarthy, *Intermediate Punishments,* 182–83.
48. Ibid., 183–84.
49. Thomas G. Blomberg, Gordon P. Waldo, and Lisa C. Burcroff, "Home Confinement and Electronic Surveillance," in McCarthy, *Intermediate Punishments,* 173.

50. Reported in Blomberg, Waldo, and Burcroff, "Home Confinement," 173.
51. Schmidt and Curtis, "Electronic Monitoring," 148–49.
52. Ibid., 205.
53. Ibid., 218.
54. United States General Accounting Office, *Prison Boot Camps: Too Early to Measure Effectiveness* (Washington, D.C.: U.S. General Accounting Office, September 1988), 3; Doris Layton MacKenzie and Dale G. Parent, "Boot Camp Prisons for Young Offenders," in *Smart Sentencing,* 103–19.
55. Dale K. Sechrest, "Prison 'Boot Camps' Do Not Measure Up," *Federal Probation* (September 1989): 19.
56. Doris Layton MacKenzie et al., "Boot Camp Prisons and Recidivism in Eight States," *Criminology* 33 (1995): 351.
57. Ibid.
58. Ibid., 353.
59. Ibid., 352–53.
60. Doris Layton MacKenzie and Robert Brame, "Shock Incarceration and Positive Adjustment During Community Supervision," *Journal of Quantitative Criminology* 11 (1995): 111–42, 138.
61. Shelcon X. Zhang, "In Search of Hopeful Glimpses: A Critique of Research Strategies in Current Boot Camp Evaluations," *Crime and Delinquency* 44 (1998): 315.
62. Sally T. Hillsman and Judith A. Greene, "The Use of Fines as an Intermediate Sanction," in *Smart Sentencing,* 124–25.
63. Michael Tonry and Kate Hamilton, eds., *Intermediate Sanctions in Overcrowded Times* (Boston: Northeastern University Press, 1995), 15.
64. Hillsman and Greene, "The Use of Fines," 125–26.
65. Ibid., 127–28.
66. Sally T. Hillsman, "Day Fines in New York," in *Intermediate Sanctions in Overcrowded Times,* 23.
67. Hillsman and Greene, "The Use of Fines," 133–34.
68. Douglas C. McDonald, "Unpaid Community Service as a Criminal Sentence," in *Smart Sentencing,* 183–84.
69. Ibid., 182.
70. Ibid., 187.
71. Ibid., 186.
72. Ibid., 189.
73. Ibid., 188–91.
74. Ibid., 191–92.
75. Dale G. Parent, "Day Reporting Centers," in *Intermediate Sanctions in Overcrowded Times,* 125.
76. *Criminal Justice Abstracts* (Monsey, N.Y.: Willow Tree Press, 1998), 105–106.
77. Joan Petersilia, "When Probation Becomes More Dreaded than Prison," *Federal Probation* 54 (1990): 23–27.
78. Ibid.

CHAPTER 14

Prisons, Jails, and Prisoners

CHAPTER OUTLINE

Should We Have Drug Prisons?

Shane Pinkerson was 16 when he started drinking. He was 18 the first time he was arrested for possession of stolen property. Five years later, he was sent away for the fifth time when he broke into a home to score some money to feed his cocaine habit. Sentenced to 4½ to 9 years for robbery, last year Mr. Pinkerson was transferred to a new prison—one the tall, soft-spoken inmate says may finally end his revolving-door ways. The State Correctional Institute in Chester, Pennsylvania, which opened its doors in August, is part of a small but growing movement in the nation's prison system to deal with the unique needs of substance abusers—and thus try to keep them from filling jail beds in the future. The medium-security facility . . . provides full-time treatment for inmates with drug or alcohol problems. It is one of three such specialized prisons in the nation. The state's experiment here, if successful, may offer a glimmer of hope for America's justice system.[1]

INTRODUCTION

A record 1.7 million Americans were behind bars on January 1, 1998 (Figure 14.1). This is more than any other country except Russia (Figure 14.2). Since 1989, the United States has added an average of 1,177 prisoners a week to the prison population. In 1997, the average incarceration rate in the United States was 445 for every 100,000 people, up from 292 in 1990. Some individual states have much higher rates than that average. For example, Texas had an incarceration rate of 717! At the other extreme, Minnesota's rate was 113. In contrast, Western European rates are not only lower than in the United States, but they are declining.[2]

PRISONS

Incarceration in the United States is expensive. The cost of building, maintaining, and operating prisons was nearly $11.5 billion in 1990. It cost an average of $15,513 to keep one prisoner confined for a year in state and federal prisons. (Some states spent much more than the average; Minnesota spent the most, $30,302. Others spent much less; Arkansas, for example, spent $7,557.) Federal and state governments are engaged in the biggest prison construction program in the history of American corrections. At present the United States has enough prison space to hold the city of Orlando, Florida. California spends as much on prisons as it does on higher education.[3]

Money spent on the steeply rising incarcerated population competes with dollars spent on other public services, such as education, health care, roads, and bridges. Why must we choose between spending money on public services for law-abiding people and spending it on convicted criminals? Why not allow taxpayers to keep more of their own money instead of spending it on building prisons and imprisoning offenders? The answer to these questions depends on the missions of prisons. The missions are similar to the purposes of sentencing discussed in Chapter 12: retribution, incapacitation, deterrence, and rehabilitation.

History of U.S. Prisons

Americans have always been schizophrenic about what to do with convicted offenders. According to sociologist and prison expert David A. Ward:

> The Bureau [Federal Bureau of Prisons] has been criticized by conservative hardliners for running "country club" prisons and by liberals and prison reformers for operating a Devil's Island or a House of Pain. Some of the citizens and their elected officials want criminals to be executed or locked up until they die and others call for understanding, the repair of damages to personalities, and preparation for the offender to reenter the free world. Dealing with any group of lawbreakers is a complicated and difficult business with much diversity of opinion even among the experts.[4]

The history of prisons is largely a history of the tensions inherent in the multiple missions of criminal punishment (see Chapter 12). The tension between the missions of retribution and rehabilitation has been particularly strong. According to the criminologist and prison expert Norval Morris:

> The long, slow, painful dance of retribution and reform, first retribution leading, then reform, with rationalization for all the ornate steps in this dance being

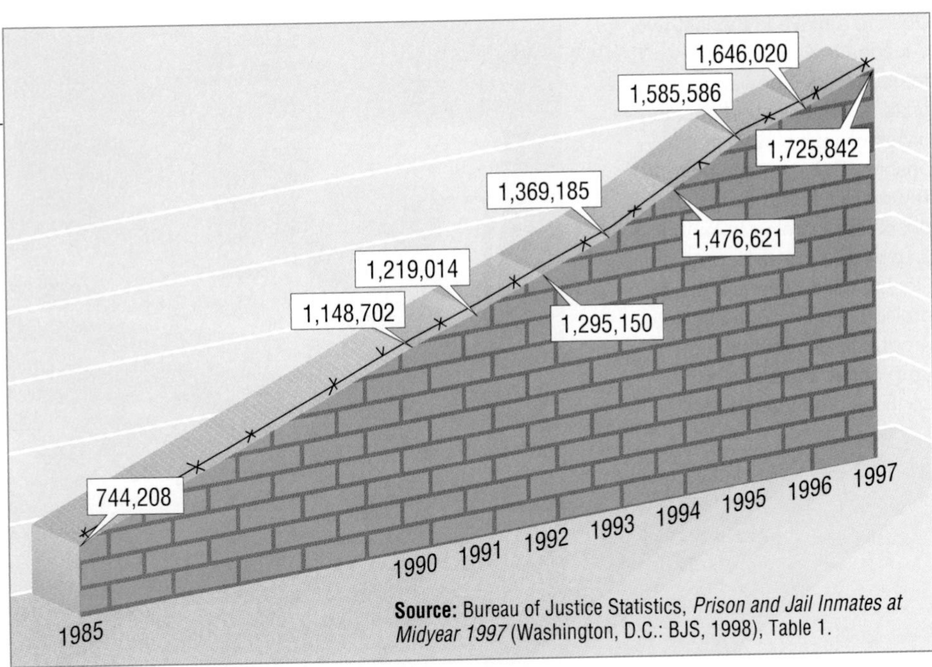

Source: Bureau of Justice Statistics, *Prison and Jail Inmates at Midyear 1997* (Washington, D.C.: BJS, 1998), Table 1.

Figure 14.1
Prisoners in Federal and State Prisons, 1985–1997

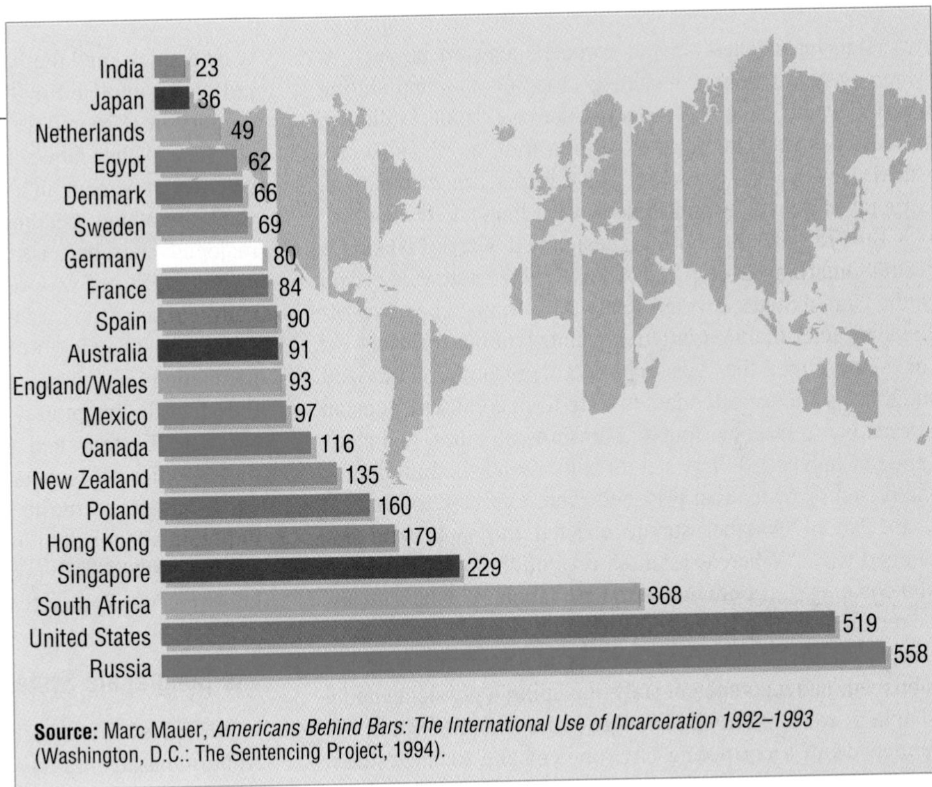

Source: Marc Mauer, *Americans Behind Bars: The International Use of Incarceration 1992–1993* (Washington, D.C.: The Sentencing Project, 1994).

Figure 14.2
International Incarceration Rates, 1993, per 100,000 Population

based on many unproved assumptions, is a performance that should be known to all who hope to understand contemporary punishments; but it is far from common knowledge.[5]

Punishment is as ancient as recorded history. One of the earliest known writings, the Code of Hammurabi, contains a list of penalties chipped in stone. These penalties strongly resemble the mandatory sentences of our own day (discussed in Chapter 12). Prisons, too, are ancient, but their mission has changed. Until well into the 1700s, prisons were used to hold suspects and defendants to ensure their appearance for trial, not to punish convicted offenders for their crimes. Punishment in colonial America took a number of forms, but prison was not one of them. Capital punishment was commonly prescribed, if not so frequently practiced. Occasionally, early

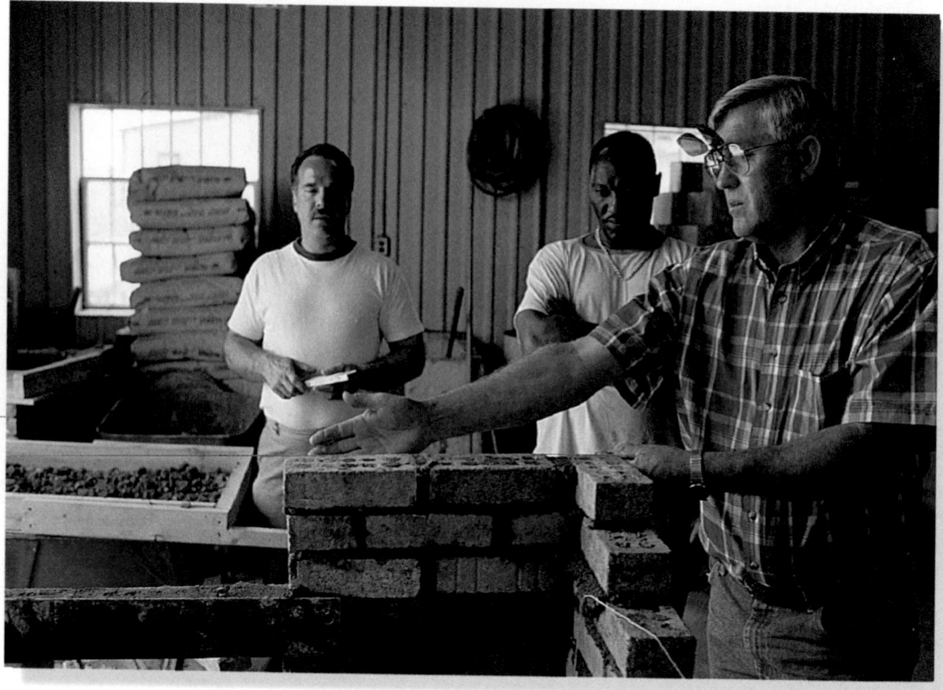

Despite a move in the last two decades toward a more retributive ideology about prisons, rehabilitation-oriented programs still survive in many prisons. These inmates of a Taylorsville, North Carolina, prison are learning to lay bricks as part of a job skills program. Do you think prisons should provide inmates with such programs as vocational training, drug abuse therapy, and continuing education?

American magistrates ordered corporal punishment, such as whipping or mutilation, including cropping ears and slitting nostrils. Public shaming—stocks, ducking stools, pillories, dunce caps, and signs such as "I am a fornicator"—also prevailed. However, far more pervasive in practice than capital, corporal, and shaming punishments were fines and restitution.[6]

In 1785, Massachusetts designated Castle Island, a fortress guarding Boston Harbor, as the first statewide prison in the United States devoted solely to confining *convicted* offenders rather than *holding* defendants waiting for trials. At the same time, the Massachusetts legislature authorized judges to sentence offenders to long-term confinement as an alternative to the older public punishments, fines, and restitution (Chapter 13). The statute authorizing the building of the prison provided that prisoners were expected to perform "hard labor." Another statute enacted the same year explained why: "Whereas idleness is often the parent of fraud and cheating . . . confinement to hard labour may be a means of reclaiming such offenders." Convicts served under military discipline; dietary and sanitary requirements were established; and a competent staff, including a physician and a chaplain, were provided. The basic idea was to remove offenders from a corrupting environment and to make them work. The isolation and the work was supposed to redeem their souls, reform their bodies, and instill in them the habits of law-abiding citizens ready, willing, and capable of doing the work of society.[7]

The Solitary System

The Pennsylvania Quakers soon stole the limelight from Massachusetts as prison innovators. The Quakers considered physical pain inflicted purely for retribution barbaric and cruel. In an enlightened effort to reform "fallen" citizens, the Quakers designed the Walnut Street Jail in Philadelphia. The jail was completed in 1790, followed by the Western Penitentiary in 1826 and the Eastern Penitentiary in 1830.

The Walnut Street Jail represented the first use of segregated confinement in America. It provided adequate food, shelter, clothing, bedding, and medical care without fees—a major advance, because these necessities had always depended on the ability of prisoners to pay for them. Prisoners made nails, cut stone, and did other work they could perform in their own cells. They had to remain silent at all times, supposedly meditating on their past wrongs and thinking about improving their lives in the future—hence, the name **penitentiary.**

The Eastern and Western penitentiaries had similar philosophies. Prisoners remained in solitary confinement performing tasks during the day—except Sunday—and meditating in silent isolation during their idle hours. This combination of solitary work and silent meditation came to be known as the **Pennsylvania system.**

The Congregate System

In 1817, New York built its own version of a new prison at Auburn, based entirely on solitary confinement in small cells and a strict rule of silence. Within a short time, however, so many prisoners committed suicide or had mental breakdowns, due to confinement in tiny cells with no exercise and no work, that authorities modified the system. The **Auburn** or **congregate system** imposed a rule of prisoners working in absolute silence as groups during the day and solitary confinement at night. Keepers flogged on the spot anyone who broke the rules.

The Pennsylvania and Auburn systems had several common features. Prisons were huge, walled fortresses in which wardens had total control over their prisoners. Violating the rules of either silence or work resulted in swift, harsh punishment. Authorities considered both prison systems more humane methods of punishment than corporal and capital punishment and mutilation—and they may well have been, initially. Both were intended to reform prisoners through the presumed salutary effects of silent meditation, hard work, healthy food, and religion. Under both systems it was assumed that following this regimen, prisoners would return to society as law-abiding, compliant citizens who worked for a living rather than preying on others.

Both systems were part of a much larger movement in nineteenth-century America: the institutionalization of life outside the home. Historically, most life activities—work, play, education, and punishment—took place in or around individuals' homes. After about 1820, the center for these activities increasingly moved from the home to large, centralized buildings—factories, gymnasiums, hospitals, schools, "reformatories," and "penitentiaries."[8]

Most observers soon noted that penitentiaries did not reform their prisoners, and they discovered that the reformation of offenders was not their sole—perhaps not even their primary—purpose. Prisons were increasingly becoming custodial warehouses for criminals, and despite the reform efforts and humanitarian rhetoric, they could also be cruel. One prisoner from the Elmira Reformatory, an institution widely hailed for its reformatory ideals, reported the results of failing to complete a work assignment:

> I knew I was in for a beating and I had a terror of what was coming. I refused to leave my cell. They stuck into the cell an iron rod with a two-foot hook on the end, heated red hot, and poked me with it. I tried to defend myself, but my clothing took fire, and the iron burned my breast. I finally succumbed, was handcuffed and taken to the bathroom. I asked Brockway [the renowned, born-again Christian reformer] if I had not been punished enough. He laughed at me. I got half a dozen blows with the paddle right across the kidneys. The pain was so agonizing that I fainted. They revived me, and when I begged for mercy, Brockway struck me on the head with a strap, knocked me insensible. The next thing I knew I was lying on a cot in the dungeon, shackled to an iron bar. The next day I was again hoisted and beaten, returned to the dungeon, and after one day's rest, beaten again. Then I was put in the cell in Murderer's Row, where I remained for twenty-one days on bread and water.[9]

The Progressive Reforms, 1890–1970

The Progressive reformers of the early twentieth century attacked the existing prisons as cruel and barbaric, just as the initiators of prisons had attacked capital, corporal, and mutilative punishments. These new reformers urged more effective means to "rehabilitate" offenders. Their methods combined humane treatment, counseling, vocational training, and discipline intended to make prisoners fit into society. The Progressives instituted many rehabilitative programs. They created the indeterminate sentence and parole boards, making imprisonment dependent on prisoners' gradual rehabilitation, not on their past crimes, and advocated separate facilities for men, women, and delinquent children.[10]

By the 1940s, the **correctional institution**—based on the penal philosophy of rehabilitation—emerged as the cruelty and harsh discipline in the custody-oriented **fortress prison** diminished. In principle and practice, correctional institutions were more humane and accommodating than "big houses," the name for old fortress prisons. They provided less intrusive discipline; more yard and recreational privileges; more liberal visitation and mail policies; more amenities, such as movies; and more rehabilitation programs, such as education, vocational training, and therapy.[11]

The Return to Punishment, 1970–Present

During the 1960s, reformers on both ends of the ideological spectrum attacked the Progressive reforms. Liberals believed prisons were stripping away prisoners' rights in exchange for what prison administrators and treatment-oriented experts considered prisoners' "needs." From the conservative side came the attack that prisons did not punish prisoners sufficiently to prevent them from committing future crimes. Academics joined the chorus of criticism by claiming that rehabilitation did not work. All were convinced that the correctional institution was not working, as indicated by prison riots, rising crime rates, and recidivism. As a result, calls came for new goals for imprisonment; new kinds of prisons; different prison populations; revised prison conditions; a new breed of prison guard—called corrections officers—and a more modern administrative system within prisons; a heightened accountability to outside authorities; and even alternatives to incarceration for some types of prisoners.[12]

Nevertheless, according to prison scholar Robert Johnson:

> The benefits of correctional institutions are easily exaggerated. To my mind, the differences between the Big Houses and correctional institutions are of degree rather than kind. Correctional institutions did not correct. Nor did they abolish the pains of imprisonment. They were, at bottom, simply more tolerable warehouses than the Big Houses they supplanted, less a departure than a toned-down imitation. Often, correctional institutions occupied the same physical plant as the Big Houses. Indeed, one might classify them as Big Houses gone soft.[13]

Today, we still call prisons *correctional* institutions. However, many criminologists maintain that since the middle of the 1960s a new type of prison has emerged to replace the correctional institution in everything but name. Criminologists call this new type of prison the **violent prison.** In Hans Toch's blunt language, the modern prison is a "human warehouse with a jungle-like underground." Extreme differences, distrust, and hatred divide prisoners. Nonwhites, particularly African Americans and Hispanics, now outnumber whites in

Despite the fact that this scene is from a movie, the violence it portrays is reflective of what criminologists call today's violent prison climate. Why do you think that tensions within prisons have increased so dramatically in the last few decades?

many prisons, and racially constituted gangs and cliques often dominate. Identities based on "macho images" encourage violence. Links between gangs in the slums outside and prisoners from the gangs inside have altered the view that prisons are isolated from the surrounding community, particularly when they are located near large cities.[14]

In the eyes of many prisoners today, prison is the ultimate test of manhood. A man in prison is able to secure what he wants and protect what he has: "In here, a man gets what he can," and "nobody can force a man to do something he don't want to," are key elements of the belief system. Any prisoner who does not meet these standards is not a man, "has no respect for himself," and is therefore not entitled to respect from others. According to Professor Robert Blecker, who, with convicted armed robber John Allen, spent hundreds of hours observing life in Lorton Central Prison outside Washington, D.C.:

> Prisoners constantly confront life-threatening situations. If you let someone cut in line in front of you, others will take greater advantage. But if you confront him, you face possible lethal retaliation. Phone lines, canteen lines, chow lines, the gym—all are dangerous spots. A new prison ethos prevails among the younger generation: Smaller slights are taken as disrespect. Today's kids no longer settle "beefs" by fists; no longer is a fair fight one-on-one with equal weapons. Routinely, now, they wear masks and attack in groups.[15]

Maximum Security Prisons

Not all U.S. prisons are alike; prisons are designed according to three security levels—maximum, medium, and minimum security. The design of prisons according to security level originated in the discovery in the 1800s that problems arose when hard-core criminals are confined in the same place with nondangerous, first-time offenders. Hence, separate prisons were created to confine different types of offenders.

Violent and repeat offenders are confined in **maximum security prisons.** Maximum security prisons hold about half of all prisoners in the United States. As the name implies, these prisons focus almost exclusively on security. Their main mission is to prevent prisoners from escaping or hurting themselves, each other, and prison staff. To prevent escape, high walls surround most maximum security prisons. Armed guards stand in observation towers watching the walls at all times, using searchlights and even electronic devices to prevent prisoner escapes. Inside maximum security prisons, supervision, surveillance, and control are extensive. Whenever prisoners move from one area of the prison to another, they do so only in groups and under close supervision by corrections officers.[16]

Traditional Maximum Security Prisons

In older maximum security prisons, large cell blocks arranged in tiers permit a single guard to observe hundreds of cells at one time. Bars replace doors and windows. Television surveillance makes it easier to watch prisoners, not only in their cells but also in the shower, at meals, and even in the toilet. Prisoners may be strip-searched before and after visits, and even visitors are subject to pat-downs. Officers take "head counts" throughout the day; anyone not accounted for prompts major efforts to locate the "missing" prisoner. Metal furniture built into the walls and floors improves security by preventing chairs and tables from being used as obstacles and weapons. Scraping, clashing, and echoing metal causes high noise levels. It is an understatement to say that prisons are not quiet places. They are also boring. Prisoners spend many hours in their cells with little or no activity.[17]

Most maximum security prisons are large and were built to last a long time. More than 40 percent of existing prisons were built before 1925; 11 percent were built before 1875! Eighty percent of all prisoners live in the oldest prisons, most of which hold more than 1,000 prisoners each. The largest prison in the United States is in Jackson, Michigan; it holds 5,000 prisoners! The oldest prisons are usually not only the largest but also have the largest populations. Maximum security prisoners are older and more violent than those incarcerated in other prisons.[18]

Super Maximum Security Prisons

The federal prison system has operated three **super maximum prisons:**

1. The legendary Alcatraz from the 1930s until 1963.
2. The federal penitentiary at Marion, Illinois, from 1964.
3. The new Administrative Maximum (ADX) security penitentiary in Florence, Colorado, since 1994.

According to the Office of Public Affairs of the Federal Bureau of Prisons:

> Florence (ADX) has been designed to operate in a humane, safe manner that is in accord with all applicable legal standards and sound correctional practices. . . . Unusually high security prisons are necessary at institutions like Marion and Florence because they confine the most serious escape and assault risks in the Bureau, as well as some equally dangerous inmates from a number of states. Most Marion inmates have demonstrated by highly assaultive, predatory, or serious escape-related behavior that they are in a stage of their institutional career where they cannot function in traditional, open population institutions of lower security. They are simply the most violent and dangerous inmates in the entire system, and most of them have proven it repeatedly.[19]

Therefore, according to the Bureau of Prisons:

> An unfortunate but real aspect of modern correctional administration in America is that many prison populations include growing numbers of extremely violent, predatory individuals. This, in part, is due to the emergence of prison gangs that seek to control internal drug trafficking and other illicit activity, and rely on threats, intimidation, assault, and murder to accomplish their objectives. Another threat to prison security comes from major offenders, who have immense outside assets, or lead sophisticated criminal organizations with resources that make violent, outside-assisted escapes a very real possibility. Furthermore, the lack of an enforceable Federal death penalty for murderous activity in prison means that, especially for inmates already serving life without parole, there is little effective deterrent to murder while incarcerated.[20]

Not all prisoners, of course, see the super maximum security prisons the same way as the Federal Bureau of Prisons does. One prisoner described life in super maximum security at Marion this way:

> Some men at Marion have grown up here in the harshest hole ever constructed. Deprived for so long of a normal existence, our measure of self-worth is gauged by our capacity to endure whatever physical or psychological torture is thrust upon us. Men along the tiers boast of surviving brutal riots, of running gauntlets of club-wielding guards, of being starved and beaten in places like San Quentin, Attica and Huntsville. It is both an indictment of society and a human tragedy that the state of imprisonment in America has been allowed to degenerate to this level.[21]

Super maximum security prisons fascinate and horrify (depending on your point of view) the press, public, and politicians. According to Professor David A. Ward, despite the small number of prisoners they have confined, Alcatraz (250 prisoners) and Marion (350 prisoners) "have been responsible for more newspaper and magazine articles, more movies and television spots, more hearings before congressional committees, and more debates among criminologists and penologists than have been produced by all other federal prisons combined." Alcatraz confined some of the most notorious crime figures in our history—Al Capone, John Dillinger, Pretty Boy Floyd, and Baby Face Nelson.

According to Professor Ward, "Marion contained a small, special unit to hold the country's high-visibility spies, an 'avowed racist' serial killer, and the country's most famous prison writer, Jack Abbott, author of *In the Belly of the Beast.*" Marion is the "end of the line" for the "worst of the worst" prisoners. At Marion, prisoners are locked in their cells for 23 hours a day. Whenever convicts leave their cells, they are handcuffed, their legs are chained, and three guards armed with nightsticks surround them. (See Chapter 15 for a discussion of life at Marion.)[22]

New-Generation Maximum Security Prisons

Not all maximum security prisons fit the description of either the traditional or the super prisons. In recent years, a new idea for both building and managing maximum security prisons has arisen. **New-generation prisons** are based on the idea that offenders are sent to prison *as* punishment, not *for* punishment. These prisons are built so that both the architecture and the style of management contribute to a safe, humane confinement where the confinement itself is supposed to be the punishment. (See the discussion on prison management styles, Prison Administration.)

New-generation prisons usually contain six to eight physically separated units within a secure perimeter. Each unit contains 40 to 50 prisoners, with a cell for each inmate.

Table 14.1
Daily Schedule and Counts, Oak Park Heights New-Generation Prison

6:30	Wake-up
6:45–6:55	Live count–must show movement
7:00–7:20	Breakfast
7:35	Report to work
7:35–11:25	Work or program–receiving and orientation
11:25–11:40	Return to unit–stand-up count
11:40–12:15	Lunch
12:15	Return to work
12:15–3:25	Work or program–receiving and orientation
1:50–2:00	Education only–down to gym
2:00–3:30	Education only–mandatory gym
2:50–3:00	Verification count
3:25–3:35	Return to unit–verification count
3:35–4:50	Free time
4:50–5:00	Stand-up count
5:00–5:30	Dinner
5:30–8:30	Evening program
8:30–9:55	Evening program–free time
10:00	Stand-up count–inmates are locked
10:55–11:55	Shift change–live count
1:00	Live count
3:00	Live count
5:00	Live count

Each also has dining rooms, a laundry, counseling offices, game rooms, and an enclosed outdoor recreation yard and work area. Because these units are only two levels high, continual surveillance from secure "bubbles" monitors all prisoners' interactions with each other and staff. These self-contained units make it possible to keep many prisoners secure within an overall large perimeter, while at the same time allowing for groups small enough to participate in congregate activities. The design also permits specialization. One unit focuses on drug dependency. Another houses prisoners attending school. A third concentrates on work projects. Another is reserved for disciplinary problems.[23]

New-generation prisons are still maximum security prisons. For example, most prisoners at Oak Park Heights, the new-generation prison in Minnesota, are violent offenders. The prison houses not only the most dangerous prisoners in Minnesota, but also federal prisoners ranked in the highest-security category. Furthermore, prisoners have a choice of programs, but they cannot choose to do nothing. They can work, go to school, or obtain treatment; but they cannot sit in their cells. Furthermore, the security is the highest. Prisoners are under constant surveillance; they do not move about unattended. Table 14.1 reproduces the daily schedule and security counts at Oak Park Heights.

Medium and Minimum Security Prisons

About one-third of all prisoners are cofined in **medium security prisons** enclosed by double fences topped with barbed wire. Outside cell blocks in units of 150 cells or fewer are common, as are dormitories and even cubicles in some facilities. Medium security prisons are not as old as maximum security prisons; more than 87 percent have been built since 1925. Although supposedly less focused on security, medium security prisons follow many practices common in maximum security prisons, such as head counts, electronic surveillance, and cell watching. Unlike maximum security prisoners, prisoners in medium security prisons work without constant supervision. The prison design, especially in newer medium security prisons, comes from campus or courtyard models.[24]

Minimum security prisons hold only 11 percent of all prisoners. **Minimum security prisons** are newer than both maximum and medium security prisons; most were built after 1950. Vocational training and treatment, not security, are the focus of minimum security prisons. Minimum security prisoners mainly comprise first-time, nonviolent, white-collar and younger offenders who are not considered dangerous or likely to escape.

The grounds of a minimum security prison resemble a college campus, with low buildings centered about a recreational area. Critics call them resorts or, in the case of the federal minimum security prison camps, "Club Fed," because the media reported that during the 1970s and 1980s, Watergate conspirators and Wall Street inside traders spent their afternoons sunbathing and playing tennis.

Minimum security prisons emphasize trust and a more normal lifestyle. Prisoners eat in small groups, often at tables for four, instead of at long rows of tables that all face in one direction, a common feature of maximum and medium security prisons. Minimum security prisoners also have a modicum of privacy. Some even have private rooms with doors that prisoners may lock.

Most minimum security prisons also provide a range of programs for prisoners, including vocational training, academic education, psychiatric treatment, and counseling. Some minimum security prisons supply family visiting facilities, where prisoners can stay with their families for up to three days at a time. A considerable number of prisoners work on the prison grounds or are released for the day on work-study programs that allow them to hold jobs or attend neighboring schools and colleges.[25]

Women's Prisons

In all societies, men convicts outnumber women convicts; hence, men's prisons also outnumber women's. Most women's prisons display little evidence of external security. However, that is changing. For example, the Ohio State Reformatory for Women at Marysville used to look like a college campus. It had no fences and only a few prisoners were considered dangerous. Now, razor-wire tops tall fences. Why? Both because the Marysville population has increased 600 percent since 1977 and the number of drug offenders incarcerated there has markedly increased.[26]

Most women's prisons are combined maximum, medium, and minimum security institutions. Often a single cottage, dormitory, or wing makes up the maximum security area of a woman's prison. "Honor cottages" confine minimum security prisoners. Separate sections exist for prisoners of various ages, disciplinary statuses, programs, and sentence lengths. Their usually rural setting, absence of security apparatus, prevalence of private rooms, and typical cottage architecture make women's prisons relatively less gloomy than men's prisons.

However, limited numbers usually mean limited educational opportunities and training. Most women's prisons focus on work that maintains the institution, such as cooking, cleaning, laundry, and sewing. Domestic work has characterized women's prisons since the separate women's prison movement in the late nineteenth and early twentieth centuries.[27]

PRISON ADMINISTRATION

Research has revealed a variety of prison management styles. Dr. George Beto, former director of the Texas Department of Corrections, adopted a **control model of management,** a style that originated in the late nineteenth century at the famous Elmira reformatory. The control model emphasized prisoner obedience, work, and education. Beto ran every prison in Texas as a maximum security prison. He believed that prisoners needed order, that only through order could they develop work and educational skills that would make their lives in prison more productive and also facilitate their later reintegration into the community.

Formal, strict paramilitary lines from the warden and assistant wardens to the most junior correctional officer defined the duties within the prison. Official rules and regulations governed most actions of both staff and prisoners. Prisoners walked between painted lines in the corridors; loud talking constituted a punishable offense. In short, daily life inside the prisons was a busy but carefully orchestrated routine of numbering, counting, checking, locking, and monitoring inmate movement to and from work activities and treatment programs.[28]

The political scientist John DiIulio, who studied prison management styles in Texas, Michigan, and California, found that under the control model of management,

> officers had a sense of mission, an esprit de corps, and an amazing knowledge of the prison's history. Treatment and work opportunities were offered on a regular basis and well administered. . . . In short, life inside the Walls [the oldest prison in Texas] was in general safe, humane, productive, calm, stable, and predictable.[29]

Prisoners who violated the rules received the swift, certain punishment of shifts of solitary confinement and extra work assignments. Prisoners who obeyed orders, worked, and "did their own time" received the carrot of the most liberal good time (time off for good behavior) provisions in American prisons—two days off for every productive, problem-free day served.[30]

However, the control model had its shortcomings. In Texas, it suffered from the **building-tender system,** which relied on prisoners to assist correctional officers in managing cell blocks. According to Dr. Beto:

> In any contemporary prison, there is bound to be some level of inmate organization, some manner of inmate society. . . . The question is this: who selects the leaders? Are the inmates to select them? Or is the administration to choose them or at least influence the choice? If the former, the extent of control over organized and semi-organized inmate life is lessened; if the latter, the measure of control is strengthened.[31]

The building-tender system led to a con-boss system in which prison gangs, organized along racial and ethnic lines, ran major parts of the Texas prison system. Violence, exploitation, fear, and disruption followed.[32]

The Michigan prison system exemplifies a **responsibility management approach.** This model stresses the responsibility of prisoners for their own actions, not administrative control to ensure prescribed behavior. Michigan adopted not a single maximum security classification, but a number of security levels. Proper classification, according to the responsibility model, permits placing prisoners in the least restrictive prison consistent with security, safety, and humane confinement. Even prisoners in maximum security prisons should not live totally regimented lives. They should be given a significant degree of freedom and then held to account for their actions. According to one Michigan administrator:

> We go by the idea that prison should be as unrestrictive as possible. Don't misunderstand. Order comes first. You have to keep control. Security is number one through one thousand. But we don't have to smother people to keep things under control. We try to show inmates respect and expect it in return. We are more willing than Texas to give them air and then hold them accountable. . . . We attempt to operate safely in the least restrictive environment possible. . . . If Texas opts for the most restrictive, we opt for the least restrictive.[33]

The responsibility model creates a better prison milieu and focuses on the importance of prisoner responsibility. It also requires enormous paperwork. Furthermore, it has generated considerable opposition from some staff; among correctional officers, it has stimulated animosity toward the "brass" at headquarters in Lansing. One disgruntled officer complained:

> Lansing plays the spoiling grandparent. They come up with all sorts of goodies to spoil. They give the inmates their own way too much and then ask us to keep order and raise them properly. Bulls—t! They reap what they sow. We are made into scapegoats for their a——e schemes. We look like some kind of bartenders' union. We got rid of the symbols of authority. But we lost more than the symbols. Property control is a nightmare.[34]

According to one 30-year veteran:

> I'd love to have a prison that could run the way the model says. But we've got a little problem: impulsive convicts and human nature. . . . This system deprives inmates of the right to safety in the name of giving them other rights. . . . A cellblock should be like a residential street. Would you want to live on a street where your neighbors were always shouting? Where most of what they shouted was vulgar and violent? Would you permit your neighbors to assault you and each other?[35]

Of course it is not perfect, but Michigan prisons have provided more humane, safe, and secure confinement than many other state prisons. The control and responsibility systems do not exist in pure form in most prisons. Some states, such as California, balance elements of control and responsibility into what DiIulio calls **consensus prison management.**[36]

Prison management to a large extent reflects the personality and management style of prison wardens. Some believe it was the personality of George Beto that accounted for much of the success of the Texas prisons under the control model. Certainly, more than just the architecture of the new-generation prison at Oak Park Heights, Minnesota, accounts for the virtual elimination of serious violent incidents, suicide, and drug use in that prison. The architecture has its counterpart in the new management philosophy that accompanies it. Warden Frank Wood (and his successors) exemplified this new management philosophy, which requires personal interaction among the warden, inmates, and staff. Wood spent more than 25 percent of his time, in his words, "eyeball to eyeball" with inmates and staff. He personally conducted the final prisoner orientation meeting that makes them "understand their responsibilities and the prison's responsibilities to them." Wood's philosophy also proposes that:

- "Staff should treat the inmates as we would want our sons, brothers, or fathers [and, presumably, in women's prisons our daughters, sisters, and mothers] treated."
- Inmates who do not work or go to school are not free to watch TV and "roam around their units" but are locked in their cells.
- The response to troublemaking is individual and not group punishment.
- Units are locked up on a random, regular basis for three to four days to "purge contraband."
- Every lock is tested every day.
- Inmates are kept very busy.
- The staff always promptly listen to inmate requests, however unimportant the requests may appear.
- Inmates are periodically rotated into the prison's mental health unit for observation and a change of environment, and for relief from nearby inmates and staff.[37]

The effects of this management philosophy are positive. Oak Park Heights has virtually eliminated serious violence, both between prisoners and toward staff.

Mark S. Fleisher, a cultural anthropologist, describes life in Lompoc, California, federal prison based on participant observation and open-ended interviews. Despite housing many violent prisoners, Lompoc has a relatively low rate of violence, due in part to management and a prison culture that rewards peace and quiet.[38]

Prison administrators are often caught in a double bind because they serve competing formal and informal goals. Prisons are supposed to both punish and rehabilitate prisoners, as well as protect society and other inmates from assaultive, escape-prone prisoners. These conflicting goals lead to actions that may offend vocal interest groups. Also, when wardens take measures ensure security or to punish prisoners, they offend counselors and other staff committed to rehabilitation. At the same time, actions taken to encourage prisoner rehabilitation can anger line officers, who have the direct responsibility of maintaining prison security, and the large segment of the public that believes prisons exist to "punish" prisoners.[39]

CORRECTIONS OFFICERS

Corrections officers used to be called called guards because of the misguided belief that their primary job was to protect the public by maintaining order and control over prisoners and preventing them from escaping. Those who are on the front line of protecting the public have to do a lot more than "merely opening and closing doors." According to Harold E. Williamson, "Corrections is a service industry. . . . Those whose primary roles are custody and surveillance . . . are actually performing paraprofessional roles involving interpersonal and technical skills."[40]

According to Stan Stojkovic and Rick Lovell, corrections officers have to play the roles of "father, mother, babysitter, counselor, priest, and police officer to prisoners."[41] Their duties include:

- Supervising living, work, dining, and recreation areas. In new-generation prisons these might be small units; in traditional prisons, they could be large cell blocks and dining halls.
- Transfering prisoners to hospitals, courts, and even to community visits with their families.
- Serving on disciplinary boards.
- Sitting in towers and protecting the gates that separate inside from outside and one area from another within the prison.[42]

The most important cell block duty is conducting the "count." That means that several times a day, officers account for every prisoner. Even one unaccounted-for prisoner leads to a halt in all operations and movement. Miscounting brings disciplinary action. In most large maximum security prisons, cell block duty is dangerous. Prisoners outnumber

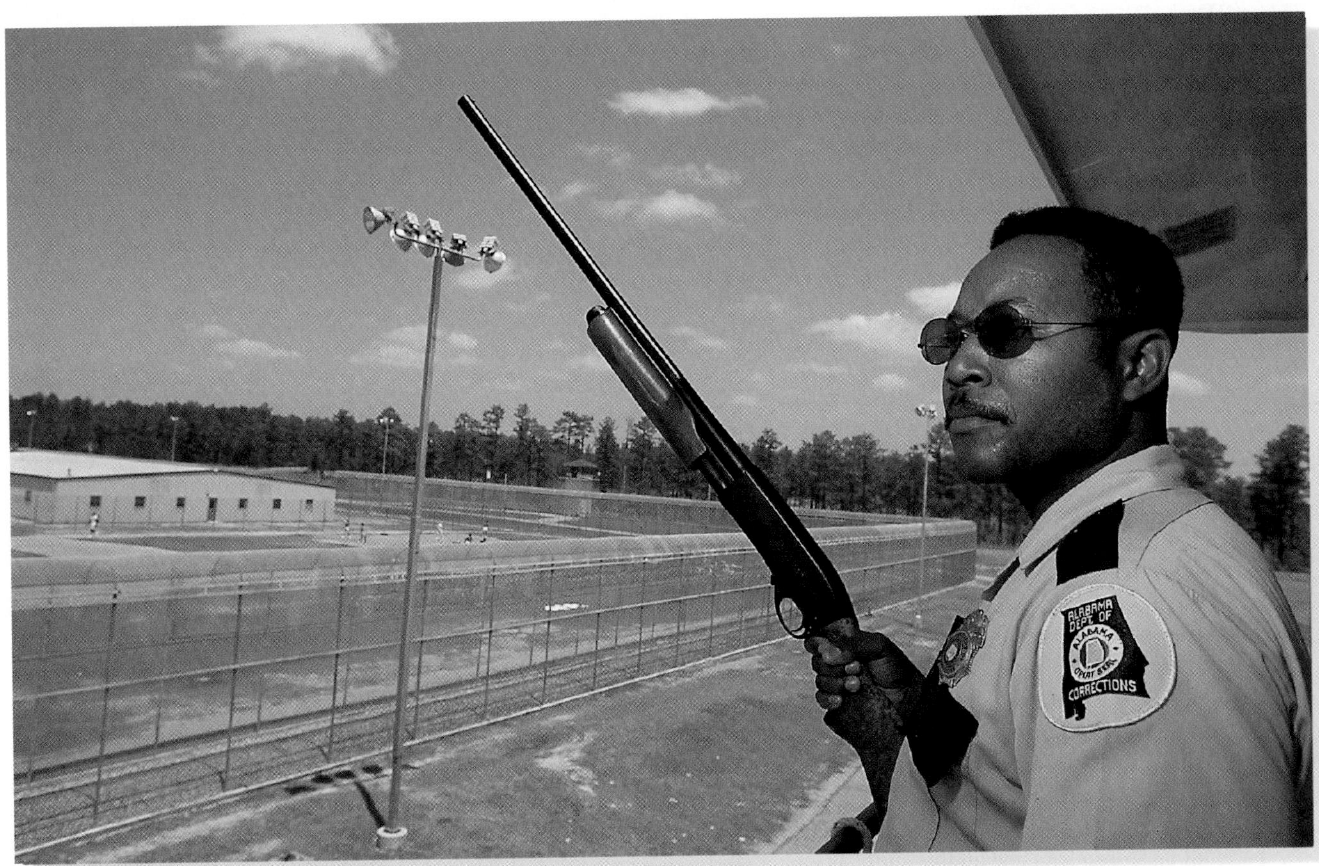

Tower duty is the loneliest guard job because the tower guards have no contact with anyone except by telephone or walkie-talkie. On tower duty, officers cannot read, listen to the radio, or watch television.

officers by as much as 50 to 1, so officers depend more on communicating authority than on power. During cell duty, particularly in large cell blocks, chances increase that prisoners will assault, overwhelm, and take officers hostage. During riots, the situation worsens—prisoners may beat, rape, and sometimes kill officers.[43]

Other officers supervise the work areas, such as stores and factories, and watch the gates. Tower duty is the loneliest guard job because tower guards have no contact with anyone except by telephone or walkie-talkie. On tower duty, officers cannot read, listen to the radio, or watch television. In the past, tower duty was regarded as highly undesirable. In violent and insecure prisons, however, officers seek the relatively safer tower duty. Tower guards remind prisoners as no one or nothing else can of the true nature of their confinement. Consequently, tower guards and prisoners share an open animosity.[44]

The Supervision Hierarchy

Above line officers in rank are sergeants, lieutenants, and captains. Sergeants supervise cell blocks, work units, kitchens, and hospitals. They check correctional officers' work, assign them to specific tasks, and even fill in for absentees. In traditional prisons, social distance separates line officers from lieutenants and captains. True to the operations of any paramilitary organization, corrections officers receive orders from their superior officers, orders that lieutenants and captains expect the officers to carry out efficiently and effectively.

Lieutenants act as prison police officers who keep the peace by stopping fights and other prison disturbances. They have to maintain order by "walking" prisoners to isolation or forcibly removing them from cells when necessary. When they are not settling disturbances, they go on preventive patrol, checking and "shaking down" prisoners for weapons and other contraband. Lieutenants police not only the prisoners but also the line officers. They search lower-ranking officers for contraband and weapons, just as they do prisoners. Lieutenants check on both prisoners and officers to make sure they are doing their jobs. Further, lieutenants write disciplinary reports, called "tickets," on officers, just as officers write them on prisoners.

The few captains manage the paperwork required by bureaucracy—personnel evaluations, budget preparations, and disciplinary committee reports. Records management is an onerous task, one that grows more ponderous as prisons turn to bureaucratic management and as courts and other outside agencies demand increasing accountability.

The "Other Prisoners"

Corrections officers are the "other prisoners," according to one expert. Their close contact with prisoners stigmatizes them. "Even close friends do not know what to make of the prevailing belief that corrections officers are sadistic, corrupt, stupid, and incompetent." Furthermore, officers, like prisoners, are often locked off from the outside world. Stateville, in Illinois, for example, supplies dormitories for guards living inside the prison, and trailer parks for married couples who live outside the prison walls. Officers also frequently become the scapegoats for prison problems and failures. Higher-echelon administrators and treatment personnel can easily blame the officers for breaches of prison discipline and failures in prisoner rehabilitation.[45]

In some places, fear and uncertainty permeate the world of corrections officers. Corrections officers carry no weapons because prisoners might overpower them and use the seized weapons:

> I was back there on the job when it broke out. I think every officer out there was frightened because we had no weapons. The tower officers—they didn't know exactly what to do. They were firing warning shots. You couldn't see clearly what they were doing, so you didn't know whether to duck, run or stand still and then you look at the inmates and they are coming with sticks, baseball bats, iron bars and all this stuff. Any man who says he wasn't afraid, I'd have to call him a liar.[46]

Women and Minority Corrections Officers

Selection of corrections officers in many prison systems gives high priority to physical standards—height, weight, and general strength. Empirical data, however, do not indicate that guard work requires this premium on physical strength. According to Gordon Hawkins:

> One thing which is quite certain is that the almost universal insistence on certain physical standards which restrict the selection of potentially qualified employees is a mistake. The fact that a man weighs 145 pounds (the Attica requirement) is no index of character or ability or indeed of anything except the extent to which he can tip the scales. The officer's control over an inmate depends primarily on his skills of persuasion and leadership. Skill in interpersonal relations [is crucial].[47]

Prior to 1972, men officers always guarded men prisoners. Due to the impetus of affirmative action lawsuits and federal and state legislation, that situation has begun to change. The number of women corrections officers varies from state to state. Nationwide, women constitute only about 6 percent of corrections officers. However, the number in some states is considerably higher. In Louisiana, Wyoming, and Kentucky, more than 15 percent of corrections officers are women.[48]

Prison administrators have historically excluded women from guard work in men's prisons, primarily because of the general belief that women's physical weakness would allow male prisoners to overpower and assault them. Although few empirical studies have examined the point, informed opinion holds that in those prisons that employ women, women and men officers experience comparable assault rates. In Illinois, none of the 39 women officers and 28 women trainees serving in medium and maximum security men's prisons have been attacked by men prisoners. Corrections officials in New York regard gender integration as a success, despite one knife attack on a woman officer in Attica.[49]

Women correctional officers encounter various reactions from prisoners and male staff, from total support to amusement to outright hostility. The warden of one maximum security prison for men reported that the "presence of women is long overdue. We're glad to see women in our facility. It adds a new dimension to corrections. It's a little too soon to say, but I tend to think that women are more respected than male guards."[50]

A female correctional officer in San Quentin suggests that despite men's reluctance to have women colleagues, women have made male correctional officers less brutal:

> [Having women in the pen] brings about a calmer setting. It also forces male officers not to act as "big, bad and tough" because here they have this little 5′2″, 115 lb. woman standing beside them, putting a guy that is 6′4″, 230 lbs. in cuffs saying, "Come on now, act right," and not having any problem doing it. Whereas he might have to go in there with two or three other guys and tackle him down to cuff him. It also forces them to recognize that they can't go home and talk about how bad and mean they are and what a tough day they have had because some little chickie can do the same thing he is doing.[51]

Some believe that adding nonwhite officers will improve guard work, but it is not clear whether this is true. Race conflicts in prisons affect officers as well as prisoners. In San Quentin, for example, although violence is missing from race relations among staff, racial conflicts and competition are still present. The Stanford Prison Experiment suggested that the role guards play is far more important than their sex or race in determining how they do their work. Students participated in an experiment in which some acted as officers and others as prisoners. Some officers enjoyed their dominant position and harassed prisoners:

> In less than a week the experience of imprisonment undid (temporarily) a lifetime of learning: human values were suspended, self-concepts were challenged and the ugliest, most base, pathological side of human nature surfaced. We were horrified because we saw some boys (guards) treat others as if they were despicable animals, taking pleasure in cruelty.[52]

Craig Haney, Curtis Banks, and Philip Zimbardo found that

> Although the black corrections officers are younger, more urban, better educated, and more liberal than

their white colleagues, there were no consistent differences in their attitudes toward prisoners, staff, correctional goals, or their occupation.[53]

Training

The U.S. Bureau of Prisons conducts a prison officer training program that some state prisons have followed. The training covers conventional matters related to custodial care, disciplinary procedures, report writing, and other people-processing duties, but it does more. It offers a 40-hour introduction to interpersonal communications, with a 12-hour segment devoted to improving staff relations. According to some experts, training also ought to include "a liberal component" to help officers "to be more tolerant, more capable of accepting difference, and generally more sympathetic (in the best sense) to the prisoner's position."[54]

However, training is not a panacea according to the Joint Commission on Correctional Manpower and Training. The commission maintains that "too often [officers] receive little useful direction from management or professionally trained staff, and they find themselves in something of a sink-or-swim situation." Gordon Hawkins says that the situation is not easily remedied because

> unfortunately, there is little scientific knowledge about handling offender populations, few principles for consistent practice, and almost no provision for assessing the value of particular measures in various situations. Custodial staff generally operate on the basis of lore which has made for continued improvements in practice in other fields and occupations. Very little has been written on group management practices with confined offenders. What there is has come mainly from social scientists and has little relevance for the line practitioner.[55]

Use *Your* Discretion

What are the advantages of working as a corrections officer?

A growing number of corrections officers are well paid and adequately trained, and they work under good conditions. Applicants eagerly seek positions in places such as Minnesota's Oak Park Heights maximum security prison. In 1993, correctional counselors—as they are called there—started at about $23,615 a year with no experience. Sergeants earned up to $36,618, lieutenants up to $44,078, and captains up to $49,235. Minnesota has no problem recruiting. Corrections officers are willing to move from other parts of the country just to work at Oak Park Heights. Many have college degrees or have nearly completed them, although they are not required.[56]

Corrections officers at Oak Park Heights receive training not only in how to use force, but also in how to implement the institution's management philosophy, which stresses treating prisoners humanely and without violence. According to former warden Frank Wood, in his message to prisoners:

> You will be interacting with a well-trained staff of professional correctional practitioners who are among the finest in the field of corrections in this country. You will be treated with courtesy, respect and the personal dignity due any reasonable and rational person. In return, we expect that you display the same maturity in your interactions with staff. We have a very fundamental philosophy that is summed up in the statement: "AS STAFF, WE TREAT INMATES AS WE WOULD WANT TO BE TREATED IF WE WERE AN INMATE OR AS WE WOULD WANT OUR FATHER, BROTHER, OR SON TO BE TREATED IF THEY WERE AN INMATE."[57]

Promotion at Oak Park Heights is at least partly based on education: completing approved courses related to human relations helps correctional counselors advance from one level to another and to supervisory positions.[58]

Working at Oak Park Heights is different from guarding at many prisons. Although it is a maximum security prison—it houses Minnesota's worst violent and repeat offenders as well as some overflow of the most dangerous offenders from the federal prison system.

The following is a description written for the author by Dan Crutchfield, a corrections officer in Minnesota:

> It's 6:30 in the morning, the beginning of another day as a corrections officer at Oak Park Heights (OPH). Arriving officers report to a designated area of the institution for their daily Watch Briefing and job assignments, which are given out by the Watch Lieutenant. The Watch Briefing consists of information from the previous shifts in the form of reports. These reports give detailed accounts of pertinent information regarding incidents that occur within the institution.
>
> After the Watch Briefing officers then embark to their designated work areas throughout the institution. Unit officers report to their units where they are briefed by the officers they relieve. The officer just arriving for duty will go into the unit and take a count of all the inmates assigned to that particular unit (fifty-two maximum). A quick inventory is also taken on essential items officers are accountable for, such as keys and various security equipment. After the officers properly relieve the previous shift they must get ready for their watch. There are log books to fill out, paperwork to be

completed, and daily activities to be scheduled. For the morning officers, the next main event will be getting the inmates "switched out" for breakfast.

Meals are served in each of the units at OPH. This is one of the security features of the institution. Instead of allowing inmates to travel through corridors in large crowds which are hard to monitor, a food cart is delivered to each unit. The food cart is prepared in the institution kitchen and is delivered to the units by inmate servers. Officers conduct a search of the food cart upon entering the units and the cart is checked for contraband, that is, anything that would be unauthorized.

When the meal is ready to be served by the inmate servers, two officers station themselves near the food cart. The officer in the security bubble (which operates all the doors electronically) will announce over a PA system that breakfast is served and announce which rooms will be switched out first. Officers by the food cart regulate the feeding, making sure there is an orderly procession through the food line and that inmates take the appropriate portions of food that is served. After everyone has gone through the food line there is a last call in which any inmates who wish to go through the line again may do so. After breakfast is served inmates sign up for sick call at the "bubble" and also for use of the phone later in the day after work.

The inmates work upstairs from where they reside. The officer in the security bubble makes an announcement over the PA system. This time the announcement is to report to work in five minutes. Inmates assigned to work in the shops upstairs gather around the flag area and proceed through various security doors. After the work switch a verification check is made by the unit officers of the inmates upstairs, downstairs, or out of the unit for sick call. It is the correctional officer's duty to have an accurate accountability of all inmates assigned to his or her unit. Not only should the officer know how many inmates are assigned to the unit, but the officer should know their location out of the unit as well.

Unit officers stationed downstairs perform random security rounds and supervise unit workers, referred to as "swampers." The swampers are the custodians of the units. It is their job to keep the units clean. Inspections are made randomly by officers, to insure the job is done properly.

Room checks and shakedowns are also performed randomly, and in cases where they are necessary. Receipts are left in rooms where articles are removed with the officer's name on them, and a description of each article removed along with the reason it was removed. At the end of the morning, the inmates working upstairs switch back downstairs into the unit. Once in the unit, the officer in the security unit bubble announces that inmates are to report to their rooms for count. The afternoon procedure is similar to the morning routine. Lunch is served in the same fashion. After lunch the inmates again switch back upstairs for work.

As an officer at OPH there are always new challenges in daily routines because of the diverse population incarcerated within the institution. Every day is different due to human nature, ultimately a tense situation is a learning experience. There is much personal satisfaction in deescalating potential situations, the experience that is acquired while working in a correctional environment enables corrections officers to meet these challenges. It is not the old stereotype guard that is 6 foot 4 and 250 pounds who deals with a crisis situation by physical force in an intense situation that gets positive results. Rather, it is the officer who uses his skills in personal relationships, that knows how to deal with people in a positive manner that will be successful as a corrections officer.

Oak Park Heights is one of the world's most secure maximum security prisons. However, the usual tension and stress that is associated with a maximum security prison does not seem to exist at OPH. This is due to the chemistry of the Minnesota Department of Corrections. Officers are paid a lucrative salary that is competitive with other law enforcement agencies. Advancement is also available with the completion of college courses in the human relations field. There exists a positive atmosphere for corrections officers and inmates alike at OPH. This creates favorable working conditions that enable an officer to strive for a better working relationship with staff and inmates alike and not have to be preoccupied about survival. However, it should be understood that OPH is a maximum security prison and there are certain hazards that could surface due to the elements that exist in such a structural environment which houses individuals who are incarcerated due to their negative behaviors.

CRITICAL THINKING

1. Describe the duties of corrections officers at Oak Park Heights.
2. What are the strengths of Officer Crutchfield's job?
3. Do you detect weaknesses? What are they?
4. Would you want Crutchfield's job? Explain.

Knowledge and Understanding CHECK

1. Describe the pattern of growth in U.S. prisons and jails how the pattern compares with other countries.
2. Trace the history of prisons in the United States.
3. Compare the Pennsylvania and Auburn, New York, systems of prison reform in the nineteenth century.
4. Describe the Progressive reforms in prisons in the late nineteenth and early twentieth centuries.
5. Why is the period 1970 to the present called "the return to punishment"?
6. Why are prisons called "correctional facilities," and why is this not an accurate term?
7. Identify and list the characteristics of the major types of prisons.
8. What is the difference between maximum and super maximum prisons?
9. List the characteristics of "new generation" prisons.
10. List the main characteristics of women's prisons, and compare them with men's prisons.
11. Identify and list the characteristics of the prison management styles in the United States.
12. Why were corrections officers called guards?
13. List the roles and duties of corrections officers, according to Stan Stojkovic and Rick Lovell.
14. Compare line officers with lieutenants and captains.
15. Why are corrections officers called the "other prisoners"?
16. Why don't corrections officers carry weapons?
17. What does empirical data tell us about the importance of physical standards in selecting officers?
18. Describe the reactions of men prisoners and corrections officers to women officers.
19. Does adding nonwhite officers improve guard work? Explain your answer.
20. Describe the nature and effectiveness of training for corrections officers.

JAILS

The predecessors of American jails originated nearly five hundred years ago. The English jail, or "gaol" as the English spell it, held only criminal suspects who could not make bail. In the United States today, jail populations, like those of prisons, are rising (Figure 14.3). At midyear 1997, the jail population in the United States hit a record high of 567,079 prisoners, a 9.4 percent increase over 1996 and nearly double the average annual increase. Why are the numbers increasing? The reasons include:

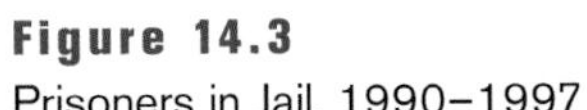
Figure 14.3
Prisoners in Jail, 1990–1997

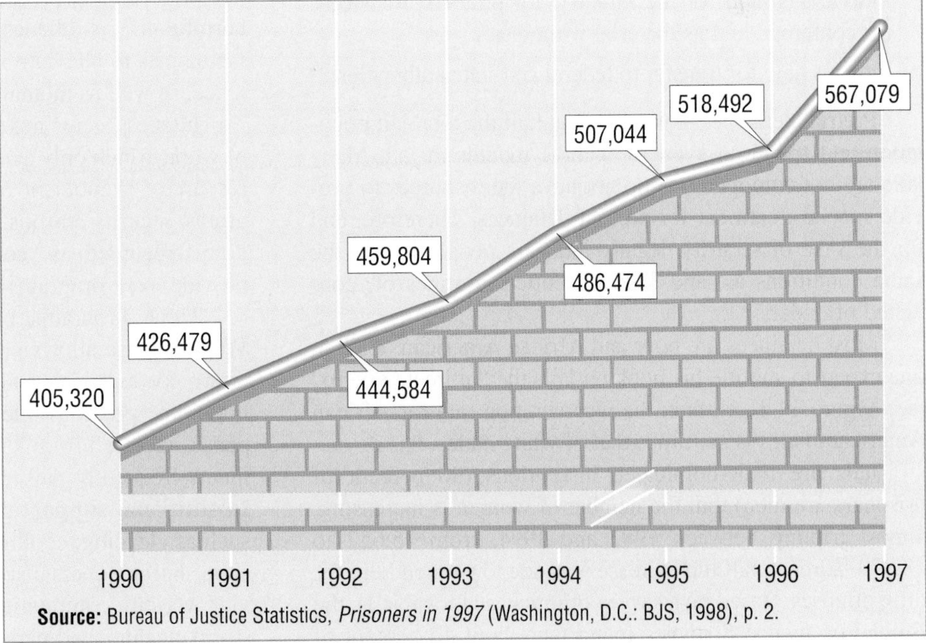

Source: Bureau of Justice Statistics, *Prisoners in 1997* (Washington, D.C.: BJS, 1998), p. 2.

Figure 14.4
Percent of Federal and State Prisoners by Race, 1996

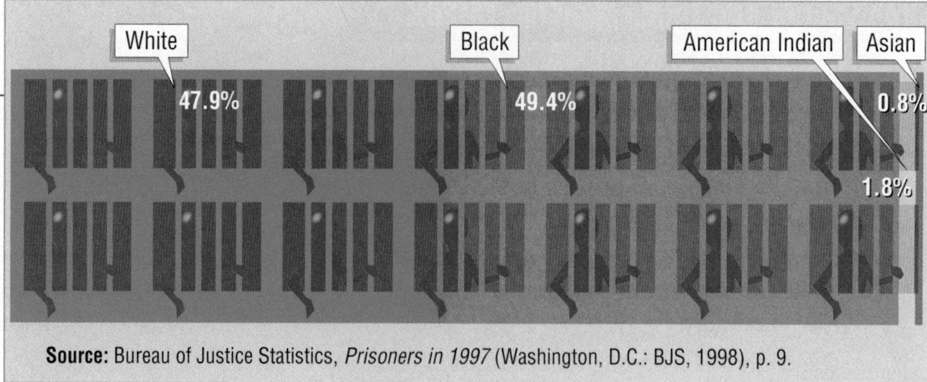

Source: Bureau of Justice Statistics, *Prisoners in 1997* (Washington, D.C.: BJS, 1998), p. 9.

- An increase in the number of arrests.
- A growth in the number of people admitted to jails.
- An increase in the number of felons sentenced to local jails.
- An increase in the number of inmates charged with or convicted of drug offenses.
- More prisoners held in jails because of crowded state and federal prisons.[59]

Jail Inmates

Jails confine people both *before* and *after* conviction. Jails contain a variety of prisoners, including:

- Defendants awaiting trial, conviction, and sentencing.
- Probation, parole, and bail-bond violators.
- Juveniles awaiting transfer to juvenile facilities.
- Mentally ill people awaiting transfer to mental health facilities.
- Individuals held for the military, for protective custody, for contempt, and as material witnesses.
- Inmates held for transfer to federal and state authorities.[60]

Pretrial detainees make up about half the total jail population and spend an average of three months in jail. Many jails are not equipped and do not have the resources to provide special treatment for pretrial detainees. Therefore, and for the sake of security, legally innocent people live in the same conditions as, and follow identical routines of, convicted offenders.

Most detainees are poor and African American, leading one expert to subtitle his book on jails the "ultimate ghetto" (see Figure 14.4). In fact, the incarceration rate for African American males is six times that of white males. [61]

Jails are male-dominated institutions (90 percent of prisoners are men), but the number of women is increasing, almost tripling between 1983 and 1994, from 15,652 to 48,879. Almost half the increase was due to women held for drug offenses. Based on a survey of inmates in local jails, the Bureau of Justice Statistics found that about 40 percent of women arrested reported that they committed their offenses while under the influence of drugs.[62]

According to the Advisory Commission on Jails, despite the increase in numbers of women in jail, they remain at a disadvantage:

> Women are frequently denied access to the cafeteria and recreational facilities and confined to a specific floor, wing, or cell for the duration of their confinement. By far the most common medical problems of incarcerated women are gynecological or obstetric. . . . Yet medical services of jails, when provided, are usually [by] physicians accustomed to and primarily concerned with men.[63]

Jail Programs

Residents in traditional jails get little recreation. On the average, they spend only two hours a day at indoor exercise and less than an hour at outdoor recreation. More than one thousand jails in the country provide no recreation at all for jail prisoners. Depriving prisoners of recreation can have harmful effects. Idleness, especially without radios and television sets to alleviate it, creates enhanced tension and violence, as well as mental and physical deterioration.[64]

Idleness stems not only from lack of recreation but lack of work, which only exacerbates the problem. Due to lack of resources, skepticism over the effectiveness of work programs, security reasons, and philosophical opposition to programs regarded as "coddling" criminals, only a few jails provide work programs for jail inmates.

Three programs provide differing degrees of work. **Work release** allows prisoners to leave jail for work and to return for evenings and weekends. Work release alleviates boredom, provides meaningful activity, and defrays expenses incurred from keeping prisoners in programs. Participants frequently pay room and board from their earnings. **Institutional support** gives prisoners work within the jail, such as cleaning, cooking and serving food, and making repairs. Jail prisoners also form **public works crews** that provide various community services, such as street cleaning, storm cleanup, and park maintenance.

Jail Conditions

Jails and jail conditions vary greatly across the country. Some jails are modern, safe, clean, and efficiently and humanely administered. Others provide inadequate living conditions for prisoners and create security and control problems for jail managers. Ronald Goldfarb, leading jail expert, describes one type of jail:

> I can recall taking a three-day trip to see a sampling of correctional institutions in Georgia. I had seen eight different prison institutions in a state which was not famous for its progressive correctional institutions. Then I asked to see the Atlanta jail. I was shocked to discover conditions so horrible I could not believe them. The jail was far worse than the state prisons I had just seen. Inside a relatively modern exterior in a modest, busy part of town was a cramped, dark, dank interior. Large four-sided cages each held sixteen men, with disheveled beds and an open toilet. Inmates are kept inside these cages twenty-four hours a day throughout their often prolonged stays at the Atlanta jail. There is no privacy . . . and artificial air and light. A dismal atmosphere, a constant din, and a wretched stench pervaded the place.[65]

After four years spent traveling around the country studying jail conditions, Goldfarb concluded that such conditions were not peculiar to the Atlanta jail:

> One shocking paradox became apparent to me. Our prisons are used to incarcerate men convicted of serious crimes and our jails (while housing some convicted men) primarily hold people who are awaiting trial, who have been convicted of nothing; yet our jails are far worse than our prisons.[66]

Perhaps no single condition has done more to bring jails into national focus than crowding. Determining the amount of crowding creates problems due to at least four standards used to measure it:

1. **Reported capacity:** whatever figure a particular jurisdiction designates as a jail's capacity.
2. **Measured capacity:** one prisoner per cell.
3. **Density:** the number of square feet of floor space per prisoner.
4. **Occupancy:** the number of prisoners for each unit of confinement.

The National Institute of Justice has put occupancy and density together and defines **crowded prisoners** as those who "live in a high density multiple occupancy confinement unit—that is, a cell or dormitory shared with one or more inmates with less than sixty square feet of floor space per inmate." Using that measure, most large jails are overcrowded. In one survey, the National Sheriff's Association reported that 795 respondents listed overcrowding as the most serious problem in their jails.[67]

Many see buildings as the solution to jail problems. This can mean three things:

1. Building new jails.
2. Renovating existing jails.
3. Acquiring additional jails.

The pro-builders consider more and improved buildings as absolutely essential to avert a crisis. Others contend that spending money on buildings foolishly wastes precious corrections dollars. Everyone agrees that buildings are expensive. New construction costs the most, averaging between $20,000 and $41,000 for every bed. Renovations are cheaper but still expensive, with estimates putting the amount at nearly $4,000 per bed. Maintaining jails is also expensive: taking care of one jail inmate costs more than $5,000 a year.

Building many more jails is unlikely—even if more jails could solve the problem of crowding—because of financial, political, and ideological reasons. Local governments, especially counties, face severe budget problems. When money is in short supply, roads and other services take priority over jails in the competition for funds. Politically, jails have no constituency—prisoners do not vote, and few voters support their cause. Ideologically, the "coddling criminals at the country club" idea hinders spending money on jails because people conclude that those who get in trouble, whether they are convicted or not, ought to be uncomfortable.

Taxpayers favor getting tough on criminals, but resist paying to do so. After the Lucas County Commissioners unveiled plans for a new jail, the *Toledo Blade* accused the commissioners of being

> undaunted, unhearing, and unswayed by common sense and moving into a position to cram down the public's craw an extravagant, over-blown jail that will cost at least 11.4 million dollars. And that amount of money does not include the small fortune that will be spent on equipment and accessories to decorate the jail in the style and comfort its three hundred or so short-term inmates can be expected to enjoy.[68]

New-Generation Jails

> The scene resembles a college dormitory with a student union lounge attached. At one end of a large, colorful room, a handful of young men are watching television; in another area, a second group watches a different set. Two inmates are playing ping-pong. A group of inmates goes up to the uniformed deputy, who is chatting amiably with someone, and asks him for the volleyball. He gives it to them, and they rush out the door to the recreation yard. Another man pads from the shower room to his private room, where he closes the door for privacy.
>
> The area is bright, sunny, and clean. The furniture—sofas and chairs—is comfortable and clean. The carpet on the floor is unstained. No one has scratched

New-generation prisons and jails may look more pleasant, but they are still prisons. Empirical evidence suggests, however, that there is less violence and other destructive behavior in these new types of prisons, based on officers' increased supervision of and interaction with inmates, as well as inmates' positive responses to a cleaner, more comfortable environment. Do you think the new generation prisons are too "soft" on prisoners?

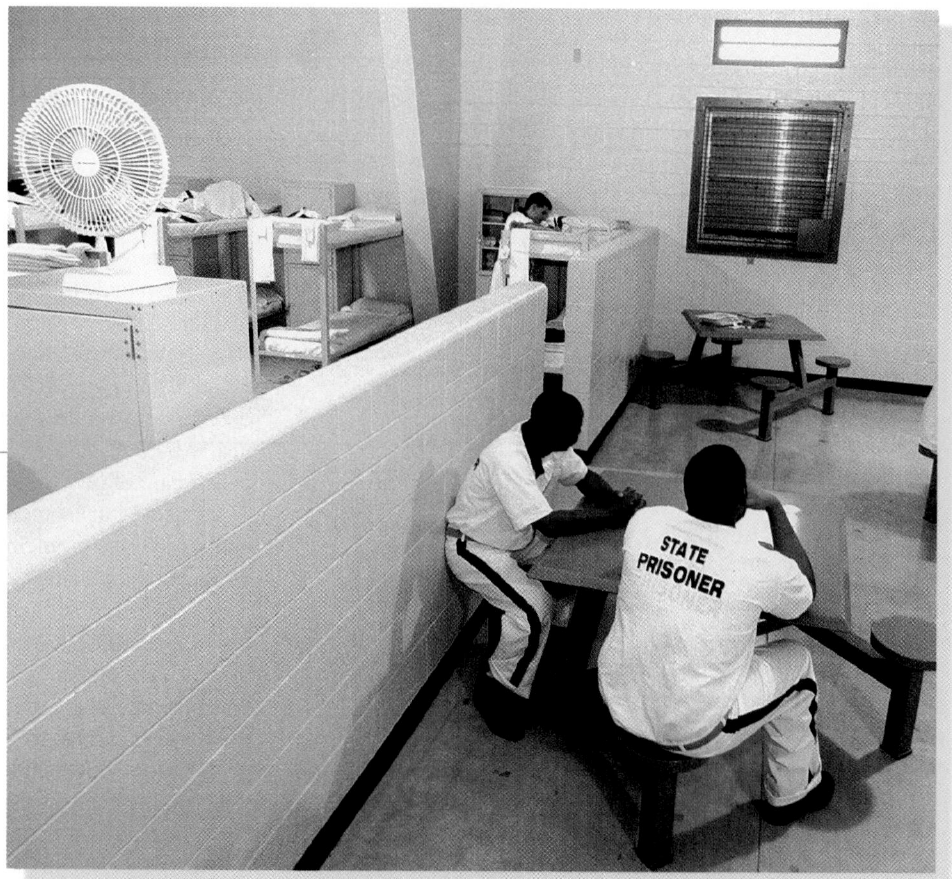

> his initials in the paint or on the butcher-block tables and desks. Windows allow a view of the outside. Despite all the activity, the room is relatively quiet. The television volume is low, and no one is shouting.[69]

This quote describes a **new-generation jail,** endorsed by prestigious bodies like the Advisory Board of the National Institute of Corrections, the American Jail Association, the American Institute of Architects' Committee on Architecture for Criminal Justice, and the American Correctional Association. New-generation jails combine architecture, management philosophy, operation, and training. This combination has produced a revolutionary change in a few jails. When the Federal Bureau of Prisons, traditionally an innovative force in American corrections, developed the new-generation jail concept, it followed the basic directive: "If you can't rehabilitate, at least do no harm." Three federal Metropolitan Correctional Centers (MCCs) were built in Chicago, New York, and San Diego to provide humane, secure detention.[70]

New-generation jails screen out violent and mentally ill inmates, and prisoners cannot come and go as they please. The differences between traditional jails and new-generation jails lie in architecture, management, and staff training. Architecturally, new-generation jails have a **podular design** (Figure 14.5). Most traditional jails, on the other hand, have a corridor lined with cells that permit only intermittent surveillance as officers periodically walk down the hallways (Figure 14.6). In these traditional facilities, officers can control only the area they can see; prisoners control the remainder. The podular design includes the following characteristics:

- Security concentration on the outside perimeter—impregnable walls and windows.
- Restricted movement inside jail—unit officers do not have keys; officer in a control booth can allow movement in and out of the unit by closed-circuit television and intercom.
- Free movement and as few barriers as possible inside living units.
- Living units with fewer than fifty prisoners to give officers an unobstructed view of the entire area.
- Private rooms for prisoners.
- Standard building materials for both cost and appearance.

At first, new-generation jails were viewed as soft on criminals; they were accused of providing inmates with a luxury motel at public expense. But the new jails report fewer violent incidents—as many as 90 percent. Homosexual rape has almost disappeared. Private rooms allow prisoners to go to their own rooms to cool off, thereby preventing violent responses to incidents. Vandalism and graffiti have nearly vanished. For example, the new jail at Pima, Arizona, reported the following:

Figure 14.5
Podular Design of New-Generation Jail

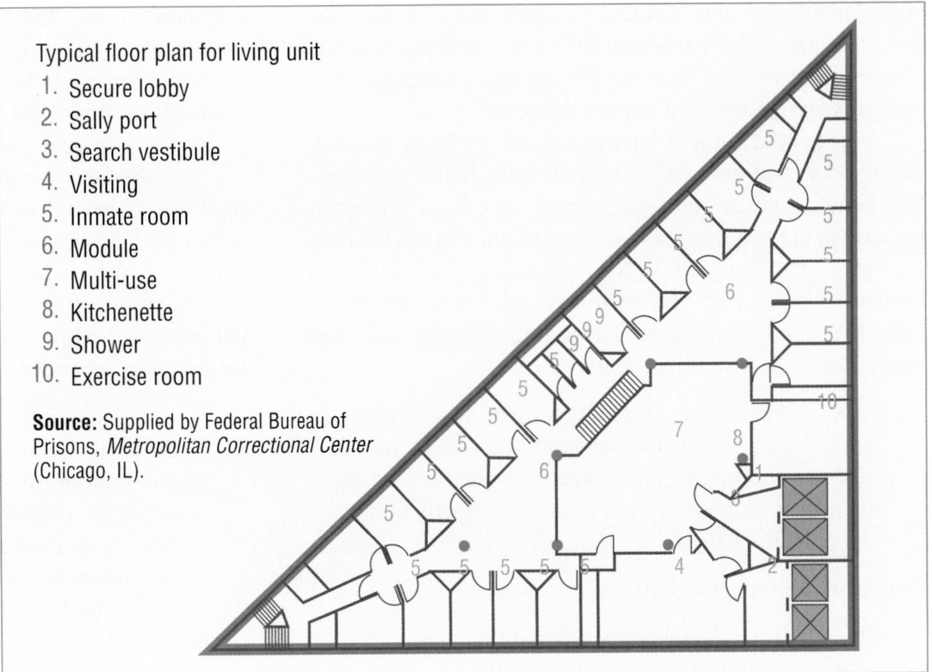

Source: Supplied by Federal Bureau of Prisons, *Metropolitan Correctional Center* (Chicago, IL).

Figure 14.6
Linear/Intermittent Surveillance

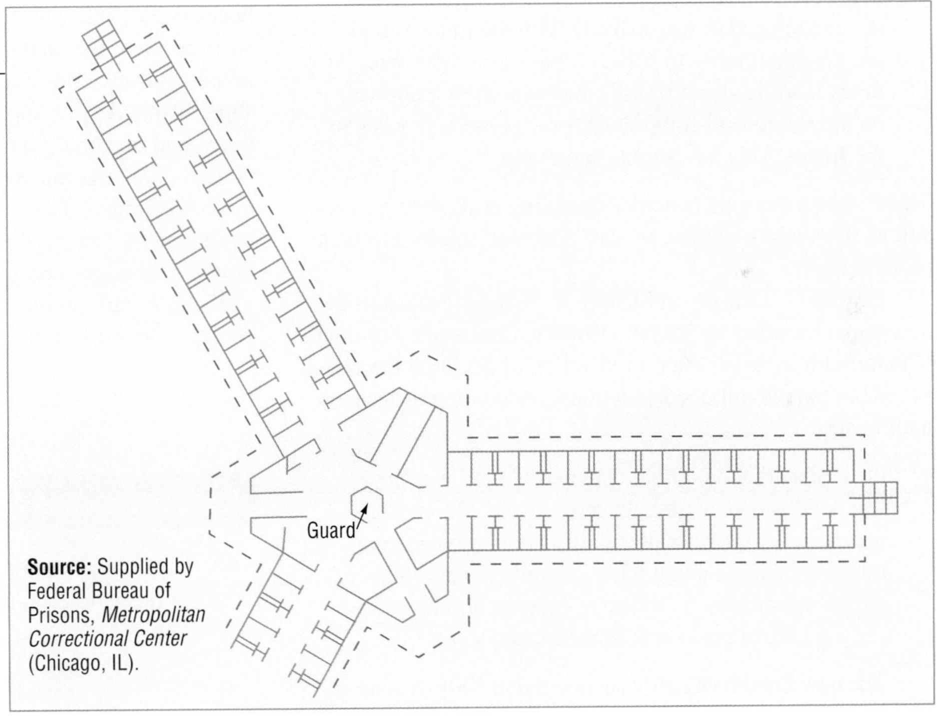

Source: Supplied by Federal Bureau of Prisons, *Metropolitan Correctional Center* (Chicago, IL).

- Reductions in the number of damaged mattresses from 150 a year to none.
- Reduction of damaged televisions sets from two repairs a week to two repairs in two years.
- Reduction from an average 99 sets of prisoners' clothes destroyed every week to 15 in two years.

All of these reductions have occurred without rises in costs of construction and maintenance. Vandal-proof materials, such as porcelain plumbing, would have cost much more than standard materials.[71]

Architecture alone does not account for the success of new-generation jails. "You can't run a new-generation jail with old-generation management," said the new commander of a major jail whose revamped podular design "had turned into a nightmare for staff and inmates." **Direct supervision** places officers in constant contact with prisoners, which allows officers to get to know prisoners and thereby recognize and respond to trouble before it escalates into violence. Negotiation and verbal communication replace physical force. Women officers, who make up 40 percent of direct supervision jails, are as effective as male officers.[72]

New-generation jails have had positive effects not only on prisoners and budgets but also on staff. Better surroundings benefit staff as much as, perhaps more than, prisoners, because in the long run staff spend more time in the jail than prisoners, who face temporary confinement. According to Richard Weiner and his associates, jails that are clean, vandalism- and graffiti-free, carpeted, less noisy, safe, and peaceful also help staff morale:

> Officers and inmates [agree] that direct supervision works better than traditional approaches. Most of the officers acknowledged that what was good for the inmates helped them as well, by improving conditions and reducing tension.[73]

Stephen H. Gettinger reports:

> The relatively pleasant atmosphere of the new-generation jail is designed with the officer in mind even more than the inmate. Without fear of assault, officers can relax and pay attention to their jobs. They are encouraged to mix actively with the inmates and are given authority to solve problems on their own. Officers learn leadership skills that will serve them well on the streets and equip them for management roles in the future. This job is more satisfying.[74]

There is a further side benefit—operating costs drop as a result of the sharp reduction in staff absenteeism, by as much as 40 percent.

Patrick G. Jackson and Cindy A. Stearns evaluated the new-generation jail in Sonoma County, California. Sonoma County built their jail after a federal court declared the conditions in the old jail unconstitutional. According to Jackson and Stearns:

> the cramped and poorly ventilated old jail was dirty, was loud, smelled, and, for most of the 225-or-so inmates and a much smaller staff, had all the negative trappings that go along with intermittent surveillance in linear facilities: a climate of fear, an absence of privacy, a lack of positive leadership, and so on.[75]

The new Sonoma County jail opened in 1991. A state-of-the art jail, it includes the two cornerstones of new-generation jails. First is podular architecture, including five two-tiered living quarters shaped in a semicircle facing an officers' station that is not enclosed by bars or glass barriers. Each "pod" contains a medical unit and a recreational area exposed to natural light, showers, carpeted floors, television, and telephones. Wall-to-wall carpet and acoustical ceilings reduce noise, pastel-painted walls improve appearance, and plenty of inexpensive wood and plastic furniture replaces the harsh metal of traditional jails. Second is direct supervision. Correctional officers are trained extensively in interpersonal communications. They manage problems proactively. Continuous, direct, and personal supervision is supposed to put control of the jail in the hands of the officers, not the inmates. Inmates are managed by positive reinforcement, not by "brute force or steel bars."[76]

Jackson and Stearns measured the attitudes, perceptions, and behaviors of inmates in the old jail before transfer, and in the new jail after transfer. They found that women experienced the conditions of confinement in the new-generation jail differently from men. Men's perceptions of jail improved while women experienced increased dissatisfaction. The researchers suspect that the reason for this difference lies in the new-generation jail philosophy that

> seeks to lessen the development, breadth, intensity, and/or continuity of interpersonal networks or peer groups that might be perceived as supportive of inmate control of an institution. It is precisely these kinds of relationships between inmates that past research suggests has been of differential importance to female and male inmates.[77]

New-generation jails are a lot more expensive than traditional jails. Besides, they are harder to "sell" to the public because they are viewed as not harsh enough and therefore susceptible to the charge that they "coddle criminals." Also, administrators and managers remain skeptical of direct supervision, despite support among hard-line corrections officers and criminal justice professors. These supporters advocate that we incarcerate people *as* punishment, not *for* punishment. They maintain that humane, safe, secure confinement is enough punishment without adding bad conditions. Besides, not just the inmates benefit from new-generation jail architecture and management; so do the people who work in the jails.[78]

Knowledge and Understanding Check

1. List the reasons why jail populations are growing.
2. During which stages in the criminal process do jails confine people?
3. Identify the major types of jail prisoners.
4. Explain why women jail inmates are at a disadvantage.
5. Describe the nature and limits of jail programs.
6. Describe the condition of jails in the United States.
7. Explain why some see construction as the solution to jail problems.
8. Describe new-generation jails.

9. List and describe the major elements of new-generation jails.
10. Describe the major characteristics of podular design.
11. List the positive effects of podular design.
12. Why are newgeneration jails difficult to "sell" to the public?

PRIVATE PRISONS AND JAILS

Private administration of criminal justice in the United States began with the establishment of the American colonies. Until 1850, police forces were private patrols, and privately hired detectives prevailed over public police forces. Until publicly funded prosecutors were established in the 1850s, victims were responsible for prosecuting their cases. Private defense attorneys are a major part of the criminal defense bar, although public defenders are common in large cities. Probation began as a private and often charitable operation in the middle of the nineteenth century. Juvenile corrections was largely a private operation as well during the nineteenth century, and about 40 percent of juvenile correctional facilities remain privately administered.

Private parties have also played their part in the history of adult corrections, although a lesser part than in other spheres of criminal justice. Until 1825, adult corrections was exclusively a public enterprise. In that year, the merchant Joel Scott offered to pay the state of Kentucky $1,000 to lease him all the prisoners in the inefficiently run and costly Frankfort prison. In return for the right to work the prisoners, Scott agreed to house, clothe, and feed them; and he promised further to pay the state half the profits made from the convict labor. This arrangement, which lasted until the 1880s, reported profits and no mistreatment of prisoners. Throughout the South and West, states followed Kentucky's example, contracting prisoners out to work in coal mines and factories and to build roads and railroads. Most states abandoned the contract labor system by 1900. Both organized labor and manufacturers who did not hire contract prison labor opposed the system because it competed unfavorably with free labor.[79]

Private business has also provided prison services, including food preparation and medical care, as well as education, training, and other programs. Private organizations also provide 70 percent of the Federal Bureau of Prisons' halfway houses. In 1986, Corrections Corporation of America broke new ground in the history of adult corrections when it opened the first private state prison in the United States. The prison, located at Marion, Kentucky, is a 300-bed minimum security facility for "clients" within three years of parole. Corrections Corporation of America in 1998 was operating 77 prisons around the world, and had contracts to build more. By July 1998, private prisons housed almost 100,000 prisoners. The old device of **privatization**—private management of correctional facilities—is being used to solve the problem of administering a rapidly growing prison population. Predictions are that the number of private correctional facilities will continue to grow.[80]

Use *Your* Discretion

Should we privatize prisons and jails?

Available research provides at best mixed answers to many questions about private prisons and jails. Contracting out medical services and staff training to the private sector *may* be cost effective, according to *some* evidence. The National Institute of Justice found that private enterprise promises the most benefits in providing work programs, but saw little participation by businesses in such programs. So, former Chief Justice of the U.S. Supreme Court Justice Warren Burger's hope for "factories with fences" instead of warehouses with walls has not come to pass. Private financing for prison construction holds *some* promise in easing the burden on general revenues and avoiding debt ceilings often placed on government unit bonding issues.

In a lengthy survey of private prisons, David Shichor found the following:

- There are no constitutional barriers to establishing private prisons.
- Privatization is not more cost-effective than public operation of prisons.
- Privately operated prisons and jails *may* provide higher-quality services for lower costs in *some* places under *special* circumstances.
- Negative consequences and hidden costs are potentially extensive.[81]

The U.S. Department of Justice has concluded that it is "too early to draw *any* conclusions on how successful privately run prisons are." According to the Department:

> There is not enough information to judge whether the cost and quality of privately run prisons equal or surpass those operated by state and local governments, Acting Assistant Attorney General L. Anthony Sutin told the Senate Judiciary Committee. . . . The report . . . found that previous studies of private prisons have been methodologically flawed. . . . Few would disagree that the potential cost savings that may result from privatization would not justify creating substantial threats to public safety or wholesale failure to prepare of-

fenders for what hopefully will be a crime-free return to the community after release from prison," the letter said.[82]

CRITICAL THINKING

1. List the major findings of the research on private prisons.
2. Which findings support privatization and which oppose it?
3. Would you recommend privatization on the basis of these findings? Defend your answer.
4. Or, would you recommend further study? What would you want to know in further study?

PRISONERS

Most prisoners in the United States are nonwhite men under 30 years old who have not graduated from high school. Many have alcohol and other drug problems (Figure 14.7). Distributions by race and ethnicity vary widely. In Stateville, the Illinois maximum security prison near Chicago, 80 percent of the prisoners are African American. In Lorten Central, the prison outside Washington, D.C., 99 percent of the prisoners are African American. And, the racial and ethnic composition of prison populations is changing. The rate of incarceration for African and Hispanic Americans has risen sharply since 1980. The number of older prisoners is also increasing. If the current practices of longer sentences and mandatory minimum sentences, particularly of the "three strikes and you're out" variety, continue (see Chapter 12), the graying of the prison population will continue to add to prison costs, particularly by contributing to a rise in geriatric costs.[83]

Most prisoners have grown up in single-parent homes, where they frequently endured sexual or physical abuse. Forty percent have immediate family members who have spent time in prison. Half have never married; 20 percent are divorced or separated. White prisoners have a much higher divorce and separation rate than African American prisoners. Even though most prisoners are not married, more than half have children, and more than one-third have three or more children, almost all under eighteen.[84]

The educational levels of prisoners fall far below the national average. In the general population, 85 percent of males between ages 20 and 29 have finished high school; only 40 percent of prisoners have done so. Prisoners have a school dropout rate three times greater than the general population. Six percent of all prisoners have had no schooling at all. Practically none have college degrees.

Educational level is closely linked to conviction offense. White prisoners with more than a high school education are more likely to commit drug offenses, fraud, embezzlement, and forgery. Public order offenses are more common among prisoners with little education. Prisoners with some college education are less likely to either commit violent crimes or to have prior criminal records.

Prisoners, on the whole, have poor work records. Most had little or no legal income before incarceration. Nearly 40 percent were unemployed. The incarceration rate for employed persons is 356 per 100,000. For the unemployed, it rises sharply to 933 per 100,000. Forty percent of prisoners have either never had legitimate jobs or worked only sporadically. Average income for half of all prisoners is at the poverty level.[85]

George Beto, former director of the Texas Department of Corrections—with his typical and welcome bluntness—depicted the character of most prisoners:

Figure 14.7
Percent of Positive Drug Tests in State Prisons, 1990

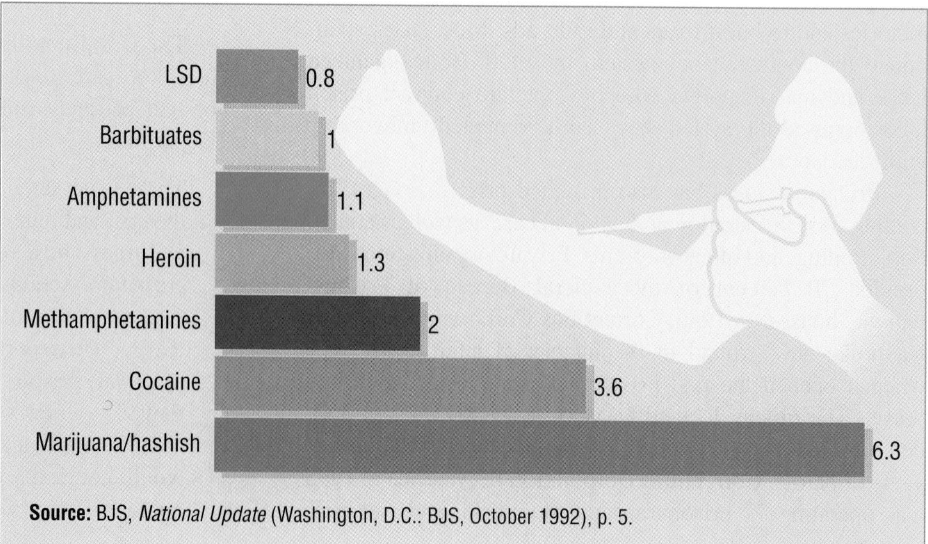

Source: BJS, *National Update* (Washington, D.C.: BJS, October 1992), p. 5.

> Not only society but also governmental leaders need to remember the character of those who come to the doors and gates of America's prisons . . . they are the poor, the stupid, the inept, the flotsam and jetsam of society. Fifteen percent are illiterate; 90% are school dropouts; 65% come from broken homes; 40% had no sustained work experience prior to their incarceration; 20% are mentally retarded . . . they stumble from one mud puddle of life to another.[86]

Women Prisoners

Men far outnumber women prisoners. Women are imprisoned at the rate of 54 for every 100,000 women in the general population, whereas the rate for men is 853 prisoners for every 100,000 men in the general population. However, the number of women prisoners is growing at a faster rate than that for men (Figure 14.8). For example, in 1997 the number of women prisoners rose 6.2 percent (from 74,970 to 79,624). This increase was double that for men. Women compose 6 percent of the prison population in the United States.

According to the American Correctional Association, women were historically imprisoned for either theft or drug offenses. Even the few violent crimes committed by women were special cases. Women convicted of murder or manslaughter had usually killed men who abused them. Women convicted of robbery did not ordinarily instigate the crime.

The traditional reasons given for the relatively small number of women prisoners compared with men have included the virtuous nature of women, their dependent status, and the code of chivalry. However, the reasons for the steep rise in the number of women prisoners since 1980 are *not* women's loss of virtue and dependence, nor the decline in chivalry, according to Barbara Owen and Barbara Bloom, who profiled women prisoners in California. It is mainly due to the growing numbers of women prosecuted and convicted of drug offenses, the increasingly harsh sentences for drug offenses, and the lack of both treatment and community sanctions for women drug offenders. In fact, Bloom and Owen argue that the "war on drugs" is really a war on women.[87]

The rise in the number of women prisoners has more to do with politics and policy than with an actual increase in the number of crimes women commit, according to Russ Immarigeon and Meda Chesney-Lind of the National Council on Crime and Delinquency:

> Women are arrested and imprisoned in greater numbers because of changes in legislative responses to the "war on drugs," law enforcement practices, and judicial decision-making rather than a shift in the nature of the crimes they commit. . . . [T]he drug war, in particular, with its emphasis on increasing the penalties for drug use and selling, may be having a significant effect on women's imprisonment. Simply put, the criminal justice system now seems more willing to incarcerate women.[88]

The National Council on Crime and Delinquency report *Women's Prisons: Overcrowded and Overused* recommends that correctional leaders avoid "build[ing] their way out of" the steep rise in the number of women convicted of crimes. As alternatives, the report recommends basing criminal sanctions on the "least restrictive alternative consistent with public safety." Women "overwhelmingly commit crimes that, while unacceptable, pose little threat to the physical safety of the community at large." Dennis Wagner observed women ex-convicts for two years after their release from Taycheedah women's prison in Wisconsin. He found that

Figure 14.8
Women Prisoners, 1985–1997

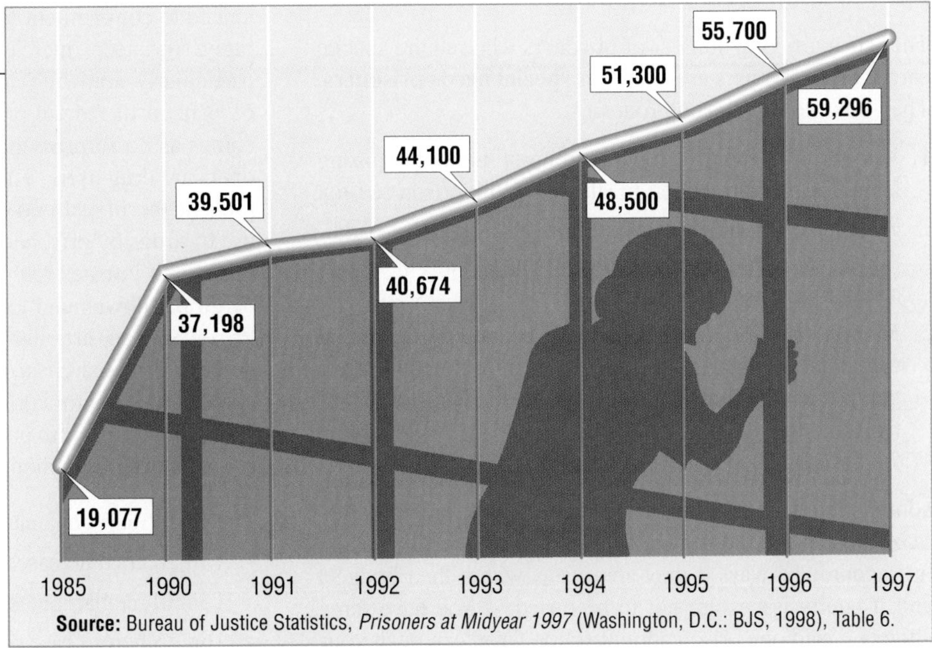

Source: Bureau of Justice Statistics, *Prisoners at Midyear 1997* (Washington, D.C.: BJS, 1998), Table 6.

Women comprise only 6 percent of the prison population in the United States. However, the number of female prisoners is growing at double the rate of that for male prisoners.

women were 44 percent less likely to commit further crimes than men. If they did recidivate, they were one-third less likely than men to commit serious crimes against persons. Joan McDermott surveyed female offenders in New York. She found that 16.9 percent of women released from prison returned, compared with 37.3 percent of men.[89]

Special Management Prisoners

There is a growing number of prisoners who require special care. These prisoners are known as **special needs prisoners.** They fall into three main groups:

1. *Vulnerable:* a rapidly growing group of inmates requiring some form of protection to survive in the prison setting.
2. *Troublemaker:* prisoners who must be subjected to additional restraints to protect other inmates, staff, or the security of the institution.
3. *Mentally abnormal:* prisoners who, because of emotional or mental problems or retardation, cannot function in the general population without assistance or who need professional treatment and medication.

Special needs prisoners create problems for the prison administration. According to a report of the Bureau of Justice Statistics, "Prisons must handle large numbers of people in standardized ways if they are to stay within their budgets and if equity issues are not to be raised." "You have three choices," said one prison administrator. "You can pitch your program to the majority of inmates, in which case the needs of special groups will not be met. You can tailor your efforts to the minority of special inmates, which means that the majority will suffer. Or you can run two separate programs."[90]

Prisoner Illegal Drug Use

The rising numbers of people arrested, prosecuted, and sentenced to confinement for drug offenses has led, not surprisingly, to steep increases in the numbers of prisoners, particularly nonwhite and female prisoners. Approximately 61 percent of federal prisoners are drug offenders. Again it comes as no surprise that substantial numbers of these prisoners are drug users. This has led to the increase in efforts to prevent the illegal entry of drugs into prisons and stop the use of drugs by prisoners. Most prisons require both new inmates and inmates returning from temporary release to undergo pat-downs and exchanges of clothing to prison garb. Prison visitors are also subject to interdiction efforts. Pat-downs, strip searches, and even body cavity searches are conducted if visitors or corrections officers are suspected of smuggling drugs into prison. The Bureau of Justice Statistics reported drug use among state prisoners as follows:

- 1 in 16 marijuana cases.
- 1 in 28 cocaine cases.
- 1 in 50 methamphetamine cases.
- 1 in 75 heroin cases.[91]

More than one-third of prisoners drink heavily, meaning at any one drinking session they consume the equivalent of eight cans of beer, seven glasses of wine, or nine ounces of 82-proof liquor. During the year before they were arrested, two-thirds of all prisoners claimed, possibly as a rationalization, that they drank this heavily every day. For most prisoners under the influence of drugs at the time they committed their offenses, the drug was marijuana, usually combined with heroin. Women are more likely than men to use heroin; white prisoners drink more heavily than black prisoners. Finally, prisoners with long criminal records are more likely to drink right before committing crimes, drink more heavily, and get drunk more often than those with fewer prior convictions.[92]

Use *Your* Discretion

Is there a "better way" than imprisoning young African Americans?

In 1990, The Sentencing Project, a national nonprofit organization that promotes sentencing reform and conducts research on criminal justice issues, released a report documenting that 23 percent of African American males between the ages of 20 and 29 were under some form of correctional supervision on any given day, either on probation or parole, or in jail or prison. In 1995, The Sentencing Project issued a follow-up report, entitled "Young Black Americans and the Criminal Justice System: Five Years Later." The new study reported that the situation had worsened considerably. The following excerpts are taken from the 1995 report:

- Almost one in three (32.2%) young black men in the age group 20–29 is under criminal justice supervision on any given day—in prison or jail, on probation or parole.
- The cost of criminal justice control for these 827,440 young African American males is about $6 billion a year.
- In recent years, African American women have experienced the greatest increase in criminal justice supervision of all demographic groups, with their rate of criminal justice supervision rising by 78% from 1989–94.
- Drug policies constitute the single most significant factor contributing to the rise in criminal justice populations in recent years, with the number of incarcerated drug offenders having risen by 510% from 1983 to 1993. The number of Black (non-Hispanic) women incarcerated in state prisons for drug offenses increased more than eight-fold—828%—from 1986 to 1991.
- African Americans and Hispanics constitute almost 90% of offenders sentenced to state prison for drug possession.

Criminal Justice Control Rates in the 1990s

Our 1990 report documented shockingly high rates of criminal justice control for young African American males in particular. We find that many of the contributing factors to these high rates endure or have worsened in the intervening years. As a result, they have failed to slow the increasing rate of criminal justice control for young black males and they have contributed to a dramatic rise in the number of black women in the criminal justice system. These factors include:

- The continuing overall growth of the criminal justice system;
- The continuing disproportionate impact of the "war on drugs" on minority populations;
- The new wave of "get tough" sentencing policies and their potential impact on criminal justice populations;
- The continuing difficult circumstances of life for many young people living in low-income urban areas in particular.

The Overrepresentation of Young Black Males in the Criminal Justice System

We have documented the dramatically high rates of criminal justice control for young black men. In many respects it would be quite surprising if these rates were not high, given the social and economic circumstances and crime rates in their communities. The growth of the criminal justice system in the past twenty years has coincided with a host of economic disruptions and changes in social policy that have had profound effects on income distribution, employment and family structure. Since the 1970s, many urban areas have witnessed the decline of manufacturing, the expansion of low-wage service industries and the loss of a significant part of the middle class tax base. Real wages have declined for most Americans during this period, with a widening of the gap between rich and poor beginning in the 1980s. For black male high school dropouts in their twenties, annual earnings fell by a full 50 percent from 1973 to 1989. Social service benefits such as mental health services and other supports have generally declined while the social problems that they address have been exacerbated.

The impact of these changes on the African American community has resulted from the intersection of race and class effects. Since African Americans are disproportionately represented in low-income urban communities, the effects of these social ills are intensified. As Douglas Massey and Nancy Denton have illustrated, the persistence of housing segregation exacerbates the difficult life circumstances of these communities, contributing to extremely high rates of unemployment, poor schooling, and high crime rates.

Over the years many researchers have examined the extent to which racial disparity within the criminal justice system can be explained by higher crime rates among blacks or other relevant factors. . . . While some studies have documented specific cases of racially unwarranted outcomes, much research has concluded that, with one significant exception, race plays a relatively minor role in sentencing and incarceration. Michael Tonry's review, for example, concludes that "for nearly a decade there has been a near consensus among scholars and policy analysts that most of the black punishment disproportions result not from racial bias or discrimination within the system but from patterns of black offending and of blacks' criminal records." Similarly, Alfred Blumstein's research has concluded that 76 percent of the racial disparity in prison populations is explained by higher rates of offending among blacks for serious offenses. But both authors find, as Tonry indicates, that drug law enforcement is the conspicuous exception. Blacks are arrested and confined in numbers grossly out of line with their use or sale of drugs. Blumstein concludes that for drug offenses, fully half of the racial disproportions in prison are not explained by higher arrest rates.

While scholars will continue to study the relative influence of race within the criminal justice system, several key issues should not go unaddressed in explaining these disparities.

First, as noted above, it is difficult to isolate the relative influence of race and class in public policy and decision making. That is, to the extent that African Americans are overrepresented in the criminal justice system, to what degree is this a function of their being disproportionately low-income? . . . Studies of sentencing practices reveal that the current offense and the offender's prior record are the most significant factors determining a prison sentence. But if low-income youth are more subject to police scrutiny and have fewer counseling and treatment resources available to them than middle class adolescents, their youthful criminal activities will more likely result in a criminal record that will affect their chances of going to prison later on. . . .

Impact of the "War on Drugs"

While debate will continue on the degree to which the criminal justice system overall contributes to racial disparities, there is increasing evidence that the set of policies and practices contained within the phrase "war on drugs" has been an unmitigated disaster for young blacks and other minorities. Whether or not these policies were consciously or unconsciously designed to incarcerate more minorities is a question that may be debated. In essence, though, what we have seen are policy choices that have not only failed to reduce the scale of the problem but have seriously eroded the life prospects of the primary targets of those policies. . . .

Looking at minorities overall, we find that African Americans and Hispanics represented almost 90% of all sentences to state prison for drug possession offenses in 1992, the most recent year for which data are available. While we have no available data regarding other factors which often correlate with a higher likelihood of incarceration, particularly prior criminal record, the findings displayed here are of such magnitude that they raise serious questions about the racial implications of current drug policies. In summing up the rationale and impact of prevailing drug policies, Professor Michael Tonry states:

> All that is left is politics. The War on Drugs and the set of harsh crime control policies in which it was enmeshed were undertaken to achieve political, not policy, objectives. It is the adoption for political purposes of policies with foreseeable disparate impacts, the use of disadvantaged black Americans as means to achieving politicians' electoral ends, that must in the end be justified. It cannot.

Impact of High Rates of Control on the African American Community

The high rate of incarceration of African American males raises concerns about its impact not only on the individuals who are incarcerated, but on their communities as well. As increasing numbers of young black men are arrested and incarcerated, their life prospects are seriously diminished. Their possibilities for gainful employment are reduced, thereby making them less attractive as marriage partners and unable to provide for children they father. This in turn contributes to the deepening of poverty in low-income communities.

The large scale rates of incarceration may contribute to the destruction of the community fabric in other ways as well. As prison becomes a common experience for young males, its stigmatizing effect is diminished. Further, gang or crime group affiliations on the outside may be reinforced within the prison only to emerge stronger as the individuals are released back to the community. With so few males in underclass communities having stable ties to the labor market, the ubiquitous ex-offenders and gang members may become the community's role models.

The cumulative impact of these high rates of incarceration has been to postpone the time at which large numbers of African American males start careers and families. While we should not ignore the fact that these men have committed crimes that led to their imprisonment, current crime control policies may actually be increasing the severity of the problem, particularly when other options for responding to crime exist.

Increasing Criminal Justice Control Rates for Women
While we have seen that criminal justice control rates for young black men are shockingly high and increasing, from 1989 to 1994 young African American women experienced the greatest increase in criminal justice control of all demographic groups studied. The 78% increase in criminal justice control rates for black women was more than double the increase for black men and for white women, and more than nine times the increase for white men.

What is causing this dramatic increase in the numbers of young black women under criminal justice control? Although research on women of color in the criminal justice system is limited, existing data and research suggest it is the combination of race and sex effects that is at the root of the trends which appear in our data. For example, while the number of blacks and Hispanics in prison is growing at an alarming rate, the rate of increase for women is even greater. Between 1980 and 1992 the female prison population increased 276%, compared to 163% for men. Unlike men of color, women of color thus belong to two groups that are experiencing particularly dramatic growth in their contact with the criminal justice system. The key factor behind this explosion in the women's prison population is the war on drugs. We see this taking place at several levels. . . .

African American Women and the War on Drugs
Looking at the criminal justice data that are available by gender and race/ethnicity a picture emerges of individuals who are doubly disadvantaged. Nationally, between 1980 and 1992 the number of black females in state or federal prisons grew 278% while the numbers of black males grew 186%; overall the inmate population increased by 168% during this period.

An enormous increase in the numbers of black women incarcerated for drug offenses is the primary factor causing this trend. Our analysis of Justice Department data shows that between 1986 and 1991, the number of black non-Hispanic women in state prisons for drug offenses nationwide increased more than eight-fold in this five-year period, from 667 to 6,193. This 828% increase was nearly double the increase for black non-Hispanic males and more than triple the increase for white non-Hispanic females. . . .

Lack of Access to Treatment
Problems caused by the limited availability of drug treatment programs and facilities, particularly for low-income individuals, are also compounded for women. Overall, while women make up 33% of the addicted population, only 20.6% of treatment resources are used for women. A 1991 Bureau of Justice Assistance report indicates that women arrestees (interviewed at 4 DUF sites) have had limited treatment experience. Nearly three-fourths (71%) had never been in treatment for substance abuse, and only 4% were in treatment at the time of their arrest. . . .

Women, Children, and the Criminal Justice System: Is There a Better Way?
While more research is needed to determine how race and gender bias may have contributed to the rise in the number of women of color under criminal justice control, it seems clear that the war on drugs has succeeded only in criminalizing women already suffering under extreme socio-economic and psychological stress. The consequences of continuing on this path are dire not only for the women involved but for future generations. The multiple negative effects of parental arrest and incarceration on children, particularly if that parent is the primary caretaker, are well- documented, and include traumatic stress, loss of self-confidence, aggression, withdrawal, depression, gang activity, and interpersonal violence. As more and more inner-city children lose not only their fathers but their mothers, most often the primary caretakers, to the criminal justice system, their own risks for future involvement in crime and incarceration increase dramatically.

In recent testimony before the U.S. Senate Judiciary Committee, Elaine Lord, the warden of New York State's maximum security prison for women, suggests a very different course:

> We need to be more honest with ourselves that the vast majority of women receiving prison sentences are not the business operatives of the drug networks. The glass ceiling seems to operate for women whether we are talking about legitimate or illegitimate business. They [women] are very small cogs in a very large system, not the organizers or backers of illegal drug empires. This, coupled with a growing mood among the American public reportedly concerned about early intervention for troubled kids and more drug treatment in preference to more prisons, should give us the opening we need to look at better and more cost-effective ways of dealing with women offenders. . . .

Recommendations

1. Revise national spending priorities. Since the mid-1980s, both Republican and Democratic administrations have directed about two-thirds of federal drug funding toward law enforcement and only one-third toward prevention and treatment. The lack of available treatment has been documented by the Department of Health and Human Services which reports that of the 2.4 million drug users who could benefit from treatment, 1 million can not have access to treatment each year.

2. Expand drug treatment within the criminal justice system. Criminal justice personnel throughout the country uniformly cite the need for expanded treatment options. New programs such as drug courts and prosecutorial diversion to treatment have met with widespread professional and community support. With the exception of treatment in prison, efforts to expand funding for drug courts and other treatment options have been folded into block grant funding where they are not likely to receive a high level of support.
3. Provide treatment programs that address the multiple and specific needs of women. Despite the fact that women involved with the criminal justice system are more likely than men to use drugs, and use more serious drugs, existing treatment models have not always been designed to incorporate the particular circumstances and multiple needs of women. Programs that accommodate children and address the range of economic, social and psychological stressors that contribute to substance abuse and drug-related crime among women should be developed and made available to women.
4. Promote a renewed dialogue on drug policy. While drug policy discussions of the 1980s were often heated and contentious, they nonetheless served to explore the range of options available to respond to substance abuse. Little such discussion exists today, as seen by the low priority given by the Justice Department to its 1994 report on mandatory sentencing or the disciplining of former Surgeon General Joycelyn Elders for advocating a discussion of drug policy. It is unconscionable to inhibit a broad discussion of a range of policy alternatives, particularly as we continue to be confronted by the tragic consequences of current policies.
5. A long-term goal clearly should be to reduce crime and the numbers of people entering the criminal justice system. An intermediate strategy, though, could reduce the severity of criminal justice control without compromising public safety by creating a broader array of sentencing options for non-violent offenders who would otherwise be sentenced to prison.
6. A variety of sentencing policies adopted nationally since 1980 have exacerbated the problems faced by women and minorities in the criminal justice system. The injustices caused by mandatory sentencing and its failure to have an impact on crime have been well documented. Of particular concern here is the disparity in sentencing between crack cocaine and powder cocaine that is present in the federal courts and many states. In addition to the racial disparities that have been demonstrated, eliminating this disparity in the federal system would lead to a long-term reduction of about 15,000 person years in the federal prisons.
7. In recent years the federal government and some state legislatures have adopted policies requiring a fiscal impact statement prior to consideration of any sentencing legislation in an effort to help legislators assess the long-term costs of any changes.
8. Criminal justice policy is often short-sighted and formulated in response to emotional appeals. The political power of the crime issue, the media sensationalism around atypical crimes, and the persistence of high crime rates join to limit discussion and planning. Unfortunately, we have seen the consequences of more than two decades of heavy investment in the criminal justice system to the detriment of other social programs.

Those who suggest that high rates of crime and drug abuse demand immediate solutions need only look back a decade to the inception of the current "drug war." Despite an enormous increase in the number of drug offenders in prison since then, little progress can be claimed for the law enforcement approach. Had a different set of choices been made at that time, the country might have been the beneficiary of more humane and effective solutions.

CRITICAL THINKING

1. Which, if any, of the recommendations would you adopt, if you were a criminal justice policymaker? Why?
2. Do any of these policy recommendations point to a "better way" to deal with young African-American men and women who are involved in drugs and crime? Explain your answer.
3. If you believe that imprisonment is the "better way," how do you justify your response, in view of the report and the recommendations of The Sentencing Project?

Prisoner Crimes of Commitment

It is commonly thought that prisons are full of violent criminals. Some people even think that the increasing public outrage over violence and drugs, the growing number of mandatory minimum sentence laws, the longer sentences judges are handing out, and the tougher sentences making their way into the sentencing guidelines have resulted in the confinement of more violent criminals. The truth is that violent criminals make up less than half of the total prison population and represent less of the total than they did in 1980. The major reason is the steep rise in the number of drug of-

Figure 14.9
Percent of Federal and State Prisoners by Their Most Serious Offense, 1980, 1993

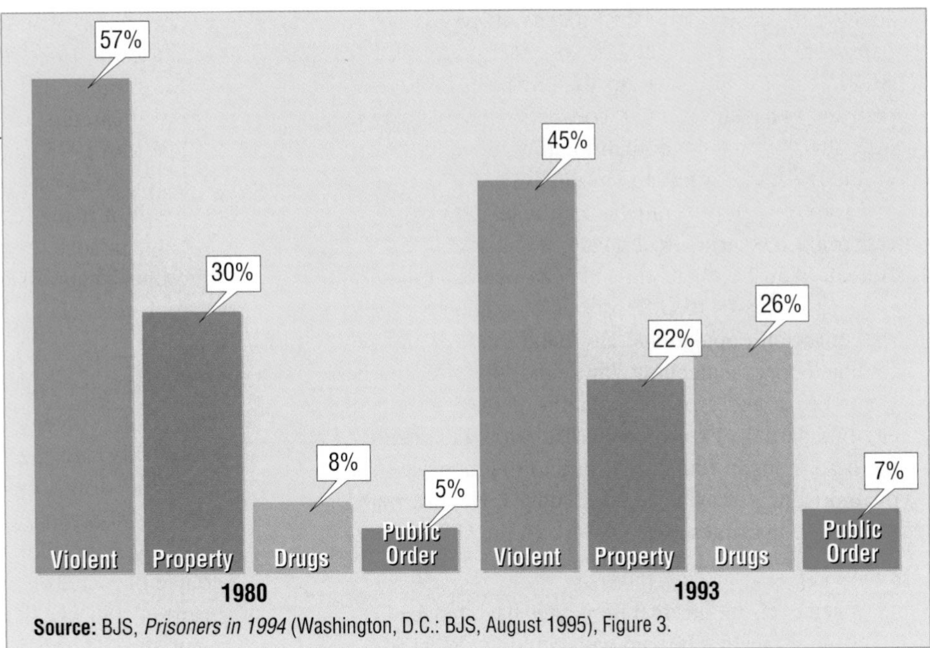

Source: BJS, *Prisoners in 1994* (Washington, D.C.: BJS, August 1995), Figure 3.

fenders committed to prison. Figure 14.9 depicts the shifting distribution of prisoners according to the crimes for which they were convicted.

Length of Imprisonment

Time actually spent in prison varies according to the region of the country and according to conviction offense. Despite sharp increases in sentences required by legislation and tougher sentencing practices by judges, the average length of time that prisoners actually serve has only increased two months between 1985 when it was 20 months and 1992 when it was 22 months. The picture in federal prisons is different. There, the average time served rose from 15 months to 24 months. Most of that increase was due to the longer time served by drug offenders. The actual time served by drug offenders rose from 22 to 33 months, compared with an increase from 50 to 56 months by violent offenders.[93]

Several factors affect the length of time prisoners serve. Judges have considerable discretion both in sending people to prison and in deciding how long they will stay once they are there. In some states, parole boards' discretionary powers can lead to the release of prisoners almost as soon as they enter prison. Other states have eliminated parole boards or curtailed their powers. All states but Hawaii, Michigan, Missouri, and Pennsylvania have **good-time laws** that allow prisoners to reduce their sentences by at least one-third—that is, one day for every three days served on good behavior. In some states, the rate of good time is as much as one-half. Prisoners can also earn good time for donating blood and for participating in education, treatment, or other programs.[94]

Prisoners also get credit for time spent in jail without bail, during trial, and after conviction waiting for sentences. Convicted murderers earn an average of 20 months for time spent in jail. For other crimes, the time earned is usually less: about 11 months for attempted murder and voluntary manslaughter, 9 months for rape, 7.6 for robbery, 5.7 for aggravated assault, 4.8 for burglary, and 4 for larceny.

Increasingly, the heavy rise in prison admissions, mandatory minimum sentences, and crowded prisons have led to the controversial practice of early release. Judges are sentencing more offenders to prison, but prisons, trying to cope with large populations, are releasing them early. The Use Your Discretion case "Is 'Lock 'em up' good public policy?" examines the problems arising from increased use of imprisonment.[95]

Use *Your* Discretion

Is "lock 'em up" good public policy?

"Lock 'em Up" Is Good Public Policy
Most of the public, whatever their gender, race, or ethnic background, believe that violent and repeat offenders belong in prison. A group of academics and professionals representing such organizations as The Sentencing Project and the National Council on Crime and Delinquency, on the other hand, advocates the greater use of alternatives to imprisonment in some cases. According to John DiIulio, imprisonment is worth the cost. DiIulio and Anne Piehl analyzed prisoner self-report surveys that showed that the typical prisoner commits about twelve crimes a year. Crime depresses local business development and erodes local economic activity. According to some estimates, each

street crime costs victims and society at least $2,300 in pain, suffering, and economic loss. At the average of twelve street crimes a year, that amounts to $27,600 per year. That means it is cheaper in most states to lock street criminals up than to allow them to be free on the street, according to DiIulio.[96]

Moreover, imprisonment may also reduce crime, according to Patrick A. Langan, a statistician for the Bureau of Justice Statistics. Langan examined admissions and releases to U.S. prisons to explain the steep rise in prison populations. He found that the increase in mandatory sentencing laws and the rise in the crime-prone age group population of the baby-boom era only partially explained the rise. More than half the increase, Langan found, was due to the increased use of imprisonment by sentencing judges. He also noted a decrease in crimes measured by victim surveys during the same period. Langan concluded:

> Whether rising incarceration rates have reduced crime . . . cannot be said with certainty. What is clear is that, since 1973, per capita prison incarceration rates have risen to their highest levels ever while crime rates measured in the National Crime Survey . . . have gradually fallen to their lowest levels ever. The changing age structure apparently does not explain most of the declines. Whatever the causes, in 1989, there were an estimated 66,000 fewer rapes, 323,000 fewer robberies, 380,000 fewer assaults, and 3.3 million fewer burglaries . . . between 1973 versus those of 1989. If only one-half or even one-fourth of the reductions were the result of rising incarceration rates, that would still leave prisons responsible for sizable reductions in crime. That possibility must be seriously weighed in debates about America's prisons.[97]

"Lock 'em Up" Is Bad Public Policy

The National Council on Crime and Delinquency examined the strategy to reduce crime by increasing the probability and the length of imprisonment, particularly for drug offenses. The research focused on Florida. According to researcher James Austin, "More than any state, Florida has dramatically followed this course of increasing the use of imprisonment for drug crimes." Florida has increased the use of imprisonment most dramatically—by over 300 percent from 1980 to 1989 (see Figure 14.10).

Despite the increase in both prison building and the number of prison admissions, the Florida prison system has released prisoners at an even greater rate during the same period. The result is shorter prison terms,

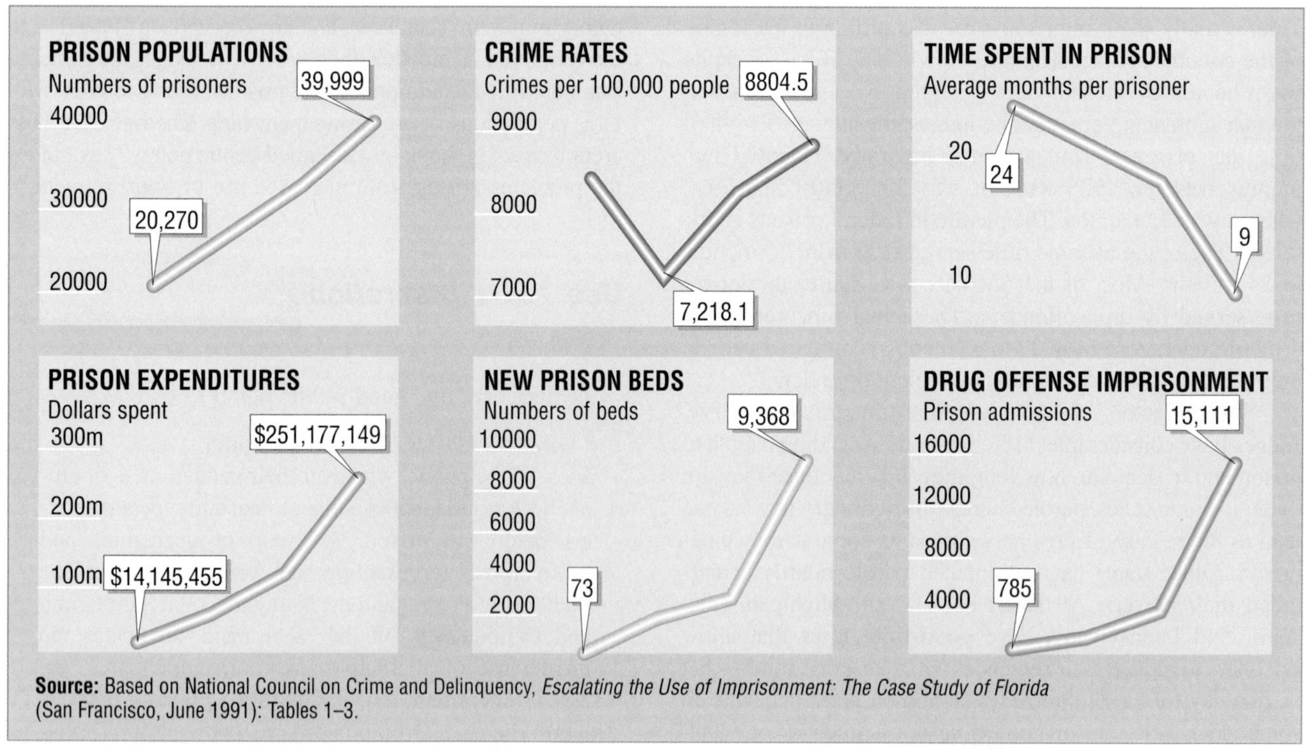

Source: Based on National Council on Crime and Delinquency, *Escalating the Use of Imprisonment: The Case Study of Florida* (San Francisco, June 1991): Tables 1–3.

Figure 14.10
Escalating the Use of Imprisonment
(Florida, 1980–1989, sampled at three-year intervals)

dropping from an average of 24 months in 1980 to 9 months in 1989 (Figure 14.10).

According to the NCCD researchers:

> Based on the theories of deterrence and incapacitation, the sharp and huge rise in imprisonment should have produced a reduction in the crime rate. Instead, the crime rate rose 5 percent during the period. In fact, the steepest rise in crime accompanied the greatest rise in imprisonment, namely, between 1986 and 1989. (Figure 14.10)

The war on drugs did not produce a reduction in drug offenses. Admissions to prison for drug offenses rose by 1,825 percent over the decade, compared with an overall admission increase of 381 percent. For female drug offenders, the rise was even greater—more than 3,000 percent. According to present data, the number of drug offenses continues to rise, not fall, despite the huge increase in prison admissions for drug offenses.

The explosion in the prison population creates a risk to public safety. Mandatory sentencing requires some prisoners to remain in prison, but it also forces the early release of ordinary prisoners. In one case, Charles Street, convicted of a violent crime, was released a year early. Following his early release, he murdered two Miami police officers. In another case, Robert and Harry Lebo were convicted for "molesting a crawfish trap." After their release, they were convicted of lobster theft. Under the habitual offender law, correctional authorities had to release two prisoners to make room for the Lebos. According to the researchers, "It is the worst of both worlds when nonviolent petty offenders are sentenced inappropriately to prison while dangerous criminals are released early."

CRITICAL THINKING

1. What is the evidence for and against a tougher imprisonment policy?
2. Is the case for imprisonment stronger or weaker than the case against it, as presented here? Explain your answer.
3. Is it possible that both are correct? Is Florida perhaps an exception to the national data that Langan and DiIulio present? Defend your answer.

Returning to Prison

Most prisoners are **recidivists;** that is, they are repeat offenders, and have served time in prison one or more previous times. Depending on the researcher, recidivism has a variety of meanings. It can include all crimes including juvenile offenses; all prior arrests; all criminal charges; all convictions; or only prior commitments to prison or jail. Nearly 85 percent of prisoners are not first-time offenders. Some time prior to their present imprisonment, they have been sentenced to either probation or incarceration as adults or juveniles. More than one-fifth of all prisoners have been convicted six or more times. More than 60 percent have already spent time incarcerated for prior offenses. More than half have been convicted of at least one violent crime.[98]

The longer former prisoners remain out of prison, the less likely they are to return. Recidivism varies according to offense. Property offenders return to prison (36.8 percent) more frequently than violent offenders (31.5 percent). Burglars return most frequently, robbers next most frequently. Drug-related crimes, forgery, embezzlement, and sexual assault follow; homicide has the lowest recidivist rates. The more times prisoners are confined, the greater the likelihood they will return to prison. About one-quarter of all prisoners with no prior record will return to prison; 37 percent of all prisoners with one or two prior prison terms will return; and 42.7 percent of those with three or more prior terms will be back in prison. Eighty percent of state prisoners in 1991 had previously served sentences either of probation or incarceration.[99]

Recidivism also varies with age, gender, and race. The younger prisoners are upon their release, the more likely they are to return to prison. In Massachusetts, for example, 31 percent of prisoners under age 25 will return to prison; between the ages of 25 and 29, 28 percent recidivate. At 30 and older, only 17 percent return to prison.

Gender also affects recidivism. Men recidivate at substantially higher rates than women. In New York State, for example, 36 percent of released men return to prison; 12.1 percent of women return. Women are less likely to recidivate when support services are available in the community. Most imprisoned women have "serious economic, medical, mental health, and social difficulties which are often overlooked and frequently intensified" in prison. Community programs more effectively enable women to lead law-abiding lives than does imprisonment. In Pennsylvania, for example, the Program for Women Offenders found that its services reduced recidivism. In a random sample of more than one thousand clients, 3.2 percent recidivated. Intermediate sanctions such as home confinement and intensive supervision may also provide alternatives to imprisonment, if they include direct services.

Whites recidivate at significantly lower levels than other races. In California, for example, 27.9 percent of released whites returned to prison. African Americans returned at a rate of 33.5 percent.[100]

Recidivism has three other critical characteristics. First, nearly 60 percent of all prisoners admitted to prison for the first time have been convicted before but were sentenced to probation instead of prison. In fact, 27 percent of all prisoners were on probation when they were sentenced to their first prison term. Second, nearly 46 percent would still have been in prison when presently admitted if they had completely served out a prior maximum prison term. Third, more than one-third of released prisoners are sent back to prison after completing the supervision period following release.

The incidence of recidivism has led to questions about the effectiveness of probation over prison, rehabilitation rograms in prison, and community-based parole systems that facilitate ex-prisoners' reentry into the community. The information about high recidivism rates has resulted in several major changes affecting prison policy: mandatory prison terms, sentence enhancements for repeat offenders, the determinate sentence, sentencing guidelines, and parole guidelines. To some extent, these changes reflect a general hardening in public attitudes toward crime; they also stem from increased knowledge about how much recidivism actually occurs. As a result, imprisonment has become the dominant form of punishment.[101]

Knowledge and Understanding CHECK

1. Describe the general characteristics of the majority of prisoners in U.S. prisoners.
2. Describe the family, educational, and occupational backgrounds of prisoners.
3. How does George Beto describe the character of most prisoners?
4. Compare women and men prisoners.
5. What are special management prisoners?
6. Describe prisoners in terms of illegal drug use.
7. What did BJS report about illegal drug use among state prisoners?
8. Summarize prisoners and alcohol use.
9. What is the truth about the number of violent prisoners?
10. How long do prisoners remain in prison?
11. Identify the main reasons for shortening prison terms.
12. How many prisoners return to prison, and why do they return?

Should We Have Drug Prisons? Consideration

With 7 of every 10 inmates having substance-abuse problems, expectations are that the repeat-offender rate could drop significantly if such prison programs become widespread. "What drives our prison growth is drugs," says Steve Amos, an official of the Department of Justice Corrections Program. "If we want to impact public safety, we need to treat those people. "Locking up inmates in prison is a short-term response. The question is, will they be back to the same behavior when they get out?" says Mr. Amos. The average treatment length is 9 to 12 months and costs $3,000. It costs $30,000 per year to lock someone up.

"[Treatment] is a cheap investment." Sonjia Paige, director of SCI-Chester's prison program, agrees, and points out another benefit of treating inmates: a captive audience. "In prison, we can do an excellent job of providing inmates with tools they need to change attitudes and behaviors."

A change in behavior is desperately needed. Inmates who do not receive adequate treatment are more likely to become repeat offenders and have caused an explosion in the prison population, found a study by the National Center on Addiction and Substance Abuse at Columbia University. From 1980 to 1996, the number of inmates in state, federal, and local prisons tripled from 500,000 to 1.7 million. . . .

The $70 million prison has a no-tolerance policy on all drugs, including nicotine. It costs $61.40 [a day] to house and treat an inmate at SCI Chester—the average for inmates in Pennsylvania state prisons. SCI-Chester contracts with Gaudenzia, a private drug-and-alcohol-treatment provider in Norristown, Pennsylvania, to treat inmates. Drug counselors are on site 12 hours a day, and treatment ranges from Alcoholics Anonymous meetings to one-on-one sessions with a counselor.

According to Paige, structure is a key component of the treatment program. Each day, 250 inmates must make their own beds and shine their shoes in addition to other chores. They spend most of the day in counseling and vocational education programs.

When inmates are ready, they move to a halfway house, where they continue treatment and take part in a work/education program. That continuity of care is a key to success. Seventy-one percent of inmates who took part in both prison treatment and a work-release program remained out of prison 18 months after release, compared with 48 percent who only had prison-based treatment, according to a study of Delaware inmates by Jim Inciardi, professor at the University of Delaware.

There are certain complexities to running such a prison, however. Paige points out that the problem with getting inmates into a treatment program like SCI-Chester is that inmates won't admit to a drug problem, which might damage their records or hurt chances of parole. Second, many of the inmates at SCI-Chester are not there voluntarily.

"Some are mad that they're here. It takes us a little while to get them to understand where they are and why," says Paige. However, she adds, the outlook is usually good if they can get inmates past the initial 35 to 40 days to a point where they can recognize their problem. Pinkerson and Bruce Jenkins, another inmate who was convicted of a drug-related assault, say their stay at SCI-Chester has given them a sense of direction. Both plan to go back to school—Pinkerson to get a degree in computer programming; Jenkins to get an associate degree that would let him work for the prison treatment center.

They say the strict schedule is a stark contrast with previous state prison experiences, where treatment is offered a few hours a week and inmates are often idle. "It gave me a reality break," says Jenkins. "We can see what we've done with our lives and the people we've hurt, and we're facing up to a lot of responsibilities. Our lives don't have to go to a complete waste."[103]

Critical Thinking

1. Summarize the arguments for and against drug prisons.
2. On the basis of the information included here, would you recommend the creation of drug prisons? Explain your answer.
3. If your answer is no, what would you want to know before you recommended the creation of drug prisons?

CHAPTER CAPSULE

- Prisons vary depending on their location and purpose.
- Prison management styles depend on whether the mission is to control prisoners or to make them responsible enough to support themselves and play by the rules when they are released.
- New-generation prisons and jails combine architecture and management to create safe, secure, and humane confinement.
- Most prisoners are nonwhite, are less than 30 years old, have not graduated from high school, and have not maintained steady work.

KEY TERMS

penitentiary
Pennsylvania system
Auburn, or congregate system
correctional institution
fortress prison
violent prison
maximum security prison
super maximum prison
new-generation prison
medium security prison
minimum security prison
control model of management
building-tender system
responsibility management approach
consensus prison management

work release
institutional support
public works crews
reported capacity
measured capacity
density
occupancy
crowded prisoners
new-generation jail
podular design
direct supervision
privatization
special needs prisoners
good-time laws
recividist

INTERNET RESEARCH EXERCISES

Exercise: Search for information on women's prisons and prisoners. What are the main concerns of women prisoners' advocacy groups? What solutions are being proposed to address these concerns?

Suggested sites:

- California Coalition for Women Prisoners, http://www.igc.org/prisons/ccwp/index.html
- The Prison Issues Desk, http://www.open.igc.org/prisons/women/

InfoTrac College Edition: Search using the key words "women prisoners"

NOTES

1. Stephanie L. Baum, "States Experiment with Specialized Drug Prisons," *Christian Science Monitor,* 3 November 1998.
2. BJS, *Prisoners, 1925–1981* (Washington, D.C.: Bureau of Justice Statistics, 1982); Elliott Currie, *Confronting Crime* (New York: Pantheon Books, 1985), 28–29; BJS, *Prisoners in 1997* (Washington, D.C.: Bureau of Justice Statistics, 1998).
3. BJS, *Prisons and Prisoners in the United States* (Washington, D.C.: Bureau of Justice Statistics, 1992), 12; BJS, *Correctional Populations in the United States—1990* (Washington, D.C.: Bureau of Justice Statistics, 1992), Table 4.20.
4. David A. Ward, "Alcatraz and Marion: Confinement in Super Maximum Custody," in *Escaping Prison Myths: Selected Topics in the History of Federal Corrections,* John W. Roberts, ed. (Washington, D.C.: American University Press, 1994), 91–92.
5. Norval Morris, "Foreword," in *Escaping Prison Myths,* vii.
6. Lee H. Bowker, *Corrections: The Science and the Art* (New York: Macmillan, 1982).
7. Adam Jay Hirsch, *The Rise of the Penitentiary* (New Haven: Yale University Press, 1992), 11.
8. David Rothman, *The Discovery of the Asylum* (Boston: Little, Brown, 1971); Gerald Grob, *Mental Institutions in America* (New York: Free Press, 1973).
9. Quoted in A. W. Pisciotta, "Scientific Reform: The 'New Penology' at Elmira, 1876–1900," *Crime and Delinquency* 29 (1983): 621.
10. David Rothman, *Conscience and Convenience: The Asylum and Its Alternatives in Progressive America* (Boston: Little, Brown, 1980).
11. John Irwin, *Prisons in Turmoil* (Boston: Little, Brown, 1980), chap. 2.
12. Willard Gaylin et al., *Doing Good: The Limits of Benevolence* (New York: Pantheon, 1981); American Friends Society, *Struggle for Justice: A Report on Crime and Punishment in America* (New York: Hill and Wang, 1971); Michael Sherman and Gordon Hawkins, *Imprisonment in America: Choosing the Future* (Chicago: University of Chicago Press, 1981); Norval Morris, *The Future of Imprisonment* (Chicago: University of Chicago Press, 1974); Robert Johnson, *Hard Time: Understanding and Reforming the Prison* (Monterey, Calif.: Brooks/Cole, 1987).
13. Johnson, *Hard Time,* 43.
14. Robert Johnson and Hans Toch, *The Pains of Imprisonment* (Beverly Hills: Sage, 1982), 41.
15. Prisoners quoted in Irwin, *Prisons in Turmoil,* 181–213; Robert Blecker, "Haven or Hell? Inside Lorton Central Prison: Experiences of Punishment Justified," *Stanford Law Review* 42 (1990): 1162.
16. Richard G. Singer, "Prisons: Typologies and Classifications," in *Encyclopedia of Crime and Justice* (New York: Free Press, 1983), 3:1202–4; *Prisoners in 1997* (Washington, D.C.: BJS, 1998).
17. Ibid.
18. BJS, *Report to the Nation on Crime and Justice,* 2d ed., 107; Singer, "Prisons: Typologies and Classifications," 1204.
19. Federal Bureau of Prisons, Office of Public Affairs, "Florence Fact Sheet" (June 16, 1993), 1.
20. Federal Bureau of Prisons, Office of Public Affairs, "Florence Background Paper" (June 16, 1993), 1.
21. T. D. Bingham, "Maximum Transfer from Marion to Florence," *Prison Life* (n.d.), 25.
22. Pete Earley, *The Hot House* (New York: Bantham Books, 1992), 30; Ward, "Alcatraz and Marion," 81, 90.
23. David A. Ward and Kenneth F. Schoen, eds., *Confinement in Maximum Custody* (Lexington, Mass.: Lexington Books, 1981), chaps. 9–11.
24. Ibid., Singer, "Prisons: Typologies and Classifications," 1204.
25. Singer, "Prisons: Typologies and Classifications," 1203–4; Earley, *The Hot House,* 30.
26. Raymond G. Wozda and Judy Rowse, *Women Behind Bars* (Washington, D.C.: American Correctional Association, 1997), 3–4.
27. Isabel C. Barrows, "The Reformatory Treatment of Women in the United States," in *Penal and Reformatory Institutions,* vol. 2,

Charles R. Henderson, ed. (New York: Russell Sage Foundation, 1910), 129–67.
28. John DiIulio, *Governing Prisons* (New York: Free Press, 1987), 105.
29. Ibid.
30. Ibid., 107.
31. Ibid., 112.
32. Steve J. Martin and Sheldon Ekland-Olson, *Texas Prisons: The Walls Came Tumbling Down* (Austin: Texas Monthly Press, 1987) recounts much of this history.
33. Quoted in DiIulio, *Governing Prisons,* 119–20.
34. Quoted ibid., 124.
35. Quoted ibid., 127.
36. Ibid.
37. David A. Ward, "Control Strategies for Problem Prisoners in American Penal Systems," in *Problems of Long-Term Imprisonment,* Anthony E. Bottoms and Roy Light, eds., (Brookfield, Vt.: Gower, 1987).
38. Mark S. Fleisher, *Warehousing Violence* (Newbury Park, Calif.: Sage Publications, 1989).
39. Bowker, *Corrections,* 208–209.
40. Harold E. Williamson, *The Corrections Profession* (Newbury Park, Calif.: Sage Publications, 1990).
41. Stan Stojkovic and Rick Lovell, *Corrections: An Introduction* (Cincinnati: Anderson, 1992).
42. James B. Jacobs, ed., *New Perspectives on Prisons and Imprisonment* (Ithaca, N.Y.: Cornell University Press, 1983), 115–32.
43. Robert R. Ross, *Prison Guard/Correctional Officer: The Use and Abuse of the Human Resources of the Prison* (Toronto: Butterworths, 1981), part I.
44. Hans B. Toch, "Is a 'Correctional Officer,' By Any Other Name, a 'Screw'?" *Criminal Justice Review* 3 (1978): 19–37.
45. Hawkins, *The Prison: Policy and Practice* (Chicago: University of Chicago Press, 1976), 81; Jacobs and Gretsky, "Prison Guard," *Urban Life* 4 (April 1975), 10.
46. Jacobs and Gretsky, "Prison Guard," 10.
47. Hawkins, *The Prison,* 96, 98.
48. Lynne E. Zimmer, *Women Guarding Men* (Chicago: University of Chicago Press, 1986), 1.
49. Susan M. Hunter, "On the Line: Working Hard with Dignity," *Corrections Today* 48, no. 4 (1986): 12–13; James B. Jacobs, "Female Guards in Men's Prisons," *New Perspectives,* 178–201.
50. Quoted in Jacobs, *New Perspectives,* 187–88.
51. Barbara A. Owen, "Race and Gender Relations Among Prison Workers," *Crime and Delinquency* 31 (1985): 158.
52. Ibid.
53. Craig Haney, Curtis Banks, and Philip Zimbardo, "Interpersonal Dynamics in a Simulated Prison," *International Journal of Criminology and Penology* 1 (1973): 163. Hawkins, *The Prison,* 101.
54. Quoted in Hawkins, *The Prison,* 105.
55. Hawkins, *The Prison,* 101.
56. I am grateful to Leanne Phinney, Human Research Director, Oak Park Heights Correctional Facility, for these figures.
57. Minnesota Correctional Facility, Oak Park Heights, *Inmate Handbook,* 2–3.
58. Ross, *Prison Guard/Correctional Officer* stresses these positive dimensions to guards and their work. I am grateful to Professor David Ward, Chairman, Department of Sociology, University of Minnesota; Warden Gordon Wood; Penny Nelson at the warden's office at Oak Park Heights; the BBC special segment about Oak Park Heights; and to Dan Crutchfield, former correctional counselor at Oak Park Heights, for this information.
59. Bureau of Justice Statistics, *Prisoners in Jails and Prisons 1997* (Washington, D.C.: BJS, 1998), 2.
60. Ibid.; Belinda R. McCarthy, "The Use of Jail Confinement in the Disposition of Felony Arrests," *Journal of Criminal Justice* 17 (1989): 241–51.
61. BJS, *Prison and Jail Inmates 1997* (Washington, D.C.: BJS, 1998), 1.
62. Ibid.
63. Advisory Commission, *Jails, Intergovernmental Dimensions of a Local Problem* (Washington, D.C.: Advisory Commission on Intergovernmental Relations, 1984), 14.
64. Ibid., 21.
65. Ronald Goldfarb, *Jails: The Ultimate Ghetto* (New York: Archer Press, 1975), 27.
66. Ibid.
67. Ibid., 21.
68. Quoted in Goldfarb, *Jails: The Ultimate Ghetto,* 32.
69. Stephen H. Gettinger, *New Generation Jails: An Innovative Approach to an Age-Old Problem* (Washington, D.C.: National Institute of Corrections, March 1984), 1.
70. Richard Weiner, William Frazier, and Jay Farbstein, "Building Better Jails," *Psychology Today* (June 1987), 40.
71. Weiner, Frazier, and Farbstein, "Building Better Jails," 42.
72. Gettinger, *New Generation Jails,* 20–21; Weiner, Frazier, and Farbstein, "Building Better Jails," 42.
73. Weiner, Frazier, and Farbstein, "Building Better Jails," 42.
74. Gettinger, *New Generation Jails,* 5.
75. Patrick G. Jackson and Cindy A. Stearns, "Gender Issues in the New Generation Jail," *Prison Journal* 75 (1995): 205–206.
76. Ibid., 207.
77. Ibid., 215.
78. Charles H. Logan and Gerald G. Gaes, "Meta-Analysis and the Rehabilitation of Punishment," *Justice Quarterly* 10 (1993): 256–57.
79. Douglas C. McDonald, "Private Penal Institutions," *Crime and Justice: A Review of Research,* vol. 16 (Chicago: University of Chicago Press, 1992), 380.
80. GAO, *Prison Crowding* (Washington, D.C.: U.S. General Accounting Office, November 1989), 27; Daniel B. Wood, "Private Prisons, Public Doubts," *Christian Science Monitor,* 21 July 1998.
81. David Shichor, *Punishment for Profit* (Thousand Oaks, Calif.: Sage Publications, 1995).
82. *Associated Press,* "Feds Still Wary on Private Prisons," 28 October 1998.
83. Marc Mauer and Tracy Huling, "Young Black Americans and the Criminal Justice System: Five Years Later" (Washington, D.C.: The Sentencing Project, October 1995), 3; Blecker, "Haven or Hell?" 1154; Peter C. Kratcoski and George A. Pownall, "Federal Bureau of Prisons Programming for Older Inmates," *Federal Probation* 53 (1989): 28–35; *Prisoners in 1997* (Washington, D.C.: BJS, 1998).
84. BJS, *Sourcebook of Criminal Justice Statistics—1988* (Washington, D.C.: Bureau of Justice Statistics, 1989); BJS, *Prisons and Prisoners in the United States,* 13.
85. BJS, *Report to the Nation on Crime and Justice,* 2d ed., 48.
86. Quoted in Fleisher, *Warehousing Violence,* 22.
87. Jane R. Chapman, *Economic Realities and the Female Offender* (Lexington, Mass.: Lexington Books, 1980), 21–75; Barbara Owen and Barbara Bloom, "Profiling Women Prisoners: Findings from National Surveys and a California Sample," *Prison Journal* 75 (1995): 166; Russ Immarigeon and Meda Chesney-Lind, *Women's Prisons: Overcrowded and Overused* (San Francisco: National Council on Crime and Delinquency, 1992), 2–3, 6; American

Correctional Association, *The Female Offender: What Does the Future Hold?* (Washington, D.C.: St. Mary's Press, 1990); BJS, *Prisoners in 1997* (Washington, D.C.: BJS, 1998); also, see Barbara Owen, *In the Mix: Struggle and Survival in a Women's Prison* (Albany: State University of NY Press, 1998), 9–10.
88. Immarigeon and Chesney-Lind, *Women's Prisons,* 3.
89. Studies cited in Immarigeon and Chesney-Lind, *Women's Prisons,* 9.
90. *The Special Management Inmate* (Washington, D.C.: National Institute of Justice, March 1985).
91. BJS, *Drugs and Crime Facts, 1994* (Washington, D.C.: BJS, 1995).
92. BJS, *Report to the Nation on Crime and Justice: The Data,* 37.
93. BJS, *Report to the Nation on Crime and Justice,* 100; BJS, *Prison Admissions and Releases, 1982* (Washington, D.C.: Bureau of Justice Statistics, 1985), Table 11; BJS, *Prisoners in 1994* (Washington, D.C.: BJS, August 1995), Tables 15, 16.
94. James B. Jacobs, "Sentencing by Prison Personnel: Good Time," *UCLA Law Review* 30 (1982): 226.
95. Koppel, *Time Served in Prison* (Washington, D.C.: Bureau of Justice Statistics, 1986).
96. John DiIulio, Jr., "The Value of Prisons," *Wall Street Journal,* 13 May 1992.
97. Patrick A. Langan, "America's Soaring Prison Population," *Science* 251 (1991): 1568, 1573.
98. Lawrence A. Greenfield, *Examining Recidivism* (Washington, D.C.: Bureau of Justice Statistics, 1985), 1; BJS, *Profile of State Prison Inmates, 1986* (Washington, D.C.: Bureau of Justice Statistics, January 1988); Allen J. Beck, *Recidivism of Prisoners Released in 1983* (Washington, D.C.: Bureau of Justice Statistics, 1989).
99. John F. Wallerstedt, *Returning to Prison* (Washington, D.C.: Bureau of Justice Statistics, 1984), 2–3; BJS, *Prisons and Prisoners in the United States,* 16; Immarigeon and Chesney-Lind, *Women's Prisons.*
100. John F. Wallerstedt, *Returning to Prison* (Washington, D.C.: Bureau of Justice Statistics, 1984), 5.
101. Greenfield, *Examining Recidivism,* 1; Wallerstedt, *Returning to Prison,* 5.

CHAPTER 15

Prison Life

CHAPTER OUTLINE

Should Prisoners Get to Lift Weights and Play Team Sports?

Several states are taking away the privileges or amenities of prisoners. For example, Georgia has removed the exercise bikes, foosball, pool and, Ping-Pong tables. "We got this all out of there," said Wayne Garner in 1995, commissioner of Georgia's Department of Corrections. Georgia Congressman Bob Barr, a Republican, supports the move: "I think prison is *for* punishment. I'm opposed to anything that detracts from the fundamental notion–one that ought to be hammered home every day–which is *they are there to be punished*" (emphasis added). Two of the most cherished privileges–team sports and weightlifting–are on the list of remaining privileges to be removed in a number of jurisdictions. Should they be removed too?[1]

INTRODUCTION

Imprisonment is the most popular response to crime. But, it is also the most expensive. What should imprisonment be like? Ask most of my own students and other students at other colleges that I have visited, and you will hear tough answers. Like "Torture chambers!" "Miserable!" "Horrible!" "Hell holes!" Listen to most people on the street and politicians who are only too happy to follow the public's lead, and their answers are similar to those of the students.

However, ask corrections professionals and you will likely get a quite different answer. They will remind you that most people locked up in prison are at some time going to get out—probably sooner than later. Will torture, misery, and deprivation make them less dangerous and more productive when they get out? Will it turn them from lawbreakers who prey on the rest of us into people who work hard, play by the rules, and pay their own way? Corrections professionals will probably also ask you about the lives of corrections officers—the "other prisoners" discussed in Chapter 14—who spend most of their time in prison too. What do you think their lives should be like? Does it matter that corrections professionals also have to spend their time in the "hell holes" that you want for prisoners? Does it concern you that if the prisoners are miserable that this makes the work of the professionals harder, too?

Unfortunately, the state of our knowledge does not help us to answer the question about whether brutal punishment makes prisoners more criminal or punishes them into becoming law-abiding, responsible people. Nor does the empirical evidence tell us that rehabilitation programs "work." However, we do know that safe, secure, humane imprisonment makes the lives of corrections officers better, and that in safe, secure, humane prisons the level of disorder, violence, and gang activity is lower.

This is the reason that a number of enlightened corrections professionals—who know a lot more about these matters than the rest of us—are recommending that we send offenders to prison *as* punishment, not *for* punishment. Disciplined, safe, secure, orderly confinement that provides only the basic necessities of life *is* punishment, even if it is also *humane*. Punishment does not require that we *add* brutal, filthy, unsafe, disorderly conditions to confinement. This chapter examines prison society and life in that society.

MALE PRISONER SUBCULTURE

Life in prison has provided fertile subject matter for fiction and sociology throughout the twentieth century. However, it was in the 1930s that a sociologist first identified a distinct **prison subculture** in a maximum security prison. Quickly, the idea of a "foreign" culture inside prisons with its own rules, customs, and language captured the way penologists thought about life in prison.

Indigenous or Imported?

Sociologists have developed two basic theories to explain prison society: the indigenous theory and the importation theory. According to the **indigenous theory** of prison society, conditions inside prisons themselves shape the nature of prison society. Donald Clemmer introduced the concept of **prisonization** in his 1940 classic *The Prison Community*. Clemmer was a former staff member of Menard Penitentiary in Illinois. Based on his detailed observations, Clemmer concluded that prisonization is the process by which inmates adapt to the customs of the prison world.[2]

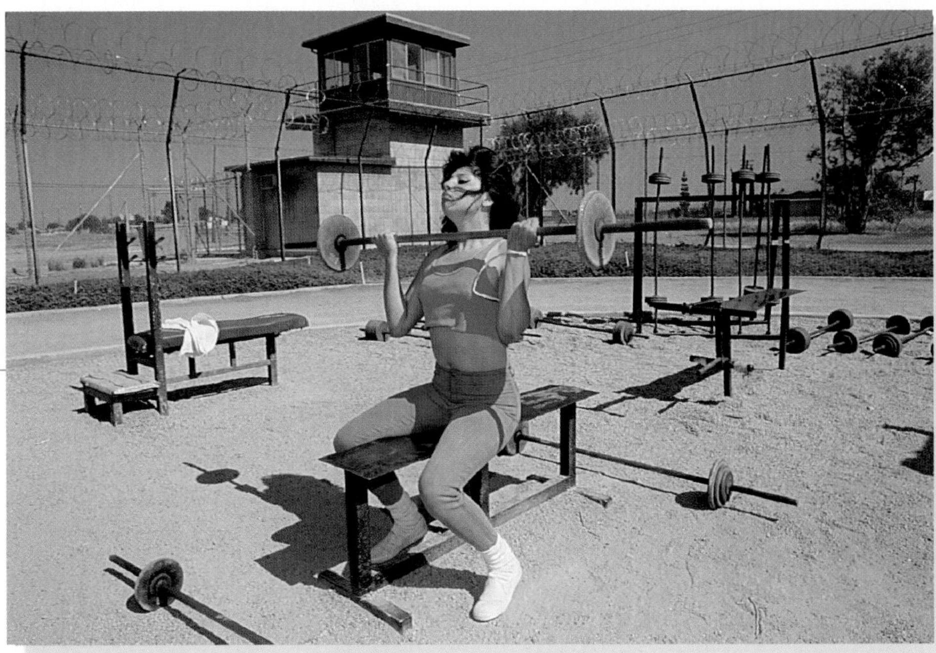

This woman, lifting weights in a prison in Chino, California, may be affected by the trend to make prisons tougher places to live in. Most of the public supports this move, but corrections officials see recreation as a means to occupy prisoners' time in nondestructive behavior, which makes life easier not only for prisoners but also for those who work in prisons as well.

Since the 1960s, however, prisons have lost much of their isolation from the "free world." With these changed conditions, and perhaps also because of a recognition that prison society was never so distinct from the society outside as the indigenous theory maintained, a new theory of prison society appeared—the **importation theory.** According to importation theory, prisoners have to adapt to life both inside and outside prison. Life outside prison, including television, magazines, music, visitors, lawsuits, friends, and gangs have all contributed to a closer relationship between prison society and society as a whole.

According to the importation theory, prison society has roots not only in conventional but also criminal culture outside prison. Former inmate turned sociologist John Irwin and the distinguished sociologist Donald Cressey found that the values held by prison newcomers affected prison society as much as the values acquired by inmates in prison.

Irwin and Cressey identified three inmate subcultures—the thief, the straight, and the convict. Only the convict was indigenous; the thief and the straight are imported. "Convicts" accept life in prison as their normal life and try to obtain power and privileges within the prison community. They are mainly **state-raised youths,** having spent most of their lives in orphanages, reform schools, and other state-operated institutions. Thieves keep to themselves, waiting to get out and resume their former lives. Straight prisoners do not consider themselves criminals at all, at least not "real criminals." White-collar offenders, for example, try to retain in prison legitimate elements of their former lives.[3]

Adaptive Prisoner Lifestyles

The choice of which subculture to join faces all inmates. According to John Irwin in his book *The Felon,* based on interviews with convicts in Soledad men's prison in California, all new inmates ask themselves, "How shall I do my time?" Or, "What shall I do in prison?" A few cannot cope; they either commit suicide or sink into psychosis. Irwin found that those who can cope fit into two basic groups:

1. Those who identify with the world outside prison.
2. Those who identify primarily with the prison world. This is called **jailing.**[4]

Jailers "who do not retain or . . . never acquired any commitment to outside social worlds tend to make a world out of prison." One such inmate told Mark Fleisher, who studied life in the maximum security federal penitentiary at Lompoc, California:

> Beating the system is the best game in town. Middle-class Americans will never understand it. You know, I feel "extracultural." I live on the same planet you do. We speak the same language, but that's where our similarity ends. That's right, I live outside this culture. This is your culture. This is your prison. You have to live with all the f———-rules in this society. I don't. You have to obey the rules, Mark. That's how you live. But, I don't have to obey anybody's f———-rules. The worst that can happen to me is that they put me back in prison. And who gives a f——! When they do that, you got to pay for me. I win. If this is all this society can do to me, then I'm gonna do whatever I want to do. How you going to stop me? I'm invincible.[5]

Another prisoner, this one in the federal prison at Leavenworth, Kansas, put it this way:

> As the years go by and you get older, you realize that your life is considered a failure by society's standards. . . . You're a jailbird. You don't have any money, no house, no job, no status. In society's eyes

> you're a worthless piece of shit, or you can say, "Fuck society, I'll live by my own rules." That's what I did. I decided to live by my own standards and rules. They aren't society's but they are mine and that's what I've done. In your society, I may not be anybody, but in here, I am.[6]

Prisoners who identify with the outside world fall into two further divisions, according to Irwin:

a. **Doing time:** those who for the most part want to maintain their former life patterns and identities.
b. **Gleaning:** those who desire to make significant changes in their life patterns and identities and see prison as a chance to do this.[7]

Time-doers try to get through their prison terms with "the least amount of suffering and the greatest amount of comfort." They avoid trouble, find activities to occupy their time, secure a few luxuries, and make a few friends. The gleaners follow a sometimes detailed plan of self-improvement. According to one gleaner:

> I got tired of losing. I had been losing all of my life. I decided that I wanted to win for a while. So I got on a different kick. I knew that I had to learn something so I went to school, got my high school diploma. I cut myself off from my old . . . buddies and started hanging around with some intelligent guys who minded their own business. We read a lot, a couple of us paint. We play a little bridge and talk, a lot of the time about what we are going to do when we get out.[8]

Deciding whether to be a time-doer, a gleaner, or a jailer is not always easy. Irwin quotes Piri Thomas, who was forced to decide whether to participate in a riot:

> I stood there watching and weighing, trying to decide whether or not I was a con first and an outsider second. I had been doing time inside yet living every mental minute I could outside; now I had to choose one or the other. I stood there in the middle of the yard. Cons passed me by, some going west to join the boppers, others going east to neutral ground. . . . I had to make a decision. *I am a con. These damn cons are my people. Your people are outside the cells, home, in the streets. No! That ain't so. . . . Look at them go toward the west wall. Why in hell am I taking so long in making up my mind?*[9]

The Inmate Code

Just as people do in the larger society outside prison, prisoners have a code. This **inmate code** is the informal system of rules that determines what is right and wrong and what is good and bad within inmate society. This code should not be confused either with formal prison rules or the informal adaptations of the written rules of the prison to the lives of prisoners. (These are discussed later in this chapter in Prisoners' Rights.) The two cardinal principles of the inmate code are:

1. Do your own time.
2. Never inform on another inmate.

Gresham Sykes, in his classic study of life in a New Jersey prison during the 1950s, *The Society of Captives,* found five fundamental principles of the inmate code and stated them in five graphic rules:

1. *Don't interfere with inmate interests:* Never rat on a con, don't be nosy, don't have a loose lip, don't put a guy on the spot.
2. *Don't quarrel with fellow inmates:* Play it cool, don't lose your head, do your own time.
3. *Don't exploit inmates:* Don't break your word, don't steal from cons, don't sell favors, don't welsh on bets.
4. *Maintain yourself:* Don't weaken, don't whine, don't cop out, be tough, be a man.
5. *Don't trust the guards or the things they stand for:* Don't be a sucker, guards are hacks and screws, the officials are wrong and the prisoners are right.[10]

No single inmate code, of course, can exist for all prisons at all times. These rules were derived from maximum security prisons for men, and they stem from the 1950s. Much has changed since then. Prisoners are younger, they are more violent, they are members of racial and ethnic gangs, and they are less tied to codes of any kind. All these changes make the management of prisons, particularly maximum and minimum security prisons for men, more difficult.

THE PRISON ECONOMY

Prisoners are not supposed to be *comfortable* in confinement. As part of their punishment, they lose their freedom, their privacy, and also the "extras" connected to what we call the "material comforts in life." They are supposed to live lives of enforced poverty. This means that the state provides only the bare essentials of plain food, clothing, and shelter. Prisons are supposed to be islands of poverty in a sea of abundance.[11]

Of course, in movies and on television, prisons are not entirely "islands of poverty." Viewers see TV sets in prison cells and prisoners working out in well-equipped exercise rooms. We also hear of "country club" minimum security prisons where "prisoners" play golf. We read of prisoners who are drunk or high on drugs. How does it happen that such comforts exist in these "islands of poverty"? Prisoners obtain some amenities legally. For example, prisoners are allowed to receive gifts from friends and relatives. Prisoners can also buy some of the comforts of life from the prison commissary. These purchases are not made with money—currency is not allowed—but with scrip or on credit drawn on accounts supplied with money from the outside or that prisoners have earned in prison. (How prisoners make money while they are in prison is discussed later in this chapter, in Programs.)

The approved list of gifts and the stock of items in the commissary are hardly enough to satisfy the wants of most prisoners. Prisoners are well aware of all the comforts of life that they are *not* allowed to have. They find it hard to satisfy their desires with available resources and within the enforced poverty of confinement. According to Susan Sheehan, most of the men she studied in a New York prison were there "precisely because they were not willing to go without on the street. They are no more willing to go without in prison, so they hustle to obtain what they cannot afford to buy."[12]

Use *Your* Discretion

Should prisoners be allowed contraband goods and services?

Hustling contraband goods and services—mainly food, clothing, weapons, drugs, and prostitution—both violates the rules of prisons and frustrates the goal of punishment by enforced poverty. Deprived of luxuries, prisoners nonetheless seek them. Obtaining them not only helps ease the pain of imprisonment but also contributes informally to prison stability. Because these contraband goods and services contribute to stability and therefore make prisons and prisoners easier to manage, they are tolerated by the authorities to some extent. Prisoners put great stake in these amenities; trouble arises when they do not receive them. Equally important, trouble brews when prisoner leaders lose the profits from and control of contraband goods and services. In some prisons, prisoner leaders who control the contraband business form symbiotic relationships with correctional officers. Both have an interest in maintaining stability, so they make trade-offs: Officers allow some illegal trafficking, usually in "nonserious" contraband such as food; prisoner leaders, in return, maintain peaceful cell blocks.[13]

CRITICAL THINKING

1. List the arguments for and against allowing prisoners to get amenities.
2. Would you recommend allowing the amenities? Back up your answer with the list you made in (1).

CONSENSUAL SEX IN PRISON

Sex is prohibited in all prisons for at least two reasons. First, prisoners are supposed to suffer hardships as part of their punishment. The prohibition of sex is one of these. Second, there is a prohibition against sexual assault to ensure that prisoners are safe and secure (see Violence). However, anecdotes about prison life for generations have told of routine consensual sex behind prison walls. Sometimes, journalists tell of these activities. The early records of Stillwater prison and the St. Cloud reformatory in Minnesota are replete with violations of the celibacy code. Despite anecdotes and some prison records, it is still not clear what exactly this sexual activity is, and how often it occurs.[14]

Empirical research reveals greatly varying estimates of how much consensual sex there is in prison. Some say it is rampant; others have found that consensual sex is infrequent. Estimates that include both consensual sex and sexual assault showed a variation of from 20 percent to 90 percent! Here are some comments from Delaware prisoners commenting on sex in prison in 1994:

- There is an unspoken ridicule of inmates who engage in sex today.
- Sex still goes on in here. People I know don't use protection because it's not available. People are knowledgeable [about HIV] but still have sex.
- Most people that do it are lifers . . . they don't care.
- Just like on the streets; you can get sex anytime if you have money.[15]

The demand for more knowledge about consensual sex in prison has grown because of the spread of AIDS. Christine A. Saum, Hilary L. Surratt, James A. Inciardi, and Rachael E. Bennett have responded to this demand in a study of sex among prisoners in Delaware. They conducted voluntary interviews with male prisoners in a medium security prison who were in a treatment program for drug abusers. They defined consensual sex as "oral or anal sex that is agreed on before the act takes place." They found:

- 51.5 percent reported that they had heard of consensual sex acts during their previous year of imprisonment.
- 35.6 percent reported that they had never heard of consensual sex acts during their previous year of imprisonment.
- 24.8 percent reported that they had actually seen a consensual sex act during their last year of imprisonment.
- 2 percent reported that they themselves had had consensual sex during their last year of imprisonment.[16]

Use *Your* Discretion

Can we really know how widespread sex in prisons is?

A major reason for the inconclusive results of research about sex in prison is methodological difficulties. According to Saum and others who surveyed the literature and completed their own research in a Delaware prison, the major drawback is inaccurate reporting because:

- Most incidents are not officially recorded.
- Definitions of sex vary.
- Prisoners underestimate the amount of sex because they are afraid they will get in trouble.
- Prisoners are embarrassed to admit that they have sex with other men.
- Prisoners are afraid of being labeled weak or gay.[17]

Saum and her colleagues tried to reduce these difficulties in their interviews with Delaware prisoners. Interviewers developed excellent rapport with the inmates that they interviewed, and this fostered honesty in the prisoners' responses. Furthermore, inmates were not asked about incidents in their present unit. Instead, they were asked about "sexual activities that they may have heard about, seen, or participated in when they were part of the general prison population." Therefore, they were not in contact with the prisoners whom they were reporting.[18]

CRITICAL THINKING

1. List the methodological problems of measuring sex in prison.
2. List the ways that Saum and her colleagues tried to reduce these problems.
3. Do you have confidence in Saum and her colleagues' findings? Support your answer.

RACE AND ETHNICITY

During the 1960s and early 1970s, increased racial and ethnic consciousness, assertiveness, confrontation, solidarity, and violence appeared in U.S. society. These developments did not bypass men's prisons; instead, they were imported into male prison society, leaving men's prisons "fragmented, tense, and often extremely violent." We speak only of men's prisons here. Women's prisons are different (as we will see in Life in Women's Prisons). Prison populations were also changing. By the late 1970s, African Americans, Latinos, Puerto Ricans, Native Americans, and other minorities in the general population became the majority in American prisons. Stateville, Illinois' maximum security prison just outside Chicago, for example has 80 percent African American prisoners (Chapter 14).[19]

Racial hatred has also increased in prisons. Prisoners tend to restrict their relationships to small friendship groups, cliques, and, increasingly, gangs in which individuals band together according to race. To be sure, other shared experiences, such as committing similar crimes, coming from the same neighborhood, doing time in another state prison or institution, and just living in the same cell block or working in the same prison workshop, contribute to cohesion. But race is the overriding element in much of today's prisoner society.[20]

The most powerful social groupings in prisons today have a racial basis, and the most volatile dynamic within prisons is the hatred between white and African American prisoners. African American prisoners are not only more numerous, but they are also more assertive than they were in the past. According to one African American prisoner at Stateville Prison in Illinois:

> In the prison, the black dudes have a little masculinity game they play. It has no name, really, but I call it whup a white boy—especially the white gangsters or syndicate men, the bad juice boys, the hit men, etc. The black dudes go out of their way to make faggots out of them. And to lose a fight to a white dude is one of the worst things that can happen to a black dude. And I know that, by and far, the white cats are faggots. They will drop their pants and bend over and touch their toes and get had before they will fight.[21]

According to another:

> Every can I been in that's the way it is. It's gettin' even I guess. You guys been cuttin' our b——s off ever since we been in this country. Now we're just gettin' even.[22]

White prisoners either become bigoted or even more bigoted if they were already racially prejudiced before coming to prison. According to a white California prisoner:

> After 10:30, the voice dropped a decibel or two, and from the morass of sound Ron began to recognize certain voices by timbre and catch snatches of conversation. Above him, perhaps on the second tier, he picked up a gumboed black voice saying he'd like to kill all white babies, while his listener agreed it was the best way to handle the beasts—before they grew up. A year earlier, Ron would have felt compassion for anyone so consumed by hate and whenever whites casually used "nigger" he was irked. Now he felt tentacles of hate spreading through himself—and half an hour later, he smiled when a batch of voices began chanting: "Sieg Heil! Sieg Heil!"[23]

African Americans and whites are not the only prisoners. According to James B. Jacobs:

> Afro-American, Caucasian-American and Mexican-American inmates lived side by side but maintained three distinct ethnic cultures. Inmates did not eat at the same table, share food, cigarettes or bathroom facilities with individuals of other ethnic groups. They would not sit in the same row while viewing television or even talk for more than brief interchanges with members of a different ethnic group.[24]

Prisoners of similar racial groups tend to stick together in prison.

GANGS

In some men's prisons, there are racial and ethnic cliques and gangs. Gang members rob, assault, and otherwise prey on members of other gangs and members of the general prison population. Prisons have always had violent prisoners, generally youths recently "graduated" from juvenile prison as well as unskilled, lower- and working-class criminals. Prior to the 1960s, a strong normative consensus against violence among most other prisoners kept such men in check. Since then, however, the number of tough young prison graduates and unskilled prisoners has increased.[25]

Unlike older, more traditional prisoners, gang members have a belligerent attitude toward all authority and its institutions when they enter prison. Little rewards, like sneaking extra cups of coffee, do not satisfy gang members as they did older prisoners. Gang members are preoccupied with status and gang rivalry. Challenging authority is commonplace. According to James Jacobs in his study of Stateville Prison outside Chicago:

> [W]hen a lieutenant was called to "walk" an inmate, he was often confronted with ten or twelve of the inmate's fellow gang members surrounding him, challenging his authority. One Stateville guard explained: "The inmate will say, 'I'm not going.' Then a group of his gang will gather around him. I'll have to call a lieutenant. Sometimes one of the leaders will just come over and tell the member to go ahead."[26]

Prison, in the eyes of the new prisoner, is the ultimate test of manhood. A man in prison is able to secure what he wants and protect what he has: "In here, a man gets what he can" and "nobody can force a man to do something he don't want to" are key elements of their belief system. Any prisoner who does not meet these standards is not a man, "has no respect for himself," and is therefore not entitled to respect from others.[27]

The influence of prison gangs can extend outside the prison. In about half the states, gangs have counterparts on the streets. In some of these states, prisons act as bases for criminal gang activity in the community. In California, the Black Guerrilla Family is allied with a gang of younger African American prisoners called "Crips" (after their reputation for crippling their victims), most of whom have been convicted of violent street crimes. According to law enforcement officers, "leaders of the Black Guerrilla Family are directing a growing effort to take over part of Southern California's lucrative cocaine trade by using Crips as their soldiers." The Crips, they say, are recruited in prison. After being paroled they are attempting, often with violence, to push out other cocaine dealers from the predominantly African American South-Central area of Los Angeles. "Investigators say [they have] fresh evidence of the influence of prison gangs beyond prison walls," a problem that a former attorney general of the United States called "serious and spreading."[28]

VIOLENCE

In some prisons, race and ethnic tensions, the growth of gangs and violent prisoners, and the prison economy have created an increase in violent crimes against other prisoners.

Assaults and homicides in maximum security prisons has grown to the point that "the possibility of being attacked or killed has loomed as the major concern of offenders incarcerated in these prisons or anticipating going to one." According to one prisoner in California during the 1990s:

> I've been on the yard watching people get shot, watching people die. You know how hard it is coming out with tears in your eyes knowing that you're going to get hit, knowing that someone is going to physically hurt you, or try to kill you. . . . Eighty-two, 83, 84, people were dropping like flies, people getting stuck. After two or three years of that, it's hard. People on the outside say, ah, that doesn't happen. You weren't there, man.[29]

Economic victimization occurs when violence or threats of it accompany the involvement of prisoners in gambling, frauds, loan sharking, theft, robbery, protection rackets, con games, delivery of misrepresented contraband (or nondelivery of contraband), and so on. When promised commodities are not delivered—or are not as promised—victims may retaliate. Drug trafficking is a good example. To get drugs into prisons requires sophisticated smuggling operations. Violence results if drugs are stolen, misrepresented, overpriced, or not delivered. Prisoners use violence to prevent these distribution irregularities from happening in the first place, or to retaliate for them if they do take place.[30]

Gangbanging

Increased violence has forced prisoners in these prisons to adopt strategies of doing time that reduce their chances of being victimized. One strategy, especially for young first-timers, is **gangbanging**—that is, affiliating with a gang or clique for protection. Some older prisoners who have reputations for being tough can circulate freely in violence-prone prisons. However, the majority of prisoners avoid most prisoners and most settings where large groups of prisoners get together. According to John Irwin and James Austin, most prisoners:

> shy away from most prisoners and settings where masses of prisoners congregate and withdraw into small groups or virtual isolation. Although they may occasionally buy from the racketeers, place bets, or trade commodities on a small scale with other unaffiliated prisoners, they stay out of the large-scale economic activities and dissociate themselves from the violent cliques and gangs. They stick to a few friends whom they have met in the cell blocks, at work, on the outside (**homeboys**), in other prisons, or through shared interests. Either alone or with their few trusted friends, they go to work and/or attend meetings of various clubs and formal organizations that the prison administration allows to exist in prison. Otherwise, they stay in their cells.[31]

Sexual Assault

Some prisoners have another problem—they are victims of sexual assault. More than 80 percent of the victims are young white men, 16 percent are African American, and 2 percent are Hispanic. Most of the attackers are African American (80 percent), some are Hispanic (14 percent), and a few are white (6 percent). Daniel Lockwood, in his *Prison Sexual Violence,* maintains that the following three statements explain the preceding figures:[32]

1. Whites are considered weak.
2. Whites are the objects of race hatred.
3. Whites are poorly organized.

According to one African American prisoner in a New York State prison:

> If you come in here alone then they [black prisoners] will try to crack on you for something. But if they know that you know people that have been here for awhile, then they know better. They try to pick on some of the weak ones. They like to pick on them.[33]

White prisoners tend to be less organized, less likely to know other whites in prison, and less willing to band together for protection. Class divisions among white prisoners are also stronger than they are among blacks. Middle-class whites look down on white prisoners whom they believe are their social inferiors. Some do not consider themselves criminals at all, which isolates them and makes them more vulnerable to attacks from violent cliques and gangs.[34]

The image of toughness is so important to the "new young prison hero," so dominating a young white prisoner only enhances his prestige. Whites who do not respond violently to unwanted sexual approaches are likely victims:

> You see a young pretty dude who doesn't come in here on a violent record. Now, he is probably in the worst situation than the guy that comes in here on a violent record. Because if you know that a guy has murdered someone on the street, and has taken a life, and is in here for life, you are going to think three or—not just once but three or four times—before you go up against him.
>
> Somebody that shows he's timid, who is real quiet. That is basically it. Someone who is real quiet and withdrawn and looks scared. He looks frightened you know. He is most apt to be approached.[35]

Whites are also seen as vulnerable because they have no group behind them. Furthermore, a higher percentage of African American prisoners are incarcerated for violent offenses than are whites. These factors, combined with African American prisoners' pent-up rage against what they perceive as white oppression outside prison, make imprisoned whites prime victims. Daniel Lockwood says:

> [I]t is surprising that, viewed as a whole, sexual aggression in prisons is not more widespread. Women rarely sexually assault other women prisoners. Women tend to join groups similar to families, where mother, father, and spousal roles are adopted, engendering strong support and protection for members. Even in men's prisons where sexual violence is most concentrated, estimates of the incidence of sexual assault run as low as less than 1 percent. In some prisons, of course, the numbers are higher. In New York State, 28 percent of the prisoners reported some form of aggression—threats, propositions, and some physical contact. Even here, however, only one prisoner reported actually being raped.[36]

Use *Your* Discretion

How much sexual assault is there?

Most empirical prison violence studies focus on mature prisoners in men's maximum security prisons. Angela S. Maitland and Richard D. Sluder turned their attention to young offenders in a medium-security state prison. Maitland and Sluder were allowed access to a midwestern prison. The medium security prison had an average daily population of 1,100 young male offenders between 17 and 25 years old. Researchers surveyed volunteers in secondary education classes at the prison. The researchers concede that their sampling procedures could only lead to exploratory findings. However, they believe that their findings raise important questions about young men's prison experience.

1. One inmate admitted that he was sexually assaulted.
2. A few inmates were subjected to sexual comments.
3. Whites were the main victims of the few "mind games."[37]

Saum and her colleagues in the study of sex in a Delaware medium security prison, also made findings regarding sexual assault among their sample:

1. 60 percent of their sample reported not hearing about even one incident of rape during the last year they were in the general prison population.
2. 88 percent said that they had never seen a rape.
3. 90 percent said that they had never seen an attempted rape.
4. 3 percent said that they had seen one rape.
5. 1 inmate reported that he had been raped.
6. 5 inmates reported that they had been victims of attempted rape.[38]

CRITICAL THINKING

1. List the findings of both studies.
2. Do they support or contradict each other? Explain.
3. On the basis of these findings, what do you conclude about sexual assault in men's prisons?
4. How do you account for the widespread belief that sexual assault occurs daily in male prison society?

Prisoner-Officer Violence

Prisoners attack not only each other but also corrections officers. Attacks on officers are sometimes spontaneous and sometimes planned in advance. Officers take great risks in attempting to break up fights, manage intoxicated prisoners, and escort prisoners to punitive segregation. Predictably, these situations provoke assaults. Much worse are the random violent acts that cannot be predicted, such as throwing dangerous objects at officers or dropping items from catwalks above as officers patrol the cell blocks below.[39]

Officers also attack prisoners. According to Todd R. Clear and George F. Cole:

> Unauthorized physical violence against inmates by officers to enforce rules, uphold the officer-prisoner relationship, and maintain order is a fact of life in many institutions. Stories abound of guards giving individual prisoners "the treatment" outside the notice of their superiors. Many guards view physical force as an everyday operating procedure and legitimize its use.[40]

The Level 6 Prison at Marion

During the 1980s, the federal maximum security prison at Marion, Illinois, was known as the most violent prison in the country (Figure 15.1). Marion housed the most dangerous prisoners from the federal prison system and a considerable number from state prisons as well. Marion (and now the growing number of super maximum prisons in both the federal and state prison systems) presents a perplexing problem for prison administrators and criminal justice policymakers: how to control violent prisoners.

Most prisons segregate violent prisoners in special units. In small- and medium-size prisons, violent prisoners can stay in these units for short periods of time with no serious management problems. However, large prisons, especially ones like Marion with many "dangerous" prisoners, pose a greater problem. Predatory prisoners go through the special units in a revolving door fashion. Because not all violent prisoners are in the special units at the same time, some prisons are operated as if every prisoner is about to explode into violence.[41]

In the 1930s, the Federal Bureau of Prisons adopted a **concentration model** of confinement, putting the most violent prisoners in one prison. The famous Alcatraz was one of

Figure 15.1
Violence at Marion

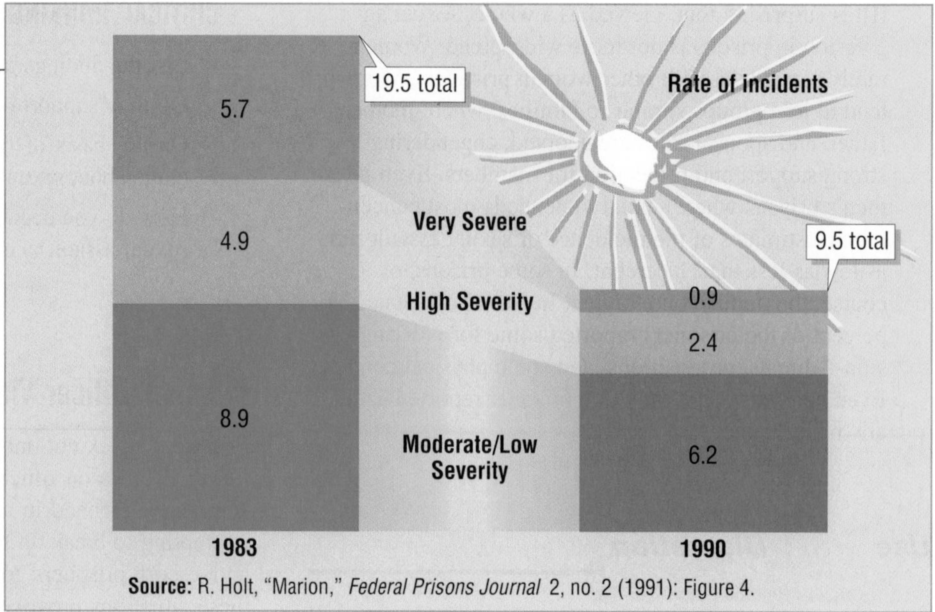

Source: R. Holt, "Marion," *Federal Prisons Journal* 2, no. 2 (1991): Figure 4.

these prisons. Alcatraz became home to the worst prisoners from the federal maximum security prisons, including Leavenworth and Atlanta. They were transferred to Alcatraz not for rehabilitation, but for incapacitation and punishment. Alcatraz was a prison run on the popular idea of "lock them up and throw away the key."

In 1962 Alcatraz was closed, a victory for reformers who sought rehabilitation in imprisonment. Most inmates were returned to Leavenworth and Atlanta for rehabilitation. As racial tension and violence increased in the 1960s and rehabilitation received more vocal criticism, the then-new federal prison at Marion's Control Unit became the most used holding center for the nation's most dangerous prisoners.

In 1978, the Federal Bureau of Prisons reformed its traditional classification system based on three levels of security—maximum, medium, and minimum—replacing it with six security levels. Marion became the first "level 6." It was the highest security federal prison in the country until the opening of the new super maximum federal prison as part of the federal prison complex in Florence, Colorado, in 1994 (discussed in Chapter 14). Marion's purpose was the same as that of its predecessor Alcatraz—to "provide long-term segregation within a highly controlling setting" for inmates from throughout the federal system who:

- Threatened or injured other inmates or staff.
- Possessed deadly weapons or dangerous drugs.
- Disrupted "the orderly operation of a prison."
- Escaped or attempted to escape in those instances in which the escape involved "injury, threat of life or use of deadly weapons."

Several reasons lie behind the decision to convert Marion to a super maximum security prison, including a series of gang-related killings at Atlanta Penitentiary, the growing power of gangs in other prisons, creation of "assassination squads" under gang auspices in a number of prisons, an increase in the number of assaults on inmates and staff in level 4 and 5 prisons, the violent deaths of three Marion prisoners, and the stabbings of the Marion associate warden and food service steward in the inmate dining room. During the late 1970s when the prison population was declining, assaults at Marion increased sharply: homicides rose 8.5 percent, assaults on inmates 15.3 percent, and assaults on officers 78.4 percent.

Assaults on staff and inmates at Marion increased sharply again in the early 1980s. Along with some group disturbances were 54 serious inmate-on-inmate assaults, 8 prisoner killings, and 28 serious assaults on staff. During 1983, the frequency and seriousness of assaults on staff increased. On July 8, 1983, two prisoners armed with knives stabbed a guard they had taken hostage. The next week, prisoners stabbed five times a **general population inmate** who had more privileges than the ordinary level 6 prisoners. Several days later, while prisoners were returning to their cells from the dining hall, two prisoners attacked two guard escorts, stabbing one officer 12 times.

Following this stabbing, the prison was put on **lockdown** status—the temporary suspension of all activities, including recreation. Prisoners received sack lunches in their cells for breakfast, lunch, and dinner. When these restrictions were lifted, one prisoner was stabbed, staff were threatened, and the lockdown was reinstated. This pattern continued, more or less—lockdowns, some letup followed by prisoner violence, and then a reinstated lockdown.[42]

This long-term lockdown and close confinement of Marion prisoners turned them from engaging in physical violence to fighting the conditions of their confinement in federal courts. The success of lockdown as a mechanism to control violence, prison managers now speak of "marionizing" their prisons.[43]

Violence at Marion declined sharply after the implementation of concentration management. Under concentration management prisoners can participate in programs and receive services, but only under a strictly controlled movement system. Prisoners start their sentences at Marion by spending most of their time in their cells or in the cell house. As they demonstrate nondangerous behavior by compliance with the rules, they progress through a graduated work and housing plan that allows more personal activities. If they continue to progress, prisoners gain more freedom and privileges.

RIOTS

Famous riots have occurred throughout the history of prisons in the United States. Even young people have probably heard of the riot at Attica State Prison in New York in the 1970s and the bloody riot at New Mexico Penitentiary in 1980. Although they are serious and deserve their notorious reputation, they are rare events in prison life. Some of these riots were spontaneous; others were planned in advance. A highly organized inmate force held together by racial solidarity and political consciousness planned and executed the famous Attica riot in 1971. To a considerable extent that riot was a product of the 1960s—a political protest against what was considered white oppression. Other riots, such as the New Mexico riot in 1980, were spontaneous, disorganized outbursts.[44]

According to its historian, Mark Colvin, the New Mexico prison riot was the most brutal, destructive, and disorganized riot in American penal history. In 36 hours, prisoners killed 33 fellow prisoners and beat and raped as many as 200 others. After drinking too much homemade whiskey, several drunk prisoners overpowered four guards. Seven guards were taken hostage, beaten, stabbed, or sodomized before being released by their captors. Without any plan, the prisoners took over the entire prison. By chance, they stumbled on an open dormitory door, an open security grill, and blow torches accidentally left behind by renovation crews. Storming through the prison, rioters tortured 12 inmates with blow torches, set them on fire, and mutilated them. They beheaded one with a shovel. Their victims were suspected "snitches" (prisoners who inform on other prisoners' misbehavior), child rapists, and "mentally disturbed" prisoners whose screaming kept their killers awake at night.[45]

Prisoners riot for complicated reasons. It has been argued that riots break out when prison administrations take actions that disrupt existing prison society. This is particularly true when administrations try to alter accommodations existing between staff and prisoners in which prisoners share power with staff, gain status based on that, and reap material benefits to the extent possible inside prison walls.

According to Colvin, these administrative disruptions generally arise out of three situations:

1. *Discovering and exposing corruption,* such as narcotics traffic inside prisons.
2. *Policy conflicts,* such as those between reformist, rehabilitation-oriented administrators and old-line, security-oriented staff.
3. *Policy changes* brought about by new prison administrations, such as wardens who decide they are going to "crack down" on minority prisoner assertiveness.[46]

Attica riots. Inmates of Attica State Prison raise their hands in clenched fist salutes as they voice demands during a negotiating session with New York's prison boss, Commissioner Russell Oswald. More than 1200 inmates rioted and took over the facility on September 9, 1971. Well-organized, the inmates armed themselves, took guards and civilian employees hostage, and issued several demands, including amnesty for their crimes. The siege ended four days later when the National Guard flew in, administering chemical agents, and nearly 200 New York State police officers stormed the facility. Ten hostages and 32 inmates were killed in the conflict.

If all three conditions occur simultaneously, trouble is almost certain to follow. Cohesion arising out of power, status, and wealth badly erodes. Conflict between prisoners' social structure and administration's control structure erupts in various forms. Prisoner protests and strikes are organized to reinstate denied privileges. If privileges are restored, order returns.

Sometimes, administrations do not respond by restoring lost privileges. Instead, for political or ideological reasons, administrations meet protest with still more restrictions. Prisoners' resentment grows; administrators find it increasingly difficult to restore lost privileges. Mutual hostility between guards and prisoners escalates; administrations change and guard turnover increases. None of these actions restore order. On the contrary, they only raise tensions. As administrative staff divide into warring bureaucratic camps, prisoners' social structure disintegrates into self-protective, hostile cliques. Eventually, rioting breaks out.

Burt Useem and Peter Kimball, in their stimulating study of prison riots, list the following eight popular theories of the causes of prison riots:

1. Violent, depraved prisoners.
2. Prison conditions.
3. Liberal judges giving prisoners too many rights.
4. Radical prisoner organizations stirring up trouble.
5. Prisoners crowded as if in cages.
6. Racism.
7. Gang plots.
8. Prisoners' "cry for help."[47]

CROWDING

One feature of prison life is not rare—crowded prisons. Crowding exacerbates hostile race relations, gang activity, and violence. According to experts, crowding is "the most critical administrative problem facing the United States criminal justice system." U.S. prison populations have skyrocketed, and to date are continuing to do so despite declines in the crime rates (outlined in Chapter 14).[48]

It is difficult to assess exactly how to determine whether prisons are crowded because definitions of crowding vary. The American Correctional Association Commission on Accreditation for Corrections defines capacity standards as one inmate for every 60-square-foot cell. This is sufficient only if inmates spend no more than ten hours a day locked in their cell; however, when confinement exceeds ten hours a day, 80 square feet of floor space are required. Not all systems have adopted this definition; so, it is necessary to know how the correctional system defines crowding to know whether there is crowding.[49]

At the end of 1997, 36 states and the federal government were operating prisons at more than 100 percent capacity, however they define capacity. California reported that it was operating at 206 percent of capacity. Overall, state systems were operating at 115 percent of capacity while the federal prison system was operating at 122 percent of capacity.[50]

One reason for crowding is shifting attitudes toward punishment and prison. Rehabilitation has lost ground to retribution and incapacitation as justifications for criminal punishment. As a result, prison sentences have grown in both frequency and length. During the 1980s and 1990s, the number of prisoners admitted to prisons significantly exceeded the number released. Judges have not ignored public opinion demanding more punishment. Increased admissions to prison at a time when street crime rates have fallen (despite increased reporting of offenses) reflect, in part, the public demand for harsher punishment.

Aggravating the demographic shift and public demand for harsher punishment is public unwillingness (and in some cases government inability) to pay for additional facilities. Some say that the public and even government officials in some jurisdictions are content to "allow inmates to pile up in prisons until the pressure they create is relieved by a federal court order or a riot focuses public attention on the problem."[51]

Use *Your* Discretion

What is the best policy for prison crowding?

Building more prisons provides only one policy option to reduce prison crowding. The easiest short-term alternative is to do nothing, an approach that permits prosecutors to demand harsh prison penalties, judges to respond to those demands, and wardens to pile prisoners two to a cell. Doing nothing carries risks. Crowding almost always leads to diminished control by prison administrators and increased control by inmates, usually the most violent. This transfer of control demoralizes staff and leaves unprotected the prisoners who most need protection. Prisoners and guards have little, if any, political clout, so the situation ordinarily remains in check, but not always. The courts could intervene, declaring the conditions unconstitutional, or prisoners might riot, in which case the public might demand changes in the do-nothing approach.[52]

Selective incapacitation combines the demand for more effective crime control with the need to reduce crowding. Identifying the most serious offenders—those who commit the worst crimes, do so most frequently, and are likely to do so in the future—and reserving scarce and costly prison space for them is an attractive idea with many pitfalls. It is difficult to predict who will commit future serious crimes. Research suggests that such predictions might discriminate racially; African Americans tend to fall into the high-risk categories much more frequently than whites. Existing research on prediction of criminal potential, sketchy and preliminary, must be tested carefully before individuals are confined in maximum security prisons for extended periods.[53]

Peter Greenwood, who conducted the most thorough study to date of selective incapacitation, makes only limited claims for its use. He reminds us that the theory "might" provide a means to utilize scarce prison space, and that selective incapacitation strategies "may" lead to reduced crime rates. Greenwood also cautions that predictive criteria are imprecise and can lead to wrong predictions. Researchers have not independently verified the results.[54]

Rudy A. Haapenan investigated the patterns of officially recorded criminal behavior over a period of 9 to 15 years for 1,300 men committed to California Youth Correctional facilities during the 1960s. Haapenan focused on changes in criminal behavior as the young men moved through their twenties and into their thirties. Race affected the kinds and rates of arrest, and both declined with age. Social influences related to ethnicity or age affected whether and how long offenders engaged in criminal careers and the year-to-year nature and intensity of careers. According to Haapenan, the instability of and measurement problems with official data greatly reduce the ability to predict which offenders will recidivate at higher rates. Furthermore, selective incapacitation would not have prevented a significant amount of crime in the sample and seems to offer only minimal potential for reducing crime in society. These difficulties suggest that selective incapacitation requires further evaluation before being adopted as a major strategy to reduce prison crowding.[55]

Crowding can be reduced either by not sending people to prison in the first place, a **front-door strategy,** or by releasing them early if they are imprisoned, a **back-door strategy.** Front-door population decreases come about when first-time property offenders and other so-called marginal offenders are channeled into alternative programs to incarceration. Probation is the most common front-door practice, but there are others. First-time property offenders, for example, might be assigned to a restitution program whereby, in promising to pay back the victim, they avoid going to prison. In recent years, the alternatives to incarceration have grown in richness and variety to include a variety of intermediate punishments.

Back-door strategies attempt to release prisoners earlier than the prescribed time when their sentences expire. Much recommends the use of back-door strategies to reduce prison populations. Research has demonstrated convincingly that sentence certainty is far more important to the prisoner than sentence severity. Thus, it seems wise to send more people to prison for shorter periods than a few for long periods. Prisoners who are incarcerated for long periods show no better rehabilitation rates than those imprisoned for short periods. Nor does long-term imprisonment ensure that, when released, prisoners will not return to crime. People seem to retire from criminal careers at about the same rate, whether they are imprisoned or not. These conclusions call for policies aimed at early release from prison, such as the commonly exercised time off for good behavior and parole.[56]

Jurisdictions have adopted three approaches to adjusting admissions and releases to alleviate prison crowding. One ties sentencing to prison population. For example, in Minnesota, by legislative mandate, sentencing guidelines have to take prison capacity into account. The sentencing guidelines are devised according to a certain prison capacity. Sentences must not overload the prisons; to date, they have not. Whether other states will replicate this self-discipline remains uncertain. Even in Minnesota, present legislation will substantially increase prison capacity to allow for growth.[57]

A second strategy is a **safety-valve policy,** such as that adopted by Michigan's legislature in 1981. A commission monitors prison population. If it exceeds capacity, the governor receives the mandate to reduce prison population by reducing the minimum sentences of all prisoners by up to 90 days. This increases the number of prisoners eligible for parole and eliminates automatic release, thereby retaining the parole board's authority and discretion to decide which eligible prisoners should be released. Of course, capacity has to have some meaningful definition if the population control measures based on it are to work. If its definition can be changed to mean two or three prisoners to a cell, for instance, strategies based on it will not make much sense.

By May 1984, under Michigan law, the governor had used the safety-valve policy to order eight sentence reductions in both men's and women's prisons. By 1985, more than 2,000 prisoners had been released under the law, at which point then-Governor James Blanchard began to balk because it was becoming increasingly difficult to avoid releasing violent criminals. Public support for the law seriously eroded when, in October 1984, a convicted murderer was released early under the law and later charged with killing a police officer.[58]

Connecticut has proposed a third strategy, called **cell rationing.** In cell rationing, judges and prosecutors in each district are assigned a certain number of cells in the state's prisons. When they have used up their ration and want to send another convicted defendant to prison, they must designate which of the cells assigned to them they want vacated to make room for this proposed new prisoner.[59]

CRITICAL THINKING

1. List all of the alternative policies on prison crowding.
2. Summarize the strengths and weaknesses of each alternative.
3. Summarize the findings on these policies.
4. Which would you adopt, if any? Give your reasons.
5. If you would not adopt any of them, what are your reasons?

Knowledge and Understanding CHECK

1. Describe the characteristics of most prisoners.
2. How did the late George Beto describe prisoners?
3. Identify and describe the two major theories explaining prison society.
4. List the major rules in the inmate code.
5. What are prisoners supposed to lose as part of their punishment?
6. What does it mean to say that prisoners are supposed to live "lives of enforced poverty"?
7. How do prisoners try to overcome their lives of enforced poverty?
8. Identify the two reasons why sex is prohibited in prisons.
9. How widespread is consensual sex in prisons?
10. Describe the racial makeup of prison populations.
11. What are the effects of race and ethnicity on prison populations?
12. Describe the major characteristics of prison gangs.
13. How prevalent are prison gangs?
14. What are some of the effects of prison gangs?
15. List the kinds of violence that occur in prison, and describe how extensive violence is in men's prisons.
16. Identify the eight popular theories of prison riots.
17. How does the American Correctional Association define "crowded" prisons?
18. List the reasons for prison crowding.
19. List the ways that crowding can be reduced.

PROGRAMS

Boredom and monotony are far more widespread in prison than fear and violence. Anyone who visits a prison cannot help but notice how many inmates are either sleeping or sitting around staring into space. So, the one thing most prisoners have plenty of is time. Nothing more clearly demonstrates the meaning of the saying "time on our hands" than the lives of prisoners. Commenting on research on prison society, Samuel Walker wrote:

> [F]or the most part, inmates have little to do, even in the form of make-work. Some have jobs, but they tend to be menial and occupy only a few hours at the most. In general, inmates don't do anything, much less anything of a productive or vocational nature.[60]

The lack of meaningful programs is a disappointing aspect of the history of prison reform. From the Elizabethan Houses of Corrections to the modern prison, there has been a constant refrain: prisoners should work, and they should work hard. In 1900, the Industrial Commission of the House of Representatives said:

> The most desirable system for employing convicts is one which provides primarily for the punishment and reformation of the prisoners and the least competition with free labor, and, secondarily, for the revenue of the state.[61]

In 1950, F. Flynn wrote:

> The modern concept of prisons as institutions for treatment does not contemplate the "busy prison factory" or the self-supporting prison as a goal. Nevertheless, in any well-rounded program directed toward the needs of those confined, some employment projects have their place.[62]

And in 1982, then–Chief Justice of the Supreme Court, Warren Burger, said:

> We can continue to have largely human "warehouses," with little or no education and training, or we can have prisons that are factories with fences around them . . . to accomplish the dual objective of training inmates in gainful occupations and lightening the enormous load of maintaining the prison system of this country.[63]

Why have prison programs? For a number of reasons, including:

- Work is a cure for what ails prisoners.
- Work can reduce the cost of imprisonment.
- Work can provide training for life outside prison.
- Work can keep prisoners out of trouble.
- Work can produce goods and services for the state.[64]

Most prison programs have focused on four main problems that most prisoners face:

- Inadequate academic education.
- Insufficient vocational training.
- Sketchy industrial employment.
- Deficient social and psychological treatment.

Despite these serious problems, only 10 percent of institutional budgets go toward rehabilitation programs. Programs include education, rehabilitation, work, recreation, and religion.[65]

We tend to think that all prison programs are supposed to rehabilitate prisoners. The National Academy of Sciences defines rehabilitation programs as "any planned intervention that reduces an offender's further criminal activity." But not all programs have rehabilitation as their goal, and even those that are labeled specifically as rehabilitation have further purposes. The purposes of correctional programs include education, rehabilitation, work, recreation, and religion.

Education

Most prisoners enter prison with less than a ninth-grade education. Although it is widely agreed that academic education for prisoners is highly desirable, too many prisons have insufficient programs. There are exceptions. For example, Minnesota and Texas have highly innovative computer-assisted instructional programs that are regarded as significant contributions to adult prisoner education. Insight Incorporated, Minnesota's private, no-profit corporation founded by two prisoners independently studying for college, provides post-secondary education for prisoners. Prisoner telemarketing and computer services industries support the cost of the program. Any prisoner who passes a battery of tests can enroll in courses as long as they maintain at least a C average. Fewer than 15 percent of former students have returned to prison. During Insight Incorporated's first 13 years of existence, 40 men at Stillwater Prison earned bachelor's degrees and two obtained master's degrees; prisoners earned more than 23,000 quarter credit hours.[66]

One purpose of education programs is, of course, rehabilitation. But education serves other purposes as well. Education in our society is valued for its own sake. Among the public and most criminal justice professionals, it also enjoys wide support as part of humane punishment. Furthermore, it contributes to smooth prison management because it gives prisoners something worthwhile to do with their time.

Rehabilitation

Rehabilitation programs cover a wide spectrum—from vocational training to individual psychotherapy. Furthermore, rehabilitation, like education, serves purposes in addition to

Most prisoners enter prison with less than a ninth-grade education. Although it is widely agreed that academic and vocational education for prisoners is highly desirable, many prisons have no such programs.

"reduc[ing] an offender's further criminal activity." These programs, too, contribute to better prison management, help to accomplish the mission of meting out humane punishment, and give prisoners something to do. We discuss here only some of the many programs aimed at the rehabilitation of offenders, including vocational training, work release, financial assistance, prison industries, and treatment.

Vocational Training

A powerful logic supports vocational training. Most prisoners have few, if any, skills qualifying them for legitimate work. Since at least 1870, vocational training has been recognized as central to rehabilitation. But as rehabilitation, according to John P. Conrad, the results of actual programs are disappointing:

> Some excellent training programs have achieved remarkable results, but they are isolated examples. For the most part, vocational training is conducted with inadequate or obsolete equipment, and instructors are poorly prepared. Too often the training is intended to meet institutional maintenance needs rather than the formal requirements of an apprenticeship.[67]

Vocational training fails for several reasons. Equipment is expensive, and prison budgets cannot support purchasing sufficient quantities of it. Many unions do not accept workers who finished apprenticeships in prison. Most prisoners are not imprisoned long enough to complete apprenticeships, or their training is too often interrupted. However, vocational training has purposes other than preparing inmates for life outside prison. It also gives prisoners something to do and satisfies the aims of humane punishment. Furthermore, vocational training enjoys perhaps even more public support than academic education programs. Rightly or wrongly, the public believes vocational training is "useful," whereas academic learning is not.[68]

Work Release

Some rehabilitation programs show more promise than vocational training. An economist, Ann D. Witte, studied work release in North Carolina and found that prisoners who participated in work-release programs were less likely to commit serious crimes than prisoners who did not. According to Witte:

> There seems to be a number of possible ways in which work release might affect the seriousness of criminal activity. First, it provides a man with a stable work record and job experience. Second, it allows a man to support his dependents while in prison and hence could aid in keeping his family together. Third, it might provide new job skills. Fourth, it provides a man with money at the time of release and often with a job. Fifth, it allows a man to maintain contacts with the free community and limits at least somewhat his immersion in the prison community. Finally, it may change a man's attitude toward himself and toward society.[69]

The results of the North Carolina experiment did not support all its possibilities. Nevertheless, Witte concluded:

> [W]ork release should be considered a successful program: successful in the sense that men who have been on the work-release program decrease the seriousness of the criminal offenses which they commit after release from prison. This project found most support for work release effecting this decrease in seriousness of criminal activity by improving the work performance and the attitudes of men who participate in the program.[70]

Financial Assistance

Some programs provide offenders released from prison with financial assistance in the form of employment compensation. One experimental program in Georgia and Texas, the Transitional Aid Research Project (TARP), gave a group of released prisoners small weekly payments, while control groups received no such payments. Released prisoners who received the aid were arrested less frequently and were also able to obtain better jobs than those who did not receive aid.[71]

Prison Industries

Prison industries were a major part of prison life from 1900 to 1925. They were considered a major element in the rehabilitation of prisoners. Work was not only useful, it was also therapeutic, according to the Progressive prison reformers. However, prison industries were scaled back because of ethical questions about using prison labor, and because they competed with private industry. Both labor unions and small businesses secured legislation that restricted prison industries. Furthermore, the programs had to compete with reasoning that was firmly planted in the public mind—the **principle of less eligibility.** This means that prisoners are supposed to suffer; they are not supposed to make as much money as people working outside. However, by 1980, prison industries had once again become at least a small part of prison life.[72]

The major justification for returning prison industries to prison life is the idea that prisoners should pay for their imprisonment. This rarely happens; only a few prisoners work in prison industries. Further, many of the prison industry programs cost taxpayers more money than they save. People in charge of prison industries say that potential profits are eaten away by security and other concerns, such as rehabilitating inmates and protecting private businesses from unfair competition. "The goal is really to create work, reduce idleness, and help manage the prison," said Pamela Jo Davis, president of Florida's PRIDE (Prison Rehabilitative Industries and Diversified Enterprises) and chair of Correctional Industries Association, a national umbrella group for prison industries.[73]

In 1997, 76,519 prisoners were working in prison industries, more than twice the number in 1980. Sales of products from prison industries more than tripled—from $392 million in 1980 to $1.62 billion in 1997. Nevertheless, according to a National State Auditors Association's evaluation of prison industries in 13 states, many prison industries are not self-sufficient. The association recommended the following to achieve the goal of self-sufficiency:

- Better planning.
- Expanded work opportunities for prisoners.
- Greater use of sound business practices.[74]

Use *Your* Discretion

Should we expand prison industry programs?

Enough empirical evidence exists to demonstrate that prison industries are not profitable. This means that working inmates are not paying for the cost of their confinement. Despite this, prison administrators say that industry programs are worth continuing because there are other benefits besides profitability, such as:

- They provide a demand for raw materials.
- They reduce cost of imprisoning; prisoners are earning something.
- They reduce disciplinary problems.
- They aid rehabilitation.
- They reduce recidivism.

Some evaluation research lends empirical support for these benefits. Florida's prison industry programs—currently operated by PRIDE, a nonprofit corporation—show great promise, according to an evaluation done for the Florida House of Representatives. According to the report, PRIDE's 1987 profits, $4,052,508, doubled the profits of correctional industry programs for the past 20 years. PRIDE employs fewer than half the available workers, but has increased prisoner employment more than 70 percent since eliminating profitless enterprises. Prison recommitment rates were lower for participants than for nonparticipants. PRIDE has reduced the cost to the state by paying more than $4,122,195 into the state's general revenue for housing prisoner workers.[75]

Timothy J. Flanagan and his associates at the Prison Industry Research Project investigated the impact of prison industry employment on offender behavior. Data were collected on 692 prisoners who had worked in prison shops in one of seven facilities for at least six continuous months, and on a comparison group of 742 prisoners in the same facilities who were not employed in prison shops. Recidivism rates were virtually identical between the two groups. However, participants had lower rates of disciplinary infractions inside prison, even when controlling for low, medium, and high risks for prison misconduct among prisoners in both groups.[76]

CRITICAL THINKING

1. Identify the benefits and drawbacks of prison industry programs.
2. List the findings of evaluation research concerning prison industry programs.
3. Do you think the benefits outweigh the costs of prison industry programs? Defend your answer.

Treatment

Treatment programs in prison fall into two broad categories: psychological treatment and behavior modification. All psychological treatment programs in prison assume that the cause of criminal behavior is an underlying emotional problem. Psychotherapy, now rare, consists mainly of talking, either individually or in groups. The therapist and the "patient" try to get to the core of the emotional "illness" that supposedly caused the offender to commit crimes. Group therapy is based on the idea that because people are "social animals," they can effectively work through their emotional problems by talking in groups.

Reality therapy is much more commonly used. Reality therapy rests on the straightforward notion that the best therapy is to *act* more responsibly, not just talk about being more responsible. Problems arise when people fail in their responsibilities in life—to work hard, play by the rules, and treat other people the way they are supposed to be treated. The job of the reality therapist is to repeatedly get offenders to see the consequences—especially the negative consequences—of irresponsible behavior. Reality therapy is popular in prisons for three reasons:

1. It accepts the proposition that the rules of society are inescapable.
2. Its techniques are easy for therapists to learn and apply.
3. The method can be applied in the short term.[77]

Behavior modification treatment programs focus on how people respond to social situations that get them "in trouble." The method operates in two stages: First, identify the conditions that cause the "acting out" problem. Second, change the conditions so that the behavior will change also. The **token economy** is one popular form of behavior modification therapy. To get benefits, such as a television set, inmates have to purchase them with tokens earned by responsible behavior, like going to work or getting good grades. Resembling reality therapy, the token economy brings inmates into constant contact with the way the real world is supposed to work—responsible behavior is rewarded and irresponsible behavior is punished.

Work

Prisons have to provide all the basic services that most communities in the outside world have to provide—and more. These include:

- Utilities (sewer and water, electricity, telephones, and so on).
- Restaurants.
- Laundry and dry cleaning.
- Bakeries.
- Hospitals.
- Mail delivery.
- Fire protection.
- Safety.
- Record keeping.
- Janitorial services.

Prisoners do most of the work required to provide these services. Obviously, the resources of prisoner labor and time are in great supply in prisons. Jobs in these services not only get the work of maintaining prisons done, but they also tell a lot about the prestige of the prisoners who hold them. The most prestigious are those jobs closest to the decision makers. Record keeping is the most prestigious because it puts inmates in charge of a valuable commodity—information, such as who is eligible for release or reclassification to lower or higher security prisons. Desk jobs are also desirable because they provide access to administrators and perhaps an opening to better food and other amenities; so are jobs that allow access to the commodities that prisoners can sell in the prison economy. The lowest prestige job is also the most available—janitorial work. This work is menial, like mopping floors; and there is virtually no access to information, goods, and services.[78]

Prison jobs are important for two reasons. First, they save taxpayers' money by using prison labor to do required work that would cost much more if it were hired out. Second, prison jobs contribute to enforcing prison discipline by providing a system of rewards and punishment and a hierarchy of prestige.[79]

Recreation

Time that is not spent working; in treatment, school, or vocational training; or just "killing time," prisoners devote to recreation. Most prisons have athletic teams; many prisoners work out in prison exercise rooms; virtually all watch movies; some participate in drama, music, art, and journalism. Recreation is an important—and of course desirable—part of prison life, filling some of prisoners' abundant time. Furthermore, recreation programs allow prisoners to maintain some of their individuality by getting together and doing things with others who share their interests. In addition, recreation also serves the interests of rehabilitation by teaching social skills, such as fair competition and working together, and by building self-esteem. Moreover, recreation programs are part of the reward and punishment system that helps to enforce prison discipline. Few inmates want to lose the privilege of recreation. Finally, recreation definitely fits in with the philosophy of humane punishment. Perhaps nothing more humanizes prisons than allowing prisoners to participate in social activities that they really enjoy. Of course, recreation programs also create safety risks. Fights can—and do—erupt during competitive sports, for example.

Religious Programs

The scholarly literature gives little attention to religious programs in prison, but they exist almost everywhere. The First Amendment guarantees freedom of religion and therefore requires prisons to provide religion programs. Like most other prison programs, religious programs help prisoners fill time, are supposed to aid in rehabilitation, and contribute to a humane punishment.

Todd Clear and his colleagues conducted one of the few national studies of religion in prison. Interviews with inmates indicated that religion helps prisoners by providing a psychological and physical "safe haven." Religion also enables inmates to maintain ties with family and with religious volunteers. The study also found that participation in religious programs contributed both to helping prisoners adjust to prison and to reducing disciplinary infractions.[80]

Evaluation of Prison Programs

Education, vocational training, prison work, and religious programs attract a broad consensus across the political and ideological spectrum and so arouse little controversy. Recreation programs stir up some controversy over the **confinement model** of imprisonment under which prisoners are sent to prison *as* punishment not for punishment. Those who believe that prisoners are supposed to suffer more than confinement resent recreation programs that allow prisoners to "work out," compete in sports, and watch movies.

Rehabilitation programs have aroused the greatest amount of controversy, both from an ideological perspective—*Should* we rehabilitate prisoners?—and from a practical standpoint—*Can* we rehabilitate prisoners? The ideological commitment to or against rehabilitation has interfered with evaluating rehabilitation programs. The late sociologist Robert Martinson caused an enormous stir in a spin-off article to a major evaluation of rehabilitation studies in 1974. The title of Martinson's article, which appeared prior to the final release of the study, was "What Works?" However, the article quickly was distorted into "nothing works," although Martinson never said that. In fact, the study reported that 48 percent of the programs surveyed showed positive outcomes.[81]

In an influential survey of the evaluation studies of rehabilitation, the admittedly pro-rehabilitation scholar Ted Palmer reviewed a wide range of prison programs. He found that 25 to 35 percent of the programs "work," meaning they reduce recidivism. But they do not work spectacularly. Some programs that combine treatment with external control reduce recidivism somewhat under some circumstances. Palmer's research suggests that like the 1960s optimism that treatment was a panacea, the deep pessimism that "nothing works" is equally unwarranted. Furthermore, a strong sense that prisons should do more than warehouse prisoners has run throughout the history of American prisons—witness the term *corrections*.[82]

Charles H. Logan of the University of Connecticut and Gerald G. Gaes of the Federal Bureau of Prisons dismiss Palmer's study and other **meta-analyses** (studies of studies) of rehabilitation programs. Because of a host of definitional, methodological, and other complicated problems, and due to the ideological bias in favor of rehabilitation possessed by most of the meta-analysis scholars, the studies of studies of rehabilitation cannot be trusted, according to Logan and Gaes.[83]

Perhaps the fairest summary of the state of our knowledge about this controversial subject is that the results of the studies evaluating rehabilitation programs are decidedly mixed if we are simply evaluating whether the programs rehabilitate the offender. But rehabilitation programs serve purposes other than preparing offenders to "work hard and play by the rules" when they leave prison. Rehabilitation programs keep prisoners busy, and keeping them busy keeps them out of trouble—even if it does not turn them into law-abiding people. Furthermore, "constructive" activity is consistent with an orderly, safe, humane confinement. Finally, according to Logan and Gaes:

> "Constructive" activity is not defined here as "contributing to the betterment of inmates" but as activity that is, on its face, consistent with the orderly, safe, secure, and humane operation of a prison. Idleness and boredom can be considered wrong from a work ethic standpoint, or as unnatural because human beings are not meant to be idle, or as so fundamentally related to mischief as to be undesirable for that reason. In any case, prison programs can be defended as forms of constructive and meaningful activity and as antidotes to idleness, without invoking claims of rehabilitative effectiveness. This is not to say that it does not matter whether the programs have any rehabilitative effects; it would be fine if they did so. But when we say that the primary purpose of the prison is to punish through confinement, we become more interested in the operation of these programs inside the prison gates and less concerned about their effects beyond.[84]

Knowledge and Understanding CHECK

1. How does boredom compare with prison violence?
2. List the major reasons for having prison programs.
3. How much of prison budgets is spent on prison programs?
4. What are the purposes of prison education programs?
5. Describe the logic of vocational training in prisons.
6. List the major limits on vocational training programs.
7. Do work release programs work? Explain.
8. Describe and explain the effectiveness of financial assistance programs.
9. Identify the limits and effectiveness of prison industry programs.
10. Identify the two categories of prison treatment programs
11. Identify the major types of prison work programs.
12. Describe the nature and the significance of prison recreation.
13. Describe the extent of and the significance of religious programs.
14. Overall, how effective are prison programs? Explain.

PRISONERS' RIGHTS

Conviction of a crime causes a fundamental change in legal status. The Thirteenth Amendment to the U.S. Constitution abolishes slavery, "*except as a punishment for crime whereof the party shall have been duly convicted.*" A Virginia court in *Ruffin v. Commonwealth* shortly after the Civil War, explained what the Thirteenth Amendment means to prisoners:

> During his term of service in the penitentiary, he is in a state of penal servitude to the State. He has, as a consequence of his crime, not only forfeited his liberty, but all his personal rights except those which the law in its humanity accords to him. He is for the time being the slave of the State.
>
> The bill of rights is a declaration of general principles to govern a society of freemen, and not of convicted felons and men civilly dead. Such men have some rights it is true, such as the law in its benignity accords to them, but not the rights of freemen. They

> are the slaves of the State undergoing punishment for heinous crimes committed against the laws of the land. While in this state of penal servitude, they must be subject to the regulations of the institution of which they are inmates, and the laws of the State to whom their service is due in expiation of their crimes.[85]

The U.S. Supreme Court has gone so far as to say that "prison brutality . . . is part of the total punishment to which the individual is being subjected for his crime." These strong words do not mean that prisoners have *no* rights. The Supreme Court has extended some rights, admittedly severely limited, to prisoners.[86]

"Hands Off" Prisons

Until the 1960s, courts followed the lead of *Ruffin v. Commonwealth.* They practically never interfered with prison life. How prisons were run and the way prisoners were treated inside them were considered matters for prison administrators, and courts kept their "hands off." This approach was called the **"hands-off" doctrine** of prison law. According to the hands-off doctrine, the law did not accompany prisoners inside the prison; it left them at the prison gate. Prison conditions and prison society were matters properly left wholly to administrative discretion; they were not the courts' business.

The main justification for this hands-off doctrine was that judges were not qualified to run prisons. They were untrained in prison administration and far from the conditions administrators were expected to manage. It made no sense for judges to substitute their own opinions for those of the experts, the prison administrators and line officers. Another argument in favor of the hands-off doctrine was the retributive nature of prisons. Prisons are for punishment; they are supposed to be unpleasant. Finally, the hands-off doctrine was necessary for prison security. Prisoners' rights backed up by judicial intervention could become an avenue for prison unrest and even riot.[87]

During the civil rights movement of the 1960s, a prisoners' rights movement arose. From that time, the courts have recognized and are willing to enforce some constitutional standards in a severely limited fashion. In defining these rights, the courts balance the limited rights of prisoners against strong needs for security, order, and discipline in prison.

A combination of forces in the 1960s put limits on the hands-off doctrine. The civil rights movement extended to the rights of prisoners. Prisoners, especially African American and Hispanic prisoners, took their grievances about prison conditions and the treatment of minority prisoners to court. Moreover, disillusionment with rehabilitation led to a shift from an emphasis on the *needs* of prisoners to a focus on their *rights.* A viable prisoners' rights movement, however, required a forum. The judicial activism of reform-minded judges gave prisoners that forum, permitting them to bring grievances to the courts. Having so respected a grievance forum as the nation's courts generated great solidarity among prisoners, and this prisoner solidarity itself enhanced the prisoners' rights movement. However, without the support of a new breed of prison lawyers, specialists who knew how to voice complaints and frame grievances in legal and constitutional terms, the prisoners' rights movement would have probably come to naught. According to James B. Jacobs, a leading scholar of prisons and the rights of prisoners:

> A platoon, eventually a phalanx, of prisoners' rights lawyers, supported by federal and foundation funding, soon appeared and pressed claims. They initiated, and won, prisoners' rights cases that implicated every aspect of prison governance. In many cases the prisoners' attorneys were more dedicated and effective than the overburdened and inexperienced government attorneys who represented the prison officials.[88]

Overview of Prisoners' Rights

Three principles explain why prisoners have highly restricted rights:

1. Restricted rights are part of just punishment.
2. Restricted rights are necessary for the safety and security of prisoners and staff.
3. Prison officials need wide discretion in managing prisons.[89]

Prisoners retain six rights in limited form:

1. Access to the courts.
2. Due process of law.
3. Equal protection of the laws.
4. First Amendment rights of free speech, association, and religion.
5. The Eighth Amendment right against "cruel and unusual punishment."
6. Fourth Amendment rights against unreasonable searches and seizures.

Access to the Courts

Prisoners retain the right to go to court, one of the most basic rights of all Americans. Access to the courts includes access to challenge the legitimacy, duration, and conditions of confinement; access to attorneys; the right to a **jailhouse lawyer** (prisoners who help ignorant, illiterate, or otherwise incompetent fellow prisoners); access to law libraries; and access to transcripts of their cases, to typewriters, and to other writing implements they need to present their claims.

Due Process of Law

The Fifth and the Fourteenth Amendments guarantee that neither the federal government nor state governments can "deprive any person of life, liberty, or property without due process of law" (Chapter 4). In determining whether state officials have deprived prison inmates of these rights, the U.S. Supreme Court looks both at how severe the deprivation was and the procedures followed to deprive inmates of life, liberty, or property.

The amount of process "due" to prisoners is considerably less than that due to law-abiding people outside prisons. The Court divides deprivations into three categories for the purposes of determining whether they violate due process rights:

1. Deprivations so trivial that they clearly do not deprive prisoners of life, liberty, or property.
2. Deprivations so serious that they clearly deprive prisoners of life, liberty, or property.
3. Deprivations that are not either clearly trivial or clearly in violation of the rights of prisoners.[90]

The Court has found that taking away "good time" clearly invades the liberty of prisoners. Therefore, prison administration cannot take away good time without following procedures that will ensure "due process of law." Prison administrators can, however, move prisoners from medium to maximum security facilities where the restrictions are much greater.[91]

Assuming that states have invaded a right, how much process are prisoners due? The Supreme Court has ruled that prisoners are clearly not entitled to the "full panoply of rights due" an ordinary citizen in a criminal trial. The state can follow a more flexible procedure that balances the rights of inmates and the needs of the prison. The state can satisfy the requirements of due process by providing four things:

1. Written notice to inmates of disciplinary charges no less than 24 hours prior to disciplinary proceedings that can deprive inmates of their rights.
2. Impartial disciplinary proceedings.
3. Written statement of the facts relied on and the reasons for the decision.
4. The right of inmates to call witnesses and present evidence.[92]

Inmates are not entitled to two fundamental parts of due process allowed to other citizens: the right to a lawyer and the right to confront the witnesses against them.[93]

Equal Protection of the Laws

The Fourteenth Amendment guarantees all citizens, including prisoners, equal protection of the laws. The most common equal protection claim that prisoners make is against racial discrimination. Although the Constitution prohibits outright racial discrimination, it does not prevent differential treatment on racial grounds. Therefore, according to the Supreme Court, prison administrators have "the right, acting in good faith and in particularized circumstances, to take into account racial tensions in maintaining security, discipline, and good order."[94]

Free Speech, Association, and Religion

Prisoners retain the First Amendment rights to expression, association, and religion to the extent that such rights do not either conflict with their status as prisoners or interfere with the objectives of the corrections system. Courts strike a balance between prisoners' rights and prison administrative needs in this area. Hence, prison administrators can censor the correspondence of prisoners for legitimate security purposes. In *Procunier v. Martinez,* the U.S. Supreme Court ruled that California's prison censorship rules were constitutional because they were designed to enhance security, order, and rehabilitation and because First Amendment freedoms were restricted only enough to ensure security, order, and rehabilitation.[95]

Right Against Cruel and Unusual Punishment

The Eighth Amendment prohibits "cruel and unusual punishments." This prohibition specifically protects prisoners. However, according to the U.S. Supreme Court, the Eighth Amendment does not extend to "every government action affecting the interests or well-being of a prisoner." According to the Court:

> [O]nly the unnecessary and wanton infliction of pain constitutes cruel and unusual punishment forbidden by the Eighth Amendment. . . . It is obduracy and wantonness, not inadvertence or error in good faith, that characterize the conduct prohibited by the Eighth Amendment clause, whether that conduct occurs in connection with establishing conditions of confinement, supplying medical needs, or restoring official control over a tumultuous cellblock. The infliction of pain in the course of a prison security, therefore, does not amount to cruel and unusual punishment simply because it may appear in retrospect that the degree of force authorized or applied for security purposes was unreasonable.[96]

The Court applied this interpretation in *Whitley v. Albers.* During a riot at the Oregon State Penitentiary, prisoners took a correctional officer hostage and held him in the upper tier of a two-tier cell block. Prison officials developed a plan to free the hostage. According to the plan, the prison security manager entered the cell block unarmed. Armed prison officials followed him. The security manager ordered one of the officers to fire a "warning shot and to shoot low at any inmates climbing the stairs to the upper tier since he would be climbing the stairs to free the hostage." Assistant Warden Harold Whitley, after firing the warning shot, shot inmate Gerald Albers in the knee when Albers tried to climb the stairs. Albers contended that shooting him was cruel and unusual punishment. Even though the Court agreed that, viewing the incident in retrospect, the use of deadly force was probably excessive, the action was not "cruel and unusual punishment." As long as the action was taken in "good faith," it was not an "intentional and wanton infliction of pain."[97]

Right Against Unreasonable Searches and Seizures

The Fourth Amendment protects against unreasonable searches and seizures by any agent of the government (see Chapter 7). But the right of prisoners against unreasonable searches and seizures is extremely limited. (Some critics say that for all practical purposes the Fourth Amendment does not protect prisoners.) Surveillance, cell and strip searches, monitored visits, censored mail, and other restrictions on privacy are basic parts of prison life, justified on the grounds that prisoners are in prison for punishment and that such intrusions are necessary to secure safe and orderly prisons.

In the leading case on the Fourth Amendment rights of prisoners, *Hudson v. Palmer,* the U.S. Supreme Court ruled that the Fourth Amendment provides no right to privacy in prison cells.

Use *Your* Discretion

Do prisoners have a right against unreasonable searches and seizures?

The following is extracted from the U.S. Supreme Court's opinion in *Hudson v. Palmer,* 468 U.S. 517 (1984).

Facts

The respondent Palmer is an inmate at the Bland Correctional Center in Bland, Virginia, serving sentences for forgery, uttering, grand larceny, and bank robbery convictions. On September 16, 1981, petitioner Hudson, an officer at the Correctional Center, with a fellow officer, conducted a "shakedown" search of respondent's prison locker and cell for contraband. During the "shakedown," the officers discovered a ripped pillowcase in a trash can near the respondent's cell bunk. Charges against Palmer were instituted under the prison disciplinary procedures for destroying state property. After a hearing, Palmer was found guilty on the charge and was ordered to reimburse the State for the cost of the material destroyed; in addition, a reprimand was entered on his prison record.

Opinion

We have repeatedly held that prisons are not beyond the reach of the Constitution. No "iron curtain" separates one from the other. Indeed, we have insisted that prisoners be accorded those rights not fundamentally inconsistent with imprisonment itself or incompatible with the objectives of incarceration. For example, we have held that invidious racial discrimination is as intolerable within a prison as outside, except as may be essential to "prison security and discipline."

However, while persons imprisoned for crime enjoy many protections of the Constitution, it is also clear that imprisonment carries with it the loss of many significant rights. These constraints on inmates, and in some cases the complete withdrawal of certain rights, are "justified by the considerations underlying our penal system." The curtailment of certain rights is necessary, as a practical matter, to accommodate a myriad of "institutional needs and objectives" of prison facilities, chief among which is internal security. Of course, these restrictions or retractions also serve, incidentally, as reminders that, under our system of justice, deterrence and retribution are factors in addition to correction.

We have not before been called upon to decide the specific question whether the Fourth Amendment applies within a prison cell. . . . [W]e hold that society is not prepared to recognize as legitimate any subjective expectation of privacy that a prisoner might have in his prison cell and that, accordingly, the Fourth Amendment proscription against unreasonable searches does not apply within the confines of the prison cell. The recognition of privacy rights for prisoners in their individual cells simply cannot be reconciled with the concept of incarceration and the needs and objectives of penal institutions.

Prisons, by definition, are places of involuntary confinement of persons who have a demonstrated proclivity for anti-social criminal, and often violent, conduct. Inmates have necessarily shown a lapse in ability to control and conform their behavior to the legitimate standards of society by the normal impulses of self-restraint; they have shown an inability to regulate their conduct in a way that reflects either a respect for law or an appreciation of the rights of others.

The administration of a prison, we have said, is "at best an extraordinarily difficult undertaking." But it would be literally impossible to accomplish the prison objectives identified above if inmates retained a right of privacy in their cells. Virtually the only place inmates can conceal weapons, drugs, and other contraband is in their cells. Unfettered access to these cells by prison officials, thus, is imperative if drugs and contraband are to be ferreted out and sanitary surroundings are to be maintained.

Determining whether an expectation of privacy is "legitimate" or "reasonable" necessarily entails a balancing of interests. The two interests here are the interest of society in the security of its penal institutions and the interest of the prisoner in privacy within his cell. The latter interest, of course, is already limited by the exigencies of the circumstances: A prison "shares none of the attributes of privacy of a home, an automobile, an office, or a hotel room."

We strike the balance in favor of institutional security, which we have noted is "central to all other corrections goals." A right of privacy in traditional Fourth Amendment terms is fundamentally incompatible with the close and continual surveillance of inmates and their cells required to ensure institutional security and internal order. We are satisfied that society would insist that the prisoner's expectation of privacy always yield to what must be considered the paramount interest in institutional security. We believe that it is accepted by our society that "[l]oss of freedom of choice and privacy are inherent incidents of confinement."

Dissent
Prison guard Hudson maliciously took and destroyed a quantity of Palmer's property, including legal materials and letters, for no reason other than harassment. Measured by the conditions that prevail in a free society, neither the possessions nor the slight residuum of privacy that a prison inmate can retain in his cell can have more than the most minimal value. From the standpoint of the prisoner, however, that trivial residuum may mark the difference between slavery and humanity.

Personal letters, snapshots of family members, a souvenir, a deck of cards, a hobby kit, perhaps a diary or a training manual for an apprentice in a new trade, or even a Bible—a variety of inexpensive items may enable a prisoner to maintain contact with some part of his past and an eye to the possibility of a better future. Are all of these items subject to unrestrained perusal, confiscation or mutilation at the hands of a possibly hostile guard? Is the Court correct in its perception that "society" is not prepared to recognize any privacy or possessory interest of the prison inmate—no matter how remote the threat to prison security may be?

It is well-settled that the discretion accorded prison officials is not absolute. A prisoner retains those constitutional rights not inconsistent with legitimate penological objectives. There can be no penological justification for the seizure alleged here. There is no contention that Palmer's property posed any threat to institutional security. Hudson had already examined the material before he took and destroyed it. The allegation is that Hudson did this for no reason save spite; there is no contention that under prison regulations the material was contraband. The need for "close and continual surveillance of inmates and their cells," in no way justifies taking and destroying non-contraband property; if material is examined and found not to be contraband, there can be no justification for its seizure.

CRITICAL THINKING

1. Which opinion do you support, the majority (which is regarded as "the law of the land") or the dissent? Explain your answer.
2. If you were deciding the law, what would you decide? What reasons would you give?

Prisoners' Rights in Operation

Beginning in the late 1970s and continuing through the 1990s, the Supreme Court placed limits on prisoners' rights, returning to prison administrators much of the discretion that they enjoyed during the "hands-off" era. Typical of this move is the important case of *Bell v. Wolfish,* in which the Court ruled that prisoners had no right to a single cell. Justice Rehnquist wrote:

> The deplorable conditions and draconian restrictions of our Nation's prisons are too well known to require recounting here, and the federal courts rightly have condemned these sordid aspects of our prison systems. But many of these same courts have, in the name of the Constitution, become increasingly enmeshed in the minutiae of prison operations. Judges, after all, are human. They, no less than others in our society, have a natural tendency to believe that their individual solutions to often intractable problems are better and more workable than those of the persons who are actually charged with the running of the particular institution under examination. But under the Constitution, the first question to be answered is not whose plan is best, but in what branch of government is lodged the authority to initially devise the plan. This does not mean constitutional rights are not to be scrupulously observed. It does mean, however, the inquiry of federal courts into prison management must be limited to the issue of whether a particular system violates any prohibition of the Constitution, or in the case of a federal prison, a statute. The wide range of "judgment calls" that meet constitutional and statutory requirements are confined to officials outside the Judiciary Branch of Government.[98]

Not only has the Supreme Court restricted the rights of prisoners and returned discretionary judgment to prison officials, but most prisoners fail in their lawsuits even when the Court has accepted that they have rights against discretionary decision making by prison administrators. Most prisoner cases never get beyond the earliest stages of the proceedings. In California, for example, the court terminated 80.4 percent of prisoner cases shortly after filing and before the court registered any response by the defendant prison administrations. Nationwide, 68 percent of all prisoner cases were dropped at this early stage. Due to early dismissal, only 4.2 percent of all cases filed ever get to trial.

However, Jack E. Call found that prisoners meet with greater success in prison crowding cases. Courts issued favorable rulings in 73.8 percent of all cases, 80 percent in federal district courts, and 66 percent in courts of appeals. According to Call, many courts have made it clear that prison administrative discretion in managing prisons will not shield prisons from litigation involving "gruesome living conditions."[99]

Even when prisoners succeed in getting their cases into court, they practically never "win." In one sample of 664 cases, only three court orders were issued regarding confinement conditions; only two prisoners were awarded minimal money damages. In a few more cases, seven temporary restraining orders and five preliminary injunctions were issued. Prisoners who win their cases almost certainly have lawyers, because cases rarely go to trial unless prisoners have attorneys. In the two cited cases awarded damages, the prisoner with a lawyer received $200; the one without a lawyer got only $6![100]

Although prisoners win few victories in lower federal courts, court cases still affect prisons. Even a lost case can lead to prison reform. Prison administrators do not want courts to intrude into their domain, so they sometimes make changes to avoid the intrusions. Jim Thomas, in his analysis of prisoner litigation, quotes one prison administrator on the effects of prisoner lawsuits:

> Where only a few years ago prisons operated without written rules and with only the most rudimentary record keeping systems, today prison authorities are engulfed in bureaucratic paper. There are regulations, guidelines, policy statements, and general orders; there are forms, files, and reports for virtually everything.[101]

Litigation has also increased centralization and oversight by correctional administrations. Although in the short term, court orders may reduce staff morale and even cause prison violence, court restrictions on crowding have increased prison and jail construction, according to Malcolm Feeley and Roger Hanson. Court orders have also mitigated the most extreme abusive conditions in prisons. A detailed study of four major prison condition cases found that compliance, although grudging, slow, and incomplete, led all four states to spend substantial amounts of money responding to court orders. In some cases, new prisons were built following litigation. It is unlikely that this would have occurred had prisoners not sued their keepers.[102]

INTERNAL GRIEVANCE MECHANISMS

Lawsuits are not the only redress for prisoners who have grievances against prison administration. Virtually every prison provides for internal grievance proceedings. Elaborate rules formulated by administrations with legal assistance govern grievance proceedings. Prison officers and sometimes outside participants, including former prisoners on occasion, operate such grievance mechanisms. Although not totally supported by either prisoners or prisons' critics, internal grievance proceedings play a significant part in prison governance and life. In the past 15 years, a spectacular growth in prison internal grievance mechanisms has taken place. In every adult correctional system in the country, some procedures exist for resolving prisoners' grievances without going to court.[103]

No two states have exactly the same grievance system, but all systems have some basic similarities. Most possess broad mandates to hear prisoner grievances. Illinois, for example, opens its Institutional Inquiry Board (IIB) to any prisoner who wants "resolution to complaints, problems, and grievances which [he or she has] not been able to resolve through other avenues available at the institution or facility."[104]

Common Grievances and Disciplinary Violations

Grievances, such as these in Illinois, are common:

- Claims for early release.
- Charges that guards issued disciplinary "tickets" improperly.
- Complaints that work or program assignments were not right.
- Claims that prisoners were classified wrong.
- Charges that property was lost, stolen, or confiscated.

Common disciplinary actions against prisoners include "tickets" for:

- Creating dangerous disturbances.
- Disobeying a direct order.
- Undertaking unauthorized movement.
- Assaulting another prisoner or an officer.
- Destroying or damaging property.
- Possessing dangerous contraband.
- Engaging in sexual misconduct.[105]

Minnesota supplies prisoners in all facilities with a written list of their rights, out of which come most grievances. The rights include:

- A published list of the charges and penalties.
- A prompt and full statement of the nature of the alleged violation not later than five days after the prisoner is charged with a prison rule violation.
- The right to adequate notice prior to the hearing.
- The opportunity for a prisoner to appear in person before the disciplinary hearing board and be heard.
- The right to bring witnesses and present evidence to the hearing.
- The right to an impartial hearing board.
- The right to counsel or substitute counsel throughout the process.
- A written notice of the board's findings.
- The right to appeal to the warden or another designated person.
- The right to a record of the proceedings at the hearing for review and appeal.[106]

Prisoners most often challenge disciplinary tickets when they affect vital prisoner interests, such as good time and classification. In Illinois, for example, prisoners get a one-day sentence reduction for every day of good time served. Discipline infractions can reduce this good time. Also in Illinois, prisoners are classified either as A, B, or C. Grade A entitles prisoners to maximum freedom and privileges; C results in maximum security and the least freedom. Disciplinary tickets might lead to downgrading in security level. A challenge to a disciplinary ticket might, therefore, be grounds to grieve reduced good time and security reclassification. For example, according to Illinois prison rules, forced sexual contacts carry maximum penalties that reduce good time by 360 days and that downgrade prisoners to grade C security for 360 days.[107]

Denying requests for protective custody also provides a ground to file a grievance. Protective custody means that prisoners—often at their own request—are put in the segregation unit, where their movement is restricted to avoid danger. One grievance arose when prison officials denied a request for protective custody to a 6'4" white man weighing 210 pounds against African American gang members. Prison officials stated that someone of the prisoner's size ought to be able to protect himself.[108]

Prisoners' property leads to another group of grievances. Most commonly, these arise because the administration has confiscated property on the ground that it is either unauthorized or contraband. Other common cases involve lost or stolen prisoner property. According to the prisoner, the administration did not carry out its responsibility either to protect the property or to compensate for its loss. Even though property cases do not ordinarily involve items worth a lot of money, they are important. First, they make up a considerable number of grievances filed. Second, items such as photographs, jewelry, and jackets may have sentimental value to the prisoner. These items may be all that provides individuality in an otherwise very impersonal and regulated place.

Grievance Procedures and Their Effects

Decisions regarding these grievances are generally two-tiered. Members of a local grievance committee, drawn entirely from within the prison, initially decide for or against the prisoner. Prisoners can appeal adverse decisions to a board drawn from outside the prison, sometimes one with private citizens as well as correctional administrators on it. The mechanism is self-contained; that is, the local board is a local prison body, and the appeals board is a statewide corrections department body.

Proceedings in grievance bodies are formal, governed by written rules and regulations. Prisoners have basic due process rights, usually including the right to be present at the hearing, sometimes the right to have witnesses and to challenge adverse evidence, and the right to have a decision in writing within a specified time period. This written decision must set forth the reasons supporting the board's ruling. Sometimes, prisoners must go through the whole grievance procedure inside the prison before taking any of their complaints to courts, in a requirement called "exhausting administrative remedies."

Prisoners rarely win their grievance cases. One prisoner overestimated the win ratio when he said, "You don't win more than 1 in 10." In fact, it is considerably less. One survey reviewed grievances in several cell blocks and showed that prisoners won only 1 case out of 12 in one block, 1 of 19 in a second, 1 of 25 in a third, and only 1 in 28 in a fourth. On appeal to a review board, the results were also low. In one maximum security prison, prisoners "won" 17 percent of the appeals and lost 75 percent. Another 7 percent had mixed results.[109]

Grievance procedures in prisons have several aims:

- They improve prison management and help to identify problems.
- They reduce inmate frustration and prison violence.
- They aid in prisoner rehabilitation.
- They reduce the number of cases prisoners take to the courts.
- They bring "justice" to prisons.

Existing grievance mechanisms may or may not substantiate these justifications. Research has raised several questions. To improve prison management by identifying problems, the first aim, prison administrations have to take the time periodically to review caseloads to determine what kinds of grievances prisoners have. Only by reviewing the grievances can something be done about them. This takes time and resources that most prisons simply do not have. To achieve this aim might require prisoners to bring grievances more selectively; instead of using grievance procedures to express "rights consciousness" or harassment, prisoners may have to make their complaints more "pure." According to prison litigation expert Jan Brakel:

> The message to inmates should be that abusing the procedures for frivolous, repetitive grievances harms the chances of other inmates, and ultimately their own, of having important things changed.[110]

Few prison officials go so far as to say that grievance procedures eliminate violence from prisons. They may provide a "safety valve" for prisoner discontent and thereby "keep the lid on" violent prison outbreaks, but there is little or no proof that this is true. No correlation seems to exist between violence levels and prison grievance mechanisms. Through grievance procedures, isolated inmates might develop more respect for, and willingness to abide by, regular procedures, thereby becoming "rehabilitated," more ready to live in society without breaking its rules. However, most prisoners do not view grievance mechanisms positively. In many cases they seem only to confirm prisoners' ideas that institutions rig decisions to maintain the establishment against dissidents—in this case, prison officials against prisoners.[111]

Proving that grievance mechanisms reduce the load of cases in courts is also difficult. Many things influence these caseloads, and it is impossible to say that grievance procedures determine them. Grievance mechanisms may even increase litigation because prisoners who are more conscious of their rights are more apt to demand them. If they do not feel satisfied at the administrative level, then they will carry on their fight in the courts.

Finally, it is not clear that grievance mechanisms bring justice to the prisons. For that to be the case, according to Jan Brakel, administrators and prisoners must use them to best advantage,

> instead of playing games with them, games of power, games of psychology, harassment games, legalistic games, passing time games, and so forth. At neither Vienna nor Stateville were the procedures used to full advantage—the staff failed to maximize both the problem-identification and the problem-disposition potential of the process, and far too many of the inmates abused the process with groundless or frivolous claims.[112]

Several recommendations attempt to bring the reality of grievance mechanisms closer to the claims made for them. One suggests changing the composition of the grievance body. Prisoners and other critics commonly complain that prison officials dominate grievance mechanisms. They call for more outside participation, either by citizens or prisoners. However, although outsiders may be impartial, they are also naive and ignorant of prison society, and can therefore be "conned" by both prisoners and administration. Prisoners do not make feasible members, either. They can be partial and subject to intimidation and physical danger if they rule against another prisoner.

Other reformers demand that procedures be made more formal, with more documentation and more bound by precedent. Some believe, however, that there already is enough paper; the real problem is how to use the documentation to achieve fair and just results. Demands for more investigation, more listening to the prisoners' side of the story, and so on accomplish little if they merely add to an already heavily burdened grievance body.[113]

Perhaps the severest criticism is that too many frivolous and trumped-up grievances, or ones brought only to harass, are filed. Grievances must be screened more carefully, but the problem of how to do this remains. How does anyone decide, before hearings begin, whether a complaint has merit or is a farce—something "cooked up to obstruct the system, harass the staff, pass dead time"? Once proceedings begin, however, frivolous claims often come to light. At that point, they could be penalized, and such penalties might take several forms. Privileges such as movies, television, or visits to the commissary could be taken away. Refiling restrictions could be imposed if present grievances are decided to be frivolous or spurious. Extreme cases might even call for the levy of fines.[114]

LIFE IN WOMEN'S PRISONS

In 1998, almost 80,000 women made up 6.4 percent of the total imprisoned population in the United States. However, their numbers are growing rapidly. Since 1990, the female prisoner population has grown at an annual rate of almost 9 percent. More than one-third of women prisoners are in California, Texas, and federal prisons. Women prisoners are mainly low-income, African American or Hispanic, undereducated, and unskilled with little or no work experience. They are also mostly young, single mothers with at least two children under 18. And, they have many medical, psychological, and financial problems and needs. According to Barbara Owen and Barbara Bloom, "Substance abuse, compounded by poverty, unemployment, physical and mental illness, physical and sexual abuse, and homelessness, often propel women through the revolving door of the criminal justice system."[115]

According to the U.S. Bureau of Justice Statistics, women are "substantially more likely than men to be serving time for a drug offense and less likely to have been sentenced for a violent crime." More than 60 percent of women prisoners are serving time for nonviolent crimes, mainly drug offenses and minor property crimes. More than half of the increase in women prisoners is due to the imprisonment of drug offenders. Since 1991, the number of women serving time for violent offenses has declined. One-third of the women serving time for either murder or manslaughter had killed relatives.[116]

Use *Your* Discretion

Does more women prisoners mean more female crime?

The debate about whether more women in prison means that women are committing more crimes is wide open. However, Barbara Owen and Barbara Bloom, two experts on female crime and women's imprisonment, maintain that "the criminality of women has not increased." How do they support their conclusion? Consider the following arguments:

- Substance abuse, physical and sexual abuse, and poverty and underemployment play a prominent role in sending women to prison.
- A significant proportion of women prisoners are not dangerous, are not career criminals, and therefore, are not a threat to the community.

- A large part of the increase in women prisoners is due to drug-related offenses. The "war on drugs" is a "war on women."
- The number of women in prison for conviction of violent crimes is definitely decreasing.
- More than half of the women prisoners are first-time offenders.

Owen and Bloom argue that "the legal response to drug-related behavior has become increasingly punitive, resulting in a flood of less serious offenders into the state and federal prison systems."

CRITICAL THINKING

1. Explain how these points support the conclusion that the criminal justice system is the reason for the increase in the number of women in prison.
2. Do they also support the conclusion that women are committing more crime? Explain how.
3. Which do you believe: that female criminality is increasing or that the criminal justice system is imprisoning more offenders? Defend your answer.
4. If you are undecided, what more would you want to know before you make up your mind?

Personal relationships are important to female prisoners trying to get through their time in prison. Besides creating family-like structures with other inmates, female inmates rely on visits from their families outside prison as well. This woman visits with her baby in a nursery program at Riker's Island, New York.

The Culture of Women Prisoners

Women cope with prison life differently than men do. David A. Ward and Gene G. Kassebaum's path-breaking study of the California Institution for Women demonstrated this difference in coping with life in prison. According to Ward and Kassebaum, women suffer from "affectional starvation," the need for personal relationships, and a "psycho-sexual" need for men. Ward and Kassebaum found that women prisoners met these needs by structuring their prison relationships around homosexual "family" relationships. But, unlike in men's prisons, female prisoners did not coerce their partners in homosexual relationships. Of course, some women are "just playing around" with these relationships while others take them seriously.[117]

Rose Giallombardo's study of the Federal Reformatory for Women supported Ward and Kassebaum's findings. Giallombardo showed that women reproduced outside family relationships in prison—father, mother, daughter, sister. Unlike the subculture of men's prisons, women's prison subculture, according to Giallombardo, fostered mutuality and harmony, not competition and dissension.

Esther Heffernen found a heterogeneous population in the women incarcerated in the District of Columbia's Reformatory. For women who grew up in foster homes, prison became the center of their lives. They continuously struggled with staff and other inmates for control of their lives and to obtain illegal food, drugs, clothing, and letters. Women imprisoned for situational offenses, such as murder of an abusive husband, rejected any criminal self-identification, attempting to recreate conventional life inside prison and maintain contacts outside. These prisoners accepted rules and regulations and identified with the staff. Professional criminals tried to keep busy to pass time quickly and avoided trouble to get released as soon as possible to their former lives of crime.[118]

Barbara Owen, in *Surviving the Mix: Struggle and Survival in a Women's Prison,* conducted a combined ethnographic and survey study of the largest women's prison in the United States and probably the world. The Central California Women's Facility holds more than 4,000 women. It has all levels of security, from the murderers on death row to the minor drug and property offenders. Two themes run through her research. First, when women enter prison, they realize the importance of developing some kind of program to help them cope with doing their time. Work assignments and personal relationships are essential elements in their program. Also important are privacy, material comforts, and acquiring skills. According to Owen:

> Most women want to do their time, leave the prison, and return to the free world. They want to avoid the mix of risky and self-defeating behaviors such as drug use and fighting or damaging relationships that interfere with one's program or limit freedom through

> placement in restrictive housing or the addition of time to one's sentence.
>
> Some dip into the mix in the beginning of their prison terms, leaving when they establish a more productive program. Others invest permanently in the destructive spiral of the mix and its attendant activities. For a small minority of women, the lure of the mix, with its emphasis on the fast life and the excitement of drug use, fighting, and volatile intimate relationships, proves too hard to resist.[119]

The second theme of Owen's research is the importance of personal relationships. The play family is one of these relationships. It contains interpersonal satisfactions, a combination of social and material responsibilities, and a sense of belonging. According to Owen, the play family "creates the sense of community and protection that the . . . cliques and gang structure provide for male prisoners."[120]

"Getting with the Program"

As we saw in the last section, a program is essential to organizing a life around doing time. "Getting with the program" is the first step in learning how to do time. According to Barbara Owen:

> Successful programming . . . involves settling down and developing a routine that provides satisfying . . . personal relationships and routine activities that offer constructive stimulation and protection from the dangers of the prison environment.[121]

Programming is to inmates what following a daily routine is to those not in prison. According to one inmate:

> Programming means to me that I get up every morning, shower, brush my teeth, and get ready for work. I come to work, do my work. I go home for lunch, I come back. I get off, go home, shower and kick back. Either I read a book, or I kick back with some of my friends and bullshit. I stay in my room sometimes, but I go to the day room. It depends on the kind of mood I am in. I got in a fight once and lost my privileges for thirty days. This changed my whole attitude . . . as far as getting in trouble, going off on people. I have been able to come to myself, to sit in my room and think about my goals and stuff in life.[122]

Some women refuse to program. These women spend their time getting around expectations. Trying to get around the program leads to loss of jobs, time spent in detention, and loss of "good time" (reduction in sentence length).

Knowledge and Understanding CHECK

1. What is the significance of *Ruffin v. Commonwealth?*
2. Identify the justifications for the "hands-off" doctrine.
3. Identify the forces that placed limits on the "hands-off" doctrine during the 1960s.
4. Identify the three principles underlying the restrictions on prisoners' rights.
5. List the six rights of prisoners, and describe each of them.
6. Describe how prisoners' rights operate in practice.
7. Identify the main grievances brought to and the procedures involved in internal grievance mechanisms.
8. What is the percentage of women prisoners?
9. What are the major types of crimes women prisoners have committed?
10. Describe the culture of women's prisons.
11. Describe what the phrase "getting with the program" means in the context of women's prisons.

Should Prisoners Get to Lift Weights and Play Team Sports? Consideration

Many prison officials believe that "sports programs help condition inmates to behave better at the risk of losing their privileges. They say the games also provide a tension release, making inmates less aggressive." "I'm sure that's absolutely true," Bobb Barr responds. "But," he adds, "Pavlov's dog can be made to respond to any number of positive stimuli."[123]

On the other hand, one commentator asks:

> Whatever happened to the constitutional provision which calls for the nation's citizens to not be submitted to cruel and unusual treatment? The state's punishment objective is accomplished by the deprivation of liberty in and of itself. If a person were held in a fabulous mansion, prohibited from leaving at any time and prohibited from seeing friends or family except at designated times, he would suffer punishment equal to any penitentiary. Those privileges sought to be terminated are minimal and only make conditions tolerable for the staff, more than the prisoners."[124]

Critical Thinking

1. Summarize the arguments for and against removing privileges for prisoners.
2. Think about what you have learned in this chapter.
3. Would you recommend the removal of privileges? Why?
4. If you answered no to (3), what would you want to know before you changed your mind?

CHAPTER CAPSULE

- Imprisonment is supposed to be painful, humane, and fair.
- Men's prisons and men prisoners differ markedly from women's prisons and women prisoners.
- There is less violence and consensual sex in men's prisons than is talked and written about.
- Prisoners try hard and to some extent succeed in getting around the "enforced poverty" that is supposed to govern prisons.
- Boredom and monotony are the dominating characteristics of most prisons.
- Prisoners retain some of their rights, but their rights are highly restricted.

KEY TERMS

prison subculture
indigenous theory
prisonization
importation theory
state-raised youths
jailing
doing time
gleaning
inmate code
gangbanging
homeboys
concentration model
general population inmate
lockdown
selective incapacitation
front-door strategy
back-door strategy
safety-valve policy
cell rationing
principle of less eligibility
reality therapy
behavior modification
token economy
confinement model
meta-analyses
"hands-off" doctrine
jailhouse lawyer

INTERNET RESEARCH EXERCISES

Exercise: What rights do prisoners presently have? Do you believe prisoners should have fewer or more rights than they presently have? Should they have no rights? Search for information about prisoners rights and explain your answers on the basis of what you find in your research.

Suggested Site:
- ACLU: Prisoners Rights, http://www.aclu.org/issues/prisons/arprisons.html

InfoTrac College Edition:
- Search using the key words "prisoners' rights"

NOTES

1. *The Atlanta Journal and Constitution,* 22 March 1998, 12E.
2. Donald Clemmer, *The Prison Community* (New York: Holt, Rinehart, & Winston, 1940).
3. *Social Problems* 10 (1962): 142–55.
4. John Irwin, "The Prison Experience: The Convict World," in *Criminal Justice,* George S. Bridges, Joseph G. Weis, and Robert D. Crutchfield, eds. (Thousand Oaks, Calif.: Pine Forge Press, 1996), 426.
5. Mark Fleisher, *Warehousing Violence* (Newbury Park, Calif.: Sage, 1989), 28–29.
6. Quoted in Robert Johnson, *Hard Time,* 2d ed. (Belmont, Calif.: Wadsworth, 1996), 164.
7. Irwin, "The Prison Experience," 426.
8. Ibid., 430–31.
9. Ibid., 426.
10. Gresham M. Sykes, *The Society of Captives: A Study of a Maximum Security Prison* (Princeton, N.J.: Princeton University Press, 1958), quoted in Todd R. Clear and George F. Cole, *American Corrections,* 3d ed. (Belmont, Calif.: Wadsworth, 1994), 259.
11. Virgil L. Williams and Mary Fish, *Convicts, Codes, and Contraband* (Cambridge, Mass.: Ballinger, 1974), 40.
12. Susan Sheehan, *A Prison and a Prisoner* (Boston: Houghton Mifflin, 1978), 91; quoted in Clear and Cole, *American Corrections,* 266.
13. David B. Kalinich, *Power, Stability, and Contraband* (Prospect Heights, Ill.: Waveland Press, 1986).
14. This section relies on Christine A. Saum, Hilary Spratt, James A. Inciardi, and Rachael E. Bennett, "Sex in Prison: Exploring Myths and Realities," *Prison Journal* 75 (1997): 413–30, and the author's unpublished research into the history of prisons in Minnesota.
15. Saum et al., "Sex in Prison," 413.
16. Ibid., 421–22, 425.
17. Ibid., 418.
18. Ibid.
19. John Irwin, *Prisons in Turmoil* (Boston: Little, Brown, 1980), 181; Samuel Jan Brakel, "Administrative Justice in the Penitentiary: Report on Inmate Grievance Procedures," *American Bar Foundation Research Journal* (1982): 113; BJS, *Prisoners in 1997* (Washington, D.C.: BJS, 1998).
20. Irwin, *Prisons in Turmoil,* 182.
21. Billy "Hands" Robinson, "Love: A Hard Legged Triangle," *Black Scholar* (September 1971): 29.
22. Quoted in James B. Jacobs, "Race Relations and the Prisoner Subculture," in *Crime and Justice: An Annual Review of Research,* Norval Morris and Michael Tonry, eds. (Chicago: University of Chicago Press, 1980), I, 16.
23. Edward Bunker, *Animal Factory* (New York: Viking Press, 1977), 92.
24. Quoted in Jacobs, "Race Relations," 13–14.
25. Irwin, *Prisons in Turmoil,* 189; figures for Illinois cited in George W. Knox, *An Introduction to Gangs* (Berrien Springs, Mich.: Van de Vere Publishing Ltd., 1991), 283.
26. James Jacobs, *Stateville: The Penitentiary in Modern Society* (Chicago: University of Chicago Press, 1977), 161.
27. Quoted in Irwin, *Prisons in Turmoil,* 193–94.
28. *New York Times,* 2 June 1985.
29. John Irwin and James Austin, *It's About Time: America's Imprisonment Binge,* 2d ed. (Belmont, Calif.: Wadsworth, 1997), 72.
30. Lee H. Bowker, "Prisons: Problems and Prospects," in *Encyclopedia of Crime and Justice,* Sanford H. Kadish, ed. (New York: Free Press, 1983), 3:1230–31.
31. Ibid., 78.
32. Daniel Lockwood, *Prison Sexual Violence* (New York: Elsevier/North Holland, Inc., 1980), 29.
33. Ibid.
34. Ibid., 30.
35. Ibid., 33–34.
36. Ibid.
37. Angela S. Maitland and Richard D. Sluder, "Victimization and Youthful Prison Inmates," *Prison Journal* 75 (1997): 68.
38. Saum et al., "Sex in Prison," 422–25.
39. Bowker, "Prisons: Problems and Prospects," 1231.
40. Clear and Cole, *American Corrections,* 275–76.
41. This account of Marion draws heavily on *The United States Penitentiary, Marion, Illinois, Consultants Report Submitted to Committee on the Judiciary, U.S. House of Representatives, Ninety-eighth Congress, Second Session* (Washington, D.C.: U.S. Government Printing Office, 1985).
42. Conversation with David A. Ward, 30 March 1990, about his research on prison management.
43. Ibid.; Raymond Holt, "Marion: Separating Fact from Fiction," *Federal Prisons Journal* 2, no. 2 (1991): 33–34.
44. Mark Colvin, "The 1980 New Mexico Prison Riot," *Social Problems* 29 (June 1982): 449.
45. Mark Colvin, *The Penitentiary in Crisis: From Accommodation to Riot in New Mexico* (Albany: State University of New York Press, 1992).
46. Colvin, "The 1980 New Mexico Prison Riot," 450.
47. Burt Useem and Peter Kimball, *States of Siege: U.S. Prison Riots, 1971–1986* (New York: Oxford University Press, 1989), 3–4.
48. Alfred Blumstein, "Prisons: Population, Capacity, and Alternatives," in *Crime and Public Policy,* James Q. Wilson, ed. (New Brunswick, N.J.: Transaction Books, 1983), 229; Bureau of Justice

Statistics, *Prisoners in 1997* (Washington, D.C.: BJS, August 1998).
49. Joan Mullen, *American Prisons and Jails* (Washington, D.C.: National Institute of Justice, 1980), 1:53.
50. BJS, *Prisoners in the United States,* 1997 (Washington, D.C.: Bureau of Justice Statistics, 1998), 8–9; U.S. Department of Justice, *State of the Bureau,* 1997.
51. Blumstein, "Prisons," 229.
52. Ibid., 242-43.
53. Peter Greenwood, *Selective Incapacitation* (Santa Monica: RAND Corporation, 1982).
54. Ibid., xix–xx.
55. Rudy A. Haapenan, *Selective Incapacitation and the Serious Offender: A Longitudinal Study of Criminal Career Patterns* (New York: Springer-Verlag, 1990).
56. Garry, *Options to Reduce Prison Crowding,* 5–12.
57. Ibid., 13.
58. Ibid., 14–16; *Criminal Justice Newsletter* (June 1, 1984), 7; *Criminal Justice Newsletter* (January 2, 1985), 1.
59. Blumstein, "Prisons," 247.
60. Samuel Walker, *Sense and Nonsense About Crime,* 2d ed., (Belmont, Calif.: Wadsworth, 1989), 183.
61. Quoted in Timothy J. Flanagan, "Prison Labor and Industry," in *The American Prison: Issues in Research and Policy,* Lynne Goodstein and Doris Layton MacKenzie, eds. (New York: Plenum Press, 1989), 135.
62. Ibid.
63. Ibid.
64. Ibid., 137–40.
65. Walker, *Sense and Nonsense About Crime,* 182.
66. John P. Conrad, "Correctional Treatment," *Encyclopedia of Crime and Justice,* 1:274; "Insight Incorporated Fact Sheet" (mimeographed, Stillwater State Prison, Minnesota).
67. Conrad, "Correctional Treatment," 275.
68. Ibid.
69. Ann Dryden Witte, *Work Release in North Carolina: An Evaluation of Its Post-Release Effects* (Chapel Hill: The University of North Carolina, 1975), 99.
70. Ibid., 100.
71. Peter H. Rossi, Richard A. Berk, and Kenneth J. Lenihan, *Money, Work, and Crime: Experimental Evidence,* (New York: Academic Press, 1980).
72. Gordon Hawkins, "Prison Labor and Prison Industries," in *Crime and Justice: An Annual Review of Research* (Chicago: University of Chicago Press, 1983), 5:98–103; Charles Hoskinson, "Prison Induustries Often in the Red," *Associated Press,* 1 December 1998.
73. Hoskinson, "Prison Industries."
74. Ibid.
75. Florida House of Representatives, *Oversight Report on PRIDE (Prison Rehabilitative Industries and Diversified Enterprises)* (Tallahassee, Fla., 1988).
76. Timothy J. Flanagan et al., *The Effect of Prison Industry Employment on Offender Behavior: Final Report of the Prison Industry Research Project* (Albany, N.Y.: Hindelang Criminal Justice Research Center, SUNY at Albany, 1988).
77. Clear and Cole, *American Corrections,* 334.
78. Ibid., 369–70.
79. Ibid., 370.
80. Todd R. Clear et al., *Prisons, Prisoners, and Religion* (final report, Rutgers University, 1992).
81. Michael Welch, "Rehabilitation: Holding Its Ground in Corrections," *Federal Probation* (December 1995): 3.
82. Ted Palmer, *The Re-Emergence of Correctional Intervention* (Newbury Park, Calif.: Sage, 1992), 1–11.
83. Charles H. Logan and Gerald G. Gaes, "Meta-Analysis and the Rehabilitation of Punishment," *Justice Quarterly* 10 (1993): 247.
84. Ibid., 261.
85. *Ruffin v. Commonwealth,* 62 Va. 790 (1871).
86. *Ingraham v. Wright,* 430 U.S. 651, 669 (1977).
87. Donald P. Baker et al., "Judicial Intervention in Corrections: The California Experience—An Empirical Study," *UCLA Law Review* 20 (1973): 454.
88. Jacobs, *New Perspectives on Prison,* 39.
89. James J. Gobert and Neil P. Cohen, *Rights of Prisoners* (New York: McGraw-Hill, 1981); *Bell v. Wolfish,* 441 U.S. 520, 547 (1979).
90. *Sandin v. Connor,* 115 S.Ct. 2293 (1995).
91. *Wolff v. McDonnell,* 418 U.S. 539; *Meachum v. Fano,* 427 U.S. 215.
92. *Wolff v. McDonnell; Sandin v. Connor,* 115 S.Ct. 2293 (1995).
93. Ibid.
94. *Lee v. Washington,* 390 U.S. 333 (1968), 334.
95. *Procunier v. Martinez,* 416 U.S. 396 (1974).
96. *Whitley v. Albers,* 475 US 312 (1986), 319.
97. Ibid., 313.
98. *Bell v. Wolfish,* 441 U.S. 520 (1979); Joachim Herrmann, "The Federal Republic of Germany," in *Major Criminal Justice Systems: A Comparative Study,* 2d ed., George F. Cole, Stansilaw J. Frankowski, and Marc G. Gertz, eds. (Newbury Park, Calif.: Sage Publications, 1987), 130–32.
99. Jack E. Call, "Lower Court Treatment of Jail and Prison Overcrowding Cases: A Second Look," *Federal Probation* 52 (1988): 34–41.
100. Jim Thomas, "The 'Reality' of Prisoner Litigation: Repackaging the Data," *New England Journal on Criminal Law and Civil Confinement* 15 (1989): 27–54.
101. Ibid.
102. Malcolm Feeley and Roger Hanson, "What We Know, Think We Know and Would Like to Know About the Impact of Court Orders on Prison Conditions and Jail Crowding," in *Prison and Jail Crowding: Workshop Proceedings,* Dale K. Sechrest, Jonathan D. Caspar, and Jeffrey A. Roth, eds. (Washington, D.C.: National Academy of Sciences, 1987); M. Kay Harris and Dudley P. Spiller, Jr., *After Decision: Implementation of Judicial Decrees in Correctional Settings* (Washington, D.C.: U.S. Department of Justice, LEAA, 1977).
103. Samuel Jan Brakel, "Ruling on Prisoners' Grievances," *American Bar Foundation Research Journal* (1983): 393–425, 394, from which most of this section is derived.
104. Ibid., 117.
105. Ibid.
106. Minnesota Department of Corrections, *Inmate Discipline Regulations* (1988).
107. Brakel, "Ruling on Prisoners' Grievances," 412.
108. Ibid., 414–15.
109. Samuel Jan Brakel, "Administrative Justice," 124–26.
110. Ibid., 129.
111. Ibid., 130.
112. Ibid., 133.
113. Ibid., 136–37.
114. Ibid., 139.

115. BJS, *Prisoners in 1997* (Washington D.C.: BJS, 1998), 1, 5; Barbara Owen and Barbara Bloom, "Profiling Women Prisoners," *The Prison Journal* 75 (1995): 167.
116. Owen and Bloom, "Profiling Women Prisoners," 168.
117. David A. Ward and Gene G. Kassebaum, *Women's Prison: Sex and Social Structure* (Chicago: Aldine, 1965).
118. Rose Giallombardo, *Society of Women: A Study of a Women's Prison* (New York: Wiley, 1966); Esther Heffernen, *Making It in Prison: The Square, the Cool, and the Life* (New York: Wiley Interscience, 1972); Raymond G. Wozda and Judy Rowse, *Women Behind Bars* (Washington, D.C.: American Correctional Association, 1997), 4.
119. Barbara Owen, *Surviving the Mix: Struggle and Survival in a Women's Prison* (Albany, N.Y.: State University of New York Press, 1998), 8.
120. Ibid.
121. Ibid., 97.
122. Quoted, ibid.
123. *The Atlanta Journal and Constitution,* "Sports in Prison," 22 March 1998, 12E.
124. *Los Angeles Times,* 12 February 1998, Part B, 8.

CHAPTER 16

Returning to Society

CHAPTER OUTLINE

Should He Go to Jail?

Dr. Gregory Johnson, a Kirkland (Washington) plastic surgeon obtained hung juries in two trials for raping a woman while she was under anesthesia. Johnson then violated at least two conditions of his community service after he was convicted for assaulting the woman–he consumed alcohol and he changed his address without consulting authorities. The judge could order Johnson to go to jail for six months. Should she issue that order?[1]

INTRODUCTION

Almost all the talk about corrections is about prisons. Nearly all the increased public spending authorized for corrections is earmarked for building more prisons. We hear talk of harsher laws, tougher sentences, and the resulting overcrowded prisons. Many of us hope that this crackdown on crime and criminals will result in *sending* more criminals to prison—and *keeping* them there. However, reality belies this hope.

In reality, almost all prisoners leave prison eventually—and probably this is the way it should be. A handful of prisoners are executed or are sentenced to life without chance of parole; and a few thousand are either murdered or otherwise die before their sentences expire. The vast majority, however, return to society. In 1996, 395,000 men and women were released from prison on **parole** (supervised release from prison). In 1997, the latest year for which numbers were available when this book went to press, more than 685,000 men and women were on parole. Figure 16.1 depicts a fairly steady increase in the number of prisoners conditionally released since 1990. Although the numbers of conditionally released prisoners have risen, the resources devoted to supervising these released prisoners has decreased.[2]

Figure 16.1
Parolees, 1990–1997

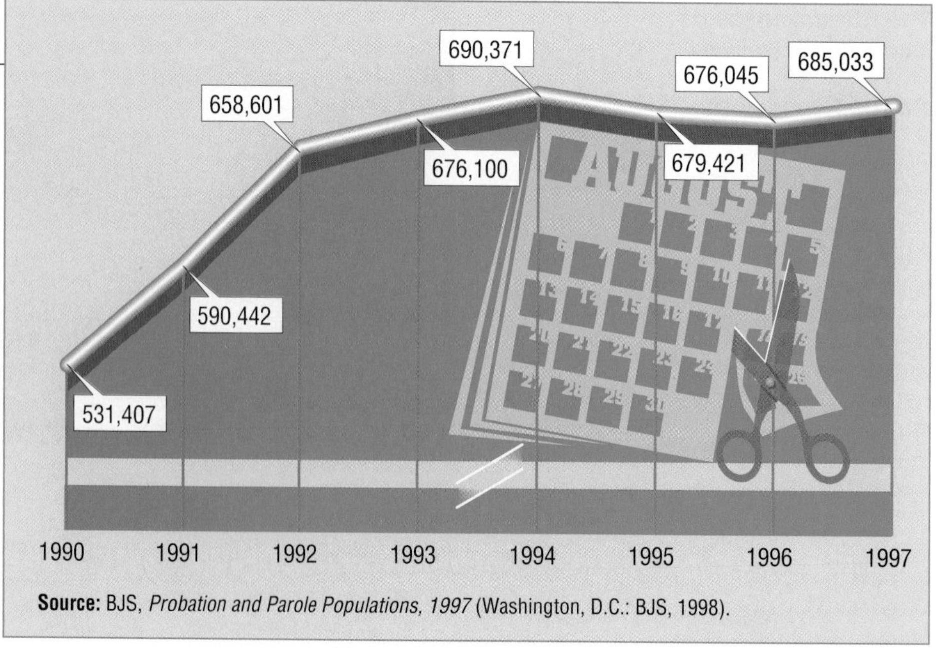

Source: BJS, *Probation and Parole Populations, 1997* (Washington, D.C.: BJS, 1998).

RELEASE FROM PRISON

The United States sentences more people to prison and keeps them there longer than almost all major countries in the world except for Russia (see Chapter 14). But, despite harsher penalties, sharply increasing prison populations, and the building of new prisons in almost every state and in the federal system, most prisoners convicted of felonies serve less than two years of their sentences before their first release from prison. Release from prison does not mean that prisoners are free. They are still in custody, meaning that they are under the supervision of parole officers. Prisoners obtain release in one of three ways:

1. **Discretionary release:** Parole boards determine the date of release from prisons. Prisoners are released conditionally and remain in state custody until the expiration of their full sentence.
2. **Mandatory release:** Legislatures and judges, not correctional authorities, determine sentences. Prisoners are released conditionally into the community by provisions of determinate sentencing laws and parole guidelines. Prisoners remain in state custody until the expiration of their terms.
3. **Expiration release:** In a few states, such as Maine and Connecticut, and in the federal government, parole has been abolished. In these jurisdictions, prisoners are released unconditionally at the end of their terms, less good time. These prisoners are no longer in state custody.[3]

Until the 1970s, prisoners were released at the discretion of parole boards. Parole boards decided when and under what conditions prisoners were ready to reenter society. The adoption of determinate sentencing (Chapter 12) and the abolition of parole boards markedly changed this practice. Mandatory release sharply reduced the discretionary decision making of some parole boards and eliminated it altogether in a few states. Despite this trend toward mandatory release mechanisms, most people still leave prison by the discretionary release of parole boards (see Figure 16.2). These released prisoners remain under the supervision of parole authorities until the expiration of their sentences.

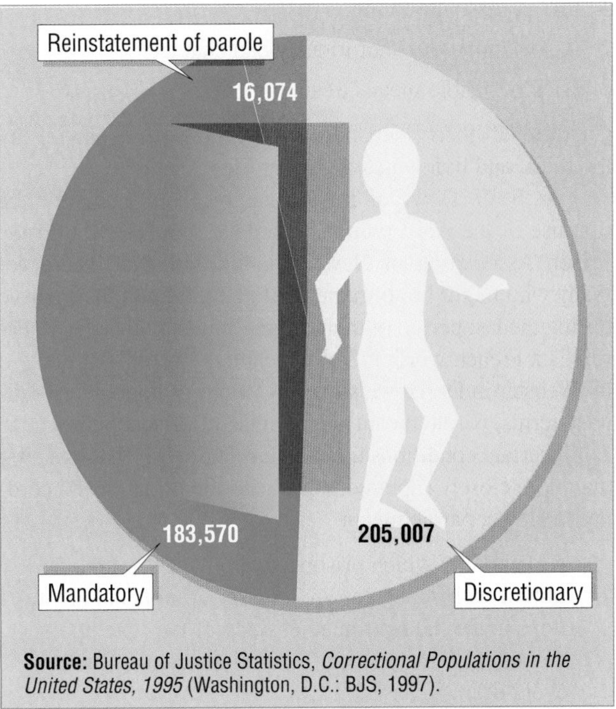

Source: Bureau of Justice Statistics, *Correctional Populations in the United States, 1995* (Washington, D.C.: BJS, 1997).

Figure 16.2
Number of Released Prisoners by Type of Release, 1995

THE HISTORY OF PAROLE

The practice of releasing prisoners before the end of their terms is ancient. It goes back at least as far as the sixteenth century when the Tudor monarchs issued general pardons releasing all people convicted of certain crimes in the hope that the act of mercy would "reform" them. The practice of conditional release was common throughout Europe in the nineteenth century, but Alexander Maconochie, a captain in the British Royal Navy, has generally received credit for beginning our modern practice of parole. Maconochie was put in charge of the infamous English penal colonies in New South Wales in 1840.

Maconochie believed that many prisoners were capable of reform. Therefore, he developed a plan to gradually prepare prisoners for their eventual return to society. He divided prisoners into three grades, each of which was progressively more like life outside prison. Prisoners could earn promotion through the grades by labor, study, and good behavior; the advance toward freedom was tied to success in prison programs that were intended to improve and reform prisoners.

The third grade in Maconochie's system was what today we call parole—conditional liberty with a "a ticket of leave." This document allowed prisoners to remain free as long as they observed the conditions of release attached to the ticket. Violating the rules of release meant returning to prison and starting all over again through the ranks. So conditional liberty, like the grades inside prison, was tied to success in living according to the rules outside prison walls.[4]

Sir Walter Crofton, director of Irish Convict Prisons, took over and developed Maconochie's idea. Named the Irish System, prisoners passed through similar stages to those designed by Maconochie. The "ticket of leave" under the Irish System was a form of conditional release. According to the ticket, prisoners were required to report to the chief of police of their home towns as soon as they arrived, and once a month thereafter until the expiration of their sentences. Conditions were attached to the ticket. Any of the following violations could lead to immediate arrest and return to prison:

1. Idle or dissolute living.
2. Association with "notoriously bad characters."
3. Lack of visible means of support.[5]

Conditional liberty depended on working hard, playing by the rules, and living a clean, sober life.

Dr. S. G. Howe of Boston has received credit for the first use of the word *parole.* "I believe," Dr. Howe told the Prison Association of New York in 1846, that "there are many who might be so trained as to be left upon their parole during the last period of their imprisonment with safety." Parole is a French word, literally meaning "word," but defined by Webster in Dr. Howe's time as "word of honour." In military terms, parole meant the promise of prisoners of war to fulfill certain conditions upon their release. It is that meaning that more closely captured Howe's notion of parole. According to Howe, parole meant

> a method by which prisoners who have served a portion of their sentences are released from penal institutions under the continued custody of the state upon conditions which permit their reincarceration in the event of misbehavior.[6]

As a result of these developments, parole came to include three elements:

1. *Conditional release* from incarceration before the expiration of the sentence.
2. *Supervision* under state custody until the end of the sentence.
3. *Revocation* for violations of the conditions of the release.

Parole was slow to catch on in American jurisdictions. Only three states had provided for parole by 1880. Then parole adoption speeded up. From 1880 to 1889, nine more states adopted parole. During the Progressive Era in the early twentieth century, most other states adopted parole. By 1940, every state and the federal government had some form of conditional release. That is still true today.[7]

Throughout its history, parole has generated controversy—usually heated controversy. Clair Wilcox, in his masterful survey of parole in Pennsylvania in the 1920s, surveyed newspapers and magazine articles about parole. He found headlines like "Turning the Criminals Loose" and "Uplifters and Politicians Free Convicts." He quotes the writer of one article, typical of those he surveyed:

> The organized efforts of well-meaning sentimentalists who are unable to see anything but the welfare of the individual criminal and are interested only in the reform of the criminal to the exclusion of any consideration of his victims or of society as a whole [have caused] desperate criminals, convicted of serious offenses and sent to prison for long terms [to be set free] wholesale [again] to prey upon society.[8]

Criticism of parole was not limited to Pennsylvania. Even former president William Howard Taft joined in the attacks. During his term as Chief Justice of the Supreme Court, Taft took the opportunity to tell an interviewer for the highly popular *Collier's Weekly* magazine:

> Paroles have been abused and should be granted with greater care. It is discouraging to read of the arrest and prosecution of one charged with a new felony who had committed some prior offense, had secured parole after a short confinement and then had used his release to begin again his criminal life.[9]

These criticisms originated in the 1920s, but they could have come from any decade. Criticisms of this nature are timeless. Every time a parolee commits a serious crime, it is major news. The reality, like so much else in criminal justice, is more complex than these criticisms of parole suggest. This chapter introduces you to the complexities—and, hopefully some of the reality—of the three major functions of parole: conditional release, supervision until final release, and revocation.

THE MISSIONS OF PAROLE

The decisions made in releasing and supervising parolees and in revoking their parole are made for a variety of reasons. Decision making is tied to the missions that parole is intended to accomplish. Among the general public, it is widely believed that the mission of parole is leniency, that parole was dreamed up by "bleeding hearts" or "sentimentalists" who care more about criminals than their victims. To others, the mission of parole is to rehabilitate offenders so that they can earn a living and obey the law. In reality, parole—like policing, courts, and prisons—is supposed to accomplish a number of complex and conflicting missions:

1. Punishment
2. Rehabilitation
3. Public safety
4. Prison management

Parolees are not in prison, but they remain in the custody of the state. From its early days the supporters of parole have had to defend it against the attack that it allowed criminals to avoid punishment for their crimes. As early as 1916, Warren F. Spalding, in an address to the American Prison Association, found it necessary to remind his audience that parole was part of punishment:

> A parole does not release the parolee from custody; it does not discharge him from the penal consequences of his act; it does not mitigate his punishment; it does not wash away the stain or remit the penalty. . . . Unlike a pardon, it is not an act of grace or mercy, of clemency or leniency. The granting of parole is merely permission to a prisoner to serve part of his sentence outside the walls of the prison. He continues to be in the custody of the authorities, both legally and actually, and is still under restraint. The sentence is in full force and at any

time when he does not comply with the conditions upon which he was released, or does not conduct himself properly, he may be returned, for his own good and in the public interest.[10]

"For his own good" points to the rehabilitation mission of parole. As we have seen from its brief history, parole was based on the idea that prisoners could reform. Parole was the last stage in the process of proving that prisoners had in fact changed from criminals into law-abiding citizens. The proof that prison programs have "worked" is in the behavior of parolees. If they find jobs and keep them, and if they obey the law, then the programs have worked. If, on the other hand, parolees cannot adapt to the outside world by "working hard and playing by the rules," then parole has not accomplished its reformative mission.

The "playing by the rules" part of reformation points to the mission of maintaining public safety. This mission involves predicting before release and ensuring by supervision during release that offenders do not commit crimes or otherwise "misbehave" while they are in custody on conditional release. Furthermore, it means revoking and possibly returning to incarceration parolees who violate the conditions of their parole that forbid them to endanger public safety.

A fourth mission of parole is to aid in the management of prisons. Parole can support the prison discipline system by denying release to "troublemakers" who repeatedly break prison rules. It can also promote order in prison by only paroling prisoners who have served the "average amount of time" for people convicted of the same offense.

Probably the most constant management mission of parole is its use in controlling prison populations. Since at least the nineteenth century, when prisons became "warehouses for the poor," releasing prisoners has been a mechanism to relieve prison crowding. Relieving prison overcrowding continues to remain one mission—if largely unstated—of parole. The record numbers of prisoners (see Chapter 14), the lag between prison construction and population growth (see Chapter 14), and the limits of public budgets have all placed pressure on release as a mechanism to reduce prison populations. Parole, by releasing prisoners before the end of their term, makes room for new prisoners who are waiting in jail or elsewhere to be transferred to prison.

As we have seen in the chapters on police, courts, and prisons and jails, varied goals are not always in harmony. The same is true of parole. Releasing more prisoners may well reduce prison populations, but perhaps at the risk of public safety. Close supervision outside prison may enhance public safety, but at the risk of interfering with rehabilitating offenders. Allowing the flexibility of rehabilitation may endanger public safety. These conflicting missions indicate the complexity and difficulty of decision making about conditional release, supervision during conditional release, and either final release from or revocation of parole.

PAROLE AUTHORITIES

The authority to grant parole varies from jurisdiction to jurisdiction. Two states, Maine and Connecticut, have abolished parole; of course, these states have no parole authority. Others have retained the indeterminate sentence. In most of these states, **parole boards** decide when to conditionally release prisoners before the end of their sentences. Nearly all parole authorities are part of the executive branch of government. They are ordinarily quite small agencies, but they have considerable power.

The Powers of Parole Boards

Parole boards determine not only when prisoners are released but also when parole conditions are violated. But the power of most parole boards extends beyond release and revocation. Depending on the jurisdiction, parole boards also have the following powers:

Parole boards have broad authority to release prisoners to the community. The membership of parole boards is determined by state and federal law. Who sits on the board affects how parole is administered.

- Rescinding a parole date that is already set.
- Issuing warrants and subpoenas.
- Setting the conditions of supervision.
- Restoring the civil rights of offenders.
- Granting final discharge from state custody.
- Ordering payment of restitution to victims.
- Ordering payment of part of the fees of prisoners' supervision.
- Granting furloughs to prisoners.
- Granting or recommending pardons and commutations of sentences.[11]

Parole Board Membership

Statutes and, in a few cases, state constitutions determine the size and the basic qualifications of parole board membership. These are important, but *who* sits on the board obviously plays a large role in how parole is administered. Most jurisdictions provide for five- to seven-member parole boards. More than half limit the terms of members to either four or six years. The average length of actual service on parole boards is a little more than four and a half years. Most jurisdictions prescribe minimum requirements for parole board membership. About half of the states require "some experience" in criminal justice. Seven states require a bachelor's degree. Twenty-three jurisdictions have no statutory requirements for board membership. Despite either the total lack of statutory requirements or the minimum requirements specified, parole board members tend to be well educated. Their average age is 53; nearly three-quarters are men; most are white.[12] (See Figures 16.3 and 16.4.)

The minimal requirements specified by statute give state governors—the central figures in the appointment of parole board members—enormous power to shape the administration of parole in individual states. Governors appoint parole board members in 44 states; and in 36 states, governors also have the power to appoint board chairs. In 11 states, either the attorney general or the state judiciary appoints the chair and members of parole boards. The president of the United States appoints both the chair and the members of the U.S. Parole Board.[13]

PAROLE RELEASE

Two basic mechanisms determine when prisoners are released—mandatory release and discretionary parole board decisions. Mandatory release was common until the 1890s, when parole boards with discretionary power to release prisoners were introduced. Discretionary release by parole boards was the major mechanism for release from prison until the revival of determinate sentences during the 1970s. (See Chapter 12.) States with determinate sentencing laws have sharply curtailed the discretionary powers of parole boards; a few have abolished parole entirely.

The process of parole begins when judges sentence defendants. In states with indeterminate sentences and traditional parole boards, judges sentence defendants to a minimum and a maximum term, such as 5 to 10 years. After inmates have served a portion of this term, less credit earned for good behavior and the performance of prison duties, they are *eligible* for parole. Parole boards decide whether to re-

Figure 16.3
Education of Parole Board Members. (Members with bachelor's degrees include those who also have graduate and law degrees.)

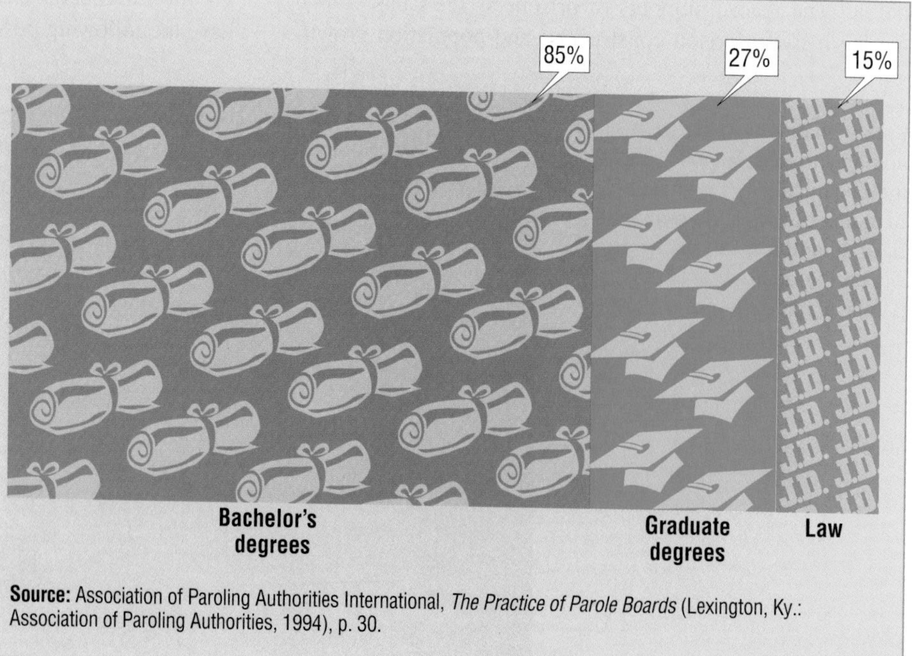

Source: Association of Paroling Authorities International, *The Practice of Parole Boards* (Lexington, Ky.: Association of Paroling Authorities, 1994), p. 30.

Figure 16.4
Race and Ethnicity of Parole Board Members

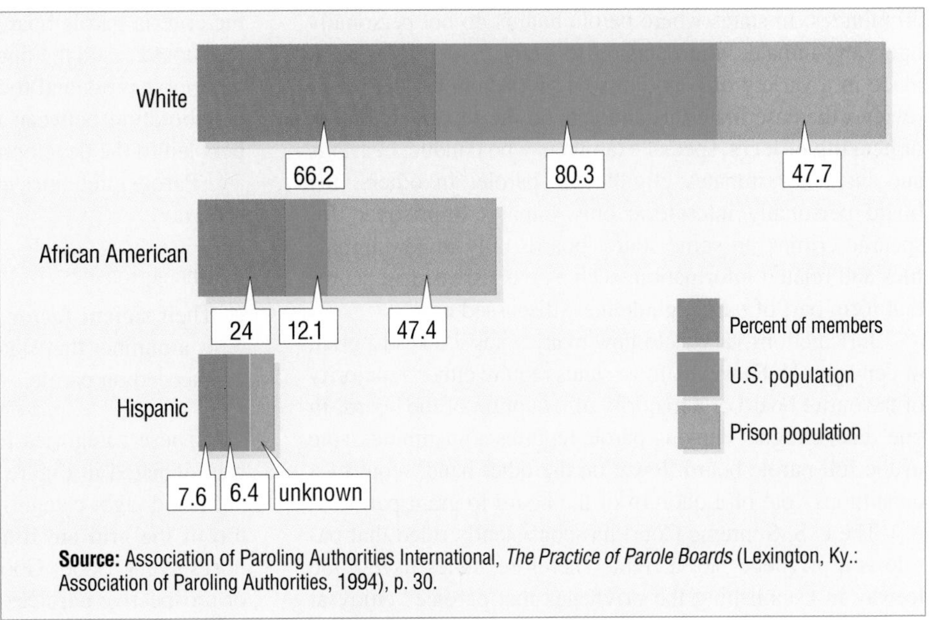

Figure 16.5
Number of States, Including the District of Columbia, and Type of Discretionary Parole

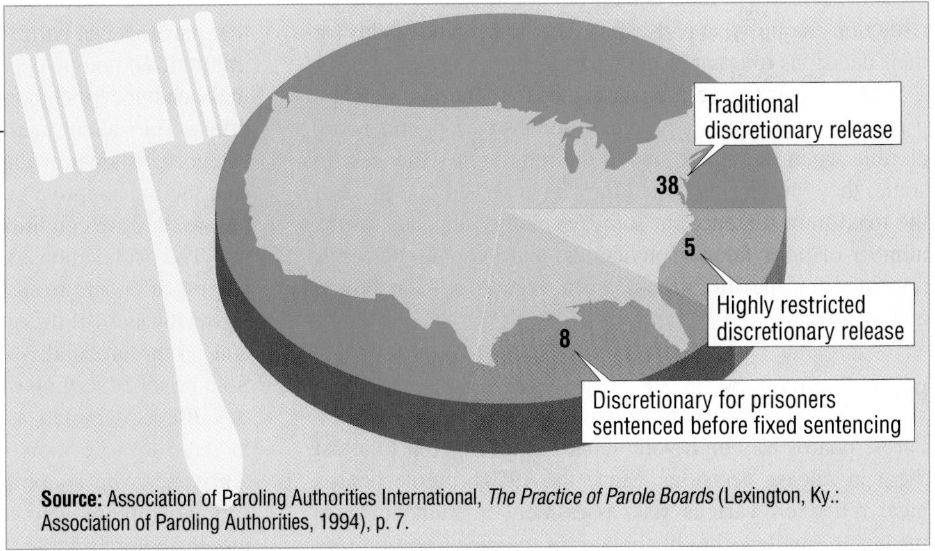

lease eligible prisoners onto parole. In states with determinate sentencing, whether in the form of mandatory minimum sentencing laws or sentencing guidelines, conditional release is mandatory. Parole authorities must release inmates onto parole when they have served a specified portion of their sentence.

Parole Board Release

Since the 1970s, critics have mounted serious challenges to the discretionary release of prisoners by parole boards. Linked with both the general hardening of public attitudes toward crime and demands for harsher punishment, the challenges to parole board discretionary release have resulted in considerable restrictions on discretionary release. Although they have received by far the most public attention, mandatory minimum sentence laws—especially the "three strikes and you're out" variety—are only one mechanism devised to limit or in some cases eliminate the discretion of parole boards to release prisoners. Sentencing guidelines have had a similar effect, particularly when their adoption is accompanied by the abolition of discretionary parole board release. However, despite the publicity surrounding mandatory minimum sentences and sentencing guidelines, parole boards remain the predominant mechanism for conditionally releasing prisoners from incarceration. (See Figure 16.5.)

Parole Release Hearing

In most jurisdictions, parole boards interview inmates in prison before granting or denying them parole. These hearings are usually brief and cursory, lasting between 15 and

30 minutes. In states where parole boards do not personally interview inmates, the decision to grant or deny parole is made in a variety of ways. In some jurisdictions, the board reviews the case materials and acts on the recommendation of **hearing officers,** special examiners who conduct hearings and interview inmates eligible for parole. In others, the board personally interviews only inmates imprisoned for specific crimes. In some states, boards only review inmate files and related information, such as risk assessment scores that form part of parole guidelines (discussed next).[14]

Jurisdictions vary as to how many votes it takes to grant or deny parole. However, most states require either a majority of the entire board or a majority of a quorum of the board. In one state, Oregon, denying parole requires a unanimous vote of the full parole board. Iowa, on the other hand, requires a unanimous vote of a quorum of the board to grant parole.[15]

The U.S. Supreme Court has consistently ruled that parole is a privilege, not a right. Therefore, states have wide leeway in establishing the privileges that parolees enjoy at parole hearings. In some states, inmates can bring lawyers to the hearings; in others, they cannot. In some states, they can present witnesses in their behalf, but not in others. Some jurisdictions require that parole boards give written reasons for their decisions to grant or deny parole.

Most states have established rules for determining when prisoners are eligible for parole. In some states, prisoners are eligible when they have served the minimum sentences; in some, they are eligible when they have served one-third of the maximum sentence; in some, eligibility depends on the number of prior felony convictions; and in some, parole is restricted for specific offenses such as murder, kidnapping, and aggravated rape.[16]

Parole Guidelines

Parole boards rely on a wide range of information to assist them in release decisions. Since the 1970s, parole boards have relied on various risk assessment instruments as a means to predict the likelihood of parolees committing crimes while on parole. Twenty-six states rely on risk assessment instruments. These instruments *guide* release decision making; they do not *determine* it. The instrument merely groups inmates according to their perceived risk of committing further crimes. If the board finds grounds to override the instrument-based prediction, it can do so; they still retain the ultimate power to grant or deny parole.[17]

Trying to predict the success of parolees during conditional release began in the 1920s, but the development of current risk assessment instruments, called **parole guidelines,** began in the 1970s. The National Council of Crime and Delinquency and the United States Parole Commission proposed to study parole decision making and turned to social scientists for help. Don Gottfredson and Leslie Wilkins became the pioneers in parole (and, by example, in bail and sentencing guidelines as well) when they headed up the Parole Decision-Making Project in the early 1970s. Relying on social science methods, Gottfredson and Wilkins examined the criteria parole boards used in their decision making. Parole boards used the findings to facilitate an evaluation of the appropriateness and the effectiveness of these criteria. This collaboration between researchers and parole board members led to the development of parole guidelines.[18]

Parole guidelines categorize offenders according to two criteria:

1. The seriousness of their offense. (See Figure 16.6.)
2. Their **salient factor score (SFS).** (See Figure 16.7.) SFS is a number that states the probability that a parolee will succeed on parole.

These categories form the two parts of the guidelines grid depicted in Figure 16.6. Along the left side of the grid are listed eight categories of offense seriousness. Along the top of the grid are listed the four parole probability prognoses (Very Good, Good, Fair, and Poor) based on the SFS of prospective parolees. Parole boards award points according to these salient factors.

Figure 16.7 depicts the salient factors included in the United States Parole Commission's guidelines and the points that parolees can earn for them. They can earn up to a maximum of 10 points, depending on their prior record of criminal behavior, prior commitments, age, and dependence on drugs. The salient factor score translates into the eight risk categories shown in Figure 16.6. The cells in the grid indicate the presumptive range of months offenders must serve before they are conditionally released.[19]

The grid demonstrates that the decision to conditionally release offenders from prison depends on a combination of the seriousness of the offense for which they are incarcerated and on the probability of their success if they are released. So a prisoner serving time for a "Category One" (least serious offense who has a "very good" SFS presumptively has to serve up to 6 months before parole. On the other hand, a prisoner who is doing time for a "Category Eight" (most serious) offense who has a "poor" SFS has to serve 150 months before release.

To their supporters, parole guidelines are appealing for a number of reasons. First, they appear to be objective. Both the seriousness of the offense and the salient factor scores derive from measurable criteria that reduce the subjective element in decision making. Second, because they are objective, they are also fairer, particularly because they reduce or eliminate unacceptable criteria such as gender, race, and class from the decision to release offenders on parole. Third, they are economical. Maintaining prisoners costs more than supervising parolees. The guidelines ranking keeps the highest-risk offenders who have committed the most serious offenses in expensive prisons longer. On the other hand, the ranking allows the less expensive release on parole of less serious offenders with the lowest risk to the community. Finally, reliance on the salient factor score releases the offenders most likely to succeed on parole. As a result, the kind and amount of supervision on parole depends on the degree of risk of the parolee.[20]

Offense Severity: Severity of Offense Behavior	Salient Factors 1981			
	Very Good (10–8 pints)	**Good (7–6 points)**	**Fair (5–4 points)**	**Poor 3–0 points)**
Category One (formerly "Low Severity")	6 months	6–9 months	9–12 months	12–16 months
Category Two (formerly "Low Moderate Severity")	8 months	8–12 months	12–16 months	16–22 months
Category Three (formerly "Moderate Severity")	10–14 months	14–18 months	18–24 months	24–32 months
Category Four (formerly "High Severity")	14–20 months	20–26 months	26–34 months	34–44 months
Category Five (formerly "Very High Severity")	24–36 months	36–48 months	48–60 months	60–72 months
Category Six (formerly "Greatest Severity")	40–52 months	52–67 months	67–78 months	78–100 months
Category Seven (formerly part of "Greatest II Severity")	52–80 months	64–92 months	78–110 months	100–148 months
Category Eight (formerly part of "Greatest II Severity")	100 months	120 months	150 months	150 months

Figure 16.6
Federal Parole Guidelines

Figure 16.7
Salient Factor Score (SFS)

A. Prior convictions/Adjudications (adult or juvenile)

None	= 3 points
One	= 2 points
Two	= 1 point
Three	= 0 points

B. Prior commitments of more than 30 days (adult or juvenile)

None	= 2 points
One or two	= 1 point
Three or more	= 0 points

C. Age at current offense/prior commitments

26 years of age or more	= 2 points*
20–25 years of age	= 1 point*
19 years of age or less	= 0 points
*Exception: If five or more prior commitments of more than 30 days (adult or juvenile) place an x here ___ and score this item	= 0 points

D. Recent commitment-free period (3 years)

No prior commitment of more than 30 days (adult or juvenile), or released to the community from last such commitment at least 3 years prior to the commencement of the current offense	= 1 point
Otherwise	= 0 points

E. Probation/parole/confinement/escape status violator this time

Neither on probation or parole, confinement, or escape status at the time of the current offense; nor committed as probation, parole, confinement, or escape status violator this time	= 1 point
Otherwise	= 0 points

F. Heroin/opiate dependence

No history of heroin or opiate dependence	= 1 point
Otherwise	= 0 points

Researchers have challenged these conclusions about the advantages of devices that predict the risk of failure of convicted offenders living outside prison. Kevin N. Wright, Todd R. Clear, and Paul Dickson studied a risk assessment instrument developed for Wisconsin that the National Institute of Corrections called a "model system" and that a number of other states adopted. Wright and his associates conducted a validation study of the system by choosing a sample of closed cases from New York, a state that had adopted the Wisconsin model. The instrument ranked *probationers* on their "potential risk to the community, thus permitting closer supervision of those who are most likely to offend again." The risk applies as well to parolees. The researchers concluded that their "analysis raises serious questions about the state-of-the-art of risk prediction." They found that risk assessment instruments developed for one population do not necessarily work with other populations. Furthermore, Wright and his colleagues confirmed other studies that showed that no matter what the instrument used, all predictions are "fairly weak."[21]

Furthermore, the degree of sophistication of the device does not appear to improve the accuracy of the predictions. Stephen D. Gottfredson and Don M. Gottfredson compared five different prediction methods of varying levels of sophistication used to predict the success of 4,500 parolees released from federal prisons. They found that simpler and easy-to-understand prediction methods worked as well as complex schemes based on advanced statistical techniques.[22]

Parole guidelines can also create legal problems. The Florida Parole Commission, for example, reported that civil litigation by adult male prisoners rose 450 percent following the introduction of parole guidelines. The increase in litigation forced the Parole Commission to increase its legal staff from two to seven lawyers during the first year of the guidelines. Civil litigation usually involved four issues:

1. Errors in computing salient factor scores.
2. Complaints about placement in offense severity levels.
3. Claims that parole examiners illegally elevated cases of aggravation.
4. Claims that the parole commission failed to consider mitigating factors.[23]

Mandatory Conditional Release

Parole guidelines restrict—but do not eliminate—the discretionary decision making of parole boards. As we saw in Chapter 12, both conservatives and liberals joined the public in demanding fixed sentences for convicted offenders during the 1970s. Along with this came the demand to restrict the discretionary power of parole boards to return prisoners to society; so the determinate sentencing statutes shifted the responsibility for fixing the release date to judges and legislatures. Determinate sentencing is based on the idea that judges—at the time of sentencing—should assign a specific amount of time the offender should serve. This replaced the indeterminate sentencing system in which judges sentenced offenders to a minimum and a maximum amount of time, such as "from 1 to 20 years," leaving it to parole boards to determine the exact date of release within that range.

States vary on how much discretion judges have. In determinate sentencing, at the time they enter prison, all offenders know how much time they have to serve. Release does not depend on participating in prison programs or on the degree of rehabilitation. Instead, prisoners are released at the end of the term fixed by the judge. However, this transfer of authority from parole boards to judges has not left corrections departments without effect on release.

All determinate sentencing states allow the deduction of "good time" from the time that prisoners are required to serve in prison. Most have also provided corrections officials with generous amounts of good time to allocate. Of course, statutes regulate both the rate of good time accumulation and the amount that officials can take away for "bad time." However, prison officers and staff have considerable discretion in interpreting the rules, in establishing procedures for the revocation of good time (see Chapter 14), and in utilizing good time to reduce prison crowding.[24]

Knowledge and Understanding CHECK

1. Compare the complaints with the reality of corrections.
2. Compare corrections in the United States with corrections in most other countries.
3. Identify the three ways prisoners obtain release from incarceration.
4. Compare parole with mandatory release.
5. Briefly trace the history of parole.
6. Identify and explain briefly the main missions of parole.
7. List the powers of parole boards.
8. Describe the membership qualification for parole board members.
9. Identify the two mechanisms for determining when to release prisoners.
10. Identify and describe some of the limits placed on discretionary release from prison.
11. Define and describe parole release hearings.
12. Describe and explain the significance of parole guidelines.
13. Are parole guidelines effective? Explain.
14. Identify four legal claims made regarding parole decisions.
15. Compare parole board release with mandatory release.

PAROLE SUPERVISION

A common misbelief among the general public is that when prisoners leave prison on parole they have "paid their debt to society" and are free to come and go as they please. The reality is, as the United States Sentencing Commission's *Federal Sentencing Guidelines Manual* puts it, judges are required to "order a term of supervised release to follow imprisonment when a sentence of imprisonment of more than one year is imposed. . . ." The period of supervised release ranges from five years for the most serious felonies to one year for the least serious offenses.[25]

Returning to society after serving time in prison is not easy, whether the release is conditional or outright (as when prisoners have served out their maximum term). People leave prison with clothes, a little cash, a list of the conditions of their parole, the name and address of their parole officer, and the *promised* job. Most are unskilled or have only minimal job skills, and they move from the regimented, controlled life of prison to life on the "outside," with all its difficulties and temptations. Todd R. Clear and George F. Cole list the following problems facing released prisoners:

- Long absence from family and friends.
- Legal and practical limits on employment.
- Suspiciousness and uneasiness of acquaintances.
- Strangeness of everyday living.[26]

According to Clear and Cole:

> No matter what the intentions of others, the former inmate always faces the cold fact that no truly "clean start" is possible. The change in status is from convict to former convict; the new status is nearly as stigmatizing as the old, and in many ways is more frustrating. In the former convict's mind, he or she is "free." Yes, the crime was a big mistake, but the prison time has paid for it and now there is a chance to turn over a new leaf. Yet most people look at the parolee askance and treat him or her as though there is still something to prove.[27]

The Conditions of Release

In addition to the practical and legal problems of adjustment and the obligation to obey the law, parolees have the added responsibility of complying with the specific conditions of

The Garden Project in San Francisco, California, is a program that provides jobs to former inmates like Phillip Limutan, seen here harvesting spinach, in raising and selling organic produce. Catherine Sneed, who started the program, had worked with inmates on learning such skills while they were still incarcerated, but had noticed that once the inmates left prison they were unable to find jobs in which they could work at their new trade. The Garden Project provides a transition in which former inmates can build structure in their lives once they have left prison.

their release. These conditions restrict their freedom, subjecting them to the monitoring of their movements, activities, and associations. This monitoring is based on the reasonable assumption that supervision is part of punishment, required by both parolees and society: society to provide public safety, parolees to avoid a return to bad habits and activities.

The conditions of release are an essential part of a **parole contract,** an agreement between the state and the offender. As its part of the contract, the state promises to release the offender on specific conditions. The offender, the other party to the contract, promises to abide by the conditions. If the offender fails to keep any of the conditions in the agreement or commits a new crime, the offender is in breach of the parole contract and the state can revoke it. (See Parole Revocation later in this chapter.)

The conditions of the parole contract are usually set out specifically in the contract, or the **certificate of parole.** Each jurisdiction determines its own conditions, and each individual agreement may have its own special conditions. However, most conditions resemble those included in the United States Parole Commission's certificate of discharge, issued to every parolee from the federal prison system. These conditions are:

1. You shall go directly to the district showing on this CERTIFICATE OF PAROLE (unless released to the custody of other authorities). Within three days after your arrival you shall report to your parole advisor if you have one, and to the United States Probation Officer whose name appears on this certificate. If in any emergency you are unable to get in touch with your parole advisor, or your probation officer or his office, you shall communicate with the United States Board of Parole, Department of Justice, Washington, D.C. 20537.
2. If you are released to the custody of other authorities, and after your release from physical custody of such authorities, you are unable to report to the United States Probation Officer to whom you are assigned within three days, you shall report instead to the nearest United States Probation Officer.
3. You shall not leave the limits of this CERTIFICATE OF PAROLE without written permission from the probation officer.
4. You shall notify your probation officer immediately of any change in your place of residence.
5. You shall make a complete and truthful written report (on a form provided for that purpose) to your probation officer between the first and third day of each month, and on the final day of parole. You shall also report to your probation officer at other times as he directs.
6. You shall not violate any law. Nor shall you associate with persons engaged in criminal activity. You shall get in touch immediately with your probation officer or his office if you are arrested or questioned by a law enforcement officer.
7. You shall not enter into any agreement to act as an "informer" or special agent for any law enforcement agency.
8. You shall work regularly, unless excused by your probation officer, and support your legal dependents, if any, to the best of your ability. You shall report immediately to your probation officer any change in employment.
9. You shall not drink alcoholic beverages to excess. You shall not purchase, possess, use, or administer marijuana or narcotic or other habit forming or dangerous drugs, unless prescribed or advised by a physician. You shall not frequent places where such drugs are illegally sold, dispensed, used, or given away.
10. You shall not associate with persons who have a criminal record unless you have the permission of your probation officer.
11. You shall not have firearms (or other dangerous weapons) in your possession without the written permission of your probation officer, following prior approval of the United States Board of Parole.
12. You shall, if ordered by the Board pursuant to Section 4203, Title 18, U. S. C., as amended October 1970, reside in and/or participate in a treatment program of a Community Treatment Center operated by the Bureau of Prisons, for a period not to exceed 120 days.[28]

Parole Programs

Most parolees are required to participate in some kind of activity as a condition of their release. This may be no more than filing regular reports with parole agencies. It can also include living in special housing, performing community service, working, going to school, getting vocational training, or participating in drug, alcohol, sex, and other treatment programs. Many of these programs resemble those in which probationers participate (see Chapter 13). In fact, probationers and parolees are often in the same programs together, and often the same correctional officers act as both probation and parole officers.

But parolees differ from probationers in some important respects. Parolees have lived in confinement, sometimes for a long time. The effects of prison life put them in special circumstances requiring major adjustment to living outside prison. Also, parolees are sometimes more serious offenders than probationers. For both these reasons, parolees generally require more intensive supervision than do probationers.[29]

Parole Officers

Parole officers are responsible for the supervision of the vast majority of parolees during the period of their conditional release. As we have seen throughout this text, most criminal justice professionals have always had to play conflicting roles to suit the multiple and conflicting missions of criminal justice. In this respect, parole officers are much like professionals in courts and police departments. Former corrections commissioner and penal reformer David Fogel succinctly described the conflict between two basic—and conflicting—roles of parole officers: counselors and law enforcement officers:

> [A] parole officer can be seen going off to his/her appointed rounds with Freud in one hand and a .38 Smith and Wesson in the other hand. It is by no means clear that Freud is as helpful as the .38 in most areas where parole officers venture. . . . Is Freud backup to the .38? Or is the .38 carried to support Freud?[30]

Supervising parolees has always meant both treatment for the rehabilitation of individual parolees and surveillance for the purpose of protecting society. The treatment mission arose from the social work approach to corrections. Social work adopts a **casework model** of treatment, in which supervision provides the basis for a treatment plan in which individual parolees are the cases. **Welfare parole officers** use all the information they can get about individual parolees ("cases") to diagnose their needs and design a treatment plan. This plan is supposed to rehabilitate parolees, which usually means reintegrate them into the community as people who "work hard and play by the rules." Or, as the President's Task Force on Corrections put it, "developing the offender's effective participation in the major social institutions of the school, business and the church . . . which offer access to a successful career."[31]

Since the 1970s, with the tougher attitude toward crime and the accompanying shift in emphasis from rehabilitation to incapacitation and punishment, the law enforcement role of parole officers has taken precedence. The National Conference on Parole offered a definition of the surveillance role of parole officers: "Surveillance is that activity of the parole officer which utilizes watchfulness, checking, and verification of certain behavior of a parolee without contributing to a helping relationship with him."[32]

Law enforcer parole officers see themselves as the guardians of middle-class morality. To safeguard ordinary, law-abiding people, such parole officers have to watch parolees to make sure they follow the rules and do not victimize innocent people. (See Chapter 13 on types of probation officers.)

The law enforcer and welfare roles do not necessarily conflict. According to Richard McCleary's *Dangerous Men,* a study of parole officers at work, parole officers sort through their caseload to identify the "dangerous men." This means identifying those parolees who "do not demonstrate willingness to accept the PO as a therapist." These parolees become candidates for surveillance instead of treatment. So parole officers "rehabilitate the offenders who are amenable to treatment, while simultaneously protecting society from those who prove to be dangerous."[33]

Daniel Glaser identified another type of parole officer—the passive officer. **Passive parole officers** are just doing a job, putting in only the minimum effort required, doing only enough to get by to keep their jobs. Charles L. Erickson offered the following satirical advice to passive officers who want to "fake" their way to a "trouble-free caseload."

> "I'm just so busy—never seem to have enough time." A truly professional execution of this ploy does require some preparation. Make sure that your desktop is always inundated with a potpourri of case files, messages, memos, unopened mail, and professional literature. . . . Have your secretary hold all your calls for a few days and schedule several appointments for the same time. When, after a lengthy wait, the . . . [parolee] is finally ushered into your presence, impress him (or her) with the volume of your business. . . . Always write while conversing with the subject, and continue to make and receive telephone calls. Interrupt your dialogue with him to attend to other important matters, such as obtaining the daily grocery list from your wife or arranging to have your car waxed. Apologize repeatedly and profusely for these necessary interruptions and appear to be distracted, weary, and slightly insane. Having experienced the full treatment, it is unlikely that the probationer will subsequently try to discuss with you any matters of overwhelming concern. He could even feel sorrier for you than he does for himself. You should henceforth be able to deal with him on an impersonal basis, if indeed he tries to report anymore at all.[34]

Parole supervision has always suffered from criticism, as has any criminal justice policy that seems to "coddle criminals." But since the 1970s, the attacks have become especially severe. Crime control supporters have—as always—attacked parole as "soft on crime." Due process advocates have hammered it for being arbitrary and unfair. Rehabilitation proponents have denounced the lack of meaningful programs to help parolees.

These attacks have led to a shift in the focus of parole in general, and of parole supervision in general, to the missions of punishment and public safety. So, although the welfare role still exists and the passive officer will always be with us, it is the law enforcer who predominates in conditional release at the end of the twentieth century.[35]

The predominance of the law enforcement mission of parole has allowed a shift in resources from the needs of parolees to the risks they pose for the community. According to Cheryl L. Ringel, Ernest L. Cowles, and Thomas C. Castellano:

> The shift in emphasis from offender treatment needs to offender risk meant that scarce resources could be directed away from treatment programs without damage to the integrity of the model. No longer was there a strong implicit assumption that the correctional agencies providing such supervision had to provide extensive programs to bring about offender change. Such treatment became more the offender's responsibility, as program participation became less often a condition of supervision and offenders were also more frequently called upon to pay the costs of such programs.[36]

THE EFFECTIVENESS OF CONDITIONAL RELEASE

The shift in emphasis in parole from the needs of offenders to the risks they pose to public safety raises the important public policy question: How effective is conditional release? In corrections, "effective" usually means lack of **recidivism,** or the return to criminal behavior. Recidivism means different things to different researchers. Usually, it consists of three measures:

1. New criminal event—arrest, conviction, or revocation of parole for a new crime.
2. Duration until return to criminal behavior.
3. Seriousness of the new criminal behavior.

The effectiveness of parole varies depending on the definition of recidivism selected. For example, effectiveness will be dramatically less if you define recidivism (as many do) as an arrest for any offense, however minor, at any time after release from prison. On the other hand, effectiveness will increase dramatically if you define recidivism (as some researchers do) as the return to prison for the commission of a felony within one or two years. For a long time, the numbers have indicated that more than half of all prisoners released on parole return to prison—*eventually* (see Figure 16.8).

However recidivism is defined, empirical research findings are decidedly mixed on how parole supervision impacts the rates of recidivism. A Connecticut court decision provided a unique opportunity for researchers Howard R. Sacks and Charles H. Logan to study the effect of parole release on recidivism. In *Szawarak v. Warden,* the Connecticut Supreme Court declared that the legislature had violated the Connecticut constitution by authorizing sentences of more than one year for Class D felonies (less serious felonies such as unarmed robbery, burglary, and possession of drugs). So, the court ordered the release of all prisoners who had served more than one year for these felonies. Under ordinary circumstances, all of these prisoners eventually would get paroled. This group of offenders became the experimental group in a natural experiment. The control group consisted of similar prisoners who were released on parole at the ordinary time. After the first year, the researchers found that parole had only modest effects on recidivism. Parolees did avoid conviction at a slightly higher rate (about 7 percent) than the discharged prisoners in the experimental group. The researchers found that parole had no significant effect on the seriousness of the offenses committed.[37]

Further, they found that the modest positive effects of parole supervision on recidivism were short-lived. According to Sacks and Logan:

> [P]arole had no preventive effects after two (or three) years following release. Parole seems to affect recidivism while the parolee is on parole (and for a short period thereafter) but these effects soon begin to dissipate and tend to disappear by the time parolees have finished two years in the community.[38]

The researchers also found no significant differences between parolees and those discharged outright in terms of the seriousness of the offenses that they committed following release. One positive finding was that parolees did remain in the community about six months longer than discharged offenders before they committed new crimes; "parole does not prevent a return to crime, but it does delay it."[39]

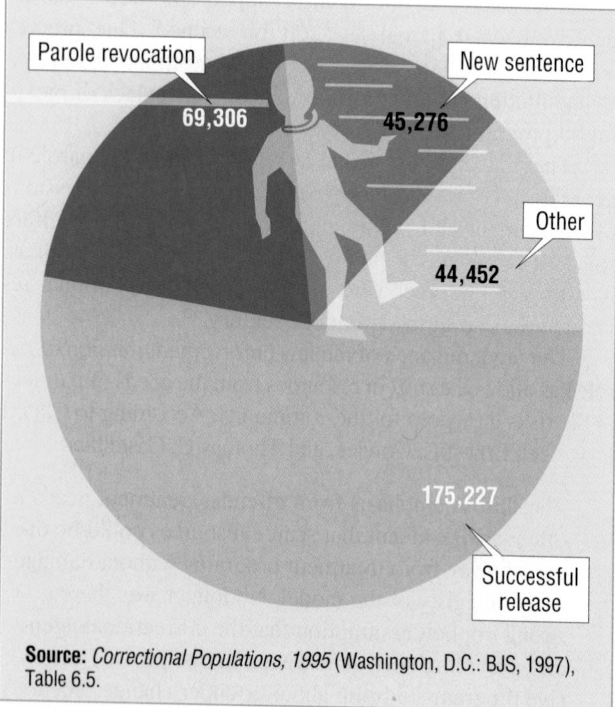

Source: *Correctional Populations, 1995* (Washington, D.C.: BJS, 1997), Table 6.5.

Figure 16.8
Number of Conditionally Released Prisoners Returning to Prison, 1995.

Use *Your* Discretion

Does the success of parole depend on the kind of parole supervision?

Some research suggests that the success of parole depends on the kind of supervision parolees receive. Mark Jay Lerner evaluated parole in the state of New York, a state in which the law enforcement mission comes first. The rehabilitation mission of helping parolees definitely is considered less important. According to the New York State Department of Correctional Services:

> The Parole officer is a professional caseworker who at no time is permitted to put the rights of the individual parolee ahead of the rights of society.

He protects society by helping the parolee become a productive member of society but at all times he takes every precaution to insure the parolee's activities are not a threat to society.[40]

In keeping with this law enforcement orientation, parole officers are "armed with .38 caliber revolvers [and] have even more extensive investigative and surveillance powers than those of policemen." This led the Citizens' Inquiry on Parole and Criminal Justice to conclude:

> [I]n New York, the designation of parole officers as peace officers—arming them with guns, using technical violations of parole rules as a basis for return to prison, and encouraging surveillance activities—were indicators of a higher emphasis on law enforcement than is found in other parole systems.[41]

Lerner sampled 195 misdemeanant parolees. About half were in the control group of inmates released at the end of their sentences; the other half were inmates released on parole. Using the electronic retrieval system in New York State, Lerner collected arrest information for two years following the release of the 195 inmates in his sample. He found that "parole supervision reduces criminal behavior of persons released from local correctional institutions." Figure 16.9 shows the results of Lerner's study. Although Lerner concedes that his study did not try to explain why parole reduced recidivism, he speculated that the "effect is probably due to the deterrent or law-enforcement effect of parole supervision and not to the popular notions of rehabilitation."[42]

Two evaluations of different levels of supervision of parolees in California confirm neither Lerner's findings about the success of parole nor his speculation that the law enforcement orientation of parole reduces recidivism. Deborah Star reported the results of two surveys of the effectiveness of parole supervision in California. In the first, a group of felons (excluding inmates convicted of murder, rape, and some other serious offenses) was randomly assigned to either an experimental group of parolees who received reduced levels of supervision or a control group that received regular parole. The experimental group had significantly fewer face-to-face contacts initiated by parole officers for the purpose of checking up on parolees than the control group on regular parole. After six months, the researchers found no significant difference in either the frequency or the severity of criminal activity between the control group on regular parole and the experimental group on reduced supervision. A follow-up study after one year confirmed the researchers' conclusions that reduced supervision had no significant effect on either the frequency or the severity of criminal activity.[43]

The High Control Project

In a second study, Star reported the results of the High Control Project, another parole experiment conducted by the California Department of Corrections. This study evaluated the effects of increased surveillance and investigation of parolees to control their criminal activities. The High Control Project differed from regular parole in the following important ways:

1. It emphasized control of, not service to, parolees.
2. It placed primary emphasis on conducting investigation of parolees' possible criminal activities *before* arrest. Traditional parole supervision focuses on investigation after arrest. (See Parole Revocation later.)

Figure 16.9
Percent of Parolees Compared with the General Population

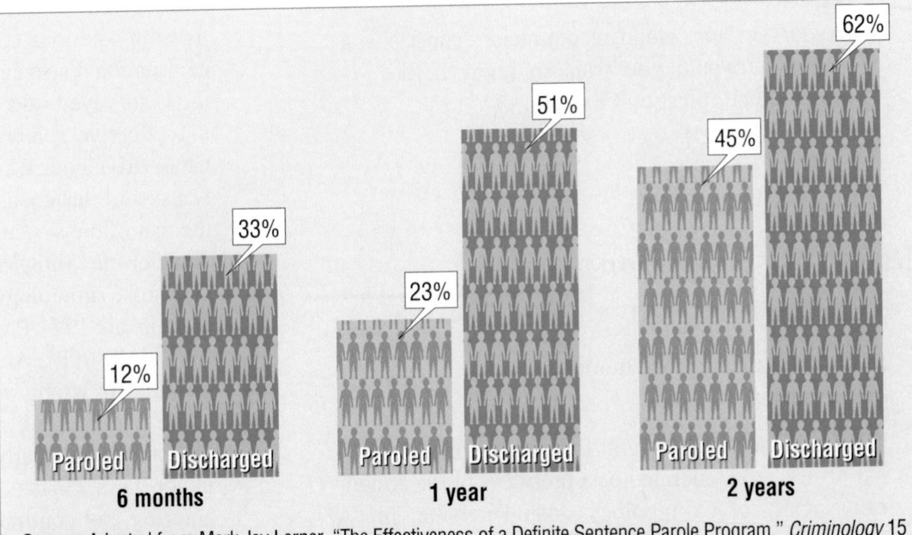

Source: Adapted from Mark Jay Lerner, "The Effectiveness of a Definite Sentence Parole Program," *Criminology* 15 (1997), Table 1m, p. 220.

3. It targeted a group of parolees selected by agents as "high risk" cases.
4. It used specialized units of parole officers who specialized in law enforcement.[44]

The High Control Project relied on two law enforcer tactics to test the effectiveness of high levels of control. The first tactic, criminal investigation, utilized high control parole officers to conduct short-term investigations of parolees suspected of current involvement in illegal activities. The purposes of the investigations were to verify the involvement, apprehend the suspected parolees, and aid in successfully prosecuting them. The second tactic, intensive supervision, utilized parole officers with reduced caseloads to closely monitor parolees with serious prior criminal records. The purpose of the close surveillance was to prevent parolees from returning to criminal activities.[45]

Using a quasi-experimental design, high control parolees were compared with regular parolees. The evaluation that followed showed that neither enhanced investigation nor intensive supervision significantly affected either the frequency or the severity of criminal behavior. The researchers concluded that "there was nothing readily apparent about intensive supervision which would suggest that a close watch may deter parolees from returning to criminal activity and thereby reduce recidivism rates." However, researchers did find that criminal investigation in the High Control Project was more successful than regular parole in verifying criminal behavior once it had occurred, even if it did not significantly affect the frequency and severity of that behavior.[46]

CRITICAL THINKING

1. Summarize the three studies described.
2. Would you recommend changing the type of parole supervision based on these findings? Explain.
3. If you said you would recommend against changing, what would you want to know before you changed your position? Explain.

Use *Your* Discretion

Should we spend more money on parole supervision?

[The following is an excerpt from the respected criminal justice researcher and past president of the American Society of Criminology, Joan Petersilia. In "A Crime Control Rationale for Reinvesting in Community Corrections," Petersilia suggests some policies for community corrections generally, and for parole especially. These suggestions are based on recent empirical research and stem from the debate over whether to spend our tax dollars on building more prisons or on crime prevention and supervision of offenders in the community.]

Last year Congress passed the most ambitious crime bill in our nation's history, the Violent Crime Control and Law Enforcement Act of 1994. It allocated $22 billion to expand prisons, impose longer sentences, hire more police, and to a lesser extent, fund prevention programs. But as part of the Republicans' "Contract with America," the House significantly revised the Act, and the money allocated to prevention programs was eliminated. The amended bill—whose price tag rose to $30 billion—shifted nearly all of the $5 billion targeted for prevention programs into prison construction and law enforcement. As a *Los Angeles Times* op-ed concluded of the whole matter: "what started out last legislative season as a harsh and punitive bill has gotten downright Draconian."

While such tough-on-crime legislation has political appeal, it finds almost no support among criminal justice practitioners and scholars. They are uniformly agreed that such efforts—which endorse an "enforcement model" to the sacrifice of all else—will do little to curb crime. In recent months, organizations as diverse as the International Association of Chiefs of Police (IACP), the U.S. Conference of Mayors, the American Bar Association (ABA), National Governors Association, the League of Cities, The RAND Corporation, the National Council on Crime and Delinquency (NCCD), the Campaign for an Effective Crime Policy (CECP), and the National Research Council have all voiced opposition to the approach.

Even prison wardens (who stand to benefit from an enforcement model) uniformly reject the crime-fighting solutions coming out of Washington. In a recent national survey of prison wardens, 85 percent of those surveyed said that elected officials are not offering effective solutions to America's crime problem. Chase Riveland, Washington State Director of Corrections, said that focusing only on prisons and ignoring the rest of the system is "drive-by legislation, at best." And Jerome Skolnick, President of the American Society of Criminology (ASC), spoke of the federal efforts in his 1994 Presidential Address and entitled it, "What *Not* to Do About Crime."

What is wrong with the current proposals? Some argue that they are racist, others argue that they cost too much, but nearly everyone agrees they have two major flaws: (1) they fail to prevent young people from entering and continuing a life of crime; and (2) they leave the vast majority of criminals, who are serving sentences on probation and parole rather than prison or jail, unaffected.

Criminologists have long observed that age 18 is the year of peak criminality. Analysis recently completed by Alfred Blumstein at Carnegie-Mellon showed that today we have the smallest cohort of 18-year-olds we will see for at least the next 15 years. Next year, the number is going to start going up, and the biggest growth will occur in the number of African American children who are now four to nine years old. Blumstein (1994) recently observed:

> These young people are being less well educated and socialized, and as a result are easy recruits for the booming crack cocaine industry, where weapons are a business accessory for an increasing number of youths. The result will be a steep increase in juvenile and young adult violent crime, unless we begin investing in community-based programs to better socialize kids when their parents are not doing so. This is a population crying out for our attention, and, as a society, we need to find a means to divert them from becoming as violent as their big brothers.

As more young people are recruited into and retained in a criminal lifestyle, the ability of back-end responses (such as imprisonment) to increase public safety is severely limited because of the replenishing supply of young people who are entering into criminal careers.

The second, and equally important, reason that current federal efforts will fail is that they focus exclusively on prisons as a corrections strategy, ignoring the fact that most criminals are serving probation and parole sentences. In 1993 there were just under five million adult (convicted) criminals—or about one in every 39 Americans. Seventy-two percent of all identified criminals were not in prison, but serving sentences in the community on probation or parole supervision. Even though we have quadrupled the number of prisoners in the past decade, prisoners are still less than of the convict population, and the vast majority of offenders remain in the community amongst us (Bureau of Justice Statistics, 1995). If we are to effectively control crime—as opposed to exacting retribution and justice—we must focus our efforts where the offenders are, which is in the community reporting to probation and parole officers.

Despite the fact that both crime bills were touted by their proponents as comprehensive approaches to the crime problem, neither the 1994 Crime Act or the 1995 "Taking Back Our Streets" proposal *even mentions* probation or parole, much less provides funding or direction for revising programs or practices. Moreover, the federal bill will likely take money away from community corrections budgets, which are already at a dangerously low level, to fund the expanded prison space required to comply with federal mandates requiring state prisoners to serve 86 percent of their sentence (so called "truth in sentencing").

This article addresses the public safety consequences of current probation and parole practices. It contends that current crime policies are neither comprehensive nor will they be effective unless we focus on the needs and risks posed by probationers and parolees. Whether we are able to control the crime propensities of *these* offenders is critical to the effectiveness of any anti-crime program.

Who Is on Probation and Parole?
A Profile of the Population

The public misunderstands the safety risks and needs posed by offenders currently under community supervision. . . . To gauge the public safety risks of probationers and parolees, it is useful to consider the population as a whole in terms of conviction crimes. . . . [A]bout 16 percent of all adult probationers were convicted of violent crimes, as were 26 percent of parolees. This means that on any given day in the U.S. in 1991, there were an estimated 435,000 probationers and 155,000 parolees residing in local communities who have been convicted of violent crime—or over a half million offenders. If we compare that to the number of violent offenders residing in prison during the same year, we see that there were approximately 372,500 offenders convicted of violent crime *in* prison, and approximately 590,000 *outside* in the community on probation and parole! Overall, we can conclude that nearly three times as many violent offenders (1.02 million) were residing in the community as were incarcerated in prison (372,000). These numbers make painfully clear why a failure to provide adequate funding for community corrections invariably places the public at risk. . . .

Despite the unprecedented growth in probation populations and their more serious clientele, probation budgets have not grown. From 1977 to 1990 prison, jail, parole, and probation populations all about tripled in size. Yet only spending for prisons and jails had accelerated growth in overall government expenditures. In 1990 prison and jail spending accounted for two cents of every state and local dollar spent—twice the amount spent in 1977. Spending for probation and parole accounted for two-tenths of one cent of every dollar spent in 1990—unchanged from what it was in 1977. Today, although nearly *three-fourths* of correctional clients are in the community, only about *one-tenth* of the correctional budget goes to supervise them.

The increase in populations, coupled with stagnant or decreasing funding, means that caseloads (the number of offenders an officer is responsible for supervising) keep increasing. . . .

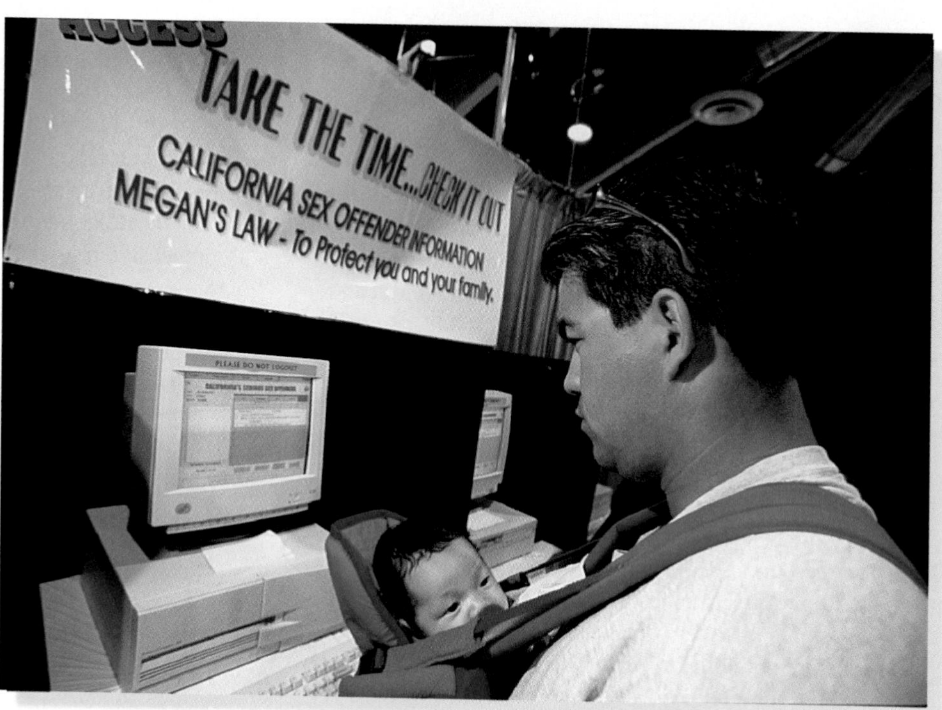

More people who have been convicted of violent crimes live within communities as probationers or parolees than are incarcerated in prisons. Yet public fears tend to revolve around certain types of criminals released into the community, especially sex offenders. This has led to legislation such as Megan's Law, which allows community members, such as this man at the Los Angeles County Fair, to view information on registered sex offenders that was once restricted. Do you think the public has a right to know this information?

But neglect in funding has had serious consequences. As caseloads rise, there is less opportunity for personal contact between officer and offender, limiting any ability of the officer to bring about positive change in the offender, or refer the offender to appropriate community-based resources and programs (which incidentally are also being reduced). Court-ordered fines and restitution don't get paid, and community service doesn't get performed. . . .

What Can We Do? A Proposal to Develop an Integrated Treatment/Control Program for Drug Offenders

The grim situation described above is known to most of those who work in the justice system or study it. Until we curb the criminal activities of the three-fourths of criminals who reside in the community, real reductions in crime or prison commitments are unlikely. But just as there is growing agreement about the nature of the problem, there is also an emerging consensus about how to address it.

We need to first regain the public's trust that probation and parole can be meaningful, credible sanctions. During the past decade, many jurisdictions developed "intermediate sanctions" as a response to prison crowding. These programs (e.g., house arrest, electronic monitoring, and intensive supervision) were designed to be community-based sanctions that were tougher than regular probation, but less stringent and expensive than prison. The program models were good and could have worked, except for one critical factor: they were usually implemented without creating an organizational capacity to ensure compliance with the court-ordered conditions. Intermediate sanctions were designed with smaller caseloads enabling officers to provide both services and monitoring for new criminal activity, but they never were given the resources needed to enforce the sanctions or provide necessary treatment. . . .

But not all programs have had this experience. In a few instances, communities invested in intermediate sanctions and made the necessary treatment and work programs available to offenders. And, most importantly, the programs worked: in programs where offenders both received surveillance (e.g., drug tests) and participated in relevant treatment, recidivism was reduced 20–30 percent. Recent program evaluations in Texas, Wisconsin, Oregon, and Colorado have found similarly encouraging results. Even in BJS's national probation follow-up study, it was found that if probationers were participating in or making progress in treatment programs, they were less likely to have a new arrest (38 percent) than either those drug offenders who had made no progress (66 percent) or those who were not ordered to be tested or treated (48 percent).

There now exists rather solid empirical evidence that ordering offenders into treatment and getting them to participate, reduces recidivism. So, the first order of business must be to allocate sufficient resources so that the designed programs (incorporating both surveillance and treatment) can be implemented. Sufficient monetary resources are essential to obtaining and sustaining judicial support, and achieving program success.

Once we have that in place, we need to create a public climate to support a reinvestment in community corrections. Good community corrections costs money, and we should be honest about that. We currently spend about $200 per year, per probationer, for supervision. It is no wonder that recidivism rates are so high. Effective treatment programs cost at least $12,000-$14,000 per year. Those resources will be forthcoming only if the public believes the programs are both effective and punitive.

Public opinion is often cited by officials as the reason for supporting expanded prison policies. According to officials, the public demands a "get tough on crime" policy, which is synonymous with sending more offenders to prison for longer terms. We must publicize recent evidence showing that offenders—whose opinion on such matters is critical for deterrence—judge some intermediate sanctions as *more* punishing than prison. Surveys of offenders in Minnesota, Arizona, New Jersey, Oregon, and Texas reveal that when offenders are asked to equate criminal sentences, they judge certain types of community punishments as *more* severe than prison.

One of the more striking examples comes from Marion County, Oregon. Selected nonviolent offenders were given the choice of serving a prison term or returning to the community to participate in the Intensive Supervision Probation (ISP) program, which imposed drug testing, mandatory community service, and frequent visits with the probation officer. About a third of the offenders given the option between ISP or prison chose prison. When Minnesota inmates and corrections staff were asked to equate a variety of criminal sentences, they rated three years of Intensive Supervision Probation as equivalent in punitiveness to one year in prison.

What accounts for this seeming aberration? Why should anyone prefer imprisonment to remaining in the community—no matter what the conditions? Some have suggested that prison has lost some of its punitive sting, and hence its ability to scare and deter.

The length of time an offender can be expected to serve in prison has also decreased—the latest statistics show that the average U.S. prison term for those released to parole is 17 months. But more to the point, for less serious offenders, the expected time served can be much less. In California, for example, more than half of all offenders entering prison in 1995 are expected to serve six months or less. Offenders on the street seem to be aware of this, perhaps because of the extensive media coverage such issues are receiving.

For convicted felons, freedom, of course, is preferable to prison. But the type of program being advocated here—combining heavy doses of surveillance and treatment—does not represent freedom. In fact, as suggested above, such community-based programs may have more punitive bite than prison. . . .

It is important to publicize these results, particularly to policymakers, who say they are imprisoning such a large number of offenders because of the public's desire to get tough on crime. But it is no longer necessary to equate criminal punishment solely with prison. The balance of sanctions between probation and prison can be shifted, and at some level of intensity and length, intermediate punishments can be the more dreaded penalty.

CRITICAL THINKING

Assume you are on the staff of a legislator. You receive a copy of this article by Joan Petersilia.

1. On the basis of the article, how would you advise your legislator to vote on a proposal to spend more of the taxpayers' money on corrections? Support your advice with specific information and arguments from this article.
2. If you cannot decide what advice to give, what questions do you want answered and what further information do you need before you advise your legislator?
3. In giving your advice, how would you use the mixed results of the empirical research discussed in the Effectiveness of Conditional Release section?

PAROLE REVOCATION

"The enforcement leverage that supports the parole conditions derives from the authority to return the parolee to prison to serve out the balance of his sentence if he fails to abide by the rules," wrote Chief Justice Warren Burger in the landmark parole revocation case, *Morrissey v. Brewer* (excerpted in the Use Your Discretion case "What process is 'due' to parolees?" later). Fifty-five percent of parolees successfully complete their parole and are released from state custody. Forty percent return to prison because of new crimes; or because they have had their parole revoked or revocation is pending.[47]

Parole revocation occurs for two reasons:

1. New crimes.
2. Technical violations—that is, they violate any of the noncriminal conditions of their release.

Parole officers have considerable discretion to decide whether they will or won't report new crimes or technical violations. Revocation actually takes place only if parolees:

- Are arrested on serious criminal charges.
- Repeatedly violate the conditions of their parole.
- Abscond or cannot otherwise be found.
- Abuse alcohol or other drugs.
- Carry weapons.[48]

The Fourteenth Amendment provides that "No state shall deprive any person of life, liberty, or property without due process of law." Parole officers and parole boards are agents of the state. As such, they cannot revoke parole (which is part of the *liberty* in the amendment) "without due process of law." But what process is "due" to parolees? Not the full, impressive array of rights afforded criminal defendants not yet convicted of crimes, and certainly not the rights afforded people who are not even suspected of committing crimes. (See Chapters 2, 6, 9, and 10 for discussions of these rights.) According to the Supreme Court, "what is needed is an informal hearing structured to assure that the finding of a parole violation will be based on verified facts and that the exercise of discretion will be informed by an accurate knowledge of the parolee's behavior."[49]

A federal statute provides for the following two-stage revocation procedure to guarantee due process:

> [A]ny alleged parole violator summoned or retaken . . . shall be accorded the opportunity to have—
>
> (A) *a preliminary hearing* at or reasonably near the place of the alleged parole violation or arrest, without unnecessary delay, to determine if there is probable cause to believe that he has violated a condition of his parole; and upon a finding of probable cause a digest shall be prepared by the Commission setting forth in writing the factors considered and the reasons for the decision, a copy of which shall be given to the parolee within a reasonable period of time; except that after a finding of probable cause the Commission may restore any parolee to parole supervision if:
> (i) continuation of revocation proceedings is not warranted; or
> (ii) incarceration of the parolee pending further revocation proceedings is not warranted by the alleged frequency or seriousness of such violation or violations;
> (iii) the parolee is not likely to fail to appear for further proceedings; and
> (iv) the parolee does not constitute a danger to himself or others.
>
> (B) upon a finding of probable cause under subparagraph (1)(A), a *revocation hearing* at or reasonably near the place of the alleged parole violation or arrest within sixty days of such determination of probable cause, except that a revocation hearing may be held at the same time and place set for the preliminary hearing.
> (2) Hearings held pursuant to subparagraph (1) of this subsection shall be conducted by the Commission in accordance with the following procedures:
> (A) notice to the parolee of the conditions of parole alleged to have been violated, and the time, place, and purposes of the scheduled hearing;
> (B) opportunity for the parolee to be represented by an attorney (retained by the parolee, or if he is financially unable to retain counsel, counsel shall be provided pursuant to section 3006A) or, if he so chooses, a representative as provided by rules and regulations, unless the parolee knowingly and intelligently waives such representation.
> (C) opportunity for the parolee to appear and testify, and present witnesses and relevant evidence on his own behalf; and
> (D) opportunity for the parolee to be apprised of the evidence against him and, if he so requests, to confront and cross-examine adverse witnesses, unless the Commission specifically finds substantial reason for not so allowing.
>
> For the purposes of subparagraph (1) of this subsection, the Commission may subpoena witnesses and evidence, and pay witness fees as established for the courts of the United States. If a person refuses to obey such a subpoena, the Commission may petition a court of the United States for the judicial district in which such parole proceeding is being conducted, or in which such person may be found, to request such person to attend, testify, and produce evidence. The court may issue an order requiring such person to appear before the Commission, when the court finds such information, or testimony directly related to a matter with respect to which the Commission is empowered to make a determination under this section. Failure to obey such an order is punishable by such court as a contempt. All process in such a case may be served in the judicial district in which such a parole proceeding is being conducted, or in which such person may be found.
>
> (b)(1) Conviction for any criminal offense committed subsequent to release on parole shall constitute probable cause for purposes of subsection (a) of this section. In cases in which a parolee has been convicted of such an offense and is serving a new sentence in an institution, a parole revocation warrant or summons issued pursuant to section 4213 may be placed against him as a detainer. Such detainer shall be reviewed by the Commission within one hundred and eighty days of notification to the Commission of placement. The parolee shall receive notice of the pending review, have an opportunity to submit a written application containing information relative to the disposition of the detainer, and, unless waived, shall have counsel as provided in subsection (a)(2)(B) of this section to assist him in the preparation of such application. . . .
>
> (d) Whenever a parolee is summoned or retaken pursuant to section 4213, and the Commission finds pursuant to the procedures of this section and by a preponderance of the evidence that the parolee has violated a condition of his parole the Commission may take any of the following actions:
> (1) restore the parolee to supervision;
> (2) reprimand the parolee;

(3) modify the parolee's conditions of the parole;
(4) refer the parolee to a residential community treatment center for all or part of the remainder of his original sentence; or
(5) formally revoke parole or release as if on parole pursuant to this title. . . .

(e) The Commission shall furnish the parolee with a written notice of its determination not later than twenty-one days, excluding holidays, after the date of the revocation hearing. If parole is revoked, a digest shall be prepared by the Commission setting forth in writing the factors considered and reasons for such action, a copy of which shall be given to the parolee.

(f) Notwithstanding any other provision of this section, a parolee who is found by the Commission to be in possession of a controlled substance shall have his parole revoked.[50]

Use *Your* Discretion

What process is "due" to parolees?
***Morrissey v. Brewer,* 408 U.S. 471 (1972)**

Chief Justice Burger delivered the opinion of the Court.

Facts
. . . Petitioner Morrissey was convicted of false drawing or uttering of checks in 1967 pursuant to his guilty plea, and was sentenced to not more than seven years' confinement. He was paroled from the Iowa State Penitentiary in June 1968. Seven months later, at the direction of his parole officer, he was arrested in his home town as a parole violator and incarcerated in the county jail. One week later, after review of the parole officer's written report, the Iowa Board of Parole revoked Morrissey's parole, and he was returned to the penitentiary located about 100 miles from his home. Petitioner asserts he received no hearing prior to revocation of his parole.

The parole officer's report on which the Board of Parole acted shows that petitioner's parole was revoked on the basis of information that he had violated the conditions of parole by buying a car under an assumed name and operating it without permission, giving false statements to police concerning his address and insurance company after a minor accident, obtaining credit under an assumed name, and failing to report his place of residence to his parole officer. The report states that the officer interviewed Morrissey, and that he could not explain why he did not contact his parole officer despite his effort to excuse this on the ground that he had been sick. Further, the report asserts that Morrissey admitted buying the car and obtaining credit under an assumed name, and also admitted being involved in the accident. The parole officer recommended that his parole be revoked because of "his continual violating of his parole rules." . . .

After exhausting state remedies, . . . petitioner filed [a] habeas corpus petition in the United States District Court for the Southern District of Iowa alleging that [he] had been denied due process because [his] parole had been revoked without a hearing. The State responded by arguing that no hearing was required. The District Court held on the basis of controlling authority that the State's failure to accord a hearing prior to parole revocation did not violate due process. . . . The Court of Appeals, dividing 4 to 3, held that due process does not require a hearing. . . . Iowa law provides that a parolee may be returned to the institution at any time. . . .

Opinion
. . . The enforcement leverage that supports . . . parole conditions derives from the authority to return the parolee to prison to serve out the balance of his sentence if he fails to abide by the rules. In practice, not every violation of parole conditions automatically leads to revocation. Typically, a parolee will be counseled to abide by the conditions of parole, and the parole officer ordinarily does not take steps to have parole revoked unless he thinks that the violations are serious and continuing so as to indicate that the parolee is not adjusting properly and cannot be counted on to avoid antisocial activity. The broad discretion accorded the parole officer is also inherent in some of the quite vague conditions, such as the typical requirement that the parolee avoid "undesirable" associations or correspondence. Yet revocation of parole is not an unusual phenomenon, affecting only a few parolees. It has been estimated that 35%–45% of all parolees are subjected to revocation and return to prison. Sometimes revocation occurs when the parolee is accused of another crime; it is often preferred to a new prosecution because of the procedural ease of recommitting the individual on the basis of a lesser showing by the State. . . . If a parolee is returned to prison, he usually receives no credit for the time "served" on parole. Thus, the returnee may face a potential of substantial imprisonment.

We begin with the proposition that the revocation of parole is not part of a criminal prosecution and thus the full panoply of rights due a defendant in such a proceeding does not apply to parole revocations. Parole arises after the end of the criminal prosecution, including imposition of sentence. Supervision is not directly by the court but by an administrative agency, which is sometimes an arm of the court and sometimes of the executive. Revocation deprives an individual, not of the absolute liberty to which every citizen is entitled, but only of the conditional liberty properly dependent on observance of special parole restrictions.

We turn, therefore, to the question whether the requirements of due process in general apply to parole revocations. . . . Whether any procedural protections are due depends on the extent to which an individual will be "condemned to suffer grievous loss." The question is . . . whether the nature of the interest is one within the contemplation of the "liberty or property" language of the Fourteenth Amendment. Once it is determined that due process applies, the question remains what process is due. It has been said so often by this Court and others as not to require citation of authority that due process is flexible and calls for such procedural protections as the particular situation demands. . . .

We turn to an examination of the nature of the interest of the parolee in his continued liberty. The liberty of a parolee enables him to do a wide range of things open to persons who have never been convicted of any crime. The parolee has been released from prison based on an evaluation that he shows reasonable promise of being able to return to society and function as a responsible, self-reliant person. Subject to the conditions of his parole, he can be gainfully employed and is free to be with family and friends and to form the other enduring attachments of normal life. Though the State properly subjects him to many restrictions not applicable to other citizens, his condition is very different from that of confinement in a prison. He may have been on parole for a number of years and may be living a relatively normal life at the time he is faced with revocation. The parolee has relied on at least an implicit promise that parole will be revoked only if he fails to live up to the parole conditions. In many cases, the parolee faces lengthy incarceration if his parole is revoked.

We see, therefore, that the liberty of a parolee, although indeterminate, includes many of the core values of unqualified liberty and its termination inflicts a "grievous loss" on the parolee and often on others. It is hardly useful any longer to try to deal with this problem in terms of whether the parolee's liberty is a "right" or a "privilege." By whatever name, the liberty is valuable and must be seen as within the protection of the Fourteenth Amendment. Its termination calls for some orderly process, however informal.

Turning to the question what process is due, we find that the State's interests are several. The State has found the parolee guilty of a crime against the people. That finding justifies imposing extensive restrictions on the individual's liberty. Release of the parolee before the end of his prison sentence is made with the recognition that with many prisoners there is a risk that they will not be able to live in society without committing additional antisocial acts. Given the previous conviction and the proper imposition of conditions, the State has an overwhelming interest in being able to return the individual to imprisonment without the burden of a new adversary criminal trial if in fact he has failed to abide by the conditions of his parole.

Yet, the State has no interest in revoking parole without some informal procedural guarantees. Although the parolee is often formally described as being "in custody," the argument cannot even be made here that summary treatment is necessary as it may be with respect to controlling a large group of potentially disruptive prisoners in actual custody. Nor are we persuaded by the argument that revocation is so totally a discretionary matter that some form of hearing would be administratively intolerable. A simple factual hearing will not interfere with the exercise of discretion. . . .

This discretionary aspect of the revocation decision need not be reached unless there is first an appropriate determination that the individual has in fact breached the conditions of parole. The parolee is not the only one who has a stake in his conditional liberty. Society has a stake in whatever may be the chance of restoring him to normal and useful life within the law. Society thus has an interest in not having parole revoked because of erroneous information or because of an erroneous evaluation of the need to revoke parole, given the breach of parole conditions. And society has a further interest in treating the parolee with basic fairness: fair treatment in parole revocations will enhance the chance of rehabilitation by avoiding reactions to arbitrariness.

Given these factors, most States have recognized that there is no interest on the part of the State in revoking parole without any procedural guarantees at all. What is needed is an informal hearing structured to assure that the finding of a parole violation will be based on verified facts and that the exercise of discretion will be informed by an accurate knowledge of the parolee's behavior.

We now turn to the nature of the process that is due, bearing in mind that the interest of both State and parolee will be furthered by an effective but informal hearing. In analyzing what is due, we see two important stages in the typical process of parole revocation.

Arrest of Parolee and Preliminary Hearing

The first stage occurs when the parolee is arrested and detained, usually at the direction of his parole officer. The second occurs when parole is formally revoked. There is typically a substantial time lag between the arrest and the eventual determination by the parole board whether parole should be revoked. Additionally, it may be that the parolee is arrested at a place distant from the state institution, to which he may be returned before the final decision is made concerning revocation.

Given these factors, due process would seem to require that some minimal inquiry be conducted at or reasonably near the place of the alleged parole violation or arrest and as promptly as convenient after arrest while information is fresh and sources are avail-

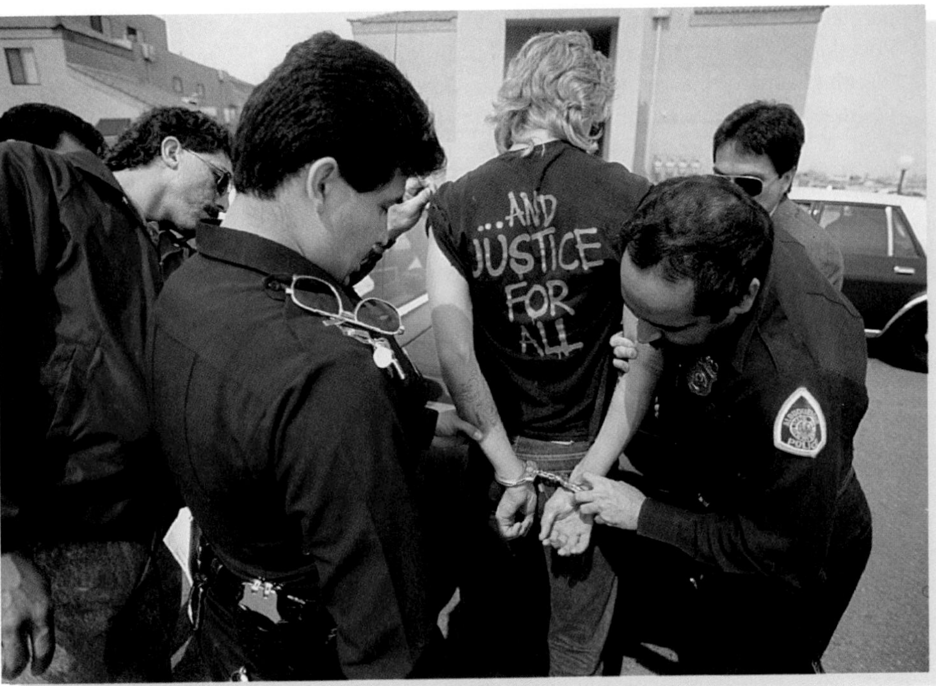

Though this man is being arrested by the Albuquerque, New Mexico, police for violating his parole, violations do not often lead to parole revocation.

able. Such an inquiry should be seen as in the nature of a "preliminary hearing" to determine whether there is probable cause or reasonable ground to believe that the arrested parolee has committed acts that would constitute a violation of parole conditions.

In our view, due process requires that after the arrest, the determination that reasonable ground exists for revocation of parole should be made by someone not directly involved in the case. It would be unfair to assume that the supervising parole officer does not conduct an interview with the parolee to confront him with the reasons for revocation before he recommends an arrest. It would also be unfair to assume that the parole officer bears hostility against the parolee that destroys his neutrality; realistically the failure of the parolee is in a sense a failure for his supervising officer. However, we need make no assumptions one way or the other to conclude that there should be an uninvolved person to make this preliminary evaluation of the basis for believing the conditions of parole have been violated. The officer directly involved in making recommendations cannot always have complete objectivity in evaluating them. *Goldberg v. Kelly* found it unnecessary to impugn the motives of the caseworker to find a need for an independent decision maker to examine the initial decision.

This independent officer need not be a judicial officer. The granting and revocation of parole are matters traditionally handled by administrative officers. In *Goldberg,* the Court pointedly did not require that the hearing on termination of benefits be conducted by a judicial officer or even before the traditional "neutral and detached" officer; it required only that the hearing be conducted by some person other than one initially dealing with the case. It will be sufficient, therefore, in the parole revocation context, if an evaluation of whether reasonable cause exists to believe that conditions of parole have been violated is made by someone such as a parole officer other than the one who has made the report of parole violations or has recommended revocation. A State could certainly choose some other independent decision maker to perform this preliminary function.

With respect to the preliminary hearing before this officer, the parolee should be given notice that the hearing will take place and that its purpose is to determine whether there is probable cause to believe he has committed a parole violation. The notice should state what parole violations have been alleged. At the hearing the parolee may appear and speak in his own behalf; he may bring letters, documents, or individuals who can give relevant information to the hearing officer. On request of the parolee, the person who has given adverse information on which parole revocation is to be based is to be made available for questioning in his presence. However, if the hearing officer determines that an informant would be subjected to risk of harm if his identity were disclosed, he need not be subjected to confrontation and cross-examination.

The hearing officer shall have the duty of making a summary, or digest, of what occurs at the hearing in terms of the responses of the parolee and the substance of the documents or evidence given in support of parole revocation and of the parolee's position. Based on the information before him, the officer should determine whether there is probable cause to hold the parolee for the final decision of the parole board on revocation. Such a determination would be sufficient to warrant the parolee's continued detention and return to the state correctional institution pending the final decision. As in *Goldberg,* "the decision maker should state the reasons for his determination and indicate the evidence he relied on . . ." but it should be remembered that this is not a final determination calling for "formal findings of fact and conclusions of law." No interest would be served by formalism in this process; informality will not lessen the utility of this inquiry in reducing the risk of error.

The Revocation Hearing

There must also be an opportunity for a hearing, if it is desired by the parolee, prior to the final decision on revocation by the parole authority. This hearing must be the basis for more than determining probable cause; it must lead to a final evaluation of any contested relevant facts and consideration of whether the facts as determined warrant revocation. The parolee must have an opportunity to be heard and to show, if he can, that he did not violate the conditions, or, if he did, that circumstances in mitigation suggest that the violation does not warrant revocation. The revocation hearing must be tendered within a reasonable time after the parolee is taken into custody. A lapse of two months, as respondents suggest occurs in some cases, would not appear to be unreasonable.

We cannot write a code of procedure; that is the responsibility of each State. Most States have done so by legislation, others by judicial decision usually on due process grounds. Our task is limited to deciding the minimum requirements of due process. They include (a) written notice of the claimed violations of parole; (b) disclosure to the parolee of evidence against him; (c) opportunity to be heard in person and to present witnesses and documentary evidence; (d) the right to confront and cross-examine adverse witnesses (unless the hearing officer specifically finds good cause for not allowing confrontation); (e) a "neutral and detached" hearing body such as a traditional parole board, members of which need not be judicial officers or lawyers; and (f) a written statement by the fact finders as to the evidence relied on and reasons for revoking parole. We emphasize there is no thought to equate this second stage of parole revocation to a criminal prosecution in any sense. It is a narrow inquiry; the process should be flexible enough to consider evidence including letters, affidavits, and other material that would not be admissible in an adversary criminal trial.

We do not reach or decide the question whether the parolee is entitled to the assistance of retained counsel or to appointed counsel if he is indigent.

We have no thought to create an inflexible structure for parole revocation procedures. The few basic requirements set out above, which are applicable to future revocations of parole, should not impose a great burden on any State's parole system. Control over the required proceedings by the hearing officers can assure that delaying tactics and other abuses sometimes present in the traditional adversary trial situation do not occur. Obviously a parolee cannot relitigate issues determined against him in other forums, as in the situation presented when the revocation is based on conviction of another crime. . . .

We reverse and remand to the Court of Appeals for further proceedings consistent with this opinion.
Reversed and remanded.

Concurring Opinion

Mr. Justice Brennan, concurring in the result.

. . . The Court . . . states that it does not now decide whether the parolee is also entitled at each hearing to the assistance of retained counsel or of appointed counsel if he is indigent. *Goldberg v. Kelly,* 397 U.S. 254, 90 S.Ct. 1011, 25 L.Ed.2d 287 (1970) nonetheless plainly dictates that he at least "must be allowed to retain an attorney if he so desires." As the Court said there, "Counsel and help delineate the issues, present the factual contentions in an orderly manner, conduct cross-examination, and generally safeguard the interests of" his client. The only question open under our precedents is whether counsel must be furnished the parolee if he is indigent.

Dissent

Mr. Justice Douglas, dissenting in part.

. . . Under modern concepts of penology, paroling prisoners is part of the rehabilitative aim of the correctional philosophy. The objective is to return a prisoner to a full family and community life. . . . That status is conditioned upon not engaging in certain activities and perhaps in not leaving a certain area or locality. Violations of conditions of parole may be technical, they may be done unknowingly, they may be fleeting and of no consequence. The parolee should, in the concept of fairness implicit in due process, have a chance to explain. Rather, under Iowa's rule revocation proceeds on the ipse dixit of the parole agent; and on his word alone each of these petitioners has already served three additional years in prison. The charges may or may not be true. Words of explanation may be adequate to transform into trivia what looms large in the mind of the parole officer.

"[T]here is no place in our system of law for reaching result of such tremendous consequences without ceremony—without hearing, without effective assistance of counsel, without a statement of reasons." Parole, while originally conceived as a judicial function, has become largely an administrative matter. The parole boards have broad discretion in formulating and imposing parole conditions.

Parole is commonly revoked on mere suspicion that the parolee may have committed a crime. Such great control over the parolee vests in a parole officer a broad discretion in revoking parole and also in counseling the parolee—referring him for psychiatric treatment or obtaining the use of specialized therapy for narcotic addicts or alcoholics. Treatment of the parolee, rather than revocation of his parole, is a common course. Counseling may include extending help to a parolee in finding a job. A parolee, like a prisoner, is a person entitled to constitutional protection, including procedural due process. At the federal level, the construction of regulations of the Federal Parole Board presents federal questions of which we have taken cognizance. At the state level, the construction of parole statutes and regulations is for the States alone. . . .

It is only procedural due process, required by the Fourteenth Amendment, that concerns us in the present cases. Procedural due process requires the following:

> If a violation of a condition of parole is involved, rather than the commission of a new offense, there should not be an arrest of the parolee and his return to the prison or to a local jail. Rather, notice of the alleged violation should be given to the parolee and a time set for a hearing. The hearing should not be before the parole officer, as he is the one who is making the charge and "there is inherent danger in combining the functions of judge and advocate." Moreover, the parolee should be entitled to counsel. As the Supreme Court of Oregon said in *Perry v. Williard,* "A hearing in which counsel is absent or is present only on behalf of one side is inherently unsatisfactory if not unfair. Counsel can see that relevant facts are brought out, vague and insubstantial allegations discounted, and irrelevancies eliminated."
>
> The hearing required is not a grant of the full panoply of rights applicable to a criminal trial. But confrontation with the informer may . . . be necessary for a fair hearing and the ascertainment of the truth. The hearing is to determine the fact of parole violation. The results of the hearing would go to the parole board—or other authorized state agency—for final action, as would cases which involved voluntary admission of violations.

The rule of law is important in the stability of society. Arbitrary actions in the revocation of paroles can only impede and impair the rehabilitative aspects of modern penology. "Notice and opportunity for hearing appropriate to the nature of the case," are the rudiments of due process which restore faith that our society is run for the many, not the few, and that fair dealing rather than caprice will govern the affairs of men.

I would not prescribe the precise formula for the management of the parole problems. We do not sit as an ombudsman, telling the States the precise procedures they must follow. I would hold that so far as the due process requirements of parole revocation are concerned:

1. the parole officer—whatever may be his duties under various state statutes—in Iowa appears to be an agent having some of the functions of a prosecutor and of the police; the parole officer is therefore not qualified as a hearing officer;
2. the parolee is entitled to a due process notice and a due process hearing of the alleged parole violations including, for example, the opportunity to be confronted by his accusers and to present evidence and argument on his own behalf; and
3. the parolee is entitled to the freedom granted a parolee until the results of the hearing are known and the parole board—or other authorized state agency—acts.

CRITICAL THINKING

1. What "liberties" do parolees have that entitle them to due process when their parole is revoked?
2. Why is less process "due" to parolees than to defendants and people not charged with crimes?
3. What process exactly is "due" to parolees in revocation of their parole?
4. If you were writing the rules regarding the revocation of parole, would you write the ones recommended by the majority of the Court as set out by Chief Justice Burger, or those of Justice Douglas in his dissent?
5. Should parolees have a right to counsel at their revocation hearings? Defend your answer.
6. Should parole officers have the authority to take parolees into custody and have them detained in jail without a hearing prior to the detention? Defend your answer.

Knowledge and Understanding CHECK

1. Identify the common misbelief concerning what happens when prisoners leave prison.
2. What is the range of time of supervised release?
3. Identify the difficulties in returning to society after imprisonment.
4. List the conditions attached to most conditional releases from prison.

5. Identify the difficulties that conditionally released prisoners encounter.
6. Identify the activities in which most conditionally released prisoners have to participate.
7. List and describe the major parole officer roles.
8. What changes in roles have occurred since the 1970s?
9. Identify the three usual measures of recidivism.
10. Summarize the state of our knowledge about the effects of parole supervision on recidivism.
11. List the two grounds for parole revocation.
12. Identify the circumstances that influence the actual revocation of parole.
13. Describe the process that is "due" to parole violators.

Should He Go to Jail? Consideration

Superior Court Judge Norma Huggins ruled that Johnson had violated his parole but stopped short of revoking his community supervision and sending him to jail, pending the results of a drug test to determine whether Johnson had also used drugs. Two previous tests showed that Johnson had used cocaine. Johnson's attorney contested the outcome of the first two tests. The lawyer asked the judge to allow Johnson to take a third test, which is now pending. Judge Johnson agreed.

- Almost all prisoners eventually leave prison.
- The United States is one of the most punitive countries in the world.
- Most prisoners are released from prison with limits on their property, liberty, and privacy.
- Predicting the behavior of parolees is weak, no matter whether discretionary assessment or risk assessment by empirical data is used.
- We don't know whether a public safety focus or rehabilitation of individually released prisoners works better.

KEY TERMS

parole
discretionary release
mandatory release
expiration release
parole boards
hearing officers
parole guidelines
salient factor score (SFS)
parole contract
certificate of parole
casework model
welfare parole officers
law enforcer parole officer
passive parole officers
recidivism
parole revocation

INTERNET RESEARCH EXERCISES

Exercise: Search for information on prisoners who are released and return to society. What are the criteria for release from prison? How many people return to society before the end of their prison sentence? How many who are released violate new laws or other conditions of their release?

Suggested Sites:

- Bureau of Justice Statistics http://www.ojp.usdoj.gov/bjs/ Click on "Publications". Click on "C". Select *Correctional Populations in the U.S.*
- State Parole Boards, Inmates, Criminal Histories, and Prison Info, http://www.inil.com/users/dguss/gator70.htm

InfoTrac College Edition: Search on key word "parole"

NOTES

1. *The Seattle Times,* 15 September 1998, B2.
2. BJS, *Nation's Probation and Parole Population Reached New High Last Year* (Washington, D.C.: BJS, 1998).
3. BJS, *Prisoners in 1994* (Washington, D.C.: BJS, August 1995), 12, and Table 15.
4. Joel Samaha, "Hanging for Felony," *Historical Journal* (1979); Clair Wilcox, *Parole from State Penal Institutions* (Philadelphia: Pennsylvania State Parole Commission, 1927), 5–6.
5. Wilcox, *Parole,* 6.
6. Ibid., 3.
7. Harry Elmer Barnes and Negley K. Teeters, *New Horizons in Criminology,* 3d ed. (Englewood Cliffs, N.J.: Prentice-Hall, 1959), 567.
8. Wilcox, *Parole,* 1.
9. Quoted in Wilcox, *Parole,* 2.
10. Ibid., 21.
11. John C. Rundt, Edward E. Rhine, and Robert E. Wetter, *The Practice of Parole Boards* (Lexington, Ky.: Association of Paroling Authorities, 1997), 1–7.
12. Ibid.
13. Ibid., 28.
14. Ibid.
15. Ibid., 9.
16. *Greenholtz v. Inmates of the Nebraska Penal and Correction Complex,* 99 S.Ct. 2100 (1979).
17. Ibid.
18. John S. Goldkamp, "Prediction in Criminal Justice Policy Development," in *Prediction and Classification: Criminal Justice Decision Making,* Don M. Gottfredson and Leslie T. Wilkins, eds. (Chicago: University of Chicago Press, 1987), 106.
19. Kevin N. Wright, Todd R. Clear, and Paul Dickson, "Universal Applicability of Probation Risk-Assessment Instruments," *Criminology* 22 (1984): 113.
20. John H. Lombardi and Donna M. Lombardi, "Objective Parole Criteria: More Harm than Good?" *Corrections Today* (February 1986): 86–87; Donald Atkinson, "Parole Can Work!" *Corrections Today* (February 1986): 54–55.
21. Wright, Clear, and Dickson, "Risk-Assessment Instruments," 122–23.
22. Stephen D. Gottfredson and Don M. Gottfredson, "Screening for Risk Among Parolees: Policy, Practice, and Method," in *Prediction in Criminology,* David P. Farrington and R. Tarling, eds. (Albany, N.Y.: State University of New York Press, 1985).
23. Lombardi and Lombardi, "Objective Parole Criteria," 87.
24. Todd R. Clear and George F. Cole, *American Corrections,* 3d ed. (Monterey, Calif.: Wadsworth, 1994), 412–13.
25. U.S. Sentencing Commission, *Federal Sentencing Guidelines Manual* (St. Paul: West, 1995), sec. 5D1.1, 2.
26. Clear and Cole, *American Corrections,* 428.
27. Ibid.
28. U.S. Department of Justice, U.S. Parole Commission, *Parole Commission Rules* 28 C.F.R. secs. 2.39, 2.40 (November 12, 1991).
29. Champion, *Probation and Parole,* 316.
30. Quoted in Harry E. Allen et al., *Probation and Parole in America* (New York: Free Press, 1985), 127.
31. Quoted in Allen et al., *Probation and Parole,* 128.
32. Ibid.
33. Cited and discussed in Allen et al., *Probation and Parole,* 129.
34. Quoted in Allen et al., *Probation and Parole,* 130.
35. Cheryl L. Ringel, Ernest L. Cowles, and Thomas C. Castellano, "Changing Patterns in Parole Supervision," in *Critical Issues in Criminal Justice,* Albert R. Roberts, ed. (Thousand Oaks, Calif.: Sage Publications, 1994), 299.
36. Ibid., 306.
37. Howard R. Sacks and Charles H. Logan, *Does Parole Make a Difference?* (Storrs, Conn.: The University of Connecticut Law School Press, 1979).
38. Howard R. Sacks and Charles H. Logan, *Parole: Crime Prevention or Crime Postponement* (Storrs, Conn.: The University of Connecticut Law School Press, 1980), 14–15.
39. Ibid., 15–17, 20.
40. Quoted in Mark Jay Lerner, "The Effectiveness of a Definite Sentence Parole Program," *Criminology* 15 (1977): 215.
41. Ibid.
42. Ibid., 220.
43. Deborah Star, *Summary Parole* (California Department of Corrections, 1979), 2–3, 52, 132.
44. Deborah Star, *Investigation and Surveillance in Parole Supervision: An Evaluation of the High Control Project* (California Department of Corrections, 1981), i.
45. Ibid., i–ii.
46. Ibid., 168, 251, 257.
47. *Morrissey v. Brewer,* 408 US 471 (1972); BJS, *Parole in 1995* (Washington, D.C.: BJS, 1997).
48. Champion, *Probation and Parole,* 172.
49. *Morrissey v. Brewer,* 484.
50. 18 United States Code Annotated, sec. 4214.

CHAPTER 17

Juvenile Justice

CHAPTER OUTLINE

Is Arrest and Criminal Prosecution the Best Response?

On December 30, 1998, a headline in the *Sarasota Herald-Tribune* read:

> CHARGE: 13-YEAR-OLD THREATENED SIBLINGS

The 13-year-old Port Charlotte boy, Rowland Lawrence Fisher, was arrested on two counts of aggravated assault with a deadly weapon. According to a Charlotte County Sheriff's Office report:

> Witnesses said Fisher was quarreling with his 16-year-old sister at about 8 A.M. Monday at their house because he refused to put his clothes away. His sister picked up the clothes, but the boy threw them back on the floor. He then ran into the kitchen and returned with a 4-inch knife. He threatened to stab his sister and one of his brothers. His sister grabbed his arm and hit it against the wall, knocking the knife out of his hand. Deputies arrived and arrested Roland Fisher. He was taken to the Charlotte County Jail, and was later transferred to the Department of Juvenile Justice in Fort Myers.[1]

INTRODUCTION

A 12-year-old-boy attacks a woman walking down the street and grabs her purse. A 16-year-old boy does the same thing to another woman on another street. A 19-year-old young man attacks a third woman and takes her purse. The police arrest all three. Do their ages make a difference in what happens to them following arrest? Yes. In all American jurisdictions, age determines which institutions will process these cases, what procedures govern their process, and what policies shape their disposition. The United States has a *dual justice system:* one set of institutions, procedures, and goals governs juveniles and another governs adults.

The agencies that deal with juveniles serve multiple formal and informal missions. Their formal missions are:

1. Supervising, protecting, and supporting juveniles.
2. Protecting society from juveniles who commit crimes or otherwise threaten social stability.
3. Preserving the constitutional rights of juveniles.

Informally, juvenile justice agencies are organizations whose goals are shaped by work-group relationships; ambitions and attitudes of personnel within particular agencies; and political, economic, and social influences from the community outside. Despite shifting emphases and conflict, the purposes of American juvenile justice encompass service to children's needs and rights and general social control on the formal level, and organizational goals at the informal level.

Three agencies that parallel adult criminal justice are responsible for the processing of juvenile cases: police, juvenile court and its supporting staff, and juvenile corrections. The juvenile justice process reflects multiple, and often conflicting, formal and informal missions.

Five primary issues in juvenile justice are hotly debated. They include the

1. Needs and rights of individual juveniles balanced against the needs and rights of society.
2. Scope of juvenile justice authority.
3. Process of juvenile justice.
4. Effectiveness of juvenile programs.
5. Reforms in defining, processing, and "correcting" juveniles.

HISTORY OF JUVENILE JUSTICE

Criminal law has treated children differently from adults for centuries. In early English history, children under 7 were not legally competent to form criminal intent; hence, they could not be tried for criminal behavior. Between 7 and 14, children were presumed incapable of forming criminal intent, but evidence showing the capacity to form criminal intent could overcome the presumption of incompetency. Children over 14 were treated as adults because by that age the law presumed that they had the mental capacity to form criminal intent. However, informally children over 14 were rarely punished as harshly as adults even though they were tried formally by criminal court judges and juries.

In branches of the law outside criminal law, the **doctrine of *parens patriae*** allowed the government to intervene in family life to protect children's estates from dishonest guardians. This principle expanded over time to include the power to intervene to protect children's welfare in general against parental neglect, incompetence, and abuse. The ancient doctrine of parens patriae and presumptions against children's capacity to form criminal intent came to America with the English colonists.[2]

Use *Your* Discretion

Should the boys be charged with attempted murder and burglary?[3]

On April 23, 1996, two 8-year-old twin boys tearfully described a burglary and assault on a 4-week-old baby that they had committed the day before in a "rough, working-class neighborhood" of Richmond, California. Police were led to the boys by a relative of the infant who recognized the tricycle they stole and took it away from them as they fled the apartment. During an interview with police, the twins admitted that they and a 6-year-old boy had entered the apartment after they found the door open and had made their way to a bedroom, where the baby, Ignacio Bermudez, was sleeping. They had entered the apartment to steal the tricycle. During the Monday burglary, the infant's bassinet was kicked over and the baby was attacked with fists, kicked in the head, and possibly struck on the head with a stick, according to Richmond Police Sgt. Michael Walter. The infant is in "critical condition on life support at the Children's Hospital in Oakland, according to hospital officials. Doctors said he likely will have permanent brain damage."

The 6-year-old boy was charged with attempted murder in the beating of the baby. According to Dennis Murphy, a senior deputy district attorney for Contra Costa County, "the juvenile's strained relations with the baby's family was only 'the tip of the iceberg' of reasons prosecutors thought they could pursue an attempted murder charge." Juvenile court referee Stephen Easton ordered the boy "to remain in a juvenile detention hall." The twins were charged with burglary.

Experts are divided over whether the justice system can cope with offenders so young. Leslie Bialik, the public defender for the 6-year-old, told Easton that she did not think the detention hall was "set up to deal with someone of this age." In a telephone interview, Deputy District Attorney Howard Jewett said, "The state has a responsibility to say this conduct is not okay." Jewett said that "with a crime of this severity, I don't think we can look the other way. When you're talking about another person's death, society must assign legal responsibility if the law permits it to." Deputy District Attorney Murphy said videotapes of police questioning the boy showed he clearly understood that the assault was wrong. "This is not to punish the child but to control the situation and remedy it," he said. "This is the route that has to be taken to get wardship." If the referee determines the allegations are true, the boys would become wards of the court. They could be placed in a foster home, rehabilitation home, or a stricter juvenile detention facility, said officials. The *Associated Press* reported that the 6-year-old's mother and grandparents attended today's hearing and that he hugged his grandparents but ignored his mother.

Crimes this vicious are so rarely committed by children this young that the justice system does not have facilities to house them. All three youngsters were kept separated from the general population at the juvenile hall, where the next-youngest resident is 13, according to Terrence Starr, chief probation officer. J. P. Trembly of the California Youth and Corrections Agency said the agency is not equipped to care for offenders younger than 11 years old. "We do not have the staffing and training to deal with these kids who are this young," he said.

Patricia Puritz, director of the American Bar Association's Juvenile Justice Center, said a child so young shouldn't have been charged. "Charging a 6-year-old with anything is beyond what a civilized society should do, even if that child is behaving in an uncivilized way." Shannan Wilber, a staff attorney at the San Francisco-based Youth Law Center, a child advocacy organization, said, "There's really no benefit to prosecuting this child. You don't need to prosecute to access services like counseling for him or his family, and that's clearly what's needed here."

In juvenile court, prosecutors must prove their case beyond a reasonable doubt. For attempted murder, they also must show intent to kill, which experts say could prove difficult given the boy's age. "We don't know if he understands the consequences of his actions," said Wilber. "Does he know that if he hits someone over the head, he'll die? Does he even know what death is?"

CRITICAL THINKING

1. List the arguments for and against charging these boys with attempted murder and burglary.
2. If you were the prosecutor, would you charge the boys with crimes? Defend your answer.
3. Identify the benefits of your decision to society, to the victim, and to the boys.

During the reform movements that swept through the United States in the nineteenth century, a romantic concern for children arose, and a "child-saving" movement grew out of that romantic concern. A general institutionalization of America took place at around the same time (Chapter 1). As a result, the child-saving movement relied on two institutions, the house of refuge and the reform school, to "save" children. Both institutions were based on the nineteenth-century idea that children's environments made them bad. So, by removing youths from bad institutions—bad homes and unhealthy associates—and putting them in good institutional homes and schools, they would give up their evil habits. Refuges and schools would "reform" bad children into law-abiding people.[4]

During the Progressive Era a century ago, attention again focused on reforming children. The Progressives believed that children were born a blank slate. Unsuitable environments, particularly "unhealthy" home lives were the cause of misbehavior. Healthy meant homes where parents lived according to middle-class values: the virtues of hard work, thrift, temperance, and deference to established authority. The Progressives maintained that families who did not have these values—particularly immigrants—should acquire these values. Further, it was the Progressives' influence that would supply the values.

The Progressives had great confidence in both the state and in experts. Hence, they called on the state to supply a battery of experts to "save" children by "curing" their "unhealthy" home lives. The Progressives distrusted traditional institutions that operated according to what they believed were outdated, inefficient, and ineffective formal rules. So, they turned away from the criminal courts, which emphasized criminal conduct. They created a new institution, the juvenile court, which focused on what children needed to make them responsible.

The juvenile court was supposed to differ from adult courts. Judges did not sit on benches above children, but next to them. Proceedings were informal. Their aim was not to affix blame, but to find out what caused children to "go wrong" so that something could be done about it. The Progressives were great fact collectors. They gathered information about children's home life, past behavior, health, and anything else that might help them diagnose and cure youth problems.

The Progressives were great optimists. They had a strong faith that government could cure delinquency by seeing to it that experts could make professional judgments not hampered by formal rules. Their optimistic faith in government led to the adoption of what came to be called a **medical model** of crime. The medical model is based on the idea that crime is a disease that experts can diagnose, treat, and cure. Based on these optimistic ideas, Chicago established the first juvenile court in 1899. By 1925, almost every jurisdiction in the country had one.[5]

During the 1960s, the professional interest in children shifted from needs to rights. This shift was due both to the general rights movement and a growing skepticism about the capacity of government to meet the needs of children. The increased fear of crime and disorder during that turbulent time led critics to attack juvenile justice generally and juvenile court specifically. In 1967, the President's Commission on Law and Enforcement and the Administration of Justice concluded:

> The juvenile court has not succeeded significantly in rehabilitating delinquent youth, in reducing or even stemming the tide of juvenile criminality, or in bringing justice to the child offender. Uncritical and unrealistic estimates of what is known can make expectation so much greater than achievement and serve to justify extensive official action, and to mask the fact that much of it may do more harm than good. Official action may help to fix and perpetuate delinquency in the child—the individual begins to think of himself as a delinquent and proceeds to organize his behaviors accordingly. The undesirable consequences of official actions are heightened in programs that rely on institutionalization of the child. The most informed and benign institutional treatment, even in well designed and staffed reformatories and training schools, thus may contain within it the seeds of its own frustration, and itself may often feed the very disorder it is designed to cure.[6]

Several landmark U.S. Supreme Court decisions restricted the informal, discretionary powers of the juvenile court and other agencies dealing with juveniles. These restrictions were made by granting to juveniles a number of rights enjoyed by adult criminal defendants. For example, in *Kent v. United States* (a 1996 case involving a 16-year-old charged with housebreaking, robbery, and rape) the Court ruled that juvenile court proceedings must afford juveniles the basic due process right to a fair hearing.[7]

In 1967, the Court further extended due process rights in juvenile court proceedings. *In re Gault* involved proceedings against a 15-year-old Arizona boy who made lewd remarks to an elderly woman on the telephone. The juvenile court committed the juvenile to a training school. The U.S. Supreme Court ruled that committing a juvenile to a correctional facility required:

1. Written notice that a hearing was scheduled.
2. Advice about the right to counsel.
3. The right to confront and cross-examine witnesses.

In *In re Winship,* a 12-year-old boy was charged with purse snatching. The U.S. Supreme Court ruled that due process required that proof beyond a reasonable doubt was required to classify juveniles as delinquent.[8]

However, juveniles do not have all the rights of adult criminal defendants; juvenile proceedings don't have to be identical to adult criminal court proceedings. In *McKeiver v. Pennsylvania,* the Court ruled, for example, that juveniles are not entitled to a jury trial in delinquency proceedings. By 1970, therefore, juveniles had gained some of the constitutional protections of adults, but not all. In the Court's words, "We do not mean to indicate that the hearing must be held to conform with all the requirements of a criminal trial but we do hold that the hearing must measure up to the essentials of due process and fair treatment."[9]

During the 1970s, the fear of crime and youth rebellion continued to rise. This fear was rising at the same time as

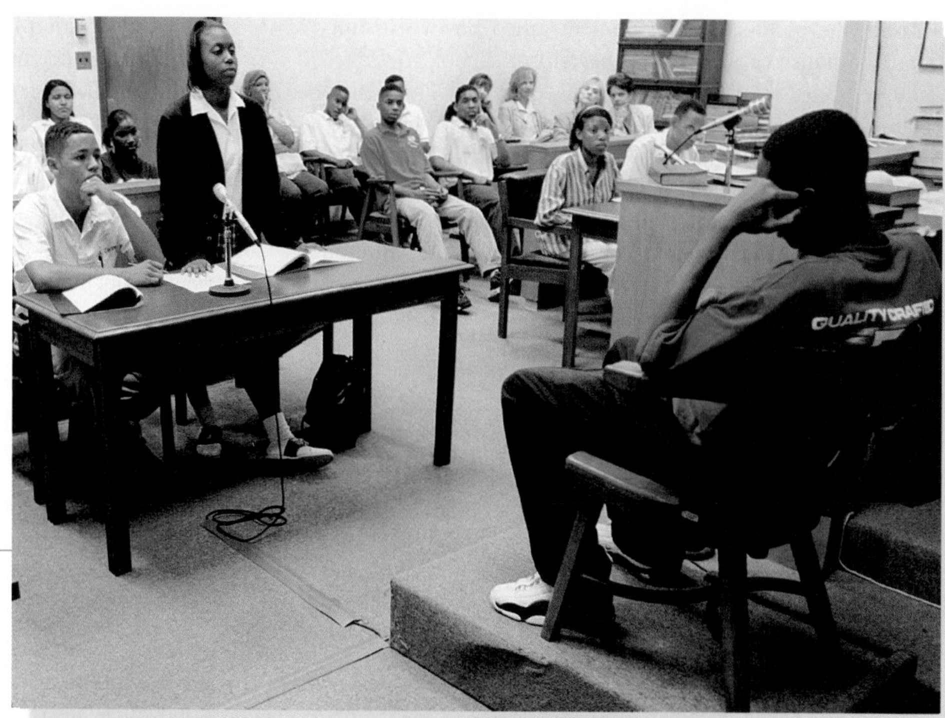

Because society has throughout history dealt with juvenile offenders differently than adult offenders, the structures for assessing and punishing juvenile crimes have evolved significantly and are often allowed to take unusual forms. Here, a defendant faces Lesley Venable, acting as prosecutor, and a court of his peers under charges of unauthorized use of a vehicle. Defendants who are sent to this Teen Court are first-time offenders who have pleaded guilty in Juvenile Court and have been sent to Teen Court for sentencing.

(and may have been partly responsible for) the disillusionment with the juvenile justice system's capacity to both meet the needs of juveniles and secure their rights. Fear and disillusionment contributed to a harsher public attitude toward youth crime and to a renewed confidence that retribution was the right response to crime and delinquency. A growing consensus among both criminal justice professionals and the public demanded that juveniles should be tried as adults.

Reflecting this consensus was a belief that if juveniles are old enough to commit crimes, they are old enough to take the consequences. Today, impressionistic evidence suggests that there is "a rising tide of anger at teen-age killers." According to juvenile justice exert, Professor Martin Guggenheim, "We've lost our faith in the rehabilitative ideal, and that loss of faith has come from both the left and the right." Since 1994, 43 states have made it easier to prosecute juveniles as adults, and half of all states no longer have a minimum age for prosecuting children as adults.[10]

DELINQUENCY

States vary considerably in their definitions of juveniles. Most states exclude children under 8 from juvenile justice jurisdiction. States differ about the upper age, some using 16 and others 18 as the dividing line between juvenile and criminal justice jurisdiction. In most states, "older" juveniles, those within a year or two of the upper age limit, qualify either as juveniles or adults, depending on the circumstances (discussed later).

Juvenile justice processes several types of juveniles: the needy, the dependent, the neglected, the delinquent, and the deviant. This chapter focuses on the delinquent and the deviant. **Delinquency** includes conduct that would be criminal if an adult engaged in it. **Status offenses** include conduct that is illegal only if children engage in it. Common examples include truancy, underage drinking, curfew violations, running away, and incorrigibility. The term **juvenile delinquent** can refer to a youth who has committed either crimes or status offenses, or both. The term is so broad that the late Paul Tappan noted that "delinquency has little specific behavioral content either in law or in fact." So, a "juvenile delinquent is a person who has been adjudicated as such by a court of proper jurisdiction."[11]

The California Welfare and Institutions Code captures the broad scope of delinquency in the nation's most populous state:

> Any person who is under the age of eighteen when he violates any law of this state or the United States or any ordinance of any city or county of this state defining crime other than an ordinance establishing a curfew based solely on age, is within the jurisdiction of the juvenile court. Any person under the age of eighteen years who persistently or habitually refuses to obey the reasonable and proper orders or directions of his parents, guardian, or custodian, or who is beyond the control of such person, or who is under the age of 18 years when he violates any ordinance of any city or county of this state establishing a curfew based solely on age is within the jurisdiction of the juvenile court.[12]

Juvenile delinquency, therefore, can include everything from serious violent crime to staying out too late at night.

Use *Your* Discretion

Should curfew laws be strictly enforced?

A number of states have enacted and called for strict enforcement of tougher nighttime and schoolday curfew laws. Defenders of the laws maintain that the laws protect youths and the public from violence and criminality and deter curfew violators from committing more serious crimes. Opponents warn that curfew laws violate constitutional rights; lead to antagonism between youths and law enforcement; and do not reduce crime.

Both opponents and supporters of the law base their support on anecdotal evidence. The U.S. Conference of Mayors surveyed cities with more than 30,000 people. The conference survey asked if law enforcement agencies credited curfews for reduced juvenile crime. Although they had no statistical evidence to back them up, 88 percent of those who returned surveys said that their curfews were responsible for reductions in juvenile crime in their cities. However, the Los Angeles Police Department reported that vigorous enforcement of curfew laws (101 task forces of 3,600 officers writing 4,800 curfew citations in six months) had *no* effect on either reported crime or violent juvenile offenses. The LAPD did not compare strict enforcement with lax enforcement areas in the city.[13]

A California group called the Justice Policy Institute examined whether year-to-year increases or decreases in curfew arrest rates correlate with youth crime in California. The institute conducted three analyses of these data:

1. Statewide curfew arrests and crime rates separated by race/ethnicity for all youths and for California's four major groups (white non-Hispanics, Hispanics, black non-Hispanics, and Asian non-Hispanics).
2. County curfew rates and youth crime for the 12 most populous counties in California.
3. Local curfew and youth crime rates and trends for all cities with populations of more than 100,000 people.[14]

The researchers found:

- Statistical analyses find no support for the proposition that stricter curfew enforcement reduces youth crime either absolutely, or relative to adults, by location, by city, or by type of crime. Curfew enforcement generally had no discernible effect on youth crime. In those few instances in which a significant effect was found, it was more likely to be positive (that is, greater curfew enforcement was associated with higher rates of juvenile crime) than negative.
- Of the 30 correlations of statewide rates of youth crime by race and ethnicity, 7 were significantly positive, none were significantly negative, and 23 showed no effect.
- Of the 30 correlations of youth crime rates with adult crime rates, 4 were significantly positive, none were negative, and 26 were not significant.
- Of 72 correlations in the 12 most populous counties, 5 were significantly positive, none were negative, and 67 were not significant.
- Cities in Los Angles and Orange counties follow dramatically different curfew enforcement practices. Some make practically no arrests, others practice high rates, and some vary from year to year. Despite these dramatic differences, "no consistent effects of curfew arrest on local youth crime" could be found.

CRITICAL THINKING

1. List the major arguments for and against strict curfew enforcement.
2. Summarize the findings of the Justice Policy Institute.
3. In view of the findings, would you favor strict enforcement of curfew laws? Defend your answer.
4. If you answered no to (3), what would you need to know before you supported strict curfew enforcement?
5. Would you change your mind if you knew that the Justice Policy Institute is known by some as a "liberal" group? Explain your answer.

Delinquency is not only difficult to define, it is also difficult to measure. As is the case with measuring adult crime, statistics concerning delinquency are not complete (Chapter 3). Most criticisms regarding crime statistics generally apply also to measures of juvenile delinquency. In fact, these measures stem mainly from the same sources: the Uniform Crime Reports, the National Crime Survey, court records, and self-reports.

Despite difficulties in measuring delinquency, several facts stand out. First, youths are substantially more "crime-prone" than adults. The juvenile arrest rate for serious property crimes exceeds the adult rate by about six to one, and for violent crimes by about two to one. Second, the majority of youth arrests are for property crimes, such as theft and burglary, and youth-only offenses, such as truancy, runaway, and curfew. Indications are that juveniles commit fewer violent crimes and more crimes against property.[15]

Furthermore, most juveniles commit crimes in groups. Younger offenders commit crimes in groups of four or more five times more often than adults. Of the total juvenile crimes charged in New York City, 90 percent of the robberies, 86 percent of the burglaries, 78 percent of the homicides,

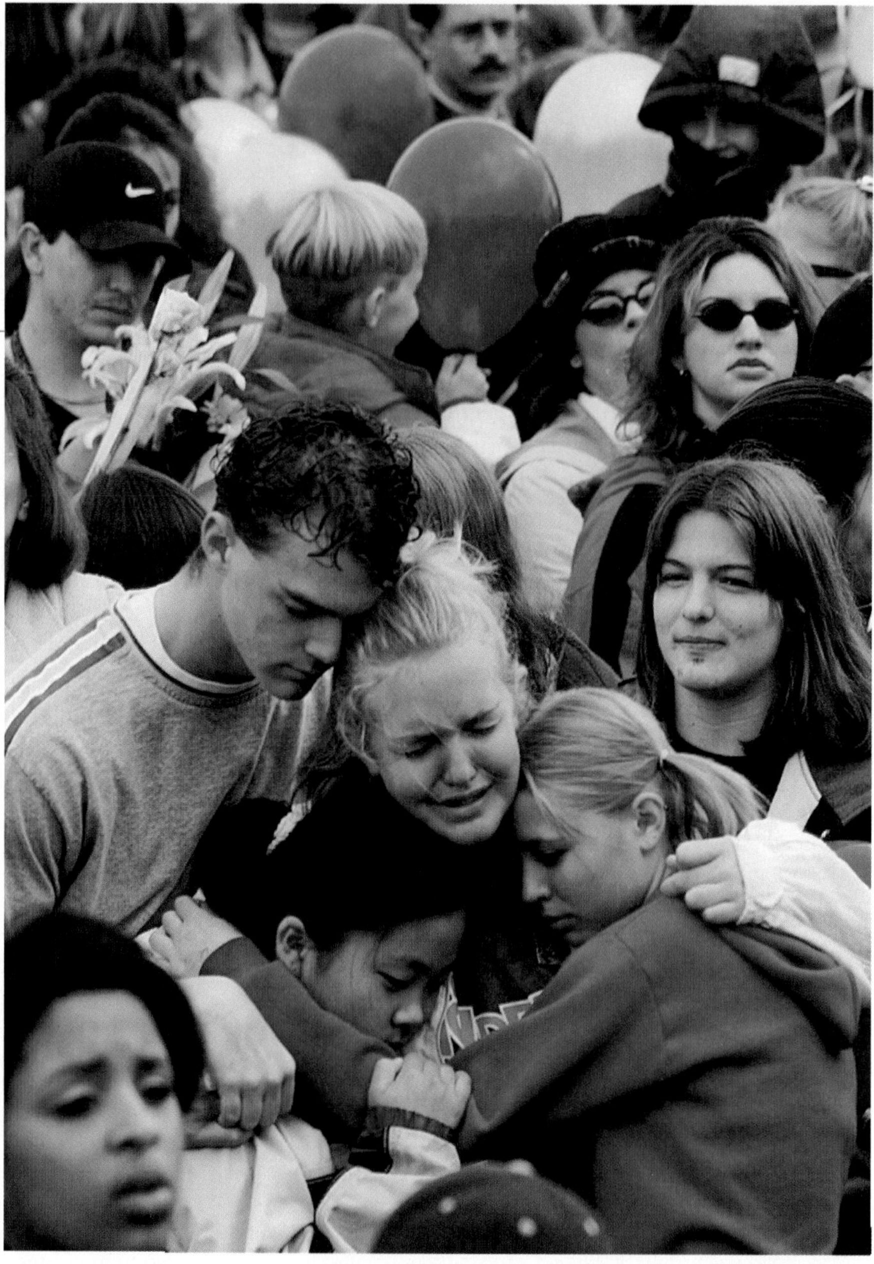

Students mourn at a memorial service for the victims of the Columbine High School shooting in April 1999. Two students, Eric Harris and Dylan Klebold, killed 12 students and one teacher and injured several others on campus before killing themselves. The incident focused attention on juvenile violence and especially on gun control. Do you think stronger gun control laws will help reduce violence?

60 percent of the assaults, and 50 percent of the rapes were committed in groups. Finally, serious juvenile crime is concentrated in urban minority group males, a population group that is increasing.[16]

Finally, youths are frequently armed. Three sociologists at Tulane University, James Wright, Joseph Sheley, and M. Dwayne Smith, interviewed male juveniles serving sentences and male students attending inner-city schools. They found that city youths can easily acquire handguns, and almost one-third have owned a gun at one time or another. They get them from friends, family, and street sources. Most guns were stolen and purchased at prices well below their retail value. Most youths claimed that they carried guns for protection. Figure 17.1 depicts the percent of the two groups answering yes to questions about obtaining guns, the type of gun obtained, whether they carry guns, and whether they own guns.[17]

Knowledge and Understanding CHECK

1. Identify the three formal missions of the agencies of juvenile justice.
2. Describe the informal missions of juvenile justice.
3. List five hotly debated issues in contemporary juvenile justice.
4. Identify the three juvenile justice agencies that parallel adult criminal justice.
5. Explain how criminal law has treated children differently from adults.
6. Describe the dominant feature and the results of the nineteenth-century reform movement.

Figure 17.1
Youths and Guns

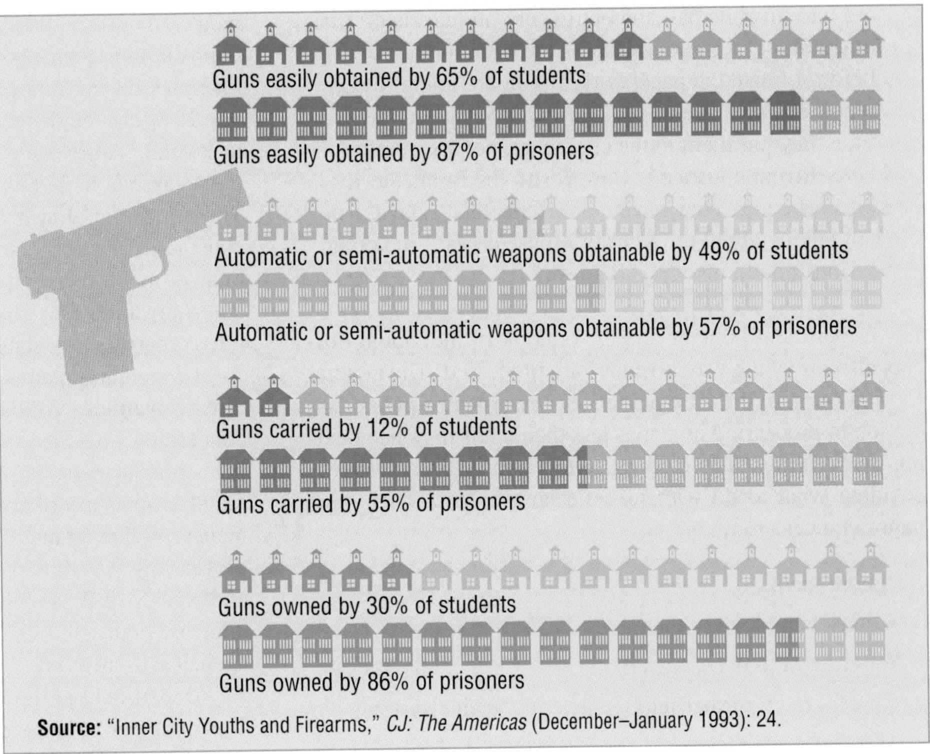
Guns easily obtained by 65% of students
Guns easily obtained by 87% of prisoners
Automatic or semi-automatic weapons obtainable by 49% of students
Automatic or semi-automatic weapons obtainable by 57% of prisoners
Guns carried by 12% of students
Guns carried by 55% of prisoners
Guns owned by 30% of students
Guns owned by 86% of prisoners

Source: "Inner City Youths and Firearms," *CJ: The Americas* (December–January 1993): 24.

7. Identify the change of focus introduced by the Progressives, and describe the elements of the Progressive formula for reform.
8. Identify and describe the shift in emphasis that occurred during the 1960s.
9. List and describe the significance of the landmark U.S. Supreme Court juvenile justice decisions.
10. Identify and explain the significance for juvenile justice of developments in the 1970s.
11. Compare the different ways in which states define delinquency.
12. List the types of juveniles.
13. What is the difference between status offenses and delinquency?
14. Explain the difficulties in measuring delinquency.
15. List the facts that stand out about juvenile delinquency, despite difficulties in measurement.

THE JUVENILE JUSTICE SYSTEM

The main agencies dealing with juvenile delinquency are legislatures, police, prosecutors, defense attorneys, courts, probation offices, detention centers, correctional facilities, treatment centers, halfway houses, and a range of social service agencies. Legislatures define the scope of these agencies' legal authority, particularly what age span and what conduct falls within the jurisdiction of the juvenile justice system. They also determine when older juveniles can be transferred to the criminal justice system as adults, in a procedure called **certification**. Legislatures determine the budgets each agency receives to administer juvenile justice.[18]

POLICE AND JUVENILES

Most large-city police departments have special units to handle juveniles. They keep records on juveniles, investigate cases involving them, and initiate referrals to the juvenile court. Police also have the power to detain some juveniles in secure facilities for brief periods. Although these special youth divisions are responsible for juveniles, regular patrol officers encounter most juveniles and make the critical decisions whether to investigate and/or arrest them. How police handle juveniles depends on a combination of internal and external influences that differ from department to department and even among individuals within departments, making generalization risky. Departments adopting a community-service approach emphasize helping juveniles, whereas departments stressing the crime-fighting role view rehabilitation very differently. As one officer put it:

> I don't want to sound like a hardass, but we have some really bad young hoodlums on the streets in L.A. These aren't the nickel and dime kid shoplifters; they are hardcore. Some of them have dozens of arrests, but they're still out there ripping off people. These pukes

> are into juvenile hall and out twenty minutes later; seriously, some of these hoodlums are back on the street before I finish the paperwork. If you are going to correct kids they have to get their hands whacked the first time they put them in the cookie jar, not six months later. Juvenile justice is slow. Jesus, the rights these kids have got. They have more rights than I have. I'm not talking about the Mickey Mouse cases; I mean the serious hoodlums.[19]

Department policies and the outlook of individual officers also affect the way juveniles are processed. The general formalization of the criminal process has affected police discretion in processing juveniles less than it has in police dealing with adults. The police have a range of options in deciding what to do with juvenile lawbreakers. Their four major choices are to:

1. Ignore them.
2. Counsel and release them.
3. Refer them to other agencies.
4. Process them further into the juvenile justice system.

Which of these four options officers choose—that is, how they exercise their discretion in processing juveniles—depends mainly on the nature of the encounter between the police and juvenile and the seriousness of the offense the officer detects or suspects. For example, if officers encounter juveniles together in a situation where the officers "sense something is wrong," they may simply pass by or stop for a brief conversation. They may go further and ask the juveniles their names, addresses, and what they are doing or where they are going. Officers may go still further and search them. They may tell the juveniles to break up the group and move on, or they may take them home and warn their parents to keep them off the street. Alternatively, they may take them to the station for further questioning, without formal arrest. In a considerable number of cases, the police take juveniles to the station house and call in their parents. If the parents seem amenable, the police then warn them and the juveniles of the consequences of further bad conduct and send them home. None of these choices involves formal police action, because the police did not make any arrests.[20]

Individual departments vary widely but in most about 50 percent of juveniles are "counseled and dismissed" informally. Informal handling might mean considerably more than the words imply. In some cases, police treat this option as an informal probation system. If juveniles who are counseled and dismissed commit further offenses, police will formally arrest them. Police also use the informal counsel-and-release option as a trade for information about other juveniles.[21]

Those juveniles who are not counseled and dismissed are either arrested and then released or **diverted** (referred to a social service agency), or are formally referred to juvenile court. According to most estimates, about 50 percent of the juveniles who come in contact with police are referred to juvenile court, but this figure varies according to the department. The police also have the authority to detain juveniles until the intake process begins. Although they release most juveniles during this period, they detain about one-third.[22]

How are the decisions to dismiss, divert, arrest, or refer to juvenile court made? The most important factor, according to research findings, is the seriousness of the offense. The police are almost certain to arrest and refer to juvenile court juveniles suspected of serious crimes, such as murder, rape, or major theft. They are much more likely to dismiss or divert juveniles they suspect have committed less serious offenses, particularly status offenses.[23]

Citizen complaints are important in police decisions to arrest juveniles. Police acquire most of their information concerning juveniles in the same way they do for adults—from private persons. If complainants are present and demand action short of arrest, police comply; if they ask for leniency, police grant it; if they demand formal arrest and processing, the officers usually accede. Hence, the presence and wishes of those who complain influence whether juveniles are counseled and released, diverted to social service agencies, or arrested.

Department policy also affects what action police take. The numbers of arrested juveniles police refer to juvenile court vary widely. Some departments refer less than 10 percent, others as many as 80 percent. In a legalistic department, to use James Q. Wilson's typology, impersonal legal standards are applied and more arrests will take place. In more service-oriented departments, or those that are less formalized, officers exercise wider discretion in releasing and diverting.

Demographic characteristics of juveniles who come in contact with police also affect police discretion. First is gender. Although most research shows that female delinquents commit fewer delinquent acts, in the main they commit the same kinds of offenses as males. They drink, shoplift, skip school, destroy property, steal, and burglarize. The police, however, use a double standard in dealing with male and female delinquents. Police are much less likely to arrest females for these offenses. However, if females violate what are considered traditional expectations—if they run away from home, disobey their parents, are sexually active—police are much more likely to take them into custody. In Honolulu, for example, only 6.1 percent of the females who committed serious criminal offenses were referred to juvenile court, whereas 33.7 percent of those arrested for status offenses were referred. Nationwide, 75 percent of the female delinquents referred to juvenile court were arrested for status, not criminal, offenses.[24]

Racial minorities and the poor are overrepresented in the arrest statistics for juveniles, just as they are for adults. To what extent this overrepresentation is due to outright prejudice or to deep structural features in American society and economy is not clear, although both certainly play a part. Naturally, inner-city dwellers and the police see matters very differently.[25] James Baldwin, African American novelist and commentator on racism, wrote about the police in the inner cities:

> Their very presence is an insult, and it would be, even if they spent their entire day feeding gum drops to children. They represent the force of the white world, and that world's criminal profit and ease, to keep the black man corralled up here, in his place. The badge, the gun in the holster, and the swinging club make vivid what will happen should his rebellion become overt.[26]

For the other side, criminologist James Q. Wilson writes:

> The patrolman believes with considerable justification that teenagers, Negroes, and lower income persons commit a disproportionate share of all reported crimes; being in those population categories at all makes one, statistically, more suspect than other persons; but to be in those categories and to behave unconventionally is to make oneself a prime suspect. Patrolmen believe they would be derelict in their duty if they did not treat such persons with suspicion, routinely question them on the street, and detain them for longer questioning if a crime has occurred in the area. To the objection of some middle-class observers that this is arbitrary or discriminatory, the police are likely to answer: "Have you ever been stopped or searched? Of course not. We can tell the difference; we have to tell the difference in order to do our job. What are you complaining about?"[27]

JUVENILE COURT

The combination of conflicting ideology, competing goals, and a colorful history infuses the juvenile court with particular vigor. Former juvenile judge H. Ted Rubin writes:

> This court is a far more complex instrument than outsiders imagine. It is law, and it is social work; it is control, and it is help; it is the good parent and, also, the stern parent; it is both formal and informal. It is concerned not only with the delinquent, but also with the battered child, the runaway, and many others. The juvenile court has been all things to all people.[28]

To fulfill its competing goals (help children in need, treat and/or punish juveniles who commit crimes, and protect society from juvenile criminality), work within its traditions, and balance conflicting ideologies, the juvenile court uses a three-step process:

1. Intake
2. Adjudication
3. Disposition

The police refer most cases to juvenile court, but parents, relatives, schools, and welfare agencies also bring juveniles to the attention of juvenile court. **Intake** is the process following police referrals to juvenile court during which several important decisions are made, including whether to:

1. Detain juveniles during case investigation.
2. File a petition for a formal court hearing.
3. Dismiss cases.

Since the creation of the juvenile court, probation officers have done most of the intake screening.

Probation officers have five options:

1. They can transfer the juvenile to criminal court for trial as an adult. Called either certification or judicial waiver, this option is increasingly heralded as the answer to rising juvenile street crime.

Proceedings in a juvenile court are less public and less formal than in an adult court. Despite a move by many courts to institute more formal procedures, the ideology that the moral and social condition of the child is more important than the crime he or she commits persists.

2. They can refer to an intake or prejudicial conference where, if the charge is not serious and the juvenile admits wrongdoing, the case is most often dropped. An intake conference also continues the case pending fulfillment of specified conditions, such as drug treatment, restitution, or psychological counseling.
3. They can refer cases to a juvenile conference committee (JCC). Juvenile conference committees comprise citizens appointed by juvenile courts to recommend dispositions for juveniles in nonserious cases. These JCC's are not common, and they apply only to first-time petty offenders.[29]
4. The probation officer or judge can dismiss the case, simply dropping it without any further action.
5. Probation officers can recommend adjudication, or a court hearing. Since about 1950, only half of all court referrals have resulted in adjudication.[30]

In one study of several hundred juvenile courts, the researchers concluded:

> The most typical pattern is either to dismiss the case or to counsel, warn, and release the youth. Only a small fraction are put on informal probation (16 percent) or referred to other social service agencies. In other words, most courts seem to cope with the inflow of cases through very minimal intervention which may, at most, produce a court record, but no significant action by court staff.[31]

Status and property offenses account for most referrals to juvenile court. Only a minor proportion are crimes against persons, and most of the crimes against persons are lesser assaults. Most research has demonstrated that the decision to dismiss, divert, or adjudicate primarily depends on the seriousness of the offense. Hence, the evidence does not support the conventional wisdom that juvenile courts adhere mainly to their original purpose: to look at juveniles, not their crimes, and consider rehabilitating them, not punishing them. Nor does it support the current complaint that juveniles are treated leniently—many offenses are either not crimes, or, if they are, are property offenses, not violent crimes.[32]

According to some experts, the evidence leads to a different conclusion. Because status and property offenders make up about 70 percent of the cases referred to adjudication, and only juveniles who commit serious crimes against persons are certain to go forward to adjudication, Lamar T. Empey believes:

> Such findings reflect in a striking way the persistence of the benevolent assumption that the moral and social condition of the child is more important than the act he or she commits. When intake personnel encounter children who are out of parental control, who are persistently truant from school, or who are habitual runaways, they often feel that formal action is required.[33]

Adjudication, following intake, is the legal process that judges conduct in juvenile court with the assistance of probation officers. Judges determine whether the allegations in the petition are proven. If they are, juveniles are formally delinquent. Since the Supreme Court opinions reviewed at the beginning of this chapter, the juvenile court's proceedings have become more formal than they were originally intended to be. Juveniles are notified of the pending delinquency charges, lawyers are more often present, evidence standards are stricter, and proceedings are more like criminal courts. Juvenile justice expert Lamar Empey noted that despite some increase in formality:

> [I]t is only in a minority of courts where attorneys and due process procedures are uniformly present. As more courts begin to adhere to this model, however, it seems likely that less attention will be paid to the moral condition of the child and more to the evidence in support of the charge. It is likely, moreover, that resistance will grow to the formal trials of status offenders, not only because they are not charged with crimes, but because status offenses are more difficult to prove.[34]

Once juveniles have been adjudicated delinquent, judges schedule **disposition hearings.** In the disposition hearings judges decide how best to resolve delinquency cases. In the meantime, probation officers conduct background investigations to assist judges in their disposition decisions. Disposition hearings resemble sentence hearings in adult criminal courts. Juvenile court judges have wide discretion to choose from a broad range of alternative dispositions, ranging from outright dismissal to commitment to secure correctional facilities resembling adult prisons.

Judges may order cases held in abeyance, or **"continuance in contemplation of dismissal."** If delinquents do not get into further trouble with the law within a specified period—often between six months and a year—judges will dismiss their cases without further action. Abeyance allows judges to keep open their option for further action if juveniles do not obey the law. Judges might continue cases until the fulfillment of specified conditions, including taking required diagnostic tests and treatment for disturbances stemming from emotional problems, substance abuse, and physical illness; observing curfew; paying restitution to victims; and providing community service. Delinquents usually receive a time period of one to six months to fulfill these conditions.[35]

Probation of delinquents strongly resembles adult probation. For delinquents confined in juvenile correctional facilities for status offenses and minor property crimes, confinement probably means training schools or camps for delinquents. Or, the confinement might consist of community-based programs, such as foster care, youth development centers, or independent living arrangements. For serious delinquency, juvenile corrections means secure facilities that resemble adult prisons.

Most juvenile cases are disposed of informally before a disposition hearing ever occurs. Of those adjudicated cases in which formal disposition takes place, most result in probation, only a few terminate in commitment to juvenile facilities, and an insignificant number are certified to adult criminal courts. Juvenile court judges exercise wide discretion in choosing among these alternatives. Some observers believe juveniles are not treated fairly; that is, that inappropriate factors weigh in judges' disposition decisions. Anthony Platt concluded that the Progressive "child savers" used dispositions to impose middle-class values on lower-class youths:

> The child saving movement had its most direct consequences on the children of the urban poor. The fact that "troublesome" adolescents were depicted as "sick" or "pathological," were "imprisoned for their own good," and were addressed in a paternalistic vocabulary, and exempted from criminal law processes did not alter the subjective experiences of control, restraint, and punishment. The "invention" of delinquency consolidated the inferior social status and dependency of lower-class youth.[36]

Sociologist Edwin Schur concurred:

> The philosophy of the juvenile court ensures that stereotypes will influence judicial dispositions. Sending the child who comes from a "broken home" in the slums to a training school, while giving probation to a youngster from a "good family" may not strike the judge as an exercise in stereotyping. [H]owever, such stereotypes tend to be self-confirming. Children from "broken homes" are likely to be committed to institutions because they are believed to be delinquency-prone; yet these very commitments, in turn, serve to reinforce that belief.[37]

Neither Platt nor Schur based their findings on empirical evidence. However, Lawrence E. Cohen made an effort to measure empirically the influences on juvenile court dispositions. He gathered information about nearly 13,000 juveniles who appeared before juvenile courts in three counties in Colorado, Tennessee, and Pennsylvania. Cohen measured the effects of juveniles' age, sex, ethnicity, socioeconomic status, family situation; the seriousness of their offenses; the number of their prior referrals to juvenile court; their referral agent; whether juveniles were in detention prior to hearings; and whether there were formal petitions against juveniles or informal dispositions.

The jurisdictions varied considerably. In Colorado, the seriousness of offense was most important. In Tennessee, offense seriousness was also most significant but was followed closely by whether the police referred the juveniles, and whether they were in detention prior to adjudication. In Pennsylvania, the most important factors were whether juveniles were idle, from broken homes, and referred by agencies other than police.[38]

Other investigators have found that minority youths are more likely to be incarcerated and less likely to be put on probation. Barry Krisberg and others took data collected nationally in a semiannual survey conducted by the U.S. Bureau of the Census, called Children in Custody, or CIC, and compared the populations in juvenile correctional facilities with the arrest statistics in the Uniform Crime Reports. They found that in 1982, for example, African American youths were incarcerated at a rate of 8.6 per 100 compared with 5.1 per 100 for whites, a ratio 69 percent higher. For Native Americans, the ratio is even higher—14.5. The researchers concluded that the reasons for this higher incarceration rate are not due to offense seriousness.[39]

Offense seriousness is an appropriate reason for incarceration, but race and ethnicity clearly are not. Equally inappropriate are idleness and broken homes, criteria that demonstrate that juveniles are incarcerated according to attitudes prejudicial to those who are not from traditional, middle-class families.[40]

Knowledge and Understanding CHECK

1. Who decides whether to arrest or release juveniles?
2. Identify the influences on how police handle juveniles.
3. Identify four options the police have in deciding what to do with juveniles.
4. List the influences that determine how officers decide which option to select.
5. Identify the conflicting missions of the juvenile court.
6. List the three steps in the juvenile court process.
7. List the major decisions made during intake.
8. List the five options probation officers have during the intake process, and identify the most typical pattern.
9. What kinds of offenses account for most referrals to juvenile court?
10. What happens during adjudication in juvenile court?
11. Describe what happens during the disposition hearing.
12. List the findings of Lawrence E. Cohen regarding the influences on juvenile court dispositions.

JUVENILE CORRECTIONS

Several approaches to juvenile crime have been taken throughout most of U.S. history. Colonial Americans assumed people were basically prone to do wrong and were, therefore, more forgiving toward juveniles who had done so, often permitting young, convicted offenders to return to the community after warning, shaming, or corporal punishment. Toward the end of the eighteenth century, the Enlightenment philosophy worked a change in this approach. Relying on the assumption that criminals chose to commit crimes out of their own free will, deterring crime through effective law enforcement, followed by certain and swift punishment, became fashionable. Corporal punishment, hard labor, and similar tactics reinforced the idea that basic human nature did not lead inevitably to crime, but rather individuals chose to commit crimes because they did not suffer sufficient pain to offset the pleasure derived from committing crimes.[41]

During the 1830s, another shift occurred. The unsettled society that resulted from deep changes in the American way of life led to the conclusion that rapidly accelerating urbanization, industrialization, and immigration caused crime. As a solution, society proposed to remove criminals from it until they could be reformed and returned to lead law-abiding lives and withstand the evils spawned by urban, industrial America. Hence, a great building spree produced adult prisons, reformatories for older youthful offenders, and industrial training schools for younger delinquents where reform could take place away from the evils afflicting general society.

Within a few years, the great hopes for institutional correction were clearly not realized. Early alternatives to institutional corrections, the roots of modern probation and parole, were created. John Augustus, a Boston bootmaker, took young children from courts and placed them under his direct care in his home (Chapter 13). If they remained free from further delinquency during the period in which they would have been incarcerated, they were released. Augustus's efforts began what would be a series of shifts between institutional and community corrections.

Shifting emphases between institutional corrections and various community alternatives to it, as well as efforts to "improve" them both, characterized the century from 1850 to 1950. In the 1950s, a great interest arose in community-based alternatives to large, state-run institutions for delinquents, exemplified in the growth of local institutions, residential youth centers, group homes, and specialized probation services. From the late 1960s to the 1970s, in a second phase of this development, diversion and deinstitutionalization programs proliferated and were touted as the panacea to youth crime and delinquency. These community-based corrections rested on the conviction that state reformatories failed to prevent delinquency and, in fact, exacerbated it by stigmatizing youths exposed to it: such youths became part of a "state youth subculture" heavily involved in patterns of both state dependence and criminality that were very difficult, if not impossible, to break.[42]

During the 1970s, the rise in reported street crime, heavy emphasis on juvenile crime, growing empirical literature questioning rehabilitation's effectiveness, the perception that retribution is the most effective response to crime, and growing public demand for retributive punishment led to a return to demands to incarcerate delinquents. The trend has produced additional demands for other reforms that generally emphasize punishment and community safety in juvenile justice. Informally, punishment and community protection have always been juvenile justice goals to some extent, even if they are not explicitly articulated. Despite changes that have brought them to a closer resemblance to adult corrections, juvenile corrections are still quite distinct. Juvenile corrections continue to emphasize rehabilitation and have a considerably richer variety of institutions and alternatives than adult corrections.

Community Corrections

The definition of community corrections is broad, and the distinction between community and institutional corrections for juveniles is blurred. The Task Force on Corrections, National Advisory Commission on Criminal Justice Standards and Goals, defines community corrections as "all correctional activities that take place in the community. The community base must be an alternative to confinement of an offender at any point in the correctional system."[43]

Sociologist Paul Lerman notes:

> In practice, the term has been treated as elastic, stretching to cover institutional "communities" in Texas housing Illinois children, institutional communities in western Massachusetts housing youths from eastern Massachusetts, a youth service bureau in a youngster's neighborhood, a residential treatment facility in a distant county, a secure mental hospital ward in a state hospital, and a group home on the grounds of a large hospital.[44]

James O. Finckenauer offers perhaps the best working definition of community-based corrections for juveniles:

> Community corrections must include, at a minimum, regular access to school or a job in the community; regular access to home, family, and friends; and regular access to recreation in the community.[45]

Perhaps nothing more clearly demonstrates the difference between adult and juvenile corrections than the heavier commitment to, and the greater variety of, community corrections as an alternative to institutions following disposition. Probation is by far the most frequently used form of community juvenile corrections. Probation and parole for juveniles strongly resemble the same practices for adults (see Chapter 13). Both probation and parole are types of community supervision. Probation is community supervision in place of incarceration in an institution; parole is community supervision following a period of incarceration. Juvenile probation is informal probation supervised by the police. Juveniles are usually required to report periodically to police departments and to follow police-established conditions for behavior.[46]

Institutional Corrections

Juvenile correctional institutions cover a broad spectrum, from small, short-term, nonsecure facilities to long-term, highly secure facilities serving large areas. Foster homes—

Wilderness camps are one type of juvenile corrections facility. Often, programs stress survival, teaching juveniles to rely on themselves and therefore build the self-esteem that will hopefully lead to them becoming strong, responsible people. In this photo juveniles brave the winter in a camp in Calwood, Colorado.

small, nonsecure facilities that are supposed to be real family substitutes—are used at all stages in the juvenile justice process. Police might temporarily place arrested juveniles who cannot be returned to their homes in foster homes instead of detention facilities. Courts might also assign juveniles to foster homes before, or after, adjudication. The National Advisory Commission (NAC) recommends foster care as the primary placement for minor delinquency. However, due to inadequate—and sometimes totally lacking—accreditation and monitoring, some persons convicted of child abuse have received or retained foster home licenses.[47]

Shelters, nonsecure residential facilities, hold juveniles temporarily assigned to them, usually in lieu of detention or returning home following arrest, or after adjudication while awaiting more permanent placement. Shelters are reserved primarily for status offenders and are not intended for either treatment or punishment.

Group homes, also nonsecure, relatively open community-based facilities, mainly hold juveniles who have been adjudicated delinquent. Group homes are larger and less familylike than foster homes. Small group homes serve from four to eight; large group homes, from eight to twelve. Residents range in age from 10 to 17, but most are between 13 and 16. Group homes permit more independent living in a more permanent setting, and they are more treatment-oriented than shelters. Group home residents usually attend school—in the home or in the community—or they work. They also participate in individual and group counseling and recreation. Group homes are intended to provide support and structure in nonrestrictive settings that facilitate reintegration into the community.[48]

Halfway houses are large, nonsecure residential centers. They provide both a place to live and a range of personal and social services. The typical halfway house serves from 12 to 20 residents, but some large programs serve as many as 40 residents. Residents' ages range from 14 to 18. "Halfway houses provide a range of services and emphasize normal group living, school attendance, securing employment, working with parents to resolve problems and general participation in the community."[49]

Camps and ranches are nonsecure facilities, almost always located in rural and remote areas. Juveniles adjudicated delinquent are generally placed in camps as an alternative to the more secure training schools. The healthful setting, small numbers of residents, and close contact between staff and juveniles are supposed to develop good work and living habits that will facilitate rehabilitation. Ranches and camps emphasize outside activity, self-discipline, and the development of vocational and interpersonal skills. Juveniles assigned to them are not only supposed to develop good work habits, but they are also to perform "useful and necessary" work that benefits the community.[50]

Detention centers are temporary custodial facilities. However, unlike shelters, detention centers are secure institutions—lockups—that hold juveniles both before and after adjudication. The three formal purposes of locking juveniles up in detention centers include:

1. To secure their presence at court proceedings.
2. To hold those who cannot be sent home.
3. To protect them from harming themselves or others or disrupting juvenile court processes.

Juveniles who have committed more serious offenses are sent to detention centers, whereas those who have committed less serious ones are sent to shelters.[51]

Before adjudication, juveniles may stay in detention centers anywhere from a day to more than two weeks, raising the troubling question of the fairness of detention prior to proven delinquency. Detention is also sometimes used as informal punishment. Judges lock juveniles up to scare them, to show them what might happen to them, or to "teach them a lesson and give them a taste of jail." Some jurisdictions have formalized detention centers as jails for children. New Jersey, for example, permits sentencing juveniles who have been adjudicated delinquent for "repetitive disorderly persons offenses" to up to 60 days in detention centers.[52]

Not all juveniles who are detained go to juvenile detention centers. Some are housed in adult jails—a situation criticized for more than a century. James O. Finckenauer visited one of these jails in Tyler, Texas, and reported the following:

> This author visited one such all purpose jail. On the upper floor of this jail (on a very humid day in late June, with the temperature soaring into triple figures) approximately a dozen juveniles were confined in a large bullpen cell. This cell was literally a "hot box," dark and without ventilation. Some of the juveniles were from out of the state, and the average stay for most was somewhere around forty-five days. Because these youth were confined in an adult facility, and because the sheriff was attempting to maintain physical separation of juveniles and adults, the youth had no place to go and nothing to do for just about the entire duration of their incarceration. The NAC referred to the jailing of juveniles as a "disconcerting phenomenon." This is certainly an understatement, to say the very least. Because they are intended to be temporary holding facilities, jails and detention centers offer little or nothing in the way of correctional treatment.[53]

Training schools exist in every state except Massachusetts, which abolished them in the 1970s. They vary greatly in size, staff, services, programs, ages, and types of residents. Most, however, house from one to several hundred juveniles committed by juvenile courts. Some training schools resemble adult prisons, with congregate-style living and emphasis on security and order, whereas others are relatively open facilities that focus on treatment and rehabilitation.

Training schools are the instrument of last resort in the juvenile correctional system. They contain the most serious delinquents: those who are security risks, have substantial prior records, or have exhausted other juvenile court dispositions. Almost all training schools are state-operated and controlled, unlike the other facilities discussed. Most legislation requires training schools to provide both safe custody and rehabilitative treatment.[54]

According to corrections expert Kenneth Wooden:

> I found basically two types of training schools. The first is a miniature penitentiary with high walls surrounding the grounds. All the buildings and cell block wings therein are interlocked by long corridors. Not only are individual cell doors secured, but each wing is also locked at all times. There is almost always a self-sufficient industrial complex on the grounds—laundry, hospital, maintenance shop and any other facility needed to keep strangers out and the children in. Dubious educational and religious services are available to the children, along with the standbys of solitary confinement and of bloodhounds to locate any who run away.
>
> The second and more common type of training school is the cottage system. Its concept was introduced in 1856 to give children the closest thing to some form of home life. Those in charge are "house parents" rather than "guards." The outside area is usually quiet and pleasant and bears little semblance to a penal facility. The cottages are usually small, aesthetically pleasing, dormlike structures. Unfortunately, those I have seen have no back or side doors, or if they do, the doors are always chained and locked. The windows are also secured with heavy wire. The cottage system always reserves one building for secure treatment, solitary confinement. Any child who acts up in solitary cottage is further isolated in a special single room for indefinite periods of time.[55]

CERTIFICATION

Every jurisdiction in the United States operates two separate systems for responding to criminal conduct, one for juveniles and one for adults. Different laws, procedures, and terminology govern each system. Furthermore, historically they operated according to distinct policies regarding the people who came before them. Age determines which system has authority to determine cases before it. Depending on the laws of a given state, for a criminal suspect younger than 16, 17, or 18, juvenile court handles the case; adult criminal courts manage the others.

This division of authority, the **dual system of justice,** has received careful scrutiny. How does this dual (or "two-track") system affect the sentencing of offenders who, while legally juveniles, have demonstrated a sustained commitment to serious predatory crime, or who have just crossed the age boundary between juvenile court and criminal court? A number of commentaries assert that these youthful offenders receive more lenient treatment than their older peers. Some people question whether such leniency is appropriate, given that sentencing criteria in the adult courts are moving away from rehabilitation and more toward punishment and community protection.[56]

This debate is not simply academic. Many jurisdictions are looking at a variety of reforms that would change the way in which serious youthful offenders are treated. They include:

- Reducing the juvenile court's maximum age limit from 18 to 16, so that older juveniles must be tried in adult courts.

- Increasing the use of juvenile records, particularly in adult courts, to help identify high-risk offenders and treat them accordingly.
- Replacing the juvenile court's rehabilitation philosophy with a get-tough policy in which the sentencing objective becomes punishment that fits the crime.
- Making sentencing of juveniles charged with specific, violent crimes mandatory.
- Prosecuting juvenile career criminals.
- Replacing the two-track system with a three-track system that would include (1) a family court for neglected and dependent youths under 14 years of age, (2) a juvenile court for 14- to 18-year-olds whose crimes are not particularly serious, and (3) a criminal court to handle offenders over 18 and juveniles whose crimes are serious.[57]

The RAND Corporation explored how youthful offenders, ages 16 to 21, are treated during that time when legal responsibility for dealing with their criminal behavior is shifting from juvenile to adult court. They found a positive relationship between age and average crime seriousness for young offenders, prompting RAND to conclude that aggregate arrest figures probably exaggerate the amount of serious crime attributable to this age group. This exaggeration also appears to inflate the leniency with which these offenders are treated. Their analysis of case disposition patterns disclosed a wide degree of variation among jurisdictions, both between offenders of the same age across sites and in the relative severity with which different age groups are treated within sites. The sentencing patterns across these sites could not be fully attributed to organizational or legal differences between them.[58]

Use *Your* Discretion

How should criminal justice treat juveniles who murder?[59]

Andre, who was born and lives in New York City, is the product of a broken home. There was never enough money at home, and he was left to fend for himself. He tried selling crack when he was 12 but found that it was too dangerous, so he turned to mugging. "I would go up to somebody and tell them to give me money. If they tried to hit me, my friends would jump in. We hardly ever used a weapon. Sometimes, my friends had a razor." By the time he was 14, Andre had pulled off more than 120 muggings. "It was fun," he said. "It's like getting away with something. It's like a high, excitement." Did he think it was wrong? "Not really," he said. "I didn't think much about it. It was like I was going through a stage."

Andre first held a gun when he was 13. He had cut school and a friend let him hold the gun in the hallway of an apartment building. When he was 14, Andre fired a friend's gun in the air at a birthday party. One afternoon, while Andre was talking to two girls, about a dozen boys rode up on bicycles and one hit Andre with a baseball bat and another punched him in the face. The next morning, Andre went to a friend who was a crack dealer and bought a chrome-plated Smith & Wesson .32. Later that day he ran into the boys from the previous day. One boy accused Andre of roughing up the boy's cousin. He danced around Andre like a prize fighter, jabbing a hand in Andre's face. Andre warned him to back away or "he would have to shoot."

Fear of youth violence is high but it is not new: Almost every generation fears the violence that juveniles are capable of. Shootings by youths not only in the streets but in schools as well are perceived as being on the rise. Here a youth at Thomas Jefferson High School in New York holds his possessions in a tray while a guard uses a metal detector to check for weapons.

The boy said, "If you shoot me, you better kill me, because I'll get you." Andre fired the gun into the boy's face, turned, and ran away, dodging traffic as he tried to avoid the victim's friends. "I didn't intend to kill him. I just wanted to scare him. I didn't know it would go off so easily."

Andre is one of an increasing number of teenagers who have murdered with guns. In 1982, 10 to 15 percent of teenagers who got into serious trouble in New York City were carrying guns. In 1992, 60 to 65 percent were carrying guns. Researchers at the Federal Center for Disease Control reported that shootings by teenagers contributed significantly to the rising homicide rate in the early 1990s. The National Crime Analysis Project at Northeastern University found that the number of 17-year-olds arrested for murder climbed 121 percent from 1985 through 1991. The number of 16-year-olds rose 158 percent. But the biggest increase—217 percent—was in the arrest of 15-year-olds. Even the number of arrests of boys 12 and under rose 100 percent.

According to James Alan Fox, dean of the College of Criminal Justice at Northeastern University, "Murder is plunging to a much younger age group. What is so dangerous about this is that a 15-year-old with a gun in his hand is a much more volatile individual than a 40-year-old or even an 18-year-old." Fox predicted that the United States is on the verge of a "vast new epidemic of murder. What we've seen in the past few years is nothing compared with what we'll see in the . . . next century as the resurging adolescent population mixes with changes in our society, our culture, and our economy." The reason is the expected increase in the numbers of adolescents in the population.

Experts point to a number of reasons for the sharp increase in killings by younger boys, including:

- The drug epidemic among the urban poor.
- The growing number and firepower of guns.
- The eroding quality of public schools.
- The glorification of violence on television and in the movies.

According to Alfred Blumstein, dean of the Heinz School of Public Policy and Management at Carnegie-Mellon University and president of the American Society of Criminology, the continued breakdown of the American family is the most important reason for increases in juvenile crime. Blumstein said that many young people are poorly socialized and are more vulnerable to drugs, violence on television, and the easy availability of guns. "The glorification of violence on television has little effect on most folks, but it has a powerful effect on kids who are poorly socialized. It dehumanizes them and becomes a self-fulfilling process." Blumstein says change requires "a considerable investment in the socialization process, which we have heretofore left to the family." However, Blumstein adds, investing in socialization is expensive and intrusive and, therefore, unpopular.

James Alan Fox is skeptical of the current policy of imprisonment. "People say, 'Let's just try these kids who kill as adults and lock them up.' But that won't work. They don't care. They don't think about the consequences, and they don't have a long-term perspective. They face death every day on the street and even at school, so why should they be afraid that maybe the police will catch them and maybe they will be executed?"

According to Marvin Wolfgang, the late distinguished professor of criminology and law at the University of Pennsylvania, and the former director of the Sellin Criminology Center, "What we're seeing is the loss of childhood. These kids are growing up too fast into the subculture of violence. They are learning at an ever younger age that violence is not only tolerated, but often expected and sometimes required. If you don't respond aggressively to a slur on your mother or your manhood, you're a coward."

The story of Andre and the comments of Fox, Blumstein, and Wolfgang point to teenagers murdering with guns in slums of large cities. However, George Butterfield, deputy director of the National School Safety Center at Pepperdine University in Malibu, California, sees a clear migration of guns to the suburbs, much the way that drugs and gangs have come to the middle class. "Teenage shootings and weapons incidents have increased across the board. It's just that in the suburbs you have a lot more denial. All over the country, people tell me, 'This was an isolated incident.'" In Westport, Connecticut, for example, a 16-year-old was charged with fatally shooting a classmate. The newspapers were deluged by critical letters when it reported on widespread drunkenness at the high school homecoming game, and on a teenage party where a youth had brandished a 9 mm pistol. "We believe Westport suffers from the disease of denial," responded an editorial in the local newspaper.

CRITICAL THINKING

1. What is the best policy to reduce the increase in murder by teenagers? Lock them up? Execute them? Intervene in the family and socialization process? Improve schools? Pass gun control legislation?
2. After reading the comments of Blumstein, Fox, and Wolfgang, what would you recommend specifically for Andre?
3. Consider the comments of Butterfield regarding the increase of shootings in suburbs. What are your recommendations for a long-term policy to deal with teenage murderers? Do you recommend the same policies for urban slums and affluent suburbs? Explain your answer.

Knowledge and Understanding CHECK

1. Identify the shifting approaches to juvenile crime taken in U.S. history.
2. Compare juvenile with adult corrections.
3. Identify and describe the major types of institutional corrections for juveniles.
4. List the major purposes of confining juveniles in detention centers.
5. According to the RAND Corporation, how are youths between 16 and 21 treated during the time when legal responsibiliy for criminal behavior is shifting from juvenile to adult court?

Is Arrest and Criminal Prosecution the Best Response? Consideration

1. List all of the alternatives presented in this chapter to charging 13-year-old Rowland Fisher with aggravated assault.
2. Which of them is the best in your judgment? Defend your answer with specific details in the chapter.

CHAPTER CAPSULE

- Society and law have always treated children differently from adults.
- History demonstrates a conflict over whether the justice system should help or punish juvenile offenders.
- At the turn of the twenty-first century, there is a trend toward treating juveniles who commit serious crimes as adults.
- There is a preoccupation with young children who commit violent crime, but the numbers who do are comparatively small.

KEY TERMS

doctrine of *parens patriae*
medical model
delinquency
status offenses
juvenile delinquent
certification
diversion
intake
adjudication
disposition hearing
continuance in contemplation of dismissal
shelters
group home
halfway house
detention center
training school
dual system of justice

INTERNET RESEARCH EXERCISES

Exercise: Search for information about correctional "boot camps" for juveniles. What are the goals of the camps? Identify the major characteristics of the camps. Summarize the findings of the evaluations of boot camps. Are correctional "boot camps" for juveniles effective? Defend your response with the results of your research.

Suggested sites:

- You will find several Internet sites related to the topic of juvenile correctional boot camps. Here is just one to get you started:
- Koch Crime Institute: Article on Juvenile Boot Camps, http://www.kci.org/newsletter/1998/nov/boot_camps.htm

Infotrac College Edition: Search on key word "juvenile boot camps"

NOTES

1. "Charge: 13-Year-Old Threatened Siblings," *Sarasota Herald-Tribune,* 30 December 1998.
2. Stephen Schlossman, *Love and the American Delinquent: The Theory and Practice of "Progressive" Juvenile Justice, 1825–1920* (Chicago: University of Chicago Press, 1977).
3. Based on Kathryn Wexler, "Prosecutors Pursue Case Against 6-Year-Old Suspect," *Washington Post,* 27 April 1996.
4. See generally Anthony Platt, *The Child Savers: The Invention of Delinquency* (Chicago: University of Chicago Press, 1969).
5. See generally, David J. Rothman, *Conscience and Convenience: The Asylum and Its Alternatives in Progressive America* (Boston: Little, Brown, 1980); Ellen Ryerson, *The Best Laid Plans: America's Juvenile Court Experiment* (New York: Hill and Wang, 1978); Platt, *Child Savers.*
6. President's Commission on Law Enforcement and the Administration of Justice, *The Challenge of Crime in a Free Society* (Washington, D.C.: U.S. Government Printing Office, 1967).
7. *Kent v. United States,* 383 U.S. 541 (1966).
8. *In re Winship,* 387 U.S. 1 (1967); 397 U.S. 358 (1970).
9. *McKeiver v. Pennsylvania,* 403 U.S. 528 (1970), 533–34.
10. Reported in William Glaberson, "Rising Tide of Anger at Teen-Aged Killers," *New York Times,* 24 May 1998.
11. H. Ted Rubin, *Juvenile Justice: Policy, Practice and Law* (Santa Monica, Calif.: Goodyear Press, 1979), 40; Tappan quoted in Malcolm W. Klein, ed., *Western Systems of Juvenile Justice* (Beverly Hills: Sage Publications, 1984), 20; Mike Males and Dan Macallair, "The Impact of Juvenile Curfew Laws in California" (San Francisco: Justice Policy Institute, June 1998).
12. Department of Youth Authority, 1981, secs. 601, 602.
13. Males and Macallair, "The Impact of Curfew Laws," 3–4.
14. Ibid., 5–6.
15. Robert A. Mathias, Paul DeMuro, and Richard S. Allinson, eds., *Violent Juvenile Offenders: An Anthology* (San Francisco: National Council on Crime and Delinquency, 1984), 8; National Institute for Juvenile Justice and Delinquency Prevention, *Reports of the National Juvenile Justice Assessment Centers: A National Assessment of Serious Crime and the Juvenile Justice System* (Washington, D.C.: Law Enforcement Assistance Administration, April 1980), 59.
16. Richard J. Lundman, *Prevention and Control of Juvenile Delinquency* (New York: Oxford University Press, 1984), 4.
17. Franklin E. Zimring, "Kids, Groups and Crime: Some Implications of a Well-Known Secret," *Journal of Criminal Law and Criminology* 72 (1981): 867–85; Franklin E. Zimring, *Confronting Youth Crime—Report of the Twentieth Century Fund Task Force on Sentencing PolicyToward Young Offenders: Background Paper* (New York: Holmes and Maier, 1978), 38.
18. Lamar T. Empey, *American Delinquency: Its Meaning and Construction* (Homewood, Ill.: The Dorsey Press, 1978), 403–84; Robert M. Carter, "The United States," in Klein, *Western Systems of Juvenile Justice,* 17–38; Jay S. Albanese, *Dealing with Delinquency: An Investigation of Juvenile Justice* (Lanham, Md.: University Press of America, 1985).
19. Robert M. Carter, "The Police View of the Justice System," in *The Juvenile Justice System,* Malcolm W. Klein, ed. (Beverly Hills: Sage Publications, 1976), 124.
20. Carter, "United States," 27.
21. Ibid., 29.
22. Empey, *American Delinquency,* 432; Patricia M. Harris, "Is the Juvenile Justice System Lenient?" *Criminal Justice Abstracts* 18 (1986):107.
23. Harris, "Is the Juvenile Justice System Lenient?" 107.
24. Empey, *American Delinquency,* 426–27.
25. Ibid., 427–28.
26. James Baldwin, *Nobody Knows My Name* (New York: Dell, 1962), 66.
27. James Q. Wilson, *Varieties of Police Behavior* (Cambridge, Mass.: Harvard University Press, 1978), 40–41.
28. H. Ted Rubin, *The Courts: Fulcrum of the Justice System* (Pacific Palisades, Calif.: Goodyear, 1976), 66.
29. Albanese, *Dealing with Delinquency,* 85.
30. Ibid., 454.
31. Yeheskel Hasenfield, "Youth in the Juvenile Court: Input and Output Patterns," in *Brought to Justice? Juveniles, the Courts and the Law,* Rosemary Sarri and Yeheskel Hasenfield, eds. (Ann Arbor: National Assessment of Juvenile Corrections, University of Michigan, 1976), 70.
32. Harris, "Is the Juvenile Justice System Lenient?" 111.
33. Empey, *American Delinquency,* 455.
34. Ibid., 457–58.
35. Albanese, *Dealing with Delinquency,* 89.
36. Platt, *Child Savers,* 176–78.
37. Edwin Schur, *Radical Non-Intervention: Rethinking the Delinquency Problem* (Englewood Cliffs, N.J.: Prentice-Hall, 1973), 44.
38. Lawrence E. Cohen, *Delinquency Dispositions: An Empirical Analysis of Processing Decisions in Three Juvenile Courts* (Washington, D.C.: U.S. Government Printing Office, 1975).
39. Barry Krisberg et al., *The Incarceration of Minority Youth* (Minneapolis: University of Minnesota, Hubert H. Humphrey Institute of Public Affairs, 1986), 23.

40. Albanese, *Dealing with Delinquency,* 91.
41. Thomas G. Blomberg, *Juvenile Court and Community Corrections* (Lanham, N.Y.: University Press of America, 1984), 1–3; Alden D. Miller and Lloyd E. Ohlin, *Delinquency and Community* (Beverly Hills: Sage Publications, 1985), 11–22.
42. Richard A. Cloward and Lloyd E. Ohlin, *Delinquency and Opportunity: A Theory of Delinquent Gangs* (New York: Free Press, 1960).
43. National Advisory Commission on Criminal Justice Standards and Goals, *Corrections* (Washington, D.C.: U.S. Government Printing Office, 1973), 222.
44. Paul Lerman, "Trends and Issues in the Deinstitutionalization of Youths in Trouble," *Crime and Delinquency* 26 (1980): 295.
45. James O. Finckenauer, *Juvenile Delinquency and Corrections: The Gap Between Theory and Practice* (Orlando: Academic Press, 1984), 126.
46. Thomas R. Collingwood et al., "Juvenile Diversion: The Dallas Police Department Youth Services Program," in *Effective Correctional Treatment,* Robert R. Ross and Paul Gendreau, eds. (Toronto: Butterworths, 1980), 93–100.
47. Finckenauer, *Juvenile Delinquency,* 151.
48. National Institute of Corrections, *Standards for Juvenile Community Residential Facilities* (Washington, D.C.: National Institute of Corrections, 1983), xvii.
49. Ibid., xvi.
50. National Advisory Committee, *Standards for Administration of Juvenile Justice* (Washington, D.C.: Government Printing Office, 1980), 487–91.
51. Finckenauer, *Juvenile Delinquency,* 152.
52. Ibid; New Jersey P.L. 1982, chap. 77, sec. 24; American Correctional Association, *Standards for Juvenile Training Schools,* 2d ed. (Washington, D.C.: National Institute of Justice, 1983), xvii.
53. Finckenauer, *Juvenile Delinquency,* 132.
54. American Correctional Association, *Standards for Juvenile Training Schools,* xvii.
55. Kenneth Wooden, *Weeping in the Playtime of Others* (New York: McGraw-Hill, 1976), 28–29.
56. RAND Corporation, *Age, Crime, and Sanctions: The Transition from Juvenile to Adult Court* (Santa Monica: RAND Corporation, 1980).
57. Ibid.
58. Ibid.
59. Based on Fox Butterfield, "Seeds of Murder Epidemic: Teenage Boys with Guns," *New York Times,* 19 October 1992; Joseph B. Treaster, "Teen-age Murderers: Plentiful Guns, Easy Power," *New York Times,* 24 May 1992; Ellen Graham, "Mainstream America Finds It Isn't Immune to Kids Killing Kids," *Wall Street Journal,* 7 February 1992.

Appendix A
Careers in Criminal Justice

According to the *Monthly Labor Review's* projections of occupational employment, the total number of jobs will continue to grow between 1988 and 2000, but at half the rate of the previous twelve-year period. Jobs that require special education and training will foreclose a growing and attractive segment of the job market to those with low educational attainment or specific practical skills. Much of the growth in employment until the year 2000 will be in the service industries, which includes the criminal justice occupations. So, criminal justice is an area of job growth for those with the education and training to compete for the jobs. This appendix describes the range of positions in criminal justice. An excellent source for more details concerning these and other positions related to criminal justice, a description of the specific qualifications for the jobs described here, and general information on how to prepare a résumé and get ready for an interview is J. Scott Harr and Kären M. Hess, *Seeking Employment in Law Enforcement, Private Security, and Related Fields.*

LAW ENFORCEMENT: FEDERAL AGENCIES

Career opportunities are available in the following agencies of the federal government:

United States Bureau of Alcohol, Tobacco, and Firearms

The Bureau of Alcohol, Tobacco, and Firearms has a unique opportunity to deter crime because of its diversified jurisdictions. Enforcement of possession laws in the areas of alcohol, tobacco, and firearms are the bureau's main concern. Investigation of arson-for-profit schemes is also an important function of ATF. Irregular hours and rigorous training are common for special agents.

- *Salary schedule:* Special agents begin at a salary level usually between $18,340 and $22,717. Employees then progress along the General Schedule for federal employees with income potential well above $60,000. *Educational qualifications:* A college degree or at least three years of general experience is necessary with an additional year of specialized experience often preferred.
- *Benefits:* Early retirement as early as 50, premiums on income potential as high as an additional 25 percent, group health and life insurance programs, and paid holidays are only a few of the benefits enjoyed by ATF employees.
- *Do you want to know more?*
  Contact Bureau of Alcohol, Tobacco, and Firearms
  Personnel Division—Employment Branch
  Washington, D.C. 20226
  Phone: (202) 927-8610

Central Intelligence Agency

Many diverse careers are available upon appointment to a position in the CIA. There is a current need for intelligence analysts and overseas analysts within the CIA. Employment can be exciting and rewarding but employees are expected to work many odd hours and days. Employees must also be able to relocate.

- *Salary schedule:* Employees earn their salary according to the General Schedule with beginning salaries dependent upon the appointment.
- *Educational qualifications:* A college degree is necessary for appointment and fluency in a foreign language is definitely preferred. A 6–9 month application process must be completed as well as polygraph, medical, and physical examinations.
- *Benefits:* Employees enjoy many benefits comparable to other federal agencies such as accumulated vacation time, health insurance, life insurance, and a quality retirement plan.
- *Do you want to know more?*
  Contact Central Intelligence Agency
  Recruitment Office
  Philadelphia, PA 12330
  Phone: (800) 562-7242

United States Department of Justice: Federal Bureau of Investigation

A wide range of employment opportunities exist within the Federal Bureau of Investigation. Careers such as special agents as well as computer programmers, laboratory technicians, and electronics technicians illustrate the diversity of opportunities within the bureau. Employees often are required to relocate many times throughout their careers in order to undertake new, challenging, and exciting assignments.

- *Salary schedule:* Employees are salaried on the General Schedule pay rates. Entry level positions offer salaries between \$18,340 and \$27,789 with many employees earning over \$50,000 annually.
- *Educational qualifications:* Most positions require a four-year college degree from an accredited institution.
- *Benefits:* Employees enjoy benefits equivalent to many programs in the private sector with vacation days, paid sick days, federal holidays, and more. It is important to note that the holidays and vacation days are often not the same as other federal employees, as careers in the FBI often require hours other than a typical 9:00 A.M. to 5:00 P.M. shift, Monday–Friday.
- *Do you want to know more?*
  Contact U.S. Department of Justice
  Federal Bureau of Investigation
  Office of Public Affairs
  10th Street and Pennsylvania Avenue, N.W.
  Washington, D.C. 20535
  Phone: (202) 324-5611

United States Department of Justice: Federal Bureau of Prisons

Within the Federal Bureau of Prisons a wide range of opportunities are available with careers in areas such as accounting and marketing analysis as well as jobs for correction officers and administrators. Many "prisoner contact" positions exist as well as behind-the-scenes careers where employees may never even meet a prisoner.

- *Salary schedule:* Correctional Treatment Specialists earn \$27,789 in their first year alone with potential to earn \$33,623 in their second year. Other careers begin at various salaries with advancement opportunities abundant.
- *Educational Qualifications:* Almost all careers require a bachelor's degree with a master's being preferred in some areas.
- *Benefits:* Employees enjoy low-cost life insurance programs, family health plans, 13–26 days of annual paid leave (based on length of employment), early retirement, and more.
- *Do you want to know more?*
  Contact U.S. Department of Justice
  Federal Bureau of Prisons
  Human Resource Management Division
  National Recruitment Office
  320 First Street, N.W., Room 446
  Washington, D.C. 20534
  Phone: (202) 307-3026, (202) 307-3204, or (202) 514-6089

United States Department of Justice: Immigration and Naturalization Service

Careers as criminal investigators, immigration inspectors, immigration examiners, deportation officers, and detention enforcement officers are some of the more common opportunities available within the INS. These are exciting and demanding careers that enforce the United States immigration laws. Hours are abnormal depending on the employee's appointment within the bureau.

- *Salary schedule:* Employees earn competitive salaries based on appointment with many earning \$30,000 in their first year alone.
- *Educational qualifications:* While qualifications may vary from department to department, law-enforcement experience, investigative experience, fluency in a foreign language, and a college degree may be beneficial.
- *Benefits:* Life and health insurance, early retirement, paid vacations, and sick leave are only a few of the many benefits the INS affords its employees.
- *Do you want to know more?*
  Contact

  Eastern Region
  INS
  70 Kimball Avenue
  South Burlington, VT
  05403-6813

  Southern Region
  INS
  7701 North Stemmons
  Freeway
  Dallas, TX 75247

  Western Region
  INS
  24000 Avila RD
  P.O. Box 30080
  Laguna Niguel, CA
  92607-8080

  Northern Region
  INS
  Bishop Henry
  Whipple Bldg.
  Room 400
  1 Federal Drive
  Ft. Snelling, MN
  55111-4007

United States Department of Justice: Probation Office

This division of the government enforces sentencing guidelines set forth by the courts. Probation is also in charge of the supervision of federal offenders as well as conducting investigations into the backgrounds of individuals. Careers are considered to be somewhat hazardous due to daily contact with criminals.

- *Salary schedule:* Employees earn excellent salaries with most beginning at approximately \$27,000 and progressing to more than \$52,000. *Educational qualifications:* A bachelor's degree with an emphasis in the social sciences is preferred and experience in related fields is desirable.
- *Benefits:* Employees enjoy early retirement, accumulated vacation time, and medical and life insurance benefits comparable to many private sector employees.

- *Do you want to know more?*
  Contact U.S. Department of Justice
  Probation
  1 Columbus Circle
  Washington, D.C. 20544
  Phone: (202) 273-1610

United States Department of Justice: United States Marshals

United States Marshals help transport federal prisoners, accompany them to court appearances, protect judges, and play a major role in the witness protection program. Marshals are, in a way, the security guard of the government.

- *Salary schedule:* Employees generally begin earning $22,717, with progression up the General Schedule.
- *Educational qualifications:* A bachelor's degree is preferred, but three years of related experience may qualify an applicant.
- *Benefits:* Marshals enjoy the same benefits as other federal employees with opportunities for early retirement. Employees must be willing to relocate.
- *Do you want to know more?*
  Contact United States Marshals
  Recruitment Center
  600 Army–Navy Drive
  Arlington, VA 22202

Department of Health and Human Services: Social Security Administration

Careers within the Social Security Administration offer a wide range of opportunities. Positions in areas of claims examination as well as "public contact" positions are always available in various locations throughout the United States.

- *Salary schedule:* Employees are salaried on the General Schedule pay rates. Most entry-level careers pay between $16,393 and $22,717 per year with top salaries exceeding $100,000 annually.
- *Educational qualifications:* A bachelor's degree or three years of progressively responsible experience or a combination of both is generally required.
- *Benefits:* Employees enjoy benefits that are comparable to if not better than those earned by employees in the private sector with 11 paid federal holidays, 13 vacation days annually with increases based upon service, 13 days of paid sick leave annually with unlimited accumulation, as well as numerous other benefits.
- *Do you want to know more?*
  Contact Department of Health and Human Services
  Regional Personnel Office
  105 West Adams
  Chicago, Illinois
  Phone: (312) 353-5175

United States Post Office: Division of Postal Inspectors

Postal inspectors are responsible for regulating the mails, regulating pornography and contraband when they are sent through the mail, and investigating mail fraud, internal theft within the post office, and external theft of the mails.

- *Salary schedule:* Postal inspectors can earn up to $70,000 annually with most starting at $47,000.
- *Educational qualifications:* Any non-postal employee must have a professional degree, preferably with an emphasis in law, accounting, or computer science, and it is desirable for applicants to be fluent in a second language.
- *Benefits:* Employees enjoy excellent retirement plans, health insurance, and can accumulate sick and vacation time.
- *Do you want to know more?*
  Contact Recruitment Program Manager
  United States Postal Inspection Service
  William F. Bolger Management Academy
  9600 Newbridge Drive
  Potomac, MD 20858-4328
  Phone: (301) 983-7340

Department of the Treasury: Internal Revenue Service

Employing over 120,000 people nationwide in careers in areas such as revenue officers, special agents, tax auditors, and computer specialists, the IRS has a wide range of career opportunities available. Enforcement of tax laws, decisions on liability of taxes, and investigation of criminal and civil violations of Internal Revenue laws are some of the main functions of the IRS.

- *Salary schedule:* Employees earn competitive salaries on the General or Special Schedules based on employment. Typical starting salaries are around $20,000 with quick progression along the schedules for dedicated employees.
- *Educational qualifications:* A bachelor's degree in accounting, liberal arts, computer science, public administration, or business is preferred.
- *Benefits:* Employees enjoy co-op educational programs in which the IRS shares the cost, retirement plans, ten paid holidays annually, 26 days of vacation each year, and more.
- *Do you want to know more?*
  Contact the District Director or IRS Recruitment Coordinator in your area.

LAW ENFORCEMENT: STATE AGENCIES

The following state government agencies offer criminal justice career opportunities:

- *State Bureaus of Investigation and Apprehension.* Many states have an agency that places investigators throughout the state to help county and municipal law enforcement agencies investigate major crimes, organized crime, and illegal drug trafficking. In addition to investigation, they provide scientific examinations of crime scenes and laboratory analysis of evidence, maintain criminal justice information and telecommunications systems, and conduct training courses for law enforcement officers.

- *State Fire Marshal Division.* State fire marshals investigate suspicious fire origins, fire fatalities, and fires that cause major losses. They also tabulate fire statistics and provide training programs for fire prevention.
- *State Departments of Natural Resources.* Conservation officers investigate complaints about nuisance wildlife, misuse of public lands and waters, violations of state parks rules, and unlawful taking of state timber. Conservation officers also issue fishing, hunting, and boat licenses.
- *Departments of Human Rights.* Departments of Human Rights enforce the states' laws that prohibit discrimination on the bases of race, religion, ethnicity, and gender in employment, education, housing, and public accommodations and services.
- *State Police and Highway Patrol.* Some state police agencies are responsible for enforcing all the laws of the state, such as crimes committed on the highways of the state. Others enforce only the traffic laws on state highways and freeways.

LAW ENFORCEMENT: COUNTY AGENCIES

County agencies offer these criminal justice opportunities:

- *County Sheriff.* Sheriffs appoint deputies who are responsible for a range of law enforcement duties, including (1) keeping the peace; (2) executing civil and criminal process, such as warrants; (3) staffing and maintaining the county jail; (4) preserving order and dignity in the courts; and (5) enforcing court orders.
- *Coroner or Medical Examiner.* The main duties of the coroner are to determine the cause of death in cases of "suspicious" deaths and to take care of the remains and the personal effects of deceased persons.

LAW ENFORCEMENT: LOCAL AGENCIES

At the local level, municipal police are by far the most numerous and best known of all the law enforcement agencies and personnel. The duties of the more than 12,000 local police departments include law enforcement, order maintenance, crime prevention, service, and civil rights and liberties protection.

LAW ENFORCEMENT: PRIVATE SECURITY

The rapidly expanding private security industry includes two basic types of entry-level positions. Private security guards control access to private property, and protect, enforce rules, and maintain order regarding private property. Private patrol officers move from location to location on foot or in vehicles, protecting property and preventing property losses. Mid-level jobs include private investigators, detectives, armed couriers, central alarm experts, and security consultants. The top jobs in private security include managing private security companies or heading security divisions in large companies.

COURTS

Career opportunities in the courtroom include the following:

- *Lawyers.* The three leading professionals in the courts are the judges, prosecutors, and defense attorneys. Judges and prosecutors all have law degrees, and most are elected to their positions. Defenders are either hired by clients who can afford to pay, are appointed by some selection system, or are employed by public defender systems. Prosecutors manage cases for the government from the time the police bring them to their attention to final disposition. Defense attorneys represent the interests of their clients from the time that either a client hires them or they are assigned a case by the court or the public defender's office. Judges preside over all of the formal proceedings in court.
- *Court Administrator.* Court administrators are in charge of running the court system. They manage cases and resources.
- *Paralegals.* Paralegals work as legal secretaries, court reporters, legal assistants to judges, prosecutors, and defense attorneys. According to the *Monthly Labor Review,* paralegals will be the fastest-growing occupation in the 1990s. The *Review* projects a 75 percent increase in the number of paralegals between 1988 and 2000.

CORRECTIONS

Career opportunities in corrections include the following:

- *Probation Officers.* Probation officers supervise offenders who are released into the community following their convictions. They act as both counselors and law enforcement officers, making sure that offenders do not commit new offenses or violate the conditions of their probation.
- *Correctional Officers.* Correctional officers spend most of their time guarding prisoners. But increasingly, they work with prisoners in such tasks as recreation, vocational training, and education. They help prisoners adjust to incarceration and prepare for release back into society. According to the *Monthly Labor Review,* the demand for correctional officers will continue to be strong throughout the 1990s. The *Review* projects an increase in correctional officers of 40 percent from 1988 to 2000.
- *Parole Officers.* Parole officers supervise prisoners following their release from prison. They help them find jobs, continue their education, and deal with family problems. They also act as law enforcement officers in preventing the violation of parole conditions and the commission of new crimes.

RESEARCH AND TEACHING

Career opportunities in research and teaching include the following:

- *Research.* Researchers contribute to the basic knowledge of criminal justice and to the assessment of the effectiveness of criminal justice policies. Many private research groups referred to in the text conduct both types of research. The federal government, some state governments, most universities, and many colleges have strong research units that provide opportunities for those who are interested in criminal justice research.
- *Teaching.* More than 600 criminal justice programs require instructors to teach the courses offered in the programs. Some are specialized criminal justice schools and departments; others are offered in connection with sociology, political science, or other social science departments. Criminal justice programs exist at all levels, including graduate programs, four-year universities and colleges, two-year junior colleges, and vocational-technical schools. Even a number of high schools offer criminal justice courses.

This appendix is based on J. Scott Harr and Kären M. Hess, *Seeking Employment in Law Enforcement, Private Security, and Related Fields* (St. Paul: West Publishing Company, 1992); George Silvestri and John Lukasiewicz, "Projections of occupational employment, 1988–2000," *Monthly Labor Review,* November 1989, 42–65.

Appendix B
Constitution of the United States

PREAMBLE

We the People of the United States, in Order to form a more perfect Union, establish Justice, insure domestic Tranquility, provide for the common defence, promote the general Welfare, and secure the Blessings of Liberty to ourselves and our Posterity, do ordain and establish this Constitution for the United States of America.

Article I

Section 1

All legislative Powers herein granted shall be vested in a Congress of the United States, which shall consist of a Senate and House of Representatives.

Section 2

The House of Representatives shall be composed of Members chosen every second Year by the People of the several States, and the Electors in each State shall have the Qualifications requisite for Electors of the most numerous Branch of the State Legislature.

No Person shall be a Representative who shall not have attained to the Age of twenty five Years, and been seven Years a Citizen of the United States, and who shall not, when elected, be an Inhabitant of that State in which he shall be chosen.

Representatives and direct Taxes shall be apportioned among the several States which may be included within this Union, according to their respective Numbers, which shall be determined by adding to the whole Number of free Persons, including those bound to Service for a Term of Years, and excluding Indians not taxed, three fifths of all other Persons. The actual Enumeration shall be made within three Years after the first Meeting of the Congress of the United States, and within every subsequent Term of ten Years, in such Manner as they shall by Law direct. The Number of Representatives shall not exceed one for every thirty Thousand, but each State shall have at Least one Representative; and until such enumeration shall be made, the State of New Hampshire shall be entitled to choose three, Massachusetts eight, Rhode Island and Providence Plantations one, Connecticut five, New York six, New Jersey four, Pennsylvania eight, Delaware one, Maryland six, Virginia ten, North Carolina five, South Carolina five, and Georgia three.

When vacancies happen in the Representation from any State, the Executive Authority thereof shall issue Writs of Election to fill such Vacancies.

The House of Representatives shall choose their Speaker and other Officers; and shall have the sole Power of Impeachment.

Section 3

The Senate of the United States shall be composed of two Senators from each State, chosen by the Legislature thereof, for six Years; and each Senator shall have one Vote.

Immediately after they shall be assembled in Consequence of the first Election, they shall be divided as equally as may be into three Classes. The Seats of the Senators of the first Class shall be vacated at the Expiration of the second Year, of the second Class at the Expiration of the fourth Year, and of the third Class at the Expiration of the sixth Year, so that one third may be chosen every second Year; and if Vacancies happen by Resignation, or otherwise, during the Recess of the Legislature of any State, the Executive thereof may make temporary Appointments until the next Meeting of the Legislature, which shall then fill such Vacancies.

No Person shall be a Senator who shall not have attained to the Age of thirty Years, and been nine Years a Citizen of the United States, and who shall not, when elected, be an Inhabitant of that State for which he shall be chosen.

The Vice President of the United States shall be President of the Senate, but shall have no Vote, unless they be equally divided.

The Senate shall choose their other Officers, and also a President pro tempore, in the Absence of the Vice President, or when he shall exercise the Office of President of the United States.

The Senate shall have the sole Power to try all Impeachments. When sitting for that Purpose, they shall be on Oath or Affirmation. When the President of the United

States is tried, the Chief Justice shall preside: And no Person shall be convicted without the Concurrence of two thirds of the Members present.

Judgment in Cases of Impeachment shall not extend further than to removal from Office, and disqualification to hold and enjoy any Office of honor, Trust, or Profit under the United States: but the Party convicted shall nevertheless be liable and subject to Indictment, Trial, Judgment, and Punishment, according to Law.

Section 4

The Times, Places and Manner of holding Elections for Senators and Representatives, shall be prescribed in each State by the Legislature thereof; but the Congress may at any time by Law make or alter such Regulations, except as to the Places of choosing Senators.

The Congress shall assemble at least once in every Year, and such Meeting shall be on the first Monday in December, unless they shall by Law appoint a different Day.

Section 5

Each House shall be the Judge of the Elections, Returns, and Qualifications of its own Members, and a Majority of each shall constitute a Quorum to do Business; but a smaller Number may adjourn from day to day, and may be authorized to compel the Attendance of absent Members, in such Manner, and under such Penalties as each House may provide.

Each House may determine the Rules of its Proceedings, punish its Members for disorderly Behavior, and, with the Concurrence of two thirds, expel a Member.

Each House shall keep a Journal of its Proceedings, and from time to time publish the same, excepting such Parts as may in their Judgment require Secrecy; and the Yeas and Nays of the Members of either House on any question shall, at the Desire of one fifth of those Present, be entered on the Journal.

Neither House, during the Session of Congress, shall, without the Consent of the other, adjourn for more than three days, nor to any other Place than that in which the two Houses shall be sitting.

Section 6

The Senators and Representatives shall receive a Compensation for their Services, to be ascertained by Law, and paid out of the Treasury of the United States. They shall in all Cases, except Treason, Felony and Breach of the Peace, be privileged from Arrest during their Attendance at the Session of their respective Houses, and in going to and returning from the same; and for any Speech or Debate in either House, they shall not be questioned in any other Place.

No Senator or Representative shall, during the Time for which he was elected, be appointed to any civil Office under the Authority of the United States, which shall have been created, or the Emoluments whereof shall have been increased during such time; and no Person holding any Office under the United States, shall be a Member of either House during his Continuance in Office.

Section 7

All Bills for raising Revenue shall originate in the House of Representatives; but the Senate may propose or concur with Amendments as on other Bills.

Every Bill which shall have passed the House of Representatives and the Senate, shall, before it become a Law, be presented to the President of the United States; If he approve he shall sign it, but if not he shall return it, with his Objections to the House in which it shall have originated, who shall enter the Objections at large on their Journal, and proceed to reconsider it. If after such Reconsideration two thirds of that House shall agree to pass the Bill, it shall be sent together with the Objections, to the other House, by which it shall likewise be reconsidered, and if approved by two thirds of that House, it shall become a Law. But in all such Cases the Votes of both Houses shall be determined by Yeas and Nays, and the Names of the Persons voting for and against the Bill shall be entered on the Journal of each House respectively. If any Bill shall not be returned by the President within ten Days (Sundays excepted) after it shall have been presented to him, the Same shall be a Law, in like Manner as if he had signed it, unless the Congress by their Adjournment prevent its Return in which Case it shall not be a Law.

Every Order, Resolution, or Vote, to which the Concurrence of the Senate and House of Representatives may be necessary (except on a question of Adjournment) shall be presented to the President of the United States; and before the Same shall take Effect, shall be approved by him, or being disapproved by him, shall be repassed by two thirds of the Senate and House of Representatives, according to the Rules and Limitations prescribed in the Case of a Bill.

Section 8

The Congress shall have Power To lay and collect Taxes, Duties, Imposts and Excises, to pay the Debts and provide for the common Defence and general Welfare of the United States; but all Duties, Imposts and Excises shall be uniform throughout the United States;

To borrow Money on the credit of the United States;

To regulate Commerce with foreign Nations, and among the several States, and with the Indian Tribes;

To establish an uniform Rule of Naturalization, and uniform Laws on the subject of Bankruptcies throughout the United States;

To coin Money, regulate the Value thereof, and of foreign Coin, and fix the Standard of Weights and Measures;

To provide for the Punishment of counterfeiting the Securities and current Coin of the United States;

To establish Post Offices and post Roads;

To promote the Progress of Science and useful Arts, by securing for limited Times to Authors and Inventors the exclusive Right to their respective Writings and Discoveries;

To constitute Tribunals inferior to the supreme Court;

To define and punish Piracies and Felonies committed on the high Seas, and Offenses against the Law of Nations;

To declare War, grant Letters of Marque and Reprisal, and make Rules concerning Captures on Land and Water;

To raise and support Armies, but no Appropriation of Money to that Use shall be for a longer Term than two Years;

To provide and maintain a Navy;

To make Rules for the Government and Regulation of the land and naval Forces;

To provide for calling forth the Militia to execute the Laws of the Union, suppress Insurrections and repel Invasions;

To provide for organizing, arming, and disciplining, the Militia, and for governing such Part of Them as may be employed in the Service of the United States, reserving to the States respectively, the Appointment of the Officers, and the Authority of training the Militia according to the discipline prescribed by Congress;

To exercise exclusive Legislation in all Cases whatsoever, over such District (not exceeding ten Miles square) as may, by Cession of particular States, and the Acceptance of Congress, become the Seat of the Government of the United States, and to exercise like Authority over all Places purchased by the Consent of the Legislature of the State in which the Same shall be, for the Erection of Forts, Magazines, Arsenals, dock-Yards, and other needful Buildings;—And

To make all Laws which shall be necessary and proper for carrying into Execution the foregoing Powers, and all other Powers vested by this Constitution in the Government of the United States, or in any Department or Officer thereof.

Section 9

The Migration or Importation of such Persons as any of the States now existing shall think proper to admit, shall not be prohibited by the Congress prior to the Year one thousand eight hundred and eight, but a Tax or duty may be imposed on such Importation, not exceeding ten dollars for each Person.

The privilege of the Writ of Habeas Corpus shall not be suspended, unless when in Cases of Rebellion or Invasion the public Safety may require it.

No Bill of Attainder or ex post facto Law shall be passed.

No Capitation, or other direct, Tax shall be laid, unless in Proportion to the Census or Enumeration herein before directed to be taken.

No Tax or Duty shall be laid on Articles exported from any State.

No Preference shall be given by any Regulation of Commerce or Revenue to the Ports of one State over those of another: nor shall Vessels bound to, or from, one State be obliged to enter, clear, or pay Duties in another.

No Money shall be drawn from the Treasury, but in Consequence of Appropriations made by Law; and a regular Statement and Account of the Receipts and Expenditures of all public Money shall be published from time to time.

No Title of Nobility shall be granted by the United States: And no Person holding any Office of Profit or Trust under them, shall, without the Consent of the Congress, accept of any present, Emolument, Office, or Title, of any kind whatever, from any King, Prince, or foreign State.

Section 10

No State shall enter into any Treaty, Alliance, or Confederation; grant Letters of Marque and Reprisal; coin Money; emit Bills of Credit; make any Thing but gold and silver Coin a Tender in Payment of Debts; pass any Bill of Attainder, ex post facto Law, or Law impairing the Obligation of Contracts, or grant any Title of Nobility.

No State shall, without the Consent of the Congress, lay any Imposts or Duties on Imports or Exports, except what may be absolutely necessary for executing it's inspection Laws: and the net Produce of all Duties and Imposts, laid by any State on Imports or Exports, shall be for the Use of the Treasury of the United States; and all such Laws shall be subject to the Revision and Control of the Congress.

No State shall, without the Consent of Congress, lay any Duty of Tonnage, keep Troops, or Ships of War in time of Peace, enter into any Agreement or Compact with another State, or with a foreign Power, or engage in War, unless actually invaded, or in such imminent Danger as will not admit of delay.

Article II

Section 1

The executive Power shall be vested in a President of the United States of America. He shall hold his Office during the Term of four Years, and, together with the Vice President, chosen for the same Term, be elected, as follows:

Each State shall appoint, in such Manner as the Legislature thereof may direct, a Number of Electors, equal to the whole Number of Senators and Representatives to which the State may be entitled in the Congress; but no Senator or Representative, or Person holding an Office of Trust or Profit under the United States, shall be appointed an Elector.

The Electors shall meet in their respective States, and vote by Ballot for two Persons, of whom one at least shall not be an Inhabitant of the same State with themselves. And they shall make a List of all the Persons voted for, and of the Number of Votes for each; which List they shall sign and certify, and transmit sealed to the Seat of the Government of the United States, directed to the President of the Senate. The President of the Senate shall, in the Presence of the Senate and House of Representatives, open all the Certificates, and the Votes shall then be counted. The Person having the greatest Number of Votes shall be the President, if such Number be a Majority of the whole Number of Electors appointed; and if there be more than one who have such Majority, and have an equal Number of Votes, then the House of Representatives shall immediately choose by Ballot one of them for President; and if no Person have a Majority, then from the five highest on the List the said House shall in like Manner choose the President. But in choosing the President, the Votes shall be taken by States, the Representation from each State having one Vote; A quorum for this Purpose shall consist of a Member or Members from two thirds of the States, and a Majority of all the States shall be necessary to a Choice. In every Case, after the Choice of the President, the Person having the greater Number of Votes of the Electors shall be the Vice President. But if there should remain two or more who have equal Votes, the Senate shall choose from them by Ballot the Vice President.

The Congress may determine the Time of choosing the Electors, and the Day on which they shall give their Votes; which Day shall be the same throughout the United States.

No person except a natural born Citizen, or a Citizen of the United States, at the time of the Adoption of this Constitution, shall be eligible to the Office of President; neither shall any Person be eligible to that Office who shall not have attained to the Age of thirty five Years, and been fourteen Years a Resident within the United States.

In Case of the Removal of the President from Office, or of his Death, Resignation or Inability to discharge the Powers and Duties of the said Office, the same shall devolve on the Vice President, and the Congress may by Law provide for the Case of Removal, Death, Resignation or Inability, both of the President and Vice President, declaring what Officer shall then act as President, and such Officer shall act accordingly, until the Disability be removed, or a President shall be elected.

The President shall, at stated Times, receive for his Services, a Compensation, which shall neither be increased nor diminished during the Period for which he shall have been elected, and he shall not receive within that Period any other Emolument from the United States, or any of them.

Before he enter on the Execution of his Office, he shall take the following Oath or Affirmation: "I do solemnly swear (or affirm) that I will faithfully execute the Office of President of the United States, and will to the best of my Ability, preserve, protect and defend the Constitution of the United States."

Section 2

The President shall be Commander in Chief of the Army and Navy of the United States, and of the Militia of the several States, when called into the actual Service of the United States: he may require the Opinion, in writing, of the principal Officer in each of the executive Departments, upon any Subject relating to the Duties of their respective Offices, and he shall have Power to grant Reprieves and Pardons for Offenses against the United States, except in Cases of Impeachment.

He shall have Power, by and with the Advice and Consent of the Senate to make Treaties, provided two thirds of the Senators present concur; and he shall nominate, and by and with the Advice and Consent of the Senate, shall appoint Ambassadors, other public Ministers and Consuls, Judges of the supreme Court, and all other Officers of the United States, whose Appointments are not herein otherwise provided for, and which shall be established by Law; but the Congress may by Law vest the Appointment of such inferior Officers, as they think proper, in the President alone, in the Courts of Law, or in the Heads of Departments.

The President shall have Power to fill up all Vacancies that may happen during the Recess of the Senate, by granting Commissions which shall expire at the End of their next Session.

Section 3

He shall from time to time give to the Congress Information of the State of the Union, and recommend to their Consideration such Measures as he shall judge necessary and expedient; he may, on extraordinary Occasions, convene both Houses, or either of them, and in Case of Disagreement between them, with Respect to the Time of Adjournment, he may adjourn them to such Time as he shall think proper; he shall receive Ambassadors and other public Ministers; he shall take Care that the Laws be faithfully executed, and shall Commission all the Officers of the United States.

Section 4

The President, Vice President and all civil Officers of the United States, shall be removed from Office on Impeachment for, and Conviction of, Treason, Bribery, or other high Crimes and Misdemeanors.

Article III

Section 1

The judicial Power of the United States, shall be vested in one supreme Court, and in such inferior Courts as the Congress may from time to time ordain and establish. The Judges, both of the supreme and inferior Courts, shall hold their Offices during good Behavior, and shall, at stated Times, receive for their Services a Compensation, which shall not be diminished during their Continuance in Office.

Section 2

The judicial Power shall extend to all Cases, in Law and Equity, arising under this Constitution, the Laws of the United States, and Treaties made, or which shall be made, under their Authority;—to all Cases affecting Ambassadors, other public Ministers and Consuls;—to all Cases of admiralty and maritime Jurisdiction;—to Controversies to which the United States shall be a Party;—to Controversies between two or more States;—between a State and Citizens of another State;—between Citizens of different States;—between Citizens of the same State claiming Lands under Grants of different States, and between a State, or the Citizens thereof, and foreign States, Citizens or Subjects.

In all Cases affecting Ambassadors, other public Ministers and Consuls, and those in which a State shall be a Party, the supreme Court shall have original Jurisdiction. In all the other Cases before mentioned, the supreme Court shall have appellate Jurisdiction, both as to Law and Fact, with such Exceptions, and under such Regulations as the Congress shall make.

The Trial of all Crimes, except in Cases of Impeachment, shall be by Jury; and such Trial shall be held in the State where the said Crimes shall have been committed; but when not committed within any State, the Trial shall be at such Place or Places as the Congress may by Law have directed.

Section 3
Treason against the United States, shall consist only in levying War against them, or, in adhering to their Enemies, giving them Aid and Comfort. No Person shall be convicted of Treason unless on the Testimony of two Witnesses to the same overt Act, or on Confession in open Court.

The Congress shall have Power to declare the Punishment of Treason, but no Attainder of Treason shall work Corruption of Blood, or Forfeiture except during the Life of the Person attainted.

Article IV

Section 1
Full Faith and Credit shall be given in each State to the public Acts, Records, and judicial Proceedings of every other State. And the Congress may by general Laws prescribe the Manner in which such Acts, Records and Proceedings shall be proved, and the Effect thereof.

Section 2
The Citizens of each State shall be entitled to all Privileges and Immunities of Citizens in the several States.

A Person charged in any State with Treason, Felony, or other Crime, who shall flee from Justice, and be found in another State, shall on Demand of the executive Authority of the State from which he fled, be delivered up, to be removed to the State having Jurisdiction of the Crime.

No Person held to Service or Labour in one State, under the Laws thereof, escaping into another, shall, in Consequence of any Law or Regulation therein, be discharged from such Service or Labor, but shall be delivered up on Claim of the Party to whom such Service or Labor may be due.

Section 3
New States may be admitted by the Congress into this Union; but no new State shall be formed or erected within the Jurisdiction of any other State; nor any State be formed by the Junction of two or more States, or Parts of States, without the Consent of the Legislatures of the States concerned as well as of the Congress.

The Congress shall have Power to dispose of and make all needful Rules and Regulations respecting the Territory or other Property belonging to the United States; and nothing in this Constitution shall be so construed as to Prejudice any Claims of the United States, or of any particular State.

Section 4
The United States shall guarantee to every State in this Union a Republican Form of Government, and shall protect each of them against Invasion; and on Application of the Legislature, or of the Executive (when the Legislature cannot be convened) against domestic Violence.

Article V

The Congress, whenever two thirds of both Houses shall deem it necessary, shall propose Amendments to this Constitution, or, on the Application of the Legislatures of two thirds of the several States, shall call a Convention for proposing Amendments, which, in either Case, shall be valid to all Intents and Purposes, as part of this Constitution, when ratified by the Legislatures of three fourths of the several States, or by Conventions in three fourths thereof, as the one or the other Mode of Ratification may be proposed by the Congress; Provided that no Amendment which may be made prior to the Year One thousand eight hundred and eight shall in any Manner affect the first and fourth Clauses in the Ninth Section of the first Article; and that no State, without its Consent, shall be deprived of its equal Suffrage in the Senate.

Article VI

All Debts contracted and Engagements entered into, before the Adoption of this Constitution shall be as valid against the United States under this Constitution, as under the Confederation.

This Constitution, and the Laws of the United States which shall be made in Pursuance thereof; and all Treaties made, or which shall be made, under the Authority of the United States, shall be the supreme Law of the Land; and the Judges in every State shall be bound thereby, any Thing in the Constitution or Laws of any State to the Contrary notwithstanding.

The Senators and Representatives before mentioned, and the Members of the several State Legislatures, and all executive and judicial Officers, both of the United States and of the several States, shall be bound by Oath or Affirmation, to support this Constitution; but no religious Test shall ever be required as a Qualification to any Office or public Trust under the United States.

Article VII

The Ratification of the Conventions of nine States shall be sufficient for the Establishment of this Constitution between the States so ratifying the Same.

Amendment I [1791]

Congress shall make no law respecting an establishment of religion, or prohibiting the free exercise thereof; or abridging the freedom of speech, or of the press; or the right of the people peaceably to assemble, and to petition the Government for a redress of grievances.

Amendment II [1791]

A well regulated Militia, being necessary to the security of a free State, the right of the people to keep and bear Arms, shall not be infringed.

Amendment III [1791]

No Soldier shall, in time of peace be quartered in any house, without the consent of the Owner, nor in time of war, but in a manner to be prescribed by law.

Amendment IV [1791]

The right of the people to be secure in their persons, houses, papers, and effects, against unreasonable searches and seizures, shall not be violated, and no Warrants shall issue, but upon probable cause, supported by Oath or affirmation, and particularly describing the place to be searched, and the persons or things to be seized.

Amendment V [1791]

No person shall be held to answer for a capital, or otherwise infamous crime, unless on a presentment or indictment of a Grand Jury, except in cases arising in the land or naval forces, or in the Militia, when in actual service in time of War or public danger; nor shall any person be subject for the same offence to be twice put in jeopardy of life or limb; nor shall be compelled in any criminal case to be a witness against himself, nor be deprived of life, liberty, or property, without due process of law; nor shall private property be taken for public use, without just compensation.

Amendment VI [1791]

In all criminal prosecutions, the accused shall enjoy the right to a speedy and public trial, by an impartial jury of the State and district wherein the crime shall have been committed, which district shall have been previously ascertained by law, and to be informed of the nature and cause of the accusation; to be confronted with the witnesses against him; to have compulsory process for obtaining witnesses in his favor, and to have the Assistance of Counsel for his defence.

Amendment VII [1791]

In Suits at common law, where the value in controversy shall exceed twenty dollars, the right of trial by jury shall be preserved, and no fact tried by jury, shall be otherwise reexamined in any Court of the United States, than according to the rules of the common law.

Amendment VIII [1791]

Excessive bail shall not be required, nor excessive fines imposed, nor cruel and unusual punishments inflicted.

Amendment IX [1791]

The enumeration in the Constitution, of certain rights, shall not be construed to deny or disparage others retained by the people.

Amendment X [1791]

The powers not delegated to the United States by the Constitution, nor prohibited by it to the States, are reserved to the States respectively, or to the people.

Amendment XI [1798]

The Judicial power of the United States shall not be construed to extend to any suit in law or equity, commenced or prosecuted against one of the United States by Citizens of another State, or by Citizens or Subjects of any Foreign State.

Amendment XII [1804]

The Electors shall meet in their respective states, and vote by ballot for President and Vice-President, one of whom, at least, shall not be an inhabitant of the same state with themselves; they shall name in their ballots the person voted for as President, and in distinct ballots the person voted for as Vice-President, and they shall make distinct lists of all persons voted for as President, and of all persons voted for as Vice-President, and of the number of votes for each, which lists they shall sign and certify, and transmit sealed to the seat of the government of the United States, directed to the President of the Senate;—The President of the Senate shall, in the presence of the Senate and House of Representatives, open all the certificates and the votes shall then be counted;—The person having the greatest number of votes for President, shall be the President, if such number be a majority of the whole number of Electors appointed; and if no person have such majority, then from the persons having the highest numbers not exceeding three on the list of those voted for as President, the House of Representatives shall choose immediately, by ballot, the President. But in choosing the President, the votes shall be taken by states, the representation from each state having one vote; a quorum for this purpose shall consist of a member or members from two thirds of the states, and a majority of all states shall be necessary to a choice. And if the House of Representatives shall not choose a President whenever the right of choice shall devolve upon them, before the fourth day of March next following, then the Vice-President shall act as President, as in the case of the death or other constitutional disability of the President.—The person having the greatest number of votes as Vice-President, shall be the Vice-President, if such number be a majority of the whole number of Electors appointed, and if no person have a majority, then from the two highest numbers on the list, the Senate shall choose the Vice-President; a quorum for the purpose shall consist of two thirds of the whole number of Senators, and a majority of the whole number shall be necessary to a choice. But no person constitutionally ineligible to the office of President shall be eligible to that of Vice-President of the United States.

Amendment XIII [1865]

Section 1
Neither slavery nor involuntary servitude, except as a punishment for crime whereof the party shall have been duly convicted, shall exist within the United States, or any place subject to their jurisdiction.

Section 2
Congress shall have power to enforce this article by appropriate legislation.

Amendment XIV [1868]

Section 1

All persons born or naturalized in the United States, and subject to the jurisdiction thereof, are citizens of the United States and of the State wherein they reside. No State shall make or enforce any law which shall abridge the privileges or immunities of citizens of the United States; nor shall any State deprive any person of life, liberty, or property, without due process of law; nor deny to any person within its jurisdiction the equal protection of the laws.

Section 2

Representatives shall be apportioned among the several States according to their respective numbers, counting the whole number of persons in each State, excluding Indians not taxed. But when the right to vote at any election for the choice of electors for President and Vice President of the United States, Representatives in Congress, the Executive and Judicial officers of a State, or the members of the Legislature thereof, is denied to any of the male inhabitants of such State, being twenty-one years of age, and citizens of the United States, or in any way abridged, except for participation in rebellion, or other crime, the basis of representation therein shall be reduced in the proportion which the number of such male citizens shall bear to the whole number of male citizens twenty-one years of age in such State.

Section 3

No person shall be a Senator or Representative in Congress, or elector of President and Vice-President, or hold any office, civil or military, under the United States, or under any State, who having previously taken an oath, as a member of Congress, or as an officer of the United States, or as a member of any State legislature, or as an executive or judicial officer of any State, to support the Constitution of the United States, shall have engaged in insurrection or rebellion against the same, or given aid or comfort to the enemies thereof. But Congress may by a vote of two thirds of each House, remove such disability.

Section 4

The validity of the public debt of the United States, authorized by law, including debts incurred for payment of pensions and bounties for services in suppressing insurrection or rebellion, shall not be questioned. But neither the United States nor any State shall assume or pay any debt or obligation incurred in aid of insurrection or rebellion against the United States, or any claim for the loss or emancipation of any slave; but all such debts, obligations and claims shall be held illegal and void.

Section 5

The Congress shall have power to enforce, by appropriate legislation, the provisions of this article.

Amendment XV [1870]

Section 1

The right of citizens of the United States to vote shall not be denied or abridged by the United States or by any State on account of race, color, or previous condition of servitude.

Section 2

The Congress shall have power to enforce this article by appropriate legislation.

Amendment XVI [1913]

The Congress shall have power to lay and collect taxes on incomes, from whatever source derived, without apportionment among the several States, and without regard to any census or enumeration.

Amendment XVII [1913]

Section 1

The Senate of the United States shall be composed of two Senators from each State, elected by the people thereof, for six years; and each Senator shall have one vote. The electors in each State shall have the qualifications requisite for electors of the most numerous branch of the State legislatures.

Section 2

When vacancies happen in the representation of any State in the Senate, the executive authority of such State shall issue writs of election to fill such vacancies: Provided, That the legislature of any State may empower the executive thereof to make temporary appointments until the people fill the vacancies by election as the legislature may direct.

Section 3

This amendment shall not be so construed as to affect the election or term of any Senator chosen before it becomes valid as part of the Constitution.

Amendment XVIII [1919]

Section 1

After one year from the ratification of this article the manufacture, sale, or transportation of intoxicating liquors within, the importation thereof into, or the exportation thereof from the United States and all territory subject to the jurisdiction thereof for beverage purposes is hereby prohibited.

Section 2

The Congress and the several States shall have concurrent power to enforce this article by appropriate legislation.

Section 3

This article shall be inoperative unless it shall have been ratified as an amendment to the Constitution by the legislatures of the several States, as provided in the Constitution, within seven years from the date of the submission hereof to the States by the Congress.

Amendment XIX [1920]

Section 1
The right of citizens of the United States to vote shall not be denied or abridged by the United States or by any State on account of sex.

Section 2
Congress shall have power to enforce this article by appropriate legislation.

Amendment XX [1933]

Section 1
The terms of the President and Vice President shall end at noon on the 20th day of January, and the terms of Senators and Representatives at noon on the 3d day of January, of the years in which such terms would have ended if this article had not been ratified; and the terms of their successors shall then begin.

Section 2
The Congress shall assemble at least once in every year, and such meeting shall begin at noon on the 3d day of January, unless they shall by law appoint a different day.

Section 3
If, at the time fixed for the beginning of the term of the President, the President elect shall have died, the Vice President elect shall become President. If the President shall not have been chosen before the time fixed for the beginning of his term, or if the President elect shall have failed to qualify, then the Vice President elect shall act as President until a President shall have qualified; and the Congress may by law provide for the case wherein neither a President elect nor a Vice President elect shall have qualified, declaring who shall then act as President, or the manner in which one who is to act shall be selected, and such person shall act accordingly until a President or Vice-President shall have qualified.

Section 4
The Congress may by law provide for the case of the death of any of the persons from whom the House of Representatives may choose a President whenever the right of choice shall have devolved upon them, and for the case of the death of any of the persons from whom the Senate may choose a Vice-President whenever the right of choice shall have devolved upon them.

Section 5
Sections 1 and 2 shall take effect on the 15th day of October following the ratification of this article.

Section 6
This article shall be inoperative unless it shall have been ratified as an amendment to the Constitution by the legislatures of three-fourths of the several States within seven years from the date of its submission.

Amendment XXI [1933]

Section 1
The eighteenth article of amendment to the Constitution of the United States is hereby repealed.

Section 2
The transportation or importation into any State, Territory, or possession of the United States for delivery or use therein of intoxicating liquors, in violation of the laws thereof, is hereby prohibited.

Section 3
This article shall be inoperative unless it shall have been ratified as an amendment to the Constitution by conventions in the several States, as provided in the Constitution, within seven years from the date of the submission hereof to the States by the Congress.

Amendment XXII [1951]

Section 1
No person shall be elected to the office of the President more than twice, and no person who has held the office of President, or acted as President, for more than two years of a term to which some other person was elected President shall be elected to the office of President more than once. But this Article shall not apply to any person holding the office of President when this Article was proposed by the Congress, and shall not prevent any person who may be holding the office of President, or acting as President, during the term within which this Article becomes operative from holding the office of President or acting as President during the remainder of such term.

Section 2
This article shall be inoperative unless it shall have been ratified as an amendment to the Constitution by the legislatures of three-fourths of the several States within seven years from the date of its submission to the States by the Congress.

Amendment XXIII [1961]

Section 1
The District constituting the seat of Government of the United States shall appoint in such manner as the Congress may direct:

A number of electors of President and Vice President equal to the whole number of Senators and Representatives in Congress to which the District would be entitled if it were a State, but in no event more than the least populous state; they shall be in addition to those appointed by the states, but they shall be considered, for the purposes of the election of President and Vice President, to be electors appointed by a state; and they shall meet in the District and perform such duties as provided by the twelfth article of amendment.

Section 2
The Congress shall have power to enforce this article by appropriate legislation.

Amendment XXIV [1964]

Section 1
The right of citizens of the United States to vote in any primary or other election for President or Vice President, for electors for President or Vice-President, or for Senator or Representative in Congress, shall not be denied or abridged by the United States, or any State by reason of failure to pay any poll tax or other tax.

Section 2
The Congress shall have power to enforce this article by appropriate legislation.

Amendment XXV [1967]

Section 1
In case of the removal of the President from office or of his death or resignation, the Vice President shall become President.

Section 2
Whenever there is a vacancy in the office of the Vice President, the President shall nominate a Vice President who shall take office upon confirmation by a majority vote of both Houses of Congress.

Section 3
Whenever the President transmits to the President pro tempore of the Senate and the Speaker of the House of Representatives his written declaration that he is unable to discharge the powers and duties of his office, and until he transmits to them a written declaration to the contrary, such powers and duties shall be discharged by the Vice President as Acting President.

Section 4
Whenever the Vice President and a majority of either the principal officers of the executive departments or of such other body as Congress may by law provide, transmit to the President pro tempore of the Senate and the Speaker of the House of Representatives their written declaration that the President is unable to discharge the powers and duties of his office, the Vice President shall immediately assume the powers and duties of the office as Acting President.

Thereafter, when the President transmits to the President pro tempore of the Senate and the Speaker of the House of Representatives his written declaration that no inability exists, he shall resume the powers and duties of his office unless the Vice President and a majority of either the principal officers of the executive department or of such other body as Congress may by law provide, transmit within four days to the President pro tempore of the Senate and the Speaker of the House of Representatives their written declaration and the President is unable to discharge the powers and duties of his office. Thereupon Congress shall decide the issue, assembling within forty-eight hours for that purpose if not in session. If the Congress, within twenty-one days after receipt of the latter written declaration, or, if Congress is not in session, within twenty-one days after Congress is required to assemble, determines by two thirds vote of both Houses that the President is unable to discharge the powers and duties of his office, the Vice President shall continue to discharge the same as Acting President; otherwise, the President shall resume the powers and duties of his office.

Amendment XXVI [1971]

Section 1
The right of citizens of the United States, who are eighteen years of age or older, to vote shall not be denied or abridged by the United States or by any State on account of age.

Section 2
The Congress shall have power to enforce this article by appropriate legislation.

Amendment XXVII [Proposed 1789; Ratified 1992]

No law, varying the compensation for the services of Senators and Representatives, shall take effect until an election of Representatives have intervened.

Glossary

abuse of force: excessive use of coercive force.

acquittal: total avoidance of criminal liability.

***actus reus*:** the criminal act or physical element in a crime.

adjudication: formal proceedings that take place in court.

admissible evidence: information that justifies government intrusions and deprivation.

adversary system: system in which criminal justice is viewed as a contest between the government and the individual.

affidavit: a sworn statement.

aggregate statistics: total counts of reported crimes and arrests.

aggressive field investigation: police take initiative in checking out suspicious circumstances, places, and persons.

alibi: defense to criminal liability that places the defendant at a different location when the crime was committed.

anomie: the weakening of social norms.

appellate courts: courts of appeal jurisdiction.

arraignment: bringing defendants into open court to read charges against them and secure a plea from them.

arrest: a detention that amounts to a Fourth Amendment seizure.

articulable facts and circumstances: explainable to a judge to justify.

assigned counsel: lawyers in private practice selected by judges to represent indigent defendants on a case-by-case basis.

attempt: taking substantial steps toward completing a crime.

Auburn, or **congregate system:** early prison system that imposed a rule of congregate work in absolute silence and solitary confinement at night.

back-door strategy: early release of prisoners to reduce crowding.

bail: release of defendants pending the final disposition of their cases.

bailiff: a court officer who keeps order and has custody of jurors and suspects.

bail point system: assigning points for employment, family, and other community ties to determine pretrial release.

balancing test of reasonableness: test to determine whether a warrantless search is reasonable.

bark-and-bite sentencing: sentencing in which the actual time served is less than the sentence imposed.

behavior modification: treatment program that focuses on actions in response to surroundings, not on how individuals feel about their environment.

bifurcated trials: multistage trials in which defendants charged with capital crimes receive a verdict in the first stage, and if convicted are sentenced during a second stage to death or life imprisonment.

bind over defendants: order that defendants stand trial.

building-tender system: prison management system that relies on prisoners to assist corrections officers in managing cell blocks.

bureaucratic probation officers: probation officers who stress following procedures, completing tasks, and making sure agencies run smoothly, efficiently, and economically.

capital felonies: crimes punishable by death or life imprisonment.

case attrition: reduction in numbers of crimes from those reported to those resulting in punishment.

casework model: parole supervision that provides the basis for a treatment plan in which individual parolees are the cases.

causation: operation of two kinds of cause: cause in fact and legal cause

cell rationing: the assignment of a specified number of prison cells to each judicial district.

certificate of parole: document that specifically sets out the conditions of the parole contract.

certification: treating juveniles as adults for criminal prosecution.

challenge for cause: the right of both sides to an unlimited number of objections to prospective jurors who decide act without bias.

charge bargaining: plea negotiation in which prosecutors drop some charges or file less serious ones in exchange for a guilty plea.

colloquy: a formal discussion in which judges attempt to determine whether defendants' guilty pleas are voluntary and knowing.

commercial bail: practice of bail bonding as a private business.

common law: the traditions, customs, and values of the English community translated into legal rules.

community service: police mission devoted to providing both information and physical assistance to people in need.

community service sentences: sentences that order offenders to work without pay at projects that benefit either the public or public charities.

community-oriented policing: citizen participation in setting police priorities and police operations.

commute: power of the executive branch to reduce criminal sentences.

concentration model: putting the most violent criminals in one prison to facilitate their management.

concurrence: union of the criminal act, or *actus reus,* and the criminal intent, or *mens rea,* in a crime.

conditional release: release of defendants subject to a range of nonmonetary conditions.

confinement model: prisoners are sent to prison as punishment, not for punishment.

conflict perspective: view of law holding that the criminal law reflects the success of the most powerful groups in society to translate their values into law.

consensus perspective: view of law holding that the criminal law reflects a general agreement regarding the values of society.

consensus prison management: prison management model that balances elements of control and responsibility.

consent search: conducted with voluntary agreement.

conspiracy: agreeing to commit a crime.

constructive intent: cases in which actors did not intend harm but whose actions caused a result the criminal law prohibits.

context explanations: explanations of criminal behavior that focus on the situations in which crimes occur.

continuance in contemplation of dismissal: case in abeyance pending good behavior.

contract attorneys: private attorneys who operate under contracts with local jurisdictions to represent indigent defendants for a fee.

control model of management: prison management model that emphasizes prisoner obedience, work, and education.

correctional boot camp: places run like military boot camps to correct the behavior of the young, first-time offenders who are sentenced there.

correctional institution: type of prison developed during the early 1900s that was based on the penal philosophy of rehabilitation.

corrections: the most widely used label for the agencies and decision making related to the supervision of convicted criminals in custody.

courthouse work group: lawyers who form a courtroom elite whose primary goal is the efficient and harmonious disposition of cases.

courts of record: courts that keep a formal written record of their proceedings.

crime control model: model that favors informal, discretionary decision making to efficiently, economically, accurately, and quickly separate the guilty from the innocent.

Crime Index: raw numbers and rates of eight serious crimes that track the movement, fluctuations, and trends in U.S. total rates.

crime-specific focus: the idea that decision making differs according to the crime being contemplated and committed.

criminal career: the history of a criminal noting beginning, duration, and frequency of criminal acts.

criminal conduct: crimes exhibiting actus reus, mens rea, and concurrence.

criminal event: a specific crime that an offender decides to commit.

criminal justice system: collection of agencies that make up the whole of criminal justice.

criminal law: the formal definition of crime and punishment, describing what behavior is prohibited and prescribing the punishment for criminal behavior; the primary source of the actions of criminal justice agencies.

criminal negligence: unconsciously creating a high risk of harm.

criminal recklessness: purposely or consciously creating a high risk of harm.

cross-examination: examination of a witness by the opposing side.

crowded prisoners: definition of prisoners who "live in a high density multiple occupancy confinement unit."

cycle-of-violence hypothesis: hypothesis that a childhood history of physical abuse, neglect, or both predisposes the survivor to later violence.

damages: money awarded in noncriminal lawsuits for injuries; money awarded to plaintiffs in successful torts.

DARE: specially trained officers go to schools to teach drug prevention.

dark figure in crime: offenses not reported or recorded.

day fines: basing the amount of a fine on the daily income of offenders.

day reporting centers: reduce jail and prison crowding by requiring offenders to report every day instead of confining them.

dead-bang cases: cases in which a guilty verdict is virtually certain.

deadly force: force that can cause serious bodily injury or death.

decision to charge: power of prosecutors to initiate formal proceedings against suspects and to decide what to charge them with.

defense of qualified immunity: protects officers in torts whose actions are "objectively reasonable."

defenses of excuse: defense to criminal liability whereby defendants admit that what they did was wrong but that under the circumstances they were not responsible.

defenses of justification: defense to criminal liability whereby the criminal behavior was justified under the circumstances.

delinquency: behavior that would be criminal in adults.

density: number of square feet of floor space per prisoner.

descriptive sentencing guidelines: guidelines for sentences based on what past sentencing practices actually were.

detention center: secure, temporary holding facility.

determinate sentencing: fixed sentencing, where legislatures fix the specific penalty for crimes.

determinist theories of crime: theories of criminal behavior positing that forces beyond the control of individuals determine how they behave.

differential association: theory that criminal behavior, like behavior in general, depends on the person's associations with other people.

differential response: police response to routine calls differs from that to emergency calls.

diminished capacity: a partial defense to criminal liability when diseases or defects short of insanity impair the capacity to form *mens rea.*

direct examination: first examination of a witness conducted by the side on whose behalf the witness was called.

direct information: facts known firsthand.

direct supervision: supervision that places officers in living units where they are in constant contact with prisoners.

Dirty Harry problem: when officers feel the need to resort to "dirty" means to catch criminals.

discovery: proceeding asking the other side to produce its evidence.

discretion: decisions based on individual judgment instead of formal rules.

discretionary release: parole boards determine the date of release from prisons.

disorder: a public breach of minimum standards of decent behavior.

displacement: criminal activity moves to another location in response to police crackdowns.

disposition hearing: determine what should follow finding of delinquency.

diversion: removal from the justice system to alternative programs; transferring defendants into some alternative to criminal prosecution.

DNA (deoxyribonucleic acid) testing: using DNA to identify or exclude suspects.

doctrine of official immunity: limits the liability of officers for torts.

doctrine of *parens patriae:* the government acts as parent.

doctrine of *respondeat superior:* imposes liability on governments for the torts of their officers.

doing time: adaptive style of maintaining one's pre-prison life pattern and identity.

dual system of justice: separate systems for adults and juveniles.

due process clauses: parts of the 5th and 14th Amendments that guarantee fair procedures in denying individuals life, liberty, or property.

due process model: model that puts the formal legal process at the heart of decision making in criminal justice.

duress: defense that a defendant was forced by another person to commit a crime.

either-or punishment: practice of either incarcerating offenders or placing them on straight probation.

entrapment: law enforcement officers' inducement of people to commit a crime for the purpose of prosecuting them.

equal protection of the laws: rule that prohibits separating persons by unacceptable criteria, such as gender, race, religion, ethnicity, and, in some instances, age.

ethnographic studies: field observations and interviews to gather data in the natural settings of the behavior under study.

***ex post facto* law:** a retroactive law.

exclusionary rule: prohibiting the use of illegally obtained evidence to prove guilt.

exclusive jurisdiction: the sole authority to hear and decide cases.

executive clemency: power of the executive branch to release prisoners or reduce their sentences.

expiration release: unconditional release at the end of the prison sentence.

express bargaining: plea negotiating in which attorneys for both sides and the defendant meet to work out specific concessions.

external review of police misconduct: civilian review of police misconduct charges.

factual guilt: the defendant did commit the crime.

felonies: crimes punishable by one year or more in prison.

field training: places rookies in the hands of experienced officers to teach them the realities of policing.

fines: payment of money as a punishment for committing a crime.

first appearance: proceedings to read charges, set initial bail, and assign attorneys.

fleeing felon doctrine: allowed use of deadly force to apprehend a fleeing suspect.

follow-up investigations: the work done to solve crimes after preliminary investigations.

foot patrol: police patrolling on foot to increase contact with residents.

formal criminal justice: the law and written rules providing the framework of criminal justice.

formalization: replacing discretion with rules.

fortress prison: large, custody-oriented prison that began in the 1800s.

front-door strategy: reducing prison crowding by not sending people to prison.

full enforcement: the principle that law enforcement officers enforce all criminal statutes with equal vigor.

fundamental fairness doctrine: due process rule that focuses on the substance of fairness, rather than on the form of procedure.

gangbanging: affiliating with a gang in prison for protection.

gender model of police attitudes: theory that suggests there is a difference in attitudes between male and female officers.

general deterrence: utilitarian philosophy of sentencing that aims to prevent those in the general population from committing crimes.

general intent: intent to do something at an undetermined time or to an unspecified object.

general jurisdiction: the authority to hear and decide all criminal cases.

general population inmate: without special conditions beyond those of ordinary confinement.

gleaning: adaptive style of using prison to make significant changes in one's life pattern and identity.

good time: the number of days deducted from sentences for good behavior.

good-time laws: statutes that allow prisoners to reduce their sentences by a certain number of days for good behavior.

grand jury: citizens who test the government's case.

gross misdemeanors: offenses punishable by jail terms from 30 days to one year.

group home: relatively open, community-based facility.

guided discretion death penalty statutes: statutes requiring juries to administer capital punishment according to statutory guidelines on mitigating and aggravating circumstances.

halfway house: large, nonsecure, community-based residential center.

"hands-off" doctrine: courts decline to interfere with the daily operations of prisons.

Hawthorne principle: the creation of a new and closely watched project produces temporary positive results.

hearing officers: special examiners who conduct parole hearings and interview inmates eligible for parole.

hearsay: information acquired through a third person.

hearsay evidence: information not directly known by the witness that is offered for its truth at trial.

homeboys: friends made outside of prison who often become newcomers' gang connection inside.

home confinement: sentencing offenders to remain in their homes except for specified times and purposes.

hostile witness: witnesses who may be uncooperative to the side that did not call them.

hot spot patrol: location differentiates police response.

hot spots: the locations where most crimes take place.

hydraulic effect: phenomenon in which discretion compressed at one point in the system expands somewhere else in the system.

illegitimate opportunity structure: availability of illegitimate opportunities according to position in the social structure.

implicit bargaining: plea negotiation in which defense counsel can assume their clients will get the "going rate" sentence for a guilty plea.

importation theory: theory that prison society has roots in criminal and convention outside prison.

incapacitation: utilitarian philosophy of sentencing aimed at preventing sentenced offenders from committing crimes.

incident reports: officer's description of a crime, witnesses, and suspects.

incident-based reporting: reporting by local police departments to the FBI of both summaries of crime figures and details of each criminal event.

indeterminate sentencing: legislatures set only the outer limits of possible penalties.

indictment: formal accusation of a crime by a grand jury.

indigenous theory: theory that conditions inside prisons shape the nature of prison society.

inducement test: test of entrapment based on the conclusion that if the government engages in conduct that would induce an ordinary, law-abiding person to commit the crime, the court should dismiss the case.

informal criminal justice: discretionary decision making in day-to-day criminal justice.

information: document allowing prosecutors to bypass grand juries and initiate criminal proceedings.

initiate formal proceedings: preliminary decision to charge based on the results of police investigations.

injunctions: court orders requiring officers and departments to cease an activity.

inmate code: informal system of rules that determines right and wrong, good and bad within inmate society.

insanity: a legal, not a medical, term in defense, which defines when some mental disease or defect renders persons not responsible for their actions.

institutional support: work program that provides for jail services by relying on the work of jail inmates.

intake: early juvenile court process.

intensive supervised probation (ISP): practice of subjecting probationers to more severe conditions and greater supervision than ordinary probation.

intermediate sanctions: punishments that are less severe than incarceration but more severe than ordinary probation.

intermittent incarceration: sentence that imposes incarceration with release for work, school, community service, and drug or other treatment during the day.

internal affairs units (IAU): units created to investigate, report, and recommend with respect to civilian complaints against police officers.

interrogation: questioning suspects.

irresistible impulse test: test of insanity that focuses on mental diseases and defects that affect defendants' willpower to control their actions.

jailhouse lawyer: prisoners who help fellow prisoners gain access to the legal process to file grievances.

jailing: adaptive style of identifying primarily with the prison world.

job model of police attitude: theory that predicts that male and female officers' attitudes converge with time on the job.

jury instructions: explanation to the jury of the law governing the case.

jury nullification: the power of juries to ignore the formal law and decide cases according to informed extralegal considerations.

jury panel: those people called for jury duty who are not excused or exempted.

just deserts: a justice model that assumes justices demands punishment for crimes.

justice model: just deserts philosophy of sentencing.

juvenile delinquent: youth who has committed either status or delinquency offense.

Kansas City Preventive Patrol Experiment: tested the effectiveness of preventive patrol and found it wanting.

knock-and-announce rule: required of police before they enter a home.

knockdown force: sufficient use of force by police to bring a suspect to the ground.

labeling theory: explanation of criminal behavior asserting that the criminal justice system creates criminals by defining people as criminals.

lack of a material element: defense to criminal liability whereby one of the elements of crime is missing.

law enforcer parole officer: role of protecting law-abiding citizens by watching parolees to make sure they keep the conditions of their parole.

law of criminal procedure: law defining the limits of government power to enforce the criminal law and prescribing consequences for official actions that violate the law.

leading questions: cross-examination questions in which witnesses are essentially told how to answer.

legal guilt: guilt that the government has proved beyond a reasonable doubt by evidence according to the Constitution.

legalistic style of policing: style of policing that emphasizes formal criminal law enforcement and the minimization of discretionary decision making.

legitimate use of force: the force sometimes required by police to do their job.

liberation hypothesis: the assertion that in close cases the value judgments of jurors unconsciously affect their finding of the facts.

lifestyle-exposure theory: differences in victims' lifestyles account for the demographic differences in criminal victimization.

limited jurisdiction: courts limited to hearing and deciding minor offenses and preliminary proceedings in felonies.

lineups: witnesses try to identify a suspect who is standing in line with other individuals.

local legal culture: attitudes, values, and expectations of a particular court or jurisdiction regarding law and the legal system.

lockdown: temporary suspension of all prison activities, including recreation.

lower criminal courts: courts of limited jurisdiction.

maintaining order: police mission devoted to keeping the peace by doing something to settle problems right now.

***mala in se*:** crimes that are inherently bad, or "evil."

***mala prohibit*:** behavior that is a crime only because the law says so.

Management-of-Demand (MOD) System: handling noncritical calls by alternatives to sending a patrol car.

mandatory minimum sentence laws: determinate sentencing laws that require offenders to serve at least some time in prison.

mandatory release: conditional release from prison according to determinate sentencing laws and parole guidelines.

material evidence: evidence that can prove the elements of a crime.

maximum security prison: prisons that focus mainly on security because they house the most dangerous and escape-prone prisoners.

measured capacity: measurement of one prisoner per cell.

medical model: based on treating instead of punishing criminals; views crime as illness and criminals as sick.

medium security prison: the second most secure prisons, which resemble maximum security prisons but with somewhat less constant supervision.

***mens rea*:** the criminal intent or mental element in a crime.

meta-analyses: studies of studies (of rehabilitation programs).

minimum security prison: the least secure prisons, where rehabilitation is stressed and relatively more freedom and privacy are allowed than in maximum and medium security prisons.

Miranda warnings: statements officers must read suspects to assure any incriminating statements made during their custody are voluntary.

misdemeanors: crimes punishable either by fines or up to one year in jail.

mistake of fact: defense that a defendant either did not know a fact or misinterpreted it.

mistake of law: defense that a defendant did not know a law or misunderstood it.

moral entrepreneurs: according to labeling theorists, those institutions that create criminals by attempting to suppress criminal behavior.

National Crime Victimization Survey (NCVS): national survey of crime victims conducted by the U.S. Census Bureau.

National Incident-Based Reporting System (NIBRS): detailed reports of crimes based on individual cases.

negotiated pleas: guilty pleas in exchange for concessions from the government.

net widening: sentencing offenders to intermediate sanctions who would otherwise receive sentences of straight probation.

new-generation jail: jail in which both the architecture and the management style focus on the safe, humane confinement of inmates.

nolo contendere: a plea of "no contest" to charges.

objective basis: the facts required to justify and back up intrusive behaviors by police.

occupancy: number of prisoners for each unit of confinement.

occupational crime: crimes committed by people who use their occupation as an opportunity to engage in criminal behavior.

offender-focused explanations: explanations of criminal behavior that focus on the individuals who commit crimes.

opportunity theory: explanation that maintains that criminal behavior depends on the opportunities available.

organizational crime: crimes committed by corporate officers and managers under the authority of the corporation.

original jurisdiction: the authority to initiate proceedings.

parole: release from incarceration while remaining in state custody according to specific conditions.

parole boards: agency that decides when to conditionally release prisoners before the end of their sentences.

parole contract: an agreement between the state and the offender in which the state promises to release the offender and the offender agrees to abide by the conditions of release.

parole guidelines: risk assessment instruments based on the seriousness of the offense and the risk of the offender to public safety.

parole revocation: cancellation of conditional release, resulting in a return to prison.

Part I offenses: those offenses reported in the Crime Index.

Part II offenses: raw numbers of offenses not reported in the Crime Index.

passive parole officers: officers who do only enough to keep their jobs.

penitentiary: early prisons in which prisoners had to remain silent to think about their crimes.

Pennsylvania system: early prison system that required solitary confinement and silence.

peremptory challenge: the right of both sides to a limited number of challenges to prospective jurors without cause or explanation.

petty misdemeanors: offenses punishable by fines or up to 30 days in jail.

photo identification: witnesses look at pictures to identify suspects.

plain-view search: object of seizure discovered inadvertently where an officer has a right to be.

plaintiffs: those suing wrongdoers (defendants) in torts.

podular design: jail design in which living units are pod-shaped, allowing officers to keep inmates under constant surveillance.

police academy: training school where police socialization begins.

police corruption: form of occupational crime in which officers use their authority for private gain.

police crackdown: proactive strategy that sharply increases police presence.

police defensiveness: distrust of outsiders.

police depersonalization: treating violence and other unpleasant experiences as matter-of-fact.

police misconduct: range of behavior including brutality, constitutional violations, corruption, and unfair treatment of citizens.

police stress: negative pressures associated with police work.

police war stories: socialization by episodes related by experienced officers to recruits.

police working personality: character traits of police officers revealed in their work.

predatory crimes: crimes committed for monetary gain.

predisposition test: test of entrapment that focuses on the intent of defendants who were not predisposed to commit crimes until the government improperly encouraged them.

preliminary hearing: held to determine whether there is probable cause to hold a revocation hearing to end an offender's probation.

preliminary investigations: collecting information at crime scenes and writing reports on what they learned.

prescriptive sentencing guidelines: development of new sentencing norms, based on what decision makers decide the type and range of penalties should be.

presentence investigation (PSI): investigation of the prior criminal record, the social history, and sometimes a psychiatric evaluation of defendants upon which sentencing partially depends.

presentence report (PSR): the report provided by the probation officer in a presentence investigation.

presumption of guilt: attitude of the crime control model that considers those that remain in the system as probably guilty.

presumptive sentencing guidelines: sentencing method in which either legislatures or special commissions set the types and ranges of sentences.

preventive detention: detention of defendants who endanger either public safety or specific individuals.

preventive patrol: moving through the streets to intercept and prevent crime.

principle of concurrence: the *actus reus* must join with the *mens rea.*

principle of less eligibility: belief that prisoners should not earn as much as people working outside prison.

prison subculture: a culture inside prisons with its own rules, customs, and language.

prisonization: process by which inmates adapt to the customs of the prison world.

privatization: private management of correctional facilities.

pro bono assistance: appointment of counsel who voluntarily assist defendants without monetary compensation.

proactive policing: police themselves initiate action to control crime.

probable cause hearing: preliminary hearing.

probable cause to arrest: the quantum of proof required to arrest.

probation: substitution for incarceration, in which those convicted face supervised release into the community.

probation bill collector: probation officers who are in charge of seeing to it that probationers pay part of the cost of their probation.

procedural due process: laws that enforce the constitutional limits on actions taken by the government to enforce the criminal law.

proof beyond a reasonable doubt: enough evidence legally obtained and properly presented that will convince an ordinary, reasonable person that a defendant is guilty.

protective probation officers: probation officers who focus on a combination of their law enforcement and social worker roles.

public defenders: defense attorneys who work full time in public defender offices to represent indigent defendants.

public works crews: jail work program in which inmates provide community services, such as street cleaning, storm cleanup, and park maintenance.

punitive probation officers: probation officers who focus on their law enforcement role.

quasi-military organizations: law enforcement agencies that resemble military organizations in having a hierarchical command structure.

rational choice perspective: explanation of criminal behavior that assumes that people choose to commit crimes because they believe it is in their self-interest to do so.

reactive policing: police respond to calls for help from victims and witnesses.

reality therapy: getting offenders to see the consequences of irresponsible behavior.

reasonable suspicion: the quantum of proof required for a stop and frisk.

recidivism: return to criminal behavior; when probationers are arrested for committing new crimes.

recidivist: repeat offender.

reform model of policing: the view that police are the front end or gatekeepers of the criminal justice system.

rehabilitation: utilitarian philosophy of punishment that aims at preventing future crimes by changing individual offenders.

release on recognizance (ROR): release of defendants solely on their promise to appear at trial.

relevant evidence: evidence that relates to the elements of the crime.

reported capacity: figure that a particular jurisdiction designates as the capacity of a jail.

response time: the time it takes the police to respond to citizens' calls.

responsibility management approach: prison management model that stresses the responsibility of prisoners for their own actions, not administrative control to ensure prescribed behavior.

restitution: paying back victims for the injuries and other losses caused by offenders; philosophy of sentencing based on requiring offenders to pay in money or service for the harm to individuals and society caused by their crimes.

retribution: philosophy of punishment that looks backward in time to punish for crimes already committed.

revocation: cancellation of probation for either technical violations or the commission of crimes.

revocation hearing: final evaluation of whether probationers have violated the conditions of their probation.

right to privacy: a Supreme Court–imputed Constitutional right of persons to be free from government intrusion into the privacy of their homes.

risk assessment instrument: used to put inmates in a particular group according to the risk of committing further crimes.

"rotten apple" theory: a single bad officer who is not reflective of the department.

routine activities theory: explanation of criminal behavior that focuses not on the motivation of offenders but on time and space.

rule of four: rule used by the Supreme Court, in which four justices must vote to issue a writ of certiorari before hearing a case.

safety-valve policy: reducing prison crowding by reducing the minimum sentences of all prisoners.

salient factor score (SFS): number that states the probability that a prisoner will succeed on parole.

search: examining persons or property to discover evidence, weapons, or contraband.

search incident to arrest: search without a warrant conducted at the time of arrest.

section 1983 actions: legal actions brought under the KKK Act permitting citizens to sue government officials for the violation of civil rights.

selective enforcement: the principle that law enforcement officers use discretionary judgment as to which laws to enforce.

selective incapacitation: identifying the most serious offenders and reserving prison space for them.

sentence bargaining: plea negotiation in which defendants plead guilty with the understanding that the judge will show leniency.

sentencing discrimination: influence on sentencing of unacceptable criteria, such as race, ethnicity, and gender.

sentencing disparity: the differences—not necessarily discrimination—in sentences among individuals.

service style of policing: style of policing that takes all requests for service seriously, regardless of whether they stem from criminal law violations, maintaining order, or simply providing information.

shelters: temporary, nonsecure, community-based holding facilities.

shock incarceration: sentence that imposes incarceration, after which offenders may petition the court to grant probation.

show-ups: witnesses try to identify suspects without other possible suspects present.

situation theories: explanations of criminal behavior based on the importance of location of targets and the movement of offenders and victims in time and space.

slow pleas: defendants plead not guilty and go to trial, but the trial is short and superficial.

social conflict theories: explanations of criminal behavior that emphasize the power structure and control of society and its institutions by the rich and powerful.

social control theories: theories that obedience to rules depends on institutions to keep the desire to break the rules in check.

social learning theories: theories that individuals at birth are blank slates and learn values and behavior.

social service brokers: probation officers who focus on finding the best social service agencies to aid probationers in reintegrating into the community.

social structure of the case: extralegal sociological considerations that affect decisions.

solicitation: asking another to commit a crime.

special deterrence: incapacitation of specific offenders.

special needs prisoners: the vulnerable, troublemakers, the mentally ill, and the elderly.

specific intent: intent to do something in addition to the *actus reus*.

split-sentence probation: sentence that includes a specific period of incarceration followed by a period of probation.

state-raised youths: inmates who have spent most of their lives in state-operated institutions.

statistical discrimination: attributing group stereotypes to individual members of the group.

status offenses: behavior that only juveniles commit.

stop and frisk: less intrusive search and seizure protected by the Fourth Amendment.

straight pleas: pleas of guilty without negotiation.

strain theory: explanation of criminal behavior that focuses on the effects of frustration experienced by those who work hard yet fail to attain the American dream.

strict liability: liability without fault; without *mens rea*.

subculture of competition: corporate culture in which the goal is success, measured in money, power, and prestige.

subculture of violence: a subculture in which recourse to violence is acceptable or favored.

subculture theories: social process theories that stress the importance of the values of groups in determining behavior.

subpoena: order of a court commanding that witnesses appear in court to present relevant testimony.

substantial capacity test: test of insanity that focuses on both reason and will.

substantial justice approach: decide according to the justice of individual cases.

substantive due process: the means by which constitutional protections of life, liberty, and property apply to the definitions of crimes and punishments.

super maximum prison: "end of the line' prisons for the "worst of the worst" prisoners.

sweet deals: practice of prosecutors' settling for less than the initial charges because the case against a defendant is weak.

technical probation violations: breaking of probation rules that do not amount to crimes.

The Uniform Crime Reports (UCR): crimes reported to the police and arrests made and reported to the FBI.

"three strikes and you're out": mandatory sentencing that seeks to lock up for life dangerous offenders who habitually prey on innocent people.

ticket of leave: a document that allowed prisoners to remain free as long as they kept the conditions of release attached to the ticket.

time-server probation officers: probation officers who are "putting in their time," avoiding hassles and collecting their salary and fringe benefits.

token economy: earning tokens to buy privileges by responsible behavior.

torts: noncriminal legal wrongs; private personal injury actions.

totality of circumstances: a look at all pertinent facts to determine the balancing test.

training school: secure detention center.

transferred intent: intent to harm one victim but instead harming another.

trial courts: courts of general jurisdiction.

undercover police operations: covert operations.

utility: philosophy of punishment that looks forward in time to prevent future crimes.

violation: petty offenses punishable by a small fine and not part of a criminal record.

violent predator: a criminal who performs violent acts for gain.

violent prison: type of prison that started in the 1960s, housing younger, more violent prisoners who often exhibit racial and ethnic hatred.

void-for-vagueness: rule that a law is invalid unless it clearly defines what it prohibits.

voir dire: examination of prospective jurors by the judge and the attorneys.

voluntary sentencing guidelines: sentencing method in which judges can but are not legally obliged to follow suggested sentences.

walling: building walls for protection.

wariness: measures to protect against suspicious strangers.

watching: keeping a lookout for suspicious persons and circumstances.

watchman style of policing: nonbureaucratic, informal style of policing in which officers focus on caretaking and maintaining order by means of discretionary decision making.

welfare parole officers: role that relies on information about individual parolees to diagnose their needs and design a treatment plan for them.

welfare probation officers: probation officers who focus on their social worker role.

work release: practice that allows prisoners to leave jail for work and to return for evenings and weekends.

writ of certiorari: order to review the proceedings of a lower court.

writ of habeas corpus: order to review the lawfulness of detention.

Table of Cases

Name Index

Subject Index

E

F

Photo Credits

1 (opener): © Mike Maple/Woodfin Camp & Associates; 10: © Robert E. Daemmrich/Tony Stone Images; 15: © Tom McHugh/ Photo Researchers; 17: AP/Wide World Photos; 20: AP/Wide World Photos; 22: © Tracie Cambre Pierce/SABA; 27 (opener): © F. M. Kearney/Impact Visuals; 30: © Richard Hutchings/Photo Researchers; 40: Photo courtesy of the Alaska State Troopers; 42: AP/Wide World Photos; 44: © Donna Ferrato/Domestic Abuse Awareness, Inc.; 46: AP/Wide World Photos; 59 (opener): © Douglas Burrows/The Liaison Agency Network; 65: © Najlah Feanny/SABA; 71: © A. Ramey/Stock Boston; 74 (above): © Enrico Ferorelli; (below): AP/Wide World Photos; 82 (opener): © Michael J. Okoniewski/The Gamma Liaison Network; 90: © Bill Biggart/Impact Visuals; 95: © J. Langevin/SYGMA; 100: AP/ Wide World Photos; 103: AP/Wide World Photos; 107: UPI/ Corbis-Bettmann; 116 (opener): © A. Ramey/Woodfin Camp & Associates; 122: © David Rae Morris/Impact Visuals; 126 © Leif Skoogfors/Woodfin Camp & Associates; 131: AP/Wide World Photos; 136: © P. Chock/Stock Boston; 140: © Christopher Brown/Stock Boston; 147 (opener): © Dan Miller/Woodfin Camp & Associates; 152: © Joel Gordon; 155: AP/Wide World Photos; 158: © Starr/Stock Boston; 162: © Jacques N. Chenet/The Gamma Liaison Network; 166: © Bob Daemmrich/The Image Works; 175 (opener): © Gene Blevins/LA Daily News/SYGMA; 177 © Stephen Agricola/Stock Boston; 189: © Kenneth Jarecke/Woodfin Camp & Associates; 192 (both): © David Frazier Photolibrary; 196: AP/Wide World Photos; 212 (opener): © Joel Gordon; 221: © A. Ramey/Woodfin Camp & Associates; 226: © Rick Gerharter/ Impact Visuals; 231: © Andrew Lichtenstein/SYGMA; 241: © Donna Ferrato/Domestic Abuse Awareness, Inc.; 252 (opener): © Joel Gordon; 261: © Aaron Haupt/David Frazier Photolibrary; 263: AP/Wide World Photos; 266: © Pool/SABA; 268: © S. Gazin/ The Image Works; 273 (opener): © Bob Daemmrich; 276: © Donna Binder/Impact Visuals; 281: AP/Wide World Photos; 283: AP/Wide World Photos; 286: © Tom McDonald/SYGMA; 295 (opener): © R. Freeda/SYGMA; 300: Tina Gerson/Los Angeles Daily News/SABA; 302: © Billy E. Barnes/Tony Stone Images; 305: © Morris Abernathy/Gamma Liaison; 324 (opener): AP/Wide World Photos; 333: Courtesy of the Treleaven family & Families Against Mandatory Minimums; 343: AP/Wide World Photos; 349: AP/Wide World Photos; 354: AP/Wide World Photos; 356: AP/Wide World Photos; 359: AP/Wide World Photos; 365 (opener): © John Livzey; 369: © A. Ramey/Stock Boston; 381: © A. Ramey/Photo Edit; 383: © John Chiasson/Gamma Liaison; 386: AP/Wide World Photos; 390: AP/Wide World Photos; 395 (opener): © Robert McElroy/Woodfin Camp & Associates; 398: © Pete Souza/Liaison International; 400: Eric Liebowitz/HBO/The Kobal Collection; 405: © A. Ramey/Photo Edit; 412: AP/Wide World Photos; 418: © A. Ramey/Photo Edit; 431 (opener): © J. Peter Mortimer/Gamma Liaison; 433: © Lester Sloan/Woodfin Camp; 437: © A. Lichtenstein/SYGMA; 441: AP/Wide World Photos; 445: © Keith Wood/Tony Stone Images; 457: © Joel Gordon; 463 (opener): AP/Wide World Photos; 467: © Bob Daemmrich/Stock Boston; 473: AP/Wide World Photos; 480: © GillesMingasson/Gamma Liaison; 485: © Jeffry Scott/Impact Visuals; 490 (opener): AP/Wide World Photos; 494: AP/Wide World Photos; 496: AP/Wide World Photos; 499: AP/Wide World Photos; 503: © C. Takagi/Impact Visuals; 505: AP/Wide World Photos